Lethbridge—Alberta

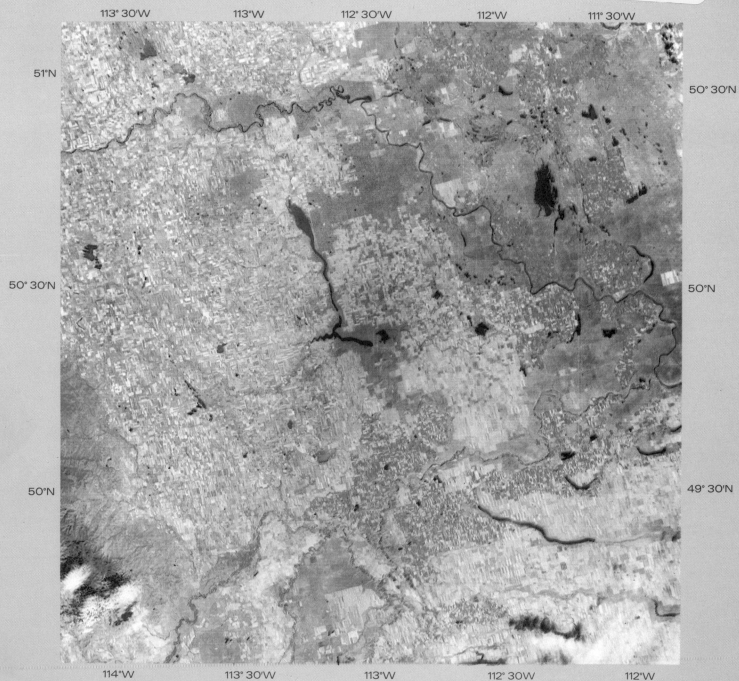

This area of southwestern Alberta is dominated by agriculture with several patterns of land-use. In the northeast, pasture and rangeland with the relative absence of field divisions is brown. The dry high plains of Alberta makes irrigation advisable where possible, and irrigation areas stand out as bright red, growing corn, sugar beet, potatoes and other green crops. Several reservoirs can be seen where rivers have been dammed for irrigation purposes. Wheat and other cereals are grown on the fields with a light tan colour, while mixed farming occupies the remainder of the agricultural area in the smaller, darker, more rectangular fields (especially in the west of the area). In the southwest are the Porcupine Hills – foothills of the Rocky Mountains – covered with forest which gives them a red colour. Lethbridge itself, not clearly visible, lies in the lower centre.

(23 August 1973)

The images shown on the endpapers were produced by the Landsat spacecraft which orbits the earth at an altitude of 900 km. (Images from NASA).

The Comprehensive
ATLAS
of CANADA
and the WORLD

Prepared under the direction of

HAROLD FULLARD
Consultant Cartographer

B. M. WILLETT
Cartographic Editor

GEORGE PHILIP

Preface

The easier and more rapid means of communication, the increase in global trade and exchanges, the growth of world organizations of all kinds and the pace of international events all demand of anyone who is careful to co-ordinate his information a convenient reference source and there is nothing better for this than an atlas. To be of the greatest use, it is essential that the maps should be detailed, accurate, legible and up-to-date; in addition, the index must enable the reader to find any place quickly. Also it is considered helpful that the detailed maps should be complemented by thematic maps, tables and illustrations to analyse and portray on the one hand the physical environment (such as geology, climate and vegetation) and on the other man and his activities, production and trade.

The COMPREHENSIVE ATLAS OF CANADA AND THE WORLD meets these needs. The Atlas is of an easily portable size, convenient for frequent use, and able to stand on a bookshelf. At the same time, the content has been arranged to give regional maps on a large scale because it is only at such scales that a precision and wealth of detail can be satisfactorily presented.

The Atlas gives firstly an overall view of the earth in space, the composition of the earth and its surrounding atmosphere, then physical, demographic, economic and political maps followed by studies in depth of the continents by means of specialized maps and the more detailed regional maps. As befits the requirements of Canadian readers, a considerable section of the Atlas is given to special maps dealing with the country as a whole, as well as with each of the provinces. Thematic maps of Canada portray in the first place the physical conditions – geology, soils, vegetation – followed by specific maps on population and economic activities in agriculture, forestry, fishing, mining, energy production and industry. Regional maps on scales of 1:7M and 1:10M are amplified by larger scale maps, 1:2.5M, of the important more densely settled parts of the provinces, with yet more detailed maps of the Metropolitan regions, whilst the larger cities and capitals are shown on maps of 1:250,000 complemented by photographs. Neighbouring countries in the North and Latin America are given special treatment e.g. Northeastern United States, the Chicago-St. Louis region, California and Washington, Mexico and the Caribbean.

The design of the maps takes advantage of new developments in map reproduction. Lighter yet clearer layer colours have made possible the inclusion of a hill-shading to bring out clearly the character of the land and relief features without impairing the legibility of names, settlements and communications.

The opportunity of new reproduction has been taken to incorporate latest changes up to the date of printing and is shown in the most recent state of boundaries, political and administrative divisions and communications. International boundaries are drawn to show the *de facto* situation where there are rival claims to territory.

Spellings of Canadian names are the forms given in the Gazetteer of Canada by the Canadian Permanent Committee on Geographic Names and in the Répertoire Géographique du Québec by the Commission de Géographie. Spellings of names in other parts of the world are in the forms given in the latest official list and generally agree with the rules of the Permanent Committee on Geographical Names and the United States Board on Geographic Names. The comprehensive index locates over 35,000 places and geographical features by coordinates of latitude and longitude.

H. FULLARD

Contents

Maps 1–136

Contents–II

Canada

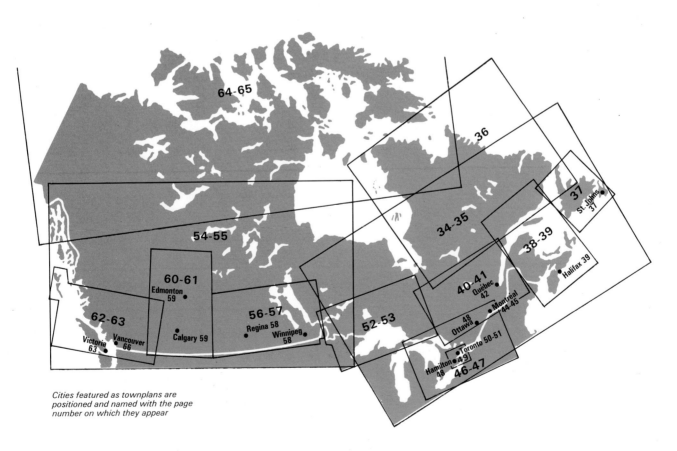

Cities featured as townplans are positioned and named with the page number on which they appear

Contents–III

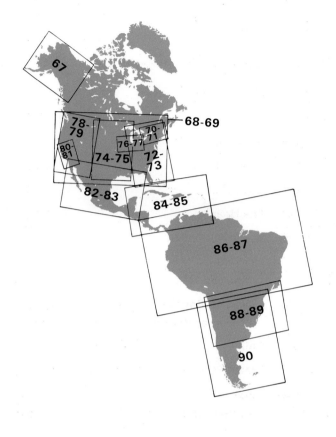
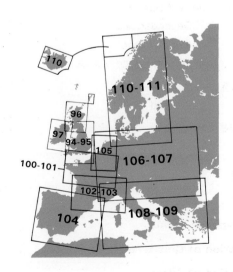

Contents–IV

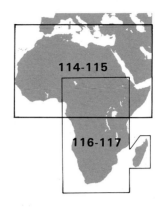

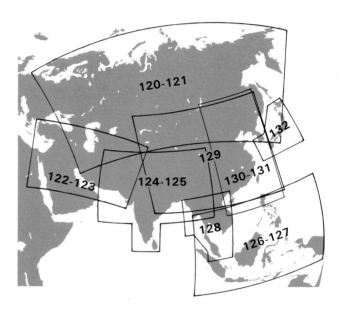

Index

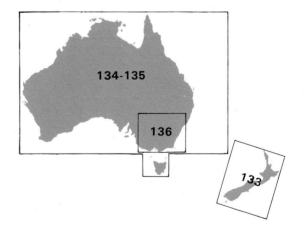

Selected References

These selected references are additional to the contents list on the previous pages and are included to take the reader directly to the page required for certain well known and used names. The list includes country names and names of large geographical features, mountains and seas for example. The page quoted will be the one where the feature appears as a whole and at the largest scale.

Chart of the Stars

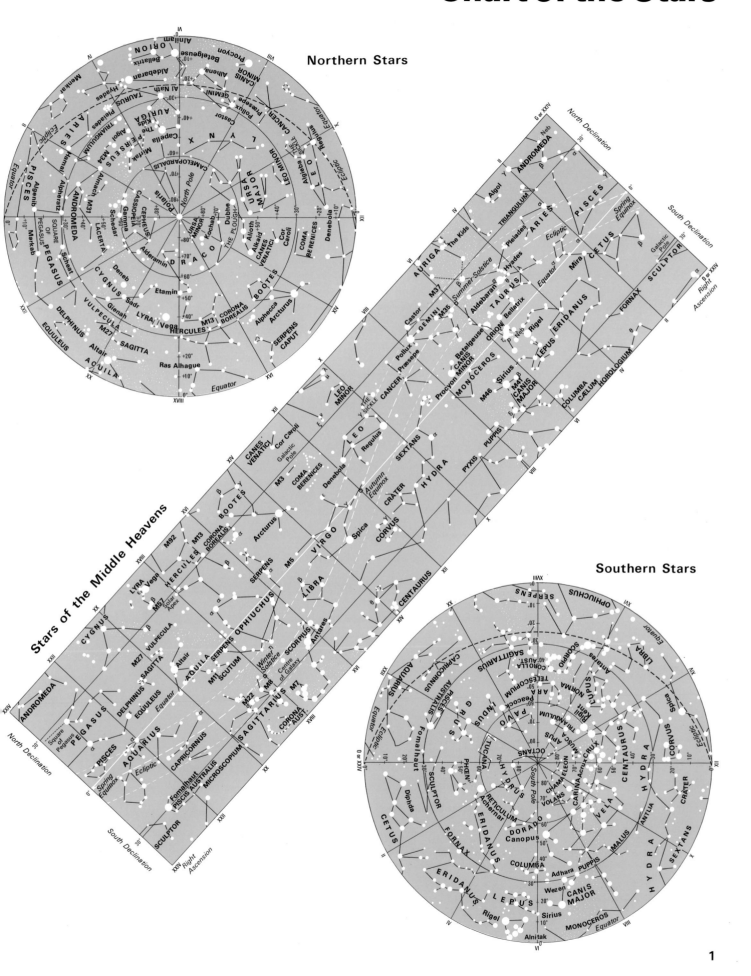

Northern Stars

Stars of the Middle Heavens

Southern Stars

1

The Solar System

The Solar System is a minute part of one of the innumerable galaxies that make up the universe. Our Galaxy is represented in the drawing to the right and The Solar System (S) lies near the plane of spiral-shaped galaxy, but 27 000 light-years from the centre. The System consists of the Sun at the centre with planets, moons, asteroids, comets, meteors, meteorites, dust and gases revolving around it. It is calculated to be at least 4 700 million years old.

The Solar System can be considered in two parts: the Inner Region planets- Mercury, Venus, Earth and Mars - all small and solid, the Outer Region planets - Jupiter, Saturn, Uranus and Neptune - all gigantic in size, and on the edge of the system the smaller Pluto.

Our galaxy

Inner region planets

Outer region planets

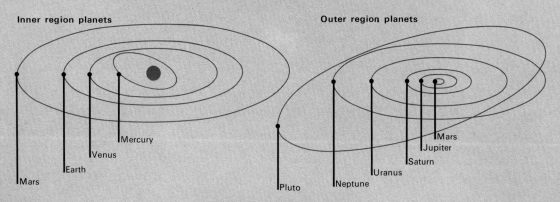

Mercury
Venus
Earth
Mars

Mars
Jupiter
Saturn
Uranus
Neptune
Pluto

The planets

All planets revolve round the Sun in the same direction, and mostly in the same plane. Their orbits are shown (left) - they are not perfectly circular paths.

The table below summarizes the dimensions and movements of the Sun and planets.

The Sun

The Sun has an interior with temperatures believed to be of several million °C brought about by continuous thermo-nuclear fusions of hydrogen into helium. This immense energy is transferred by radiation into surrounding layers of gas the outer surface of which is called the chromosphere. From this "surface" with a temperature of many thousands °C "flames" (solar prominences) leap out into the diffuse corona which can best be seen at times of total eclipse (see photo right). The bright surface of the Sun, the photosphere, is calculated to have a temperature of about 6 000 °C, and when viewed through a telescope has a mottled appearance, the darker patches being called sunspots - the sites of large disturbances of the surface.

Total eclipse of the sun

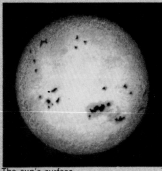

The sun's surface

	Equatorial diameter in km	Mass (earth=1)	Mean distance from sun in millions km	Mean radii of orbit (earth = 1)	Orbital inclination	Mean sidereal period (days)	Mean period of rotation on axis (days)	Number of satellites
Sun	1 392 000	332 946	—	—	—	—	25·38	—
Mercury	4 878	0·05	57·9	0·38	7°	87·9	58·6	0
Venus	12 104	0·81	108·2	0·72	3°23'	224·7	243	0
Earth	12 756	1·00	149·6	1·00	—	365·2	0·99	1
Mars	6 794	0·10	227·9	1·52	1°50'	686·9	1·02	2
Jupiter	142 800	317·9	778·3	5·20	1°18'	4332·5	0·41	14 ?
Saturn	120 000	95·1	1 427	9·53	2°29'	10759·2	0·42	11
Uranus	52 000	14·5	2 869	19·17	0°46'	30684·8	0·45	5
Neptune	48 400	17·2	4 496	30·05	1°46'	60190·5	0·67	2
Pluto	3 000 ?	0·001	5 900	39·43	17°1'	91628·6	6·38	1 ?

The Sun's diameter is 109 times greater than that of the Earth.

Distances from sun in millions km

9 — Mercury
2 — Venus
6 — Earth
9 — Mars

3 — Jupiter

7 — Saturn

9 — Uranus

6 — Neptune

0 — Pluto

Mercury is the nearest planet to the Sun. It is composed mostly of high density metals and probably has an atmosphere of heavy inert gases.

Venus is similar in size to the Earth, and probably in composition. It is, however, much hotter and has a dense atmosphere of carbon dioxide which obscures our view of its surface.

Earth is the largest of the inner planets. It has a dense iron-nickel core surrounded by layers of silicate rock. The surface is approximately $\frac{3}{8}$ land and $\frac{5}{8}$ water, and the lower atmosphere consists of a mixture of nitrogen, oxygen and other gases supplemented by water vapour. With this atmosphere and surface temperatures usually between $-50°C$ and $+40°C$, life is possible.

Mars, smaller than the Earth, has a noticeably red appearance. Photographs taken by the Mariner probes show clearly the cratered surface and polar ice caps, probably made from frozen carbon dioxide.

The Asteroids orbit the Sun mainly between Mars and Jupiter. They consist of thousands of bodies of varying sizes with diameters ranging from yards to hundreds of miles.

Jupiter is the largest planet of the Solar System. Photographs taken by Voyager I and II have revealed an equatorial ring system and shown the distinctive Great Red Spot and rotating cloud belts in great detail.

Saturn, the second largest planet consists of hydrogen, helium and other gases. The equatorial rings are composed of small ice particles.

Uranus is extremely remote but just visible to the naked eye and has a greenish appearance. A faint equatorial ring system was discovered in 1977. The planet's axis is tilted through 98° from its orbital plane, therefore it revolves in a retrograde manner.

Neptune, yet more remote than Uranus and larger. It is composed of gases and has a bluish green appearance when seen in a telescope. As with Uranus, little detail can be observed on its surface.

Pluto. No details are known of its composition or surface. The existence of this planet was firstly surmised in a computed hypothesis, which was tested by repeated searches by large telescopes until in 1930 the planet was found. Latest evidence seems to suggest that Pluto has one satellite, provisionally named Charon.

The Earth

Seasons, Equinoxes and Solstices

The Earth revolves around the Sun once a year and rotates daily on its axis, which is inclined at $66\frac{1}{2}°$ to the orbital plane and always points into space in the same direction. At midsummer (N.) the North Pole tilts towards the Sun, six months later it points away and half way between the axis is at right angles to the direction of the Sun (right).

Earth data

Maximum distance from the Sun (Aphelion) 152 007 016 km
Minimum distance from the Sun (Perihelion) 147 000 830 km
Obliquity of the ecliptic 23° 27′ 08″
Length of year - tropical (equinox to equinox) 365.24 days
Length of year - sidereal (fixed star to fixed star) 365.26 days
Length of day - mean solar day 24h 03m 56s
Length of day - mean sidereal day 23h 56m 04s

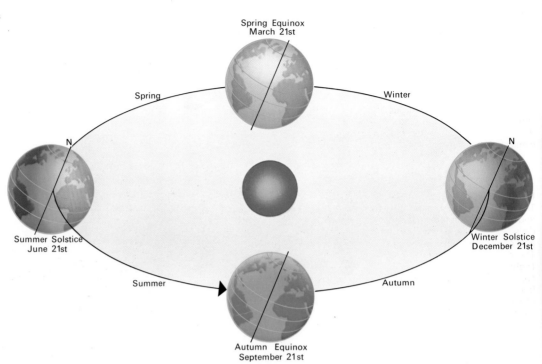

Length of day and night

At the summer solstice in the northern hemisphere, the Arctic has total daylight and the Antarctic total darkness. The opposite occurs at the winter solstice. At the equator, the length of day and night are almost equal all the year, at 30° the length of day varies from about 14 hours to 10 hours and at 50° from about 16 hours to 8 hours.

Apparent path of the Sun

The diagrams (right) illustrate the apparent path of the Sun at A the equator, B in mid latitudes say 45°N, C at the Arctic Circle $66\frac{1}{2}°$ and D at the North Pole where there is six months continuous daylight and six months continuous night

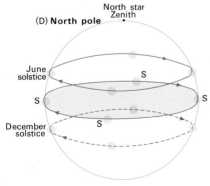

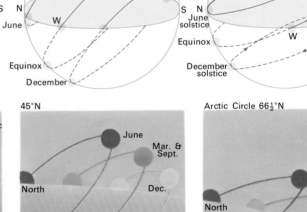

The Moon

The Moon rotates slowly making one complete turn on its axis in just over 27 days. This is the same as its period of revolution around the Earth and thus it always presents the same hemisphere ('face') to us. Surveys and photographs from space-craft have now added greatly to our knowledge of the Moon, and, for the first time, views of the hidden hemisphere.

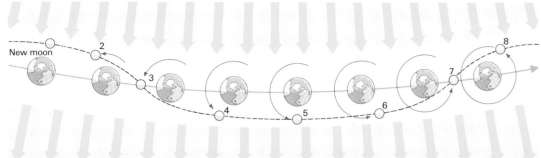

New moon 2 3 4 5 6 7 8

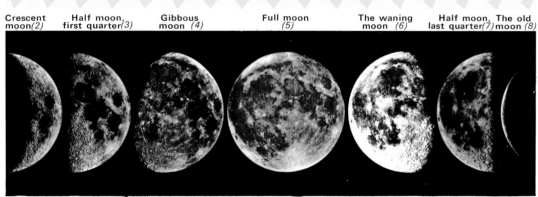

| Crescent moon(2) | Half moon, first quarter(3) | Gibbous moon (4) | Full moon (5) | The waning moon (6) | Half moon, last quarter(7) | The old moon (8) |

Phases of the Moon
The interval between one full Moon and the next is approximately $29\frac{1}{2}$ days - thus there is one new Moon and one full Moon every month. The diagrams and photographs (right) show how the apparent changes in shape of the Moon from new to full arise from its changing position in relation to the Earth and both to the fixed direction of the Sun's rays.

Moon data
Distance from Earth 356 410 km
to 406 685 km
Mean diameter 3 473 km
Mass approx. $\frac{1}{81}$ of that of Earth
Surface gravity $\frac{1}{6}$ of that of Earth
Atmosphere - none, hence no clouds, no weather, no sound.
Diurnal range of temperature at the Equator +200°C

Landings on the Moon
Left are shown the landing sites of the U.S. Apollo programme.
Apollo 11 Sea of Tranquility (1°N 23°E) 1969
Apollo 12 Ocean of Storms (3°S 24°W) 1969
Apollo 14 Fra Mauro (4°S 17°W) 1971
Apollo 15 Hadley Rill (25°N 4°E) 1971
Apollo 16 Descartes (9°S 15°E) 1972
Apollo 17 Sea of Serenity (20°N 31°E) 1972

Eclipses of Sun and Moon
When the Moon passes between Sun and Earth it causes a partial eclipse of the Sun *(right 1)* if the Earth passes through the Moon's outer shadow *(P)*, or a total eclipse *(right 2)*, if the inner cone shadow crosses the Earth's surface.
In a lunar eclipse, the Earth's shadow crosses the Moon and gives either total or partial eclipses.

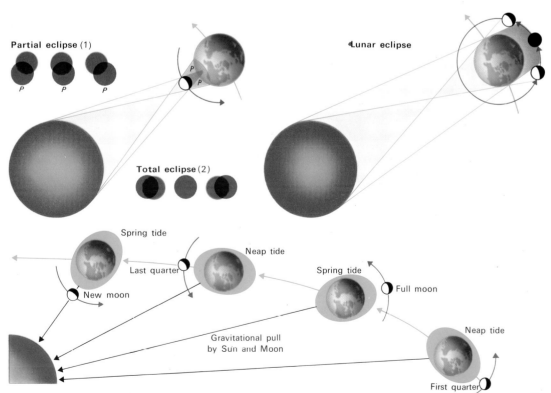

Partial eclipse (1)

P P P

Lunar eclipse

Total eclipse (2)

Tides
Ocean water moves around the Earth under the gravitational pull of the Moon, and, less strongly, that of the Sun. When solar and lunar forces pull together - near new and full Moon - high spring tides result. When solar and lunar forces are not combined - near Moon's first and third quarters - low neap tides occur.

Spring tide
Neap tide
Last quarter
Spring tide
New moon
Full moon
Neap tide
Gravitational pull by Sun and Moon
First quarter

Time

Time measurement
The basic unit of time measurement is the day, one rotation of the earth on its axis. The subdivision of the day into hours and minutes is arbitrary and simply for our convenience. Our present calendar is based on the solar year of $365\frac{1}{4}$ days, the time taken for the earth to orbit the sun. A month was anciently based on the interval from new moon to new moon, approximately $29\frac{1}{2}$ days - and early calendars were entirely lunar.

Rotation of the Earth

The International Date Line
When it is 12 noon at the Greenwich meridian, 180° east it is midnight of the same day while 180° west the day is only just beginning. To overcome this the International Date Line was established, approximately following the 180° meridian. Thus, for example, if one travelled eastwards from Japan (140° East) to Samoa (170° West) one would pass from Sunday night into Sunday morning.

Time zones
The world is divided into 24 time zones, each centred on meridians at 15° intervals which is the longitudinal distance the sun appears to travel every hour. The meridian running through Greenwich passes through the middle of the first zone. Successive zones to the east of Greenwich zone are ahead of Greenwich time by one hour for every 15° of longitude, while zones to the west are behind by one hour.

Night and day
As the earth rotates from west to east the sun appears to rise in the east and set in the west: when the sun is setting in Shanghai on the directly opposite side of the earth New York is just emerging into sunlight. Noon, when the sun is directly overhead, is coincident at all places on the same meridian with shadows pointing directly towards the poles.

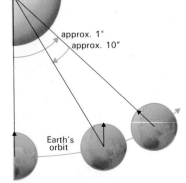
Greenwich Observatory

Prime Meridian

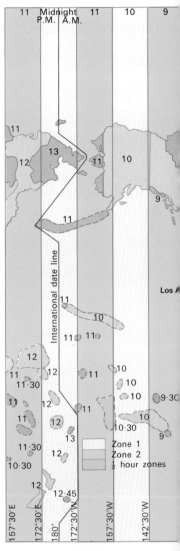

Solar time
The time taken for the earth to complete one rotation about its own axis is constant and defines a day but the speed of the earth along its orbit around the sun is inconstant. The length of day, or 'apparent solar day', as defined by the apparent successive transits of the sun is irregular because the earth must complete more than one rotation before the sun returns to the same meridian.

Sidereal time
The constant sidereal day is defined as the interval between two successive apparent transits of a star, or the first point of Aries, across the same meridian. If the sun is at the equinox and overhead at a meridian on one day, then the next day the sun will be to the east by approximately 1°; thus the sun will not cross the meridian until about 4 minutes after the sidereal noon.

Astronomical clock, Delhi

Sundials
The earliest record of sundials dates back to 741 BC but they undoubtedly existed as early as 2000 BC although probably only as an upright stick or obelisk. A sundial marks the progress of the sun across the sky by casting the shadow of a central style or gnomon on the base. The base, generally made of stone, is delineated to represent the hours between sunrise and sunset.

Kendall's chronometer

Chronometers
With the increase of sea traffic in the 18th century and the need for accurate navigation clockmakers were faced with an intriguing problem. Harrison, an English carpenter, won a British award for designing a clock which was accurate at sea to one tenth of a second per day. He compensated for the effect of temperature changes by incorporating bi-metallic strips connected to thin wires and circular balance wheels.

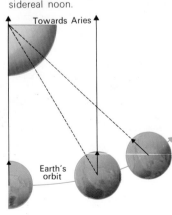

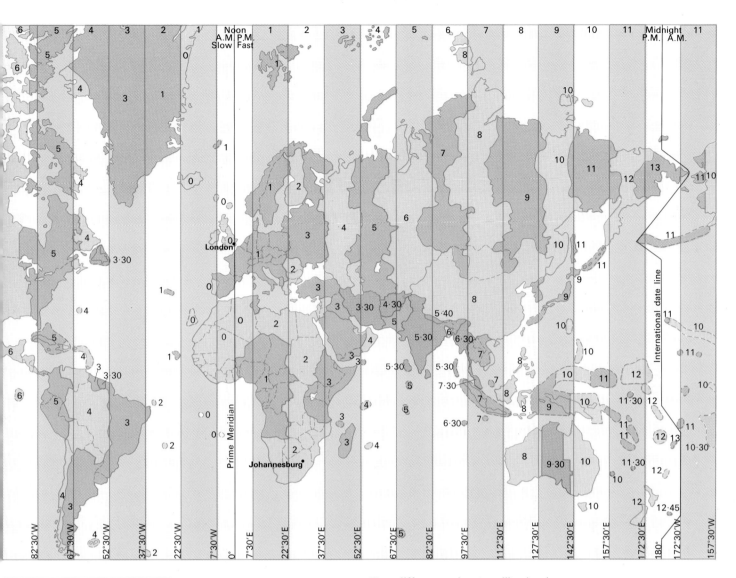

Map labels (time zones across the top):

| 6 | 5 | 4 | 3 | 2 | 1 | Noon A.M P.M. Slow Fast | 1 | 2 | 3 | 4 | 5 | 6 | 7 | 8 | 9 | 10 | 11 | Midnight P.M. A.M. | 11 |

London · Johannesburg · Prime Meridian

Longitude labels (bottom): 82°30'W · 67°30'W · 52°30'W · 37°30'W · 22°30'W · 7°30'W · 0° · 7°30'E · 22°30'E · 37°30'E · 52°30'E · 67°30'E · 82°30'E · 97°30'E · 112°30'E · 127°30'E · 142°30'E · 157°30'E · 172°30'E · 180° · 172°30'W · 157°30'W

International date line

Progress of the accuracy of timekeepers

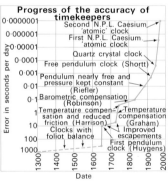

Error in seconds per day:
0·0000001 — Second N.P.L. Caesium 'atomic' clock
0·000001 — First N.P.L. Caesium 'atomic' clock
0·00001 — Quartz crystal clock
0·0001 — Free pendulum clock (Shortt)
0·001 —
0·01 — Pendulum nearly free and pressure kept constant (Riefler)
0·1 — Barometric compensation (Robinson)
1 — Temperature compensation and reduced friction (Harrison) / Temperature compensation (Graham)
10 — Improved escapements
100 — Clocks with foliot balance
1000 — First pendulum clock (Huygens)

Date: 1300 1400 1500 1600 1700 1800 1900 2000

Vibration of quartz ring

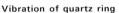
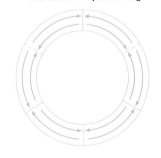

Time difference when travelling by air

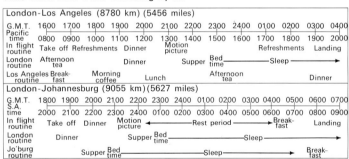

London–Los Angeles (8780 km) (5456 miles)

G.M.T.	1600	1700	1800	1900	2000	2100	2200	2300	2400	0100	0200	0300	0400
Pacific time	0800	0900	1000	1100	1200	1300	1400	1500	1600	1700	1800	1900	2000
In flight routine	Take off	Refreshments	Dinner		Motion picture						Refreshments		Landing
London routine	Afternoon tea			Dinner			Supper	Bed time		Sleep			
Los Angeles routine	Break-fast		Morning coffee		Lunch			Afternoon tea			Dinner		

London–Johannesburg (9055 km) (5627 miles)

G.M.T.	1800	1900	2000	2100	2200	2300	2400	0100	0200	0300	0400	0500	0600	0700
S.A. time	2000	2100	2200	2300	2400	0100	0200	0300	0400	0500	0600	0700	0800	0900
In flight routine	Take off	Dinner	Motion picture		← Rest period →					Break-fast		Landing		
London routine	Dinner				Supper	Bed time	Sleep							
Jo'burg routine		Supper	Bed time			Sleep				Break-fast				

Chronographs

The invention of the chronograph by Charles Wheatstone in 1842 made it possible to record intervals of time to an accuracy of one sixtieth of a second. The simplest form of chronograph is the stop-watch. This was developed to a revolving drum and stylus and later electrical signals. A recent development is the cathode ray tube capable of recording to less than one ten-thousadth of a second.

Quartz crystal clocks

The quartz crystal clock, designed originally in America in 1929, can measure small units of time and radio frequencies. The connection between quartz clocks and the natural vibrations of atoms and molecules mean that the unchanging frequencies emitted by atoms can be used to control the oscillator which controls the quartz clock. A more recent version of the atomic clock is accurate to one second in 300 years.

International date line

Gain a day

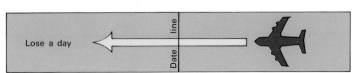

Lose a day

The Atmosphere and Clouds

Earth's thin coating *(right)*
The atmosphere is a blanket of protective gases around the earth providing insulation against otherwise extreme alternations in temperature. The gravitational pull increases the density nearer the earth's surface so that 5/6ths of the atmospheric mass is in the first 15 kms. It is a very thin layer in comparison with the earth's diameter of 12 680 kms., like the cellulose coating on a globe.

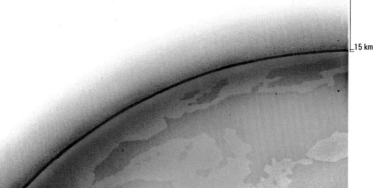
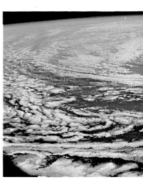

Exosphere*(1)*
The exosphere merges with the interplanetary medium and although there is no definite boundary with the ionosphere it starts at a height of about 600 kms. The rarified air mainly consists of a small amount of atomic oxygen up to 600 kms. and equal proportions of hydrogen and helium with hydrogen predominating above 2 400 kms.

Ionosphere*(2)*
Air particles of the ionosphere are electrically charged by the sun's radiation and congregate in four main layers, D, E, F1 and F2, which can reflect radio waves. Aurorae, caused by charged particles deflected by the earth's magnetic field towards the poles, occur between 65 and 965 kms. above the earth. It is mainly in the lower ionosphere that meteors from outer space burn up as they meet increased air resistance.

Stratosphere*(3)*
A thin layer of ozone contained within the stratosphere absorbs ultra-violet light and in the process gives off heat. The temperature ranges from about -55°C at the tropopause to about -60°C in the upper part, known as the mesosphere, with a rise to about 2°C just above the ozone layer. This portion of the atmosphere is separated from the lower layer by the tropopause.

Troposphere*(4)*
The earth's weather conditions are limited to this layer which is relatively thin, extending upwards to about 8 kms. at the poles and 15 kms. at the equator. It contains about 85% of the total atmospheric mass and almost all the water vapour. Air temperature falls steadily with increased height at about 1°C for every 100 metres above sea level.

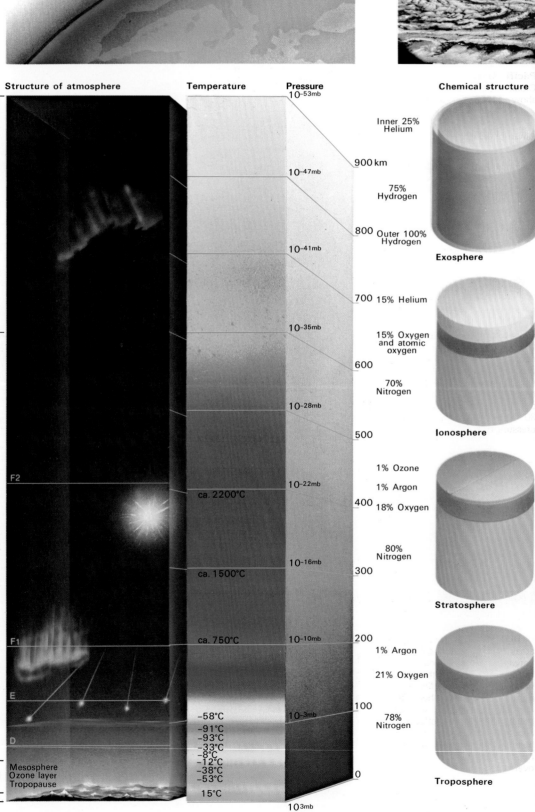

Structure of atmosphere

Temperature

Pressure

Chemical structure

600 km	
15 km	

10⁻⁵³mb → $10^{-53}mb$

Inner 25% Helium

900 km — 10⁻⁴⁷mb → $10^{-47}mb$

75% Hydrogen

800 — Outer 100% Hydrogen

Exosphere

10⁻⁴¹mb → $10^{-41}mb$

700 — 15% Helium

10⁻³⁵mb → $10^{-35}mb$

15% Oxygen and atomic oxygen

600

70% Nitrogen

10⁻²⁸mb → $10^{-28}mb$

500

Ionosphere

F2

ca. 2200°C

10⁻²²mb → $10^{-22}mb$

1% Ozone

1% Argon

400 — 18% Oxygen

ca. 1500°C

10⁻¹⁶mb → $10^{-16}mb$

80% Nitrogen

300

Stratosphere

F1

ca. 750°C

10⁻¹⁰mb → $10^{-10}mb$

200

1% Argon

21% Oxygen

E

100

10⁻³mb → $10^{-3}mb$

78% Nitrogen

D

-58°C
-91°C
-93°C
-33°C
-8°C
-12°C
-38°C
-53°C

Mesosphere
Ozone layer
Tropopause

15°C

0

10³mb → $10^{3}mb$

Troposphere

Pacific Ocean
Cloud patterns over the Pacific show the paths of prevailing winds.

Circulation of the air

Circulation of the air
Owing to high temperatures in equatorial regions the air near the ground is heated, expands and rises producing a low pressure belt. It cools, causing rain, spreads out then sinks again about latitudes 30° north and south forming high pressure belts.

High and low pressure belts are areas of comparative calm but between them, blowing from high to low pressure, are the prevailing winds. These are deflected to the right in the northern hemisphere and to the left in the southern hemisphere (Corolis effect). The circulations appear in three distinct belts with a seasonal movement north and south following the overhead sun.

Cloud types

Clouds form when damp air is cooled, usually by rising. This may happen in three ways: when a wind rises to cross hills or mountains; when a mass of air rises over, or is pushed up by another mass of denser air; when local heating of the ground causes convection currents.

Cirrus *(1)* are detached clouds composed of microscopic ice crystals which gleam white in the sun resembling hair or feathers. They are found at heights of 6 000 to 12 000 metres.

Cirrostratus *(2)* are a whitish veil of cloud made up of ice crystals through which the sun can be seen often producing a halo of bright light.

Cirrocumulus *(3)* is another high altitude cloud formed by turbulence between layers moving in different directions.

Altostratus *(4)* is a grey or bluish striated, fibrous or uniform sheet of cloud producing light drizzle.

Altocumulus *(5)* is a thicker and fluffier version of cirro cumulus, it is a white and grey patchy sheet of cloud.

Nimbostratus *(6)* is a dark grey layer of cloud obscuring the sun and causing almost continuous rain or snow.

Cumulus *(7)* are detached heaped up, dense low clouds. The sunlit parts are brilliant white while the base is relatively dark and flat.

Stratus *(8)* forms dull overcast skies associated with depressions and occurs at low altitudes up to 1500 metres.

Cumulonimbus *(9)* are heavy and dense clouds associated with storms and rain. They have flat bases and a fluffy outline extending up to great altitudes.

High clouds

Middle clouds

Low clouds

Thousands of metres

1 Cirrus

2 Cirrostratus

3 Cirrocumulus

4 Altostratus

5 Altocumulus

6 Nimbostratus

7 Cumulus

8 Stratus

9 Cumulonimbus

Climate and Weather

All weather occurs over the earth's surface in the lowest level of the atmosphere, the troposphere. Weather has been defined as the condition of the atmosphere at any place at a specific time with respect to the various' elements: temperature, sunshine, pressure, winds, clouds, fog, precipitation. Climate, on the other hand, is the average of weather elements over previous months and years.

Climate graphs *right*
Each graph typifies the kind of climatic conditions one would experience in the region to which it is related by colour to the map. The scale refers to degrees Celsius for temperature and millimetres for rainfall, shown by bars. The graphs show average observations based over long periods of time, the study of which also compares the prime factors for vegetation differences.

Development of a depression *below*
In an equilibrium front between cold and warm air masses (i) a wave disturbance develops as cold air undercuts the warm air (ii). This deflects the air flow and as the disturbance progresses a definite cyclonic circulation with warm and cold fronts is created (iii). The cold front moves more rapidly than the warm front eventually overtaking it, and occlusion occurs as the warm air is pinched out (iv).

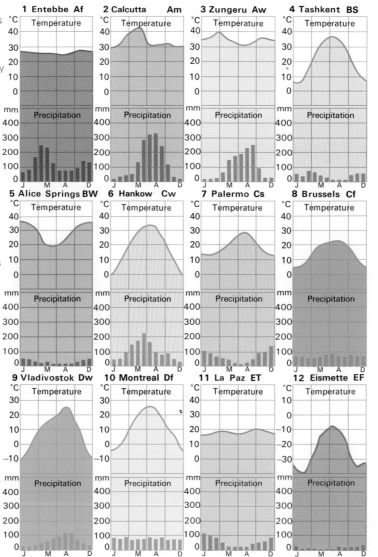

1 Entebbe Af   2 Calcutta Am   3 Zungeru Aw   4 Tashkent BS
5 Alice Springs BW   6 Hankow Cw   7 Palermo Cs   8 Brussels Cf
9 Vladivostok Dw   10 Montreal Df   11 La Paz ET   12 Eismette EF

Af Equatorial forest
Am Monsoon forest
Aw Savanna

Tropical climates

| Af | Am | Aw |

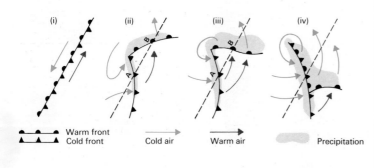

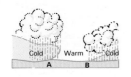
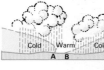
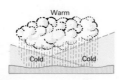

Warm front
Cold front   Cold air   Warm air   Precipitation

Frontal cloud

Precipitation

The upper diagrams show in plan view stages in the development of a depression.
The cross sections below correspond to stages (ii) to (iv).

Kinds of precipitation
Rain The condensation of water vapour on microscopic particles of dust, sulphur, soot or ice in the atmosphere forms water particles. These combine until they are heavy enough to fall as rain.

Hail Water particles, carried to a great height, freeze into ice particles which fall and become coated with fresh moisture. They are swept up again and refrozen. This may happen several times before falling as hail-stones.

Frost Hoar, the most common type of frost, is precipitated instead of dew when water vapour changes directly into ice crystals on the surface of ground objects which have cooled below freezing point.

Snow is the precipitation of ice in the form of flakes, or clusters, of basically hexagonal ice crystals. They are formed by the condensation of water vapour directly into ice.

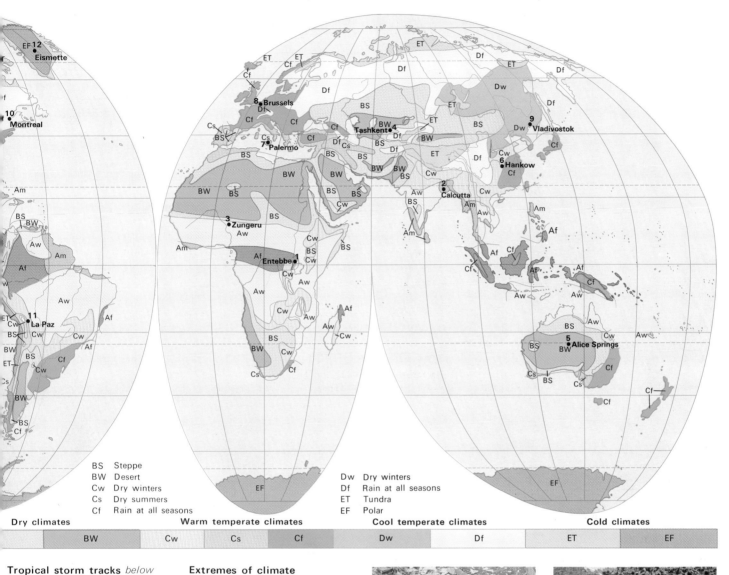

BS	Steppe	
BW	Desert	
Cw	Dry winters	
Cs	Dry summers	
Cf	Rain at all seasons	
	Dw	Dry winters
	Df	Rain at all seasons
	ET	Tundra
	EF	Polar

Dry climates	Warm temperate climates	Cool temperate climates	Cold climates

BW	Cw	Cs	Cf	Dw	Df	ET	EF

Tropical storm tracks *below*

A tropical cyclone, or storm, is designated as having winds of gale force (60 kph) but less than hurricane force (120 kph). It is a homogenous air mass with upward spiralling air currents around a windless centre, or eye. An average of 65 tropical storms occur each year, over 50% of which reach hurricane force. They originate mainly during the summer over tropical oceans.

Extremes of climate & weather *right*

Tropical high temperatures and polar low temperatures combined with wind systems, altitude and unequal rainfall distribution result in the extremes of tropical rain forests, inland deserts and frozen polar wastes. Fluctuations in the limits of these extreme zones and extremes of weather result in occasional catastrophic heat-waves and drought, floods and storms, frost and snow.

Hurricane devastation

Hot desert

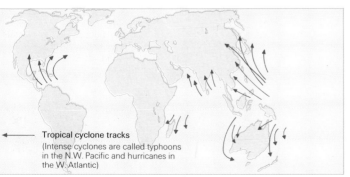

Tropical cyclone tracks
(Intense cyclones are called typhoons in the N.W. Pacific and hurricanes in the W. Atlantic)

Tornado

Arctic dwellings

11

The Earth from Space

Mount Etna, Sicily *left*
Etna is at the top of the photograph, the Plain of Catania in the centre and the Mediterranean to the right. This is an infra-red photograph; vegetation shows as red, water as blue/black and urban areas as grey. The recent lava flows, as yet with no vegetation, show up as blue/black unlike the cultivated slopes which are red and red/pink.

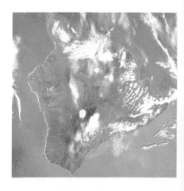

Hawaii, Pacific Ocean *above*
This is a photograph of Hawaii, the largest of the Hawaiian Islands in the Central Pacific. North is at the top of the photograph. The snowcapped craters of the volcanoes Mauna Kea (dormant) in the north centre and Mauna Loa (active) in the south centre of the photograph can be seen. The chief town, Hilo, is on the north east coast.

River Brahmaputra, India *left*
A view looking westwards down the Brahmaputra with the Himalayas on the right and the Khasi Hills of Assam to the left.

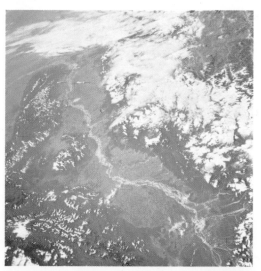

Szechwan, China *right*
The River Tachin in the mountainous region of Szechwan, Central China. The lightish blue area in the river valley in the north east of the photograph is a village and its related cultivation.

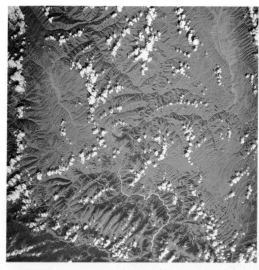

New York, U.S.A. *left*
This infra-red photograph shows the western end of Long Island and the entrance to the Hudson River. Vegetation appears as red, water as blue/black and the metropolitan areas of New York, through the cloud cover, as grey.

The Great Barrier Reef, Australia *right*
The Great Barrier Reef and the Queensland coast from Cape Melville to Cape Flattery. The smoke from a number of forest fires can be seen in the centre of the photograph.

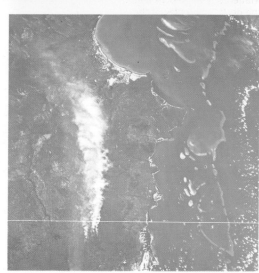

Eastern Himalayas, Asia
above left
A view from Apollo IX looking north-westwards over the snowcapped, sunlit mountain peaks and the head waters of the Mekong, Salween, Irrawaddy and, in the distance, with its distinctive loop, the Brahmaputra.

Atacama Desert, Chile
above right
This view looking eastwards from the Pacific over the Mejillones peninsula with the city of Antofagasta in the southern bay of that peninsula. Inland the desert and salt-pans of Atacama, and beyond, the Andes.

The Alps, Europe *right*
This vertical photograph shows the snow-covered mountains and glaciers of the Alps along the Swiss-Italian-French border. Mont Blanc and the Matterhorn are shown and, in the north, the Valley of the Rhône is seen making its sharp right-hand bend near Martigny. In the south the head waters of the Dora Baltea flow towards the Po and, in the north-west, the Lac d'Annecy can be seen.

The Evolution of the Continents

The origin of the earth is still open to much conjecture although the most widely accepted theory is that it was formed from a solar cloud consisting mainly of hydrogen. Under gravitation the cloud condensed and shrank to form our planets orbiting around the sun. Gravitation forced the lighter elements to the surface of the earth where they cooled to form a crust while the inner material remained hot and molten. Earth's first rocks formed over 3500 million years ago but since then the surface has been constantly altered.

Until comparatively recently the view that the primary units of the earth had remained essentially fixed throughout geological time was regarded as common sense, although the concept of moving continents has been traced back to references in the Bible of a break up of the land after Noah's floods. The continental drift theory was first developed by Antonio Snider in 1858 but probably the most important single advocate was Alfred Wegener who, in 1915, published evidence from geology, climatology and biology. His conclusions are very similar to those reached by current research although he was wrong about the speed of break-up.

The measurement of fossil magnetism found in rocks has probably proved the most influential evidence. While originally these drift theories were openly mocked, now they are considered standard doctrine.

The jigsaw
As knowledge of the shape and structure of the earth's surface grew, several of the early geographers noticed the great similarity in shape of the coasts bordering the Atlantic. It was this remarkable similarity which led to the first detailed geological and structural comparisons. Even more accurate fits can be made by placing the edges of the continental shelves in juxtaposition.

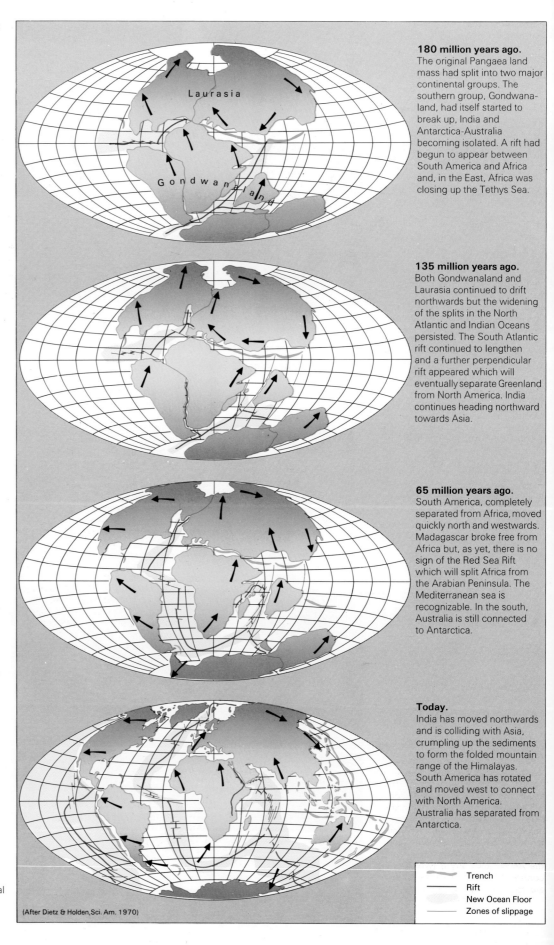

(After Dietz & Holden, Sci. Am. 1970)

180 million years ago.
The original Pangaea land mass had split into two major continental groups. The southern group, Gondwana-land, had itself started to break up, India and Antarctica-Australia becoming isolated. A rift had begun to appear between South America and Africa and, in the East, Africa was closing up the Tethys Sea.

135 million years ago.
Both Gondwanaland and Laurasia continued to drift northwards but the widening of the splits in the North Atlantic and Indian Oceans persisted. The South Atlantic rift continued to lengthen and a further perpendicular rift appeared which will eventually separate Greenland from North America. India continues heading northward towards Asia.

65 million years ago.
South America, completely separated from Africa, moved quickly north and westwards. Madagascar broke free from Africa but, as yet, there is no sign of the Red Sea Rift which will split Africa from the Arabian Peninsula. The Mediterranean sea is recognizable. In the south, Australia is still connected to Antarctica.

Today.
India has moved northwards and is colliding with Asia, crumpling up the sediments to form the folded mountain range of the Himalayas. South America has rotated and moved west to connect with North America. Australia has separated from Antarctica.

﹏﹏	Trench
——	Rift
▨	New Ocean Floor
══	Zones of slippage

Plate tectonics

The original debate about continental drift was only a prelude to a more radical idea; plate tectonics. The basic theory is that the earth's crust is made up of a series of rigid plates which float on a soft layer of the mantle and are moved about by convection currents in the earth's interior. These plates converge and diverge along margins marked by earthquakes, volcanoes and other seismic activity. Plates diverge from mid-ocean ridges where molten lava pushes upwards and forces the plates apart at a rate of up to 30 mm a year. Converging plates form either a trench, where the oceanic plate sinks below the lighter continental rock, or mountain ranges where two continents collide. This explains the paradox that while there have always been oceans none of the present oceans contain sediments more than 150 million years old.

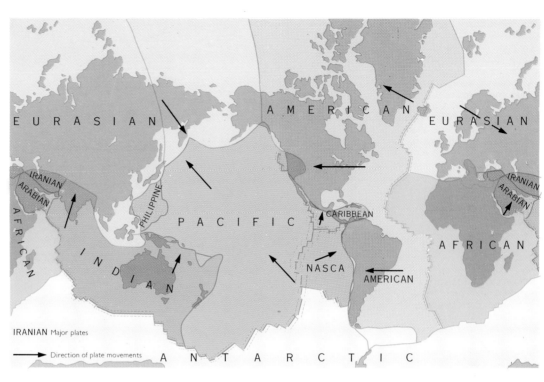

IRANIAN Major plates

→ Direction of plate movements

Trench boundary

The present explanation for the comparative youth of the ocean floors is that where an ocean and a continent meet the ocean plate dips under the less dense continental plate at an angle of approximately 45°. All previous crust is then ingested by downward convection currents. In the Japanese trench this occurs at a rate of about 120 mm a year.

Transform fault

The recent identification of the transform, or transverse, fault proved to be one of the crucial preliminaries to the investigation of plate tectonics. They occur when two plates slip alongside each other without parting or approaching to any great extent. They complete the outline of the plates delineated by the ridges and trenches and demonstrate large scale movements of parts of the earth's surface

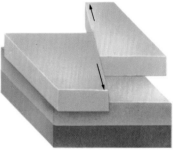

Ridge boundary

Ocean rises or crests are basically made up from basaltic lavas for although no gap can exist between plates, one plate can ease itself away from another. In that case hot, molten rock instantly rises from below to fill in the incipient rift and forms a ridge. These ridges trace a line almost exactly through the centre of the major oceans.

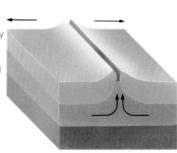

Destruction of ocean plates.

As the ocean plate sinks below the continental plate some of the sediment on its surface is scraped off and piled up on the landward side. This sediment is later incorporated in a folded mountain range which usually appears on the edge of the continent, such as the Andes. Similarly if two continents collide the sediments are squeezed up into new mountains.

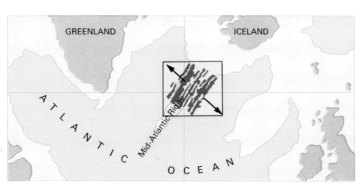

Sea floor spreading

Reversals in the earth's magnetic field have occured throughout history. As new rock emerges at the ocean ridges it cools and is magnetised in the direction of the prevailing magnetic field. By mapping the magnetic patterns either side of the ridge a symmetrical stripey pattern of alternating fields can be observed (see inset area in diagram). As the dates of the last few reversals are known the rate of spreading can be calculated.

The Unstable Earth

The earth's surface is slowly but continually being rearranged. Some changes such as erosion and deposition are extremely slow but they upset the balance which causes other more abrupt changes often originating deep within the earth's interior. The constant movements vary in intensity, often with stresses building up to a climax such as a particularly violent volcanic eruption or earthquake.

The crust *(below and right)*
The outer layer or crust of the earth consists of a comparatively low density, brittle material varying from 5 km to 50 km deep beneath the continents. This consists predominately of silica and aluminium; hence it is called 'sial'. Extending under the ocean floors and below the sial is a basaltic layer known as 'sima', consisting mainly of silica and magnesium.

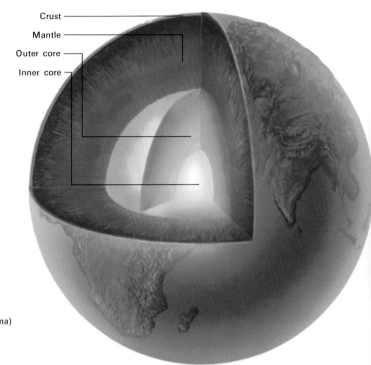

Crust
Mantle
Outer core
Inner core

Continental crust   Ocean crust

Sediment
Granite rock (sial)
Basaltic layer (sima)
Mantle

Volcanoes *(right, below and far right)*
Volcanoes occur when hot liquefied rock beneath the crust reaches the surface as lava. An accumulation of ash and cinders around a vent forms a cone. Successive layers of thin lava flows form an acid lava volcano while thick lava flows form a basic lava volcano. A caldera forms when a particularly violent eruption blows off the top of an already existing cone.

The mantle *(above)*
Immediately below the crust, at the mohorovicic discontinuity line, there is a distinct change in density and chemical properties. This is the mantle - made up of iron and magnesium silicates - with temperatures reaching 1 600 °C. The rigid upper mantle extends down to a depth of about 1 000 km below which is the more viscous lower mantle which is about 1 900 km thick.

The core *(above)*
The outer core, approximately 2 100 km thick, consists of molten iron and nickel at 2 000 °C to 5 000 °C possibly separated from the less dense mantle by an oxidised shell. About 5 000 km below the surface is the liquid transition zone, below which is the solid inner core, a sphere of 2 740 km diameter where rock is three times as dense as in the crust.

Shield volcano   **Cinder cone**   **Hornit cone**   **Caldera**

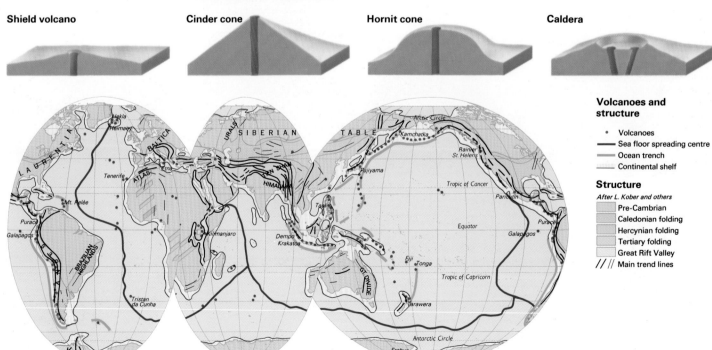

Volcanoes and structure

- Volcanoes
— Sea floor spreading centre
— Ocean trench
— Continental shelf

Structure
After L. Kober and others

Pre-Cambrian
Caledonian folding
Hercynian folding
Tertiary folding
Great Rift Valley
// /// Main trend lines

Major earthquakes in the last 100 years and numbers killed

Year	Location	Killed	Year	Location	Killed	Year	Location	Killed	Year	Location	Killed
1896	Japan (tsunami)	22 000	1923	Japan, Tokyo	143 000	1939/40	Turkey, Erzincan	30 000	1966	U.S.S.R., Tashkent	destroyed
1906	San Francisco	destroyed	1930	Italy, Naples	2 100	1948	Japan, Fukui	5 100	1970	N. Peru	66 800
1906	Chile, Valparaiso	22 000	1931	New Zealand, Napier	destroyed	1956	N. Afghanistan	2 000	1972	Nicaragua, Managua	7 000
1908	Italy, Messina	77 000	1931	Nicaragua, Managua	destroyed	1957	W. Iran	10 000	1974	N. Pakistan	10 000
1920	China, Kansu	180 000	1932	China, Kansu	70 000	1960	Morocco, Agadir	12 000	1976	China, Tangshan	650 000
			1935	India, Quetta	60 000	1962	N.W. Iran	10 000	1978	Iran, Tabas	11 000
			1939	Chile, Chillan	20 000	1963	Yugoslavia, Skopje	1 000	1980	Algeria, El Asnam	20 000

World distribution of earthquakes

Major earthquake zones
Areas experiencing frequent earthquakes

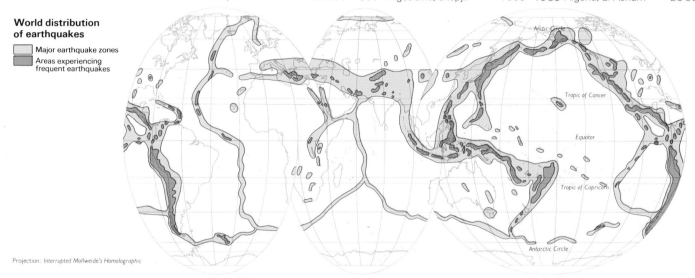

Projection: *Interrupted Mollweide's Homolographic*

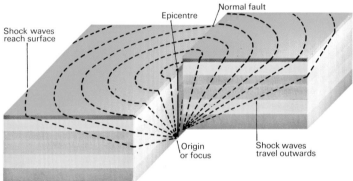

Normal fault
Epicentre
Shock waves reach surface
Origin or focus
Shock waves travel outwards

Earthquakes *(right and above)*

Earthquakes are a series of rapid vibrations originating from the slipping or faulting of parts of the earth's crust when stresses within build up to breaking point. They usually happen at depths varying from 8 km to 30 km. Severe earthquakes cause extensive damage when they take place in populated areas destroying structures and severing communications. Most loss of life occurs due to secondary causes i.e. falling masonry, fires or tsunami waves.

Alaskan earthquake, 1964

Seismic Waves *(right)*

The shock waves sent out from the focus of an earthquake are of three main kinds each with distinct properties. Primary (P) waves are compressional waves which can be transmitted through both solids and liquids and therefore pass through the earth's liquid core. Secondary (S) waves are shear waves and can only pass through solids. They cannot pass through the core and are reflected at the core-mantle boundary taking a concave course back to the surface. The core also refracts the P waves causing them to alter course, and the net effect of this reflection and refraction is the production of a shadow zone at a certain distance from the epicentre, free from P and S waves. Due to their different properties P waves travel about 1,7 times faster than S waves. The third main kind of wave is a long (L) wave, a slow wave which travels along the earth's surface, its motion being either horizontal or vertical.

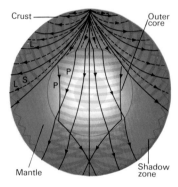

Crust
Outer core
Mantle
Shadow zone

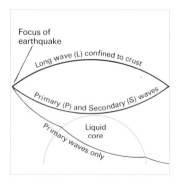

Focus of earthquake
Long wave (L) confined to crust
Primary (P) and Secondary (S) waves
Primary waves only
Liquid core

Tsunami waves *(left)*

A sudden slump in the ocean bed during an earthquake forms a trough in the water surface subsequently followed by a crest and smaller waves. A more marked change of level in the sea bed can form a crest, the start of a Tsunami which travels up to 600 km/h with waves up to 60 m high. Seismographic detectors continuously record earthquake shocks and warn of the Tsunami which may follow it.

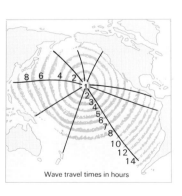

Wave travel times in hours

Horizontal
D M P

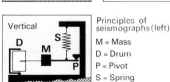

Vertical
D M S P

Principles of seismographs (left)
M = Mass
D = Drum
P = Pivot
S = Spring

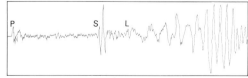

P S L

Seismographs

are delicate instruments capable of detecting and recording vibrations due to earthquakes thousands of kilometres away. P waves cause the first tremors. S the second, and L the main shock.

The Making of Landscape

The making of landscape

The major forces which shape our land would seem to act very slowly in comparison with man's average life span but in geological terms the erosion of rock is in fact very fast. Land goes through a cycle of transformation. It is broken up by earthquakes and other earth movements, temperature changes, water, wind and ice. Rock debris is then transported by water, wind and glaciers and deposited on lowlands and on the sea floor. Here it builds up and by the pressure of its own weight is converted into new rock strata. These in turn can be uplifted either gently as plains or plateaux or more irregularly to form mountains. In either case the new higher land is eroded and the cycle recommences.

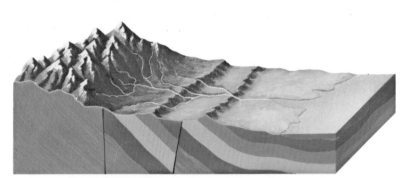

A Peneplain

Uplifted peneplain

Rivers

Rivers shape the land by three basic processes : erosion, transportation and deposition. A youthful river flows fast eroding downwards quickly to form a narrow valley (1) As it matures it deposits some debris and erodes laterally to widen the valley (2). In its last stage it meanders across a wide flat flood plain depositing fine particles of alluvium (3).

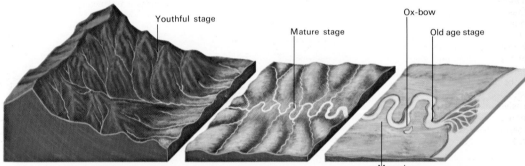

Youthful stage

Mature stage

Ox-bow

Old age stage

Meanders

Underground water

Water enters porous and permeable rocks from the surface moving downward until it reaches a layer of impermeable rock. Joints in underground rock, such as limestone, are eroded to form underground caves and caverns. When the roof of a cave collapses a gorge is formed. Surface entrances to joints are often widened to form vertical openings called swallow holes.

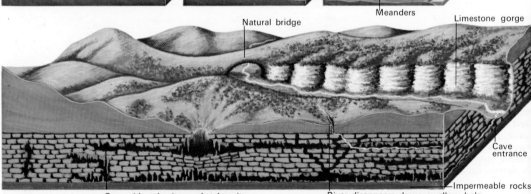
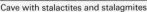

Natural bridge

Limestone gorge

Cave entrance

Cave with stalactites and stalagmites

River disappears down swallow hole

Impermeable rocks

Wind

Wind action is particularly powerful in arid and semi-arid regions where rock waste produced by weathering is used as an abrasive tool by the wind. The rate of erosion varies with the characteristics of the rock which can cause weird shapes and effects (right). Desert sand can also be accumulated by the wind to form barchan dunes (far right) which slowly travel forward, horns first.

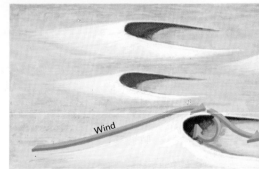

Wind

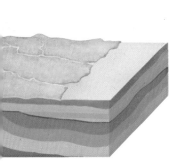

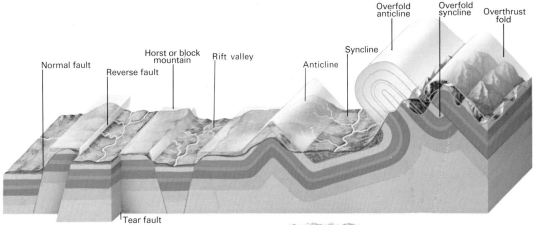

Normal fault · Reverse fault · Horst or block mountain · Rift valley · Anticline · Syncline · Overfold anticline · Overfold syncline · Overthrust fold

Tear fault

Folding and faulting

A vertical displacement in the earth's crust is called a fault or reverse fault; lateral displacement is a tear fault. An uplifted block is called a horst, the reverse of which is a rift valley. Compressed horizontal layers of sedimentary rock fold to form mountains. Those layers which bend up form an anticline, those bending down form a syncline : continued pressure forms an overfold.

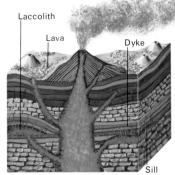

Laccolith · Lava · Dyke · Sill

Volcanic activity

When pressure on rocks below the earth's crust is released the normally semi-solid hot rock becomes liquid magma. The magma forces its way into cracks of the crust and may either reach the surface where it forms volcanoes or it may collect in the crust as sills dykes or laccoliths. When magma reaches the surface it cools to form lava.

Waves

Coasts are continually changing, some retreat under wave erosion while others advance with wave deposition. These actions combined form steep cliffs and wave cut platforms. Eroded debris is in turn deposited as a terrace. As the water becomes shallower the erosive power of the waves decreases and gradually the cliff disappears. Wave action can also create other features (far right).

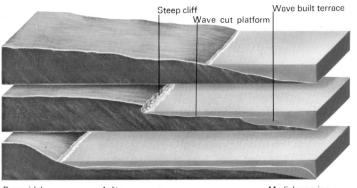

Steep cliff · Wave cut platform · Wave built terrace

Ice

These diagrams *(right)* show how a glaciated valley may have formed. The glacier deepens, straightens and widens the river valley whose interlocking spurs become truncated or cut off. Intervalley divides are frost shattered to form sharp aretes and pyramidal peaks. Hanging valleys mark the entry of tributary rivers and eroded rocks form medial moraine. Terminal moraine is deposited as the glacier retreats.

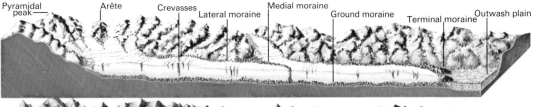

Pyramidal peak · Arête · Crevasses · Lateral moraine · Medial moraine · Ground moraine · Terminal moraine · Outwash plain

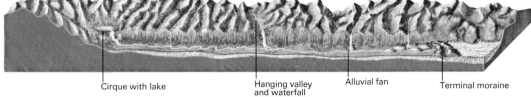

Cirque with lake · Hanging valley and waterfall · Alluvial fan · Terminal moraine

Subsidence and uplift

As the land surface is eroded it may eventually become a level plain - a peneplain, broken only by low hills, remnants of previous mountains. In turn this peneplain may be uplifted to form a plateau with steep edges. At the coast the uplifted wave platform becomes a coastal plain and in the rejuvenated rivers downward erosion once more predominates.

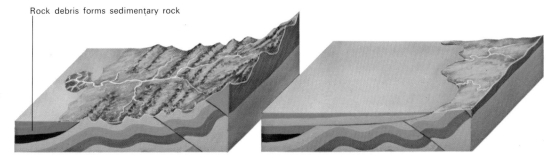

Rock debris forms sedimentary rock

The Earth: Physical Dimensions

Its surface

Highest point on the earth's
surface: Mt. Everest, Tibet -
Nepal boundary   8 848 m
Lowest point on the earth's
surface: The Dead Sea,
Jordan   below sea level 395 m
Greatest ocean depth.:
Challenger Deep, Mariana
Trench   11 022 m
Average height of land   840 m
Average depth of seas
and oceans   3 808 m

Dimensions

Superficial area	510 000 000 km²
Land surface	149 000 000 km²
Land surface as % of total area	29·2 %
Water surface	361 000 000 km²·
Water surface as % of total area	70·8 %
Equatorial circumference	40 077 km
Meridional circumference	40 009 km
Equatorial diameter	12 756·8 km
Polar diameter	12 713·8 km
Equatorial radius	6 378·4 km
Polar radius	6 356·9 km
Volume of the Earth	1 083 230 x 10⁶ km³
Mass of the Earth	5·9 x 10²¹ tonnes

The Figure of Earth

An imaginary sea-level surface is
considered and called a geoid. By
measuring at different places the
angles from plumb lines to a fixed
star there have been many
determinations of the shape of parts
of the geoid which is found to be an
oblate spheriod with its axis along
the axis of rotation of the earth.
Observations from satellites have
now given a new method of more
accurate determinations of the
figure of the earth and its local
irregularities.

Land and Sea Hemispheres.

About 85% of the total land area
is contained in the hemisphere
centred on a point between
Paris and Brussels.

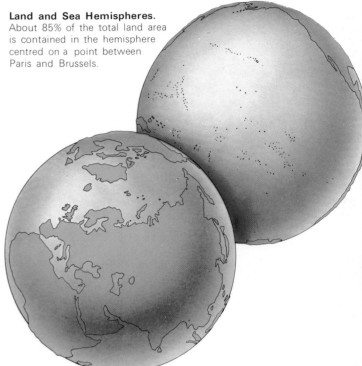

Oceans and Seas
Area in 1000 km²

Pacific Ocean	165 721	North Sea	575
Atlantic Ocean	81 660	Black Sea	448
Indian Ocean	73 442	Red Sea	440
Arctic Ocean	14 351	Baltic Sea	422
Mediterranean Sea	2 966	The Gulf	238
Bering Sea	2 274	St. Lawrence, Gulf of	236
Caribbean Sea	1 942	English Channel & Irish Sea	179
Mexico, Gulf of	1 813	California, Gulf of	161
Okhotsk, Sea of	1 528		
East China Sea	1 248		
Hudson Bay	1 230		
Japan, Sea of	1 049		

Lakes and Inland Seas
Areas in 1000 km²

Caspian Sea, Asia	424·2	Lake Ontario, N.America	19·5
Lake Superior, N.America	82·4	Lake Ladoga, Europe	18·4
Lake Victoria, Africa	69·5	Lake Balkhash, Asia	17·3
Aral Sea (Salt), Asia	63·8	Lake Maracaibo, S.America	16·3
Lake Huron, N.America	59·6	Lake Onega, Europe	9·8
Lake Michigan, N.America	58·0	Lake Eyre (Salt), Australia	9·6
Lake Tanganyika, Africa	32·9	Lake Turkana (Salt), Africa	9·1
Lake Baikal, Asia	31·5	Lake Titicaca, S.America	8·3
Great Bear Lake, N.America	31·1	Lake Nicaragua, C.America	8·0
Great Slave Lake, N.America	28·9	Lake Athabasca, N.America	7·9
Lake Nyasa, Africa	28·5	Reindeer Lake, N.America	6·3
Lake Erie, N.America	25·7	Issyk-Kul, Asia	6·2
Lake Winnipeg, N.America	24·3	Lake Torrens (Salt), Australia	6·1
Lake Chad, Africa	20·7	Koko Nor (Salt), Asia	6·0
		Lake Urmia, Asia	6·0
		Vänern, Europe	5·6

Longest rivers

	km.
Nile, Africa	6 690
Amazon, S.America	6 280
Mississippi-Missouri,N.America	6 270
Yangtze, Asia	4 990
Zaïre, Africa	4 670
Amur. Asia	4 410
Hwang Ho (Yellow), Asia	4 350
Lena, Asia	4 260
Mekong, Asia	4 180
Niger, Africa	4 180
Mackenzie, N.America	4 040
Ob, Asia	4 000
Yenisei, Asia	3 800

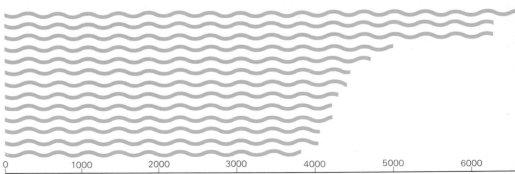

0	1000	2000	3000	4000	5000	6000

The Highest Mountains and the Greatest Depths.

Mount Everest defied the world's greatest mountaineers for 32 years and claimed the lives of many men. Not until 1920 was permission granted by the Dalai Lama to attempt the mountain, and the first successful ascent came in 1953. Since then the summit has been reached several times. The world's highest peaks have now been climbed but there are many as yet unexplored peaks in the Himalayas some of which may be over 7600 m

The greatest trenches are the Puerto Rico deep (9200 m). The Tonga (10 822 m) and Mindanao (10 497 m) trenches and the Mariana Trench (11 022 m) in the Pacific. The trenches represent less than 2% of the total area of the sea-bed but are of great interest as lines of structural weakness in the Earth's crust and as areas of frequent earthquakes.

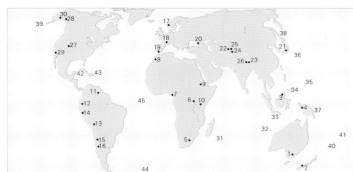

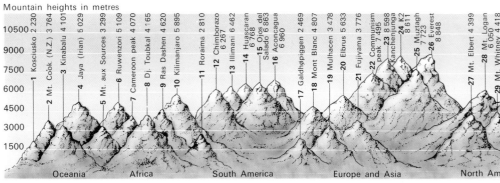

Mountain heights in metres

1 Kosciusko 2 230 · 2 Mt. Cook (N.Z.) 3 764 · 3 Kinabalu 4 101 · 4 Jaya (Irian) 5 029 · 5 Mt. aux Sources 3 299 · 6 Ruwenzori 5 109 · 7 Cameroon peak 4 070 · 8 Dj. Toubkal 4 165 · 9 Ras Dashen 4 620 · 10 Kilimanjaro 5 895 · 11 Roraima 2 810 · 12 Chimborazo 6 267 · 13 Illiman 6 462 · 14 Huascaran 6 768 · 15 Ojos del Salado 6 863 · 16 Aconcagua 6 960 · 17 Galdhøpiggen 2 469 · 18 Mont Blanc 4 807 · 19 Mulhacen 3 478 · 20 Elbrus 5 633 · 21 Fujiyama 3 776 · 22 Communism peak 7 495 · 23 Kanchenjunga 8 598 · 24 K2 8 611 · 25 Muztagh 7 723 · 26 Everest 8 848 · 27 Mt. Elbert 4 399 · 28 Mt. Logan 6 050 · 29 Mt. Whitney 4 418 · 30 Mt. McKinley 6 194

Oceania — Africa — South America — Europe and Asia — North America

Ocean depths in metres — Sea level

31 Mauritius basin 6 400 · 32 W. Australian basin 6 459 · 33 Java trench 7 450 · 34 Mindanao trench 10 497 · 35 Mariana trench 11 022 · 36 Japan trench 10 554 · 37 Bougainville deep 9 140 · 38 Kuril trench 10 542 · 39 Aleutian trench 7 822 · 40 Kermadec trench 10 047 · 41 Tonga trench 10 822 · 42 Cayman trough 7 680 · 43 Puerto Rico trough 9 200 · 44 S. Sandwich trench 8 428 · 45 Romanche deep 7 758

Indian Ocean — Pacific Ocean — Atlantic Ocean

High mountains

Bathyscaphe

Waterfall

Dam

Notable Waterfalls heights in metres

Angel, Venezuela	980
Tugela, S. Africa	853
Mongefossen, Norway	774
Yosemite, California	738
Mardalsfossen, Norway	655
Cuquenan, Venezuela	610
Sutherland, N.Z.	579
Reichenbach, Switzerland	548
Wollomombi, Australia	518
Ribbon, California	491
Gavarnie, France	422
Tyssefallene, Norway	414
Krimml, Austria	370
King George VI, Guyana	366
Silver Strand, California	356
Geissbach, Switzerland	350
Staubbach, Switzerland	299
Trümmelbach, Switzerland	290
Chirombo, Zambia	268
Livingstone, Zaïre	259
King Edward VIII, Guyana	256
Gersoppa, India	253
Vettifossen Norway	250
Kalambo, Zambia	240
Kaieteur, Guyana	226
Maletsunyane, Lesotho	192
Terui, Italy	180
Kabarega, Uganda	122
Victoria, Zimbabwe-Zambia	107
Cauvery, India	97
Boyoma, Zaïre	61
Niagara, N.America	51
Schaffhausen, Switzerland	30

Notable Dams heights in metres

Africa

Cabora Bassa, Zambezi R.	168
Akosombo Main Dam, Volta R.	141
Kariba, Zambezi R.	128
Aswan High Dam, Nile R.	110

Asia

Nurek, Vakhsh R., U.S.S.R.	317
Bhakra, Sutlej R., India	226
Kurobegawa, Kurobe R., Jap.	186
Charvak, Chirchik R., U.S.S.R.	168
Okutadami, Tadami R., Jap.	157
Bratsk, Angara R., U.S.S.R.	125

Oceania

Warragamba, N.S.W., Australia	137
Eucumbene, N.S.W., Australia	116

Europe

Grande Dixence, Switz.	284
Vajont, Vajont, R., Italy	261
Mauvoisin, Drance R., Switz.	237
Contra, Verzasca R., Switz.	230
Luzzone, Brenno R., Switz.	208
Tignes, Isère R., France	180
Amir Kabir, Karadj R., U.S.S.R.	180
Vidraru, Arges R., Rom.	165
Kremasta, Acheloos R., Greece	165

North America

Mica, Columbia R., Can.	242
Oroville, Feather R.,	235
Hoover, Colorado R.,	221
Glen Canyon, Colorado R.,	216
Daniel Johnson, Can.	214
New Bullards Bar, N. Yuba R.	194
Mossyrock, Cowlitz R.,	184
Shasta, Sacramento R.,	183
W.A.C. Bennett, Canada.	183
Don Pedro, Tuolumne R.,	178
Grand Coulee, Columbia R.,	168

Central and South America

Guri, Caroni R., Venezuela.	106

Distances

Kms

(Lower-left triangle values are in Kms; upper-right triangle values are in miles. Diagonal = city name.)

	Berlin	Bombay	Buenos Aires	Cairo	Calcutta	Caracas	Chicago	Copenhagen	Darwin	Hong Kong	Honolulu	Johannesburg	Lagos	Lisbon
Berlin	—	3907	7400	1795	4370	5241	4402	222	8044	5440	7310	5511	3230	1436
Bombay	6288	—	9275	2706	1034	9024	8048	3990	4510	2683	8024	4334	4730	4982
Buenos Aires	11909	14925	—	7341	10268	3167	5599	7498	9130	11481	7558	5025	4919	5964
Cairo	2890	4355	11814	—	3541	6340	6127	1992	7216	5064	8838	3894	2432	2358
Calcutta	7033	1664	16524	5699	—	9609	7978	4395	3758	1653	7048	5256	5727	5639
Caracas	8435	14522	5096	10203	15464	—	2502	5215	11221	10166	6009	6847	4810	4044
Chicago	7084	12953	9011	3206	12839	4027	—	4250	9361	7783	4247	8689	5973	3992
Copenhagen	357	6422	12067	9860	7072	8392	6840	—	8017	5388	7088	5732	3436	1540
Darwin	12946	7257	14693	11612	6047	18059	15065	12903	—	2654	5369	6611	8837	9391
Hong Kong	8754	4317	18478	8150	2659	16360	12526	8671	4271	—	5543	6669	7360	6853
Honolulu	11764	12914	12164	14223	11343	9670	6836	11407	8640	8921	—	11934	10133	7821
Johannesburg	8870	6974	8088	6267	8459	11019	13984	9225	10639	10732	19206	—	2799	5089
Lagos	5198	7612	7916	3915	9216	7741	9612	5530	14222	11845	16308	4505	—	2360
Lisbon	2311	8018	9600	3794	9075	6501	6424	2478	15114	11028	12587	8191	3799	—
London	928	7190	11131	3508	7961	7507	6356	952	13848	9623	11632	9071	5017	1588
Los Angeles	9311	14000	9852	12200	13120	5812	2804	9003	12695	11639	4117	16676	12414	9122
Mexico City	9732	15656	7389	12372	15280	3586	2726	9514	14631	14122	6085	14585	11071	8676
Moscow	1610	5031	13477	2902	5534	9938	8000	1561	11350	7144	11323	9161	6254	3906
Nairobi	6370	4532	10402	3536	6179	11544	12883	6706	10415	8776	17282	2927	3807	6461
New York	6385	12541	8526	9020	12747	3430	1145	6188	16047	12950	7980	12841	8477	5422
Paris	876	7010	11051	3210	7858	7625	6650	1026	13812	9630	11968	8732	4714	1454
Peking	7822	4757	19268	7544	3269	14399	10603	7202	6011	1963	8160	11710	11457	9668
Reykjavik	2385	8335	11437	5266	8687	6915	4757	2103	13892	9681	9787	10938	6718	2948
Rio de Janeiro	10025	13409	1953	9896	15073	4546	8547	10211	16011	17704	13342	7113	6035	7734
Rome	1180	6175	11151	2133	7219	8363	7739	1531	13265	9284	12916	7743	4039	1861
Singapore	9944	3914	15879	8267	2897	18359	15078	9969	3349	2599	10816	8660	11145	11886
Sydney	16096	10160	11800	14418	9138	15343	14875	16042	3150	7374	8168	11040	15519	18178
Tokyo	8924	6742	18362	9571	5141	14164	10137	8696	5431	2874	6202	13547	13480	11149
Toronto	6497	12488	9093	9233	12561	3873	700	6265	15498	12569	7465	13374	8948	5737
Wellington	18140	12370	9981	16524	11354	13122	13451	17961	5325	9427	7513	11761	16050	19575

City	Mexico City	Moscow	Nairobi	New York	Paris	Peking	Reykjavik	Rio de Janeiro	Rome	Singapore	Sydney	Tokyo	Toronto	Wellington
Berlin	6047	1000	3958	3967	545	4860	1482	6230	734	6179	10002	5545	4037	11272
Bombay	9728	3126	2816	7793	4356	2956	5179	8332	3837	2432	6313	4189	7760	7686
Buenos Aires	4591	8374	6463	5298	6867	11972	7106	1214	6929	9867	7332	11410	5650	6202
Cairo	7687	1803	2197	5605	1994	4688	3272	6149	1325	5137	8959	5947	5737	10268
Calcutta	9494	3438	3839	7921	4883	2031	5398	9366	4486	1800	5678	3195	7805	7055
Caracas	2228	6175	7173	2131	4738	8947	4297	2825	5196	11407	9534	8801	2406	8154
Chicago	1694	4971	8005	711	4132	6588	2956	5311	4809	9369	9243	6299	435	8358
Copenhagen	5912	970	4167	3845	638	4475	1306	6345	951	6195	9968	5403	3892	11160
Darwin	9091	7053	6472	9971	8582	3735	8632	9948	8243	2081	1957	3375	9630	3309
Hong Kong	8775	4439	5453	8047	5984	1220	6015	11001	5769	1615	4582	1786	7810	5857
Honolulu	3781	7036	10739	4958	7437	5070	6081	8290	8026	6721	5075	3854	4638	4669
Johannesburg	9063	5692	1818	7979	5426	7276	6797	4420	4811	5381	6860	8418	8310	7308
Lagos	6879	3886	2366	5268	2929	7119	4175	3750	2510	6925	9643	8376	5560	9973
Lisbon	5391	2427	4015	3369	903	6007	1832	4805	1157	7385	11295	6928	3565	12163
London	5552	1552	4237	3463	212	5057	1172	5778	889	6743	10558	5942	3545	11691
Los Angeles	1549	6070	9659	2446	5645	6251	4310	6310	6331	8776	7502	5475	2170	6719
Mexico City		6664	9207	2090	5717	7742	4635	4780	6365	10321	8058	7024	2018	6897
Moscow			3942	4666	1545	3600	2053	7184	1477	5237	9008	4651	4637	10283
Nairobi				7358	4029	5727	5395	5548	3350	4635	7552	6996	7570	8490
New York					3626	6828	2613	4832	4280	9531	9935	6741	356	8951
Paris						5106	1384	5708	687	6671	10539	6038	3738	11798
Peking	10724						4897	10773	5049	2783	5561	1304	6557	6700
Reykjavik	14818	6344						6135	2048	7155	10325	5469	2600	10725
Rio de Janeiro	3364	7510	11842						5725	9763	8389	11551	5180	7367
Rome	9200	2486	6485	5836						6229	10143	6127	4399	11523
Singapore	12460	5794	9216	10988	8217						3915	3306	9350	5298
Sydney	7460	3304	8683	4206	2228	7882						4861	9800	1383
Tokyo	7693	11562	8928	7777	9187	17338	9874						6410	5762
Toronto	10243	2376	5391	6888	1105	8126	3297	9214						8820
Wellington	16610	8428	7460	15339	10737	4478	11514	15712	10025					
	12969	14497	12153	15989	16962	8949	16617	13501	16324	6300				
	11304	7485	11260	10849	9718	2099	8802	18589	9861	5321	7823			
	3247	7462	12183	574	6015	10552	4184	8336	7080	15047	15772	10316		
	11100	16549	13664	14405	18987	10782	17260	11855	18545	8526	2226	9273	14194	

Miles

Water Resources and Vegetation

Water resources and vegetation

Fresh water is essential for life on earth and in some parts of the world it is a most precious commodity. On the other hand it is very easy for industrialised temperate states to take its existence for granted, and man's increasing demand may only be met finally by the desalination of earth's 1250 million cubic kilometres of salt water. 70% of the earth's fresh water exists as ice.

The hydrological cycle

Water is continually being absorbed into the atmosphere as vapour from oceans, lakes, rivers and vegetation transpiration. On cooling the vapour either condenses or freezes and falls as rain, hail or snow. Most precipitation falls over the sea but one quarter falls over the land of which half evaporates again soon after falling while the rest flows back into the oceans.

Distribution of water

Oceans and seas 97·29%
Ice caps and glaciers 2·09%
Underground aquifers 0·6054%
Lakes and rivers 0·01362%
Atmosphere 0·00094%
Biosphere 0·00004%

Tundra

Mediterranean scrub

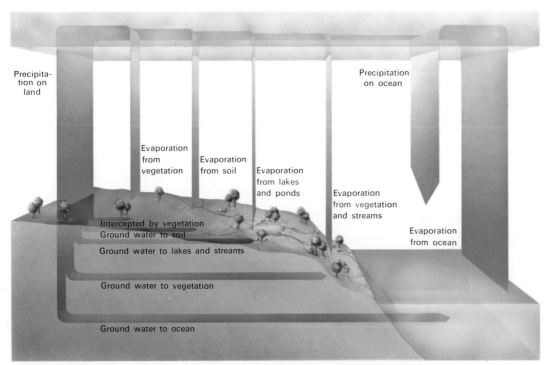

Precipitation on land

Precipitation on ocean

Evaporation from vegetation

Evaporation from soil

Evaporation from lakes and ponds

Evaporation from vegetation and streams

Evaporation from ocean

Intercepted by vegetation
Ground water to soil

Ground water to lakes and streams

Ground water to vegetation

Ground water to ocean

Domestic consumption of water

An area's level of industrialisation, climate and standard of living are all major influences in the consumption of water. On average Europe consumes 636 litres per head each day of which 180 litres is used domestically. In the U.S.A. domestic consumption is slightly higher at 270 litres per day. The graph (right) represents domestic consumption in the U.K.

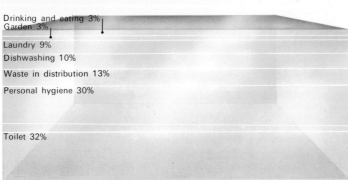

Drinking and eating 3%
Garden 3%
Laundry 9%
Dishwashing 10%
Waste in distribution 13%
Personal hygiene 30%
Toilet 32%

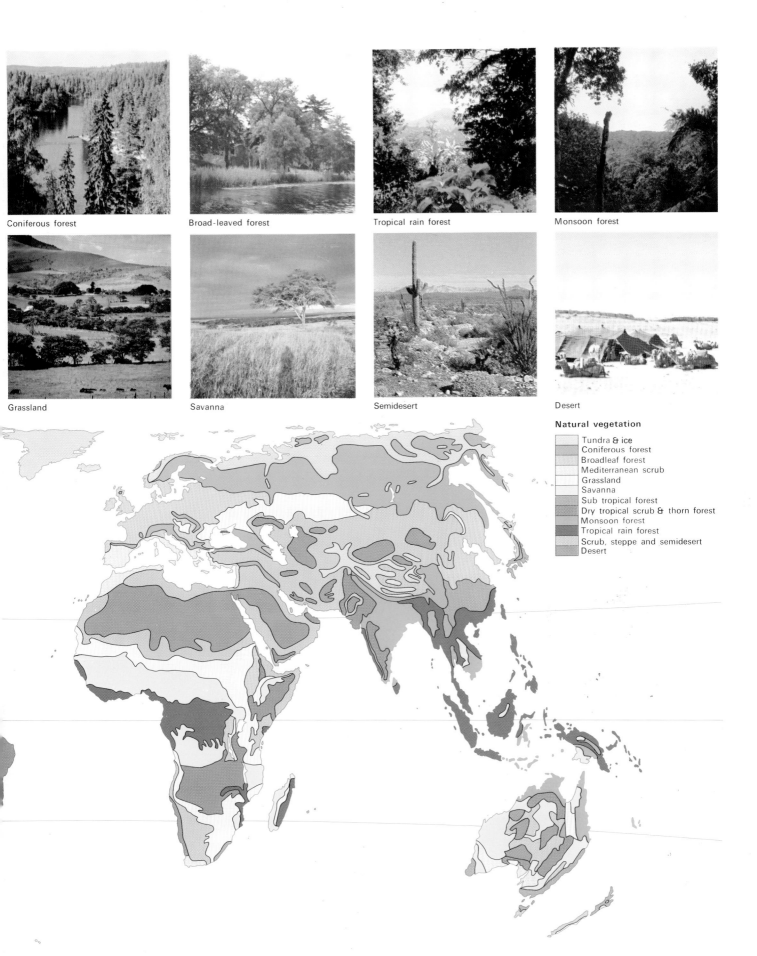

Coniferous forest

Broad-leaved forest

Tropical rain forest

Monsoon forest

Grassland

Savanna

Semidesert

Desert

Natural vegetation

Tundra & ice
Coniferous forest
Broadleaf forest
Mediterranean scrub
Grassland
Savanna
Sub tropical forest
Dry tropical scrub & thorn forest
Monsoon forest
Tropical rain forest
Scrub, steppe and semidesert
Desert

Population

Population distribution
(right and lower right)
People have always been unevenly distributed in the world. Europe has for centuries contained nearly 20% of the world's population but after the 16-19th century explorations and consequent migrations this proportion has rapidly reduced. In 1750 the Americas had 2% of the world's total: in 2000 AD they are expected to contain 16%.

The most densely populated regions are in India, China and Europe where the average density is between 100 and 200 per square km. although there are pockets of extremely high density elsewhere. In contrast Australia has only 1·5 people per square km. The countries in the lower map have been redrawn to make their areas proportional to their populations.

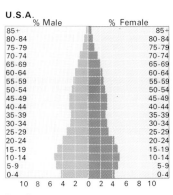

U.S.A.

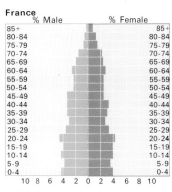

France

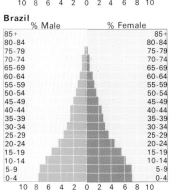

Brazil

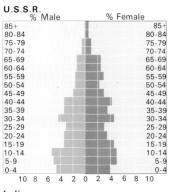

U.S.S.R.

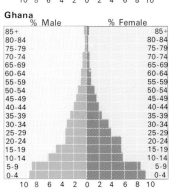

Ghana

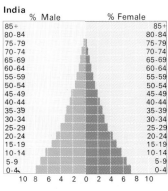

India

Age distribution
France shows many demographic features characteristic of European countries. Birth and death rates have declined with a moderate population growth - there are nearly as many old as young. In contrast, India and several other countries have few old and many young because of the high death rates and even higher birth rates. It is this excess that is responsible for the world's population explosion.

World population increase
Until comparatively recently there was little increase in the population of the world. About 6000 BC it is thought that there were about 200 million people and in the following 7000years an increase of just over 100 million. In the 1800's there were about 1000 million; at present there are over 4500 million and by the year 2000 if present trends continue there would be at least 6100 million.

1650 1700 1750 1800

World population distribution

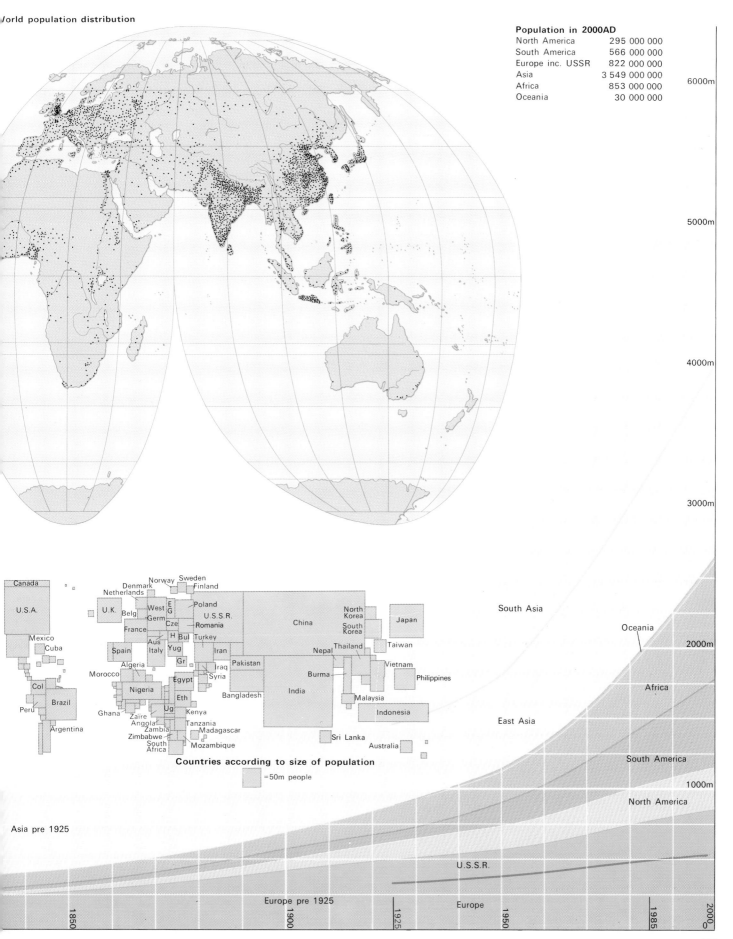

Population in 2000AD	
North America	295 000 000
South America	566 000 000
Europe inc. USSR	822 000 000
Asia	3 549 000 000
Africa	853 000 000
Oceania	30 000 000

6000m

5000m

4000m

3000m

Canada

U.S.A.

Mexico
Cuba

Col
Peru   Brazil

Argentina

Norway Sweden
Denmark Finland
Netherlands
U.K. Belg West E Poland
Germ G
France Cze U.S.S.R.
Romania
Spain Aus H Bul Turkey
Italy Yug
Algeria Gr
Morocco Iran Pakistan
Egypt Iraq
Syria
Nigeria Bangladesh
Ghana Eth India
Zaire Ug Kenya
Angola Tanzania
Zambia Madagascar
Zimbabwe
South Mozambique
Africa

China

North
Korea
South
Korea

Japan

Taiwan

Nepal Thailand
Burma Vietnam
Philippines

Malaysia

Indonesia

Sri Lanka

Australia

South Asia

Oceania 2000m

Africa

East Asia

South America

1000m

North America

Countries according to size of population

=50m people

Asia pre 1925

U.S.S.R.

Europe pre 1925   Europe

1850   1900   1925   1950   1985 2000
0

Language

Languages may be blamed partly for the division and lack of understanding between nations. While a common language binds countries together it in turn isolates them from other countries and groups. Thus beliefs, ideas and inventions remain exclusive to these groups and different cultures develop.

There are thousands of different languages and dialects spoken today. This can cause strife even within the one country, such as India, where different dialects are enough to break down the country into distinct groups.

As a result of colonization and the spread of internationally accepted languages, many countries have superimposed a completely unrelated language in order to combine isolated national groups and to facilitate international understanding, for example Spanish in South America, English in India.

Related languages

Certain languages showing marked similarities are thought to have developed from common parent languages for example Latin. After the retreat of the Roman Empire wherever Latin had been firmly established it remained as the new nation's language. With no unifying centre divergent development took place and Latin evolved into new languages.

Calligraphy

Writing was originally by a series of pictures, and these gradually developed in styles which were influenced by the tools generally used. Carved alphabets, such as that used by the Sumerians, tended to be angular, while those painted or written tended to be curved, as in Egyptian hieroglyphics development of which can be followed through the West Semitic, Greek and Latin alphabets to our own.

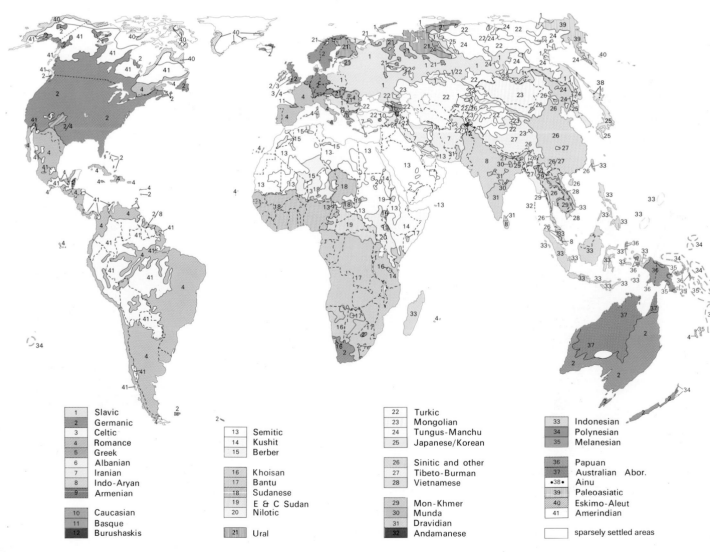

1	Slavic	22	Turkic
2	Germanic	23	Mongolian
3	Celtic	24	Tungus-Manchu
4	Romance	25	Japanese/Korean
5	Greek		
6	Albanian	26	Sinitic and other
7	Iranian	27	Tibeto-Burman
8	Indo-Aryan	28	Vietnamese
9	Armenian		
		29	Mon-Khmer
10	Caucasian	30	Munda
11	Basque	31	Dravidian
12	Burushaskis	32	Andamanese
13	Semitic	33	Indonesian
14	Kushit	34	Polynesian
15	Berber	35	Melanesian
16	Khoisan	36	Papuan
17	Bantu	37	Australian Abor.
18	Sudanese	•38•	Ainu
19	E & C Sudan	39	Paleoasiatic
20	Nilotic	40	Eskimo-Aleut
21	Ural	41	Amerindian
			sparsely settled areas

Religion

Throughout history man has had beliefs in supernatural powers based on the forces of nature which have developed into worship of a god and some cases gods.

Hinduism honours many gods and goddesses which are all manifestations of the one divine spirit, Brahma, and incorporates beliefs such as reincarnation, worship of cattle and the caste system.

Buddhism, an offshoot of Hinduism, was founded in north east India by Gautama Buddha (563-483 BC) who taught that spiritual and moral discipline were essential to achieve supreme peace.

Confucianism is a mixture of Buddhism and Confucius' teachings which were elaborated to provide a moral basis for the political structure of Imperial China and to cover the already existing forms of ancestor worship.

Judaism dates back to c. 13th century B.C. The Jews were expelled from the Holy Land in AD70 and only reinstated in Palestine in 1948.

Christian monastery

Jewish holy place

Hindu temple

Islam, founded in Mecca by Muhammad (570-632 AD) spread across Asia and Africa and in its retreat left isolated pockets of adherent communities.

Christianity was founded by Jesus of Nazareth in the 1st century AD The Papal authority, established in the 4th century, was rejected by Eastern churches in the 11th century. Later several other divisions developed eg. Roman Catholicism, Protestantism.

Mohammedan mosque

Buddhist temple

- Roman Catholicism
- Orthodox and other Eastern Churches
- Protestantism
- Sunni Islam
- Shiah Islam
- Buddhism
- Hinduism
- Confucianism
- Judaism
- Shintoism
- Primitive religions
- Uninhabited

The Growth of Cities

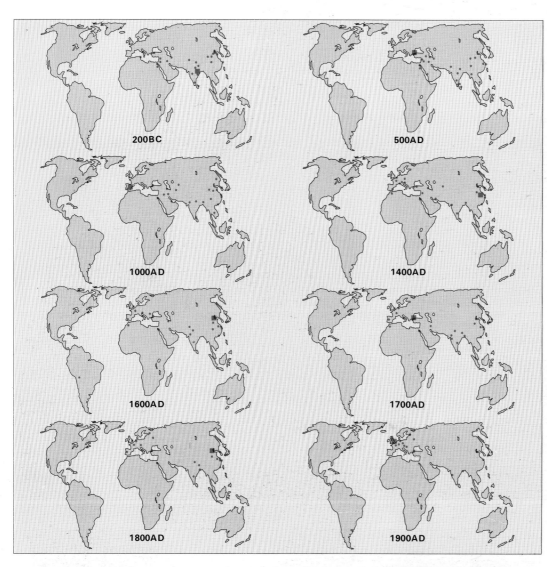

200BC

500AD

1000AD

1400AD

1600AD

1700AD

1800AD

1900AD

Sao Paulo

Increase in urbanisation
The increase in urbanisation is a result primarily of better sanitation and health resulting in the growth of population and secondarily to the movement of man off the land into industry and service occupations in the cities. Generally the most highly developed industrial nations are the most intensely urbanised although exceptions such as Norway and Switzerland show that rural industrialisation can exist.

Increase in urbanisation
The figures on the vertical columns show the urban population as a percentage of the total population for each country in the year shown.

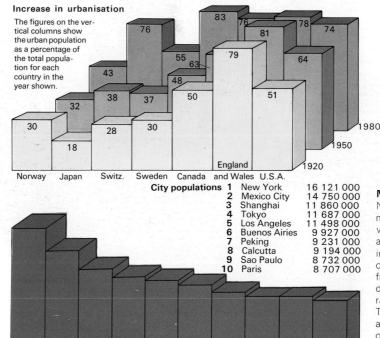

Norway   Japan   Switz.   Sweden   Canada and Wales   U.S.A.
England
1980
1950
1920

Metropolitan areas
A metropolitan area can be defined as a central city linked with surrounding communities by continuous built-up areas controlled by one municipal government. With improved communications the neighbouring communities generally continue to provide the city's work-force. The graph (right) compares the total populations of the world's ten largest cities.

City populations		
1	New York	16 121 000
2	Mexico City	14 750 000
3	Shanghai	11 860 000
4	Tokyo	11 687 000
5	Los Angeles	11 498 000
6	Buenos Airies	9 927 000
7	Peking	9 231 000
8	Calcutta	9 194 000
9	Sao Paulo	8 732 000
10	Paris	8 707 000

Major cities
Normally these are not only major centres of population and wealth but also of political power and trade. They are the sites of international airports and characteristically are great ports from which imported goods are distributed using the roads and railways which focus on the city. Their staple trades and industries are varied and flexible and depend on design and fashion rather than raw material production.

30

York

Sydney

Moscow

Tokyo

Hong Kong

Bombay

London

Cairo

Rio de Janeiro

Rome

Cities over 5 000 000 inhabitants

2 000 000-5 000 000 inhabitants

1 000 000-2 000 000 inhabitants

250 000-1 000 000 inhabitants

Food Resources: Vegetable

Cocoa, tea , coffee
These tropical or sub-tropical crops are grown mainly for export to the economically advanced countries. Tea and coffee are the world's principal beverages. Cocoa is used more in the manufacture of chocolate.

Cocoa
Tea
Coffee

Cocoa
Tea
Coffee

Sugar beet, sugar cane
Cane Sugar - a tropical crop - accounts for the bulk of the sugar entering into international trade. Beet Sugar, on the other hand, demands a temperate climate and is produced primarily for domestic consumption.

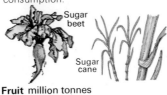
Sugar beet
Sugar cane

Sugar beet
Sugar cane

Fruit million tonnes

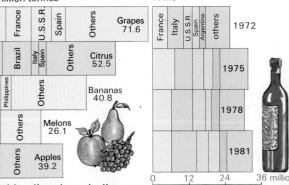

					Grapes 71.6
Italy	France	U.S.S.R.	Spain	Others	
U.S.A.	Brazil	Italy/Spain	Others		Citrus 52.5
Brazil	India	Philippines	Others		Bananas 40.8
China	Turkey	U.S.S.R.	Others		Melons 26.1
U.S.S.R.	U.S.A.	Others			Apples 39.2

Wine

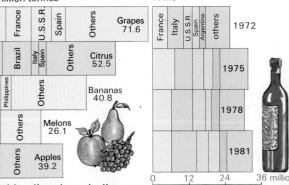

France / Italy / U.S.S.R. / Spain / Argentina / others

1972
1975
1978
1981

0   12   24   36 million tonnes

Vegetable oilseeds and oils
Despite the increasing use of synthetic chemical products and animal and marine fats, vegetable oils extracted from these crops grow in quantity, value and importance. Food is the major use- in margarine and cooking fats.

Groundnut
Soya bean

Groundnuts are also a valuable subsistence crop and the meal is used as animal feed. Soya-bean meal is a growing source of protein for humans and animals. The Mediterranean lands are the prime source of olive oil.

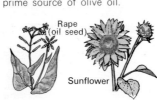
Rape (oil seed)
Sunflower

Fruit, wine
With the improvements in canning, drying and freezing, and in transport and marketing, the international trade and consumption of deciduous and soft fruits, citrus fruits and tropical fruits has greatly increased. Recent developments in the use of the peel will give added value to some of the fruit crops.

Over 80% of grapes are grown for wine and over a half in countries bordering the Mediterranean.

Groundnuts
Soya beans

Rape seed
Sunflower seed

Cereals
Cereals include those members of the grain family with starchy edible seeds - wheat, maize, barley, oats, rye, rice, millets and sorghums.

Cereals and potatoes (not a cereal but starch-producing) are the principal source of food for our modern civilisations because of their high yield in bulk and food value per unit of land and labour required. They are also easy to store and transport, and provide food also for animals producing meat, fat, milk and eggs. Wheat is the principal bread grain of the temperate regions in which potatoe are the next most important food source. Rice is the principal cereal in the hotter. humid regions. especially in Asia. Oats, barley and maize are grown mainly for animal feed; millets and sorghums as main subsistence crops in Africa and India.

Maize (or Corn) Needs plenty of sunshine, summer rain or irrigation and frost free for 6 months. Important as animal feed and for human food in Africa, Latin America and as a vegetable and breakfast cereal.

World production 339·8 million tonnes

Barley  Has the widest range of cultivation requiring only 8 weeks between seed time and harvest. Used mainly as animal-feed and by the malting industry.

World production 169·3 million tonnes

Oats  Widely grown in temperate regions with the limit fixed by early autumn frosts. Mainly fed to cattle. The best quality oats are used for oatmeal, porridge and breakfast foods.

World production 43·8 million tonnes

Rice  Needs plains or terraces which can be flooded and abundant water in the growing season. The staple food of half the human race. In the husk, it is known as paddy.

World production 427·2 million tonnes

Wheat 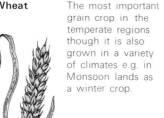 The most important grain crop in the temperate regions though it is also grown in a variety of climates e.g. in Monsoon lands as a winter crop.

World production 495·6 million tonnes

Rye 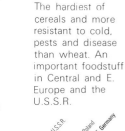 The hardiest of cereals and more resistant to cold, pests and disease than wheat. An important foodstuff in Central and E. Europe and the U.S.S.R.

World production 30·8 million tonnes

Millets  The name given to a number of related members of the grass family, of which sorghum is one of the most important. They provide nutritious grain.

World production 95·6 million tonnes

Potato An important food crop though less nutritious weight for weight than grain crops.

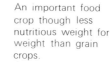

World production 258·8 million tonnes

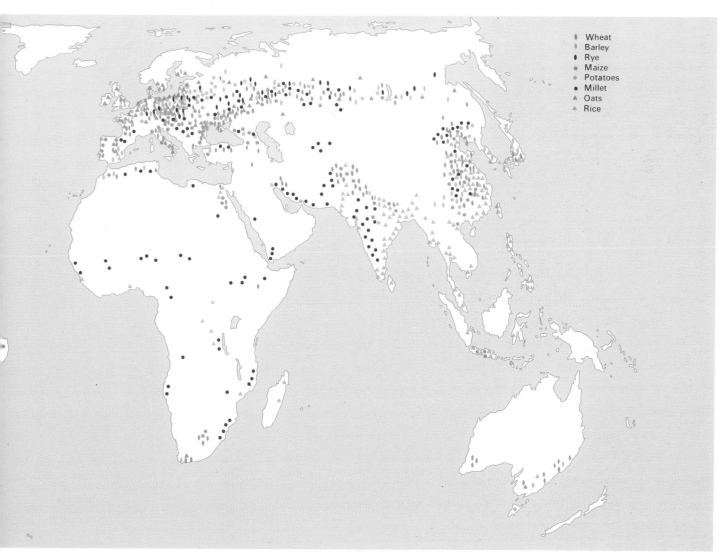

- ◆ Wheat
- ◆ Barley
- ◆ Rye
- ● Maize
- ● Potatoes
- ● Millet
- ▲ Oats
- ▲ Rice

Food Resources: Animal

Food resources: Animal
Meat, milk and allied foods are prime protein-providers and are also sources of essential vitamins. Meat is mainly a product of continental and savannah grasslands and the cool west coasts, particularly in Europe. Milk and cheese, eggs and fish - though found in some quantity throughout the world - are primarily a product of the temperate zones.

Beef cattle Australia, New Zealand and Argentina provide the major part of international beef exports. Western U S.A. and Europe have considerable production of beef for their local high demand.

World production 1002 million head

Dairy Cattle The need of herds for a rich diet and for nearby markets result in dairying being characteristic of densely-populated areas of the temperate zones - U.S.A., N.W. Europe, N. Zealand and S.E. Australia.

World production 224·0 million head

Cheese The principal producers are the U.S.A., W. Europe, U.S.S.R., and New Zealand with principal exporters Netherlands, New Zealand, Denmark and France.

World production 12·0 million tonn

Sheep Raised mostly for wool and meat, the skins and cheese from their milk are important products in some countries. The merino yields a fine wool and crossbreds are best for meat.

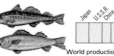
World production 1157·7 million head

Pigs Can be reared in most climates from monsoon to cool temperate. They are abundant in China, the corn belt of the U.S.A. N.W. and C. Europe, Brazil and U.S.S.R.

World production 763·8 million head

Fish Commercial fishing requires large shoals of fish of one species within reach of markets. Freshwater fishing is also important. A rich source of protein, fish will become an increasingly valuable food source.

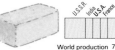
World production 74·8 million tonnes

Butter (includes Ghee) The biggest producers are U.S.S.R., India, U.S.A. and France.

World production 7·3 million tonne

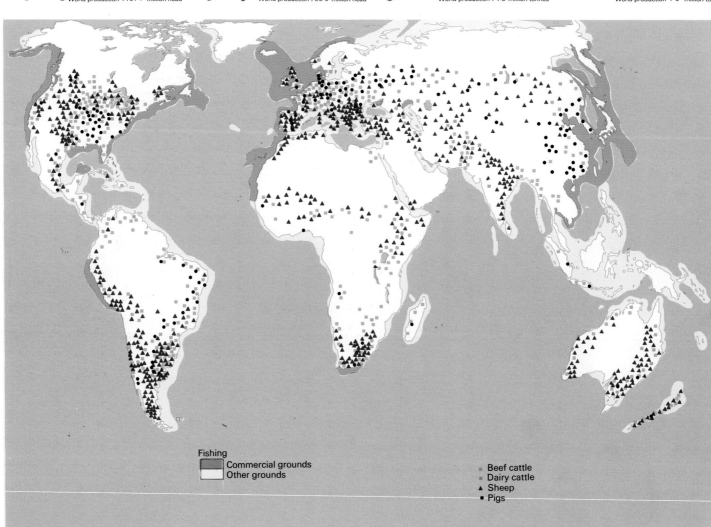

Fishing
Commercial grounds
Other grounds

■ Beef cattle
■ Dairy cattle
▲ Sheep
● Pigs

Nutrition

Foodstuffs fall, nutritionally, into three groups - providers of energy, protein and vitamins. Cereals and oil-seeds provide energy and second-class protein'; milk, meat and allied foods provide protein and vitamins, fruit and vegetables provide vitamins, especially Vitamin C, and some energy. To avoid malnutrition, a minimum level of these three groups of foodstuffs is required: the maps and diagrams show how unfortunately widespread are low standards of nutrition and even malnutrition.

Comparison of daily diets

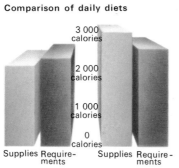

3 000 calories
2 000 calories
1 000 calories
0 calories

Supplies Requirements — Far East, Near East, Africa & Latin America

Supplies Requirements — Europe, Oceania & North America

Malnutrition

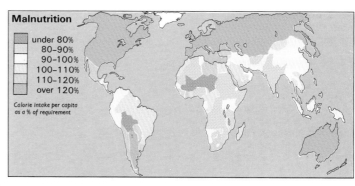

- under 80%
- 80–90%
- 90–100%
- 100–110%
- 110–120%
- over 120%

Calorie intake per capita as a % of requirement

Proportions of calories

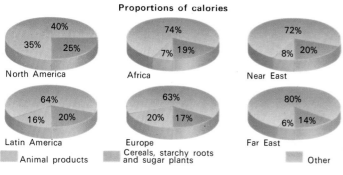

North America — 40% / 35% / 25%

Africa — 74% / 7% / 19%

Near East — 72% / 8% / 20%

Latin America — 64% / 16% / 20%

Europe — 63% / 20% / 17%

Far East — 80% / 6% / 14%

- Animal products
- Cereals, starchy roots and sugar plants
- Other

People and tractors engaged in agriculture

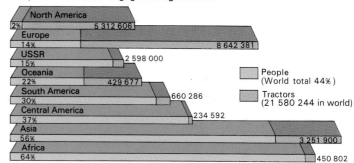

Region	%	Value
North America	2%	5 312 606
Europe	14%	8 642 381
USSR	15%	2 598 000
Oceania	22%	429 677
South America	30%	660 286
Central America	37%	234 592
Asia	56%	3 251 900
Africa	64%	450 802

- People (World total 44%)
- Tractors (21 580 244 in world)

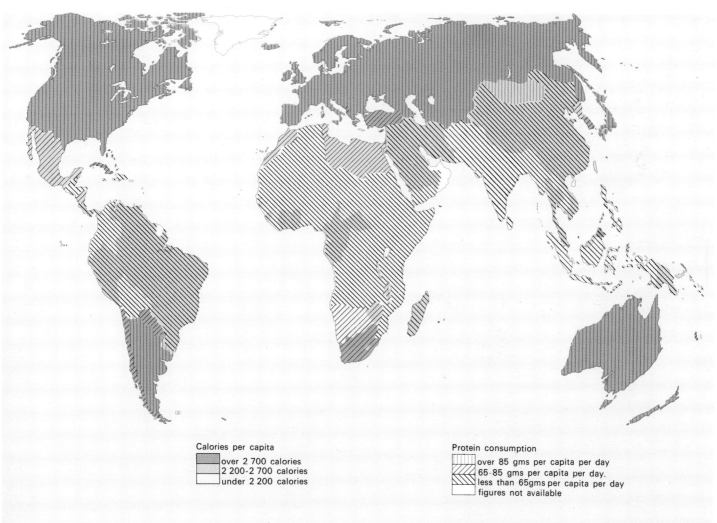

Calories per capita
- over 2 700 calories
- 2 200-2 700 calories
- under 2 200 calories

Protein consumption
- over 85 gms per capita per day
- 65-85 gms per capita per day.
- less than 65gms per capita per day
- figures not available

Mineral Resources I

Primitive man used iron for tools and vessels and its use extended gradually until iron, and later steel, became the backbone of the Modern World with the Industrial Revolution in the late 18th Century. At first, local ores were used, whereas today richer iron ores in huge deposits have been discovered and are mined on a large scale, often far away from the areas where they are used; for example, in Western Australia, Northern Sweden, Venezuela and Liberia. Iron smelting plants are today increasingly located at coastal sites, where the large ore carriers can easily discharge their cargo.

Steel is refined iron with the addition of other minerals, ferro-alloys, giving to the steel their own special properties; for example, resistance to corrosion (chromium, nickel, cobalt), hardness (tungsten, vanadium), elasticity (molybdenum), magnetic properties (cobalt), high tensile strength (manganese) and high ductility (molybdenum).

Production of Ferro-alloy metals

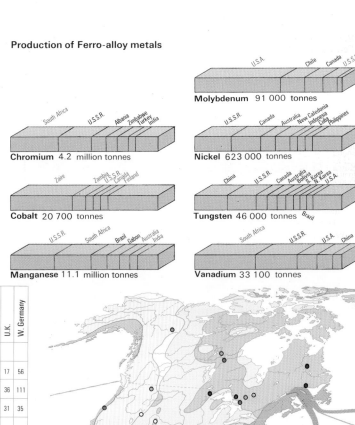

Molybdenum 91 000 tonnes
Chromium 4.2 million tonnes
Cobalt 20 700 tonnes
Nickel 623 000 tonnes
Tungsten 46 000 tonnes
Manganese 11.1 million tonnes
Vanadium 33 100 tonnes

Iron and Steel Industry of Western Europe

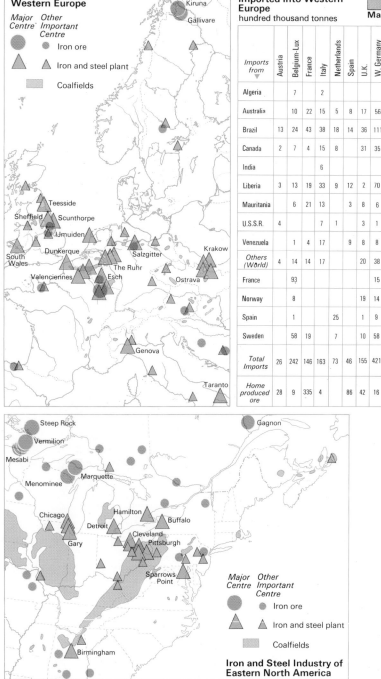

Major Centre / *Other Important Centre*
- ● / ● Iron ore
- ▲ / ▲ Iron and steel plant
- ▨ Coalfields

Sources of Iron ore imported into Western Europe
hundred thousand tonnes

Imports from ▼	Austria	Belgium-Lux	France	Italy	Netherlands	Spain	U.K.	W. Germany
Algeria		7		2				
Australia		10	22	15	5	8	17	56
Brazil	13	24	43	38	18	14	36	111
Canada	2	7	4	15	8		31	35
India				6				
Liberia	3	13	19	33	9	12	2	70
Mauritania		6	21	13		3	8	6
U.S.S.R.	4		7	1		3	1	
Venezuela		1	4	17		9	8	8
Others (World)	4	14	14	17			20	38
France	93							15
Norway	8						19	14
Spain	1			25			1	9
Sweden		58	19		7		10	58
Total Imports	26	242	146	163	73	46	155	421
Home produced ore	28	9	335	4		86	42	16

Iron and Steel Industry of Eastern North America

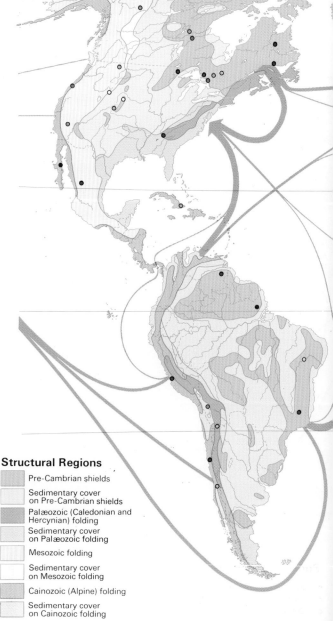

Major Centre / *Other Important Centre*
- ● / ● Iron ore
- ▲ / ▲ Iron and steel plant
- ▨ Coalfields

Structural Regions

- Pre-Cambrian shields
- Sedimentary cover on Pre-Cambrian shields
- Palæozoic (Caledonian and Hercynian) folding
- Sedimentary cover on Palæozoic folding
- Mesozoic folding
- Sedimentary cover on Mesozoic folding
- Cainozoic (Alpine) folding
- Sedimentary cover on Cainozoic folding

World production of Pig iron and Ferro-alloys
Total World production 451 million tonnes

- Others 9.9%
- U.S.S.R. 24%
- Japan 17%
- U.S.A. 9%
- China 8%
- W. Germany 6%
- France 3%
- Italy 2.5%
- Brazil 2.5%
- Czech. 2.1%
- Poland 1.9%
- India 2.1%
- Romania 1.9%
- S. Korea 1.9%
- U.K. 1.9%
- Canada 1.8%
- Belgium 1.7%
- S. Africa 1.5%

Growth of World production of Pig iron and Ferro-alloys

million tonnes

1938 1946 1951 1961 1971 1981 1982

World production of Iron ore (Fe content)
Total World production 480 million tonnes

U.S.S.R. 146.4 Australia 55.2 Brazil 42.7 China 36.0 India 25.7 U.S.A. 23.7 Canada 20.2 S. Africa 16.0 Liberia 13.4 Sweden 10.0 Venezuela 7.5 France 5.8 Others

50 25 10 5 1 million tonnes

Principal Sources of Iron ore and ferro-alloys

- Iron
- Chrome
- Cobalt
- Manganese
- Molybdenum
- Nickel
- Tungsten
- Vanadium
- Iron ore trade flow

Mineral Resources II

Antimony – imparts hardness when alloyed to other metals, especially lead.
Uses: type metal, pigments to paints, glass and enamels, fireproofing of textiles

World production 50 196 tonnes

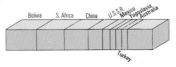

Lead – heavy, soft, malleable, acid resistant.
Uses: storage batteries, sheeting and piping, cable covering, ammunition, type metal, weights, additive to petrol.

World production 3.57 million tonnes

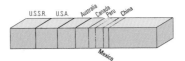

Tin – resistant to attacks by organic acids, malleable.
Uses: canning, foils, as an alloy to other metals (brass and bronze).

World production 222 500 tonnes

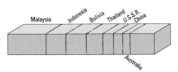

Aluminium – light, resists corrosion, good conductor.
Uses: aircraft, road and rail vehicles, domestic utensils, cables, makes highly tensile and light alloys.

World production 78.2 million tonnes (of Bauxite)

Gold – untarnishable and resistant to corrosion, highly ductile and malleable, good conductor. The pure metal is soft and it is alloyed to give it hardness.
Uses: bullion, coins, jewellery, gold-leaf, electronics.

World production 1 396 tonnes

Copper – excellent conductor of electricity and heat, durable, resistant to corrosion, strong and ductile.
Uses: wire, tubing, brass (with zinc and tin), bronze (with tin), (compounds) – dyeing.

World production 8.7 million tonnes

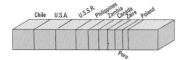

Mercury – the only liquid metal, excellent conductor of electricity
Uses: thermometers, electrical industry, gold and silver ore extraction, (compounds) – drugs, pigments, chemicals, dentistry.

World production 6 533 tonnes

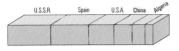

Zinc – hard metal, low corrosion factor.
Uses: brass (with copper and tin), galvanising, diecasting, medicines, paints and dyes.

World production 6.5 million tonnes

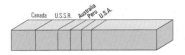

Diamonds – very hard and resistant to chemical attack, high lustre, very rare.
Uses: jewellery, cutting and abrading other materials.

World production 41.9 million carats

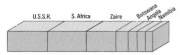

Silver – ductile and malleable, a soft metal and must be alloyed for use in coinage.
Uses: coins, jewellery, photography, electronics, medicines.

World production 11 531 tonnes

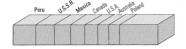

World consumption of non-ferrous metals

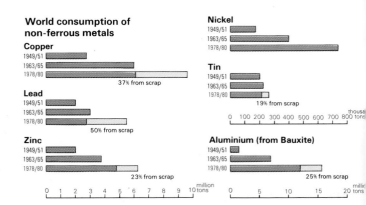

Structural Regions

- Pre-Cambrian shields
- Sedimentary cover on Pre-Cambrian shields
- Palæozoic (Caledonian and Hercynian) folding
- Sedimentary cover on Palæozoic folding
- Mesozoic folding
- Sedimentary cover on Mesozoic folding
- Cainozoic (Alpine) folding
- Sedimentary cover on Cainozoic folding

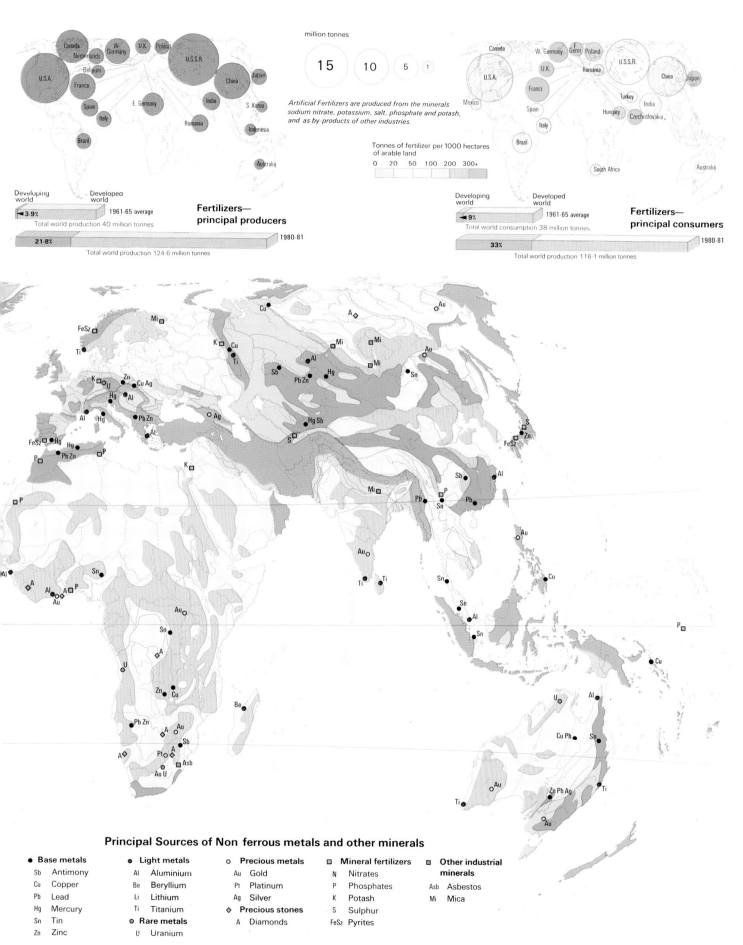

million tonnes

15   10   5   1

Artificial Fertilizers are produced from the minerals
sodium nitrate, potassium, salt, phosphate and potash,
and as by-products of other industries.

Tonnes of fertilizer per 1000 hectares
of arable land

0   20   50   100   200   300+

Fertilizers— principal producers

Developing world   Developed world

◄3·9%   1961-65 average
Total world production 40 million tonnes

21·8%   1980-81
Total world production 124·6 million tonnes

Fertilizers— principal consumers

Developing world   Developed world

◄9%   1961-65 average
Total world consumption 38 million tonnes

33%   1980-81
Total world production 116·1 million tonnes

Principal Sources of Non-ferrous metals and other minerals

● **Base metals**
Sb   Antimony
Cu   Copper
Pb   Lead
Hg   Mercury
Sn   Tin
Zn   Zinc

● **Light metals**
Al   Aluminium
Be   Beryllium
Li   Lithium
Ti   Titanium

◉ **Rare metals**
U   Uranium

○ **Precious metals**
Au   Gold
Pt   Platinum
Ag   Silver

◇ **Precious stones**
A   Diamonds

▣ **Mineral fertilizers**
N   Nitrates
P   Phosphates
K   Potash
S   Sulphur
FeSz   Pyrites

▣ **Other industrial minerals**
Asb   Asbestos
Mi   Mica

Fuel and Energy

Coal

Coal is the result of the accumulation of vegetation over millions of years. Later under pressure from overlying sediments, it is hardened through four stages: peat, lignite, bituminous coal, and finally anthracite. Once the most important source of power, coal's importance now lies in the production of electricity and as a raw material in the production of plastics, heavy chemicals and disinfectants.

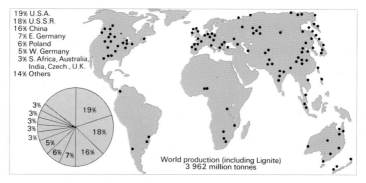

19% U.S.A.
18% U.S.S.R.
16% China
7% E. Germany
6% Poland
5% W. Germany
3% S. Africa, Australia, India, Czech., U.K.
14% Others

World production (including Lignite) 3 962 million tonnes

Coal mine

Oil

Oil is derived from the remains of marine animals and plants, probably as a result of pressure, heat and chemical action. It is a complex mixture of hydrocarbons which are refined to extract the various constituents. These include products such as gasolene, kerosene and heavy fuel oils. Oil is rapidly replacing coal because of easier handling and reduced pollution.

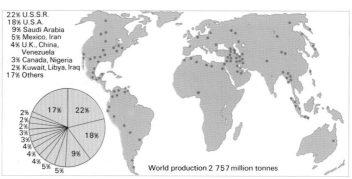

22% U.S.S.R.
18% U.S.A.
9% Saudi Arabia
5% Mexico, Iran
4% U.K., China, Venezuela
3% Canada, Nigeria
2% Kuwait, Libya, Iraq
17% Others

World production 2 757 million tonnes

Oil derrick

Natural gas

Since the early 1960's natural gas (methane) has become one of the largest single sources of energy. By liquefaction its volume can be reduced to 1/600 of that of gas and hence is easily transported. It is often found directly above oil reserves and because it is both cheaper than coal gas and less polluting it has great potential.

33% U.S.S.R.
33% U.S.A.
5% Netherlands, Canada
2% U.K., Romania, Mexico, Norway
1.5% Indonesia
14.5% Others

World production 1 517 million m³

North sea gas rig

Water

Hydro-electric power stations use water to drive turbines which in turn generate electricity. The ideal site is one in which a consistently large volume of water falls a considerable height, hence sources of H.E.P. are found mainly in mountainous areas. Potential sources of hydro-electricity using waves or tides are yet to be exploited widely.

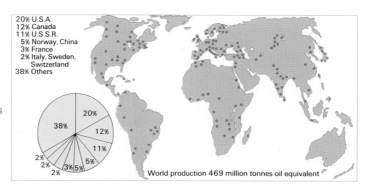

20% U.S.A.
12% Canada
11% U.S.S.R.
5% Norway, China
3% France
2% Italy, Sweden, Switzerland
38% Others

World production 469 million tonnes oil equivalent

Water power

Nuclear energy

The first source of nuclear power was developed in Britain in 1956. Energy is obtained from heat generated by the reaction from splitting atoms of certain elements, of which uranium and plutonium are the most important. Although the initial installation costs are very high the actual running costs are low because of the slow consumption of fuel.

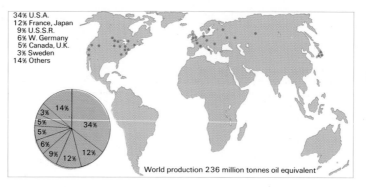

34% U.S.A.
12% France, Japan
9% U.S.S.R.
6% W. Germany
5% Canada, U.K.
3% Sweden
14% Others

World production 236 million tonnes oil equivalent

Nuclear power station

40

In a short space of time these two diagrams can change markedly; there can be a cut-back in supply owing to internal political change (Iran), or in consumption by vigorous government action (U.S.A.). The production of North Sea oil has changed the balance of oil trade in the U.K. and Norway but it is very costly to extract, relatively short-lived and is small on a world scale.

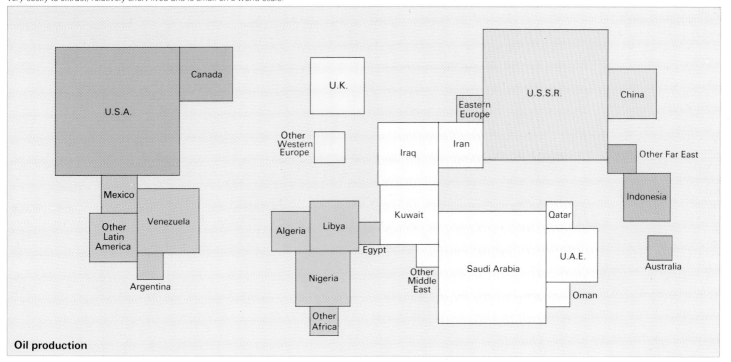

Oil production

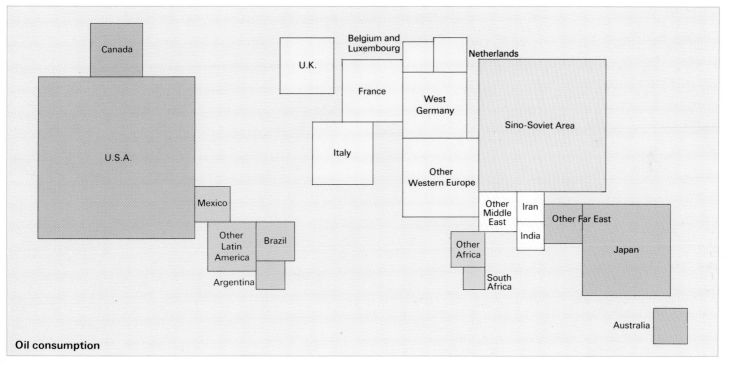

Oil consumption

Oil's new super-powers *above*
When countries are scaled according to their production and consumption of oil they take on new dimensions. At present, large supplies of oil are concentrated in a few countries of the Caribbean, the Middle East and North Africa, except for the vast indigenous supplies of the U.S.A. and U.S.S.R. The Middle East, with 58% of the world's reserves, produces 35% of the world's supply and yet consumes less than 3%. The U.S.A.,

despite its great production, has a deficiency of nearly 415 million tons a year, consuming 30% of the world's total. The U.S.S.R., with 11% of world reserves, produces 19% of world output and consumes 13%. Soviet production continues to grow annually although at a decreased rate since the mid-1970's. Japan, one of the largest oil importers, increased its consumption by 440% during the period 1963-73. Since then, total imports have decreased slightly.

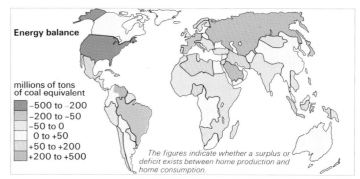

Energy balance

millions of tons
of coal equivalent

- −500 to −200
- −200 to −50
- −50 to 0
- 0 to +50
- +50 to +200
- +200 to +500

The figures indicate whether a surplus or deficit exists between home production and home consumption.

Occupations

Proportion employed in

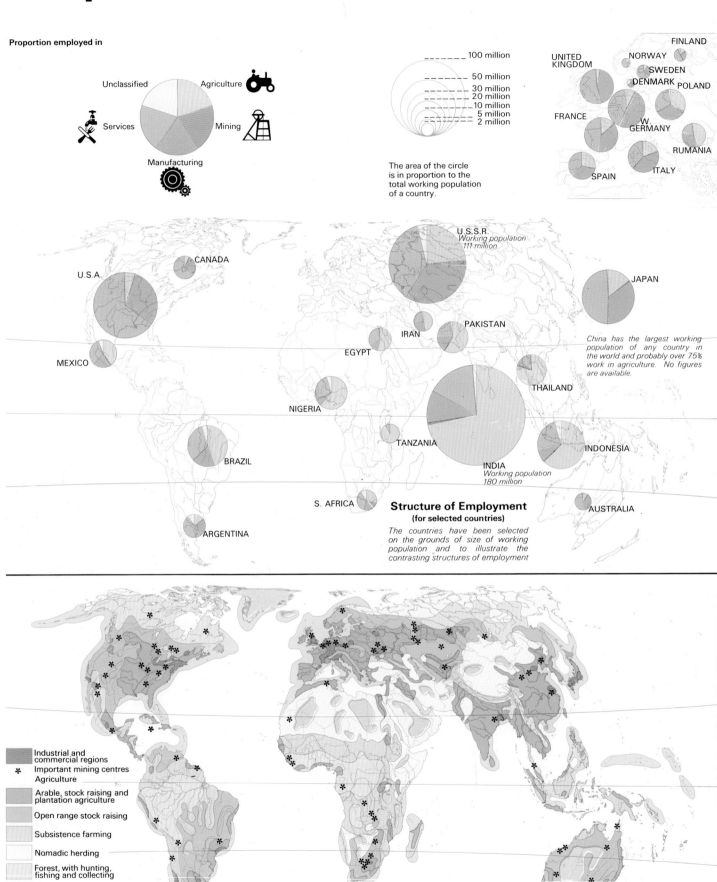

Unclassified
Agriculture
Services
Mining
Manufacturing

— — — — — — 100 million
— — — — — 50 million
— — — — 30 million
— — — 20 million
— — 10 million
— 5 million
— 2 million

The area of the circle is in proportion to the total working population of a country.

FINLAND
UNITED KINGDOM
NORWAY
SWEDEN
DENMARK
POLAND
FRANCE
W. GERMANY
RUMANIA
SPAIN
ITALY

CANADA
U.S.A.
MEXICO

U.S.S.R.
Working population 111 million

JAPAN

IRAN
PAKISTAN
EGYPT

China has the largest working population of any country in the world and probably over 75% work in agriculture. No figures are available.

THAILAND

NIGERIA

TANZANIA

INDONESIA

INDIA
Working population 180 million

BRAZIL

S. AFRICA

Structure of Employment
(for selected countries)

The countries have been selected on the grounds of size of working population and to illustrate the contrasting structures of employment

AUSTRALIA

ARGENTINA

Industrial and commercial regions
* Important mining centres
Agriculture
Arable, stock raising and plantation agriculture
Open range stock raising
Subsistence farming
Nomadic herding
Forest, with hunting, fishing and collecting
Forest, with lumbering
Fishing
Little or no economic activity

Predominant Economies

Industry

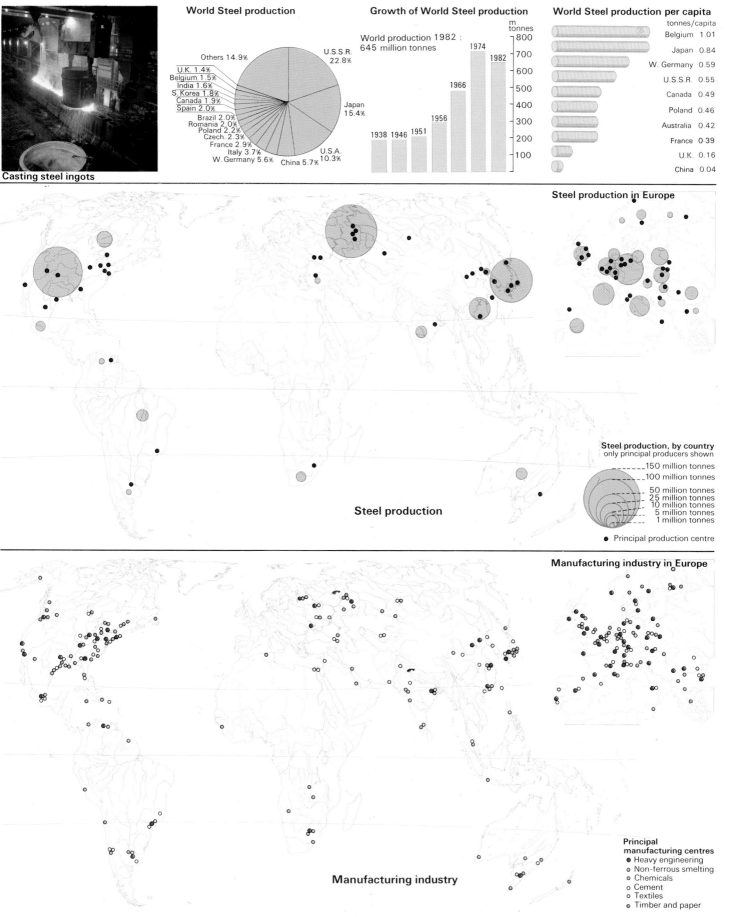

Casting steel ingots

World Steel production

- U.S.S.R. 22.8%
- Japan 15.4%
- U.S.A. 10.3%
- China 5.7%
- W. Germany 5.6%
- Italy 3.7%
- France 2.9%
- Czech. 2.3%
- Poland 2.2%
- Romania 2.0%
- Brazil 2.0%
- Spain 2.0%
- Canada 1.9%
- S. Korea 1.8%
- India 1.6%
- Belgium 1.5%
- U.K. 1.4%
- Others 14.9%

Growth of World Steel production

World production 1982 : 645 million tonnes

m tonnes

- 1938
- 1946
- 1951
- 1956
- 1966
- 1974
- 1982

(scale: 100–800)

World Steel production per capita

tonnes/capita

	tonnes/capita
Belgium	1.01
Japan	0.84
W. Germany	0.59
U.S.S.R.	0.55
Canada	0.49
Poland	0.46
Australia	0.42
France	0.39
U.K.	0.16
China	0.04

Steel production in Europe

Steel production

Steel production, by country
only principal producers shown

- 150 million tonnes
- 100 million tonnes
- 50 million tonnes
- 25 million tonnes
- 10 million tonnes
- 5 million tonnes
- 1 million tonnes

● Principal production centre

Manufacturing industry in Europe

Manufacturing industry

Principal manufacturing centres
- Heavy engineering
- Non-ferrous smelting
- Chemicals
- Cement
- Textiles
- Timber and paper

43

Transport

Shipyards

Japan 8 300	
S. Korea 1 531	
W. Germany 682	
Spain 613	
U.K. 525	
Brazil 469	
Denmark 419	World production
Yugoslavia 407	17.2 million tonnes
France 321	
Norway 304	**Shipbuilding**
Poland 302	tonnage launched
U.S.A. 282	in thousand gross registered tons

Principal shipbuilding centres

Europe

Japan

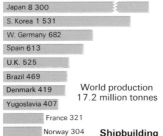

Concorde and Boeing 747

Aircraft Industry

In 1982 there were approximately 10 000 civil passenger airliners in service. This diagram shows where they were built.

U.S.A. 53%	U.S.S.R. 33%	U.K. 6% Netherlands 3% France 2%

Trade in Aircraft and Aircraft Engines

Exports	*million U.S. $*		Imports		
	Aircraft	Engines		Aircraft	Engines
U.S.A.	5893	789	W. Germ.	1218	136
France	995	262	U.K.	651	543
W. Germ.	915	227	U.S.A.	604	132
U.K.	861	721	France	472	278
Canada	303		Canada	264	149
Neth.	288	836	Neth.	210	132
Italy	279	88	Japan	201	151

Principal aircraft manufacturing centres

Motor vehicles World production 35.3 million vehicles

Production *thousand units*	Exports *million U.S. $*	Imports *million U.S. $*
Japan 10 732	21 601	737
U.S.A. 6 975	15 034	25 008
W. Germany 4 062	24 539	8 000
France 3 149	11 824	5 820
U.S.S.R. 2 173	1 831	1 164
Italy 1 453	5 582	4 645
Canada 1 277	9 593	11 598
U.K. 1 157	6 329	8 182
Spain 1 070	1 771	695

Europe

Locomotive works

Railway vehicles

Exports *million U.S. $*		Imports *million U.S. $*	
Japan	496·9	Brazil	151·8
France	353·9	Mexico	95·3
W. Germany	329·3	U.S.A.	81·7
U.S.A.	306·0	S. Korea	69·6
U.K.	78·6	S. Africa	67·5
Italy	62·6	Egypt	53·0
Yugoslavia	57·5	W. Germany	52·7
Canada	48·5	Yugoslavia	52·2
S. Korea	41·7	Netherlands	48·1
Sweden	37·7	Sweden	44·4
Belg.-Lux.	27·8	U.K.	40·5
Switzerland	37·5	Belg.-Lux.	33·6
Spain	18·5	France	30·3
		Italy	30·0

Principal locomotive building centres

Car assembly line

Principal motor vehicle plants

Merchant Shipping

Gross Registered Tonnage of merchant fleets registered in each country

2 5 10 20 30 40

Millions of G.R.T.

Weight of goods loaded and unloaded in each country's external trade, per inhabitant

Dry cargo only, petroleum excluded

1 2 3 4 5 6 7 8 9

Metric tons/inhabitant

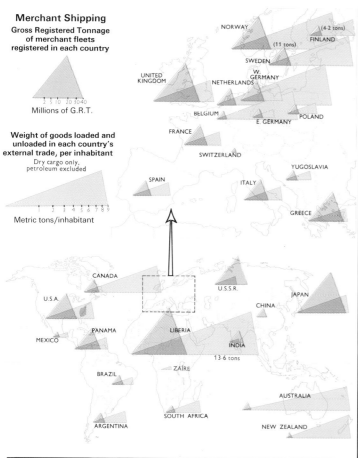

NORWAY (4·2 tons) FINLAND (11 tons) SWEDEN W. GERMANY UNITED KINGDOM NETHERLANDS BELGIUM POLAND FRANCE E. GERMANY SWITZERLAND YUGOSLAVIA SPAIN ITALY GREECE CANADA U.S.S.R. JAPAN CHINA U.S.A. PANAMA LIBERIA INDIA 13·6 tons MEXICO BRAZIL ZAÏRE AUSTRALIA ARGENTINA SOUTH AFRICA NEW ZEALAND

Density of Transport Networks

Density of network in km/100 km²

Road	Rail	Inland Waterway
100	20	10
75	15	5
50	10	4
		3
25	5	2
		1
0	0	0

Strict comparisons between the transport networks of different nations cannot be made due to differences in the gauges of railways, sizes of inland waterways and in the criteria used to designate roads

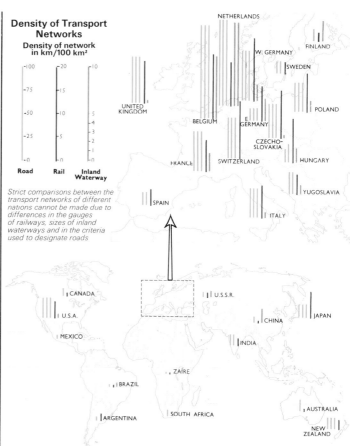

NETHERLANDS W. GERMANY FINLAND SWEDEN UNITED KINGDOM BELGIUM E. GERMANY POLAND FRANCE SWITZERLAND CZECHO-SLOVAKIA HUNGARY SPAIN YUGOSLAVIA ITALY CANADA U.S.S.R. U.S.A. CHINA JAPAN MEXICO INDIA ZAÏRE BRAZIL ARGENTINA SOUTH AFRICA AUSTRALIA NEW ZEALAND

Motor Vehicles and Passenger Transport

Private vehicles per 1000 inhabitants

250 200 150 100 50 0

Commercial vehicles per 1000 inhabitants

100 75 50 25 0

Passenger-km. travelled by air and by rail, per 100 inhabitants

Air   Rail

75 000 50 000 25 000 250 000 10 000 150 000 5000 100 000 1000 25 000

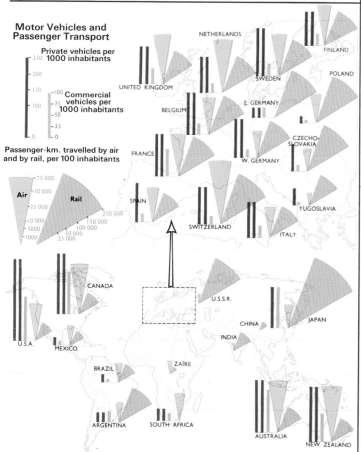

NETHERLANDS FINLAND SWEDEN POLAND UNITED KINGDOM BELGIUM E. GERMANY CZECHO-SLOVAKIA FRANCE W. GERMANY SPAIN YUGOSLAVIA SWITZERLAND ITALY CANADA U.S.S.R. CHINA JAPAN INDIA U.S.A. MEXICO BRAZIL ZAÏRE ARGENTINA SOUTH AFRICA AUSTRALIA NEW ZEALAND

Freight Carried

3000 2000 1000 500 100 **Freight carried by air**

100 tonne-km./100 inhabitants

Freight carried by rail

750 000 500 000 250 000 100 000 50 000 25 000 tonne-km./100 inhabitants

Freight carried by inland waterway

300 000 200 000 100 000 50 000 25 000 tonne-km./100 inhabitants

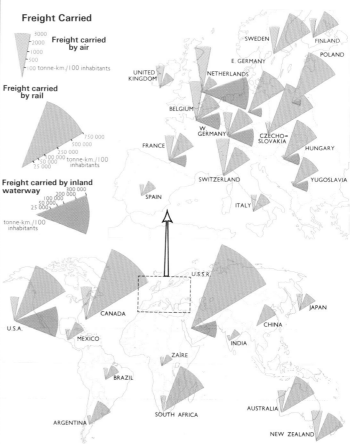

SWEDEN FINLAND E. GERMANY POLAND UNITED KINGDOM NETHERLANDS BELGIUM W. GERMANY CZECHO-SLOVAKIA HUNGARY FRANCE SWITZERLAND YUGOSLAVIA SPAIN ITALY U.S.S.R. CANADA JAPAN U.S.A. CHINA MEXICO INDIA ZAÏRE BRAZIL AUSTRALIA ARGENTINA SOUTH AFRICA NEW ZEALAND

45

Trade

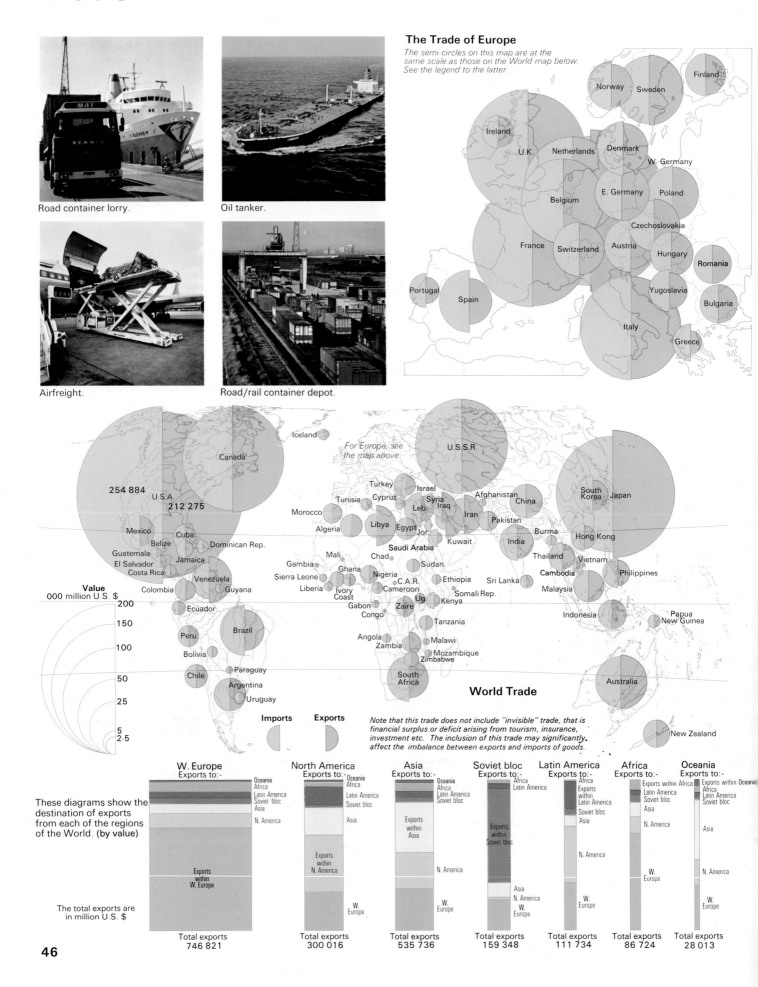

Road container lorry.

Oil tanker.

Airfreight.

Road/rail container depot.

The Trade of Europe

The semi-circles on this map are at the same scale as those on the World map below. See the legend to the latter.

Norway · Sweden · Finland · Ireland · U.K. · Netherlands · Denmark · W. Germany · Belgium · E. Germany · Poland · France · Switzerland · Austria · Czechoslovakia · Hungary · Romania · Portugal · Spain · Yugoslavia · Bulgaria · Italy · Greece

Iceland · Canada · *For Europe, see the map above* · U.S.S.R.

254 884
U.S.A.
212 275

Mexico · Cuba · Belize · Dominican Rep. · Guatemala · Jamaica · El Salvador · Costa Rica · Venezuela · Guyana · Colombia

Turkey · Israel · Tunisia · Cyprus · Syria · Afghanistan · China · South Korea · Japan · Leb. · Iraq · Morocco · Iran · Algeria · Libya · Egypt · Jor. · Pakistan · Burma · Hong Kong · Kuwait · India · Saudi Arabia · Thailand · Vietnam · Mali · Chad · Sudan · Cambodia · Philippines · Gambia · Ghana · Nigeria · Sri Lanka · Malaysia · Sierra Leone · C.A.R. · Ethiopia · Liberia · Ivory Coast · Cameroon · Somali Rep. · Ug. · Kenya · Gabon · Zaire · Congo · Tanzania · Indonesia · Papua New Guinea

Value
000 million U.S. $

Ecuador · Peru · Brazil · Bolivia · Angola · Malawi · Zambia · Mozambique · Zimbabwe · Paraguay · Chile · South Africa · Australia · Argentina · Uruguay

World Trade

Value
200
150
100
50
25
5
2·5

Imports **Exports**

Note that this trade does not include "invisible" trade, that is financial surplus or deficit arising from tourism, insurance, investment etc. The inclusion of this trade may significantly affect the imbalance between exports and imports of goods.

New Zealand

These diagrams show the destination of exports from each of the regions of the World. (by value)

The total exports are in million U.S. $

W. Europe	North America	Asia	Soviet bloc	Latin America	Africa	Oceania
Exports to:-	Exports to:-	Exports to:-	Exports to:-	Exports to:-	Exports to:-	Exports to:-
Oceania	Oceania	Oceania	Africa	Africa	Exports within Africa	Exports within Oceania
Africa	Africa	Africa	Latin America	Latin America	Latin America	Africa
Latin America	Latin America	Latin America	Soviet bloc	Exports within Latin America	Soviet bloc	Latin America
Soviet bloc	Soviet bloc	Soviet bloc		Soviet bloc	Asia	Soviet bloc
Asia	Asia	Exports within Asia	Exports within Soviet bloc	Asia	N. America	Asia
N. America	Exports within N. America	N. America	Asia	N. America	W. Europe	N. America
Exports within W. Europe	W. Europe	W. Europe	N. America · Asia · N. America · W. Europe	W. Europe		W. Europe
Total exports 746 821	Total exports 300 016	Total exports 535 736	Total exports 159 348	Total exports 111 734	Total exports 86 724	Total exports 28 013

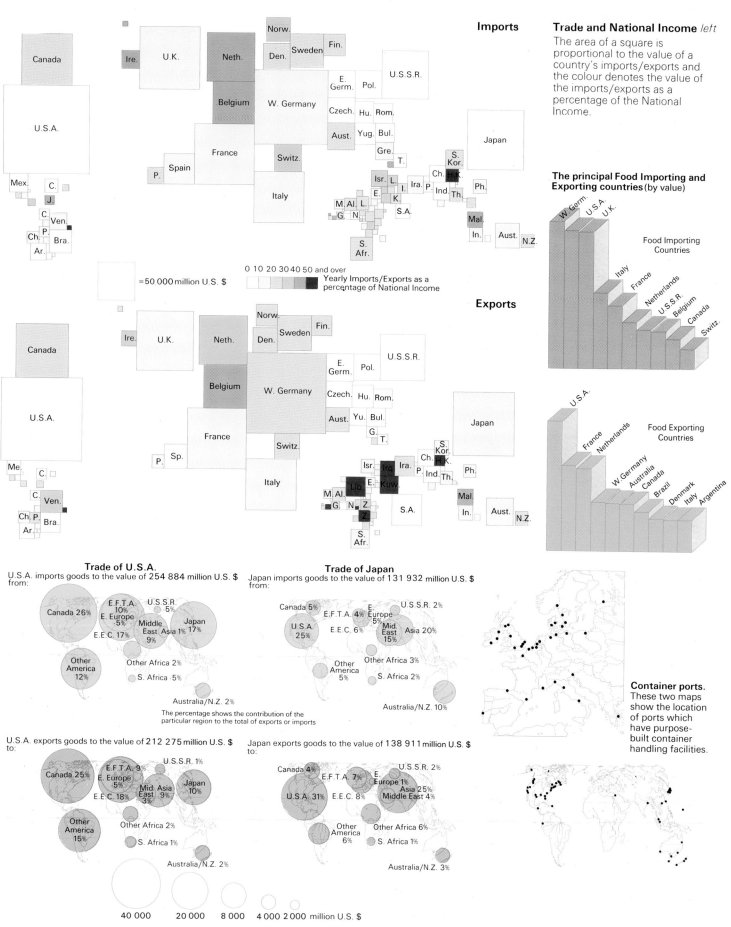

Imports

Trade and National Income *left*
The area of a square is proportional to the value of a country's imports/exports and the colour denotes the value of the imports/exports as a percentage of the National Income.

Canada
U.S.A.
Mex.
C.
J.
C.
Ven.
Ch. P.
Bra.
Ar.

Ire.
U.K.
Neth.
Norw.
Den.
Sweden
Fin.
E. Germ.
Pol.
U.S.S.R.
Belgium
W. Germany
Czech.
Hu.
Rom.
Aust.
Yug.
Bul.
France
Switz.
Gre.
T.
Japan
P.
Spain
Italy
Isr.
L.
I.
Ira.
P.
Ch.
S. Kor.
H.K.
Ind.
Th.
Ph.
E.
K.
M. Al. L.
G. N.
S.A.
Mal.
In.
Aust.
N.Z.
S. Afr.

= 50.000 million U.S. $

0 10 20 30 40 50 and over
Yearly Imports/Exports as a percentage of National Income

Exports

Canada
U.S.A.
Me.
C.
C.
Ven.
Ch. P.
Bra.
Ar.

Ire.
U.K.
Neth.
Norw.
Den.
Sweden
Fin.
E. Germ.
Pol.
U.S.S.R.
Belgium
W. Germany
Czech.
Hu.
Rom.
Aust.
Yu.
Bul.
France
Switz.
G.
T.
Japan
P.
Sp.
Italy
Isr.
Irq.
Ira.
Ch.
S. Kor.
H.K.
P.
Ind.
Th.
Ph.
Lib.
E.
Kuw.
M. Al.
G. N. Z.
Z.
S.A.
Mal.
In.
Aust.
N.Z.
S. Afr.

The principal Food Importing and Exporting countries (by value)

W. Germ.
U.S.A.
U.K.
Italy
France
Netherlands
U.S.S.R.
Belgium
Canada
Switz.

Food Importing Countries

U.S.A.
France
Netherlands
W. Germany
Australia
Canada
Brazil
Denmark
Italy
Argentina

Food Exporting Countries

Trade of U.S.A.
U.S.A. imports goods to the value of 254 884 million U.S. $ from:

Canada 26%
E.F.T.A. 10%
E. Europe 5%
U.S.S.R. 5%
E.E.C. 17%
Middle East 9%
Asia 1%
Japan 17%
Other America 12%
Other Africa 2%
S. Africa 5%
Australia/N.Z. 2%

The percentage shows the contribution of the particular region to the total of exports or imports

U.S.A. exports goods to the value of 212 275 million U.S. $ to:

Canada 25%
E.F.T.A. 9%
E. Europe 5%
U.S.S.R. 1%
E.E.C. 18%
Mid. East 3%
Asia 9%
Japan 10%
Other America 15%
Other Africa 2%
S. Africa 1%
Australia/N.Z. 2%

Trade of Japan
Japan imports goods to the value of 131 932 million U.S. $ from:

Canada 5%
E.F.T.A. 4%
E. Europe 5%
U.S.S.R. 2%
U.S.A. 25%
E.E.C. 6%
Mid. East 15%
Asia 20%
Other America 5%
Other Africa 3%
S. Africa 2%
Australia/N.Z. 10%

Japan exports goods to the value of 138 911 million U.S. $ to:

Canada 4%
E.F.T.A. 7%
E. Europe 1%
U.S.S.R. 2%
U.S.A. 31%
E.E.C. 8%
Middle East 4%
Asia 25%
Other America 6%
Other Africa 6%
S. Africa 1%
Australia/N.Z. 3%

40 000 20 000 8 000 4 000 2 000 million U.S. $

Container ports.
These two maps show the location of ports which have purpose-built container handling facilities.

47

Wealth

The living standard of a few highly developed, urbanised, industrialised countries is a complete contrast to the conditions of the vast majority of economically undeveloped, agrarian states. It is this contrast which divides mankind into rich and poor, well fed and hungry. The developing world is still an over-whelmingly agricultural world: over 70% of all its people live off the land and yet the output from that land remains pitifully low. Many Africans, South Americans and Asians struggle with the soil but the bad years occur only too frequently and they seldom have anything left over to save. The need for foreign capital then arises.

National Income
The gap between developing and developed worlds is in fact widening eg. in 1938 the incomes for the United States and India were in the proportions of 1:15; now they are 1:53.

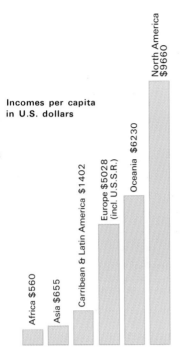

Incomes per capita in U.S. dollars

Africa $560
Asia $655
Carribean & Latin America $1402
Europe $5028 (incl. U.S.S.R.)
Oceania $6230
North America $9660

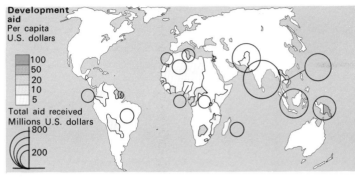

Development aid
Per capita U.S. dollars

100
50
20
10
5

Total aid received Millions U.S. dollars
800
200

Development aid
The provision of foreign aid, defined as assistance on con-cessional terms for promoting development, is today an accepted, though controversial aspect of the economic policies of most advanced countries towards less developed countries. Aid for development is based not merely on economic considerations but also on social, political and historical factors. The most important international committee set up after the war was that of the U.N.; practically all aid however has been given bi-laterally direct from an industrialised country to an under-developed country. Although aid increased during the 1950's the donated proportion of industrialised countries GNP has diminished from 0·5 to 0·4%. Less developed countries share of world trade also decreased and increased population invalidated any progress made:

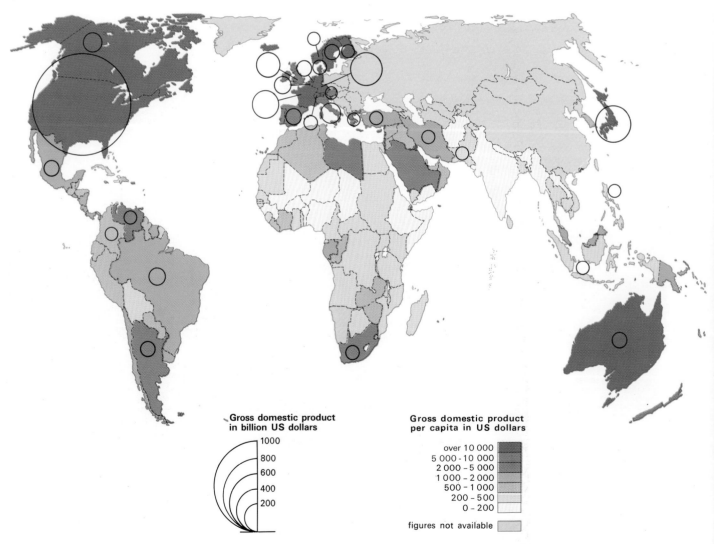

Gross domestic product in billion US dollars

1000
800
600
400
200

Gross domestic product per capita in US dollars

over 10 000
5 000 - 10 000
2 000 - 5 000
1 000 - 2 000
500 - 1 000
200 - 500
0 - 200

figures not available

SETTLEMENTS

Settlement symbols in order of size

LONDON
MONTRÉAL

■Stuttgart
Hamilton

●Sevilla
Moose Jaw

◎Bergen
Prince Rupert

○Bath
Gaspé

○Biarritz
Banff

○Srikolayatji
Miquelon

Settlement symbols and type styles vary according to the scale of each map and indicate the importance of towns on the map rather than specific population figures

∴ Sites of Archæological or Historical importance

BOUNDARIES

——— International Boundaries

— — — International Boundaries (Undemarcated or Undefined)

········· Internal Boundaries

International boundaries show the *de facto* situation where there are rival claims to territory

National and Provincial Parks

COMMUNICATIONS

═══ Freeways

━━━ Principal Railways

·········· Principal Canals

========= Freeways under construction

⌒⌒ Other Railways

━━━━ Principal Oil Pipelines

━○━ Trans-Canada Highway

`---` Railways under construction

_3386_ Principal Shipping Routes (Distances in Nautical Miles)

——— Principal Roads

╡---╞ Railway Tunnels

——— Principal Air Routes

⌒⌒ Other Roads

╡---╞ Road Tunnels

✈ ✛ ✿ Airports

`----` Tracks and Seasonal Roads

‿ Passes

PHYSICAL FEATURES

⌒⌒ Perennial Streams

Seasonal Lakes, Salt Flats

Permanent Ice

`-----` Seasonal Streams

Swamps, Marshes

‿ Wells in Desert

▲ 8848 Spot Height in metres

▼ 8050 Sea Depths. in metres

1134 Height of Lake Surface Above Sea Level, in metres

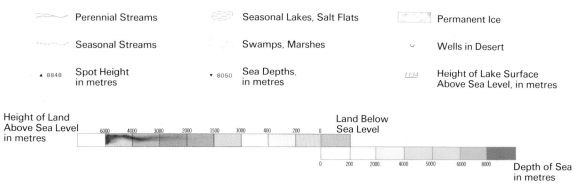

Height of Land Above Sea Level in metres — 6000 4000 3000 2000 1500 1000 400 200 0 — Land Below Sea Level

0 200 2000. 4000 5000 6000 8000 Depth of Sea in metres

Some of the maps have different contours to highlight and clarify the principal relief features

Abbreviations of measures used   mm Millimetres   m Metres   km Kilometres   °C Degrees Celsius   mb Millibars

STRUCTURE

1:95 000 000

Structural Regions of the Land

- Pre-Cambrian shields
- Sedimentary cover on Pre-Cambrian shields
- Palæozoic (Caledonian and Hercynian) folding
- Sedimentary cover on Palæozoic folding
- Mesozoic folding
- Sedimentary cover on Mesozoic folding
- Cainozoic folding
- Sedimentary cover on Cainozoic folding
- Intensive Mesozoic and Cainozoic vulcanism
- Oceanic-type crust raised above sea level

Structural Regions of the Oceans

- Regions of continental-type crust
- —— Limit of continental shelf
- Oceanic marginal troughs
- Mid-oceanic volcanic ridges
- Rift valleys in mid-oceanic ridges
- —— Principal faults
- +++ Frontal line of overthrust folds

GEOLOGICAL TIME SCALE

Era	System	Orogeny	Millions of years before present
Cainozoic (Tertiary, Quaternary)	Quaternary / Pliocene	ALPINE FOLDING	
	Miocene		
	Oligocene		
	Eocene		— 50
	Paleocene	LARAMIDE FOLDING	
Mesozoic (Secondary)	Cretaceous		— 100
	Jurassic		— 150
	Triassic		— 200
Palæozoic (Primary) Upper	Permian		— 250
	Carboniferous	HERCYNIAN FOLDING	— 300
	Devonian		— 350
Palæozoic (Primary) Lower	Silurian	CALEDONIAN FOLDING	— 400
	Ordovician		— 450
	Cambrian		— 500 / — 550
Pre-Cambrian	Pre-Cambrian		— 600

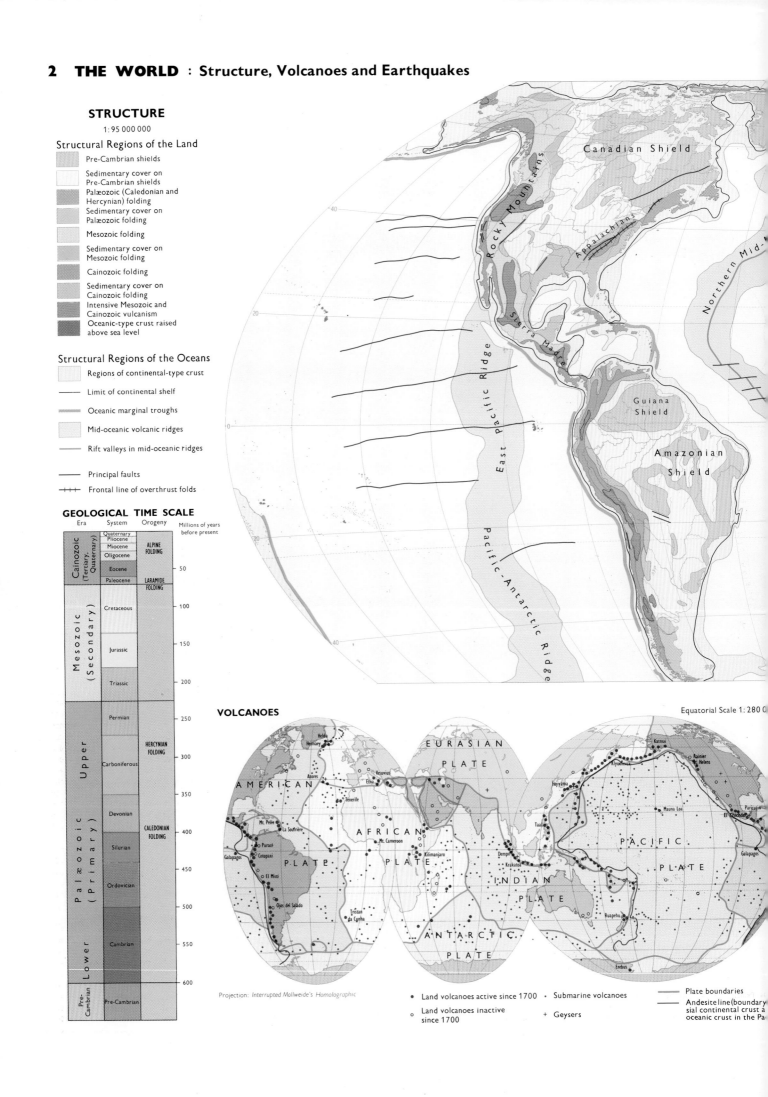

Canadian Shield
Rocky Mountains
Appalachians
Sierra Madre
Northern Mid-
East Pacific Ridge
Guiana Shield
Amazonian Shield
Pacific-Antarctic Ridge

VOLCANOES

Equatorial Scale 1:280 0

EURASIAN PLATE
AMERICAN PLATE
AFRICAN PLATE
PACIFIC PLATE
INDIAN PLATE
ANTARCTIC PLATE

Hekla, Heimaey, Azores, Vesuvius, Etna, Tenerife, Mt. Pelée, La Soufrière, Puracé, Galapagos, Cotopaxi, El Misti, Ojos del Salado, Tristan da Cunha, Mt. Cameroon, Kilimanjaro, Dempo, Krakatoa, Taal, Fujiyama, Miyoshima, Katmai, Rainier, St. Helens, Mauna Loa, Paricutin, El Chichon, Galapagos, Ruapehu, Erebus

Projection: *Interrupted Mollweide's Homolographic*

- • Land volcanoes active since 1700
- ○ Land volcanoes inactive since 1700
- · Submarine volcanoes
- + Geysers
- —— Plate boundaries
- —— Andesite line (boundary sial continental crust a oceanic crust in the Pa

1 : 95 000 000

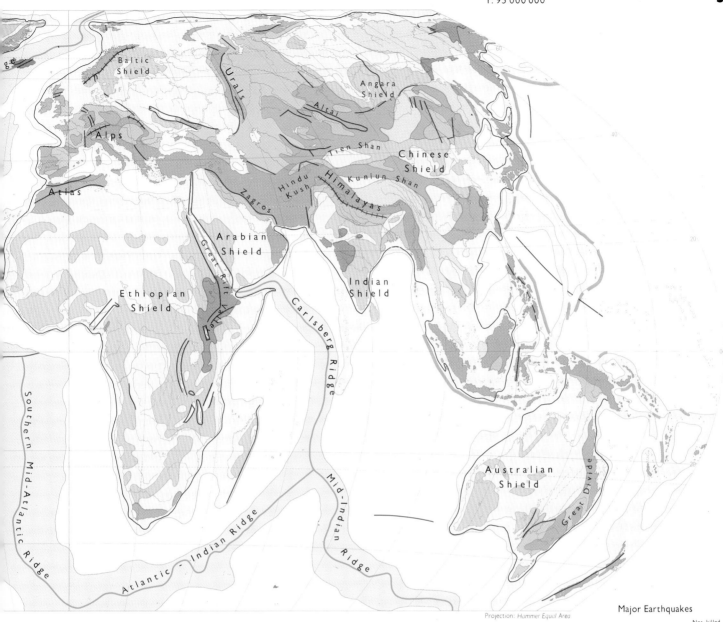

Baltic Shield

Urals

Angara Shield

Altai

Alps

Tien Shan

Chinese Shield

Atlas

Hindu Kush

Himalayas

Kunlun Shan

Zagros

Arabian Shield

Great Rift Valley

Ethiopian Shield

Carlsberg Ridge

Indian Shield

Southern Mid-Atlantic Ridge

Atlantic – Indian Ridge

Mid-Indian Ridge

Australian Shield

Great Divide

Projection: *Hammer Equal Area*

Major Earthquakes

RTHQUAKES

Equatorial Scale 1 . 280 000 000

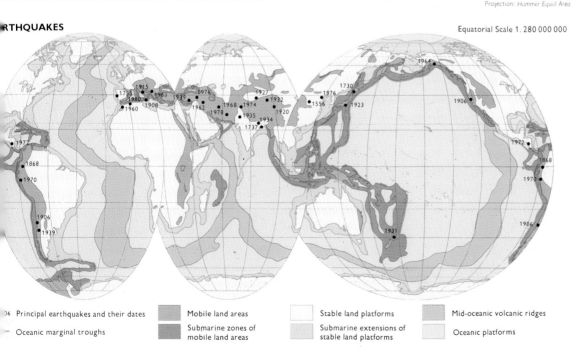

		Nos. killed
1556	Shensi, China	830 000
1730	Hokkaido, Japan	137 000
1737	Calcutta, India	300 000
1755	Lisbon, Portugal	60 000
1868	Ecuador and N. Peru	40 000
1906	Valparaiso, Chile	22 000
1906	San Francisco, U.S.A.	450
1908	Messina, Italy	77 000
1915	Avezzano, Italy	30 000
1920	Kansu, China	180 000
1923	Yokohama, Japan	143 000
1927	Nan Shan, China	200 000
1931	Napier, N. Zealand	250
1932	Kansu, China	70 000
1934	Nepal	11 700
1935	Quetta, Pakistan	30 000
1939	Erzincan, Turkey	30 000
1960	Agadir, Morocco	12 000
1962	Khorasan, Iran	10 000
1963	Skopje, Yugoslavia	1 000
1964	Anchorage, Alaska	100
1968	N.E. Iran	12 000
1970	N. Peru	67 000
1972	Managua, Nicaragua	7 000
1974	N. Pakistan	10 000
1976	Tangshan, China	650 000
1976	Lice, Turkey	3 800
1978	Tabas, Iran	11 000
1980	**El Asnam, Algeria**	**20 000**

06 Principal earthquakes and their dates

Oceanic marginal troughs

Mobile land areas

Submarine zones of mobile land areas

Stable land platforms

Submarine extensions of stable land platforms

Mid-oceanic volcanic ridges

Oceanic platforms

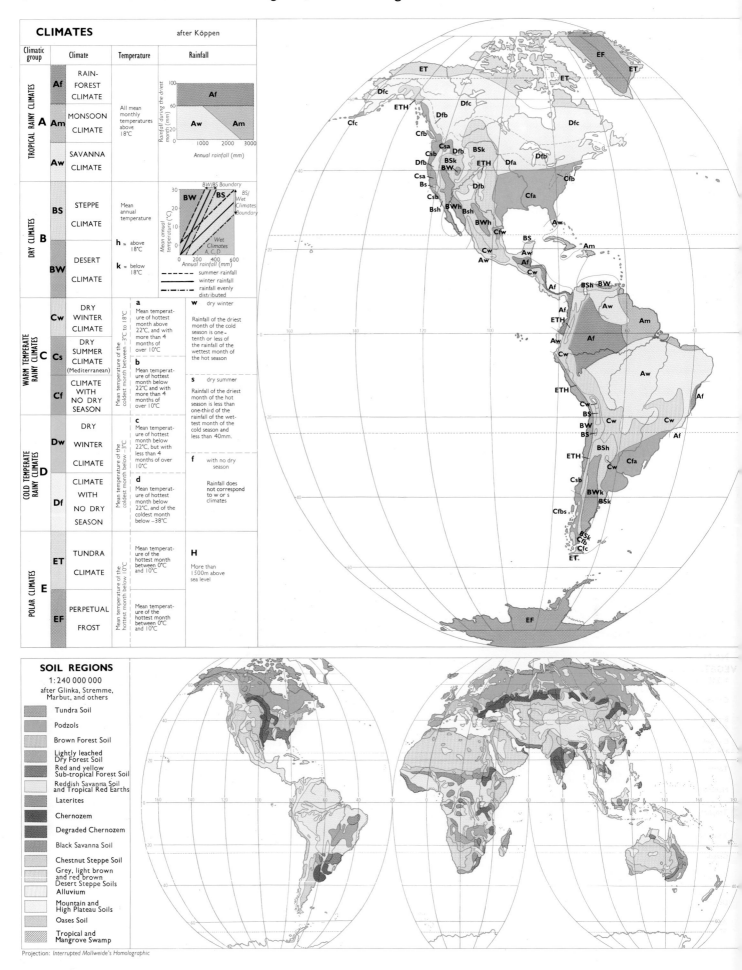

CLIMATES

after Köppen

Climatic group	Climate		Temperature	Rainfall
TROPICAL RAINY CLIMATES **A**	**Af**	RAIN-FOREST CLIMATE	All mean monthly temperatures above 18°C	
	Am	MONSOON CLIMATE		
	Aw	SAVANNA CLIMATE		
DRY CLIMATES **B**	**BS**	STEPPE CLIMATE	Mean annual temperature	
			h = above 18°C	
	BW	DESERT CLIMATE	**k** = below 18°C	
WARM TEMPERATE RAINY CLIMATES **C**	**Cw**	DRY WINTER CLIMATE	Mean temperature of the coldest month between −3°C to 18°C	**a** Mean temperature of hottest month above 22°C, and with more than 4 months of over 10°C
	Cs	DRY SUMMER CLIMATE (Mediterranean)		**b** Mean temperature of hottest month below 22°C and with more than 4 months of over 10°C
	Cf	CLIMATE WITH NO DRY SEASON		
COLD TEMPERATE RAINY CLIMATES **D**	**Dw**	DRY WINTER CLIMATE	Mean temperature of the coldest month below −3°C	**c** Mean temperature of hottest month below 22°C, but with less than 4 months of over 10°C
	Df	CLIMATE WITH NO DRY SEASON		**d** Mean temperature of hottest month below 22°C, and of the coldest month below −38°C
POLAR CLIMATES **E**	**ET**	TUNDRA CLIMATE	Mean temperature of the hottest month between 0°C and 10°C	
	EF	PERPETUAL FROST	Mean temperature of the hottest month between 0°C and 10°C	

Rainfall column notes:
w dry winter — Rainfall of the driest month of the cold season is one-tenth or less of the rainfall of the wettest month of the hot season

s dry summer — Rainfall of the driest month of the hot season is less than one-third of the rainfall of the wettest month of the cold season and less than 40mm.

f with no dry season — Rainfall does not correspond to w or s climates

H More than 1500m above sea level

Af / Aw / Am rainfall chart: *Rainfall during the driest month (mm)* vs *Annual rainfall (mm)* — 0, 1000, 2000, 3000

BW/BS chart: *Mean annual temperature* — BW/BS Boundary, BS/Wet Climates Boundary, Wet Climates A,C,D — *Annual rainfall (mm)* 0 200 400 600
- - - - summer rainfall
– – – winter rainfall
–·–·– rainfall evenly distributed

SOIL REGIONS

1:240 000 000
after Glinka, Stremme, Marbut, and others

- Tundra Soil
- Podzols
- Brown Forest Soil
- Lightly leached Dry Forest Soil
- Red and yellow Sub-tropical Forest Soil
- Reddish Savanna Soil and Tropical Red Earths
- Laterites
- Chernozem
- Degraded Chernozem
- Black Savanna Soil
- Chestnut Steppe Soil
- Grey, light brown and red brown Desert Steppe Soils
- Alluvium
- Mountain and High Plateau Soils
- Oases Soil
- Tropical and Mangrove Swamp

Projection: *Interrupted Mollweide's Homolographic*

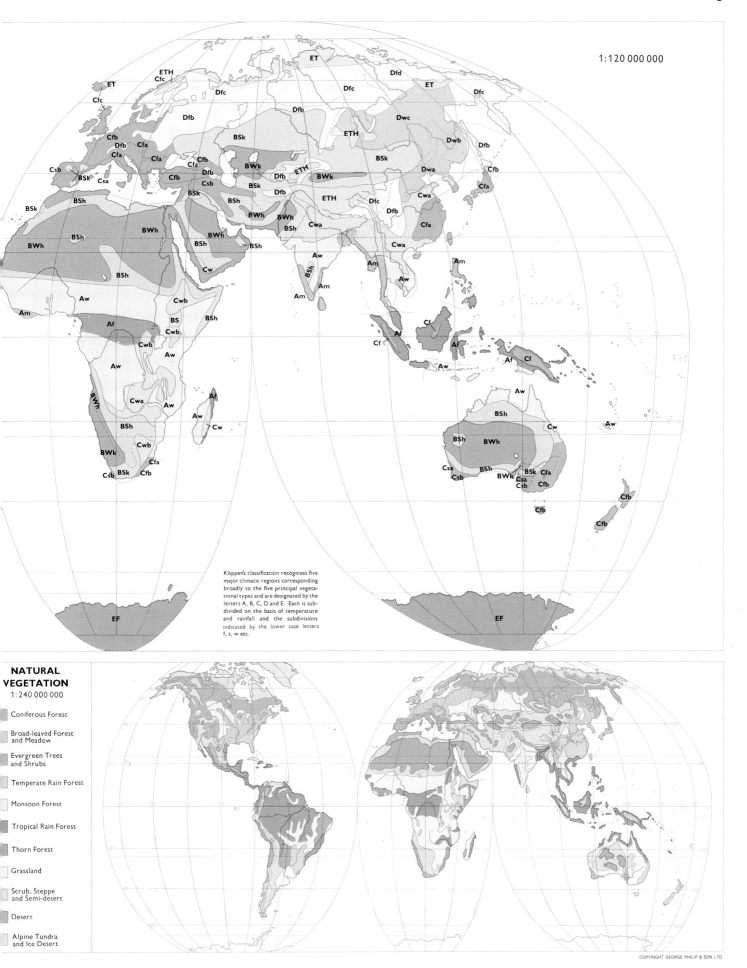

1:120 000 000

Köppen's classification recognises five major climatic regions corresponding broadly to the five principal vegetational types and are designated by the letters A, B, C, D and E. Each is subdivided on the basis of temperature and rainfall and the subdivisions indicated by the lower case letters f, s, w etc.

NATURAL VEGETATION
1:240 000 000

- Coniferous Forest
- Broad-leaved Forest and Meadow
- Evergreen Trees and Shrubs
- Temperate Rain Forest
- Monsoon Forest
- Tropical Rain Forest
- Thorn Forest
- Grassland
- Scrub, Steppe and Semi-desert
- Desert
- Alpine Tundra and Ice Desert

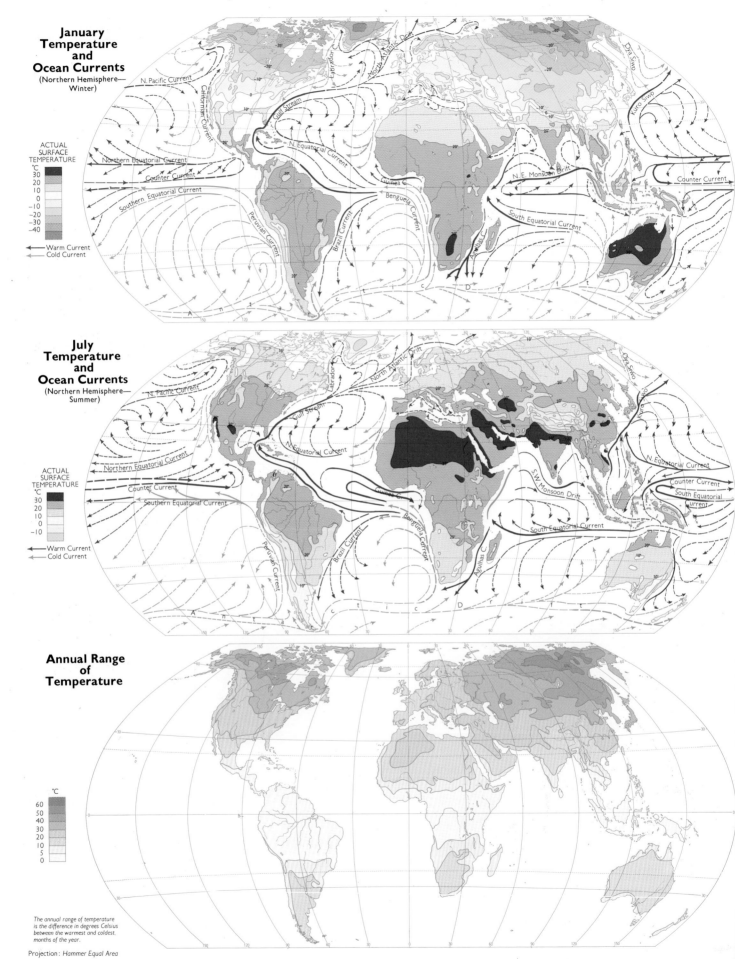

January Temperature and Ocean Currents
(Northern Hemisphere—Winter)

ACTUAL
SURFACE
TEMPERATURE
°C
30
20
10
0
−10
−20
−30
−40

→ Warm Current
→ Cold Current

N. Pacific Current
Californian Current
Gulf Stream
Labrador C.
North Atlantic Drift
N. Equatorial Current
Counter Current
Southern Equatorial Current
Guinea C.
Benguela Current
Peruvian Current
Brazil Current
Agulhas C.
South Equatorial Current
N.E. Monsoon Drift
Counter Current
Kuro Siwo
Oya Siwo

July Temperature and Ocean Currents
(Northern Hemisphere—Summer)

ACTUAL
SURFACE
TEMPERATURE
°C
30
20
10
0
−10

→ Warm Current
→ Cold Current

N. Pacific Current
Labrador
Gulf Stream
North Atlantic Drift
N. Equatorial Current
Northern Equatorial Current
Counter Current
Southern Equatorial Current
Guinea Cr.
Benguela Current
Peruvian Current
Brazil Current
Agulhas C.
S.W. Monsoon Drift
South Equatorial Current
N. Equatorial Current
Counter Current
South Equatorial Current
Kuro Siwo
Oya Siwo

Annual Range of Temperature

°C
60
50
40
30
20
10
5
0

The annual range of temperature is the difference in degrees Celsius between the warmest and coldest months of the year.

Projection: *Hammer Equal Area*

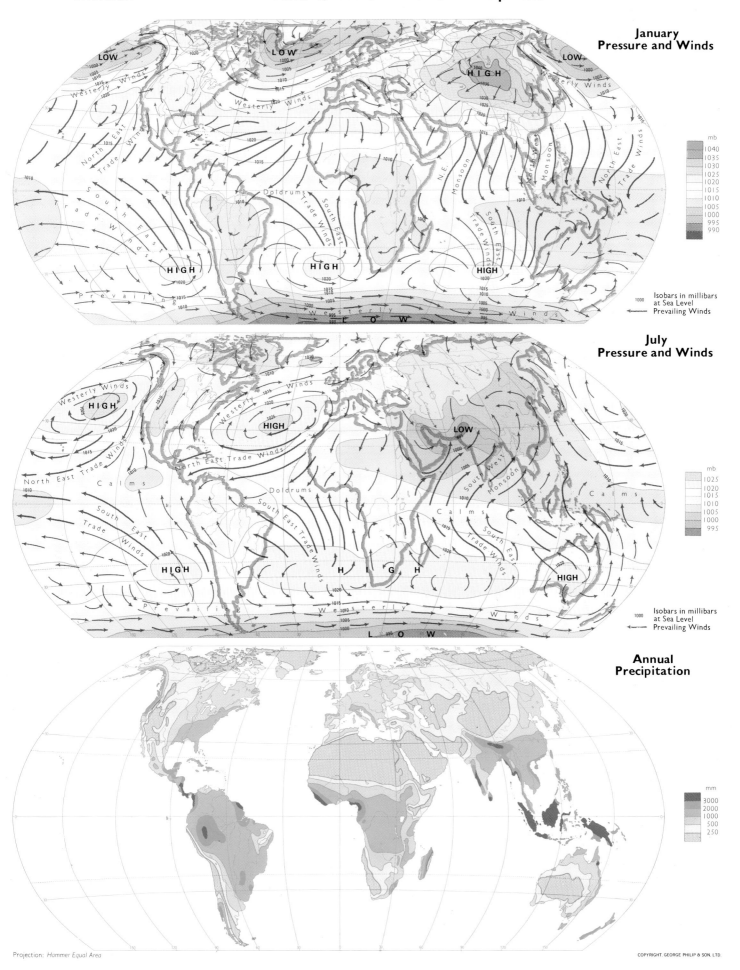

**January
Pressure and Winds**

mb
1040
1035
1030
1025
1020
1015
1010
1005
1000
995
990

1000 Isobars in millibars
at Sea Level
Prevailing Winds

**July
Pressure and Winds**

mb
1025
1020
1015
1010
1005
1000
995

1000 Isobars in millibars
at Sea Level
Prevailing Winds

**Annual
Precipitation**

mm
3000
2000
1000
500
250

Projection: *Hammer Equal Area*

COPYRIGHT. GEORGE PHILIP & SON. LTD.

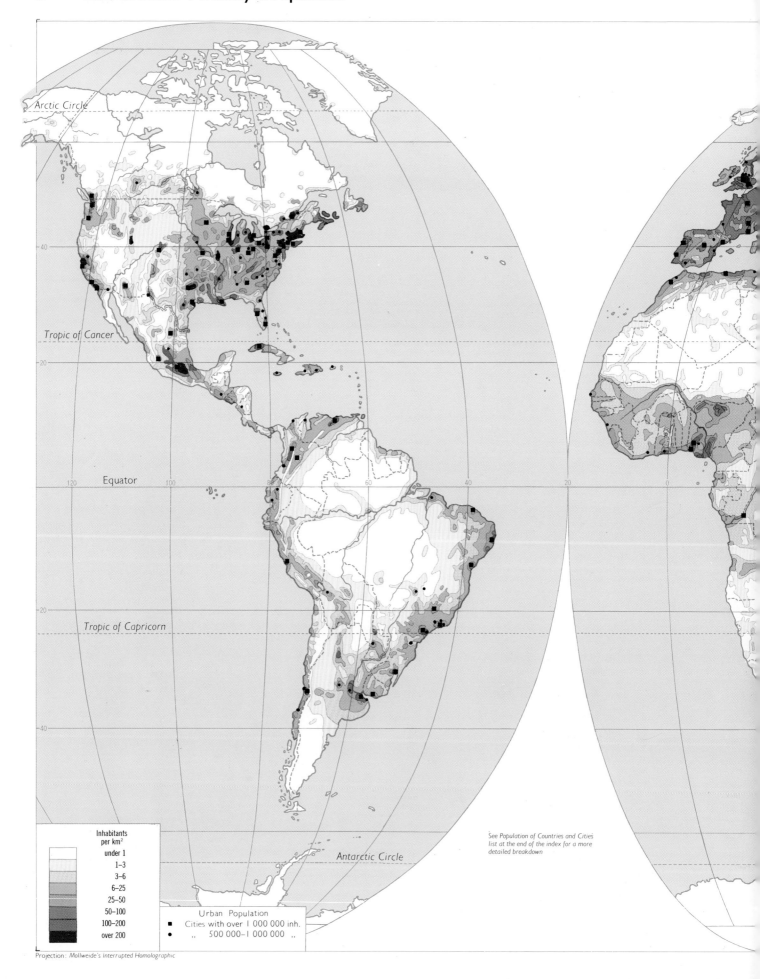

Arctic Circle

Tropic of Cancer

Equator

Tropic of Capricorn

Antarctic Circle

Inhabitants per km²	
	under 1
	1–3
	3–6
	6–25
	25–50
	50–100
	100–200
	over 200

Urban Population
■ Cities with over 1 000 000 inh.
● „ 500 000–1 000 000 „

See Population of Countries and Cities
list at the end of the index for a more
detailed breakdown

Projection: Mollweide's Interrupted Homolographic

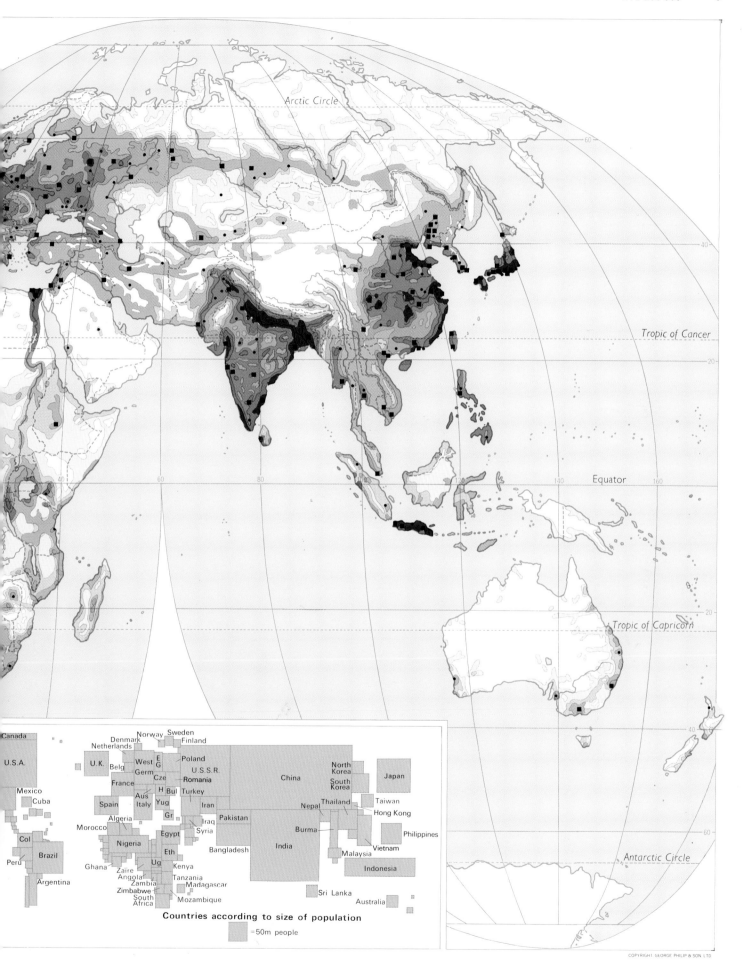

Arctic Circle

Tropic of Cancer

Equator

Tropic of Capricorn

Antarctic Circle

Countries according to size of population

=50m people

Canada
Norway Sweden
Denmark Finland
Netherlands
U.S.A. U.K. Belg West E G Poland
Germ Cze U.S.S.R. China North Korea Japan
France Romania South Korea
Mexico Spain Aus H Bul Turkey Taiwan
Cuba Italy Yug Iran Thailand Hong Kong
Algeria Gr Nepal
Morocco Iraq Pakistan Philippines
Col Nigeria Egypt Syria Burma Vietnam
Brazil Eth Bangladesh India Malaysia
Peru Ghana Ug Kenya Indonesia
Argentina Zaïre Tanzania Sri Lanka
Angola Zambia Madagascar Australia
Zimbabwe Mozambique
South Africa

Projection: Hammer Equal Area

ARCTIC OCEAN

Franz Joseph Ld.

Novaya Zemlya

Barents Sea

Kara Sea

Laptev Sea

Severnaya Zemlya

New Siberian Is.

Kotelny

Bolshevik

L. Taymyr

C. Chelyuskin

East Siberian Sea

Taymyr

Arctic Circle

FINLAND

Stockholm

Helsinki

Leningrad

Moskva

Gorkiy

Sverdlovsk

Novosibirsk

Tomsk

Krasnoyarsk

Irkutsk

UNION OF SOVIET SOCIALIST REPUBLICS

RUSSIAN SOVIET FEDERATIVE SOCIALIST REPUBLIC

Siberia

KAZAKHSTAN

MONGOLIA

Ulan Bator

Ulan Ude

Chita

Blagoveshchensk

Komsomolsk

Khabarovsk

Sea of Okhotsk

Nikolayevsk

Kamchatka

Petropavlovsk-Kamchatskiy

Bering Sea

Sakhalin

Kuril Islands

Vladivostok

Harbin

Changchun

Shenyang

Peking

Tientsin

Lu-ta

Taiyuan

Tsinan

Tsingtao

Sapporo

Hokodate

Sendai

Sea of Japan

JAPAN

Kyōto

Tōkyō

Yokohama

Nagoya

Ōsaka

Kōbe

Kitakyūshū

Pusan

Sŏul

P'yŏngyang

Nanking

Shanghai

East China Sea

CHINA

Lanchow

Sian

Chengtu

Chungking

Changsha

Wuhan

Foochow

Kwangchow

Hong Kong

Taipei

TAIWAN

PACIFIC

OCEAN

Tropic of Cancer

Ogasawara-gunto

Mariana or Ladrone Is.

Wake I. (U.S.)

Guam (U.S.)

Yap

Belau

Caroline Is.

(U. S. Trust Territory)

Truk

Ponape

Jaluit

Marshall Is.

Kiribati

Nauru

LIBYA

EGYPT

SAUDI ARABIA

Nejd

YEMEN

SOUTH YEMEN

Arabian Sea

OMAN

U.A.E.

QATAR

IRAN

(PERSIA)

Tehrān

PAKISTAN

Karachi

INDIA

Ahmadabad

Bombay

Pune

Hyderabad

Bangalore

Madras

Colombo

SRI LANKA (CEYLON)

Maldive Is.

Delhi

Agra

Kanpur

Lucknow

Varanasi

Nagpur

Calcutta

Bay of Bengal

Dhaka

BURMA

Rangoon

THAILAND (SIAM)

Bangkok

CAMBODIA

Phnom Penh

Thanh Bho Ho Chi Minh (Saigon)

VIET-NAM

Hanoi

Hainan

South China Sea

Manila

Quezon City

Cebu

PHILIPPINES

MALAYSIA

Kuala Lumpur

Singapore

Borneo

SABAH

Kuching

SARAWAK

Medan

Sumatra

Palembang

Jakarta

Bandung

Java

Surabaya

Banjarmasin

INDONESIA

Ujung Pandang

Sulawesi

Moluccas

Irian Jaya

PAPUA NEW GUINEA

New Britain

New Ireland

Admiralty Is.

Rabaul

Solomon Is.

Timor

Timor Sea

Arafura Sea

Darwin

NORTHERN TERRITORY

Alice Springs

WESTERN AUSTRALIA

Perth

Fremantle

Kalgoorlie

Geraldton

SOUTH AUSTRALIA

L. Eyre

QUEENSLAND

Cairns

Townsville

Mt. Isa

Rockhampton

Brisbane

AUSTRALIA

NEW SOUTH WALES

Sydney

Newcastle

Canberra

VICTORIA

Melbourne

Adelaide

Great Australian Bight

TASMANIA

Hobart

Tasman Sea

NEW ZEALAND

North I.

Auckland

Wellington

South I.

Christchurch

Dunedin

New Caledonia

Fiji Is.

Vanuatu

Tuvalu (Ellice Is.)

INDIAN

OCEAN

Seychelles

Chagos Arch. (Br.)

Diego Garcia (Br.)

Cocos (Keeling) Is. (Australia)

Christmas I. (Australia)

Equator

MADAGASCAR

Antananarivo

Comoro Is.

Réunion (Fr.)

MAURITIUS

Rodriguez

Amsterdam I. (Fr.)

St. Paul (Fr.)

Crozet Is. (Fr.)

Kerguelen (Fr.)

Heard I. (Australia)

McDonald I. (Australia)

Pr. Edward Is. (South Africa)

Tropic of Capricorn

SOUTHERN OCEAN

Antarctic Circle

Enderby Land

Wilkes Land

AUSTRALIAN DEPENDENCY

DEPENDENCY

from Greenwich

Ross Sea

TERRE ADÉLIE

Balleny Is.

Macquarie I. (Australia)

Campbell I. (N.Z.)

Auckland Is. (N.Z.)

Antipodes Is. (N.Z.)

Bounty Is.

Stewart I.

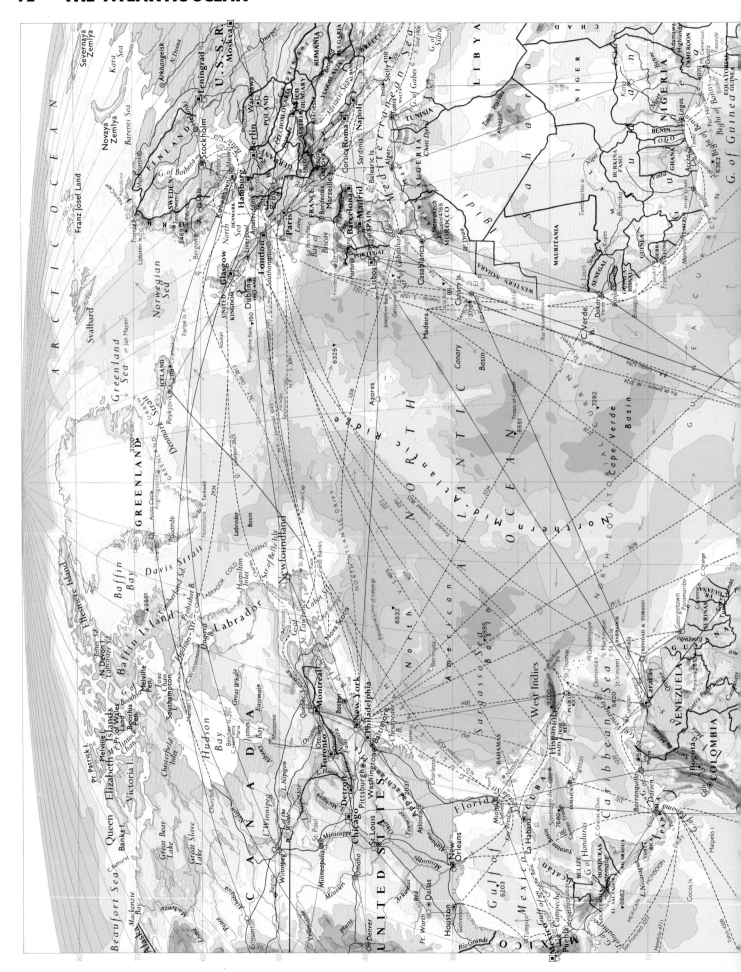

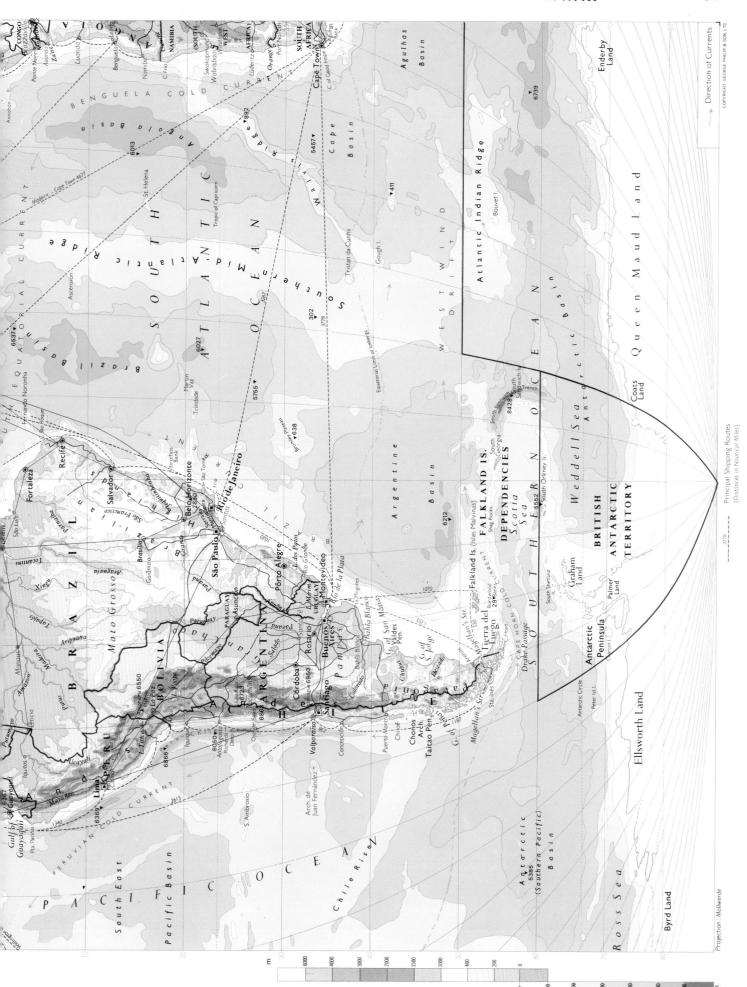

PACIFIC OCEAN

SOUTH ATLANTIC OCEAN

SOUTHERN OCEAN

BRAZIL

ARGENTINA

CHILE

BOLIVIA

PERU

Andes

Amazon

Mato Grosso

Pampas

Patagonia

ANGOLA

NAMIBIA

SOUTH WEST AFRICA

SOUTH AFRICA

Cape Town

BENGUELA COLD CURRENT

SOUTH EQUATORIAL CURRENT

PERUVIAN COLD CURRENT

CAPE HORN COLD CURRENT

WEST WIND DRIFT

Angola Basin

Cape Basin

Agulhas Basin

Brazil Basin

Argentine Basin

Scotia Sea

Weddell Sea

Southern Mid-Atlantic Ridge

Mid-Atlantic Ridge

Atlantic Indian Ridge

Walvis Ridge

Chile Rise

South East Pacific Basin

South Pacific Basin

Antarctic (Southern Pacific) Basin

Enderby Land

Queen Maud Land

Coats Land

Ellsworth Land

Byrd Land

Ross Sea

BRITISH ANTARCTIC TERRITORY

Antarctic Peninsula

Graham Land

Palmer Land

FALKLAND IS. (Islas Malvinas)

DEPENDENCIES

South Georgia

South Sandwich Is.

South Orkney Is.

South Shetland Is.

Tierra del Fuego

Drake Passage

Magellan's Str.

Rio de la Plata

Buenos Aires

Montevideo

Córdoba

Rosario

Santiago

Valparaíso

Concepción

Asunción

PARAGUAY

URUGUAY

São Paulo

Rio de Janeiro

Belo Horizonte

Brasília

Salvador

Recife

Fortaleza

Pôrto Alegre

Lima

La Paz

Iquique

Antofagasta

St. Helena

Ascension

Tristan da Cunha

Gough I.

Bouvet I.

Martin Vaz

Trindade

Fernando Noronha

Projection: Mollweide

COPYRIGHT GEORGE PHILIP & SON LTD

Direction of Currents

Principal Shipping Routes
(Distances in Nautical Miles)

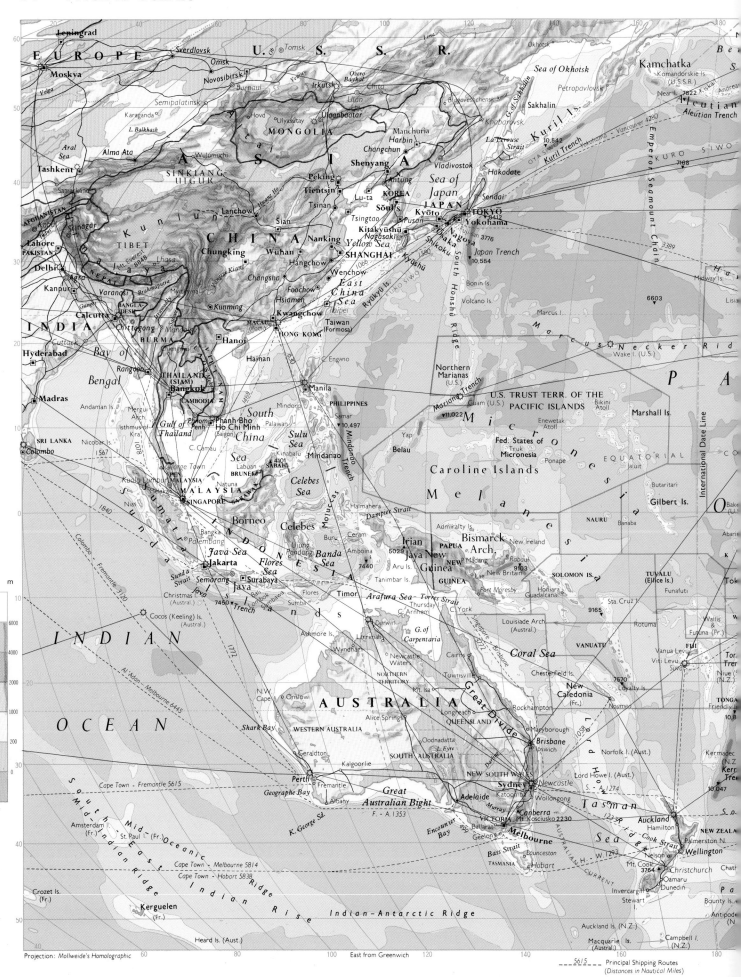

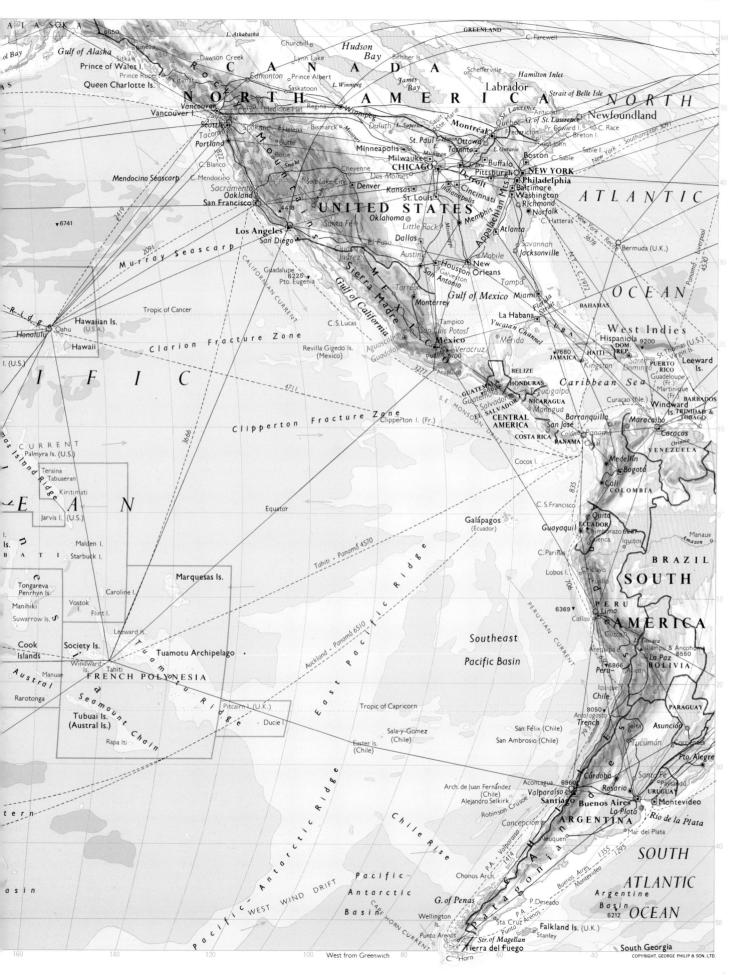

ALASKA
6050
Gulf of Alaska
Juneau
Prince of Wales I.
Kitimat
Prince Rupert
Queen Charlotte Is.
L. Athabaska
Churchill
Dawson Creek
GREENLAND
C. Farewell
Hudson Bay
Belcher Is.
Scheffeville
Hamilton Inlet
Labrador
Strait of Belle Isle
NORTH

R O C K Y   CANADA
NORTH   AMERICA
Edmonton
Prince Albert
L. Winnipeg
James Bay
St. Lawrence
Anticosti I.
Newfoundland
Vancouver
Vancouver I.
Victoria
Seattle
Tacoma
Portland
Spokane
Helena
Bismarck
Saskatoon
Regina
Winnipeg
Duluth
L. Superior
Ste. Marie
Montréal
Québec
G. of St. Lawrence
Fredericton
Pr. Edward I.
C. Breton I.
C. Race
Southampton 3091

Mountains
Butte
Boise
Snake
Cheyenne
Des Moines
Minneapolis
Milwaukee
St. Paul
L. Huron
Ottawa
Toronto
L. Ontario
Boston
Sable I.
New York
Liverpool

C. Blanco
C. Mendocino
Mendocino Seascarp
Sacramento
Oakland
San Francisco
4418
Salt Lake City
Denver
Kansas
CHICAGO
Detroit
Erie
Buffalo
Pittsburgh
Philadelphia
Washington
Baltimore
Richmond
Cincinnati
Indianapolis
St. Louis
UNITED   STATES
Santa Fe
Oklahoma
Little Rock
Memphis
Atlanta
Norfolk
C. Hatteras
ATLANTIC

6741
Los Angeles
San Diego
El Paso
Cd.
Juárez
Dallas
Austin
Houston
San Antonio
New Orleans
Galveston
Mobile
Jacksonville
Savannah
Tampa
Miami
Florida
Bermuda (U.K.)
OCEAN
New York 3678
N.Y.C. 1972

Murray Seascarp
2091
Guadalupe
6225
Pto. Eugenia
Sierra Madre
Gulf of California
Torreón
Monterrey
Tampico
San Luis Potosí
Gulf of Mexico
La Habana
CUBA
BAHAMAS
West Indies
Hispaniola
9200
DOM. REP.
St. Thomas (U.S.)
Virgin Is.
Leeward Is.
Panamá 4530
Tropic of Cancer
CALIFORNIAN CURRENT
C.S. Lucas
Clarion Fracture Zone
Revilla Gigedo Is. (Mexico)
Aguascalientes
Guadalajara
México
Puebla
5700
Veracruz
Mérida
Yucatán Channel
7680
JAMAICA
Kingston
HAITI
Santo Domingo
PUERTO RICO
Guadeloupe (Fr.)
Martinique (Fr.)
BARBADOS

Hawaiian Is. (U.S.A.)
Oahu
Honolulu
Hawaii
I. (U.S.)
4711
3277
Acapulco
BELIZE
GUATEMALA
Guatemala 3902
HONDURAS
Tegucigalpa
SALVADOR
NICARAGUA
Managua
CENTRAL AMERICA
San José
COSTA RICA
Caribbean Sea
Barranquilla
Curaçao (Ne.)
Windward Is.
TRINIDAD & TOBAGO

PACIFIC
Clipperton Fracture Zone
Clipperton I. (Fr.)
S.E. MONSOON DRIFT
3666
Cocos I.
San José
Colón
PANAMA
Panamá Canal
Medellín
Bogotá
Caracas
Orinoco
VENEZUELA

CURRENT
Palmyra Is. (U.S.)
Teraina
Tabuaeran
Kiritimati
OCEAN
Cali
COLOMBIA
C.S. Francisco
835

Christmas Island Ridge
Malden I.
Starbuck I.
Jarvis I. (U.S.)
Equator
Galápagos (Ecuador)
Guayaquil
Quito
ECUADOR
Chimborazo 6267
Cuenca
Iquitos
Manaus
Amazon
BRAZIL

KIRIBATI
Tongareva
Penrhyn Is.
Manihiki
Suwarrow Is.
Vostok I.
Flint I.
Caroline I.
Marquesas Is.
Tahiti - Panamá 4570
C. Pariñas
Lobos I.
706
Chiclayo
Trujillo
SOUTH
PERU
Lima
Callao
6369
AMERICA

Cook Islands
Society Is.
Windward Is.
Leeward Is.
Tahiti
Tuamotu Archipelago
FRENCH POLYNESIA
Auckland - Panamá 6510
East Pacific Ridge
Southeast
Pacific Basin
Cuzco
PERUVIAN CURRENT
Arequipa
Illampu & Ancohuma 6550
La Paz
BOLIVIA
Iquique
Antofagasta
8050
Trench
Manuae
Austral
Rarotonga
Tubuai Is. (Austral Is.)
Rapa Iti
Seamount Chain
Pitcairn I. (U.K.)
Ducie I.
Tropic of Capricorn
Sala-y-Gomez (Chile)
Easter Is. (Chile)
San Félix (Chile)
San Ambrosio (Chile)
Chile
PARAGUAY
Salta
Asunción
Tucumán
Corrientes
Pto. Alegre

Pacific - Antarctic Ridge
Tuamotu Ridge
Arch. de Juan Fernández (Chile)
Alejandro Selkirk
Robinson Crusoe
Aconcagua 6960
Valparaíso
Santiago
Córdoba
Rosario
Santa Fé
Paysandú
URUGUAY
Montevideo
P.A. Valparaíso
1474
Concepción
Neuquén
ARGENTINA
La Plata
Buenos Aires
Río de la Plata
Mar del Plata

Chile Rise
Chonos Arch.
Pacific
Antarctic
Basin
Wellington I.
G. of Penas
Sta. Cruz Arenas
P. Deseado
Buenos Aires 1355
Montevideo 1295
Patagonian
SOUTH
ATLANTIC
Argentine Basin
6212
OCEAN

Eastern
Basin
WEST WIND DRIFT
CAPE HORN CURRENT
Punta Arenas
Str. of Magellan
Tierra del Fuego
C. Horn
P.A. Sta. Cruz Arenas
Punta Arenas
Stanley
Falkland Is. (U.K.)
South Georgia

160   140   120   100   West from Greenwich   80   60   40

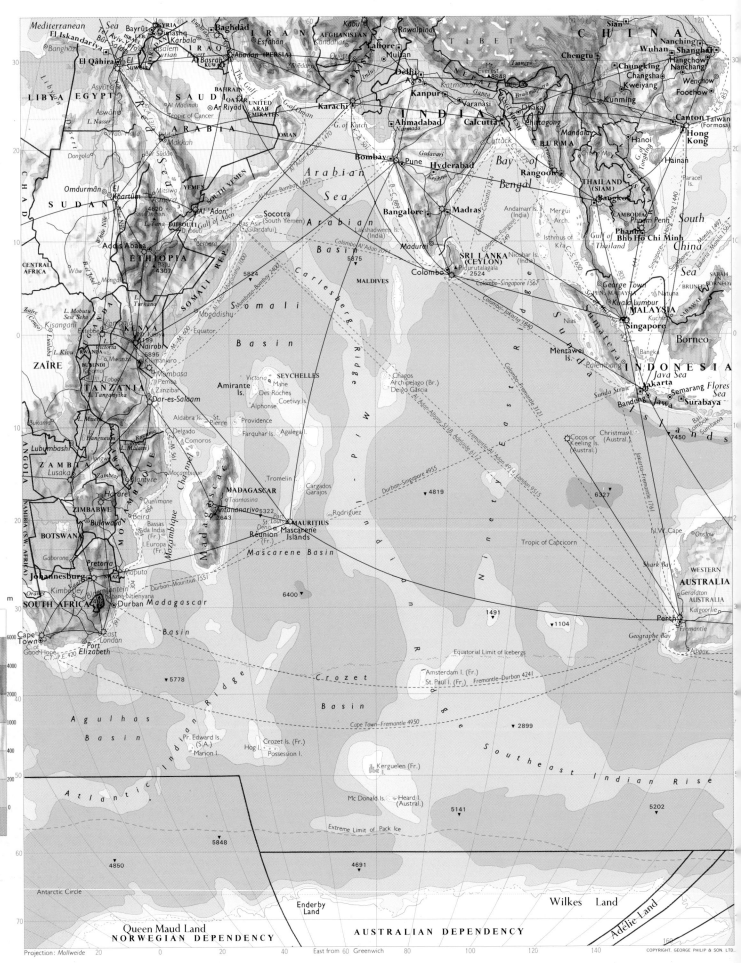

Projection: Mollweide

East from 60 Greenwich

1 : 35 000 000

400   0   400   800   1200 km

RCTIC REGIONS

EUREKA

TEMPERATURE
Range 51.7°C

Eureka
80°00'N
85°56'W

PRESSURE
M.S.L.

ANNUAL
PRECIPITATION
Total 58.2mm.

J F M A M J J A S O N D

PACIFIC OCEAN

Aleutian Islands

Near Is.

JAPAN
Hakodate
Hokkaido

Dutch Harbor

Mys Lopatka

Kurilskiye Ostrova

La Perouse Str.

Unimak I.

Bering Sea

Kamandorskiye
Ostrova

Petropavlovsk-
Kamchatskiy

Vlk. Klyuchevskaya
4850

Sakhalin

Pribilof Is.

Mys
Olyutorski

Poluostrov Kamchatka

Sea of
Okhotsk

Tatarskiy Proliv

Sovetskaya
Gavan

Bristol Bay

St. Matthew
(U.S.A.)

Ostrov
Karaginskiy

Penzhinskaya G.

Gizhiginskaya
Guba

Tauiskaya
Guba

Amur

Khabarovsk

Ussuri

Kodiak I.

G. of Alaska

Nunivak

St. Lawrence I.
(U.S.A.)

Mys Navarin

Penzhina

Nikolayevsk

Ulbanskiy
Sahv

Udskaya
Guba

Ussuri

Seward

Kuskokwim

Anadyrskiy
Zaliv

Anadyr

Okhotsk

Pr. William Sd.
Anchorage

St. Michael

Nome

Bering Str.

Mys
Chukotskiy

Omolon

Mt. St. Elias
5489

Cordova Mt. McKinley
6194

Copper

Fairbanks

Tanana

Yukon

Norton Sd.

Pr. of Wales

Okhotsko
Kolymskoye

Chukotskiy
Khrebet

Stanovoy Khrebet

Aldan

Mt. Logan
6050

Skagway

ALASKA

Circle

Yukon

Koyukuk

Kotzebue Sd.

Pt. Hope
C. Lisburne

Proliv Longa

Nizhne

Kolyma

Sredne Kolymsk

Alazeya

Indigirka

Yana

Yakutsk

Lena

Olekma

Whitehorse

Lewes

Fort Yukon

Noatak

C. Belcher

Cook 1778
Rodgers
1855

Ostrova
Vrangelya

Chaunskaya

Ostrova
Medvezhi

Zashiversk

Verkhoyansk

Verkhoyanskiy Khrebet

Olekma

ky Mountains

Dawson Creek

Stewart

Dawson

Peel

Porcupine

Coville

C. Halkett
Pt. Barrow
Kellett 1849
Harrison Bay
Franklin 1826
Collinson 1850

Berry 1881

Wrangell 1822

Russkoye
Ustie

Postnik 1640

Verkhoyansk

Yana

Zhigansk

Fort
Simpson

Fort
Norman

Mackenzie

Fort
Good Hope

Herschel
Mackenzie 1789
Mackenzie
Bay

Novosibirskiye
O. Novaya
Sibir

O-va
Lyakhovskiye
Ostrova

Kazache

Bulun

Olenek

NORTH

Great Bear
Lake

Liverpool B.
C. Bathurst
Darnley B.

Beaufort Sea

O. Bennetta

O. Delong
1881
Jeannette

O. Kotelnyy

Guba Buor-Khaya

Tiksi

Fort
Resolution

Gt. Slave
Lake

Coppermine

Franklin B.

ARCTIC

O. Faddeyevskiy

Baron Toll
1901

Laptev
Sea

Ofenek

asca
L.

Coppermine

C. Kellett

Banks
I.

Pr.
Albert
Pen.

M'Clure 1851

O C E A N

Khatangskiy Sdliv

O-va Petra

Nordvik

Anabar

Vilyuy

MERICA

Dubawnt
L.

Victoria
Island

Melville I.

Melville I.

Pr. Patrick
I.

Borden I.

Mys Chelyuskin

O. Bolshevik

Poluostrov
Taymyr

Oz. Taymyr

Kotuy

Kheta

Plato
Putorana

Podkamennaya Tunguska

Nizhnyaya Tunguska

Back

King William
I.

Boothia
Pen.

Bathurst
I.

Cornwallis
I.

Ellef Ringnes I.

Amund Ringnes I.

Sverdrup Is.

Axel
Heiberg

Aldrich 1875

Severnaya Zemlya
O. Oktyabrskoy Revolyutsii

Nansen 1895 O. Komsomolets

Proliv Vilkitskogo

Pyasina

Golchikha

Dudinka

Turukhansk

Yenisey

Igarka

son
ay

southampton I.

ats I.

ansel

Melville
Pen.

Foxe
Channel Pr.
Charles I.

Pr. of
Wales
I.

Devon I.

Ellesmere I.

C. Columbia
Markham 1876

Lincoln
Sea

Markham I.

Lockwood 1882

NORTH
POLE

Peary 1909
Byrd 1926
Amundsen 1926;
Herbert 1969
Cagni 1900

O. Uedineniya

O. Vise

Ostrov
Graham Bell
Z. Vilcheka

Payer 1872

Kara
Sea

Ostrov
Belyy

Poluostrov
Yamal

Ob

Surgut

Baffin
Bay

Davis 1585

Smith Sd.
Thule

Kane
Basin

Robeson Ch.

McKinley
Sea

Peary 1900

Markham I.

Byrd 1926

Zemlya Frantsa
Iosifa
Alexandra Ld.

Parry 1827

Leigh Smith 1871

Novaya

Zemlya

Baydaratskaya
Guba

Nadym

Foxe
Basin

Fury
and
Hecla
Str.

Byrd

Lancaster Sd.

Pond Inlet

K. York

Knud

Rasmussen
Land

Peary 1892

Vills Land

Independence Fj.

Hinlopenstredet

Hudson
1607

Nordaustlandet

Olgastretet

Barents
1594

Novy Port

Salekhard

O. Vaygach

P. Karskiy Vorota

Khabarovo

Berezovo

Amadjuak

Nettilling

Baffin

Cumberland
Sd.

Upernavik

Kong Frederik
VIII.s.Land

Kong
Christian
X.s.Land

Shannon

Svalbard

Edgeøya

Zemlya

Barents

Sørkapp

Ostrov
Kolguyev

Mys
Kanin
Nos

Pechora

Narodnaya

Uralskie

Tobolsk

C. Dyer

Disko

Umanak

Disko B.
Godhavn

Greenland
Sea

Bjørnøya

Matochkin Sh.

Kolskiy
Poluostrov

Belove

Sev. Dvina

Arkhangelsk

Ob

Resolution I.

C. Chidley

pedale

Julianehab
Sydprøven

K. Farvel

Frederikshåb

Goathåb

GREENLAND
(To Denmark)

Kong Frederik
IX.s.Kyst

Kong
Christian IX.s. Land

Mont Forel
3360

Kong
Christian IX.s. Land

K. Franz Joseph Fd.
Hudson 1607

Kong Oscar Fj.

Scoresbysund

K. Brewster

Jan Mayen

Nordkapp

Hammerfest

Vadsø Varangerfjord

Polyarny

Murmansk

Nordkapp

Onega

Mezen

Onezhskoye
Ozero

Sverdlovsk

Perm

Chelyabinsk

Gory

Ufa

m

4000

3000

2000

1000

400

200

0

mton Inlet

arles

Angmagssalik

Kangerdlugssuak

Denmark
Strait

Horn

Fontur

Norwegian

Tromsø

Lofoten

Torne

Tornio

Vatangerfjord

Kem

Arctic Circle

Breidafjørdur

Reykjavik ICELAND
Hekla
1491

Orajojøkull

Sea

Trondheim

Ume

Pite

Gulf of Bothnia

FINLAND

Ladozhskoye
Ozero

Vologda

Volga

Kuybyshev

Seas open all year

Extreme limits of
drift-ice

Seas covered by
pack-ice in Spring

Seas permanently
covered by pack-ice

Ice-caps and
permanent ice shelf

Arctic Explorers

— Cook 1778
— Franklin 1826–47
— McClure 1850–53
— Nansen ("Fram") 1893–96
+ Sverdrup 1902
+ Peary 1892–1906
— Amundsen 1903–6 & 1926
+++ Bernier 1906–1913
— Peary 1908–9
— Knud Rasmussen 1912
— Stefánsson 1914–15
→ Byrd 1926 (by air)
→ Wilkins 1928 (by air)
— Lindsay 1934
— Papanin (Drift of Soviet
      Expedition) 1937–8
— Sedov 1937–40

— Knuth (Danish Pearyland
      Expedition) 1948–49
→ Skate (Nuclear submarine)
                  1959
|—| Manhattan (Tanker) 1969

n: Zenithal Equidistant

Faroe Is.

Shetland Is.

Rockall

Hebrides

Orkney Is.

BRITISH
ISLES

SCOTLAND
Glasgow Edinburgh

North
Sea

Bergen

Oslo

Helsinki

Stockholm

Leningrad

Moskvá

EST.
Chudskoye
Ozero

LATVIA

LITH.

Faeroe Is.

Riga

Vilnius

Kaliningrad

Helsingfors

ATLANTIC
OCEAN

C. Clear

Cork

London

Amsterdam

GERMANY

Hamburg

Berlin POLAND

Köln

Praha

Gdansk

Szczecin

Warszawa

Wisla

Łódz

Wrocław

NORTH SEA

Rockall

WALES
ENGLAND

IRELAND
Dublin

Liverpool

Skagerrak

DENMARK
København

SWEDEN

Gulf of Finland

Nemen

Oder

Baltic Sea

Tallinn

Zap.

Progress of Exploration

Coasts explored before   1800
    „   „   between 1800 & 1850
    „   „   between 1850 & 1900
    „   „   since   1900
+ Byrd   Highest latitudes reached by explorers
  1926   with date

© GEORGE PHILIP & SON, LTD.

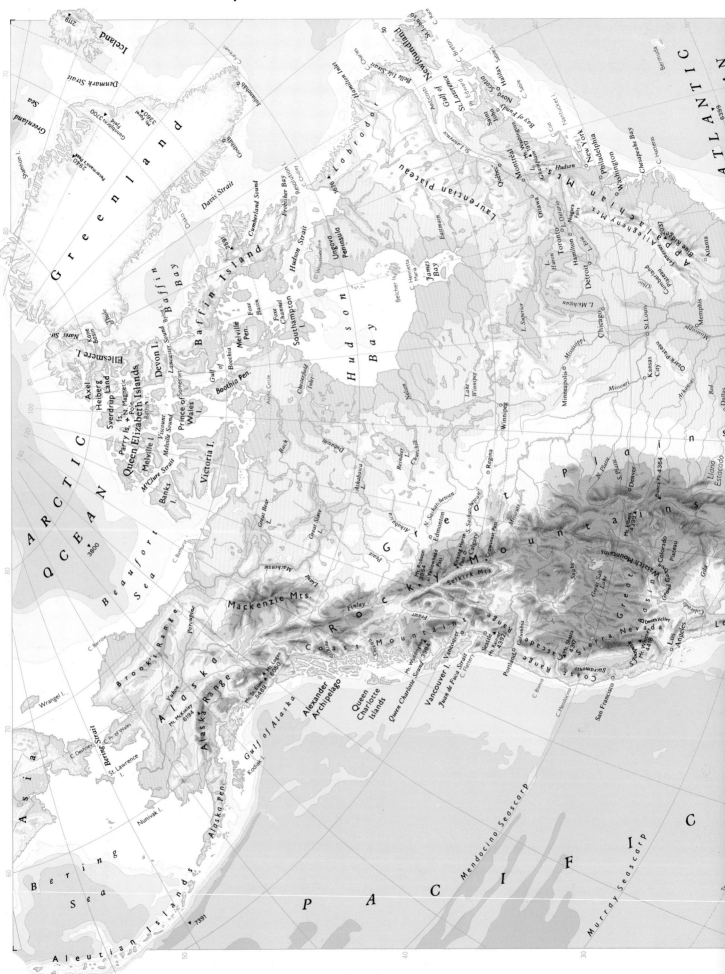

ATLANTIC

Iceland

Greenland Sea

Denmark Strait

2119

Kap Farvel

3700

Gunnbjörn Fjeld 3380

Petermann Peak 2940

Shannon I.

G r e e n l a n d

Davis Strait

Disko I.

Godthåb

Julianehåb

Holsteinsborg

Newfoundland

St John's

Race

Belle Isle Strait

Gulf of St. Lawrence

Anticosti

Cabot Strait

Nova Scotia

Halifax

Cape Sable I.

Bay of Fundy

Sable I.

Bermuda

6399

C. Cod

Nantucket I.

Long I.

New York

Philadelphia

Washington 1907

Chesapeake Bay

C. Hatteras

Atlanta

Memphis

L a b r a d o r

L a u r e n t i a n   P l a t e a u

1676

Ungava Peninsula

Cumberland Sound

Frobisher Bay

Resolution I.

Hudson Strait

Charles

Hamilton Inlet

A p p a l a c h i a n   M t s.

Blue Ridge

Allegheny Mts.

Cumberland Plateau

Quebec

Montreal Mt. 1917

Ottawa

Hudson

Toronto

Hamilton

Niagara Falls

Detroit

L. Ontario

Lake Erie

Ohio

B a f f i n   B a y

Baffin Island

Devon I.

Ellesmere I.

Axel Heiberg

Sverdrup Land

Parry Is. ★ N. Magnetic Pole

N. Pole

Bathurst I.

Melville I.

Viscount Melville Sound

Prince of Wales

Lancaster Sound

Boothia Pen.

Gulf of Boothia

Melville Pen.

Foxe Basin

Foxe Channel

Southampton

Belcher Is.

James Bay

C. Henrietta Maria

Eastmain

Great Whale

W. Wolstenholme

Arctic Circle

Chesterfield Inlet

H u d s o n   B a y

Nelson

Churchill

Reindeer L.

Winnipeg

Lake Winnipeg

L. Nipigon

L. Superior

L. Michigan

Chicago

St. Louis

Minneapolis

Kansas City

Missouri

Mississippi

Ozark Plateau

Dallas

Red

Arkansas

Queen Elizabeth Islands

M'Clure Strait

Banks I.

Victoria I.

Great Bear L.

Great Slave L.

Back

Dubawnt

G r e a t   P l a i n s

N. Platte

S. Platte

Denver

Mt. Elbert 4399

Blanca Pk. 4364

Colorado Plateau

Llano Estacado

Gila

Colorado

Grand Canyon

Great Salt Lake

Wasatch Mountains

Spanish Pk.

Death Valley

Sierra Nevada

Los Angeles

A R C T I C

O C E A N

3800

Beaufort Sea

C. Bathurst

C. Barrow

Mackenzie

Liard

Mackenzie Mts.

Finlay

Peace

Athabasca

L. Athabasca

N. Saskatchewan

S. Saskatchewan

Edmonton

Calgary

Regina

Crowfoot Pass

Kicking Horse Pass

Yellowhead Pass

Mt. Robson 3954

Selkirk Mts.

Fraser

R o c k y   M o u n t a i n s

C o a s t   M o u n t a i n s

Mt. Waddington 3994

Columbia

G r e a t   B a s i n

Cascade Range

Mt. Rainier 4392

Mt. Shasta 4317

Mt. Whitney 4418

Seattle

Portland

Sacramento

San Francisco

Coast Range

C. Mendocino

C. Blanco

Juan de Fuca Strait

Vancouver I.

Queen Charlotte Islands

Queen Charlotte Sound

Alexander Archipelago

Gulf of Alaska

Mt. St. Elias 5489

Mt. Logan 6050

Mt. McKinley 6194

Alaska Range

Yukon

A l a s k a

Brooks Range

Porcupine

Wrangel I.

C. Deshnev

Bering Strait

Pr. of Wales

St. Lawrence I.

Nunivak I.

Kodiak I.

Alaska Pen.

A l e u t i a n   I s l a n d s

7391

A s i a

B e r i n g   S e a

P A C I F I C

Mendocino Seascarp

Murray Seascarp

C

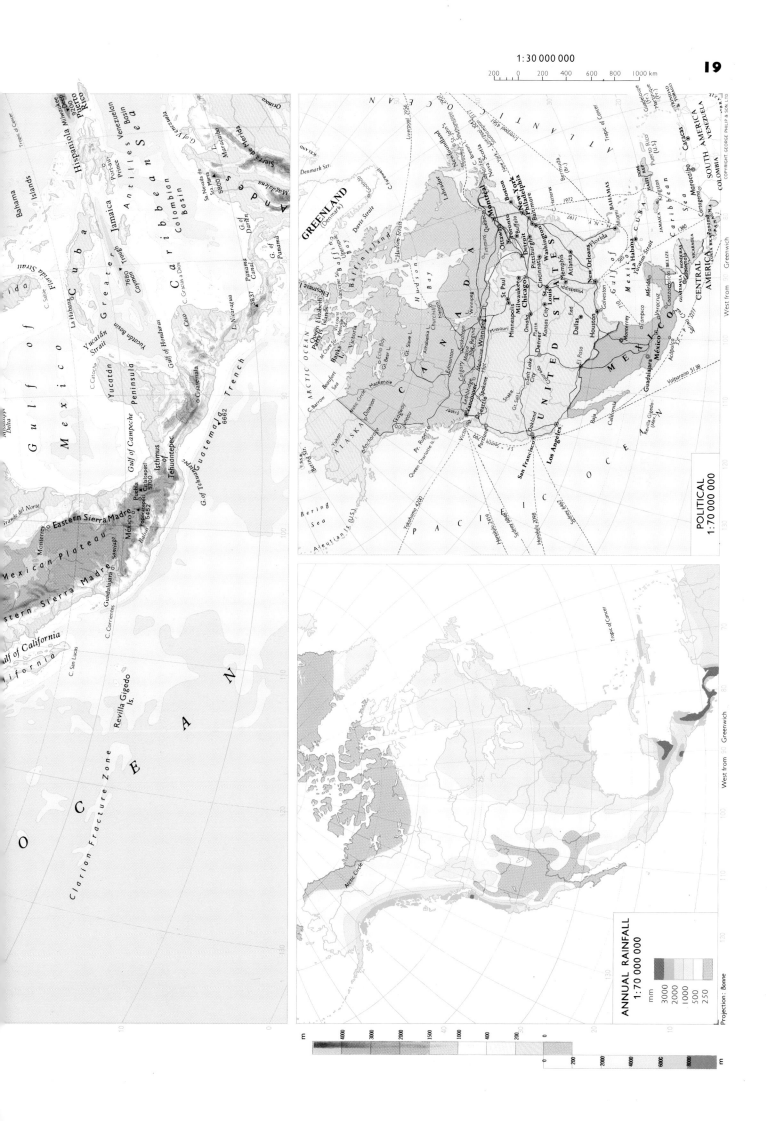

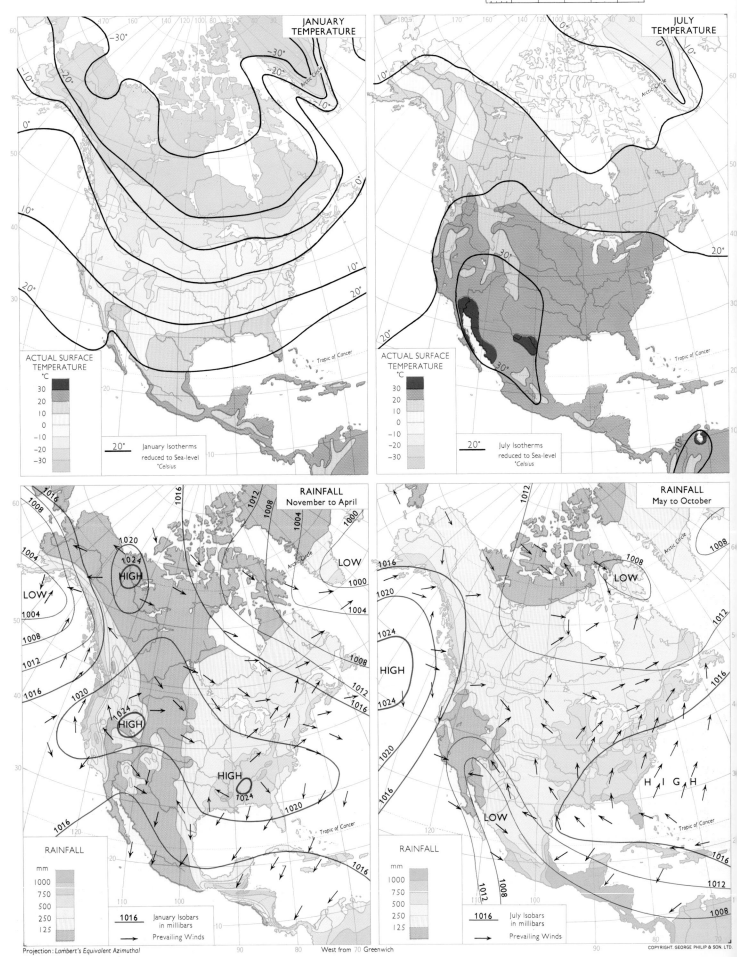

1 : 70 000 000

500 0 500 1000 1500 2000 2500 km

JANUARY TEMPERATURE

JULY TEMPERATURE

ACTUAL SURFACE TEMPERATURE
°C
30
20
10
0
-10
-20
-30

20° January Isotherms reduced to Sea-level °Celsius

ACTUAL SURFACE TEMPERATURE
°C
30
20
10
0
-10
-20
-30

20° July Isotherms reduced to Sea-level °Celsius

RAINFALL November to April

RAINFALL May to October

RAINFALL
mm
1000
750
500
250
125

1016 January Isobars in millibars
→ Prevailing Winds

RAINFALL
mm
1000
750
500
250
125

1016 July Isobars in millibars
→ Prevailing Winds

Projection: Lambert's Equivalent Azimuthal

West from Greenwich

COPYRIGHT. GEORGE PHILIP & SON. LTD.

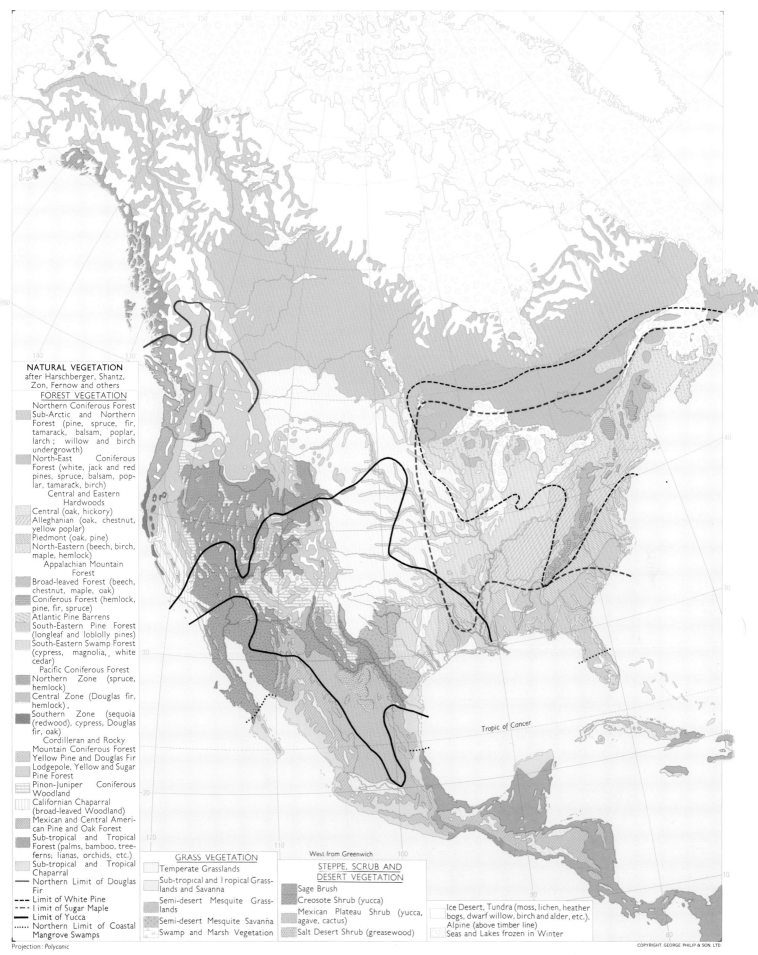

1:32 000 000

400 0 400 800 1200 km

NATURAL VEGETATION
after Harschberger, Shantz,
Zon, Fernow and others
FOREST VEGETATION
Northern Coniferous Forest
Sub-Arctic and Northern
Forest (pine, spruce, fir,
tamarack, balsam, poplar,
larch; willow and birch
undergrowth)
North-East Coniferous
Forest (white, jack and red
pines, spruce, balsam, pop-
lar, tamarack, birch)
Central and Eastern
Hardwoods
Central (oak, hickory)
Alleghanian (oak, chestnut,
yellow poplar)
Piedmont (oak, pine)
North-Eastern (beech, birch,
maple, hemlock)
Appalachian Mountain
Forest
Broad-leaved Forest (beech,
chestnut, maple, oak)
Coniferous Forest (hemlock,
pine, fir, spruce)
Atlantic Pine Barrens
South-Eastern Pine Forest
(longleaf and loblolly pines)
South-Eastern Swamp Forest
(cypress, magnolia, white
cedar)
Pacific Coniferous Forest
Northern Zone (spruce,
hemlock)
Central Zone (Douglas fir,
hemlock).
Southern Zone (sequoia
(redwood), cypress, Douglas
fir, oak)
Cordilleran and Rocky
Mountain Coniferous Forest
Yellow Pine and Douglas Fir
Lodgepole, Yellow and Sugar
Pine Forest
Pinon-Juniper Coniferous
Woodland
Californian Chaparral
(broad-leaved Woodland)
Mexican and Central Ameri-
can Pine and Oak Forest
Sub-tropical and Tropical
Forest (palms, bamboo, tree-
ferns, lianas, orchids, etc.)
Sub-tropical and Tropical
Chaparral
—— Northern Limit of Douglas
Fir
––– Limit of White Pine
–·–· Limit of Sugar Maple
—— Limit of Yucca
······ Northern Limit of Coastal
Mangrove Swamps

Projection: Polyconic

GRASS VEGETATION
Temperate Grasslands
Sub-tropical and Tropical Grass-
lands and Savanna
Semi-desert Mesquite Grass-
lands
Semi-desert Mesquite Savanna
Swamp and Marsh Vegetation

West from Greenwich

STEPPE, SCRUB AND
DESERT VEGETATION
Sage Brush
Creosote Shrub (yucca)
Mexican Plateau Shrub (yucca,
agave, cactus)
Salt Desert Shrub (greasewood)

Ice Desert, Tundra (moss, lichen, heather
bogs, dwarf willow, birch and alder, etc.),
Alpine (above timber line)
Seas and Lakes frozen in Winter

Tropic of Cancer

Projection: *Bonne*

West from Greenwich

1:17 500 000

200 0 200 400 600 km

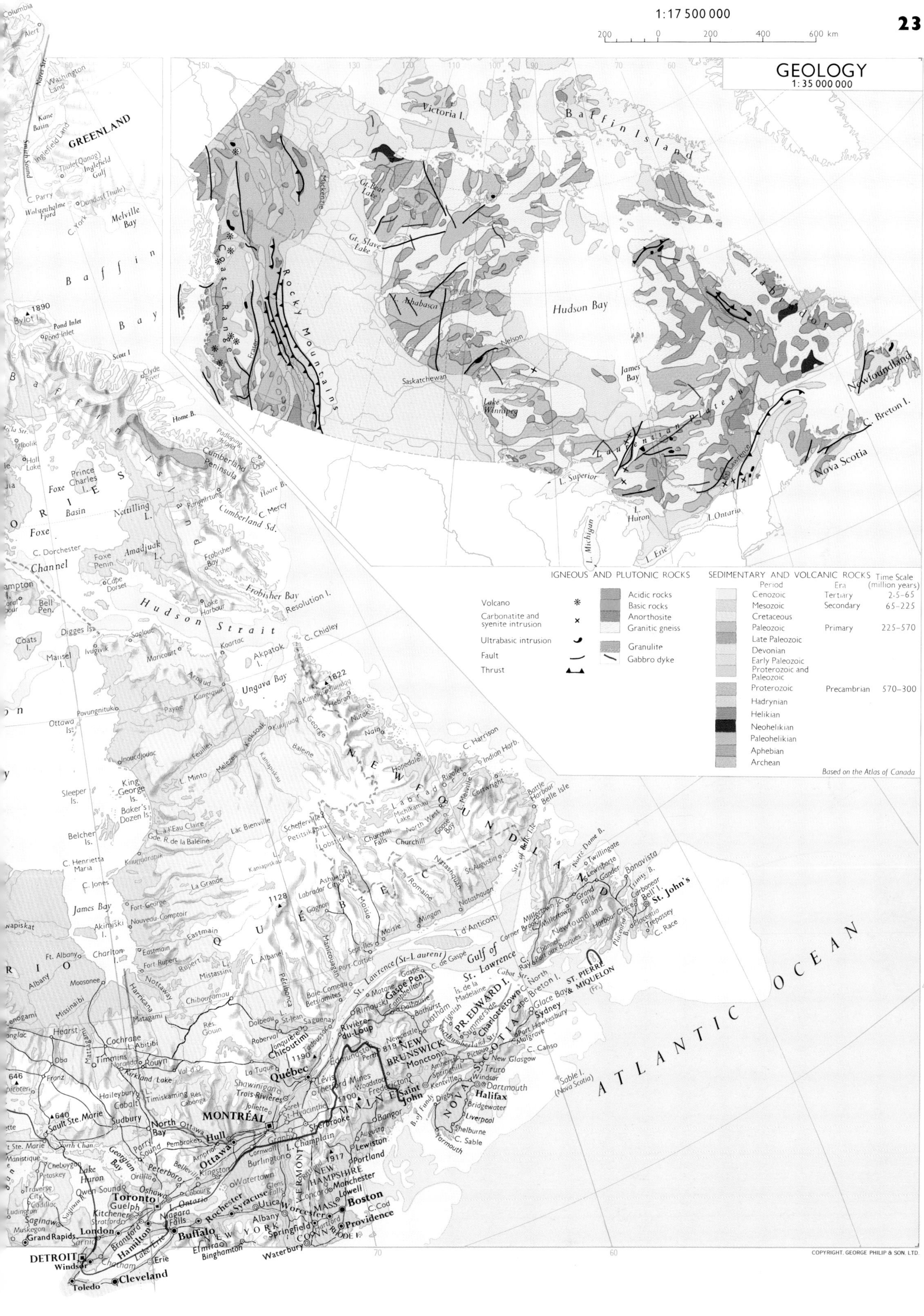

GEOLOGY
1:35 000 000
IGNEOUS AND PLUTONIC ROCKS
Volcano
Carbonatite and syenite intrusion
Ultrabasic intrusion
Fault
Thrust
Acidic rocks
Basic rocks
Anorthosite
Granitic gneiss
Granulite
Gabbro dyke
SEDIMENTARY AND VOLCANIC ROCKS
Period
Era
Time Scale (million years)
Cenozoic
Tertiary 2·5-65
Mesozoic
Secondary 65-225
Cretaceous
Paleozoic
Primary 225-570
Late Paleozoic
Devonian
Early Paleozoic
Proterozoic and Paleozoic
Proterozoic
Precambrian 570-300
Hadrynian
Helikian
Neohelikian
Paleohelikian
Aphebian
Archean
Based on the Atlas of Canada
Victoria I.
Baffin Island
Hudson Bay
Labrador
Rocky Mountains
Coast Range
Gt. Bear Lake
Gt. Slave Lake
L. Athabasca
Lake Winnipeg
James Bay
Laurentian Plateau
Newfoundland
C. Breton I.
Nova Scotia
L. Superior
L. Huron
L. Ontario
L. Erie
L. Michigan
GREENLAND
Baffin Bay
Melville Bay
Hudson Strait
Ungava Bay
Foxe Basin
Foxe Channel
Frobisher Bay
Cumberland Sd.
NEWFOUNDLAND
QUÉBEC
Gulf of St. Lawrence
ATLANTIC OCEAN
NEW BRUNSWICK
NOVA SCOTIA
PR. EDWARD I.
ST. PIERRE & MIQUELON (Fr.)
MONTRÉAL
Québec
Ottawa
Toronto
Halifax
St. John's
Boston
Buffalo
DETROIT
Cleveland
MAINE
VERMONT
NEW HAMPSHIRE
NEW YORK
Sable I. (Nova Scotia)
COPYRIGHT, GEORGE PHILIP & SON, LTD.

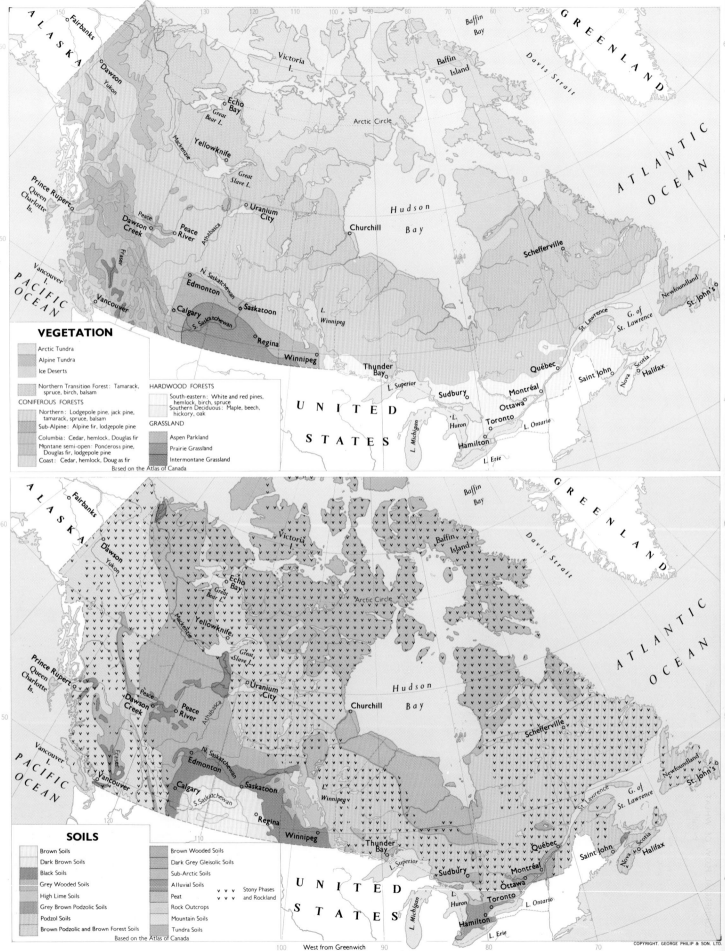

1:30 000 000

200 0 200 400 600 800 1000 km

VEGETATION

Arctic Tundra

Alpine Tundra

Ice Deserts

Northern Transition Forest: Tamarack, spruce, birch, balsam

CONIFEROUS FORESTS

Northern: Lodgepole pine, jack pine, tamarack, spruce, balsam

Sub-Alpine: Alpine fir, lodgepole pine

Columbia: Cedar, hemlock, Douglas fir

Montane semi-open: Ponderosa pine, Douglas fir, lodgepole pine

Coast: Cedar, hemlock, Douglas fir

HARDWOOD FORESTS

South-eastern: White and red pines, hemlock, birch, spruce

Southern Deciduous: Maple, beech, hickory, oak

GRASSLAND

Aspen Parkland

Prairie Grassland

Intermontane Grassland

Based on the Atlas of Canada

SOILS

Brown Soils

Dark Brown Soils

Black Soils

Grey Wooded Soils

High Lime Soils

Grey Brown Podzolic Soils

Podzol Soils

Brown Podzolic and Brown Forest Soils

Brown Wooded Soils

Dark Grey Gleisolic Soils

Sub-Arctic Soils

Alluvial Soils

Peat

Rock Outcrops

Mountain Soils

Tundra Soils

v v v Stony Phases
v v v and Rockland

Based on the Atlas of Canada

100 West from Greenwich 90 80 70

COPYRIGHT. GEORGE PHILIP & SON. LTD.

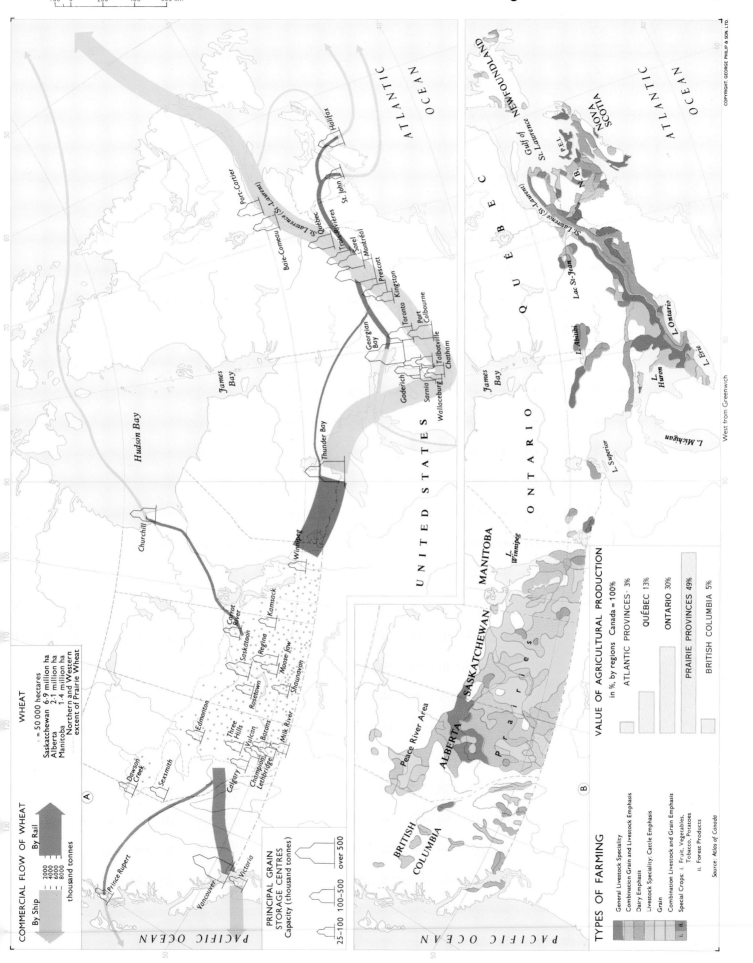

COPYRIGHT GEORGE PHILIP & SON. LTD.

1 : 22 500 000

100 0   200   400   600 km

COMMERCIAL FLOW OF WHEAT

By Ship   By Rail

thousand tonnes
8000
6000
4000
2000

WHEAT

= 50 000 hectares

Saskatchewan 6.9 million ha
Alberta   2.1 million ha
Manitoba   1.4 million ha
— — — Northern and Western
      extent of Prairie Wheat

PRINCIPAL GRAIN STORAGE CENTRES
Capacity (thousand tonnes)

25–100   100–500   over 500

Source: Atlas of Canada

TYPES OF FARMING

General Livestock Speciality
Combination Grain and Livestock Emphasis
Dairy Emphasis
Livestock Speciality: Cattle Emphasis
Grain
Combination Livestock and Grain Emphasis
Special Crops: i. Fruit, Vegetables,
                  Tobacco, Potatoes
               ii. Forest Products

VALUE OF AGRICULTURAL PRODUCTION

in % by regions Canada = 100%

ATLANTIC PROVINCES 3%
QUÉBEC 13%
ONTARIO 30%
PRAIRIE PROVINCES 49%
BRITISH COLUMBIA 5%

West from Greenwich

PACIFIC OCEAN
ATLANTIC OCEAN
Hudson Bay
James Bay
UNITED STATES

Prince Rupert
Vancouver
Victoria
Dawson Creek
Sexsmith
Edmonton
Three Hills
Vulcan
Barons
Calgary
Champion
Lethbridge
Milk River
Shaunavon
Rosetown
Moose Jaw
Regina
Saskatoon
Kamsack
Carrot River
Churchill
Winnipeg
Thunder Bay
Goderich
Sarnia
Wallaceburg
Chatham
Talbotville
Port Colbourne
Toronto
Georgian Bay
Kingston
Prescott
Montréal
Sorel
Trois-Rivières
Québec
Baie-Comeau
Port-Cartier
St. Lawrence (St-Laurent)
St. John
Halifax

BRITISH COLUMBIA
Peace River Area
ALBERTA
SASKATCHEWAN
MANITOBA
Prairies
L. Winnipeg
ONTARIO
QUÉBEC
NEWFOUNDLAND
NOVA SCOTIA
P.E.I.
N.B.
Gulf of St. Lawrence
Lac St-Jean
St. Lawrence (St-Laurent)
L. Abitibi
L. Ontario
L. Erie
L. Huron
L. Michigan
L. Superior
ATLANTIC OCEAN
James Bay

A
B

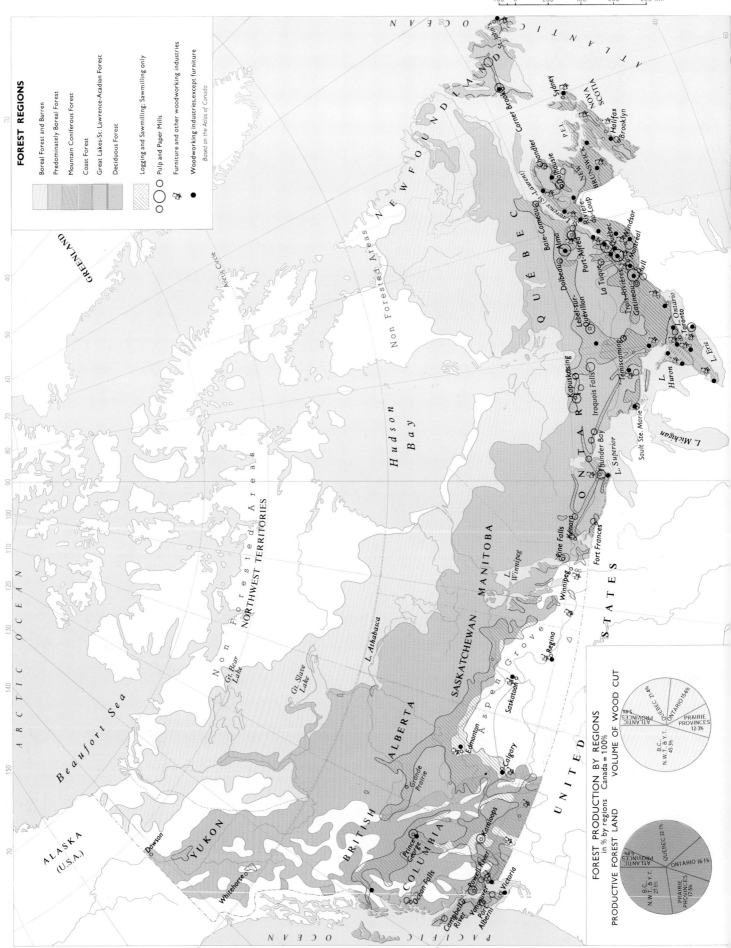

1 : 22 000 000

100 0   200   400   600   800 km

FOREST REGIONS

Boreal Forest and Barren
Predominately Boreal Forest
Mountain Coniferous Forest
Coast Forest
Great Lakes-St. Lawrence-Acadian Forest
Deciduous Forest

Logging and Sawmilling: Sawmilling only
Pulp and Paper Mills
Furniture and other woodworking industries
Woodworking industries, except furniture

Based on the Atlas of Canada

ATLANTIC OCEAN

Arctic Circle

ARCTIC OCEAN

Beaufort Sea

ALASKA
(U.S.A.)

YUKON

NORTHWEST TERRITORIES

Non Forested Areas

Gt. Bear Lake

Gt. Slave Lake

L. Athabasca

Hudson Bay

Non Forested Areas

NEWFOUNDLAND

St. John's

Corner Brook

Sydney
NOVA SCOTIA
Halifax
Brooklyn
P.E.I.
NEW BRUNSWICK

Chandler

St. Lawrence (R.)
Rivière-du-Loup
Baie-Comeau
Alma
Windsor
Quebec
Montreal
Hull
Port-Alfred
Dolbeau
La Tuque
Trois-Rivières
Gatineau
Lebel-sur-Quévillon
Quévillon
Témiscaming
L. Ontario
Toronto
L. Erie
L. Huron
Kapuskasing
Iroquois Falls
Sault Ste. Marie
L. Michigan
L. Superior
Thunder Bay

QUEBEC

ONTARIO

Kenora
Fort Frances
Pine Falls

MANITOBA

L. Winnipeg
Winnipeg

SASKATCHEWAN

Saskatoon
Aspen Grove
Regina

ALBERTA

Edmonton
Grande Prairie
Calgary

UNITED STATES

BRITISH COLUMBIA

Prince George
Kamloops
Powell River
Ocean Falls
Campbell River
Vancouver
Victoria
Port Alberni

Dawson

Whitehorse

PACIFIC OCEAN

FOREST PRODUCTION BY REGIONS
in % by regions   Canada = 100%

PRODUCTIVE FOREST LAND

QUEBEC 32·1%
ONTARIO 16·1%
ATLANTIC PROVINCES
PRAIRIE PROVINCES 17·5%
B.C. N.W.T. & Y.T. 27·5%

VOLUME OF WOOD CUT

ATLANTIC PROVINCES 5·4%
QUEBEC 21·4%
ONTARIO 15·6%
PRAIRIE PROVINCES 12·3%
B.C. N.W.T. & Y.T. 45·3%

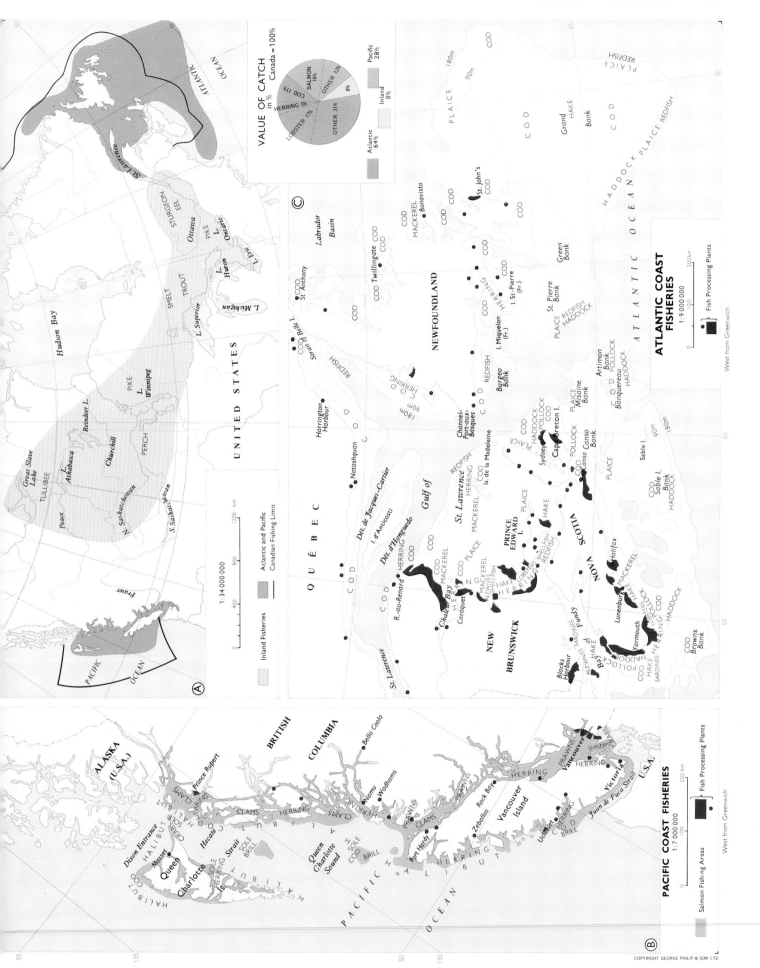

VALUE OF CATCH
in % Canada = 100%

SALMON 16%
OTHER 12%
COD 11%
HERRING 5%
LOBSTER 17%
OTHER 31%

Pacific 28%
Inland 8%
Atlantic 64%

Ⓒ **ATLANTIC COAST FISHERIES**
1:9 000 000
■ Fish Processing Plants
West from Greenwich

Ⓐ
1:34 000 000

Inland Fisheries
Atlantic and Pacific
Canadian Fishing Limit

Ⓑ **PACIFIC COAST FISHERIES**
1:7 000 000
Salmon Fishing Areas
Fish Processing Plants
West from Greenwich

COPYRIGHT GEORGE PHILIP & SON LTD

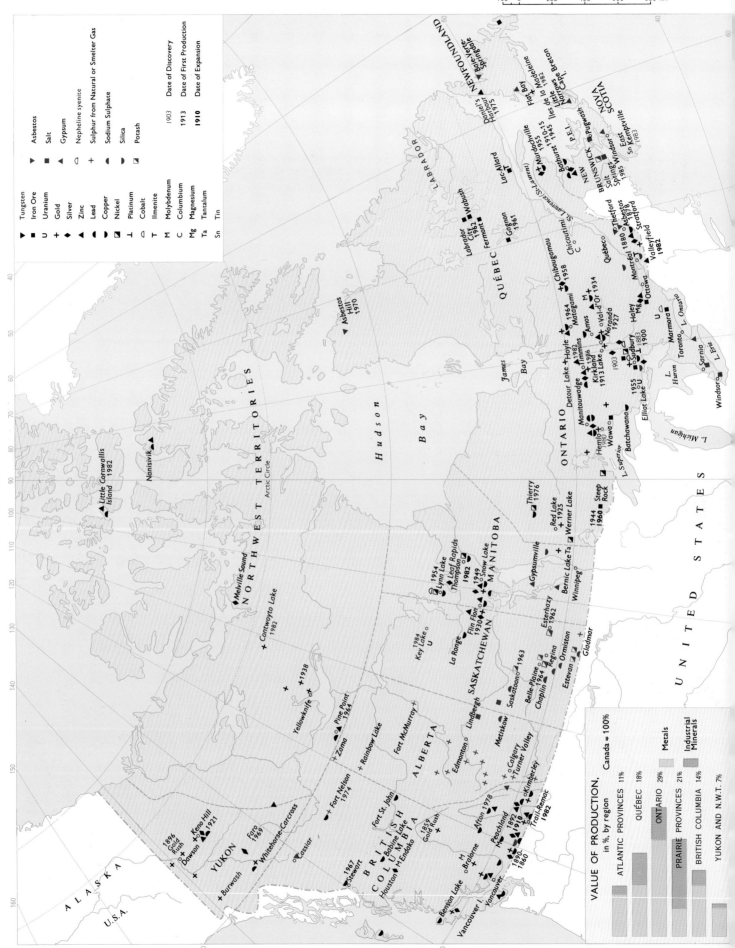

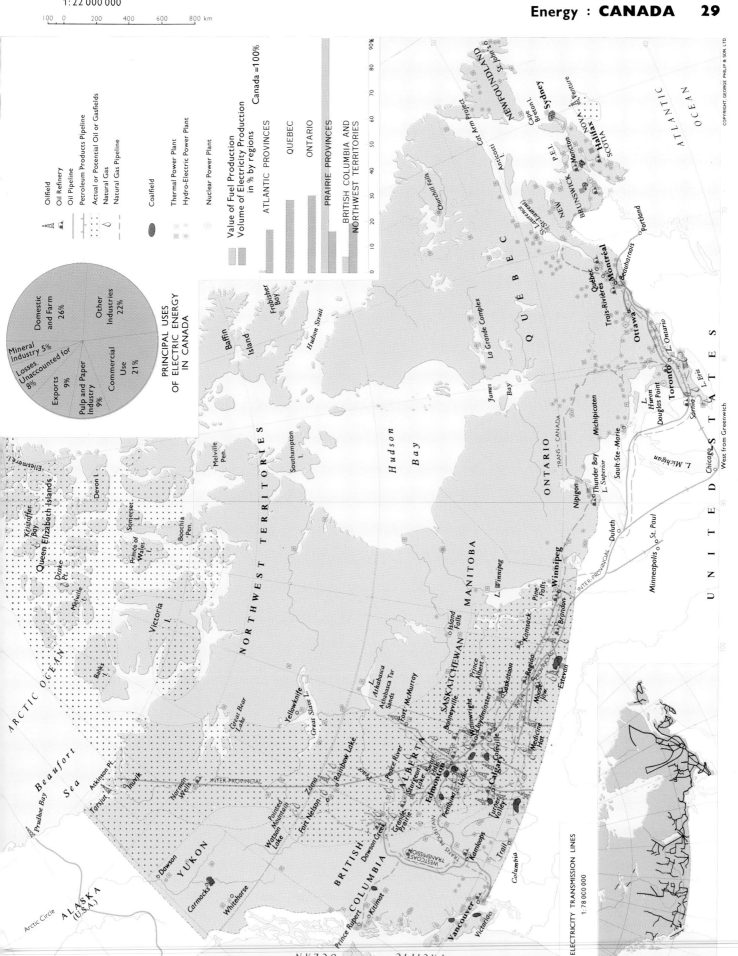

1 : 22 000 000

100 0   200   400   600   800 km

COPYRIGHT GEORGE PHILIP & SON LTD.

Legend:

Oilfield
Oil Refinery
Oil Pipeline
Petroleum Products Pipeline
Actual or Potential Oil or Gasfields
Natural Gas
Natural Gas Pipeline

Coalfield

Thermal Power Plant
Hydro-Electric Power Plant

Nuclear Power Plant

Value of Fuel Production
Volume of Electricity Production
in % by regions
Canada = 100%

ATLANTIC PROVINCES
QUEBEC
ONTARIO
PRAIRIE PROVINCES
BRITISH COLUMBIA AND
NORTHWEST TERRITORIES

PRINCIPAL USES
OF ELECTRIC ENERGY
IN CANADA

Domestic and Farm 26%
Other Industries 22%
Mineral Industry 5%
Losses Unaccounted for 8%
Exports 9%
Pulp and Paper Industry 9%
Commercial Use 21%

ELECTRICITY TRANSMISSION LINES
1 : 78 000 000

West from Greenwich

ATLANTIC OCEAN

PACIFIC OCEAN

ARCTIC OCEAN

UNITED STATES

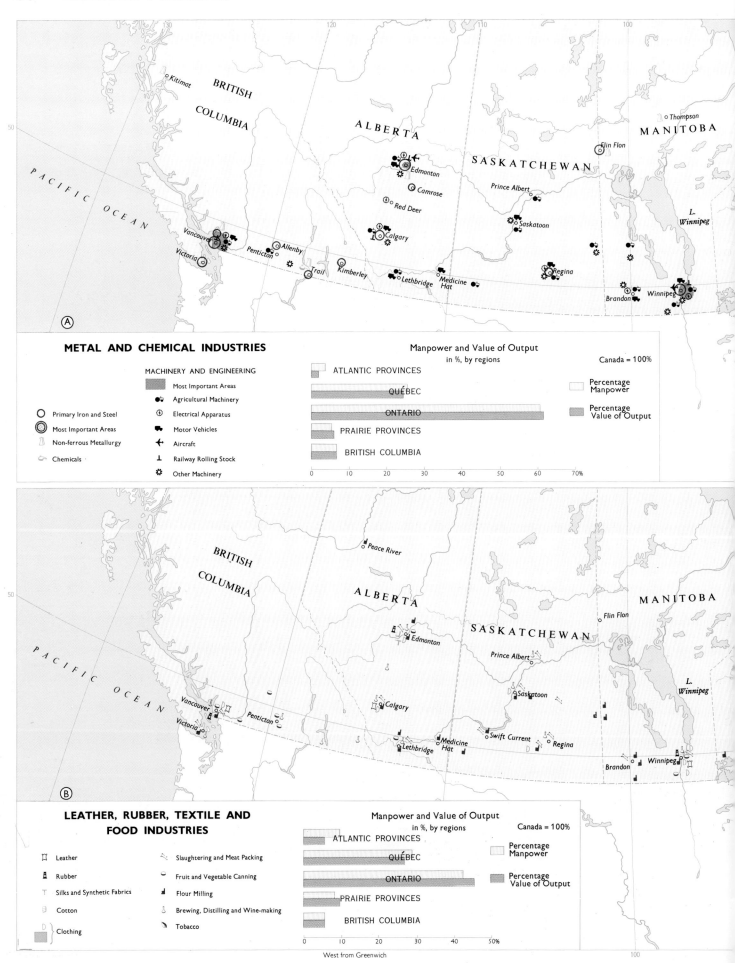

Ⓐ

METAL AND CHEMICAL INDUSTRIES

MACHINERY AND ENGINEERING

	Most Important Areas
◒	Agricultural Machinery
⊕	Electrical Apparatus
🚛	Motor Vehicles
✦	Aircraft
⊥	Railway Rolling Stock
✿	Other Machinery

○ Primary Iron and Steel
◉ Most Important Areas
🗊 Non-ferrous Metallurgy
⌇ Chemicals

Manpower and Value of Output
in %, by regions

Canada = 100%

ATLANTIC PROVINCES
QUÉBEC
ONTARIO
PRAIRIE PROVINCES
BRITISH COLUMBIA

☐ Percentage Manpower
▨ Percentage Value of Output

0 10 20 30 40 50 60 70%

Ⓑ

LEATHER, RUBBER, TEXTILE AND FOOD INDUSTRIES

◫	Leather	⤸	Slaughtering and Meat Packing
🅰	Rubber	⌣	Fruit and Vegetable Canning
⊤	Silks and Synthetic Fabrics	⬛	Flour Milling
▤	Cotton	⌁	Brewing, Distilling and Wine-making
⫘	Clothing	⟍	Tobacco

Manpower and Value of Output
in %, by regions

Canada = 100%

ATLANTIC PROVINCES
QUÉBEC
ONTARIO
PRAIRIE PROVINCES
BRITISH COLUMBIA

☐ Percentage Manpower
▨ Percentage Value of Output

0 10 20 30 40 50%

West from Greenwich

1:15 000 000

100   0   100   200   300   400   500   600 km

Hudson Bay

NEWFOUNDLAND

✿ St. John's

QUÉBEC

Murdochville

Baie-
Comeau

St. Lawrence (St-Laurent)

Sydney   Cape Breton I.

ONTARIO

Arvida

Belledune

P.E.I.

NEW

BRUNSWICK

Moncton

NOVA SCOTIA

Timmins

Rouyn

Shawinigan
Trois-Rivières

Québec

Saint John

Halifax

Thunder Bay

L. Superior

Sudbury

North Bay

Montréal

Sherbrooke

ATLANTIC OCEAN

Sault-
Ste-Marie

Ottawa

L.
Huron

Kingston

L.
Ontario

Kitchener

Toronto

Sarnia

Hamilton

London

Niagara

Windsor

L. Erie

Hudson Bay

NEWFOUNDLAND

St. John's

QUÉBEC

St. Lawrence (St-Laurent)

ONTARIO

Sydney   Cape Breton I.

P.E.I.

NEW

BRUNSWICK

Fredericton

NOVA SCOTIA

Chicoutimi

Halifax

Thunder Bay

L. Superior

Montmorency

Québec

Shawinigan

Drummondville

Montréal

Sherbrooke

ATLANTIC OCEAN

Granby

Ottawa

Cornwall

Kingston

L.
Huron

L.
Ontario

Kitchener

Toronto

Hamilton

Welland

London

Brantford

Sarnia

Chatham

Windsor

L. Erie

West from Greenwich

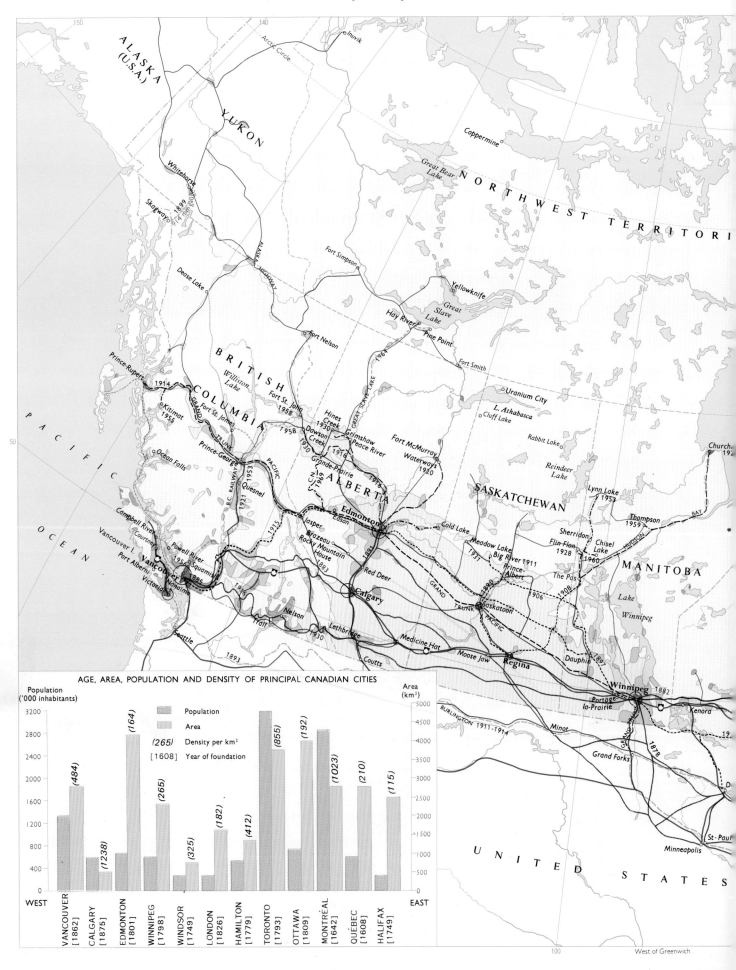

AGE, AREA, POPULATION AND DENSITY OF PRINCIPAL CANADIAN CITIES

Population
('000 inhabitants)

Area
(km²)

Population
Area
(265)   Density per km²
[1608]   Year of foundation

WEST

VANCOUVER [1862] (4484)
CALGARY [1875] (1238)
EDMONTON [1801] (164)
WINNIPEG [1798] (265)
WINDSOR [1749] (325)
LONDON [1826] (182)
HAMILTON [1779] (412)
TORONTO [1793] (855)
OTTAWA [1809] (192)
MONTRÉAL [1642] (1023)
QUÉBEC [1608] (210)
HALIFAX [1749] (115)

EAST

West of Greenwich

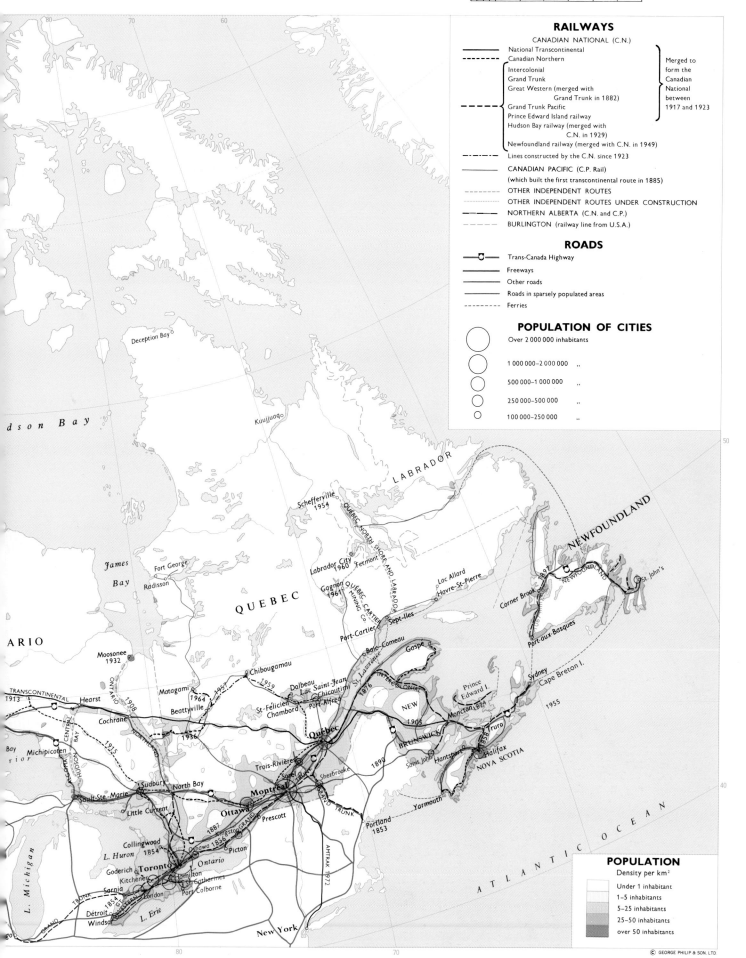

1:15 000 000

100   0   100   200   300   400   500   600 km

RAILWAYS

CANADIAN NATIONAL (C.N.)

National Transcontinental
Canadian Northern
Intercolonial
Grand Trunk
Great Western (merged with
                Grand Trunk in 1882)
Grand Trunk Pacific
Prince Edward Island railway
Hudson Bay railway (merged with
                C.N. in 1929)
Newfoundland railway (merged with C.N. in 1949)

} Merged to form the Canadian National between 1917 and 1923

Lines constructed by the C.N. since 1923

CANADIAN PACIFIC (C.P. Rail)

(which built the first transcontinental route in 1885)

OTHER INDEPENDENT ROUTES
OTHER INDEPENDENT ROUTES UNDER CONSTRUCTION
NORTHERN ALBERTA (C.N. and C.P.)
BURLINGTON (railway line from U.S.A.)

ROADS

Trans-Canada Highway
Freeways
Other roads
Roads in sparsely populated areas
Ferries

POPULATION OF CITIES

Over 2 000 000 inhabitants
1 000 000–2 000 000   ,,
500 000–1 000 000   ,,
250 000–500 000   ,,
100 000–250 000   ,,

POPULATION

Density per km²

Under 1 inhabitant
1–5 inhabitants
5–25 inhabitants
25–50 inhabitants
over 50 inhabitants

© GEORGE PHILIP & SON, LTD

Hudson Bay

Deception Bay

LABRADOR

NEWFOUNDLAND

St. John's

Schefferville 1954

QUEBEC NORTH SHORE AND LABRADOR

Labrador City 1960   Fermont

Gagnon 1961   QUEBEC-CARTIER MINING Co.

Lac Allard
Havre-St-Pierre

Corner Brook 1897   NEWFOUNDLAND

James Bay

Fort George

Radisson

QUEBEC

Sept-Iles

Port-Cartier

Port-aux-Basques

Baie-Comeau

Gaspé

Sydney   Cape Breton I.   1955

Moosonee 1932

Chibougamau

ONTARIO

Matagami 1964   1957   1959   Dolbeau   Lac Saint-Jean   St-Laurence

Baie-Comeau

INTERCOLONIAL

Prince Edward I.

TRANSCONTINENTAL 1913   Hearst   1908   Beattyville   St-Félicien   Chicoutimi   1876

St. Lawrence

Cochrane   NORTHLAND   1936   Chambord   Port-Alfred

1905   Moncton 1874

Sydney

Michipicoten   1915   CENTRAL   HUDSON BAY   Québec

Truro   1858

Bay

Superior

Trois-Rivières   1890   Saint John   Hantsport   Halifax

NEW BRUNSWICK

NOVA SCOTIA

Sudbury   North Bay   Sorel   Sherbrooke   1890

Sault-Ste-Marie   Little Current   Montreal

Yarmouth

Ottawa   Prescott   Portland 1853

ATLANTIC OCEAN

Collingwood   1887   Kingston   GRAND TRUNK

L. Huron   1854   Oshawa 1856   Picton

Goderich   Ontario

Toronto

Kitchener   Hamilton   St. Catharines

GRAND TRUNK   Sarnia   London   Port Colborne

1854

Détroit   L. Erie

Windsor

AMTRAK 1972

New York

L. Michigan

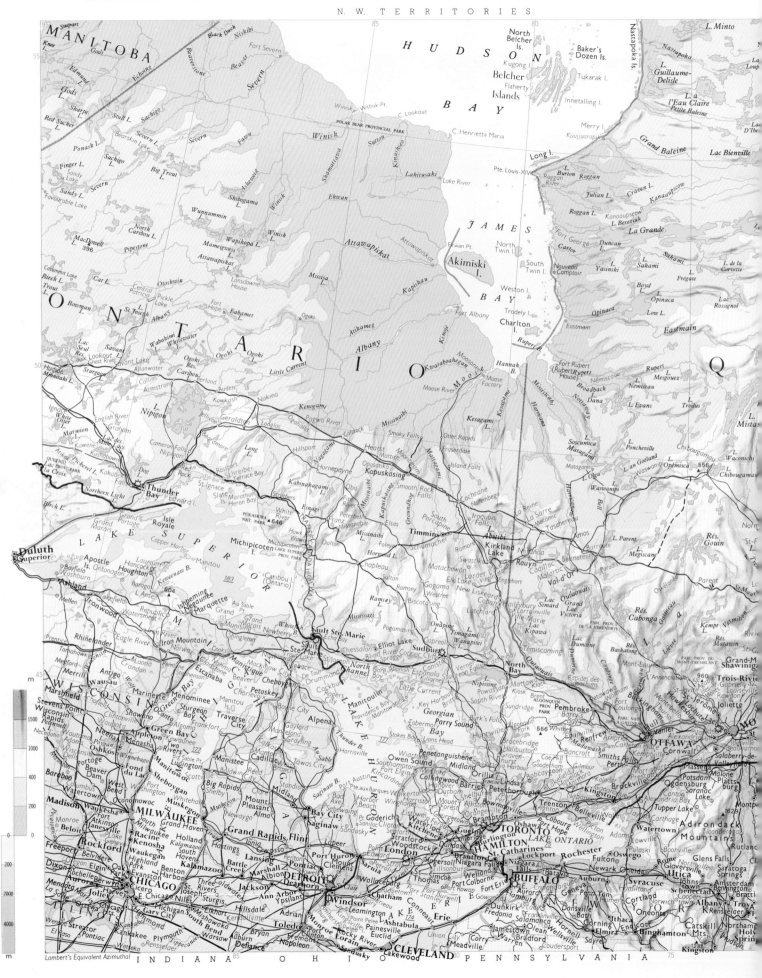

1:7 000 000

50   0   50   100   150   200   250   300 km

West from Greenwich

COPYRIGHT GEORGE PHILIP & SON LTD

1 : 7 000 000

50   0   50   100   150   200   250   300 km

COPYRIGHT GEORGE PHILIP & SON Ltd.

Projection: Lambert's Equivalent Azimuthal

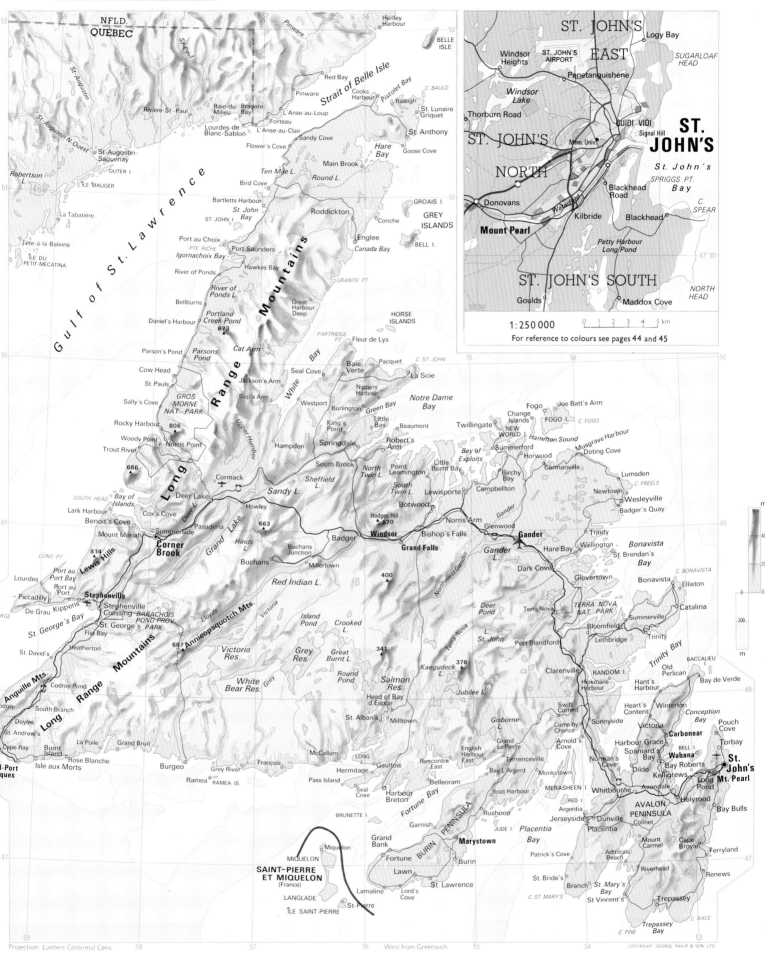

1:2 500 000

10 0 10 20 30 40 50 60 70 80 90 100 km

NFLD.
QUEBEC

Henley Harbour

BELLE ISLE

Pinware

Strait of Belle Isle

Red Bay

C. BAULD

Cooks Harbour

Pistolet Bay

Raleigh

St. Lunaire Griquet

St. Anthony

Forteau

L'Anse-au-Loup

Baie-du- Bradore Bay

Milieu

Rivière-St-Paul

Lourdes-de- L'Anse-au-Clair

Blanc-Sablon Sandy Cove

Goose Cove

Flower's Cove

Hare Bay

Main Brook

Ten Mile L.

Round L.

Bird Cove

OUTER I.

ÎLE MAUGER

Robertson L.

St-Augustin N. Ouest

ST. JOHN I.

Bartletts Harbour

St. John Bay

Roddickton

GROAIS I.

GREY ISLANDS

St-Augustin- Saguenay

La Tabatière

Conche

Englee

BELL I.

Tête-à-la-Baleine

ÎLE DU PETIT-MÉCATINA

Port au Choix

PTE. RICHE

Igornachoix Bay

Port Saunders

Canada Bay

HORSE ISLANDS

River of Ponds

Hawkes Bay

GRANITE PT.

Bellburns

River of Ponds L.

Portland Creek Pond

673

Great Harbour Deep

PARTRIDGE PT.

Fleur de Lys

Daniel's Harbour

Cat Arm

PT.

Parson's Pond

Parsons Pond

Pacquet

C. ST. JOHN

Cow Head

Seal Cove

Baie Verte

La Scie

St. Pauls

Jackson's Arm

White Bay

Nippers Harbour

GROS MORNE NAT. PARK

Sop's Arm

Westport

Burlington

Green Bay

Notre Dame Bay

Fogo

Joe Batt's Arm

Sally's Cove

Rocky Harbour

806

King's Point

Little Bay

Beaumont

Change Islands

FOGO I.

C. FOGO

Woody Point

Norris Point

Hampden

Springdale

Robert's Arm

Twillingate

NEW WORLD I.

Hamilton Sound

Musgrave Harbour

Trout River

686

South Brook

Sheffield L.

North Twin L.

Point Leamington

Little Burnt Bay

Bay of Exploits

Summerford

Horwood

Doting Cove

Cormack

Sandy L.

South Twin L.

Lewisporte

Birchy Bay

Carmanville

SOUTH HEAD

Bay of Islands

Deer L.

Howley

Botwood

Campbellton

Lumsden

Lark Harbour

Cox's Cove

Pasadena

663

Norris Arm

Gander

C. FREELS

Newtown

Benoit's Cove

Deer L.

Hodges Hill 570

Glenwood

Wesleyville

Mount Moriah

Summerside

Grand Lake

Hinds L.

Badger

Windsor

Bishop's Falls

Gander L.

Trinity

Badger's Quay

Corner Brook

814

Lewis Hills

Buchans Junction

Grand Falls

Hare Bay

Wellington

Bonavista Bay

LONG PT.

Buchans

Millertown

Gander

Dark Cove

St. Brendan's

Port au Port Bay

Stephenville

Red Indian L.

400

Glovertown

Bonavista

C. BONAVISTA

Lourdes

Port au Port

Stephenville Crossing

BARACHOIS POND PROV. PARK

Victoria

Island Pond

TERRA NOVA NAT. PARK

Elliston

Piccadilly

De Grau Kippens

Lloyds

Crooked L.

341

Deer Pond

Terra Nova

Summerville

Catalina

St. George's Bay

St. George's

Flat Bay

687

Annieopsquotch Mts.

Victoria Res.

Grey Res.

Great Burnt L.

Kaegudeck L.

376

L. St. John

Port Blandford

Lethbridge

Trinity

Trinity Bay

ORGE

Heatherton

Round Pond

Salmon Res.

Clarenville

RANDOM I.

BACCALIEU

St. David's

White Bear Res.

Grey

Head of Bay d'Espoir

Jubilee L.

Hickman's Harbour

Old Perlican

Anguille Mts.

Codroy Pond

St. Alban's

Milltown

Gisborne L.

Swift Current

Hant's Harbour

Heart's Content

Winterton

Bay de Verde

Codroy

South Branch

LONG RANGE Mountains

Come by Chance

Sunnyside

Conception Bay

Doyles

St. Andrew's

Gaultois

Grand Le Pierre

Arnold's Cove

Victoria

Carbonear

Pouch Cove

Cape Ray

Burnt Island

La Poile

Grand Bruit

McCallum

LONG

Rencontre East

Terrenceville

English Harbour East

Norman's Cove

Harbour Grace

Spaniard's Bay

BELL I.

Torbay

Wabana

St. John's

Isle aux Morts

Rose Blanche

Burgeo

Grey River

Francois

Hermitage

Seal Cove

Pass Island

Belleoram

Bay L'Argent

Boat Harbour

Monkstown

MERASHEEN I.

Dildo

Bay Roberts

Kelligrews

Mt. Pearl

el-Port sques

Ramea

RAMEA IS.

Harbour Breton

Fortune Bay

BURIN PENINSULA

Rushoon

RED I.

Whitbourne

Avondale

Long Pond

Holyrood

Garnish

Garnish

JUDE I.

Placentia Bay

Argentia

Dunville

AVALON PENINSULA

Bay Bulls

BRUNETTE I.

Grand Bank

Jerseyside

Colinet

Placentia

MIQUELON

Miquelon

Fortune

Lawn

Patrick's Cove

Mount Carmel

Cape Broyle

SAINT-PIERRE ET MIQUELON (France)

Lamaline

Lord's Cove

Burin

St. Lawrence

St. Bride's

Branch

St. Mary's Bay

Admiral's Beach

Riverhead

Ferryland

LANGLADE

ÎLE SAINT-PIERRE

St-Pierre

C. ST. MARY'S

St Vincent's

St. Mary's Bay

Trepassey

C. PINE

Trepassey Bay

C. RACE

Projection: Lambert Conformal Conic

West from Greenwich

COPYRIGHT GEORGE PHILIP & SON LTD

Inset map — St. John's

ST. JOHN'S EAST

Logy Bay

Windsor Heights

ST. JOHN'S AIRPORT

Penetanguishene

SUGARLOAF HEAD

Windsor Lake

Thorburn Road

QUIDI VIDI

Signal Hill

ST. JOHN'S

ST. JOHN'S NORTH

Mem. Univ.

St. John's

SPRIGGS PT.

Bay

Donovans

Waterford

Blackhead Road

C. SPEAR

Mount Pearl

Kilbride

Blackhead

Petty Harbour Long Pond

ST. JOHN'S SOUTH

Goulds

Maddox Cove

NORTH HEAD

52°50'

52°40'

1:250 000

0 1 2 3 4 5 km

For reference to colours see pages 44 and 45

m

400

200

0

200

m

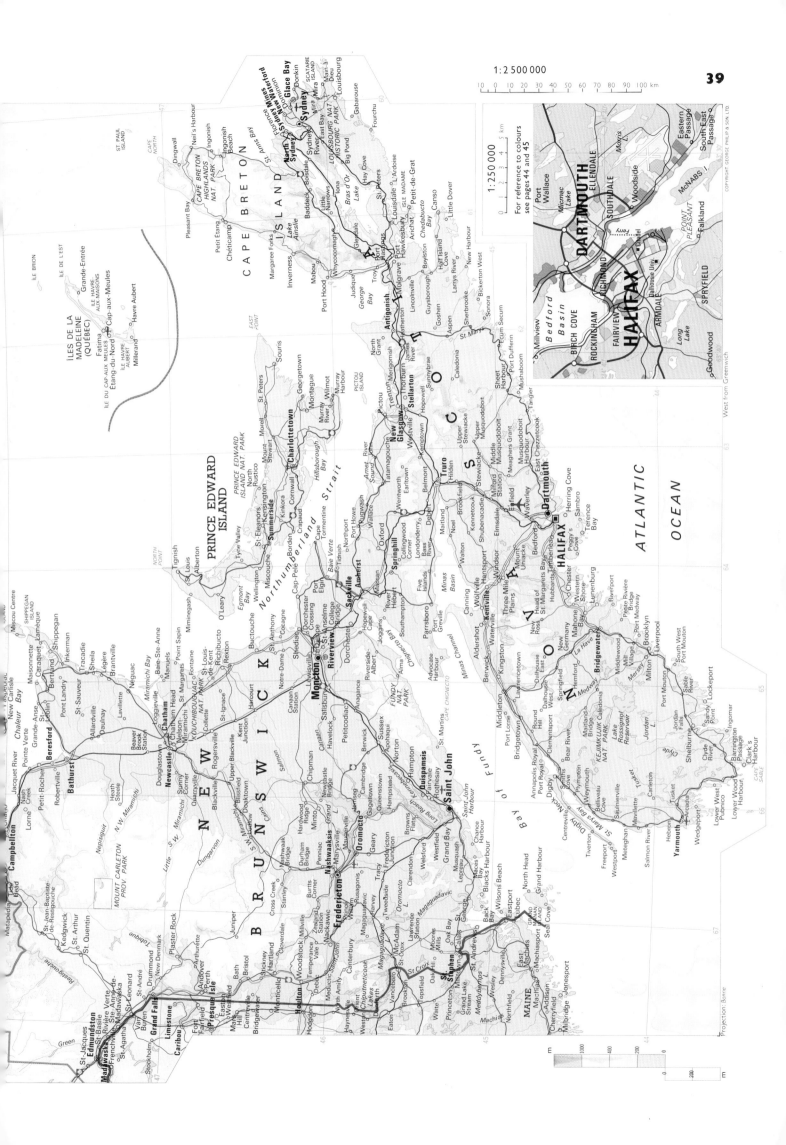

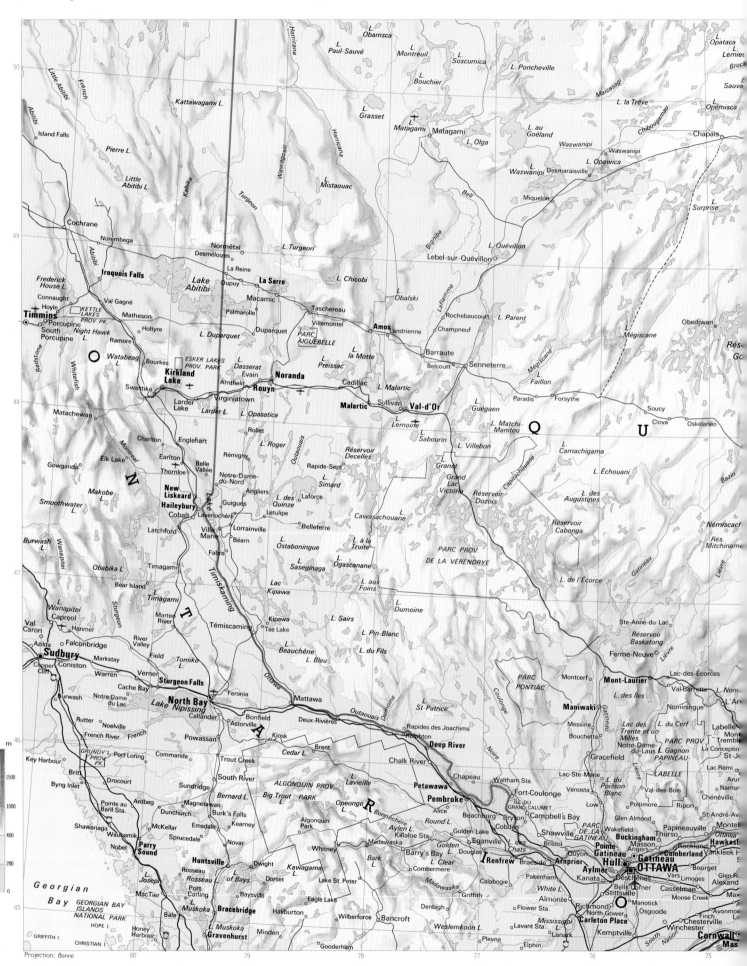

Projection: Bonne

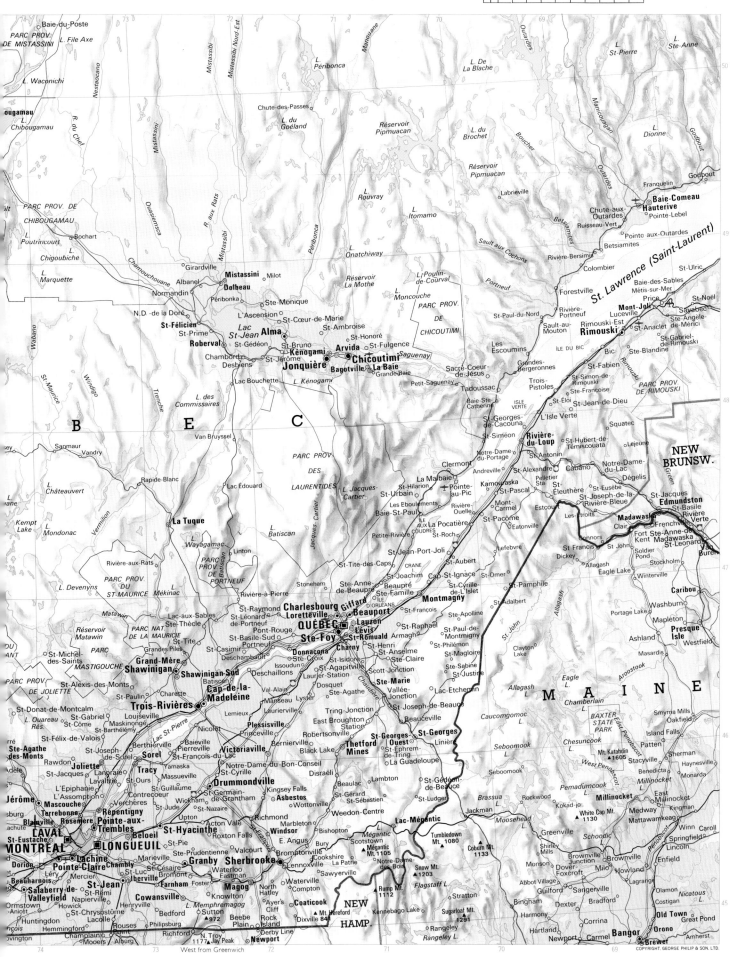

1:2 500 000

10 0 10 20 30 40 50 60 70 80 90 100 km

PARC PROV. DE MISTASSINI

L. Waconichi

ougamau
Chibougamau

L. File Axe
Baie-du-Poste

R. du Chef

PARC PROV. DE CHIBOUGAMAU

L. Poutrincourt
Bochart
Chigoubiche
L. Marquette

Nestaocano

Ouasiemsca

Mistassibi Nord Est
Mistassibi

Mistassini

Chute-des-Passes

L. du Goéland

L. Péribonca

Réservoir Pipmuacan

Péribonca

L. De La Blache

L. du Brochet

L. Ste-Anne
L. St-Pierre

Manouane

Outardes

Manicouagan

L. Dionne
Godbout

Franquelin
Godbout

Baie-Comeau
Hauterive
Pointe-Lebel

Chute-aux-Outardes
Ruisseau-Vert
Pointe aux Outardes
Betsiamites

Labrieville

St. Lawrence (Saint-Laurent)

Betsiamites
Rivière-Bersimis

Portneuf
Sault aux Cochons

Colombier

Forestville
Baie-des-Sables
Métis-sur-Mer
Price

St-Ulric
St-Noël
Mont-Joli
Sayabec
Luceville
Rimouski-Est
St-Anaclet-de-Mérici
Rimouski

Girardville
Mistassini
Milot
Albanel
Normandin
Péribonka
Ste-Monique
L'Ascension
St-Cœur-de-Marie
St-Ambroise

N.D.-de-la-Doré
St-Félicien
St-Prime
Roberval
St-Gédéon
Chambord
Desbiens

Lac St-Jean
Alma
St-Bruno
St-Jérôme
Kénogami
Jonquière
Bagotville
La Baie

Dolbeau

Réservoir La Mothe
Moncouche

PARC PROV. DE CHICOUTIMI

St-Honoré
St-Fulgence
Arvida
Chicoutimi
Grande-Baie

Saguenay
Sacré-Cœur-de-Jésus
Petit-Saguenay
Tadoussac

Les Escoumins
Grandes-Bergeronnes

St-Simon-de-Rimouski
Ste-Françoise

St-Fabien
Bic
Ste-Blandine
St-Gabriel-de-Rimouski

ÎLE DU BIC
PARC PROV. DE RIMOUSKI

Lac Bouchette
L. Kénogami

Onatchiway

L. Poulin-de-Courval

Baie-Ste-Catherine

ISLE VERTE
St-Éloi
L'Isle Verte
St-Jean-de-Dieu

Squatec

Trois-Pistoles

B E C

Van Bruyssel

St-Georges-de-Cacouna
St-Siméon

Rivière-du-Loup

St-Hubert-de-Témiscouata
Lejeune

NEW BRUNSW.

Sanmaur
Vandry
Rapide-Blanc

Windigo

St-Maurice

PARC PROV. DES LAURENTIDES

L. des Commissaires

Notre-Dame-du-Portage
St-Antonin

Clermont
Andreville
St-Alexandre
Cabano
Notre-Dame-du-Lac
Dégelis

La Malbaie
Pointe-au-Pic
St-Hilarion
St-Urbain

Pelletier Sta.
St-Éleuthère
St-Joseph-de-la-Rivière-Bleue
St-Eusèbe

St-Jacques
Edmundston
St-Basile

Châteauvert

Lac Édouard

L. Jacques-Cartier
St-Pascal
Mont-Carmel

Les-Troits
Estcourt
Clair
Connors
Madawaska
St-Léonard

Rivière-Verte

Kempt Lake
Mondonac

Trenche

Jacques-Cartier

Baie-St-Paul
Les Eboulements
Rivière-Ouelle

Kamouraska

Fort Ste-Anne-de-Madawaska
Frenchville

La Tuque

L. Wayagamac
Linton

L. Batiscan

ÎLE AUX COUDRES
La Pocatière
Petite-Rivière
St-Roch

St-Pacôme
Eatonville

St-John
Dickey
St-Francis
Allagash

Soldier Pond
Stockholm

Buren

Rivière-aux-Rats

PARC PROV. DE PORTNEUF

St-Jean-Port-Joli
St-Aubert

Eagle Lake
Winterville

Caribou

L. Devenyns

PARC PROV. DU ST-MAURICE
Mékinac

Rivière-à-Pierre

Stoneham

St-Tite-des-Caps
CRANE

St-Joachim
Ste-Anne-de-Beaupré
Beaupré
Ste-Famille

Cap-St-Ignace
St-Cyrille-de-L'Islet
St-Omer

St-Pamphile

St-Adalbert

Washburn
Portage Lake
Mapleton
Ashland

Presque Isle
Westfield

Matawin

Réservoir Matawin

PARC NAT. DE LA MAURICIE

Lac-aux-Sables
Ste-Thècle
St-Léonard-de-Portneuf

St-Raymond
Charlesbourg
Giffard
Loretteville
Beauport

ÎLE D'ORLEANS
St-François

Montmagny

St-Apolline
St-Raphaël
St-Paul-de-Montminy

St-John

Clayton Lake

Masardis

PARC MASTIGOUCHE

Grandes Piles
St-Tite

QUÉBEC
Ste-Foy
Lévis
Lauzon
St-Romuald

St-Henri
St-Anselme

St-Magloire
St-Philémon

Eagle L.

M A I N E

St-Michel-des-Saints

St-Basile-Sud
Pont-Rouge
Portneuf
St-Casimir

Donnacona
Charny
Ste-Croix
St-Isidore
St-Agapitville

Ste-Claire
Scott-Jonction

Ste-Sabine
St-Justine

Allagash L.
Chamberlain

PARC PROV. DE JOLIETTE

Grand-Mère
Shawinigan
Shawinigan-Sud

Deschambault
Issoudun
Laurier-Station

Ste-Marie
Lac-Etchemin

Caucomgomoc

BAXTER STATE PARK

St-Alexis-des-Monts
St-Paulin
Charette

Cap-de-la-Madeleine
Trois-Rivières
Batiscan
Val-Alain
Manseau
Lyster
Dosquet
Ste-Agathe

Vallée-Jonction

St-Joseph-de-Beauce
Beauceville

Seboomook

Mt. Katahdin
1605

Smyrna Mills
Oakfield
Island Falls
Patten
Sherman
Haynesville

ST-MAURICE

St-Donat-de-Montcalm
St-Gabriel
Louiseville
Maskinongé
Lac St-Pierre

Nicolet
Lemieux
Laurierville

Tring-Jonction

East Broughton Station

Linière
St-Georges

Chesuncook
Seboomook L.

Monarda

L. Ouareau Rés.
St-Côme
St-Barthélemy

Berthierville
Pierreville
St-François-du-Lac

Plessisville
Princeville
Bernierville

Robertsonville

St-Georges-Ouest
St-Ephrem-de-Tring
La Guadeloupe

Brassua
Rockwood

West Penobscot

White Cap Mt.
1130

Stacyville

Millinocket
East Millinocket
Kingman

Ste-Agathe-des-Monts
Rawdon
Joliette
Lanoraie
Lavaltrie
St-Ours

Victoriaville
Sorel
Tracy
Yamaska
Massueville
St-Cyrille

Black Lake
Thetford Mines
Disraëli

Beaulac
St-Gérard

Kokad-jo

Pemadumcook

Medway

St-Jacques
St-Félix-de-Valois

Drummondville
St-Germain-de-Grantham
Asbestos
Wottonville
Weedon-Centre

Lambton
St-Sébastien

St-Gédéon-de-Beauce
St-Ludger

Jackman

Moosehead

Greenville

Winn Caroll

Jérôme
sburg
Mascouche
Terrebonne
Rosemère
Repentigny
Contrecœur
Verchères
St-Jude
Upton

Kingsey Falls
Wickham
Richmond
Marbleton
Bishopton

Lac-Mégantic

Mégantic
Scotstown
Mégantic Mt. 1105

Tumbledown Mt. 1080
Coburn Mt. 1133

Shirley Mills
Rockwood
Monson
Abbot Village

Brownville Junction
Dover-Foxcroft
Milo

Brownville
Enfield
Lincoln
Springfield

LAVAL
MONTRÉAL
St-Eustache
LONGUEUIL
Blainville
Pointe-aux-Trembles
St-Hyacinthe
St-Pie

Acton Vale
Roxton Falls
Windsor
E. Angus
Bury

La Patrie
Notre-Dame-des-Bois

Snow Mt.
1203

Flagstaff L.

Guilford
Sangerville

Howland
Lagrange
Olamon
Costigan

Lachine
Pointe-Claire
Chambly
St-Luc
Iberville

Granby
Sherbrooke
Waterloo
Eastman
Lennoxville
Sawyerville

Rump Mt.
1112

Stratton
Bingham

Dexter
Bradford

Old Town

Dorion
Mercier
St-Césaire
Bromont
Farnham
Foster

Magog
Knowlton
North Hatley
Waterville
Compton

Corrina

Orono

Beauharnois
Salaberry-de-Valleyfield
St-Rémi
Napierville
Henryville

Cowansville
Bedford
Sutton
972

L. Memphremagog
Ayer's Cliff
Beebe Plain
Rock Island

Coaticook
Mt. Hereford 844
Dixville

Kennebago Lake
Sugarloaf Mt.
1291

Harmony
Hartland
Newport
Carmel

Bangor
Brewer
Great Pond
Amherst

Huntingdon
Hemmingford
Ormstown
Anicet
çois
ovington

Champlain
Mooers
Alburg
Rouses Point
Philipsburg
Richford
N. Troy
1177
Jay Peak
Derby Line
Newport

NEW HAMP.

Rangeley
Rangeley L.

Nicatous
L.

COPYRIGHT. GEORGE PHILIP & SON. LTD.

74
73
West from Greenwich
72
71
70
69

1 : 250 000

5 4 3 2 1 0 5 10 km

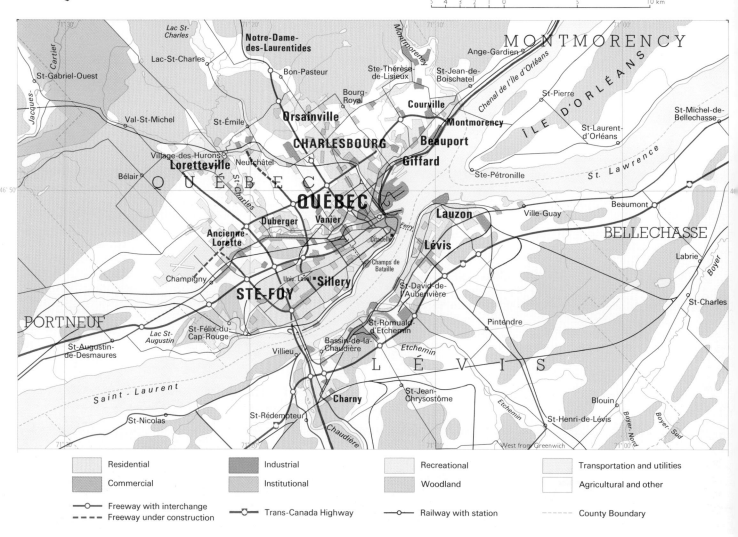

MONTMORENCY

Lac St-Charles

Notre-Dame-des-Laurentides

Lac-St-Charles

Ange-Gardien

St-Gabriel-Ouest

Bon-Pasteur

Ste-Thérèse-de-Lisieux

St-Jean-de-Boischatel

Chenal de l'Île d'Orléans

ÎLE D'ORLÉANS

Bourg-Royal

St-Pierre

St-Michel-de-Bellechasse

Val-St-Michel

St-Émile

Orsainville

Courville

Montmorency

St-Laurent-d'Orléans

Village-des-Hurons

Loretteville

Neufchâtel

CHARLESBOURG

Beauport

Giffard

Ste-Pétronille

St. Lawrence

Bélair

QUÉBEC

46° 50

Duberger

Vanier

QUÉBEC

Ancienne-Lorette

Citadelle

Lauzon

Ville-Guay

Beaumont

BELLECHASSE

Ferry

Lévis

Labrie

Boyer

Champigny

Univ. Laval

Sillery

Champs de Bataille

St-David-de-Aubervière

St-Charles

Champigny

STE-FOY

St-Félix-du-Cap-Rouge

Lac St-Augustin

St-Romuald-d'Etchemin

Pintendre

PORTNEUF

St-Augustin-de-Desmaures

Villieu

Bassin-de-la-Chaudière

Etchemin

L É V I S

St-Nicolas

Charny

St-Jean-Chrysostôme

Blouin

Boyer-Nord

Boyer-Sud

Saint - Laurent

St-Rédempteur

Etchemin

St-Henri-de-Lévis

Chaudière

West from Greenwich

Residential	Industrial	Recreational	Transportation and utilities
Commercial	Institutional	Woodland	Agricultural and other

—○— Freeway with interchange —▽— Trans-Canada Highway —○— Railway with station - - - - - County Boundary

- - - Freeway under construction

Québec looking south-east across the St. Lawrence River

Montréal looking south-east across the city centre towards the St. Lawrence River

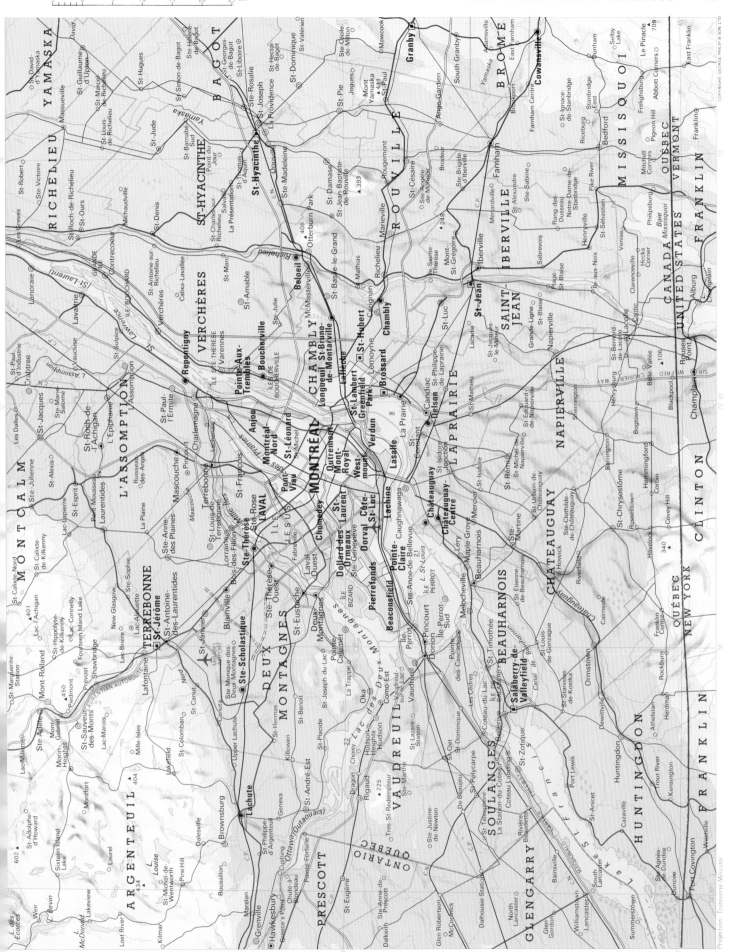

1 : 600 000

5   0   5   10   15   20   25 km

COPYRIGHT GEORGE PHILIP & SON LTD

Projection Transverse Mercator

m   500   200   100   0

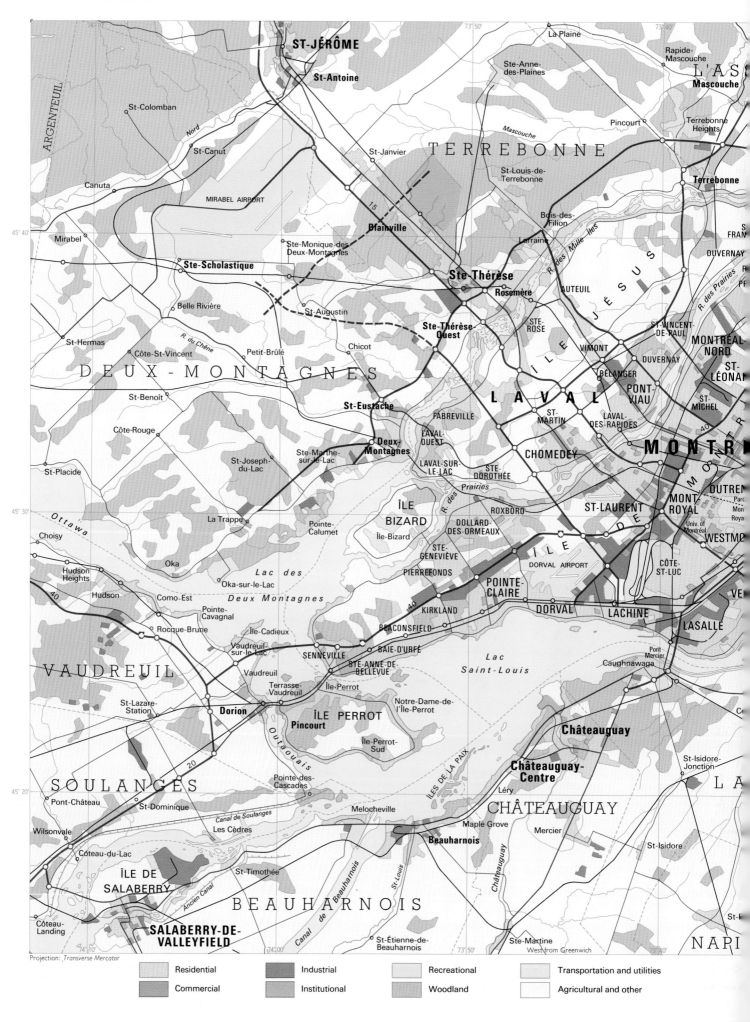

Residential	Industrial	Recreational	Transportation and utilities
Commercial	Institutional	Woodland	Agricultural and other

Projection: Transverse Mercator

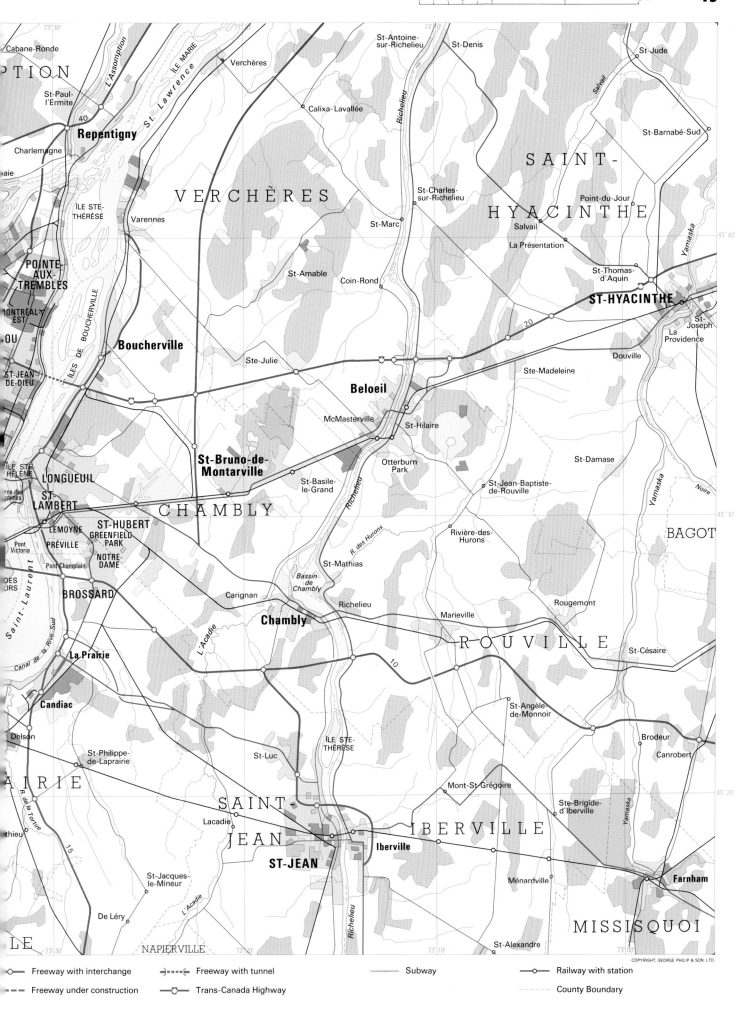

1:250 000

45

5 4 3 2 1 0   5   10 km

Cabane-Ronde

St-Paul-
l'Ermite

40

Repentigny

Charlemagne

L'Assomption

ÎLE MARIE

Verchères

Calixa-Lavallée

St-Antoine-
sur-Richelieu

St-Denis

St-Jude

POINTE-
AUX-
TREMBLES

ÎLE STE-
THÉRÈSE

V E R C H È R E S

St-Charles-
sur-Richelieu

St-Barnabé-Sud

S A I N T -

Varennes

St-Marc

Salvail

H Y A C I N T H E

MONTRÉAL-
EST

ÎLES DE BOUCHERVILLE

St-Amable

Coin-Rond

La Présentation

Point-du-Jour

St-Thomas-
d'Aquin

Yamaska

Salvail

ST-JEAN-
DE-DIEU

Boucherville

Ste-Julie

20

ST-HYACINTHE

St-
Joseph
La
Providence

ÎLE STE-
HÉLÈNE

Beloeil

Ste-Madeleine

Douville

McMasterville

St-Hilaire

L'ONGUEUIL

ST-
LAMBERT

**St-Bruno-de-
Montarville**

St-Basile-
le-Grand

Otterburn
Park

St-Damase

Yamaska

Noire

LEMOYNE

ST-HUBERT
GREENFIELD
PARK

C H A M B L Y

St-Jean-Baptiste-
de-Rouville

Pont
Victoria

PRÉVILLE

NOTRE-
DAME

R. des Hurons

Richelieu

Rivière-des-
Hurons

45° 30'

B A G O T

Pont Champlain

BROSSARD

St-Mathias

Bassin
de
Chambly

Carignan

Richelieu

Marieville

Rougemont

La Prairie

Chambly

R O U V I L L E

St-Césaire

Canal de la Rive-Sud

L'Acadie

10

Candiac

Delson

St-Angèle-
de-Monnoir

Brodeur

St-Philippe-
de-Laprairie

St-Luc

ÎLE STE-
THÉRÈSE

Canrobert

A I R I E

R. de la Tortue

S A I N T -

Mont-St-Grégoire

Ste-Brigide-
d'Iberville

45° 20'

thieu

15

Lacadie

J E A N

**St-Jacques-
le-Mineur**

L'Acadie

Iberville

I B E R V I L L E

Yamaska

Ménardville

Farnham

ST-JEAN

De Léry

L'Acadie

Richelieu

St-Alexandre

M I S S I S Q U O I

LE

NAPIERVILLE

73° 30'   73° 20'   73° 10'   73° 00'

COPYRIGHT. GEORGE PHILIP & SON. LTD.

○—○ Freeway with interchange   ⇥·····⇤ Freeway with tunnel   —— Subway   —○— Railway with station

‒ ‒ ‒ Freeway under construction   —○— Trans-Canada Highway   ‒ ‒ ‒ ‒ County Boundary

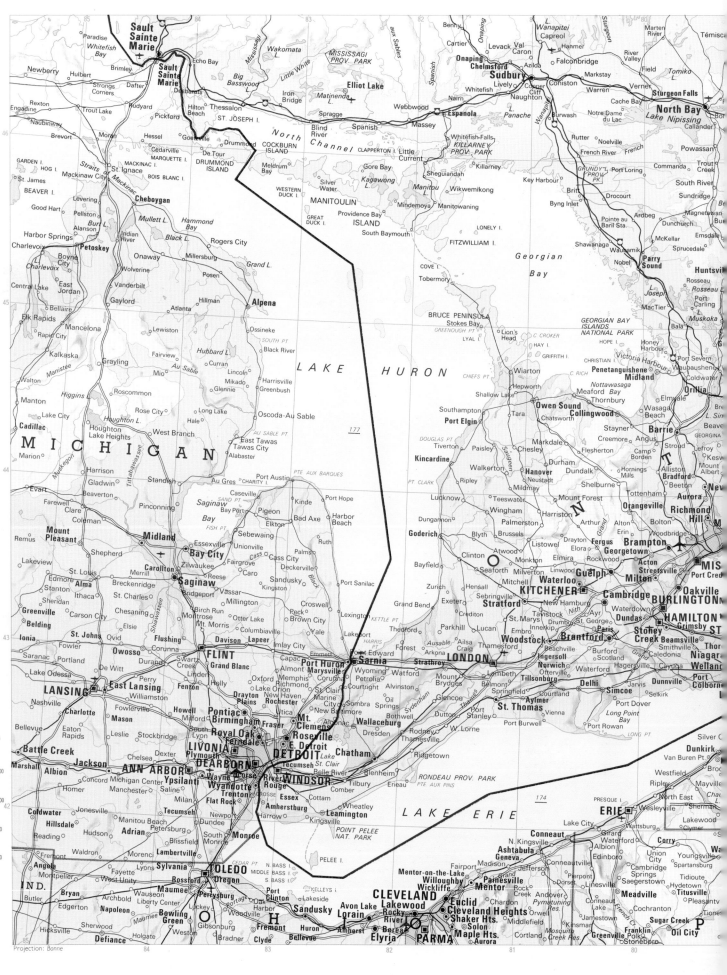

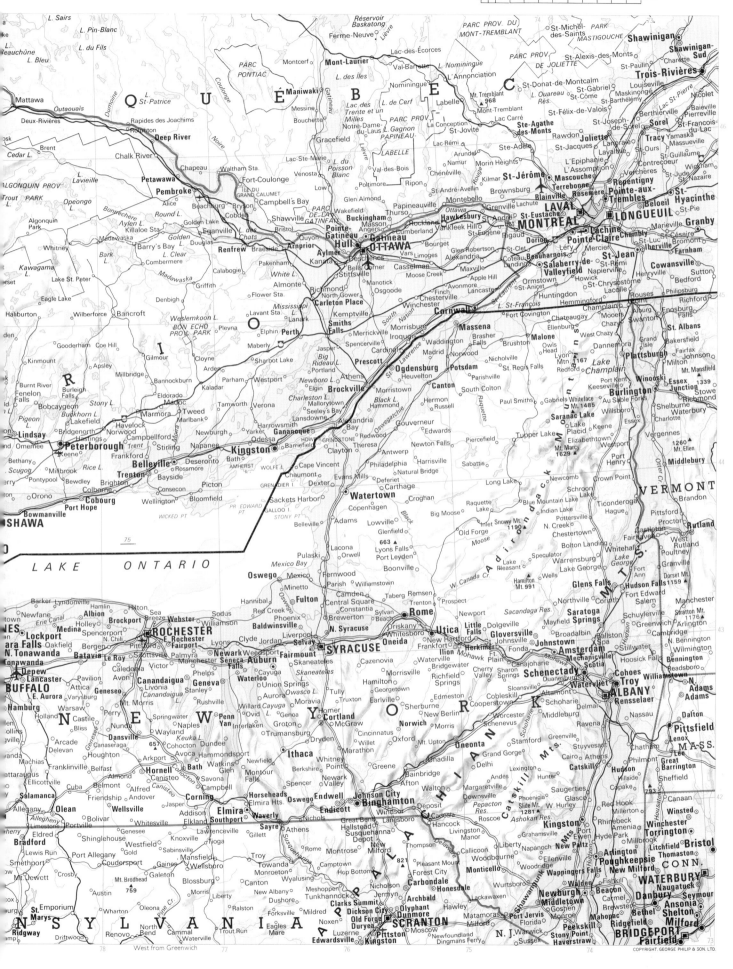

L. Sairs
L. Pin-Blanc
L. Bleu
L. du Fils
Réservoir Baskatong
Ferme-Neuve
Lièvre
PARC PROV. DU MONT-TREMBLANT
PARC PROV. MASTIGOUCHE
St-Michel-des-Saints
PARK
St-Alexis-des-Monts
Shawinigan
Shawinigan-Sud

Beauchêne
Montcerf
Mont-Laurier
Val-Barrette
L. Nominingue
DE JOLIETTE
St-Paulin
Charette
Trois-Rivières
Nicolet

Mattawa
QUÉBEC
Maniwaki
Nominingue
L'Annonciation
Labelle
Mt. Tremblant ▲ 968
Mont-Tremblant
St-Donat-de-Montcalm
L. Ouareau Rés.
St-Gabriel
St-Côme
St-Pierre
Maskinongé
Louiseville
St-Barthélémy
Baieville
Pierreville

Outaouais
Dumoine
Deux-Rivières
L. St-Patrice
Gatineau
Messine
Bouchette
L. des Trente et un Milles
Notre-Dame-du-Laus
PAPINEAU
La Conception
Lac Carré
Ste-Agathe-des-Monts
Rawdon
Joliette
L'Assomption
Lanoraie
Lavaltrie
Contrecoeur
Verchères
St-Ours
St-Guillaume
Wickham
St-Nazaire
Sorel
Yamaska

Rapides des Joachims
Holphton
ALGONQUIN PROV.
Trout PARK
Cedar L.
Brent
Deep River
Chalk River
Chapeau
Waltham Sta.
Lac-Ste-Marie
L. du Poisson Blanc
Val-des-Bois
Ripon
Poltimore
Chénéville
St-André-Avellin
Namur
Morin Heights
St-Jovite
Ste-Adèle
St-Jacques
L'Épiphanie
Repentigny
Terrebonne
Rosemère
Pointe-aux-Trembles
St-Hyacinthe
Beloeil
Granby

Petawawa
Pembroke
Alice
Beachburg
Bryson
Campbell's Bay
ÎLE DU GRAND CALUMET
PARC DE-LA GATINEAU
Gracefield
Buckingham
Thurso
Papineauville
Montebello
Rockland
Grenville
Lachute
St-André
Brownsburg
Blainville
St-Eustache
LAVAL
MONTRÉAL
Pointe-Claire
Lachine
LONGUEUIL
Chambly
Marieville
Césaire
Bromont
Farnham
Cowansville
Sutton

Bonnechere
Round L.
Golden Lake
Cobden
Shawville
Quyon
L. des Chats
Pointe-Gatineau
Hull
Ottawa
Hawkesbury
Cumberland
Yankleek Hill
St-Eugène
Coteau-Landing
Dorion
Mercier
St-Rémi
St-Jean
Iberville
Napierville
Bedford
Philipsburg
Richford

Algonquin Park
Aylen L.
Killaloe Sta.
Douglas
L. Clear
Eganville
Renfrew
Braeside
Arnprior
Aylmer
Deschênes
Kanata
Stittsville
Bells Corner
Casselman
Maxville
St-Clet
Léry
Pointe-Claire
Salaberry-de-Valleyfield
St-Chrysostôme
Henryville
Lacolle
Rouses Point
Enosburg Falls
Sheldon

Whitney
Madawaska
Barry's Bay
Combermere
Calabogie
Pakenham
Almonte
White L.
Richmond
North Gower
Manotick
Osgoode
Winchester
Finch
Avonmore
Apple Hill
Howick
St-Anicet
Huntingdon
Hemmingford
Mooers
Alburg
Swanton
Grand Isle
Fairfax
Bakersfield
Johnson
Mt. Mansfield

Kawagama L.
Lake St. Peter
Opeongo
Eagle Lake
Kinmount
Wilberforce
Bancroft
Weslemkoon L.
BON ECHO PROV. PARK
Plevna
ONTARIO
Elphin
Lavant Sta.
Lanark
Carleton Place
Kemptville
Merrickville
Spencerville
South Nation
Chesterville
Morrisburg
Iroquois
Waddington
Brasher Falls
Brushton
Malone
Chazy
West Chazy
Owls Head
Dannemora
Lyon Mtn. ▲ 1167
Redford
Fairfield
Milton
Plattsburgh

Haliburton
Gooderham
Coe Hill
Gilmour
Cloyne
Sharbot Lake
Big Rideau L.
Jasper
Smiths Falls
Perth
Maberly
Arden
Portland
Athens
Prescott
Ogdensburg
Madrid
Norwood
Nicholville
St. Regis Falls
Paul Smiths
Gabriels
Whiteface
Keeseville
Port Kent
Au Sable Forks
Lake Placid
Essex 1339
Winooski
Burlington
Richmond
Stowe
Waterbury

Apsley
Burnt River
Millbridge
Eldorado
Madoc
Tweed
Verona
Charleston L.
Newboro L.
Elgin
Newboro
Brockville
Morristown
Heuvelton
Canton
Hermon
Russell
South Colton
Edwards
Pierrefield
Saranac Lake
Keene
Elizabethtown
Willsboro
Shelburne
Charlotte
Essex

Fenelon Falls
Bobcaygeon
Buckhorn L.
Pigeon L.
Stony L.
Marmora
Marlbank
Newburgh
Yarker
Harrowsmith
Seeley's Bay
Lansdowne
Black L.
Hammond
Gouverneur
Newton Falls
Tupper Lake
Mt. Marcy ▲ 1629
1260 Mt. Ellen

Lindsay
Bridgenorth
Norwood
Campbellford
Stirling
Havelock
Napanee
Odessa
Kingston
Barriefield
HOWE I.
Alexandria Bay
Clayton
Redwood
Theresa
Antwerp
Harrisville
Sabattis
Newcomb
Schroon Lake
Elizabethtown
Westport
Port Henry
Middlebury

Bethany
Omemee
Keene
Frankford
Belleville
Deseronto
Rossmore
Bath
AMHERST I.
WOLFE I.
Cape Vincent
GRENADIER I.
Chaumont
Philadelphia
Natural Bridge
Carthage
Deferiet
Long Lake
Crown Point
Ticonderoga
Hague
VERMONT
Brandon

Scugog
Millbrook
Pontypool
Bewdley
Rice L.
Trenton
Bayside
Picton
Bloomfield
Dexter
Evans Mills
Croghan
Copenhagen
Raquette Lake
Blue Mountain Lake
Indian Lake
N. Creek
Newcomb
Pottersville
Bolton Landing
Pittsford
Proctor
Rutland

Orono
Cobourg
Port Hope
Wellington
Consecon
PR. EDWARD PT.
GALLOO I.
STONY PT.
WICKED PT.
Sackets Harbor
Watertown
Big Moose
Old Forge
Speculator
Warrensburg
Lake George
Fort Ann
West Rutland
Poultney
Granville
Whitehall

Bowmanville
OSHAWA
Colborne
Brighton
Bloomfield
Belleville
Adams
Lowville
Port Leyden
Lyons Falls
663 ▲
Inlet Snowy Mt. ▲ 1190
Moose
Lake Pleasant
Wells
Lake George
Hamilton Mt. ▲ 991
Glens Falls
Hudson Falls 1159
Fort Edward
Dorset Mt. ▲
Manchester

LAKE ONTARIO
75
Mexico Bay
Pulaski
Orwell
Boonville
Oswego
Mexico
Fernwood
Parish
Williamstown
W. Canada Cr.
Newport
Sacandaga Res.
Northville
Mayfield
Saratoga Springs
Schuylerville
Stratton Mt. ▲ 1176
Arlington
Greenwich
Cambridge
N. Bennington
Wilmington

Barker
Lyndonville
Hamlin
Hilton
Sea Breeze
Red Creek
Sodus
Hannibal
Camden
Central Square
Constantia
Sylvan Beach
Taberg
Remsen
Prospect
Dolgeville
Broadalbin
Ballston Spa
Stillwater
Bennington
Readsboro

Newfane
Medina
Albion
Brockport
Holley
Spencerport
N. Chili
Webster
Phoenix
Brewerton
Rome
Little Falls
Gloversville
Johnstown
Fonda
Amsterdam
Mechanicville
Schuylerville
Saratoga Springs

Lockport
N. Tonawanda
Niagara Falls
Oakfield
Batavia
Bergen
ROCHESTER
E. Rochester
Pittsford
Lyons
Clyde
Jordan
Liverpool
N. Syracuse
Driskany
Whitesboro
Utica
New Hartford
Frankfort
Herkimer
Canajoharie
Fonda
Broadalbin
Ballston Spa

Tonawanda
Depew
Lancaster
Caledonia
Le Roy
Scottsville
Palmyra
Manchester
Newark
Weedsport
Fairmount
SYRACUSE
Oneida
Ilion
Mohawk
Ft. Plain
Cobleskill
Schoharie
Amsterdam
Scotia
Schenectady
Cohoes
Troy
Williamstown
N. Adams

BUFFALO
E. Aurora
Avon
Pavilion
Victor
Canandaigua
Geneva
Waterloo
Seneca Falls
Auburn
Skaneateles
Cazenovia
Morrisville
Bridgewater
Waterville
Richfield Springs
Cherry Valley
Sharon Springs
Duanesburg
Watervliet
ALBANY
Rensselaer
Pittsfield

Hamburg
Holland
Castile
Perry
Geneseo
Livonia
Canandaigua L.
Stanley
Cayuga L.
Union Springs
Aurora
Hamilton
Georgetown
Edmeston
Sloansville
Altamont
Delmar
Nassau
Adams

N. Collins
Arcade
Warsaw
Mt. Morris
Nunda
Springwater
Naples
Penn Yan
Ovid L.
Interlaken
Groton
Tully
Truxton
Cortland
McGraw
Homer
Cincinnatus
Oxford
Norwich
New Berlin
Sherburne
Schenevus
Middleburgh
Ravena
Schoharie
Cooperstown
Pittsfield
Lenox
Lee
MASS.

NEW YORK
Delevan
Castile
Bliss
Perry
Canaseraga
Dansville
657 ▲
Wayland
Cohocton
Dundee
Keuka L.
Dundee
Avoca
Hammondsport
Trumansburg
Dryden
Willet
Marathon
Greene
Oneonta
Mt. Upton
Unadilla
New Berlin
Grand Gorge
Stamford
Greenville
Stuyvesant
Cairo
Athens
Philmont
Great Barrington
Sheffield

Franklinville
Machias
Arcade
Houghton
Belfast
Canaseraga
Arkport
Hornell
Canisteo
Almond
Alfred
Andover
Bath
Savona
Campbell
Avoca
Ithaca
Newfield
Spencer
Whitney Point
Berkshire
Newark Valley
Afton
Bainbridge
Delhi
Andes
Margaretville
Lexington
Catskill
Hunter
Cairo
Catskill Mts.
Hudson
Hillsdale
Copake
793 ▲
Canaan

Cattaraugus
Salamanca
Ellicottville
Cuba
Friendship
Belmont
Wellsville
Whitesville
Addison
Jasper
Corning
Elmira
Elmira Hts.
Horseheads
Oswego
Endwell
Endicott
Johnson City
Binghamton
Deposit
Downsville
Pepacton Res.
Slide Mt. ▲ 1281
W. Hurley
Ashokan Res.
Kingston
Glasco
Saugerties
Red Hook
Milton
Rhinebeck
Winsted
Torrington

Allegany
Olean
Bolivar
Shinglehouse
Genesee
Knoxville
Lawrenceville
Gillett
Troy
Tioga
Sayre
Waverly
Nichols
Owego
Vestal
Great Bend
Windsor
Langsboro
Hallstead
Hancock
Livingston Manor
Roscoe
Callicoon
Liberty
Grahamsville
Napanoch
Ellenville
New Paltz
Poughkeepsie
Hyde Park
Amenia
Millbrook
Wappingers Falls
Litchfield
Bristol
CONN.

Eldred
Bradford
Lewis Run
Port Allegany
Westfield
Gold
Sabinsville
Mansfield
Wellsboro
Canton
Towanda
Monroeton
Wyalusing
Camptown
Hop Bottom
Montrose
New Milford
Susquehanna
Thompson
Pleasant Mount
Forest City
Honesdale
Woodbourne
Woodridge
Monticello
Wurtsboro
Middletown
Newburgh
Beacon
New Windsor
Cornwall
New Paltz
Wassaic
Amenia
Sharon
Cornwall
Torrington
Thomaston
Waterbury

St. Marys
Emporium
Austin
Mt. Brodhead ▲ 759
Wharton
Oleona
Pine Cr.
Galeton
Blossburg
Morris
Liberty
Ralston
Canton
New Albany
Dushore
Mildred
Noxen
Meshoppen
Tunkhannock
Nicholson
Hallstead
Callicoon
Woodbourne
Forest City
Carbondale
Hawley
Lackawaxen
Matamoras
Port Jervis
Monroe
Goshen
Florida
Middletown
Warwick
Brewster
Mahopac
Peekskill
Danbury
Bethel
Naugatuck
Ansonia
Seymour
Shelton
Milford

Ridgway
Driftwood
Renovo
North Bend
Cammal
Trout Run
Eagles Mare
Luzerne
Edwardsville
Kingston
Clarks Summit
Dickson City
Old Forge
Duryea
Dunmore
Duryea
SCRANTON
Olyphant
Archbald
Jermyn
Moscow
Newfoundland
Dingmans Ferry
Sussex
Warwick
N. J.
Stony Point
Haverstraw
BRIDGEPORT
Fairfield

PENNSYLVANIA
West from Greenwich

Parliament Hill, seen from the Rideau Canal.

1 : 250 000

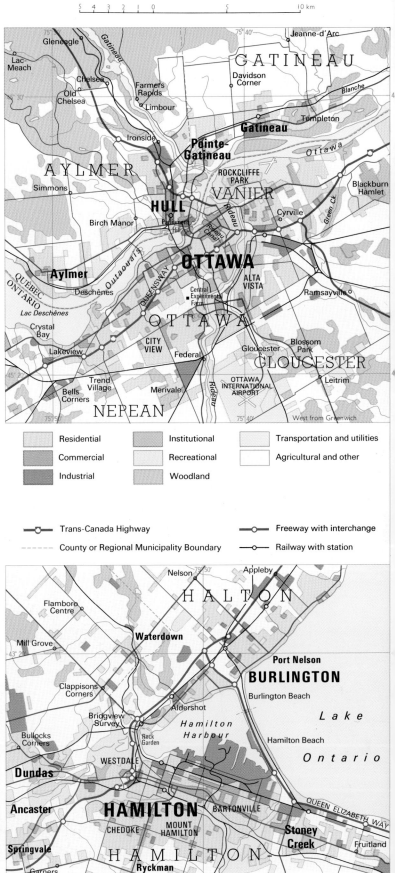

Residential	Institutional	Transportation and utilities
Commercial	Recreational	Agricultural and other
Industrial	Woodland	

Trans-Canada Highway — Freeway with interchange

County or Regional Municipality Boundary — Railway with station

The centre of Hamilton seen from the mountain brow.

1 : 600 000

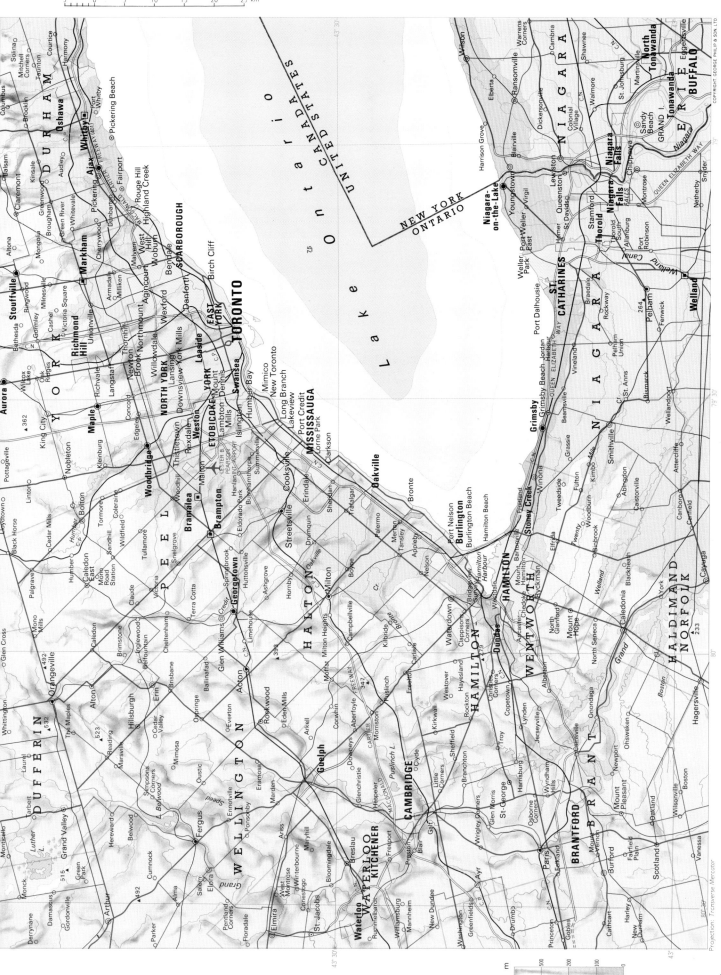

Projection: Transverse Mercator

m
Lake
Depths

SIMCOE CO.

44° 00'

Lloydtown • Pottageville • Snowball • **Aurora** • **Stouffville** • Altona

Linton • Wilcox Lake • Bethesda • Ringwood

Wilcocks Lake • Oak Ridges • Gormley • Cashel • Milnesville

Nobleton • **King City** • Victoria Square • Green River

Bolton • Y O R K • **RICHMOND HILL** • Y O R K • **MARKHAM**

Humber • **Maple** • **Unionville** Buttonville • *Rouge*

Tormore • Kleinburg • Richvale • Armadale

43° 50' • Coleraine • Langstaff • Milliken

Wildfield • *West Don* • *East Don* • Thornhill

West Humber • Edgeley • Concord • **NEWTON BROOK**

Tullamore • Pine Grove • **WILLOWDALE** • Malvern

Woodbridge • York Univ. • **NORTHMOUNT** • AGINCOURT • WOBURN

Woodhill • *Mimico Cr.* • LANSING • YORK MILLS • WEXFORD • **SCARBOROUGH** • WES HILL

THISTLETOWN • **N O R T H Y O R K** • *West Don* • **DON MILLS** • SCARBOROUGH

DOWNSVIEW • *East Don* • BENDALE

BRAMALEA • REXDALE • T O R O N T O • DANFORTH

Malton • **ETOBICOKE** • **WESTON** • **LEASIDE**

BRAMPTON • LESTER B. PEARSON INTERNATIONAL AIRPORT • **FOREST HILL** • **EAST YORK** • BIRCH CLIFF

43° 40' • *Etobicoke Cr.* • *Humber* • MOUNT DENNIS • **YORK** • *Don*

Hanlan • **LAMBTON MILLS** • Univ. of Toronto • Kew Gardens

Eldorado Park • *Mimico Cr.* • **SWANSEA** • City Hall

Credit • ISLINGTON • High Park • C.N. Tower

Etobicoke Cr. • **HUMBER BAY** • Exhibition Park • *Toronto Harbour* • **TORONTO**

Burnhamthorpe • Summerville • *Humber Bay* • Centre Island Park

TORONTO ISLAND

MIMICO

NEW TORONTO

P E E L • **LONG BRANCH**

Cooksville • Lakeview

Streetsville • *L a k e*

MISSISSAUGA

Erindale • *Credit* • **Port Credit**

Lorne Park

43° 30' • Clarkson

Sheridan

Trafalgar

H A L T O N

OAKVILLE

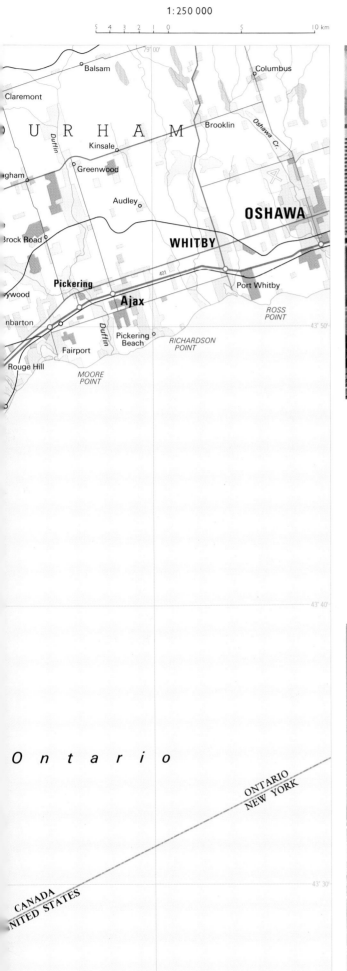

1 : 250 000

5 4 3 2 1 0   5   10 km

Balsam
Columbus
Claremont
D U R H A M
Brooklin
Oshawa Cr.
Kinsale
Duffin
gham
Greenwood
Audley
OSHAWA
Brock Road
WHITBY
Pickering
401
Port Whitby
ywood
Ajax
ROSS
POINT
nbarton
Duffin
Pickering
Beach
43° 50'
RICHARDSON
POINT
Fairport
Rouge Hill
MOORE
POINT

43° 40'

O n t a r i o

ONTARIO
NEW YORK

43° 30'

CANADA
NITED STATES

79° 00'

The City Hall area, Toronto.

▨	Residential	▨	Institutional	▢	Transportation and utilities
▨	Commercial	▨	Recreational	▢	Agricultural and other
▨	Industrial	▨	Woodland		

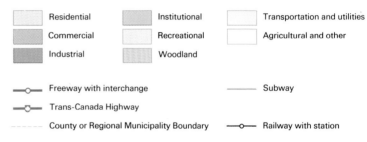

—○— Freeway with interchange   ——— Subway

—○— Trans-Canada Highway

- - - County or Regional Municipality Boundary   —○— Railway with station

The C.N. Tower (553 metres high) seen from Lake Ontario.

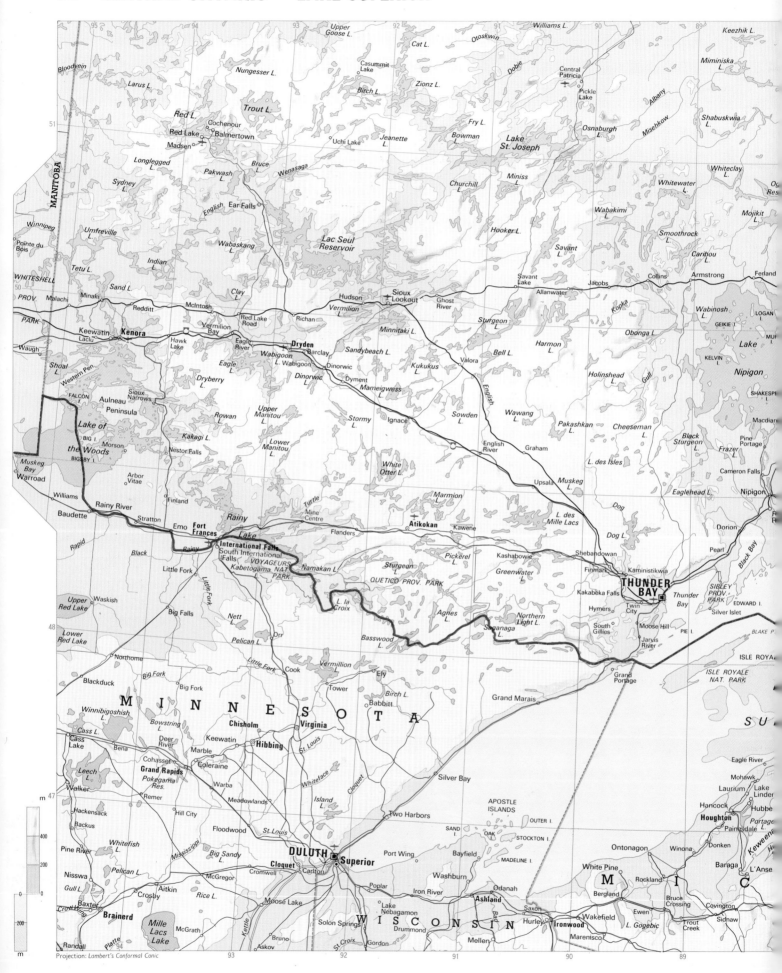

Projection: Lambert's Conformal Conic

1:2 500 000

10 0 10 20 30 40 50 60 70 80 90 100 km

53

James
Bay

Moosonee
Moose
Factory

Wabassi
Albany
Ogoki
Atikameg
Albany
Kinoje
Lakes
Kinoje
Galeton

Eabamet
L.
Washi L.
Wabimeig
L.
Cheepay
Stooping
Kwataboahegan
North French

Makokibatan
L.
Dusey
Albany
Jaab L.
Sandbank
L.
Renison
51

Kagianagami
L.
Ogoki
Little Current
Pledger
L.
Cheepash
Moose River
Onakawana

Kapikotongwa
Abamasagi
L.
Drowning
Ridge
Kenogami
Missinaibi
Ranoke

Ara L.
O'Sullivan
L.
Esnagami
L.
Otter Rapids

Kowkash
Nakina
Kenogami
Otasawian
Pivabiska
Smoky Falls
Foxville
Abitibi
50

Chipman
Ogahalla
Pagwa River
Calstock
Shannon L.
Opasatika
Fraserdale
Little Abitibi
Island Falls

Onaman
L.
Burrows
L.
Longlac
Pagwachuan
Naagagami
Hearst
Hallebourg
Mattice
Opasatika
REMI LAKE PROV. PK.
Abitibi

Wildgoose L.
Geraldton
Caramat
Osawin
Nagagamisis
L.
Jogues
Lowther
Opasatika
Harty
Kapuskasing
Smooth
Rock Falls

Jellicoe
Parks
McKay
L.
Stevens
Hillsport
Nagagami
Kabinakagami
Mattawitchewan
Valrita
Moonbeam
Fauquier
49

Wintering
Kagiano
L.
Obakamiga
L.
Cameron
L.
Oba
Opasatika
L.
Saganash
L.
Kapuskasing

Barbara
L.
Killala L.
Manitouwadge
Hornepayne
Brunswick L.
Mattagami

Little Pic
Kabinakagami
L.
Akron
Fire River
Dunrankin

Rossport
White
L.
Mosher
Peterbell
Elsas
Timmins
Porcupine

Schreiber
Terrace Bay
Marathon
Struthers
Esnagi
L.
Oba L.
Missinaibi L.
Schumacher
South Porcupine

SIMPSON
SLATE IS.
PIC I.
Heron Bay
White River
Amyot
Franz
Wabatongushi
L.
Missanabie
MISSINAIBI LAKE PROV. PARK
Foleyet
Redstone

PUKASKWA NAT. PARK
OBATANGA PROV. PARK
University
Magpie
Dog L.
Dalton
Racine
Nemegosenda
Horwood
L.
Palomar
Groundhog
48

Hawk Junction
Windermere
L.
Rush L.
Mattagami L.

Wawa
SHOALS PROV. PARK
Chapleau
Borden
L.
Gogama

Michipicoten
Nagasin L.
Jerome

C A N A D A
Michipicoten Bay
Agawa
Sideburned
L.
Sultan
Westree

U N I T E D   S T A T E S
MICHIPICOTEN
ISLAND
LAKE SUPERIOR PROV. PARK
Kormak
Ramsey
Biscotasing
Ruel

per Harbor
MANITOU I.
CARIBOU I.
LEACH L.
Wenebegon
L.
White
Owl L.
Ramsey
L.
Biscotasi L.
Onaping L.

Grise
MONTREAL I.
Montreal
Goulais
Wenebegon
Mazhabong
L.
Pogamasing
Benny

Ranger L.
Rocky
Island L.
Cartier
Capreol
Val
Caron

Batchawana
Bay
Batchawana
Bay
Searchmont
aux Sables
Benny
Levack
Azilda

Whitefish
Point
**Sault
Sainte
Marie**
Onaping
Chelmsford
Sudbury

M I C H I G A N
AU SABLE PT.
GRAND I.
Grand
Marais
Paradise
Whitefish
Bay
Echo Bay
Mississagi
Wakomata
L.
Little White
MISSISSAGI PROV. PARK
Whitefish
Copper
Lively

Marquette
Grand I.
**Sault
Sainte
Marie**
Brimley
Elliot Lake
Nairn
Cliff
Naughton
Panache

Negaunee
Skandia
Munising
Newberry
Hulbert
Dafter
Echo Bay
Thessalon
Big
Basswood
L.
Iron
Bridge
Matinenda
Webbwood
Espanola

Gwinn
Chatham
Shingleton
Seney
McMillan
Strongs
Corners
Rudyard
Hilton
Beach
ST. JOSEPH I.
Blind
River
Spragge
Spanish
Massey
Whitefish Falls

87   86   West from Greenwich   85   84   83   82
COPYRIGHT. GEORGE PHILIP & SON LTD.

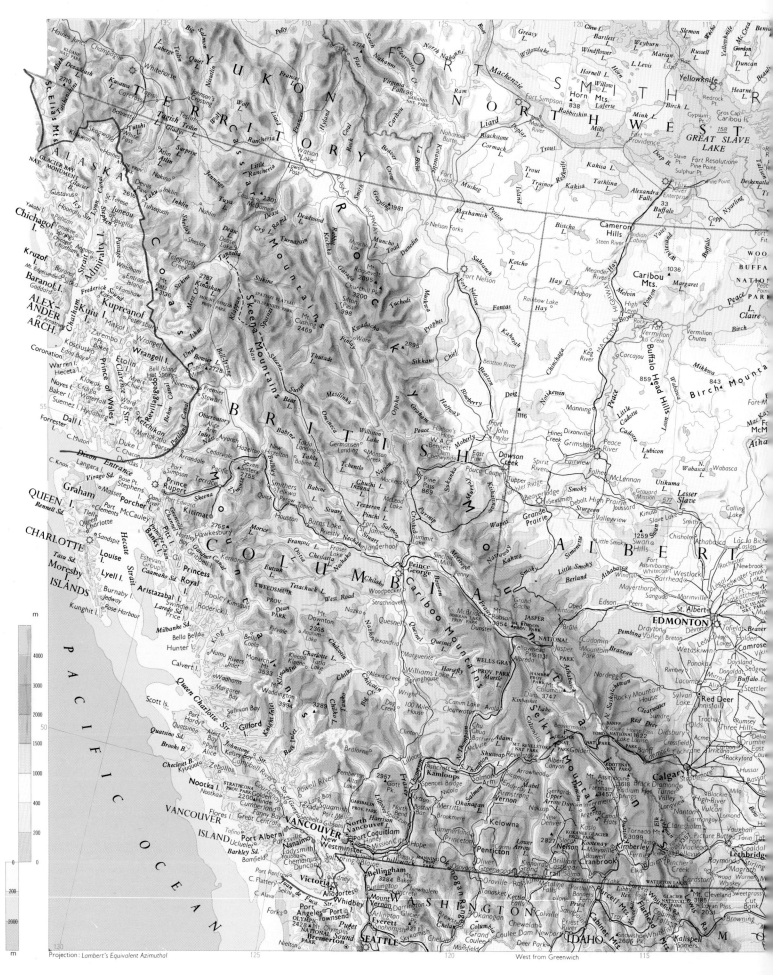

Projection: Lambert's Equivalent Azimuthal   West from Greenwich

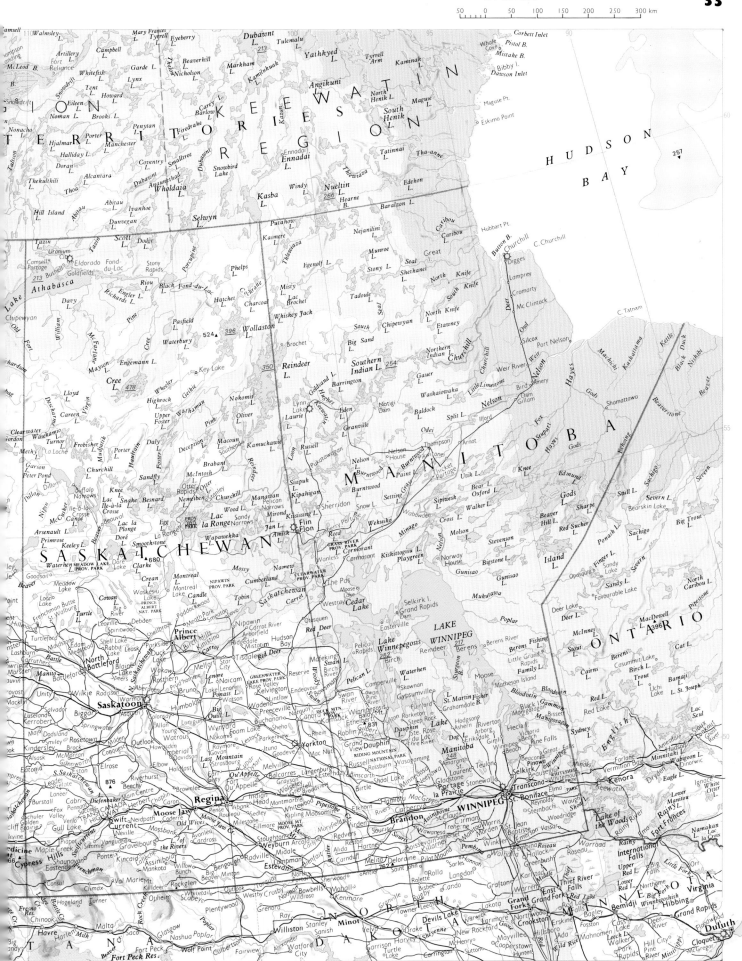

50   0   50   100   150   200   250   300 km

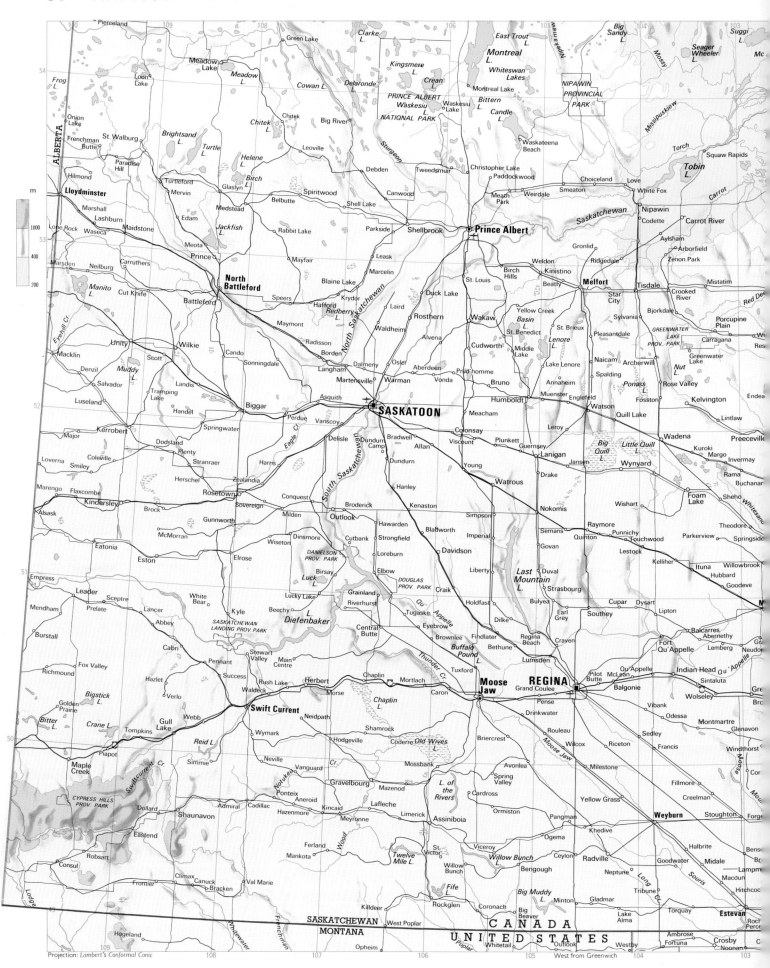

Projection: Lambert's Conformal Conic

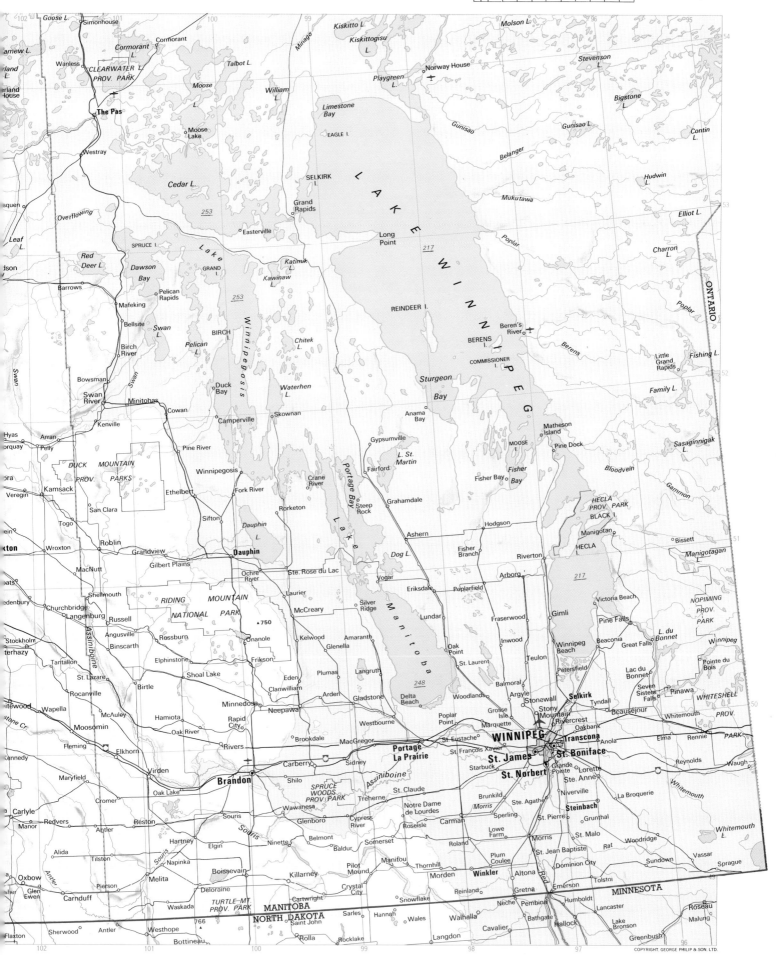

ONTARIO

MINNESOTA

MANITOBA

NORTH DAKOTA

LAKE WINNIPEG

Lake Winnipegosis

Lake Manitoba

Goose L.   Simonhouse   101   100   99   98   96   95   54

Cormorant   Cormorant   *Talbot L.*   *Kiskitto L.*   *Kiskittogisu L.*   *Molson L.*

Wanless   CLEARWATER L. PROV. PARK   *Moose L.*   *William L.*   Norway House   *Stevenson L.*

The Pas   *Moose Lake*   Playgreen L.   *Bigstone L.*

Westray   *Cedar L.*   EAGLE I.   Limestone Bay   *Gunisao L.*   *Contin L.*

SPRUCE I.   SELKIRK   Belanger   *Hudwin L.*

Overflowing   *Red Deer L.*   *Dawson Bay*   Grand Rapids   Mukutawa   *Elliot L.*

Barrows   GRAND I.   253   Long Point   217   Poplar   *Charron L.*

Mafeking   253   *Katimik*   *Kawinaw L.*   REINDEER I.   Beren's River   *Poplar*

Bellsite   Pelican Rapids   BIRCH   *Chitek L.*   BERENS   Berens   *Little Grand Rapids*   *Fishing L.*

Birch River   *Swan L.*   *Pelican L.*   COMMISSIONER I.   *Family L.*

Bowsman   Duck Bay   *Waterhen L.*   Sturgeon Bay   *Sasaginnigak L.*

Swan River   Minitonas   Camperville   Skownan   Anama Bay   Matheson Island   MOOSE   Pine Dock   *Gammon*

Hyas   Arran   Kenville   Cowan   Gypsumville   L. St. Martin   Fisher Bay   *Fisher Bay*   *Bloodvein*

Pelly   Pine River   Winnipegosis   Crane River   Fairford   HECLA PROV. PARK   BLACK I.   *Manigotagan L.*

Kamsack   DUCK MOUNTAIN PROV. PARKS   Ethelbert   Fork River   Portage Bay   Grahamdale   Hodgson   BLACK I.   Bissett

Veregin   San Clara   Rorketon   Steep Rock   Ashern   Fisher Branch   Riverton   HECLA   217   Manigotagan

Togo   Roblin   *Dauphin L.*   Dog L.   NOPIMING PROV. PARK

Wroxton   Grandview   Ochre River   Ste. Rose du Lac   Vogar   Eriksdale   Poplarfield   Arborg   Victoria Beach

MacNutt   Gilbert Plains   Dauphin   Laurier   Silver Ridge   Lundar   Fraserwood   Gimli   Pine Falls

Churchbridge   Shellmouth   RIDING MOUNTAIN   McCreary   Oak Point   Inwood   Winnipeg Beach   Beaconia   Great Falls   WHITESHELL

Langenburg   Russell   NATIONAL PARK   ▲750   Kelwood   Amaranth   St. Laurent   Teulon   Petersfield   Lac du Bonnet   L. du Bonnet   *Winnipeg*

Angusville   Rossburn   Onanole   Glenella   Oak Point   Balmoral   Seven Sisters Falls   Pinawa   PROV. PARK

Tantallon   Binscarth   Elphinstone   Frikson   Eden   Plumas   Langruth   248   Woodlands   Argyle   Stonewall   Selkirk   Tyndall   Beauséjour   Pointe du Bois

St. Lazare   Birtle   Shoal Lake   Clanwilliam   Arden   Gladstone   Delta Beach   Grosse Isle   Stony Mountain   Rivercrest   Oakbank   Whitemouth   PROV.

Rocanville   Minnedosa   Neepawa   Westbourne   Poplar Point   Marquette   PARK   50

Wapella   McAuley   Hamiota   Rapid City   Woodlands   WINNIPEG   Transcona   Anola   Elma   Rennie

Moosomin   Oak River   Brookdale   MacGregor   St. Eustache   St. James   St. Boniface   Reynolds   Waugh

Fleming   Elkhorn   Rivers   Sidney   St. François Xavier   St. Norbert   Grande Pointe   Lorette   Whitemouth

Virden   Carberry   Portage La Prairie   Starbuck   Ste. Anne

Maryfield   Shilo   Assiniboine   St. Claude   Brunkild   Niverville   La Broquerie   *Whitemouth L.*

Brandon   Oak Lake   SPRUCE WOODS PROV. PARK   Treherne   Notre Dame de Lourdes   Morris   Ste. Agathe   St. Pierre   Steinbach

Cromer   Wawanesa   Cypress River   Roseisle   Carman   Sperling   Grunthal   Woodridge

Carlyle   Redvers   Antler   Reston   Souris   Glenboro   Somerset   Roland   Lowe Farm   Morris   St. Malo

Manor   Hartney   Elgin   Baldur   Pilot   Manitou   Plum Coulee   St. Jean Baptiste   Rat   Vassar

Alida   Tilston   Napinka   Ninette   Belmont   Mound   Thornhill   Morden   Winkler   Altona   Dominion City   Sundown   Sprague

Oxbow   Glen Ewen   Carnduff   Pierson   Melita   Boissevain   Killarney   Crystal City   Snowflake   Reinland   Gretna   Emerson   Tolstoi   *Whitemouth L.*

Flaxton   Sherwood   Antler   Waskada   TURTLE MT. PROV. PARK   Cartwright   Saint John   Sarles   Hannah   Wales   Walhalla   Neche   Pembina   Humboldt   Lancaster   Roseau

Westhope   766   Bottineau   Rolla   Rocklake   Langdon   Cavalier   Bathgate   Hallock   Lake Bronson   Greenbush   Malung

102   101   100   99   98   97   96

1:250 000

5 4 3 2 1 0 5 10 km

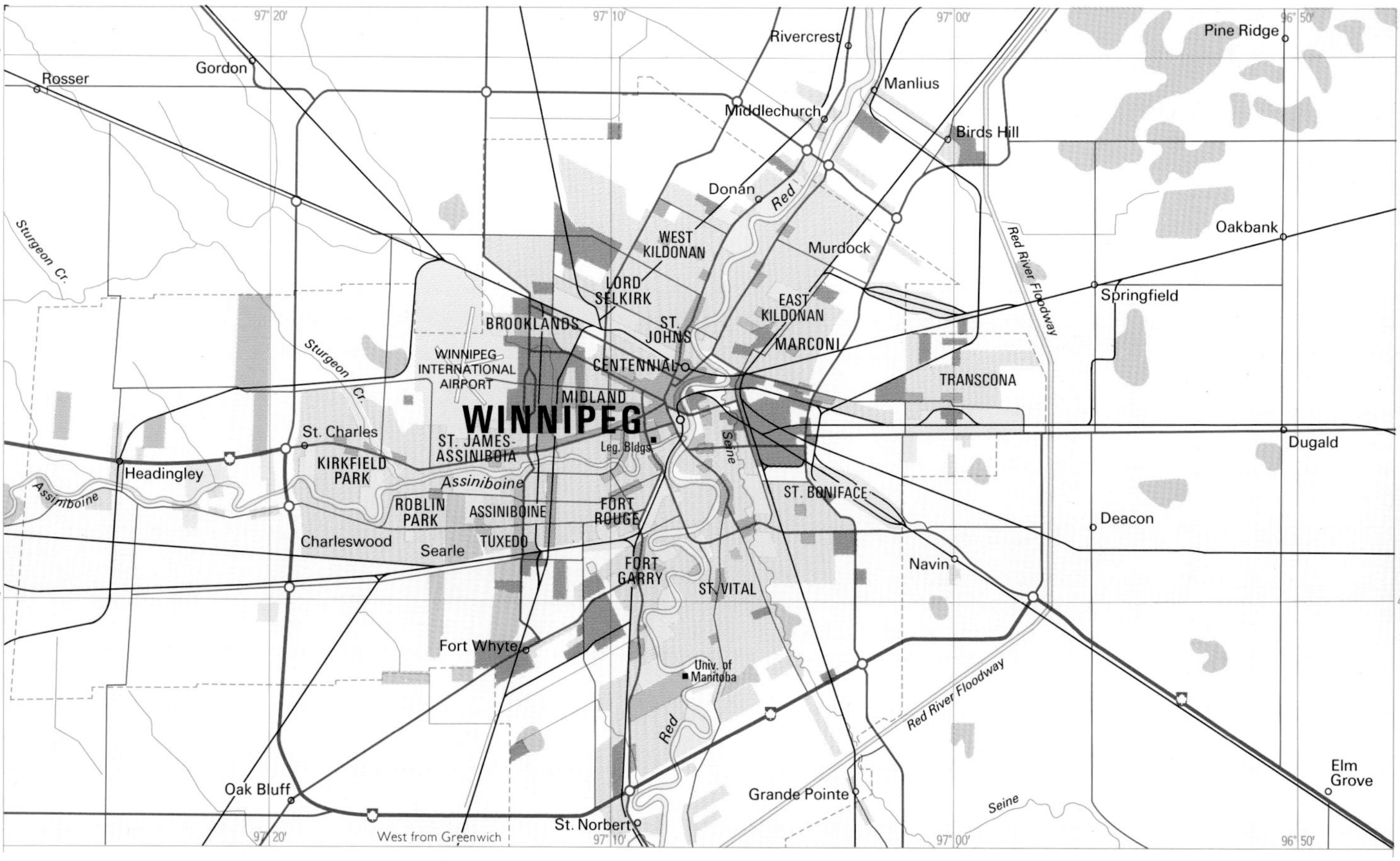

Winnipeg map

Rosser
Gordon
Rivercrest
Pine Ridge
Middlechurch
Manlius
Birds Hill
Donán
Red
WEST KILDONAN
Murdock
Oakbank
LORD SELKIRK
Springfield
BROOKLANDS
ST JOHNS
EAST KILDONAN
WINNIPEG INTERNATIONAL AIRPORT
CENTENNIAL
MARCONI
TRANSCONA
St. Charles
MIDLAND
WINNIPEG
Leg. Bldgs
Steine
KIRKFIELD PARK
ST. JAMES-ASSINIBOIA
Dugald
Headingley
Assiniboine
Assiniboine
ROBLIN PARK
ASSINIBOINE
FORT ROUGE
ST. BONIFACE
Deacon
Charleswood
Searle
TUXEDO
Navin
FORT GARRY
ST. VITAL
Fort Whyte
Univ. of Manitoba
Red
Red River Floodway
Oak Bluff
West from Greenwich
St. Norbert
Grande Pointe
Seine
Elm Grove

Legend

Residential	Industrial	Recreational	Transportation and utilities
Commercial	Institutional	Woodland	Agricultural and other

○ Freeway with interchange   ○ Trans-Canada Highway   ○ Railway with station   - - - City Boundary

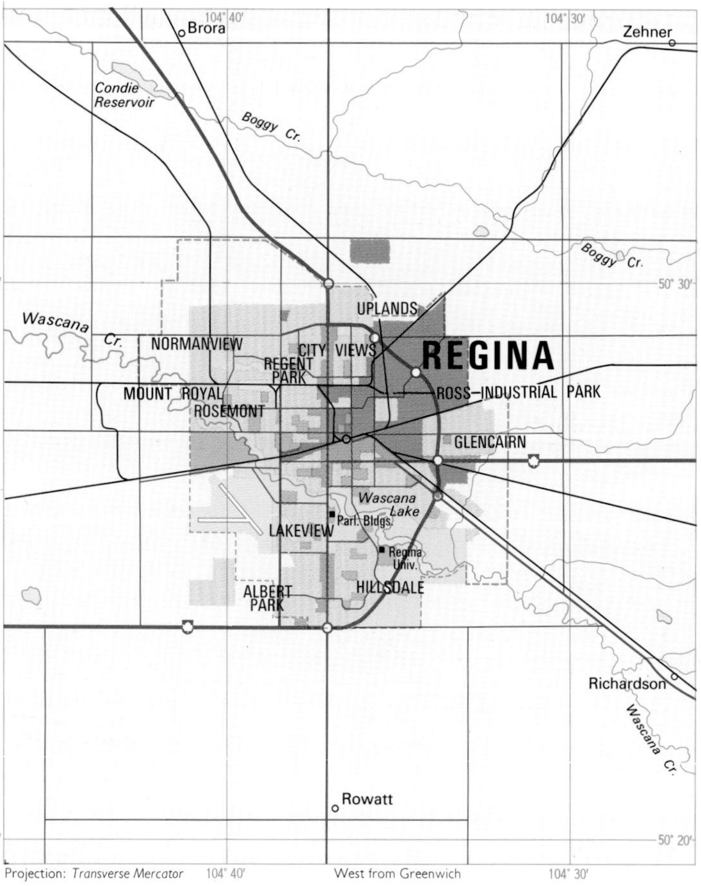

Regina map

Brora
Zehner
Condie Reservoir
Boggy Cr.
Boggy Cr.
Wascana Cr.
UPLANDS
NORMANVIEW
CITY VIEWS
REGINA
REGENT PARK
MOUNT ROYAL
ROSEMONT
ROSS INDUSTRIAL PARK
GLENCAIRN
Wascana Lake
LAKEVIEW
Parl. Bldgs
Regina Univ.
ALBERT PARK
HILLSDALE
Richardson
Wascana Cr.
Rowatt

Projection: *Transverse Mercator*   104° 40'   West from Greenwich   104° 30'

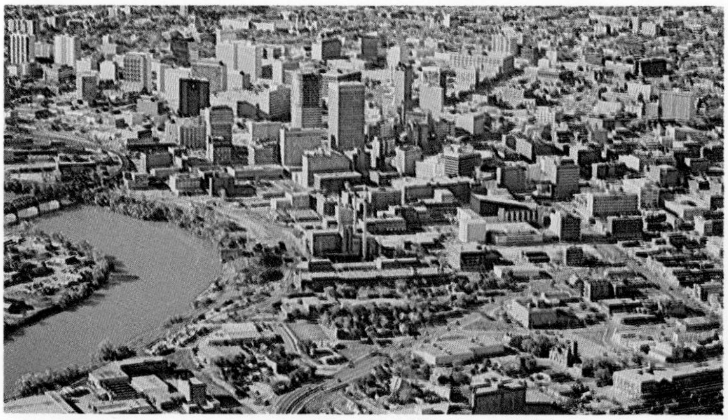

Winnipeg aerial view looking south

Regina looking north across Wascana L

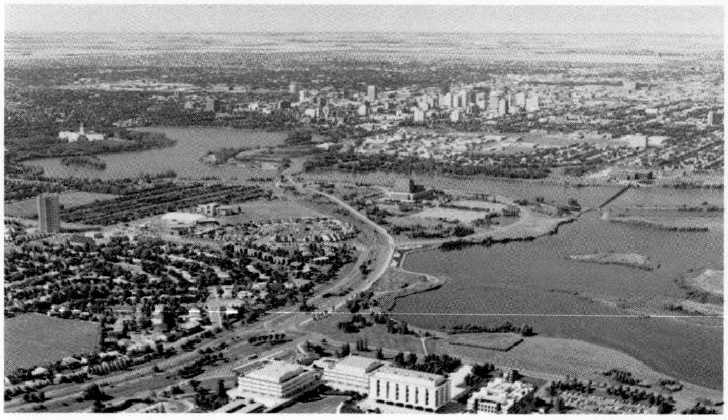

1:250 000

5 4 3 2 1 0   5   10 km

Edmonton city centre

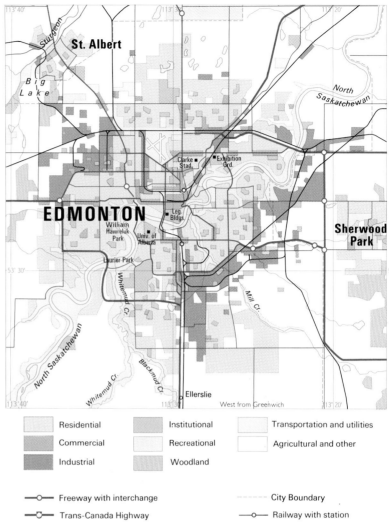

	Residential		Institutional		Transportation and utilities
	Commercial		Recreational		Agricultural and other
	Industrial		Woodland		

───○─── Freeway with interchange   ────── City Boundary

───○─── Trans-Canada Highway   ───○─── Railway with station

Calgary city centre looking south across Bow River, with Calgary Tower (188 metres high) at left.

Projection: *Transverse Mercator*

West from Greenwich   COPYRIGHT. GEORGE PHILIP & SON. LTD

1:2 500 000

10 0 10 20 30 40 50 60 70 80 90 100 km

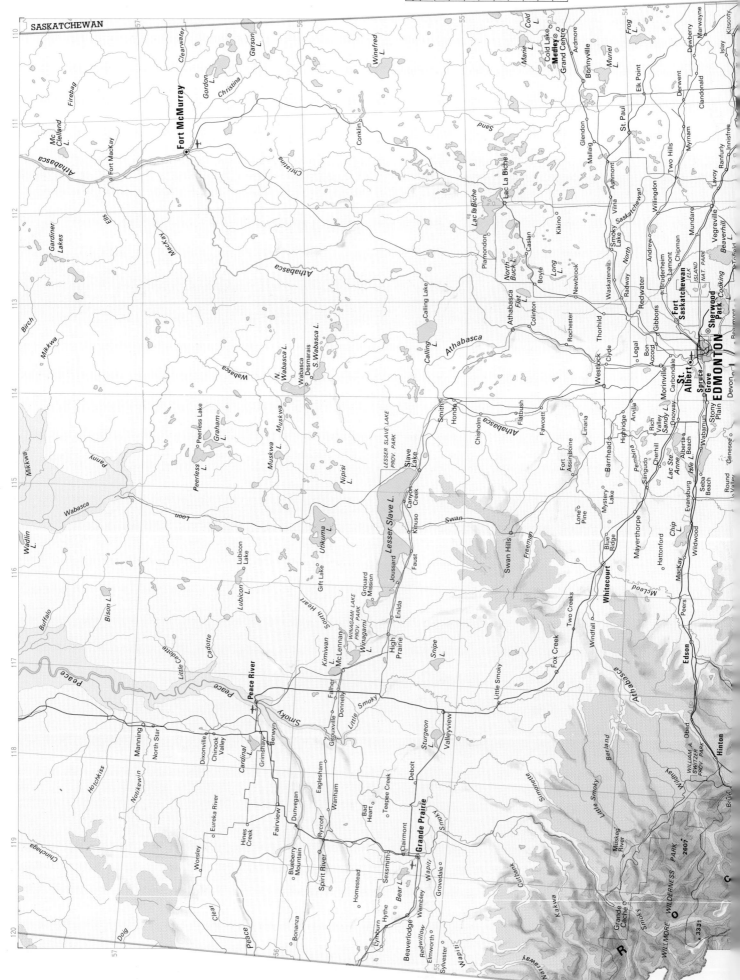

COPYRIGHT GEORGE PHILIP & SON LTD.

Projection Lambert's Conformal Conic

West from Greenwich

111   112   113   114   115   116   117   118

52   52

51   51

50   50

Medicine Hat
Lethbridge
Calgary
Red Deer
Drumheller
Brooks
Wetaskiwin
Ponoka
Lacombe
Innisfail
Airdrie
Camrose
Taber
Cranbrook
Kimberley
Nelson
Trail

MONTANA

WASHINGTON

IDAHO

BRITISH COLUMBIA

ALBERTA

Cariboo Mountains

m   3000   2000   1500   1000   400   200

Projection: Lambert's Conformal Conic

West from Greenwich

1 : 2 500 000

10 0 10 20 30 40 50 60 70 80 90 100 km

Victoria inset

GORDON HEAD

Royal Oak

Colquitz

Lake Hill

SAANICH

Mt. Tolmie

Cadboro Bay

Craigflower

Langford

Belmont Park

VICTORIA

OAK BAY

Colwood

ESQUIMALT

DISCOVERY I.

MACAULAY PT.

Beacon Hill Park

Victoria Harb.

CLOVER PT. 123° 20'

1 : 250 000

0 1 2 3 4 5 km

For reference to colours see page 66

COPYRIGHT. GEORGE PHILIP & SON. LTD.

Shelley

Prince George

Pineview

Red Rock

Stoner

Woodpecker

Hixon

Strathnaver

Dunkley

Moose Heights

Quesnel

Kersley

Alexandria

Castle Rock

Marguerite

Macalister

ex Graham

Riske Creek

Hanceville

Chilcotin

Big Creek

Gang Ranch

Springhouse

Williams Lake

150 Mile House

Meldrum Creek

Wright

Dog Creek

Big Bar Creek

Carpenter L.

Bralorne

Shalalth

Anderson L.

Seton Portage

Birken

Lillooet L.

Pemberton

Alta Lake

GARIBALDI

Mt. Garibaldi 2678

PROV. PARK

endale

Squamish

Britannia Beach

Howe

Bowen Island

North Vancouver

VANCOUVER

New Westminster

Langley

White Rock

ROBERTS

Mayne

Saturna

Fulford Harbour

Sidney

Friday Harbor

SAN JUAN

ORCAS I.

LOPEZ

Anacortes

VICTORIA

WHIDBEY

Oak Harbor

Coupeville

CAMANO

Penny

Dome Creek

2074

Crescent Spur

Fraser

Lamming Mills

McBride

Dunster

Bowron

Cariboo

BOWRON LAKE PROV. PARK

Wells

1783

Mitchell L.

Hobson L.

Azure L.

Quesnel L.

Likely

Horsefly L.

Horsefly

Clearwater L.

WELLS GRAY

Murtle L.

Blue River

PROVINCIAL PARK

Hendrix Lake

Mahood L.

Canim L.

Mahood Falls

Lac la Hache

Forest Grove

Canim Lake

Tatton

Buffalo Creek

100 Mile House

Lone Butte

Sheridan L.

Little Fort

70 Mile House

Bonaparte L.

Chasm

2243

Clinton

2877

Lillooet

2329

Ashcroft

Spences Bridge

Thompson

Lytton

Thompson

Lower Nicola

Nicola L.

Nicola

Merritt

Skihist Mt. 2944

North Bend

Boston Bar

2385

Spuzzum

Yale

Hope

GOLDEN EARS PROV. PARK

Harrison Lake

Stave L.

Pitt L.

Port Moody

Coquitlam

Haney

Port Coquitlam

Stave Falls

Deroche

Mission City

Fort Langley

Abbotsford

Sardis

Chilliwack

Yarrow

Lindell Beach

Sumas

Blaine

Lynden

Ferndale

Maple Falls

Whatcom

Mt. Baker 3284

Shannon L.

Bellingham

East Sound

LUMMI

Hamilton

Concrete

2703

Marblemount

Rockport

Sedro Woolley

Burlington

Mount Vernon

Stanwood

Arlington

Darrington

Glacier Peak 3211

Silverton

Holden

Lucerne

WILLMORE WILDERNESS PARK

2607

ROCKY

3331

ALTA

B.C.

Mt. Robson 3954

MT. ROBSON

Red Pass

PROV.

PARK

Lucerne

Yellowhead Pass

Valemount

3505

Albreda

North Thompson

Murtle L.

2577

Avola

Clearwater

Clearwater

Birch Island

Vavenby

Adams

Chu Chua

Barrière

Louis Creek

McLure

Black Pines

Rayleigh

Westsyde

Kamloops

Cache Creek

Walhachin

Savona

Cherry Creek

South Thompson

Kamloops

Valleyview

Quilchena

Aspen Grove

Brookmere

Coalmont

Princeton

Similkameen

Hedley

Keremeos

Cathedral PROV. PARK 2593

MANNING PROV. PARK

Manning Park

Silvertip Mt. 2606

Laidlaw

Cheam View

Agassiz

Harrison Hot Springs

Rosedale

CASCADES

NORTH

NATIONAL PARK

Newhalem

Mazama

Methow

Winthrop

Twisp

Carlton

Stehekin

Chelan

Chewuch Creek

Conconully

Riverside

Okanogan

Omak

Malott

Tonasket

Republic

Kettle Falls

Colville

Springdale

Chewelah

Newport

Priest L.

IDAHO

Pend Oreille

Ione

Metaline Falls

Northport

Columbia

WASHINGTON

Grand Forks

Christina

Rock Creek

Midway

Greenwood

Eholt

2304

Oliver

Osoyoos

Osoyoos L.

Oroville

Okanogan

Okanagan

Mica Dam

Mica Creek

Mt. Chapman 3075

Seymour Arm

Mt. Sir Sandford 3522

HAMBER PROV. PARK

Kinbasket Lake

Mt. Columbia 3747

3491

BANFF

3612

NATIONAL

Bow Pass

YOHO

Beavermouth

Donald

Kicking Horse Pass

NATIONAL PARK

Lake Louise

3312

Vermilion Pass

Columbia

Parson

GLACIER NAT'L PARK

Glacier

Golden

Albert Canyon

Revelstoke

MT. REVELSTOKE NAT'L PARK

BUGABOO GLACIER PROV. PARK

Mt. Templeman 3070

3468

Duncan

Gerrard

Duncan L.

Toby Creek

Marblehead

Duncan Dam

Trout Lake

Arrowhead

Upper Arrow Lake

Nakusp

New Denver

Silverton

Kaslo

Riondel

Slocan L.

KOKANEE GLACIER PROV. PARK

Kootenay

Procter

Boswell

Nelson

Kootenay

Kootenay L.

Salmo

Ymir

Fruitvale

Trail

Montrose

Warfield

Rossland

H. Keenleyside Dam

Brilliant

Kinnaird

Castlegar

Renata

Edgewood

Fauquier

Burton

Lower Arrow L.

Carmi

Beaverdell

Granby

Kettle

Columbia

Adams L. 2303

Shuswap L.

Sicamous

Canoe

Hupel

Enderby

Salmon Arm

Mabel L.

MONASHEE PROV. PARK

2972

Armstrong

SILVER STAR PROV. PARK

Vernon

Cherryville

Sugar L.

Oyama

Okanagan L.

Kelowna

Okanagan Mission

Wilson Landing

Peachland

OKANAGAN MOUNTAIN PROV. PARK

Summerland

Penticton

Chase

Arrow Park

Columbia

Hanville

Quesnel

Buffalo

Castle

Wells

Dunster

Fraser

Cariboo

Mountains

Monashee

Kootenay

Selkirk

Projection: Bonne

1:10 000 000

100   0   100   200   300   400 km

United States Range

Barbeau Pk. 2604

C. Thomas Hubbard

Nansen Sd.

Princess Margaret Range

Eureka

Greely Fd.

Victoria and Albert Mts.

Kennedy Str.

Kane Basin

Humboldt Glacier

Knud Rasmussen Land

Inglefield Land

G R E E N L A N D

(DENMARK)

2140 Axel Heiberg I.

Fosheim Pen.

Smith Sound

Thule (Qanaq)

Inglefield Gulf

drup Is.

Amund Ringnes

Norwegian Bay

Raanes Pen.

Smith B.

C. Parry

Wolstenholme Fjord

Dundas (Thule)

C. York

Melville Bay

Kraulshavn

Upernavik

Prøven

Cornwall I.

Belcher Channel

Graham

Simmons Pen.

Grise Fiord

Coburg I.

Lady Ann Str.

Magnetic

Penny Str.

E l i z a b e t h   I s .

Jones Sound

Treuter Mts. 1887

Hyde Inlet

C. Cockburn

Svartenhuk Peninsula

Umanak

Nugssuaq Pen.

Jakobshavn

hurst I.

Devon I.

C. Warrender

B a f f i n

B a y

Disko I.

Godhavn

Disko B.

Corn- wallis I.

Wellington Chan.

Resolute

Lancaster Sound

C. Liverpool

Davis Strait

Holsteinsborg

Russell I.

Barrow Str.

R E G I O N

Crauford

2134 Bylot I.

C. Hunter

Nova Zembla I.

C. Jameson

Bruce Mts.

Scott Inlet

Clyde River

C. Hewett

C. Raper

Home B.

FFIN

Somerset I.

Brodeur Peninsula

Arctic Bay

Nanisivik

Borden Peninsula

Eclipse Sd.

Pond Inlet

Pond Inlet

C. Henry Kater

Prince of Wales I.

Admiralty Inlet

B a f f i n

Barnes Icecap

Kivitoo

Broughton Island

Padloping Island

Cape Dyer

Franklin Str.

Ft. Ross

C. Farrand

Prince Regent Inlet

Peninsula

Steensby Inlet

Baird Pen.

AUYUITTUQ Penny Highland NAT. 2591 PARK

Ponds Inlet

Pangnirtung

Cumberland Peninsula

Hoare B.

Gateshead I.

Boothia Peninsula

Gulf of Boothia

Bernier B.

I s l a n d

C. Mercy

EOT

573

Fury & Hecla Str.

C. Englefield

Rowley I.

Foley I.

Air Force I.

Cumberland Sound

Lemieux Islands

Thom Bay

Igloolik

Prince Charles I.

Nettilling L.

Spence Bay

Hall Beach

King William

Gjoa Haven

Simpson Pen.

Pelly Bay

Melville

Wales Peninsula

Foxe Basin

Foxe Basin

C. Dominion

Amadjuak L.

Frobisher Bay

Hall Pen.

miralty

Chantrey Inlet

Committee B.

T E R R I T O R I E S

Amadjuak

Everett Mts.

Frobisher Bay

Resolution I.

Adelaide Pen.

Rae Isthmus

Repulse Bay

Arctic Circle

Vansittart I.

C. Dorchester

Foxe Pen.

Cape Dorset

Salisbury

Lake Harbour

Big I.

C. Chidley

Gulf

Macdougall L.

Wager Wager B. Bay

Roes Welcome Sd.

Torsill Mts.

Foxe Channel

H u d s o n   S t r a i t

Port Burwell

garry L.

Southampton I.

Coral Harbour

Bell Pen.

Nottingham I.

Nottingham Island

Salisbury

Wolstenholme

Saglouc

Maricourt (Wakeham)

Kootac C. Hopes Advance

Akpatok

Baker Lake

Baker

Chesterfield Inlet

Fisher Strait

Coats I.

Digges Is.

C. Wolstenholme

Ivugivik

St. Louis Mts.

Kugisgiuk

Arnaud (Payne)

Kuujjuaq

Ungava Bay

K E E W A T I N

Dubawnt L.

Rankin Inlet

Chesterfield Inlet

Mansel I.

Payne L.

Koksoak

R E G I O N

Kaminak L.

Whale Cove

Cape Smith

Pavungnituk

Feuilles (Leaf)

Mélèzes (Larch)

Yathkyed L.

Padlei

Tavani

H u d s o n   B a y

Portland Promontory

Nueltin L.

Eskimo Point

Thlewiaza

Ottawa Is.

Inoucdjouac Port Harrison

I. Minto

1 : 250 000

5 4 3 2 1 0   5   10 km

BOWYER I.

Eastcap Cr.

Cathedral Mt.
1732 ▲

Seymour
Lake

Mt. Burwell
1532 ▲

Mt. Bishop
1507 ▲

MT. SEYMOUR

PROV.

Capilano

Mt. Strachan
▲ 1454

PARK

Black Mt.
▲ 1217

Hollyburn Mt.
▲ 1324

Grouse Mt. ▲
1211

Mt. Seymour
▲ 1453

CYPRESS
PROV. PARK

Capilano
Lake

Horseshoe
Bay

Eagle Harbour

WEST
VANCOUVER

Sherman   Wadsley

Caulfield

DUNDARAVE

PARK
ROYAL

NORTH
LONSDALE

Lynn
Creek

Buntzen
Lake

49° 20'

LOWER
CAPILANO

NORTH
VANCOUVER

Deep
Cove

49° 20'

First Narrows

Lion's Gate
Bridge

LYNNMOUR

Seymour
Heights

Dollarton

Ioco

Coquitlam

Stanley
Park

Burrard Inlet

Vancouver
Harbour

Second Narrows

Barnet

Port Moody

English Bay

False Creek

NORTH
BURNABY

LOCHDALE

Simon Fraser
Univ.

Port Moody

Port
Coquitlam

Spanish
Banks

POINT GREY
Univ. of B.C.■

HASTINGS
ROAD

BURQUITLAM

MAILLARDVILLE

Pitt

Chatham Reach

VANCOUVER

BURNABY

Burnaby L.

Essondale

SOUTH
BURNABY

EDMONDS

NEW
WESTMINSTER

Fraser

DOUGLAS I.

Pitt Meadows

SEA
ISLAND

MITCHELL I.

ELSONA

Port Mann

SURREY

Port
Hammond

VANCOUVER
INTERNATIONAL
AIRPORT

Bridgeport

QUEENSBOROUGH

SOUTH
WESTMINSTER

BARNSTON
I.

Fraser

49° 10'

LULU ISLAND

ANNACIS
I.

ANNIEVILLE

Kennedy

Port Kells

49° 10'

Brighouse

RICHMOND

S U R R E Y

Steveston

Sunbury

Strawberry
Hill

Newton

PELLY POINT

Fraser

D E L T A

Colebrook

Sullivan

Surrey
Centre

WESTHAM
ISLAND

Port
Guichon

Ladner

Cloverdale

Langley

Serpentine

Nicomekl

Mud Bay

Elgin

Crescent
Beach

Hazelmere

Boundary Bay

Beach Grove

Ocean Park

Campbell

ROBERTS BANK
SUPERPORT

Tsawassen

White Rock

CANADA

Semiahmoo Bay

BRITISH COLUMBIA

49° 00'

UNITED STATES

Blaine

WASHINGTON

49° 00'

Point Roberts

Drayton
Harbor

Strait of Georgia

123° 10'   123° 00'   West from Greenwich   122° 50'   122° 40'

Vancouver looking north east towards
Vancouver Harbour and Mount Seymour.

Residential	Industrial	Recreational	Transportation and utilities
Commercial	Institutional	Woodland	Agricultural and other

Freeway with interchange   Trans-Canada Highway   Railway with station   City Boundary

Projection: Transverse Mercator

COPYRIGHT. GEORGE PHILIP & SON. LTD

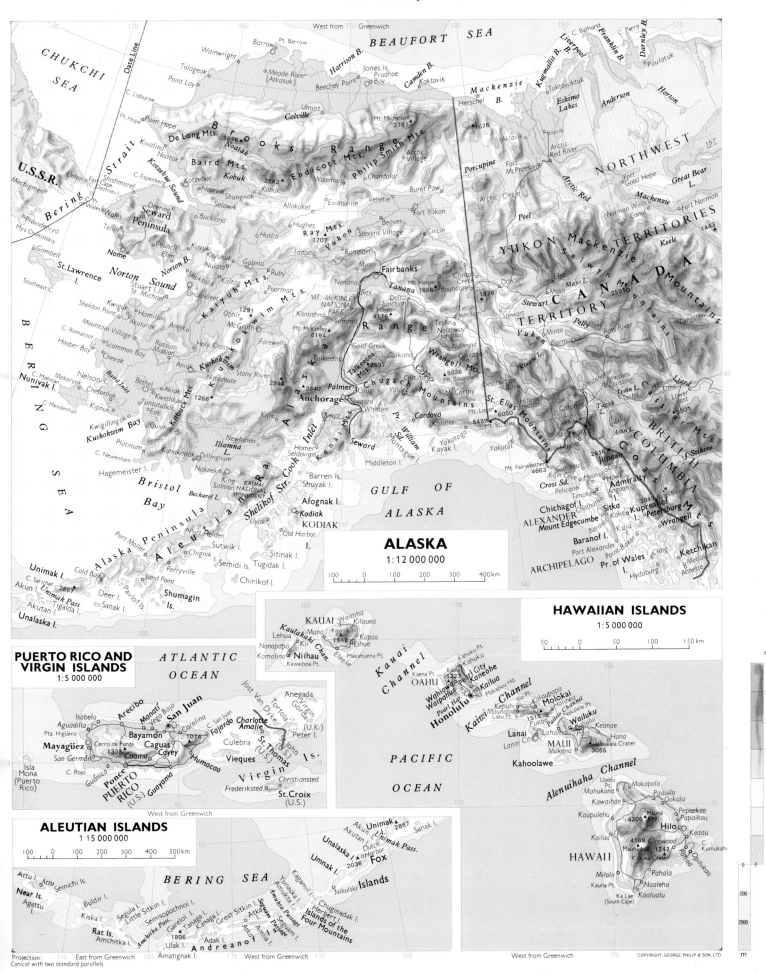

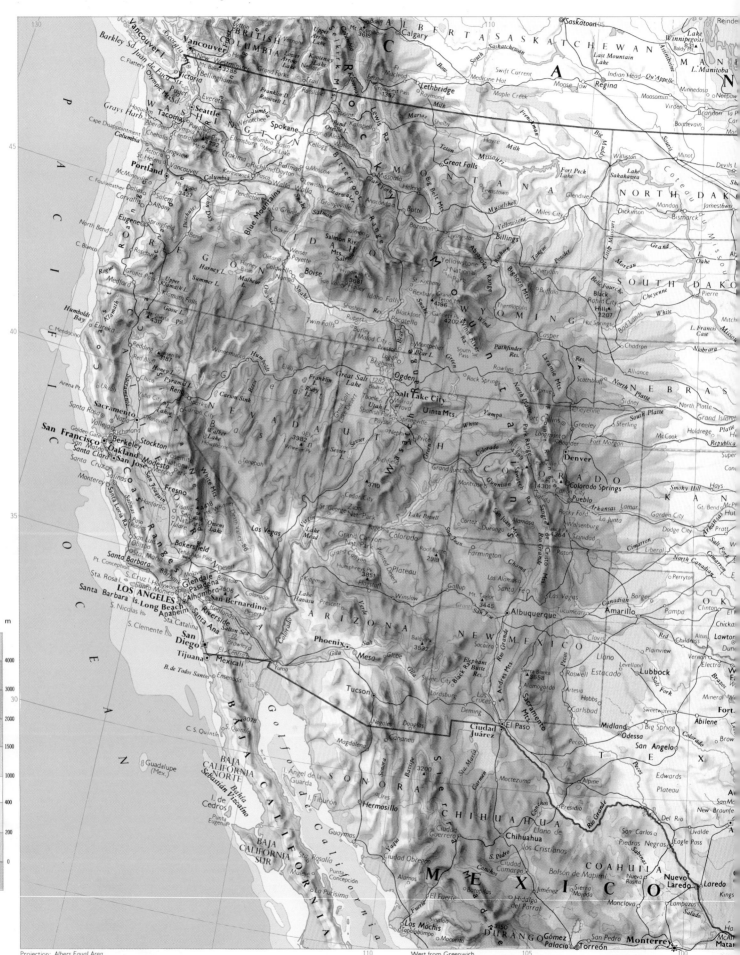

Projection: Albers Equal Area

West from Greenwich

1:12 000 000

100   0   100   200   300   400   500 km

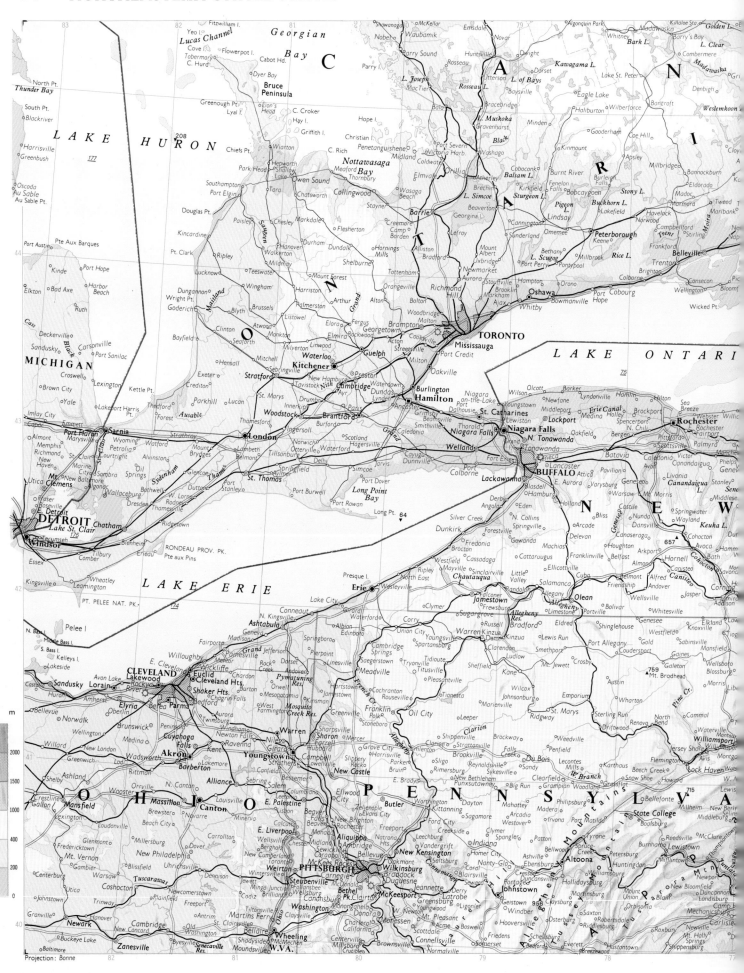

1 : 2 500 000

10 0 10 20 30 40 50 60 70 80 90 100 km

ATLANTIC OCEAN

Long Island

COPYRIGHT. GEORGE PHILIP & SON. LTD.

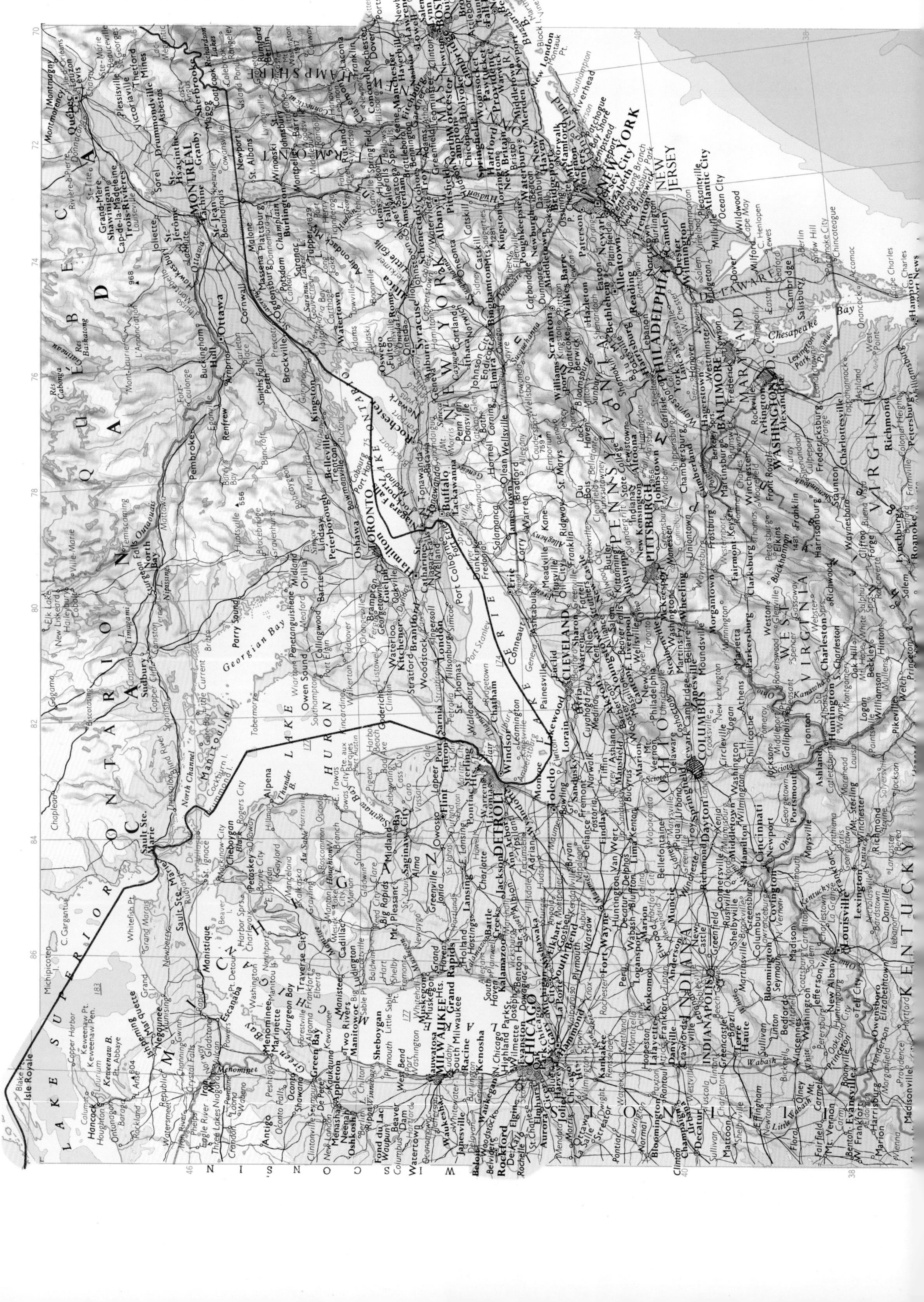
LAKE SUPERIOR
LAKE HURON
LAKE ONTARIO
LAKE ERIE
Georgian Bay
ONTARIO
QUEBEC
CANADA
MICHIGAN
WISCONSIN
ILLINOIS
INDIANA
OHIO
PENNSYLVANIA
NEW YORK
NEW JERSEY
MARYLAND
DELAWARE
WEST VIRGINIA
VIRGINIA
KENTUCKY
NEW HAMPSHIRE
VERMONT
MASS.
CHICAGO
MILWAUKEE
DETROIT
TORONTO
MONTREAL
Ottawa
CLEVELAND
PITTSBURGH
COLUMBUS
INDIANAPOLIS
PHILADELPHIA
BALTIMORE
WASHINGTON
NEW YORK
BOSTON
Quebec
Buffalo
Cincinnati
Louisville

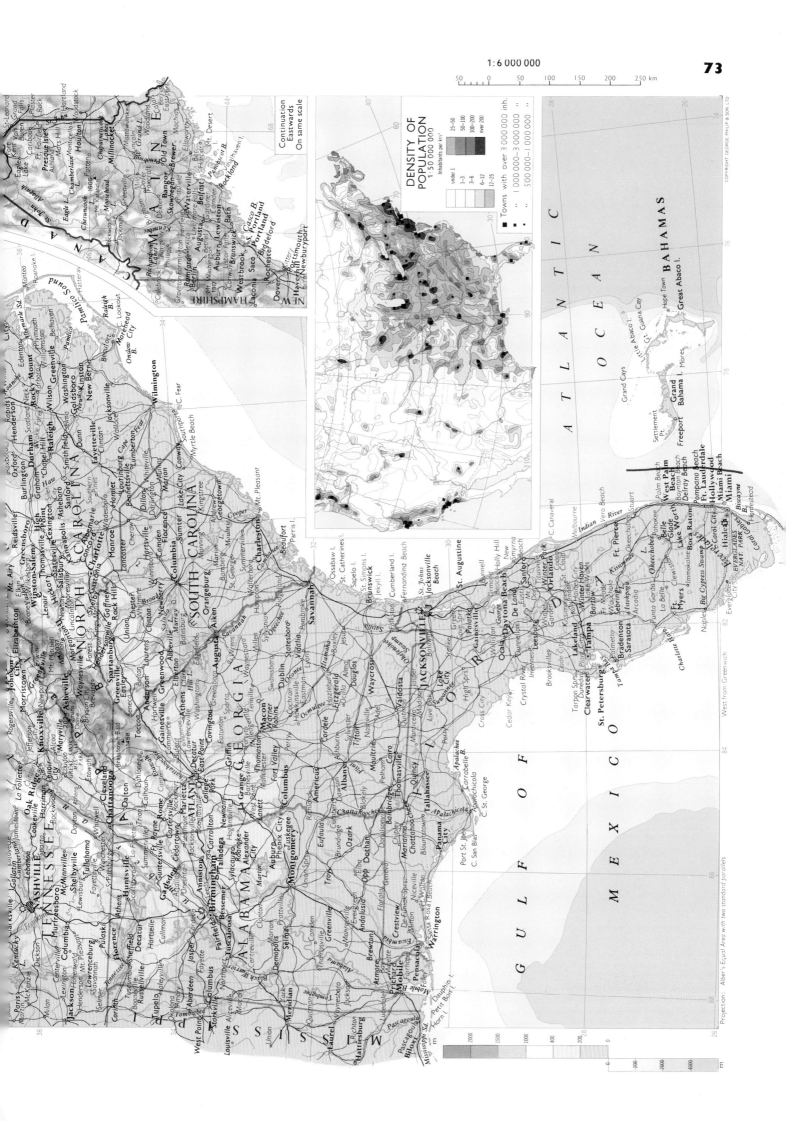

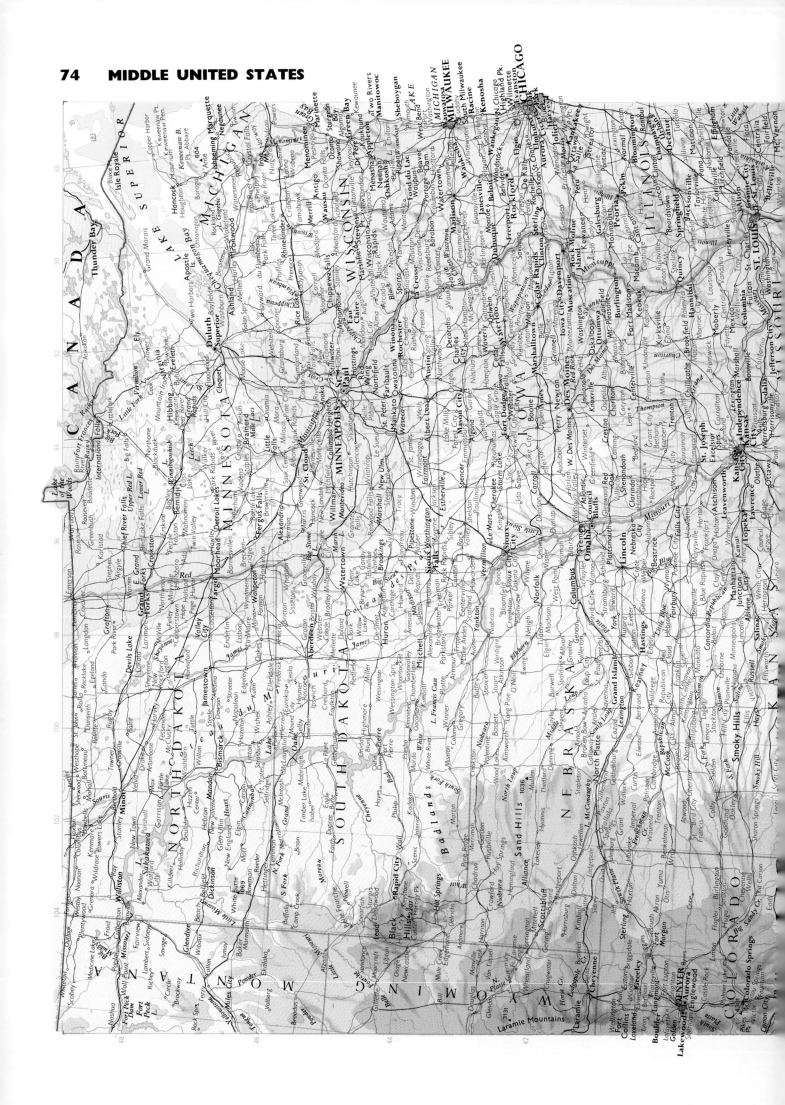

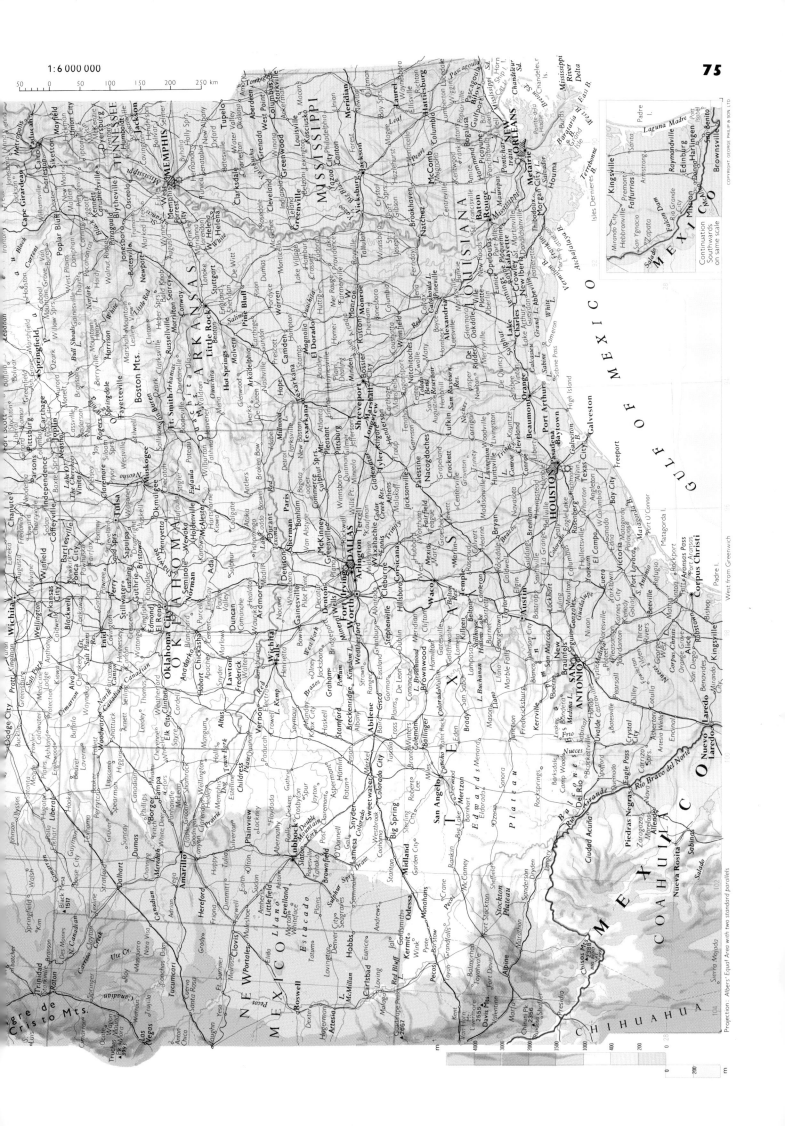

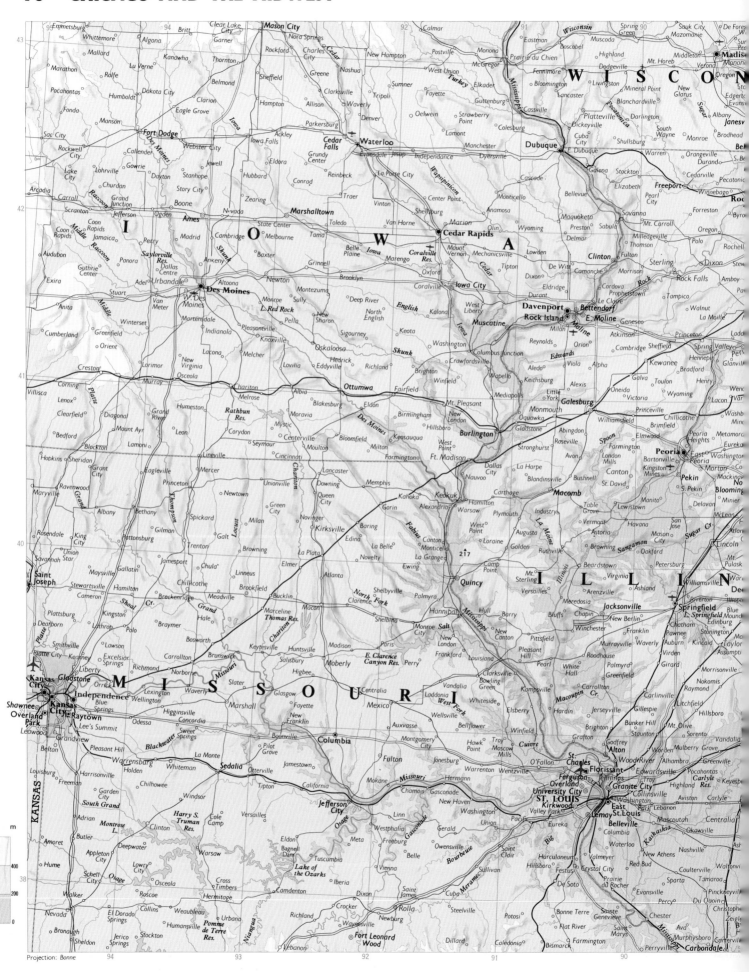

Projection: Bonne

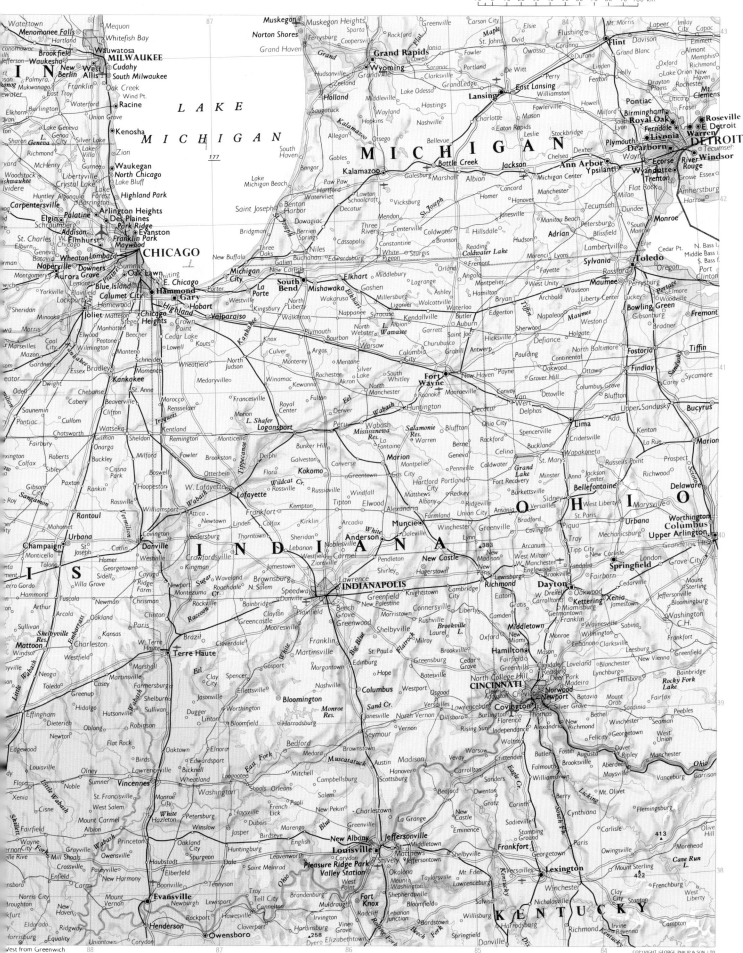

1 : 2 500 000

10 0 10 20 30 40 50 60 70 80 90 100 km

1:6 000 000

UNITED STATES
SOILS
after Marbut
1:50 000 000

PEDOCALS (LIME ACCUMULATING SOILS)
Northern chernozem soils
Southern chernozem soils
Northern dark brown soils
Southern dark brown soils
Brown soils
Northern grey desert soils
Southern grey desert soils
Soil of Pacific valleys (grey-brown, slightly podsolized)

PEDALFERS (NON-LIME ACCUMULATING SOILS)
Podsol soils
Grey-brown podsolic soils
Red and yellow soils
Soils of the northern Prairies
Soils of the southern Prairies
Mountainous areas
Sandhills of Nebraska

Projection: Alber's Equal Area with two standard parallels

COPYRIGHT GEORGE PHILIP & SON LTD

SEATTLE-PORTLAND
REGION
On same scale

PACIFIC OCEAN

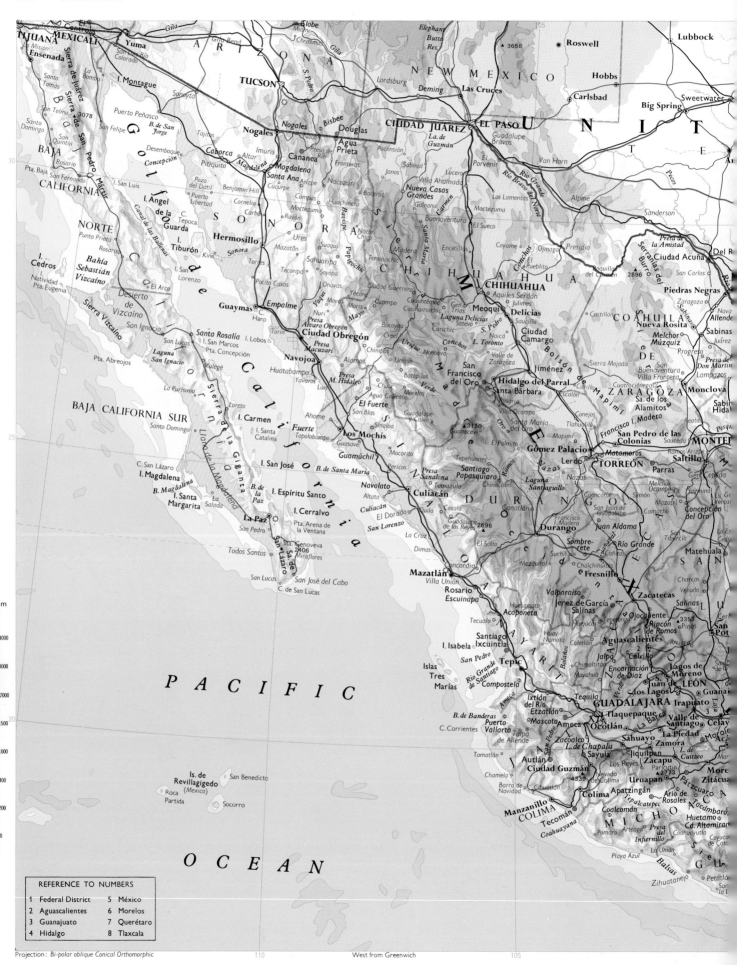

REFERENCE TO NUMBERS

1	Federal District	5	México
2	Aguascalientes	6	Morelos
3	Guanajuato	7	Querétaro
4	Hidalgo	8	Tlaxcala

Projection: Bi-polar oblique Conical Orthomorphic

West from Greenwich

1 : 8 000 000

50 0 50 100 150 200 250 300 km

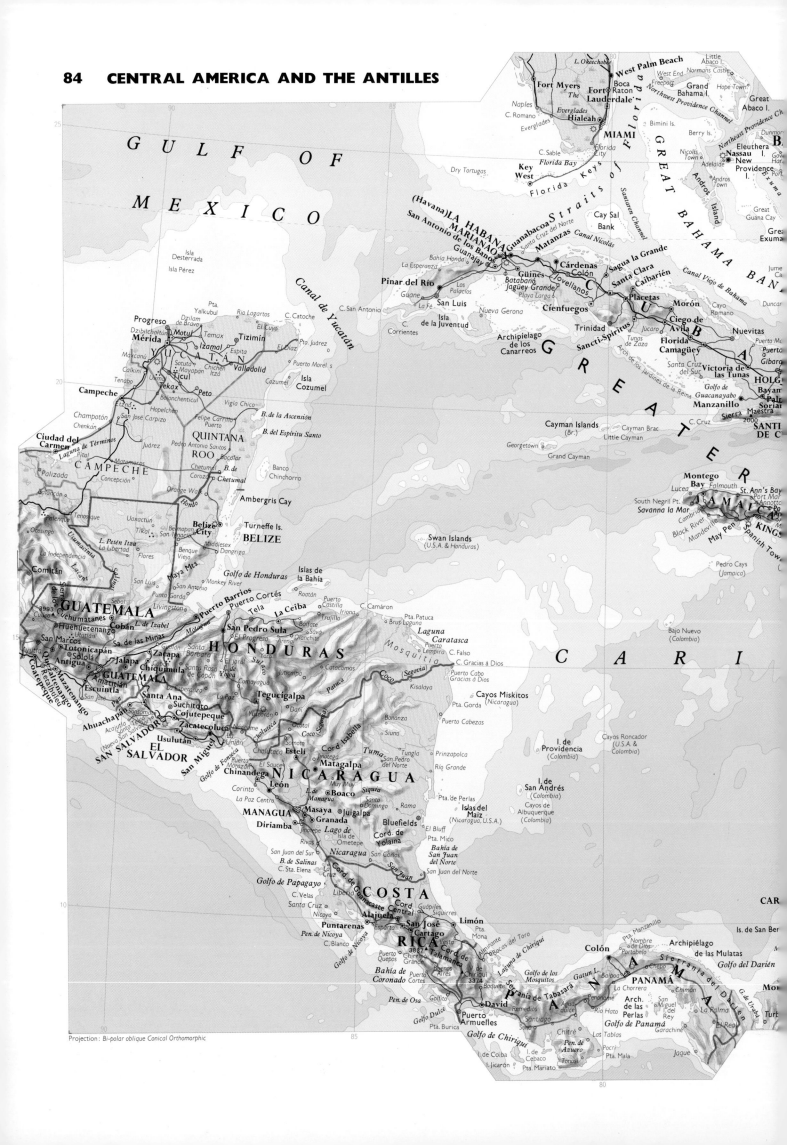

GULF OF

MEXICO

Projection: Bi-polar oblique Conical Orthomorphic

1 : 8 000 000

50   0   50   100   150   200   250   300 km

ATLANTIC

OCEAN

Tropic of Cancer

MAS

's Town

Cat I.

The Bight

San Salvador
(Watling I., Guanahani)

Conception I.

Rum Cay

Long I.

Clarence Town

Crooked I. Passage   Atwood or Samana Cay

Crooked I.

Albert Town   Snug Corner

Acklins I.

Mayaguana I.

Verde

Mira por vos Cay

Hogsty Reef

Little Inagua I.

Caicos Passage

Caicos Islands (Br.)

Turks I. Passage

Turks Islands (Br.)

Lake Rose

Great Inagua I.

Matthew Town

Moa

Baracoa

Pta. de Maisí

Paso de los Vientos (Windward Passage)

Î. de la Tortue

Port-de-Paix

Cap-Haïtien

Fort-Liberté

Monte Cristi

La Isabela

Puerto Plata

C. Frances Viejo

San Francisco de Macorís

Sánchez

Sabana de La Mar

Cap-à-Foux

Jean-Rabel

Santiago de Cabelleros

Vega

Nagua

SAN JUAN

Virgin Gorda

Anegada

Sombrero (Anguilla)

Golfe de la Gonâve

Gonaïves

Hinche

Cord. Central

3175

Bayamón

Arecibo

Aguadilla

Virgin Is. (Br.)

St. Thomas

Virgin Is. (U.S.A.)

Road Town

Anguilla (Br.)

St.-Martin (Guad.)

St.-Barthélemy (Fr.)

HAITI

DOMINICAN REP.

Hato Mayor

C. Engano

Fajardo

Angada Passage

St. Maarten (Neth.)

Saba (Neth.)

Barbuda

St.-Marc

PORT-AU-PRINCE

San Juan

San Pedro de Macorís

Higuey

La Romana

1338

Ponce

Caguas

Virgin Is. (U.S.A.)

St. Eustatius (Neth.)

Basseterre

ST. KITTS-NEVIS

Nevis

ANTIGUA & BARBUDA

St. Johns

Antigua

Jérémie

Î. de la Gonâve

B. de Yuma

I. Saona

Mayagüez

Guayama

Charlotte Amalie

St. Croix

Redonda

Massif de la Hotte

Dame Marie

2280

Enriquillo

San Cristóbal

Baní

Isla Mona (U.S.A.)

PUERTO RICO (U.S.A.)

Frederiksted

Christiansted

Montserrat

C. Carcasse

Les Cayes

Aquin

Jacmel

Barahona

Canal de la Mona

Guadeloupe Passage

Pointe-à-Gravois

Î.-à-Vache

Pedernales

San José de Ocoa

I. Beata   C. Beata

Ste-Rose

Moule

Désirade

HISPANIOLA

ANTILLES

Basse-Terre

GUADELOUPE (Fr.)

Pointe-à-Pitre

Marie-Galante (Fr.)

Grand-Bourg

I. des Saintes (Guad.)

I. de Aves (Bird I.) (Venezuela)

Portsmouth

Dominica Passage

Roseau

DOMINICA

Martinique Passage

BEAN   SEA

Mt. Pelée   Ste-Marie

1397

François

Fort-de-France

Rivière-Pilot

MARTINIQUE

St. Lucia Channel (Fr.)

Castries

Soufrière

ST. LUCIA

St. Vincent Passage

Soufrière 1234

ST. VINCENT

Speightstown

Kingstown

Bridgetown

BARBADOS

Hillsborough

LESSER ANTILLES

St. George's

GRENADA

Neth. Antilles

Aruba (Neth.)

Curaçao (Neth.)

Bonaire (Neth.)

I. Blanquilla (Ven.)

I. Los Hermanos (Ven.)

I. Los Testigos (Ven.)

Tobago

Pta. Gallinas

Willemstad

Is. de Aves (Ven.)

I. Orchila (Ven.)

Scarborough

Galera Pt.

C. San Román

Pen. de la Guajira

Pta. Espada

Pen. de Paraguaná

Punto Fijo

Is. Los Roques (Ven.)

I. Margarita

La Asunción

Pta. Peñas

Pen. de Paria

Port of Spain

Arima

Trinidad

Ríohacha

Uribia

Golfo de Venezuela

Puerto Cardón

Coro

La Vela de Coro

Tucacas

Maiquetía

La Guaira

CARACAS

DISTRITO FEDERAL

I. La Tortuga (Ven.)

NUEVA ESPARTA

Porlamar

Carúpano

Río Caribe

Golfo de Paria

Río Claro

TRINIDAD & TOBAGO

Santa Marta

C. San Juan de Guía

GUAJIRA

Punta Cardón

San Rafael

Altagracia

Mene de Mauroa

FALCON

Tocuyo

Puerto Cabello

Maracay

MIRANDA

Los Teques

C. Codera

Higuerote

Río Chico

Puerto La Cruz

Cumaná

SUCRE

Caripito

San Fernando

Serpent's Mouth

Pta. Mejillones

Pen. de Paria

Dragon's Mouth

Cienaga

Sa. Nevada de Santa Marta 5800

MARACAIBO

La Concepción

Santa Rita

Baragua

San Felipe

YARACUY

Villa de Cura

S. Juan de los Morros de Orituco

Altagracia

Aragua de Barcelona

Barcelona

Caicara

Caripe

Maturín

MONAGAS

DELTA AMACUR

Soledad

Sabanalarga

Fundación

Cabimas

Ciudad Ojeda

Mene Grande

LARA

BARQUISIMETO

Yaritagua de los Morros

Valencia

Valencia

Ocumare del Tuy

Anaco

Cantaura

El Tigre

Tucupita

Calamar

Agustín Codazzi

Valledupar

Villa del Rosario

MAGDALENA

Plato

Zambrano

CÉSAR

ZULIA

La Ceiba

Lago de Maracaibo

TRUJILLO

Acarigua

Valera

El Tocuyo

San Carlos

COJEDES

El Sombrero

Valle de la Pascua

GUARICO

Santa María de Ipire

ANZOÁTEGUI

Pariaguán

Soledad

El Pao

Sierra Imataca

Magangué

Mompós

El Banco

Machiques

San Carlos del Zulia

Trujillo

PORTUGUESA

Guanare

Portuguesa

El Baúl

Calabozo

Manapire

Ciudad Guayana

Upata

Corozal

Ayapel

El Barco

Ocaña

Agua Clara

Betijoque

MERIDA

Barinas

Ciudad Bolivia

Libertad

Fío de Nutrias

BARINAS

San Fernando de Apure

Apure

Orinoco

Mapire

Ciudad Bolivar

Emb. de Guri

Guasipati

El Callao

Tumeremo

BOLÍVAR

Simití

Ocaña

SANTANDER

TACHIRA

Santa Bárbara

Bruzual

Achaguas

Caicara

Caroní

Cúcuta

VENEZUELA

West from Greenwich

m

4000

3000

2000

1500

1000

400

200

0

200

2000

4000

6000

8000

m

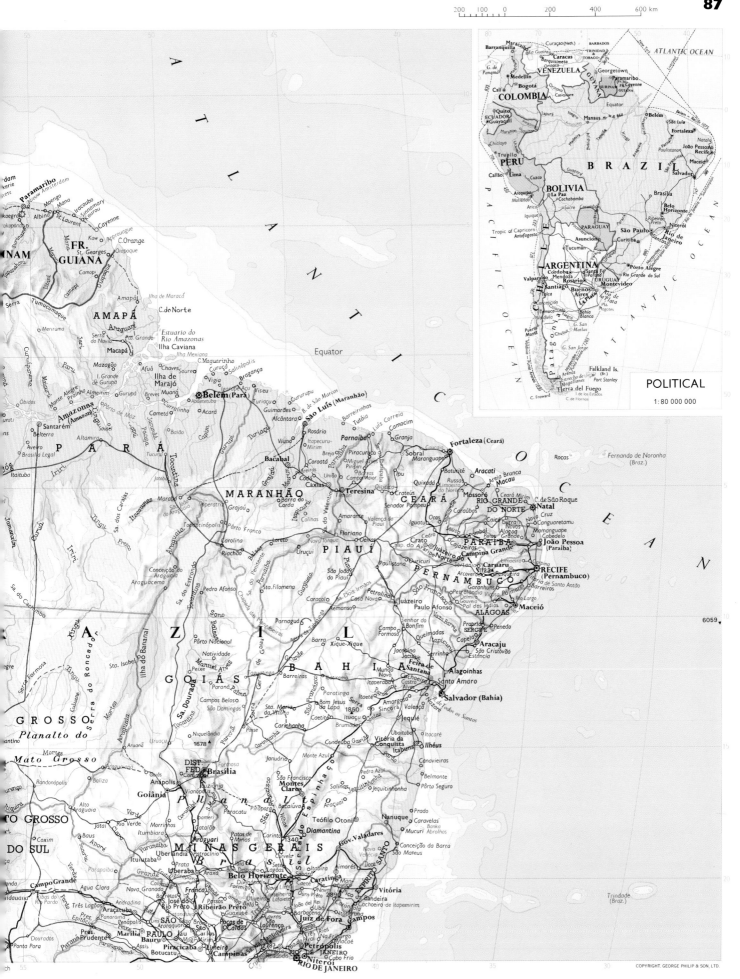

1:16 000 000

200 100 0   200   400   600 km

87

ATLANTIC OCEAN

POLITICAL

1:80 000 000

COPYRIGHT. GEORGE PHILIP & SON, LTD.

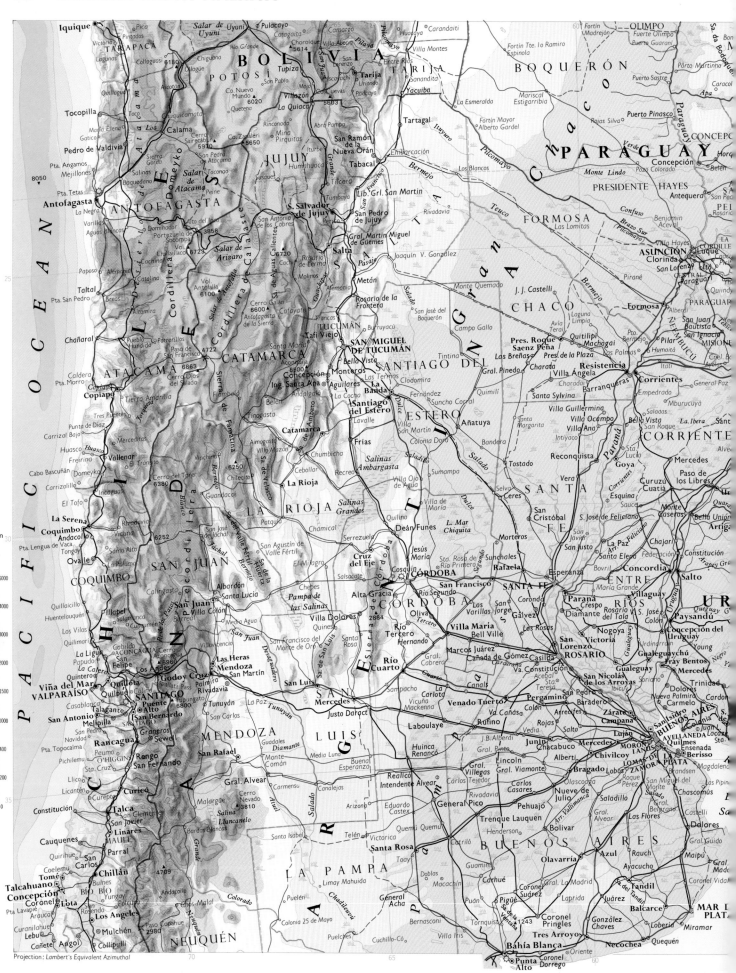

Projection: Lambert's Equivalent Azimuthal

1:8 000 000

50 0 50 100 150 200 250 300 km

BELO HORIZONTE

VITÓRIA

ATLANTIC

OCEAN

B R A Z I L

SÃO PAULO

PARANÁ

SANTA CATARINA

RIO GRANDE DO SUL

RIO DE JANEIRO

MISIONES

Tropic of Capricorn

5304

1:16 000 000

Projection: Sanson-Flamsteed's Sinusoidal

60 West from Greenwich 55

COPYRIGHT GEORGE PHILIP & SON LTD.

1 : 20 000 000

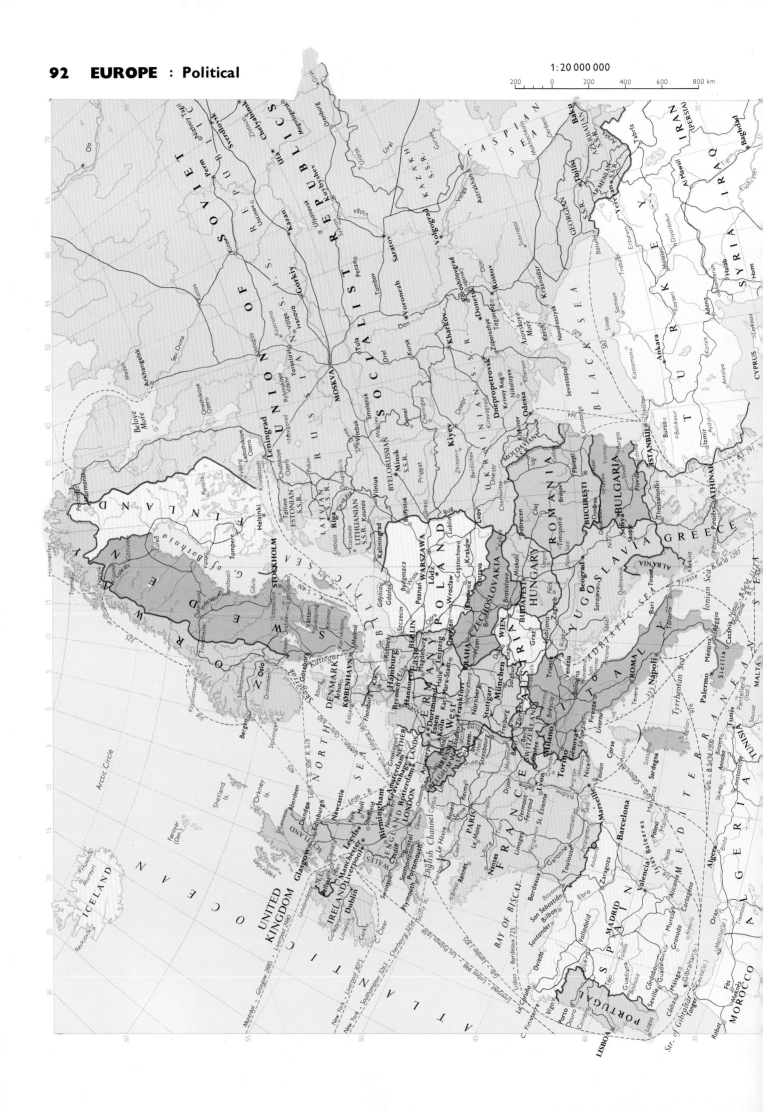

1:20 000 000

200   0   200   400   600   800 km

Ob

Ural Mountains

Narodnaya 1894

Pechora

Obshchi Syrt

Kama

Ural

Volga

CASPIAN SEA −28

Caucasus

Elbruz 5633

Armenia

Ararat 5165

Arax

Kurdistan

Tundra

Mezen

Kanin Peninsula

Kola Peninsula

White Sea

Onega

L. Onega

Ladoga

Volga Uplands

Don

Rybinsk Res.

Oka

Volga

Tsimlyansk Res.

Manych

Don

Sea of Azov

Crimea

Kerch

Terek

Rion

BLACK SEA

2211

Anatolia

Taurus

Erzurum 3770

Euphrates

Cyprus 1951

Lapland

Chenkovskoye

L. Inari

L. Torne 2123

Finland

Gulf of Finland

Neva

Chudskoye

W. Dvina

Pripyat (Pripet) Marshes

Dnepr (Dnieper)

Ukraine

Bug

Dnestr (Dniester)

Prut

Danube

Mambra

Carpathians 2655

Transylvanian Alps

Wallachia

Danube

Balkan Peninsula

Rhodope

Balkans

Aegean Sea

Crete

Scandinavia

Kjolen Mts.

Galdhopiggen 2469

BALTIC SEA

Gulf of Bothnia

Gotland

Malaren

Vanern

Vattern

Niemen

Wisła (Vistula)

North European Plain

Odra (Oder)

Sudetes

Morava

Tatra

Danube

Plain of Hungary

Tisza

Drava

Sava

Danube

Morava

Mures

Pindus

5121

C. Matapan

Morea

Ionian Is.

Dinaric Alps

ADRIATIC SEA

Str. of Otranto

Ionian Sea

Iceland

Hekla 1491

Cerro Jökull 2119

NORWEGIAN SEA

3734

Arctic Circle

Faroe Is.

Shetland Is.

Orkney Is.

Hebrides

Fisher Bank

Rockall

NORTH SEA

Dogger Bank

Jutland

Skagerrak

Kattegat

Helgoland

Elbe

Weser

Harz 1142

Erz Geb.

Bohemian For.

Moravian Hts.

Black For.

Danube

Donau

Taunus

Vosges

Jura

Alps

Mt. Blanc 4807

Great Britain

Ben Nevis 1344

Snowdon 1085

British Isles

Ireland

Irish Sea

Thames

English Channel

Land's End

Valentia

C. Clear

Brittany

Seine

Loire

Bay of Biscay

Gironde

Garonne

Rhone

Central Massif 1886

Cevennes

Pyrenees 3404

G. of Lions

Ligurian Sea

Corsica

Sardinia

Str. of Bonifacio

Apennines 2914

Tiber

Tyrrhenian Sea

Vesuvius 1277

Sicily 3263

Etna

Str. of Messina

Calabria

C. Bon

Malta

MEDITERRANEAN SEA

Iberian Peninsula

Cantabrian Mts.

Old Castile

New Castile

Douro

Pico de Aneto 3404

Sa. de Guadarrama

Sa. da Estrela

Tejo (Tagus)

Guadiana

Sierra Morena

Andalusia

Sa. Nevada 3478

Guadalquivir

C. Finisterre

C. Roca

C. St. Vincent

C. Trafalgar

Str. of Gibraltar

C. Spartel

Maritime Atlas

Plateau of the Shotts

ATLANTIC OCEAN

West from Greenwich   East from Greenwich

Projection Bonne

m   4000   2000   1000   400   200   0

0   200   2000   4000   m

1:2 000 000

10   0   10   20   30   40   50   60   70   80 km

FRANCE

ENGLISH CHANNEL

SCILLY ISLES
On same Scale

Isles of Scilly

Projection: Conical with two standard parallels.

1 : 2 000 000

10 0 10 20 30 40 50 60 70 80 km

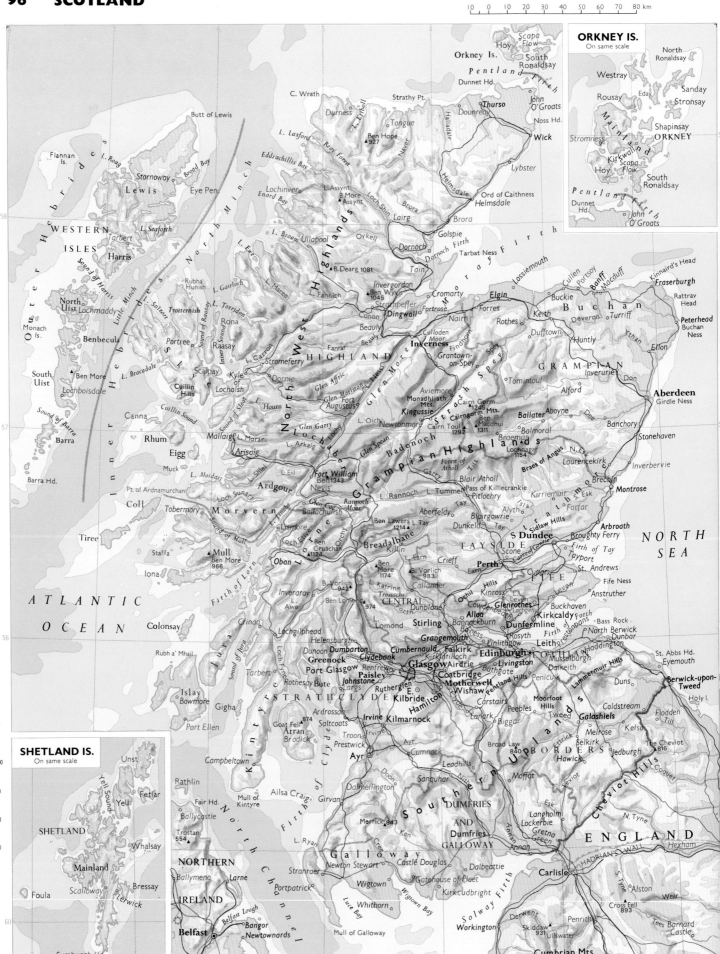

ORKNEY IS.
On same scale

SHETLAND IS.
On same scale

Projection : Conical with two standard parallels.

West from Greenwich

COPYRIGHT. GEORGE PHILIP & SON, LTD.

1:2 000 000

10 0 10 20 30 40 50 60 70 80 km

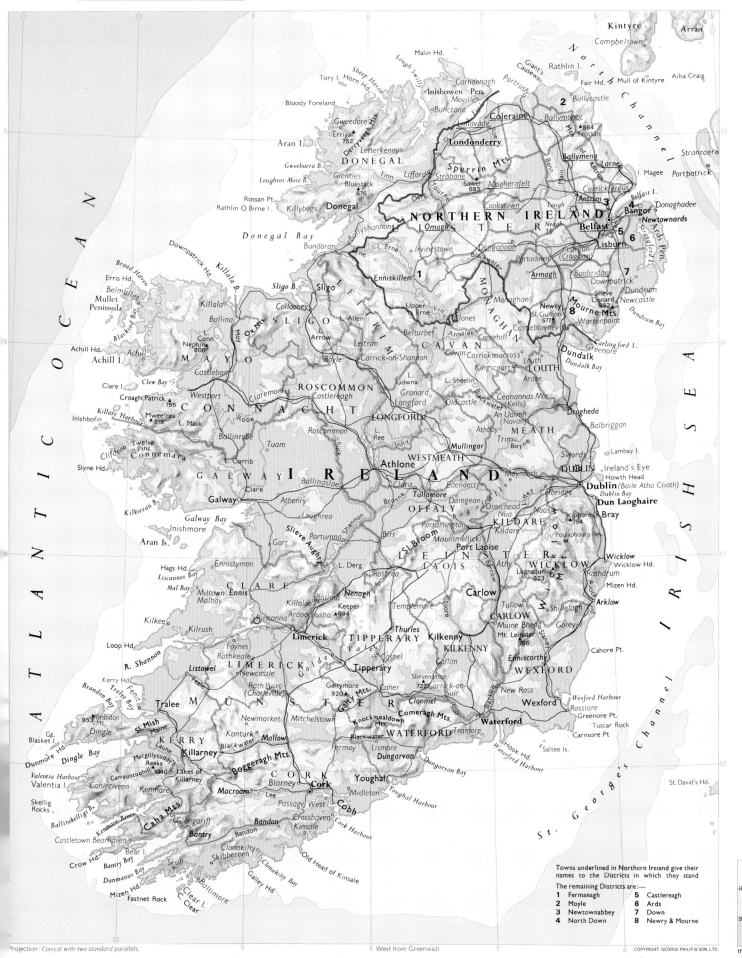

Towns underlined in Northern Ireland give their
names to the Districts in which they stand

The remaining Districts are:—

1	Fermanagh	5	Castlereagh
2	Moyle	6	Ards
3	Newtownabbey	7	Down
4	North Down	8	Newry & Mourne

Projection: Conical with two standard parallels.

8 West from Greenwich

COPYRIGHT. GEORGE PHILIP & SON, LTD.

1 : 4 000 000

Projection: Conical with two standard parallels

West from Greenwich   East from Greenwich

COPYRIGHT. GEORGE PHILIP & SON. LTD.

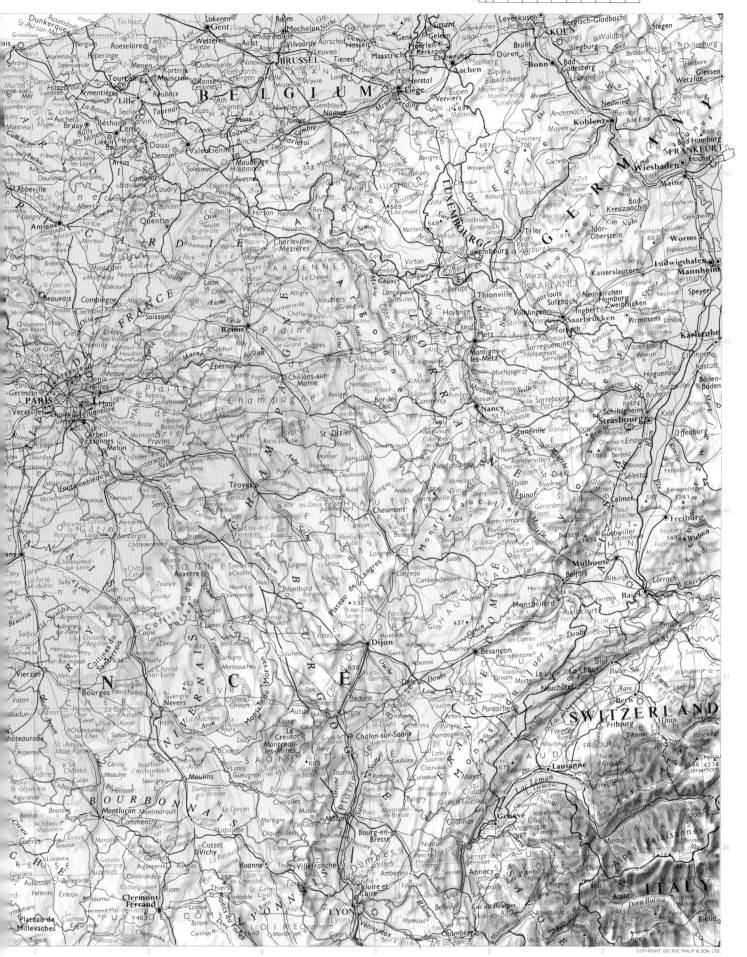

1 : 2 500 000

10 0 10 20 30 40 50 60 70 80 90 100 km

BELGIUM

GERMANY

LUXEMBOURG

FRANCE

PARIS

SWITZERLAND

ITALY

COPYRIGHT GEORGE PHILIP & SON LTD.

1:2 500 000

10 0 0 10 20 30 40 50 60 70 80 90 100 km

SWITZERLAND

ITALY

MILANO
(Milan)

TORINO
(Turin)

GENOVA
(Genoa)

Golfo di Génova

LIGURIAN SEA

LYON

Grenoble

MARSEILLE

Toulon

Nice
MONACO
Monte-Carlo

Côte d'Azur

ILES D'HYÈRES

MEDITERRANEAN SEA

CORSICA

HAUTE-CORSE

CORSE DU SUD

Ajaccio

Bastia

Elba

Lion

COPYRIGHT. GEORGE PHILIP & SON. LTD.

1:5 000 000

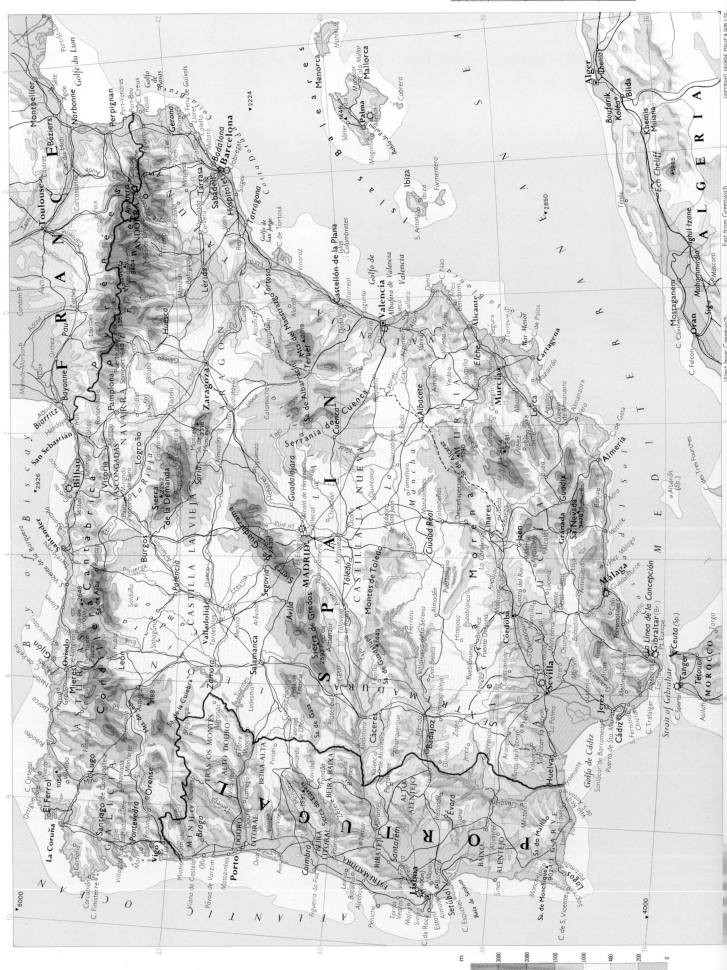

1:2 000 000

10 0 10 20 30 40 50 60 70 80 km

NORTH SEA

WESTFRIESCHE EILANDEN

Terschelling Ameland Schiermonnikoog

Vlieland Waddenzee

Texel Den Oever Leeuwarden Groningen Emden Oldenburg

Den Helder FRIESLAND Assen DRENTHE Meppen

Alkmaar IJsselmeer Zwolle Nordhorn Münster

Haarlem AMSTERDAM Deventer OVERIJSSEL Enschede Osnabrück

Leiden UTRECHT Amersfoort Arnhem GELDERLAND

s'GRAVENHAGE (The Hague) Utrecht Zeist

Delft ROTTERDAM Nijmegen Kleve NORDRHEIN

Hoek van Holland Dordrecht 's-Hertogenbosch Wesel DORTMUND

Goeree Breda Tilburg Eindhoven Venlo ESSEN Düsseldorf

Walcheren Middelburg Bergen-op-Zoom Roosendaal Roermond Mönchen-Gladbach KÖLN

Oostende (Ostend) Brugge (Bruges) ANTWERPEN Antwerpen Mechelen Maastricht Aachen Bonn

Ghent (Gand) BRUSSEL/Bruxelles BRABANT Liège Verviers

BELGIUM HAINAUT Namur Koblenz

Lille Roubaix Tournai Mons Charleroi Dinant LUXEMBOURG RHEINLAND PFALZ

Arras Cambrai ARDENNES Bastogne Trier Wiesbaden / Mainz

FRANCE PICARDIE Charleville-Mézières Sedan LUXEMBOURG Saarbrücken

Reims MARNE Verdun MOSELLE Metz

Projection: Conical with two standard parallels

East from Greenwich

COPYRIGHT GEORGE PHILIP & SON. LTD.

Projection: Conical with two standard parallels   East from Greenwich

1 : 5 000 000

50   0   50   100   150   200 km

CENTRAL
EUROPE
POLITICAL
1 : 25 000 000

DENMARK

København

's-Gravenhage
The
Hague   NETH.

BELGIUM   Berlin
Brussel   WEST   EAST   POLAND   Warszawa   U.S.S.R.
LUX.   GERMANY
Bonn
FRANCE   Praha
CZECHOSLOVAKIA
Bern   Wien
SWITZ.   LIECHT.   AUSTRIA   Budapest   HUNGARY
MONACO   ITALY   Beograd   București   ROMANIA
SAN MARINO
Roma   YUGOSLAVIA
BULGARIA
Sofiya

POLAND

EA   Zatoka
Gdańska   Zelenogradsk   Kaliningrad (Königsberg)   Chernyakhovsk   Vilnius
ejherowo   Gdynia   Pregolya   LITHUANIAN
Sopot   R.   S. F. S. R.   Gusev   S. S. R.
Gdańsk   Braniewo   Lyna   Varena
(Danzig)   Elbląg   ▲309   Suwałki   Alitus
Starogard   Malbork   Kętrzyn   Gizycko   Augustów
zcz   Chełmno   Kwidzyń   Ostróda   Olsztyn   Grodno
Grudziądz   Jezierze   Mazurski   Neman   Novogrudok
Iława   Mława   Sokółka   ▲238   BYELORUSSIAN
Toruń   Lipno   Ciechanów   Ostrów   Brańsk   Bereza
Włocławek   Płock   Pułtusk   Mazowiecka   Hajnówka   S. S. R.
Konin   Kutno   Łowicz   Warszawa   Mińsk   Shchara   Slonim
LAND   Łęczyca   Pruszków   (Warsaw)   Mazowiecki   Zhabinka   Pripyat
Kalisz   Zduńska   Skierniewice   Siedlce   Biała   Brest
Wola   Łódź   Grójec   Łuków   Podlaska
Ostrów   Pilica   Kozienice   Międzyrzec   Kovel   Sarny
Wielkopolski   Tomaszów   Włodawa   Podlaska
Piotrków   Mazowiecki   Puławy   Bug
Trybunalski   Radom   Lublin   Chełm   Vladimir   Lutsk   Korosten
Wieluń   Końskie   Krasnik   Volynskiy   Rovno
Radomsko   Ostrowiec   Zamość   Sokal   Dubno   Ostrog   Kiyev
Opole   Częstochowa   Kielce   Świętokrzyski   Sandomierz   Zhitomir
Tarnowskie   Jedrzejów   Pinczów   Tarnobrzeg   ▲390   Kamenka   Radekhov   Shepetovka   Berdichev   Fastov   Belaya Tserkov
Góry   Zawiercie   Przeworsk   Bugskaya   Brody   Kremenets   Kazatin
Zabrze   Bytom   Dabrowa   Tarnowska   Jarosław   Zolochev   Starokonstantinov
Gliwice   Sosnowiec   Wisła (Vistula)   Rzeszów   Lvov   UKRAINIAN
Chorzów   Katowice   Tarnów   Przemyśl   Gorodok   ▲471   Ternopol   Khmelnitskiy   S. S. R.   Vinnitsa
Kraków   Wieliczka   Sambor   Dnestr   U.   S.   S.   R.   ▲384
Bielsko-   Nowy   Jasło   Drogobych   Stryi   Buchach   Zhmerinka
Biała   Sącz   Krosno   Sanok   Borislav   Chortkov   Uman
Frydek   Czeski Těšin   1725   Dukelský Pr.   502   Turka   Ivano-Frankovsk   Zaleshchiki   Kamenets-Podolskiy
Místek   Jablunkovsky Pr.   Vychodné Beskydy   Nadvornaya   Kolomyya   Snyatyn   Khotin
550   Západné Beskydy   Prešov   ▲1881   Yablonitse   Mogilev-Podolskiy   Pervomaisk
VAKIA   Žilina   Tatry   2655   Ružomberok   Uzhgorod   931   Chernovtsy   Yedintsy
Nízke Tatry   Košice   Mukachevo   ▲2061   Storozhinets   MOLDAVIA   Kotovsk
Kremnica   Banska Bystrica   Beregovo   Khust   Dorohoi   Soroki
Nitra   Zvolen   Slovenské Rudohorie   Sátoraljaújhely   Botoșani   Beltsy
Banská Štiavnica   Lučenec   Hernad   Sighet   Radauti   Beltsy
N. Zámky   Hron   Miskolc   Tokaj   Satu Mare   Pietrosul   Suceava   Iași   ▲429   Kishinev   Tiraspol
Komárno   Vác   Gyöngyös   Nyíregyháza   Carei   ▲2305   Vatra-Dornei   Bendery
Eger   Mezőkövesd   Hajdúböszörmény   Baia Mare   Benderý   Odessa
Esztergom   Hatvan   Someș   2102   Bistrita   Roman
Tatabánya   Újpest   Jászberény   Debrecen   Dej   Pietrosul   Piatra   Bacău   Belgorod
Hegyseg   BUDAPEST   Karcag   Oradea   Cluj   Târgu   Neamt   Dnestrovskiy
Székesfehérvár   Cegléd   Szolnok   Mezőtúr   Turda   Mures   Praid   Odorhei   Bârlad   Kagul
UNGARY   Kecskemét   Salonta   Negru   Miercurea   Vaslui
Dunaújváros   Kiskunfélegyháza   Körös   Mții Bihor   ▲1848   Aiud   Ciuc
Dunaföldvár   Kalocsa   Békéscsaba   Gyula   Crișul   Abrud   Transilvania   Sfântu Gheorghe   Tecuci
vár   Szekszárd   Kiskunhalas   Szentes   Hódmezővásárhely   Alba-Iulia   Medias   Sighișoara   Bretcu   Focșani   Galati
Bataszek   Baja   Szeged   Mikó   Arad   Brad   Deva   Simeria   Sibiu   Brașov   Rîmnicu Sarat   Reni   Ismail
Pécs   Subotica   ROMANIA   Mureș   Hunedoara   Meridionali   Vf. Omul   Cîmpina   Galati   Bolgrad   Kiliya
Mohács   Kikinda   Lugoj   Carpații   ▲2535   Vf. Negoiu   ▲2507   Brăila   ▲467   Tulcea   Ozero
Timișoara   Caransebeș   Turnu Roșu   Petroșani   350   Sulina   Sasyk
Novi Sad   Bečej   Banat   Peleaga   2518   Paringul Mare   Cîmpulung   Buzău   Dunărea   Sulina
Petrovaradin   Zrenjanin   Reșita   2509   Poarta Orientalis   Tîrgu-Jiu   Rîmnicu Vîlcea   Tîrgoviste   Ploiești   Cernavoda
Sremska   (Petrovgrad)   Vršac   Mehadia   Pitești   Constanța
Mitrovica   Porțile de Fier   Jiu   Arges   București   BLACK
Osijek   Bela Crkva   Orșova   Turnu-   Dîmbovița   (Bucharest)
Brod   Pančevo   Severin   Oltenita   Mamaia
Zemun   Smederevo   Craiova   Silistra   SEA
GOSLAVIA   (Belgrade)   Požarevac   Slatina   Olt   Mangalia
Beograd   Vidin   Vedea
Sava   Morava   Negotin   Timok   Turnu   Giurgiu   Ruse (Ruschuk)   Tolbukhin
Sarajevo   1340   Valjevo   Čačak   Zaječar   Măgurele   Corabia   Zimnicea   BULGARIA
INA   Titovo Užice   Kragujevac   Lom Dunărea (Danube)

COPYRIGHT. GEORGE PHILIP & SON LTD.

MALTA
1:1 000 000

S.E. EUROPE
POLITICAL
1:25 000 000

Projection: Conical with two standard parallels

ICELAND
on the same scale
as general map

1:5 000 000

50 0 50 100 150 200 km

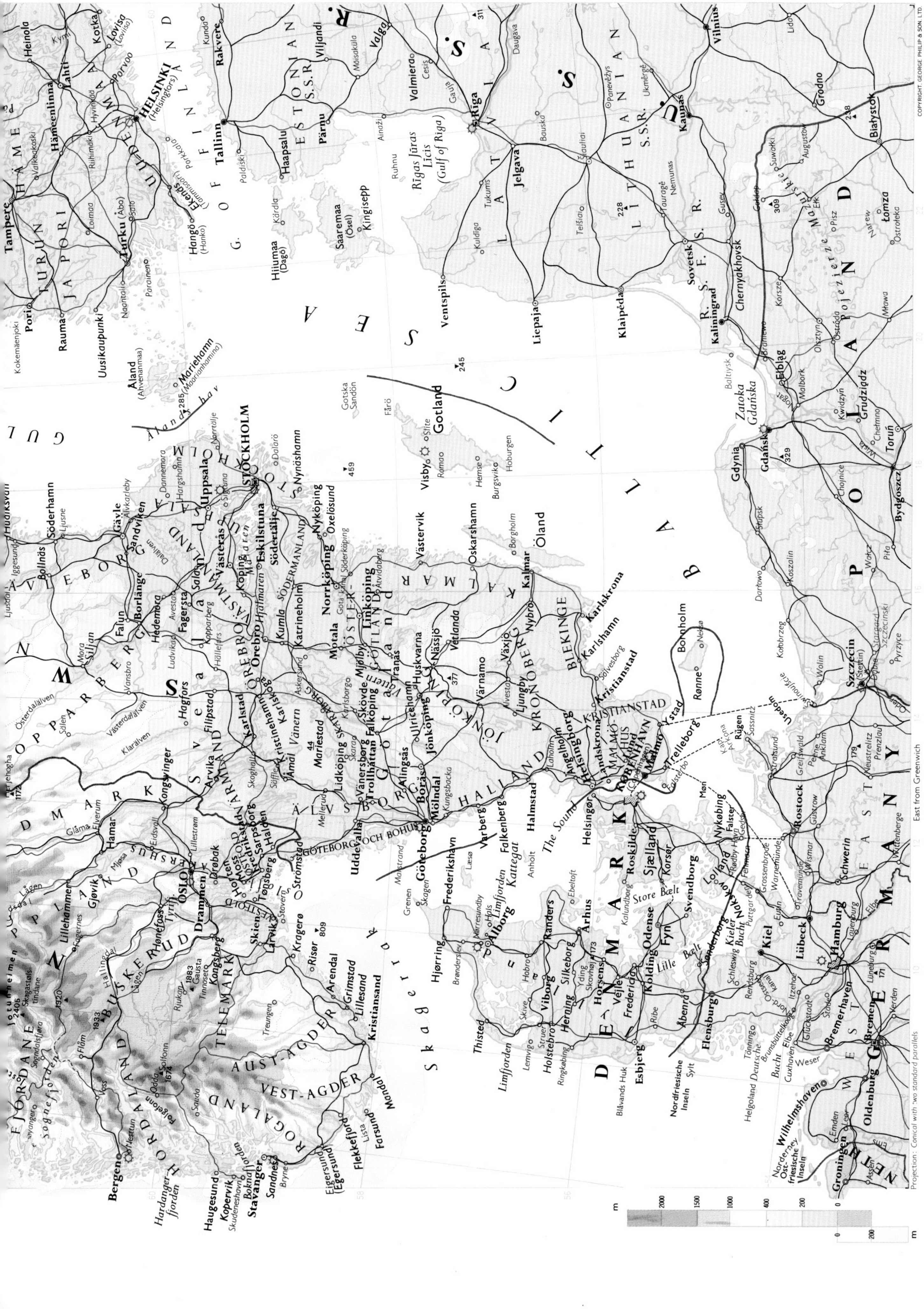

Heinola · Lahti · Kotka (Lovisa) · Lovisa
Tampere · Hämeenlinna · HELSINKI (Helsingfors) · Porvoo · Kotka
TURUN JA PORI · Turku (Åbo) · Tallinn
Pori · Raumo · Hangö (Hanko)
Uusikaupunki · Åland (Ahvenanmaa) · Mariehamn (Maarianhamina)

ESTONIAN S.S.R. · Rakvere · Viljandi · Valga · R.
Haapsalu · Pärnu · Valmiera · Cēsis · RIGA · S.
Hiiumaa (Dagö) · Saaremaa (Ösel) · Kingisepp · Rīgas Jūras Līcis (Gulf of Riga)
LATVIAN S.S.R. · Bauska · Šiauliai · Panevėžys · Vilnius
Ventspils · Kuldīga · Jelgava · LITHUANIAN S.S.R. · Kaunas
Liepāja · Klaipėda · Sovetsk · S.S.R. · Chernyakhovsk
R.S.F.S.R. · Kaliningrad · Grodno · Białystok

BALTIC SEA
Gotska Sandön · Gotland · Fårö · Visby · Gdynia · Gdańsk · Grudziądz
STOCKHOLM · Uppsala · Nynäshamn · Öland · Szczecin (Stettin) · Bydgoszcz · Toruń
Gävle · Söderhamn · Västerås · Eskilstuna · Norrköping · Oskarshamn · Kalmar · POLAND
Borlänge · Falun · Örebro · Linköping · Västervik · Karlskrona · Bornholm · Rønne
Mora · KOPPARBERG · ÖREBRO · Motala · Jönköping · BLEKINGE · Kristianstad · Rostock
NORWAY · VÄRMLAND · Karlstad · Vänern · Skövde · Växjö · Halmstad · Rügen · GERMANY
Kongsvinger · Arvika · Vättern · Nässjö · KRONOBERG · Helsingborg · København · Kiel
OSLO · Drammen · GÖTEBORG · Borås · HALLAND · MALMÖ · Trelleborg · Lübeck · Hamburg
BUSKERUD · TELEMARK · Uddevalla · Varberg · Falkenberg · The Sound · Rostock · Schwerin
AUST-AGDER · VEST-AGDER · Kristiansand · Kattegat · Frederikshavn · Ålborg · Odense · Kiel
Bergen · Stavanger · Haugesund · Skagerrak · Århus · Randers · DENMARK · Flensburg · Bremen
HORDALAND · ROGALAND · Esbjerg · Horsens · Kolding · NETHERLANDS · Groningen · Wilhelmshaven

Projection: Conical with two standard parallels · East from Greenwich

COPYRIGHT GEORGE PHILIP & SON LTD.

m 2000 1500 1000 400 200 0
0 200 m

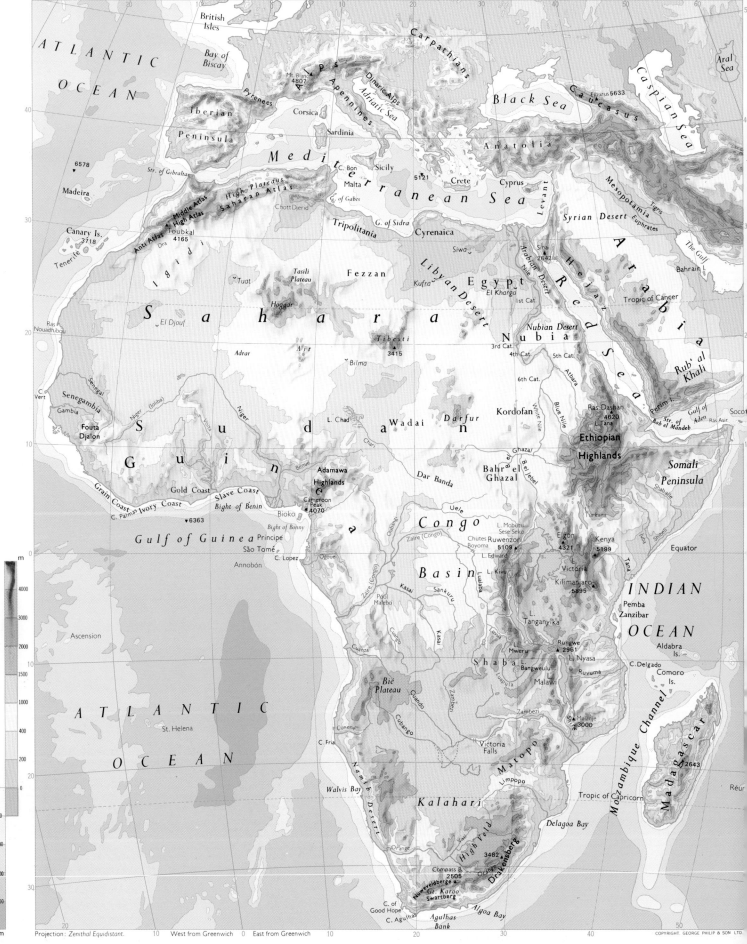

1 : 40 000 000

400   0   400   800   1200   1600 km

ATLANTIC OCEAN

British Isles

Bay of Biscay

Carpathians

Aral Sea

Caspian Sea

Black Sea

Caucasus Elburus 5633

▲Mt. Blanc 4807 Alps

Dinaric Alps

Adriatic Sea

Pyrenees

Apennines

Iberian Peninsula

Corsica

Sardinia

Anatolia

Mesopotamia

6578▼

Madeira

Str. of Gibraltar

C. Bon

Sicily

Malta

Mediterranean Sea

5121

Crete

Cyprus

Levant

Tigris

Euphrates

The Gulf

Syrian Desert

Arabia

Bahrain I.

Canary Is. 3718

Tenerife

Middle Atlas High Plateaus

High Atlas Saharan Atlas

Anti Atlas Toubkal 4165

Dra

Chott Djerid

G. of Gabes

Tripolitania

G. of Sidra

Cyrenaica

Siwa

Libyan Desert

Egypt

Arabian Desert

El Kharga

1st Cat.

Sinai 2642

Hejaz

Red Sea

Tropic of Cancer

Ras Nouadhibou

Igidi

Sahara

El Djouf

Tuat

Tasili Plateau

Hoggar

Fezzan

Adrar

Air

Tibesti 3415

Bilma

Kufra

Nile

Nubian Desert

Nubia

3rd Cat.

4th Cat.

5th Cat.

Atbara

Ras Dashan 4620 L. Tana

Perim I.

Str. of Bab el Mandeb Gulf of Aden Ras Asir

Socotra

Rub' al Khali

6th Cat.

Senegal

C. Vert

Senegambia

Gambia

Fouta Djalon

Niger (Joliba)

Volta

Niger

Sudan

Guinea

L. Chad

Chari

Wadai

Darfur

Kordofan

White Nile

Blue Nile

Bel el Ghazal

Ethiopian Highlands

Somali Peninsula

Shabelle

Grain Coast Ivory Coast

Gold Coast Slave Coast

C. Palmas

Bight of Benin

6363▼

Bioko

Adamawa Highlands

Cameroon Peak 4070

Benue

Dar Banda

Bahr el Ghazal

Oubangui

Uele

Turkana

Gulf of Guinea Principe

São Tomé

C. Lopez

Annobón

Ascension

Ogoué

Zaïre (Congo)

Congo

Basin

L. Mobutu Sese Seko

Chutes Boyoma Ruwenzori 5109

L. Edward

L. Kivu

Elgon 4321

Kenya 5199

Equator

Victoria

Kilimanjaro 5895

INDIAN OCEAN

Pemba

Zanzibar

Kasai

Sankuru

Lualaba

Pool Malebo

Kasai

L. Tanganyika

Lavua

Rungwe 2961

Mweru

Aldabra Is.

Cuango

Cuanza

Zaïre (Congo)

Shaba

Bangweulu

L. Nyasa

Malawi

Ruvuma

C. Delgado

Comoro Is.

ATLANTIC OCEAN

St. Helena

Biè Plateau

Cuando

Cubango

Cunene

Zambezi

Luapula

Victoria Falls

Malanje 3000

Shire

Madagascar

Mozambique Channel

2643▲

Réur

Walvis Bay

Namib Desert

Kalahari

Orange

C. Fria

Limpopo

Matopo

Victoria Falls

Tropic of Capricorn

Delagoa Bay

High Veld

3482▲

Drakensberg

Compass B. 2505

Orange

Algoa Bay

Niewveldberge Gr. Karoo Swartberg

C. of Good Hope

C. Agulhas

Agulhas Bank

m
4000
3000
2000
1500
1000
400
200
0
200
2000
4000
6000
m

Projection: Zenithal Equidistant.   10   West from Greenwich   0   East from Greenwich   10   20   30   40   50

COPYRIGHT. GEORGE PHILIP & SON LTD.

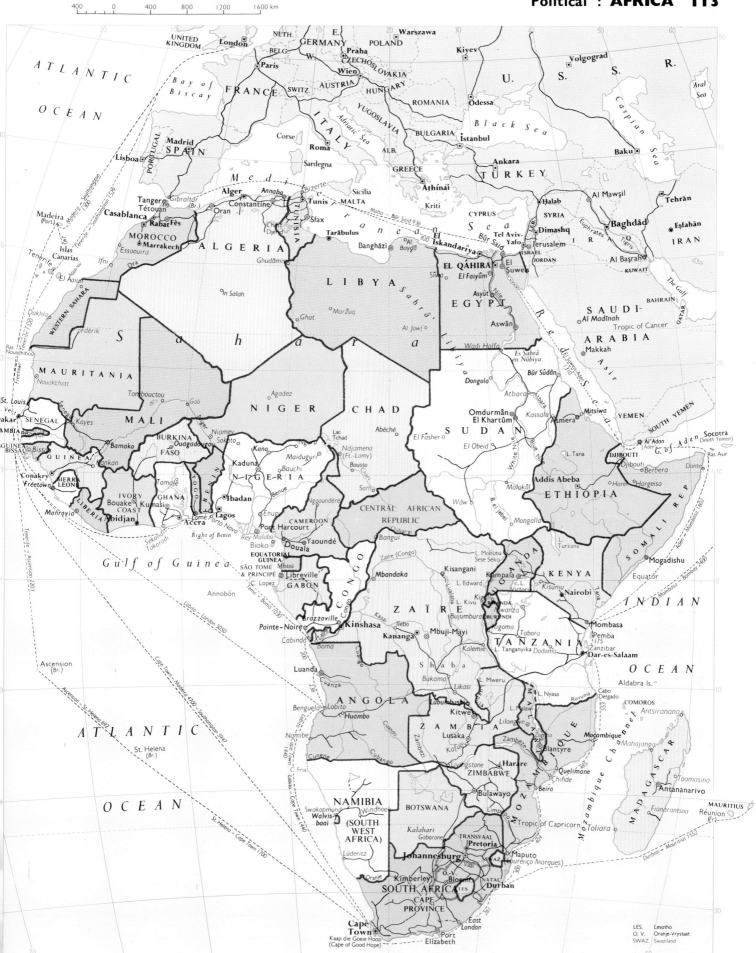

1 : 40 000 000

400   0   400   800   1200   1600 km

ATLANTIC

OCEAN

UNITED
KINGDOM
London
NETH.
BELG.
GERMANY
POLAND
Warszawa
Praha
Wien
CZECHOSLOVAKIA
Kiyev
Volgograd
Paris
FRANCE
SWITZ.
AUSTRIA
HUNGARY
ROMANIA
U. S. S. R.
Bay of
Biscay
Odessa
Black Sea
Aral
Sea
Madrid
SPAIN
Lisboa
PORTUGAL
Corse
Roma
ITALY
Adriatic Sea
YUGOSLAVIA
BULGARIA
İstanbul
Caspian Sea
Baku
Sardegna
GREECE
Athínai
Ankara
TURKEY
Tehrān
Tanger
Tétouan
Casablanca
Rabat
Fès
Gibraltar
(Br.)
Oran
Alger
Constantine
Annaba
Bizerte
Tunis
TUNISIA
Sicilia
MALTA
Kriti
Mediterranean Sea
Bûr Saîd
Al Mawşil
Ḥalab
SYRIA
Tel Aviv-
Yafo
Dimashq
Baghdād
Eşfahān
Madeira
(Port.)
MOROCCO
Marrakech
Essaouira
Ifni
Chott
Djerid
Sfax
Tarābulus
Banghāzi
El Bayda
El Iskandarîya
El QÂHIRA
El Suweis
Jerusalem
ISRAEL
JORDAN
KUWAIT
Al Başrah
IRAN
Islas
Canarias
Tenerife
El Aaiún
WESTERN SAHARA
Dakhla
Fdérik
In Salah
ALGERIA
LIBYA
Ghudāmis
Ghat
Marzûq
Al Jawf
Sahrâ' Libya
EGYPT
Sîwa
El Faiyûm
Asyût
Aswân
Wâdî Halfa
Nile
Es Sahrâ
en Nûbîya
Bûr Sûdân
SAUDI
ARABIA
Al Madînah
Makkah
Tropic of Cancer
BAHRAIN
QATAR
The Gulf
Ras
Nouadhibou
MAURITANIA
Nouakchott
Sahara
Tombouctou
Agadez
NIGER
CHAD
Dongola
Atbara
Kassala
Asmera
Mitsiwa
YEMEN
SOUTH YEMEN
Socotra
(South Yemen)
Ras Asir
St. Louis
Dakar
GAMBIA
SENEGAL
Kayes
MALI
Bamako
Gaô
Niamey
BURKINA
FASO
Sokoto
Kano
N-I-G-E-R-I-A
Ndjamena
(Ft.-Lamy)
Bousso
Abéché
El Fasher
SUDAN
El Khartûm
Omdurmân
El Obeid
L. Tana
DJIBOUTI
Djibouti
Berbera
Hargeisa
G. of Aden
Dante
GUINEA
BISSAU
Bissau
Conakry
Freetown
GUINEA
Kankan
SIERRA
LEONE
LIBERIA
Monrovia
IVORY
COAST
Bouake
Kumasi
GHANA
Tamale
Ouagadougou
TOGO
BENIN
Kaduna
Bauchi
Maiduguri
Benue
Garoua
Sarh
Bel Jebel
Mālakāl
Wâw
Wôu
Addis Abeba
Harer
ETHIOPIA
SOMALI REP
Mogadishu
Tamale
Abidjan
Sekondi-
Takoradi
Lomé
Porto Novo
Accra
Ibadan
Lagos
Bight of Benin
Enugu
Port Harcourt
CAMEROON
Ngaoundéré
Rey Malabo
Bioko
Yaoundé
CENTRAL AFRICAN
REPUBLIC
Bangui
Oubangi
L. Mobutu
Sese Seko
L. Turkana
Equator
INDIAN
Gulf of Guinea
EQUATORIAL
GUINEA
SÃO TOMÉ
& PRINCIPE
Mbini
Libreville
GABON
C. Lopez
Tama
Annobón
Ascension
(Br.)
CONGO
Brazzaville
Pointe-Noire
Cabinda
Boma
Mbandaka
ZAÏRE
Zaïre (Congo)
Kisangani
Kampala
UGANDA
L. Edward
L. Victoria
RWANDA
Kigali
BURUNDI
Bujumbura
L. Kivu
Mwanza
Kisumu
Nairobi
KENYA
Mombasa
ATLANTIC
St. Helena
(Br.)
OCEAN
Kinshasa
Ilebo
Kasai
Kananga
Mbuji-Mayi
Shaba
Kalemie
L. Tanganyika
Kigoma
Tabora
Dodoma
TANZANIA
Pemba
Zanzibar
Dar-es-Salaam
OCEAN
Aldabra Is.
Luanda
Cuanza
Bukama
Lubumbashi
Likasi
L. Mweru
Kitwe
ZAMBIA
Lusaka
L. Nyasa
L. Malawi
MALAWI
Lilongwe
Blantyre
Ruvuma
Cabo
Delgado
COMOROS
Antsiranana
Mahajanga
ANGOLA
Benguela
Lobito
Huambo
Namibe
Cuando
Cunene
Cubango
Zambezi
Kafue
Livingstone
Harare
ZIMBABWE
Bulawayo
Zambeze
MOZAMBIQUE
Chinde
Quelimane
Beira
Mozambique Channel
MADAGASCAR
Antananarivo
Toamasina
MAURITIUS
Réunion
(Fr.)
NAMIBIA
(SOUTH
WEST
AFRICA)
Windhoek
Swakopmund
Walvis-
baai
Lüderitz
Kalahari
BOTSWANA
Gaborone
Tropic of Capricorn
Limpopo
Maputo
Lourenço Marques
Toliara
Fianarantsoa
Oranje
Kimberley
Bloem.
O.V.
Johannesburg
TRANSVAAL
Pretoria
Vaal
NATAL
Durban
SOUTH AFRICA
CAPE
PROVINCE
Cape
Town
Kaap die Goeie Hoop
(Cape of Good Hope)
East
London
Port
Elizabeth

Projection : Zenithal Equidistant.

West from Greenwich   East from Greenwich

LES.   Lesotho
O. V.   Oranje-Vrystaat
SWAZ.   Swaziland

COPYRIGHT. GEORGE PHILIP & SON. LTD.

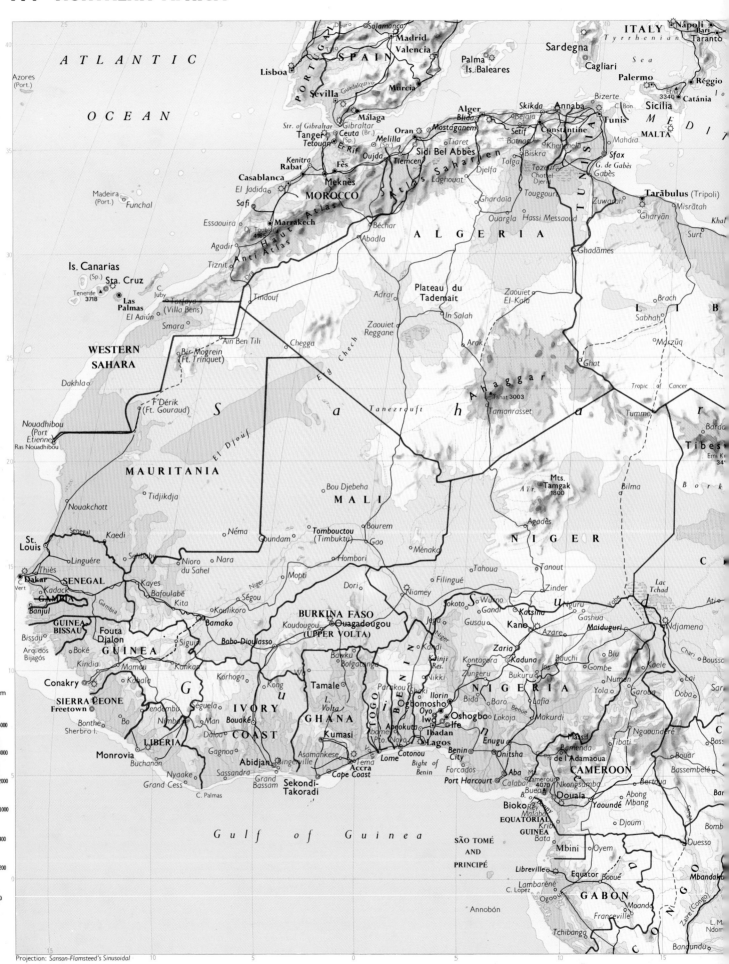

ATLANTIC

OCEAN

Azores
(Port.)

ITALY

Tyrrhenian

Sea

Sardegna

Cagliari

Palermo

Sicilia

MALTA

M E D I

SPAIN

Madrid
Valencia

Lisboa

Palma
Is. Baleares

PORTUGAL

Sevilla

Murcia

Guadalquivir

Málaga

Str. of Gibraltar

Gibraltar

Tanger
Tetouan

Ceuta (Sp.)

El Rif

Melilla
(Sp.)

Oran

Mostaganem

Tiaret

Alger
Blida

Skikda

Setif

Bejaia

Annaba

Bizerte

C. Bon

Tunis

Constantine

Batna

Khenchela

Biskra

TUNISIA

Mahdia

Sfax

G. de Gabès
Gabès

Tarābulus (Tripoli)

Misrātah

Surt

Kenitra
Rabat

Fès

Meknès

Oujda

Tlemcen

Sidi Bel Abbès

Tolga

Tozeur

Chott el
Djerid

Zuwārah

Casablanca

El Jadida

Safi

MOROCCO

Djelfa

Laghouat

Ghardaïa

Touggour

Hassi Messaoud

Ouargla

Gharyān

Khal

Essaouira

Marrakech

Béchar

ALGERIA

Ghadāmes

LIB

Agadir

Dj. Toubkal
4165

Haut Atlas

Abadla

Anti Atlas

Tiznit

Tindouf

Adrar

Plateau du
Tademait

In Salah

Zaouiet
El-Kala

Brach

Sabhah

Is. Canarias

Sta. Cruz

Tenerife
3718

C.
Juby

Tarfaya
(Villa Bens)

El Aaiún

Smara

WESTERN
SAHARA

Dakhla

Las
Palmas

Aïn Ben Tili

Chegga

Zaouiet
Reggane

Araki

Ahaggar

Tahat 3003

Ghat

Tropic of Cancer

Marzūq

Bir Mogrein
(Ft. Trinquet)

Eg Chech

Tamanrasset

Tummo

Barda

F'Dérik
(Ft. Gouraud)

S

a

Tanezrouft

h

a

r

Tibes

Emi Ke
34°

Nouadhibou
(Port
Etienne)

Ras Nouadhibou

El Djouf

MAURITANIA

Bou Djebeha

Mts.
Tamgak
1800

Aïr

Bilma

Bork

Tidjikdja

MALI

Agadès

NIGER

C

Nouakchott

Néma

Goundam

Tombouctou
(Timbuktu)

Bourem

Gao

Ménaka

Tahoua

Tanout

Lac
Tchad

Ati

St.
Louis

Senegal

Kaedi

Selibaby

Nioro
du Sahel

Nara

Hombori

Zinder

Nguru

Yobe

Ndjamena

Linguére

Thiès

Dakar
Vert

SENEGAL

Kayes

Bafoulabé

Kita

Koulikoro

Ségou

Niger

Mopti

Dori

Filingué

Niamey

Sokoto

Gandi

Wurno

Katsina

Gashua

Maiduguri

Kadack

GAMBIA

Banjul

Bamako

Koudougou

BURKINA FASO

Ouagadougou
(UPPER VOLTA)

Gusau

Kano

Azare

Chari

GUINEA
BISSAU

Bissau

Fouta
Djalon

Siguiri

Bobo-Dioulasso

Bawku

Bolgatanga

Zungeru

Kontagora

Zaria

Kaduna

Bauchi

Biu

Gombe

Numan

Kaele

Lai

Boussa

Boké

GUINEA

Kindia

Mamou

Kankan

Korhogo

Kong

W. Volta

Choki

Kandi

Kainji
Res.

Nikki

Jega

Bukuru

Jos

Lafia

Yola

Garoua

Doba

Conakry

Kabala

G

u

Tamale

Parakou

BENIN

Ilorin

NIGERIA

Baro

Benue

Makurdi

Massif
de l'Adamaoua

Ngaoundéré

Tibati

Bouar

Bassembelé

SIERRA LEONE

Freetown

Séguéla

IVORY
COAST

L.
Volta

Ogbomosho

Oyo

Iwo

Oshogbo

Lokoja

Enugu

Bamenda

CAMEROON

Boss

Bonthe

Sherbro I.

Bo

Daloa

GHANA

Kumasi

Abeokuta

Ibadan

Ife

Onitsha

Aba

Mt.
Cameroun
4070

Bertoua

Vendembu

Nimba

Man

Bouaké

Segou

Abomey

Pto. Novo

Lagos

Benin
City

Port Harcourt

Calabar

Buea

Nkongsamba

Doula

Abong Mbang

Bar

LIBERIA

Monrovia

Gagnoa

Asamankese

Tema

Lome

Cotonou

Bight of
Benin

Forcados

Bioko

Malabo

Yaoundé

Djoum

Buchanan

Bingerville

Accra

Cape Coast

EQUATORIAL
GUINEA

Krib

Bata

Bomb

Nyaake

Sassandra

Grand
Bassam

Sekondi-
Takoradi

SÃO TOMÉ
AND
PRINCIPÉ

Mbini

Oyem

Ouesso

Grand Cess

C. Palmas

Libreville

Equator

Booué

Mbandaka

Gulf   of   Guinea

Annobón

GABON

Ogooué

Moanda

C. Lopez

Lambaréné

Franceville

L. M.

Ndom

Tchibanga

Bangundu

Projection: Sanson-Flamsteed's Sinusoidal

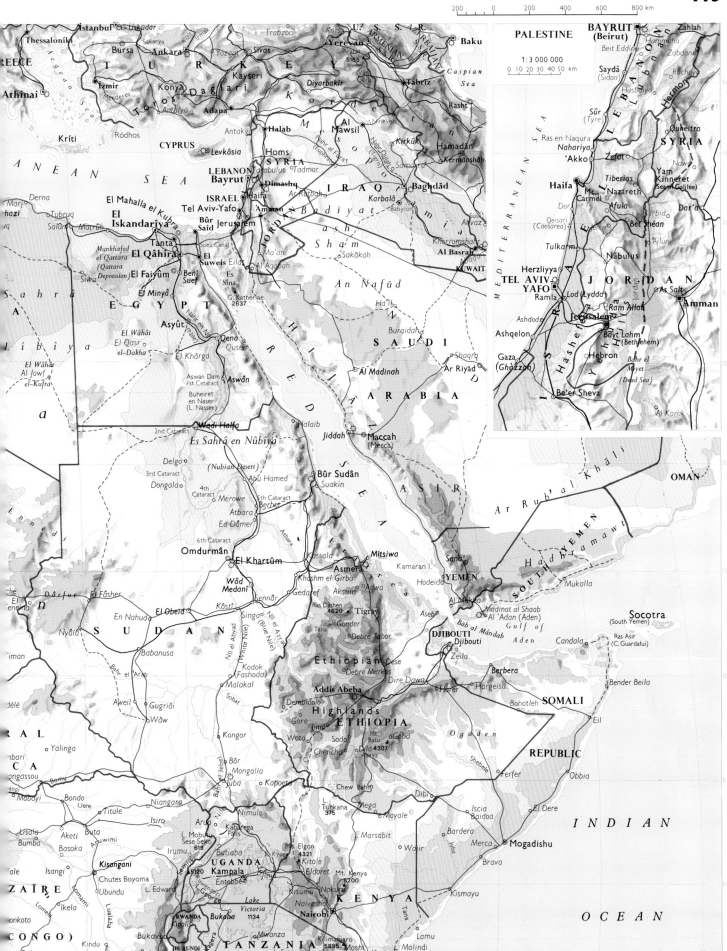

1 : 20 000 000

200 0 200 400 600 800 km

PALESTINE

BAYRUT
(Beirut)

1 : 3 000 000

0 10 20 30 40 50 km

Zahlah

Beit Eddine

Hammana

Zabdani

Sayda
(Sidon)

Rachaya

Hasbaiya

LEBANON

Hermon

Ras en Naqura

Nahariya

SYRIA

Quneitra

'Akko

Žefat

Naw

Haifa

Tiberias

Yam
Kinneret
(Sea of Galilee)

Mt.
Carmel

Nazareth

Dor

Afula

Irbid

Dar'a

(Qeisari)
(Caesarea)

Jenin

Bet Shean

'Ajlun

Herzliyya

Tulkarm

Nâbulus

As Salt

**TEL AVIV
YAFO**

Lod (Lydda)

Ram Allah

Amman

Ramla

Jerusalem

Ashdod

Bayt Lahm
(Bethlehem)

Ashqelon

Hebron

Gaza
(Ghazzon)

Bahr el
Mayet
(Dead Sea)

Be'er Sheva

Al Karak

MEDITERRANEAN SEA

MEDITERRANEAN SEA

Thessaloníki

Istanbul

Üsküdar

Sakarya

Yeşil Irmak

Trabzon

Yerevan

Baku

Bursa

Ankara

TURKEY

Yozgat

Sivas

ARMENIAN

S.S.R.

AZERBAIJAN

İzmir

Konya

Kayseri

Diyarbakir

Tabriz

**Caspian
Sea**

Rasht

GREECE

Athínai

Toros
Dağları

Antalya

Adana

Antakya

Ninveh

Kirkûk

Hamadân

Kermânshâh

Kríti

Ródhos

CYPRUS

Levkôsia

Halab

Al
Mawsil

Homs

Baghdad

SYRIA

Tarabulus

Tadmor

Nahr el Firat
(Euphrates)

Samarra

LEBANON

Bayrut

Dimashq

IRAQ

Karbalā

Babylon

Derna

Marj

ISRAEL

Haifa

Tel Aviv-Yafo

Amman

Ar Rutbah

Ahvaz

Khorramshahr

Tubruq

El Mahalla el Kubra

**El
Iskandariya**

Bûr
Saîd

Jerusalem

JORDAN

Badiyat
ash
Sham

Al Basrah

KUWAIT

Salûm

Matrûh

Tanta

Suez Canal

Ma'an

Sakâkah

Munkhafed
el Qattara
(Qattara
Depression)

El Qâhira

El Faiyûm

El Suweis

Eilat

Al 'Aqabah

An Nafûd

Benî
Suef

Es Sîna

Ha'il

Siwa

El Minyâ

Es Sîna

St. Katherine
2637

SAUDI

Buraidah

Sahrâ

Lîbîya

El Wâhât
El Qasr
el-Dakha

Asyût

Nahr en Nil
(Nile)

Qena
Quseir

El Khârga

Ar Riyad

Shaqra

a

El Wâhât
Al Jawf
el-Kufra

Aswan Dam
1st Cataract

Aswân

Buheiret
en Naser
(L. Nasser)

Al Madinah

ARABIA

Wadi Halfa

2nd Cataract

Halaib

Jiddah

Maccah
(Mecca)

ASIR

**RED
SEA**

HIJAZ

Es Sahrâ en Nûbiya

Delgo

(Nubian Desert)

Abú Hamed

Bûr Sudân

OMAN

3rd Cataract

Dongala

4th
Cataract

Merowe

5th Cataract

Suakin

Ennedi

Berber

Atbara

Ar Rub' al Khāli

Ed Dâmer

SUDAN

6th Cataract

Kassala

Mitsiwa

Kamaran I.

YEMEN

SOUTH

Hadhramawt

Omdurmân

El Khartûm

Khashm el Girba

Asmera

Sana'

Mukalla

Dârfur

El Fâsher

Wâd
Medanî

Gedaref

Aksum

Adwa

Hodeida

Al Mukha

YEMEN

Madinat al Shaab
Al 'Adan (Aden)

Socotra
(South Yemen)

En Nahuda

El Obeid

Sennar

Ras Dashen
4620

Tigray

Aseb

Bâb al Mándab

Gulf of

Candala

Ras Asir
(C. Guardafui)

Nyâlâ

Singa

Nil el Azra
(Blue Nile)

Tana

Gonder

Debre Tabor

DJIBOUTI
Djibouti

Aden

Bender Beila

Babanusa

Nil el Abyad
(White Nile)

Kodok
(Fashoda)

Malakal

Ethiopian

Dese

Debre Markos

Zeila

Berbera

Bahr el 'Arab

Aweil

Gugriâl

Waw

Sobat

Highlands

Addis Abeba

ETHIOPIA

Dembidolo

Jima

Dire Dawa

Harer

Hargeisa

SOMALI

Eil

Bohotleh

Kongor

Bôr

Mongalla

Mt.
Batu

Goba

Ogaden

Shebele

Ferfer

Obbia

REPUBLIC

Juba

Kapoeta

Chew Bahir

Dibi

Iscia
Baidoa

El Dere

Dembidolo

Wota

Sodo

Dila 4307

Abaya

Chencha

Omo

INDIAN

Titule

Niangara

Nimule

Aru

Kabarega
Falls

L. Turkana
375

Mega

Moyale

Marsabit

Bardera

Merca

Isiro

UGANDA

Butiaba

Mt. Elgon
4321

Kitale

Eldoret

Wajir

Mogadishu

Kisangani

L. Mobutu
Sese Seko
619

Kampala
Entebbe

Jinja

Kisumu

Mt. Kenya
5200

Brava

Chutes Boyoma

L. Edward

Kyoga

Nakuru

KENYA

Kismayu

ZAÏRE

L. George

Lake
Victoria
1134

Naivasha

Nairobi

Tana

Lamu

OCEAN

RWANDA
Kigali

Bukoba

Mwanza

(CONGO)

BURUNDI

Bujumbura

TANZANIA

Kilimanjaro
5895

Moshi

Arusha

Voi

Malindi

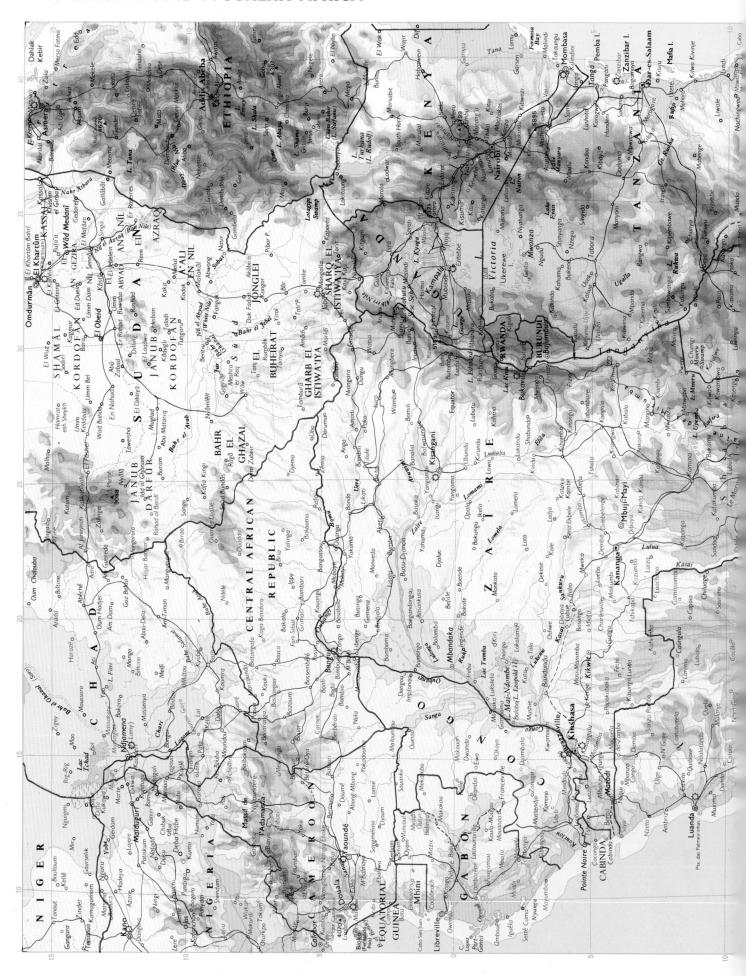

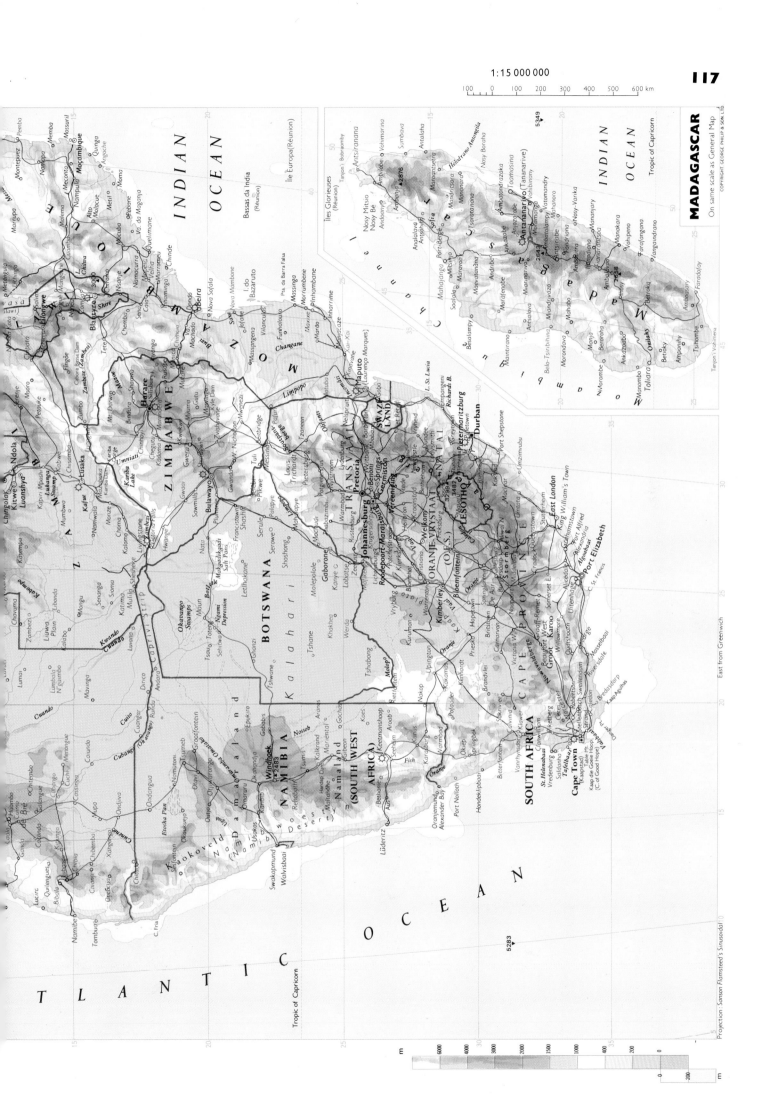

1:15 000 000

100   0   100   200   300   400   500   600 km

MADAGASCAR
On same scale as General Map

COPYRIGHT GEORGE PHILIP & SON LTD.

Projection: Sanson Flamsteed's Sinusoidal

East from Greenwich

m
6000
4000
3000
2000
1500
1000
400
200
0

m
200
0

1:50 000 000

500 0 500 1000 1500 2000 km

ARCTIC OCEAN

PACIFIC OCEAN

INDIAN OCEAN

m
6000
4000
2000
1000
400
200
0
200
2000
4000
6000

1 : 50 000 000

500   0   500   1000   1500   2000 km

Projection: Bonne

Projection: Conical Orthomorphic with two standard parallels

East from Greenwich

1 : 20 000 000

200   0   200   400   600   800 km

OCEAN

Mys Dezhneva
(East C.)

St. Lawrence I.
(U.S.A.)

Severnaya
Zemlya

Laptev Sea

East Siberian Sea

Chukotskoye
More

Bering
Sea

POLUOSTROV
KAMCHATKA

Petropavlovsk-
Kamchatskiy

Magadan

Okhotsk

Sea
of
Okhotsk

Sakhalin

YAKUT A.S.S.R.

SOCIALIST   REPUBLIC

Verkhoyansk

Khrebet Cherskogo

Yakutsk

Vilyuysk

Olekminsk

Krasnoyarsk

Nizhneudinsk

Bratsk

Irkutsk

Ulan Ude

Chita

Komsomolsk

Khabarovsk

Sovetskaya Gavan

Yuzhno-Sakhalinsk

Blagoveshchensk

Harbin

Ussuriysk

Vladivostok

Nakhodka

Hokkaidō

Sapporo

Hakodate

SEA of JAPAN

Honshū

Ni-igata

Hinan Ling

Tsitsihar

Changchun

Kirin

Shenyang

Fushun

Anshan

Chongjin

Wŏnsan

North

Korea

Pyongyang

Lu-ta

Peking

Paotow

Changkiakow
(Kalgan)

MONGOLIA

Ulaanbaatar
(Ulan Bator)

Hangayn Nuruu

INNER MONGOLIAN REPUBLIC

Sŏul

Inchŏn   South   Taejŏn

Pusan

Boundaries of U.S.S.R.
Boundaries of S.S.R.
Boundaries of A.S.S.R.

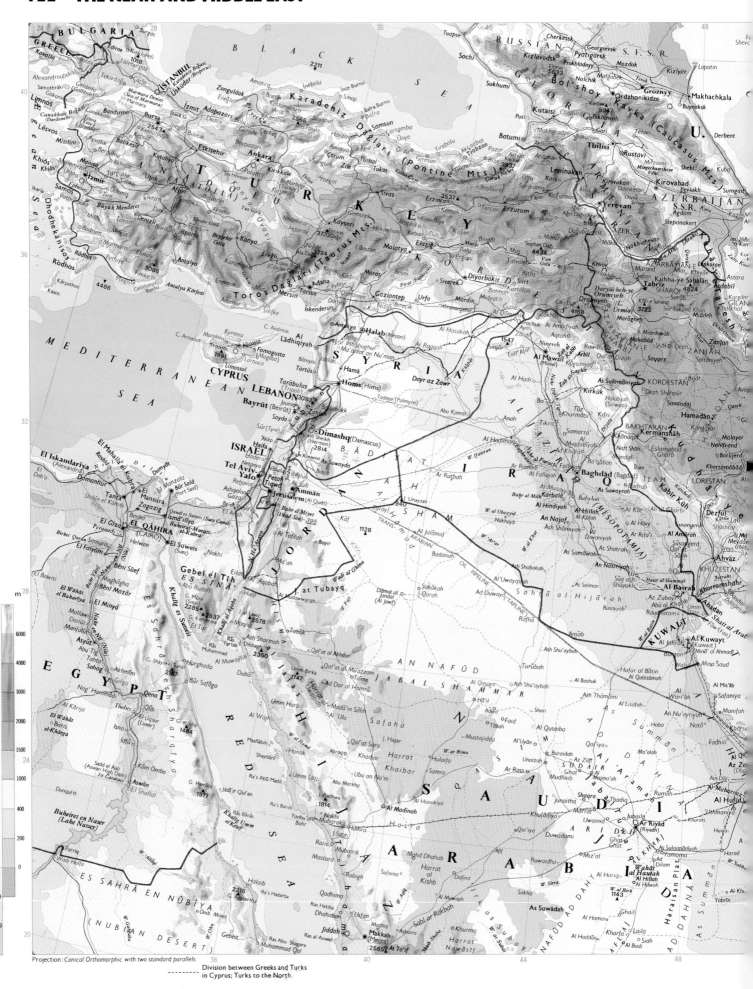

m
6000
4000
3000
2000
1500
1000
400
200
0
0
200
2000
m

Projection: Conical Orthomorphic with two standard parallels

Division between Greeks and Turks
in Cyprus; Turks to the North.

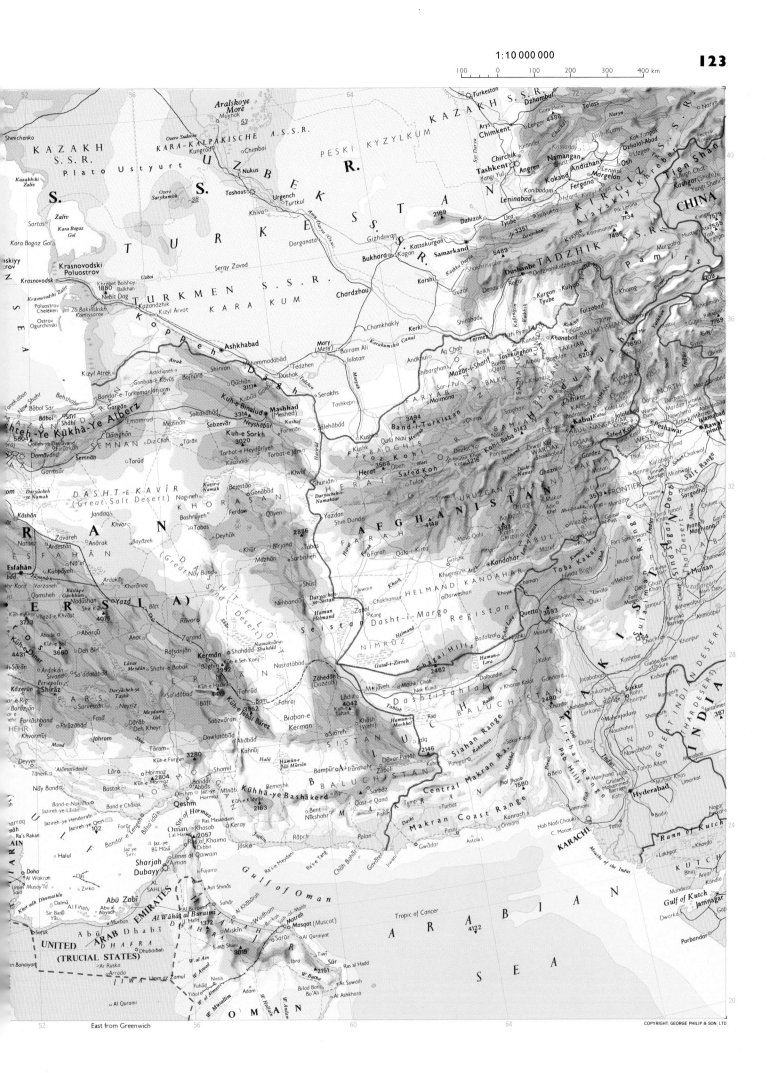

1:10 000 000

100   0   100   200   300   400 km

KAZAKH
S.S.R.

Aralskoye
More

KARA-KALPAKISCHE A.S.S.R.

PESKI KYZYLKUM   KAZAKH S.S.R.

U Z B E K   S.S.R.

Plato Ustyurt

Shevchenko

Kazakhski
Zaliv

Sartas

Kara Bogaz
Gol

Kara Bogaz Gol

Krasnovodski
Poluostrov

Krasnovodsk

Poluostrov
Cheleken

Ostrov
Ogurchinski

T U R K M E N   S.S.R.

KARA KUM

Nebit Dag

Kizyl Arvat

Ashkhabad

K o p p e h   D a g h

TADZHIK
S.S.R.

Dushanbe

KIRGIZ
S.S.R.

Tien Shan

CHINA

Pamirs

7134

7690

7789

HINDU KUSH

Mashhad

Kuh-e Binalud
3314

Kuh-e Sorkh
3020

I R A N

DASHT-E KAVIR
(Great Salt Desert)

KHORASAN

A F G H A N I S T A N

Kabul

Peshawar

Islamabad

P A K I S T A N

Herat

Kandahar

Quetta

DASHT-I-LUT
(Great Sand Desert)

Dasht-i-Margo

Registon

BALUCHISTAN

Kerman

Shiraz

Esfahan

Yazd

F A R S

Bam

Zahedan

Bandar Abbas

Strait of Hormuz

Qeshm

Gwadar

Karachi

Makran Coast Range

Gulf of Oman

O M A N

Masqat (Muscat)

Abu Zabi

UNITED ARAB EMIRATES
(TRUCIAL STATES)

Dubayy

Sharjah

Doha

Tropic of Cancer

A R A B I A N

S E A

Gulf of Kutch

I N D I A

GREAT INDIAN DESERT

Hyderabad

East from Greenwich

COPYRIGHT. GEORGE PHILIP & SON. LTD.

U.S.S.R.

HINDU KUSH

AFGHANISTAN

HERAT · GHOR · HELMAND · KANDAHAR · ZABUL · PAKTYA · GHAZNI · URUZGAN · WARDAK · LOGAR · NANGARHAR · KUNAR · PAKTIKA · CHAKHANSUR · FARAH · BADGHIS · FARYAB · JOUZJAN · SAMANGAN · BALKH · BAGHLAN · TAKHAR · BADAKHSHAN · KAPISA

Herat · Kabul · Kandahar · Quetta · Ghazni

IRAN (PERSIA)

Zāhedān (Duzdab)

BALUCHISTAN

Central Makran Range · Makran Coast Range · Siahan Range · Kirthar Range · Chagai Hills

PAKISTAN

Peshawar · Rawalpindi · Islamabad · Lahore · Faisalabad · Multan · Bahawalpur · Sukkur · Hyderabad · KARACHI

JAMMU AND KASHMIR · Srinagar · Karakoram Mountains · Nanga Parbat

HIMACHAL PRADESH · Simla · Chandigarh

PUNJAB · Amritsar · Ludhiana · Ambala · Patiala

HARYANA · DELHI · Meerut · Moradabad

RAJASTHAN · Bikaner · Jodhpur · Jaipur · Ajmer · Udaipur · Kota · Jaisalmer

Great Indian Desert (Thar Desert)

ARABIAN SEA

Tropic of Cancer

Rann of Kutch · Little Rann · Gulf of Kutch · Gulf of Cambay

GUJARAT · Ahmadabad · Rajkot · Jamnagar · Vadodara (Baroda) · Surat · Bhavnagar · Junagadh · Kathiawar

Diu · Daman · DADRA & NAGAR HAVELI

MADHYA PRADESH · Indore · Bhopal · Ujjain · Ratlam · Sagar · Jhansi

BIHAR · Gwalior

Satpura Range · Ajanta Range · Gawilgarh Hills

MAHARASHTRA · BOMBAY · Pune (Poona) · Nasik · Thana · Ulhasnagar · Aurangabad · Sholapur · Kolhapur · Nagpur · Amraoti · Akola · Wardha · Satara · Sangli

ANDHRA PRADESH · Hyderabad · Secunderabad · Gulbarga · Bidar · Nizamabad · Bijapur · Raichur

Godavari · Krishna

GOA · Panaji (Panjim) · Marmagao

KARNATAKA · Bangalore · Hubli · Gadag · Bellary · Mangalore · Mysore · Shimoga · Davangere · Hospet · Kolar

KERALA · Calicut (Kozhikode) · Coimbatore · Ernakulam · Mattancheri · Alleppey · Quilon · Trivandrum · Nagercoil · Cape Comorin · Malabar Coast · Cardamon Hills · Palni Hills

TAMIL NADU · Madras · Vellore · Salem · Erode · Tiruchchirappalli · Madurai · Thanjavur · Pondicherry · Cuddalore · Tirunelveli · Kanchipuram (Conjeeveram)

Eastern Ghats · Western Ghats · Nilgiri Hills · Nallamalai Hills

Pulicat Lake · Palk Strait · Palk Bay · Gulf of Mannar · Adam's Bridge · Point Pedro

SRI LANKA (CEYLON) · Colombo · Kandy · Jaffna · Trincomalee · Negombo · Moratuwa · Galle · Adam's Peak 2243 · Mt. Lavinia · Dondra Head

Continuation Southwards on same scale

m
6000
4000
3000
2000
1500
1000
400
200
0
200

Projection: Conical with two standard parallels

NKIANG-
lui-gur-Shan
Koko Shili
TSINGHAI

Sumpa Kangri
6300

Ngoring Nor
Amne
Machin Shan
6094

Toghral Omba
Polur

Kashum Tso

Mani

Mantekomu Hu

Dungbuva La
4930

Tsaring Nor

Chabrun La
4526

Chatsam La
4593

Doyung

Joma
6800

Achak Gomba

Iyekundo
(Yushu)

Tengko

CHINESE   REPUBLIC

Ating

CHINESE   REPUBLIC

Khetinsiring

Angenong

Denchin

Tsing

TIBET

Tang La
5180

Tang la

Shaba Gomba

Ed Dzong

Shan

Nagchu Dzong

Lantsien

Tungbo

Kantse

ng Kangri
7315

Nagrong

Tangri

Zilling Tso

Nam Tso

Pondo Dzong

Giamda Dzong

Chamdo

Paiyu

Tsunga

SZECHWAN
4959

Yoking

Lhasa

Tsangpo (Brahmaputra)

BAY   OF   BENGAL

INDIAN   OCEAN

Projection: Mercator

East from Greenwich

1:12 500 000

100   0   100   200   300   400   500 km

JAVA AND MADURA

1:7 500 000

50   0   50   100   150   200   250   300 km

COPYRIGHT. GEORGE PHILIP & SON. LTD.

1:10 000 000

PENINSULAR MALAYSIA AND SINGAPORE
1:6 000 000

Projection: Conical with two standard parallels

East from Greenwich

1:20 000 000

200 0 200 400 600 800 km

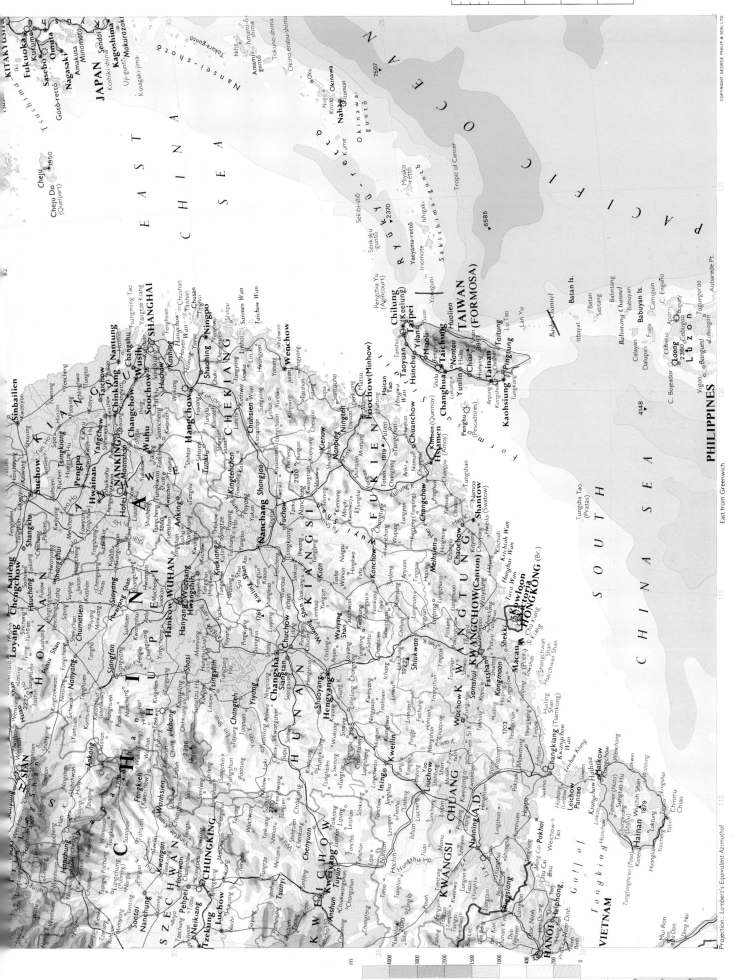

1:10 000 000

100   0   100   200   300   400 km

COPYRIGHT GEORGE PHILIP & SON LTD

P A C I F I C   O C E A N

PHILIPPINES

S O U T H   C H I N A   S E A

E A S T   C H I N A   S E A

JAPAN

SHANGHAI

TAIWAN (FORMOSA)

Taipei

HONGKONG (Br.)

Macau

VIETNAM

HANOI

Haiphong

HAINAN

SZECHWAN

CHUNGKING

KWEICHOW

YUNNAN

KWANGSI - CHUANG A.D.

KWANGTUNG

HUNAN

KIANGSI

FUKIEN

CHEKIANG

ANHWEI

KIANGSU

NANKING

WUHAN

Hankow

Wuchang

Hanyang

HONAN

HUPEH

SHENSI

Projection: Lambert's Equivalent Azimuthal   East from Greenwich

m
4000
3000
2000
1500
1000
400
200

m
200
2000
4000
6000

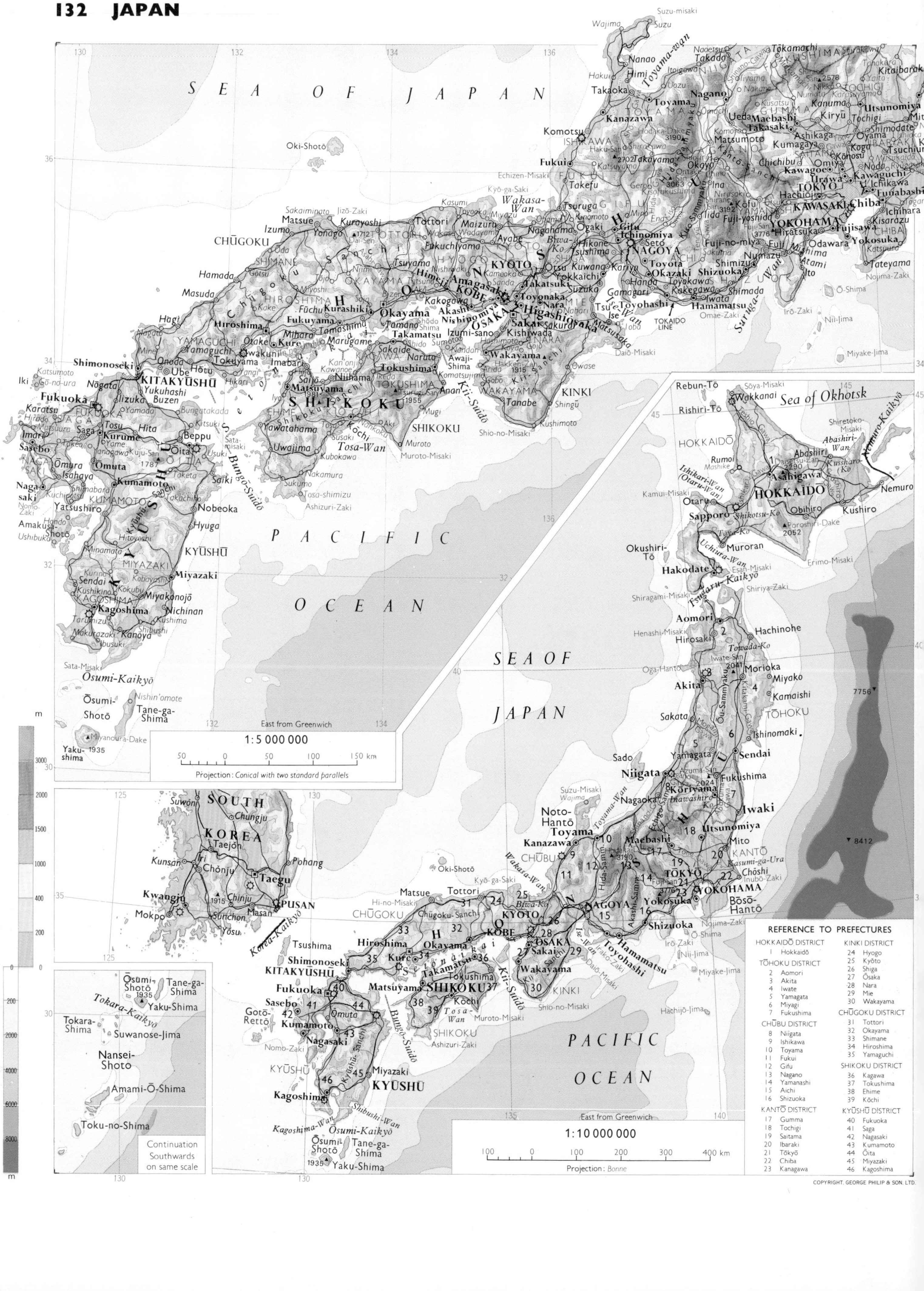

SEA OF JAPAN

PACIFIC OCEAN

SEA OF JAPAN

CHŪGOKU

SHIKOKU

KYŪSHŪ

HOKKAIDO

Sea of Okhotsk

TŌHOKU

CHŪBU

KANTŌ

KINKI

SOUTH KOREA

1:5 000 000

East from Greenwich

50 0 50 100 150 km

Projection: Conical with two standard parallels

1:10 000 000

East from Greenwich

100 0 100 200 300 400 km

Projection: Bonne

Continuation Southwards on same scale

Nansei-Shoto

Ōsumi-Shotō

Tane-ga-Shima

Yaku-Shima

Tokara-Kaikyō

Tokara-Shima

Suwanose-Jima

Amami-Ō-Shima

Toku-no-Shima

REFERENCE TO PREFECTURES

HOKKAIDŌ DISTRICT	KINKI DISTRICT
1 Hokkaidō	24 Hyogo
TŌHOKU DISTRICT	25 Kyōto
2 Aomori	26 Shiga
3 Akita	27 Ōsaka
4 Iwate	28 Nara
5 Yamagata	29 Mie
6 Miyagi	30 Wakayama
7 Fukushima	**CHŪGOKU DISTRICT**
CHŪBU DISTRICT	31 Tottori
8 Niigata	32 Okayama
9 Ishikawa	33 Shimane
10 Toyama	34 Hiroshima
11 Fukui	35 Yamaguchi
12 Gifu	**SHIKOKU DISTRICT**
13 Nagano	36 Kagawa
14 Yamanashi	37 Tokushima
15 Aichi	38 Ehime
16 Shizuoka	39 Kōchi
KANTŌ DISTRICT	**KYŪSHŪ DISTRICT**
17 Gumma	40 Fukuoka
18 Tochigi	41 Saga
19 Saitama	42 Nagasaki
20 Ibaraki	43 Kumamoto
21 Tōkyō	44 Ōita
22 Chiba	45 Miyazaki
23 Kanagawa	46 Kagoshima

1:6 000 000

50   0   50   100   150   200   250 km

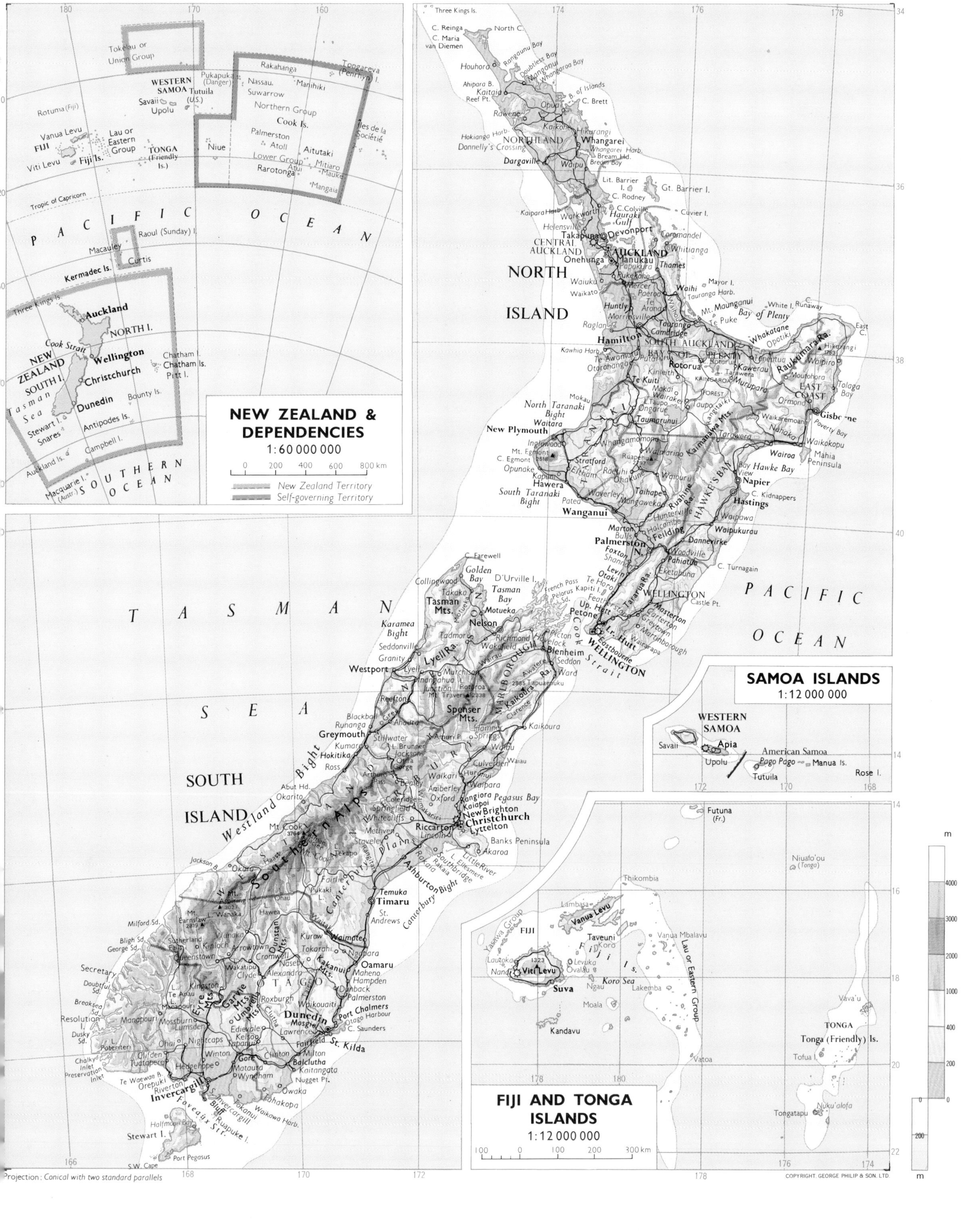

NEW ZEALAND & DEPENDENCIES

1:60 000 000

0   200   400   600   800 km

New Zealand Territory
Self-governing Territory

Tokelau or
Union Group

WESTERN
SAMOA
Savaii
Upolu   Tutuila (U.S.)

Rotuma (Fiji)

Vanua Levu
FIJI
Viti Levu   Fiji Is.

TONGA
(Friendly
Is.)

Niue

Pukapuka
(Danger)   Nassau
Suwarrow

Rakahanga
Manihiki

Tongareva
(Penrhyn) I.

Northern Group
Cook Is.

Palmerston
Atoll   Aitutaki
Lower Group   Mitiaro
Rarotonga   Mauke
Mangaia

Îles de la
Société

PACIFIC   OCEAN

Tropic of Capricorn

Macauley
Curtis

Raoul (Sunday) I.

Kermadec Is.

Three Kings Is.

Auckland

NORTH I.

Cook Strait

NEW
ZEALAND
SOUTH I.

Wellington

Christchurch

Dunedin

Chatham Is.
Chatham I.
Pitt I.

Bounty Is.

Tasman
Sea

Stewart I.
Snares
Antipodes Is.

Campbell I.

Auckland Is.

Macquarie
(Austr.)

SOUTHERN
OCEAN

NORTH ISLAND

Three Kings Is.
C. Reinga
C. Maria
van Diemen
North C.

Houhora
Ahipara B.
Kaitaia
Reef Pt.
Rawene

Rangaunu Bay
Doubtless Bay
Mangonui
Whangaroa Bay

NORTHLAND

Hokianga Harb.
Donnelly's Crossing
Dargaville

Kaikohe
Hikurangi
Whangarei

Opua
C. Brett
B. of Islands

Waipu   Whangarei Harb.
Bream Hd.
Bream Bay

Lit. Barrier I.
Gt. Barrier I.
C. Rodney
Cuvier I.

Kaipara Harb.
Waikworth
C. Colville

Helensville
Hauraki
Gulf
Coromandel
Whitianga

Takapuna   Devonport
CENTRAL
AUCKLAND
AUCKLAND
Onehunga   Manukau
Papakura
Waiuku   Pukekohe
Mercer

Mayor I.

Whakatane
Opotiki

Waihi
Tauranga Harb.

NORTH
ISLAND

Waikato
Huntly
Morrinsville
Te Aroha
Raglan   Cambridge
Hamilton
SOUTH AUCKLAND
Kawhia Harb.
Te Awamutu   Putaruru
Otorohanga
Te Kuiti
BAY OF PLENTY
Te Puke
Rotorua

White I. Runaway
Bay of Plenty

Waihi
Kawerau

Raukumara Ra.
Waipiro

East
C.

Mokau
North Taranaki
Bight
Waitara
New Plymouth
Mt. Egmont
C. Egmont
Opunake

Makai
Taupo
Ongarue
Taumarunui

Waiotapu
Murupara

Kaingaroa
FOREST

Gisborne
Poverty Bay

Waikaremoana
Nuhaka
Waikokopu

Mahia
Peninsula

Inglewood
Stratford
Eltham
Kaponga

Raurimu
Ohakune

Ruapehu

Taihape

Wairoa

Bay Hawke Bay
Napier
C. Kidnappers

Hawera
South Taranaki
Bight
Patea
Waverley
Wanganui
Mangaweka

Waiouru

Hastings
Waipawa

Marton
Bulls
Halcombe
Feilding

Waipukurau

C. Turnagain

Foxton
Shannon

Palmerston N.
Danevirke
Woodville
Pahiatua

Levin
Otaki

Eketahuna

Up. Hutt   Masterton
Otaki   Carterton
Lr. Hutt   Greytown
Petone   Martinborough
WELLINGTON

Castle Pt.

PACIFIC

OCEAN

SOUTH ISLAND

C. Farewell
Collingwood   Golden
Takaka   Bay
Tasman
Mts.
Motueka

D'Urville I.
Tasman
Bay

French Pass
Pelorus Sd.
Picton

Karamea
Bight
Tadmor
Richmond
Wakefield
Nelson

Blenheim
Seddon
Ward

Seddonville
Granity
Westport

Lyell Ra.
Lyell

Murchison
Rotoiti
MARLBOROUGH

TASMAN

SEA

Reefton
Blackball

Ruanga
Greymouth
Stillwater
Kumara
Hokitika
Ross

Spenser
Mts.

Hanmer
Springs

Kaikoura

Arthur's P.
Otira

SOUTH

ISLAND

Abut Hd.
Okarito

Hokitika

Waikari
Oxford
Coleridge

Culverden
Waiau
Hurunui
Waipara
Rangiora
Kaiapoi

Pegasus Bay

Jackson B.

Mt. Cook

SOUTHERN ALPS

WESTLAND

Mt.
Aspiring

Mt. Earnslaw

Milford Sd.
Bligh Sd.
George Sd.
Sutherland
Kaikoura
Wanaka

Haast

New Brighton
Christchurch
Riccarton   Lyttelton
Lincoln
Little River
Akaroa

Banks Peninsula

Whitecliffs
Springfield
Methven
Darfield
Rakaia

Geraldine
Temuka
Timaru

Canterbury
Plains

L. Ellesmere

Ashburton

Canterbury Bight

Secretary
Doubtful Sd.

Queenstown
Arrowtown
Cromwell
Clyde
Alexandra

Kurow
Tokarahi
Ngapara

Fairlie
Pukaki

St.
Andrews

Waimate

Breaksea
Sd.
Resolution I.
Dusky Sd.

Te Anau
Manapouri
Lumsden

Roxburgh
Ettrick

Kakanui
Mts.

Maheno
Dunback
Hampden
Palmerston

Oamaru

Chalky
Inlet
Preservation
Inlet

Ohai
Nightcaps
Winton

Edievale
Kelso
Lawrence

Waikouaiti
Port Chalmers
Otago Harbour

Te Waewae B.
Orepuki
Riverton
Invercargill
Bluff

Clinton
Milton
Mataura
Gore
Wyndham
Balclutha
Kaitangata
Nugget Pt.

Dunedin
Mosgiel
St. Kilda
Fairfield

Owaka

Stewart I.
S.W. Cape
Port Pegasus

Paterson Inlet
Ruapuke I.
Foveaux Str.

SAMOA ISLANDS

1:12 000 000

WESTERN
SAMOA
Savaii   Apia
Upolu

American Samoa
Pago Pago   Manua Is.
Tutuila   Rose I.

FIJI AND TONGA ISLANDS

1:12 000 000

100   0   100   200   300 km

Futuna
(Fr.)

Niuafo'ou
(Tonga)

Thikombia

Lambasa
Vanua Levu
Taveuni
Koro
FIJI
Nandi   Levuka
Viti Levu   Ovalau
Suva
Koro Sea

Lau or Eastern Group

TONGA
Tonga (Friendly) Is.

Vava'u

Kandavu

Moala

Lakemba

Vatoa

Tongatapu   Nuku'alofa
Tofua

Projection: Conical with two standard parallels

COPYRIGHT. GEORGE PHILIP & SON LTD.

m
4000
3000
2000
1000
400
200
0
200
m

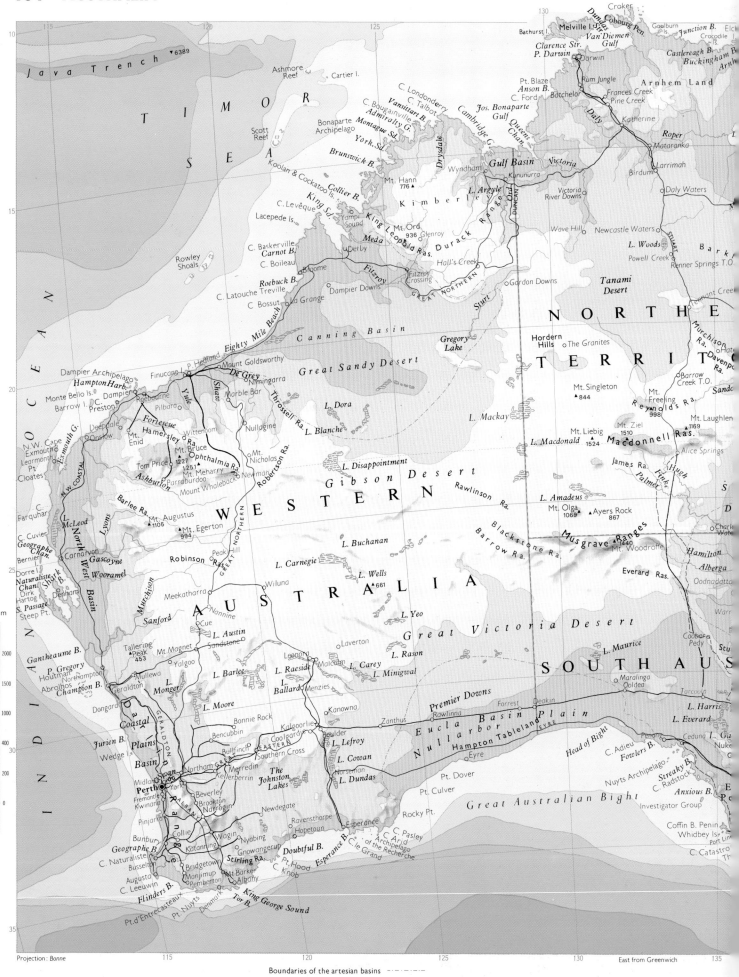

Projection: Bonne

East from Greenwich

Boundaries of the artesian basins - - - - -

T I M O R   S E A

Java Trench ▼6389

I N D I A N   O C E A N

W E S T E R N   A U S T R A L I A

N O R T H E R N   T E R R I T O R Y

SOUTH AUS

Croker
Cobourg Pen.
Goulburn Is.
Junction B.
Melville I.
Dundas Str.
Van Diemen Gulf
Bathurst I.
Clarence Str.
P. Darwin
Darwin
Pt. Blaze
Anson B.
C. Ford
Batchelor
Rum Jungle
Frances Creek
Pine Creek
Katherine
Daly
Roper
Mataranka
Larrimah
Birdum
Daly Waters
Victoria River Downs
Wave Hill
Newcastle Waters
Powell Creek
Renner Springs T.O.
Tennant Creek
Barrow Creek T.O.
Mt. Singleton ▲844
Reynolds Ra.
Mt. Freeling 998
Mt. Liebig
Mt. Ziel 1510
Mt. Laughlen ▲1169
Macdonnell Ras.
L. Macdonald 1524
Alice Springs
James Ra.
Hugh
Finke
Palmer
Mt. Olga 1069 ▲Ayers Rock 867
Musgrave Ranges
Mt. Woodroffe ▲1440
Everard Ras.
Hamilton
Alberga
Oodnadatta
Cooper Pedy
L. Maurice
Maralinga
Ooldea
Tarcoola
L. Harris
L. Everard
Ceduna
Streaky B.
Anxious B.

Ashmore Reef
Cartier I.
Scott Reef
C. Londonderry
C. Talbot
Vansittart B.
C. Bougainville
Admiralty G.
Bonaparte Archipelago
Montague Sd.
York Sd.
Brunswick B.
Cambridge Gulf
Jos. Bonaparte Gulf
Wyndham
Kununurra
Drysdale
L. Argyle
Ord
Duncan
Victoria
Gulf Basin
Mt. Hann 776 ▲
K i m b e r l e y
L. Leopold Ras.
Mt. Ord 936 Glenroy
Hall's Creek
Gordon Downs
Hordern Hills
The Granites
Tanami Desert
Koolan & Cockatoo Is.
King Sd.
C. Lévêque
Lacepede Is.
C. Baskerville
Carnot B.
C. Boileau
Derby
Meda
Broome
Yampi Sound
Durack Range
Fitzroy
Fitzroy Crossing
Roebuck B.
C. Latouche Treville
C. Bossut
La Grange
Dampier Downs
Sturt
Gregory Lake
Rowley Shoals
Eighty Mile Beach
C a n n i n g   B a s i n
G r e a t   S a n d y   D e s e r t
L. Dora
L. Mackay
Great Northern
P. Hedland
Mount Goldsworthy
Finucane
Nimingarra
De Grey
Marble Bar
Shaw
Yule
Nullagine
Throssell Ra.
L. Blanche
Dampier Archipelago
Hampton Harb.
Monte Bello Is.
Barrow I.
Dampier
Preston
Roebourne
Pilbara
Fortescue
Hamersley Ra.
Wittenoom
Mt. Enid
Mt. Bruce
Ophthalmia Ra.
Mt. Nicholas
Robertson Ra.
L. Disappointment
G i b s o n   D e s e r t
Rawlinson Ra.
L. Amadeus
Blackstone Ra.
Barrow Ra.
N.W. Cape
Exmouth G.
Learmonth
Pt. Cloates
Deepdale
Onslow
Tom Price 1227
Mt. Meharry 1251
Parraburdoo
Ashburton
Mount Whaleback
Newman
L. Buchanan
C. Farquhar
C. Cuvier
Geographe Chan.
Bernier
Dorre I.
Naturaliste Chan.
Dirk Hartog I.
Denham
Shark B.
S. Passage
Steep Pt.
L. McLeod
North West Basin
Carnarvon
Gascoyne
Wooramel
Lyons
Barlee Ra.
Mt. Augustus ▲1105
Mt. Egerton 994
Peak Hill
Ras.
Robinson
Great Northern
Murchison
Sanford
Meekatharra
Nannine
Cue
Sandstone
L. Austin
L. Carnegie
L. Wells 661
L. Yeo
G r e a t   V i c t o r i a   D e s e r t
L. Maurice
L. Rason
L. Minigwal
L. Carey
Laverton
Leonora
Malcolm
L. Raeside
L. Ballard
Menzies
Kanowna
Premier Downs
Rawlinna
Forrest
Deakin
E u c l a   B a s i n
N u l l a r b o r
Hampton Tableland Plain
EYRE
Head of Bight
Great Australian Bight
Gantheaume B.
P. Gregory
Houtman
Abrolhos
Northampton
Champion B.
Geraldton
Dongara
Coastal Plains Basin
Jurien B.
Wedge I.
Dandaragan
Mullewa
Yalgoo
Mt. Magnet
Tallering Peak 453
L. Moore
L. Monger
L. Barlee
Bonnie Rock
Bencubbin
Bullfinch
Southern Cross
Merredin
Kellerberrin
The Johnston Lakes
Coolgardie
Boulder
Kalgoorlie
Zanthus
Rawlinna
L. Lefroy
L. Cowan
L. Dundas
Norseman
Eyre
Pt. Dover
Pt. Culver
Rocky Pt.
Swan
Perth
Fremantle
Kwinana
Midland
York
Northam
Beverley
Brookton
Narrogin
Pinjarra
Newdegate
Ravensthorpe
Hopetoun
Esperance
C. Pasley
C. Arid
Archipelago of the Recherche
C. le Grand
Bunbury
Collie
Wagin
Nyabing
Gnowangerup
Doubtful B.
Esperance B.
Pt. Hood
C. le Grand
Geographe B.
C. Naturaliste
Busselton
Bridgetown
Manjimup
Pemberton
Stirling Ra.
Mt. Barker
Albany
Augusta
C. Leeuwin
Flinders B.
Pt. d'Entrecasteaux
Pt. Nuyts
Denmark
Tor B.
King George Sound
Nuyts Archipelago
Investigator Group
Coffin B. Penin.
Whidbey Is.
Fowlers B.
C. Adieu
Streaky B.
C. Radstock

m
2000
1500
1000
400
200
0
0
200
2000
4000
6000
m

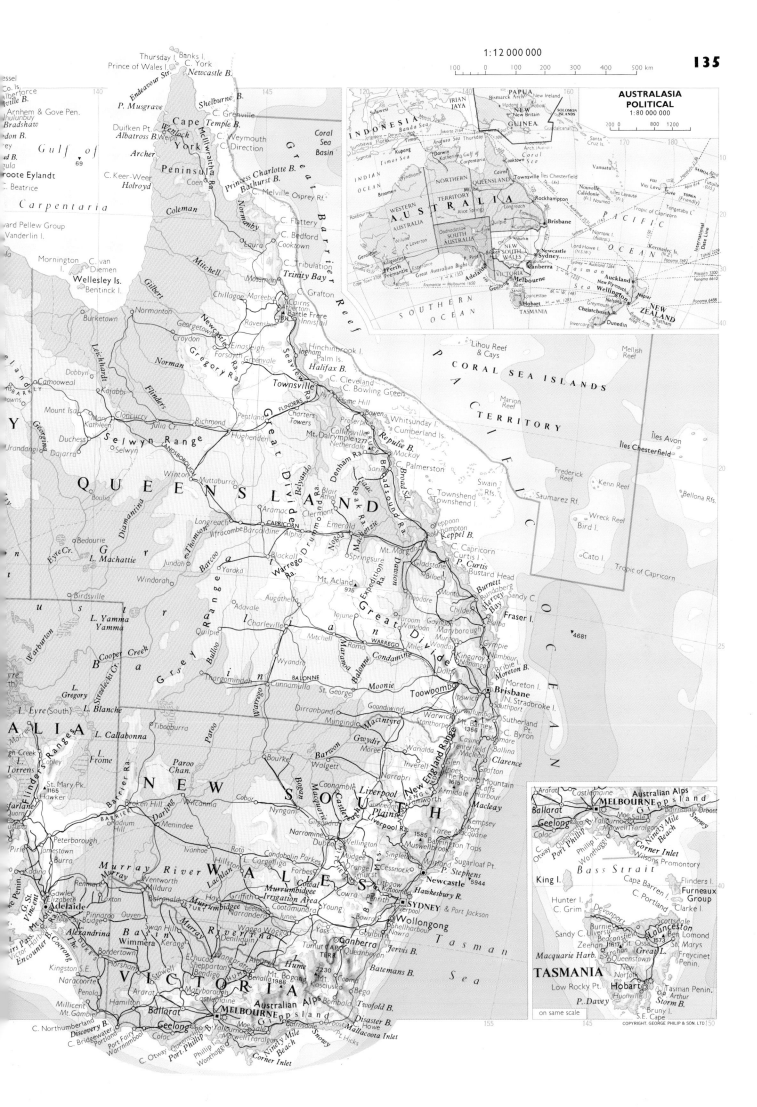

1:12 000 000

100   0   100   200   300   400   500 km

AUSTRALASIA
POLITICAL
1:80 000 000

200 0   800   1200

INDONESIA

IRIAN
JAYA

PAPUA
NEW
GUINEA

NORTHERN
TERRITORY

QUEENSLAND

WESTERN
AUSTRALIA

SOUTH
AUSTRALIA

AUSTRALIA

NEW
SOUTH
WALES

VICTORIA

TASMANIA

PACIFIC
OCEAN

NEW
ZEALAND

SOUTHERN
OCEAN

Gulf of
Carpentaria

Cape
York
Peninsula

Q U E E N S L A N D

CORAL SEA ISLANDS
TERRITORY

Great Barrier Reef

P A C I F I C   O C E A N

Great Dividing Range

N E W   S O U T H   W A L E S

Murray River

V I C T O R I A

Australian Alps

MELBOURNE

TASMANIA

Tasman Sea

Bass Strait

on same scale

COPYRIGHT. GEORGE PHILIP & SON, LTD

on same scale

1:4 500 000

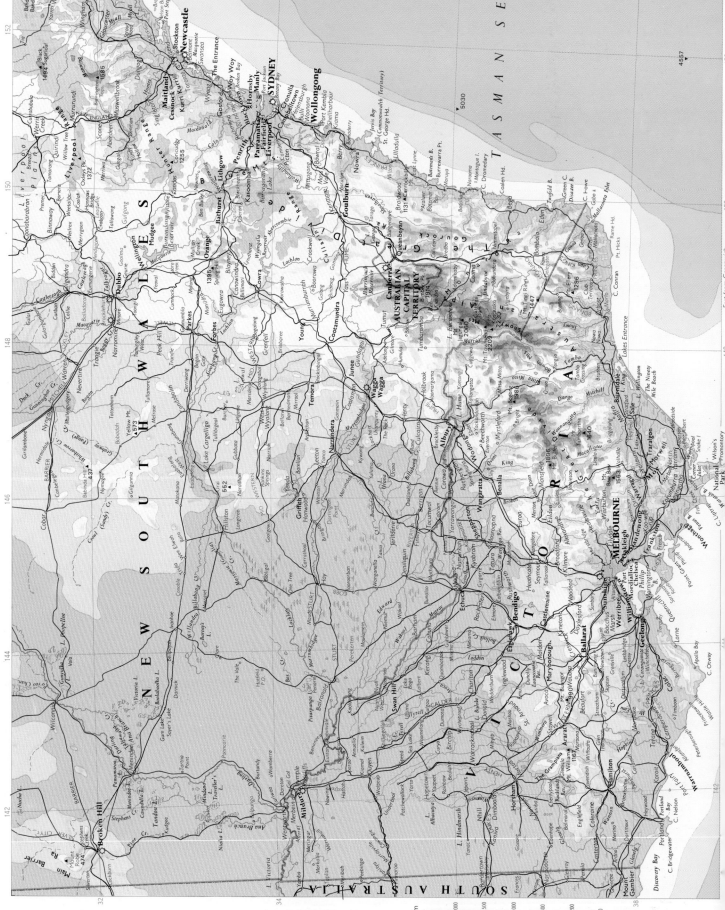

Index

The number printed in bold type against each index entry indicates the map page where the feature will be found. The geographical coordinates which follow the name are sometimes only approximate but are close enough for the place name to be located.

An open square □ signifies that the name refers to an administrative subdivision of a country while a solid square ■ follows the name of a country.

The alphabetical order of names composed of two or more words is governed primarily by the first word and then by the second. This rule applies even if the second word is a description or its abbreviation, R.,L.,I. for example. Names composed of a proper name (St. Lawrence) and a description (Gulf of) are positioned alphabetically by the proper name. If the same place name occurs twice or more times in the index and all are in the same country, each is followed by the name of the administrative subdivision in which it is located. The names are placed in the alphabetical order of the subdivisions. If the same place name occurs twice or more in the index and the places are in different countries they will be followed by their country names, the latter governing the alphabetical order. In a mixture of these situations the primary order is fixed by the alphabetical sequence of the countries and the secondary order by that of the country subdivisions.

A. C. T. – Australian Capital Territory
A. R. – Autonomous Region
A. S. S. R. – Autonomous Soviet Socialist Republic
Afghan. – Afghanistan
Afr. – Africa
Ala. – Alabama
Alas. – Alaska
Alg. – Algeria
Alta. – Alberta
Amer. – America
And. P. – Andhra Pradesh
Ang. – Angola
Arch. – Archipelago
Argent. – Argentina
Ariz. – Arizona
Ark. – Arkansas
Atl. Oc. – Atlantic Ocean
Austral. – Australia
B. – Baie, Bahía, Bay, Bucht, Bugt
B.A. – Buenos Aires
B.C. – British Columbia
Bangla. – Bangladesh
Barr. – Barrage
Bay. – Bayern
Belg. – Belgium
Bol. – Bolshoi
Bots. – Botswana
Br. – British
Bri. – Bridge
Bt. – Bight
Bulg. – Bulgaria
C. – Cabo, Cap, Cape
C. Prov. – Cape Province
C. Rica – Costa Rica
Calif. – California
Camb. – Cambodia
Cambs. – Cambridgeshire
Can. – Canada
Cat. – Cataract, Cataracta
Cent. – Central
Chan. – Channel
Co. – Country
Colo. – Colorado
Conn. – Connecticut
Cord. – Cordillera
Cr. – Creek
Cumb. – Cumbria
Cy. – City
Czech. – Czechoslovakia
D.C. – District of Columbia
Del. – Delaware
Dep. – Dependency
Des. – Desert
Dist. – District
Dj. – Djebel
Dom. Rep. – Dominican Republic
E. – East
Eng. – England
Eq. Guinea – Equatorial Guinea

Fed. – Federal, Federation
Fla. – Florida
For. – Forest
Fr. – France, French
Fr. Gui. – French Guiana
Fs. – Falls
Ft. – Fort
G. – Golf, Golfo, Gulf, Guba
Ga. – Georgia
Germ. – Germany
Gib. – Gibraltar
Gr. – Grande, Great, Greater, Group
Guat. – Guatemala
H.K. – Hong Kong
H.P. – Himachal Pradesh
Hants. – Hampshire
Harb. – Harbor, Harbour
Hd. – Head
Hung. – Hungary
I. of W. – Isle of Wight
I.(s). – Île, Ilha, Insel, Isla, Island
Id. – Idaho
Ill. – Illinois
Ind. – Indiana
Ind. Oc. – Indian Ocean
Ivory C. – Ivory Coast
J. – Jabal, Jabel, Jazira
Junc. – Junction
K. – Kap, Kapp
K. – Kuala
Kal. – Kalmyk A.S.S.R.
Kans. – Kansas
Kor. – Korea
Kpl. – Kapell
Ky. – Kentucky
L. – Lac, Lacul, Lago, Lagoa, Lake, Limni, Loch, Lough
La. – Louisiana
Lancs. – Lancashire
Leb. – Lebanon
Lincs. – Lincolnshire
Lit. – Little
Lr. – Lower
Lt. Ho. – Light House
Mad. P. – Madhya Pradesh
Madag. – Madagascar
Malay. – Malaysia
Man. – Manitoba
Mass. – Massachusetts
Md. – Maryland
Me. – Maine
Mend. – Mendoza
Mer. – Méridionale
Mich. – Michigan
Mid. – Middle
Minn. – Minnesota
Miss. – Mississippi
Mo. – Missouri
Mong. – Mongolia
Mont. – Montana
Moroc. – Morocco
Mozam. – Mozambique

Mt.(e). – Mont, Monte, Monti, Montaña, Mountain
Mys. – Mysore
N. – North, Northern, Nouveau
N.B. – New Brunswick
N.C. – North Carolina
N.D. – North Dakota
N.H. – New Hampshire
N.I. – North Island
N.J. – New Jersey
N. Mex. – New Mexico
N.S. – Nova Scotia
N.S.W. – New South Wales
N.T. – Northern Territory
N.W.T. – North West Territory
N.Y. – New York
N.Z. – New Zealand
Nat. – National
Nat. Mon. – National Monument
Nat. Park. – National Park
Nebr. – Nebraska
Neth. – Netherlands
Nev. – Nevada
Newf. – Newfoundland
Nic. – Nicaragua
Northants. – Northamptonshire
O. – Oued, ouadi
O.F.S. – Orange Free State
Okla. – Oklahoma
Ont. – Ontario
Or. – Orientale
Oreg. – Oregon
Os. – Ostrov
Oz. – Ozero
P. – Pass, Passo, Pasul, Pulau
P.E.I. – Prince Edward Island
P.N.G. – Papua New Guinea
P.O. – Post Office
P. Rico – Puerto Rico
Pa. – Pennsylvania
Pac. Oc. – Pacific Ocean
Pak. – Pakistan
Parc Prov. – Parc Provincial
Pass. – Passage
Pen. – Peninsula, Peninsule
Phil. – Philippines
Pk. – Park, Peak
Plat. – Plateau
P-ov. – Poluostrov
Port. – Portugal, Portuguese
Prom. – Promontory
Prov. – Province, Provincial
Pt. – Point
Pta. – Ponta, Punta
Pte. – Pointe
Qué. – Québec
Queens. – Queensland
R. – Rio, River
R.I. – Rhode Island
R.S.F.S.R. – Russian Soviet Federative Socialist Republic
Ra.(s). – Range(s)

Raj. – Rajasthan
Reg. – Region
Rep. – Republic
Res. – Reserve, Reservoir, Reservation
S. – San, South, Southern
S. Afr. – South Africa
Si. Arab. – Saudi Arabia
S. Austral. – South Australia
S.C. – South Carolina
S.D. – South Dakota
S.I. – South Island
S. Leone – Sierra Leone
S.S.R. – Soviet Socialist Republic
Sa. – Serra, Sierra
Sard. – Sardinia
Sask. – Saskatchewan
Scot. – Scotland
Sd. – Sound
Sept. – Septentrionale
Sib. – Siberia
Span. – Spanish
Sprs. – Springs
St. – Saint
Sta. – Santa, Station
Ste. – Sainte
Sto. – Santo
Str. – Strait, Stretto
Switz. – Switzerland
T.O. – Telegraph Office
Tanz. – Tanzania
Tas. – Tasmania
Tenn. – Tennessee
Terr. – Territory
Tex. – Texas
Tg. – Tanjung
Thai. – Thailand
Trans. – Transvaal
Trin. – Trinidad
U.K. – United Kingdom
U.S.A. – United States of America
U.S.S.R. – Union of Soviet Socialist Republics
Ukr. – Ukraine
Ut.P. – Uttar Pradesh
Va. – Virginia
Vdkhr. – Vodokhranilishche
Venez. – Venezuela
Vic. – Victoria
Viet. – Vietnam
Vol. – Volcano
Vt. – Vermont
W. – Wadi, West
W.A. – Western Australia
W. Isles – Western Isles
Wash. – Washington
Wis. – Wisconsin
Wlkp. – Wielkopolski
Wyo. – Wyoming
Yorks. – Yorkshire
Yugo. – Yugoslavia

Aachen Al Madīnah

A

Aachen 105 50 47N 6 4E
Aadorf 13 47 30N 8 55E
Aalsmeer 105 52 17N 4 43E
Aalst, Neth. 54 50 57N 4 20E
Aalst, Neth. 105 51 23N 5 29E
Aalten 105 51 56N 6 35E
Aarau 106 47 23N 8 4E
Aare, R. 106 47 33N 8 14E
Aarschot 105 50 59N 4 49E
Aba 114 5 10N 7 19E
Abadan 122 30 22N 48 20E
Abade 123 31 8N 52 40E
Abadla 114 31 2N 2 45W
Abaetetuba 87 1 40S 48 50W
Abai 89 25 58S 55 54W
Abakan 121 53 40N 91 10E
Aballetuba 87 1 40S 51 15W
Abamasagi L. 53 50 28N 87 15W
Abarqū 123 31 10N 53 20E
Abashiri 132 44 0N 144 15E
Abaya L. 115 6 30N 37 50E
Abbaye, Pt. 72 46 58N 88 4W
Abbeville, France 101 50 6N 1 49E
Abbeville, La., U.S.A. 75 30 0N 92 7W
Abbeville, S.C., U.S.A. 73 34 12N 82 21W
Abbey 56 50 44N 108 45W
Abbotabad 124 34 10N 73 15E
Abbotsford, B.C., Can. 63 49 5N 122 20W
Abbotsford, Que., Can. 71 45 25N 72 53W
Abbotsford, U.S.A. 74 44 55N 90 20W
Abbott Corners 43 45 3N 72 48W
Abéché 115 13 50N 20 35E
Åbenrå 111 55 3N 9 25E
Abeokuta 114 7 3N 3 19E
Aberaeron 95 52 15N 4 16W
Aberayron = Aberaeron 95 52 15N 4 16W
Abercorn = Mbala 116 8 46S 31 17E
Abercrombie, R. 136 33 54S 149 8E
Aberdare 95 51 43N 3 27W
Aberdaron 95 52 48N 4 41W
Aberdeen, Austral. 136 32 9S 150 56E
Aberdeen, Can. 56 52 20N 106 8W
Aberdeen, U.K. 96 57 9N 2 6W
Aberdeen, Ohio, U.S.A. 77 38 39N 83 46W
Aberdeen, S.D., U.S.A. 74 45 30N 98 30W
Aberdeen, Wash., U.S.A. 80 47 0N 123 50W
Aberdovey 95 52 33N 4 3W
Aberfeldy 96 56 37N 3 50W
Aberfoyle 49 43 28N 80 9W
Abernathy 75 33 49N 101 49W
Abernethy 56 50 45N 103 25W
Aberystwyth 95 52 25N 4 6W
Abidjan 114 5 26N 3 58W
Abilene, Kans., U.S.A. 74 39 0N 97 16W
Abilene, Texas, U.S.A. 75 32 22N 99 40W
Abingdon, Can. 49 43 5N 79 41W
Abingdon, U.K. 95 51 40N 1 17W
Abingdon, Ill., U.S.A. 76 40 53N 90 23W
Abingdon, Va., U.S.A. 73 36 46N 81 56W
Abitau L. 55 60 27N 107 15W
Abitau, R. 55 59 53N 109 3W
Abitibi L. 34 48 40N 79 40W
Abitibi, R. 53 51 3N 80 55W
Abkhaz A.S.S.R. □ 120 43 0N 41 0E
Abkit 121 64 10N 157 10E
Åbo = Turku 111 60 27N 22 14E
Abohar 124 30 10N 74 10E
Abomey 114 7 10N 2 5E
Abondance 103 46 18N 6 42E
Abong Mbang 116 4 0N 13 8E
Aboyne 96 57 4N 2 48W
Abqaiq 122 26 0N 49 45E
Abra Pampa 88 22 43S 65 42W
Abrantes 104 39 24N 8 7W
Abreojos, Pta. 82 26 50N 113 40W
Abreschviller 101 48 39N 7 6E
Abrets, Les 103 45 32N 5 35E
Abrolhos, Arquipélago dos 87 18 0S 38 30W
Abrud 107 46 19N 23 5E
Abruzzi □ 108 42 15N 14 0E
Absaroka Ra. 78 44 40N 110 0W
Abū al Khasib 122 30 25N 48 0E
Abū 'Alī 122 27 20N 49 27E
Abū Dhabī 123 24 28N 54 36E
Abu Hamed 115 19 32N 33 13E
Abu Kamal 122 34 30N 41 0E
Abu Markha 122 25 4N 38 22E
Abû Zabad 116 12 25N 29 10E
Abukumagawa 132 37 30N 140 30E
Abunã 86 9 40S 65 20W
Abunã, R. 86 9 41S 65 20W
Abut Hd. 133 43 7S 170 15E
Acacias 86 3 59N 73 46W
Acadia 59 50 58N 114 4W
Acadia Valley 61 51 8N 110 13W
Acadie, L', R. 45 45 29N 73 16W
Acajutla 84 13 36N 89 50W
Acámbaro 82 20 0N 100 40W
Acaponeta 82 22 30N 105 20W
Acapulco de Juárez 83 16 51N 99 56W
Acarai, Serra 87 1 50N 57 50W
Acarigua 86 9 33N 69 12W
Acatlan 83 18 10N 98 3W
Acayucán 83 17 59N 94 58W
Accomac 72 37 43N 75 40W
Accra 114 5 35N 0 6W
Accrington 94 53 46N 2 22W
Acebal 88 33 20S 60 50W
Aceh □ 126 4 0N 97 30E
Achaguas 86 7 46N 68 14W
Achalpur 124 21 22N 77 32E
Achill 97 53 56N 9 55W
Achill Hd. 97 53 59N 10 15W
Achill I. 97 53 58N 10 5W
Achill Sd. 97 53 53N 9 55W
Achinsk 121 56 20N 90 20E
Ackerman 75 33 20N 89 8W
Ackley 76 42 33N 93 3W
Acklin's I. 85 22 30N 74 0W
Acland, Mt. 135 24 50S 148 20E
Acme 61 51 33N 113 30W
Aconcagua 88 32 50S 70 0W
Aconcagua □ 88 32 15S 70 30W
Aconcagua, Cerro 88 32 39S 70 0W
Aconquija, Mt. 88 27 0S 66 0W
Açores, Is. dos 12 38 44N 29 0W
Acre = 'Akko 115 32 35N 35 4E
Acre □ 86 9 1S 71 0W
Acre, R. 86 10 45S 68 25W
Actinolite 70 44 34N 77 20W
Acton 49 43 38N 80 3W
Acton Vale 41 45 39N 72 34W
Ad Dammam 122 26 20N 50 5E
Ad Dar al Hamrā 122 27 20N 37 45E
Ad Dawhah 123 25 15N 51 35E
Ad Dilam 122 23 55N 47 10E
Ada, Minn., U.S.A. 74 47 20N 96 30W
Ada, Ohio, U.S.A. 77 40 46N 83 49W
Ada, Okla., U.S.A. 75 34 50N 96 45W
Adair C. 17 71 50N 71 0W
Adaja, R. 104 41 15N 4 50W
Adam 123 22 15N 57 28E
Adamaoua, Massif de l' 114 7 20N 12 20E
Adamawa Highlands = Adamaoua 114 7 20N 12 20E
Adamello, Mt. 108 46 10N 10 34E
Adaminaby 136 36 0S 148 45E
Adams, Mass., U.S.A. 71 42 38N 73 8W
Adams, N.Y., U.S.A. 71 43 50N 76 3W
Adams, Wis., U.S.A. 74 43 59N 89 50W
Adam's Bridge 124 9 15N 79 40E
Adams Center 71 43 51N 76 1W
Adams L. 63 51 10N 119 40W
Adams Mt. 80 46 10N 121 28W
Adam's Peak 124 6 55N 80 45E
Adams, R. 63 51 25N 119 27W
Adamsville 43 45 17N 72 47W
Adana 122 37 0N 35 16E
Adapazari 122 40 48N 30 25E
Adare, C. 91 71 0S 171 0E
Adavale 135 25 52S 144 32E
Adda, R. 108 45 25N 9 30E
Addie 61 48 55N 116 10W
Addis Ababa = Addis Abeba 115 9 2N 38 42E
Addis Abeba 115 9 2N 38 42E
Addison, Ill., U.S.A. 77 41 56N 87 59W
Addison, N.Y., U.S.A. 70 42 9N 77 15W
Addison, Vt., U.S.A. 71 44 6N 73 18W
Addu Atoll 119 0 30S 73 0E
Addyston 77 39 8N 84 43W
Adel, Ga., U.S.A. 73 31 10N 83 28W
Adel, Iowa, U.S.A. 76 41 37N 94 1W
Adelaide, Austral. 135 34 52S 138 30E
Adelaide, Bahamas 84 25 0N 77 31W
Adelaide I. 91 67 15S 68 30W
Adelaide Pen. 65 68 15N 97 30W
Adelanto 81 34 35N 117 22W
Adélie, Terre 91 67 0S 140 0E
Aden 115 12 50N 45 0E
Aden, G. of 115 13 0N 50 0E
Adi 127 4 15S 133 30E
Adieu, C. 134 32 0S 132 10E
Adige, R. 108 45 9N 11 25E
Adilabad 124 19 33N 78 35E
Adin 78 41 10N 121 0W
Adin Khel 124 32 45N 68 5E
Adirondack Mts. 71 44 0N 74 15W
Adlavik Is. 36 55 2N 58 45W
Admiral 56 49 43N 108 1W
Admiral's Beach 37 47 1N 53 39W
Admiralty B. 91 62 0S 59 0W
Admiralty G. 134 14 20S 125 55E
Admiralty I., Can. 65 69 25N 101 10W
Admiralty I., U.S.A. 67 57 40N 134 35W
Admiralty In. 65 72 30N 86 0W
Admiralty Inlet 78 48 0N 122 40W
Admiralty Ra. 91 72 0S 164 0E
Adonara 127 8 15S 123 5E
Adoni 124 15 33N 77 18W
Adour, R. 102 43 32N 1 32W
Adra 104 36 43N 3 3W
Adrano 108 37 40N 14 49E
Adrar 114 27 51N 0 11W
Adrian, Mich., U.S.A. 77 41 55N 84 0W
Adrian, Mo., U.S.A. 76 38 24N 94 21W
Adrian, Tex., U.S.A. 75 35 19N 102 37W
Adriatic Sea 108 43 0N 16 0E
Adua 127 1 45S 129 50E
Advocate Harbour 39 45 20N 64 47W
Adwa, Ethiopia 115 14 15N 38 52E
Adwa, Si Arab. 122 27 15N 42 35E
Adzhar A.S.S.R. □ 120 42 0N 42 0E
Ægean Sea 109 37 0N 25 0E
Aerht'ai Shan 129 46 40N 92 45E
*Afars & Issas, Terr. of ■ 115 11 30N 42 15E
Affric, R. 96 57 15N 4 50W
Afghanistan ■ 124 33 0N 65 0E
Afif 122 23 53N 42 56E
Afognak I. 67 58 10N 152 50W
Africa 112 10 0N 20 0E
Afton 71 42 14N 75 31W
Afuá 87 0 15S 50 10W
Afula 115 32 37N 35 17E
Afyon Karahisar 122 38 45N 30 33E
Agadès 114 16 58N 7 59E
Agadir 114 30 28N 9 35W
Agano, R. 132 37 50N 139 30E
Agapa 121 71 27N 89 15E
Agartala 125 23 50N 91 23E
Agassiz 63 49 14N 121 46W
Agattu I. 67 52 25N 172 30E
Agawa, R. 53 47 23N 84 40W
Agde 102 43 19N 3 28E
Agde, C. d' 102 43 16N 3 28E
Agen 102 44 12N 0 38E
Aghil Mts. 124 36 0N 77 0E
Aghil Pass 124 36 15N 76 35E
Agincourt 50 43 47N 79 17W
Aginskoye 121 51 6N 114 32E
Agly, R. 102 42 46N 3 3E
Agnes L. 52 48 15N 91 20W
Agon 100 49 2N 1 34W
Agout, R. 102 43 47N 1 41E
Agra 124 27 17N 77 58E
Agrado 86 2 15N 75 46W
Ağri Daği 122 39 50N 44 15E
Agri, R. 108 40 17N 16 15E
Agrigento 108 37 19N 13 33E
Agrinion 109 38 37N 21 27E
Agua Caliente, Mexico 82 26 30N 108 20W
Agua Caliente, U.S.A. 81 32 29N 116 59W
Agua Caliente Springs 81 32 56N 116 19W
Agua Clara 87 20 25S 52 45W
Agua Hechicero 81 32 26N 116 14W
Agua Prieta 82 31 20N 109 32W
Aguadas 86 5 40N 75 38W
Aguadilla 85 18 27N 67 10W
Aguadulce 84 8 15N 80 32W
Aguanaval, R. 82 23 45N 103 10W
Aguanga 81 33 27N 116 51W
Aguanus, R. 38 50 13N 62 5W
Aguapey, R. 88 29 7S 56 36W
Aguaray Guazú, R. 88 24 47S 57 19W
Aguarico, R. 86 0 0 77 30W
Aguas Blancas 88 24 15S 69 55W
Aguas Calientes, Sierra de 88 25 26S 67 27W
Aguascalientes 82 22 0N 102 12W
Aguascalientes □ 82 22 0N 102 20W
Aguilares 88 27 26S 65 35W
Aguilas 104 37 23N 1 35W
Aguja, C. de la 86 11 18N 74 12W
Aguja, Pta. 86 6 0S 81 0W
Agulhas Basin 16 45 0S 25 0E
Agulhas, Kaap 117 34 52S 20 0E
Agung 126 8 20S 115 28E
Agusan, R. 127 9 20N 125 50E
Ahaggar 114 23 0N 6 30E
Ahar 122 38 35N 47 0E
Ahaura 133 42 20S 171 32E
Ahimanawa Ra. 14 39 5S 176 30E
Ahipara B. 133 35 5S 173 5E
Ahiri 124 19 30N 80 0E
Ahlen 105 51 45N 7 52E
Ahmadabad (Ahmedabad) 124 23 0N 72 40E
Ahmadnagar (Ahmednagar) 124 19 7N 74 46E
Ahmadpur 124 29 12N 71 10E
Ahome 82 25 55N 109 11W
Ahsā, Wahatā al 122 25 50N 49 0E
Ahuachapán 84 13 54N 89 52W
Ahvāz 122 31 20N 48 40E
Ahvenanmaa 111 60 15N 20 0E
Aibaq 123 36 15N 68 5E
Aichi-ken □ 132 35 0N 137 15E
Aignay-le-Duc 101 47 40N 4 43E
Aigre 102 45 54N 0 1E
Aigua 89 34 13S 54 46W
Aiguebelle, Parc 40 48 30N 78 45W
Aigueperse 102 46 3N 3 13E
Aigues-Mortes 103 43 35N 4 12E
Aiguilles 103 44 47N 6 51E
Aiguillon 102 44 18N 0 21E
Aiguillon, L' 102 46 20N 1 16W
Aigurande 102 46 27N 1 49E
Aihun 130 49 55N 127 30E
Aija 86 9 50S 77 45W
Aijal 125 23 40N 92 44E
Aiken 73 33 34N 81 50W
Aillant-sur-Tholon 101 47 52N 3 20E
Aillik 36 55 11N 59 18W
Ailly-sur-Noye 101 49 45N 2 20E
Ailsa Craig 46 43 8N 81 33W
Ailsa Craig, I. 96 55 15N 5 7W
Aim 121 59 0N 133 55E
Aimere 127 8 45S 121 3E
Aimogasta 88 28 33S 66 50W
Aimorés 87 19 30S 41 4W
Aimorés, Serra dos 87 17 50S 40 30W
Ain □ 103 46 5N 5 20E
Ain Banaiyan 123 23 0N 51 0E
Ain Dār 122 25 55N 49 10E
Ain, R. 103 45 52N 5 11E
Ainslie, L. 39 46 8N 61 11W
Ainsworth 74 42 33N 99 52W
Aion 121 69 50N 169 0E
Aipe 86 3 13N 75 15W
Aïr 114 18 30N 8 0E
Air Force I. 65 67 58N 74 5W
Airaines 101 49 58N 1 55E
Aird, The, C. 96 57 26N 4 30W
Airdrie, Can. 61 51 18N 114 2W
Airdrie, U.K. 96 55 53N 3 57W
Aire 101 50 37N 2 22E
Aire, R., France 101 49 18N 5 0E
Aire, R., U.K. 94 53 42N 1 30W
Aire-sur-l'Adour 102 43 42N 0 15W
Airvault 100 46 50N 0 8W
Aishihik 67 61 40N 137 46W
Aisne □ 101 49 42N 3 40E
Aisne, R. 101 49 26N 2 50E
Aitkin 52 46 32N 93 43W
Aitush 129 39 54N 75 40E
Aiud 107 46 19N 23 44E
Aix-en-Provence 103 43 32N 5 27E
Aix-la-Chapelle = Aachen 105 50 47N 6 4E
Aix-les-Bains 103 45 41N 5 53E
Aix-sur-Vienne 102 45 48N 1 8E
Aiyansh 54 55 17N 129 2W
Aiyina 109 37 45N 23 26E
Aiyion 109 38 15N 22 5E
Aizenay 100 46 44N 1 38W
Ajaccio 103 41 55N 8 40E
Ajaccio, G. d' 103 41 52N 8 40E
Ajalpán 83 18 22N 97 15W
Ajanta Ra. 124 20 28N 75 50E
Ajax 51 43 50N 79 1W
'Ajlun 115 32 18N 35 47E
Ajman 123 25 25N 55 30E
Ajmer 124 26 28N 74 37E
Ajo 79 32 18N 112 54W
Ak Dağ 122 36 30N 30 0E
Akaroa 133 43 49S 172 59E
Akaroa Harb. 15 43 54S 172 59E
Akashi 132 34 45N 135 0E
Akelamo 127 1 35N 129 40E
Akershus Fylke □ 111 60 10N 11 15E
Aketi 116 2 38N 23 47E
Akhelóös, R. 109 39 5N 21 25E
Akhisar 122 38 56N 27 48E
Akiak 67 60 50N 161 12W
Akimiski I. 34 52 50N 81 30W
Akita 132 39 45N 140 0E
Akita-ken □ 132 39 40N 140 30E
'Akko 115 32 35N 35 4E
Akkol 120 43 36N 70 45E
Aklavik 64 68 12N 135 0W
Akola 124 20 40N 77 2E
Akpatok I. 36 60 25N 68 8W
Akranes 110 64 19N 22 6W
Akron, Can. 53 48 55N 84 7W
Akron, Colo., U.S.A. 74 40 13N 103 15W
Akron, Ind., U.S.A. 77 41 2N 86 1W
Akron, Ohio, U.S.A. 70 41 7N 81 31W
Akrotiri, Ákra 109 40 26N 25 27W
Aksaray 122 38 25N 34 2E
Aksarka 120 66 31N 67 50E
Aksehir 122 38 18N 31 30E
Aksenovo Zilovskoye 121 53 20N 117 40E
Aksu 129 41 4N 80 5E
Aksum 115 14 5N 38 40E
Aktogay 120 44 25N 76 44E
Aktyubinsk 120 50 17N 57 10E
Akulurak 67 62 40N 164 35W
Akun I. 67 54 15N 165 30W
Akureyri 110 65 40N 18 6W
Akutan I. 67 53 30N 166 0W
Al Amādiyah 122 37 5N 43 30E
Al Amārah 122 31 55N 47 15E
Al 'Aqabah 122 29 37N 35 0E
Al Ashkhara 123 21 50N 59 30E
Al Badi 122 22 0N 46 35E
Al Basrah 122 30 30N 47 50E
Al Dīwaniyah 122 32 0N 45 0E
Al Fallujah 122 33 20N 43 55E
Al Fāw 122 30 0N 48 30E
Al Hadithan 122 34 0N 41 13E
Al Hāmad 122 31 30N 39 30E
Al Hamar 122 22 23N 46 6E
Al Hariq 122 23 29N 46 27E
Al Hasakah 122 36 35N 40 45E
Al Havy 122 32 5N 46 5E
Al Hillah, Iraq 122 32 30N 44 25E
Al Hillah, Si Arab. 122 23 35N 46 50E
Al Hilwah 122 23 24N 46 48E
Al Hindiyah 122 32 30N 44 10E
Al Hūfuf 122 25 25N 49 45E
Al Ittihad = Madinat al Shaab 115 12 50N 45 0E
Al Jahrah 122 29 25N 47 40E
Al Jalāmid 122 31 20N 39 45E
Al Jawf 115 24 10N 23 24E
Al Jubail 122 27 0N 49 50E
Al Khābūrah 123 23 57N 57 5E
Al Kūt 122 32 30N 46 0E
Al Kuwayt 122 29 20N 48 0E
Al Lādhiqiyah 122 35 30N 35 45E
Al Madīnah 122 24 35N 39 52E

* *Renamed Djibouti* ■

Al Majma'ah	122	25 57N	45 22 E	Albuquerque, Cayos de	84	12 10N	81 50W	Algonquin Prov. Pk.	47	45 50N	78 30W	Alsásua	104	42 54N	2 10W
Al Manamāh	123	26 10N	50 30 E	Alburg	43	44 58N	73 19W	Alhama de Murcia	104	37 51N	1 25W	Alsdorf	105	50 53N	6 10 E
Al Marj	115	32 25N	20 30 E	Alburquerque	104	39 15N	6 59W	Alhambra, Can.	61	52 20N	114 40W	Alsten	110	65 58N	12 40 E
Al Mawsil	122	36 15N	43 5 E	Alcalá de Henares	104	40 28N	3 22W	Alhambra, Calif., U.S.A.	81	34 8N	118 10W	Alta	110	69 57N	23 10 E
Al Miqdadīyah	122	34 0N	45 0 E	Alcalá la Real	104	37 27N	3 57W	Alhambra, Ill., U.S.A.	76	38 52N	89 45W	Alta Gracia	88	31 40 S	64 30W
Al Mubarraz	122	25 30N	49 40 E	Alcamo	108	37 59N	12 55 E	Ali al Gharbi	122	32 30N	46 45 E	Alta Lake	63	50 10N	123 0W
Al Muharraq	123	26 15N	50 40 E	Alcañiz	104	41 2N	0 8W	Ali Khel	124	33 56N	69 35 E	Alta Sierra	81	35 42N	118 33W
Al Musayyib	122	32 40N	44 25 E	Alcântara	87	2 20 S	44 30W	Aliābād	123	28 10N	57 35 E	Alta Vista	48	45 23N	75 40W
Al Muwaylih	122	27 40N	35 30 E	Alcántara	104	39 41N	6 57W	Aliakmon, R.	109	40 10N	22 0 E	Altaelva	110	69 46N	23 45 E
Al Qāmishli	122	37 10N	41 10 E	Alcantara L.	55	60 57N	108 9W	Alicante	104	38 23N	0 30W	Altafjorden	110	70 5N	23 5 E
Al Qatif	122	26 35N	50 0 E	Alcaraz, Sierra de	104	38 40N	2 20W	Alice, Can.	47	45 47N	77 14W	Altagracia	86	10 45N	71 30W
Al Quaisūmah	122	28 10N	46 20 E	Alcaudete	104	37 35N	4 5W	Alice, U.S.A.	75	27 47N	98 1W	Altai	129	48 6N	87 2 E
Al Quraiyat	123	23 17N	58 53 E	Alcázar de San Juan	104	39 24N	3 12W	Alice Arm	54	55 29N	129 31W	Altai = Aerhatai Shan	129	46 40N	92 45 E
Al Qurnah	122	31 1N	47 25 E	Alcira	104	39 9N	0 30W	Alice Springs	134	23 40 S	135 50 E	Altamaha, R.	73	31 50N	82 0W
Al 'Ula	122	26 35N	38 0 E	Alcoa	73	35 50N	84 0W	Alicedale	117	33 15 S	26 4 E	Altamira, Brazil	87	3 0 S	52 10W
Al Uqayr	122	25 40N	50 15 E	Alcobaça	104	39 32N	9 0W	Aliceville	73	33 9N	88 10W	Altamira, Chile	88	25 47 S	69 51W
Al' Uwayqilah	122	30 30N	42 10 E	Alcova	78	42 37N	106 52W	Alida	57	49 25N	101 55W	Altamira, Colomb.	86	2 3N	75 47W
Al 'Uyūn	122	26 30N	43 50 E	Alcoy	104	38 43N	0 30W	Aligarh	124	27 55N	78 10 E	Altamira, Mexico	83	22 24N	97 55W
Al Wakrah	123	25 10N	51 40 E	Aldabra Is.	16	9 22 S	46 28 E	Aligudarz	122	33 25N	49 45 E	Altamont, Ill., U.S.A.	77	39 4N	88 45W
Al Warī 'ah	122	27 50N	47 30 E	Aldama	83	22 25N	98 4W	Aling Kangri,Range	125	31 45N	84 45 E	Altamont, N.Y., U.S.A.	71	42 43N	74 3W
Ala Shan	129	40 0N	104 0 E	Aldan	121	58 40N	125 30 E	Alingsas	111	57 56N	12 31 E	Altanbulag	130	50 16N	106 30 E
Alabama □	73	33 0N	87 0W	Aldan, R.	121	62 30N	135 10 E	Alipur	124	29 25N	70 55 E	Altar	82	30 40N	111 50W
Alabama, R.	73	31 30N	87 35W	Aldeburgh	95	52 9N	1 35 E	Alipur Duar	125	26 30N	89 35 E	Altario	61	51 55N	110 9W
Alabaster	46	44 10N	83 33W	Alder	78	45 27N	112 3W	Aliquippa	70	40 38N	80 18W	Altata	82	24 30N	108 0W
Alagôa Grande	87	7 3 S	35 35W	Alder Pk.	80	35 53N	121 22W	Aliwal North	117	30 45 S	26 45 E	Altavista	72	37 9N	79 22W
Alagôas □	87	9 0 S	36 0W	Alderney, I.	100	49 42N	2 12W	Alix	61	52 24N	113 11W	Altkirch	101	47 37N	7 15 E
Alagoinhas	87	12 0 S	38 20W	Aldershot, N.S., Can.	39	45 6N	64 31W	Aljustrel	104	37 55N	8 10W	Alto Araguaia	87	17 15 S	53 20W
Alajuela	84	10 2N	84 8W	Aldershot, Ont., Can.	48	43 18N	79 51W	Alkmaar	105	52 37N	4 45 E	Alto Cuchumatanes	82	15 30N	91 10W
Alameda, Can.	57	49 16N	102 17W	Aldershot, U.K.	95	51 15N	0 43W	All American Canal	79	32 45N	115 0W	Alto del Inca	88	24 10 S	68 10W
Alameda, Calif., U.S.A.	80	37 46N	122 15W	Aldersyde	54	50 40N	113 53W	Allahabad	125	25 25N	81 58 E	Alto Molocue	117	15 50 S	37 35 E
Alameda, Idaho, U.S.A.	78	43 2N	112 30W	Aledo	76	41 10N	90 50W	Allakaket	67	66 30N	152 45W	Alto Paraná □	89	25 0 S	54 50W
Alameda, N. Mex., U.S.A.	79	35 10N	106 43W	Alegre	89	20 50 S	41 30W	Allakh Yun	121	60 50N	137 5 E	Alto Uruguay, R.	89	27 0 S	53 30W
Alamitos, Sierra de los	82	26 30N	102 20W	Alegrete	89	29 40 S	56 0W	Allan	56	51 53N	106 4W	Alton, Can.	49	43 54N	80 5W
Alamo	81	37 21N	115 10W	Aleisk	120	52 40N	83 0 E	Allanburg	49	43 5N	79 12W	Alton, U.S.A.	76	38 55N	90 5W
Alamo Crossing	81	34 16N	113 33W	Alejandro Selkirk, I.	15	33 50 S	80 15W	Allanche	102	45 14N	2 57 E	Altona, Austral.	136	37 51 S	144 50 E
Alamogordo	79	32 59N	106 0W	Aleksandrov Gay.	120	50 15N	48 35 E	Allanwater	52	50 14N	90 10W	Altona, Man., Can.	57	49 6N	97 33W
Alamos	82	27 0N	109 0W	Aleksandrovsk-Sakhaliniskiy	121	50 50N	142 20 E	Allard, L.	38	50 32N	63 31W	Altona, Ont., Can.	50	43 58N	79 12W
Alamosa	79	37 30N	106 0W	Aleksandrovskiy Zavod	121	50 40N	117 50 E	Allardville	39	47 28N	65 29W	Altona, Ger.	106	53 32N	9 56 E
Åland	111	60 15N	20 0 E	Aleksandrovskoye	120	60 35N	77 50 E	Allassac	102	45 15N	1 29 E	Altoona, Iowa, U.S.A.	76	41 39N	93 28W
Ålands hav	111	60 10N	19 30 E	Além Paraiba	89	21 52 S	42 41W	Allegan	77	42 32N	85 52W	Altoona, Pa., U.S.A.	70	40 32N	78 24W
Alanson	46	45 27N	84 47W	Alemania, Argent.	88	25 40 S	65 30W	Allegany	70	41 30N	78 30W	Alturas	78	41 36N	120 37W
Alanya	122	36 38N	32 0 E	Alemania, Chile	88	25 10 S	69 55W	Alleghany Mts.	72	38 0N	80 0W	Altus	75	34 30N	99 25W
Alapayevsk	120	57 52N	61 42 E	Alençon	100	48 27N	0 4 E	Allegheny, R.	70	41 14N	79 50W	Altyn Tagh	129	39 0N	90 0 E
Alashanchih	130	38 58N	105 14 E	Alentejo, Alto-	104	39 0N	7 40W	Allegheny Res.	70	42 0N	78 55W	Alunite	81	35 59N	114 55W
Alaska □	67	65 0N	150 0W	Alentejo, Baixo-	104	38 0N	8 30W	Allègre	102	45 12N	3 41 E	Alusi	127	7 35 S	131 40 E
Alaska, G. of	67	58 0N	145 0W	Alenuihaha Chan.	67	20 25N	156 0W	Allen, Bog of	97	53 15N	7 0W	Alva	75	36 50N	98 50W
Alaska Highway	54	60 0N	130 0W	Aleppo	122	36 10N	37 15 E	Allen, L.	97	54 30N	8 5W	Alvarado, Mexico	83	18 40N	95 50W
Alaska Pen.	67	56 0N	160 0W	Aléria	103	42 5N	9 26 E	Allende	82	28 20N	100 50W	Alvarado, U.S.A.	75	32 25N	97 15W
Alaska Range	67	62 50N	151 0W	Alert	65	83 2N	60 0W	Allentown	71	40 36N	75 30W	Alvaro Obregón, Presa	82	27 55N	109 52W
Alatyr	120	54 45N	46 35 E	Alert B.	62	50 30N	127 35W	Alleppey	124	9 30N	76 28 E	Alvear	88	29 5 S	56 30W
Alausi	86	2 0 S	78 50W	Alès	103	44 9N	4 5 E	Allevard	103	45 24N	6 5 E	Alvena	56	52 31N	106 1W
Alava, C.	78	48 10N	124 40W	Alessándria	108	44 54N	8 37 E	Alliance, Can.	61	52 26N	111 47W	Alvesta	111	56 54N	14 35 E
Alba	108	44 41N	8 1 E	Ålesund	111	62 28N	6 12 E	Alliance, Nebr., U.S.A.	74	42 10N	102 50W	Alvin	75	29 23N	95 12W
Alba-Iulia	107	46 8N	23 39 E	Alet-les-Bains	102	43 0N	2 14 E	Alliance, Ohio, U.S.A.	70	40 53N	81 7W	Alvinston	46	42 49N	81 52W
Albacete	104	39 0N	1 50W	Aleutian Is.	67	52 0N	175 0W	Allier □	102	46 25N	3 0 E	Alvkarleby	111	60 32N	17 40 E
Albanel	41	48 53N	72 27W	Aleutian Ra.	67	55 0N	155 0W	Allier, R.	101	46 57N	3 4 E	Älvsborgs län □	111	58 30N	12 30 E
Albanel, L.	36	50 55N	73 12W	Alex Graham, Mt.	63	52 4N	122 52W	Alliford Bay	62	53 12N	131 58W	Alvsbyn	110	65 40N	20 0 E
Albania ■	109	41 0N	20 0 E	Alexander	74	47 51N	103 40W	Allison	76	42 45N	92 48W	Alwar	124	27 38N	76 34 E
Albany, Austral.	134	35 1 S	117 58 E	Alexander Arch.	67	57 0N	135 0W	Allison Harbour	62	51 2N	127 29W	Alyangula	135	13 55 S	136 30 E
Albany, Ga., U.S.A.	73	31 40N	84 10W	Alexander B.	117	28 36 S	16 33 E	Alliston	46	44 9N	79 52W	Alyaskitovyy	121	64 45N	141 30 E
Albany, Ind., U.S.A.	77	40 18N	85 13W	Alexander City	73	32 58N	85 57W	Alloa	96	56 7N	3 49W	Alzada	74	45 3N	104 22W
Albany, Minn., U.S.A.	74	45 37N	94 38W	Alexander I.	91	69 0 S	70 0W	Allos	103	44 15N	6 38 E	Am Timan	115	11 0N	20 10 E
Albany, Mo., U.S.A.	76	40 15N	94 20W	Alexandra, Austral.	136	37 8 S	145 40 E	Alluviaq, Fj.	36	59 27N	65 10W	Amadeus, L.	134	24 54 S	131 0 E
Albany, N.Y., U.S.A.	71	42 35N	73 47W	Alexandra, N.Z.	133	45 14 S	169 25 E	Alma, N.B., Can.	39	45 36N	64 57W	Amadi	116	3 40N	26 40 E
Albany, Oreg., U.S.A.	78	44 41N	123 0W	Alexandra Falls	54	60 29N	116 18W	Alma, Ont., Can.	49	43 44N	80 30W	Amadia	122	37 6N	43 30 E
Albany, Tex., U.S.A.	75	32 45N	99 20W	Alexandretta = Iskenderun	129	36 32N	36 10 E	Alma, Qué., Can.	41	48 35N	71 40W	Amadjuak	65	64 0N	72 39W
Albany, Wis., U.S.A.	76	42 43N	89 26W	Alexandria, B.C., Can.	63	52 35N	122 27W	Alma, Kans., U.S.A.	74	39 1N	96 22W	Amadjuak L.	65	65 0N	71 8W
Albany, R.	34	52 17N	81 31W	Alexandria, Ont., Can.	47	45 19N	74 38W	Alma, Mich., U.S.A.	46	43 25N	84 40W	Amadore	70	43 12N	82 36W
Albardón	88	31 20 S	68 30W	Alexandria, S. Afr.	117	33 38 S	26 28 E	Alma, Nebr., U.S.A.	74	40 10N	99 25W	Amaga	86	6 3N	75 42W
Albarracin, Sierra de	104	40 30N	1 30W	Alexandria, Ind., U.S.A.	77	40 18N	85 40W	Alma, Wis., U.S.A.	74	44 19N	91 54W	Amagasaki	132	34 42N	135 20 E
Albatross B.	135	12 45 S	141 30 E	Alexandria, Ky., U.S.A.	77	38 58N	84 23W	Alma Ata	120	43 15N	76 57 E	Amakusa-Shotō	132	32 15N	130 10 E
Albemarle	73	35 27N	80 15W	Alexandria, La., U.S.A.	75	31 20N	92 30W	Almada	104	38 40N	9 9W	Amål	111	59 2N	12 40 E
Albemarle Sd.	73	36 0N	76 30W	Alexandria, Minn., U.S.A.	74	45 50N	95 20W	Almadén	104	38 49N	4 52W	Amalfi	86	6 55N	75 4W
Alberche, R.	104	40 10N	4 30W	Alexandria, Mo., U.S.A.	76	40 27N	91 28W	Almanor, L.	78	40 15N	121 11W	Amalner	124	21 5N	75 5 E
Alberdi	88	26 14 S	58 20W	Alexandria, S.D., U.S.A.	74	43 40N	97 45W	Almansa	104	38 51N	1 5W	Amambai	89	23 5 S	55 13W
Alberga, R.	134	26 50 S	133 40 E	Alexandria, Va., U.S.A.	72	38 47N	77 1W	Almanzor, Pico de	104	40 15N	5 18W	Amambai, R.	89	23 22 S	53 56W
Alberni	54	49 20N	124 50W	Alexandria = El Iskandarīya	115	31 0N	30 0 E	Almanzora, R.	104	37 22N	2 21W	Amambay □	89	23 0 S	56 0W
Albert, Can.	35	45 51N	64 38W	Alexandria Bay	71	44 20N	75 52W	Almazán	104	41 30N	2 30W	Amambay, Cordillera de	89	20 30 S	56 0W
Albert, France	101	50 0N	2 38 E	Alexandrina, L.	135	35 25 S	139 10 E	Almeirim	87	1 30 S	52 0W	Amami-guntō	131	28 0N	129 0 E
Albert Canyon	63	51 8N	117 41W	Alexandroúpolis	109	40 50N	25 54 E	Almelo	105	52 22N	6 42 E	Amanda Park	80	47 28N	123 55W
Albert L.	78	42 40N	120 8W	Alexis	76	41 4N	90 33W	Almendralejo	104	38 41N	6 26W	Amangeldy	120	50 10N	65 10 E
Albert Lea	74	43 32N	93 20W	Alexis Creek	62	52 10N	123 20W	Almeria	104	36 52N	2 32W	Amapá	87	2 5N	50 50W
Albert, L. = Mobutu Sese Seko, L.	116	1 30N	31 0 E	Alexis, R.	36	52 33N	56 8W	Almirante	84	9 10N	82 30W	Amapá □	87	1 40N	52 0W
Albert Nile, R.	116	3 16N	31 38 E	Alfenas	89	21 40 S	44 0W	Almont	46	42 55N	83 2W	Amara	122	31 57N	47 12 E
Albert Park	58	50 24N	104 38W	Alford	96	57 13N	2 42W	Almonte	47	45 14N	76 12W	Amarante	87	6 14 S	42 50W
Albert Town	85	22 37N	74 33 E	Alfred, Me., U.S.A.	71	43 28N	70 40W	Almora	124	29 38N	79 4 E	Amaranth	57	50 36N	98 43W
Alberta □	54	54 40N	115 0W	Alfred, N.Y., U.S.A.	70	42 15N	77 45W	Alnwick	94	55 25N	1 42W	Amaravati = Amraoti	124	20 55N	77 45 E
Alberta Beach	60	53 40N	114 21W	Alfreton	94	53 6N	1 22W	Alo Tau, mts.	129	45 30N	80 40 E	Amargosa	87	13 2 S	39 36W
Alberti	88	35 1 S	60 16W	Alftanes	110	64 29N	22 10W	Alon	125	22 12N	95 5 E	Amargosa, R.	81	36 14N	116 51W
Alberton, Ont., Can.	49	43 11N	80 5W	Alga	120	49 53N	57 20 E	Alonsa	55	50 50N	99 0W	Amargosa Ra., mts	81	36 25N	116 40W
Alberton, P.E.I., Can.	39	46 50N	64 0W	Alganac	70	42 36N	82 34W	Alor, I.	127	8 15 S	124 30 E	Amarillo	75	35 14N	101 46W
Albertville	103	45 40N	6 22 E	Algarve	104	37 15N	8 10W	Alor Setar	128	6 7N	100 22 E	Amaro, Mt.	108	42 5N	14 6 E
Albertville = Kalemie	116	5 55 S	29 9 E	Algeciras	104	36 9N	5 28W	Alpaugh	80	35 53N	119 29W	Amarpur	125	23 30N	91 45 E
Alberz, Reshteh-Ye Kūkhā-Ye	123	36 0N	52 0 E	Algemesi	104	39 11N	0 27W	Alpena	46	45 6N	83 24W	Amasra	122	41 45N	32 30 E
Albi	102	43 56N	2 9 E	Alger	114	36 42N	3 8 E	Alpes-de-Haute-Provence □	103	44 8N	6 10 E	Amasya	122	40 40N	35 50 E
Albia	76	41 0N	92 50W	Algeria ■	114	35 10N	3 11 E	Alpes-Maritimes □	103	43 55N	7 10 E	Amatignak I.	67	51 19N	179 10W
Albina	87	5 37N	54 15W	Alghero	108	40 34N	8 20 E	Alpha, Austral.	135	23 39 S	146 37 E	Amatitlán	84	14 29N	90 38W
Albion, Idaho, U.S.A.	78	42 21N	113 37W	Algiers = Alger	114	36 42N	3 8 E	Alpha, U.S.A.	76	41 11N	90 23W	Amazon, R.	87	2 0 S	53 30W
Albion, Ill., U.S.A.	77	38 23N	88 4W	Algoabaai	117	33 50 S	25 45 E	Alphen	105	51 29N	4 58 E	Amazonas □, Brazil	86	4 20 S	64 0W
Albion, Ind., U.S.A.	77	41 24N	85 25W	Algoma, Oreg., U.S.A.	78	42 25N	121 54W	Alphonse, I.	16	7 0 S	52 45 E	Amazonas □, Colomb.	86	1 0 S	72 0W
Albion, Mich., U.S.A.	77	42 15N	84 45W	Algoma, Wis., U.S.A.	72	44 35N	87 27W	Alpi Craie	101	45 40N	7 0 E	Amazonas □, Venez.	86	3 30N	66 0W
Albion, Nebr., U.S.A.	74	41 47N	98 0W	Algona	76	43 1N	94 10W	Alpine, Ariz., U.S.A.	79	33 57N	109 4W	Amazonas, R.	87	2 0 S	53 30W
Albion, Pa., U.S.A.	70	41 53N	80 21W	Algonac	46	42 37N	82 32W	Alpine, Calif., U.S.A.	81	32 50N	116 46W	Ambala	124	30 23N	76 56 E
Ålborg	111	57 2N	9 54 E	Algonquin	77	42 10N	88 17W	Alpine, Tex., U.S.A.	75	30 25N	103 35W	Ambalavao	117	21 50 S	46 56 E
Albreda	63	52 35N	119 10W					Alps	106	47 0N	8 0 E	Ambam	116	2 20N	11 15 E
Albuquerque	79	35 5N	106 47W					Alsace	101	48 15N	7 25 E	Ambarchik	121	69 40N	162 20 E
								Alsask	56	51 21N	109 59W	Ambato	86	1 5 S	78 42W

3

Ambato, Sierra de **Aquiles Serdán**

Name	Page	Lat.	Long.
Ambato, Sierra de	**88**	28 25N	66 10W
Ambatolampy	**117**	19 20S	47 35E
Ambatondrazaka	**117**	17 55S	48 28E
Ambeno	**127**	9 20S	124 30E
Amberg	**106**	49 25N	11 52E
Ambergris Cay	**83**	18 0N	88 0W
Ambérieu-en-Bugey	**103**	45 57N	5 20E
Amberley	**133**	43 9S	172 44E
Ambert	**102**	45 33N	3 44E
Ambikapur	**125**	23 15N	83 15E
Ambilobé	**117**	13 10S	49 3E
Ambleside	**94**	54 26N	2 58W
Ambo	**86**	10 5S	76 10W
Ambon	**127**	3 35S	128 20E
Ambositra	**117**	20 31S	47 25E
Amboy, Calif., U.S.A.	**81**	34 33N	115 51W
Amboy, Ill., U.S.A.	**76**	41 44N	89 20W
Amboy, N.J., U.S.A.	**71**	40 31N	74 18W
*Ambre, C. d'	**117**	12 40S	49 10E
Ambre, Mt. d'	**117**	12 30S	49 10E
Ambridge	**70**	40 36N	80 15W
Ambriz	**116**	7 48S	13 8E
†Ambrizete	**116**	7 10S	12 52E
Ambrose	**56**	48 57N	103 29W
Amchitka I.	**67**	51 30N	179 0W
Amchitka P.	**67**	51 30N	179 0W
Amderma	**120**	69 45N	61 30E
Ameca	**82**	20 30N	104 0W
Ameca, R.	**82**	20 40N	105 15W
Amecameca	**83**	19 10N	98 57W
Ameland	**105**	53 27N	5 45E
Amélie-les-Bains-Palalda	**102**	42 29N	2 41E
Amen	**121**	68 45N	180 0E
American Falls	**78**	42 46N	112 56W
American Falls Res.	**78**	43 0N	112 50W
American Highland	**91**	73 0S	75 0E
American Samoa	**133**	14 20S	170 40W
Americana	**89**	22 45S	47 20W
Americus	**73**	32 0N	84 10W
Amersfoort	**105**	52 9N	5 23E
Amery	**55**	56 34N	94 3W
Ames	**76**	42 0N	93 40W
Amesbury	**71**	42 50N	70 52W
Amesdale	**55**	50 2N	92 55W
Ameson	**34**	49 50N	84 35W
Amet Sound	**39**	45 47N	63 10W
Amga, R.	**121**	61 0N	132 0E
Amgu	**121**	45 45N	137 15E
Amgun, R.	**121**	52 50N	138 0E
Amherst, Burma	**125**	16 2N	97 20E
Amherst, Can.	**39**	45 48N	64 8W
Amherst, Mass., U.S.A.	**71**	42 21N	72 30W
Amherst, Ohio, U.S.A.	**70**	41 23N	82 15W
Amherst, Tex., U.S.A.	**75**	34 0N	102 24W
Amherst I.	**47**	44 8N	76 43W
Amherstburg	**46**	42 6N	83 6W
Amiata Mte.	**108**	42 54N	11 40E
Amiens	**101**	49 54N	2 16E
Amirante Is.	**16**	6 0S	53 0E
Amisk	**61**	52 33N	111 4W
Amisk L.	**55**	54 35N	102 15W
Amistati, Presa	**82**	29 24N	101 0W
Amite	**75**	30 47N	90 31W
Amlia I.	**67**	52 5N	173 30W
Amlwch	**94**	53 24N	4 21W
'Ammān	**115**	32 0N	35 52E
Amne Machin Shan	**129**	34 25N	99 40E
Amnéville	**101**	49 16N	6 9E
Amoret	**76**	38 15N	94 35W
Amorgós	**109**	36 50N	25 57E
Amos	**40**	48 35N	78 5W
Amoy = Hsiamen	**131**	24 25N	118 4E
Amoy = Hsiamen	**131**	24 25N	118 4E
Amozoc	**83**	19 2N	98 3W
Ampanihy	**117**	24 40S	44 45E
Amqui	**38**	48 28N	67 27W
Amraoti	**124**	20 55N	77 45E
Amreli	**124**	21 35N	71 17E
Amritsar	**124**	31 35N	74 57E
Amroha	**124**	28 53N	78 30E
Amsterdam, Neth.	**105**	52 23N	4 54E
Amsterdam, U.S.A.	**71**	42 58N	74 10W
Amsterdam, I.	**16**	37 30S	77 30E
Amu Darya, R.	**120**	37 50N	65 0E
Amuay	**86**	11 50N	70 10W
Amukta I.	**67**	52 29N	171 20W
Amund Ringnes I.	**65**	78 20N	96 25W
Amundsen Gulf	**64**	71 0N	124 0W
Amundsen Sea	**91**	72 0S	115 0W
Amuntai	**126**	2 28S	115 25E
Amur, R.	**121**	53 30N	122 30E
Amurang	**127**	1 5N	124 40E
Amuri Pass	**133**	42 31S	172 11E
Amurzet	**121**	47 50N	131 5E
Amyot	**53**	48 29N	84 57W
An Nafūd	**122**	28 15N	41 0E
An Najaf	**122**	32 3N	44 15E
An Nasiriyah	**122**	31 0N	46 15E
An Nhon (Binh Dinh)	**128**	13 55N	109 7E
An Nu'ayriyah	**122**	27 30N	48 30E
An Uaimh, Ireland	**97**	53 39N	6 40W
An Uaimh, Ireland	**97**	53 39N	6 40W
Ana Branch, R.	**136**	32 20S	143 0E
Anaco	**86**	9 27N	64 28W
Anaconda	**78**	46 7N	113 0W
Anacortes	**80**	48 30N	122 40W
Anadarko	**75**	35 4N	98 15W
Anadolu	**122**	38 0N	29 0E
Anadyr	**121**	64 35N	177 20E
Anadyr, R.	**121**	66 50N	171 0E
Anadyrskiy Zaliv	**121**	64 0N	180 0E
Anah	**122**	34 25N	42 0E
Anaheim	**81**	33 50N	118 0W
Anahim Lake	**62**	52 28N	125 18W
Anáhuac	**82**	27 14N	100 9W
Anakapalle	**125**	17 42N	83 06E
Analalava	**117**	14 35S	48 0E
Anama Bay	**57**	51 58N	98 4W
Anambas, Kepulauan	**126**	3 20N	106 30E
Anamoose	**74**	47 55N	100 20W
Anamosa	**76**	42 7N	91 30W
Anamur	**122**	36 8N	32 58E
Anan	**132**	33 54N	134 40E
Anantnag	**124**	33 45N	75 10E
Anápolis	**87**	16 15S	48 50W
Anar	**123**	30 55N	55 13E
Anārak	**123**	33 25N	53 40E
Anatolia = Anadolu	**122**	38 0N	29 0E
Anatone	**78**	46 9N	117 4W
Añatuya	**88**	28 20S	62 50W
Anaunethad L.	**55**	60 55N	104 25W
Ancaster	**48**	43 13N	79 59W
Ancenis	**100**	47 21N	1 10W
Anchor Bay	**80**	38 48N	123 34W
Anchorage	**67**	61 10N	149 50W
Ancien Canal	**44**	45 19N	74 2W
Ancienne-Lorette	**42**	46 48N	71 21W
Ancohuma, Nevada	**86**	16 0S	68 50W
Ancon	**82**	8 57N	79 33W
Ancón	**86**	11 50S	77 10W
Ancona	**108**	43 37N	13 30E
Ancud	**90**	42 0S	73 50W
Ancud, G. de	**90**	42 0S	73 0W
Andacollo, Argent.	**88**	37 10S	70 42W
Andacollo, Chile	**88**	30 15S	71 10W
Andalgalá	**88**	27 40S	66 30W
Åndalsnes	**110**	62 35N	7 43E
Andalucia	**104**	37 35N	5 0W
Andalusia	**73**	31 25N	86 30W
Andalusia = Andalucia	**104**	37 35N	5 0W
Andaman Is.	**128**	12 30N	92 30E
Andaman Sea	**128**	13 0N	96 0E
Andaman Str.	**128**	12 15N	92 20E
Andara	**117**	18 2S	21 9E
Andelot	**101**	46 51N	5 56E
Andelys, Les	**100**	49 15N	1 25E
Anderlues	**105**	50 25N	4 16E
Andernach	**105**	50 24N	7 25E
Andernos-les-Bains	**102**	44 44N	1 6W
Anderson, Calif., U.S.A.	**78**	40 30N	122 19W
Anderson, Ind., U.S.A.	**77**	40 5N	85 40W
Anderson, Mo., U.S.A.	**75**	36 43N	94 29W
Anderson, S.C., U.S.A.	**73**	34 32N	82 40W
Anderson L.	**63**	50 37N	122 25W
Anderson, R.	**64**	69 42N	129 0W
Andes, mts.	**86**	20 0S	68 0W
Andfjorden	**110**	69 10N	16 20E
Andhra Pradesh □	**124**	15 0N	80 0E
Andikithira	**109**	35 52N	23 15E
Andizhan	**120**	41 10N	72 0E
Andkhui	**123**	36 52N	65 8E
Ando	**136**	36 43S	149 16E
Andorra ■	**104**	42 30N	1 30E
Andorra La Vella	**104**	42 31N	1 32E
Andover, Can.	**39**	46 45N	67 42W
Andover, U.K.	**95**	51 13N	1 29W
Andover, N.Y., U.S.A.	**70**	42 11N	77 48W
Andover, Ohio, U.S.A.	**70**	41 35N	80 35W
Andreanof Is.	**67**	51 0N	178 0W
Andreville	**41**	47 41N	69 44W
Andrew	**60**	53 53N	112 21W
Andrews, S.C., U.S.A.	**73**	33 29N	79 30W
Andrews, Tex., U.S.A.	**75**	32 18N	102 33W
Andria	**108**	41 13N	16 17E
Andriba	**117**	17 30S	46 58E
Androka	**117**	24 58S	44 2E
Andros	**109**	37 50N	24 50E
Andros I.	**84**	24 30N	78 0W
Andros Town	**84**	24 43N	77 47W
Andújar	**104**	38 3N	4 5W
Anegada I.	**85**	18 45N	64 20W
Aneroid	**56**	49 43N	107 18W
Aneto, Pico de	**104**	42 37N	0 40E
Ang Thong	**128**	14 35N	100 31E
Anga	**121**	60 35N	132 0E
Angamos, Punta	**88**	23 1S	70 32W
Angangki	**130**	47 9N	123 48E
Angara, R.	**121**	58 30N	97 0E
Angarsk	**121**	52 30N	104 0E
Ånge	**110**	62 31N	15 35E
Ange-Gardien	**42**	45 22N	72 57W
Angel de la Guarda, I.	**82**	29 30N	113 30W
Ängelholm	**111**	56 15N	12 58E
Angels Camp	**80**	38 8N	120 30W
Ångermanälven	**110**	62 40N	18 0E
Angers, Can.	**40**	45 31N	75 29W
Angers, France	**100**	47 30N	0 35W
Angerville	**101**	48 19N	2 0E
Ångesån	**110**	66 50N	22 15E
Angikuni L.	**55**	62 0N	100 0W
Angkor	**128**	13 22N	103 50E
Anglesey, I.	**94**	53 17N	4 20W
Anglet	**102**	43 29N	1 31W
Angleton	**75**	29 12N	95 23W
Angliers	**40**	47 33N	79 14W
Anglure	**101**	48 35N	3 50E
Angmagssalik	**17**	65 40N	37 20W
Ango	**116**	4 10N	26 5E
Angoche, I.	**117**	16 20S	39 50E
Angol	**88**	37 56S	72 45W
Angola, Ind., U.S.A.	**77**	41 40N	85 0W
Angola, N.Y., U.S.A.	**70**	42 38N	79 2W
Angola ■	**117**	12 0S	18 0E
Angoon	**67**	57 40N	134 40W
Angoulême	**102**	45 39N	0 10E
Angoumois	**102**	45 50N	0 25E
Angra dos Reis	**89**	23 0S	44 10W
Angran	**120**	80 59N	69 3E
Anguilla, I.	**85**	18 14N	63 5W
Anguille Mts.	**37**	48 0N	59 11W
Angus	**46**	44 19N	79 53W
Angus, Braes of	**96**	56 51N	3 0W
Angusville	**57**	50 44N	101 1W
Anhandui, R.	**89**	21 46S	52 9W
Anholt	**111**	56 42N	11 33E
Anhwa	**131**	28 18N	111 25E
Ani	**131**	28 50N	115 29E
Aniak	**67**	61 58N	159 50W
Animas	**79**	31 58N	108 58W
Anin	**128**	15 36N	97 50E
Anita	**76**	41 27N	94 46W
Anjen	**131**	26 42N	113 19E
Anjidiv I.	**124**	14 40N	74 10E
Anjou, Can.	**43**	45 36N	73 33W
Anjou, France	**100**	47 20N	0 15W
Anjozorobe	**117**	18 22S	47 52E
Anju	**130**	39 40N	125 45E
Ankang	**131**	32 38N	109 5E
Ankara	**122**	40 0N	32 54E
Ankazoabo	**117**	22 18S	44 31E
Ankazobé	**117**	18 20S	47 10E
Ankeny	**76**	41 44N	93 36W
Anki	**131**	25 1N	118 4E
Anking	**131**	30 34N	117 1E
Ankoro	**116**	6 45S	26 55E
Anlu	**131**	31 12N	113 38E
Ann Arbor	**46**	42 17N	83 45W
Ann C., Antarct.	**91**	66 30S	50 30E
Ann C., U.S.A.	**71**	42 39N	70 37W
Anna, Ill., U.S.A.	**75**	37 28N	89 10W
Anna, Ohio, U.S.A.	**77**	40 24N	84 11W
Annaba	**114**	36 50N	7 46E
Annacis I.	**66**	49 10N	122 57W
Annaheim	**56**	52 19N	104 49W
Annalee, R.	**97**	54 3N	7 15W
Annalera Telegraph Office	**136**	41 16S	143 59E
Annam = Trung-Phan	**128**	16 30N	107 30E
Annamitique, Chaîne	**128**	17 0N	106 0E
Annan	**96**	55 0N	3 17W
Annan, R.	**96**	54 58N	3 18W
Annapolis Royal	**39**	44 44N	65 32W
Annecy	**103**	45 55N	6 8E
Annecy, L. d'	**103**	45 52N	6 10E
Annemasse	**103**	46 12N	6 16E
Annette	**67**	55 2N	131 35W
Annieopsquotch Mts.	**37**	48 20N	57 30W
Annieville	**66**	49 11N	122 55W
Anning	**129**	24 58N	102 30E
Anniston	**73**	33 45N	85 50W
Annobón	**112**	1 35S	3 35E
Annonay	**103**	45 15N	4 40E
Annonciation, L', Can.	**34**	46 25N	74 55W
Annonciation, L', Qué., Can.	**40**	46 25N	74 55W
Annot	**103**	43 58N	6 38E
Annotto Bay	**84**	18 17N	77 3W
Annville	**71**	40 18N	76 32W
Anoka	**74**	45 10N	93 26W
Anola	**57**	49 53N	96 38W
Anping	**131**	23 0N	120 6E
Ansbach	**106**	49 17N	10 34E
Anse-au-Clair, L'	**37**	51 25N	57 5W
Anse au Loup, L'	**37**	51 32N	56 50W
Anse, L'	**52**	46 47N	88 28W
Anserma	**86**	5 13N	75 48W
Anshun	**131**	26 2N	105 57E
Ansi	**130**	40 21N	96 10E
Ansley	**74**	41 19N	99 24W
Anson	**75**	32 46N	99 54W
Anson B.	**134**	13 20S	130 6E
Ansonia, Conn., U.S.A.	**71**	41 21N	73 6W
Ansonia, Ohio, U.S.A.	**77**	40 13N	84 38W
Ansonville	**34**	48 46N	80 43W
Anstruther	**96**	56 14N	2 40W
Anstruther, E. and W.	**96**	56 14N	2 40W
Ansudu	**127**	2 11S	139 22E
Anta	**130**	46 18N	125 34E
Antabamba	**86**	14 40S	73 0W
Antakya	**122**	36 14N	36 10E
Antalaha	**117**	14 57S	50 20E
Antalya	**122**	36 52N	30 45E
Antalya Körfezi	**122**	36 15N	31 30E
Antananrivo	**117**	18 55S	47 35E
Antarctic Pen.	**91**	67 0S	60 0W
Antarctica	**91**	90 0S	0 0
Antequera, Parag.	**88**	24 8S	57 7W
Antequera, Spain	**104**	37 5N	4 33W
Antero Mt.	**79**	38 45N	106 15W
Anthony, Kans., U.S.A.	**75**	37 8N	98 2W
Anthony, N. Mex., U.S.A.	**79**	32 1N	106 37W
Anti Atlas, Mts.	**114**	30 30N	6 30W
Antibes	**103**	43 34N	7 6E
Antibes, C. d'	**103**	43 31N	7 7E
Anticosti, Î. d'	**38**	49 30N	63 0W
Antifer, C. d'	**100**	49 41N	0 10E
Antigo	**74**	45 8N	89 5W
Antigonish	**39**	45 38N	61 58W
Antigua & Barbuda ■	**84**	14 34N	90 41W
Antigua Bahama, Canal de la	**84**	22 10N	77 30W
Antigua, I.	**85**	17 0N	61 50W
Antilla	**84**	20 40N	75 50W
Antimony	**79**	38 7N	112 0W
Antioch	**80**	38 7N	121 45W
Antioche, Pertuis d'	**102**	46 6N	1 20W
Antioquia	**86**	6 40N	75 55W
Antioquia □	**86**	7 0N	75 30W
Antipodes Is.	**14**	49 45S	178 40E
Antler, Can.	**57**	49 34N	101 27W
Antler, U.S.A.	**57**	48 58N	101 18W
Antler, R.	**57**	49 8N	101 0W
Antlers	**75**	34 15N	95 35W
Antofagasta	**88**	23 50S	70 30W
Antofagasta □	**88**	24 0S	69 0W
Antofagasta de la Sierra	**88**	26 5S	67 20W
Antofallá	**88**	25 30S	68 5W
Antofalla, Salar de	**88**	25 40S	67 45W
Anton	**75**	33 49N	102 5W
Anton Chico	**79**	35 12N	105 5W
Antongil, B. d'	**117**	15 30S	49 50E
Antonina	**89**	25 26S	48 42W
Antonito	**79**	37 4N	106 1W
Antrain	**100**	48 28N	1 30W
Antrim	**97**	54 43N	6 13W
Antrim □	**97**	54 42N	6 20W
Antrim Co.	**97**	54 58N	6 20W
Antrim, Mts. of	**97**	54 57N	6 8W
Antsalova	**117**	18 40S	44 37E
Antsirabé	**117**	19 55S	47 2E
Antsohihy	**117**	14 50S	47 50E
Antung	**130**	40 10N	124 18E
Antwerp, N.Y., U.S.A.	**71**	44 12N	75 36W
Antwerp, Ohio, U.S.A.	**77**	41 11N	84 45W
Antwerp = Antwerpen	**105**	51 13N	4 25E
Antwerpen	**105**	51 13N	4 25E
Antwerpen □	**105**	51 15N	4 40E
Anupgarh	**124**	29 10N	73 10E
Anuradhapura	**124**	8 22N	80 28E
Anvers I.	**91**	64 30S	63 40W
Anvik	**67**	62 37N	160 20W
Anxious B.	**134**	33 24S	134 45E
Anyang	**130**	36 7N	114 26E
Anyer-Lor	**127**	6 6S	105 56E
Anyi	**131**	35 0N	110 44E
Anyuan	**131**	24 59N	115 31E
Anza	**81**	33 35N	116 39W
Anzhero-Sudzhensk	**120**	56 10N	83 40E
Ánzio	**108**	41 28N	12 37E
Aomori	**132**	40 45N	140 45E
Aomori-ken □	**132**	40 45N	140 40E
Aosta	**108**	45 43N	7 20E
Apa, R.	**88**	22 6S	58 2W
Apache, Ariz., U.S.A.	**79**	31 46N	109 6W
Apache, Okla., U.S.A.	**75**	34 53N	98 22W
Apalachee B.	**73**	30 0N	84 0W
Apalachicola	**73**	29 40N	85 0W
Apaporis, R.	**86**	0 30S	70 30W
Aparri	**127**	18 22N	121 38E
Aparurén	**86**	5 6N	62 8W
Apatzingán	**82**	19 0N	102 20W
Apeldoorn	**105**	52 13N	5 57E
Apenam	**126**	8 35S	116 13E
Apennines	**93**	44 20N	10 20E
Apia	**86**	5 5N	75 58W
Apia	**133**	13 50S	171 50W
Apiacás, Serra dos	**86**	9 50S	57 0W
Apiai	**86**	24 31S	48 50W
Apizaco	**83**	19 26N	98 9W
Aplao	**86**	16 0S	72 40W
Apo, Mt.	**127**	6 53N	125 14E
Apohaqui	**39**	45 42N	65 36W
Apollo Bay	**136**	38 45S	143 40E
Apolo	**86**	14 30S	68 30W
Apostle Is.	**52**	47 0N	90 30W
Apóstoles	**89**	28 0S	56 0W
Apoteri	**86**	4 2N	58 32W
Appalachian Mts.	**72**	38 0N	80 0W
Appalachicola, R.	**73**	30 0N	85 0W
Appennini	**108**	41 0N	15 0E
Appingedam	**105**	53 19N	6 51E
Apple Hill	**47**	45 13N	74 46W
Apple Valley	**81**	34 30N	117 11W
Appleby, Can.	**48**	43 23N	79 46W
Appleby, U.K.	**94**	54 35N	2 29W
Appleton	**72**	44 17N	88 25W
Appleton City	**76**	38 11N	94 2W
Approuague	**87**	4 20N	52 0W
Apsley	**47**	44 45N	78 6W
Apt	**103**	43 53N	5 24E
Apucarana	**89**	23 55S	51 33W
Apulia = Puglia	**108**	41 0N	16 30E
Apure □	**86**	7 10N	68 50W
Apure, R.	**86**	8 0N	69 20W
Apurimac, R.	**86**	12 10S	73 30W
Apurito, R.	**86**	7 50N	67 0W
Aq Chah	**123**	37 0N	66 5E
'Aqaba, Khalīj al	**122**	28 15N	33 20E
'Aqrah	**122**	36 46N	43 45E
Aqsu	**129**	41 10N	80 15E
Aquanish	**38**	50 14N	62 2W
Aquidauana	**87**	20 30S	55 50W
Aquila, L'	**108**	42 21N	13 24E
Aquiles Serdán	**82**	28 37N	105 54W

* *Renamed Bobraomby, T.'i*

† *Renamed Nzeto*

Aquin **Assis**

Aquin **85** 18 16N 73 24W
Ar Ramadi **122** 33 25N 43 20E
Ar Raqqah **122** 36 0N 38 55E
Ar Rass **122** 25 50N 43 40E
Ar Rifai **122** 31 50N 46 10E
Ar Riyāḍ **122** 24 41N 46 42E
Ar Rub 'al Khālī **115** 21 0N 51 0E
Ar Ruṭbah **122** 33 0N 40 15E
Ara L. **53** 50 33N 87 28W
Arab, Shatt al **122** 30 0N 48 31E
Arabelo **86** 4 55N 64 13W
Arabia **118** 25 0N 45 0E
Arabian Sea **118** 16 0N 65 0E
Aracajú **87** 10 55S 37 4W
Aracataca **86** 10 38N 74 9W
Aracati **87** 4 30S 37 44W
Araçatuba **89** 21 10S 50 30W
Aracena **104** 37 53N 6 38W
Aracruz **87** 19 49S 40 16W
Araçuai **87** 16 52S 42 4W
Arad **107** 46 10N 21 20E
Arafura Sea **127** 10 0S 135 0E
Aragón **104** 41 25N 1 0W
Aragón, R. **104** 42 35N 0 50W
Aragua □ **86** 10 0N 67 10W
Aragua de Barcelona **86** 9 28N 64 49W
Araguacema **87** 8 50S 49 20W
Araguaia, R. **87** 7 0S 49 15W
Araguari **87** 18 38S 48 11W
Araguari, R. **87** 1 0N 51 40W
Arak **114** 25 20N 3 45E
Arāk **122** 34 0N 49 40E
Arakan Coast **125** 19 0N 94 0E
Arakan Yoma **125** 20 0N 94 30E
Araks, R. = Aras, Rud-e **122** 39 10N 47 10E
Aral Sea = Aralskoye More **120** 44 30N 60 0E
Aralsk **120** 46 50N 61 20E
Aralskoye More **120** 44 30N 60 0E
Aramac **135** 22 58S 145 14E
Aran, I. **97** 55 0N 8 30W
Aran Is. **97** 53 5N 9 42W
Aranjuez **104** 40 1N 3 40W
Aranos **117** 24 9S 19 7E
Aransas Pass **75** 27 55N 97 9W
Aranyaprathet **128** 13 41N 102 30E
Aranzazu **86** 5 16N 75 30W
Arapahoe **74** 40 22N 99 53W
Arapawa I. **15** 41 13S 174 20E
Arapey Grande, R. **88** 30 55S 57 49W
Arapkir **122** 39 5N 38 30E
Arapongas **89** 23 29S 51 28W
Arapuni **14** 38 3S 175 37E
Araranguá **89** 29 0S 49 30W
Araraquara **87** 21 50S 48 0W
Araras **89** 5 15S 60 35W
Ararás, Serra dos **89** 25 0S 53 10W
Ararat **136** 37 16S 143 0E
Ararat, Mt. = Ağri Daği **122** 39 50N 44 15E
Araruama, Lagoa de **89** 22 53S 42 12W
Aras, Rud-e **122** 39 10N 47 10E
Arauca **86** 7 0N 70 40W
Arauca □ **86** 6 40N 71 0W
Arauca, R. **86** 7 30N 69 0W
Arauco **88** 37 16S 73 25W
Arauco □ **88** 37 40S 73 25W
Arauquita **86** 7 2N 71 25W
Araure **86** 9 34N 69 13W
Araxá **87** 19 35S 46 55W
Araya, Pen. de **86** 10 40N 64 0W
Arbatax **108** 39 57N 9 42E
Arbeláez **86** 4 17N 74 26W
Arbil **122** 36 15N 44 5E
Arbois **101** 46 55N 5 46E
Arbor Vitae **52** 48 54N 94 18W
Arborfield **56** 53 6N 103 39W
Arborg **57** 50 54N 97 13W
Arbresle, L' **103** 45 50N 4 26E
Arbroath **96** 56 34N 2 35W
Arbuckle **80** 39 3N 122 2W
Arc **101** 47 28N 5 34E
Arcachon **102** 44 40N 1 10W
Arcachon, Bassin d' **102** 44 42N 1 10W
Arcade **70** 42 34N 78 25W
Arcadia, Can. **39** 43 50N 66 4W
Arcadia, Fla., U.S.A. **73** 27 20N 81 50W
Arcadia, Ind., U.S.A. **77** 40 10N 86 1W
Arcadia, Iowa, U.S.A. **76** 42 5N 95 3W
Arcadia, La., U.S.A. **75** 32 34N 92 53W
Arcadia, Nebr., U.S.A. **74** 41 29N 99 4W
Arcadia, Pa., U.S.A. **70** 40 46N 78 54W
Arcadia, Wis., U.S.A. **74** 44 13N 91 29W
Arcanum **77** 39 59N 84 33W
Arcata **78** 40 55N 124 4W
Arcen **131** 51 29N 6 11E
Archangel = Arkhangelsk **120** 64 40N 41 0E
Archbald **71** 41 30N 75 31W
Archbold **77** 41 31N 84 18W
Archer, R. **135** 13 25S 142 50E
Archerwill **56** 52 26N 103 51W
Arcis-sur-Aube **101** 48 32N 4 10E
Arco **78** 43 45N 113 16W
Arcola, Can. **57** 49 40N 102 30W
Arcola, U.S.A. **77** 39 41N 88 19W
Arcos **104** 41 12N 2 16W
Arcot **124** 12 53N 79 20E
Arcoverde **87** 8 25S 37 4W
Arctic B. **65** 73 1N 85 7W
Arctic Ocean **17** 78 0N 160 0W
Arctic Red, R. **67** 66 0N 132 0W
Arctic Red River **64** 67 15N 134 0W
Arctic Village **67** 68 5N 145 45W
Arda, R. **109** 41 40N 25 40E
Ardabrīl **122** 38 15N 48 18E
Ardakan **123** 30 20N 52 5E
Ardbeg **46** 45 38N 80 5W
Ardèche □ **103** 44 42N 4 16E
Ardee **97** 53 51N 6 32W
Arden, Man., Can. **57** 50 17N 99 16W
Arden, Ont., Can. **47** 44 43N 76 56W
Arden, U.S.A. **81** 36 1N 115 14W
Ardennes **106** 49 30N 5 10E
Ardennes □ **101** 49 35N 4 40E
Ardentes **101** 46 45N 1 50E
Ardestān **123** 33 20N 52 25E
Ardgour **96** 56 45N 5 25W
Ardlethan **136** 34 22S 146 53E
Ardmore, Can. **60** 54 20N 110 29W
Ardmore, Okla., U.S.A. **75** 34 10N 97 5W
Ardmore, Pa., U.S.A. **71** 39 58N 75 18W
Ardmore, S.D., U.S.A. **74** 43 0N 103 40W
Ardnacrusha **97** 52 43N 8 38W
Ardnamurchan Pt. **96** 56 44N 6 14W
Ardoise, L' **39** 45 37N 60 45W
Ardres **101** 50 50N 2 0E
Ardrossan **96** 55 39N 4 50W
Ards □ **97** 54 35N 5 30W
Ards Pen. **97** 54 30N 5 25W
Arecibo **85** 18 29N 66 42W
Areia Branca **87** 5 0S 37 0W
Arena de la Ventana, Punta **82** 24 4N 109 52W
Arena, Pt. **80** 38 57N 123 44W
Arenales, Cerro **90** 47 5S 73 40W
Arenas, Pta. **86** 10 20N 62 39W
Arendal **111** 58 28N 8 46E
Arendonk **105** 51 19N 5 5E
Arenzville **76** 39 53N 90 22W
Arequipa **86** 16 20S 71 30W
Arès **102** 44 47N 1 8W
Arévalo **104** 41 3N 4 43W
Arezzo **108** 43 28N 11 50E
Argelès-Gazost **102** 43 0N 0 6W
Argelès-sur-Mer **102** 42 34N 3 1E
Argent-sur-Sauldre **101** 47 33N 2 25E
Argenta, Can. **54** 50 20N 116 55W
Argenta, U.S.A. **77** 39 59N 88 49W
Argentan **100** 48 45N 0 1W
Argentário, Mte. **108** 42 23N 11 11E
Argentat **102** 45 6N 1 56E
Argenteuil **101** 48 57N 2 14E
Argenteuil □ **43** 45 50N 74 30W
Argentia **37** 47 18N 53 58W
Argentina **86** 0 34N 74 17W
Argentina ■ **90** 35 0S 66 0W
Argentino, L. **90** 50 10S 73 0W
Argenton-sur-Creuse **102** 46 36N 1 30E
Argentré **100** 48 5N 0 40W
Argeş, R. **107** 44 30N 25 50E
Arghandab, R. **124** 32 15N 66 23E
Argolikós Kólpos **109** 37 20N 22 52E
Argonne **101** 49 0N 5 20E
Argos **109** 37 40N 22 43E
Argos **77** 41 14N 86 15W
Argostólion **109** 38 12N 20 33E
Arguello, Pt. **81** 34 34N 120 40W
Argun, R. **121** 53 20N 121 28E
Argus Pk. **81** 35 52N 117 26W
Argyle, Can. **57** 50 11N 97 27W
Argyle, U.S.A. **74** 48 23N 96 49W
Århus **111** 56 8N 10 11E
Ariake-wan **132** 31 30N 131 10E
Arica, Chile **86** 18 32S 70 20W
Arica, Colomb. **86** 2 0S 71 50W
Arica, Peru **86** 1 30S 75 30W
Arichat **39** 45 31N 61 1W
Arid, C. **134** 34 1S 123 10E
Ariège □ **102** 42 56N 1 30E
Ariège, R. **102** 43 30N 1 25E
Arima **85** 10 38N 61 17W
Arinos, R. **86** 11 15S 57 0W
Ario de Rosales **82** 19 12N 101 42W
Aripuanã **86** 9 25S 60 30W
Aripuanã, R. **86** 7 30S 60 25W
Ariquemes **86** 9 55S 63 6W
Arisaig **96** 56 55N 5 50W
Arismendi **86** 8 29N 68 22W
Ariss **49** 43 35N 80 22W
Aristazabal, I. **62** 52 40N 129 10W
Arivaca **79** 31 37N 111 25W
Arizaro, Salar de **88** 24 40S 67 50W
Arizona **88** 35 45S 65 25W
Arizona □ **79** 34 20N 111 30W
Arizpe **82** 30 20N 110 11W
Arjeplog **110** 66 3N 18 2E
Arjona **86** 10 14N 75 22W
Arjuno **127** 7 49S 112 19E
Arka **121** 60 15N 142 0E
Arka Tagh **129** 36 30N 90 0E
Arkadelphia **75** 34 5N 93 0W
Arkaig, L. **96** 56 58N 5 10W
Arkansas □ **75** 35 0N 92 30W
Arkansas City **75** 37 4N 97 3W
Arkansas, R. **75** 35 20N 93 30W
Arkell **49** 43 32N 80 10W
Arkhangelsk **120** 64 40N 41 0E
Arklow **97** 52 48N 6 10W
Arkona **46** 43 4N 81 50W
Arkticheskiy, Mys **121** 81 10N 95 0E
Arlanc **102** 45 25N 3 42E
Arlanzón, R. **104** 42 12N 4 0W
Arlberg Pass **106** 49 9N 10 12E
Arlee **78** 47 10N 114 4W
Arles **103** 43 41N 4 40E
Arlington, Oreg., U.S.A. **78** 45 48N 120 6W
Arlington, S.D., U.S.A. **74** 44 25N 97 4W
Arlington, Wash., U.S.A. **80** 48 11N 122 4W
Arlington Heights **77** 42 5N 87 59W
Arlon **105** 49 42N 5 49E
Armadale **50** 43 50N 79 15W
Armagh, Can. **41** 46 41N 70 32W
Armagh, U.K. **97** 54 22N 6 40W
Armagh □ **97** 54 18N 6 37W
Armagh Co. **97** 54 16N 6 35W
Armagnac **102** 43 44N 0 10E
Armançon, R. **101** 47 59N 3 30E
Armavir **120** 45 2N 41 7E
Armenia **86** 4 35N 75 45W
Armentières **101** 50 40N 2 50E
Armero **86** 4 58N 74 54W
Armidale, Austral. **135** 30 30S 151 40E
Armidale, Can. **39** 44 37N 63 38W
Armour **74** 43 20N 98 25W
Arms **34** 49 34N 86 3W
Armstead **78** 45 0N 112 56W
Armstrong, B.C., Can. **63** 50 25N 119 10W
Armstrong, Ont., Can. **52** 50 18N 89 4W
Armstrong, U.S.A. **75** 26 59N 97 48W
Arnarfjörður **110** 65 48N 23 40W
Arnaud, R. **36** 59 59N 69 46W
Arnay-le-Duc **101** 47 10N 4 27E
Arnes **110** 66 1N 21 31W
Arnett **75** 36 9N 99 44W
Arnhem **105** 51 58N 5 55E
Arnhem B. **134** 12 20S 136 10E
Arnhem, C. **135** 12 20S 137 0E
Arnhem Ld. **134** 13 10S 135 0E
Arno, R. **108** 43 44N 10 20E
Arnold, Calif., U.S.A. **80** 38 15N 120 20W
Arnold, Nebr., U.S.A. **74** 41 29N 100 10W
Arnold, Pa., U.S.A. **70** 40 36N 79 44W
Arnot **55** 55 56N 96 41W
Arnøy **110** 70 9N 20 40E
Arnprior **47** 45 26N 76 21W
Arntfield **40** 48 12N 79 15W
Aroa **86** 10 26N 68 54W
Aroab **117** 26 41S 19 39E
Arpajon, Cantal, France **102** 44 54N 2 28E
Arpajon, Seine et Oise, France **101** 48 37N 2 12E
Arrah **125** 25 35N 84 32E
Arraiján **84** 8 56N 79 36W
Arran **57** 51 53N 101 43W
Arran, I. **96** 55 34N 5 12W
Arrandale **54** 54 57N 130 0W
Arras **101** 50 17N 2 46E
Arreau **102** 42 54N 0 22E
Arrecifes **88** 34 06S 60 9W
Arrée, Mts. d' **100** 48 26N 3 55W
Arriaga, Chiapas, Mexico **83** 16 15N 93 52W
Arriaga, San Luis de Potosi, Mexico **82** 21 55N 101 23W
Arromanches-les-Bains **100** 49 20N 0 38W
Arrou **100** 48 6N 1 8E
Arrow L. **97** 54 3N 8 20W
Arrow Park **63** 50 6N 117 57W
Arrow Rock Res. **78** 43 45N 115 50W
Arrowhead **63** 50 40N 117 55W
Arrowhead, L. **81** 34 16N 117 10W
Arrowtown **133** 44 57S 168 50E
Arrowwood **61** 50 44N 113 9W
Arroyo Grande **81** 35 9N 120 32W
Ars **102** 46 13N 1 30W
Ars-sur-Moselle **101** 49 5N 6 4E
Arsenault L. **55** 55 6N 108 32W
Arshan **130** 46 59N 120 0E
Arta **109** 39 8N 21 2E
Arteaga **82** 18 50N 102 20W
Artenay **101** 48 5N 1 50E
Artesia **75** 32 55N 104 25W
Artesia Wells **75** 28 17N 99 18W
Artesian **74** 44 2N 97 54W
Arthez-de-Béarn **102** 43 29N 0 38W
Arthur, Can. **49** 43 50N 80 32W
Arthur, U.S.A. **77** 39 43N 88 28W
Arthurette **39** 46 47N 67 29W
Arthur's Pass **133** 42 54S 171 35E
Arthur's Town **85** 24 38N 75 42W
Artigas **88** 30 20S 56 30W
Artillery L. **55** 63 9N 107 52W
Artois **101** 50 20N 2 30E
Arts Bogd Uul, mts. **130** 44 40N 102 20E
Artvin **122** 41 14N 41 44E
Aru, Kepulauan **127** 6 0S 134 30E
Arua **116** 3 1N 30 58E
Aruanã **87** 15 0S 51 10W
Aruba I. **85** 12 30N 70 0W
Arudy **102** 43 7N 0 28W
Arunachal Pradesh □ **125** 28 0N 95 0E
Arundel **40** 45 58N 74 37W
Arusha **116** 3 20S 36 40E
Aruwimi, R. **116** 1 30N 25 0E
Arvada **78** 44 43N 106 6W
Arvayheer **130** 46 15N 102 45E
Arve, R. **103** 46 11N 6 8E
Arvert, L. **38** 52 18N 61 45W
Arvida **41** 48 25N 71 14W
Arvidsjaur **110** 65 35N 19 10E
Arvika **111** 59 40N 12 36E
Arvilla **60** 53 59N 114 0W
Arvin **81** 35 12N 118 50W
Arys **120** 42 26N 68 48E
Arzamas **120** 55 27N 43 55E
As Salt **115** 32 2N 35 43E
As Samāwah **122** 31 15N 45 15E
As Shatrah **122** 31 30N 46 10E
As Sulaimānīyah **122** 35 35N 45 29E
As Suwaih **123** 22 10N 59 33E
As Suwayda **122** 32 40N 36 30E
As Suwayrah **122** 32 55N 45 0E
Asadabad **122** 34 50N 48 10E
Asahi-dake, mt. **132** 43 42N 142 54E
Asahigawa **132** 43 45N 142 30E
Asahikawa **132** 43 45N 142 30E
Asamankese **114** 5 50N 0 40W
Asansol **125** 23 40N 87 1E
Asbestos **35** 45 47N 71 58W
Asbury Park **71** 40 15N 74 1W
Ascensión **82** 31 6N 107 59W
Ascensión, B. de la **83** 19 50N 87 20W
Ascension, I. **13** 8 0S 14 15W
Aschaffenburg **106** 49 58N 9 8E
Ascoli Piceno **108** 42 51N 13 34E
Ascope **86** 7 46S 79 8W
Ascotán **88** 21 45S 68 17W
Aseb **115** 13 0N 42 40E
Asfeld **101** 49 27N 4 5E
Ash Fork **79** 35 14N 112 32W
Ash Grove **75** 37 21N 93 36W
Ash Shām, Bādiyat **122** 31 30N 40 0E
Ash Shāmīyah **122** 31 55N 44 35E
Ashan **130** 41 3N 122 58E
Ashburn **73** 31 42N 83 40W
Ashburton **133** 43 53S 171 48E
Ashburton, R., Austral. **134** 21 40S 114 56E
Ashburton, R., N.Z. **15** 44 2S 171 50E
Ashby-de-la-Zouch **94** 52 45N 1 29W
Ashcroft **63** 50 40N 121 20W
Ashdod **115** 31 49N 34 35E
Asheboro **73** 35 43N 79 46W
Ashern **57** 51 11N 98 21W
Asherton **75** 28 25N 99 43W
Asheville **73** 35 39N 82 30W
Asheweig, R. **34** 54 17N 87 12W
Ashford, U.K. **95** 51 8N 0 53E
Ashford, U.S.A. **78** 46 45N 122 2W
Ashgrove **49** 43 36N 79 53W
Ashikaga **132** 36 28N 139 29E
Ashizuri-Zaki **132** 32 35N 132 50E
Ashkhabad **120** 38 0N 57 50E
Ashland, U.S.A. **76** 39 53N 90 0W
Ashland, Kans., U.S.A. **75** 37 13N 99 43W
Ashland, Ky., U.S.A. **72** 38 25N 82 40W
Ashland, Me., U.S.A. **35** 46 34N 68 26W
Ashland, Mont., U.S.A. **78** 45 41N 106 12W
Ashland, Nebr., U.S.A. **74** 41 5N 96 27W
Ashland, Ohio, U.S.A. **70** 40 52N 82 20W
Ashland, Oreg., U.S.A. **78** 42 10N 122 38W
Ashland, Pa., U.S.A. **71** 40 45N 76 22W
Ashland, Va., U.S.A. **72** 37 46N 77 30W
Ashland, Wis., U.S.A. **52** 46 40N 90 52W
Ashley, Ill., U.S.A. **76** 38 20N 89 11W
Ashley, Ind., U.S.A. **77** 41 32N 85 4W
Ashley, Mich., U.S.A. **77** 43 11N 84 29W
Ashley, N.D., U.S.A. **74** 46 3N 99 23W
Ashley, Pa., U.S.A. **71** 41 12N 75 55W
Ashmont **60** 54 7N 111 35W
Ashmore Reef **134** 12 14S 123 5E
Ashquelon **115** 31 42N 34 55E
Ashtabula **70** 41 52N 80 50W
Ashton **78** 44 6N 111 30W
Ashton-u.-Lyne **94** 53 30N 2 8E
Ashuanipi, L. **38** 52 45N 66 15W
Ashun **131** 25 10N 106 0E
Asia **118** 45 0N 75 0E
Asia, Kepulauan **127** 1 0N 131 13E
Asifabad **124** 19 30N 79 24E
Asinara, G. dell' **108** 41 0N 8 30E
Asinara I. **108** 41 5N 8 15E
Asino **120** 57 0N 86 0E
Asir **115** 18 40N 42 30E
Asir, Ras **115** 11 55N 51 10E
Askersund **111** 58 53N 14 55E
Askja **110** 65 3N 16 48W
Askov **52** 46 12N 92 51W
Asmar **123** 35 10N 71 27E
Asmara = Asmera **115** 15 19N 38 55E
Asmera **115** 15 19N 38 55E
Aso **132** 33 0N 130 42E
Aspen, Can. **39** 45 18N 62 3W
Aspen, U.S.A. **79** 39 12N 106 56W
Aspen Grove **63** 49 57N 120 37W
Aspermont **75** 33 11N 100 15W
Aspiring, Mt. **133** 44 23S 168 46E
Aspres **103** 44 32N 5 44E
Asquith **56** 52 8N 107 13W
Assam □ **125** 25 45N 92 30E
Assen **105** 53 0N 6 35E
Assigny, L. **38** 52 0N 65 20W
Assiniboia **56** 49 40N 105 59W
Assiniboine, R. **58** 49 53N 97 8W
Assinica L. **34** 50 30N 75 20W
Assis **89** 22 40S 50 20W

Assisi Bagan Siapiapi

Assisi 108 43 4N 12 36 E
Assomption, L' 43 45 50N 73 25W
Assomption, L' □ 43 45 49N 73 30W
Assomption, L', R. 43 45 43N 73 29W
Assumption 76 39 31N 89 3W
Assynt 96 58 25N 5 10W
Assynt, L. 96 58 25N 5 15W
Astaffort 102 44 4N 0 40 E
Asti 108 44 54N 8 11 E
Astipálaia 109 36 32N 26 22 E
Astorga 104 42 29N 6 8W
Astoria, Ill., U.S.A. 76 40 14N 90 21W
Astoria, Oreg., U.S.A. 80 46 16N 123 50W
Astorville 46 46 11N 79 17W
Astrakhan 120 46 25N 48 5 E
Asturias 104 43 15N 6 0W
Asunción 88 25 21 S 57 30W
Asunción, La 86 11 2N 63 53W
Aswân 115 24 4N 32 57 E
Aswân Dam 115 24 5N 32 57 E
Asyût 115 27 11N 31 4 E
At Tafilah 122 30 45N 35 30 E
Atacama 88 25 40 S 67 40W
Atacama □ 88 27 30 S 70 0W
Atacama, Desierto de 90 24 0 S 69 20W
Atacama, Salar de 88 24 0 S 68 20W
Ataco 86 3 35N 75 23W
Atalaia 112 9 25 S 36 0W
Atalaya 86 10 45 S 73 50W
Atami 132 35 0N 139 55 E
Atara 121 63 10N 129 10 E
Atascadero 81 35 32N 120 44W
Atasu 120 48 30N 71 0 E
Atauro 127 8 10 S 125 30 E
Atbara, R. 115 17 40N 33 56 E
Atchafalaya B. 75 29 30N 91 20W
Atchison 74 39 40N 95 10W
Ath 105 50 38N 3 47 E
Ath Thamami 122 27 45N 35 30 E
Athabasca 60 54 45N 113 20W
Athabasca, L. 55 59 15N 109 15W
Athabasca, R. 55 58 40N 110 50W
Athboy 97 53 37N 6 55W
Athelstan 43 45 2N 74 10W
Athenry 97 53 18N 8 45W
Athens, Can. 47 44 38N 75 57W
Athens, Ala., U.S.A. 73 34 49N 86 58W
Athens, Ga., U.S.A. 73 33 56N 83 24W
Athens, N.Y., U.S.A. 71 42 15N 73 48W
Athens, Ohio, U.S.A. 72 39 25N 82 6W
Athens, Pa., U.S.A. 71 41 57N 76 36W
Athens, Tex., U.S.A. 75 32 11N 95 48W
Athens = Athinai 109 37 58N 23 46 E
Atherly 70 44 37N 79 20W
Atherton 135 17 17 S 145 30 E
Athinai 109 37 58N 23 46 E
Athlone 97 53 26N 7 57W
Atholl, Forest of 96 56 51N 3 50W
Athólville 39 47 59N 66 43W
Athos, Mt. 109 40 9N 24 22 E
Athy 97 53 0N 7 0W
Ati 114 13 5N 29 2 E
Atico 86 16 14 S 73 40W
Aticonipi, L. 38 51 52N 59 22W
Atikokan 52 48 45N 91 37W
Atikonak L. 38 52 40N 64 32W
Atikonak, R. 38 52 51N 65 16W
Atka, U.S.A. 67 52 5N 174 40W
Atka, U.S.S.R. 121 60 50N 151 48 E
Atkasuk (Meade River) 67 70 30N 157 20W
Atkinson, Ill., U.S.A. 76 41 25N 90 1W
Atkinson, Nebr., U.S.A. 74 42 35N 98 59W
Atlanta, Ga., U.S.A. 73 33 50N 84 24W
Atlanta, Ill., U.S.A. 76 40 16N 89 14W
Atlanta, Mich., U.S.A. 46 45 0N 84 9W
Atlanta, Mo., U.S.A. 76 39 54N 92 29W
Atlanta, Tex., U.S.A. 75 33 7N 94 8W
Atlantic 74 41 25N 95 0W
Atlantic City 72 39 25N 74 25W
Atlantic Ocean 12 0 0 20 0W
Atlántico □ 86 10 45N 75 0W
Atlas, Great, Mts. 112 33 0N 5 0W
Atlas Saharien 114 33 30N 1 0 E
Atlin 67 59 31N 133 41W
Atlin, L. 67 59 26N 133 45W
Atmore 73 31 2N 87 30W
Atnarko 54 52 25N 126 0W
Atoka 75 34 22N 96 10W
Atolia 81 35 19N 117 37W
Atotonilco el Alto 82 20 20N 98 40W
Atoyac, R. 83 16 30N 97 31W
Atrak, R. 123 37 50N 57 0 E
Atrato, R. 86 6 40N 77 0W
Attalla 73 34 2N 86 5W
Attawapiskat 34 52 56N 82 24W
Attawapiskat, L. 34 52 18N 87 54W
Attawapiskat, R. 34 52 57N 82 18W
Attercliffe 49 42 59N 79 36W
Attica 77 40 20N 87 15W
Attichy 101 49 25N 3 3 E
Attigny 101 49 28N 4 35 E
Attikamagen L. 36 55 0N 66 30W
Attleboro 71 41 56N 71 18W
Attock 124 33 52N 72 20 E
Attopeu 128 14 48N 106 50 E
Attu 67 52 55N 173 10W
Attur 124 11 35N 78 30 E
Attwood, R 52 51 15N 88 30W
Atuel, R. 88 36 17 S 66 50W
Atunze = Tehtsin 129 28 45N 98 58 E
Atvidaberg 111 58 12N 16 0 E
Atwater 80 37 21N 120 37W
Atwood, Can. 46 43 40N 81 1W
Atwood, U.S.A. 74 39 52N 101 3W
Au Gres 46 44 3N 83 42W
Au Sable Pt., U.S.A. 46 44 20N 83 20W
Au Sable Pt., U.S.A. 53 46 40N 86 10W
Au Sable, R. 46 44 25N 83 20W
Aubagne 103 43 17N 5 37 E
Aubarede Pt. 127 17 15N 122 20 E
Aube □ 101 48 15N 4 0 E
Aubel 105 50 42N 5 51 E
Aubenas 103 44 37N 4 24 E
Aubenton 101 49 50N 4 12 E
Auberry 81 37 7N 119 29W
Aubigny-sur-Nère 101 47 30N 2 24 E
Aubin 102 44 33N 2 15 E
Aubrac, Mts. d' 102 44 38N 2 58 E
Aubry L. 64 67 23N 126 30W
Auburn, Ala., U.S.A. 73 32 37N 85 30W
Auburn, Calif., U.S.A. 80 38 50N 121 4W
Auburn, Ill., U.S.A. 76 39 36N 89 45W
Auburn, Ind., U.S.A. 77 41 20N 85 0W
Auburn, Nebr., U.S.A. 74 40 25N 95 50W
Auburn, N.Y., U.S.A. 71 42 57N 76 39W
Auburn, Wash., U.S.A. 80 47 18N 122 13W
Auburndale 73 28 5N 81 45W
Aubusson 102 45 57N 2 11 E
Auch 102 43 39N 0 36 E
Auchel 101 50 30N 2 29 E
Auckland 133 36 52 S 174 46 E
Auckland □ 133 38 35 S 177 0 E
Auckland Is. 133 51 0 S 166 0 E
Aude □ 102 43 8N 2 28 E
Aude, R. 102 44 13N 3 15 E
Auden 53 50 14N 87 53W
Auderville 100 49 43N 1 57W
Audierne 100 48 1N 4 34W
Audincourt 101 47 30N 6 50 E
Audley 51 43 54N 79 1W
Audubon 76 41 43N 94 56W
Auffay 100 49 43N 1 07 E
Augathella 135 25 48 S 146 35 E
Augsburg 106 48 22N 10 54 E
Augusta, Italy 108 37 14N 15 12 E
Augusta, U.S.A. 76 40 14N 90 57W
Augusta, U.S.A. 77 38 47N 84 0W
Augusta, Ark., U.S.A. 75 35 17N 91 25W
Augusta, Ga., U.S.A. 73 33 29N 81 59W
Augusta, Kans., U.S.A. 75 37 40N 97 0W
Augusta, Me., U.S.A. 35 44 20N 69 46 E
Augusta, Mont., U.S.A. 78 47 30N 112 29W
Augusta, Wis., U.S.A. 74 44 41N 91 8W
Augustines, L. des 40 47 37N 75 56W
Augusto Cardosa 117 12 40 S 34 50 E
Augustów 107 53 51N 23 00 E
Augustus, Mt. 134 24 20 S 116 50 E
Aukum 80 38 34N 120 43W
Aulnay 102 46 2N 0 22W
Aulne, R. 100 48 17N 4 16W
Aulneau Pen. 52 49 23N 94 29W
Ault 74 40 40N 104 42W
Ault-Onival 100 50 5N 1 29 E
Aulus-les-Bains 102 42 49N 1 19 E
Aumale 101 49 46N 1 46 E
Aumont-Aubrac 102 44 43N 3 17 E
Aunis 102 46 0N 0 50W
Auponhia 127 1 58 S 125 27 E
Aups 103 43 37N 6 15 E
Aurangabad, Bihar, India 125 24 45N 84 18 E
Aurangabad, Maharashtra, India 124 19 50N 75 23 E
Auray 100 47 40N 3 0W
Aurillac 102 44 55N 2 26 E
Aurora, Can. 49 44 0N 79 30 E
Aurora, Colo., U.S.A. 74 39 44N 104 55W
Aurora, Ill., U.S.A. 77 41 42N 88 12W
Aurora, Mo., U.S.A. 75 36 58N 93 42W
Aurora, Nebr., U.S.A. 74 40 55N 98 0W
Aurora, Ohio, U.S.A. 70 41 21N 81 20W
Aus 117 26 35 S 16 12 E
Ausable, R. 46 43 19N 81 46W
Aust-Agder fylke □ 111 58 55N 7 40 E
Austerlitz = Slavikov 106 49 10N 16 52 E
Austin, Ind., U.S.A. 77 38 45N 85 49W
Austin, Minn., U.S.A. 74 43 37N 92 59W
Austin, Nev., U.S.A. 78 39 30N 117 1W
Austin, Pa., U.S.A. 70 41 40N 78 7W
Austin, Tex., U.S.A. 75 30 20N 97 45W
Austin Chan. 65 75 35N 103 25W
Austin, L. 134 27 40 S 118 0 E
Austral Downs 135 20 30 S 137 45 E
Austral Is. = Tubouai, Îles 15 25 0 S 150 0W
Australia ■ 135 23 0 S 135 0 E
Australian Alps 136 36 30 S 148 8 E
Australian Cap. Terr. □ 136 35 15 S 149 8 E
Australian Dependency 91 73 0 S 90 0 E
Austria ■ 106 47 0N 14 0 E
Austvågøy 110 68 20N 14 40 E
Auterive 102 43 21N 1 29 E
Auteuil 44 45 38N 73 46W
Auteuil, L.d' 38 50 38N 61 17W
Authie, R. 101 50 22N 1 38 E
Autlan 82 19 40N 104 30W
Autun 101 46 58N 4 17 E
Auvergne 102 45 20N 3 0 E
Auxerre 101 47 48N 3 32 E
Auxi-le-Château 101 50 15N 2 8 E
Auxonne 101 47 10N 5 20 E
Auxvasse 76 39 1N 91 54W
Auzances 102 46 2N 2 30 E
Ava 76 37 53N 89 30W
Avallon 101 47 30N 3 53 E
Avalon 81 33 21N 118 20W
Avalon Pen. 37 47 30N 53 20W
Avalon Res. 75 32 30N 104 30W
Avaré 89 23 4 S 48 58W
Avawata Mts 81 35 30N 116 20W
Aveiro, Brazil 87 3 10 S 55 5W
Aveiro, Port. 104 40 37N 8 38W
Avej 122 35 40N 49 15 E
Avellaneda 88 34 50 S 58 10W
Avellino 108 40 54N 14 46 E
Avenal 80 36 0N 120 8W
Aversa 108 40 58N 14 11 E
Avery 78 47 22N 115 56W
Aves, Islas de 86 12 0N 67 40W
Avesnes-sur-Helpe 101 50 8N 3 55 E
Avesta 111 60 9N 16 10 E
Aveyron □ 102 44 22N 2 45 E
Aviá Terai 88 26 45 S 60 50W
Avignon 103 43 57N 4 50 E
Ávila 104 40 39N 4 43W
Avila Beach 81 35 11N 120 44W
Avilés 104 43 35N 5 57W
Aviston 76 38 36N 89 36W
Avize 101 48 59N 4 0 E
Avoca, Austral. 136 37 5 S 143 26 E
Avoca, U.S.A. 70 42 24N 77 25W
Avoca, R., Austral. 136 35 40 S 143 43 E
Avoca, R., Ireland 97 52 48N 6 10W
Avola 63 51 45N 119 19W
Avon, Ill., U.S.A. 76 40 40N 90 26W
Avon, N.Y., U.S.A. 70 43 0N 77 42W
Avon, S.D., U.S.A. 74 43 0N 98 3W
Avon □ 95 51 30N 2 40W
Avon Downs 135 19 58 S 137 25 E
Avon Is. 135 19 37 S 158 17 E
Avon Lake 70 41 28N 82 3W
Avon, R., Avon, U.K. 95 51 30N 2 43W
Avon, R., Hants., U.K. 95 50 44N 1 45W
Avon, R., Warwick, U.K. 95 52 0N 2 9W
Avondale 37 47 25N 53 12W
Avonlea 56 50 0N 105 0W
Avonmore 47 45 10N 74 58W
Avonmouth 95 51 30N 2 42W
Avranches 100 48 40N 1 20W
Avrillé 102 46 28N 1 28W
Awali 123 26 0N 50 30 E
Awatere, R. 133 41 37 S 174 10 E
Awe, L. 96 56 15N 5 15W
Aweil 115 8 42N 27 20 E
Ax-les-Thermes 102 42 44N 1 50 E
Axarfjörður 110 66 15N 16 45W
Axel Heiberg I. 65 80 0N 90 0W
Axminster 95 50 47N 3 1W
Ay 101 49 3N 4 0 E
Ayabaca 86 4 40 S 79 53W
Ayabe 132 35 20N 135 20 E
Ayacucho, Argent. 88 37 5 S 58 20W
Ayacucho, Peru 86 13 0 S 74 0W
Ayaguz 120 48 10N 80 0 E
Ayamonte 104 37 12N 7 24W
Ayan 121 56 30N 138 16 E
Ayapel 86 8 19N 75 9W
Ayapel, Sa. de 86 7 45N 75 30W
Ayaviri 86 14 50 S 70 35W
Aydın □ 122 37 40N 27 40 E
Ayeritam 128 5 24N 100 15 E
Ayer's Cliff 41 45 10N 72 3W
Ayers Rock 134 25 23 S 131 5 E
Áyios Evstrátios 109 39 34N 24 58 E
Aylen L. 47 45 37N 77 51W
Aylesbury 95 51 48N 0 49W
Aylmer, Ont., Can. 46 42 46N 80 59W
Aylmer, Ont., Can. 48 45 23N 75 50W
Aylmer, Qué., Can. 40 45 24N 75 51W
Aylmer L. 64 64 0N 110 8W
Aylsham 56 53 12N 103 49W
Ayn Zālah 122 36 45N 42 35 E
Ayolas 88 27 10 S 56 59W
Ayon, Ostrov 121 69 50N 169 0 E
Ayr, Austral. 135 19 35 S 147 25 E
Ayr, Can. 49 43 17N 80 27W
Ayr, U.K. 96 55 28N 4 37W
Ayr, R. 96 55 29N 4 40W
Ayre, Pt. of I.o.M. 94 54 27N 4 21W
Aytos 109 42 47N 27 16 E
Ayu, Kepulauan 127 0 35N 131 5 E
Ayutla, Guat. 84 14 40N 92 10W
Ayutla, Mexico 83 16 58N 99 17W
Ayutthaya = Phra Nakhon Si A. 128 14 25N 100 30 E
Ayvalık 122 39 20N 26 46 E
Az Zahrān 122 26 10N 50 7 E
Az-Zilfī 122 26 12N 44 52 E
Az Zubayr 122 30 20N 47 50 E
Azamgarh 125 26 35N 83 13 E
Azārbāijān □ 122 37 0N 44 30 E
Azare 114 11 55N 10 10 E
Azay-le-Rideau 100 47 16N 0 30 E
Azbine = Aïr 114 18 0N 8 0 E
Azerbaijan S.S.R. □ 120 40 20N 48 0 E
Azilda 46 46 33N 81 6W
Azogues 86 2 35 S 78 0W
Azores, Is. 12 38 44N 29 0W
Azov Sea = Azovskoye More 120 46 0N 36 30 E
Azovskoye More 120 46 0N 36 30 E
Azovy 120 64 55N 64 35 E
Aztec 79 36 54N 108 0W
Azúa de Compostela 85 18 25N 70 44W
Azuaga 104 38 16N 5 39W
Azúcar, Presa del 83 26 0N 99 5W
Azuero, Pen. de 84 7 30N 80 30W
Azul 88 36 42 S 59 43W
Azure L. 63 52 23N 120 3W
Azusa 81 34 8N 117 52W

B

Ba Don 128 17 45N 106 26 E
Ba Ngoi = Cam Lam 128 11 50N 109 10 E
Baa 127 10 50 S 123 0 E
Baarle Nassau 105 51 27N 4 56 E
Baarn 105 52 12N 5 17 E
Bāb el Māndeb 115 12 35N 43 25 E
Babahoyo 86 1 40 S 79 30W
Babar, I. 127 8 0 S 129 30 E
Babb 78 48 56N 113 27W
Babbitt 52 47 43N 91 57W
Babinda Hill 136 31 55 S 146 28 E
Babine L. 54 54 48N 126 0W
Babine, R. 54 55 45N 127 44W
Babo 127 2 30 S 133 30 E
Bābol 123 36 40N 52 50 E
Bābol Sar 123 36 45N 52 45 E
Babuyan Is. 131 19 10N 121 40 E
Babylon, Iraq 122 32 40N 44 30 E
Babylon, U.S.A. 71 40 42N 73 20W
Bac Kan 128 22 5N 105 50 E
Bac Lieu = Vinh Loi 128 9 17N 105 43 E
Bac Ninh 128 21 13N 106 4 E
Bac Phan 128 22 0N 105 0 E
Bac Quang 128 22 30N 104 48 E
Bacabal 87 4 15N 44 45W
Bacalar 83 18 12N 87 53W
Bacan,Pulau 127 0 50 S 127 30 E
Bacarès, Le 102 42 47N 3 3 E
Bacarra 127 18 15N 120 37 E
Bacău 107 46 35N 26 55 E
Baccalieu I. 37 48 8N 52 48W
Baccarat 101 48 28N 6 42 E
Bacchus Marsh 136 37 43 S 144 27 E
Bacerac 82 30 18N 108 50W
Bachaquero 86 9 56N 71 8W
Bacharach 105 50 3N 7 46 E
Bachclina 120 57 45N 67 20 E
Back Bay 39 45 3N 66 52W
Back, R. 64 67 15N 95 15W
Backstairs Passage 135 35 40 S 138 5 E
Backus 52 46 51N 94 31W
Bacolod 127 10 40N 122 57 E
Bacqueville 100 49 47N 1 0 E
Bacuit 127 11 20N 119 20 E
Bad Axe 46 43 48N 82 59W
Bad Godesberg 105 50 41N 7 4 E
Bad Heart 60 55 30N 118 18W
Bad Ischl 106 47 44N 13 38 E
Bad Kreuznach 105 49 47N 7 47 E
Bad Lands 74 43 40N 102 10W
Bad, R., U.S.A. 52 46 38N 90 40W
Bad, R., U.S.A. 74 44 10N 100 50W
Badagara 124 11 35N 75 40 E
Badajoz 104 38 50N 6 59W
Badakhshan □ 123 36 30N 71 0 E
Badalona 104 41 26N 2 15 E
Badampahar 125 22 10N 86 10 E
Badanah 122 30 58N 41 30 E
Badas 126 4 33N 114 25 E
Badas, Kepulauan 126 0 45N 107 5 E
Baddeck 39 46 6N 60 45W
Baddo, R. 124 28 15N 65 0 E
Bade 127 7 10 S 139 35 E
Baden, Austria 106 48 1N 16 13 E
Baden, Can. 70 43 14N 80 40W
Baden-Baden 106 48 45N 8 15 E
Baden-Württemberg □ 106 48 40N 9 0 E
Badenoch 96 58 16N 4 5W
Badgastein 106 47 7N 13 9 E
Badger, Can. 37 49 0N 56 4W
Badger, U.S.A. 80 36 38N 119 1W
Badger's Quay 37 49 7N 53 35W
Badghis □ 124 35 0N 63 0 E
Badin 124 24 38N 68 54 E
Badrinath 124 30 45N 79 30 E
Badulla 124 7 1N 81 7 E
Baetas 86 6 5 S 62 15W
Baeza, Ecuador 86 0 25 S 77 45W
Baeza, Spain 104 37 57N 3 25W
Baffin Bay 65 72 0N 64 0W
Baffin I. 65 68 0N 75 0W
Bafia 116 4 40N 11 10 E
Bafoulabé 114 13 50N 10 55W
Bafq 123 31 40N 55 20 E
Bafra 122 41 34N 35 54 E
Bāft, Iran 123 29 15N 56 38 E
Bāft, Iran 123 31 40N 55 25 E
Bafwasende 116 1 3N 27 5 E
Bagamoyo 116 6 28 S 38 55 E
Bagan Siapiapi 126 2 12N 100 50 E

Baganga Barkah

Baganga	127	7 34N	126 33E
Bagdad	81	34 35N	115 53W
Bagdarin	121	54 26N	113 36E
Bagé	89	31 20S	54 15W
Baggs	78	41 8N	107 46W
Baghdād	122	33 20N	44 30E
Bāghīn	123	30 12N	56 45E
Baghlan	124	36 12N	69 0E
Baghlan □	123	36 0N	68 30E
Bagley	74	47 30N	95 22W
Bagnell Dam	76	38 14N	92 36W
Bagnères-de-Bigorre	102	43 5N	0 9E
Bagnères-de-Luchon	102	42 47N	0 38E
Bagnoles-de-l'Orne	100	48 32N	0 25W
Bagnols-les-Bains	102	44 30N	3 40E
Bagnols-sur-Cèze	103	44 10N	4 36E
Bagot □	45	45 35N	72 45W
Bagotville	41	48 22N	70 54W
Bagrash Kol	129	42 0N	87 0E
Baguio	127	16 26N	120 34E
Bahama, Canal Viejo de	84	22 10N	77 30W
Bahama Is.	85	24 40N	74 0W
Bahamas ■	85	24 0N	74 0W
Bahau	128	2 48N	102 26E
Bahawalpur	124	29 37N	71 40E
Bahawalpur □	124	29 5N	71 3E
Bahia = Salvador	87	13 0S	38 30W
Bahia Blanca	88	38 35S	62 13W
Bahia de Caráquez	86	0 40S	80 27W
Bahia Honda	84	22 54N	83 10W
Bahia, Islas de la	84	16 45N	86 15W
Bahia Laura	90	48 10S	66 30W
Bahia Negra	86	20 5S	58 5W
Bahr el 'Arab, R.	115	10 0N	26 0E
Bahr el Ghazâl □	116	7 0N	28 0E
Bahr el Jebel	115	7 30N	30 30E
Bahra	122	21 25N	39 32E
Bahraich	125	27 38N	81 50E
Bahrain ■	123	26 0N	50 35E
Bahramabad	123	30 28N	56 2E
Bahu Kalat	123	25 50N	61 20E
Baia-Mare	107	47 40N	23 17E
Baie Comeau	38	49 12N	68 10W
Baie de l'Abri	35	50 3N	67 0W
Baie-des-Sables	38	48 43N	67 54W
Baie-du-Poste	41	50 24N	73 56W
Baie-du-Renard	38	49 17N	61 50W
Baie Johan Beetz	35	50 18N	62 50W
Baie-St-Paul	41	47 28N	70 32W
Baie-Ste-Anne	39	47 3N	64 58W
Baie-Ste-Catherine	41	48 6N	69 44W
Baie-Ste-Claire	38	49 54N	64 30W
Baie Trinité	38	49 25N	67 20W
Baie Verte, N.B., Can.	39	46 1N	64 6W
Baie Verte, Newf., Can.	37	49 55N	56 12W
Baieville	41	46 8N	72 43W
Baignes	102	45 28N	0 25W
Baigneux-les-Juifs	101	47 31N	4 39E
Ba'iji	122	35 0N	43 30E
Baikal, L.	121	53 0N	108 0E
Baile Atha Cliath = Dublin	97	53 20N	6 18W
Bailleul	101	50 44N	2 41E
Bain-de-Bretagne	100	47 50N	1 40W
Bainbridge, Ga., U.S.A.	73	30 53N	84 34W
Bainbridge, Ind., U.S.A.	77	39 46N	86 49W
Bainbridge, N.Y., U.S.A.	71	42 17N	75 29W
Bainbridge, Ohio, U.S.A.	77	39 14N	83 16W
Baing	127	10 14S	120 34E
Bainsville	43	45 10N	74 25W
Bainville	74	48 8N	104 10W
Baird	75	32 25N	99 25W
Baird Inlet	67	64 49N	164 18W
Baird Mts.	67	67 10N	160 15W
Baird Pen.	65	68 55N	76 4W
Bairnsdale	136	37 48S	147 36E
Baissoklyn	130	47 55N	102 20E
Baitadi	125	29 35N	80 25E
Baja	107	46 12N	18 59E
Baja California	82	32 10N	115 12W
Baja, Pta.	82	29 50N	116 0W
Bajo Boquete	85	8 49N	82 27W
Bakala	116	6 15N	20 20E
Baker, Calif., U.S.A.	81	35 16N	116 8W
Baker, Mont., U.S.A.	74	46 22N	104 12W
Baker, Nev., U.S.A.	78	38 59N	114 7W
Baker, Oreg., U.S.A.	78	44 50N	117 55W
Baker Is.	14	0 10N	176 35E
Baker, L.	65	64 0N	96 0W
Baker Lake	65	64 20N	96 3W
Baker Mt.	63	48 50N	121 49W
Baker's Dozen Is.	36	56 45N	78 45W
Bakersfield, Calif., U.S.A.	81	35 25N	119 0W
Bakersfield, Vt., U.S.A.	71	44 46N	72 48W
Bakhtiari □	122	32 0N	49 0E
Bakinskikh Komissarov	122	39 20N	49 15E
Bakkafjörðr	110	66 2N	14 48W
Bakkagerði	110	65 31N	13 49W
Bakony Forest = Bakony Hegység	107	47 10N	17 30E
Bakony Hegység	107	47 10N	17 30E
Bakouma	116	5 40N	22 56E
Baku	120	40 25N	49 45E
Bala, Can.	46	45 1N	79 37W
Bala, U.K.	94	52 54N	3 36W
Bala, L. = Tegid, L.	94	52 53N	3 38W
Balabac I.	126	8 0N	117 0E
Balabac, Selat	126	7 53N	117 5E
Balabakk	122	34 0N	36 10E
Balabalangan, Kepulauan	126	2 20S	117 30E
Balaghat	124	21 49N	80 12E
Balaghat Ra.	124	18 50N	76 30E
Balaguer	104	41 50N	0 50E
Balakovo	120	52 4N	47 55E
Balancán	83	17 48N	91 32W
Balasore	125	21 35N	87 3E
Balaton	107	46 50N	17 40E
Balboa	84	9 0N	79 30W
Balboa Hill	84	9 6N	79 44W
Balbriggan	97	53 35N	6 10W
Balcarce	88	38 0S	58 10W
Balcarres	56	50 50N	103 35W
Balchik	109	43 28N	28 11E
Balclutha	133	46 15S	169 45E
Bald Knob	75	35 20N	91 35W
Baldock L.	55	56 33N	97 57W
Baldur	57	49 23N	99 15W
Baldwin, Fla., U.S.A.	72	30 15N	82 10W
Baldwin, Mich., U.S.A.	72	43 54N	85 53W
Baldwinsville	71	43 10N	76 19W
Baleares, Islas	104	39 30N	3 0E
Balearic Is. = Baleares, Islas	104	39 30N	3 0E
Baler	127	15 46N	121 34E
Balfate	84	15 48N	86 25W
Balgonie	56	50 29N	104 16W
Bali □	126	8 20S	115 0E
Bali, I.	126	8 20S	115 0E
Bali, Selat	127	8 30S	114 35E
Balikesir	122	39 35N	27 58E
Balikpapan	126	1 10S	116 55E
Balimbing	127	5 10N	120 3E
Baling	128	5 41N	100 55E
Balintang Chan.	131	19 50N	122 0E
Balintang Is.	131	19 55N	122 0E
Balipara	125	26 50N	92 45E
Baliston Spa	71	43 0N	73 52W
Baliza	87	16 0S	52 20W
Balkan Mts. = Stara Planina	109	43 15N	23 0E
Balkan Pen.	93	42 0N	22 0E
Balkh = Wazirabad	123	36 44N	66 47E
Balkh □	123	36 30N	67 0E
Balkhash	120	46 50N	74 50E
Balkhash, Ozero	120	40 0N	74 50E
Balla	125	24 10N	91 35E
Ballachulish	96	56 40N	5 10W
Balladoran	136	31 52S	148 39E
Ballarat	136	37 33S	143 50E
Ballard, L.	134	29 20S	120 10E
Ballater	96	57 2N	3 2W
Ballenas, Canal de las	82	29 10N	113 45W
Balleny Is.	91	66 30S	163 0E
Ballina, Austral.	135	28 50S	153 31E
Ballina, Mayo, Ireland	97	54 7N	9 10W
Ballina, Tipp., Ireland	97	52 49N	8 27W
Ballinafad	49	43 42N	80 1W
Ballinasloe	97	53 20N	8 12W
Ballinger	75	31 45N	99 58W
Ballinrobe	97	53 36N	9 13W
Ballinskelligs	97	51 50N	10 17W
Ballinskelligs B.	97	51 46N	10 11W
Ballivian	88	22 41S	62 10W
Ballycastle	97	55 12N	6 15W
Ballymena	97	54 53N	6 18W
Ballymena □	97	54 53N	6 18W
Ballymoney	97	55 5N	6 30W
Ballymoney □	97	55 5N	6 23W
Ballyshannon	97	54 30N	8 10W
Balmaceda	90	46 0S	71 50W
Balmertown	52	51 4N	93 41W
Balmoral, Austral.	136	37 15S	141 48E
Balmoral, Can.	57	50 15N	97 19W
Balmoral, U.K.	96	57 3N	3 13W
Balmorhea	75	31 2N	103 41W
Balonne, R.	135	28 47S	147 56E
*Balovale	117	13 30S	23 15E
Balpunga	136	33 46S	141 45E
Balrampur	125	27 30N	82 20E
Balranald	136	34 38S	143 33E
Balsam	51	43 59N	79 4W
Balsam L.	70	44 35N	78 50W
Balsas	83	18 0N	99 40W
Balsas, R.	82	18 30N	101 20W
Balta	74	48 12N	100 7W
Baltic Sea	111	56 0N	20 0E
Baltimore, Can.	70	44 2N	78 10W
Baltimore, Ireland	97	51 29N	9 22W
Baltimore, U.S.A.	72	39 18N	76 37W
Baluchistan □	124	27 30N	65 0E
Balygychan	121	63 56N	154 12E
Bam	123	29 7N	58 14E
Bamako	114	12 34N	7 55W
Bambari	116	5 40N	20 35E
Bamberg, Ger.	106	49 54N	10 53E
Bamberg, U.S.A.	73	33 19N	81 1W
Bambili	116	3 40N	26 0E
Bamfield	62	48 45N	125 10W
Bamian □	124	35 0N	67 0E
Bampūr	123	27 15N	60 21E
Bampur, R.	123	27 20N	59 30E
Ban Ban	128	19 31N	103 15E
Ban Bua Chum	128	15 11N	101 12E
Ban Bua Yai	128	15 33N	102 26E
Ban Houei Sai	128	20 22N	100 32E
Ban Kantang	128	7 25N	99 31E
Ban Khe Bo	128	19 10N	104 39E
Ban Khun Yuam	128	18 49N	97 57E
Ban Me Thuot	128	12 40N	108 3E
Ban Phai	128	16 4N	102 44E
Ban Takua Pa	128	8 55N	98 25E
Ban Thateng	128	15 25N	106 27E
†† Banadar Daryay Oman □	123	25 30N	56 0E
Banadia	86	6 54N	71 49W
Banalia	116	1 32N	25 5E
Banam	128	11 20N	105 17E
Bananal, I. do	87	11 30S	50 30W
Banaras = Varanasi	125	25 22N	83 8E
Banat □	107	45 45N	21 15E
Banbridge	97	54 21N	6 17W
Banbridge □	97	54 21N	6 16W
Banbury	95	52 4N	1 21W
Banchory	96	57 3N	2 30W
Bancroft	47	45 3N	77 51W
Bancroft = Chililabombwe	117	12 18S	27 43E
Band-i-Turkistan, Ra.	123	35 2N	64 0E
Banda	124	25 30N	80 26E
Banda Aceh	126	5 35N	95 20E
Banda Banda, Mt.	136	31 10S	152 28E
Banda Elat	127	5 40S	133 5E
Banda, Kepulauan	127	4 37S	129 50E
Banda, La	88	27 45S	64 10W
Banda, Punta	82	31 47N	116 50W
Banda Sea	127	6 0S	130 0E
Bandar = Masulipatnam	125	16 12N	81 12E
Bandār 'Abbās	123	27 15N	56 15E
Bandar-e Būshehr	123	28 55N	50 55E
Bandar-e Chārak	123	26 45N	54 20E
Bandar-e Deylam	122	30 5N	50 10E
Bandar-e Lengeh	123	26 35N	54 58E
Bandar-e Ma'shur	122	30 35N	49 10E
Bandar-e-Nakhīlū	123	26 58N	53 30E
Bandar-e Rīg	123	29 30N	50 45E
* Bandar-e Shāh	123	37 0N	54 10E
** Bandar-e-Shāhpūr	122	30 30N	49 5E
† Bandar-i-Pahlavi	122	37 30N	49 30E
Bandar Maharani = Muar	128	2 3N	102 34E
Bandar Penggaram = Batu Pahat	128	1 50N	102 56E
Bandar Seri Begawan	126	4 52N	115 0E
Bandawe	117	11 58S	34 5E
Bandeira, Pico da	89	20 26S	41 47W
Bandera, Argent.	88	28 55S	62 20W
Bandera, U.S.A.	75	29 45N	99 3W
Banderas, Bahia de	82	20 40N	105 30W
Bandi-San	132	37 36N	140 4E
Bandirma	122	40 20N	28 0E
Bandon	97	51 44N	8 45W
Bandon, R.	97	51 40N	8 11W
Bandundu	116	3 15S	17 22E
Bandung	127	6 36S	107 48E
Banes	85	21 0N	75 42W
Banff, Can.	61	51 10N	115 34W
Banff, U.K.	96	57 40N	2 32W
Banff Nat. Park	61	51 30N	116 15W
Bang Hieng, R.	128	16 24N	105 40E
Bang Lamung	128	13 3N	100 56E
Bang Saphan	128	11 14N	99 28E
Bangala Dam	117	21 7S	31 25E
Bangalore	124	12 59N	77 40E
Bangassou	116	4 55N	23 55E
Banggai	127	1 40S	123 30E
Banggi, P.	126	7 50N	117 0E
Banghāzī	115	32 11N	20 3E
Bangil	127	7 36S	112 50E
Bangka, Pulau, Celebes, Indon.	127	1 50N	125 5E
Bangka, Pulau, Sumatera, Indon.	126	2 0S	105 50E
Bangka, Selat, Indon.	126	2 30S	105 30E
Bangka, Selat, Indon.	126	3 30S	105 30E
Bangkalan	127	7 2S	112 46E
Bangkinang	126	0 18N	100 5E
Bangko	126	2 5S	102 9E
Bangkok	128	13 45N	100 31E
Bangladesh ■	125	24 0N	90 0E
Bangor, Me., U.S.A.	35	44 48N	68 42W
Bangor, Mich., U.S.A.	77	42 18N	86 7W
Bangor, Pa., U.S.A.	71	40 51N	75 13W
Bangor, N.I., U.K.	97	54 40N	5 40W
Bangor, Wales, U.K.	94	53 13N	4 9W
Bangued	127	17 40N	120 37E
Bangui	116	4 23N	18 35E
Bangweulu, L.	116	11 0S	30 0E
Bangweulu Swamp	116	11 20S	30 15E
Bani	85	18 16N	70 22W
Bāniyas	122	35 10N	36 0E
Banja Luka	108	44 49N	17 26E
Banjak, Kepulauan	126	2 10N	97 10E
Banjar	127	7 24S	108 30E
Banjarmasin	126	3 20S	114 35E
Banjarnegara	127	7 24S	109 42E
Banjul	114	13 28N	16 40W
Bankipore	125	25 35N	85 10E
Banks I., B.C., Can.	62	53 20N	130 0W
Banks I., N. W. Terr., Can.	64	73 15N	121 30W
Banks I., P.N.G.	135	10 10S	142 15E
Banks Peninsula	133	43 45S	173 15E
Bankura	125	23 11N	87 18E
Bann, R.	97	55 2N	6 35W
Bann R.	97	54 30N	6 31W
Bannalec	100	47 57N	3 42W
Banning, Can.	34	48 44N	91 56W
Banning, U.S.A.	81	33 58N	116 58W
Banningville = Bandundu	116	3 15S	17 22E
Bannockburn, Can.	47	44 39N	77 33W
Bannockburn, U.K.	96	56 5N	3 55W
Bannu	124	33 0N	70 18E
Banon	103	44 2N	5 38E
Banská Bystrica	107	48 46N	19 14E
Banská Stiavnica	107	48 25N	18 55E
Banswara	124	23 32N	74 24E
Banten	127	6 5S	106 8E
Bantry	97	51 40N	9 28W
Bantry, B.	97	51 35N	9 50W
Bantul	127	7 55S	110 19E
Banu	124	35 35N	69 5E
Banyuls	102	42 29N	3 8E
Banyumas	127	7 32S	109 18E
Banyuwangi	127	8 13S	114 21E
Banzare Coast	91	66 30S	125 0E
Bapatla	125	15 55N	80 30E
Bapaume	101	50 7N	2 50E
Baqūbah	122	33 45N	44 50E
Baquedano	88	23 20S	69 52W
Bar	109	42 8N	19 8E
Bar Harbor	35	44 15N	68 20W
Bar-le-Duc	101	48 47N	5 10E
Bar-sur-Aube	101	48 14N	4 40E
Bar-sur-Seine	101	48 7N	4 20E
Barabai	126	2 32S	115 34E
Barabinsk	120	55 20N	78 20E
Baraboo	74	43 28N	89 46W
Barachois-de-Malbaie	38	48 37N	64 17W
Barachois Pond Prov. Park	37	48 28N	58 15W
Baracoa	85	20 20N	74 30W
Baradero	88	33 52S	59 29W
Baraga	52	46 49N	88 29W
Barahona	85	18 13N	71 7W
Barail Range	125	25 15N	93 20E
Barakhola	125	25 0N	92 45E
Baralzon L.	55	60 0N	98 3W
Baramula	124	34 15N	74 20E
Baran	124	25 9N	76 40E
Baranoa	86	10 48N	74 55W
Baranof I.	67	57 0N	135 10W
Baranovichi	120	53 10N	26 0E
Barão de Melgaço	86	11 50S	60 45W
Barapasi	127	2 15S	137 5E
Barat Daya, Kepulauan	127	7 30S	128 0E
Barataria B.	75	29 15N	89 45W
Baraya	86	3 10N	75 4W
Barbacena	89	21 15S	43 56W
Barbacoas, Colomb.	86	1 45N	78 0W
Barbacoas, Venez.	86	9 29N	66 58W
Barbados ■	85	13 0N	59 30W
Barbara L.	53	49 20N	87 47W
Barbeau Pk.	65	81 54N	75 1W
Barbel, L.	38	51 55N	68 13W
Barberton, S. Afr.	117	25 42S	31 2E
Barberton, U.S.A.	70	41 0N	81 40W
Barbourville	73	36 57N	83 52W
Barbuda I.	85	17 30N	61 40W
Barca, La	82	20 20N	102 40W
Barcaldine	135	23 33S	145 13E
Barce = Al Marj	115	32 25N	20 40E
Barcelona, Spain	104	41 21N	2 10E
Barcelona, Venez.	86	10 10N	64 40W
Barcelonette	103	44 23N	6 40E
Barcelos	86	1 0S	63 0W
Barclay	52	49 47N	92 43W
Barcoo, R.	135	28 29S	137 46E
Bardai	114	21 25N	17 0E
Bardas Blancas	88	35 49S	69 45W
Bardera	115	2 20N	42 27E
Bardoux, L.	38	51 9N	67 50W
Bardsey, I.	94	52 46N	4 47W
Bardstown	77	37 50N	85 29W
Bareilly	124	28 22N	79 27E
Barentin	100	49 33N	0 58E
Barenton	100	48 38N	0 50W
Barents Sea	17	73 0N	39 0E
Barfleur	100	49 40N	1 17W
Barge, La	78	42 12N	110 4W
Barguzin	121	53 37N	109 37E
Barham	136	35 36S	144 8E
Barhi	125	24 15N	85 25E
Bari	108	41 6N	16 52E
Bari Doab	124	30 20N	73 0E
Baria = Phuoc Le	128	10 39N	107 19E
Barinas	86	8 36N	70 15W
Barinas □	86	8 10N	69 50W
Baring	76	40 15N	92 12W
Baring C.	64	70 0N	117 30W
Baringo	116	0 47N	36 16E
Baringo, L.	116	0 47N	36 16E
Barinitas	86	8 45N	70 25W
Barisal	125	22 30N	90 20E
Barisan, Bukit	126	3 30S	102 15E
Barito, R.	126	2 50S	114 50E
Barjac	103	44 20N	4 22E
Barjols	103	43 34N	6 2E
Bark L	47	45 27N	77 51W
Bark L.	34	46 58N	82 25W
Barkah	123	23 40N	58 0E

* Renamed Zambezi

†† Renamed Hormozgan

* Renamed Bandar-e Torkeman

** Renamed Bandar-e Khomeyni

† Renamed Bandar-e Anzali

Barker **Bédarieux**

Barker **70** 43 20N 78 35W
Barkha **129** 31 0N 81 10E
Barkley Sound **62** 48 50N 125 10W
Barkly Tableland **135** 19 50S 138 40E
Barkol **129** 43 37N 93 2E
Barksdale **75** 29 47N 100 2W
Barlee, L. **134** 29 15S 119 30E
Barlee Ra. **134** 23 30S 116 0E
Barlett **80** 36 29N 118 2W
Barletta **108** 41 20N 16 17E
Barlow L. **55** 62 00N 103 0W
Barmedman **136** 34 9S 147 21E
Barmer **124** 25 45N 71 20E
Barmouth **94** 52 44N 4 3W
Barnard Castle **94** 54 33N 1 55W
Barnaul **120** 53 20N 83 40E
Barne Inlet **91** 80 15S 160 0E
Barnes Icecap **65** 70 0N 73 15W
Barnesville **73** 33 6N 84 9W
Barnet, Can. **66** 49 17N 122 55W
Barnet, U.K. **95** 51 37N 0 15W
Barneveld, Neth. **105** 52 7N 5 36E
Barneveld, U.S.A. **71** 43 16N 75 14W
Barneville **100** 49 23N 1 46W
Barney, Mt. **135** 28 17S 152 44E
Barnhart **75** 31 10N 101 8W
Barnsley **94** 53 33N 1 29W
Barnstaple **95** 51 5N 4 3W
Barnston I. **66** 49 12N 122 42W
Barnsville **74** 46 43N 96 28W
Barnwell **61** 49 46N 112 15W
Baro **114** 8 35N 6 18E
Baroda = Vadodara **124** 22 20N 73 10E
Barons **61** 50 0N 113 5W
Barpeta **125** 26 20N 91 10E
Barques, Pte. aux **46** 44 5N 82 55W
Barquisimeto **86** 9 58N 69 13W
Barr **101** 48 25N 7 28E
Barra **87** 11 5S 43 10W
Barra de Navidad **82** 19 12N 104 41W
Barra do Corda **87** 5 30S 45 10W
Barra do Piraí **89** 22 30S 43 50W
Barra Falsa, Pta. da **117** 22 58S 35 37E
Barra Hd. **96** 56 47N 7 40W
Barra, I. **96** 57 0N 7 30W
Barra Mansa **89** 22 35S 44 12W
Barra, Sd. of **96** 57 4N 7 25W
Barrackpur **125** 22 44N 88 30E
Barranca, Lima, Peru **86** 10 45S 77 50W
Barranca, Loreto, Peru **86** 4 50S 76 50W
Barrancabermeja **86** 7 0N 73 50W
Barrancas, Colomb. **86** 10 57N 72 50W
Barrancas, Venez. **86** 8 55N 62 5W
Barrancos **104** 38 10N 6 58W
Barranqueras **88** 27 30S 59 0W
Barranquilla, Atlántico, Colomb. **86** 11 0N 74 50W
Barranquilla, Vaupés, Colomb. **86** 1 39N 72 19W
Barras **86** 1 45S 73 13W
Barraute **40** 48 26N 77 38W
Barre **71** 44 15N 72 30W
Barreal **88** 31 33S 69 28W
Barreiras **87** 12 8S 45 0W
Barreirinhas **87** 2 30S 42 50W
Barreiro **104** 38 40N 9 6W
Barreiros **87** 8 49S 35 12W
Barrême **103** 43 57N 6 23E
Barren I. **128** 12 17N 95 50E
Barren Is. **67** 58 45N 152 0W
Barretos **87** 20 30S 48 35W
Barrhead **60** 54 10N 114 24W
Barrie **46** 44 24N 79 40W
Barriefield **47** 44 14N 76 28W
Barrière **63** 51 12N 120 7W
Barrington, Austral. **135** 31 58S 151 55E
Barrington, Can. **43** 45 6N 73 35W
Barrington, Ill., U.S.A. **77** 42 8N 88 5W
Barrington, R.I., U.S.A. **71** 41 43N 71 20W
Barrington L. **55** 56 55N 100 15W
Barrington Passage **39** 43 30N 65 38W
Barrington Tops. **136** 32 6S 151 28E
Barrow **67** 71 16N 156 50W
Barrow Creek T.O. **134** 21 30S 133 55E
Barrow I. **134** 20 45S 115 20E
Barrow-in-Furness **94** 54 8N 3 15W
Barrow, Pt. **67** 71 22N 156 30W
Barrow Ra. **134** 26 0S 127 40E
Barrow Strait **65** 74 20N 95 0W
Barrows **57** 52 50N 101 27W
Barry, U.K. **95** 51 23N 3 19W
Barry, U.S.A. **76** 39 42N 91 2W
Barry's Bay **47** 45 29N 77 41W
Barsi **124** 18 10N 75 50E
Barsoi **125** 25 48N 87 57E
Barstow, Calif., U.S.A. **81** 34 58N 117 2W
Barstow, Tex., U.S.A. **87** 31 30N 103 25W
Bartica **86** 6 25N 58 40W
Bartle Frere, Mt. **135** 17 27S 145 50E
Bartlesville **75** 36 50N 95 58W
Bartlett **75** 30 46N 97 30W
Bartlett, L. **54** 63 5N 118 20W
Bartletts Harbour **37** 50 57N 57 0W
Barton-upon-Humber **94** 53 41N 0 27W
Bartonville, Can. **48** 43 14N 79 48W
Bartonville, U.S.A. **76** 40 39N 89 39W
Bartow **73** 27 53N 81 49W
Barú, I. de **86** 10 15N 75 35W
Baruun Urt **130** 46 46N 113 15E
Bas-Rhin □ **101** 48 40N 7 30E
Bâsa'idū **123** 26 35N 55 20E
Basankusa **116** 1 5N 19 50E
Bascuñán, C. **88** 28 52S 71 35W
Basel (Basle) **106** 47 35N 7 35E
Bashaw **61** 52 35N 112 58W
Bashi Channel **131** 21 15N 122 0E
Bashkir A.S.S.R. □ **120** 54 0N 57 0E
Basilan, I. **127** 6 35N 122 0E
Basilan, Selat **127** 6 50N 122 0E
Basildon **95** 51 34N 0 29E
Basilicata □ **108** 40 30N 16 0E
Basim **124** 20 3N 77 0E
Basin **78** 44 22N 108 2W
Basin L. **56** 52 38N 105 17W
Basingstoke **95** 51 15N 1 5W
Baskatong Res. **34** 46 46N 75 50W
Baskerville C. **134** 17 10S 122 15E
Basle = Basel **106** 47 35N 7 35E
Basoka **116** 1 16N 23 40E
Basongo **116** 4 15S 20 20E
Basque Provinces = Vascongadas **104** 42 50N 2 45W
Basra = Al Basrah **122** 30 30N 47 50E
Bass River **39** 45 25N 63 47W
Bass Rock **96** 56 5N 2 40W
Bassano **61** 50 48N 112 20W
Bassano, del Grappa **108** 45 45N 11 45E
Bassas da India **117** 22 0S 39 0E
Basse-Terre, I. **85** 16 0N 61 40W
Bassée, La **101** 50 31N 2 49E
Bassein **125** 16 30N 94 30E
Basseterre **85** 17 17N 62 43W
Bassett, Nebr., U.S.A. **74** 42 37N 99 30W
Bassett, Va., U.S.A. **73** 36 48N 79 59W
Bassigny **101** 48 0N 5 10E
Bassin-de-la-Chaudière **42** 46 44N 71 16W
Basswood L. **52** 48 6N 91 52W
Bastak **123** 27 15N 54 25E
Bastar **125** 19 25N 81 40E
Basti **125** 26 52N 82 55E
Bastia **103** 42 40N 9 30E
Bastide, La **102** 44 35N 3 55E
Bastille, L. **38** 51 46N 61 11W
Bastion, C. = Chinmu Chiao **131** 18 10N 109 35E
Bastogne **105** 50 1N 5 43E
Bastrop **75** 30 5N 97 22W
Bata, Eq. Guin. **116** 1 57N 9 50E
Bata, Rumania **114** 46 1N 22 4E
Bataan **127** 14 40N 120 25E
Bataan Pen. **127** 14 38N 120 30E
Batabanó **84** 22 40N 82 20W
Batabanó, G. de **85** 22 30N 82 30W
Batac **127** 18 3N 120 34E
Batagoy **121** 67 38N 134 38E
Batalha **104** 39 40N 8 50W
Batamay **121** 63 30N 129 15E
Batan I. **131** 20 58N 122 5E
Batan Is. **131** 20 25N 121 59E
Batanes Is. **129** 20 30N 122 0E
Batang **127** 6 55S 109 40E
Batangafo **116** 7 25N 18 20E
Batangas **127** 13 35N 121 10E
Batanta, I. **127** 0 55N 130 40E
Bataszék **107** 46 10N 18 44E
Batatais **89** 20 54S 47 37W
Batavia, Ind., U.S.A. **77** 41 55N 88 17W
Batavia, N.Y., U.S.A. **70** 43 0N 78 10W
Batavia, Ohio, U.S.A. **77** 39 5N 84 11W
Batchawana B. **53** 46 53N 84 30W
Batchawana Bay **53** 46 55N 84 37W
Bateman's B. **135** 35 40S 150 12E
Batemans Bay **136** 35 44S 150 11E
Batesburg **73** 33 54N 81 32W
Batesville, Ark., U.S.A. **75** 35 48N 91 40W
Batesville, Ind., U.S.A. **77** 39 18N 85 13W
Batesville, Miss., U.S.A. **75** 34 17N 89 58W
Batesville, Tex., U.S.A. **75** 28 59N 99 38W
Bath, N.B., Can. **39** 46 31N 67 36W
Bath, Ont., Can. **47** 44 11N 76 47W
Bath, U.K. **95** 51 22N 2 22W
Bath, Maine, U.S.A. **35** 43 50N 69 49W
Bath, N.Y., U.S.A. **70** 42 20N 77 17W
Bathgate, U.K. **96** 55 54N 3 38W
Bathgate, U.S.A. **57** 48 53N 97 29W
Bathurst, Austral. **136** 33 25S 149 31E
Bathurst, Can. **35** 47 37N 65 43W
Bathurst B. **135** 14 16S 144 25E
Bathurst, C. **64** 70 34N 128 0W
Bathurst, Gambia = Banjul **114** 13 28N 16 40W
Bathurst I., Austral. **134** 11 30S 130 10E
Bathurst I., Can. **65** 76 0N 100 30W
Bathurst In. **64** 68 10N 108 50W
Bathurst Inlet **64** 66 50N 108 1W
Batiscan **41** 46 30N 72 15W
Batiscan, L. **41** 47 22N 71 55W
Batiscan, R. **41** 46 16N 72 15W
Batman **122** 37 55N 41 5E
Batna **114** 35 34N 6 15E
Baton Rouge **75** 30 30N 91 5W
Batopilas **82** 27 45N 107 45W
Batouri **116** 4 30N 14 25E
Battambang **128** 13 7N 103 12E
Batticaloa **124** 7 43N 81 45E
Battle, Can. **61** 52 58N 110 52W
Battle, U.K. **95** 50 55N 0 30E
Battle Creek **77** 42 20N 85 6W
Battle Ground **80** 45 47N 122 32W
Battle Harbour **36** 52 16N 55 35W
Battle Lake **74** 46 20N 95 43W
Battle Mountain **78** 40 45N 117 0W
Battle, R. **56** 52 43N 108 15W
Battleford **56** 52 45N 108 15W
Batu Gajah **128** 4 28N 101 3E
Batu, Kepulauan **126** 0 30S 98 25E
Batu, Mt. **115** 6 55N 39 45E
Batu Pahat **128** 1 50N 102 56E
Batuata, P. **127** 6 30S 122 20E
Batulaki **127** 5 40N 125 30E
Batumi **120** 41 30N 41 30E
Baturaja **126** 4 11S 104 15E
Baturité **87** 4 28S 38 45W
Baturité, Serra de **87** 4 25S 39 0W
Baubau **127** 5 25S 123 50E
Bauchi **114** 10 22N 9 48E
Baud **100** 47 52N 3 1W
Baudette **52** 48 46N 94 35W
Baugé **100** 47 31N 0 8W
Bauld, C. **37** 51 38N 55 26W
Baule, La **100** 47 18N 2 23W
Baume les Dames **101** 47 22N 6 22E
Bauru **89** 22 10S 49 0W
Baús **87** 18 22S 52 47W
Bautzen **106** 51 11N 14 25E
Baux, Les **103** 43 45N 4 51E
Bavaria = Bayern **106** 49 7N 11 30E
Bavispe, R. **82** 29 30N 109 11W
Baw Baw, Mt. **136** 37 49S 146 19E
Bawdwin **125** 23 5N 97 50E
Bawean **126** 5 46S 112 35E
Bawku **114** 11 3N 0 19W
Bawlake **125** 19 11N 97 21E
Bawlf **61** 52 55N 112 28W
Baxley **73** 31 43N 82 23W
Baxter, Iowa, U.S.A. **76** 41 49N 93 9W
Baxter, Minn., U.S.A. **52** 46 20N 94 16W
Baxter Springs **75** 37 3N 94 45W
Bay Bulls **37** 47 19N 52 50W
Bay City, Mich., U.S.A. **46** 43 35N 83 51W
Bay City, Oreg., U.S.A. **78** 45 45N 123 58W
Bay City, Tex., U.S.A. **75** 28 59N 95 55W
Bay de Verde **37** 48 5N 52 54W
Bay, Laguna de **127** 14 20N 121 11E
Bay L'Argent **37** 47 33N 54 54W
Bay Port **46** 43 51N 83 23W
Bay Roberts **37** 47 36N 53 16W
Bay St. Louis **75** 30 18N 89 22W
Bay Shore **71** 40 44N 73 15W
Bay Springs **75** 31 58N 89 18W
Bay View **133** 39 25S 176 50E
Bayamo **84** 20 20N 76 40W
Bayamón **85** 18 24N 66 10W
Bayan **130** 47 20N 107 55E
Bayan Agt **130** 48 32N 101 16E
Bayan Kara Shan **129** 34 0N 98 0E
Bayan-Ovoo **130** 47 55N 112 0E
Bayan-Uul **130** 49 6N 112 12E
Bayanaul **120** 50 45N 75 45E
Bayandalay **130** 43 30N 103 29E
Bayandelger **130** 47 45N 108 7E
Bayantsogt **130** 47 58N 105 1E
Bayanzürh **130** 47 48N 107 15E
Bayard **74** 41 48N 103 17W
Baybay **127** 10 40N 124 55E
Bayburt **122** 40 15N 40 20E
Bayern □ **106** 49 7N 11 30E
Bayeux **100** 49 17N 0 42W
Bayfield, Can. **46** 43 34N 81 42W
Bayfield, U.S.A. **52** 46 50N 90 48W
Bayir **122** 30 45N 36 55E
Baykal, Oz. **121** 53 0N 108 0E
Baykit **121** 61 50N 95 50E
Baykonur **120** 47 48N 65 50E
Bayombong **127** 16 30N 121 10E
Bayon **101** 48 30N 6 20E
Bayonne **102** 43 30N 1 28W
Bayovar **86** 5 50S 81 0W
Bayram-Ali **120** 37 37N 62 10E
Bayreuth **106** 49 56N 11 35E
Bayrüt **115** 33 53N 35 31E
Bays, L. of **46** 45 15N 79 4W
Bayside **47** 44 7N 77 30W
Baysville **46** 45 9N 79 7W
Bayt Lahm **115** 31 43N 35 12E
Baytown **75** 29 42N 94 57W
Baza **104** 37 30N 2 47W
Bazaruto, I. do **117** 21 40S 35 28E
Bazas **102** 44 27N 0 13W
Bazin, R. **40** 47 29N 75 22W
Beach **74** 46 57N 104 0W
Beach City **70** 40 38N 81 35W
Beach Grove **66** 49 2N 123 3W
Beachburg **47** 45 44N 76 51W
Beachville **46** 43 5N 80 49W
Beachy Head **95** 50 44N 0 16E
Beacon **71** 41 32N 73 58W
Beaconia **57** 50 25N 96 31W
Beaconsfield, Austral. **135** 41 11S 146 48E
Beaconsfield, Can. **44** 45 26N 73 50W
Beagle, Canal **90** 55 0S 68 30W
Beale, C. **62** 48 47N 125 13W
Bealey **133** 43 2S 171 36E
Beamsville **47** 43 12N 79 28W
Bear I. **97** 51 38N 9 50W
Bear I. (Nor.) **17** 74 30N 19 0E
Bear L., Alta., Can. **60** 55 9N 119 4W
Bear L., B.C., Can. **54** 56 10N 126 52W
Bear L., Man., Can. **55** 55 8N 96 0W
Bear L., Ont., Can. **70** 45 28N 79 34W
Bear L., U.S.A. **78** 42 0N 111 20W
Bear, R. **80** 38 56N 121 36W
Bear River **39** 44 34N 65 39W
Bearcreek **78** 45 11N 109 6W
Beardmore **53** 49 36N 87 57W
Beardmore Glacier **91** 84 30S 170 0E
Beardstown **76** 40 0N 90 25W
Bearhaven **97** 51 40N 9 54W
Béarn, Can. **40** 47 17N 79 20W
Béarn, France **102** 43 28N 0 36W
Bearpaw Mt. **78** 48 15N 109 55W
Bearskin Lake **34** 53 58N 91 2W
Beata, C. **85** 17 40N 71 30W
Beata, I. **85** 17 34N 71 31W
Beatrice **74** 40 20N 96 40W
Beatrice, C. **135** 14 20S 136 55E
Beatton, R. **54** 56 15N 120 45W
Beatton River **54** 57 26N 121 20W
Beatty, Can. **56** 52 54N 104 48W
Beatty, U.S.A. **80** 36 58N 116 46W
Beattyville **77** 37 35N 83 42W
Beaucaire **103** 43 48N 4 39E
Beauce, Plaines de **101** 48 10N 1 45E
Beauceville **41** 46 13N 70 46W
Beauchûne, L. **40** 46 35N 78 55W
Beaufort, Austral. **136** 37 25S 143 25E
Beaufort, Malay. **126** 5 30N 115 40E
Beaufort, N.C., U.S.A. **73** 34 45N 76 40W
Beaufort, S.C., U.S.A. **73** 32 25N 80 40W
Beaufort Sea **64** 72 0N 140 0W
Beaufort-West **117** 32 18S 22 36E
Beaugency **101** 47 47N 1 38E
Beauharnois **44** 45 20N 73 52W
Beauharnois □ **44** 45 15N 74 0W
Beauharnois, Canal de **44** 45 19N 73 54W
Beaujeu **103** 46 10N 4 35E
Beaujolais **103** 46 0N 4 25E
Beaulac **41** 45 50N 71 23W
*Beaulieu, Can. **42** 46 51N 71 8W
Beaulieu, France **103** 46 41N 1 37W
Beaulieu, R. **54** 62 3N 113 11W
Beauly **96** 57 29N 4 27W
Beauly, R. **96** 57 26N 4 28W
Beaumaris **94** 53 16N 4 7W
Beaumetz-les-Loges **101** 50 15N 2 40E
Beaumont, Alta., Can. **60** 53 21N 113 25W
Beaumont, Newf., Can. **37** 49 37N 55 41W
Beaumont, Qué., Can. **42** 46 50N 71 1W
Beaumont, France **102** 44 45N 0 46E
Beaumont, Calif., U.S.A. **81** 33 56N 116 58W
Beaumont, Tex., U.S.A. **75** 30 5N 94 8W
Beaumont-le-Roger **100** 49 4N 0 47E
Beaumont-sur-Oise **101** 49 9N 2 17E
Beaune **101** 47 2N 4 50E
Beaune-la-Rolande **101** 48 4N 2 25E
Beauport **42** 46 52N 71 11W
Beaupré **41** 47 3N 70 54W
Beauséjour **57** 50 5N 96 35W
Beausset, Le **103** 43 10N 5 46E
Beauvais **101** 49 25N 2 8E
Beauval **55** 55 9N 107 37W
Beauvoir, Deux Sèvres, France **102** 46 12N 0 30W
Beauvoir, Vendée, France **100** 46 55N 2 1W
Beaver, Alaska, U.S.A. **67** 66 20N 147 30W
Beaver, Okla., U.S.A. **75** 36 52N 100 31W
Beaver, Pa., U.S.A. **70** 40 40N 80 18W
Beaver, Utah, U.S.A. **79** 38 20N 112 45W
Beaver Brook Station **39** 47 8N 65 36W
Beaver City **74** 40 13N 99 50W
Beaver Creek **64** 63 0N 141 0W
Beaver Dam **74** 43 28N 88 50W
Beaver Falls **70** 40 44N 80 20W
Beaver I. **46** 45 40N 85 31W
Beaver, R. **54** 59 52N 124 20W
Beaver, R **34** 55 55N 87 48W
Beaver, R. **55** 55 26N 107 45W
Beaverdell **63** 49 27N 119 6W
Beaverhill L., Alta., Can. **60** 53 27N 112 32W
Beaverhill L., Man., Can. **55** 54 5N 94 50W
Beaverhill L., N.W.T., Can. **55** 63 2N 111 22W
Beaverlodge **60** 55 11N 119 29W
Beavermouth **63** 51 32N 117 23W
Beaverstone, R. **34** 54 59N 89 25W
Beaverton, Can. **46** 44 26N 79 9W
Beaverton, Mich., U.S.A. **46** 43 53N 84 29W
Beaverton, Oreg., U.S.A. **80** 45 29N 122 48W
Beaverville **77** 40 57N 87 39W
Beawar **124** 26 3N 74 18E
Bebedouro **89** 21 0S 48 25W
Beccles **95** 52 27N 1 33E
Bečej **109** 45 36N 20 3E
Béchar **114** 31 38N 2 18E
Becharof L. **67** 58 0N 156 30W
Bechuanaland = Botswana **117** 23 0S 24 0E
Beckley **72** 37 50N 81 8W
Bécon **100** 47 30N 0 50W
Bédarieux **102** 43 37N 3 10E

* *Renamed Ste-Pétronille*

Bédarrides Beuil

Bédarrides **103** 44 2N 4 54 E
Beddington Cr. **59** 51 9N 114 3W
Bedford, N.S., Can. **39** 44 44N 63 40W
Bedford, Qué., Can. **43** 45 7N 72 59W
Bedford, S. Afr. **117** 32 40 S 26 10 E
Bedford, U.K. **95** 52 8N 0 29W
Bedford, Ind., U.S.A. **77** 38 50N 86 30W
Bedford, Iowa, U.S.A. **76** 40 40N 94 41W
Bedford, Ky., U.S.A. **77** 38 36N 85 19W
Bedford, Ohio, U.S.A. **70** 41 23N 81 32W
Bedford, Pa., U.S.A. **70** 40 1N 78 30W
Bedford, Va., U.S.A. **72** 37 25N 79 30W
Bedford □ **95** 52 4N 0 28W
Bedford Basin **39** 44 42N 63 38W
Bedford, C. **135** 15 14 S 145 21 E
Bednesti **54** 53 50N 123 10W
Bedourie **135** 24 30 S 139 30 E
Beebe Plain **41** 45 1N 72 9W
Beech Forest **136** 38 37 S 143 37 E
Beech Fork, R. **77** 37 55N 85 50W
Beech Grove **77** 39 40N 86 2W
Beecher **77** 41 21N 87 38W
Beechey Hd. **63** 48 10N 123 30W
Beechey Point **67** 70 27N 149 18W
Beechworth **136** 36 22 S 146 43 E
Beechy **56** 50 53N 107 24W
Beemunnel **136** 31 40 S 147 51 E
Be'er Sheva' **115** 31 15N 34 48 E
Beeston **94** 52 55N 1 11W
Beeton **46** 44 5N 79 47W
Beetz, L. **38** 50 34N 62 42W
Beeville **75** 28 27N 97 44W
Befale **116** 0 25N 20 45 E
Befandriana **117** 21 55 S 44 0 E
Bega **136** 36 41 S 149 51 E
Béhagle = Lai **114** 9 25N 16 30 E
* Behara **117** 24 55 S 46 20 E
Behbehan **122** 30 30N 50 15 E
Behshahr **123** 36 45N 53 35 E
Beilen **105** 52 52N 6 27 E
Beira **117** 19 50 S 34 52 E
Beira-Alta **104** 40 35N 7 35W
Beira-Baixa **104** 40 2N 7 30W
Beira-Litoral **104** 40 5N 8 30W
Beirut = Bayrūt **115** 33 53N 35 31 E
Beiseker **61** 51 23N 113 32W
Beitbridge **117** 22 12 S 30 0 E
Beja **104** 38 2N 7 53W
Béjaïa **114** 36 42N 5 2 E
Bejestān **123** 34 30N 58 5 E
Bekasi **127** 6 20 S 107 0 E
Békéscsaba **107** 46 40N 21 10 E
Bekok **128** 2 20N 103 7 E
Bela, India **125** 25 50N 82 0 E
Bela, Pak. **124** 26 12N 66 20 E
Bela Crkva **109** 44 55N 21 27 E
Bela Vista, Brazil **89** 22 12 S 56 20W
Bela Vista, Mozam. **117** 26 10 S 32 44 E
Bélâbre **102** 46 34N 1 8 E
Bélair **42** 46 51N 71 26W
Bélanger **44** 45 36N 73 43W
Belanger, R. **57** 53 27N 97 41W
Belawan **126** 3 33N 98 32 E
Belaya Tserkov **120** 49 45N 30 10 E
Belbutte **56** 53 22N 107 49W
Belcher, C. **17** 75 0N 160 0W
Belcher Chan. **65** 77 15N 95 0W
Belcher Is. **36** 56 15N 78 45W
Belcourt **40** 48 24N 77 21W
Belden **80** 40 2N 121 17W
Belém (Pará) **87** 1 20 S 48 30W
Belén, Argent. **88** 27 40 S 67 5W
Belén, Colomb. **86** 1 26N 75 56W
Belén, Parag. **88** 23 30 S 57 6W
Belen **79** 34 40N 106 50W
Bélesta **102** 42 55N 1 56 E
Belfair **80** 47 27N 122 50W
Belfast, S. Afr. **117** 25 42 S 30 2 E
Belfast, U.K. **97** 54 35N 5 56W
Belfast, Maine, U.S.A. **35** 44 30N 69 0W
Belfast, N.Y., U.S.A. **70** 42 21N 78 9W
Belfast □ **97** 54 35N 5 56W
Belfast, L. **97** 54 40N 5 50W
Belfield **74** 46 54N 103 11W
Belfort **101** 47 38N 6 50 E
Belfort □ **101** 47 38N 6 52 E
Belfountain **49** 43 48N 80 1W
Belfry **78** 45 10N 109 2W
Belgaum **124** 15 55N 74 35 E
Belgium ■ **105** 51 30N 5 0 E
Belgorod **120** 50 35N 36 35 E
Belgrade **78** 45 50N 111 10W
Belgrade = Beograd **109** 44 50N 20 37 E
Belhaven **73** 35 34N 76 35W
Beli Drim, R. **109** 42 25N 20 34 E
Belinga **116** 1 10N 13 2 E
Belinyu **126** 1 35 S 105 50 E
Belitung, P. **126** 3 10 S 107 50 E
Belize ■ **83** 17 0N 88 30W
Belize City **83** 17 25N 88 0W
Belize Inlet **62** 51 8N 127 20W
Bell I., Newf., Can. **37** 47 38N 52 58W
Bell I., Newf., Can. **37** 50 46N 55 35W
Bell Irving, R. **54** 56 12N 129 5W
Bell L. **52** 49 48N 90 58W
Bell Peninsula **65** 63 50N 82 0W
Bell, R. **40** 49 48N 77 38W
Bell Ville **88** 32 40 S 62 40W
Bella Bella **62** 52 10N 128 10W
Bella Coola **62** 52 25N 126 40W
Bella Unión **88** 30 15 S 57 40W
Bella Vista, Corrientes, Argent. **88** 28 33 S 59 0W
Bella Vista, Tucuman, Argent. **88** 27 10 S 65 25W
Bellaire, Mich., U.S.A. **46** 44 59N 85 13W
Bellaire, Ohio, U.S.A. **70** 40 1N 80 46W
Bellary **124** 15 10N 76 56 E
Bellburns **37** 50 20N 57 32W
Belle **76** 38 17N 91 43W
Belle Fourche **74** 44 43N 103 52W
Belle Fourche, R. **74** 44 25N 105 0W
Belle Glade **73** 26 43N 80 38W
Belle-Ile **100** 47 20N 3 10W
Belle Isle **37** 51 57N 55 25W
Belle-Isle-en-Terre **100** 48 33N 3 23W
Belle Isle, Str. of **37** 51 30N 56 30W
Belle, La, Fla., U.S.A. **73** 26 45N 81 22W
Belle, La, Mo., U.S.A. **76** 40 7N 91 55W
Belle Plaine, Iowa, U.S.A. **76** 41 51N 92 18W
Belle Plaine, Minn., U.S.A. **74** 44 35N 93 48W
Belle Rive **77** 38 14N 88 45W
Belle River **46** 42 18N 82 43W
Belle Rivière **44** 45 37N 74 6W
Belle-Vallée **43** 45 4N 73 26W
Bellechasse □ **42** 46 47N 71 14W
Belledonne **103** 45 11N 6 0 E
Belledune **35** 47 55N 65 50W
Bellefontaine **77** 40 20N 83 45W
Bellefonte **70** 40 56N 77 45W
Bellegarde, Ain, France **103** 46 4N 5 49 E
Bellegarde, Creuse, France **101** 45 59N 2 19 E
Bellegarde, Loiret, France **101** 48 0N 2 26 E
Belleoram **37** 47 31N 55 25W
Bellerive **43** 45 15N 74 10W
Belleterre **40** 47 25N 78 41W
Belleville, Can. **47** 44 10N 77 23W
Belleville, Rhône, France **103** 46 7N 4 45 E
Belleville, Vendée, France **100** 46 48N 1 28W
Belleville, Ill., U.S.A. **77** 38 30N 90 0W
Belleville, Kans., U.S.A. **74** 39 51N 97 38W
Belleville, N.Y., U.S.A. **71** 43 46N 76 10W
Bellevue, Can. **61** 49 35N 114 22W
Bellevue, Idaho, U.S.A. **78** 43 25N 144 23W
Bellevue, Iowa, U.S.A. **76** 42 16N 90 26W
Bellevue, Mich., U.S.A. **77** 42 27N 85 1W
Bellevue, Ohio, U.S.A. **70** 41 20N 82 48W
Bellevue, Pa., U.S.A. **70** 40 29N 80 3W
Bellevue, Wash., U.S.A. **80** 47 37N 122 12W
Belley **103** 45 46N 5 41 E
Bellflower **76** 39 0N 91 21W
* Bellin (Payne Bay) **36** 60 0N 70 0W
Bellingham **80** 48 45N 122 27W
Bellingshausen Sea **91** 66 0 S 80 0W
Bellinzona **106** 46 11N 9 1 E
Belliveau Cove **39** 44 23N 66 4W
Bello **86** 6 20N 75 33W
Bellona Reefs **135** 21 26 S 159 0 E
Bellows Falls **71** 43 10N 72 30W
Bells Corners **48** 45 19N 75 50W
Bellsite **57** 52 35N 101 4W
Belluno **108** 46 8N 12 6 E
Bellville, Ohio, U.S.A. **70** 40 38N 82 32W
Bellville, Tex., U.S.A. **75** 29 58N 96 18W
Bellwood **70** 40 36N 78 21W
Belly, R. **61** 49 46N 113 2W
Belmar **71** 40 10N 74 2W
Bélmez **104** 38 17N 5 17W
Belmond **76** 42 51N 93 37W
Belmont, Austral. **136** 33 4 S 151 42 E
Belmont, Man., Can. **57** 49 25N 99 27W
Belmont, N.S., Can. **39** 45 25N 63 23W
Belmont, Ont., Can. **46** 42 53N 81 5W
Belmont, U.S.A. **70** 42 14N 78 3W
Belmont Park **63** 48 27N 123 27W
Belmonte **87** 16 0 S 39 0W
Belmopan **83** 17 18N 88 30W
Belmullet **97** 54 13N 9 58W
Belo Horizonte **87** 19 55 S 43 56W
Belo Tsiribihana **117** 19 40 S 43 30 E
Beloeil **45** 45 34N 73 12W
Belogorsk **121** 51 0N 128 20 E
Beloit, Kans., U.S.A. **74** 39 32N 98 9W
Beloit, Wis., U.S.A. **76** 42 35N 89 0W
Belomorsk **120** 64 35N 34 30 E
Belonia **125** 23 15N 91 30 E
Belot, L. **64** 66 53N 126 16W
Belovo **120** 54 30N 86 0 E
Beloye Ozero **120** 45 15N 46 50 E
Belozersk **120** 60 0N 37 30 E
Belterra **87** 2 45 S 55 0W
Belton, S.C., U.S.A. **73** 34 31N 82 39W
Belton, Tex., U.S.A. **75** 31 4N 97 30W
Belturbet **97** 54 6N 7 28W
Belukha **120** 49 50N 86 50 E
Beluran **126** 5 48N 117 35 E
Belvès **102** 44 46N 1 0 E
Belvidere, Ill., U.S.A. **77** 42 15N 88 55W
Belvidere, N.J., U.S.A. **71** 40 48N 75 5W
Belwood **49** 43 47N 80 19W
Belwood, L. **49** 43 46N 80 20W
Belyando, R. **135** 21 38 S 146 50 E
Belyj Jar **120** 58 26N 84 39 E
Belyy, Ostrov **120** 73 30N 71 0 E
Belzoni **75** 33 12N 90 30W
Bement **77** 39 55N 88 34W
Bemidji **74** 47 30N 94 50W
Ben Cruachan, Mt. **96** 56 26N 5 8W
Ben Dearg, mt. **96** 56 54N 3 49W
Ben Hope, mt. **96** 58 24N 4 36W
Ben Lawers, mt. **96** 56 33N 4 13W
Ben Lomond **135** 41 38 S 147 42 E
Ben Lomond, mt. **96** 56 12N 4 39W
Ben Macdhui **96** 57 4N 3 40W
Ben Mhor **96** 57 16N 7 21W
Ben More, Mull, U.K. **96** 56 26N 6 2W
Ben More, Perth, U.K. **96** 56 23N 4 31W
Ben More Assynt **96** 58 7N 4 51W
Ben Nevis, mt. **96** 56 48N 5 0W
Ben Vorlich, Strathclyde, U.K. **96** 56 17N 4 47W
Ben Vorlich, Tayside, U.K. **96** 56 22N 4 15W
Ben Wyvis, mt. **96** 57 40N 4 35W
Bena **52** 47 19N 94 8W
Bena Dibele **116** 4 4 S 22 50 E
Benalla **136** 36 30 S 146 0 E
Benambra, Mt. **136** 36 31 S 147 34 E
Benares = Varanasi **125** 25 22N 83 8 E
Benavides **75** 27 35N 98 28W
Benbecula, I. **96** 57 26N 7 21W
Bencubbin **134** 30 48 S 117 52 E
Bend **78** 44 2N 121 15W
Bendale **50** 43 46N 79 14W
Bender Beila **115** 9 30N 50 48 E
Bendigo **136** 36 40 S 144 15 E
Bénestroff **101** 48 54N 6 45 E
Benet **102** 46 22N 0 35W
Benevento **108** 41 7N 14 45 E
Benfeld **101** 48 22N 7 34 E
Bengal, Bay of **125** 15 0N 00 90 E
Bengawan Solo **127** 7 5 S 112 25 E
Benghazi = Banghāzī **115** 32 11N 20 3 E
Bengkalis **126** 1 30N 102 10 E
Bengkulu **126** 3 50 S 102 12 E
Bengkulu □ **126** 3 48 S 102 16 E
Bengough **56** 49 25N 105 10W
Benguela **117** 12 37 S 13 25 E
Beni **116** 0 30N 29 27 E
Beni, R. **86** 10 30 S 66 0W
Benī Suēf **115** 29 5N 31 6 E
Beniah L. **54** 63 23N 112 17W
Benicia **80** 38 3N 122 9W
Benidorm **104** 38 33N 0 9W
Benin ■ **114** 10 0N 2 0 E
Benin, Bight of **114** 5 0N 3 0 E
Benin City **114** 6 20N 5 31 E
Benjamin Aceval **88** 24 58 S 57 34W
Benjamin Constant **86** 4 40 S 70 15W
Benjamin Hill **82** 30 10N 111 10W
Benkelman **74** 40 7N 101 32W
Bennett **67** 59 56N 134 53W
Bennettsville **73** 34 38N 79 39W
Bennington **71** 42 52N 73 12W
Benny **46** 46 47N 81 38W
Benoa **126** 8 50 S 115 20 E
Bénodet **100** 47 53N 4 7W
Benoit's Cove **37** 49 1N 58 7W
Benoni **117** 26 11 S 28 18 E
Benque Viejo **83** 17 5N 89 8W
Benson, Can. **56** 49 27N 103 1W
Benson, U.S.A. **79** 31 59N 110 19W
Bent **123** 26 20N 59 25 E
Benteng **127** 6 10 S 120 30 E
Bentinck I. **135** 17 3 S 139 35 E
Bentley **61** 52 28N 114 4W
Bento Gonçalves **89** 29 10 S 51 31W
Benton, Ark., U.S.A. **75** 34 30N 92 35W
Benton, Calif., U.S.A. **80** 37 48N 118 32W
Benton, Ill., U.S.A. **76** 38 0N 88 55W
Benton Harbor **77** 42 10N 86 28W
Bentong **128** 3 31N 101 55 E
Benue, R. **114** 7 50N 6 30 E
Beo **127** 4 25N 126 50 E
Beograd **109** 44 50N 20 37 E
Beowawe **78** 40 45N 116 30W
Beppu **132** 33 15N 131 30 E
Berber **115** 18 0N 34 0 E
Berbera **115** 10 30N 45 2 E
Berbérati **116** 4 15N 15 40 E
Berbice, R. **86** 5 20N 58 10W
Berck-sur-Mer **101** 50 25N 1 36 E
Berdsk **120** 54 47N 83 2 E
Berea, Kentucky, U.S.A. **72** 37 35N 84 18W
Berea, Ohio, U.S.A. **70** 41 21N 81 50W
Berebere **127** 2 25N 128 45 E
Berens I. **57** 52 18N 97 18W
Berens, R. **57** 52 25N 96 55W
Berens River **57** 52 25N 97 0W
Beresford **39** 47 42N 65 42W
Bereziuk, L. **36** 54 0N 76 18W
Berezniki **120** 59 24N 56 46 E
Berezovo **120** 64 0N 65 0 E
Bergama **122** 39 8N 27 15 E
Bérgamo **108** 45 42N 9 40 E
Bergen, Norway **111** 60 23N 5 20 E
Bergen, U.S.A. **70** 43 5N 77 56W
Bergen-Binnen **105** 52 40N 4 43 E
Bergen-op-Zoom **105** 51 30N 4 18 E
Bergerac **102** 44 51N 0 30 E
Bergisch-Gladbach **105** 50 59N 7 9 E
Bergland **52** 46 35N 89 34W
Bergues **101** 50 58N 2 24 E
Bergum **105** 53 13N 5 59 E
Berhala, Selat **126** 1 0 S 104 15 E
Berhampore **125** 24 2N 88 27 E
Berhampur **125** 19 15N 84 54 E
Bering Sea **14** 58 0N 167 0 E
Bering Str. **67** 66 0N 170 0W
Beringovskiy **121** 63 3N 179 19 E
Berisso **88** 34 40 S 58 0W
Berja **104** 36 50N 2 56W
Berkeley **80** 37 52N 122 20W
Berkeley Springs **72** 39 38N 78 12W
Berkner I. **91** 79 30 S 50 0W
Berkshire □ **95** 51 30N 1 20W
Berkshire Downs **95** 51 30N 1 30W
Berlaar **105** 51 7N 4 39 E
Berland, R. **60** 54 0N 116 50W
Berlin, Ger. **106** 52 32N 13 24 E
Berlin, Md., U.S.A. **72** 38 19N 75 12W
Berlin, N.H., U.S.A. **71** 44 29N 71 10W
Bermejo, R., Formosa, Argent. **88** 26 30 S 58 50W
Bermejo, R., San Juan, Argent. **88** 30 0 S 68 0W
Bermen, L. **36** 53 35N 68 55W
Bermuda, I. **10** 32 45N 65 0W
Bern (Berne) **106** 46 57N 7 28 E
Bernalillo **79** 35 17N 106 37W
Bernam, R. **128** 3 45N 101 5 E
Bernard L. **46** 45 45N 79 23W
Bernardo de Irigoyen **89** 26 15 S 53 40W
Bernasconi **88** 37 55 S 63 44W
Bernay **100** 49 5N 0 35 E
Bernburg **106** 51 40N 11 42 E
Berne **77** 40 39N 84 57W
Berne = Bern **106** 46 57N 7 28 E
Bernier B. **65** 71 5N 88 15W
Bernier I. **134** 24 50 S 113 12 E
Bernierville **41** 46 6N 71 34W
Beroroha **117** 21 40 S 45 10 E
Beroun **106** 49 57N 14 5 E
Berowra **136** 33 35 S 151 12 E
Berre **103** 43 28N 5 11 E
Berre, Étang de **103** 43 27N 5 5 E
Berrien Springs **77** 41 57N 86 20W
Berrigan **136** 35 38 S 145 49 E
Berry, France **101** 47 0N 2 0 E
Berry, U.S.A. **77** 38 31N 84 23W
Berry Cr. **61** 50 50N 111 37W
Berry Is. **84** 25 40N 77 50W
Berryessa, L. **80** 38 31N 122 6W
Berryville **75** 36 23N 93 35W
Berthaund **74** 40 21N 105 5W
Berthierville **41** 46 5N 73 10W
Berthold **74** 48 19N 101 45W
Bertincourt **101** 50 5N 2 58 E
Bertoua **116** 4 30N 13 45 E
Bertrand, Can. **39** 47 45N 65 4W
Bertrand, U.S.A. **74** 40 35N 99 38W
Berufjörður **110** 64 48N 14 29W
Berwick, N.B., Can. **39** 45 47N 65 36W
Berwick, N.S., Can. **39** 45 3N 64 44W
Berwick, U.S.A. **71** 41 4N 76 17W
Berwick-upon-Tweed **94** 55 47N 2 0W
Berwyn **60** 56 9N 117 44W
Berwyn Mts. **94** 52 54N 3 26W
Besalampy **117** 16 43 S 44 29 E
Besançon **101** 47 9N 6 0 E
Besar **126** 2 40 S 116 0 E
Beserah **128** 3 50N 103 21 E
Besnard L. **55** 55 25N 106 0W
Bessèges **103** 44 18N 4 8 E
Bessemer **74** 46 27N 90 0W
Bessin **100** 49 21N 1 0W
Bessines-sur-Gartempe **100** 46 6N 1 22 E
Bet She'an **115** 32 30N 35 30 E
Bete Grise B. **53** 47 26N 87 53W
Bethanien **117** 26 31 S 17 8 E
Bethany, Can. **47** 44 11N 78 34W
Bethany, Ill., U.S.A. **77** 39 39N 88 45W
Bethany, Mo., U.S.A. **76** 40 18N 94 0W
Bethel, Alaska, U.S.A. **67** 60 50N 161 50W
Bethel, Ohio, U.S.A. **77** 38 58N 84 5W
Bethel, Pa., U.S.A. **70** 40 20N 80 2W
Bethel, Vt., U.S.A. **71** 43 50N 72 37W
Bethesda **50** 43 58N 79 21W
Bethlehem, S. Afr. **117** 28 14 S 28 18 E
Bethlehem, U.S.A. **71** 40 39N 75 24W
Bethlehem = Bayt Lahm **115** 31 43N 35 12 E
Bethulie **117** 30 30 S 25 59 E
Bethune **56** 50 43N 105 13W
Béthune **101** 50 30N 2 38 E
Béthune, R. **100** 49 56N 1 5 E
Betijoque **86** 9 23N 70 44W
Betioky **117** 23 48 S 44 20 E
Beton Bazoches **101** 48 42N 3 15 E
Betong **128** 5 45N 101 5 E
Betroka **117** 23 16 S 46 0 E
Betsiamites **41** 48 56N 68 40W
Betsiamites, R. **41** 48 56N 68 38W
Bettendorf **76** 41 32N 90 30W
Bettiah **125** 26 48N 84 33 E
Bettles **67** 66 54N 150 50W
Betul **124** 21 48N 77 59 E
Betung **126** 2 0 S 103 10 E
Beuil **103** 44 6N 7 0 E

Beulah **Blåvands Huk**

Beulah, Can. **55** 50 16N 101 02W
Beulah, U.S.A. **74** 47 18N 101 47W
Beverley, Austral. **134** 32 9S 116 56E
Beverley, U.K. **94** 53 52N 0 26W
Beverly, Can. **54** 53 36N 113 21W
Beverly, Mass., U.S.A. **71** 42 32N 70 50W
Beverly, Wash., U.S.A. **78** 46 55N 119 59W
Beverly Hills **81** 34 4N 118 29W
Beverwijk **105** 52 28N 4 38E
Bevin, L. **43** 45 57N 74 35W
Bewdley **47** 44 5N 78 19W
Beynat **102** 45 8N 1 44E
Beyneu **120** 45 10N 55 3E
Beypazarı **122** 40 10N 31 48E
Beyşehir Gölü **122** 37 40N 31 45E
Bezhitsa **120** 53 19N 34 17E
Béziers **102** 43 20N 3 12E
Bezwada = Vijayawada **125** 16 31N 80 39E
Bhachau **124** 23 20N 70 16E
Bhadrakh **125** 21 10N 86 30E
Bhadravati **124** 13 49N 76 15E
Bhagalpur **125** 25 10N 87 0E
Bhakra Dam **124** 31 30N 76 45E
Bhamo **125** 24 15N 97 15E
Bhandara **124** 21 5N 79 42E
Bhanrer Ra. **124** 23 40N 79 45E
Bharat = India **124** 24 0N 78 0E
Bharatpur **124** 27 15N 77 30E
Bhatpara **125** 22 50N 88 25E
Bhaunagar = Bhavnagar **124** 21 45N 72 10E
Bhavnagar **124** 21 45N 72 10E
Bhawanipatna **125** 19 55N 83 30E
Bhilsa = Vidisha **124** 23 28N 77 53E
Bhilwara **124** 25 25N 74 38E
Bhima, R. **124** 17 20N 76 30E
Bhimvaram **125** 16 30N 81 30E
Bhind **124** 26 30N 78 46E
Bhiwandi **124** 19 15N 73 0E
Bhiwani **124** 28 50N 76 9E
Bhola **125** 22 45N 90 35E
Bhopal **124** 23 20N 77 53E
Bhubaneswar **125** 20 15N 85 50E
Bhuj **124** 23 15N 69 49E
Bhusaval **124** 21 15N 69 49E
Bhutan ■ **125** 27 25N 89 50E
Biafra, B. of = Bonny, Bight of **116** 3 30N 9 20E
Biak **127** 1 0S 136 0E
Biała Podlaska **107** 52 4N 23 6E
Białystok **107** 53 10N 23 10E
Biaro **127** 2 5N 125 26E
Biarritz **102** 43 29N 1 33W
Bibby I. **55** 61 55N 93 0W
Biberach **106** 48 5N 9 49E
Bic **41** 48 20N 68 41W
Bic, Île du **41** 48 24N 68 52W
Bicester **95** 51 53N 1 9W
Biche, L. la **60** 54 50N 112 3W
Biche, La, R. **54** 59 57N 123 50W
Bickerton West **39** 45 6N 61 44W
Bicknell, Ind., U.S.A. **77** 38 50N 87 20W
Bicknell, Utah, U.S.A. **79** 38 16N 111 35W
Bida **114** 9 3N 5 58E
Bidar **124** 17 55N 77 35E
Biddeford **35** 43 30N 70 28W
Bideford **95** 51 1N 4 13W
Bidor **128** 4 6N 101 15E
Bié, Planalto de **117** 12 0S 16 0E
Bieber **78** 41 4N 121 6W
Biel (Bienne) **106** 47 8N 7 14E
Bielé Karpaty **107** 49 5N 18 0E
Bielefeld **106** 52 2N 8 31E
Biella **108** 45 33N 8 3E
Bielsko-Biała **107** 49 50N 19 8E
Bien Hoa **128** 10 57N 106 49E
Bienfait **56** 49 10N 102 50W
Bienne = Biel **106** 47 8N 7 14E
Bienville, L. **36** 55 5N 72 40W
Big B. **36** 55 43N 60 35W
Big Bar Creek **63** 51 12N 122 7W
Big Basswood L. **46** 46 25N 83 23W
Big Bay **53** 46 49N 87 44W
Big Bear City **81** 34 16N 116 51W
Big Bear L. **81** 34 15N 116 56W
Big Beaver **56** 49 10N 105 10W
Big Beaver House **34** 52 59N 89 50W
Big Belt Mts. **78** 46 50N 111 30W
Big Bend Nat. Park **75** 29 15N 103 15W
Big Bend Res. **61** 52 59N 115 30W
Big Black, R. **75** 32 35N 90 30W
Big Blue, R., Ind., U.S.A. **77** 39 12N 85 56W
Big Blue, R., Kans., U.S.A. **74** 40 20N 96 40W
Big Cr. **63** 51 42N 122 41W
Big Creek, Can. **63** 51 43N 123 2W
Big Creek, U.S.A. **80** 37 11N 119 14W
Big Cypress Swamp **73** 26 12N 81 10W
Big Delta **67** 64 15N 145 0W
Big Falls **52** 48 11N 93 48W
Big Fork **52** 47 45N 93 39W
Big Fork, R. **52** 48 31N 93 43W
Big Horn **78** 46 11N 107 25W
Big Horn Dam **61** 52 20N 116 20W
Big Horn Mts. = Bighorn Mts. **78** 44 30N 107 30W
Big Horn R. **78** 45 30N 108 10W
Big I., N.W.T., Can. **65** 62 43N 70 43W
Big I., Ont., Can. **52** 49 9N 94 40W
Big L. **59** 53 37N 113 42W
Big Lake **75** 31 12N 101 25W
Big Moose **71** 43 49N 74 58W
Big Muddy L. **56** 49 9N 104 51W
Big Muddy, R **76** 38 0N 89 0W
Big Muddy, R. **74** 48 25N 104 45W
Big Pine **80** 37 12N 118 17W
Big Piney **78** 42 32N 110 3W
Big Pond **39** 45 57N 60 32W
Big Quill L. **56** 51 55N 104 22W
Big, R., Can. **36** 54 50N 58 55W
Big, R., U.S.A. **76** 38 27N 90 37W
Big Rapids **72** 43 42N 85 27W
Big Rideau L. **47** 44 40N 76 15W
Big River **56** 53 50N 107 0W
Big Run **70** 40 57N 78 55W
Big Sable Pt. **72** 44 5N 86 30W
Big Salmon **67** 61 50N 136 0W
Big Sand L. **55** 57 45N 99 45W
Big Sandy **78** 48 12N 110 9W
Big Sandy Cr. **74** 38 52N 103 11W
Big Sandy L., Can. **56** 54 27N 104 6W
Big Sandy L., U.S.A. **52** 46 45N 93 20W
Big Sioux, R. **74** 44 20N 96 53W
Big Snowy Mt. **78** 46 50N 109 15W
Big Spring **75** 32 10N 101 25W
Big Springs **74** 41 4N 102 3W
Big Stone City **74** 45 20N 96 30W
Big Stone Gap **73** 36 52N 82 45W
Big Stone L. **74** 45 30N 96 35W
Big Sur **80** 36 15N 121 48W
Big Trout L., Ont., Can. **34** 53 40N 90 0W
Big Trout L., Ont., Can. **47** 45 46N 78 37W
Big Valley **61** 52 2N 112 46W
Biganos **102** 44 39N 0 59W
Bigfork **78** 48 3N 114 2W
Biggar **56** 52 4N 108 0W
Biggs **80** 39 24N 121 43W
Bighorn Mts. **78** 44 30N 107 30W
Bigniba, R. **40** 49 18N 77 20W
Bigot, L. **38** 50 50N 65 39W
Bigsby I **52** 49 4N 94 34W
Bigstick L. **56** 50 16N 109 20W
Bigstone L. **57** 53 42N 95 44W
Bigtimber **78** 45 53N 110 0W
Bihać **108** 44 49N 15 57E
Bihar **125** 25 5N 85 40E
Bihar □ **125** 25 0N 86 0E
Bihé Plateau **117** 12 0S 16 0E
Bihor, Munţii **107** 46 29N 22 47E
Bijagós, Arquipélago dos **114** 11 15N 16 10W
Bijapur, Mad. P., India **125** 18 50N 80 50E
Bijapur, Mysore, India **124** 16 50N 75 55E
Bijār **122** 35 52N 47 35E
Bijeljina **109** 44 46N 19 17E
Bijnor **124** 29 27N 78 11E
Bikaner **124** 28 2N 73 18E
Bikin **121** 46 50N 134 20E
Bikini, atoll **14** 12 0N 167 30E
Bikoro **116** 0 48S 18 15E
Bilād Banī Bū 'Alt **123** 22 0N 59 20E
Bilara **124** 26 14N 73 53E
Bilaspur **125** 22 2N 82 15E
Bilauk Taungdan **128** 13 0N 99 0E
Bilbao **104** 43 16N 2 56W
Bildudalur **110** 65 41N 23 36W
Bilecik **122** 40 5N 30 5E
Bilibino **121** 68 3N 166 20E
Bilir **121** 65 40N 131 20E
Bill **74** 43 18N 105 18W
Billabong Creek **136** 35 5S 144 2E
Billingham **94** 54 36N 1 18W
Billings **78** 45 43N 108 29W
Billiton Is = Belitung **126** 3 10S 107 50E
Billom **102** 45 43N 3 20E
Bilma **114** 18 50N 13 30E
Biloxi **75** 30 30N 89 0W
Bima **127** 8 22S 118 49E
Bimberi Peak, mt. **136** 35 44S 148 51E
Bimbo **116** 4 15N 18 33E
Bina-Etawah **124** 24 13N 78 14E
Binalbagan **127** 10 12N 122 50E
Binalong **136** 34 40S 148 39E
Binatang **126** 2 10N 111 40E
Binbrook **49** 43 7N 79 48W
Binche **105** 50 26N 4 10E
Bindura **117** 17 18S 31 18E
Bingen **105** 49 57N 7 53E
Bingerville **114** 5 18N 3 49W
Bingham **35** 45 5N 69 50W
Bingham Canyon **78** 40 31N 112 10W
Binghamton **71** 42 9N 75 54W
Bingöl **122** 39 20N 41 0E
Binh Dinh = An Nhon **128** 13 55N 109 7E
Binh Son **128** 15 20N 108 40E
Binjai **126** 3 50N 98 30E
Binnaway **136** 31 28S 149 24E
Binongko **127** 5 55S 123 55E
Binscarth **57** 50 37N 101 17W
Bint **123** 26 22N 59 25E
Bintan **126** 1 0N 104 0E
Bintulu **126** 3 10N 113 0E
Binzert = Bizerte **114** 37 15N 9 50E
Bio-Bio □ **88** 37 35S 72 0W
Bir **124** 19 0N 75 54E
Bir Mogreïn, (Fort Trinquet) **114** 25 10N 11 25W
Bira **127** 2 3S 132 2E
Birch Cliff, Ont., Can. **49** 43 41N 79 18W
Birch Cliff, Ont., Can. **50** 43 41N 79 17W
Birch Cove **39** 44 42N 63 41W
Birch Hills **56** 52 59N 105 25W
Birch I. **57** 52 26N 99 54W
Birch Island **63** 51 37N 119 54W
Birch L., Alta., Can. **60** 53 19N 111 35W
Birch L., N.W.T., Can. **54** 62 4N 116 33W
Birch L., Ont., Can. **52** 51 23N 92 18W
Birch L., Sask., Can. **56** 53 27N 108 10W
Birch L., U.S.A. **52** 47 48N 91 43W
Birch Manor **48** 45 26N 75 46W
Birch Mts. **54** 57 30N 113 10W
Birch River **57** 52 24N 101 6W
Birch Run **46** 43 15N 83 48W
Birchip **136** 35 56S 142 55E
Birchy Bay **37** 49 21N 54 44W
Bird **55** 56 30N 94 13W
Bird City **74** 39 48N 101 33W
Bird Cove **37** 51 3N 56 56W
Bird I. **135** 22 10S 155 28E
Birds **77** 38 50N 87 40W
Birds Hill **58** 49 59N 97 0W
Birdseye **77** 38 19N 86 42W
Birdsville **135** 25 51S 139 20E
Birdum **134** 15 39S 133 13E
Birecik **122** 37 0N 38 0E
Bireuen **126** 5 14N 96 39E
Birigui **89** 21 18S 50 16W
Birjand **123** 32 57N 59 10E
Birken **63** 50 28N 122 37W
Birkenhead **94** 53 24N 3 1W
Bîrlad **107** 46 15N 27 38E
Birmingham, U.K. **95** 52 30N 1 55W
Birmingham, U.S.A. **46** 42 33N 83 15W
Birmingham, Ala., U.S.A. **73** 33 31N 86 50W
Birmingham, Iowa, U.S.A. **76** 40 53N 91 57W
Birmitrapur **125** 22 30N 84 10E
Birobidzhan **121** 48 50N 132 50E
Biron **38** 48 12N 66 16W
Birr **97** 53 7N 7 55W
Birsay **56** 51 6N 106 59W
Birsk **120** 55 25N 55 30E
Birtle **57** 50 30N 101 5W
Birur **124** 13 30N 75 55E
Bisa **127** 1 10S 127 40E
Bisbee **79** 31 30N 110 0W
Biscay, B. of **12** 45 0N 2 0W
Biscayne B. **73** 25 40N 80 12W
Bischwiller **101** 48 41N 7 50E
Biscoe I. **91** 66 0S 67 0W
Biscostasing **53** 47 18N 82 9W
Biscotasi L. **53** 47 22N 82 1W
Biscucuy **86** 9 22N 69 59W
Bishop, Calif., U.S.A. **80** 37 20N 118 26W
Bishop, Tex., U.S.A. **75** 27 35N 97 49W
Bishop Auckland **94** 54 40N 1 40W
Bishop, Mt. **66** 49 26N 122 56W
Bishop's Falls **37** 49 2N 55 30W
Bishop's Stortford **95** 51 52N 0 11E
Bishopton **41** 45 35N 71 35W
Biskra **114** 34 50N 5 44E
Bislig **127** 8 15N 126 27E
Bismarck, Can. **49** 43 3N 79 30W
Bismarck, Mo., U.S.A. **76** 37 46N 90 38W
Bismarck, N.Dak., U.S.A. **74** 46 49N 100 49W
Bismarck Arch. **14** 2 30S 150 0E
Bison **74** 45 34N 102 28W
Bison L. **60** 57 12N 116 8W
Bispfors **110** 63 1N 16 39E
Bissagos = Bijagós **114** 11 15N 16 10W
Bissau **114** 11 45N 15 45W
Bissett **57** 51 2N 95 41W
Bistcho L. **54** 59 45N 118 50W
Bistrita **107** 47 9N 24 35E
Bistriţa, R. **107** 47 10N 24 30E
Bitam **116** 2 5N 11 25E
Bitche **101** 48 58N 7 25E
Bitlis **122** 38 20N 42 3E
Bitola (Bitolj) **109** 41 5N 21 10E
Bitter Creek **78** 41 39N 108 36W
Bitter L. **56** 50 7N 109 48W
Bitterfontein **117** 31 0S 18 32E
Bittern L., Alta., Can. **61** 53 3N 113 5W
Bittern L., Sask., Can. **56** 53 56N 105 45W
Bitteroot, R. **78** 46 30N 114 20W
Bitterroot Range **78** 46 0N 114 20W
Bitterwater **80** 36 23N 121 0W
Bitumount **54** 57 26N 111 40W
Biu **114** 10 40N 12 3E
Biwa-Ko **132** 35 15N 135 45E
Biwabik **74** 47 33N 92 19W
Biysk **120** 52 40N 85 0E
Bizard, Île **44** 45 29N 73 54W
Bizerte (Binzert) **114** 37 15N 9 50E
Bjargtangar **110** 65 30N 24 30W
Bjelovar **108** 45 56N 16 49E
Bjorkdale **56** 52 43N 103 39W
Blache, L. de la **41** 50 5N 69 29W
Black B. **52** 48 40N 88 25W
Black Creek **62** 49 49N 125 7W
Black Diamond **61** 50 45N 114 14W
Black Hills **74** 44 0N 103 50W
Black Horse **49** 43 59N 79 49W
Black I. **57** 51 12N 96 30W
Black L., Can. **55** 59 12N 105 15W
Black L., U.S.A. **46** 45 28N 84 15W
Black Lake **41** 46 1N 71 22W
Black Mesa, Mt. **75** 36 57N 102 55W
Black Mt. **66** 49 23N 123 13W
Black Mt. = Mynydd Du **95** 51 45N 3 45W
Black Mts. **95** 51 52N 3 5W
Black Pines **63** 50 57N 120 15W
Black, R., Can. **46** 44 42N 79 19W
Black, R., Ark., U.S.A. **75** 36 15N 90 45W
Black, R., Mich., U.S.A. **46** 43 3N 82 37W
Black, R., Minn., U.S.A. **52** 48 32N 93 51W
Black, R., N.Y., U.S.A. **71** 43 59N 76 40W
Black, R., Wis., U.S.A. **74** 44 18N 90 52W
Black Range, Mts. **79** 33 30N 107 55W
Black River, Jamaica **84** 18 0N 77 50W
Black River, U.S.A. **46** 44 53N 83 18W
Black Rock Pt. **36** 60 2N 64 10W
Black Sea **92** 43 30N 35 0E
Black Sturgeon L. **52** 49 20N 88 53W
Black Sugarloaf, Mt. **136** 31 18S 151 35E
Black Warrior, R. **73** 33 0N 87 45W
Blackall **135** 24 25S 145 45E
Blackball **133** 42 22S 171 26E
Blackburn **94** 53 44N 2 30W
Blackburn Hamlet **48** 45 26N 75 33W
Blackburn, Mt. **67** 61 5N 142 3W
Blackduck **52** 47 43N 94 32W
Blackfalds **61** 52 23N 113 47W
Blackfoot, Can. **60** 53 17N 110 10W
Blackfoot, U.S.A. **78** 43 13N 112 12W
Blackfoot, R. **78** 47 0N 113 35W
Blackhead **37** 47 32N 52 39W
Blackhead Road **37** 47 33N 52 43W
Blackheath **49** 43 4N 79 49W
Blackie **61** 50 36N 113 37W
Blackmud Cr. **59** 53 27N 113 33W
Blackpool, Can. **43** 45 1N 73 28W
Blackpool, U.K. **94** 53 48N 3 3W
Blackriver **70** 44 46N 83 17W
Blacks Harbour **39** 45 3N 66 49W
Blacksburg **72** 37 17N 80 23W
Blacksod B. **97** 54 6N 10 0W
Blackstone **72** 37 6N 78 0W
Blackstone, R. **54** 61 5N 122 55W
Blackstone Ra. **134** 26 00S 129 00E
Blackville **39** 46 44N 65 50W
Blackwater **54** 53 20N 123 0W
Blackwater, R., Cork, Ireland **97** 52 5N 9 3W
Blackwater, R., Limerick, Ireland **97** 51 55N 7 50W
Blackwater, R., Meath, Ireland **97** 53 46N 7 0W
Blackwater, R., U.K. **97** 54 31N 6 35W
Blackwater, R., U.S.A. **76** 38 59N 92 59W
Blackwell **75** 36 55N 97 20W
Blackwells Corner **81** 35 37N 119 47W
Bladworth **56** 51 22N 106 8W
Blaenau Ffestiniog **94** 53 0N 3 57W
Blagnac **102** 43 38N 1 24E
Blagoveshchensk **121** 50 20N 127 30E
Blaine **66** 48 59N 122 43W
Blaine Lake **56** 52 51N 106 52W
Blainville, Can. **44** 45 40N 73 52W
Blainville, France **101** 48 33N 6 23E
Blair, Can. **49** 43 23N 80 23W
Blair, U.S.A. **74** 41 33N 96 10W
Blair Athol **135** 22 42S 147 31E
Blair Atholl **96** 56 46N 3 50W
Blairgowrie **96** 56 36N 3 20W
Blairmore **61** 49 40N 114 25W
Blairs Mills **70** 40 17N 77 45W
Blairsden **80** 39 47N 120 37W
Blairsville **70** 40 27N 79 15W
Blairville **49** 43 14N 79 2W
Blake Pt. **52** 48 12N 88 27W
Blakely **73** 31 22N 85 0W
Blakesburg **76** 40 58N 92 38W
Blâmont **101** 48 35N 6 50E
Blanc, Le **102** 46 37N 1 3E
Blanc, Mont **103** 45 48N 6 50E
Blanca, Bahia **90** 39 10S 61 30W
Blanca Peak **79** 37 35N 105 29W
Blanchard **75** 35 8N 97 40W
Blanchardville **76** 42 48N 89 52W
Blanche L., S. Austral., Austral. **134** 29 15S 139 40E
Blanche L., W. Austral., Austral. **135** 22 25S 123 17E
Blanche, R. **48** 45 30N 75 33W
Blanchester **77** 39 17N 83 59W
Blanco **75** 30 7N 98 30W
Blanco, C., C. Rica **84** 9 34N 85 8W
Blanco, C., Peru **86** 4 10S 81 10W
Blanco, C., U.S.A. **78** 42 50N 124 40W
Blanco, R. **88** 31 54S 69 42W
Blanda **110** 65 20N 19 40W
Blandford Forum **95** 50 52N 2 10W
Blanding **79** 37 35N 109 30W
Blandinsville **76** 40 33N 90 52W
Blankenberge **105** 51 20N 3 9E
Blanquefort **102** 44 55N 0 38W
Blanquilla, La **86** 11 51N 64 37W
Blanquillo **89** 32 53S 55 37W
Blantyre **117** 15 45S 35 0E
Blarney **97** 51 57N 8 35W
Blåvands Huk **111** 55 33N 8 4E

Blaydon Bowbells

Blaydon 94 54 56N 1 47W
Blaye 102 45 8N 0 40W
Blaye-les-Mines 102 44 1N 2 8E
Blayney 136 33 32S 149 14E
Blaze, Pt. 134 12 56S 130 11E
Blednaya, Gora 120 65 50N 65 30E
Bleiburg 106 46 35N 14 49E
Blekinge län □ 111 56 20N 15 20E
Blenheim, Can. 46 42 20N 82 0W
Blenheim, N.Z. 133 41 38S 174 5E
Bléone, R. 103 44 5N 6 0E
Bletchley 95 51 59N 0 44W
Bleu, L. 40 46 35N 78 24W
Bleymard, Le 102 44 30N 3 42E
Blida 114 36 30N 2 49E
Bligh Sound 133 44 47S 167 32E
Blind River 46 46 10N 82 58W
Blissfield, Can. 39 46 36N 66 5W
Blissfield, U.S.A. 77 41 50N 83 52W
Blitar 127 8 5S 112 11E
Block I., U.S.A. 71 41 11N 71 35W
Block I., U.S.A. 71 41 13N 71 35W
Block Island Sound 71 41 17N 71 35W
Blockton 76 40 37N 94 29W
Bloemfontein 117 29 6S 26 14E
Bloemhof 117 27 38S 25 32E
Blois 100 47 35N 1 20E
Blönduós 110 65 40N 20 12W
Bloodvein, R. 57 51 47N 96 43W
Bloody Foreland 97 55 10N 8 18W
Bloomer 74 45 8N 91 30W
Bloomfield, Newf., Can. 37 48 23N 53 54W
Bloomfield, Ont., Can. 47 43 59N 77 14W
Bloomfield, Ind., U.S.A. 77 39 1N 86 57W
Bloomfield, Iowa, U.S.A. 76 40 44N 92 26W
Bloomfield, Ky., U.S.A. 77 37 55N 85 19W
Bloomfield, N. Mexico, U.S.A. 79 36 46N 107 59W
Bloomfield, Nebr., U.S.A. 74 42 38N 97 40W
Bloomingburg 77 39 36N 83 24W
Bloomingdale 49 43 31N 80 27W
Bloomington, Ill., U.S.A. 76 40 49N 89 0W
Bloomington, Ind., U.S.A. 77 39 10N 86 30W
Bloomington, Wis., U.S.A. 76 42 53N 90 55W
Bloomsburg 71 41 0N 76 30W
Blora 127 6 57S 111 25E
Blossburg 70 41 40N 77 4W
Blossom Park 48 45 21N 75 37W
Blouin 42 46 2N 71 0W
Blountstown 73 30 28N 85 5W
Blubber Bay 62 49 47N 124 37W
Blue Hills 64 75 34N 114 30W
Blue I. 77 41 40N 87 40W
Blue Lake 78 40 53N 124 0W
Blue Mesa Res. 79 38 30N 107 15W
Blue Mound 76 39 42N 89 7W
Blue Mountain Peak 85 18 0N 76 40W
Blue Mts., Austral. 136 33 40S 150 0E
Blue Mts., Jamaica 85 18 0N 76 40W
Blue Mts., Ore., U.S.A. 78 45 15N 119 0W
Blue Mts., Pa., U.S.A. 71 40 30N 76 0W
Blue Mud B. 135 13 30S 136 0E
Blue Nile, R. = Nîl el Azraq 114 10 30N 35 0E
Blue, R. 77 38 11N 86 18W
Blue Ridge 60 54 8N 115 22W
Blue Ridge, Mts. 73 36 30N 80 15W
Blue River 63 52 6N 119 18W
Blue Springs 76 39 1N 94 17W
Blue Stack Mts. 97 54 46N 8 5W
Blueberry Mountain 60 55 56N 119 9W
Blueberry, R. 54 56 45N 120 49W
Bluefield 72 37 18N 81 14W
Bluefields 84 12 0N 83 50W
Bluenose L. 64 68 30N 119 35W
Bluestack, mt. 97 54 46N 8 5W
Bluff, N.Z. 133 46 37S 168 20E
Bluff, U.S.A. 67 64 50N 147 15W
Bluffs 76 39 45N 90 32W
Bluffton, Can. 61 52 45N 114 17W
Bluffton, Ind., U.S.A. 77 40 43N 85 9W
Bluffton, Ohio, U.S.A. 77 40 54N 83 54W
Bluford 77 38 20N 88 45W
Blumenau 89 27 0S 49 0W
Blunt 74 44 32N 100 0W
Bly 78 42 23N 121 0W
Blyth, Can. 46 43 44N 81 26W
Blyth, U.K. 94 55 8N 1 32W
Blythe 81 33 40N 114 33W
Blytheswood 70 42 8N 82 37W
Bo 114 7 55N 11 50W
Bo Duc 128 11 58N 106 50E
Boa Vista 86 2 48N 60 30W
Boaco 84 12 29N 85 35W
Boat Harbour 37 47 24N 54 50W
Bobbili 125 18 35N 83 30E
Bobcaygeon 47 44 33N 78 33W
Bobo-Dioulasso 114 11 8N 4 13W
Bóbr, R. 106 51 50N 15 15E
Bobruysk 120 53 10N 29 15E
Bobundara 136 36 32S 148 59E
Bobures 86 9 15N 71 11W
Boca de Uracoa 86 9 8N 62 20W
Bôca do Acre 86 8 50S 67 27W
Boca, La 84 9 0N 79 30W
Bocage 99 49 0N 1 0W
Bocaiúva 87 17 7S 43 49W
Bocaranga 116 7 0N 15 35E
Bocas del Dragon 86 11 0N 61 50W
Bocas del Toro 84 9 15N 82 20W
Bochart 41 49 10N 73 30W
Bocholt 106 51 50N 6 35E
Bochum 105 51 28N 7 12E
Bocoyna 82 27 52N 107 35W
Boda 116 4 19N 17 26E
Bodaybo 121 57 50N 114 0E
Bodega Bay 80 38 20N 123 3W
Boden 110 65 50N 21 42E
Bodensee 106 47 35N 9 25E
Bodhan 124 18 40N 77 55E
Bodmin 95 50 28N 4 44W
Bodmin Moor 95 50 33N 4 36W
Bodrog, R. 107 48 15N 21 35E
Bodrum 122 37 5N 27 30E
Boën 103 45 44N 4 0E
Boende 116 0 24S 21 12E
Boerne 75 29 48N 98 41W
Bogalusa 75 30 50N 89 55W
Bogan Gate 136 33 7S 147 49E
Bogan, R. 136 32 45S 148 8E
Bogandyera, Mt. 136 35 50S 147 5E
Bogata 75 33 26N 95 10W
Bogenfels 117 27 25S 15 25E
Boggeragh Mts. 97 52 2N 8 55W
Boggy Cr. 58 50 40N 104 50W
Bognor Regis 95 50 47N 0 40W
Bogo 127 11 3N 124 0E
Bogor 127 6 36S 106 48E
Bogoro 116 9 37N 9 29E
Bogorodskoye 121 52 22N 140 30E
Bogotá 86 4 34N 74 0W
Bogotol 120 56 15N 89 50E
Bogra 125 24 51N 89 22E
Bogtown 43 45 5N 73 31W
Boguchany 121 58 40N 97 30E
Bohain 101 49 59N 3 28E
Bohemian Forest = Böhmerwald 106 49 30N 12 40E
Böhmerwald 106 49 30N 12 40E
Boholl, I. 127 9 50N 124 10E
Bohotleh 115 8 20N 46 25E
Boi, Pta. de 89 23 55S 45 15W
Boiestown 35 46 27N 66 26W
Boileau, C. 134 17 40S 122 7E
Bois Blanc I. 46 45 50N 84 30W
Bois-des-Filion 44 45 40N 73 45W
Bois, L. des 64 66 50N 125 9W
Boisdale 39 46 6N 60 30W
Boise 78 43 43N 116 9W
Boise City 75 36 45N 102 30W
Boissevain 57 49 15N 100 5W
Bojana, R. 109 41 52N 19 22E
Bojnürd 123 37 30N 57 20E
Bojonegoro 127 7 11S 111 54E
Boké 114 10 56N 14 17W
Boknafjorden 111 59 14N 5 40E
Bokote 116 0 12S 21 8E
Bokpyin 128 11 18N 98 42E
Bokungu 116 0 35S 22 50E
Bolan Pass 124 29 50N 67 20E
Bolaños, R. 82 22 0N 104 10W
Bolbec 100 49 30N 0 30E
Bolchereche 120 56 4N 74 45E
Bolesławiec 106 51 17N 15 37E
Bolgatanga 114 10 44N 0 53W
Bolinao C. 127 16 30N 119 55E
Bolivar, Argent. 88 36 15S 60 53W
Bolivar, Antioquía, Colomb. 86 5 50N 76 1W
Bolivar, Cauca, Colomb. 86 2 0N 77 0W
Bolivar, Mo., U.S.A. 75 37 38N 93 22W
Bolivar, Tenn., U.S.A. 75 35 14N 89 0W
Bolivar □ 86 9 0N 74 40W
Bolivia ■ 86 17 6S 64 0W
Bollène 103 44 18N 4 45E
Bollnäs 111 61 21N 16 24E
Bolobo 116 2 6S 16 20E
Bologna 108 44 30N 11 20E
Bologne 101 48 10N 5 8E
Bologoye 120 57 55N 34 0E
Bolomba 116 0 35N 19 0E
Bolonchenticul 83 20 0N 89 49W
Bolong 127 6 6N 122 16E
Boloven, Cao Nguyen 128 15 10N 106 30E
Bolsena, L. di 108 42 35N 11 55E
Bolshereche 120 56 5N 74 40E
Bolshevik, Ostrov 121 78 30N 102 0E
Bolshoi Kavkas 120 42 50N 44 0E
Bolshoy Atlym 120 62 25N 66 50E
Bolsward 105 53 3N 5 32E
Bolton, Can. 50 43 54N 79 45W
Bolton, U.K. 94 53 35N 2 26W
Bolu 122 40 45N 31 35E
Bolvadin 122 38 45N 31 57E
Bolzano (Bozen) 108 46 30N 11 20E
Bom Despacho 87 19 43S 45 15W
Bom Jesus da Lapa 87 13 15S 43 25W
Boma 116 5 50S 13 4E
Bomaderry 136 34 52S 150 37E
Bomba, La 82 31 53N 115 2W
Bombay 124 18 55N 72 50E
Bomboma 116 2 25N 18 55E
Bomda 129 29 59N 96 25E
Bomili 116 1 45N 27 5E
Bomongo 116 1 27N 18 21E
Bomu, R. 116 4 40N 23 30E
Bon Accord 60 53 50N 113 25W
Bon C. 114 37 1N 11 2E
Bon Echo Prov. Pk. 47 45 0N 77 20W
Bon-Pasteur 42 46 54N 71 18W
Bonaduz 13 46 49N 9 25E
Bonaire, I. 85 12 10N 68 15W
Bonanza, Can. 60 55 55N 119 49W
Bonanza, Nic. 84 13 54N 84 35W
Bonaparte Archipelago 134 14 0S 124 30E
Bonaparte L. 63 51 15N 120 34W
Bonaventure 39 48 5N 65 32W
Bonavista 37 48 40N 53 5W
Bonavista B. 37 48 45N 53 25W
Bonavista, C. 37 48 42N 53 5W
Bondo 116 3 55N 23 53E
Bone Rate, I. 127 7 25S 121 5E
Bone Rate, Kepulauan 127 6 30S 121 10E
Bone, Teluk 127 4 10S 120 50E
Bo'ness 96 56 0N 3 38W
Bonfield 46 46 14N 79 9W
Bong Son = Hoai Nhon 128 14 26N 109 1E
Bongandanga 116 1 24N 21 3E
Bonham 75 33 30N 96 10W
Bonifacio 103 41 24N 9 10E
Bonifacio, Bouches de 108 41 12N 9 15E
Bonilla I. 62 53 28N 130 37W
Bonin Is. 14 27 0N 142 0E
Bonn 105 50 43N 7 6E
Bonnat 102 46 20N 1 53E
Bonne B. 35 40 31N 58 0W
Bonne Espérance, I. 35 51 24N 57 40W
Bonne Terre 76 37 57N 90 33W
Bonnechere, R. 47 45 35N 77 50W
Bonners Ferry 61 48 38N 116 21W
Bonnet, Lac du 57 50 22N 95 55W
Bonnétable 100 48 11N 0 25E
Bonneuil Matours 100 46 41N 0 34E
Bonneville 103 46 5N 6 24E
Bonnie Rock 134 30 29S 118 22E
Bonny 101 47 34N 2 50E
Bonny, Bight of 116 3 30N 9 20E
Bonnyville 60 54 20N 110 45W
Bonoi 127 1 45S 137 41E
Bonsall 81 33 16N 117 14W
Bontang 126 0 10N 117 30E
Bonthain 127 5 34S 119 56E
Bonthe 114 7 30N 12 33W
Booker 75 36 29N 100 30W
Boolaboolka, L. 136 32 38S 143 10E
Boom 105 51 6N 4 20E
Boone, Iowa, U.S.A. 76 42 5N 93 53W
Boone, N.C., U.S.A. 73 36 14N 81 43W
Booneville, Ark., U.S.A. 75 35 10N 93 54W
Booneville, Miss., U.S.A. 73 34 39N 88 34W
Boonville, Calif., U.S.A. 80 39 1N 123 22W
Boonville, Ind., U.S.A. 77 38 3N 87 13W
Boonville, Mo., U.S.A. 76 38 57N 92 45W
Boonville, N.Y., U.S.A. 71 43 31N 75 20W
Boorowa 136 34 28S 148 44E
Boothia, Gulf of 65 71 0N 91 0W
Boothia Pen. 65 71 0N 94 0W
Bootle, Cumb., U.K. 94 54 17N 3 24W
Bootle, Merseysude, U.K. 94 53 28N 3 1W
Booué 116 0 5S 11 55E
Boquete 84 8 46N 82 27W
Boquillas 82 29 17N 102 53W
Bôr 115 6 10N 31 40E
Bor 109 44 8N 22 7E
Borah, Mt. 78 44 19N 113 46W
Borås 111 57 43N 12 56E
Borāzjan 123 29 22N 51 10E
Borba 86 4 12S 59 34W
Bordeaux 102 44 50N 0 36W
Borden, P.E.I., Can. 39 46 18N 63 47W
Borden, Sask., Can. 56 52 27N 107 14W
Borden I. 64 78 30N 111 30W
Borden L. 53 47 50N 83 17W
Borden Pen. 65 73 0N 83 0W
Borders □ 96 55 45N 2 50W
Bordertown 136 36 19S 140 45E
Borðeyri 110 65 12N 21 6W
Borgarnes 110 64 32N 21 55W
Borgefjellet 110 65 20N 13 45E
Borger, Neth. 105 52 54N 6 33E
Borger, U.S.A. 75 35 40N 101 20W
Borgholm 111 56 52N 16 39E
Borisoglebsk 120 51 27N 42 5E
Borja 86 4 20S 77 40W
Borkou 114 18 15N 18 50E
Borkum I. 106 53 38N 6 41E
Borlänge 111 60 29N 15 26E
Borley, C. 91 66 15S 52 30E
Borneo, I. 126 1 0N 115 0E
Bornholm, I. 111 55 10N 15 0E
Borogontsy 121 62 42N 131 8E
Boron 81 35 0N 117 39W
Borongan 127 11 37N 125 26E
Borrego Springs 81 33 15N 116 23W
Borroloola 135 16 4S 136 17E
Bort-les-Orgues 102 45 24N 2 29E
Borujerd 122 33 55N 48 50E
Borzya 121 50 24N 116 31E
Bos. Gradiška 108 45 10N 17 15E
Bosa 108 40 17N 8 32E
Boscobel 76 43 8N 90 42W
Boshrūyeh 123 33 50N 57 30E
Bosna i Hercegovina □ 108 44 0N 18 0E
Bosna, R. 109 44 50N 18 10E
Bosnik 127 1 5S 136 10E
Bōsō-Hantō 132 35 20N 140 20E
Bosobolo 116 4 15N 19 50E
Bosporus = Karadeniz Boğazı 122 41 10N 29 10E
Bossangoa 116 6 35N 17 30E
Bossekop 110 69 57N 23 15E
Bossembélé 114 5 25N 17 40E
Bossier City 75 32 28N 93 48W
Bossut C. 134 18 42S 121 35E
Boston, Can. 49 42 59N 80 16W
Boston, U.K. 94 52 59N 0 2W
Boston, U.S.A. 71 42 20N 71 0W
Boston Bar 63 49 52N 121 30W
Boston Cr. 49 43 2N 79 56W
Boswell, Can. 63 49 28N 116 45W
Boswell, Ind., U.S.A. 77 40 30N 87 23W
Boswell, Okla., U.S.A. 75 34 1N 95 50W
Boswell, Pa., U.S.A. 70 40 9N 79 2W
Bosworth 76 39 28N 93 20W
Bothnia, G. of 110 63 0N 21 0E
Bothwell, Ont., Can. 46 42 38N 81 52W
Bothwell, Ont., Can. 46 42 38N 81 52W
Botletle R. 117 20 10S 24 10E
Botoşani 107 47 42N 26 41E
Botswana ■ 117 22 0S 24 0E
Bottineau 57 48 49N 100 25W
Bottrop 105 51 34N 6 59E
Botucatu 89 22 55S 48 30W
Botwood 37 49 6N 55 23W
Bou Djébéha 114 18 25N 2 45W
Bouaké 114 7 40N 5 2W
Bouar 116 6 0N 15 40E
Bouca 116 6 45N 18 25E
Boucau 102 43 32N 1 29W
Bouchard, Ile 43 45 49N 73 21W
Boucher, R. 41 49 10N 69 6W
Boucherville 45 45 36N 73 27W
Boucherville, Is. de 45 45 37N 73 28W
Bouches-du-Rhône □ 103 43 37N 5 2E
Bouchette 40 46 12N 75 57W
Bouchier, L. 40 50 6N 77 48W
Bougainville C. 134 13 57S 126 4E
Bougie = Béjaïa 114 36 42N 5 2E
Boulder, Austral. 134 30 46S 121 30E
Boulder, Colo., U.S.A. 74 40 3N 105 10W
Boulder, Mont., U.S.A. 78 46 14N 112 4W
Boulder City 81 36 0N 114 50W
Boulder Creek 80 37 7N 122 7W
Boulder Dam = Hoover Dam 79 36 0N 114 45W
Bouleau, Lac au 34 47 40N 77 35W
Boulia 135 22 52S 139 51E
Bouligny 101 49 17N 5 45E
Boulogne, R. 100 46 50N 1 25W
Boulogne-sur-Gesse 102 43 18N 0 38E
Boulogne-sur-Mer 101 50 42N 1 36E
Boundary 67 64 11N 141 2W
Boundary B. 66 49 2N 122 57W
Boundary Bay 66 49 0N 123 2W
Boundary Pk. 80 37 51N 118 21W
Bountiful 78 40 57N 111 58W
Bounty I. 14 46 0S 180 0E
Bour Khaya 121 71 50N 133 10E
Bourbeuse, R. 76 38 24N 90 54W
Bourbon 77 41 18N 86 7W
Bourbon-l'Archambault 102 46 36N 3 4E
Bourbon-Lancy 102 46 37N 3 45E
Bourbonnais 102 46 28N 3 0E
Bourbonne 101 47 59N 5 45E
Bourem 114 17 0N 0 24W
Bourg 102 45 3N 0 34W
Bourg-Argental 103 45 18N 4 32E
Bourg-de-Péage 103 45 2N 5 3E
Bourg-en-Bresse 103 46 13N 5 12E
Bourg-Royal 42 46 53N 71 15W
Bourg-St.-Andéol 103 44 23N 4 39E
Bourg-St.-Maurice 103 45 35N 6 46E
Bourganeuf 102 45 57N 1 45E
Bourges 101 47 9N 2 25E
Bourget 47 45 26N 75 9W
Bourget, L. du 103 45 44N 5 52E
Bourgneuf 100 47 2N 1 58W
Bourgneuf, B. de 100 47 3N 2 10W
Bourgneuf, Le 100 48 10N 0 59W
Bourgogne 101 47 0N 4 30E
Bourgoin-Jallieu 103 45 36N 5 17E
Bourlamaque 34 48 5N 77 56W
Bournemouth 95 50 43N 1 53W
Bourriot-Bergonce 102 44 7N 0 14W
Bouscat, Le 102 44 53N 0 32W
Bouse 81 33 55N 114 0W
Boussac 102 46 22N 2 13E
Boussens 102 43 12N 0 58E
Bousso 114 10 34N 16 52E
Bouthillier, Le 35 47 47N 64 55W
Bouvet I. 13 55 0S 3 30E
Bouzonville 101 49 17N 6 32E
Bovigny 105 50 12N 5 55E
Bovill 78 46 58N 116 27W
Bow Island 61 49 50N 111 23W
Bow Pass 61 51 43N 116 30W
Bow, R. 61 49 57N 111 41W
Bowbells 74 48 47N 102 19W

Bowden **Bruce Crossing**

Bowden 61 51 55N 114 2W
Bowdle 74 45 30N 99 40W
Bowen 135 20 0S 148 16E
Bowen Island 63 49 23N 123 20W
Bowie, Ariz., U.S.A. 79 32 15N 109 30W
Bowie, Tex., U.S.A. 75 33 33N 97 50W
Bowland, Forest of 94 54 0N 2 30W
Bowling Green, Ky., U.S.A. 72 37 0N 86 25W
Bowling Green, Mo., U.S.A. 76 39 21N 91 12W
Bowling Green, Ohio, U.S.A. 77 41 22N 83 40W
Bowling Green, C. 135 19 19S 147 25E
Bowman 74 46 12N 103 21W
Bowman, I. 91 65 0S 104 0E
Bowman L. 52 51 10N 91 25W
Bowmanville 47 43 55N 78 41W
Bowmore 96 55 45N 6 18W
Bowness 59 51 5N 114 10W
Bowral 136 34 26S 150 27E
Bowron Lake Prov. Park 63 53 10N 121 5W
Bowron, R. 63 54 3N 121 50W
Bowser 62 49 27N 124 40W
Bowser L. 54 56 30N 129 30W
Bowsman 57 52 14N 101 12W
Bowstring L. 52 47 34N 93 52W
Bowyer I. 66 49 26N 123 16W
Boxelder Creek 78 47 20N 108 30W
Boxtel 105 51 36N 5 9E
Boyacá □ 86 5 30N 72 30W
Boyce 75 31 25N 92 39W
Boyd L. 36 52 46N 76 42W
Boyer-Nord, R. 42 46 44N 70 58W
Boyer, R., Alta., Can. 54 58 27N 115 57W
Boyer, R., Qué., Can. 42 46 53N 70 52W
Boyer-Sud, R. 42 46 44N 70 58W
Boyle, Can. 60 54 35N 112 49W
Boyle, Ireland 97 53 58N 8 19W
Boylston 39 45 26N 61 30W
Boyne 49 43 29N 79 50W
Boyne City 46 45 13N 85 1W
Boyne, R. 97 53 40N 6 34W
Boynton Beach 73 26 31N 80 3W
Bozeman 78 45 40N 111 0W
Bozouls 102 44 28N 2 43E
Bozoum 116 6 25N 16 35E
Brabant □ 105 50 46N 4 30E
Brabant L. 55 55 58N 104 5W
Brač 108 43 20N 16 40E
Bracadale, L. 96 57 20N 6 30W
Bracciano, L. di 108 42 8N 12 11E
Bracebridge 46 45 2N 79 19W
Brach 114 27 31N 14 20E
Bracieux 101 47 30N 1 30E
Bräcke 110 62 45N 15 26E
Bracken 56 49 11N 108 6W
Brackendale 63 49 48N 123 8W
Brackenridge 70 40 38N 79 44W
Brackettville 75 29 21N 100 20W
Brad 107 46 10N 22 50E
Braddock 70 40 24N 79 51W
Bradenton 73 27 25N 82 35W
Bradford, Can. 46 44 7N 79 34W
Bradford, U.K. 94 53 47N 1 45W
Bradford, Ill., U.S.A. 76 41 11N 89 39W
Bradford, Ohio, U.S.A. 77 40 8N 84 27W
Bradford, Pa., U.S.A. 70 41 58N 78 41W
Bradford, Vt., U.S.A. 71 43 59N 72 9W
Bradley, Ark., U.S.A. 75 33 7N 93 39W
Bradley, Calif., U.S.A. 80 35 52N 120 48W
Bradley, Ill., U.S.A. 77 41 9N 87 52W
Bradley, S.D., U.S.A. 74 45 10N 97 40W
Bradore Bay 37 51 27N 57 18W
Bradshaw 135 15 21S 130 16E
Bradwell 56 51 57N 106 14W
Brady 75 31 8N 99 25W
Braedale 49 43 8N 79 14W
Braeside 47 45 28N 76 24W
Braga 104 41 35N 8 25W
Bragado 88 35 2S 60 27W
Bragança, Brazil 87 1 0S 47 2W
Bragança, Port. 104 41 48N 6 50W
Bragança Paulista 89 22 55S 46 32W
Bragg Creek 61 50 57N 114 35W
Brahmanbaria 125 23 50N 91 15E
Brahmani, R. 125 21 0N 85 15E
Brahmaputra, R. 125 26 30N 93 30E
Brahmaur 124 32 28N 76 32E
Braich-y-Pwll 94 52 47N 4 46W
Braidwood 136 35 27S 149 49E
Brăila 107 45 19N 27 59E
Brainerd 52 46 20N 94 10W
Braintree, U.K. 95 51 53N 0 34E
Braintree, U.S.A. 71 42 11N 71 0W
Bralorne 63 50 50N 123 45W
Bramalea 50 43 44N 79 43W
Brampton 50 43 45N 79 45W
Branch 37 46 53N 53 57W
Branchton 49 43 18N 80 15W
Branco, R. 86 0 0 61 15W
Brandenburg, Ger. 106 52 24N 12 33E
Brandenburg, U.S.A. 77 38 0N 86 10W
Brandon, Can. 57 49 50N 99 57W
Brandon, U.S.A. 71 43 48N 73 4W
Brandon B. 97 52 17N 10 8W
Brandon, Mt. 97 52 15N 10 15W
Brandsen 88 35 10S 58 15W
Brandvlei 117 30 25S 20 30E
Branford 71 41 15N 72 48W
Braniewo 107 54 25N 19 50E
Bransfield Str. 91 63 0S 59 0W
Brańsk 107 52 45N 22 50E
Branson, Colo., U.S.A. 75 37 4N 103 53W
Branson, Mo., U.S.A. 75 36 40N 93 18W
Brant □ 49 43 10N 80 20W
Brantford 49 43 10N 80 15W
Brantôme 102 45 22N 0 39E
Brantville 39 47 22N 64 58W
Bras d'or, L. 39 45 50N 60 50W
Brasiléia 86 11 0S 68 45W
Brasilia 87 15 47S 47 55E
Braşov 107 45 38N 25 35E
Brasschaat 105 51 19N 4 27E
Brassey, Barisan 126 5 0N 117 15E
Brasstown Bald, Mt. 73 34 54N 83 45W
Bratislava 106 48 10N 17 7E
Bratsk 121 56 10N 101 30E
Brattleboro 71 42 53N 72 37W
Braunschweig 106 52 17N 10 28E
Brava 115 1 20N 44 8E
Bravo del Norte, R. 82 30 30N 105 0W
Brawley 81 32 58N 115 30W
Bray 97 53 12N 6 6W
Bray, Pays de 101 49 15N 1 40E
Bray-sur-Seine 101 48 25N 3 14E
Braymer 76 39 35N 93 48W
Brazeau, R. 61 52 55N 115 14W
Brazil 77 39 32N 87 8W
Brazil ■ 86 10 0S 50 0W
Brazilian Highlands 87 18 0S 46 30W
Brazo Sur, R. 88 25 30S 58 0W
Brazos, R. 75 30 30N 96 20W
Brazzaville 116 4 9S 15 12E
Brčko 109 44 54N 18 46E
Breadalbane 96 56 30N 4 15W
Breaksea Sd. 133 45 35S 166 35E
Bream Bay 133 35 56S 174 28E
Bream Head 133 35 51S 174 36E
Breas 88 25 29S 70 24W
Brebes 127 6 52S 109 3E
Brechin, Can. 46 44 32N 79 10W
Brechin, U.K. 96 56 44N 2 40W
Breckenridge, Colo., U.S.A. 78 39 30N 106 2W
Breckenridge, Mich., U.S.A. 46 43 24N 84 29W
Breckenridge, Minn., U.S.A. 74 46 20N 96 36W
Breckenridge, Mo., U.S.A. 76 39 46N 93 48W
Breckenridge, Tex., U.S.A. 75 32 48N 98 55W
Breckland 98 52 30N 0 40E
Brecon 95 51 57N 3 23W
Brecon Beacons 95 51 53N 3 27W
Breda 105 51 35N 4 45E
Bredasdorp 117 34 33S 20 2E
Bredenbury 57 50 57N 102 3W
Bregenz 106 47 30N 9 45E
Brèhal 100 48 53N 1 30W
Bréhat, I. de 100 48 51N 3 0W
Breiðafjörður 110 65 15N 23 15W
Breil 103 43 56N 7 31E
Bremen 106 53 4N 8 47E
Bremerhaven 106 53 34N 8 35E
Bremerton 80 47 30N 122 38W
Brenham 75 30 5N 96 27W
Brenner Pass 106 47 0N 11 30E
Brent, Can. 47 46 2N 78 29W
Brent, U.K. 95 51 33N 0 18W
Brentwood 59 51 7N 114 9W
Bréscia 108 45 33N 10 13E
Breslau 49 43 28N 80 25W
Breslau = Wrocław. 106 51 5N 17 5E
Bresle, R. 100 50 4N 1 21E
Bresles 101 49 25N 2 13E
Bressanone 108 46 43N 11 40E
Bressay I. 96 60 10N 1 5W
Bresse, La 101 48 0N 6 53E
Bresse, Plaine de 101 46 50N 5 10E
Bressuire 100 46 51N 0 30W
Brest, France 100 48 24N 4 31W
Brest, U.S.S.R. 120 52 10N 23 40E
Bretagne 100 48 0N 3 0W
Bretçu 107 46 7N 26 18E
Breteuil, Eur, France 100 48 50N 0 53E
Breteuil, Oise, France 101 49 38N 2 18E
Breton 61 53 7N 114 28W
Breton, Le, L. 38 51 53N 60 9W
Breton, Pertuis 102 46 17N 1 25W
Breton Sd. 75 29 40N 89 12W
Brett, C. 133 35 10S 174 20E
Brevard 73 35 19N 82 42W
Brevort 46 46 2N 85 2W
Brewer 35 44 43N 68 50W
Brewer, Mt. 80 36 44N 118 28W
Brewster, N.Y., U.S.A. 71 41 23N 73 37W
Brewster, Wash., U.S.A. 78 48 10N 119 51W
Brewster, Kap 17 70 7N 22 0W
Brewton 73 31 9N 87 2W
Bria 116 6 30N 21 58E
Briançon 103 44 54N 6 39E
Briare 101 47 38N 2 45E
Bribie I. 135 27 0S 152 58E
Brickaville 117 18 49S 49 4E
Bricon 101 48 5N 5 0E
Briçonnet, L. 38 51 27N 60 10W
Bricquebec 100 49 29N 1 39W
Bridge River 54 50 50N 122 40W
Bridgehampton 71 40 56N 72 19W
Bridgeman 77 41 57N 86 33W
Bridgend 95 51 30N 3 35W
Bridgenorth 47 44 23N 78 23W
Bridgeport, B.C., Can. 66 49 12N 123 8W
Bridgeport, Ont., Can. 46 43 29N 80 29W
Bridgeport, Calif., U.S.A. 80 38 14N 119 15W
Bridgeport, Conn., U.S.A. 71 41 12N 73 12W
Bridgeport, Mich., U.S.A. 46 43 22N 83 53W
Bridgeport, Nebr., U.S.A. 74 41 42N 103 10W
Bridgeport, Tex., U.S.A. 75 33 15N 97 45W
Bridger 78 45 20N 108 58W
Bridgeton 72 39 29N 75 10W
Bridgetown, Austral. 134 33 58S 116 7E
Bridgetown, Barbados 85 13 0N 59 30W
Bridgetown, Can. 39 44 55N 65 18W
Bridgeview Survey 48 43 18N 79 54W
Bridgewater, Can. 39 44 25N 64 31W
Bridgewater, Mass., U.S.A. 71 41 59N 70 56W
Bridgewater, S.D., U.S.A. 74 43 34N 97 29W
Bridgewater, C. 136 38 23S 141 23E
Bridgnorth 95 52 33N 2 25W
Bridgton 71 44 5N 70 41W
Bridgwater 95 51 7N 3 0W
Bridlington 94 54 6N 0 11W
Bridport 95 50 43N 2 45W
Brie-Comte-Robert 101 48 40N 2 35E
Brie, Plaine de 101 48 35N 3 10E
Briec 100 48 6N 4 0W
Brienne-le-Château 101 48 24N 4 30E
Brienon 101 48 0N 3 35E
Briercrest 56 50 10N 105 16W
Briey 101 49 14N 5 57E
Brig 106 46 18N 7 59E
Brigg 94 53 33N 0 30W
Briggsdale 74 40 40N 104 20W
Brigham City 78 41 30N 112 1W
Brighouse 66 49 10N 123 8W
Bright 136 36 42S 146 56E
Brighton, Can. 47 44 2N 77 44W
Brighton, U.K. 95 50 50N 0 9W
Brighton, Colo., U.S.A. 74 39 59N 104 50W
Brighton, Ill., U.S.A. 76 39 2N 90 8W
Brighton, Iowa, U.S.A. 76 41 10N 91 49W
Brighton, Pa., U.S.A. 70 40 42N 80 19W
Brightsand L. 56 53 36N 108 53W
Brignogan-Plage 100 48 40N 4 20W
Brignoles 103 43 25N 6 5E
Brilliant, Can. 63 49 19N 117 38W
Brilliant, U.S.A. 70 40 15N 80 39W
Brimfield 76 40 50N 89 53W
Brimley 46 46 25N 84 41W
Brimstone 49 43 48N 80 0W
Brindisi 109 40 39N 17 55E
Brinkley 75 34 55N 91 15W
Brinnon 80 47 41N 122 54W
Brion I. 39 47 46N 61 26W
Brionne 100 49 11N 0 43E
Brioude 102 45 18N 3 23E
Briouze 100 48 42N 0 23W
Brisbane, Austral. 135 27 25S 153 2E
Brisbane, Can. 49 43 44N 80 4W
Bristol, N.B., Can. 39 46 28N 67 35W
Bristol, Qué., Can. 40 45 32N 76 28W
Bristol, U.K. 95 51 26N 2 35W
Bristol, Conn., U.S.A. 71 41 44N 72 57W
Bristol, R.I., U.S.A. 71 41 40N 71 15W
Bristol, S.D., U.S.A. 74 45 25N 97 43W
Bristol B. 67 58 0N 160 0W
Bristol Channel 95 51 18N 4 30W
Bristol I. 91 58 45S 28 0W
Bristol L. 79 34 23N 116 50W
Bristow 75 35 55N 96 28W
Britannia Beach 63 49 38N 123 12W
British Antarctic Territory 91 66 0S 45 0W
British Columbia □ 54 55 0N 125 15W
British Guiana = Guyana 86 5 0N 59 0W
British Honduras = Belize 83 17 0N 88 30W
British Isles 93 55 0N 4 0W
British Mts. 64 68 50N 140 0W
Britstown 117 30 37S 23 30E
Britt, Can. 46 45 46N 80 34W
Britt, U.S.A. 76 43 6N 93 48W
Brittany = Bretagne 100 48 0N 3 0W
Britton 74 45 50N 97 47W
Brive-la-Gaillarde 102 45 10N 1 32E
Brlik 120 44 0N 74 5E
Brno 106 49 10N 16 35E
Broach, L. 38 50 45N 67 59W
Broad B. 96 58 14N 6 16W
Broad Haven 97 54 20N 9 55W
Broad Law, Mt. 96 55 30N 3 22W
Broad, R. 73 34 30N 81 26W
Broad Sd. 135 22 0S 149 45E
Broadback, R. 36 51 21N 78 52W
Broadford 136 37 14S 145 4E
Broads, The 94 52 45N 1 30E
Broadsound Ra. 135 22 50S 149 30E
Broadus 74 45 28N 105 27W
Broadview 56 50 22N 102 35W
Brochet, Man., Can. 55 57 53N 101 40W
Brochet, Québec, Can. 34 47 12N 72 42W
Brochet, L. 55 58 36N 101 35W
Brochet, L. du 41 49 40N 69 37W
Brock 56 51 26N 108 43W
Brock I. 64 77 52N 114 19W
Brock, R. 40 50 0N 75 5W
Brock Road 51 43 53N 79 5W
Brocken 106 51 48N 10 40E
Brockport 70 43 12N 77 56W
Brockton 71 42 8N 71 2W
Brockville 47 44 35N 75 41W
Brockway 74 47 18N 105 46W
Brockwayville 70 41 14N 78 48W
Brocton 70 42 25N 79 26W
Brod 109 41 35N 21 17E
Broderick 56 51 30N 106 55W
Brodeur 45 45 22N 72 59W
Brodeur Pen. 65 72 30N 88 10W
Brodhead 76 42 37N 89 22W
Brodick 96 55 34N 5 9W
Brogan 78 44 14N 117 32W
Broglie 100 49 0N 0 30E
Broken Bay 136 33 30S 151 15E
Broken Bow, Nebr., U.S.A. 74 41 25N 99 35W
Broken Bow, Okla., U.S.A. 75 34 2N 94 43W
Broken Hill 136 31 58S 141 29E
Broken, R. 136 36 24S 145 24E
Bromhead 55 49 18N 103 40W
Bromley 95 51 20N 0 5E
Bromont 41 45 17N 72 39W
Bromptonville 41 45 28N 71 57W
Bronaugh 76 37 41N 94 28W
Brønderslev 111 57 16N 9 57E
Bronson 77 41 52N 85 12W
Bronte, Can. 49 43 24N 79 43W
Bronte, U.S.A. 75 31 54N 100 18W
Bronte Cr. 49 43 24N 79 43W
Brookdale 57 50 3N 99 34W
Brookfield, Can. 39 45 15N 63 17W
Brookfield, Ill., U.S.A. 77 41 50N 87 51W
Brookfield, Mo., U.S.A. 76 39 50N 92 55W
Brookhaven 75 31 40N 90 25W
Brookings, Oreg., U.S.A. 78 42 4N 124 10W
Brookings, S.D., U.S.A. 74 44 20N 96 45W
Brooklands 58 49 55N 97 12W
Brooklin 51 43 55N 78 55W
Brooklyn, Can. 39 44 3N 64 42W
Brooklyn, Iowa, U.S.A. 76 41 44N 92 27W
Brooklyn, N.Y., U.S.A. 71 40 45N 73 58W
Brookmere 63 49 52N 120 53W
Brookport 43 45 15N 72 50W
Brooks 61 50 35N 111 55W
Brooks B. 62 50 15N 127 55W
Brooks L. 55 61 55N 106 35W
Brooks Ra. 67 68 40N 147 0W
Brookston 77 40 36N 86 52W
Brooksville, Fla., U.S.A. 73 28 32N 82 21W
Brooksville, Ky., U.S.A. 77 38 41N 84 4W
Brookton 134 32 22S 116 57E
Brookville, Ind., U.S.A. 77 39 25N 85 0W
Brookville, Pa., U.S.A. 70 41 10N 79 6W
Broom, L. 96 57 55N 5 15W
Broome 134 18 0S 122 15E
Broons 100 48 20N 2 16W
Brora 58 50 35N 104 41W
Brora, R. 96 58 4N 3 52W
Brosna, R. 97 53 8N 8 0W
Brossard 45 45 26N 73 29W
Brothers 78 43 56N 120 39W
Brougham 51 43 55N 79 6W
Broughton 77 37 56N 88 27W
Broughton I. 62 50 48N 126 42W
Broughton Island 65 67 33N 63 0W
Broughty Ferry 96 56 29N 2 50W
Browerville 74 46 3N 94 50W
Brown City 46 43 13N 82 59W
Brown Willy, Mt. 95 50 35N 4 34W
Brownfield 75 33 10N 102 15W
Browning, Can. 56 49 27N 102 38W
Browning, Ill., U.S.A. 76 40 7N 90 22W
Browning, Mo., U.S.A. 76 40 3N 93 12W
Browning, Mont., U.S.A. 78 48 35N 113 0W
Brownlee 56 50 43N 106 1W
Browns Flats 39 45 28N 66 8W
Browns Line 50 43 36N 79 32W
Brownsburg, Can. 43 45 41N 74 25W
Brownsburg, U.S.A. 77 39 50N 86 24W
Brownstown 77 38 53N 86 3W
Brownsville, Oreg., U.S.A. 78 44 29N 123 0W
Brownsville, Tenn., U.S.A. 75 35 35N 89 15W
Brownsville, Tex., U.S.A. 75 25 56N 97 25W
Brownwood 75 31 45N 99 0W
Brownwood, L. 75 31 51N 98 35W
Bruas 128 4 31N 100 46E
Bruay-en-Artois 101 50 29N 2 33E
Bruce 61 53 10N 112 2W
Bruce Crossing 52 46 38N 89 9W

Bruce L Cáceres

Bruce L. 52 50 49N 93 20W
Bruce Mines 34 46 20N 83 45W
Bruce, Mt. 134 22 37S 118 8E
Bruce Mts. 65 71 12N 72 15W
Bruce Pen. 46 45 0N 81 30W
Bruck a.d. Leitha 106 48 1N 16 47E
Bruderheim 60 53 47N 112 56W
Brue, R. 95 51 10N 2 59W
Bruges = Brugge 105 51 13N 3 13E
Brugge 105 51 13N 3 13E
Brühl 105 50 49N 6 51E
Brûlé 60 53 15N 117 58W
Brûlé, L. 38 52 30N 63 40W
Brûlon 100 47 58N 0 15W
Brumado 87 14 14S 41 40W
Brumath 101 48 43N 7 40E
Brundidge 73 31 43N 85 45W
Bruneau 78 42 57N 115 55W
Bruneau, R. 78 42 45N 115 50W
Brunei = Bandar Seri Begawan 126 4 52N 115 0E
Brunei ■ 126 4 50N 115 0E
Brunette I. 37 47 16N 55 55W
Brunkild 57 49 36N 97 35W
Brunner 133 42 27S 171 20E
Brunner, L. 133 42 27S 171 20E
Bruno, Can. 56 52 20N 105 30W
Bruno, U.S.A. 52 46 17N 92 44W
Brunsbüttelkoog 106 53 52N 9 13E
Brunswick, Ga., U.S.A. 73 31 10N 81 30W
Brunswick, Md., U.S.A. 72 39 20N 77 38W
Brunswick, Me., U.S.A. 35 43 53N 69 50W
Brunswick, Mo., U.S.A. 76 39 26N 93 10W
Brunswick, Ohio, U.S.A. 70 41 15N 81 50W
Brunswick = Braunschweig 106 52 17N 10 28E
Brunswick B. 134 15 15S 124 50E
Brunswick L. 53 48 58N 83 23W
Brunswick, Pen. de 90 53 30S 71 30W
Bruny I. 135 43 20S 147 15E
Brus Laguna 84 15 47N 84 35W
Brush 74 40 17N 103 33W
Brushton 71 44 50N 74 62W
Brusque 89 27 5S 49 0W
Brussel 105 50 51N 4 21E
Brussels, Can. 70 43 45N 81 25W
Brussels, Ont., Can. 46 43 44N 81 15W
Brussels = Bruxelles 105 50 51N 4 21E
Bruxelles 105 50 51N 4 21E
Bruyères 101 48 10N 6 40E
Bryan, Ohio, U.S.A. 77 41 30N 84 30W
Bryan, Texas, U.S.A. 75 30 40N 96 27W
Bryansk 120 53 13N 34 25E
Bryne 111 58 44N 5 38E
Bryson 40 45 41N 76 37W
Bryson City 73 35 28N 83 25W
Bryte 80 38 35N 121 33W
Buapinang 127 4 40S 121 30E
Buayan 127 5 3N 125 28E
Bucaramanga 86 7 0N 73 0W
Buchan 96 57 32N 2 8W
Buchan Ness 96 57 29N 1 48W
Buchanan, Can. 56 51 40N 102 45W
Buchanan, Liberia 114 5 57N 10 2W
Buchanan, U.S.A. 77 41 50N 86 22W
Buchanan, L., Austral. 134 25 33S 123 2E
Buchanan, L., U.S.A. 75 30 50N 98 25W
Buchans 37 48 50N 56 52W
Buchans Junction 37 48 51N 56 28W
Bucharest = Bucureşti 107 44 27N 26 10E
Buchon, Pt. 80 35 15N 120 54W
Buck L. 61 52 59N 114 46W
Buck Lake 61 52 57N 114 47W
Buckeye 79 33 28N 112 40W
Buckhannon 72 39 2N 80 10W
Buckhaven 96 56 10N 3 2W
Buckhorn L. 47 44 29N 78 23W
Buckie 96 57 40N 2 58W
Buckingham, Can. 40 45 37N 75 24W
Buckingham, U.K. 95 52 0N 0 59W
Buckingham □ 95 51 50N 0 55W
Buckingham B. 134 12 10S 135 40E
Buckland, Alaska, U.S.A. 67 66 0N 161 5W
Buckland, Ohio, U.S.A. 77 40 37N 84 16W
Buckland Newton 70 50 50N 2 57W
Buckley, Ill., U.S.A. 77 40 35N 88 2W
Buckley, Wash., U.S.A. 78 47 10N 122 2W
Bucklin, Kans., U.S.A. 75 37 37N 99 40W
Bucklin, Mo., U.S.A. 76 39 47N 92 53W
Bucks L. 80 39 54N 121 12W
Bucquoy 101 50 9N 2 43E
Buctouche 39 46 30N 64 45W
Bucureşti 107 44 27N 26 10E
Bucyrus 77 40 48N 83 0W
Budacul, Munte 99 47 5N 25 40E
Budalin 125 22 20N 95 10E
Budapest 107 47 29N 19 5E
Budaun 124 28 5N 79 10E
Budd Coast 91 67 0S 112 0E
Bude 95 50 49N 4 33W
Búdir 110 64 49N 23 23W
Budjala 116 2 50N 19 40E
Buea 114 4 10N 9 9E
Buellton 81 34 37N 120 12W
Buena Vista, Colo., U.S.A. 79 38 56N 106 6W
Buena Vista, Va., U.S.A. 72 37 47N 79 23W
Buena Vista L. 81 35 15N 119 21W
Buenaventura 82 29 50N 107 30W
Buenaventura, B. de 86 3 48N 77 17W
Buenos Aires, Argent. 88 34 30S 58 20W
Buenos Aires, Colomb. 86 1 36N 73 18W
Buenos Aires, C. Rica 84 9 10N 83 20W
Buenos Aires □ 88 36 30S 60 0W
Buenos Aires, Lago 90 46 35S 72 30W
Buesaco 86 1 23N 77 9W
Buffalo, Can. 55 50 49N 110 42W
Buffalo, Mo., U.S.A. 76 37 40N 93 5W
Buffalo, N.Y., U.S.A. 49 42 55N 78 50W
Buffalo, Okla., U.S.A. 75 36 55N 99 42W
Buffalo, S.D., U.S.A. 75 45 39N 103 31W
Buffalo, Wyo., U.S.A. 78 44 25N 106 50W
Buffalo Center 67 64 2N 145 50W
Buffalo Creek 63 51 44N 121 9W
Buffalo Head Hills 54 57 25N 115 55W
Buffalo L. 61 52 27N 112 54W
Buffalo Narrows 55 55 51N 108 29W
Buffalo Pound L. 56 50 39N 105 30W
Buffalo, R. 54 60 5N 115 5W
Buford 73 34 5N 84 0W
Bug, R. 107 51 20N 23 40E
Buga 86 4 0N 77 0W
Bugeat 102 45 36N 1 55E
Buggs I. L. 73 36 20N 78 30W
Bugsuk, I. 126 8 15N 117 15E
Bugue, Le 102 44 55N 0 56E
Bugun Shara 130 49 0N 104 0E
Buguruslan 120 53 39N 52 26E
Buhl, Idaho, U.S.A. 78 42 35N 114 54W
Buhl, Minn., U.S.A. 74 47 30N 92 46W
Buick 75 37 38N 91 2W
Builth Wells 95 52 10N 3 26W
Buina Qara 123 36 20N 67 0E
Buis-les-Baronnies 103 44 17N 5 16E
Buit, L. 38 50 59N 63 13W
Buitenpost 105 53 15N 6 9E
Bujnurd 123 37 35N 57 15E
Bujumbura (Usumbura) 116 3 16S 29 18E
Bukachacha 121 52 55N 116 50E
Bukama 116 9 10S 25 50E
Bukavu 116 2 20S 28 52E
Bukene 116 4 15S 32 48E
Bukhara 120 39 48N 64 25E
Bukittinggi 126 0 20S 100 20E
Bukoba 116 1 20S 31 49E
Bukuru 114 9 42N 8 48E
Bulak 129 45 2N 82 5E
Bulan 127 12 40N 123 52E
Bulandshahr 124 28 28N 77 58E
Bulawayo 117 20 7S 28 32E
Buldir I. 67 52 20N 175 55E
Bulgan 130 48 45N 103 34E
Bulgaria ■ 109 42 35N 25 30E
Buli, Teluk 127 1 5N 128 25E
Buliluyan, C. 126 8 20N 117 15E
Bulkley, R. 54 55 15N 127 40W
Bulkur 121 71 50N 126 30E
Bull, R. 62 49 18N 115 18W
Bull Shoals L. 75 36 40N 93 5W
Buller, Mt. 136 37 10S 146 28E
Bullfinch 134 30 58S 119 3E
Bullhead City 81 35 11N 114 33W
Bullocks Corners 48 43 17N 79 59W
Bulls 133 40 10S 175 24E
Bully-les-Mines 101 50 27N 2 44E
Bulnes 88 36 42S 72 19W
Bulsar 124 20 40N 72 58E
Bulu Karakelong 127 4 35N 126 50E
Buluan 127 9 0N 125 30E
Bulukumba 127 5 33S 120 11E
Bulun 121 70 37N 127 30E
Bulun Tokhai = Puluntohai 129 47 2N 87 29E
Bulyea 56 50 59N 104 52W
Bumba 116 2 13N 22 30E
Bumble Bee 79 34 8N 112 18W
Bumhpa Bum 125 26 51N 97 14E
Buna 116 2 58N 39 30E
Bunaiyin 122 23 10N 51 8E
Bunaloo 136 35 47S 144 35E
Bunbury 134 33 20S 115 35E
Buncrana 97 55 8N 7 28W
Bundaberg 135 24 54S 152 22E
Bundi 124 25 30N 75 35E
Bundoran 97 54 24N 8 17W
Bundure 136 35 10S 146 1E
Bungendore 136 35 14S 149 30E
Bungō-Suidō 132 33 0N 132 15E
Bunguran N. Is. 126 4 45N 108 0E
Bungwahl 136 32 25S 153 0E
Bunia 116 1 35N 30 20E
Bunji 124 35 45N 74 40E
Bunju 126 3 35N 117 50E
Bunker Hill, Ill., U.S.A. 76 39 3N 89 57W
Bunker Hill, Ind., U.S.A. 77 40 40N 86 6W
Bunkerville 79 36 47N 114 6W
Bunkie 75 31 1N 92 12W
Bunnell 73 29 28N 81 12W
Buntok 126 1 40S 114 58E
Buntzen L. 66 49 21N 122 52W
Búoareyri 110 65 2N 14 13W
Buol 127 1 15N 121 32E
Buorkhaya, Mys 121 71 50N 133 10E
Bûr Sa'îd 115 31 16N 32 18E
Bûr Sûdân 115 19 32N 37 9E
Bura 116 1 4S 39 58E
Buraidah 122 26 20N 44 8E
Buraimī, Al Wāhāt al 123 24 15N 55 43E
Buras 75 29 20N 89 33W
Burbank 81 34 9N 118 23W
Burcher 136 33 30S 147 16E
Burchun 129 48 0N 86 7E
Burdett 61 49 50N 111 32W
Burdur 122 37 45N 30 22E
Burdwan 125 23 16N 87 54E
Bure, R. 94 52 38N 1 45E
Burford 49 43 7N 80 27W
Burgan 122 29 0N 47 57E
Burgas 109 42 33N 27 29E
Burgenland □ 106 47 20N 16 20E
Burgeo 37 47 37N 57 38W
Burgersdorp 117 31 0S 26 20E
Burgos 104 42 21N 3 41W
Burgsvik 111 57 3N 18 19E
Burgundy = Bourgogne 101 47 0N 4 30E
Burhou Rocks 100 49 45N 2 15W
Burias, I. 127 12 55N 123 5E
Burica, Punta 84 8 3N 82 51W
Burin 37 47 1N 55 14W
Burin Peninsula 37 47 0N 55 40W
Buriram 128 15 0N 103 0E
Burkburnett 75 34 7N 98 35W
Burke 78 47 31N 115 56W
Burke Chan. 62 52 10N 127 30W
Burketown 135 17 45S 139 33E
Burkina Faso ■ 114 12 0N 0 30W
Burk's Falls 46 45 37N 79 24W
Burleigh Falls 47 44 33N 78 12W
Burley 78 42 37N 113 55W
Burlingame 80 37 35N 122 21W
Burlington, Newf., Can. 37 49 45N 56 1W
Burlington, Ont., Can. 48 43 18N 79 45W
Burlington, Colo., U.S.A. 74 39 21N 102 18W
Burlington, Ill., U.S.A. 77 42 43N 88 33W
Burlington, Iowa, U.S.A. 76 40 50N 91 5W
Burlington, Kans., U.S.A. 74 38 15N 95 47W
Burlington, Ky., U.S.A. 77 39 2N 84 43W
Burlington, N.C., U.S.A. 73 36 7N 79 27W
Burlington, N.J., U.S.A. 71 40 5N 74 50W
Burlington, Vt., U.S.A. 71 44 27N 73 14W
Burlington, Wash., U.S.A. 80 48 29N 122 19W
Burlington, Wis., U.S.A. 72 42 41N 88 18W
Burlington Beach 48 43 18N 79 48W
Burlyu-Tyube 120 46 30N 79 10E
Burma ■ 125 21 0N 96 30E
Burnaby 66 49 15N 123 0W
Burnaby I. 62 52 25N 131 19W
Burnaby L. 66 49 14N 122 56W
Burnet 75 30 45N 98 11W
Burnett, R. 135 24 45S 152 23E
Burney 78 40 56N 121 41W
Burnham 70 40 37N 77 34W
Burnhamthorpe 50 43 37N 79 36W
Burnie 135 41 4S 145 56E
Burnley 94 53 47N 2 15W
Burns, Oreg., U.S.A. 78 43 40N 119 4W
Burns, Wyo., U.S.A. 74 41 13N 104 18W
Burns Lake 54 54 20N 125 45W
Burnside, R. 64 66 51N 108 4W
Burnt Island 37 47 36N 58 53W
Burnt L. 36 53 35N 64 4W
Burnt Paw 67 67 2N 142 43W
Burnt, R. 70 44 40N 78 42W
Burnt River 47 44 41N 78 42W
Burntwood L. 55 55 22N 100 26W
Burntwood, R. 55 56 8N 96 34W
Burquitlam 66 49 16N 122 54W
Burra 135 33 40S 138 55E
Burragorang, L. 136 33 52S 150 37E
Burrard Inlet 66 49 18N 123 15W
Burrendong Res. 136 32 45S 149 10E
Burrewarra Pt. 136 35 50S 150 15E
Burrinjuck Dam 136 35 0S 148 34E
Burrinjuck Res. 136 35 0S 148 36E
Burro, Serranias del 82 29 0N 102 0W
Burrows L. 53 49 57N 86 44W
Burruyacú 88 26 30S 64 40W
Bursa 122 40 15N 29 5E
Burstall 56 50 39N 109 54W
Burt L. 46 45 27N 84 40W
Burton 63 50 0N 117 53W
Burton L. 36 54 45N 78 20W
Burton-upon-Trent 94 52 48N 1 39W
Burtts Corner 39 46 3N 66 52W
Buru, I. 127 3 30S 126 30E
Burujird 122 33 58N 48 41E
Burundi ■ 116 3 15S 30 0E
Burung 126 0 21N 108 25E
Burwash 46 46 14N 80 51W
Burwash Landing 67 61 21N 139 0W
Burwell 74 41 49N 99 8W
Burwell, Mt. 66 49 27N 123 1W
Bury, Can. 41 45 28N 71 30W
Bury, U.K. 94 53 36N 2 19W
Bury St. Edmunds 95 52 15N 0 42E
Buryat A.S.S.R. □ 121 53 0N 110 0E
Busayyah 122 30 0N 46 10E
Busby 54 53 55N 114 0W
Bushell 55 59 31N 108 45W
Bushnell, Ill., U.S.A. 74 40 32N 90 30W
Bushnell, Nebr., U.S.A. 74 41 18N 103 50W
Businga 116 3 16N 20 59E
Buskerud fylke □ 111 60 13N 9 0E
Busra 122 32 30N 36 25E
Bussang 101 47 50N 6 50E
Busselton 134 33 42S 115 15E
Bussum 105 52 16N 5 10E
Bustard Hd. 135 24 0S 151 48E
Busto Arsizio 108 45 40N 8 50E
Busu-Djanoa 116 1 50N 21 5E
Busuangal, I. 127 12 10N 120 0E
Buta 116 2 50N 24 53E
Butare 116 2 31S 29 52E
Bute Inlet 62 50 40N 124 53W
Butedale 62 53 8N 128 42W
Butembo 116 0 9N 29 18E
Butiaba 116 1 50N 31 20E
Butler, Ind., U.S.A. 77 41 26N 84 52W
Butler, Ky., U.S.A. 77 38 47N 84 22W
Butler, Mo., U.S.A. 76 38 17N 94 18W
Butler, Pa., U.S.A. 70 40 52N 79 52W
Butte, Mont., U.S.A. 78 46 0N 112 31W
Butte, Nebr., U.S.A. 74 42 56N 98 54W
Butte Creek, R. 80 39 12N 121 56W
Butterworth 128 5 24N 100 23E
Buttle L. 62 49 42N 125 33W
Button B. 55 58 45N 94 23W
Button Is. 36 60 38N 64 40W
Buttonville 50 43 51N 79 21W
Buttonwillow 81 35 24N 119 28W
Butuan 127 8 57N 125 33E
Butung, I. 127 5 0S 122 45E
Buxton 94 53 16N 1 54W
Buxy 101 46 44N 4 40E
Buyaga 121 59 50N 127 0E
Buyr Nuur 130 47 50N 117 35E
Büyük Menderes, R. 122 37 45N 27 40E
Buzançais 100 46 54N 1 25E
Buzău 107 45 10N 26 50E
Buzău, R. 107 45 10N 27 20E
Buzen 132 33 35N 131 5E
Buzi, R. 117 19 52S 34 30E
Buzuluk 120 52 48N 52 12E
Buzzards Bay 71 41 45N 70 38W
Byam Martin I. 64 75 15N 104 15W
Bydgoszcz 107 53 10N 18 0E
Byelorussian S.S.R. □ 120 53 30N 27 0E
Byers 74 39 46N 104 13W
Byesville 70 39 56N 81 32W
Byhalia 75 34 53N 89 41W
Bylas 79 33 11N 110 9W
Bylot I. 65 73 13N 78 34W
Byng Inlet 46 45 46N 80 33W
Byrd Land = Marie Byrd Land 91 79 30S 125 0W
Byrd Sub-Glacial Basin 91 82 0S 120 0W
Byron 76 42 8N 89 15W
Byron B. 35 54 42N 57 40W
Byron, C. 135 28 38S 153 40E
Byrranga, Gory 121 75 0N 100 0E
Byske 110 64 57N 21 11E
Byske, R. 110 65 20N 20 0E
Bytom 107 50 25N 19 0E

C

Ca Mau = Quan Long 128 9 7N 105 8E
Ca Mau, Mui = Bai Bung 128 8 35N 104 42E
Caacupé 88 25 23N 57 5W
Caamano Sd. 62 52 55N 129 25W
Caatingas 87 7 0S 52 30W
Caazapá 88 26 8S 56 19W
Caazapá □ 89 26 10S 56 0W
Cabanatuan 127 15 30N 121 5E
Cabane-Ronde 45 45 47N 73 33W
Cabano 41 47 40N 68 56E
Cabazon 81 33 55N 116 47W
Cabedelo 87 7 0S 34 50W
Cabery 77 41 0N 88 12W
Cabildo 88 32 30S 71 5W
Cabimas 86 10 30N 71 25W
Cabinda 116 5 40S 12 11E
Cabinda □ 116 5 0S 12 30E
Cabinet Mts. 78 48 0N 115 30W
Cabo Blanco 90 47 56S 65 47W
Cabo Frio 89 22 51S 42 3W
Cabo Pantoja 86 1 0S 75 10W
Cabonga Réservoir 40 47 20N 76 40W
Cabool 75 37 10N 92 8W
Cabora Bassa Dam 117 15 20S 32 50E
Caborca (Heroica) 82 30 40N 112 10W
Cabot Hd. 70 45 14N 81 18W
Cabot, Mt. 71 44 30N 71 25W
Cabot Strait 35 47 15N 59 40W
Cabrera, I. 104 39 6N 2 59E
Cabri 56 50 35N 108 25W
Cabriel, R. 104 39 20N 1 20W
Cabruta 86 7 50N 66 10W
Caburan 127 6 3N 125 45E
Cabuyaro 86 4 18N 72 49W
Čačak 109 43 54N 20 20E
Cáceres, Brazil 86 16 5S 57 40W

Cáceres Canyon Creek

Cáceres, Colomb. 86 7 35N 75 20W
Cáceres, Spain 104 39 26N 6 23W
Cache B. 34 46 26N 80 1W
Cache Bay 46 46 22N 80 0W
Cache Cr. 80 38 45N 121 43W
Cache Creek 63 50 48N 121 19W
Cachi 88 25 5S 66 10W
Cachimbo, Serra do 87 9 30S 55 0W
Cáchira 86 7 21N 73 17W
Cachoeira 87 12 30S 39 0W
Cachoeira de Itapemirim 89 20 51S 41 7W
Cachoeira do Sul 89 30 3S 52 53W
Cacolo 116 10 9S 19 21E
Caconda 117 13 48S 15 8E
Cadboro Bay 63 48 28N 123 17W
Caddo 75 34 8N 96 18W
Cader Idris 94 52 43N 3 56W
Cadereyta Jiménez 83 25 40N 100 0W
Cadillac, Qué., Can. 40 48 14N 78 23W
Cadillac, Sask., Can. 56 49 44N 107 44W
Cadillac, France 102 44 38N 0 20W
Cadillac, U.S.A. 46 44 16N 85 25W
Cadiz 127 11 30N 123 15E
Cádiz 104 36 30N 6 20W
Cadiz 70 40 13N 81 0W
Cádiz, G. de 104 36 40N 7 0W
Cadomin 61 53 2N 117 20W
Cadotte, R. 60 56 43N 117 10W
Cadours 102 43 44N 1 2E
Caen 100 49 10N 0 22W
Caergwrle 95 53 6N 3 3W
Caernarfon 94 53 8N 4 17W
Caernarfon B. 94 53 4N 4 40W
Caernarvon = Caernarfon 94 53 8N 4 17W
Cæsarea = Qesari 115 32 30N 34 53E
Caeté 87 20 0S 43 40W
Caetité 87 13 50S 42 50W
Cafayate 88 26 2S 66 0W
Cagayan de Oro 127 8 30N 124 40E
Cagayan, R. 127 18 25N 121 42E
Cágliari 108 39 15N 9 6E
Cágliari, G. di 108 39 8N 9 10E
Cagnes-sur-Mer 103 43 40N 7 9E
Caguas 85 18 14N 66 4W
Caha Mts. 97 51 45N 9 40W
Cahir 97 52 23N 7 56W
Cahirciveen 97 51 57N 10 13W
Cahore Pt. 97 52 34N 6 11W
Cahors 102 44 27N 1 27E
Cahuapanas 86 5 15S 77 0W
Caibarién 84 22 30N 79 30W
Caicara 86 7 38N 66 10W
Caicó 87 6 20S 37 0W
Caicos Is. 85 21 40N 71 40W
Caicos Passage 85 22 45N 72 45W
Caihaique 90 45 30S 71 45W
Cains, R. 39 46 40N 65 47W
Cainsville 49 43 9N 80 15W
Caird Coast 91 75 0S 25 0W
Cairn Gorm 96 57 7N 3 40W
Cairn Toul 96 57 3N 3 44W
Cairngorm Mts. 96 57 6N 3 42W
Cairns 135 16 57S 145 45E
Cairnside 43 45 7N 73 54W
Cairo, Ga., U.S.A. 73 30 52N 84 12W
Cairo, Illinois, U.S.A. 75 37 0N 89 10W
Cairo = El Qâhira 115 30 1N 31 14E
Caistorville 49 43 3N 79 44W
Caithness, Ord of, C. 96 58 35N 3 37W
Caiundo 117 15 50S 17 52E
Caiza 86 20 2S 65 40W
Cajamarca 86 7 5S 78 28W
Cajarc 102 44 29N 1 50E
Cajàzeiros 87 7 0S 38 30W
Calabar 114 4 57N 8 20E
Calabogie 47 45 18N 76 43W
Calabozo 86 9 0N 67 20W
Calábria □ 108 39 24N 16 30E
Calafate 90 50 25S 72 25W
Calahorra 104 42 18N 1 59W
Calais, France 101 50 57N 1 56E
Calais, U.S.A. 35 45 5N 67 20W
Calais, Pas de 78 50 57N 1 20E
Calalaste, Sierra de 88 25 0S 67 0W
Calama, Brazil 86 8 0S 62 50W
Calama, Chile 88 22 30S 68 55W
Calamar, Bolívar, Colomb. 86 10 15N 74 55W
Calamar, Vaupés, Colomb. 86 1 58N 72 32W
Calamian Group 127 11 50N 119 55E
Calamocha 104 40 50N 1 17W
Calanaque 86 0 5S 64 0W
Calang 126 4 30N 95 43E
Calapan 127 13 25N 121 7E
Calatayud 104 41 20N 1 40W
Calauag 127 13 55N 122 15E
Calavite, Cape 127 13 26N 120 10E
Calayan, I. 131 19 20N 121 30E
Calca 86 13 10S 72 0W
Calcutta 125 22 36N 88 24E
Caldas □ 86 5 15N 75 30W
Calder, R. 94 53 44N 1 21W
Caldera 88 27 5S 70 55W
Caldiran 122 39 7N 44 0E
Caldwell, Idaho, U.S.A. 78 43 45N 116 42W
Caldwell, Kans., U.S.A. 75 37 5N 97 37W
Caldwell, Texas, U.S.A. 75 30 30N 96 42W
Caledon, Can. 49 43 52N 80 0W
Caledon, S. Afr. 117 34 14S 19 26E
Caledon B. 135 12 45S 137 0E
Caledon East 49 43 52N 79 52W
Caledon, R. 117 30 0S 26 46E
Caledonia, N.S., Can. 39 44 22N 65 2W
Caledonia, N.S., Can. 39 45 17N 62 33W
Caledonia, Ont., Can. 49 43 7N 79 58W
Caledonia, Mo., U.S.A. 76 37 45N 90 46W
Caledonia, N.Y., U.S.A. 70 42 57N 77 54W
Calella 104 41 37N 2 40E
Calera, La 88 32 50S 71 10W
Calexico 81 32 40N 115 33W
Calf of Man 94 54 4N 4 48W
Calgary 59 51 0N 114 10W
Calgary International Airport 59 51 4N 114 1W
Calhoun 73 34 30N 84 55W
Cali 86 3 25N 76 35W
Calicoan, I. 127 10 59N 125 50E
Calicut, (Kozhikode) 124 11 15N 75 43E
Caliente 79 37 43N 114 34W
California, Mo., U.S.A. 76 38 37N 92 30W
California, Pa., U.S.A. 70 40 4N 79 55W
California □ 78 37 25N 120 0W
California, Baja 82 32 10N 115 12W
California, Baja, T.N. □ 82 30 0N 115 0W
California, Baja, T.S. □ 82 25 50N 111 50W
California City 81 35 7N 117 57W
California, Golfo de 82 27 0N 111 0W
California Hot Springs 81 35 51N 118 41W
California, Lr. = California, Baja 82 25 50N 111 50W
Calilegua 88 23 45S 64 42W
Calingasta 88 31 15S 69 30W
Calipatria 81 33 8N 115 30W
Calistoga 80 38 36N 122 32W
Calixa-Lavallée 45 45 45N 73 17W
Calkini 83 20 21N 90 3W
Callabonna, L. 135 29 40S 140 5E
Callac 100 48 25N 3 27W
Callan 97 52 33N 7 25W
Callander 46 46 13N 79 22W
Callao 86 12 0S 77 0W
Callaway 74 41 20N 99 56W
Callender 76 42 22N 94 17W
Calles 83 23 2N 98 42W
Calling L. 60 55 15N 113 20W
Calling Lake 60 55 15N 113 12W
Calmar, Can. 60 53 16N 113 49W
Calmar, U.S.A. 76 43 11N 91 52W
Calpella 80 39 14N 123 12W
Calpine 80 39 40N 120 27W
Calstock 53 49 47N 84 9W
Caltagirone 108 37 13N 14 30E
Caltanissetta 108 37 30N 14 3E
Caluire-et-Cuire 103 45 49N 4 51E
Calulo 116 10 1S 14 56E
Calumbo 116 9 0S 13 20E
Calumet City 77 41 37N 87 32W
Calvados □ 100 49 5N 0 15W
Calvert 75 30 59N 96 50W
Calvert C. 62 51 25N 127 53W
Calvert I. 62 51 30N 128 0W
Calvi 108 42 34N 8 45E
Calvillo 82 21 51N 102 43W
Calvinia 117 31 28S 19 45E
Calwa 80 36 42N 119 46W
Cam Lam 128 11 54N 109 10E
Cam, R. 95 52 21N 0 16E
Cam Ranh 128 11 54N 109 12E
Camabatela 116 8 20S 15 26E
Camachigama, L. 40 47 50N 76 19W
Camacho 82 24 25N 102 18W
Camaguán 86 8 6N 67 36W
Camagüey 84 21 20N 78 0W
Camaná 86 16 30S 72 50W
Camanche 76 41 47N 90 15W
Camano I. 63 48 10N 122 30W
Camaquã, R. 89 30 50S 52 50W
Camaret 100 48 16N 4 37W
Camargo 86 20 38S 65 15E
Camargue 103 43 34N 4 34E
Camarillo 81 34 13N 119 2W
Camarón, C. 84 16 0N 85 0W
Camarones, Argent. 90 44 50S 65 40W
Camarones, Chile 86 19 0S 69 58W
Camas 80 45 35N 122 24W
Camas Valley 78 43 0N 123 46W
Cambará 89 23 2S 50 5W
Cambay 124 22 23N 72 33E
Cambay, G. of 124 20 45N 72 30E
Cambo-les-Bains 102 43 22N 1 23W
Cambodia ■ 128 12 15N 105 0E
Camborne 95 50 13N 5 18W
Cambrai 101 50 11N 3 14E
Cambria, Calif., U.S.A. 80 35 44N 121 6W
Cambria, N.Y., U.S.A. 49 43 11N 78 49W
Cambrian Mts. 95 52 25N 3 52W
Cambridge, N.B., Can. 39 45 50N 65 58W
Cambridge, Ont., Can. 49 43 23N 80 15W
Cambridge, Jamaica 84 18 18N 77 54W
Cambridge, N.Z. 133 37 54S 175 29E
Cambridge, U.K. 95 52 13N 0 8E
Cambridge, Idaho, U.S.A. 78 44 36N 116 52W
Cambridge, Ill., U.S.A. 76 41 18N 90 12W
Cambridge, Iowa, U.S.A. 76 41 54N 93 32W
Cambridge, Mass., U.S.A. 72 42 20N 71 8W
Cambridge, Md., U.S.A. 72 38 33N 76 2W
Cambridge, Minn., U.S.A. 74 45 34N 93 15W
Cambridge, Nebr., U.S.A. 74 40 20N 100 12W
Cambridge, N.Y., U.S.A. 71 43 2N 73 22W
Cambridge, Ohio, U.S.A. 70 40 1N 81 22W
Cambridge Bay 64 69 10N 105 0W
Cambridge City 77 39 49N 85 10W
Cambridge Gulf 134 14 45S 128 0E
Cambridge Springs 70 41 47N 80 4W
Cambridgeshire □ 95 52 12N 0 7E
Cambuci 89 21 35S 41 55W
Camden, Ala., U.S.A. 73 31 59N 87 15W
Camden, Ark., U.S.A. 75 33 40N 92 50W
Camden, Me., U.S.A. 35 44 14N 69 6W
Camden, N.J., U.S.A. 72 39 57N 75 1W
Camden, Ohio, U.S.A. 77 39 38N 84 39W
Camden, S.C., U.S.A. 73 34 17N 80 34W
Camden, B. 67 71 0N 145 0W
Camdenton 76 38 1N 92 45W
Camembert 100 48 53N 0 10E
Cameron, Ariz., U.S.A. 79 35 55N 111 31W
Cameron, La., U.S.A. 75 29 50N 93 18W
Cameron, Mo., U.S.A. 76 39 42N 94 14W
Cameron, Tex., U.S.A. 75 30 53N 97 0W
Cameron Falls 52 49 8N 88 19W
Cameron Highlands 128 4 27N 101 22E
Cameron Hills 54 59 48N 118 0W
Cameron L. 53 49 1N 84 17W
Cameroon ■ 114 3 30N 12 30E
Cameroun, Mt. 116 4 45N 8 55E
Cametá 87 2 0S 49 30W
Camiguin, I. 131 19 55N 122 0E
Caminha 104 41 50N 8 50W
Camino 80 38 47N 120 40W
Camlachie 70 43 3N 82 9W
Cammal 70 41 24N 77 28W
Camocim 87 2 55S 40 50W
Camooweal 135 19 56S 138 7E
Camopi, R. 87 3 12N 52 17W
Camp Borden 46 44 18N 79 56W
Camp Crook 74 45 36N 103 59W
Camp Nelson 81 36 8N 118 39W
Camp Point 76 40 3N 91 4W
Camp Wood 75 29 47N 100 0W
Campagna 108 40 40N 15 5E
Campana 88 34 10S 58 55W
Campana, I. 90 48 20S 75 10W
Campania □ 108 40 50N 14 45E
Campania I. 62 53 5N 129 25W
Campbell 80 37 17N 121 57W
Campbell Island 62 52 8N 128 12W
Campbell L. 55 63 14N 106 55W
Campbell, R. 66 49 1N 122 47W
Campbell River 62 50 5N 125 20W
Campbellford 47 44 18N 77 48W
Campbell's Bay 40 45 44N 76 36W
Campbellsburg, Ind., U.S.A. 77 38 39N 86 16W
Campbellsburg, Ky., U.S.A. 77 38 31N 85 12W
Campbellsville 72 37 23N 85 12W
Campbellton, Alta., Can. 54 53 32N 113 15W
Campbellton, N.B., Can. 39 47 57N 66 43W
Campbellton, Newf., Can. 37 49 17N 54 56W
Campbelltown 136 34 4S 150 49E
Campbellville 49 43 29N 79 59W
Campbeltown 96 55 25N 5 36W
Campeche 83 19 50N 90 32W
Campeche □ 83 19 50N 90 32W
Campeche, Golfo de 83 19 30N 93 0W
Camperdown 136 38 14S 143 9E
Camperville 57 51 59N 100 9W
Campina Grande 87 7 20S 35 47W
Campinas 89 22 50S 47 0W
Campinho 87 14 30S 39 10W
Campo 116 2 15N 9 58E
Campo Beló 87 21 0S 45 30W
Campo Formoso 87 10 30S 40 20W
Campo Grande 87 20 25S 54 40W
Campo Maior 87 4 50S 42 12W
Campoalegre 86 2 41N 75 20W
Campobasso 108 41 34N 14 40E
Campos 89 21 50S 41 20W
Campos Belos 87 13 10S 46 45W
Campos Novos 89 27 21S 51 20W
Campsie Fells 98 56 2N 4 20W
Campton 77 37 44N 83 33W
Camptonville 80 39 27N 121 3W
Campuya, R. 86 1 10S 74 0W
Camrose 61 53 0N 112 50W
Camsall L. 55 72 32N 106 47W
Camsell Portage 55 59 37N 109 15W
Can Tho 128 10 2N 105 46E
Canaan 71 42 1N 73 20W
Canaan, R. 39 45 55N 65 47W
Canaan Station 39 46 15N 65 4W
Canada ■ 22 60 0N 100 0W
Canada B. 37 50 43N 56 8W
Canadian 75 35 56N 100 25W
Canadian Pacific Irrigation Canal 59 51 0N 114 0W
Canadian, R. 75 36 0N 98 45W
Canakkale 122 40 8N 26 30E
Canakkale Boğazi 109 40 0N 26 0E
Canal de l'Est 101 48 45N 5 35E
Canal Flats 61 50 10N 115 48W
Canal latéral à la Garonne 102 44 25N 0 15E
Canalejas 88 35 15S 66 34W
Canals 88 33 35S 62 40W
Canandaigua 70 42 55N 77 18W
Cananea 82 31 0N 110 20W
Canarias, Islas 114 29 30N 17 0W
Canarreos, Arch. de los 84 21 35N 81 40W
Canary Is. = Canarias, Islas 114 29 30N 17 0W
Canatlán 82 24 31N 104 47W
Canaveral, C. 73 28 28N 80 31W
Canavieiras 87 15 39S 39 0W
Canberra 136 35 15S 149 8E
Canboro 49 42 59N 79 41W
Canby, Calif., U.S.A. 78 41 26N 120 58W
Canby, Minn., U.S.A. 74 44 44N 96 15W
Canby, Ore., U.S.A. 80 45 16N 122 42W
Cancale 100 48 40N 1 50W
Candala 115 11 30N 49 58E
Candé 100 47 34N 1 0W
Candelaria 89 27 29S 55 44W
Candiac 45 45 23N 73 31W
Candle L. 56 53 50N 105 18W
Cando, Can. 56 52 23N 108 14W
Cando, U.S.A. 74 48 30N 99 14W
Canelones 88 34 32S 56 10W
Canet-Plage 102 42 41N 3 2E
Cañete, Chile 88 37 50S 73 30W
Cañete, Cuba 85 20 36N 74 43W
Cañete, Peru 86 13 0S 76 30W
Canfield 49 42 58N 79 45W
Cangamba 117 13 40S 19 54E
Cangas 104 42 16N 8 47W
Canguaretama 87 6 20S 35 5W
Canguçu 89 31 22S 52 43W
Canicado 117 24 2S 33 2E
Canim, L. 63 51 45N 120 50W
Canim Lake 63 51 47N 120 54W
Canipaan 126 8 33N 117 15E
Canisteo 70 42 17N 77 37W
Canisteo, R. 70 42 15N 77 30W
Cañitas 82 23 36N 102 43W
Cankırı 122 40 40N 33 30E
Canlaon, Mt. 127 9 27N 118 25E
Canmore 61 51 7N 115 18W
Canna I. 96 57 3N 6 33W
Cannanore 124 11 53N 75 27E
Cannelton 77 37 55N 86 45W
Cannes 103 43 32N 7 0E
Canning 39 45 9N 64 25W
Canning Basin 134 19 50S 124 0E
Cannington 70 44 20N 79 2W
Cannock 94 52 42N 2 2W
Cannock Chase, hills 98 52 43N 2 0W
Cannon Ball, R. 74 46 20N 101 20W
Caño Colorado 86 2 18N 68 22W
Canoe 63 50 45N 119 13W
Canoe L. 55 55 10N 108 15W
Canol 67 65 15N 126 50W
Canon City 74 39 30N 105 20W
Canonba 136 31 21S 147 22E
Canora 57 51 40N 102 30W
Canourgue, Le 102 44 26N 3 13
Canowindra 136 33 35S 148 38
Canrobert 45 45 21N 72 56W
Canso 39 45 20N 61 0W
Cantabrian Mts. = Cantábrica 104 43 0N 5 10W
Cantábrica, Cordillera 104 43 0N 5 10W
Cantal □ 102 45 4N 2 45
Cantaura 86 9 19N 64 21W
Canterbury, Can. 39 45 53N 67 29W
Canterbury, U.K. 95 51 17N 1 5
Canterbury □ 133 43 45S 171 19
Canterbury Bight 133 44 16S 171 55
Canterbury Plains 133 43 55S 171 22
Cantic 43 45 4N 73 21W
Cantil 81 35 18N 117 58W
Canton, Ga., U.S.A. 73 34 13N 84 29W
Canton, Ill., U.S.A. 76 40 32N 90 0W
Canton, Mass., U.S.A. 71 42 8N 71 8W
Canton, Miss., U.S.A. 75 32 40N 90 1W
Canton, Mo., U.S.A. 76 40 10N 91 33W
Canton, N.Y., U.S.A. 71 44 32N 75 3W
Canton, Ohio, U.S.A. 70 40 47N 81 22W
Canton, Okla., U.S.A. 75 36 5N 98 36W
Canton, S.D., U.S.A. 74 43 20N 96 35W
Canton = Kwangchow 131 23 10N 113 10
*Canton I. 14 2 30S 172 0W
Canton L. 75 36 12N 98 40W
Canuck 56 49 12N 108 13W
Canudos 86 7 13S 58 5W
Canulloit 79 31 58N 106 36W
Canuta 44 45 42N 74 9W
Canutama 86 6 30S 64 20W
Canwood 56 53 22N 106 36W
Canyon, Can. 67 47 25N 84 36W
Canyon, Texas, U.S.A. 75 35 0N 101 57W
Canyon, Wyo., U.S.A. 78 44 43N 110 36W
Canyon Creek 60 55 22N 115 5W

* Renamed Abariringa

Canyonlands Nat. Park

Canyonlands Nat. Park	**79**	38 25N	109 30W
Canyonville	**78**	42 55N	123 14W
Caopacho, L.	**38**	52 0N	66 9W
Caopacho, R.	**38**	51 18N	66 18W
Caotibi, L.	**38**	50 45N	67 34W
Cap-aux-Meules	**39**	47 23N	61 52W
Cap-aux Meules, Î. du	**39**	47 23N	61 54W
Cap-Chat	**38**	49 6N	66 40W
Cap-de-la-Madeleine	**41**	46 22N	72 31W
Cap-des-Rosiers	**38**	48 52N	64 13W
Cap d'Espoir	**38**	48 26N	64 20W
Cap Haïtien	**85**	19 40N	72 20W
Cap-Pelé	**39**	46 13N	64 18W
Cap-St-Ignace	**41**	47 2N	70 28W
Capac	**46**	43 1N	82 56W
Capaia	**116**	8 27S	20 13E
Capanaparo, R.	**86**	7 0N	67 30W
Caparo, R.	**86**	7 30N	70 30W
Capatárida	**86**	11 11N	70 37W
Capbreton	**102**	43 39N	1 26W
Capdenac	**102**	44 34N	2 5E
Cape Barren I.	**135**	40 25S	148 15E
Cape Breton Highlands Nat. Park	**39**	46 50N	60 40W
Cape Breton I.	**39**	46 0N	60 30W
Cape Broyle	**37**	47 6N	52 57W
Cape Charles	**72**	37 15N	75 59W
Cape Coast	**114**	5 5N	1 15W
Cape Dorset	**65**	64 14N	76 32W
Cape Dyer	**65**	66 40N	61 22W
Cape Fear, R.	**73**	34 30N	78 25W
Cape Girardeau	**75**	37 20N	89 30W
Cape May	**72**	39 1N	74 53W
Cape Montague	**35**	46 5N	62 25W
Cape Province □	**117**	32 0S	23 0E
Cape Ray	**37**	47 38N	59 17W
Cape Scott Prov. Park	**62**	50 45N	128 20W
Cape Tormentine	**39**	46 8N	63 47W
Cape Town (Kaapstad)	**117**	33 55S	18 22E
Cape Verde Is.	**12**	17 10N	25 20W
Cape Vincent	**71**	44 9N	76 21W
Cape York Peninsula	**135**	33 34S	115 33E
Capela	**87**	10 30S	37 0W
Capelle, La	**101**	49 59N	3 50E
Capendu	**102**	43 11N	2 31E
Capestang	**102**	43 20N	3 2E
Capilano L.	**66**	49 23N	123 7W
Capilano, R.	**66**	49 19N	123 7W
Capim, R.	**87**	3 0S	48 0W
Capitachouane, R.	**40**	47 36N	76 54W
Capitan	**79**	33 40N	105 41W
Capitola	**80**	36 59N	121 57W
Caplan	**39**	48 6N	65 40W
Capraia, I.	**108**	43 2N	9 50E
Capreol	**46**	46 43N	80 56W
Caprera, I.	**108**	41 12N	9 28E
Capri, I.	**108**	40 34N	14 15E
Capricorn, C.	**135**	23 30S	151 13E
Caprivi Strip	**117**	18 0S	23 0E
Captain's Flat	**136**	35 35S	149 27E
Captieux	**102**	44 18N	0 16W
Capulin	**75**	36 48N	103 59W
Caquetá □	**86**	1 0N	74 0W
Caquetá, R.	**86**	1 0N	76 20W
Cáqueza	**86**	4 25N	73 57W
Carabobo	**86**	10 10N	68 5W
Caracal	**107**	44 8N	24 22E
Caracarai	**86**	1 50N	61 8W
Caracas	**86**	10 30N	66 55W
Caracol, Piaui, Brazil	**87**	9 15S	43 45W
Caracol, Rondonia, Brazil	**86**	9 15S	64 20W
Carajás, Serra dos	**87**	6 0S	51 30W
Caramanta	**86**	5 33N	75 38W
Caramat	**53**	49 37N	86 9W
Carangola	**89**	20 50S	42 5W
Caransebeş	**107**	45 28N	22 18E
Carantec	**100**	48 40N	3 55W
Caraquet	**39**	47 48N	64 57W
Caratasca, Laguna	**84**	15 30N	83 40W
Caratunk	**35**	45 13N	69 55W
Caraúbas	**87**	7 43S	36 31W
Caravaca	**104**	38 8N	1 52W
Caravelas	**87**	17 45S	39 15W
Caraveli	**86**	15 45S	73 25W
Caràzinho	**89**	28 0S	53 0W
Carballo	**104**	43 13N	8 41W
Carberry	**57**	49 50N	99 25W
Carbó	**82**	29 42N	110 58W
Carbon	**61**	51 30N	113 9W
Carbonara, C.	**108**	39 8N	9 30E
Carbondale, Can.	**60**	53 45N	113 32W
Carbondale, Colo, U.S.A.	**78**	39 30N	107 10W
Carbondale, Ill., U.S.A.	**76**	37 45N	89 10W
Carbondale, Pa., U.S.A.	**71**	41 37N	75 30W
Carbonear	**37**	47 42N	53 13W
Carbonia	**108**	39 10N	8 30E
Carcajou	**54**	57 47N	117 6W
Carcasse, C.	**85**	18 30N	74 28W
Carcassonne	**102**	43 13N	2 20E
Carcross	**22**	60 13N	134 45W
Cardamom Hills	**124**	9 30N	77 15E
Cárdenas, Cuba	**84**	23 0N	81 30W
Cárdenas, San Luis Potosí, Mexico	**84**	22 0N	99 41W
Cárdenas, Tabasco, Mexico	**83**	17 59N	93 21W
Cardiff	**95**	51 28N	3 11W
Cardiff-by-the-Sea	**81**	33 1N	117 17W
Cardigan	**95**	52 6N	4 41W
Cardigan B.	**95**	52 30N	4 30W
Cardinal	**47**	44 47N	75 23W
Cardinal L.	**60**	56 14N	117 44W
Cardón	**86**	11 37N	70 14W
Cardona, Spain	**104**	41 56N	1 40E
Cardona, Uruguay	**88**	33 53S	57 18W
Cardross	**56**	49 50N	105 40W
Cardston	**61**	49 15N	113 20W
Careen L.	**55**	57 0N	108 11W
Carei	**107**	47 40N	22 29E
Carentan	**100**	49 19N	1 15W
Carey, Idaho, U.S.A.	**78**	43 19N	113 58W
Carey, Ohio, U.S.A.	**77**	40 58N	83 22W
Carey, L.	**134**	29 0S	122 15E
Carey L.	**55**	62 12N	102 55W
Cargados Garajos, Is.	**16**	17 0S	59 0E
Cargèse	**103**	42 7N	8 35E
Carhaix-Plouguer	**100**	48 18N	3 36W
Carheil, L.	**38**	52 40N	67 5W
Carhué	**88**	37 10S	62 50W
Cariaco	**86**	10 29N	63 33W
Caribbean Sea	**85**	15 0N	75 0W
Cariboo Mts.	**63**	53 0N	121 0W
Cariboo, R.	**63**	53 3N	121 20W
Caribou, Can.	**55**	53 15N	121 55W
Caribou, U.S.A.	**35**	46 55N	68 0W
Caribou I.	**53**	47 22N	85 49W
Caribou Is.	**54**	61 55N	113 15W
Caribou L., Man., Can.	**55**	59 21N	96 10W
Caribou L., Ont., Can.	**52**	50 25N	89 5W
Caribou Mts.	**54**	59 12N	115 40W
Caribou, R., Man., Can.	**55**	59 20N	94 44W
Caribou, R., N.W.T., Can.	**54**	61 27N	125 45W
Carichic	**82**	27 56N	107 3W
Carignan, Can.	**45**	45 27N	73 19W
Carignan, France	**101**	49 38N	5 10E
Carillo	**82**	26 50N	103 55W
Carinhanha	**87**	14 15S	44 0W
Caripito	**86**	10 8N	63 6W
Caritianas	**86**	9 20S	63 0W
Carleton, N.-S., Can.	**39**	44 0N	65 56W
Carleton, N.B., Can.	**39**	48 5N	66 4W
Carleton Place	**47**	45 8N	76 9W
Carlin	**78**	40 50N	116 5W
Carlingford, L.	**97**	54 0N	6 5W
Carlinville	**76**	39 20N	89 55W
Carlisle, Can.	**49**	43 23N	79 59W
Carlisle, U.K.	**94**	54 54N	2 55W
Carlisle, Ky., U.S.A.	**77**	38 18N	84 1W
Carlisle, Pa., U.S.A.	**70**	40 12N	77 10W
Carlitte, Pic	**102**	42 35N	1 43E
Carlos Casares	**88**	35 53S	61 20W
Carlos Tejedor	**88**	35 25S	62 25W
Carlota, La	**88**	33 30S	63 20W
Carlow	**97**	52 50N	6 58W
Carlow □	**97**	52 43N	6 50W
Carlsbad, Calif., U.S.A.	**81**	33 11N	117 25W
Carlsbad, N. Mex., U.S.A.	**75**	32 20N	104 7W
Carlton, Minn., U.S.A.	**52**	46 40N	92 25W
Carlton, Wash., U.S.A.	**63**	48 14N	120 5W
Carlyle, Can.	**57**	49 40N	102 20W
Carlyle, U.S.A.	**74**	38 38N	89 23W
Carlyle Resr.	**76**	38 37N	89 21W
Carmacks	**67**	62 5N	136 16W
Carman	**57**	49 30N	98 0W
Carmangay	**61**	50 10N	113 10W
Carmanville	**37**	49 23N	54 19W
Carmarthen	**95**	51 52N	4 20W
Carmarthen B.	**95**	51 40N	4 30W
Carmaux	**102**	44 3N	2 10E
Carmel, Calif., U.S.A.	**80**	36 38N	121 55W
Carmel, Ind., U.S.A.	**77**	39 59N	86 8W
Carmel, N.Y., U.S.A.	**71**	41 25N	73 38W
Carmel Mt.	**115**	32 45N	35 3E
Carmel Valley	**80**	36 29N	121 43W
Carmelo	**88**	34 0S	58 10W
Carmen, Colomb.	**86**	9 43N	75 8W
Carmen, Parag.	**89**	27 13S	56 12W
Carmen de Patagones	**90**	40 50S	63 0W
Carmen, I.	**82**	26 0N	111 20W
Carmen, R.	**82**	30 42N	106 29W
Carmensa	**88**	35 15S	67 40W
Carmi, Can.	**63**	49 36N	119 8W
Carmi, U.S.A.	**77**	38 6N	88 10W
Carmichael	**80**	38 38N	121 19W
*Carmona	**104**	37 28N	5 42W
Carnarvon, Austral.	**134**	24 51S	113 42E
Carnarvon, S. Afr.	**117**	30 56S	22 8E
Carnation	**80**	47 39N	121 55W
Carndonagh	**97**	55 15N	7 16W
Carnduff	**57**	49 10N	101 50W
Carnegie	**70**	40 24N	80 4W
Carnegie, L.	**134**	26 5S	122 30E
Carniche, Alpi	**108**	46 34N	13 0E
Carnon	**102**	43 32N	3 59E
Carnot	**116**	4 59N	15 56E
Carnot B.	**134**	17 20S	121 30E
Carnsore Pt.	**97**	52 10N	6 20W
Carnwood	**61**	53 11N	114 38W
Caro	**46**	43 29N	83 27W
Carolina	**87**	7 10S	47 30W
Carolina, La	**104**	38 17N	3 38W
Caroline	**61**	52 5N	114 45W
Caroline I.	**15**	9 15S	150 3W
Caroline Is.	**14**	8 0N	150 0E
Carollton	**76**	39 22N	93 30W
Carolside	**54**	51 20N	111 40W
Carolville	**76**	41 42N	91 34W
Carolville Res.	**76**	41 50N	91 40W
Caron	**56**	50 30N	105 50W
Caron, L.	**38**	50 57N	67 44W
Caroni, R.	**86**	6 0N	62 40W
Carora	**86**	10 11N	70 5W
Carp	**71**	45 20N	76 5E
Carpathians, Mts.	**107**	46 20N	26 0E
Carpaţii Meridionali	**107**	45 30N	25 0E
Carpentaria, G. of	**135**	14 0S	139 0E
Carpenter L.	**63**	50 53N	122 37W
Carpentersville	**77**	42 6N	88 17W
Carpentras	**103**	44 3N	5 2E
Carpinteria	**81**	34 25N	119 31W
Carpolac	**136**	36 43S	141 18E
Carrabelle	**73**	29 52N	84 40W
Carragana	**56**	52 35N	103 6W
Carraipia	**86**	11 16N	72 22W
Carrara	**108**	44 5N	10 7E
Carrauntohill, Mt.	**97**	52 0N	9 49W
Carriacou, I.	**85**	12 30N	61 28W
Carrick-on-Shannon	**97**	53 57N	8 7W
Carrick-on-Suir	**97**	52 22N	7 30W
Carrickfergus	**97**	54 43N	5 50W
Carrickfergus □	**97**	54 43N	5 49W
Carrickmacross	**97**	54 0N	6 43W
Carrington	**74**	47 30N	99 7W
Carrizal	**86**	12 1N	72 11W
Carrizal Bajo	**88**	28 5S	71 20W
Carrizalillo	**88**	29 0S	71 30W
Carrizo Cr.	**75**	36 30N	103 40W
Carrizo Springs	**75**	28 28N	99 50W
Carrizozo	**79**	33 40N	105 57W
Carroll	**76**	42 2N	94 55W
Carrollton, Ga., U.S.A.	**73**	33 36N	85 5W
Carrollton, Ill., U.S.A.	**74**	39 20N	90 25W
Carrollton, Ky., U.S.A.	**77**	38 40N	85 10W
Carrollton, Mo., U.S,A.	**76**	39 19N	93 24W
Carrollton, Ohio, U.S.A.	**70**	40 31N	81 9W
Carron L.	**96**	57 22N	5 35W
Carron R.	**96**	57 30N	5 30W
Carrot, R.	**57**	53 50N	101 17W
Carrot River	**56**	53 17N	103 35W
Carrouges	**100**	48 34N	0 10W
Carruthers	**56**	52 52N	109 16W
Çarşamba	**122**	41 15N	36 45E
Carson	**74**	46 27N	101 29W
Carson City, U.S.A.	**46**	43 11N	84 51W
Carson City, Nev., U.S.A.	**80**	39 12N	119 46W
Carson, R.	**80**	39 12N	119 20W
Carson Sink	**78**	39 50N	118 40W
Carsonville	**72**	43 25N	82 39W
Carstairs, Can.	**61**	51 34N	114 6W
Carstairs, U.K.	**96**	55 42N	3 41W
Cartagena, Colomb.	**86**	10 25N	75 33W
Cartagena, Spain	**104**	37 38N	0 59W
Cartago, Colomb.	**86**	4 45N	75 55W
Cartago, C. Rica	**84**	9 50N	84 0W
Carteret	**100**	49 23N	1 47W
Cartersville	**73**	34 11N	84 48W
Carterton	**133**	41 2S	175 31E
Carterville	**76**	37 46N	89 5W
Carthage, Ark., U.S.A.	**75**	34 4N	92 32W
Carthage, Ill., U.S.A.	**76**	40 25N	91 10W
Carthage, Mo., U.S.A.	**75**	37 10N	94 20W
Carthage, N.Y., U.S.A.	**71**	43 59N	75 37W
Carthage, S.D., U.S.A.	**74**	44 14N	97 38W
Carthage, Texas, U.S.A.	**75**	32 8N	94 20W
Cartier	**46**	46 42N	81 33W
Cartier I.	**134**	12 31S	123 29E
Cartwright, Man., Can.	**57**	49 6N	99 20W
Cartwright, Newf., Can.	**36**	53 41N	56 58W
Cartwright Sd.	**62**	53 13N	132 38W
Caruaru	**87**	8 15S	35 55W
Carúpano	**86**	10 45N	63 15W
Caruthersville	**75**	36 10N	89 40W
Carvin	**101**	50 30N	2 57E
Carvoeiro	**86**	1 30S	61 59W
Casa Agapito	**86**	2 3N	73 58W
Casa Grande	**79**	32 53N	111 51W
Casa Nova	**87**	9 10S	41 5W
Casablanca, Chile	**88**	33 20S	71 25W
Casablanca, Moroc.	**114**	33 36N	7 36W
Casale Monferrato	**108**	45 8N	8 28E
Casanare, R.	**86**	6 30N	71 20W
Casas Grandes	**82**	30 22N	108 0W
Cascade, Idaho, U.S.A.	**78**	44 30N	116 2W
Cascade, Iowa, U.S.A.	**76**	42 18N	91 1W
Cascade, Mont., U.S.A.	**78**	47 16N	111 46W
Cascade Locks	**80**	45 44N	121 54W
Cascade Ra.	**80**	45 0N	121 30W
Caserta	**108**	41 5N	14 20E
Caseville	**46**	43 56N	83 16W
Casey	**41**	47 53N	74 11W
Cashel, Can.	**50**	43 55N	79 19W
Cashel, Ireland	**97**	52 31N	7 53W
Cashmere	**78**	47 31N	120 30W
Casigua	**86**	11 2N	71 1W
Casiguran	**127**	16 15N	122 15E
Casilda	**88**	33 10S	61 10W
Casino	**135**	28 52S	153 3E
Casiquiare, R.	**86**	2 45N	66 20W
Caslan	**60**	54 38N	112 31W
Casma	**86**	9 30S	78 20W
Casmalia	**81**	34 50N	120 32W
Caspe	**104**	41 14N	0 1W
Casper	**78**	42 52N	106 27W
Caspian Sea	**120**	43 0N	50 0E
Casquets	**100**	49 46N	2 15W
Cass City	**46**	43 34N	83 15W
Cass Lake	**52**	47 23N	94 38W
Cass, R.	**46**	43 23N	83 59W
Cassel	**101**	50 48N	2 30E
Casselman	**47**	45 19N	75 5W
Casselton	**74**	47 0N	97 15W
Cassiar	**54**	59 16N	129 40W
Cassiar Mts.	**54**	59 30N	130 30W
Cassils	**54**	50 29N	112 15W
Cassinga	**117**	15 5S	16 23E
Cassiporé, C.	**87**	3 50N	51 5W
Cassis	**103**	43 14N	5 32E
Cassopolis	**77**	41 55N	86 1W
Cassville, Mo., U.S.A.	**75**	36 45N	93 59W
Cassville, Wisc., U.S.A.	**76**	42 43N	90 59W
Castaic	**81**	34 30N	118 38W
Castanheiro	**86**	0 17S	65 38W
Casteljaloux	**102**	44 19N	0 6E
Castellammare del Golfo	**108**	38 2N	12 53E
Castellammare di Stábia	**108**	40 47N	14 29E
Castellane	**103**	43 50N	6 31E
Castelli	**88**	36 7S	57 47W
Castellón de la Plana	**104**	39 58N	0 3W
Castelnau-de-Médoc	**102**	45 2N	0 48W
Castelnaudary	**102**	43 20N	1 58E
Castelo	**89**	20 53S	41 42E
Castelo Branco	**104**	39 50N	7 31W
Castelsarrasin	**102**	44 2N	1 7E
Castelvetrano	**108**	37 40N	12 46E
Casterton	**136**	37 30S	141 30E
Castets	**102**	43 52N	1 6W
Castilla La Nueva	**104**	39 45N	3 20W
Castilla La Vieja	**104**	41 55N	4 0W
Castille = Castilla	**104**	40 0N	3 30W
Castilletes	**86**	11 51N	71 19W
Castillón	**82**	28 20N	103 38W
Castillon-en-Couserans	**102**	42 56N	1 1E
Castillon-la-Bataille	**102**	44 51N	0 2W
Castillonès	**102**	44 39N	0 37E
Castillos	**89**	34 12S	53 52W
Castle Dale	**78**	39 11N	111 1W
Castle Douglas	**96**	54 57N	3 57W
Castle Mountain	**61**	51 16N	115 55W
Castle Point	**133**	40 54N	176 15E
Castle Rock, Can.	**63**	52 32N	122 29W
Castle Rock, Colo., U.S.A.	**74**	39 26N	104 50W
Castle Rock, Wash., U.S.A.	**80**	46 20N	122 58W
Castlebar	**97**	53 52N	9 17W
Castleblayney	**97**	54 7N	6 44W
Castlegar	**63**	49 20N	117 40W
Castlegate	**78**	39 45N	110 57W
Castlemaine	**136**	37 2S	144 12E
Castlereagh	**97**	53 47N	8 30W
Castlereagh □	**97**	54 33N	5 33W
Castlereagh B.	**134**	12 10S	135 10E
Castlereagh, R.	**135**	30 12S	147 32E
Castleton	**71**	42 33N	73 44W
Castletown	**94**	54 4N	4 40W
Castletown Bearhaven	**97**	51 40N	9 54W
Castor	**61**	52 15N	111 50W
Castor, R.	**36**	53 24N	78 58W
Castres	**102**	43 37N	2 13E
Castricum	**105**	52 33N	4 40E
Castries	**85**	14 0N	60 50W
Castro, Brazil	**89**	24 45S	50 0W
Castro, Chile	**90**	42 30S	73 50W
Castro Alves	**87**	12 46S	39 26W
Castro del Rio	**104**	37 41N	4 29W
Castroville, Calif., U.S.A.	**80**	36 46N	121 45W
Castroville, Tex, U.S.A.	**75**	29 20N	98 53W
Casummit Lake	**52**	51 29N	92 22W
Cat I., Bahamas	**85**	24 30N	75 30W
Cat I., U.S.A.	**75**	30 15N	89 7W
Cat L.	**52**	51 40N	91 50W
Catacamas	**84**	14 54N	85 56W
Catacaos	**86**	5 20S	80 45W
Cataguases	**89**	21 23S	42 39W
Catahoula L.	**75**	31 30N	92 5W
Catalão	**87**	18 10S	47 57W
Çatalca	**122**	41 9N	28 28E
Catalina	**37**	48 31N	53 4W
Catalonia = Cataluña	**104**	41 40N	1 15E
Cataluña	**104**	41 40N	1 15E
Catamarca	**88**	28 30S	65 50W
Catamarca □	**88**	28 30S	65 50W
Catanduanas, Is.	**127**	13 50N	124 20E
Catanduva	**89**	21 5S	48 58W
Catánia	**108**	37 31N	15 4E
Catanzaro	**108**	38 54N	16 38E
Catarman	**127**	12 28N	124 1E
Catastrophe C.	**134**	34 59S	136 0E
Cateau, Le	**101**	50 6N	3 30E
Cateel	**127**	7 47N	126 24E
Cathcart	**49**	43 6N	80 31W
Cathedral Mt.	**66**	49 28N	123 1W
Cathedral Prov. Park	**63**	49 5N	120 0W
Cathlamet	**80**	46 15N	123 29W
Catine	**99**	46 30N	0 15W
Catismiña	**86**	4 5N	63 52W
Cativá	**84**	9 21N	79 49W
Catlettsburg	**72**	38 23N	82 38W

* Renamed N'Gage

Catlin Charleswood

Catlin 77 40 4N 87 42W
Cato I. 135 23 15S 155 32E
Catoche, C. 83 21 40N 87 0W
Catrimani 86 0 27N 61 41W
Catskill 71 42 14N 73 52W
Catskill Mts. 71 42 15N 74 15W
Cattaraugus 70 42 22N 78 52W
Cauca □ 86 2 30N 76 50W
Cauca, R. 86 7 25N 75 30W
Caucasia 86 8 0N 75 12W
Caucasus Mts. = Bolshoi Kavkas 120 42 50N 44 0E
Cauchy, L. 38 50 36N 60 46W
Caudebec-en-Caux 100 49 30N 0 42E
Caudry 101 50 7N 3 22E
Caughnawaga 44 45 25N 73 41W
Caulfield 66 49 21N 123 15W
Caulnes 100 48 18N 2 10W
Caungula 116 8 15S 18 50E
Cáuquenes 88 36 0S 72 30W
Caura, R. 86 6 20N 64 30W
Causapscal 38 48 19N 67 12W
Causapscal, Parc Prov. de 38 48 15N 67 0W
Caussade 102 44 10N 1 33E
Cauterets 102 42 52N 0 8W
Caution C. 62 51 10N 127 47W
Cauvery, R. 124 12 0N 77 45E
Caux, Pays de 100 49 38N 0 35E
Cavaillon 103 43 50N 5 2E
Cavalaire-sur-Mer 103 43 10N 6 33E
Cavalerie, La 102 44 0N 3 10E
Cavalier 57 48 50N 97 39W
Cavallo, I. de 103 41 22N 9 16E
Cavan 97 54 0N 7 22W
Cavan □ 97 53 58N 7 10W
Cave City 72 37 13N 85 57W
Cavers 34 48 55N 87 41W
Caviana, Ilha 87 0 15N 50 0W
Cavite 127 14 20N 120 55E
Cawasachouane, L. 40 47 27N 77 45W
Caxias 86 5 0S 43 27W
Caxias do Sul 89 29 10S 51 10W
Cay Sal Bank 84 23 45N 80 0W
Cayambe 86 0 3N 78 22W
Cayce 73 33 59N 81 2W
Caycuse 62 48 53N 124 22W
Cayenne 87 5 0N 52 18W
Cayes, Les 85 18 15N 73 46W
Cayeux-sur-Mer. 101 50 10N 1 30E
Cayey 67 18 7N 66 10W
Cayley 61 50 27N 113 51W
Caylus 102 44 15N 1 47E
Cayman Brac, I. 84 19 43N 79 49W
Cayman Is. 84 19 40N 79 50W
Cayo 83 17 10N 89 0W
Cayo Romano, I. 85 22 0N 78 30W
Cayuga, Can. 49 42 59N 79 50W
Cayuga, Ind., U.S.A. 77 39 57N 87 38W
Cayuga, N.Y., U.S.A. 71 42 54N 76 44W
Cayuga L. 71 42 45N 76 45W
Cazaux et de Sanguinet, Étang de 102 44 29N 1 10W
Cazaville 43 45 5N 74 22W
Cazères 102 43 13N 1 5E
Cazombo 117 12 0S 22 48E
Cazorla 86 8 1N 67 0W
Ceanannas Mor 97 53 42N 6 53W
Ceará □ 87 5 0S 40 0W
Ceará Mirim 87 5 38S 35 25W
Cebaco, I. 84 7 33N 81 9W
Cebollar 88 29 10S 66 35W
Cebú 127 10 18N 123 54E
Cebú, I. 127 10 15N 123 40E
Cedar City 79 37 41N 113 3W
Cedar Creek Res. 75 32 15N 96 0W
Cedar Falls, Iowa, U.S.A. 76 42 39N 92 29W
Cedar Falls, Wash., U.S.A. 80 47 25N 121 45W
Cedar Grove 77 39 22N 84 56W
Cedar Key 73 29 9N 83 5W
Cedar L., Man., Can. 57 53 20N 100 10W
Cedar L., Ont., Can. 47 46 2N 78 30W
Cedar Lake 77 41 20N 87 25W
Cedar Mills 49 43 55N 79 48W
Cedar Point 77 41 44N 83 21W
Cedar, R. 76 41 17N 91 21W
Cedar Rapids 76 42 0N 91 38W
Cedar Springs 77 43 13N 85 33W
Cedar Valley 49 43 46N 80 10W
Cedarburg 72 43 18N 87 55W
Cedartown 73 34 1N 85 15W
Cedarvale 54 55 1N 128 22W
Cedarville, Calif., U.S.A. 78 41 37N 120 13W
Cedarville, Ill., U.S.A. 76 42 23N 89 38W
Cedarville, Mich., U.S.A. 46 46 0N 84 22W
Cedarville, Ohio, U.S.A. 77 39 44N 83 49W
Cedral 82 23 50N 100 42W
Cèdres, Les 44 45 18N 74 3W
Cedro 87 6 34S 39 3W
Cedros, I. de 82 28 10N 115 20W
Ceduna 134 32 7S 133 46E
Ceepeecee 54 49 52N 126 42W
Cefalù 108 38 3N 14 1E
Cegléd 107 47 11N 19 47E
Cehegín 104 38 6N 1 48W
Ceiba, La 84 15 40N 86 50W
Celaya 82 20 31N 100 37W
Celbridge 97 53 20N 6 33W
Celebes I. = Sulawesi 127 2 0S 120 0E
Celebes Sea 127 3 0N 123 0E
Celina 77 40 32N 84 31W
Celje 108 46 16N 15 18E
Celle 106 52 37N 10 4E
Cement 75 34 56N 98 8W
Cenis, Col du Mt. 103 45 15N 6 55E
Cenon 102 44 50N 0 33W
Centennial 58 49 54N 97 9W
Center, N.D., U.S.A. 74 47 9N 101 17W
Center, Texas, U.S.A. 75 31 50N 94 10W
Center Point 76 42 12N 91 46W
Centerfield 78 39 9N 111 56W
Centerville, Ala., U.S.A. 73 32 55N 87 7W
Centerville, Calif., U.S.A. 80 36 44N 119 30W
Centerville, Iowa, U.S.A. 76 40 45N 92 57W
Centerville, Mich., U.S.A. 77 41 55N 85 32W
Centerville, Miss., U.S.A. 75 31 10N 91 3W
Centerville, Pa., U.S.A. 70 40 3N 79 59W
Centerville, S.D., U.S.A. 74 43 10N 96 58W
Centerville, Tenn., U.S.A. 73 35 46N 87 29W
Centerville, Tex., U.S.A. 75 31 15N 95 56W
Central □ 96 56 0N 4 30W
Central African Republic ■ 116 7 0N 20 0E
Central Butte 56 50 48N 106 31W
Central City, Ky., U.S.A. 72 37 20N 87 7W
Central City, Nebr., U.S.A. 74 41 8N 98 0W
Central, Cordillera, C. Rica 84 10 10N 84 5W
Central, Cordillera, Dom. Rep. 85 19 15N 71 0W
Central Islip 71 40 49N 73 13W
Central Lake 46 45 4N 85 16W
Central Makran Range 124 26 30N 64 15E
Central Patricia 52 51 30N 90 9W
Central Russian Uplands 93 54 0N 36 0E
Central Siberian Plateau 121 65 0N 105 0E
Centralia, Ill., U.S.A. 76 38 32N 89 5W
Centralia, Mo., U.S.A. 76 39 12N 92 6W
Centralia, Wash., U.S.A. 80 46 46N 122 59W
Centreville, N.B., Can. 39 46 26N 67 43W
Centreville, N.S., Can. 39 44 33N 66 1W
Ceram I. = Seram I. 127 3 10S 129 0E
Ceram Sea = Seram Sea 127 2 30S 128 30E
Cerbère 102 42 26N 3 10E
Cerbicales, Îles 103 41 33N 9 22E
Cereal 61 51 25N 110 48W
Ceres, Argent. 88 29 55S 61 55W
Ceres, S. Afr. 117 33 21S 19 18E
Ceres, U.S.A. 80 37 35N 120 57W
Céret 102 42 30N 2 42E
Cereté 86 8 53N 75 48W
Cerf, L. de 40 46 16N 75 30W
Cerfontaine 105 50 11N 4 26E
Cerignola 108 41 17N 15 53E
Cérilly 102 46 37N 2 50E
Cerisiers 101 48 8N 3 30E
Cerizay 100 46 50N 0 40W
Çerkeş 122 40 40N 32 58E
Cerknica 108 45 48N 14 21E
Cernavodă 107 44 22N 28 3E
Cernay 101 47 44N 7 10E
Cerralvo, I. 82 24 20N 109 45E
Cerritos 82 22 20N 100 20W
Cerro 79 36 47N 105 36W
Cerro de Punta, Mt. 67 18 10N 67 0W
Cerro Gordo 77 39 53N 88 44W
Cervera 104 41 40N 1 16E
Cervera del Rio Alhama 104 42 2N 1 58W
Cervione 103 42 20N 9 29E
César □ 86 9 0N 73 30W
Cesena 108 44 9N 12 14E
Česke Budějovice 106 48 55N 14 25E
Český Těšín 107 49 45N 18 39E
Cessnock 136 32 50S 151 21E
Cetinje 109 42 23N 18 59E
Ceuta 114 35 52N 5 18W
Cévennes, mts. 102 44 10N 3 50E
Ceylon 56 49 27N 104 36W
Ceylon = Sri Lanka ■ 124 7 30N 80 50E
Cha Pa. 128 22 20N 103 47E
Chaati I. 62 53 7N 132 30W
Chabeuil 103 44 54N 5 1E
Chablais 103 46 20N 6 36E
Chablis 101 47 47N 3 48E
Chacabuco 88 34 40S 60 27W
Chachapoyas 86 6 15S 77 50W
Chachran 124 28 55N 70 30E
Chaco □ 88 25 0S 61 0W
Chaco Austral 90 27 30S 61 40W
Chaco Boreal 88 22 30S 60 10W
Chaco Central 90 24 0S 61 0W
Chad ■ 114 12 30N 17 15E
Chad, L. = Tchad, L. 114 13 30N 14 30E
Chadan 121 51 17N 91 35E
Chadileuvú, R. 88 37 0S 65 55W
Chadron 74 42 50N 103 0W
Chafurray 86 3 10N 73 14W
Chagai 123 29 30N 63 0E
Chagai Hills 124 29 30N 63 0E
Chagda 121 58 45N 130 30E
Chagny 101 46 57N 4 45E
Chagos Arch. 16 6 0S 72 0E
Chágres, R. 84 9 5N 79 40W
Châh Bahâr 123 25 20N 60 40E
Chahar Buriak 124 30 15N 62 0E
Châhr-e Babak 123 30 10N 55 20E
Chaibasa 125 22 42N 85 49E
Chaillé-les-Marais 102 46 25N 1 2W
Chaise-Dieu, La 102 45 20N 3 40E
Chaize-le-Vicomté, La 100 46 40N 1 18W
Chajari 88 30 42N 58 0W
Chakhansur 124 31 10N 62 0E
Chakonipau, L. 36 56 18N 68 30W
Chakradharpur 125 22 45N 85 40E
Chakwal 124 32 50N 72 45E
Chala 86 15 48S 74 20W
Chalainor 130 49 31N 117 30E
Chalais 102 45 16N 0 3E
Chalantun = Putehachi 130 48 4N 122 45E
Chalcatongo 83 17 4N 97 34W
Chalchihuites 82 23 29N 103 53W
Chaleur B. 39 47 55N 65 30W
Chalfant 80 37 32N 118 21W
Chalhuanca 86 14 15S 73 5W
Chaling 131 26 47N 113 35E
Chalisgaon 124 20 30N 75 10E
Chalk River 47 46 1N 77 27W
Chalky Inlet 133 46 3S 166 31E
Challans 100 46 50N 1 52W
Challapata 86 19 0S 66 50W
Challerange 101 49 18N 4 46E
Challis 78 44 32N 114 25W
Chalon-sur-Saône 101 46 48N 4 50E
Chalonnes 100 47 20N 0 45W
Châlons-sur-Marne 101 48 58N 4 20E
Châlus 102 45 39N 0 58E
Chaman 124 30 58N 66 25E
Chamba, India 124 32 35N 76 10E
Chamba, Tanz. 117 11 37S 37 0E
Chambal, R. 124 26 0N 76 55E
Chamberlain 74 43 50N 99 21W
Chambers 79 35 13N 109 30W
Chambersburg 72 39 53N 77 41W
Chambéry 103 45 34N 5 55E
Chambeshi, R. 116 10 20S 31 58E
Chambly 45 45 27N 73 17W
Chambly □ 45 45 30N 73 30W
Chambly, Bassin de 45 45 27N 73 17W
Chambois 100 48 48N 0 6E
Chambon-Feugerolles, Le 103 45 24N 4 18E
Châmbon, Le 103 45 35N 4 26E
Chambord 41 48 25N 72 6W
Chamboulive 102 45 26N 1 42E
Chamdo 129 31 21N 97 2E
Chamela 82 19 32N 105 5W
Chamical 88 30 22S 66 27W
Chamois 76 38 41N 91 46W
Chamonix 103 45 55N 6 51E
Chamouchouane, R. 41 48 37N 72 20W
Champagne, Can. 54 60 49N 136 30W
Champagne, France 101 49 0N 4 40E
Champagnole 101 46 45N 5 55E
Champaign 77 40 8N 88 14W
Champain, L. 43 44 45N 73 15W
Champaubert 101 48 50N 3 45E
Champdeniers 102 46 29N 0 25W
Champdoré, L. 36 55 55N 65 49W
Champeix 102 45 37N 3 8E
Champerico 84 14 18N 91 55W
Champigny 42 46 47N 71 21W
Champion, Can. 61 50 14N 113 9W
Champion, U.S.A. 53 46 31N 87 58W
Champion B. 134 28 44S 114 36E
Champlain, Can. 35 46 27N 72 24W
Champlain, U.S.A. 43 44 59N 73 27W
Champlain, L. 71 44 30N 73 20W
Champneuf 40 48 35N 77 30W
Champotón 83 19 20N 90 50W
Chan-chŏsujigjin 130 40 21N 127 20E
Chañaral 88 26 15S 70 50W
Chance Harbour 39 45 7N 66 21W
Chanda 124 19 57N 79 25E
Chandalar 67 67 30N 148 35W
Chandeleur Sd. 75 29 58N 88 40W
Chandigarh 124 30 30N 76 58E
Chandler, Can. 38 48 18N 64 46W
Chandler, Ariz., U.S.A. 79 33 20N 111 56W
Chandler, Okla., U.S.A. 75 35 43N 97 20W
Chandmani 129 45 22N 98 2E
Chandpur 125 22 8N 90 55E
Changanacheri 124 9 25N 76 31E
Changane, R. 117 23 30S 33 50E
Changchow, Fukien, China 131 24 32N 117 44E
Changchow, Shantung, China 130 36 55N 118 3E
Changchun 130 43 58N 125 19E
Change Islands 37 49 40N 54 25W
Changhua 131 24 2N 120 30E
Changkiakow 130 40 52N 114 45E
Changkiang 131 21 7N 110 21E
Changkiang (Shihlu) 131 19 25N 108 57E
Changkwansai Ling 130 44 40N 129 0E
Changlo 131 24 0N 115 33E
Changning 131 26 25N 112 15E
Changpai Shan, mts. 130 42 25N 129 0E
Changping 130 40 15N 116 15E
Changpu 131 24 2N 117 31E
Changsha 131 28 5N 113 1E
Changshow 131 29 49N 107 10E
Changshu 131 31 33N 120 45E
Changtai 131 24 34N 117 50E
Changteh 131 29 12N 111 43E
Changting 131 25 52N 116 20E
Changwu 130 42 21N 122 45E
Changyeh 129 38 56N 100 37E
Chankiang (Tsamkong) 131 21 7N 110 21E
Channapatna 124 12 40N 77 15E
Channel Is. 100 49 30N 2 40W
Channel Islands 81 33 30N 119 0W
Channel-Port aux Basques 37 47 30N 59 9W
Channing, Mich., U.S.A. 72 46 9N 88 1W
Channing, Tex., U.S.A. 75 35 45N 102 20W
Chantada 104 42 36N 7 46W
Chanthaburi 128 12 38N 102 12E
Chantilly 101 49 12N 2 29E
Chantonnay 100 46 40N 1 3W
Chantrey Inlet 65 67 48N 96 20W
Chanute 75 37 45N 85 25W
Chanyi 129 25 56N 104 1E
Chao Phraya, R. 128 13 32N 100 36E
Chaoan 131 23 41N 116 38E
Chaochow 131 23 45N 116 32E
Chaohwa 131 32 16N 105 41E
Chaoping 131 24 1N 110 59E
Chaotung 129 27 19N 103 42E
Chaoyan 130 37 23N 120 29E
Chaoyang, Kwangtung, China 131 23 10N 116 30E
Chaoyang, Liaoning, China 130 41 46N 120 16E
Chap Kuduk 120 48 45N 55 5E
Chapais 40 49 47N 74 51W
Chapala, Lago de 82 20 10N 103 20W
Chapayevo 120 50 25N 51 10E
Chapayevsk 120 53 0N 49 40E
Chapeau 40 45 54N 77 4W
Chapecó 89 27 14S 52 41W
Chapel Hill 73 35 53N 79 3W
Chapelle-d'Angillon, La 101 47 21N 2 25E
Chapelle Glain, La 100 47 38N 1 11W
Chapleau 53 47 50N 83 24W
Chaplin, Can. 56 50 28N 106 40W
Chaplin, U.S.A. 76 39 46N 90 24W
Chaplin L. 56 50 22N 106 36W
Chapman, Mt. 63 51 56N 118 20W
Chapra 125 25 48N 84 50E
Chara 121 56 54N 118 12E
Charadai 88 27.35S 60 0W
Charagua 86 19 45S 63 10W
Charak 123 26 46N 54 18E
Charalá 86 6 17N 73 10W
Charaña 86 17 30S 69 35W
Charapita 86 0 37S 74 21W
Charata 88 27 13S 61 14W
Charcas 82 23 10N 101 20W
Charchan 129 38 4N 85 16E
Charcoal L. 55 58 49N 102 22W
Charcot I. 91 70 0S 75 0W
Chard, Can. 55 55 55N 111 10W
Chard, U.K. 95 50 52N 2 59W
Chardara 120 41 16N 67 59E
Chardon 70 41 34N 81 17W
Chardzhou 120 39 6N 63 34E
Charente-Maritime □ 102 45 30N 0 35W
Charente □ 102 45 50N 0 16E
Charente, R. 102 45 41N 0 30W
Charette 41 46 27N 72 56W
Chari, R. 114 13 0N 15 20E
Charikar 124 35 0N 69 10E
Charité, La 101 47 10N 3 0E
Chariton 76 41 1N 93 19W
Chariton R. 76 39 19N 92 58W
Charity I. 46 44 3N 83 27W
Charkhlikh 129 39 16N 88 17E
Charlemagne 45 45 43N 73 29W
Charleroi 105 50 24N 4 27E
Charlerol 70 40 8N 79 54W
Charles, C. 72 37 10N 75 52W
Charles City 76 43 2N 92 41W
Charles L. 55 59 50N 110 33W
Charles Town 72 39 20N 77 50W
Charlesbourg 42 46 51N 71 16W
Charleston, Ill., U.S.A. 77 39 30N 88 10W
Charleston, Miss., U.S.A. 75 34 2N 90 3W
Charleston, Mo., U.S.A. 75 36 52N 89 20W
Charleston, S.C., U.S.A. 73 32 47N 79 56W
Charleston, W. Va., U.S.A. 73 38 24N 81 36W
Charleston L. 47 44 32N 76 0W
Charleston Park 81 36 17N 115 37W
Charleston Pk., mt. 81 36 16N 115 42W
Charlestown 77 38 29N 85 40W
Charlesville 116 5 27S 20 59E
Charleswood 58 49 51N 97 17W

Charleville Chinmu Chiao

Charleville 135 26 24 S 146 15 E
Charleville-Mézières 101 49 44N 4 40 E
Charleville = Rath Luirc 97 52 21N 8 40W
Charlevoix 46 45 19N 85 14W
Charlevoix, L. 46 45 15N 85 8W
Charlieu 103 46 10N 4 10 E
Charlo 39 47 59N 66 17W
Charlotte, Mich., U.S.A. 77 42 36N 84 48W
Charlotte, N.C., U.S.A. 73 35 16N 80 46W
Charlotte Amalie 85 18 22N 64 56W
Charlotte Harb. 73 26 45N 82 10W
Charlotte L. 62 52 12N 125 19W
Charlotte Waters 134 25 56 S 134 54 E
Charlottesville 72 38 1N 78 30W
Charlottetown 39 46 14N 63 8W
Charlton, Austral. 136 36 16 S 143 24 E
Charlton, U.S.A. 74 40 59N 93 20W
Charlton I. 36 52 0N 79 20W
Charmes 101 48 22N 6 17 E
Charnwood Forest 98 52 43N 1 18W
Charny 42 46 43N 71 15W
Charolles 103 46 27N 4 16 E
Charost 101 47 0N 2 7 E
Charron L. 57 52 44N 95 15W
Charroux 102 46 9N 0 25 E
Charters Towers 135 20 5 S 146 13 E
Chartre, La 100 47 42N 0 34 E
Chartres 100 48 29N 1 30 E
Chascomús 88 35 30 S 58 0W
Chase 63 50 50N 119 41W
Chasm 63 51 13N 121 30W
Chasseneuil-sur-Bonnieure 102 45 52N 0 29 E
Châtaigneraie, La 100 46 38N 0 45W
Château-Chinon 101 47 4N 3 56 E
Château-du-Loir 100 47 40N 0 25 E
Château Gontien 100 47 50N 0 42W
Château-la-Vallière 100 47 30N 0 20 E
Château-Landon 101 48 8N 2 40 E
Château, Le 102 45 52N 1 12W
Château Porcien 101 49 31N 4 13 E
Château Renault 100 47 36N 0 56 E
Château-Salins 101 48 50N 6 30 E
Château-Thierry 101 49 3N 3 20 E
Châteaubourg 100 48 7N 1 25W
Châteaubriant 100 47 43N 1 23W
Châteaudun 100 48 3N 1 20 E
Châteaugiron 100 48 3N 1 30W
Châteauguay 44 45 23N 73 45W
Châteauguay □ 44 45 11N 73 45W
Châteauguay-Centre 44 45 21N 73 45W
Châteauguay, L. 36 56 26N 70 3W
Châteauguay, R. 44 45 23N 73 45W
Châteaulin 100 48 11N 4 8W
Châteaumeillant 102 46 35N 2 12 E
Châteauneuf 100 48 35N 1 15 E
Châteauneuf-du-Faou 100 48 11N 3 50W
Châteauneuf-sur-Charente 102 45 36N 0 3W
Châteauneuf-sur-Cher 101 46 52N 2 18 E
Châteauneuf-sur-Loire 101 47 52N 2 13 E
Châteaurenard 103 43 53N 4 51 E
Châteauroux 101 46 50N 1 40 E
Châteauvert, L. 41 47 39N 73 56W
Châtelaillon-Plage 102 46 5N 1 5W
Châtelaudren 100 48 33N 2 59W
Chatelet 105 50 24N 4 32 E
Châtelet, Le, Cher, France 102 46 40N 2 20 E
Châtelet, Le, Seine-et-Marne, France 101 48 30N 2 47 E
Châtelguyon 102 45 55N 3 4 E
Châtellerault 100 46 50N 0 30 E
Châtelus-Malvaleix 102 46 18N 2 1 E
Chatham, N.B., Can. 39 47 2N 65 28W
Chatham, Ont., Can. 46 42 24N 82 11W
Chatham, U.K. 95 51 22N 0 32 E
Chatham, Alaska, U.S.A. 67 57 30N 135 0W
Chatham, Ill., U.S.A. 76 39 40N 89 42W
Chatham, La., U.S.A. 75 32 22N 92 26W
Chatham, Mich., U.S.A. 53 46 20N 86 56W
Chatham, N.Y., U.S.A. 71 42 21N 73 32W
Chatham Head 39 47 0N 65 33W
Chatham Is. 14 44 0 S 176 40W
Chatham Reach 66 49 15N 122 44W
Chatham Str. 54 57 0N 134 40W
Châtillon, Loiret, France 101 47 36N 2 44 E
Châtillon, Marne, France 101 49 5N 3 43 E
Châtillon-Coligny 101 47 50N 2 51 E
Châtillon-en-Bazois 101 47 3N 3 39 E
Châtillon-en-Diois 103 44 41N 5 29 E
Châtillon-sur-Seine 101 47 50N 4 33 E
Châtillon-sur-Sèvre 100 46 56N 0 45W
Chatrapur 125 19 22N 85 2 E
Châtre, La 102 46 35N 1 59 E
Chats, L. des 47 45 30N 76 20W
Chatsworth, Can. 46 44 27N 80 54W
Chatsworth, U.S.A. 77 40 45N 88 18W
Chattahoochee 73 30 43N 84 51W
Chattanooga 73 35 2N 85 17W
Chaudes-Aigues 102 44 51N 3 1 E
Chaudière, R. 41 46 45N 71 17W
Chauffailles 103 46 13N 4 20 E
Chaukan La 125 27 0N 97 15 E
Chaulnes 101 49 48N 2 47 E
Chaumont, France 101 48 7N 5 8 E
Chaumont, U.S.A. 71 44 4N 76 9W
Chaumont-en-Vexin 101 49 16N 1 53 E
Chaumont-sur-Loire 100 47 29N 1 11 E
Chaunay 102 46 13N 0 9 E
Chauny 101 49 37N 3 12 E
Chausey, Îs. 100 48 52N 1 49W
Chaussin 101 46 59N 5 22 E
Chautauqua 70 42 17N 79 30W
Chauvin 61 52 45N 110 10W
Chaux de Fonds, La 106 47 7N 6 50 E
Chaves, Brazil 87 0 15 S 49 55W
Chaves, Port. 104 41 45N 7 32W
Chavigny, L. 36 58 12N 75 8W
Chavuma 117 13 10 S 22 55 E
Chazelles-sur-Lyon 103 45 39N 4 22 E
Chazy 71 44 52N 73 28W
Cheam View 63 49 15N 121 40W
Cheb (Eger) 106 50 9N 12 20 E
Chebanse 77 41 0N 87 54W
Cheboksary 120 56 8N 47 30 E
Cheboygan 46 45 38N 84 29W
Checheng 131 34 4N 115 33 E
Checheno-Ingush, A.S.S.R. □ 120 43 30N 45 29 E
Checleset B. 62 50 5N 127 35W
Checotah 75 35 31N 95 30W
Chedabucto B. 39 45 25N 61 8W
Chedoke 48 43 14N 79 53W
Cheepash, R. 53 51 3N 80 59W
Cheepay, R. 53 51 25N 83 26W
Cheeseman L. 52 49 27N 89 20W
Chef-Boutonne 102 46 7N 0 4W
Chef, R. du 41 49 21N 73 25W
Chefornak 67 60 10N 164 15W
Chegdomyn 121 51 7N 132 52 E
Chegga 114 25 15N 5 40W
Chehalis 80 46 44N 122 59W
Cheju 131 33 28N 126 30 E
Cheju Do 131 33 29N 126 34 E
Chekiang □ 131 29 30N 120 0 E
Chelan, Can. 55 52 38N 103 22 E
Chelan, U.S.A. 78 47 49N 120 0W
Chelan, L. 63 48 5N 120 30W
Cheleken 120 39 26N 53 7 E
Chelforó 90 39 0 S 66 40W
Chelkar 120 47 40N 59 32 E
Chelkar Tengiz, Solonchak 120 48 0N 62 30 E
Chelles 101 48 52N 2 33 E
Chełm 107 51 8N 23 30 E
Chełmno 107 53 20N 18 30 E
Chelmsford 95 51 44N 0 29 E
Chełmża 107 53 10N 18 39 E
Chelsea, Austral. 136 38 5 S 145 8 E
Chelsea, Can. 48 45 30N 75 47W
Chelsea, Mich., U.S.A. 77 42 19N 84 1W
Chelsea, Okla., U.S.A. 75 36 35N 95 35W
Chelsea, Vermont, U.S.A. 71 43 59N 72 27W
Cheltenham, Can. 49 43 45N 79 55W
Cheltenham, U.K. 95 51 55N 2 5W
Chelyabinsk 120 55 10N 61 24 E
Chelyuskin, C. 118 77 30N 103 0 E
Chemainus 63 48 55N 123 48W
Chemillé 100 47 14N 0 45W
Chemnitz = Karl-Marx-Stadt 106 50 50N 12 55 E
Chemor 128 4 44N 101 6 E
Chemult 78 43 14N 121 54W
Chemung 71 42 2N 76 37W
Chen, Gora 121 65 10N 141 20 E
Chenab, R. 124 30 40N 73 30 E
Chenango Forks 71 42 15N 75 51W
Chencha 115 6 15N 37 32 E
Chêne, R. du 44 45 33N 73 54W
Chénéville 40 45 53N 75 3W
Cheney 78 47 38N 117 34W
Chenfeng 131 25 25N 105 51 E
Chengan 131 28 30N 107 30 E
Chengchow 131 34 47N 113 46 E
Chengho 131 27 25N 118 46 E
Chenghsien 131 29 30N 120 40 E
Chengkiang 129 24 58N 102 59 E
Chengkung 131 27 8N 108 57 E
Chengpu 131 26 12N 110 5 E
Chengteh 130 41 0N 117 55 E
Chengtu 129 30 45N 104 0 E
Chenhsien 131 25 46N 112 59 E
Chenil, L. 38 51 51N 59 41W
Chenkán 83 19 8N 90 58W
Chenki 131 28 1N 110 2 E
Chenning 131 25 57N 105 51 E
Chenoa 77 40 45N 88 42W
Chentung 130 46 2N 123 1 E
Chenyuan, Kansu, China 130 35 59N 107 2 E
Chenyuan, Kweichow, China 131 27 0N 108 20 E
Cheo Reo = Hau Bon 128 13 25N 108 28 E
Cheom Ksan 128 14 13N 104 56 E
Chepén 86 7 10 S 79 15W
Chepes 88 31 20 S 66 35W
Chepo 84 9 10N 79 6W
Chequamegon B. 74 46 40N 90 30W
Cher □ 101 47 10N 2 30 E
Chér, R. 101 47 10N 2 10 E
Cheraw 73 34 42N 79 54W
Cherbourg 100 49 39N 1 40W
Cherdyn 120 60 24N 56 29 E
Cheremkhovo 121 53 32N 102 40 E
Cherepanovo 120 54 15N 83 30 E
Cherepovets 120 59 5N 37 55 E
Cherhill 60 53 49N 114 41W
Cherkassy 120 49 30N 32 0 E
Cherlak 120 54 15N 74 55 E
Chernigov 120 51 28N 31 20 E
Chernogorsk 121 54 5N 91 10 E
Chernovtsy 120 48 0N 26 0 E
Chernoye 121 70 30N 89 10 E
Chernyakhovsk 120 54 29N 21 48 E
Chernyshevskiy 121 62 40N 112 30 E
Cherokee, Iowa, U.S.A. 74 42 40N 95 30W
Cherokee, Okla., U.S.A. 75 36 45N 98 25W
Cherokees, L. O'The 75 36 50N 95 12W
Cherquenco 90 38 35 S 72 0W
Cherrapunji 125 25 17N 91 47 E
Cherry Creek, Can. 63 50 43N 120 40W
Cherry Creek, Nev., U.S.A. 78 39 50N 114 58W
Cherry Creek, N.Y., U.S.A. 70 42 18N 79 6W
Cherry Valley 81 33 59N 116 57W
Cherryvale 75 37 20N 95 33W
Cherryville 63 50 15N 118 37W
Cherrywood 51 43 52N 79 8W
Cherskiy 121 68 45N 161 18 E
Cherskogo Khrebet 121 65 0N 143 0 E
Cherwell, R. 95 51 46N 1 18W
Chesaning 46 43 11N 84 7W
Chesapeake Bay 72 38 0N 76 12W
Chesha B. = Cheshskaya G. 120 67 20N 47 0 E
Cheshire □ 94 53 14N 2 30W
Chesil Beach 98 50 37N 2 33W
Cheslatta 62 53 48N 125 48W
Cheslatta L. 62 53 49N 125 20W
Chesley 46 44 17N 81 5W
Chesne, Le 101 49 30N 4 45 E
Chester, Can. 39 44 33N 64 15W
Chester, U.K. 94 53 12N 2 53W
Chester, Calif., U.S.A. 78 40 22N 121 22W
Chester, Ill., U.S.A. 76 37 58N 89 50W
Chester, Mont., U.S.A. 78 48 31N 111 0W
Chester, N.Y., U.S.A. 71 41 22N 74 16W
Chester, Pa., U.S.A. 72 39 54N 75 20W
Chester, S.C., U.S.A. 73 34 44N 81 13W
Chesterfield 94 53 14N 1 26W
Chesterfield I. 117 16 20 S 43 58 E
Chesterfield, Îles 135 19 52 S 158 15 E
Chesterfield In. 65 63 25N 90 45W
Chesterfield Inlet 65 63 30N 90 45W
Chesterville 47 45 6N 75 14W
Chesuncook L. 35 46 0N 69 10W
Chéticamp 39 46 37N 60 59W
Chetumal 83 18 30N 88 20W
Chetumal, Bahia de 83 18 40N 88 10W
Chetwynd 54 55 45N 121 45W
Chevanceaux 102 45 18N 0 14W
Cheviot 77 39 10N 84 37W
Cheviot Hills 94 55 20N 2 30W
Cheviot, The 94 55 29N 2 8W
Chew Bahir 115 4 40N 30 50 E
Chewelah 63 48 17N 117 43W
Cheyenne, Okla., U.S.A. 75 35 35N 99 40W
Cheyenne, Wyo., U.S.A. 74 41 9N 104 49W
Cheyenne, R. 74 44 50N 101 0W
Cheyenne Wells 74 38 51N 102 23W
Cheylard, Le 103 44 55N 4 25 E
Chezacut 62 52 24N 124 1W
Chhang 126 12 15N 104 14 E
Chhatarpur 124 24 55N 79 43 E
Chhindwara 124 22 2N 78 59 E
Chhlong 128 12 15N 105 58 E
Chi, R. 128 15 11N 104 43 E
Chiai 131 23 29N 120 25 E
Chiang Mai 128 18 47N 98 59 E
Chianie 117 15 35 S 13 40 E
Chiapa de Corzo 83 16 42N 93 0W
Chiapa, R. 83 16 42N 93 0W
Chiapas □ 83 17 0N 92 45W
Chiautla 83 18 18N 98 34W
Chiba 132 35 30N 140 7 E
Chiba-ken □ 132 35 30N 140 20 E
Chibemba 117 15 48 S 14 8 E
Chibougamau 41 49 56N 74 24W
Chibougamau L. 41 49 50N 74 20W
Chibougamau, Parc Prov. de 41 49 15N 73 45W
Chibougamau, R. 40 49 42N 75 57W
Chic-Chocs, Mts. 38 48 55N 66 0W
Chic-Chocs, Parc Prov. des 38 48 55N 66 20W
Chicago 77 41 53N 87 40W
Chicago Heights 77 41 29N 87 37W
Chichagof I. 54 58 0N 136 0W
Chichén Itzá 83 20 40N 88 32W
Chichester 95 50 50N 0 47W
Chichibu 132 36 5N 139 10 E
Chichirin 130 50 35N 123 45 E
Chichiriviche 86 10 56N 68 16W
Chichow 130 38 30N 115 25 E
Chickasha 75 35 0N 98 0W
Chicken Hd. 94 58 10N 6 15W
Chiclana de la Frontera 104 36 26N 6 9W
Chiclayo 86 6 42 S 79 50W
Chico 80 39 45N 121 54W
Chico, R., Chubut, Argent. 78 44 0 S 67 0W
Chico, R., Santa Cruz, Argent. 90 49 30 S 69 30W
Chicoa 117 15 35 S 32 20 E
Chicobi, L. 40 48 53N 78 30W
Chicontepec 83 20 58N 98 10W
Chicopee 71 42 6N 72 37W
Chicot 44 45 36N 73 56W
Chicoutimi 35 48 28N 71 5W
Chicoutimi, Parc Prov. de 41 48 30N 70 20W
Chidambaram 124 11 20N 79 45 E
Chidley C. 36 60 23N 64 26W
Chiefs Pt. 46 44 41N 81 18W
Chiengi 116 8 45 S 29 10 E
Chiese, R. 108 45 45N 10 35 E
Chieti 108 42 22N 14 10 E
Chignecto B. 39 45 30N 64 40W
Chignecto, Cape 39 45 20N 64 57W
Chignik 67 56 15N 158 27W
Chigorodó 86 7 41N 76 42W
Chigoubiche, L. 41 49 7N 73 30W
Chiguana 88 21 0 S 67 50W
Chihfeng 130 42 18N 118 57 E
Chihing 131 25 2N 113 45 E
Chihkiang, Hunan, China 131 27 21N 109 45 E
Chihkiang, Hupei, China 131 30 25N 111 30 E
Chihkin 131 26 30N 105 45 E
Chihli, G. of (Po Hai) 130 38 30N 119 0 E
Chihsien (Weihwei) 131 35 29N 114 1 E
Chihuahua 82 28 40N 106 3W
Chihuahua □ 82 28 40N 106 3W
Chihuatlán 82 19 14N 104 35W
Chik Ballapur 124 13 25N 77 45 E
Chikmagalur 124 13 15N 75 45 E
Chilac 83 18 20N 97 24W
Chilako, R. 62 53 53N 122 57W
Chilanko Forks 62 52 7N 124 5W
Chilanko, R. 62 52 7N 123 41W
Chilapa 83 17 40N 99 20W
Chilas 124 35 25N 74 5 E
Chilaw 124 7 30N 79 50 E
Chilco 62 54 3N 123 49W
Chilcotin, R. 63 51 44N 122 23W
Childers 135 25 15 S 152 17 E
Childress 75 34 30N 100 15W
Chile ■ 90 35 0 S 71 15W
Chilecito 88 29 0 S 67 40W
Chilete 86 7 10 S 78 50W
Chilhowee 76 38 36N 93 51W
Chililabombwe (Bancroft) 117 12 18 S 27 43 E
Chilka L. 125 19 40N 85 25 E
Chilko, L. 62 51 20N 124 10W
Chilko, R. 62 52 6N 123 40W
Chillagoe 135 17 14 S 144 33 E
Chillán 88 36 40 S 72 10W
Chillicothe, Ill., U.S.A. 76 40 55N 89 32W
Chillicothe, Mo., U.S.A. 76 39 45N 93 30W
Chillicothe, Ohio, U.S.A. 72 39 20N 82 58W
Chilliwack 63 49 10N 122 0W
Chiloé, I. de 90 42 50 S 73 45W
Chilpancingo 83 17 30N 99 40W
Chiltern Hills 95 51 44N 0 42W
Chilton 72 44 1N 88 12W
Chiluage 116 9 15 S 21 42 E
Chilung 131 25 3N 121 45 E
Chilwa, L. (Shirwa) 117 15 15 S 35 40 E
Chimacum 78 48 1N 122 53W
Chimai 129 33 35N 102 10 E
Chimaltitán 82 21 46N 103 50W
Chimán 84 8 45N 78 40W
Chimay 105 50 3N 4 20 E
Chimbay 120 42 57N 59 47 E
Chimborazo 86 1 29 S 78 55W
Chimbote 86 9 0 S 78 35W
Chimkent 120 42 18N 69 36 E
Chin □ 125 22 0N 93 0 E
Chin Chai 131 31 58N 115 59 E
China 82 25 40N 99 20W
China ■ 129 30 0N 110 0 E
China Lake 81 35 44N 117 37W
Chinacates 82 25 0N 105 14W
Chinacota 86 7 37N 72 36W
Chinandega 84 12 30N 87 0W
Chinati Pk. 75 30 0N 104 25W
Chincha Alta 86 13 20 S 76 0W
Chinchaga, R. 60 58 53N 118 20W
Chinchón 104 40 9N 3 26W
Chinchorro, Banco 83 18 35N 87 20W
Chinchow 130 41 10N 121 2 E
Chincoteague 72 37 58N 75 21W
Chinde 117 18 45 S 36 30 E
Chindwin, R. 125 21 26N 95 15 E
Ching Ho, R. 131 34 20N 109 0 E
Chinghai □ 129 36 0N 97 0 E
Chingola 117 12 31 S 27 53 E
Chinguar 117 12 18 S 16 45 E
Chiniot 124 31 45N 73 0 E
Chinipas 82 27 22N 108 32W
Chinkiang 131 32 2N 119 29 E
Chinle 79 36 14N 109 38W
Chinmu Chiao 131 18 10N 109 35 E

Name	Page	Lat	Long
Chinnampo	130	38 52N	125 28 E
Chino	81	34 1N	117 41W
Chino Valley	79	34 54N	112 28W
Chinon	100	47 10N	0 15 E
Chinook, Can.	61	51 28N	110 59W
Chinook, U.S.A.	78	48 35N	109 19W
Chinook Valley	60	56 29N	117 39W
Chinsali	116	10 30 S	32 2 E
Chinwangtao	130	40 0N	119 31 E
Chióggia	108	45 13N	12 15 E
Chip L.	60	53 40N	115 23W
Chip Lake	54	53 35N	115 35W
*Chipai L.	34	52 56N	87 53W
Chipata (Ft. Jameson)	117	13 38 S	32 28 E
Chipewyan L.	55	58 0N	98 27W
Chipley	73	30 45N	85 32W
Chipman, Alta., Can.	60	53 42N	112 38W
Chipman, N.B., Can.	39	46 6N	65 53W
Chipman L.	53	49 58N	86 15W
Chippawa	49	43 5N	79 2W
Chippenham	95	51 27N	2 7W
Chippewa Falls	74	44 55N	91 22W
Chippewa, R.	74	44 45N	91 55W
Chiputneticook Lakes	39	45 37N	67 40W
Chiquian	86	10 10 S	77 0W
Chiquimula	84	14 51N	89 37W
Chiquinquirá	86	5 37N	73 50W
Chirala	124	15 50N	80 20 E
Chiras	123	35 14N	65 40 E
Chirchik	120	41 29N	69 35 E
Chiricahua Pk.	79	31 53N	109 14W
Chirikof I.	67	55 50N	155 40W
Chiriqui, Golfo de	84	8 0N	82 0W
Chiriqui, Lago de	84	9 10N	82 0W
Chiriqui, Vol.	84	8 55N	82 35W
Chirmiri	125	23 15N	82 20 E
Chiromo	117	16 30 S	35 7 E
Chirripó Grande, cerro	84	9 29N	83 29W
Chisamba	117	14 55 S	28 20 E
Chisapani Garhi	125	27 30N	84 2 E
Chishan	131	22 44N	120 31 E
Chisholm, Can.	60	54 55N	114 10W
Chisholm, U.S.A.	52	47 29N	92 53W
Chisos Mts.	75	29 20N	103 15W
Chistopol	120	55 25N	50 38 E
Chita, Colomb.	86	6 11N	72 28W
Chita, U.S.S.R.	121	52 0N	113 25 E
Chitado	117	17 10 S	14 8 E
Chitek	56	53 48N	107 45W
Chitek L., Man., Can.	57	52 25N	99 25W
Chitek L., Sask., Can.	56	53 45N	107 47W
Chitembo	117	13 30 S	16 50 E
Chitina	67	61 30N	144 30W
Chitokoloki	117	13 43 S	23 4 E
Chitorgarh	124	24 52N	74 43 E
Chitral	124	35 50N	71 56 E
Chitré	85	7 59N	80 27W
Chittagong	125	22 19N	91 55 E
Chittagong □	125	24 5N	91 25 E
Chittoor	124	13 15N	79 5 E
Chiusi	108	43 1N	11 58 E
Chivasso	108	45 10N	7 52 E
Chivilcoy	88	35 0 S	60 0W
Chkalov = Orenburg	120	52 0N	55 5 E
Chloride	81	35 25N	114 12W
Choahsien	130	37 48N	114 46 E
Chocó □	86	6 0N	77 0W
Chocontá	86	5 9N	73 41W
Choele Choel	90	39 11 S	65 40W
Choelquoit L.	62	51 42N	124 12W
Choiceland	56	53 29N	104 29W
Choiseul I.	14	7 0 S	156 40 E
Choisy	44	45 29N	74 13W
Choisy-le-Roi	101	48 45N	2 24 E
Choix	82	26 40N	108 10W
Chojnice	107	53 42N	17 40 E
Chokurdakh	121	70 38N	147 55 E
Cholame	80	35 44N	120 18W
Cholet	100	47 4N	0 52W
Choluteca	84	13 20N	87 14W
Choluteca, R.	84	13 5N	87 20W
Choma	117	16 48 S	26 59 E
Chomedey	44	45 32N	73 45W
Chomutov	106	50 28N	13 23 E
Chonan	130	36 48N	127 9 E
Chonburi	128	13 21N	101 1 E
Chone	86	0 40 S	80 0W
Chongjin	130	41 47N	129 50 E
Chóngju	130	36 39N	127 27 E
Chónju	130	35 50N	127 4 E
Chonos, Arch. de los	90	45 0 S	75 0W
Chopim, R.	89	25 35 S	53 5W
Chorley	94	53 39N	2 39W
Chorolque, Cerro	88	20 59 S	66 5W
Chorrera, La	84	8 50N	79 50W
Chórwón	130	38 15N	127 10 E
Chorzów	107	50 18N	19 0 E
Chos-Malal	88	37 15 S	70 5W
Choshi	132	35 45N	140 45 E
Choszczno	106	53 7N	15 25 E
Choteau	78	47 50N	112 10W
Chotila	124	22 30N	71 15 E
Chow Hu	131	31 35N	117 30 E
Chowchilla	80	37 11N	120 12W
Choybalsan	130	48 3N	114 28 E
Choyr	130	46 24N	108 30 E
Chrisman	77	39 48N	87 41W
Christchurch, N.Z.	133	43 33 S	172 47 E
Christchurch, U.K.	95	50 44N	1 47W
Christian I.	46	44 50N	80 12W
Christiana	117	27 52 S	25 8 E
Christiansted	85	17 45N	64 42W
Christie B.	55	62 32N	111 10W
Christies Corners	49	43 16N	80 2W
Christina, L.	63	49 3N	118 12W
Christina, R.	60	56 40N	111 3W
Christmas I., Ind. Oc.	16	10 0 S	105 40 E
*Christmas I., Pac. Oc.	15	1 58N	157 27W
Christopher Lake	56	53 32N	105 48W
Chu	120	43 36N	73 42 E
Chu Chua	63	51 22N	120 10W
Chu Kiang	131	22 15N	113 45 E
Chu, R.	128	19 53N	105 45 E
Chuanchow	131	24 57N	118 31 E
Chuanhsien	131	25 50N	111 12 E
Chūbu □	132	36 45N	137 30 E
Chubut, R.	90	43 0 s	70 0W
Chuchi L.	54	55 12N	124 30W
Chuchow	131	27 56N	113 3 E
Chuchow (Lishui)	131	28 30N	119 50 E
Chugach Mts.	67	62 0N	146 0W
Chugiak	67	61 7N	149 10W
Chuginadak I.	67	52 50N	169 45W
Chūgoku □	132	35 0N	133 0 E
Chūgoku-Sanchi	132	35 0N	133 0 E
Chugwater	74	41 48N	104 47W
Chuho = Shangchih	130	45 10N	127 59 E
Chuhsien, Chekiang, China	130	28 57N	118 58 E
Chuhsien, Shantung, China	131	35 31N	118 45 E
Chuhsien, Szechwan, China	131	30 51N	107 1 E
Chukai	128	4 13N	103 25 E
Chuki, Chekiang, China	131	29 30N	120 4 E
Chuki, Hupei, China	131	32 26N	110 0 E
Chukotskiy Khrebet	121	68 0N	175 0 E
Chukotskiy, Mys	121	66 10N	169 3 E
Chukotskoye More	121	68 0N	175 0W
Chula	76	39 55N	93 29W
Chula Vista	81	32 39N	117 8W
Chulucanas	86	5 0 S	80 0W
Chumatien	131	33 0N	114 4 E
Chumbicha	88	29 0 s	66 10W
Chumikan	121	54 40N	135 10 E
Chumphon	128	10 35N	99 14 E
Chunchón	130	37 58N	127 44 E
Chungan	131	27 45N	118 0 E
Chunghsien	131	30 17N	108 4 E
Chungking	131	29 30N	106 30 E
Chungsiang	131	31 14N	112 42 E
Chunya	116	8 30 S	33 27 E
Chuquibamba	86	15 47N	72 44W
Chuquicamata	88	22 15 S	69 0W
Chuquisaca □	88	23 30 S	63 30W
Chur	106	46 52N	9 32 E
Churachandpur	125	24 20N	93 40 E
Church House	54	50 20N	125 10W
Churchbridge	57	50 54N	101 54W
Churchill	55	58 47N	94 11W
Churchill, C.	55	58 46N	93 12W
Churchill Falls	36	53 36N	64 19W
Churchill L., Ont., Can.	53	50 55N	94 49W
Churchill L., Sask., Can.	55	55 55N	108 20W
Churchill Pk.	54	58 10N	125 10W
Churchill, R., Man., Can.	55	58 47N	94 12W
Churchill, R., Newf., Can.	36	53 19N	60 10W
Churchill, R., Sask., Can.	55	58 47N	94 12W
Churdan	76	42 9N	94 29W
Churu	124	28 20N	75 0 E
Churubusco	77	41 14N	85 19W
Churuguaro	86	10 49N	69 32W
Chusan	130	30 0N	122 20 E
Chushul	124	33 40N	78 40 E
Chusnan	131	32 14N	110 30 E
Chusovoy	120	58 15N	57 40 E
Chute-à-Blondeau	43	45 35N	74 28W
Chute-aux-Outardes	41	49 7N	68 24W
Chute-des-Passes	41	49 52N	71 16W
Chuting	131	27 28N	113 1 E
Chuvash A.S.S.R.□	120	55 30N	48 0 E
Chwangho	130	39 41N	123 2 E
Cibola	81	33 17N	114 9W
Cicero	72	41 48N	87 48W
Ciechanów	107	52 52N	20 38 E
Ciego de Avila	84	21 50N	78 50W
Ciénaga	86	11 1N	74 15W
Ciénaga de Oro	86	8 53N	75 37W
Cienfuegos	84	22 10N	80 30W
Cierp	102	42 55N	0 40 E
Cieszyn	107	49 45N	18 35 E
Cieza	104	38 17N	1 23W
Cijulang	127	7 42 S	108 27 E
Cikampek	127	6 23 S	107 28 E
Cilacap	127	7 43 S	109 0 E
Cilician Gates P.	122	37 20N	34 52 E
Cilician Taurus	122	36 40N	34 0 E
Cima	81	35 14N	115 30W
Cimarron, Kans., U.S.A.	75	37 50N	100 20W
Cimarron, N. Mex., U.S.A.	75	36 30N	104 52W
Cimarron, R.	75	37 10N	102 10W
Cimone, Mte.	108	44 10N	10 40 E
Cimpina	107	45 10N	25 45 E
Cîmpulung	107	45 17N	25 3 E
Cinca, R.	104	42 20N	0 9 E
Cinch, R.	73	36 0N	84 15W
Cincinnati, Iowa, U.S.A.	76	40 38N	92 56W
Cincinnati, Ohio, U.S.A.	77	39 10N	84 26W
Cinto, Mt.	103	42 24N	8 54 E
Ciotat, La	103	43 12N	5 36 E
Circle, Alaska, U.S.A.	67	65 50N	144 10W
Circle, Montana, U.S.A.	74	47 26N	105 35W
Circleville, Ohio, U.S.A.	72	39 35N	82 57W
Circleville, Utah, U.S.A.	79	38 12N	112 24W
Cirebon	127	6 45 S	108 32 E
Cirencester	95	51 43N	1 59W
Cirey-sur-Vezouze	101	48 35N	6 57 E
Cisco	75	32 25N	99 0W
Cisne	77	38 31N	88 26W
Cisneros	86	6 33N	75 4W
Cissna Park	77	40 34N	87 54W
Citlaltépetl, mt.	83	19 0N	97 20W
City View, Ont., Can.	48	45 21N	75 45W
City View, Sask., Can.	58	50 28N	104 37W
Ciudad Acuña	82	29 20N	101 10W
Ciudad Altamirano	82	18 20N	100 40W
Ciudad Bolívar	86	8 5N	63 30W
Ciudad Camargo	82	27 41N	105 10W
Ciudad de Valles	83	22 0N	98 30W
Ciudad del Carmen	83	18 20N	97 50W
Ciudad Delicias = Delicias	82	28 10N	105 30W
Ciudad Guerrero	82	28 33N	107 28W
Ciudad Guzmán	82	19 40N	103 30W
Ciudad Juárez	82	31 40N	106 28W
Ciudad Madero	83	22 19N	97 50W
Ciudad Mante	83	22 50N	99 0W
Ciudad Obregón	82	27 28N	109 59W
Ciudad Piar	86	7 27N	63 19W
Ciudad Real	104	38 59N	3 55W
Ciudad Rodrigo	104	40 35N	6 32W
Ciudad Trujillo = Sto. Domingo	85	18 30N	70 0W
Ciudad Victoria	83	23 41N	99 9W
Civitanova Marche	108	43 18N	13 41 E
Civitavécchia	108	42 6N	11 46 E
Civray	102	46 10N	0 17 E
Çivril	122	38 20N	29 55 E
Cizre	122	37 19N	42 10 E
Clacton-on-Sea	95	51 47N	1 10 E
Clairambault, L.	36	54 29N	69 0W
Claire	41	47 15N	68 40W
Claire, L.	54	58 35N	112 5W
Claire, Le	76	41 36N	90 21W
Clairemont	75	33 9N	100 44W
Clairmont	60	55 16N	118 47W
Clairton	70	40 18N	79 54W
Clairvaux-les-Lacs	103	46 35N	5 45 E
Clallam Bay	80	48 15N	124 16W
Clamecy	101	47 28N	3 30 E
Clandonald	60	53 34N	110 44W
Clanton	73	32 48N	86 36W
Clanwilliam, Can.	57	50 22N	99 49W
Clanwilliam, S. Afr.	117	32 11 S	18 52 E
Clapperton I.	46	46 0N	82 14W
Clappisons Corners	48	43 18N	79 55W
Clara	97	53 20N	7 38W
Claraville	81	35 24N	118 20W
Clare, Austral.	136	33 50 S	138 37 E
Clare, U.S.A.	46	43 47N	84 45W
Clare □	97	52 20N	7 38W
Clare I.	97	53 48N	10 0W
Clare, R.	97	53 20N	9 0W
Claremont, Can.	51	43 58N	79 7W
Claremont, U.S.A.	71	43 23N	72 20W
Claremore	75	36 40N	95 20W
Claremorris	97	53 45N	9 0W
Clarence	76	39 45N	92 16W
Clarence I.	91	61 30 S	53 50W
Clarence, I.	90	54 0 S	72 0W
Clarence, R., Austral.	135	29 25 S	153 22 E
Clarence, R., N.Z.	133	42 10 S	173 56 E
Clarence Str., Austral.	134	12 0 S	131 0 E
Clarence Str., U.S.A.	54	55 40N	132 10W
Clarence Town	85	23 6N	74 59W
Clarenceville	43	45 4N	73 15W
Clarendon, Can.	39	45 29N	66 26W
Clarendon, Ark., U.S.A.	75	34 41N	91 20W
Clarendon, Tex., U.S.A.	75	34 58N	100 54W
Clarenville	37	48 10N	54 1W
Claresholm	61	50 0N	113 45W
Clarie Coast	91	67 0 S	135 0 E
Clarinda	76	40 45N	95 0W
Clarion, Iowa, U.S.A.	76	42 41N	93 46W
Clarion, Pa., U.S.A.	70	41 12N	79 22W
Clarion, R.	70	41 19N	79 10W
Clark	74	44 55N	97 45W
Clark Fork	78	48 9N	116 9W
Clark Fork, R.	78	48 0N	115 40W
Clark Hill Res.	73	33 45N	82 20W
Clark, Pt.	46	44 4N	81 45W
Clarkdale	79	34 53N	112 3W
Clarke City	38	50 12N	66 38W
Clarke, I.	135	40 32 S	148 10 E
Clarke L.	56	54 24N	106 54W
Clarkefield	136	37 30 S	44 40 E
Clark's Fork, R.	78	45 0N	109 30W
Clark's Harbour	39	43 25N	65 38W
Clarks Summit	71	41 31N	75 44W
Clarksburg	72	39 18N	80 21W
Clarksdale	75	34 12N	90 33W
Clarkson	50	43 31N	79 37W
Clarkston	78	46 28N	117 2W
Clarksville, Ark., U.S.A.	75	35 29N	93 27W
Clarksville, Iowa, U.S.A.	76	42 47N	92 40W
Clarksville, Mich., U.S.A.	77	42 50N	85 15W
Clarksville, Ohio, U.S.A.	77	39 24N	83 59W
Clarksville, Tenn., U.S.A.	73	36 32N	87 20W
Clarksville, Tex., U.S.A.	75	33 37N	94 59W
Clatskanie	80	46 9N	123 12W
Claude, Can.	49	43 47N	79 54W
Claude, U.S.A.	75	35 8N	101 22W
Claveria	127	18 37N	121 15 E
Clay	80	38 17N	121 10W
Clay Center	74	39 27N	97 9W
Clay City, Ind., U.S.A.	77	39 17N	87 7W
Clay City, Ky., U.S.A.	77	37 52N	83 55W
Clay L.	52	50 3N	93 30W
Clayette, La	103	46 17N	4 19 E
Claypool	79	33 27N	110 55W
Claysville	70	40 5N	80 25W
Clayton, Idaho, U.S.A.	78	44 12N	114 31W
Clayton, Ind., U.S.A.	77	39 41N	86 31W
Clayton, N. Mex., U.S.A.	75	36 30N	103 10W
Cle Elum	78	47 15N	120 57W
Clear L.	80	39 5N	122 47W
Clear C.	97	51 26N	9 30W
Clear I.	97	51 26N	9 30W
Clear, L.	47	45 26N	77 12W
Clear Lake, S.D., U.S.A.	74	44 48N	96 41W
Clear Lake, Wash., U.S.A.	78	48 27N	122 15W
Clear Lake City	76	43 8N	93 23W
Clear Lake Res.	78	41 55N	121 10W
Clear, R.	60	56 11N	119 42W
Clearfield, Iowa, U.S.A.	76	40 48N	94 29W
Clearfield, Pa., U.S.A.	72	41 0N	78 27W
Clearfield, Utah, U.S.A.	78	41 10N	112 0W
Clearlake Highlands	80	38 57N	122 38W
Clearmont	78	44 43N	106 29W
Clearwater, Can.	63	51 38N	120 2W
Clearwater, U.S.A.	73	27 58N	82 45W
Clearwater Cr.	54	61 36N	125 30W
Clearwater L.	63	52 15N	120 13W
Clearwater, Mts.	78	46 20N	115 30W
Clearwater Prov. Park	57	54 0N	101 0W
Clearwater, R., Alta., Can.	60	56 44N	111 23W
Clearwater, R., Alta., Can.	61	52 22N	114 57W
Clearwater, R., B.C., Can.	63	51 38N	120 3W
Cleburne	75	32 18N	97 25W
Clee Hills	98	52 26N	2 35W
Cleethorpes	94	53 33N	0 2W
Cleeve Cloud	95	51 56N	2 0W
Cleeve Hill	95	51 54N	2 0W
Clelles	103	44 50N	5 38 E
Clementsport	39	44 40N	65 37W
Clendale	77	39 16N	84 28W
Clerks Rocks	91	56 0 S	36 30W
Clermont, Austral.	135	22 49 S	147 39 E
Clermont, Can.	41	47 41N	70 14W
Clermont-en-Argonne	101	49 5N	5 4 E
Clermont-Ferrand	102	45 46N	3 4 E
Clermont-l'Hérault	102	43 38N	3 26 E
Clerval	101	47 25N	6 30 E
Cléry-Saint-André	101	47 50N	1 46 E
Cleveland, U.K.	94	54 29N	1 0W
Cleveland, Miss., U.S.A.	75	33 43N	90 43W
Cleveland, Ohio, U.S.A.	70	41 28N	81 43W
Cleveland, Okla., U.S.A.	75	36 21N	96 33W
Cleveland, Tenn., U.S.A.	73	35 9N	84 52W
Cleveland, Tex., U.S.A.	75	30 18N	95 0W
Cleveland □	94	54 35N	1 8 E
Cleveland, C.	135	19 11 S	147 1 E
Cleveland Heights	70	41 32N	81 30W
Clevelándia	89	26 24 S	52 23W
Cleves	77	39 10N	84 45W
Clew Bay	97	53 54N	9 50W
Clewiston	73	26 44N	80 50W
Clifden, Ireland	97	53 30N	10 2W
Clifden, N.Z.	133	46 1 S	167 42 E
Cliff	79	33 0N	108 44W
Cliffdell	80	46 44N	120 42W
Clifton, Ariz., U.S.A.	79	33 8N	109 23W
Clifton, Ill., U.S.A.	77	40 56N	87 56W
Clifton, Tex., U.S.A.	75	31 46N	97 35W
Clifton Forge	72	37 49N	79 51W
Climax	56	49 10N	108 20W
Clingmans Dome	73	35 35N	83 30W
Clint	79	31 37N	106 11W
Clinton, B.C., Can.	63	51 6N	121 35W
Clinton, Ont., Can.	46	43 37N	81 32W
Clinton, N.Z.	133	46 12 S	169 23 E

Clinton, Ark., U.S.A.	**75**	35 37N	92 30W
Clinton, Ill., U.S.A.	**74**	40 8N	89 0W
Clinton, Ind., U.S.A.	**77**	39 40N	87 22W
Clinton, Iowa, U.S.A.	**76**	41 50N	90 12W
Clinton, Mass., U.S.A.	**71**	42 26N	71 40W
Clinton, Mo., U.S.A.	**76**	38 20N	93 46W
Clinton, N.C., U.S.A.	**73**	35 5N	78 15W
Clinton, Okla., U.S.A.	**75**	35 30N	99 0W
Clinton, S.C., U.S.A.	**73**	34 30N	81 54W
Clinton, Tenn., U.S.A.	**73**	36 6N	84 10W
Clinton, Wash., U.S.A.	**80**	47 59N	122 22W
Clinton, Wis., U.S.A.	**77**	42 34N	88 52W
Clinton Colden L.	**64**	64 58N	107 27W
Clinton Creek	**64**	64 25N	140 37W
Clintonville	**74**	44 35N	88 46W
Clisson	**100**	47 5N	1 16W
Clive	**61**	52 28N	113 27W
Clive L.	**54**	63 13N	118 54W
Clodomira	**88**	27 35 S	64 14W
Clonakilty	**97**	51 37N	8 53W
Clonakilty B.	**97**	51 33N	8 50W
Cloncurry	**135**	20 40 S	140 28 E
Clones	**97**	54 10N	7 13W
Clonmel	**97**	52 22N	7 42W
Cloquet	**52**	46 40N	92 30W
Cloquet, R.	**52**	46 52N	92 35W
Clorinda	**88**	25 16 S	57 45W
Cloud Peak	**78**	44 30N	107 10W
Cloudcroft	**79**	33 0N	105 48W
Clova	**40**	48 7N	75 22W
Clover Pt.	**63**	48 24N	123 21W
Cloverdale, B.C., Can.	**66**	49 7N	122 44W
Cloverdale, N.B., Can.	**39**	46 17N	67 22W
Cloverdale, Calif., U.S.A.	**80**	38 49N	123 0W
Cloverdale, Ind., U.S.A.	**77**	39 31N	86 47W
Cloverport	**77**	37 50N	86 38W
Clovis, Calif., U.S.A.	**80**	36 54N	119 45W
Clovis, N. Mex., U.S.A.	**75**	34 20N	103 10W
Cloyne	**47**	44 49N	77 11W
Cluculz L.	**62**	53 53N	123 33W
Cluj	**107**	46 47N	23 38 E
Cluny	**103**	46 26N	4 38 E
Cluses	**103**	46 5N	6 35 E
Clutha, R.	**133**	46 20 S	169 49 E
Clwyd □	**94**	53 5N	3 20W
Clwyd, R.	**94**	53 12N	3 30W
Clyde, Alta., Can.	**60**	54 9N	113 39W
*Clyde, N.W.T., Can.	**65**	70 30N	68 30W
Clyde, Ont., Can.	**49**	43 22N	80 14W
Clyde, N.Z.	**133**	45 12 S	169 20 E
Clyde, N.Y., U.S.A.	**70**	43 8N	76 52W
Clyde, Ohio, U.S.A.	**76**	41 18N	82 59W
Clyde, Firth of	**96**	55 20N	5 0W
Clyde, R., Can.	**39**	43 35N	65 27W
Clyde, R., U.K.	**96**	55 46N	4 58W
Clyde River	**39**	43 38N	65 29W
Clydebank	**96**	55 54N	4 25W
Clymer	**70**	42 3N	79 39W
Coachella	**81**	33 44N	116 13W
Coachella Canal	**81**	32 43N	114 57W
Coachman's Cove	**35**	50 6N	56 20W
Coacoachou, L.	**38**	50 25N	60 14W
Coahoma	**75**	32 17N	101 20W
Coahuayana, R.	**82**	18 41N	103 45W
Coahuayutla	**82**	18 19N	101 42W
Coahuila □	**82**	27 0N	112 30W
Coal City	**77**	41 17N	88 17W
Coal Creek	**61**	49 30N	114 59W
Coal Harbour	**62**	50 36N	127 35W
Coal, R.	**54**	59 39N	126 57W
Coalcomán	**82**	18 40N	103 10W
Coaldale	**61**	49 45N	112 35W
Coalgate	**75**	34 35N	96 13W
Coalhurst	**61**	49 45N	112 56W
Coalinga	**80**	36 10N	120 21W
Coalmont	**63**	49 32N	120 42W
Coalspur	**54**	53 15N	117 0W
Coalville, U.K.	**94**	52 43N	1 21W
Coalville, U.S.A.	**78**	40 58N	111 24W
Coamo	**67**	18 5N	66 22W
Coari	**86**	4 8 S	63 7W
Coast Mts.	**62**	52 0N	126 0W
Coast Range	**80**	40 0N	124 0W
Coastal Plains Basin	**134**	30 10 S	115 30 E
Coatbridge	**96**	55 52N	4 2W
Coatepec	**83**	19 27N	96 58W
Coatepeque	**84**	14 46N	91 55W
Coatesville	**72**	39 59N	75 55W
Coaticook	**41**	45 10N	71 46W
Coats I.	**65**	62 30N	83 0W
Coats Land	**91**	77 0 S	25 0W
Coatzacoalcos	**83**	18 7N	94 35W
Cobalt	**34**	47 25N	79 42W
Cobán	**84**	15 30N	90 21W
Cobar	**136**	31 27 S	145 48 E
Cobaz, L.	**38**	51 15N	60 21W
Cobden	**47**	45 38N	76 53W
Cóbh	**97**	51 50N	8 18W
Cobija	**86**	11 0 S	68 50W
Cobleskill	**71**	42 40N	74 30W
Coboconk	**47**	44 39N	78 48W
Cobourg	**47**	43 58N	78 10W
Cobourg Pen.	**134**	11 20 S	132 15 E
Cobram	**136**	35 54 S	145 40 E
Cobre	**78**	41 6N	114 25W
Cóbué	**117**	12 0 S	34 58 E
Coburg	**106**	50 15N	10 58 E
Coburg I.	**65**	75 57N	79 26W
Coca, R.	**86**	0 25 S	77 5W
Cocagne	**39**	46 20N	64 37W
Cocha, La	**88**	27 50 S	65 40W
Cochabamba	**86**	17 15 S	66 20W
Coche, I.	**86**	10 47N	63 56W
Cochenour	**52**	51 5N	93 48W
Cochilha Grande de Albardão	**89**	28 30 S	51 30W
Cochin China = Nam-Phan	**128**	10 30N	106 0 E
Cochise	**79**	32 6N	109 58W
Cochran	**73**	32 25N	83 23W
Cochrane, Alta., Can.	**61**	51 11N	114 30W
Cochrane, Ont., Can.	**34**	49 0N	81 0W
Cochrane, L.	**90**	47 10 S	72 0W
Cochrane, R.	**55**	57 53N	101 34W
Cockatoo I.	**134**	16 6 S	123 37 E
Cockburn	**136**	32 5 S	141 0 E
Cockburn, Canal	**90**	54 30 S	72 0W
Cockburn, C.	**65**	74 52N	79 24W
Cockburn I.	**46**	45 55N	83 22W
Coco Chan.	**128**	13 50N	93 25 E
Coco, Pta.	**86**	2 58N	77 43W
Coco, R. (Wanks)	**84**	14 10N	85 0W
Coco Solo	**84**	9 22N	79 53W
Cocoa	**73**	28 22N	80 40W
Cocobeach	**116**	0 59N	9 34 E
Cocos, Is.	**16**	12 10 S	96 50 E
Cocos (Keeling) Is.	**11**	12 12 S	96 54 E
Cod, C.	**72**	42 8N	70 10W
Cod I.	**36**	57 47N	61 47W
Codajás	**86**	3 40 S	62 0W
Codera, C.	**86**	10 35N	66 4W
Coderre	**56**	50 11N	106 31W
Codette	**56**	53 16N	104 0W
Codó	**87**	4 30 S	43 55W
Codroy	**37**	47 53N	59 24W
Codroy Pond	**37**	48 4N	58 52W
Cody	**78**	44 35N	109 0W
Coe Hill	**47**	44 52N	77 50W
Coelemu	**88**	36 30 S	72 48W
Coen	**135**	13 52 S	143 12 E
Coesfeld	**105**	51 56N	7 10 E
Coetivy Is.	**16**	7 8 S	56 16 E
Coeur d'Alene	**78**	47 45N	116 51W
Coffeyville	**75**	37 0N	95 40W
Coffs Harbour	**135**	30 16 S	153 5 E
Cofre de Perote, Cerro	**83**	19 30N	97 10W
Coghinas, R.	**108**	40 55N	8 48 E
Cognac	**102**	45 41N	0 20W
Cohagen	**78**	47 2N	106 45W
Cohasset	**52**	47 18N	93 39W
Cohoes	**71**	42 47N	73 42W
Cohuna	**136**	35 45 S	144 15 E
Coiba I.	**84**	7 30N	81 40W
Coig, R.	**90**	51 0 S	70 20W
Coimbatore	**124**	11 2N	76 59 F
Coimbra	**104**	40 15N	8 27W
Coín	**104**	36 40N	4 48W
Coin-Rond	**45**	45 38N	73 13W
Cojedes □	**86**	9 20N	68 20W
Cojimies	**86**	0 20N	80 0W
Cojutepequé	**84**	13 41N	88 54W
Cokeville	**78**	42 4N	111 0W
Colac	**136**	38 21 S	143 35 E
Colbinabbin	**136**	36 38 S	144 48 E
Colborne	**47**	44 0N	77 53W
Colby	**74**	39 27N	101 2W
Colchagua □	**88**	34 30 S	71 0W
Colchester	**95**	51 54N	0 55 E
Cold L.	**60**	54 33N	110 5W
Cold Lake	**60**	54 27N	110 10W
Coldstream	**96**	55 39N	2 14W
Coldwater, Can.	**46**	44 42N	79 40W
Coldwater, Kans., U.S.A.	**75**	37 18N	99 24W
Coldwater, Mich., U.S.A.	**77**	41 57N	85 0W
Coldwater, Ohio, U.S.A.	**77**	40 29N	84 38W
Coldwater, L.	**77**	41 48N	84 59W
Coldwell	**34**	48 45N	86 30W
Cole Camp	**76**	38 28N	93 12W
Colebrook, Can.	**66**	49 6N	122 52W
Colebrook, U.S.A.	**71**	44 54N	71 29W
Coleman, Can.	**61**	49 40N	114 30W
Coleman, Mich., U.S.A.	**46**	43 46N	84 35W
Coleman, Tex., U.S.A.	**75**	31 52N	99 30W
Coleman, R.	**135**	15 6 S	141 38 E
Coleraine, Austral.	**136**	37 36 S	141 40 E
Coleraine, Can.	**50**	43 49N	79 41W
Coleraine, U.K.	**97**	55 8N	6 40 E
Coleraine, U.S.A.	**52**	47 17N	93 27W
Coleraine □	**97**	55 8N	6 40 E
Coleridge, L.	**133**	43 17 S	171 30 E
Colesberg	**117**	30 45 S	25 5 E
Colesburg	**76**	42 38N	91 12W
Coleville, Can.	**56**	51 43N	109 15W
Coleville, U.S.A.	**80**	38 44N	119 30W
Colfax, Calif., U.S.A.	**80**	39 6N	120 57W
Colfax, Ill., U.S.A.	**77**	40 34N	88 37W
Colfax, Ind., U.S.A.	**77**	40 12N	86 40W
Colfax, La., U.S.A.	**75**	31 35N	92 39W
Colfax, Wash., U.S.A.	**78**	46 57N	117 28W
Colhué Huapi, L.	**90**	45 30 S	69 0W
Colima	**82**	19 10N	103 40W
Colima □	**82**	19 10N	103 40W
Colima, Nevado de	**82**	19 30N	103 40W
Colina	**88**	33 13 S	70 45W
Colinas	**87**	6 0 S	44 10W
Colinet	**37**	47 13N	53 33W
Colinton, Austral.	**136**	35 50 S	149 10 E
Colinton, Can.	**60**	54 37N	113 15W
Coll, I.	**96**	56 40N	6 35W
Collaguasi	**88**	21 5 S	68 45W
Collbran	**79**	39 16N	107 58W
College Bridge	**39**	45 59N	64 33W
College Heights	**61**	52 28N	113 45W
College Park	**73**	33 42N	84 27W
Collette	**35**	46 40N	65 30W
Colleymount	**62**	54 2N	126 19W
Collie	**134**	33 22 S	116 8 E
Collier B.	**134**	16 10 S	124 15 E
Collingwood, Can.	**46**	44 29N	80 13W
Collingwood, N.Z.	**133**	40 25 S	172 40 E
Collingwood Corner	**39**	45 37N	63 56W
Collins, Can.	**52**	50 17N	89 27W
Collins, U.S.A.	**76**	37 54N	93 37W
Collinson Pen	**65**	69 58N	101 24W
Collinsville, Austral.	**135**	20 30 S	147 56 E
Collinsville, U.S.A.	**76**	38 40N	89 59W
Collipulli	**88**	37 55 S	72 30W
Collonges	**103**	46 9N	5 52 E
Collooney	**97**	54 11N	8 28W
Colmar	**101**	48 5N	7 20 E
Colmars	**103**	44 11N	6 39 E
Colmor	**75**	36 18N	104 36W
Colne	**94**	53 51N	2 11W
Colnett, Cabo	**82**	31 0N	116 20W
Colo, R.	**136**	33 25 S	150 52 E
Cologne = Koln	**105**	50 56N	9 58 E
Colombey-les-Belles	**101**	48 32N	5 54 E
Colombey-les-Deux Églises	**101**	48 20N	4 50 E
Colombia	**86**	3 24N	79 49W
Colombia ■	**86**	3 45N	73 0W
Colombier	**41**	48 52N	68 51W
Colombo	**124**	6 56N	79 58 E
Colombus, Kans., U.S.A.	**75**	37 15N	94 30W
Colombus, Nebr., U.S.A.	**74**	41 30N	97 25W
Colombus, N.Mex., U.S.A.	**79**	31 54N	107 43W
Colome	**74**	43 20N	99 44W
Colón, Argent.	**88**	32 12 S	58 30W
Colón, Cuba	**84**	22 42N	80 54W
Colón, Panama	**84**	9 20N	80 0W
Colonel Hill	**85**	22 50N	74 21W
Colonia del Sacramento	**89**	34 25 S	57 50W
Colonia Dora	**88**	28 34 S	62 59W
Colonia Las Heras	**90**	46 30 S	69 0W
Colonia Sarmiento	**90**	45 30 S	68 15W
Colonial Hts.	**72**	37 19N	77 25W
Colonial Village	**49**	43 12N	78 59W
Colonsay	**56**	51 59N	105 52W
Colonsay, I.	**96**	56 4N	6 12W
Colorado □	**68**	37 40N	106 0W
Colorado Aqueduct	**81**	34 17N	114 10W
Colorado City	**75**	32 25N	100 50W
Colorado Desert	**68**	34 20N	116 0W
Colorado, I.	**84**	9 12N	79 50W
Colorado Plateau	**79**	36 40N	110 30W
Colorado, R., Argent.	**88**	37 30 S	69 0W
Colorado, R., Ariz., U.S.A.	**79**	33 30N	114 30W
Colorado, R., Calif., U.S.A.	**79**	34 0N	114 33W
Colorado, R., Tex., U.S.A.	**75**	29 40N	96 30W
Colorado Springs	**74**	38 55N	104 50W
Colotepec	**83**	15 47N	97 3W
Colotlán	**82**	22 6N	103 16W
Colquitz	**63**	48 29N	123 24W
Colton, Calif., U.S.A.	**81**	34 4N	117 20W
Colton, N.Y., U.S.A.	**71**	44 34N	74 58W
Colton, Wash., U.S.A.	**78**	46 41N	117 6W
Coluna	**80**	38 49N	120 53W
Columbia, Ill., U.S.A.	**76**	38 26N	90 12W
Columbia, La., U.S.A.	**75**	32 7N	92 5W
Columbia, Miss., U.S.A.	**75**	31 16N	89 50W
Columbia, Mo., U.S.A.	**76**	38 58N	92 20W
Columbia, Pa., U.S.A.	**71**	40 2N	76 30W
Columbia, S.C., U.S.A.	**73**	34 0N	81 0W
Columbia, Tenn., U.S.A.	**73**	35 40N	87 0W
Columbia, C.	**17**	83 0N	70 0W
Columbia City	**77**	41 8N	85 30W
Columbia, District of □	**72**	38 55N	77 0W
Columbia Falls	**78**	48 25N	114 16W
Columbia Heights	**74**	45 5N	93 10W
Columbia L.	**61**	50 15N	115 52W
Columbia, Mt.	**63**	52 8N	117 20W
Columbia Basin	**78**	47 30N	118 30W
Columbia, R.	**78**	45 49N	120 0W
Columbiana	**70**	40 53N	80 40W
Columbiaville	**46**	43 9N	83 25W
Columbretes, Is.	**104**	39 50N	0 50 E
Columbus, Can.	**51**	43 59N	78 55W
Columbus, Ga., U.S.A.	**73**	32 30N	84 58W
Columbus, Ind., U.S.A.	**72**	39 14N	85 55W
Columbus, Miss., U.S.A.	**73**	33 30N	88 26W
Columbus, Mont., U.S.A.	**78**	45 45N	109 14W
Columbus, N.D., U.S.A.	**56**	48 52N	102 48W
Columbus, Ohio, U.S.A.	**77**	39 57N	83 1W
Columbus, Tex., U.S.A.	**75**	29 42N	96 33W
Columbus, Wis., U.S.A.	**74**	43 20N	89 2W
Columbus Grove	**77**	40 55N	84 4W
Columbus Junction	**76**	41 17N	91 22W
Colusa	**80**	39 15N	122 1W
Colville	**63**	48 33N	117 54W
Colville, C.	**133**	36 29 S	175 21 E
Colville Lake	**64**	67 2N	126 7W
Colville, R.	**67**	69 15N	152 0W
Colwood	**63**	48 26N	123 29W
Colwyn Bay	**94**	53 17N	3 44W
Com-Est	**44**	45 27N	74 7W
Comácchio	**108**	44 41N	12 10 E
Comalcalco	**83**	18 16N	93 13W
Comallo	**90**	41 0 S	70 5W
Comanche, Okla., U.S.A.	**75**	34 27N	97 58W
Comanche, Tex., U.S.A.	**75**	31 55N	98 35W
Comayagua	**84**	14 25N	87 37W
Combahee, R.	**73**	32 45N	80 50W
Combeaufontaine	**101**	47 38N	5 54 E
Comber	**46**	42 14N	82 33W
Combermere	**47**	45 22N	77 37W
Comblain	**105**	50 29N	5 35 E
Combles	**101**	50 0N	2 50 E
Combourg	**100**	48 25N	1 46W
Combronde	**102**	45 58N	3 5 E
Come by Chance	**37**	47 51N	54 0W
Comeragh Mts.	**97**	52 17N	7 35W
Comilla	**125**	23 28N	91 10 E
Comino I.	**108**	36 0N	14 22 E
Comitán	**83**	16 18N	92 9W
Commanda	**46**	45 57N	79 36W
Commentry	**102**	46 20N	2 46 E
Commerce, Ga., U.S.A.	**73**	34 10N	83 25W
Commerce, Tex., U.S.A.	**75**	33 15N	95 50W
Commercy	**101**	48 40N	5 34 E
Commissaires, L. des	**41**	48 10N	72 16W
Commissioner I.	**57**	52 10N	97 16W
Committee B.	**65**	68 30N	86 30W
Commonwealth B.	**91**	67 0 S	144 0 E
Communism Pk. = Kommunisma, Pk.	**123**	38 40N	72 20 E
Como	**108**	45 48N	9 5 E
Como, L. di	**108**	46 5N	9 17 E
Comodoro Rivadavia	**90**	45 50 S	67 40W
Comores, Arch. des	**11**	10 0 S	50 0 E
Comores, Is.	**11**	12 10 S	44 15 E
Comorin, C.	**124**	8 3N	77 40 E
Comoro Is.	**11**	12 10 S	44 15 E
Comox	**62**	49 42N	124 55W
Compeer	**61**	51 52N	110 0W
Compiègne	**101**	49 24N	2 50 E
Compostela	**82**	21 15N	104 53W
Comprida, I.	**89**	24 50 S	47 42W
Compton, Can.	**41**	45 14N	71 49W
Compton, U.S.A.	**81**	33 54N	118 13W
Côn Dao	**128**	8 45N	106 45 E
Conakry	**114**	9 29N	13 49W
Conatlán	**82**	24 30N	104 42W
Concarneau	**100**	47 52N	3 56W
Conceição da Barra	**87**	18 35 S	39 45W
Conceição do Araguaia	**87**	8 0 S	49 2W
Concepción, Argent.	**88**	27 20 S	65 35W
Concepción, Boliv.	**86**	15 50 S	61 40W
Concepción, Chile	**88**	36 50 S	73 0W
Concepción, Colomb.	**86**	0 5N	75 37W
Concepción, Mexico	**83**	18 15N	90 5W
Concepción, Parag.	**88**	23 30 S	57 20W
Concepción, Venez.	**86**	10 48N	71 46W
Concepción □	**88**	37 0 S	72 30W
Concepcion, C.	**68**	34 30N	120 34W
Concepción del Oro	**82**	24 40N	101 30W
Concepción del Uruguay	**88**	32 35 S	58 20W
Concepción, L.	**86**	17 20 S	61 10W
Concepción, Punta	**82**	26 55N	111 50W
Concepción, R.	**82**	30 32N	113 2W
Conception B., Can.	**37**	47 45N	53 0W
Conception B., Namibia	**117**	23 55 S	14 22 E
Conception I.	**85**	23 52N	75 9W
Conception, La	**40**	46 9N	74 42W
Conchas Dam	**75**	35 25N	104 10W
Conche	**37**	50 48N	55 58W
Concho	**79**	34 32N	109 43W
Concho, R.	**75**	31 30N	100 8W
Conchos, R., Chihuahua, Mexico	**82**	29 20N	105 0W
Conchos, R., Tamaulipas, Mexico	**83**	25 0N	97 32W
Concon	**88**	32 56 S	71 33W
Conconully	**63**	48 31N	119 45W
Concord, Can.	**50**	43 48N	79 29W
Concord, Calif., U.S.A.	**80**	37 59N	122 2W
Concord, Mich., U.S.A.	**77**	42 11N	84 38W
Concord, N.C., U.S.A.	**73**	35 28N	80 35W
Concord, N.H., U.S.A.	**71**	43 12N	71 30W
Concórdia, Argent.	**88**	31 20 S	58 2W
Concórdia, Brazil	**86**	4 36 S	66 36W
Concordia, Colomb.	**86**	2 39N	72 47W
Concordia, Mexico	**82**	23 18N	106 2W
Concordia, U.S.A.	**76**	38 59N	93 34W
Concordia, Kans., U.S.A.	**74**	39 35N	97 40W
Concordia, La	**83**	16 8N	92 38W
Concots	**102**	44 26N	1 40 E

* *Renamed Clyde River*

Concrete Craon

Concrete **63** 48 35N 121 49W
Condamine, R. **135** 27 7S 149 48E
Condat **102** 45 21N 2 46E
Condé **101** 50 26N 3 34E
Conde **74** 45 13N 98 5W
Condé-sur-Noireau **100** 48 51N 0 33W
Condeúba **87** 15 0S 42 0W
Condie Res. **58** 50 34N 104 43W
Condobolin **136** 33 4S 147 6E
Condom **102** 43 57N 0 22E
Condon **78** 45 15N 120 8W
Conejos **82** 26 14N 103 53W
Conemaugh, R. **70** 40 24N 79 0W
Conestogo **49** 43 32N 80 30W
Conflans-en-Jarnisy **101** 49 10N 5 52E
Confolens **102** 46 2N 0 40E
Confuso, R. **88** 24 10S 59 0W
Congleton **94** 53 10N 2 12W
Congnarauya **36** 58 35N 68 1W
Congo ■ **116** 1 0S 16 0E
Congo Basin **112** 0 10S 24 30E
Congo (Kinshasa) ■ = Zaïre ■ **116** 1 0S 16 0E
Congo, R. = Zaïre, R. **116** 1 30N 28 0E
Congonhas **89** 20 30S 43 52W
Congress **79** 34 11N 112 56W
Congucu **113** 31 25S 52 30W
Coniston **46** 46 29N 80 51W
Conjeevaram = Kanchipuram **124** 12 52N 79 45E
Conklin **60** 55 38N 111 5W
Conn, L. **97** 54 3N 9 15W
Connacht **97** 53 23N 8 40W
Conneaut **70** 41 55N 80 32W
Connecticut □ **71** 41 40N 72 40W
Connecticut, R. **71** 41 17N 72 21W
Connell **78** 46 45N 118 58W
Connemara **97** 53 29N 9 45W
Conner, La **78** 48 22N 122 27W
Connersville **77** 39 40N 85 10W
Connolsville **70** 40 5N 79 32W
Connors **41** 47 10N 68 52W
Conoble **136** 32 55S 144 42E
Conon, R. **96** 57 33N 4 45W
Cononaco, R. **86** 1 20S 76 30W
Conquest **56** 51 32N 107 14W
Conquet, Le **100** 48 21N 4 46W
Conrad, Iowa, U.S.A. **76** 42 14N 92 52W
Conrad, Mont., U.S.A. **78** 48 11N 112 0W
Conroe **75** 30 15N 95 28W
Consecon **47** 44 0N 77 31W
Conselheiro Lafaiete **89** 20 40S 43 48W
Conshohocken **71** 40 5N 75 18W
Consort **61** 52 1N 110 46W
Constanţa **107** 44 14N 28 38E
Constantina **104** 37 51N 5 40W
Constantine, Alg. **114** 36 25N 6 42E
Constantine, U.S.A. **77** 41 50N 85 40W
Constitución, Chile **88** 35 20S 72 30W
Constitución, Uruguay **88** 31 0S 58 10W
Consul **56** 49 20N 109 30W
Contact **78** 41 50N 114 56W
Contai **125** 21 54N 87 55E
Contamana **86** 7 10S 74 55W
Contas, R. **87** 13 5S 41 53W
Contes **103** 43 49N 7 19E
Contin L. **57** 53 25N 95 10W
Continental **77** 41 6N 84 16W
Contoocook **71** 43 13N 71 45W
Contrecoeur **43** 45 51N 73 14W
Contres **100** 47 24N 1 26E
Contrexéville **101** 48 6N 5 53E
Contwoyto L. **64** 65 42N 110 50W
Convención **86** 8 28N 73 21W
Converse **77** 40 34N 85 52W
Convoy **77** 40 55N 84 43W
Conway, Ark., U.S.A. **75** 35 5N 92 30W
Conway, N.H., U.S.A. **71** 43 58N 71 8W
Conway, S.C., U.S.A. **73** 33 49N 79 2W
Conway = Conwy **94** 53 17N 3 50W
Conway, R. = Conwy **94** 53 10N 3 50W
Conwy **94** 53 17N 3 50W
Conwy, R. **94** 53 18N 3 50W
Coober Pedy **134** 29 1S 134 43E
Cooch Behar **125** 26 22N 89 29E
Cook **52** 47 49N 92 39W
Cook, Bahia **90** 55 10S 70 0W
Cook Inlet **67** 59 0N 151 0W
Cook Is. **15** 20 0S 160 0W
Cook, Mt. **133** 43 36S 170 9E
Cook Strait **133** 41 15S 174 29E
Cookeville **73** 36 12N 85 30W
Cooking L. **60** 53 26N 113 2W
Cook's Harbour **37** 51 36N 55 52W
Cookshire **41** 45 25N 71 38W
Cookstown **97** 54 40N 6 43W
Cookstown □ **97** 54 40N 6 43W
Cooksville **50** 43 36N 79 35W
Cooktown **135** 15 30S 145 16E
Coolah **136** 31 48S 149 41E
Coolamon **136** 34 46S 147 8E
Coolgardie **134** 30 55S 121 8E
Coolidge **79** 33 1N 111 35W
Coolidge Dam **79** 33 10N 110 30W
Cooma **136** 36 12S 149 8E
Coombs **62** 49 18N 124 25W
Coon Rapids **76** 41 53N 94 41W
Coonabarabran **136** 31 14S 149 18E
Coonamble **135** 30 56S 148 27E
Coondapoor **124** 13 42N 74 40E
Cooper **75** 33 20N 95 40W
Cooper, R. **73** 33 0N 79 55W
Cooperstown, N.D., U.S.A. **74** 47 30N 98 14W
Cooperstown, N.Y., U.S.A. **71** 42 42N 74 57W
Coopersville **77** 43 4N 85 57W
Coorong, The **135** 35 50S 139 20E
Coos Bay **78** 43 26N 124 7W
Cootamundra **136** 34 36S 148 1E
Cootehill **97** 54 5N 7 5W
Copahué, Paso **88** 37 49S 71 8W
Copainalá **83** 17 8N 93 11W
Copán **84** 14 50N 89 9W
Cope **74** 39 44N 102 50W
Copenhagen = København **111** 55 41N 12 34E
Copetown **49** 43 14N 80 4W
Copiapó **88** 27 15S 70 20E
Copiapó, R. **88** 27 19S 70 56W
Copp L. **54** 60 14N 114 40W
Copper Center **67** 62 10N 145 25W
Copper Cliff **46** 46 28N 81 4W
Copper Harbor **53** 47 31N 87 55W
Copper Mountain **54** 49 20N 120 30W
Copper R. **67** 61 30N 144 30W
Coppermine **64** 67 50N 115 5W
Coppermine, R. **64** 67 49N 115 4W
Copperopolis **80** 37 58N 120 38W
Coquet, R. **94** 55 18N 1 45W
Coquille **78** 43 15N 124 6W
Coquimbo **88** 30 0S 71 20W
Coquimbo □ **88** 31 0S 71 0W
Coquitlam, R. **66** 49 13N 122 48W
Corabia **107** 43 48N 24 30E
Coracora **86** 15 5S 73 45W
Coral Harbour **65** 64 8N 83 10W
Coral Rapids **34** 50 20N 81 40W
Coral Sea **135** 15 0S 150 0E
Coral Sea Islands Terr. **135** 20 0S 155 0E
Corangamite, L. **136** 38 0S 143 30E
Coraopolis **70** 40 30N 80 10W
Corato **108** 41 12N 16 22E
Corbeil-Essonnes **101** 48 36N 2 26E
Corbie **101** 49 54N 2 30E
Corbières, mts. **102** 42 55N 2 35E
Corbigny **101** 47 16N 3 40E
Corbin, Can. **43** 45 3N 73 41W
Corbin, U.S.A. **72** 37 0N 84 3W
Corby, Lincs., U.K. **95** 52 49N 0 31W
Corby, Northants., U.K. **95** 52 29N 0 41W
Corcoran **80** 36 6N 119 35W
Corcubión **104** 42 56N 9 12W
Cord. de Caravaya **86** 14 0S 70 30W
Cordele **73** 31 55N 83 49W
Cordell **75** 35 18N 99 0W
Cordes **102** 44 5N 1 57E
Cordillera Oriental **86** 5 0N 74 0W
Córdoba, Argent. **88** 31 20S 64 10W
Córdoba, Mexico **83** 18 50N 97 0W
Córdoba, Spain **104** 37 50N 4 50W
Córdoba □, Argent. **88** 31 22S 64 15W
Córdoba □, Colomb. **86** 8 20N 75 40W
Córdoba, Sierra de **88** 31 10S 64 25W
Cordon **127** 16 42N 121 32E
Cordova, Ala., U.S.A. **73** 33 45N 87 12W
Cordova, Alaska, U.S.A. **67** 60 36N 145 45W
Cordova, Ill., U.S.A. **76** 41 41N 90 19W
Corfu = Kerkira **109** 39 38N 19 50E
Coricudgy, Mt. **136** 32 51S 150 24E
Corigliano Cálabro **108** 39 36N 16 31E
Corinth, Ky., U.S.A. **77** 38 30N 84 34W
Corinth, Miss., U.S.A. **73** 34 54N 88 30W
Corinth, N.Y., U.S.A. **71** 43 15N 73 50W
Corinto, Brazil **87** 18 20S 44 30W
Corinto, Nic. **84** 12 30N 87 10W
Cork **97** 51 54N 8 30W
Cork □ **97** 51 50N 8 50W
Cork Harbour **97** 51 46N 8 16W
Corlay **100** 48 20N 3 5W
Çorlu **122** 41 11N 27 49E
Cormack **37** 49 18N 57 23W
Cormack L. **54** 60 56N 121 37W
Cormorant **57** 54 14N 100 35W
Cormorant L. **57** 54 15N 100 50W
Corn Is. **85** 12 0N 83 0W
Cornelio **82** 29 55N 111 8W
Cornélio Procópio **89** 23 7S 50 40W
Cornell, U.S.A. **74** 45 10N 91 8W
Cornell, U.S.A. **77** 40 58N 88 43W
Corner Brook **37** 48 57N 57 58W
Corner Inlet **136** 38 45S 146 20E
Corning, Can. **56** 49 58N 102 58W
Corning, Ark., U.S.A. **75** 36 27N 90 34W
Corning, Calif., U.S.A. **78** 39 56N 122 9W
Corning, Iowa, U.S.A. **76** 40 57N 94 40W
Corning, N.Y., U.S.A. **70** 42 10N 77 3W
Cornwall, Can. **39** 46 14N 63 13W
Cornwall, Ont., Can. **47** 45 2N 74 44W
Cornwall □ **95** 50 26N 4 40W
Cornwall I. **65** 77 37N 94 38W
Cornwallis I. **65** 75 8N 95 0W
Coro **86** 11 25N 69 41W
Coroatá **87** 4 20S 44 0W
Corocoro **86** 17 15S 69 19W
Coroico **86** 16 0S 67 50W
Coromandel **133** 36 45S 175 31E
Coromandel Coast **124** 12 30N 81 0E
Corona, Calif., U.S.A. **81** 33 49N 117 36W
Corona, N. Mex., U.S.A. **79** 34 15N 105 32W
Coronach **56** 49 7N 105 31W
Coronada B. **84** 9 0N 83 40W
Coronadas, Is. de **81** 32 25N 117 15W
Coronado **81** 32 45N 117 9W
Coronado, Bahía de **84** 9 0N 83 40W
Coronation **61** 52 5N 111 27W
Coronation Gulf **64** 68 25N 112 0W
Coronation I., Antarct. **91** 60 45S 46 0W
Coronation I., U.S.A. **54** 55 52N 134 20W
Coronda **88** 31 58S 60 56W
Coronel **88** 37 0S 73 10W
Coronel Bogado **88** 27 11S 56 18W
Coronel Dorrego **88** 38 40S 61 10W
Coronel Oviedo **88** 25 24S 56 30W
Coronel Pringles **88** 38 0S 61 30W
Coronel Suárez **88** 37 30S 62 0W
Coronel Vidal **88** 37 28S 57 45W
Coronie **87** 5 55N 56 25W
Corowa **136** 35 58S 146 21E
Corozal, Belize **83** 18 30N 88 30W
Corozal, Colomb. **86** 9 19N 75 18W
Corozal, Pan. C. Z. **84** 8 59N 79 34W
Corps **103** 44 50N 5 56E
Corpus **89** 27 10S 55 30W
Corpus Christi **75** 27 50N 97 28W
Corpus Christi L. **75** 28 5N 97 54W
Corque **86** 18 10S 67 50W
Corrèze □ **102** 45 20N 1 45E
Corrib, L. **97** 53 25N 9 10W
Corrientes **88** 27 30S 58 45W
Corrientes □ **88** 28 0S 57 0W
Corrientes, C., Colomb. **86** 5 30N 77 34W
Corrientes, C., Cuba **84** 21 43N 84 30W
Corrientes, C., Mexico **82** 20 25N 105 42W
Corrientes, R., Argent. **88** 30 21S 59 33W
Corrientes, R., Colomb. **86** 3 15S 75 58W
Corrigan **75** 31 0N 94 48W
Corry **70** 41 55N 79 39W
Corse, C. **103** 43 1N 9 25E
Corse-du-Sud □ **103** 41 45N 9 0E
Corse, Î **103** 42 0N 9 0E
Corsica = Corse **103** 42 0N 9 0E
Corsicana **75** 32 5N 96 30W
Corté **103** 42 19N 9 11E
Cortez **79** 37 24N 108 35W
Cortland **71** 42 35N 76 11W
Cortona **108** 43 16N 12 0E
Çorum **122** 40 30N 35 5E
Corumbá, Goias, Brazil **87** 16 0S 48 50W
Corumbá, Mato Grosso, Brazil **86** 19 0S 57 30W
Coruña, La **104** 43 20N 8 25W
Corunna, Can. **46** 42 53N 82 26W
Corunna, U.S.A. **46** 42 59N 84 7W
Corunna = La Coruña **104** 43 20N 8 25W
Coruripe **87** 10 5S 36 10W
Corvallis **78** 44 36N 123 15W
Corvette, L. de la **36** 53 25N 74 3W
Corwhin **49** 43 31N 80 6W
Corydon, Ind., U.S.A. **77** 38 13N 86 7W
Corydon, Iowa, U.S.A. **76** 40 42N 93 22W
Corydon, Ky., U.S.A. **77** 37 44N 87 43W
Cosalá **82** 24 28N 106 40W
Cosamaloapán **83** 18 23N 95 50W
Cosenza **108** 39 17N 16 14E
Coshocton **70** 40 17N 81 51W
Cosne-s.-Loire **101** 47 24N 2 54E
Coso Junction **81** 36 3N 117 57W
Coso Pk. **81** 36 13N 117 44W
Cosquín **88** 31 15S 64 30W
Cossé-le-Vivien **100** 47 57N 0 54W
Costa Blanca **104** 38 25N 0 10W
Costa Brava **104** 41 30N 3 0E
Costa del Sol **104** 36 30N 4 30W
Costa Dorada **104** 40 45N 1 15E
Costa Mesa **81** 33 39N 117 55W
Costa Rica **82** 31 20N 112 40W
Costa Rica ■ **84** 10 0N 84 0W
Costebelle, L. **38** 50 19N 62 23W
Costilla **79** 37 0N 105 30W
Cosumnes, R. **80** 38 14N 121 25W
Cotabato **127** 7 14N 124 15E
Cotagaita **88** 20 45S 65 30W
Côte d'Azur **103** 43 25N 6 50E
Côte d'Or **101** 47 10N 4 50E
Côte d'Or □ **101** 47 30N 4 50E
Côte-Rouge **44** 45 33N 74 6W
Côte-St. André, La **103** 45 24N 5 15E
Côte-St-Luce **44** 45 28N 73 40W
Côte-St-Vincent **44** 45 36N 74 8W
Coteau des Prairies **74** 44 30N 97 0W
Coteau-du-Lac **44** 45 18N 74 11W
Coteau du Missouri, Plat. du **68** 47 0N 101 0W
Coteau Landing **43** 45 15N 74 13W
Coteau Sta. **71** 45 17N 74 14W
Cotentin **100** 49 30N 1 30W
Côtes de Meuse **101** 49 15N 5 22E
Côtes-du-Nord □ **100** 48 25N 2 40W
Cotonou **114** 6 20N 2 25E
Cotopaxi, Vol. **86** 0 30S 78 30W
Cotswold Hills **95** 51 42N 2 10W
Cottage Grove **78** 43 48N 123 2W
Cottam **46** 42 8N 82 45W
Cottbus **106** 51 44N 14 20E
Cottonwood, Can. **54** 53 5N 121 50W
Cottonwood, U.S.A. **79** 34 48N 112 1W
Coubre, Pte. de la **102** 45 42N 1 15W
Couches **101** 46 53N 4 30E
Coudersport **70** 41 45N 77 40W
Coudres, Île aux **41** 47 24N 70 23W
Couëron **100** 47 13N 1 44W
Couesnon, R. **100** 48 20N 1 15W
Couhé-Vérac **102** 46 18N 0 12E
Coulanges **101** 47 30N 3 30E
Coulee City **78** 47 44N 119 12W
Coulman I. **91** 73 35S 170 0E
Coulommiers **101** 48 50N 3 3E
Coulonge, R. **40** 45 52N 76 46W
Coulonges **102** 46 58N 0 35W
Coulterville, Calif., U.S.A. **80** 37 42N 120 12W
Coulterville, Ill., U.S.A. **76** 38 11N 89 36W
Council **67** 64 55N 163 45W
Council Bluffs **74** 41 20N 95 50W
Council Grove **74** 38 41N 96 30W
Coupeaux, L. **38** 51 27N 63 58W
Coupeville **80** 48 13N 122 41W
Courantyne, R. **86** 5 0N 57 45W
Courçon **102** 46 15N 0 50W
Cours **103** 46 7N 4 19F
Courseulles **100** 49 20N 0 29W
Courtenay **62** 49 45N 125 0W
Courtice **49** 43 55N 78 46W
Courtine, La **102** 45 43N 2 16E
Courtland, Can. **46** 42 51N 80 38W
Courtland, U.S.A. **80** 38 20N 121 34W
Courtright **46** 42 49N 82 28W
Courville, Can. **42** 46 53N 71 10W
Courville, France **100** 48 28N 1 15E
Coutances **100** 49 3N 1 28W
Couterne **100** 48 30N 0 25W
Coutras **102** 45 3N 0 8W
Coutts **61** 49 0N 111 57W
Couture, L. **36** 60 7N 75 20W
Couvin **105** 50 3N 4 29E
Cove I. **46** 45 17N 81 44W
Coventry **95** 52 25N 1 31W
Coventry L. **55** 61 15N 106 15W
Covey Hill **43** 45 1N 73 46W
Covilhã **104** 40 17N 7 31W
Covina **81** 34 5N 117 52W
Covington, Ga., U.S.A. **73** 33 36N 83 50W
Covington, Ind., U.S.A. **77** 40 9N 87 24W
Covington, Ky., U.S.A. **77** 39 5N 84 30W
Covington, Mich., U.S.A. **52** 46 30N 88 35W
Covington, Ohio, U.S.A. **77** 40 8N 84 20W
Covington, Okla., U.S.A. **75** 36 21N 97 36W
Covington, Tenn., U.S.A. **75** 35 34N 89 39W
Cow Head **37** 49 55N 57 48W
Cowal, L. **136** 33 40S 147 25E
Cowan **57** 52 5N 100 45W
Cowan, L. **134** 31 45S 121 45E
Cowan L., Can. **56** 54 0N 107 0W
Cowan L., Sask., Can. **55** 54 0N 107 15W
Cowansville **43** 45 14N 72 46W
Cowden **77** 39 15N 88 52W
Cowdenbeath **96** 56 7N 3 20W
Cowes **95** 50 45N 1 18W
Cowichan L. **62** 48 53N 124 17W
Cowley **61** 49 34N 114 5W
Cowlitz, R **80** 46 5N 122 53W
Cowra **136** 33 49S 148 42E
Cox I. **62** 50 48N 128 36W
Coxim **87** 18 30S 54 55W
Cox's Bazar **125** 21 26N 91 59E
Cox's Cove **37** 49 7N 58 5W
Coyame **82** 29 28N 105 6W
Coyote Wells **81** 32 44N 115 58W
Coyuca de Benítez **83** 17 1N 100 8W
Coyuca de Catalán **82** 18 58N 100 41W
Cozad **74** 40 55N 99 57W
Cozumel **83** 20 31N 86 55W
Cozumel, Isla de **83** 20 30N 86 40W
Craboon **136** 32 3S 149 30E
Crabtree **43** 45 58N 73 28W
Cracroft Is. **62** 50 32N 126 25W
Cradock **117** 32 8S 25 36E
Crafton **70** 40 25N 80 4W
Craig, Alaska, U.S.A. **67** 55 30N 133 5W
Craig, Colo., U.S.A. **78** 40 32N 107 44W
Craigavon = Portadown **97** 54 27N 6 26W
Craigavon □ **97** 54 30N 6 25W
Craigavon = Lurgan **97** 54 28N 6 20W
Craigflower **63** 48 27N 123 26W
Craigmyle **61** 51 40N 112 15W
Craik **56** 51 3N 105 49W
Craiova **107** 44 21N 23 48E
Crampel **116** 7 8N 19 81E
Cranberry Portage **55** 54 35N 101 23W
Cranbrook **61** 49 30N 115 46W
Crandon **74** 45 32N 88 52W
Crane, Oregon, U.S.A. **78** 43 21N 118 39W
Crane, Texas, U.S.A. **75** 31 26N 102 27W
Crane I. **41** 47 4N 70 33W
Crane L. **56** 50 5N 109 5W
Crane River **57** 51 30N 99 14W
Cranston **71** 41 47N 71 27W
Craon **100** 47 50N 0 58W

Craonne **Dâmboviţa, R**

Craonne	**101**	49 27N	3 46 E
Crapaud	**39**	46 14N	63 30W
Crater, L.	**78**	42 55N	122 3W
Crateús	**87**	5 10 S	40 50W
Crato	**87**	7 10 S	39 25W
Crau	**103**	43 32N	4 40 E
Crauford, C.	**65**	73 44N	84 51W
Craven	**56**	50 42N	104 49W
Craven, L.	**36**	54 20N	76 56W
Crawford	**74**	42 40N	103 25W
Crawfordsville	**77**	40 2N	86 51W
Crawley	**95**	51 7N	0 10W
Crazy Mts.	**78**	46 14N	110 30W
Crean L.	**56**	54 5N	106 9W
Crèche, La	**102**	46 23N	0 19W
Crécy-en-Brie	**101**	48 50N	2 53 E
Crécy-en-Ponthieu	**101**	50 15N	1 53 E
Crécy-sur-Serre	**101**	49 40N	3 32 E
Credit, R.	**50**	43 33N	79 35W
Crediton	**46**	43 17N	81 33W
Cree L.	**55**	57 30N	106 30W
Cree, R., Can.	**55**	58 57N	105 47W
Cree, R., U.K.	**96**	54 51N	4 24W
Creede	**79**	37 56N	106 59W
Creel	**82**	27 45N	107 38W
Creelman	**56**	49 49N	103 18W
Creemore	**46**	44 19N	80 6W
Creighton	**74**	42 30N	97 52W
Creil	**101**	49 15N	2 34 E
Cremona, Can.	**61**	51 33N	114 29W
Cremona, Italy	**108**	45 8N	10 2 E
Crépy	**101**	49 37N	3 32 E
Crépy-en-Valois	**101**	49 14N	2 54 E
Cres	**108**	44 58N	14 25 E
Cresbard	**74**	45 13N	98 57W
Crescent, Okla., U.S.A.	**75**	35 58N	97 36W
Crescent, Oreg., U.S.A.	**78**	43 30N	121 37W
Crescent Beach	**66**	49 3N	122 53W
Crescent City	**78**	41 45N	124 12W
Crescent Spur	**63**	53 34N	120 42W
Crespo	**88**	32 2 S	60 19W
Cressman	**34**	47 40N	72 55W
Cressy	**136**	38 2 S	143 40 E
Crest	**103**	44 44N	5 2 E
Crested Butte	**79**	38 57N	107 0W
Crestline, Calif., U.S.A.	**81**	34 14N	117 18W
Crestline, Ohio, U.S.A.	**70**	40 46N	82 45W
Creston, Can.	**61**	49 10N	116 31W
Creston, Calif., U.S.A.	**80**	35 32N	120 33W
Creston, Iowa, U.S.A.	**76**	41 0N	94 20W
Creston, Wash., U.S.A.	**78**	47 47N	118 36W
Creston, Wyo., U.S.A.	**78**	41 46N	107 50W
Crestone	**79**	35 2N	106 0W
Crestview, Calif., U.S.A.	**80**	37 46N	118 58W
Crestview, Fla., U.S.A.	**73**	30 45N	86 35W
Creswick	**136**	37 25 S	143 51 E
Crete	**74**	40 38N	96 58W
Crete, La	**54**	58 11N	116 24W
Creus, C.	**104**	42 20N	3 19 E
Creuse □	**102**	46 0N	2 0 E
Creuse, R.	**102**	47 0N	0 34 E
Creusot, Le	**101**	46 50N	4 24 E
Crèvecœur-le-Grand	**101**	49 37N	2 5 E
Crewe	**94**	53 6N	2 28W
Criciúma	**89**	28 40 S	49 23W
Cridersville	**77**	40 39N	84 9W
Crieff	**96**	56 22N	3 50W
Crillon, Mt.	**54**	58 39N	137 14W
Crimea = Krymskaya	**120**	45 0N	34 0 E
Crimson Lake	**61**	52 27N	115 2W
Crimson Lake Prov. Park	**61**	52 28N	114 54W
Crinan	**96**	56 6N	5 34W
Cristóbal	**84**	9 10N	80 0W
Crişul Alb, R.	**107**	46 25N	21 40 E
Crişul Negru, R.	**107**	46 38N	22 26 E
Crittenden	**77**	38 47N	84 36W
Crna Gora □	**109**	42 40N	19 20 E
Crna Gora, Mts.	**109**	42 10N	21 30 E
Crna, R.	**109**	41 20N	21 59 E
Croagh Patrick, mt.	**97**	53 46N	9 40W
Crocker	**76**	37 57N	92 16W
Crocker, Barisan	**126**	5 0N	116 30 E
Crockett	**75**	31 20N	95 30W
Crocodile Is.	**134**	11 43 S	135 8 E
Crocq	**102**	45 52N	2 21 E
Crofton	**63**	48 52N	123 38W
Croisic, Le	**100**	47 18N	2 30W
Croisic, Pte. du.	**100**	47 19N	2 31W
Croix, La, L.	**52**	48 20N	92 15W
Croker, C.	**46**	44 58N	80 59W
Croker, I.	**134**	11 12 S	132 32 E
Cromarty, Can.	**55**	58 3N	94 9W
Cromarty, U.K.	**96**	57 40N	4 2W
Cromer, Can.	**57**	49 44N	101 14W
Cromer, U.K.	**94**	52 56N	1 18 E
Cromwell, N.Z.	**133**	45 3 S	169 14 E
Cromwell, U.S.A.	**52**	46 42N	92 51W
Cronat	**101**	46 43N	3 40 E
Cronulla	**136**	34 3 S	151 8 E
Crooked I.	**85**	22 50N	74 10W
Crooked Island Passage	**85**	23 0N	74 30W
Crooked L.	**37**	48 24N	56 17W
Crooked, R., Can.	**54**	54 10N	122 35W
Crooked, R., U.S.A.	**78**	44 30N	121 0W
Crooked River	**56**	52 51N	103 44W
Crookston, Minn., U.S.A.	**74**	47 50N	96 40W
Crookston, Nebr., U.S.A.	**74**	42 56N	100 45W
Crooksville	**72**	39 45N	82 8W
Crookwell	**136**	34 28 S	149 24 E
Crosby, Minn., U.S.A.	**52**	46 28N	93 57W
Crosby, N.D., U.S.A.	**56**	48 55N	103 18W
Crosby, Pa., U.S.A.	**70**	41 45N	78 23W
Crosbyton	**75**	33 37N	101 12W
Cross City	**73**	29 35N	83 5W
Cross Creek	**39**	46 19N	66 43W
Cross Fell	**94**	54 44N	2 29W
Cross L.	**55**	54 45N	97 30W
Cross Plains	**75**	32 8N	99 7W
Cross, R.	**95**	4 46N	8 20 E
Cross Sound	**67**	58 20N	136 30W
Cross Timbers	**76**	38 1N	93 14W
Crosse, La, Kans., U.S.A.	**74**	38 33N	99 20W
Crosse, La, Wis., U.S.A.	**74**	43 48N	91 13W
Crossett	**75**	33 10N	91 57W
Crossfield	**61**	51 25N	114 0W
Crosshaven	**97**	51 48N	8 19W
Crossville	**77**	38 10N	88 4W
Croswell	**46**	43 16N	82 37W
Croton-on-Hudson	**71**	41 12N	73 55W
Crotone	**108**	39 5N	17 6 E
Crow Agency	**78**	45 40N	107 30W
Crow Hd.	**97**	51 34N	10 9W
Crow, R.	**54**	59 41N	124 20W
Crow Wing R.	**52**	46 19N	94 20W
Crowell	**75**	33 59N	99 45W
Crowes	**136**	38 43 S	143 24 E
Crowley	**75**	30 15N	92 20W
Crowley, L.	**80**	37 53N	118 42W
Crown Point	**77**	41 24N	87 23W
Crows Landing	**80**	37 23N	121 6W
Crowsnest Pass	**61**	49 40N	114 40W
Croydon, Austral.	**135**	18 13 S	142 14 E
Croydon, U.K.	**95**	51 18N	0 5W
Crozet Basin	**16**	46 0 S	52 0 E
Crozet, Île	**16**	46 27 S	52 0 E
Crozon	**100**	48 15N	4 30W
Cruz, C.	**84**	19 50N	77 50W
Cruz del Eje	**88**	30 45 S	64 50W
Cruz, La, Colomb.	**86**	1 35N	76 58W
Cruz, La, C. Rica	**84**	11 4N	85 39W
Cruz, La, Mexico	**82**	23 55N	106 54W
Cruzeiro	**89**	22 50 S	45 0W
Cruzeiro do Oeste	**89**	23 46 S	53 4W
Cruzeiro do Sul	**86**	7 35 S	72 35W
Cry L.	**54**	58 45N	128 5W
Crystal Bay, Can.	**48**	45 22N	75 51W
Crystal Bay, U.S.A.	**80**	39 15N	120 0W
Crystal City, Can.	**57**	49 9N	98 57W
Crystal City, Mo., U.S.A.	**76**	38 15N	90 23W
Crystal City, Tex., U.S.A.	**75**	28 40N	99 50W
Crystal Falls	**72**	46 9N	88 11W
Crystal Lake	**77**	42 14N	88 19W
Crystal River	**73**	28 54N	82 35W
Crystal Springs	**75**	31 59N	90 25W
Csongrád	**107**	46 43N	20 12 E
Ctesiphon	**122**	33 9N	44 35 E
Cu Lao Hon	**128**	10 54N	108 18 E
Cuamba = Nova Freixo	**117**	14 45 S	36 22 E
Cuando, R.	**117**	14 0 S	19 30 E
Cuango	**116**	6 15 S	16 35 E
Cuarto, R.	**88**	33 25 S	63 2W
Cuatrociénegas de Carranza	**82**	26 59N	102 5W
Cuauhtémoc	**82**	28 25N	106 52W
Cuba, Mo., U.S.A.	**76**	38 4N	91 24W
Cuba, N. Mex., U.S.A.	**79**	36 0N	107 0W
Cuba, N.Y., U.S.A.	**70**	42 12N	78 18W
Cuba ■	**84**	22 0N	79 0W
Cuba City	**76**	42 36N	90 26W
Cubango, R.	**117**	16 15 S	17 45 E
Cuchi	**117**	14 37 S	17 10 E
Cuchumatanes, Sierra de los	**84**	15 35N	91 25W
Cucurpe	**82**	30 20N	110 43W
Cucurrupí	**86**	4 23N	76 56W
Cúcuta	**86**	7 54N	72 31W
Cudahy	**77**	42 54N	87 50W
Cuddalore	**124**	11 46N	79 45 E
Cuddapah	**124**	14 30N	78 47 E
Cudworth	**56**	52 30N	105 44W
Cue	**134**	27 25 S	117 54 E
Cuenca, Ecuador	**86**	2 50 S	79 9W
Cuenca, Spain	**104**	40 5N	2 10W
Cuenca, Serrania de	**104**	39 55N	1 50W
Cuencamé	**82**	24 53N	103 41W
Cuernavaca	**83**	18 50N	99 20W
Cuero	**75**	29 5N	97 17W
Cuers	**103**	43 14N	6 5 E
Cuervo	**75**	35 5N	104 25W
Cuevas del Almanzora	**104**	37 18N	1 58W
Cuevo	**86**	20 25N	63 30W
Cuhimbre	**86**	0 10 S	75 23W
Cuiabá	**87**	15 30 S	56 0W
Cuiabá, R.	**87**	16 50 S	56 30W
Cuidad Bolivar	**86**	8 21N	70 34W
Cuilco	**84**	15 24N	91 58W
Cuillin Hills	**96**	57 14N	6 15W
Cuillin Sd.	**96**	57 4N	6 20W
Cuima	**117**	13 0 S	15 45 E
Cuiseaux	**103**	46 30N	5 22 E
Cuito, R.	**117**	16 50 S	19 30 E
Cuitzeo, L.	**82**	19 55N	101 5W
Cuivre, R.	**76**	38 55N	90 44W
Culan	**102**	46 34N	2 20 E
Cŭlaraşi	**101**	44 14N	27 23 E
Culbertson	**74**	48 9N	104 30W
Culcairn	**136**	35 41 S	147 3 E
Culebra, I.	**67**	18 19N	65 17W
Culebra, Sierra de la	**104**	41 55N	6 20W
Culiacán	**82**	24 50N	107 40W
Culiacán, R.	**82**	24 30N	107 42W
Culion, I.	**127**	11 54N	120 1 E
Cullarin Range	**136**	34 30 S	149 30 E
Cullen	**96**	57 45N	2 50W
Cullera	**104**	39 9N	0 17W
Cullman	**73**	34 13N	86 50W
Culloden Moor	**96**	57 29N	4 7W
Cullom	**77**	40 53N	88 16W
Culoz	**103**	45 47N	5 46 E
Culpeper	**72**	38 29N	77 59W
Culuene, R.	**87**	12 15 S	53 10W
Culver	**77**	41 13N	86 25W
Culver, Pt.	**134**	32 54 S	124 43 E
Culverden	**133**	42 47 S	172 49 E
Cumaná	**86**	10 30N	64 5W
Cumberland, B.C., Can.	**62**	49 40N	125 0W
Cumberland, Ont., Can.	**47**	45 29N	75 24W
Cumberland, Qué., Can.	**71**	45 30N	75 24W
Cumberland, Iowa, U.S.A.	**76**	41 16N	94 52W
Cumberland, Md., U.S.A.	**72**	39 40N	78 43W
Cumberland, Wis., U.S.A.	**74**	45 32N	92 3W
Cumberland House	**57**	53 58N	102 16W
Cumberland I.	**73**	30 52N	81 30W
Cumberland Is.	**135**	20 35 S	149 10 E
Cumberland L.	**57**	54 3N	102 18W
Cumberland Pen.	**65**	67 0N	64 0W
Cumberland Plat.	**73**	36 0N	84 30W
Cumberland, R.	**73**	36 15N	87 0W
Cumberland Sound	**65**	65 30N	67 0W
Cumbria □	**94**	54 35N	2 55W
Cumbrian Mts.	**94**	54 30N	3 0W
Cumbum	**124**	15 40N	79 10 E
Cummings Mt.	**81**	35 2N	118 34W
Cumnock	**49**	43 46N	80 27W
Cumpas	**82**	30 0N	109 48W
Cumshewa Inlet	**62**	53 3N	131 50W
Cumuruxatiba	**87**	17 6 S	39 13W
Cuñaré	**86**	0 49N	72 32W
Cuncumén	**88**	31 53 S	70 38W
Cundinamarca □	**86**	5 0N	74 0W
Cunene, R.	**117**	17 0 S	15 0 E
Cúneo	**108**	44 23N	7 31 E
Cunlhat	**102**	45 38N	3 32 E
Cunnamulla	**135**	28 2 S	145 38 E
Cupar, Can.	**56**	50 57N	104 10W
Cupar, U.K.	**96**	56 20N	3 0W
Cupica	**86**	6 50N	77 30W
Cupica, Golfo de	**86**	6 25N	77 30W
Curaçao, I.	**85**	12 10N	69 0W
Curanilahue	**88**	37 29 S	73 28W
Curaray, R.	**86**	1 30 S	75 30W
Curatabaca	**86**	6 19N	62 51W
Curbarado	**86**	7 3N	76 54W
Curepto	**88**	35 8 S	72 1W
Curiapo	**86**	8 33N	61 5W
Curicó	**88**	34 55 S	71 20W
Curicó □	**88**	34 50 S	71 15W
Curiplaya	**86**	0 16N	74 52W
Curitiba	**89**	25 20 S	49 10W
Curlwaa	**136**	34 2 S	141 59 E
Currais Novos	**87**	6 13 S	36 30W
Curralinho	**87**	1 35 S	49 30W
Curran	**46**	44 41N	83 47W
Currant	**78**	38 51N	115 32W
Current, R.	**75**	37 15N	91 10W
Currie	**78**	40 16N	114 45W
Currituck Sd.	**73**	36 20N	75 50W
Currockbilly Mt.	**136**	35 25 S	150 0 E
Curtis	**74**	40 41N	100 32W
Curtis, I.	**135**	23 35 S	151 10 E
Curtis, Pt.	**135**	23 53 S	151 21 E
Curuapanema, R.	**87**	7 0 S	54 30W
Curuçá	**87**	0 35 S	47 50W
Curuguaty	**89**	24 19 S	55 49W
Curundu	**84**	8 59N	79 38W
Curupira, Serra	**86**	1 25N	64 30W
Cururupu	**87**	1 50 S	44 50W
Curuzú Cuatiá	**88**	29 50 S	58 5W
Curvelo	**87**	18 45 S	44 27W
Cushing	**43**	45 36N	74 28W
Cushing, Mt.	**54**	57 35N	126 57W
Cusihuiriáchic	**82**	28 10N	106 50W
Cusset	**102**	46 8N	3 28 E
Cusson, Pte.	**36**	60 23N	77 46W
Custer	**74**	43 45N	103 38W
Cut Bank	**61**	48 40N	112 15W
Cut Knife	**56**	52 45N	109 1W
Cutbank	**56**	51 18N	106 51W
Cutbank, R.	**60**	54 43N	118 32W
Cuthbert	**73**	31 47N	84 47W
Cutler	**80**	36 31N	119 17W
Cuttack	**125**	20 25N	85 57 E
Cuvier, C.	**134**	23 14 S	113 22 E
Cuvier I.	**133**	36 27 S	175 50 E
Cuxhaven	**106**	53 51N	8 41 E
Cuyabeno	**86**	0 16 S	75 53W
Cuyahoga Falls	**70**	41 8N	81 30W
Cuyahoga, R.	**70**	41 20N	81 35W
Cuyo	**127**	10 50N	121 5 E
Cuyuni, R.	**87**	7 0N	59 30W
Cuzco	**86**	13 32 S	72 0W
Cuzco, Mt.	**86**	20 0 S	66 50W
Cynthia	**60**	53 17N	115 25W
Cynthiana	**77**	38 23N	84 10W
Cypress Hills	**55**	49 40N	109 30W
Cypress Hills Prov. Park	**56**	49 40N	109 30W
Cypress River	**57**	49 34N	99 5W
Cyprus ■	**122**	35 0N	33 0 E
Cyrville	**48**	45 25N	75 38W
Czar	**61**	52 27N	110 50W
Czech S.R. □	**106**	49 30N	15 0 E
Czechoslovakia ■	**106**	49 0N	17 0 E
Czeremcha	**107**	52 32N	23 20 E
Częstochowa	**107**	50 49N	19 7 E

D

Da Lat	**128**	11 56N	108 25 E
Da Nang	**128**	16 4N	108 13 E
Da, R.	**128**	21 15N	105 20 E
Dabajuro	**86**	11 2N	70 40W
Dabie	**106**	53 27N	14 45 E
Dabrowa Tarnówska	**107**	50 10N	20 59 E
*Dacca	**125**	23 43N	90 26 E
Dacca □	**125**	24 0N	90 25 E
Dadanawa	**86**	3 0N	59 30W
Dade City	**73**	28 20N	82 12W
Dadra and Nagar Haveli □	**124**	20 5N	73 0 E
Dadu	**124**	26 45N	67 45 E
Daet	**127**	14 2N	122 55 E
Dafter	**46**	46 21N	84 27W
Dagestan, A.S.S.R. □	**120**	42 30N	47 0 E
Daggett	**81**	34 43N	116 52W
Dagupan	**127**	16 3N	120 20 E
Dagus Mines	**70**	41 20N	78 36W
Dahlgren	**77**	38 12N	88 41W
Dahlonega	**73**	34 35N	83 59W
Dahomey ■ = Benin ■	**114**	8 0N	2 0 E
Daingean	**97**	53 18N	7 15W
Daintree	**97**	16 20 S	145 20 E
Daiō-Misaki	**132**	34 15N	136 45 E
Dairen = Lu-ta	**130**	39 0N	121 31 E
Dakar	**114**	14 34N	17 29W
Dakhla	**114**	23 50N	15 53W
Dakhla, El Wâhât el-	**115**	25 30N	28 50 E
Dakota City, Iowa, U.S.A.	**76**	42 43N	94 12W
Dakota City, Nebr., U.S.A.	**74**	42 27N	96 28W
Đakovica	**109**	42 22N	20 26 E
Dalälven, L.	**111**	61 27N	17 15 E
Dalandzadgad	**130**	43 37N	104 30 E
Dalarö	**111**	59 8N	18 24 E
Dalat	**128**	12 3N	108 32 E
Dalbandin	**124**	29 0N	64 23 E
Dalbeattie	**96**	54 55N	3 50W
Dalby	**135**	27 10 S	151 17 E
Dale	**77**	38 10N	86 59W
Dalesville	**43**	45 42N	74 24W
Daleville	**77**	40 7N	85 33W
Dalhart	**75**	36 10N	102 30W
Dalhousie	**39**	48 5N	66 26W
Dalhousie East	**39**	44 43N	64 48W
Dalhousie Station	**43**	45 18N	74 27W
Dalhousie West	**39**	44 43N	65 13W
Dalj	**86**	45 28N	18 58 E
Dalkeith, Can.	**43**	45 27N	74 32W
Dalkeith, U.K.	**96**	55 54N	3 5W
Dall I.	**54**	54 59N	133 25W
Dallas, Oregon, U.S.A.	**78**	45 0N	123 15W
Dallas, Texas, U.S.A.	**75**	32 50N	96 50W
Dallas Center	**76**	41 41N	93 58W
Dallas City	**76**	40 38N	91 10W
Dalles, Les	**43**	45 59N	73 31W
Dalmacija	**108**	43 20N	17 0 E
Dalmatia = Dalmacija	**108**	43 20N	17 0 E
Dalmeny	**56**	52 20N	106 46W
Dalneretchensk	**121**	45 50N	133 40 E
Daloa	**114**	7 0N	6 30W
Dalrymple, Mt.	**135**	21 1 S	148 39 E
Dalton, Can.	**53**	48 11N	84 1W
Dalton, Ga., U.S.A.	**127**	34 45N	85 0W
Dalton, Mass., U.S.A.	**71**	42 28N	73 11W
Dalton, Nebr., U.S.A.	**74**	41 27N	103 0W
Dalton Post	**54**	66 42N	137 0W
Dalupuri, I.	**131**	19 2N	121 8 E
Dalvik	**110**	65 58N	18 32W
Daly City	**80**	37 42N	122 28W
Daly L.	**55**	56 32N	105 39W
Daly, R.	**134**	13 21 S	130 18 E
Daly Waters	**134**	16 15 S	133 24 E
Dam	**87**	4 45N	55 0W
Daman	**124**	20 25N	72 57 E
Daman □	**124**	20 25N	72 58 E
Damar, I.	**127**	7 15 S	128 30 E
Damaraland	**117**	21 0 S	17 0 E
Damascus	**49**	43 55N	80 29W
Damascus = Dimashq	**122**	33 30N	36 18 E
Damävand	**123**	36 0N	52 0 E
Damävand, Qolleh-ye	**123**	35 45N	52 10 E
Damba	**116**	6 44 S	15 29 E
Dâmboviţa, R.	**107**	44 40N	26 0 E

* *Renamed Dhaka*

Dame Marie — Deva

Dame Marie	85	18 36N	74 26W
Dāmghān	123	36 10N	54 17E
Damin	123	27 30N	60 40E
Damman	122	26 25N	50 2E
Dammarie	101	48 20N	1 30E
Dammartin	101	49 3N	2 41E
Damme	105	52 32N	8 12E
Damoh	124	23 50N	79 28E
Dampier	134	20 41S	116 42E
Dampier Arch.	134	20 38S	116 32E
Dampier Downs	134	18 24S	123 5E
Dampier, Selat	127	0 40S	131 0E
Damville	100	48 51N	1 5E
Damvillers	101	49 20N	5 21E
Dana	127	11 0S	122 52E
Dana, Lac	36	50 53N	77 20W
Dana, Mt	80	37 54N	119 12W
Danao	127	10 31N	124 1E
Danbury	71	41 23N	73 29W
Danby L.	79	34 17N	115 0W
Dandeldhura	125	29 20N	80 35E
Dandeli	124	15 5N	74 30E
Dandenong	136	38 0S	145 15E
Danforth, Can.	50	43 43N	79 15W
Danforth, U.S.A.	35	45 39N	67 57W
Dang Raek	128	14 40N	104 0E
Danger Is.	15	10 53S	165 49W
Danger Pt.	117	34 40S	19 17E
Daniel	78	42 56N	110 2W
Daniel's Harbour	37	50 13N	57 35W
Danielson	71	41 50N	71 52W
Danielson Prov. Park	56	51 16N	106 50W
Dankhar Gompa	124	32 10N	78 10E
Danlí	84	14 4N	86 35W
Dannemora, Sweden	111	60 12N	17 51E
Dannemora, U.S.A.	71	44 41N	73 44W
Dannevirke	133	40 12S	176 8E
Dansalan	127	8 2N	124 30E
Danskin	62	53 59N	125 47W
Dansville	70	42 32N	77 41W
Danube, R.	106	45 0N	28 20W
Danvers	71	42 34N	70 55E
Danville, Ill., U.S.A.	77	40 10N	87 40W
Danville, Ind., U.S.A.	77	39 46N	86 32W
Danville, Ky., U.S.A.	77	37 40N	84 45W
Danville, Va., U.S.A.	73	36 40N	79 20W
Danzig = Gdansk	107	54 22N	18 40E
Dão	127	10 30N	122 6E
Daoulas	100	48 22N	4 17W
Dar al Hamrā, Ad	122	27 22N	37 43E
Dar es Salaam	116	6 50S	39 12E
Dar'á	115	32 36N	36 7E
Dārāb	123	28 50N	54 30E
Darband	124	34 30N	72 50E
Darbhanga	125	26 15N	86 8E
Darby	78	46 2N	114 7W
D'Arcy	54	50 35N	122 30W
Dardanelle	80	38 2N	119 50W
Dardanelles = Canakkale Bğazi	122	40 0N	26 20E
Dardenelle	75	35 12N	93 9W
Dargai	124	34 25N	71 45E
Dargan Ata	120	40 40N	62 20E
Dargaville	133	35 57S	173 52E
Darhan	130	49 27N	105 57E
Darién	84	9 7N	79 46W
Darién, G. del	86	9 0N	77 0W
Darién, Serranía del	86	8 30N	77 30W
Darjeeling	125	27 3N	88 18E
Dark Cove	37	48 47N	54 13W
Darling, R.	136	34 4S	141 54E
Darling Ra.	134	32 30S	116 0E
Darlington, U.K.	94	54 33N	1 33W
Darlington, S.C., U.S.A.	73	34 18N	79 50W
Darlington, Wis., U.S.A.	76	42 43N	90 7W
Darlington Point	136	34 37S	146 1E
Darłowo	106	54 25N	16 25E
Darmstadt	106	49 51N	8 40E
Darnétal	100	49 25N	1 10E
Darney	101	48 5N	6 0E
Darnick	136	32 48S	143 38E
Darnley B.	67	69 30N	123 30W
Darnley, C.	91	68 0S	69 0E
Darrington	63	48 14N	121 37W
Dart, R.	95	50 24N	3 36W
Dartmoor	95	50 36N	4 0W
Dartmouth, Can.	39	44 40N	63 30W
Dartmouth, U.K.	95	50 21N	3 35W
Dartmouth, R.	38	48 53N	64 34W
Darvel Bay	127	4 50N	118 20E
Darwha	124	20 15N	77 45E
Darwin, Austral.	134	12 25S	130 51E
Darwin, U.S.A.	81	36 15N	117 35W
Daryacheh-ye-Sistan	123	31 0N	61 0E
Dashinchilen	130	48 0N	105 59E
Dasht-e Kavīr	123	34 30N	55 0E
Dasht-e Lūt	123	31 30N	58 0E
Dasht-i-Khash	124	32 0N	62 0E
Dasht-i-Margo	124	30 40N	62 30E
Dasht, R.	124	25 40N	62 20E
Dasserat, L.	40	48 16N	79 25W
Datia	124	25 39N	78 27E
Datteln	105	51 39N	7 23E
Daugavpils	120	55 53N	26 32E
Daulat Yar	123	34 30N	65 45E
Daulnay	39	47 25N	65 28W
Dauphin	57	51 9N	100 5W
Dauphin I.	73	30 16N	88 10W
Dauphin L.	57	51 20N	99 45W
Dauphiné	103	45 15N	5 25E
Davangere	124	14 25N	75 50E
Davao	127	7 0N	125 40E
Davao, G. of	127	6 30N	125 48E
Dāvar Panāh	123	27 25N	62 15E
Davenport, Calif., U.S.A.	80	37 1N	122 12W
Davenport, Iowa, U.S.A.	76	41 30N	90 40W
Davenport, Wash., U.S.A.	78	47 40N	118 5W
Davenport Ra.	134	20 28S	134 0E
Daventry	95	52 16N	1 10W
David	84	8 30N	82 30W
David City	74	41 18N	97 10W
David, R.	43	45 58N	72 54W
Davidson	56	51 16N	105 59W
Davis	80	38 33N	121 45W
Davis Dam	81	35 11N	114 35W
Davis Inlet	36	55 50N	60 59W
Davis Mts.	75	30 42N	104 15W
Davis Str.	65	65 0N	58 0W
Davison	46	43 2N	83 31W
Davisson, L.	80	46 30N	122 20W
Davos	106	46 48N	9 49E
Davy L.	56	58 53N	108 18W
Dawson, Can.	64	64 10N	139 30W
Dawson, Ga., U.S.A.	73	31 45N	84 28W
Dawson, N.D., U.S.A.	74	46 56N	99 45W
Dawson B.	57	52 53N	100 49W
Dawson Creek	54	55 45N	120 15W
Dawson, I.	90	53 50S	70 50W
Dawson Inlet	55	61 50N	93 25W
Dawson, R.	135	23 25S	150 10E
Daylesford	136	37 21S	144 9E
Dayr az Zawr	122	35 20N	40 5E
Daysland	61	52 50N	112 20W
Dayton, Iowa, U.S.A.	76	42 14N	94 6W
Dayton, Ky., U.S.A.	77	39 7N	84 28W
Dayton, Nev., U.S.A.	80	39 15N	119 34W
Dayton, Ohio, U.S.A.	72	39 45N	84 10W
Dayton, Pa., U.S.A.	70	40 54N	79 18W
Dayton, Tenn., U.S.A.	73	35 30N	85 1W
Dayton, Wash., U.S.A.	78	46 20N	118 10W
Daytona Beach	73	29 14N	81 0W
Dayville	78	44 33N	119 37W
De Aar	117	30 39S	24 0E
De Beaujeu	43	45 19N	74 20W
De Forest	76	43 15N	89 20W
De Funiak Springs	73	30 42N	86 10W
De Grau	37	48 29N	59 9W
De Grey	134	20 12S	119 12E
De Land	73	29 1N	81 19W
De Leon	75	32 9N	98 35W
De Léry	45	45 15N	73 26W
De Long Mts.	67	68 10N	163 0W
De Long, Ostrova	121	76 40N	149 20E
De Morhiban, L.	38	51 50N	62 54W
De Pere	72	44 28N	88 1W
De Queen	75	34 3N	94 24W
De Quincy	75	30 30N	93 27W
De Ridder	75	30 48N	93 15W
De Smet	74	44 25N	97 35W
De Soto	76	38 7N	90 33W
De Tour	46	45 59N	83 56W
De Witt, Ark., U.S.A.	75	34 19N	91 20W
De Witt, Iowa, U.S.A.	76	41 49N	90 33W
De Witt, Mich., U.S.A.	77	42 50N	84 33W
Deacon	58	49 51N	96 56W
Dead Sea = Miyet, Bahr el	115	31 30N	35 30E
Deadwood L.	54	59 10N	128 30W
Deakin	134	30 46S	129 58E
Deal	95	51 13N	1 25E
Dean Chan.	62	52 30N	127 15W
Dean, Forest of	95	51 50N	2 35W
Deán Funes	88	30 20S	64 20W
Dean, R.	62	52 49N	126 58W
Dearborn, U.S.A.	46	42 18N	83 15W
Dearborn, U.S.A.	76	39 32N	94 46W
Dease Arm	106	66 52N	119 37W
Dease L.	54	58 40N	130 5W
Dease Lake	54	58 25N	130 6W
Dease, R.	54	59 56N	128 32W
Death Valley	81	36 27N	116 52W
Death Valley Junc.	81	36 21N	116 30W
Death Valley Nat. Monument	81	36 30N	117 0W
Deauville	100	49 23N	0 2E
Debar	109	41 21N	20 37E
Debden	56	53 30N	106 50W
Debec	39	46 4N	67 41W
Debert	39	45 26N	63 28W
Debolt	60	55 12N	118 1W
Debre Markos	115	10 20N	37 40E
Debre Tabor	115	11 50N	38 26E
Debrecen	107	47 33N	21 42E
Decatur, Ala., U.S.A.	73	34 35N	87 0W
Decatur, Ga., U.S.A.	73	33 47N	84 17W
Decatur, Ill., U.S.A.	76	39 50N	89 0W
Decatur, Ind., U.S.A.	72	40 52N	85 28W
Decatur, Ind., U.S.A.	77	40 50N	84 56W
Decatur, Mich., U.S.A.	77	42 7N	85 58W
Decatur, Texas, U.S.A.	75	33 15N	97 35W
Decazeville	102	44 34N	2 15E
Deccan	124	14 0N	77 0E
Decelles, Rés	40	47 42N	78 8W
Déception, B.	36	62 8N	74 41W
Deception I.	91	63 0S	60 15W
Deception L.	55	56 33N	104 13W
Decize	101	46 50N	3 28E
Deckerville	46	43 33N	82 46W
Decorah	74	43 20N	91 50W
Dedham	71	42 14N	71 10W
Dee, R., Scot., U.K.	96	57 4N	2 7W
Dee, R., Wales, U.K.	94	53 15N	3 7W
Deep B.	54	61 15N	116 35W
Deep Cove	66	49 20N	122 56W
Deep River	76	41 35N	92 22W
Deepdale	134	26 22S	114 20E
Deepwater	76	38 18N	93 46W
Deer I.	67	54 55N	162 20W
Deer, L.	37	49 6N	57 35W
Deer Lake, Newf., Can.	37	49 11N	57 27W
Deer Lake, Ontario, Can.	55	52 36N	94 20W
Deer Lodge	78	46 25N	112 40W
Deer Park, Ohio, U.S.A.	77	39 13N	84 23W
Deer Park, Wash., U.S.A.	78	47 55N	117 21W
Deer Pond	37	48 30N	54 45W
Deer, R.	55	58 23N	94 13W
Deer River	52	47 21N	93 44W
Deering	67	66 5N	162 50W
Deesa	124	24 18N	72 10E
Defiance	77	41 20N	84 20W
Dégelis	41	47 30N	68 35W
Deggendorf	106	48 49N	12 59E
Deh Bīd	123	30 39N	53 11E
Deh Kheyr	123	28 45N	54 40E
Deh Titan	124	33 45N	63 50E
Dehkareqan	122	37 50N	45 55E
Dehra Dun	124	30 20N	78 4E
Deinze	105	50 59N	3 32E
Dej	107	47 10N	23 52E
Dekalb	77	41 55N	88 45W
Dekese	116	3 24S	21 24E
Del Mar	81	32 58N	117 16W
Del Norte	79	37 47N	106 27W
Del Rio, Mexico	82	29 22N	100 54W
Del Rio, U.S.A.	75	29 15N	100 50W
Delagua	75	32 35N	104 40W
Delano	81	35 48N	119 13W
Delaronde L.	56	54 3N	107 3W
Delavan, Ill., U.S.A.	76	40 22N	89 33W
Delavan, Wis., U.S.A.	77	42 40N	88 39W
Delaware	77	40 20N	83 0W
Delaware □	72	39 0N	75 40W
Delaware, R.	71	39 20N	75 25W
Delburne	61	52 12N	113 14W
Delft	105	52 1N	4 22E
Delgado, C.	116	10 45S	40 40E
Delgo	115	20 6N	30 40E
Delhi, Can.	46	42 51N	80 30W
Delhi, India	124	28 38N	77 17E
Delhi, U.S.A.	71	42 17N	74 56W
Delia	61	51 38N	112 23W
Delice, R.	122	39 45N	34 15E
Delicias	82	28 10N	105 30W
Delicias, Laguna	82	28 7N	105 40W
Delisle	56	51 55N	107 8W
Dell City	79	31 58N	105 19W
Dell Rapids	74	43 53N	96 44W
Delle	101	47 30N	7 2E
Delmar, Iowa, U.S.A.	76	42 0N	90 37W
Delmar, N.Y., U.S.A.	71	42 37N	73 47W
Delmiro	87	9 24S	38 6W
Deloraine	57	49 15N	100 29W
Delorme, L.	36	54 31N	69 52W
Delphi	77	40 37N	86 40W
Delphos	77	40 51N	84 17W
Delray Beach	73	26 27N	80 4W
Delson	45	45 22N	73 33W
Delta, Colo., U.S.A.	79	38 44N	108 5W
Delta, Utah, U.S.A.	78	39 21N	112 29W
Delta □	66	49 7N	123 0W
Delta Amacuro □	86	8 30N	61 30W
Delta Beach	57	50 11N	98 19W
Demak	127	6 50S	110 40E
Demanda, Sierra de la	104	42 15N	3 0W
Demba	116	5 28S	22 15E
Dembidolo	115	8 34N	34 50E
Demer, R.	105	51 0N	5 8E
Demerais, L.	34	47 35N	77 0W
Demerara, R.	86	7 0N	58 0W
Deming, N.Mex., U.S.A.	79	32 10N	107 50W
Deming, Wash., U.S.A.	80	48 49N	122 13W
Demini, R.	86	0 46N	62 56W
Demmit	54	55 20N	119 50W
Demopolis	73	32 30N	87 48W
Dempo, Mt.	126	4 10S	103 15E
Den Burg	105	53 3N	4 47E
Den Haag = 's Gravenhage	105	52 7N	4 17E
Den Helder	105	52 57N	4 45E
Den Oever	105	52 56N	5 2E
Denain	101	50 20N	3 22E
Denair	80	37 32N	120 48W
Denau	120	38 16N	67 54E
Denbigh, Can.	47	45 8N	77 15W
Denbigh, U.K.	94	53 12N	3 26W
Dendang	126	3 7S	107 56E
Denham	134	25 56S	113 31E
Denham Ra.	135	21 55S	147 46E
Denholm	55	52 40N	108 0W
Denia	104	38 49N	0 8E
Deniliquin	136	35 30S	144 58E
Denison, Iowa, U.S.A.	74	42 0N	95 18W
Denison, Texas, U.S.A.	75	33 50N	96 40W
Denison Range	135	28 30S	136 5E
Denizli	122	37 42N	29 2E
Denman Island	62	49 33N	124 48W
Denmark	134	34 59S	117 18E
Denmark ■	111	55 30N	9 0E
Denmark Str.	12	66 0N	30 0W
Dennison	70	40 21N	81 21W
Denpasar	126	8 45S	115 5E
Denton, Mont., U.S.A.	78	47 25N	109 56W
Denton, Texas, U.S.A.	75	33 12N	97 10W
Denver, Colo., U.S.A.	74	39 45N	105 0W
Denver, Ind., U.S.A.	77	40 52N	86 5W
Denver, Iowa, U.S.A.	76	42 40N	92 20W
Denver City	75	32 58N	102 48W
Denzil	56	52 14N	109 39W
Deoghar	125	24 30N	86 59E
Deolali	124	19 50N	73 50E
Deoria	125	26 31N	83 48E
Deosai, Mts.	124	35 40N	75 0E
Departure Bay	62	49 13N	123 57W
Depew	70	42 55N	78 43W
Deposit	71	42 5N	75 23W
Depot Harbour	70	45 18N	80 5W
Deputatskiy	121	69 18N	139 54E
Dera Ghazi Khan	124	30 5N	70 43E
Dera Ismail Khan	124	31 50N	70 50E
* Dera Ismail Khan □	124	32 30N	70 0E
Derbent	120	42 5N	48 15E
Derby, Austral.	134	17 18S	123 38E
Derby, U.K.	94	52 55N	1 28W
Derby, Conn., U.S.A.	71	41 20N	73 5W
Derby, N.Y., U.S.A.	70	42 40N	78 59W
Derby, Ohio, U.S.A.	77	39 46N	83 13W
Derby □	94	52 55N	1 28W
Derg, L.	97	53 0N	8 20W
Derg, R.	97	54 42N	7 26W
Dergaon	125	26 45N	94 0E
Derna	115	32 40N	22 35E
Dernieres Isles	75	29 0N	90 45W
Deroche	63	49 12N	122 4W
Derrynane	49	43 56N	80 35W
Derryveagh Mts.	97	55 0N	8 40W
Derval	100	47 40N	1 41W
Derwent	60	53 41N	110 58W
Derwent, R., Cumb., U.K.	94	54 42N	3 22W
Derwent, R., Derby, U.K.	94	52 53N	1 17W
Derwent, R., N. Yorks., U.K.	94	53 45N	0 57W
Derwentwater, L.	94	53 34N	3 9W
Des Moines, Iowa, U.S.A.	76	41 35N	93 37W
Des Moines, N. Mex., U.S.A.	75	36 50N	103 51W
Des Moines, R.	74	40 23N	91 25W
Des Plaines	77	42 3N	87 52W
Des Plaines, R.	77	41 23N	88 15W
Desaguadero, R., Argent.	88	33 28S	67 15W
Desaguadero, R., Boliv.	86	17 30S	68 0W
Desbarats	46	46 20N	83 56W
Desbiens	41	48 25N	71 57W
Descanso	81	32 12N	116 58W
Descanso, Pta.	81	32 21N	117 3W
Deschaillons	41	46 32N	72 7W
Deschambault	41	46 39N	71 56W
Descharme, R.	55	56 51N	109 13W
Deschênes, Ont., Can.	48	45 25N	75 49W
Deschênes, Qué., Can.	40	45 23N	75 48W
Deschênes, L.	48	45 22N	75 51W
Deschutes, R.	78	45 30N	121 0W
Dese	115	11 5N	39 40E
Deseado, R.	90	40 0S	69 0W
Desemboque	82	30 30N	112 27W
Deseronto	47	44 12N	77 3W
Desert Center	81	33 45N	115 27W
Desert Hot Springs	81	33 58N	116 30W
Désirade, I.	85	16 18N	61 3W
Deskenatlata L.	54	60 55N	112 3W
Desmarais	60	55 56N	113 49W
Desmaraisville	40	49 32N	76 9W
Desméloizes	40	48 57N	79 29W
Desolación, I.	90	53 0S	74 0W
Desolation Sound Prov. Marine Park	62	50 5N	124 25W
Despeñaperros, Paso	104	38 24N	3 30W
Dessau	106	51 49N	12 15E
Destruction Bay	64	61 15N	138 48W
Desvrès	101	50 40N	1 48E
Detmold	106	51 55N	8 50E
Detour Pt.	72	45 37N	86 35W
Detroit, Mich., U.S.A.	46	42 13N	83 22W
Detroit, Tex., U.S.A.	75	33 40N	95 10W
Detroit Lakes	74	46 50N	95 50W
Dettifoss	110	65 49N	16 24W
Deurne, Belg.	105	51 12N	4 24E
Deurne, Neth.	105	51 27N	5 49E
Deutsche Bucht	106	54 10N	7 51E
Deux-Loutres, L. aux	38	51 31N	62 28W
Deux Montagnes	44	45 32N	73 53W
Deux Montagnes □	44	45 40N	74 0W
Deux Montagnes, Lac des	44	45 28N	73 59W
Deux-Sèvres □	100	46 35N	0 20W
Deva	107	45 53N	22 55E

* *Now part of N.W. Frontier Province*

Devakottai **Dover Plains**

Devakottai 124 9 55N 78 45 E
Devastation Chan. 62 53 40N 128 50W
Deventer 105 52 15N 6 10 E
Devenyns, L. 41 47 5N 73 50W
Deveron, R. 96 57 40N 2 31W
Devils Den 80 35 46N 119 58W
Devils Lake 74 48 5N 98 50W
Devils Paw, mt. 54 58 47N 134 0W
Devizes 95 51 21N 2 0W
Devon 60 53 24N 113 44W
Devon I. 65 75 47N 88 0W
Devonport, Austral. 135 41 10 S 146 22 E
Devonport, N.Z. 133 36 49 S 174 49 E
Devonport, U.K. 95 50 23N 4 11W
Devonshire □ 95 50 50N 3 40W
Dewas 124 22 59N 76 3 E
Dewberry 60 53 35N 110 32W
Dewittville 43 45 7N 74 5W
Dewsbury 94 53 42N 1 38W
Dexter, U.S.A. 77 42 20N 83 53W
Dexter, Mo., U.S.A. 75 36 50N 90 0W
Dexter, N. Mex., U.S.A. 75 33 15N 104 25W
Deyhūk 123 33 15N 57 30 E
Deyyer 123 27 55N 51 55 E
Dezadeash L. 54 60 28N 136 58W
Dezfūl 122 32 20N 48 30 E
Dezh Shāhpūr 122 35 30N 46 25 E
Dezhneva, Mys 121 66 10N 169 3 E
Dhaba 122 27 25N 35 40 E
Dhahran 122 26 9N 50 10 E
Dhamtari 125 20 42N 81 35 E
Dhanbad 125 23 50N 86 30 E
Dhangarhi 125 28 55N 80 40 E
Dhankuta 125 26 55N 87 20 E
Dhar 124 22 35N 75 26 E
Dharmapuri 124 12 10N 78 10 E
Dhaulagiri Mt. 125 28 45N 83 45 E
Dhenkanal 125 20 45N 85 35 E
Dhidhimótikhon 109 41 22N 26 29 E
Dhikti, Mt. 109 35 8N 25 29 E
Dhirfis, Mt. 109 38 40N 23 54 E
Dhodhekánisos 109 36 35N 27 0 E
Dholpur 124 26 45N 77 59 E
Dhrol 124 22 40N 70 25 E
Dhubaibah 123 23 25N 54 35 E
Dhubri 125 26 2N 90 2 E
Dhulia 124 20 58N 74 50 E
Di Linh, Cao Nguyen 128 11 30N 108 0 E
Diable, Mt. 80 37 53N 121 56W
Diablo Heights 84 8 58N 79 34W
Diablo Range 80 37 0N 121 5W
Diagonal 76 40 49N 94 20W
Diamante 88 32 5 S 60 40W
Diamante, R. 88 34 31 S 66 56W
Diamantina 87 18 5 S 43 40W
Diamantina, R. 135 22 25 S 142 20 E
Diamantino 87 14 30 S 56 30W
Diamond City 61 49 48N 112 51W
Diamond Harbour 125 22 11N 88 14 E
Diamond Mts. 78 40 0N 115 58W
Diamond Springs 80 38 42N 120 49W
Diamondville 78 41 51N 110 30W
Diana B. 36 61 20N 70 0W
Diaole, Ī. du. 87 5 15N 52 45W
Dibai (Dubai) 123 25 15N 55 20 E
Dibaya 116 6 20 S 22 0 E
Dibaya Lubue 116 4 12 S 19 54 E
Dibba 123 25 45N 56 16 E
Dibega 122 35 50N 43 46 E
Dibi 115 4 10N 41 52 E
Dibrugarh 125 27 29N 94 55 E
Dibulla 86 11 17N 73 19W
Dickersonville 49 43 14N 78 53W
Dickeyville 76 42 38N 90 36W
Dickinson 74 46 50N 102 40W
Dickson 73 36 5N 87 22W
Dickson City 71 41 29N 75 40W
Didsbury 61 51 35N 114 10W
Die 103 44 47N 5 22 E
Diefenbaker L. 55 51 0N 106 55W
Diego Garcia, I. 16 9 50 S 75 0 E
*Diégo Suarez 117 12 25 S 49 20 E
Diekirch 105 49 52N 6 10 E
Diélette 100 49 33N 1 52W
Diên Biên Phu 128 21 20N 103 0 E
Diepenbeek 105 50 54N 5 25 E
Dieppe, Can. 39 46 6N 64 45W
Dieppe, France 100 49 54N 1 4 E
Dieren 105 52 3N 6 6 E
Dierks 75 34 9N 94 0W
Diest 105 50 58N 5 4 E
Dieterich 77 39 4N 88 23W
Dieulefit 103 44 32N 5 4 E
Dieuze 101 48 30N 6 40 E
Differdange 105 49 81N 5 54 E
Digby 39 44 38N 65 50W
Digby Neck 39 44 30N 66 5W
Digges 55 58 40N 94 0W
Digges Is. 36 62 40N 77 50W
Dighinala 125 23 15N 92 5 E
Dighton 74 38 30N 100 26W
Digne 103 44 5N 6 12 E
Digoin 102 46 29N 3 58 E
Digos 127 6 45N 125 20 E
Digranes 110 66 4N 14 44 E
Dihang, R. 125 27 30N 96 30 E
Dijlah 122 37 0N 42 30 E
Dijon 101 47 20N 5 0 E
Diksmuide 105 51 2N 2 52 E
Dikson 120 73 40N 80 5 E
Dila 115 6 14N 38 22 E
Dilam 122 23 55N 47 10 E
Dildo 37 47 34N 53 33W
Dili 127 8 39 S 125 34 E
Dilke 56 50 52N 105 15W
Dillard 76 37 44N 91 13W
Dilley 75 28 40N 99 12W
Dillingham 67 59 5N 158 30W
Dillon, Can. 55 55 56N 108 56W
Dillon, Mont., U.S.A. 78 45 9N 112 36W
Dillon, S.C., U.S.A. 73 34 26N 79 20W
Dillon, R. 55 55 56N 108 56W
Dillsboro 77 39 1N 85 4W
Dilolo 12 10 28 S 22 18 E
Dimas 82 23 43N 106 47W
Dimashq 122 33 30N 36 18 E
Dimbelenge 116 4 30N 23 0 E
Dimboola 136 36 28 S 142 0 E
Dimitriya Lapteva, Proliv 121 73 0N 140 0 E
Dimitrovgrad 109 42 5N 25 35 E
Dimmitt 75 34 36N 102 16W
Dinagat I. 127 10 10N 125 40 E
Dinajpur 125 25 33N 88 43 E
Dinan 100 48 28N 2 2W
Dinant 105 50 16N 4 55 E
Dinar 122 38 5N 30 15 E
Dinara Planina, mts. 108 44 0N 16 30 E
Dinard 100 48 38N 2 6W
Dinaric Alps 93 44 0N 17 30 E
Dindigul 124 10 25N 78 0 E
Dingle 97 52 9N 10 17W
Dingle B. 97 52 3N 10 20W
Dingmans Ferry 71 41 13N 74 55W
Dingwall, Can. 39 46 54N 60 28W
Dingwall, U.K. 96 57 36N 4 26W
Dinorwic 52 49 41N 92 30W
Dinorwic L. 52 49 37N 92 33W
Dinosaur National Monument 78 40 30N 108 45W
Dinosaur Prov. Park 61 50 47N 111 30W
Dinsmore 56 51 20N 107 26W
Dinuba 80 36 37N 119 22W
Dionne, L. 38 49 26N 67 55W
Dipolog 127 8 36N 123 20 E
Dir 124 35 08N 71 59 E
Dire Dawa 115 9 35N 41 45 E
Direction, C. 135 12 51 S 143 32 E
Diriamba 84 11 51N 86 19W
Dirico 117 17 50 S 20 42 E
Dirk Hartog I. 134 25 50 S 113 5 E
Dirranbandi 135 28 33 S 148 17 E
Disappointment, C. 78 46 20N 124 0W
Disappointment L. 134 23 20 S 122 40 E
Disaster B. 135 37 15 S 150 0 E
Discovery B. 136 38 10 S 140 40 E
Disko 17 69 45N 53 30W
Disko Bugt 65 69 10N 52 0W
Disko I. 65 69 30N 54 30W
Disraëli 41 45 54N 71 21W
Disteghil Sar 124 36 20N 75 5 E
Distrito Federal □ 86 10 30N 66 55W
Diu, I. 124 20 45N 70 58 E
Diver 34 46 44N 79 30W
Dives, R. 100 49 18N 0 7W
Dives-sur-Mer 100 49 18N 0 8W
Divide 78 45 48N 112 47W
Dix, R. 77 37 49N 84 44W
Dixie 78 45 37N 115 27W
Dixie Mt. 80 39 55N 120 16W
Dixon, Calif., U.S.A. 80 38 27N 121 49W
Dixon, Ill., U.S.A. 76 41 50N 89 30W
Dixon, Iowa, U.S.A. 76 41 45N 90 47W
Dixon, Mo., U.S.A. 76 37 59N 92 6W
Dixon, Mont., U.S.A. 78 47 19N 114 25W
Dixon, N. Mex., U.S.A. 79 36 15N 105 57W
Dixon Entrance 54 54 30N 132 0W
Dixonville 60 56 32N 117 40W
Dixville 41 45 4N 71 46W
Diyarbakir 122 37 55N 40 18 E
Djakarta = Jakarta 127 6 9 S 106 49 E
Djambala 116 2 20 S 14 30 E
Djawa = Jawa 127 7 0 S 110 0 E
Djelfa 114 34 40N 3 15 E
Djema 116 6 9N 25 15 E
Djibouti 115 11 30N 43 5 E
Djibouti ■ 115 11 30N 42 15 E
Djirlange 128 11 44N 108 15 E
Djolu 116 0 45N 22 5 E
Djoum 116 2 41N 12 35 E
Djugu 116 1 55N 30 35 E
Djúpivogur 110 64 39N 14 17W
Dmitriya Lapteva, Proliv 121 73 0N 140 0 E
Dneiper, R. = Dnepr 120 52 29N 35 10 E
Dnepr, R. 120 50 0N 31 0 E
Dneprodzerzhinskoye Vdkhr. 121 49 0N 34 0 E
Dnepropetrovsk 120 48 30N 35 0 E
Dnestr, R. 120 48 30N 26 30 E
Dniester = Dnestr 120 48 30N 26 30 E
Doaktown 39 46 33N 66 8W
Doba 114 8 40N 16 50 E
Dobbyn 135 19 44 S 139 59 E
Doberai, Jazirah 127 1 25 S 133 0 E
Dobie, R. 52 51 41N 90 29W
Doblas 88 37 5 S 64 0W
Dobo 127 5 45 S 134 15 E
Dobruja, reg. 107 44 30N 28 30 E
Dodecanese = Dhodhekánisos 109 36 35N 27 0 E
Dodge Center 74 44 1N 92 57W
Dodge City 75 37 42N 100 0W
Dodge L. 55 59 50N 105 36W
Dodgeville 76 42 55N 90 8W
Dodoma 116 6 8 S 35 45 E
Dodsland 56 51 50N 108 45W
Dodson 78 48 23N 108 4W
Doesburg 105 52 1N 6 9 E
Doetinchem 105 51 59N 6 18 E
Dog Creek 63 51 35N 122 14W
Dog L., Man., Can. 54 51 2N 98 31W
Dog L., Ont., Can. 52 48 40N 89 30W
Dog L., Ont., Can. 53 48 17N 84 8W
Dog, R. 52 48 32N 89 39W
Dogi 124 32 20N 62 50 E
Dohad 124 22 50N 74 15 E
Dohazari 125 22 10N 92 5 E
Doheny 34 47 4N 72 35W
Doherty 34 46 58N 79 44W
Doi, I. 127 2 21N 127 49 E
Doi Luang 128 18 20N 101 30 E
Doig, R., Alta., Can. 54 56 57N 120 0W
Doig, R., B.C., Can. 54 56 25N 120 40W
Dojran 109 41 10N 22 45 E
Dokkum 105 53 20N 5 59 E
Dol 100 48 34N 1 47W
Dolak, Pulau = Kolepom, P. 127 8 0 S 138 30 E
Doland 74 44 55N 98 5W
Dolbeau 41 48 53N 72 18W
Dole 101 47 7N 5 31 E
Dolgellau 94 52 44N 3 53W
Dolgelly = Dolgellau 94 52 44N 3 53W
Dolisie 116 4 0 S 13 10 E
Dollard 56 49 37N 108 35W
Dollard-des-Ormeaux 44 45 29N 73 49W
Dollarton 66 49 18N 122 57W
Dolomites = Dolomiti 108 46 30N 11 40 E
Dolomiti 108 46 30N 11 40 E
Dolores, Argent. 88 36 20 S 57 40W
Dolores, Mexico 82 28 53N 108 27W
Dolores, Uruguay 88 33 34 S 58 15W
Dolores, Colo., U.S.A. 79 37 30N 108 30W
Dolores, Tex., U.S.A. 75 27 40N 99 38W
Dolores, R. 75 38 30N 108 55W
Dolphin and Union Str. 64 69 5N 114 45W
Dolphin C. 90 51 10 S 50 0W
Dom Pedrito 89 31 0 S 54 40W
Dombarovskiy 120 50 46N 59 32 E
Dombås 111 62 6N 9 4 E
Dombasle 101 49 8N 5 10 E
Dombe Grande 117 12 56 S 13 8 E
Dombes 103 46 3N 5 0 E
Dome Creek 63 53 44N 121 1W
Domel, I = Letsok-aw-kyun 128 11 30N 98 25 E
Domérat 102 46 21N 2 32 E
Domeyko 88 29 0 S 71 30W
Domeyko, Cordillera 88 24 30 S 69 0W
Domfront 100 48 37N 0 40W
Dominador 88 24 21 S 69 20W
Dominica I. 85 15 20N 61 20W
Dominica Passage 85 15 10N 61 20W
Dominican Rep. ■ 85 19 0N 70 30W
Dominion 39 46 13N 60 1W
Dominion, C. 65 65 30N 74 28W
Dominion City 57 49 9N 97 9W
Dominion L. 38 52 40N 61 45W
Domme 102 44 48N 1 12 E
Domodossóla 106 46 6N 8 19 E
Dompaire 101 48 14N 6 14 E
Dompierre-sur-Besbre 102 46 31N 3 41 E
Domrémy 101 48 26N 5 40 E
Don Benito 104 38 53N 5 51W
Don Martín, Presá de 82 27 30N 100 50W
Don Mills 50 43 42N 79 21W
Don Pedro Res. 80 37 43N 120 24W
Don Pen. 62 52 25N 128 12W
Don, R., Can. 50 43 39N 79 21W
Don, R., Eng., U.K. 94 53 41N 0 51W
Don, R., Scot., U.K. 96 57 14N 2 5W
Don, R., U.S.S.R. 120 49 35N 41 40 E
Donaghadee 97 54 38N 5 32W
Donald, Austral. 136 36 23 S 143 0 E
Donald, Can. 63 51 29N 117 10W
Donalda 61 52 35N 112 34W
Donaldsonville 75 30 2N 91 0W
Donalsonville 73 31 3N 84 52W
Donan 58 49 57N 97 6W
Donau, R. 107 47 55N 17 20 E
Donauwörth 106 48 42N 10 47 E
Doncaster 94 53 31N 1 9W
Dondo, Angola 110 9 45 S 14 25 E
Dondo, Mozam. 116 19 33 S 34 46 E
Dondo, Teluk 127 0 29N 120 45 E
Dondra Head 124 5 55N 80 40 E
Donegal 97 54 39N 8 8W
Donegal □ 97 54 53N 8 0W
Donegal B. 97 54 30N 8 35W
Donetsk 120 48 0N 37 45 E
Dongara 134 29 14 S 114 57 E
Dongen 105 51 38N 4 56 E
Donges 100 47 18N 2 4W
Donggala 127 0 30 S 119 40 E
Dongou 116 2 0N 18 5 E
Doniphan 75 36 40N 90 50W
Donjon, Le 102 46 22N 3 48 E
Donken 52 46 58N 88 51W
Donkin 39 46 11N 59 52W
Donna 110 66 6N 12 30 E
Donna 75 26 12N 98 2W
Donnaconna 41 46 41N 71 41W
Donnelly 60 55 44N 117 6W
Donnelly's Crossing 133 35 42 S 173 38 E
Donora 70 40 11N 79 50W
Donovans 37 47 32N 52 50W
Donzère-Mondragon 103 44 28N 4 43 E
Donzy 101 47 20N 3 6 E
Doon, R. 96 55 26N 4 41W
Dor (Tantura) 115 32 37N 34 55 E
Dora Báltea, R. 108 45 42N 7 25 E
Dora, L. 134 22 0 S 123 0 E
Dorada, La 86 5 30N 74 40W
Doran L. 55 61 13N 108 6W
Dorat, Le 102 46 14N 1 5 E
Dorchester, Can. 39 45 54N 64 31W
Dorchester, U.K. 95 50 42N 2 28W
Dorchester, C. 65 65 27N 77 27W
Dorchester Crossing 39 46 10N 64 34W
Dordogne □ 102 45 5N 0 40 E
Dordogne, R. 102 45 2N 0 36W
Dordrecht 105 51 48N 4 39 E
Doré L. 55 54 46N 107 17W
Doré Lake 55 54 38N 107 54W
Doré, Le, L. 38 51 17N 61 23W
Dore, Mt. 102 45 32N 2 50 E
Dore, R. 102 45 59N 3 28 E
Dori 114 14 3N 0 2W
Dorion, Ont., Can. 52 48 47N 88 39W
Dorion, Qué., Can. 44 45 23N 74 3W
Dorion-Vaudreuil 71 45 25N 75 4W
Dornes 101 46 48N 3 18 E
Dornoch 96 57 52N 4 0W
Dornoch Firth 96 57 52N 4 0W
Dorohoi 107 47 56N 26 30 E
Döröö Nuur 129 48 0N 93 0 E
Dorre I. 134 25 13 S 113 12 E
Dorris 78 41 59N 121 58W
Dorset, Can. 47 45 14N 78 54W
Dorset, U.S.A. 70 41 41N 8 42W
Dorset □ 95 50 48N 2 25W
Dorsten 105 51 40N 6 55 E
Dortmund 105 51 32N 7 28 E
Dörtyol 122 36 52N 36 12 E
Doruma 116 4 42N 27 33 E
Dorval 44 45 27N 73 44W
Dorval Airport 44 45 28N 73 44W
Dos Bahías, C. 90 44 58 S 65 32W
Dos Cabezas 79 32 10N 109 37W
Dos Palos 80 36 59N 120 37W
Doshi 123 35 35N 68 50 E
Dosquet 41 46 28N 71 32W
Dot 54 50 12N 121 25W
Dothan 73 31 10N 85 25W
Doting Cove 37 49 27N 53 57W
Doty 80 46 38N 123 17W
Douai 101 50 21N 3 4 E
Douala 116 4 0N 9 45 E
Douarnenez 100 48 6N 4 21W
Doubs □ 101 47 10N 6 20 E
Doubs, R. 101 46 53N 5 1 E
Doubtful B. 134 34 15 S 119 28 E
Doubtful Sd. 133 45 20 S 166 49 E
Doubtless B. 133 34 55 S 173 26 E
Doucet 34 48 15N 76 35W
Doudeville 100 49 43N 0 47 E
Doué 100 47 11N 0 20W
Douglas, Can. 47 45 31N 76 56W
Douglas, U.K. 94 54 9N 4 29W
Douglas, Alaska, U.S.A. 67 58 23N 134 32W
Douglas, Ariz., U.S.A. 79 31 21N 109 30W
Douglas, Ga., U.S.A. 73 31 32N 82 52W
Douglas, Wyo., U.S.A. 74 42 45N 105 20W
Douglas Chan. 62 53 40N 129 20W
Douglas I. 66 49 13N 122 47W
Douglas Pt. 46 44 19N 81 37W
Douglas Prov. Park 56 51 3N 106 28W
Douglastown, N.B., Can. 38 48 46N 64 24W
Douglastown, N.B., Can. 39 47 1N 65 30W
Douglasville 73 33 46N 84 43W
Doulevant 101 48 22N 4 53 E
Doullens 101 50 10N 2 20 E
Doumé 116 4 15N 13 25 E
Dounreay 96 58 40N 3 28W
Dourados 89 22 9 S 54 50W
Dourados, R. 89 21 58 S 54 18W
Dourdan 101 48 30N 2 0 E
Douro Litoral □ 104 41 10N 8 20W
Douro, R. 104 41 1N 8 16W
Douvaine 103 46 19N 6 16 E
Douville 45 45 36N 72 59W
Dove Creek 79 37 53N 108 59W
Dove, R., N. Yorks, U.K. 94 54 20N 0 55W
Dove, R., Staffs., U.K. 94 52 51N 1 36W
Dover, U.K. 95 51 7N 1 19 E
Dover, Del., U.S.A. 72 39 10N 75 31W
Dover, Ky., U.S.A. 77 38 43N 83 52W
Dover, N.H., U.S.A. 71 43 5N 70 51W
Dover, N.J., U.S.A. 71 40 53N 74 34W
Dover, Ohio, U.S.A. 70 40 32N 81 30W
Dover-Foxcroft 35 45 14N 69 14W
Dover Plains 71 41 43N 73 35W

* *Renamed Antsiranana*

Dover, Pt **Eatonia**

Dover, Pt.	**134**	32 32 S	125 32 E
Dover, Str. of	**93**	51 0N	1 30 E
Dovey, R.	**95**	52 32N	4 0W
Dovrefjell	**110**	62 15N	9 33 E
Dowa	**117**	13 38 S	33 58 E
Dowager I.	**62**	52 25N	128 22W
Dowagiac	**77**	42 0N	86 8W
Dowlatabad	**123**	28 20N	50 40 E
Down □	**97**	54 20N	6 0W
Downers Grove	**77**	41 49N	88 1W
Downey	**78**	42 29N	112 3W
Downeys	**49**	43 29N	80 14W
Downham Market	**95**	52 36N	0 22 E
Downieville	**80**	39 34N	120 50W
Downing	**76**	40 29N	92 22W
Downpatrick	**97**	54 20N	5 43W
Downpatrick Hd.	**97**	54 20N	9 21W
Downsview	**50**	43 43N	79 29W
Downton, Mt.	**62**	52 42N	124 52W
Doyle	**80**	40 2N	120 6W
Doyles	**37**	47 50N	59 12W
Doylestown	**71**	40 21N	75 10W
Dozois, Rés	**40**	47 30N	77 5W
Drachten	**105**	53 7N	6 5 E
Dragoman, P.	**109**	43 0N	22 57 E
Dragon	**43**	45 29N	74 16W
Dragon's Mouth	**86**	11 0N	61 50W
Draguignan	**103**	43 30N	6 27 E
Drain	**78**	43 45N	123 17W
Drake, Can.	**56**	51 45N	105 1W
Drake, U.S.A.	**74**	47 56N	100 31W
Drake Passage	**91**	58 0 S	68 0W
Drakensberg	**117**	31 0 S	25 0 E
Dráma	**109**	41 9N	24 10 E
Drammen	**111**	59 42N	10 12 E
Drangajökull	**110**	66 9N	22 15W
Drava, R.	**107**	45 50N	18 0 E
Draveil	**101**	48 41N	2 25 E
Drayton	**46**	43 46N	80 40W
Drayton Harb.	**66**	48 58N	122 46W
Drayton Plains	**77**	42 42N	83 23W
Drayton Valley	**60**	53 12N	114 58W
Drenthe □	**105**	52 52N	6 40 E
Dresden, Can.	**46**	42 35N	82 11W
Dresden, Ger.	**106**	51 2N	13 45 E
Dreux	**100**	48 44N	1 23 E
Drexel	**77**	39 45N	84 18W
Driffield	**94**	54 0N	0 25W
Driftwood, Can.	**34**	49 8N	81 23 E
Driftwood, U.S.A.	**70**	41 22N	78 9W
Driggs	**78**	43 50N	111 8W
Drina, R.	**109**	44 30N	19 10 E
Drinkwater	**56**	50 18N	105 8W
Dröbak	**111**	59 39N	10 48 E
Drocourt	**46**	45 46N	80 21W
Drogheda	**97**	53 45N	6 20W
Droichead Nua	**97**	53 11N	6 50W
Droitwich	**95**	52 16N	2 10W
Drôme □	**103**	44 38N	5 15 E
Drôme, R.	**103**	44 46N	4 46 E
Dromedary, C.	**136**	36 17 S	150 10 E
Dromore	**136**	32 25 S	143 55 E
Drowning, R.	**53**	50 54N	84 34W
Drumbo	**49**	43 16N	80 35W
Drumheller	**61**	51 25N	112 40W
Drummond, Can.	**39**	47 2N	67 41W
Drummond, Mich., U.S.A.	**46**	46 1N	83 50W
Drummond, Mont., U.S.A.	**78**	46 46N	113 4W
Drummond, Wis., U.S.A.	**52**	46 20N	91 15W
Drummond I.	**46**	46 0N	83 40W
Drummond Ra.	**135**	23 45 S	147 10 E
Drummondville	**41**	45 55N	72 25W
Drumquin	**49**	43 32N	79 47W
Drumright	**75**	35 59N	96 38W
Druzhina	**121**	68 14N	145 18 E
Dry Tortugas	**84**	24 38N	82 55W
Dryberry L.	**52**	49 33N	93 53W
Dryden, Can.	**52**	49 47N	92 50W
Dryden, U.S.A.	**75**	30 3N	102 3W
Drygalski I.	**91**	66 0 S	92 0 E
Drysdale, R.	**134**	13 59 S	126 51 E
Du Bois	**70**	41 8N	78 46W
Du Gas, L.	**38**	51 55N	75 12W
Du Gué, R.	**36**	57 21N	70 45W
Du Quoin	**76**	38 0N	89 10W
Duanesburg	**71**	42 45N	74 11W
Dubā	**122**	27 10N	35 40 E
Dubai = Dubayy	**123**	25 18N	55 20 E
Dubawnt, L.	**55**	63 4N	101 42W
Dubawnt, R.	**55**	64 33N	100 6W
Dubayy	**123**	25 18N	55 20 E
Dubbo	**136**	32 11 S	148 35 E
Duberger	**42**	46 49N	71 18W
Dublin, Can.	**70**	43 32N	81 18W
Dublin, Ireland	**97**	53 20N	6 18W
Dublin, Ga., U.S.A.	**73**	32 30N	83 0W
Dublin, Tex., U.S.A.	**75**	32 0N	98 20W
Dublin □	**97**	53 24N	6 20W
Dublin, B.	**97**	53 24N	6 20W
Dubois, Idaho, U.S.A.	**78**	44 7N	112 9W
Dubois, Ind., U.S.A.	**77**	38 26N	86 48W
Dubreuilville	**53**	48 21N	84 32W
Dubrovnik	**109**	42 39N	18 6 E
Dubrovskoye	**121**	58 55N	111 0 E
Dubuc	**57**	50 41N	102 28W
Dubuque	**76**	42 30N	90 41W
Duchesne	**78**	40 14N	110 22W
Duchess, Austral.	**135**	21 20 S	139 50 E
Duchess, Can.	**61**	50 43N	111 55W
Ducie I.	**15**	24 47 S	124 40W
Duck Bay	**57**	52 10N	100 9W
Duck Lake	**56**	52 50N	106 16W
Duck, Mt.	**55**	51 27N	100 35W
Duck Mt. Prov. Parks	**57**	51 45N	101 0W
Duckwall ,Mt.	**80**	37 58N	120 7W
Dudhi	**125**	24 15N	83 10 E
Dudinka	**121**	69 30N	86 0 E
Dudley	**95**	52 30N	2 5W
Duero, R.	**104**	41 37N	4 25W
Duffel	**105**	51 6N	4 30 E
Dufferin □	**49**	43 55N	80 15W
Duffin, R.	**51**	43 49N	79 2W
Dufrost, Pte.	**36**	60 4N	77 39W
Dugald	**58**	49 53N	96 51W
Dugger	**77**	39 4N	87 16W
Dugi Otok	**108**	44 0N	15 0 E
Duhak	**123**	33 20N	57 30 E
Duifken Pt.	**135**	12 33 S	141 38 E
Duisburg	**105**	51 27N	6 42 E
Duitama	**86**	5 50N	73 2W
Duke I.	**54**	54 50N	131 20W
Dukhan	**123**	25 25N	50 50 E
Duki	**124**	30 14N	68 25 E
Dulawan	**127**	7 5N	124 20 E
Dulce, Golfo	**84**	8 40N	83 20W
Dulce, R.	**88**	29 30 S	63 0W
Duluth	**52**	46 48N	92 10W
Dum Duma	**125**	27 40N	95 40 E
Dumaguete	**127**	9 17N	123 15 E
Dumai	**126**	1 35N	101 20 E
Dumaran I.	**127**	10 33N	119 50 E
Dumaring	**127**	1 46N	118 10 E
Dumas, Ark., U.S.A.	**75**	33 52N	91 30W
Dumas, Tex., U.S.A.	**75**	35 50N	101 58W
Dūmat al Jandal	**122**	29 55N	39 40 E
Dumbarton	**96**	55 58N	4 35W
Dumbell L.	**38**	52 28N	65 45W
Dumfries	**96**	55 4N	3 37W
Dumfries & Galloway □	**96**	54 30N	4 0W
Dumoine L.	**40**	46 55N	77 55W
Dumoine, R.	**40**	46 13N	77 51W
Dun Laoghaire, (Dunleary)	**97**	53 17N	6 9W
Dun-le-Palestel	**102**	46 18N	1 39 E
Dun-sur-Auron	**101**	46 53N	2 33 E
Dunaföldvár	**107**	46 50N	18 57 E
Dunback	**133**	45 23 S	170 36 E
Dunbar	**96**	56 0N	2 32W
Dunbarton	**51**	43 50N	79 7W
Dunblane	**96**	56 10N	3 58W
Duncan, Can.	**63**	48 45N	123 40W
Duncan, Ariz., U.S.A.	**79**	32 46N	109 6W
Duncan, Okla., U.S.A.	**75**	34 25N	98 0W
Duncan Dam	**63**	50 15N	116 56W
Duncan L.	**54**	62 51N	113 58W
Duncan, L.	**54**	53 29N	77 58W
Duncan, L.B.C.	**34**	50 20N	116 57W
Duncan Pass.	**128**	11 0N	92 30 E
Duncan Town	**84**	22 15N	75 45W
Duncannon	**70**	40 23N	77 2W
Dunchurch	**46**	45 39N	79 51W
Dundalk, Can.	**46**	44 10N	80 24W
Dundalk, Ireland	**97**	53 55N	6 45W
Dundalk, B.	**97**	53 55N	6 15W
Dundarave	**66**	49 20N	123 10W
Dundas, Can.	**48**	43 17N	79 59W
Dundas, Greenl.	**65**	77 0N	69 0W
Dundas I.	**54**	54 30N	130 50W
Dundas, L.	**134**	32 35 S	121 50 E
Dundas Pen.	**64**	74 50N	111 36W
Dundas Str.	**134**	11 15 S	131 35 E
Dundee, Can.	**43**	45 0N	74 30W
Dundee, S. Afr.	**117**	28 11 S	30 15 E
Dundee, U.K.	**96**	56 29N	3 0W
Dundee, U.S.A.	**77**	41 57N	83 40W
Dundrum	**97**	54 17N	5 50W
Dundrum B.	**97**	54 12N	5 40W
Dundurn	**56**	51 49N	106 30W
Dundurn Camp	**56**	51 51N	106 34W
Dunedin, N.Z.	**133**	45 50 S	170 33 E
Dunedin, U.S.A.	**73**	28 1N	82 45W
Dunedin, R.	**54**	59 30N	124 5W
Dunfermline	**96**	56 5N	3 28W
Dungannon, Can.	**46**	43 51N	81 36W
Dungannon, U.K.	**97**	54 30N	6 47W
Dungannon □	**97**	54 30N	6 55W
Dungarvan	**97**	52 6N	7 40W
Dungarvan Bay	**97**	52 5N	7 35W
Dungarvan Harb.	**97**	52 5N	7 35W
Dungarvon, R.	**39**	46 49N	65 54W
Dungbure Shan	**129**	35 0N	90 0 E
Dungeness	**95**	50 54N	0 59 E
Dungog	**136**	32 22 S	151 40 E
Dungu	**116**	2 32N	28 22 E
Dunham	**43**	45 8N	72 48W
Dunière, Parc Prov. de	**38**	48 45N	66 41W
Dunières	**103**	45 13N	4 20 E
Dunkeld	**96**	56 34N	3 36W
Dunkerque	**101**	51 2N	2 20 E
Dunkery Beacon	**95**	51 15N	3 37W
Dunkirk	**70**	42 30N	79 18W
Dunkirk = Dunkerque	**101**	51 2N	2 20 E
Dunkley	**63**	53 17N	122 28W
Dunlap	**74**	41 50N	95 30W
Dunmanus B.	**97**	51 31N	9 50W
Dunmore, Can.	**61**	49 58N	110 36W
Dunmore, U.S.A.	**71**	41 27N	75 38W
Dunmore Town	**84**	25 30N	76 39W
Dunn	**73**	35 18N	78 36W
Dunnellon	**73**	29 4N	82 28W
Dunnet Hd.	**96**	58 38N	3 22W
Dunning	**74**	41 52N	100 4W
Dunnville	**46**	42 54N	79 36W
Dunoon	**96**	55 57N	4 56W
Dunrankin, R.	**53**	48 47N	82 51W
Duns	**96**	55 47N	2 20W
Dunseith	**74**	48 49N	100 2W
Dunsmuir	**78**	41 10N	122 10W
Dunstable	**95**	51 53N	0 31W
Dunstan Mts.	**133**	44 53 S	169 35 E
Dunster	**63**	53 8N	119 50W
Dunărea, R.	**107**	45 0N	29 40 E
Dunvegan	**60**	55 55N	118 36W
Dunvegan L.	**55**	60 8N	107 10W
Dunville	**37**	47 16N	53 54W
Duparquet	**40**	48 30N	79 14W
Duparquet, L.	**40**	48 28N	79 16W
Dupree	**74**	45 4N	101 35W
Dupuy	**40**	48 50N	79 21W
Dupuyer	**78**	48 11N	112 31W
Duque de Caxias	**89**	22 45 S	43 19W
Duquesne	**70**	40 22N	79 55W
Durack Ra.	**134**	16 50 S	127 40 E
Durance, R.	**103**	43 55N	4 45 E
Durand, Ill., U.S.A.	**76**	42 26N	89 20W
Durand, Mich., U.S.A.	**77**	42 54N	83 58W
Durango, Mexico	**82**	24 3N	104 39W
Durango, Spain	**104**	43 13N	2 40W
Durango, U.S.A.	**79**	37 10N	107 50W
Durango □	**82**	25 0N	105 0W
Durant, Iowa, U.S.A.	**76**	41 36N	90 54W
Durant, Okla., U.S.A.	**75**	34 0N	96 25W
Durazno	**88**	33 25 S	56 38W
Durban, France	**102**	43 0N	2 49 E
Durban, S. Afr.	**117**	29 49 S	31 1 E
Düren	**105**	50 48N	6 30 E
Durg	**125**	21 15N	81 22 E
Durham, Can.	**46**	44 10N	80 49W
Durham, U.K.	**94**	54 47N	1 34W
Durham, Calif., U.S.A.	**80**	39 39N	121 48W
Durham, N.C., U.S.A.	**73**	36 0N	78 55W
Durham □, Can.	**51**	43 57N	79 5W
Durham □, U.K.	**94**	54 42N	1 45W
Durham Bridge	**39**	46 7N	66 36W
Durmitor Mt.	**109**	43 10N	19 0 E
Durocher, L.	**38**	50 52N	61 12W
Durrës	**109**	41 19N	19 28 E
Durtal	**100**	47 40N	0 18W
D'Urville Island	**133**	40 50 S	173 55 E
Duryea	**71**	41 20N	75 45W
Dusey, R.	**53**	51 11N	86 21W
Dushak	**120**	37 20N	60 10 E
Dushanbe	**120**	38 33N	68 48 E
Dusky Sd.	**133**	45 47 S	166 30 E
Düsseldorf	**105**	51 15N	6 46 E
Dutch Harbour	**67**	53 54N	166 35W
Dutton	**46**	42 39N	81 30W
Duval	**56**	51 9N	104 59W
Duvernay	**44**	45 35N	73 40W
Duwadami	**122**	24 35N	44 15 E
Duzdab = Zāhedān	**123**	29 30N	60 50 E
Dwarka	**124**	22 18N	69 8 E
Dwight, Can.	**47**	45 20N	79 1W
Dwight, U.S.A.	**77**	41 5N	88 25W
Dyer	**77**	37 24N	86 13W
Dyer's B.	**70**	45 9N	81 24W
Dyersburg	**75**	36 2N	89 20W
Dyersville	**76**	42 29N	91 8W
Dyfed □	**95**	52 0N	4 30W
Dyment	**52**	49 37N	92 18W
Dysart	**56**	50 57N	104 2W
Dzerzhinsk	**120**	53 40N	27 7 E
Dzhailma	**120**	51 30N	61 50 E
Dzhalinda	**121**	53 40N	124 0 E
Dzhambul	**120**	42 54N	71 22 E
Dzhardzhan	**121**	68 10N	123 5 E
Dzhelinde	**121**	70 0N	114 20 E
Dzhetygara	**120**	52 11N	61 12 E
Dzhezkazgan	**120**	47 10N	67 40 E
Dzhizak	**120**	40 6N	67 50 E
Dzhugdzur, Khrebet	**121**	57 30N	138 0 E
Dzhungarskiye Vorota	**120**	45 0N	82 0 E
Dzibilchaltún	**83**	21 5N	89 36W
Dzilam de Bravo	**83**	21 24N	88 53W
Dzungaria	**129**	44 10N	88 0 E
Dzuunbulag	**130**	46 58N	115 30 E
Dzuunmod	**130**	47 45N	106 58 E

E

Eabamet, L.	**53**	51 30N	87 46W
Eads	**74**	38 30N	102 46W
Eagle, Alaska, U.S.A.	**67**	64 44N	141 29W
Eagle, Colo., U.S.A.	**78**	39 45N	106 55W
Eagle Butt	**74**	45 1N	101 12W
Eagle Cr.	**56**	52 20N	107 30W
Eagle Creek, R.	**77**	38 36N	85 46W
Eagle Grove	**76**	42 37N	93 53W
Eagle I.	**57**	53 40N	98 55W
Eagle L., B.C., Can.	**62**	51 55N	124 23W
Eagle L., Ont., Can.	**52**	49 42N	93 13W
Eagle L., Calif., U.S.A.	**78**	40 35N	120 50W
Eagle L., Me., U.S.A.	**35**	46 23N	69 22W
Eagle Lake, Can.	**47**	45 8N	78 29W
Eagle Lake, U.S.A.	**75**	29 35N	96 21W
Eagle Mountain	**81**	33 52N	115 26W
Eagle Nest	**79**	36 33N	105 13W
Eagle Pass	**75**	28 45N	100 35W
Eagle Pk.	**80**	38 10N	119 25W
Eagle, R.	**36**	53 36N	57 26W
Eagle River, Can.	**52**	49 47N	93 12W
Eagle River, Mich., U.S.A.	**52**	47 24N	88 18W
Eagle River, Wis., U.S.A.	**74**	45 55N	89 17W
Eaglehawk	**136**	36 43 S	144 16 E
Eaglehead L.	**52**	49 2N	89 12W
Eaglesham	**60**	55 47N	117 53W
Eagleville	**76**	40 28N	93 59W
Ealing	**95**	51 30N	0 19W
Ear Falls	**52**	50 38N	93 13W
Earl Grey	**56**	50 57N	104 43W
Earle	**75**	35 18N	90 26W
Earlimart	**81**	35 53N	119 16W
Earls Cove	**62**	49 45N	124 0W
Earltown	**39**	45 35N	63 8W
Earlville	**77**	41 35N	88 55W
Earn, L.	**96**	56 23N	4 14W
Earn, R.	**96**	56 20N	3 19W
Earnslaw, Mt.	**133**	44 32 S	168 27 E
Earth	**75**	34 18N	102 30W
Easley	**73**	34 52N	82 35W
East Angus	**41**	45 30N	71 40W
East Aurora	**70**	42 46N	78 38W
East, B.	**75**	29 2N	89 16W
East Bathurst	**35**	47 35N	65 40W
East Bay	**39**	46 1N	60 25W
East Bengal	**125**	24 0N	90 0 E
East Brady	**70**	40 59N	79 36W
East Broughton Station	**41**	46 14N	71 5W
East C.	**133**	37 42 S	178 35 E
East Chezzetcook	**39**	44 43N	63 14W
East Chicago	**77**	41 40N	87 30W
East China Sea	**131**	30 5N	126 0 E
East Coulee	**61**	51 23N	112 27W
East Detroit	**46**	42 28N	82 56W
East Don, R.	**50**	43 39N	79 21W
East Dubuque	**76**	42 29N	90 39W
East Falkland	**90**	51 30 S	58 30W
East Farnham	**43**	45 14N	72 46W
East Florenceville	**35**	46 26N	67 36W
East Fork, R.	**77**	38 33N	87 14W
East Franklin	**43**	44 59N	72 48W
East Grand Forks	**74**	47 55N	97 5W
East Greenwich	**71**	41 39N	71 27W
East Harbour	**66**	49 22N	123 16W
East Hartford	**71**	41 45N	72 39W
East Helena	**78**	46 37N	111 58W
East Humber, R.	**50**	43 48N	79 35W
East Indies	**126**	0 0	120 0 E
East Jordan	**46**	45 10N	85 7W
East Kildonan	**58**	49 55N	97 5W
East Lansing	**77**	42 44N	84 29W
East Liverpool	**70**	40 39N	80 35W
East London	**117**	33 0 S	27 55 E
East Los Angeles	**81**	34 1N	118 9W
East Moline	**76**	41 31N	90 25W
East P.	**39**	46 27N	61 58W
East Palestine	**70**	40 50N	80 32W
East Peoria	**76**	40 40N	89 34W
East Pine	**54**	55 48N	120 5W
East Point	**73**	33 40N	84 28W
East Providence	**71**	41 48N	71 22W
East Retford	**94**	53 19N	0 55W
East St. Louis	**76**	38 37N	90 9W
East Sd.	**63**	48 45N	123 0W
E. Siberian Sea	**121**	73 0N	160 0 E
East Stroudsburg	**71**	41 1N	75 11W
East Suffolk □	**95**	52 15N	1 20 E
East Sussex □	**95**	50 55N	0 20 E
East Tawas	**46**	44 17N	83 31W
East Thurlow I.	**62**	50 24N	125 25W
East Trout L.	**56**	54 22N	105 5W
East Troy	**77**	42 47N	88 24W
East Walker, R.	**80**	38 52N	119 10W
East York	**50**	43 42N	79 20W
Eastbourne, N.Z.	**133**	41 19 S	174 55 E
Eastbourne, U.K.	**95**	50 46N	0 18 E
Eastcap Cr.	**66**	49 27N	123 6W
Eastend	**56**	49 32N	108 50W
Eastern Ghats	**124**	15 0N	80 0 E
Eastern Passage	**39**	44 37N	63 30W
Easterville	**57**	53 8N	99 49W
Easthampton	**71**	42 15N	72 41W
Eastland	**75**	32 26N	98 45W
Eastleigh	**95**	50 58N	1 21W
Eastmain (East Main)	**36**	52 20N	78 30W
Eastmain, R.	**36**	52 27N	72 26W
Eastman, Can.	**41**	45 18N	72 19W
Eastman, Ga., U.S.A.	**73**	32 13N	83 20W
Eastman, Wis., U.S.A.	**76**	43 10N	91 1W
Easton, Md., U.S.A.	**72**	38 47N	76 7W
Easton, Pa., U.S.A.	**71**	40 41N	75 15W
Easton, Wash., U.S.A.	**80**	47 14N	121 8W
Eastport	**35**	44 57N	67 0W
Eastsound	**80**	48 42N	122 55W
Eastview	**34**	45 27N	75 40W
Eaton, Colo., U.S.A.	**74**	40 35N	104 42W
Eaton, Ohio, U.S.A.	**77**	39 45N	84 38W
Eaton Rapids	**77**	42 31N	84 39W
Eatonia	**56**	51 13N	109 25W

Eatonton Emmeloord

Eatonton 73 33 22N 83 24W
Eatonville, Can. 41 47 20N 69 41W
Eatonville, U.S.A. 80 46 52N 122 16W
Eau Claire, S.C., U.S.A. 73 34 5N 81 2W
Eau Claire, Wis., U.S.A. 74 44 46N 91 30W
Eau-Claire, L. à l' 38 52 36N 65 50W
Eau Claire, L. à l' 36 56 10N 74 25W
Eauze 102 43 53N 0 7E
Ebbw Vale 95 51 47N 3 12W
Ebeltoft 111 56 12N 10 41E
Ebensburg 70 40 29N 78 43W
Eberswalde 106 52 49N 13 50E
Eboli 108 40 39N 15 2E
Ebolowa 116 2 55N 11 10E
Eboulements, Les 41 47 28N 70 21W
Ebro, R. 104 41 49N 1 5W
Éceuillé 100 47 10N 1 19E
Echaneni 121 27 33S 32 6E
Echelles, Les 103 45 27N 5 45E
Echo Bay 46 46 29N 84 4W
Echo Bay (Port Radium) 64 66 05N 117 55W
Echoing, R. 55 55 51N 92 5W
Échouani, L. 40 47 46N 75 42W
Echternach 105 49 49N 6 3E
Echuca 136 36 3S 144 46E
Ecija 104 37 30N 5 10W
Eckville 61 52 21N 114 22W
Eclipse Sd. 65 72 38N 79 0W
Écommoy 100 47 50N 0 17E
Écorce, L. de l' 40 47 5N 76 24W
Ecorces, L. des 43 46 0N 74 32W
Ecorse 77 42 14N 83 10W
Écos 101 49 9N 1 35E
Écouché 100 48 42N 0 10W
Ecuador ■ 86 2 0S 78 0W
Ecueils, Pte. aux 36 59 47N 77 50W
Ecum Secum 39 44 58N 62 8W
Ed Damer 115 17 27N 34 0E
Edam, Can. 56 53 11N 108 46W
Edam, Neth. 105 52 31N 5 3E
Eday, I. 96 59 11N 2 47W
Edberg 61 52 47N 112 47W
Eddrachillis B. 96 58 16N 5 10W
Eddystone 95 50 11N 4 16W
Eddyville 76 41 9N 92 38W
Ede 105 52 4N 5 40E
Edea 116 3 51N 10 9E
Edehon L. 55 60 25N 97 15W
Eden, Austral. 136 37 3S 149 55E
Eden, Can. 57 50 23N 99 28W
Eden, N.Y., U.S.A. 70 42 39N 78 55W
Eden, Tex., U.S.A. 75 31 16N 99 50W
Eden, Wyo., U.S.A. 78 42 2N 109 27W
Eden L. 55 56 38N 100 15W
Eden Mills 49 43 35N 80 9W
Eden, R. 94 54 57N 3 2W
Edenderry 97 53 21N 7 3W
Edenton 73 36 5N 76 36W
Edgar 74 40 25N 98 0W
Edgartown 71 41 22N 70 28W
Edge Hill 95 52 7N 1 28W
Edge I. 17 77 45N 22 30E
Edgefield 73 33 43N 81 59W
Edgeley, Can. 50 43 48N 79 31W
Edgeley, U.S.A. 74 46 27N 98 41W
Edgemont 74 43 15N 103 53W
Edgeøya 17 77 45N 22 30E
Edgerton, Can. 61 52 45N 110 27W
Edgerton, Ohio, U.S.A. 77 41 27N 84 45W
Edgerton, Wis., U.S.A. 76 42 50N 89 4W
Edgewater 61 50 42N 116 5W
Edgewood, Can. 63 49 47N 118 8W
Edgewood, U.S.A. 77 38 55N 88 40W
Edgington 70 45 24N 79 46W
Edhessa 109 40 48N 22 5E
Edievale 133 45 49S 169 22E
Edina 76 40 6N 92 10W
Edinburg, Ill., U.S.A. 76 39 39N 89 23W
Edinburg, Ind., U.S.A. 77 39 21N 85 58W
Edinburg, Tex., U.S.A. 75 26 22N 98 10W
Edinburgh 96 55 57N 3 12W
Edirne 109 41 40N 26 45E
Edison, Calif., U.S.A. 81 35 21N 118 52W
Edison, Wash., U.S.A. 80 48 33N 122 27W
Edmeston 71 42 42N 75 15W
Edmond 75 35 37N 97 30W
Edmonds, Can. 66 49 13N 122 57W
Edmonds, U.S.A. 80 47 47N 122 22W
Edmonton 59 53 30N 113 30W
Edmore 46 43 25N 85 3W
Edmund L. 55 54 45N 93 17W
Edmundston 39 47 23N 68 20W
Edna 75 29 0N 96 40W
Edna Bay 54 55 55N 133 40W
Edremit 122 39 40N 27 0E
Edsel Ford Ra. 91 77 0S 143 0W
Edson 60 53 35N 116 28W
Eduardo Castex 88 35 50S 64 25W
Edward I. 52 48 22N 88 37W
Edward, L. (Idi Amin Dada, L.) 116 0 25S 29 40E
Edward, R. 136 35 0S 143 30E
Edward VII Pen. 91 80 0S 160 0W
Edwards 81 34 55N 117 51W
Edwards Plat. 75 30 30N 101 5W
Edwards, R. 76 41 10N 90 59W
Edwardsburg 77 41 48N 86 6W
Edwardsport 77 38 49N 87 15W
Edwardsville, Ill., U.S.A. 76 38 49N 89 57W
Edwardsville, Pa., U.S.A. 71 41 15N 75 56W
Edzo 54 62 49N 116 4W
Eek 67 60 10N 162 0W
Eekloo 105 51 11N 3 33E
Eel, R., Ind., U.S.A. 77 39 7N 86 58W
Eel, R., Ind., U.S.A. 77 40 45N 86 22W
Eel River Crossing 39 48 1N 66 25W
Eernegem 105 51 8N 3 2E
Effingham 77 39 8N 88 30W
Égadi, Ísole 108 37 55N 12 10E
Eganville 47 45 32N 77 5W
Egeland 74 48 42N 99 6W
Egenolf L. 55 59 3N 100 0W
Eger 107 47 53N 20 27E
Egersund = Eigersund 111 58 26N 6 1E
Egerton, Mt. 134 24 42S 117 44E
Egg L. 55 55 5N 105 30W
Eggertsville 49 42 58N 78 46W
Égletons 102 45 24N 2 3E
Eglington I. 64 75 48N 118 30W
Egmont 62 49 45N 123 56W
Egmont B. 39 46 29N 64 6W
Egmont, C. 133 39 16S 173 45E
Egmont, Mt. 133 39 17S 174 5E
Eğridir Gölü 122 37 53N 30 50E
Egua 86 5 5N 68 0W
Éguzon 102 46 27N 1 33E
Egvekinot 121 66 19N 179 50W
Egypt ■ 115 28 0N 31 0E
Ehime-ken □ 132 33 30N 132 40E
Eholt 63 49 10N 118 34W
Ehrenburg 81 33 36N 114 31W
Eidsvoll 111 60 19N 11 14E
Eifel 105 50 10N 6 45E
Eigersund 111 58 26N 6 1E
Eigg, I. 96 56 54N 6 10W
Eighty Mile Beach 134 19 30S 120 40E
Eil 115 8 0N 49 50E
Eil, L. 96 56 50N 5 15W
Eilat 122 29 30N 34 56E
Eildon, L. 136 37 10S 146 0E
Eileen L. 55 62 16N 107 37W
Einasleigh 135 18 32S 144 5E
Eindhoven 105 51 26N 5 30E
Eiríksjökull 110 64 46N 20 24W
Eirunepé 86 6 35S 70 0W
Eisenach 106 50 58N 10 18E
Eisenerz 106 47 32N 14 54E
Ejido 86 8 33N 71 14W
Ejutla 83 16 34N 96 44W
Ekalaka 74 45 55N 104 30W
Eketahuna 133 40 38S 175 43E
Ekibastuz 120 51 40N 75 22E
Ekimchan 121 53 0N 133 0W
Ekwan Pt. 34 53 16N 82 7W
Ekwan, R. 34 53 12N 82 15W
El Baúl 86 8 57N 68 17W
El Bluff 84 11 59N 83 40W
El Cajon 81 32 49N 117 0W
El Callao 86 7 25N 61 50W
El Campo 75 29 10N 96 20W
El Carmen 86 1 16N 66 52W
El Centro 81 32 50N 115 40W
El Cerro 86 17 30S 61 40W
El Cocuy 86 6 25N 72 27W
El Compadre 81 32 20N 116 14W
El Cuy 90 39 55S 68 25W
El Cuyo 83 21 30N 87 40W
El Dátil 82 30 7N 112 15W
El Dere 115 3 50N 47 8E
El Diaz 83 21 1N 87 17W
El Dificul 86 9 51N 74 14W
El Dios 82 20 40N 87 20W
El Diviso 86 1 22N 78 14W
El Djouf 114 20 0N 11 30E
El Dorado, Colomb. 86 1 11N 71 52W
El Dorado, Ark., U.S.A. 75 33 10N 92 40W
El Dorado, Kans., U.S.A. 75 37 55N 96 56W
El Dorado, Venez. 86 6 55N 61 30W
El Dorado Springs 76 37 54N 93 59W
El Escorial 104 40 35N 4 7W
El Faiyûm 115 29 19N 30 50E
El Fâsher 115 13 33N 25 26E
El Ferrol 104 43 29N 3 14W
El Fuerte 82 26 30N 108 40W
El Iskandarîya 115 31 0N 30 0E
El Khârga 115 25 30N 30 33E
El Khartûm 115 15 31N 32 35E
El Ladhiqiya 122 35 20N 35 30E
El Mahalla el Kubra 115 31 0N 31 0E
El Mansûra 122 31 0N 31 19E
El Mantico 86 7 27N 62 32W
El Miamo 86 7 39N 61 46W
El Milagro 88 30 59S 65 59W
El Minyâ 115 28 7N 30 33E
El Monte 81 34 4N 118 2W
El Obeid 115 13 8N 30 10E
El Oro = Sta. Maria del Oro 82 25 50N 105 20W
El Oro de Hidalgo 83 19 48N 100 8W
El Palmar 86 7 58N 61 53W
El Palmito, Presa 82 25 40N 105 3W
El Pao 86 9 38N 68 8W
El Paso, Ill., U.S.A. 76 40 44N 89 1W
El Paso, Tex., U.S.A. 79 31 50N 106 30W
El Paso Robles 80 35 38N 120 41W
El Pilar 86 10 32N 63 9W
El Portal 80 37 44N 119 49W
El Porvenir, Mexico 82 31 15N 105 51W
El Porvenir, Venez. 86 4 42N 71 19W
El Progreso 84 15 26N 87 51W
El Pueblito 82 29 3N 105 4W
El Qahira 115 30 1N 31 14E
El Qasr 115 25 44N 28 42E
El Reno 75 35 30N 98 0W
El Rio 81 34 14N 119 10W
El Salado 86 8 56N 73 55W
El Salto 82 23 47N 105 22W
El Salvador ■ 84 13 50N 89 0W
El Sauce 84 13 0N 86 40W
El Suweis 115 29 58N 32 31E
El Temblador 86 8 59N 62 44W
El Tigre 86 8 55N 64 15W
El Tocuyo 86 9 47N 69 48W
El Tofo 88 29 22S 71 18W
El Tránsito 88 28 52S 70 17W
El Turbio 90 51 30S 72 40W
El Vigía 86 8 38N 71 39W
El Wak 116 2 49N 40 56E
Elaho, R. 62 50 7N 123 23W
Elat 127 5 40S 133 5E
Elâziğ 122 38 37N 39 22E
Elba 73 31 27N 86 4W
Elba, I. 108 42 48N 10 15E
Elbasani 109 41 9N 20 9E
Elbe 80 46 45N 121 49W
Elbe, R. 106 53 15N 10 7E
Elberfeld 77 38 10N 87 27W
Elbert, Mt. 79 39 12N 106 36W
Elberta, Mich., U.S.A. 72 44 35N 86 14W
Elberta, N.Y., U.S.A. 49 43 16N 78 52W
Elberton 73 34 7N 82 51W
Elbeuf 100 49 17N 1 2E
Elblag 107 54 10N 19 25E
Elbow 56 51 7N 106 35W
Elbow, R. 59 51 3N 114 2W
Elbrus, Mt. 120 43 30N 42 30E
Elburg 105 52 26N 5 50E
Elburn 77 41 54N 88 28W
Elburz Mts. = Alborz 123 36 0N 52 0E
Elche 104 38 15N 0 42W
Elcho I. 134 11 55S 135 45E
Eldon, Iowa, U.S.A. 76 40 50N 92 12W
Eldon, Mo., U.S.A. 76 38 20N 92 38W
Eldora 76 42 20N 93 5W
Eldorado, Argent. 89 26 28S 54 43W
Eldorado, Ont., Can. 47 44 35N 77 31W
Eldorado, Sask., Can. 55 59 35N 108 30W
Eldorado, Mexico 82 24 0N 107 30W
Eldorado, Ill., U.S.A. 77 37 50N 88 25W
Eldorado, Tex., U.S.A. 75 30 52N 100 35W
Eldorado Park 50 43 39N 79 46W
Eldoret 116 0 30N 35 25E
Eldred 70 41 57N 78 24W
Eldridge 76 41 39N 90 35W
Electra 75 34 0N 99 0W
Eleele 67 21 54N 159 35W
Elephant Butte Res. 79 33 45N 107 30W
Elephant I. 91 61 0S 55 0W
Eleuthera I. 84 25 0N 76 20W
Elfin Cove 67 58 11N 136 20W
Elfrida 48 43 10N 79 47W
Elgin, B.C., Can. 66 49 4N 122 49W
Elgin, Man., Can. 57 49 27N 100 16W
Elgin, N.B., Can. 35 45 48N 65 10W
Elgin, Ont., Can. 47 44 36N 76 13W
Elgin, Ont., Can. 71 44 37N 76 15W
Elgin, U.K. 96 57 39N 3 20W
Elgin, Ill., U.S.A. 77 42 0N 88 20W
Elgin, N.D., U.S.A. 74 46 24N 101 46W
Elgin, Nebr., U.S.A. 74 41 58N 98 3W
Elgin, Nev., U.S.A. 79 37 27N 114 36W
Elgin, Oreg., U.S.A. 78 45 37N 118 0W
Elgin, Texas, U.S.A. 75 30 21N 97 22W
Elgon, Mt. 116 1 10N 34 30E
Eliase 127 8 10S 130 55E
Elida 75 33 56N 103 41W
Elie 55 49 48N 97 52W
Elim 67 64 35N 162 20W
Elisabethville = Lubumbashi 117 11 32S 27 38E
Elista 120 46 16N 44 14E
Elizabeth, Austral. 135 34 42S 138 41E
Elizabeth, Ill., U.S.A. 76 42 19N 90 13W
Elizabeth, N.J., U.S.A. 71 40 37N 74 12W
Elizabeth City 73 36 18N 76 16W
Elizabethton 73 36 20N 82 13W
Elizabethtown, Ill., U.S.A. 77 37 27N 88 18W
Elizabethtown, Ky., U.S.A. 72 37 40N 85 54W
Elizabethtown, N.Y., U.S.A. 71 44 13N 73 36W
Elizabethtown, Pa., U.S.A. 71 40 8N 76 36W
Elk City 75 35 25N 99 25W
Elk Creek 80 39 36N 122 32W
Elk Grove 80 38 25N 121 22W
Elk Island Nat. Park 60 53 35N 112 59W
Elk Lake 34 47 40N 80 25W
Elk Lakes Prov. Pzrk 61 50 30N 115 10W
Elk Point 60 53 54N 110 55W
Elk, R. 61 49 11N 115 14W
Elk Rapids 46 44 54N 85 25W
Elk River, Idaho, U.S.A. 78 46 50N 116 8W
Elk River, Minn., U.S.A. 74 45 17N 93 34W
Elkader 76 42 51N 91 24W
Elkford 61 49 52N 114 53W
Elkhart, Ind., U.S.A. 77 41 42N 85 55W
Elkhart, Kans., U.S.A. 75 37 3N 101 54W
Elkhart, R. 77 41 41N 85 58W
Elkhorn, Can. 57 49 59N 101 14W
Elkhorn, U.S.A. 77 42 40N 88 33W
Elkhorn, R. 74 42 0N 98 15W
Elkhovo 109 42 10N 26 40E
Elkin 73 36 17N 80 50W
Elkins 72 38 53N 79 53W
Elko, Can. 61 49 20N 115 10W
Elko, U.S.A. 78 40 50N 115 50W
Elkton 46 43 49N 83 11W
Ellef Ringnes I. 65 78 30N 102 2W
Ellen, Mt. 79 38 4N 110 56W
Ellendale, Can. 39 44 41N 63 33W
Ellendale, U.S.A. 74 46 3N 98 30W
Ellensburg 78 47 0N 120 30W
Ellenville 71 41 42N 74 23W
Ellerslie 59 53 26N 113 30W
Ellery, Mt. 136 37 28S 148 40E
Ellesmere I. 65 79 30N 80 0W
Ellesmere, L. 15 43 46S 172 27E
Ellesworth Land 91 74 0S 85 0W
Ellettsville 77 39 14N 86 38W
*Ellice Is. 14 8 0S 176 0E
Ellinwood 74 38 27N 98 37W
Elliot L. 57 52 54N 95 18W
Elliot Lake 46 46 25N 82 35W
Ellis 74 39 0N 99 39W
Elliston 37 48 38N 53 3W
Ellisville 73 31 38N 89 12W
Ellon 96 57 21N 2 5W
Ellore = Eluru 125 16 48N 81 8E
Ells, R. 60 57 18N 111 40W
Ellsworth 74 38 47N 98 15W
Ellsworth Land 91 76 0S 89 0W
Ellwood City 70 40 52N 80 19W
Elm Grove 58 49 47N 96 49W
Elma, Can. 57 49 52N 95 55W
Elma, U.S.A. 80 47 0N 123 30E
Elmer 76 39 57N 92 39W
Elmhurst 77 41 52N 87 58W
Elmira, Ont., Can. 49 43 36N 80 33W
Elmira, P.E.I., Can. 35 46 30N 61 59W
Elmira, U.S.A. 70 42 8N 76 49W
Elmore, Austral. 136 36 30S 144 37E
Elmore, Calif., U.S.A. 81 33 7N 115 49W
Elmore, Minn., U.S.A. 77 41 29N 83 18W
Elmsdale 39 44 58N 63 30W
Elmvale 46 44 35N 79 52W
Elmwood, Can. 70 44 14N 81 3W
Elmwood, U.S.A. 76 40 47N 89 58W
Elmworth 60 55 3N 119 37W
Elnora, Can. 61 51 59N 113 12W
Elnora, U.S.A. 77 38 53N 87 5W
Elora 49 43 41N 80 26W
Elorza 86 7 3N 69 31W
Eloy 79 32 46N 111 46W
Éloyes 101 48 6N 6 36E
Elphin 47 44 55N 76 37W
Elphinstone 57 50 32N 100 30W
Elrose 56 51 12N 108 0W
Elsa 64 63 55N 135 29W
Elsas 53 48 32N 82 55W
Elsie, Mich., U.S.A. 46 43 5N 84 23W
Elsie, Oreg., U.S.A. 80 45 52N 123 35W
Elsinore, Cal., U.S.A. 81 33 40N 117 15W
Elsinore, Utah, U.S.A. 79 38 40N 112 2W
Elson 80 47 32N 123 4W
Elsona 66 49 12N 122 57W
Elst 105 51 55N 5 51E
Eltham 133 39 26S 174 19E
Eluru 125 16 48N 81 8E
Elvas 104 38 50N 7 17W
Elven 100 47 44N 2 36W
Elverum 111 60 53N 11 34E
Elvire, Mt. 136 29 14S 119 33E
Elwood, Ill., U.S.A. 77 41 24N 88 7W
Elwood, Ind., U.S.A. 77 40 20N 85 50W
Elwood, Nebr., U.S.A. 74 40 38N 99 51W
Ely, U.K. 95 52 24N 0 16E
Ely, Minn., U.S.A. 52 47 54N 91 52W
Ely, Nev., U.S.A. 78 39 10N 114 50W
Elyria 70 41 22N 82 8W
Emba 120 48 50N 58 8E
Emba, R. 120 48 0N 56 0E
Embarcación 88 23 10S 64 0W
Embarras Portage 55 58 27N 111 28W
Embarrass, R. 77 38 39N 87 37W
Embro 46 43 9N 80 54W
Embrun 103 44 34N 6 30E
Embu 116 0 32S 37 38E
Emden 105 53 22N 7 12E
Emerald 135 23 32S 148 10E
Emeril 36 47 26N 75 47W
Emerson 57 49 0N 97 10W
Emery 79 38 59N 111 17W
Emery Park 79 32 10N 110 59W
Emi Koussi, Mt. 114 20 0N 18 55E
Emilia-Romagna □ 108 44 33N 10 40E
Eminence 77 38 22N 85 11W
Emlenton 70 41 11N 79 41W
Emmeloord 105 52 44N 5 46E

** Renamed Tuvalu ■*

Emmen Eyre Pen

Emmen 105 52 48N 6 57E
Emmerich 105 51 50N 6 12E
Emmetsburg 76 43 3N 94 40W
Emmett, Idaho, U.S.A. 78 43 51N 116 33W
Emmett, Mich., U.S.A. 46 42 59N 82 46W
Emo 52 48 38N 93 50W
Empalme 82 28 1N 110 49W
Empangeni 117 28 50S 31 52E
Empedrado 88 28 0S 58 46W
Emporia, Kans., U.S.A. 74 38 25N 96 16W
Emporia, Va., U.S.A. 73 36 41N 77 32W
Emporium 70 41 30N 78 17W
Empress 61 50 57N 110 0W
Ems, R. 105 52 37N 7 16E
Emsdale 46 45 32N 79 19W
Emsdetten 105 52 11N 7 31E
En Nahud 115 12 45N 28 25E
Enambú 86 1 1N 70 17W
Enard B. 96 58 5N 5 20W
Encantadas, Serra 89 30 40S 53 0W
Encanto, Cape 127 15 44N 121 40E
Encarnación 89 27 15S 56 0W
Encarnación de Diaz 82 21 30N 102 20W
Encinal 75 28 3N 99 25W
Encinillas 82 33 3N 117 17W
Encinitas 81 33 3N 117 17W
Encino 79 34 38N 105 40W
Encounter B. 135 35 45S 138 45E
Endako 62 54 6N 125 2W
Endau 128 2 40N 103 38E
Endau, R. 128 2 30N 103 30E
Ende 127 8 45S 121 30E
Endeavour 56 52 10N 102 39W
Endeavour Str. 135 10 45S 142 0E
Enderbury I. 15 3 8S 171 5W
Enderby 63 50 35N 119 10W
Enderby Land 91 66 0S 53 0E
Enderlin 74 46 45N 97 41W
Endicott, N.Y., U.S.A. 71 42 6N 76 2W
Endicott, Wash., U.S.A. 78 47 0N 117 45W
Endicott Mts. 67 68 0N 152 30W
Enez 109 40 45N 26 5E
Enfield, Can. 39 44 56N 63 32W
Enfield, U.K. 95 51 39N 0 4W
Enfield, U.S.A. 77 38 56N 88 20W
Engadin 106 46 45N 10 10E
Engadine 46 46 4N 85 38W
Engano, C. 85 18 30N 68 20W
Engaño, C. 127 18 35N 122 23E
Engels 120 51 28N 46 6E
Engemann L. 55 58 0N 106 55W
Enggano, I. 126 5 20S 102 40E
Enghien 105 50 37N 4 2E
Engkilili 126 1 3N 111 42E
England 75 34 30N 91 58W
England □ 94 53 0N 2 0W
Englee 37 50 45N 56 5W
Englefeld 56 52 10N 104 39W
Englefield, C. 65 69 49N 85 34W
Englehart 34 47 49N 79 52W
Engler L. 55 59 8N 106 52W
Englewood, U.S.A. 77 39 53N 84 18W
Englewood, Colo., U.S.A. 74 39 40N 105 0W
Englewood, Kans., U.S.A. 75 37 7N 99 59W
English 77 38 20N 86 28W
English B. 66 49 17N 123 11W
English Bazar 125 24 58N 88 21E
English Channel 95 50 0N 2 0W
English Company Is. 135 12 0S 137 0E
English Harbour East 37 47 38N 54 54W
English, R., Ont., Can. 52 50 35N 93 30W
English, R., Ont., Can. 52 49 12N 91 5W
English, R., U.S.A. 76 41 29N 91 32W
English River 52 49 20N 91 0W
Engteng (Yungting) 131 24 46N 116 45E
Enid 75 36 26N 97 52W
Enilda 60 55 25N 116 18W
*Eniwetok 15 11 30N 152 16E
Enkhuizen 105 52 42N 5 17E
Enna 108 37 34N 14 15E
Ennadai 55 61 8N 100 53W
Ennadai L. 55 61 0N 101 0W
Ennedi, reg. 115 19 20N 28 0E
Ennis, Ireland 97 52 51N 8 59W
Ennis, Mont., U.S.A. 78 45 27N 111 48W
Ennis, Texas, U.S.A. 75 32 15N 96 40W
Enniscorthy 97 52 30N 6 35W
Enniskillen 97 54 20N 7 40W
Ennistimon 97 52 56N 9 18W
Ennotville 49 43 39N 80 20W
Enns, R. 106 48 8N 14 27E
Enontekiö 110 68 23N 23 37E
Enriquillo, L. 85 18 20N 72 5W
Enschede 105 52 13N 6 53E
Ensenada, Argent. 88 34 55S 57 55W
Ensenada, Mexico 82 31 50N 116 50W
Enshih 131 30 18N 109 27E
Ensisheim 101 47 50N 7 20E
Entebbe 116 0 4N 32 28E
Enterprise, Can. 54 60 47N 115 45W
Enterprise, Oreg., U.S.A. 78 45 30N 117 11W
Enterprise, Utah, U.S.A. 79 37 37N 113 36W
Entiako L. 62 53 13N 125 31W
Entrance 54 53 25N 117 50W
Entre Rios, Boliv. 88 21 30S 64 25W

* *Renamed Enewetak*

* Entre Ríos, Mozam. 117 14 57S 37 20E
Entre Ríos □ 88 30 30S 58 30W
Entrecasteaux, Pt. d' 134 34 50S 115 56E
Entwistle 54 53 30N 115 0W
Enugu 114 6 30N 7 30E
Enumclaw 80 47 12N 122 0W
Envermeu 100 49 53N 1 15E
Envigado 86 6 10N 75 35W
Eólie o Lipari, Is. 108 38 30N 14 50E
Epe 105 52 21N 5 59E
Épernay 101 49 3N 3 56E
Épernon 101 48 35N 1 40E
Ephesus 122 38 0N 27 30E
Ephraim 78 39 30N 111 37W
Ephrata 78 47 28N 119 32W
Épinac-les-Mines 101 46 59N 4 31E
Épinal 101 48 19N 6 27E
Epiphanie, L' 43 45 51N 73 29W
Epping 95 51 42N 0 8E
Epukiro 117 21 30S 19 0E
Equality 77 37 44N 88 20W
Equatorial Guinea ■ 116 2 0S 78 0W
Équeurdreville-Hainneville 100 49 40N 1 40W
Er Rif 114 35 1N 4 1W
Eramosa 49 43 37N 80 13W
Ercha 121 69 45N 147 20E
Erciyas Daği 122 38 30N 35 30E
Erdene 130 44 30N 111 10E
Erdenedalay 130 46 3N 105 1E
Erebus, Mt. 91 77 35S 167 0E
Erechim 89 27 35S 52 15W
Ereğli 122 41 15N 31 30E
Eresma, R. 104 41 13N 4 30W
Erewadi Myitwanya 125 15 30N 95 0E
Erfurt 106 50 58N 11 2E
Erg Chech, dist. 114 50 59N 11 0E
Ergani 122 38 26N 39 49E
Ergene, R. 109 41 20N 27 0E
Erhlien 130 43 42N 112 2E
Erhtao Kiang 130 42 40N 127 10E
Eriboll, L. 96 58 28N 4 41W
Eric 36 51 56N 65 45W
Eric L. 38 51 55N 65 36W
Érice 108 38 4N 12 34E
Erie, Mich., U.S.A. 77 41 47N 83 31W
Erie, Pa., U.S.A. 70 42 10N 80 7W
Erie □ 49 42 58N 78 56W
Erie Canal 70 43 15N 78 0W
Erie, L. 46 42 15N 81 0W
Erieau 46 42 16N 81 57W
Eriksdale 57 50 52N 98 7W
Erimanthos 109 37 57N 21 50E
Erimo-misaki 132 41 50N 143 15E
Erin 49 43 45N 80 7W
Erindale 50 43 32N 79 39W
Erith 54 53 25N 116 46W
Eritrea □ 115 14 0N 41 0E
Erlandson, L. 36 57 3N 68 28W
Erlangen 106 49 35N 11 0E
Ermenak 122 36 44N 33 0E
Ermoúpolis = Siros 109 37 28N 24 57E
Ernakulam 124 9 59N 76 19E
Erne, Lough 97 54 26N 7 46W
Erne, R. 97 54 30N 8 16W
Ernée 100 48 18N 0 56W
Erode 124 11 24N 77 45E
Erquy 100 48 38N 2 29W
Erquy, Cap d' 100 48 39N 2 29W
Erramala Hills 124 15 30N 78 15E
Errigal, Mt. 97 55 2N 8 8W
Erris Hd. 97 54 19N 10 0W
Erskine, Can. 61 52 20N 112 53W
Erskine, U.S.A. 74 47 37N 96 0W
Erstein 101 48 25N 7 38E
Ervy-le-Châtel 101 48 2N 3 55E
Erwin 73 36 10N 82 28W
Erzgebirge 106 50 25N 13 0E
Erzin 121 50 15N 95 10E
Erzincan 122 39 46N 39 30E
Erzurum 122 39 57N 41 15E
Es Sînâ' 115 29 0N 34 0E
Esan-misaki 132 41 40N 141 10E
Esbjerg 111 55 29N 8 29E
Escalante 79 37 47N 111 37W
Escalante, R. 79 37 45N 111 0W
Escalón 82 26 40N 104 20W
Escambia, R. 73 30 45N 87 15W
Escanaba 72 45 44N 87 5W
Esch 105 51 37N 5 17E
Eschweiler 105 50 49N 6 14E
Escobal 84 9 6N 80 1W
Escondida, La 82 24 6N 99 55W
Escondido 81 33 9N 117 4W
Escoumins, Les 41 48 21N 69 24W
Escuinapa 82 22 50N 105 50W
Escuintla 84 14 20N 90 48W
Escuminac 35 48 0N 67 0W
Escutillas = Ceba 86 6 33N 70 24W
Esfahān □ 123 33 0N 53 0E
Esh Sham = Dimashq 122 33 30N 36 18E
Esk, R., Dumfries, U.K. 96 54 58N 3 4W
Esk, R., N. Yorks., U.K. 94 54 27N 0 36W
Esker 36 53 53N 66 25W
Eskifjördur 110 65 3N 13 55W
Eskilstuna 111 59 22N 16 32E
Eskimo Ls. 67 69 15N 132 17W
Eskimo Pt. 55 61 10N 94 3W
Eskişehir 122 39 50N 30 35E

* *Renamed Malema*

Esla, R. 104 41 45N 5 50W
Esmeralda, La 88 22 16S 62 33W
Esmeraldas 86 1 0N 79 40W
Esnagami L. 53 50 19N 86 51W
Esnagi L. 53 48 36N 84 33W
Espada, Pta. 86 12 5N 71 7W
Espalion 102 44 32N 2 47E
Espanola 46 46 15N 81 46W
Esparta 84 9 59N 84 40W
Espenberg, C. 67 66 35N 163 40W
Esperance 134 33 45S 121 55E
Esperance B. 134 33 48S 121 55E
Esperanza, Argent. 88 31 29S 61 3W
Esperanza, Can. 62 49 52N 126 43W
Esperanza Inlet 62 49 51N 126 55W
Esperanza, La, Argent. 88 24 9S 64 52W
Esperanza, La, Boliv. 86 14 20S 62 0W
Esperanza, La, Cuba 84 22 46N 83 44W
Esperanza, La, Hond. 84 14 15N 88 10W
Espéraza 102 42 56N 2 14E
Espichel, C. 104 38 22N 9 16W
Espigão, Serra do 89 26 35S 50 30W
Espinal 86 4 9N 74 53W
Espinilho, Serra do 89 28 30S 55 0W
Espino 86 8 34N 66 1W
Espíritu Santo, B. del 83 19 15N 79 40W
Espíritu Santo, I. 82 24 30N 110 23W
Espita 83 21 1N 88 19W
Espungabera 117 20 29S 32 45E
Esquel 90 42 40S 71 20W
Esquimalt 63 48 26N 123 25W
Esquina 88 30 0S 59 30W
Essaouira 114 31 32N 9 42W
Essarts, Les 100 46 47N 1 12W
Essen, Belg. 105 51 28N 4 28E
Essen, Ger. 105 51 28N 6 59E
Essequibo, R. 86 5 45N 58 50W
Essex, Can. 46 42 10N 82 49W
Essex, Calif., U.S.A. 81 34 44N 115 15W
Essex, Ill., U.S.A. 77 41 11N 88 11W
Essex, N.Y., U.S.A. 71 44 17N 73 21W
Essex □ 95 51 48N 0 30E
Essexville 46 43 37N 83 50W
Esslingen 106 48 43N 9 19E
Essondale 66 49 14N 122 48W
Essonne □ 101 48 30N 2 20E
Est, L.del' 39 47 37N 61 23W
Estados, I. de los 90 54 40S 64 30W
Estagel 102 42 47N 2 40E
Estância 87 11 16S 37 26W
Estancia 79 34 50N 106 1W
Estats, Pic d' 102 42 40N 1 40E
Estcourt 41 47 28N 69 14W
Esteli 84 13 9N 86 22W
Estelline, S.D., U.S.A. 74 44 39N 96 52W
Estelline, Texas, U.S.A. 75 34 35N 100 27W
Esterhazy 57 50 37N 102 5W
Esternay 101 48 44N 3 33E
Estevan 56 49 10N 102 59W
Estevan Group 62 53 3N 129 38W
Estevan Sd. 62 53 5N 129 34W
Estherville 74 43 25N 94 50W
Estissac 101 48 16N 3 48E
Eston 56 51 8N 108 40W
Estonian S.S.R. □ 120 48 30N 25 30E
Estoril 104 38 42N 9 23W
Estrada, La 104 42 43N 8 27W
Estrêla, Serra da 104 40 10N 7 45W
Estremadura 104 39 0N 9 0W
Estrondo, Serra do 87 7 20S 48 0W
Esztergom 107 47 47N 18 44E
Étables-sur-Mer 100 48 38N 2 51W
Étain 101 49 13N 5 38E
Etamamu 38 50 18N 59 59W
Étampes 101 48 26N 2 10E
Étang 101 46 52N 4 10E
Étang-du-Nord 39 47 22N 61 57W
Étaples 101 50 30N 1 39E
Etawah 124 26 48N 79 6E
Etawah, R. 73 34 20N 84 15W
Etawney L. 55 57 50N 96 50W
Etchemin, R. 42 46 46N 71 14W
Ethel 80 46 32N 122 46W
Ethelbert 57 51 32N 100 25W
Ethiopia ■ 115 8 0N 40 0E
Ethiopian Highlands 112 10 0N 37 0E
Etive, L. 96 56 30N 5 12W
Etna, Mt. 108 37 45N 15 0E
Etobicoke 50 43 42N 79 34W
Etobicoke Cr. 50 43 35N 79 32W
Etolin I. 54 56 5N 132 20W
Etoshapan 117 18 40S 16 30E
Etowah 73 35 20N 84 30W
Étrépagny 100 49 18N 1 36E
Étretat 100 49 42N 0 12E
Étroits, Les 41 47 24N 68 54W
Ettelbrüch 105 49 50N 6 5E
Ettrick Water 96 55 31N 2 55W
Etzatlán 82 20 48N 104 5W
Etzikom 61 49 29N 111 6W
Etzna 83 19 35N 90 15W
Eu 100 50 3N 1 26E
Euabalong West 136 33 3S 146 23E
Euboea = Évvoia 109 38 40N 23 40E
Eucla Basin 134 31 19S 126 9E
Euclid 70 41 32N 81 31W
Eucumbene, L. 136 36 2S 148 40E
Eudistes, L. des 38 50 30N 65 15W
Eudora 75 33 5N 91 17W
Eufaula, Ala., U.S.A. 73 31 55N 85 11W
Eufaula, Okla., U.S.A. 75 35 20N 95 33W
Eufaula, L. 75 35 15N 95 28W
Eugene 78 44 0N 123 8W
Eugenia, Punta 82 27 50N 115 5W
Eugowra 136 33 22S 148 24E
Eunice, La., U.S.A. 75 30 35N 92 28W
Eunice, N. Mex., U.S.A. 75 32 30N 103 10W
Eupen 105 50 37N 6 3E
Euphrates = Furat, Nahr al 122 33 30N 43 0E
Eure □ 100 49 6N 1 0E
Eure-et-Loir □ 100 48 22N 1 30E
Eureka, Can. 65 80 0N 85 56W
Eureka, Calif., U.S.A. 78 40 50N 124 0W
Eureka, Ill., U.S.A. 76 40 43N 89 16W
Eureka, Kans., U.S.A. 75 37 50N 96 20W
Eureka, Mo., U.S.A. 76 38 30N 90 38W
Eureka, Mont., U.S.A. 61 48 53N 115 6W
Eureka, Nev., U.S.A. 78 39 32N 116 2W
Eureka, S.D., U.S.A. 74 45 49N 99 38W
Eureka, Utah, U.S.A. 78 40 0N 112 0W
Eureka River 60 56 27N 118 44W
Euroa 136 36 44S 145 35E
Europa, Île 117 22 20S 40 22E
Europa, Picos de 104 43 10N 5 0W
Europa Pt. 104 36 2N 6 32W
Europe 93 20 0N 20 0E
Europoort 105 51 57N 4 10E
Eustis 73 28 54N 81 36W
Eutsuk L. 62 53 20N 126 45W
Évain 40 48 14N 79 8W
Evans 74 40 25N 104 43W
Evans L. 36 50 50N 77 0W
Evans Mills 71 44 6N 75 48W
Evans P. 74 41 0N 105 35W
Evansburg 60 53 36N 114 59W
Evansdale 76 42 30N 92 17W
Evanston, Ill., U.S.A. 77 42 0N 87 40W
Evanston, Wy., U.S.A. 78 41 10N 111 0W
Evansville, Ill., U.S.A. 76 38 5N 89 56W
Evansville, Ind., U.S.A. 77 38 0N 87 35W
Evansville, Wis., U.S.A. 76 42 47N 89 18W
Évart 46 43 54N 85 8W
Évaux-les-Bains 102 46 12N 2 29E
Eveleth 74 47 29N 92 30W
Evensk 121 61 57N 159 14E
Everard, C. 136 37 49S 149 17E
Everard, L. 134 31 30S 135 0E
Everard Ras. 134 27 5S 132 28E
Everest, Mt. 125 28 5N 86 58E
Everett, Pa., U.S.A. 70 40 2N 78 24W
Everett, Wash., U.S.A. 80 48 0N 122 10W
Everglades 73 26 0N 80 30W
Evergreen 73 31 28N 86 55W
Everrett Mts. 65 62 45N 67 12W
Everson 78 48 57N 122 22W
Everton 49 43 40N 80 9W
Evesham 95 52 6N 1 57W
Evian-les-Bains 103 46 24N 6 35E
Evinayong 116 1 50N 10 35E
Évisa 103 42 15N 8 48E
Évora 104 38 33N 7 57W
Évreux 100 49 0N 1 8E
Évron 100 48 23N 1 58W
Évvoia 109 38 30N 24 0E
Ewe, L. 96 57 49N 5 38W
Ewen 52 46 32N 89 17W
Ewing, Mo., U.S.A. 76 40 6N 91 43W
Ewing, Nebr., U.S.A. 74 42 18N 98 22W
Ewo 116 0 48S 14 45E
Exaltación 86 13 10S 65 20W
Excelsior Springs 76 39 20N 94 10W
Excideuil 102 45 20N 1 4E
Exe, R. 95 50 38N 3 27W
Exeter, Can. 46 43 21N 81 29W
Exeter, U.K. 95 50 43N 3 31W
Exeter, Calif., U.S.A. 80 36 17N 119 9W
Exeter, Nebr., U.S.A. 74 40 43N 97 30W
Exeter, N.H., U.S.A. 71 43 0N 70 58W
Exira 76 41 35N 94 52W
Exmes 100 48 45N 0 10E
Exmoor 95 51 10N 3 59W
Exmouth, Austral. 134 22 6S 114 0E
Exmouth, U.K. 95 50 37N 3 26W
Exmouth G. 134 22 15S 114 15E
Expedition Range 135 24 30S 149 12E
Exploits, B. of 37 49 20N 55 0W
Exshaw 61 51 3N 115 9W
Extremadura 104 39 30N 6 5W
Exuma Sound 84 24 30N 76 20W
Eyasi, L. 116 3 30S 35 0E
Eyeberry L. 55 63 8N 104 43W
Eyebrow 56 50 48N 106 9W
Eyehill Cr., Alta., Can. 61 52 14N 110 0W
Eyehill Cr., Sask., Can. 56 52 40N 109 39W
Eyemouth 96 55 53N 2 5W
Eygurande 102 45 40N 2 26E
Eyjafjorður 110 66 15N 18 30W
Eymet 102 44 40N 0 25E
Eymoutiers 102 45 40N 1 45E
Eyrarbakki 110 63 52N 21 9W
Eyre 134 32 15S 126 18E
Eyre Cr. 135 26 40S 139 0E
Eyre, L. 135 29 30S 137 26E
Eyre Mts. 133 45 25S 168 25E
Eyre Pen. 134 33 30S 137 17E

F

Fabens	79	31 30N	106 8W
Fabre	40	47 12N	79 22W
Fabreville	44	45 34N	73 51W
Fabriano	108	43 20N	12 52E
Fabrizia	101	38 29N	16 19E
Facatativá	86	4 49N	74 22W
Facture	102	44 39N	0 58W
Faddeyevski, Ostrov	121	76 0N	150 0E
Fadhili	122	26 55N	49 10E
Faenza	108	44 17N	11 53E
Făgăraş	107	45 48N	24 58E
Fagatogo	133	14 17S	170 41W
Fagernes	111	60 59N	9 14E
Fagersta	111	60 1N	15 46E
Fagnano, L.	90	54 30S	68 0W
Fagnières	101	48 58N	4 20E
Fahraj	123	29 0N	59 0E
Fahsien	131	21 19N	110 33E
Fahūd	123	22 18N	56 28E
Faid	122	27 1N	42 52E
Faillon, L.	40	48 21N	76 39W
Fair Harbour	62	50 4N	127 10W
Fair Hd.	97	55 14N	6 10W
Fair Isle	98	59 30N	1 40W
Fair Oaks	80	38 39N	121 16W
Fair Play	76	37 38N	93 35W
Fairbank	79	31 44N	110 12W
Fairbanks	67	64 59N	147 40W
Fairborn	77	39 42N	84 2W
Fairbury, U.S.A.	77	40 45N	88 31W
Fairbury, Nebr., U.S.A.	74	40 5N	97 5W
Fairfax, Ohio, U.S.A.	77	39 5N	83 37W
Fairfax, Okla., U.S.A.	75	36 37N	96 45W
Fairfield, Austral.	136	33 53S	150 57E
Fairfield, Ala., U.S.A.	73	33 30N	87 0W
Fairfield, Calif., U.S.A.	80	38 14N	122 1W
Fairfield, Conn., U.S.A.	71	41 8N	73 16W
Fairfield, Idaho, U.S.A.	78	43 27N	114 52W
Fairfield, Ill., U.S.A.	77	38 20N	88 20W
Fairfield, Iowa, U.S.A.	76	41 0N	91 58W
Fairfield, Mont., U.S.A.	78	47 40N	112 0W
Fairfield, Ohio, U.S.A.	77	39 21N	84 34W
Fairfield, Texas, U.S.A.	75	31 40N	96 0W
Fairfield Plain	49	43 3N	80 24W
Fairford	57	51 37N	98 38W
Fairgrove	46	43 31N	83 33W
Fairhope	73	30 35N	87 50W
Fairlie	133	44 5S	170 49E
Fairmead	80	37 5N	120 10W
Fairmont, Minn., U.S.A.	74	43 37N	94 30W
Fairmont, W. Va., U.S.A.	72	39 29N	80 10W
Fairmont Hot Springs	54	50 20N	115 56W
Fairmount	81	34 45N	118 26W
Fairplay	79	39 9N	105 40W
Fairport, Can.	51	43 49N	79 5W
Fairport, N.Y., U.S.A.	70	43 8N	77 29W
Fairport, Ohio, U.S.A.	70	41 45N	81 17W
Fairvale	39	45 25N	66 0W
Fairview, Can.	39	44 40N	63 38W
Fairview, Alta., Can.	60	56 5N	118 25W
Fairview, Mich., U.S.A.	46	44 44N	84 3W
Fairview, N. Dak., U.S.A.	74	47 49N	104 7W
Fairview, Okla., U.S.A.	75	36 19N	98 30W
Fairview, Utah, U.S.A.	78	39 50N	111 0W
Fairweather, Mt.	67	58 55N	137 45W
Faith	74	45 2N	102 4W
Faizabad, Afghan.	123	37 7N	70 33E
Faizabad, India	125	26 45N	82 10E
Fajardo	85	18 20N	65 39W
Fakfak	127	3 0S	132 15E
Fakiya	87	42 10N	27 4E
Falaise	100	48 54N	0 12W
Falcón □	86	11 0N	69 50W
Falcon Dam	75	26 50N	99 20W
Falcon I.	52	49 23N	94 45W
Falconbridge	46	46 35N	80 45W
Falconer	70	42 7N	79 13W
Falfurrias	75	27 8N	98 8W
Falher	60	55 44N	117 15W
Falkenberg, Can.	70	45 9N	79 21W
Falkenberg, Sweden	111	56 54N	12 30E
Falkirk	96	56 0N	3 47W
Falkland, N.S., Can.	39	44 37N	63 34W
Falkland, Ont., Can.	49	43 10N	80 26W
Falkland Is.	90	51 30S	59 0W
Falkland Is. Dep.	91	57 0S	40 0W
Falkland Sd.	90	52 0S	60 0W
Falköping	111	58 12N	13 33E
Fall Brook	79	33 25N	117 12W
Fall River	71	41 45N	71 5W
Fall River Mills	78	41 1N	121 30W
Failbrook	81	33 23N	117 15W
Fallon, Mont., U.S.A.	74	46 52N	105 8W
Fallon, Nev., U.S.A.	78	39 31N	118 51W
Falls City, Nebr., U.S.A.	74	40 0N	95 40W
Falls City, Oreg., U.S.A.	78	44 54N	123 29W
Falls Creek	70	41 8N	78 49W
Falmouth, Jamaica	84	18 30N	77 40W
Falmouth, U.K.	95	50 9N	5 5W
Falmouth, U.S.A.	77	38 40N	84 20W
Falmouth B.	95	50 7N	5 3E
False Cr.	66	49 15N	123 8W
Falso, C.	84	15 12N	83 21W
Falsterbo	111	55 23N	12 50E
Falun	111	60 37N	15 37E
Famagusta	122	35 8N	33 55E
Famatina, Sierra, de	88	29 5S	68 0W
Family L.	57	51 54N	95 27W
Famoso	81	35 37N	119 12W
Fancheng	131	31 2N	118 13E
Fandriana	117	20 14S	47 21E
Fangcheng	131	33 16N	112 59E
Fankiatun	130	43 50N	125 6E
Fannich, L.	96	57 40N	5 0W
*Fanning I.	15	3 51N	159 22W
Fanny Bay	62	49 27N	124 48W
Fano	108	43 50N	13 0E
Fanshaw	54	57 11N	133 30W
Fao (Al Fāw)	122	30 0N	48 30E
Far Mt.	62	52 47N	125 20W
Faraday Seamount Group	12	50 0N	27 0W
Faradje	116	3 50N	29 45E
Farafangana	117	22 49S	47 50E
Farah	124	32 20N	62 7E
Farah □	124	32 25N	62 10E
Fareham	95	50 52N	1 11W
Farewell, Alaska, U.S.A.	67	62 30N	154 0W
Farewell, Mich., U.S.A.	46	43 52N	84 55W
Farewell, C.	133	40 29S	172 43E
Farewell C. = Farvel, K.	17	59 48N	43 55W
Farfán	86	0 16N	76 41W
Fargeville, La	71	44 12N	75 58W
Fargo	74	47 0N	97 0W
Faribault	74	44 15N	93 19W
Faride, L.	38	50 58N	59 55W
Faridpur	125	18 14N	79 34E
Farimān	123	35 40N	60 0E
Farmer City	77	40 15N	88 39W
Farmers Rapids	48	45 30N	75 45W
Farmersburg	77	39 15N	87 23W
Farmerville	75	32 48N	92 23W
Farmington, Calif., U.S.A.	80	37 56N	121 0W
Farmington, Ill., U.S.A.	76	40 42N	90 0W
Farmington, Iowa, U.S.A.	76	40 38N	91 44W
Farmington, Mo., U.S.A.	76	37 47N	90 25W
Farmington, N. Mex., U.S.A.	79	36 45N	108 28W
Farmington, N.H., U.S.A.	71	43 25N	71 7W
Farmington, Utah, U.S.A.	78	41 0N	111 58W
Farmington, R.	71	41 51N	72 38W
Farmland	77	40 15N	85 5W
Farmville	72	37 19N	78 22W
Farnborough	95	51 17N	0 46W
Farne Is.	94	55 38N	1 37W
Farnham	45	45 17N	72 59W
Farnham Centre	43	45 15N	72 50W
Farnham, Mt.	54	45 20N	72 55W
Faro, Brazil	87	2 0S	56 45W
Faro, Can.	64	62 11N	133 22W
Faro, Port.	104	37 2N	7 55W
Fårö	111	58 0N	19 10E
Faroe Is.	93	62 0N	7 0W
Farquhar, C.	134	23 38S	113 36E
Farquhar Is.	16	11 0S	52 0E
Farrand, C.	65	71 45N	90 0W
Farrāshband	123	28 57N	52 5E
Farrell	70	41 13N	80 29W
Fars □	123	29 30N	55 0E
Fársala	109	39 17N	22 23E
Farsund	111	58 5N	6 55E
Fartura, Serra da	89	26 21S	52 52W
Farvel, Kap	17	59 48N	43 55W
Farwell	75	34 25N	103 0W
Faryab	124	28 7N	57 14E
Fasā	123	29 0N	53 32E
Fastnet Rock	97	51 22N	9 37W
Fatehgarh	124	27 25N	79 35E
Fatehpur, Raj., India	124	28 0N	75 4E
Fatehpur, Ut. P., India	125	27 8N	81 7E
Fati	131	23 10N	113 10E
Fatima	39	47 24N	61 53W
Fatkeng	131	23 58N	113 29E
Fatshan	131	23 0N	113 4E
Faucilles, Monts	101	48 5N	5 50E
Faulkton	74	45 4N	99 8W
Faulquemont	101	49 3N	6 36E
Fauquembergues	101	50 36N	2 5E
Fauquier, B.C., Can.	63	49 52N	118 5W
Fauquier, Ont., Can.	53	49 18N	82 3W
Fauresmith	117	29 44S	25 17E
Fauske	110	67 17N	15 25E
Faust	60	55 19N	115 38W
Favara	108	37 19N	13 39E
Favignana	108	37 56N	12 18E
Favone	103	41 47N	9 26E
Favourable Lake	34	52 50N	93 39W
Fawcett	60	54 32N	114 5W
Fawn, R.	34	52 22N	88 20W
Fawnskin	81	34 16N	116 56W
Faxaflói	110	64 29N	23 0W
Fayence	103	43 38N	6 42E
Fayette, Ala., U.S.A.	73	33 40N	87 50W
Fayette, Iowa, U.S.A.	76	42 51N	91 48W

* Renamed Tabuaeran

Fayette, Mo., U.S.A.	76	39 10N	92 40W
Fayette, Ohio, U.S.A.	77	41 40N	84 20W
Fayette, La.	72	40 22N	86 52W
Fayetteville, Ark., U.S.A.	75	36 0N	94 5W
Fayetteville, N.C., U.S.A.	73	35 0N	78 58W
Fayetteville, Tenn., U.S.A.	73	35 20N	86 50W
Fazilka	124	30 27N	74 2E
F'Derik	114	22 40N	12 45W
Fé, La	84	22 2N	84 15W
Feale, R.	97	52 26N	9 28W
Fear, C.	73	33 45N	78 0W
Feather Falls	80	39 36N	121 16W
Feather, R.	78	39 30N	121 20W
Featherston	133	41 6S	175 20E
Fécamp	100	49 45N	0 22E
Federación	88	31 0S	57 55W
Federal	48	45 20N	75 42W
Fehmarn	106	54 26N	11 10E
Fehmarn Bælt	106	54 35N	11 20E
Feilding	133	40 13S	175 35E
*Feira	117	15 35S	30 16E
Feldkirch	106	47 15N	9 37E
Felicity	77	38 51N	84 6W
Felipe Carrillo Puerto	83	19 38N	88 3W
Felixstowe	95	51 58N	1 22W
Felletin	102	45 53N	2 11E
Felton	80	37 3N	122 4W
Femunden	110	62 10N	11 53E
Fen Ho, R.	130	35 25N	110 30E
Fenelon Falls	47	44 32N	78 45W
Fénérive	117	17 22S	49 25E
Fengcheng, Heilungkiang, China	130	45 41N	128 54E
Fengcheng, Kiangsi, China	131	28 2N	115 46E
Fengcheng, Liaoning, China	130	40 28N	124 4E
Fengfeng	130	36 40N	114 24E
Fenghsien	131	33 56N	106 41E
Fenghwa	131	29 37N	121 29E
Fengkieh (Kweichow)	131	31 0N	109 33E
Fenglo	131	31 30N	112 29E
Fengsiang	131	34 27N	107 30E
Fengsin	131	28 41N	115 11E
Fengtai	130	39 57N	116 21E
Fengtu	131	29 58N	107 59E
Fengy	131	23 48N	106 50E
Fengyi	131	25 31N	100 13E
Fengyuan	131	24 10N	120 45E
Fenit	97	52 17N	9 51W
Fennimore	76	42 58N	90 41W
Feno, C. de	103	41 58N	8 33E
Fens, The	94	52 45N	0 2E
Fenton, Can.	55	53 0N	105 35W
Fenton, U.S.A.	46	42 47N	83 44W
Fenwick	49	43 1N	79 22W
Fenyang	130	37 19N	111 46E
Feodosiya	120	45 2N	35 28E
Ferdows	123	33 58N	58 2E
Fère-Champenoise	101	48 45N	4 0E
Fère-en-Tardenois	101	49 10N	3 30E
Fère, La	101	49 40N	3 20E
Ferfer	115	5 18N	45 20E
Fergana	120	40 23N	71 46E
Fergus	49	43 43N	80 24W
Fergus Falls	74	46 25N	96 0W
Ferguson, Can.	34	47 50N	73 30W
Ferguson, U.S.A.	76	38 45N	90 18W
Ferintosh	61	52 46N	112 58W
Ferland, Ont., Can.	52	50 19N	88 27W
Ferland, Sask., Can.	56	49 27N	106 57W
Fermanagh (□)	97	54 21N	7 40W
Ferme-Neuve	40	46 42N	75 27W
Fermoy	97	52 4N	8 18W
Fernández	88	27 55S	63 50W
Fernandina Beach	73	30 40N	81 30W
Fernando de Noronha, I.	87	4 0S	33 10W
Fernando do Noronho □	87	4 0S	33 10W
Fernando Póo = Bioko, I.	113	3 30N	8 40E
Ferndale, U.S.A.	46	42 26N	83 6W
Ferndale, Calif., U.S.A.	78	40 37N	124 12W
Ferndale, Wash., U.S.A.	80	48 51N	122 41W
Fernie	61	49 30N	115 5W
Fernley	78	39 42N	119 20W
Feronia	46	46 22N	79 19W
Ferozepore	124	30 55N	74 40E
Ferrara	108	44 50N	11 36E
Ferreñafe	86	6 35S	79 50W
Ferret, C.	102	44 38N	1 15W
Ferrette	101	47 30N	7 20E
Ferriday	75	31 35N	91 33W
Ferrières	101	48 5N	2 48E
Ferron	78	39 3N	111 3W
Ferryland	37	47 2N	52 53W
Ferrysburg	77	43 5N	86 13W
Ferté Bernard, La	100	48 10N	0 40E
Ferté, La	101	48 57N	3 6E
Ferté-Mace, La	100	48 35N	0 21W
Ferté-St. Aubin, La	101	47 42N	1 57E
Ferté-Vidame, La	100	48 37N	0 53E
Fertile	74	47 37N	96 18W
Fès	114	34 0N	5 0W
Feshi	116	6 0S	18 10E

* Renamed Luangwa

Fessenden	74	47 42N	99 44W
Festus	76	38 13N	90 24W
Fethiye	122	36 36N	29 10E
Fetlar, I.	96	60 36N	0 52W
Feuilles, B. aux	36	58 55N	69 20W
Feuilles, R.	36	58 47N	70 4W
Feurs	103	45 45N	4 13E
Ffestiniog	94	52 58N	3 56W
Fiambalá	88	27 45S	67 37W
Fianarantsoa	117	21 20S	46 45E
Fichtelgebirge	106	50 10N	12 0E
Field	46	46 31N	80 1W
Fife □	96	56 13N	3 2W
Fife L.	56	49 14N	105 53W
Fife Ness	96	56 17N	2 35W
Figeac	102	44 37N	2 2E
Figueira da Foz	104	40 7N	8 54W
Figueras	104	42 18N	2 58E
Fiji ■	133	17 20S	179 0E
Fiji Is.	133	17 20S	179 0E
Filadelfia	88	22 25S	60 0W
Filchner Ice Shelf	91	78 0S	60 0W
File Axe, L.	41	50 18N	73 34W
Filer	78	42 30N	114 35W
Filey	94	54 13N	0 18W
Filiatrá	109	37 9N	21 35E
Filipstad	111	59 43N	14 9E
Fillmore, Can.	56	49 50N	103 25W
Fillmore, U.S.A.	81	34 23N	118 58W
Fils, L. du	40	46 37N	78 7W
Filyos çayi	122	41 35N	32 10E
Finch	47	45 11N	75 7W
Findhorn, R.	96	57 38N	3 38W
Findlater	56	50 47N	105 24W
Findlay	77	41 0N	83 41W
Finger L.	62	53 33N	124 18W
Fingõe	117	15 12S	31 50E
Finike	122	36 21N	30 10E
Finistère □	100	48 20N	4 0W
Finisterre, C.	104	42 50N	9 19W
Finke, R.	134	24 54S	134 16E
Finland	52	48 51N	93 55W
Finland ■	111	64 0N	27 0E
Finland, G. of	111	60 0N	26 0E
Finlay, R.	54	56 50N	125 10W
Finley, Austral.	136	35 38S	145 35E
Finley, U.S.A.	74	47 35N	97 50W
Finmark	52	48 35N	89 45W
Finn, R.	97	54 50N	7 55W
Finnmark fylke □	110	69 30N	25 0E
Finucane I.	134	20 19S	118 30E
Fiora, R.	108	42 25N	11 35E
Fire River	53	48 47N	83 36W
Firebag, R.	60	57 45N	111 21W
Firebaugh	80	36 52N	120 27W
Firedrake L.	55	61 25N	104 30W
Firenze	108	43 47N	11 15E
Firmi	102	44 32N	2 19E
Firminy	103	45 23N	4 18E
Fīroz Kohi	124	34 45N	63 0E
Firozabad	124	27 10N	78 25E
First Narrows	66	49 19N	123 8W
Fīrūzābād	123	28 52N	52 35E
Fīrūzkūh	123	35 50N	52 40E
Firvale	62	52 27N	126 13W
Fish Cr.	59	50 54N	114 1W
Fish Pt.	46	43 43N	83 38W
Fish, R.	117	27 40S	17 30E
Fisher B.	57	51 35N	97 13W
Fisher Bay	57	51 29N	97 18W
Fisher Branch	57	51 5N	97 13W
Fisher Str.	65	63 15N	83 30W
Fishguard	95	51 59N	4 59W
Fishing L.	57	52 10N	95 24W
Fiskivötn	110	64 50N	20 45W
Fismes	101	49 20N	3 40E
Fitchburg	71	42 35N	71 47W
Fitz Hugh Sd.	62	51 40N	127 55W
Fitz Roy	90	47 10S	67 0W
Fitzgerald, Can.	54	59 51N	111 36W
Fitzgerald, U.S.A.	73	31 45N	83 10W
Fitzpatrick	34	47 29N	72 46W
Fitzroy Crossing	134	18 9S	125 38E
Fitzroy, R.	134	17 25S	124 0E
Fitzwilliam I.	46	45 30N	81 45W
Fiume = Rijeka	108	45 20N	14 21E
Five Islands	39	45 25N	64 6W
Five Points	80	36 26N	120 6W
Fizi	116	4 17S	28 55E
Flagler	74	39 20N	103 4W
Flagstaff	79	35 10N	111 40W
Flagstone	54	49 4N	115 10W
Flaherty, I.	36	56 15N	79 15W
Flåm	111	60 52N	7 14E
Flambeau, R.	74	45 40N	90 50W
Flamboro Centre	48	43 22N	79 56W
Flamborough Hd.	94	54 8N	0 4W
Flaming Gorge Dam	78	40 50N	109 25W
Flaming Gorge L.	78	41 15N	109 30W
Flamingo, Teluk	127	5 30S	138 0E
Flanagan	77	40 53N	88 52W
Flanders	52	48 44N	92 5W
Flandre	106	51 10N	3 15E
Flandre Occidental □	105	51 0N	3 0E
Flandreau	74	44 5N	96 38W
Flanigan	80	40 10N	119 53W
Flannan Is.	96	58 9N	7 52W
Flåsjön	110	64 5N	15 50E
Flat Bay	37	48 24N	58 36W

Name	Map	Lat	Long
Flat L.	60	54 38N	112 54W
Flat, R., Can.	54	61 51N	128 0W
Flat, R., U.S.A.	77	42 56N	85 15W
Flat River	75	37 50N	90 30W
Flat Rock, Ill., U.S.A.	77	38 54N	87 40W
Flat Rock, Mich., U.S.A.	46	42 6N	83 18W
Flatbush	60	54 42N	114 9W
Flatey, Barðastrandarsýsla, Iceland	110	66 10N	17 52W
Flatey, Suður-þingeyjarsýsla, Iceland	110	65 22N	22 56W
Flathead L.	78	47 50N	114 0W
Flatrock, R.	77	38 46N	85 10W
Flattery, C.	80	48 21N	124 43W
Flavy-le-Martel	101	49 43N	3 12 E
Flaxcombe	56	51 29N	109 36W
Flaxton	57	48 52N	102 24W
Flèche, La	100	47 42N	0 5W
Fleetwood	94	53 55N	3 1W
Fleming	57	50 4N	101 31W
Flemingsburg	77	38 25N	83 45W
Flemington	70	41 7N	77 28W
Flensburg	106	54 46N	9 28 E
Flers	100	48 47N	0 33W
Flesherton	46	44 16N	80 33W
Fletton	95	52 34N	0 13W
Fleur de Lys	37	50 7N	56 8W
Fleur-de-May, L.	38	52 0N	65 5W
Fleurance	102	43 52N	0 40 E
Flin Flon	55	54 46N	101 53W
Flinders I.	135	40 0 S	148 0 E
Flint, U.K.	94	53 15N	3 7W
Flint, U.S.A.	46	43 5N	83 40W
Flint, I.	15	11 26 S	151 48W
Flint L.	53	49 52N	85 53W
Flint, R.	73	31 20N	84 10W
Flixecourt	101	50 0N	2 5 E
Flodden	94	55 37N	2 8W
Floodwood	52	46 55N	92 55W
Flora, Ill., U.S.A.	72	38 40N	88 30W
Flora, Ind., U.S.A.	77	40 33N	86 31W
Florac	102	44 20N	3 37 E
Floradale	49	43 37N	80 35W
Florala	73	31 0N	86 20W
Florence, Can.	39	46 16N	60 16W
Florence, Ala., U.S.A.	73	34 50N	87 50W
Florence, Ariz., U.S.A.	79	33 0N	111 25W
Florence, Colo., U.S.A.	74	38 26N	105 0W
Florence, Ky., U.S.A.	77	39 0N	84 38W
Florence, Oreg., U.S.A.	78	44 0N	124 3W
Florence, S.C., U.S.A.	73	34 5N	79 50W
Florence = Firenze	108	43 47N	11 15 E
Florensac	102	43 23N	3 28 E
Flores, Azores	93	39 13N	31 13W
Flores, Guat.	84	16 50N	89 40W
Flores I.	62	49 20N	126 10W
Flores, I.	127	8 35 S	121 0 E
Flores Sea	126	6 30 S	124 0 E
Floresville	75	29 10N	98 10W
Floriano	87	6 50 S	43 0W
Florianópolis	89	27 30 S	48 30W
Florida, Cuba	84	21 32N	78 14W
Florida, Uruguay	89	34 7 S	56 10W
Florida □	73	28 30N	82 0W
Florida B.	85	25 0N	81 20W
Florida Keys	85	25 0N	80 40W
Florida, Strait of	85	25 0N	80 0W
Florissant	76	38 48N	90 20W
Florø	111	61 35N	5 1 E
Flower Sta.	47	45 10N	76 41W
Flower's Cove	37	51 14N	56 46W
Floydada	75	33 58N	101 18W
Fluk	127	1 42 S	127 38 E
Flushing	46	43 4N	83 51W
Flushing = Vlissingen	105	51 26N	3 34 E
Foam Lake	56	51 40N	103 32W
Fogo	37	49 43N	54 17W
Fogo, C.	37	49 40N	54 0W
Fogo I.	37	49 40N	54 5W
Foins, L. aux	40	47 5N	78 11W
Foix	102	42 58N	1 38 E
Folda, Nord-Trøndelag, Norway	110	64 41N	10 50 E
Folda, Nordland, Norway	110	67 38N	14 50 E
Folette, La	73	36 23N	84 9W
Foley I.	65	68 32N	75 5W
Foleyet	53	48 15N	82 25W
Folkestone	95	51 5N	1 11 E
Folkston	73	30 55N	82 0W
Follett	75	36 30N	100 12W
Folsom	80	38 41N	121 7W
Folsom Res.	80	38 42N	121 9W
Fond-du-Lac	55	59 19N	107 12W
Fond du lac	74	43 46N	88 26W
Fond-du-Lac, R.	55	59 17N	106 0W
Fonda, Iowa, U.S.A.	76	42 35N	94 50W
Fonda, N.Y., U.S.A.	71	42 57N	74 23W
Fonseca, G. de	84	13 10N	87 40W
Fontaine	101	47 32N	5 21 E
Fontaine-Française	101	47 32N	5 21 E
Fontaine, La	77	40 40N	85 43W
Fontainebleau	101	48 24N	2 40 E
Fontas, R.	54	58 14N	121 48W
Fonte Boa	86	2 25 S	66 0W
Fontenay-le-Comte	102	46 28N	0 48W
Fonteneau, L.	38	51 55N	61 30W
Fontenelle	35	48 54N	64 33W
Fontur	110	66 23N	14 32W
Foochow (Minhow)	131	26 2N	119 25 E
Foothills	61	53 4N	116 47W
Forbach	101	49 10N	6 52 E
Forcalquier	103	43 58N	5 47 E
Ford City, Calif., U.S.A.	81	35 9N	119 27W
Ford City, Pa., U.S.A.	70	40 47N	79 31W
Fording	61	50 12N	114 52W
Fordongianus	102	40 0N	8 50 E
Fordyce	75	33 50N	92 20W
Forel	17	66 52N	36 55W
Foremost	61	49 26N	111 25W
Forest, Can.	46	43 6N	82 0W
Forest, U.S.A.	75	32 21N	89 27W
Forest City, Iowa, U.S.A.	74	43 12N	93 39W
Forest City, N.C., U.S.A.	73	35 23N	81 50W
Forest City, Pa., U.S.A.	71	41 39N	75 29W
Forest Grove, Can.	63	51 46N	121 5W
Forest Grove, U.S.A.	80	45 31N	123 4W
Forest Hill	50	43 42N	79 25W
Forest Lawn	59	51 2N	113 58W
Forestburg	61	52 35N	112 1W
Foresthill	80	39 1N	120 49W
Forestville, Can.	41	48 48N	69 2W
Forestville, Calif., U.S.A.	80	38 28N	122 54W
Forestville, Wis., U.S.A.	72	44 41N	87 29W
Forez, Mts. du	102	45 40N	3 50 E
Forfar	96	56 40N	2 53W
Forges-les-Eaux	101	49 37N	1 30 E
Forget	56	49 39N	102 52W
Forillon, Parc National	38	48 46N	64 12W
Fork River	57	51 31N	100 1W
Forks	80	47 56N	124 23W
Forlì	108	44 14N	12 2 E
Forman	74	46 9N	97 43W
Formby Pt.	94	53 33N	3 7W
Formentera, I.	104	38 40N	1 30 E
Formiguères	102	42 37N	2 5 E
Formosa	88	26 15 S	58 10W
Formosa = Taiwan ■	131	24 0N	121 0 E
Formosa □	88	26 5 S	58 10W
Formosa Bay	116	2 40 S	40 20 E
Formosa Str.	131	24 40N	120 0 E
Forres	96	57 37N	3 38W
Forrest City	75	35 0N	90 50W
Forreston	76	42 8N	89 35W
Forsyth, Ga., U.S.A.	73	33 4N	83 55W
Forsyth, Mont., U.S.A.	78	46 14N	106 37W
Forsythe	40	48 14N	76 26W
Fort Albany	34	52 15N	81 35W
Fort Amador	84	8 56N	79 32W
Fort Apache	79	33 50N	110 0W
Fort Assiniboine	60	54 20N	114 45W
Fort Atkinson	77	42 56N	88 50W
Fort Augustus	96	57 9N	4 40W
Fort Babine	54	55 22N	126 37W
Fort Benton	78	47 50N	110 40W
Fort Bragg	78	39 28N	123 50W
Fort Bridger	78	41 22N	110 20W
*Fort Chimo	36	58 6N	68 25W
Fort Chipewyan	55	58 42N	111 8W
Fort Clayton	84	9 0N	79 35W
Fort Collins	74	40 30N	105 4W
Fort-Coulonge	40	45 50N	76 45W
Fort Covington	43	44 59N	74 30W
†Fort-Dauphin	117	25 2 S	47 0 E
Fort Davis, Pan.	84	9 17N	79 56W
Fort Davis, U.S.A.	75	30 38N	103 53W
Fort-de-France	85	14 36N	61 2W
Fort Defiance	79	35 47N	109 4W
Fort Dodge	74	42 29N	94 10W
Fort Edward	71	43 16N	73 35W
Fort Frances	52	48 36N	93 24W
Fort Fraser	62	54 4N	124 33W
Fort Garland	79	37 28N	105 30W
Fort Garry	58	49 50N	97 9W
Fort George	36	53 50N	79 0W
Fort George, R.	34	53 50N	77 0W
Fort Good-Hope	67	66 14N	128 40W
Fort Grahame	54	56 30N	124 35W
Fort Hancock	79	31 19N	105 56W
Fort Hauchuca	79	31 32N	110 30W
Fort Hertz (Putao)	125	27 28N	97 30 E
Fort Hope	53	51 30N	88 0W
Fort Irwin	81	35 16N	116 34W
Fort Jameson = Chipata	117	13 38 S	32 28 E
Fort Kent	35	47 12N	68 30W
Fort Klamath	78	42 45N	122 0W
Fort Knox	77	38 50N	85 0W
Fort Langley	63	49 10N	122 35W
Fort Laramie	74	42 15N	104 30W
Fort Lauderdale	73	26 10N	80 5W
Fort Leonard Wood	76	37 46N	92 11W
Fort Liard	54	60 20N	123 30W
Fort Liberté	85	19 42N	71 51W
Fort Lupton	74	40 8N	104 48W
Fort Mackay	60	57 12N	111 41W
Fort McKenzie	36	57 20N	69 0W
Fort Macleod	61	49 45N	113 30W
Fort McMurray	60	56 44N	111 23W
Fort McPherson	67	67 30N	134 55W
Fort Madison	74	40 39N	91 20W
Fort Meade	73	27 45N	81 45W
Fort Morgan	74	40 10N	103 50W
Fort Myers	73	26 30N	81 50W
Fort Nelson	54	58 50N	122 38W
Fort Nelson, R.	54	59 32N	124 0W
Fort Norman	67	64 57N	125 30W
Fort Payne	73	34 25N	85 44W
Fort Peck	78	48 1N	106 30W
Fort Peck Dam	78	48 0N	106 20W
Fort Peck L.	78	47 40N	107 0W
Fort Pierce	74	27 29N	80 19W
Fort Pierre	74	44 25N	100 25W
Fort Plain	71	42 56N	74 39W
Fort Portal	116	0 40N	30 20 E
Fort Providence	54	61 21N	117 40W
Fort Qu'Appelle	56	50 45N	103 50W
Fort Randall	67	55 10N	162 48W
Fort Randolph	84	9 23N	79 53W
Fort Recovery	77	40 25N	84 47W
Fort Resolution	54	61 10N	113 40W
Fort Ross, Can.	65	72 0N	94 14W
Fort Ross, U.S.A.	80	38 32N	123 13W
Fort Rouge	58	49 52N	97 9W
Fort Rupert	62	50 42N	127 23W
Fort Rupert (Rupert House)	36	51 30N	78 40W
Fort St. James	54	54 30N	124 10W
Fort St. John	54	56 15N	120 50W
Fort Sandeman	124	31 20N	69 25 E
Fort Saskatchewan	60	53 40N	113 15W
Fort Scott	75	37 50N	94 40W
Fort Selkirk	67	62 43N	137 22W
Fort Severn	34	56 0N	87 40W
Fort Sherman	84	9 22N	79 56W
Fort Shevchenko	120	44 30N	50 10W
Fort Simpson	54	61 45N	121 23W
Fort Smith, Can.	54	60 0N	111 51W
Fort Smith, U.S.A.	75	35 25N	94 25W
Fort Stanton	79	33 33N	105 36W
Fort Stockton	75	30 48N	103 2W
Fort Sumner	75	34 24N	104 8W
Fort Thomas, Ariz., U.S.A.	79	33 2N	109 59W
Fort Thomas, Ky., U.S.A.	77	39 5N	84 27W
Fort Valley	73	32 33N	83 52W
Fort Vermilion	54	58 24N	116 0W
*Fort Victoria	117	20 8 S	30 55 E
Ft. Walton Beach	73	30 25N	86 40W
Fort Wayne	72	41 5N	85 10W
Fort Whyte	58	49 49N	97 13W
Fort William	96	56 48N	5 8W
Fort William = Thunder Bay	34	48 20N	89 10W
Fort Worth	75	32 45N	97 25W
Fort Yates	74	46 8N	100 38W
Fort Yukon	67	66 35N	145 12W
Fortaleza	87	3 35 S	38 35W
Forte Coimbra	86	19 55 S	57 48W
Forteau	36	51 28N	56 58W
Forth, Firth of	96	56 5N	2 55W
Forth, R.	96	56 9N	4 18W
Fortín Corrales	86	22 21 S	60 35W
Fortín Guachalla	86	22 2 S	62 23W
Fortín, L.	38	50 50N	67 46W
Fortín Rojas Silva	88	22 40 S	59 3W
Fortín Siracuas	86	21 3 S	61 46W
Fortín Teniente Montania	88	22 1 S	59 45W
Fortrose	96	57 35N	4 10W
Fortuna, Cal., U.S.A.	78	48 38N	124 8W
Fortuna, N.D., U.S.A.	56	48 55N	103 48W
Fortune	37	47 4N	55 50W
Fortune B.	37	47 30N	55 22W
Forty Mile	67	64 20N	140 30W
Forûr	123	26 20N	54 30 E
Fos do Jordâo	86	9 30 S	72 14W
Fos-sur-Mer	103	43 26N	4 56 E
Fosheim Pen.	65	80 0N	85 0W
Fossil	78	45 0N	120 9W
Fosston, Can.	56	52 12N	103 49W
Fosston, U.S.A.	74	47 33N	95 39W
Foster, Can.	41	45 17N	72 30W
Foster, U.S.A.	77	38 48N	84 13W
Foster, R.	55	55 47N	105 49W
Fostoria	72	41 8N	83 25W
Fougamou	116	1 38 S	11 39 E
Fougères	100	48 21N	1 14W
Foul Pt.	124	8 35N	81 25 E
Foula, I.	96	60 10N	2 5W
Fountain, Colo., U.S.A.	74	38 42N	104 40W
Fountain, Utah, U.S.A.	78	39 41N	111 50W
Fountain Springs	81	35 54N	118 51W
Four Mts., Is. of the	67	52 0N	170 30W
Fourchambault	101	47 0N	3 3 E
Fourchu	39	45 43N	60 17W
Fourmies	101	50 1N	4 2 E
Fourmont, L.	38	52 5N	60 27W
Fournier, L.	38	51 33N	65 25W
Fours	101	46 50N	3 42 E
Fourteen Island Lake	43	45 54N	74 2W
Fouta Djalon	114	11 20N	12 10W
Foux, Cap-à-	85	19 43N	73 27W
Foveaux Str.	133	46 42 S	168 10 E
Fowler, Calif., U.S.A.	80	36 41N	119 41W
Fowler, Colo., U.S.A.	74	38 10N	104 0W
Fowler, Ind., U.S.A.	77	40 37N	87 19W
Fowler, Kans., U.S.A.	75	37 28N	100 7W
Fowler, Mich., U.S.A.	77	43 0N	84 45W
Fowlerton	75	28 26N	98 50W
Fowlerville	77	42 40N	84 4W
Fowliang	131	27 8N	117 12 E
Fowling	131	29 39N	107 29 E
Fox Creek	60	54 24N	116 48W
Fox Is.	67	52 30N	166 0W
Fox, R., Can.	55	56 3N	93 18W
Fox, R., U.S.A.	76	40 21N	91 28W
Fox Valley	56	50 30N	109 25W
Foxe Basin	65	66 0N	77 0W
Foxe Chan.	65	65 0N	80 0W
Foxe Pen.	65	65 0N	76 0W
Foxpark	78	41 4N	106 6W
Foxton	133	40 29 S	175 18 E
Foxville	53	50 4N	81 38W
Foyle, Lough	97	55 6N	7 8W
Foynes	97	52 30N	9 5W
Foz do Gregório	86	6 47 S	71 0W
Foz do Iguaçu	89	25 30 S	54 30W
Frackville	71	40 46N	76 15W
Framlingham	71	42 18N	71 26W
Franca	87	20 25 S	47 30W
Francavilla Fontana	109	40 32N	17 35 E
France ■	99	47 0N	3 0 E
Frances Creek	134	13 25 S	132 3 E
Frances L.	54	61 23N	129 30W
Frances, R.	54	60 16N	129 10W
Francés Viejo, C.	85	19 40N	70 0W
Francesville	77	40 59N	86 53W
Franceville	116	1 40 S	13 32 E
Franche Comté	101	46 30N	5 50 E
Francis	56	50 6N	103 52W
Francis Harbour	35	52 34N	55 44W
Francisco I. Madero, Coahuila, Mexico	82	25 48N	103 18W
Francisco I. Madero, Durango, Mexico	82	24 32N	104 22W
Francistown	117	21 7 S	27 33 E
François	37	47 35N	56 45W
François L.	62	54 0N	125 30W
François, Le	85	14 38N	60 57W
Franeker	105	53 12N	5 33 E
Frankford, Can.	47	44 12N	77 36W
Frankford, U.S.A.	76	39 29N	91 19W
Frankfort, Ind., U.S.A.	77	40 20N	86 33W
Frankfort, Kans., U.S.A.	74	39 42N	96 26W
Frankfort, Ky., U.S.A.	77	38 12N	84 52W
Frankfort, Mich., U.S.A.	72	44 38N	86 14W
Frankfort, Ohio, U.S.A.	77	39 24N	83 11W
Frankfurt am Main	106	50 7N	8 40 E
Frankfurt an der Oder	106	52 50N	14 31 E
Fränkische Alb	106	49 20N	11 30 E
Franklin, Ill., U.S.A.	76	39 37N	90 3W
Franklin, Ind., U.S.A.	77	39 29N	86 3W
Franklin, Ky., U.S.A.	73	36 40N	86 30W
Franklin, La., U.S.A.	75	29 45N	91 30W
Franklin, Mass., U.S.A.	71	42 4N	71 23W
Franklin, Nebr., U.S.A.	74	40 9N	98 55W
Franklin, N.H., U.S.A.	71	43 28N	71 39W
Franklin, N.J., U.S.A.	71	41 9N	74 38W
Franklin, Ohio, U.S.A.	77	39 34N	84 18W
Franklin, Pa., U.S.A.	70	41 22N	79 45W
Franklin, Tenn., U.S.A.	73	35 54N	86 53W
Franklin, Va., U.S.A.	73	36 40N	76 58W
Franklin, W. Va., U.S.A.	72	38 38N	79 21W
Franklin, Wis., U.S.A.	77	42 53N	88 1W
*Franklin □	64	71 0N	99 0W
Franklin B.	67	69 45N	126 0W
Franklin Centre	43	45 2N	73 55W
Franklin D. Roosevelt L.	78	48 30N	118 16W
Franklin I.	91	76 10 S	168 30 E
Franklin, L.	78	40 20N	115 26W
Franklin Mts.	64	65 0N	125 0W
Franklin Park	77	41 56N	87 51W
Franklin River	62	49 7N	124 48W
Franklin Str.	65	72 0N	96 0W
Franklinton	75	30 53N	90 10W
Franklinville	70	42 21N	78 28W
Franks Peak	78	43 50N	109 5W
Frankston	136	38 8 S	145 8 E
Franquelin	38	49 18N	67 54W
Frantsa Josifa, Zemlya	120	79 0N	62 0 E
Franz	53	48 25N	84 30W
Franz Josef Fd.	17	73 20N	22 0 E
Franz Josef Land = Frantsa Josifa	120	76 0N	62 0 E
Fraser	46	42 32N	82 57W
Fraser I.	135	25 15 S	153 10 E
Fraser Lake	62	54 0N	124 50W
Fraser, R., B.C., Can.	66	49 7N	123 11W
Fraser, R., Newf., Can.	36	56 39N	62 10W
Fraserburgh	96	57 41N	2 0W
Fraserdale	53	49 55N	81 37W
Fraserwood	57	50 38N	97 13W
Frasne	101	46 50N	6 10 E
Frater	34	47 20N	84 25W
Fray Bentos	88	33 10 S	58 15W
Frazer L.	52	49 15N	88 40W
Fredericia	111	55 34N	9 45 E
Frederick, Md., U.S.A.	72	39 25N	77 23W
Frederick, Okla., U.S.A.	75	34 22N	99 0W
Frederick, S.D., U.S.A.	74	45 55N	98 29W
Frederick Reef	135	20 58 S	154 23 E
Frederick Sd.	54	57 10N	134 0W

* Renamed Kuujjuaq
† Renamed Faradofay

* Renamed Masvingo

* Now Baffin Region and Kitikmeot Region

Fredericksburg Gatun

Name	Page	Lat.	Long.
Fredericksburg, Tex., U.S.A.	75	30 17N	98 55W
Fredericksburg, Va., U.S.A.	72	38 16N	77 29W
Frederickstown	75	37 35N	90 15W
Fredericton	39	45 57N	66 40W
Fredericton Junc.	39	45 41N	66 40W
Frederikshåb	17	62 0N	49 30W
Frederikshavn	111	57 28N	10 31E
Frederiksted	85	17 43N	64 53W
Fredonia, Ariz., U.S.A.	79	36 59N	112 36W
Fredonia, Kans., U.S.A.	75	37 34N	95 50W
Fredonia, N.Y., U.S.A.	70	42 26N	79 20W
Fredrikstad	111	59 13N	10 57E
Freeburg	76	38 19N	91 56W
Freehold	71	40 15N	74 18W
Freel Pk.	80	38 52N	119 53W
Freeland	71	41 3N	75 48W
Freeling, Mt.	134	22 35S	133 06E
Freels, C.	37	49 15N	53 30W
Freelton	49	43 24N	80 2W
Freeman, Calif., U.S.A.	81	35 35N	117 53W
Freeman, Mo., U.S.A.	76	38 37N	94 30W
Freeman, S.D., U.S.A.	74	43 25N	97 20W
Freeman, R.	60	54 19N	114 47W
Freeport, Bahamas	85	25 45N	88 30E
Freeport, N.S., Can.	39	44 15N	66 20W
Freeport, Ont., Can.	49	43 25N	80 25W
Freeport, Ill., U.S.A.	76	42 18N	89 40W
Freeport, Tex., U.S.A.	75	28 55N	95 22W
Freetown	114	8 30N	13 10W
Frégate, L.	36	53 15N	74 45W
Fréhel, C.	100	48 40N	2 20W
Freiberg	106	50 55N	13 20E
Freire	90	39 0S	72 50W
Freirina	88	28 30S	70 27W
Freising	106	48 24N	11 47E
Freistadt	106	48 30N	14 30E
Fréjus	103	43 25N	6 44E
Frelighsburg	43	45 3N	72 50W
Fremantle	134	32 1S	115 47E
Fremont, Calif., U.S.A.	80	37 32N	122 57W
Fremont, Ind., U.S.A.	77	41 44N	84 56W
Fremont, Mich., U.S.A.	72	43 29N	85 59W
Fremont, Nebr., U.S.A.	74	41 30N	96 30W
Fremont, Ohio, U.S.A.	77	41 20N	83 5W
Fremont, L.	78	43 0N	109 50W
Fremont, R.	79	38 15N	110 20W
French Camp	80	37 53N	121 16W
French Cr.	70	41 30N	80 2W
French Guiana ■	87	4 0N	53 0W
French I.	136	38 20S	145 22E
French Lick	77	38 33N	86 37W
French, R., Ont., Can.	46	46 2N	80 34W
French, R., Ont., Can.	53	50 40N	80 59W
French River	46	46 2N	80 34W
French Terr. of Afars & Issas □ = Djibouti ■	115	11 30N	42 15E
Frenchburg	77	37 57N	83 38W
Frenchglen	78	42 56N	119 0W
Frenchman Butte	56	53 35N	109 38W
Frenchman Creek, R.	74	40 34N	101 35W
Frenchman, R.	78	49 25N	108 20W
Fresco, R.	87	7 15S	51 30W
Freshfield, C.	91	68 25S	151 10E
Fresnillo	82	23 10N	103 0W
Fresno	80	36 47N	119 50W
Fresno Res.	78	48 47N	110 0W
Frévent	101	50 15N	2 17E
Freycinet Pen.	135	42 10S	148 25E
Fria, La	86	8 13N	72 15W
Friant	80	36 59N	119 43W
Frias	88	28 40S	65 5W
Fribourg	106	48 0N	7 52E
Friday Harbor	80	48 32N	123 1W
Friedberg	10	50 19N	8 45E
Friedrichshafen	106	47 39N	9 29E
Friendly (Tonga) Is.	133	19 50S	174 30W
Friesland □	105	53 5N	5 50E
Frigate, L.	34	53 15N	74 45W
Frijoles	84	9 11N	79 48W
Frikson	57	50 30N	99 55W
Frio, C.	117	18 0S	12 0E
Frio, R.	75	29 40N	99 40W
Friona	75	34 40N	102 42W
Fritch	75	35 40N	101 35W
Friuli-Venezia Giulia □	108	46 0N	13 0E
Frobisher	57	49 12N	102 26W
Frobisher B.	65	63 0N	67 0W
Frobisher Bay	65	63 44N	68 31W
Frobisher L.	55	56 20N	108 15W
Frog L.	60	53 55N	110 20W
Frohavet	110	64 5N	9 35E
Froid	74	48 20N	104 29W
Fromberg	78	45 19N	108 58W
Frome	95	51 16N	2 17W
Frome, L.	135	30 45S	139 45E
Fromentine	100	46 53N	2 9W
Front Range	78	40 0N	105 10W
Front Royal	72	38 55N	78 10W
Frontera	83	18 30N	92 40W
Frontier	56	49 12N	108 34W
Frontignan	102	43 27N	3 45E
Frosinone	108	41 38N	13 20E
Frostburg	72	39 43N	78 57W
Frostisen	110	68 14N	17 10E
Frouard	101	48 47N	6 8E
Fröya I.	110	63 45N	8 45E
Fruges	101	50 30N	2 8E
Fruitland	48	43 13N	79 43W
Fruitvale	63	49 7N	117 33W
Frunze	120	42 54N	74 36E
Frutal	87	20 0S	49 0W
Fry L.	52	51 14N	91 19W
Frýdek-Místek	107	49 40N	18 20E
Fuchin	130	47 10N	132 0E
Fuchow, Kiangsi, China	131	27 50N	116 14E
Fuchow, Liaoning, China	130	39 45N	121 45E
Fuchun K.	131	30 1N	120 1E
Fuchung	131	24 25N	110 16E
Fucino, L.	102	42 0N	13 30E
Fuente Ovejuna	104	38 15N	5 25W
Fuentes de Oñoro	104	40 33N	6 52W
Fuerte Olimpo	88	21 0S	58 0W
Fuerte, R.	82	26 0N	109 0W
Fuga, I.	131	19 55N	121 10E
Fugløysund	110	70 15N	20 20E
Fujaira	123	25 7N	56 18E
Fuji-no-miya	132	35 20N	138 40E
Fuji-San	132	35 22N	138 44E
Fujisawa	132	35 22N	139 29E
Fukien □	131	26 0N	117 30E
Fukow	131	34 11N	114 36E
Fukuchiyama	132	35 25N	135 9E
Fukui	132	36 0N	136 10E
Fukui-ken □	132	36 0N	136 12E
Fukuoka	132	33 30N	130 30E
Fukuoka-ken □	132	33 30N	131 0E
Fukushima-ken □	132	37 30N	140 15E
Fukuyama	132	34 35N	133 20E
Fulda	106	50 32N	9 41E
Fulda, R.	106	50 37N	9 40E
Fulford Harbour	63	48 47N	123 27W
Fullerton, Calif., U.S.A.	81	33 52N	117 58W
Fullerton, Nebr., U.S.A.	74	41 25N	98 0W
Fulton, Can.	49	43 8N	79 40W
Fulton, Ill., U.S.A.	76	41 52N	90 11W
Fulton, Ind., U.S.A.	77	40 57N	86 16W
Fulton, Mo., U.S.A.	76	38 50N	91 55W
Fulton, N.Y., U.S.A.	71	43 20N	76 22W
Fumay	101	50 0N	4 40E
Fumel	102	44 30N	0 58E
Funabashi	132	35 45N	140 0E
Funafuti, I.	14	8 30S	179 0E
Funchal	114	32 45N	16 55W
Fundación	86	10 31N	74 11W
Fundão	104	40 8N	7 30W
Fundy, B. of	39	45 0N	66 0W
Fundy Nat. Park	39	45 35N	65 10W
Funes	86	1 0N	77 28W
Fungchun	131	23 27N	111 30E
Funing	131	23 45N	105 30E
Furat, Nahr al	122	33 30N	43 0E
Furbero	83	20 22N	97 31W
Furnas, Représa de	89	20 50S	45 0W
Furneaux Group	135	40 10S	147 50E
Furness	94	54 14N	3 8W
Furness, Pen.	94	54 12N	3 10W
Fürth	106	49 29N	11 0E
Fury and Hecla Str.	65	69 56N	84 0W
Fusagasugá	86	4 21N	74 22W
Fuse	132	34 40N	135 37E
Fushun	130	41 50N	123 55E
Fusin	130	42 12N	121 33E
Fusui	131	22 35N	107 58E
Futing	131	27 15N	120 10E
Futsing	131	25 46N	119 29E
Futuna I.	14	14 25S	178 20E
Fuyang Ho	131	38 14N	116 5E
Fuyuan	130	48 9N	134 3E
Fwaka	117	12 5S	29 25E
Fyekundo = Yushu	129	33 6N	96 48E
Fylde	94	53 50N	2 58W
Fyn	111	55 20N	10 30E
Fyne, L.	96	56 0N	5 20W
G			
Gabarouse	39	45 50N	60 9W
Gabela	116	11 0S	14 37E
Gaberones = Gaborone	117	24 37S	25 57E
Gabès	114	33 53N	10 2E
Gabès, Golfe de	114	34 0N	10 30E
Gabon ■	116	0 10S	10 0E
Gaborone	117	24 37S	25 57E
Gabriels	71	44 26N	74 12W
Gabriola I.	63	49 9N	123 47W
Gabrovo	109	42 52N	25 27E
Gacé	100	48 49N	0 20E
Gach Sārān	123	30 15N	50 45E
Gadag	124	15 30N	75 45E
Gadarwara	124	22 50N	78 50E
Gadhada	124	22 0N	71 35E
Gadsden, Ala., U.S.A.	73	34 1N	86 0W
Gadsden, Ariz., U.S.A.	79	32 35N	114 47W
Gadwal	124	16 10N	77 50E
Gaffney	73	35 10N	81 31W
Gagetown	39	45 46N	66 10W
Gagnoa	114	6 4N	5 55W
Gagnon	38	51 50N	68 5W
Gagnon, L., N.W.T., Can.	55	62 3N	110 27W
Gagnon, L., Qué., Can.	40	46 7N	75 7W
Gail	75	32 48N	101 25W
Gaillac	102	43 54N	1 54E
Gaillarbois, L.	38	52 0N	67 27W
Gaillon	100	49 10N	1 20E
Gaines	70	41 45N	77 35W
Gainesville, Fla., U.S.A.	73	29 38N	82 20W
Gainesville, Ga., U.S.A.	73	34 17N	83 47W
Gainesville, Mo., U.S.A.	75	36 35N	92 26W
Gainesville, Tex., U.S.A.	75	33 40N	97 10W
Gainsborough	94	53 23N	0 46W
Gairdner L.	134	31 30S	136 0E
Gairloch L.	96	57 43N	5 45W
Galahad	61	52 31N	111 56W
Galán, Cerro	88	25 55S	66 52W
Galangue	117	13 48S	16 3E
Galápagos, Is.	15	0 0	89 0W
Galas, R.	128	4 55N	101 57E
Galashiels	96	55 37N	2 50W
Galaţi	107	45 27N	28 2E
Galatina	109	40 10N	18 10E
Galax	73	36 42N	80 57W
Galdhøpiggen	111	61 38N	8 18E
Galeana	82	24 50N	100 4W
Galela	127	1 50N	127 55E
Galena, Alaska, U.S.A.	67	64 42N	157 0W
Galena, Ill., U.S.A.	76	42 25N	90 26W
Galeota Point	85	10 8N	61 0W
Galera, Pta. de la	86	10 48N	75 16W
Galesburg, Ill., U.S.A.	76	40 57N	90 23W
Galesburg, Mich., U.S.A.	77	42 17N	85 26W
Galeton, Can.	53	51 8N	80 55W
Galeton, U.S.A.	70	41 43N	77 40W
Galicia	104	42 43N	8 0W
Galien	77	41 48N	86 30W
Galilee, S. of = Kinneret, L.	115	32 49N	35 36E
Galion	70	40 43N	82 48W
Galissonnière, La, L.	38	51 25N	62 0W
Galiuro Mts.	79	32 40N	110 30W
Gallatin, Mo., U.S.A.	76	39 55N	93 58W
Gallatin, Tenn., U.S.A.	73	36 24N	86 27W
Galle	124	6 5N	80 10E
Gallego	82	29 49N	106 22W
Gállego, R.	104	42 23N	0 30W
Gallegos, R.	90	51 50S	71 0W
Galley Hd.	97	51 32N	8 56W
Gallinas, Pta.	86	12 28N	71 40W
Gallipoli	109	40 8N	18 0E
Gallipoli = Gelibolu	109	40 28N	26 43E
Gallipolis	72	38 50N	82 10W
Gallitzin	70	40 28N	78 32W
Gällivare	110	67 9N	20 40E
Galloway	96	55 0N	4 25W
Galloway, Mull of	96	54 38N	4 50W
Gallup	79	35 30N	108 54W
Galoya	124	8 10N	80 55E
Galt, Can.	49	43 22N	80 19W
Galt, Calif., U.S.A.	80	38 15N	121 18W
Galt, Mo., U.S.A.	76	40 8N	93 23W
Galty Mts.	97	52 22N	8 10W
Galtymore, Mt.	97	52 22N	8 12W
Galva	76	41 10N	90 0W
Galveston, Ind., U.S.A.	77	40 35N	86 11W
Galveston, Tex., U.S.A.	75	29 15N	94 48W
Galveston B.	75	29 30N	94 50W
Gálvez	88	32 0S	61 20W
Galway	97	53 16N	9 4W
Galway □	97	53 16N	9 3W
Galway B.	97	53 10N	9 20W
Gamarra	86	8 20N	73 45W
Gambell	67	63 55N	171 50W
Gambia ■	114	13 25N	16 0W
Gambia, R.	114	13 20N	15 45W
Gambier I.	63	49 30N	123 23W
Gamboa	84	9 8N	79 42W
Gamboma	116	1 55S	15 52E
Gameleira	87	7 50S	50 0W
Gamerco	79	35 33N	108 56W
Gammelgarn	87	57 24N	18 49E
Gammon, R.	57	51 24N	95 44W
Gan	102	43 12N	0 27W
Gan (Addu Atoll)	119	0 10S	71 10E
Ganado, Ariz., U.S.A.	79	35 46N	109 41W
Ganado, Tex., U.S.A.	75	29 4N	96 31W
Gananoque	47	44 20N	76 10W
Ganaveh	123	29 35N	50 35E
Gand	105	51 2N	3 37E
Gandak, R.	125	27 0N	84 8E
Gandava	124	28 32N	67 32E
Gander	37	48 58N	54 35W
Gander L.	37	48 58N	54 35W
Gander, R.	37	49 16N	54 30W
Gand = Gent	105	51 2N	3 37E
Gandhi Sagar	124	24 40N	75 40E
Gandi	114	12 55N	5 49E
Ganedidalem = Gani	127	0 48S	128 14E
Gang Ranch	63	51 33N	122 20W
Ganga, R.	125	25 0N	88 0E
Ganganagar	124	29 56N	73 56E
Gangaw	125	22 5N	94 15E
Ganges	102	43 56N	3 42E
Ganges = Ganga, R.	125	25 0N	88 0E
Ganges, Mouth of the	125	21 30N	90 0E
Gangtok	125	27 20N	88 37E
Gannat	102	46 7N	3 11E
Gannett Pk.	78	43 15N	109 47W
Gannvalley	74	44 3N	98 57W
Gantheaume B.	134	27 40S	114 10E
Gao	114	16 15N	0 5W
Gao Bang	128	22 37N	106 18E
Gap	103	44 33N	6 5E
Gar Dzong	124	32 20N	79 55E
Garachiné	84	8 0N	78 12W
Garanhuns	87	8 50S	36 30W
Garber	75	36 30N	97 36W
Garberville	78	40 11N	123 50W
Gard □	103	44 2N	4 10E
Garda, L. di	108	45 40N	10 40E
Gardanne	103	43 27N	5 27E
Garde L.	55	62 50N	106 13W
Garden City, Kans., U.S.A.	75	38 0N	100 45W
Garden City, Mo., U.S.A.	76	38 34N	94 12W
Garden City, Tex., U.S.A.	75	31 52N	101 28W
Garden Grove	81	33 47N	117 55W
Garden I.	46	45 49N	85 30W
Gardez	124	33 31N	68 59E
Gardiner, Can.	34	49 19N	81 2W
Gardiner, Mont., U.S.A.	78	45 3N	110 53W
Gardiner, N. Mex., U.S.A.	75	36 55N	104 29W
Gardiner Ls.	60	57 32N	112 30W
Gardiners I.	71	41 4N	72 5W
Gardner, Ill., U.S.A.	77	41 12N	88 17W
Gardner, Mass., U.S.A.	71	42 35N	72 0W
Gardner Canal	62	53 27N	128 8W
Gardnerville	80	38 59N	119 47W
Gareloi I.	67	51 49N	178 50W
Garey	81	34 53N	120 19W
Garfield, Utah, U.S.A.	78	40 45N	112 15W
Garfield, Wash., U.S.A.	78	47 3N	117 8W
Gargano, Mte.	108	41 43N	15 43E
Gargans, Mt.	102	45 37N	1 39E
Gargantua, C.	34	47 35N	85 0W
Garibaldi	54	49 56N	123 15W
Garibaldi, Mt.	63	49 51N	123 0W
Garibaldi Prov. Park	63	49 50N	122 40W
Garies	117	30 32S	17 59E
Garigliano, R.	108	41 13N	13 44E
Garland	78	41 47N	112 10W
Garm	120	39 0N	70 20E
Garmsār	123	35 20N	52 25E
Garneau, L.	38	51 43N	63 22W
Garner	76	43 4N	93 37W
Garners Corners	48	43 12N	79 57W
Garnett	74	38 18N	95 12W
Garnish	37	47 14N	55 22W
Garonne, R.	102	45 2N	0 36W
Garoua	114	9 19N	13 21E
Garrett	77	41 21N	85 8W
Garrigues	102	43 40N	3 30E
Garrison, Ky., U.S.A.	77	38 36N	83 10W
Garrison, Mont., U.S.A.	78	46 37N	112 56W
Garrison, N.D., U.S.A.	74	31 50N	94 28W
Garrison, Tex., U.S.A.	75	47 39N	101 27W
*Garrison Res.	74	47 30N	102 0W
Garry, Glen	96	57 3N	5 7W
Garry L., Can.	65	65 58N	100 18W
Garry L., U.K.	96	57 5N	4 52W
Garry, R.	96	56 47N	3 47W
Garsen	116	2 20S	40 5E
Garson L.	60	56 19N	110 2W
Garson, R..	55	56 20N	110 1W
Gartempe, R.	102	46 47N	0 49E
Gartok	129	31 59N	80 30E
Garupá	87	1 25S	51 35W
Garut	127	7 14S	107 53E
Garvie Mts.	133	45 30S	168 50E
Gary	77	41 35N	87 20W
Garzón	86	2 10N	75 40W
Gas City	77	40 29N	85 36W
Gasan Kuli	120	37 40N	54 20E
Gascogne	102	43 45N	0 20E
Gasconade	76	38 40N	91 33W
Gasconade R.	76	38 41N	91 33W
Gascons	38	48 11N	64 51W
Gascony = Gascogne	102	43 45N	0 20E
Gascoyne, R.	134	24 52S	113 37E
Gashiun Nor	129	42 20N	100 40E
Gashua	114	12 54N	11 0E
Gaspé	38	48 52N	64 30W
Gaspé, Baie de	38	48 46N	64 17W
Gaspé, C.	38	48 48N	64 7W
Gaspé Pen.	38	48 45N	65 40W
Gaspé, Péninsule de	38	48 30N	65 30W
Gaspésie, Parc Prov. de la	38	48 55N	65 50W
Gassaway	72	38 42N	80 43W
Gastonia	73	35 17N	81 10W
Gastre	90	42 10S	69 15W
Gata, C. de	104	36 41N	2 13W
Gata, Sierra de	104	40 20N	6 20W
Gataga, R.	54	58 35N	126 59W
Gateshead	94	54 57N	1 37W
Gateshead I.	65	70 36N	100 26W
Gatesville	75	31 29N	97 45W
Gatico	88	22 40S	70 20W
Gâtinais	101	48 5N	2 40E
Gâtine, Hauteurs de	102	46 35N	0 45W
Gatineau, Ont., Can.	48	45 29N	75 39W
Gatineau, Qué., Can.	40	45 29N	75 39W
Gatineau, Parc de la	40	45 40N	76 0W
Gatineau, R.	48	45 27N	75 42W
†Gatooma	117	18 20S	29 52E
Gatun	84	9 16N	79 55W

* *Renamed Lake Sakakawea*

† *Renamed Kadoma*

Gatun Dam Gobles

Gatun Dam 84 9 16N 79 55W
Gatun, L. 84 9 7N 79 56W
Gatun Locks 84 9 16N 79 55W
Gaud-i-Zirreh 124 29 45N 62 0E
Gauer L. 55 57 0N 97 50W
Gauhati 125 26 10N 91 45E
Gaula, R. 110 62 57N 11 0E
Gaultois 37 47 36N 55 54W
Gaussberg, Mt. 91 66 45S 89 0E
Gausta, Mt. 111 59 48N 8 40E
Gavarnie 102 42 44N 0 3W
Gaväter 123 25 10N 61 23E
Gaviota 81 34 29N 120 13W
Gavle 111 60 41N 17 13E
Gävleborgs Lan □ 111 61 20N 16 15E
Gavray 100 48 55N 1 20W
Gawilgarh Hills 124 21 15N 76 45E
Gawler 135 34 30S 138 42E
Gawler Ranges 134 32 30S 135 45E
Gaya 125 24 47N 85 4E
Gaylord 46 45 1N 84 35W
Gayndah 135 25 35S 151 39E
Gayot, L. 36 55 43N 70 50W
Gaza 115 31 30N 34 28E
Gaziantep 122 37 6N 37 23E
Gdansk 107 54 22N 18 40E
Gdanska, Zatoka 107 54 30N 19 20E
Gdynia 107 54 35N 18 33E
Geary 39 45 46N 66 29W
Gebe, I. 127 0 5N 129 25E
Gedaref 115 14 2N 35 28E
Gèdre 102 42 47N 0 2E
Gedser 111 54 35N 11 55E
Geel 105 51 10N 4 59E
Geelong 136 38 10S 144 22E
Geikie I. 52 50 0N 88 35W
Geikie, R. 55 57 45N 103 52W
Geita 116 2 48S 32 12E
Gela 108 37 6N 14 18E
Gelderland □ 105 52 5N 6 10E
Geldermalsen 105 51 53N 5 17E
Geldrop 105 51 25N 5 32E
Geleen 105 50 57N 5 49E
Gelibolu 109 40 28N 26 43E
Gelsenkirchen 105 51 30N 7 5E
Gem 61 50 57N 112 11W
Gemas 128 2 37N 102 36E
Gembloux 105 50 34N 4 43E
Gemena 116 3 20N 19 40E
Gemerek 122 39 15N 36 10E
Gemert 105 51 33N 5 41E
Gemlik 122 40 28N 29 13E
Gençay 102 46 23N 0 23E
General Acha 88 37 20S 64 38W
General Alvear, B. A., Argent. 88 36 0S 60 0W
General Alvear, Mend., Argent. 88 35 0S 67 40W
General Artigas 88 26 52S 56 16W
General Belgrano 88 36 0S 58 30W
General Cabrera 88 32 53S 63 58W
General Cepeda 82 25 23N 101 27W
General Guido 88 36 40S 57 50W
General Juan Madariaga 88 37 0S 57 0W
General La Madrid 88 37 30S 61 10W
General MacArthur 127 11 18N 125 28E
General Martin Miguel de Güemes 88 24 50S 65 0W
General Paz 88 27 45S 57 36W
General Paz, L. 90 44 0S 72 0W
General Pico 88 35 45S 63 50W
General Pinedo 88 27 15S 61 30W
General Pinto 88 34 45S 61 50W
General Roca 90 30 0S 67 40W
General Santos 127 6 12N 125 14E
General Treviño 83 26 14N 99 29W
General Trias 82 28 21N 106 22W
General Viamonte 88 35 1S 61 3W
General Villegas 88 35 0S 63 0W
Genesee, Can. 60 53 21N 114 20W
Genesee, Idaho, U.S.A. 78 46 31N 116 59W
Genesee, Mich., U.S.A. 70 43 7N 83 38W
Genesee, Pa., U.S.A. 70 42 0N 77 54W
Genesee, R. 70 41 35N 78 0W
Geneseo, Ill., U.S.A. 76 41 25N 90 10W
Geneseo, Kans., U.S.A. 74 38 32N 98 8W
Geneseo, N.Y., U.S.A. 70 42 49N 77 49W
Geneva, Can. 43 45 36N 74 20W
Geneva, Ala., U.S.A. 73 31 2N 85 52W
Geneva, Ill., U.S.A. 77 41 53N 88 18W
Geneva, Nebr., U.S.A. 74 40 35N 97 35W
Geneva, N.Y., U.S.A. 70 42 53N 77 0W
Geneva, Ohio, U.S.A. 70 41 49N 80 58W
Geneva = Genève 106 46 12N 6 9E
Geneva, L. 77 42 38N 88 30W
Geneva, L. = Léman, Lac 106 46 26N 6 30E
Genève 106 46 12N 6 9E
Geneve 77 40 36N 84 57W
Genil, R. 104 37 12N 3 50W
Génissiat, Barrage de 103 46 1N 5 48E
Genk 105 50 58N 5 32E
Genlis 101 47 15N 5 12E
Gennargentu, Mt. del 108 40 0N 9 10E
Gennes 100 47 20N 0 17W
Genoa, Ill., U.S.A. 77 42 6N 88 42W
Genoa, Nebr., U.S.A. 74 41 31N 97 44W
Genoa, Nev., U.S.A. 80 39 2N 119 50W
Genoa, N.Y., U.S.A. 71 42 40N 76 32W
Genoa = Génova 108 44 24N 8 57E
Genoa City 77 42 30N 88 20W
Génova 108 44 24N 8 56E
Génova, Golfo di 108 44 0N 9 0E
Gent 105 51 2N 3 37E
Genteng 127 7 25S 106 23E
Geographe B. 134 33 30S 113 20E
Geographe Chan. 134 24 30S 113 0E
George, Can. 35 46 12N 62 32W
George, S. Afr. 117 33 58S 22 29E
George B. 39 45 45N 61 45W
George, L., N.S.W., Austral. 136 35 10S 149 25E
George, L., S. Austral., Austral. 136 37 25S 140 0E
George, L., Uganda 116 0 5N 30 10E
George, L., Fla., U.S.A. 73 29 15N 81 35W
George, L., N.Y., U.S.A. 71 43 30N 73 30W
George, R., Qué., Can. 35 58 49N 66 10W
George, R., Qué., Can. 36 49 21N 67 59W
George River = Port Nouveau-Québec 36 58 32N 65 54W
George Sound 133 44 52S 167 25E
George Town, Bahamas 84 23 33N 75 47W
George Town, Malay. 128 5 25N 100 19E
George V Coast 91 67 0S 148 0E
George West 75 28 18N 98 5W
Georgetown, Austral. 135 18 17S 143 33E
Georgetown, Ont., Can. 49 43 40N 79 56W
Georgetown, P.E.I., Can. 39 46 13N 62 24W
Georgetown, Cay. Is. 84 19 20N 81 24W
Georgetown, Guyana 86 6 50N 58 12W
Georgetown, Calif., U.S.A. 80 38 54N 120 50W
Georgetown, Colo., U.S.A. 78 39 46N 105 49W
Georgetown, Ill., U.S.A. 77 39 59N 87 38W
Georgetown, Ky., U.S.A. 77 38 13N 84 33W
Georgetown, Ohio, U.S.A. 72 38 50N 83 50W
Georgetown, S.C., U.S.A. 73 33 22N 79 15W
Georgetown, Tex., U.S.A. 75 30 40N 97 45W
Georgia □ 72 32 0N 82 0W
Georgia, Str. of 62 49 25N 124 0W
Georgian B. 46 45 15N 81 0W
Georgian S.S.R. □ 120 41 0N 45 0E
Georgievsk 120 44 12N 43 28E
Georgina I. 46 44 22N 79 17W
Georgina, R. 135 23 30S 139 47E
Georgiu-Dezh 120 51 3N 39 20E
Gera 106 50 53N 12 5E
Geraardsbergen 105 50 45N 3 53E
Geral de Goias, Serra 87 12 0S 46 0W
Geral, Serra 89 26 25S 50 0W
Gerald 76 38 24N 91 21W
Geraldine 78 47 45N 110 18W
Geraldton, Austral. 134 28 48S 114 32E
Geraldton, Can. 53 49 44N 86 59W
Gérardmer 101 48 3N 6 50E
Gerdine, Mt. 67 61 32N 152 30W
Gerede 122 40 45N 32 10E
Gerik 128 5 25N 100 8E
Gering 74 41 51N 103 40W
Gerlach 78 40 43N 119 27W
Germain, Grand L. 38 51 12N 66 41W
Germansen Landing 54 55 43N 124 40W
Germantown 77 39 38N 84 22W
Germany, East ■ 106 52 0N 12 0E
Germany, West ■ 106 52 0N 9 0E
Germiston 117 26 11S 28 10E
Gerona 104 41 58N 2 46E
Gerrard 63 50 30N 117 17W
Gers □ 102 43 35N 0 38E
Gerze 122 41 45N 35 10E
Geser 127 3 50N 130 35E
Gethsémani 36 50 13N 60 40W
Gettysburg, Pa., U.S.A. 72 39 47N 77 18W
Gettysburg, S.D., U.S.A. 74 45 3N 99 56W
Getz Ice Shelf 91 75 0S 130 0W
Gévaudan 102 44 40N 3 40E
Gevelsberg 105 51 21N 7 7E
Gex 103 46 21N 6 3E
Geyser 78 47 17N 110 30W
Geyserville 80 38 42N 122 54W
Geysir 110 64 19N 20 18W
Ghaghara, R. 125 26 0N 84 20E
Ghail 122 21 40N 46 20E
Ghana ■ 114 6 0N 1 0W
Ghanzi 117 21 50S 21 45E
Ghardaïa 114 32 31N 3 37E
Gharyān 114 32 10N 13 0E
Ghāt 114 24 59N 10 19E
Ghat Ghat 122 24 40N 46 15E
Ghawdex = Gozo, I. 108 36 0N 14 13E
Ghaziabad 124 28 42N 77 35E
Ghazipur 125 25 38N 83 35E
Ghazni 124 33 30N 68 17E
Ghazni □ 124 33 0N 68 0E
Ghent = Gand 105 51 4N 3 43E
Ghisonaccia 103 42 1N 9 26E
Ghizao 124 33 30N 65 59E
Ghorat □ 124 34 0N 64 20E
Ghost River 52 50 12N 91 30W
Ghugus 124 20 0N 79 0E
Ghurian 124 34 17N 61 25E
Gia Lai = Pleiku 128 14 3N 108 0E
Gia Nghia 128 12 0N 107 42E
Giant Forest 80 36 36N 118 43W
Giant's Causeway 97 55 15N 6 30W
Giarre 108 37 44N 15 10E
Gibara 84 21 0N 76 20W
Gibbon 74 40 49N 98 45W
Gibbons 60 53 50N 113 20W
Gibeon 117 25 7S 17 45E
Gibraltar 104 36 7N 5 22W
Gibraltar, Str. of 104 35 55N 5 40W
Gibson City 77 40 28N 88 22W
Gibson Des. 134 24 0S 126 0E
Gibsonburg 77 41 23N 83 19W
Gibsons 63 49 24N 123 32W
Gibsonville 80 39 46N 120 54W
Gida. G. 17 72 30N 77 0E
Giddings 75 30 11N 96 58W
Gien 101 47 40N 2 36E
Giessen 106 50 34N 8 40E
Giffard 42 46 51N 71 12W
Gift Lake 60 55 53N 115 49W
Gifu 132 35 30N 136 45E
Gifu-ken □ 132 36 0N 137 0E
Gig Harbor 80 47 20N 122 35W
Giganta, Sa. de la 82 25 30N 111 30W
Gigha, I. 96 55 42N 5 45W
Gignac 102 43 39N 3 32E
Gijón 104 43 32N 5 42W
Gil I. 62 53 12N 129 15W
Gila Bend 79 33 0N 112 46W
Gila Bend Mts. 79 33 15N 113 0W
Gila, R. 79 33 5N 108 40W
*Gilbert Is. 14 1 0S 176 0E
Gilbert, Mt. 62 50 52N 124 16W
Gilbert Plains 57 51 9N 100 28W
Gilbert, R. 135 16 35S 141 15E
Gilford I. 62 50 40N 126 30W
Gilgandra 136 31 43S 148 39E
Gilgit 124 35 50N 74 15E
Gillam 55 56 20N 94 40W
Gillespie 76 39 7N 89 49W
Gillette 74 44 20N 105 38W
Gillies Bay 62 49 42N 124 29W
Gillingham 95 51 23N 0 34E
Gilman, Ill., U.S.A. 77 40 46N 88 0W
Gilman, Mo., U.S.A. 76 40 8N 93 53W
Gilmer 75 32 44N 94 55W
Gilmour 47 44 48N 77 37W
Gilroy 80 37 1N 121 37W
Gimli 55 50 40N 97 10W
Gimont 102 43 38N 0 52E
Gióna, Óros 109 38 38N 22 14E
Giong, Teluk 127 4 50N 118 20E
Giovi, P. dei 103 44 30N 8 55E
Gippsland 135 37 45S 147 15E
Girard, Ill., U.S.A. 76 39 27N 89 48W
Girard, Kans., U.S.A. 75 37 30N 94 50W
Girard, Ohio, U.S.A. 70 41 10N 80 42W
Girard, Pa., U.S.A. 70 42 1N 80 21W
Girardot 86 4 18N 74 48W
Girardville 41 49 0N 72 32W
Girdle Ness 96 57 9N 2 2W
Giresun 122 40 45N 38 30E
Giridih 125 24 10N 86 21E
Girishk 124 31 47N 64 24E
Giromagny 101 47 44N 6 50E
Gironde □ 102 44 45N 0 30W
Gironde, R. 102 45 27N 0 53W
Girouxville 60 55 45N 117 20W
Girvan 96 55 15N 4 50W
Gisborne 133 38 39S 178 5E
Gisborne L. 37 47 48N 54 49W
Gisenyi 116 1 41S 29 30E
Gisors 101 49 15N 1 40E
Giurgiu 107 43 52N 25 57E
Givet 101 50 8N 4 49E
Givors 103 45 35N 4 45E
Givry 101 46 41N 4 46E
Gizhiga 121 62 0N 150 27E
Gizhiginskaya, Guba 121 61 0N 158 0E
Gizycko 107 54 2N 21 48E
Gjirokastër 109 40 7N 20 16E
Gjoa Haven 65 68 38N 95 53W
Gjøvik 111 60 47N 10 43E
Glace Bay 39 46 11N 59 58W
Glacier B. 54 58 30N 136 10W
Glacier Nat. Park 63 51 15N 117 30W
Glacier National Park 61 48 35N 113 40W
Glacier Peak Mt. 63 48 7N 121 7W
Glacier Str. 65 76 12N 79 15W
Gladewater 75 32 30N 94 58W
Gladmar 56 49 10N 104 27W
Gladstone, Austral. 136 23 52S 151 16E
Gladstone, Can. 57 50 13N 98 57W
Gladstone, Mich., U.S.A. 72 45 52N 87 1W
Gladstone, Mo., U.S.A. 76 39 13N 94 35W
Gladwin 46 43 59N 84 29W
Gladys L. 54 59 50N 133 0W
Gláma 110 65 48N 23 0W
Gláma, R. 111 60 30N 12 8E
Glamis 81 33 0N 115 4W
Glamorgan (□) 95 51 37N 3 35W
Glamorgan, Vale of 98 50 45N 3 15W
Glan 127 5 45N 125 20E
Glanville 76 41 17N 89 15W
Glasco, Kans., U.S.A. 74 39 25N 97 50W
Glasco, N.Y., U.S.A. 71 42 3N 73 57W
Glasgow, U.K. 96 55 52N 4 14W
Glasgow, Ky., U.S.A. 72 37 2N 85 55W
Glasgow, Mo., U.S.A. 76 39 14N 92 51W
Glasgow, Mont., U.S.A. 78 48 12N 106 35W
Glaslyn 56 53 22N 108 21W
Glastonbury, U.K. 95 51 9N 2 42W
Glastonbury, U.S.A. 71 41 42N 72 27W
Glauchau 106 50 50N 12 33E
Glazov 120 58 9N 52 40E
Gleichen 54 50 50N 113 0W
Glen 71 44 7N 71 10W
Glen Affric 96 57 15N 5 0W
Glen Almond 40 45 42N 75 29W
Glen Canyon Dam 79 37 0N 111 25W
Glen Canyon Nat. Recreation Area 79 37 30N 111 0W
Glen Coe 98 56 40N 5 0W
Glen Cove 71 40 51N 73 37W
Glen Cross 49 43 59N 80 3W
Glen Ewen 57 49 12N 102 1W
Glen Garry 96 57 3N 5 7W
Glen Gordon 43 45 10N 74 32W
Glen Innes 135 29 40S 151 39E
Glen Lyon 71 41 10N 76 7W
Glen Mor 96 57 12N 4 37E
Glen Moriston 96 57 10N 4 58W
Glen Morris 49 43 16N 80 21W
Glen Robertson 43 45 22N 74 30W
Glen Thompson 136 37 38S 142 35E
Glen Ullin 74 46 48N 101 46W
Glen Williams 49 43 40N 79 55W
Glénans, Îs. de 100 47 42N 4 0W
Glenavon 56 50 12N 103 8W
Glenboro 57 49 33N 99 17W
Glenbrook 133 33 46S 150 37E
Glenburnie 136 37 51S 140 50E
Glencairn 58 50 26N 104 33W
Glenchristie 49 43 28N 80 17W
Glencoe, Can. 46 42 45N 81 43W
Glencoe, U.S.A. 74 44 45N 94 10W
Glendale, Alta., Can. 59 51 2N 114 9W
Glendale, N.S., Can. 39 45 49N 61 18W
Glendale, Ariz., U.S.A. 79 33 40N 112 8W
Glendale, Calif., U.S.A. 81 34 7N 118 18W
Glendale, Oreg., U.S.A. 78 42 44N 123 29W
Glendive 74 47 7N 104 40W
Glendo 74 42 30N 105 0W
Glendon 60 54 15N 111 10W
Glendora 81 34 8N 117 52W
Gleneagle 48 45 32N 75 48W
Glenelg, R. 136 38 4S 140 59E
Glenella 57 50 33N 99 11W
Glengariff 97 51 45N 9 33W
Glengarry □ 43 45 15N 74 30W
Glenmoor Res. 59 50 59N 114 8W
Glenmora 75 31 1N 92 34W
Glenn 80 39 31N 122 1W
Glennie 46 44 32N 83 39W
Glennie's Creek 136 32 30S 151 8E
Glenns Ferry 78 43 0N 115 15W
Glenrock 78 42 53N 105 55W
Glenroy 134 26 23S 28 17E
Glens Falls 71 43 20N 73 40W
Glenties 97 54 48N 8 18W
Glenville 72 38 56N 80 50W
Glenwood, Alta., Can. 61 49 21N 113 31W
Glenwood, Newf., Can. 37 49 0N 54 47W
Glenwood, Ark., U.S.A. 75 34 20N 93 30W
Glenwood, Hawaii, U.S.A. 67 19 29N 155 10W
Glenwood, Iowa, U.S.A. 74 41 7N 95 41W
Glenwood, Minn., U.S.A. 74 45 38N 95 21W
Glenwood, Wash., U.S.A. 80 46 1N 121 17W
Glenwood Sprs. 78 39 39N 107 15W
Glettinganes 110 65 30N 13 37W
Gliwice 107 50 22N 18 41E
Globe 79 33 25N 110 53W
Głogów 106 51 37N 16 5E
Gloria, La 86 8 37N 73 48W
Glorieuses, Îs. 117 11 30S 47 20E
Glossop 94 53 27N 1 56W
Gloucester, Can. 48 45 21N 75 39W
Gloucester, U.K. 95 51 52N 2 15W
Gloucester, U.S.A. 71 42 38N 70 39W
Gloucestershire □ 95 51 44N 2 10W
Gloversville 71 43 5N 74 18W
Glovertown 35 48 40N 54 03W
Glückstadt 106 53 46N 9 28E
Gmünd 106 48 45N 15 0E
Gmunden 106 47 55N 13 48E
Gniezno 107 52 30N 17 35E
Gnowangerup 134 33 58S 117 59E
Go Cong 128 10 22N 106 40E
Goa 124 15 33N 73 59E
Goa □ 124 15 33N 73 59E
Goalen Hd. 136 36 33S 150 4E
Goalpara 125 26 10N 90 40E
Goat Fell 96 55 37N 5 11W
Goba, Ethiopia 115 7 1N 39 59E
Goba, Mozam. 117 26 15S 32 13E
Gobabis 117 22 16S 19 0E
Gobi, desert 129 44 0N 111 0E
Gobles, Can. 49 43 9N 80 34W

* *Now part of Kiribati*

Gobles Great Central

Gobles, U.S.A. 77 42 22N 85 53W
Gochas 117 24 59S 19 25E
Godavari Point 125 17 0N 82 20E
Godavari, R. 125 19 5N 79 0E
Godbout 38 49 20N 67 38W
Godbout, R. 38 49 19N 67 36W
Goderich 46 43 45N 81 41W
Goderville 100 49 38N 0 22E
Godfrey 76 38 57N 90 11W
Godham 65 60 55N 60 40W
Godhavn 17 69 15N 53 38W
Godhra 124 22 49N 73 40E
Godoy Cruz 88 32 56S 68 52W
Gods L. 55 54 40N 94 15W
Gods, R. 55 56 22N 92 51W
Godthåb 17 64 10N 51 46W
Goeie Hoop, Kaap die 117 34 24S 18 30E
Goéland, L. du 41 49 47N 71 43W
Goéland, L.au 40 49 50N 76 48W
Goeree 105 51 50N 4 0E
Goes 105 51 30N 3 55E
Goetzville 46 46 3N 84 5W
Gogama 53 47 35N 81 43W
Gogebic, L. 52 46 30N 89 34W
Gogriâl 115 8 30N 28 0E
Goiânia 87 16 35S 49 20W
Goiás 87 15 55S 50 10W
Goiás □ 87 12 10S 48 0W
Goirle 105 51 31N 5 4E
Gojra 124 31 10N 72 40E
Gokteik 125 22 26N 97 0E
Golchikha 17 71 45N 84 0E
Golconda 78 40 58N 117 32W
Gold Beach 78 42 25N 124 25W
Gold Creek 67 62 45N 149 45W
Gold Hill 78 42 28N 123 2W
Gold River 62 49 40N 126 10E
Golden, Can. 63 51 20N 117 59W
Golden, Colo., U.S.A. 74 39 42N 105 30W
Golden, Ill., U.S.A. 76 40 7N 91 1W
Golden Bay 133 40 40S 172 50E
Golden Ears Prov. Park 63 49 30N 122 25W
Golden Gate 78 37 54N 122 30W
Golden Hinde, mt. 62 49 40N 125 44W
Golden Lake 47 45 34N 77 21W
Golden Prairie 56 50 13N 109 37W
Golden Vale 97 52 33N 8 17W
Goldendale 78 45 53N 120 48W
Goldfield 79 37 45N 117 13W
Goldfields 55 59 28N 108 29W
Goldpines 55 50 45N 93 05W
Goldsand L. 55 57 2N 101 8W
Goldsboro 73 35 24N 77 59W
Goldsmith 75 32 0N 102 40W
Goldthwaite 75 31 25N 98 32W
Goleniów 106 53 35N 14 50E
Goleta 81 34 27N 119 50W
Golfito 84 8 41N 83 5W
Goliad 75 28 40N 97 22W
Golmo 129 36 30N 95 10E
Golo, R. 103 42 31N 9 32E
Golspie 96 57 58N 3 58W
Goma 116 2 11S 29 18E
Gombe 114 10 19N 11 2E
Gomel 120 52 28N 31 0E
Gómez Palacio 82 25 40N 104 40W
Gomogomo 127 6 25S 134 53E
Gomoh 125 23 52N 86 10E
Gonâbâd 123 34 15N 58 45E
Gonaïves 85 19 20N 72 50W
Gonâve, G. de la 85 19 29N 72 42W
Gonâve, I. de la 85 18 45N 73 0W
Gonda 125 27 9N 81 58E
Gondab-e Kāvūs 123 37 20N 55 25E
Gonder 115 12 23N 37 30E
Gondia 124 21 30N 80 10E
Gondrecourt-le-Château 101 48 26N 5 30E
Gonno-Altaysk 120 51 50N 86 5E
Gonzales, Calif., U.S.A. 80 36 35N 121 30W
Gonzales, Tex., U.S.A. 75 29 30N 97 30W
González Chaves 88 38 02S 60 05W
Goobang Cr. 136 33 20S 147 50E
Good Hart 46 45 34N 85 7W
Good Hope, C. of = Goeie Hoop 117 34 24S 18 30E
Good Hope Mt. 62 51 9N 124 10W
Good Spirit L. 56 51 34N 102 40W
Gooderham 47 44 54N 78 21W
Goodeve 56 51 4N 103 10W
Gooding 78 43 0N 114 50W
Goodland 74 39 22N 101 44W
Goodnight 75 35 4N 101 13W
Goodsoil 55 54 24N 109 13W
Goodsprings 79 35 51N 115 30W
Goodwater 56 49 24N 103 42W
Goodwood 39 44 37N 63 40W
Goole 94 53 42N 0 52W
Goolgowi 136 33 58S 145 41E
Goolma 136 32 18S 149 10E
Goondiwindi 135 28 30S 150 21E
Goose Bay 36 53 15N 60 20W
Goose Cove 37 51 18N 55 38W
Goose I. 62 51 57N 128 26W
Goose L., Can. 57 54 28N 101 30W
Goose L., U.S.A. 78 42 0N 120 30W
Goose R. 36 53 20N 60 35W
Gop 124 22 5N 69 50E
Gorakhpur 125 26 47N 83 32E
Gorda 80 35 53N 121 26W
Gorda, Punta 84 14 10N 83 10W
Gordon, Can. 58 50 0N 97 21W
Gordon, Nebr., U.S.A. 74 42 49N 102 6W
Gordon, Wis., U.S.A. 52 46 15N 91 48W
Gordon Downs 134 18 48S 128 40E
Gordon Hd. 63 48 29N 123 18W
Gordon L., Alta., Can. 60 56 30N 110 25W
Gordon L., N.W.T., Can. 54 63 5N 113 11W
Gordonville 49 43 54N 80 33W
Gore, Ethiopia 115 8 12N 35 32E
Gore, N.Z. 133 46 5S 168 58E
Gore Bay 46 45 57N 82 28W
Gorey 97 52 41N 6 18W
Gorgān 123 36 55N 54 30E
Gorgona, I. 86 3 0N 78 10W
Gorham 71 44 23N 71 10W
Gorham Mt. 71 43 42N 70 37W
Gorin 76 40 22N 92 1W
Gorinchem 105 51 50N 4 59E
Gorizia 108 45 56N 13 37E
Gorki = Gorkiy 120 56 20N 44 0E
Gorkiy 120 56 20N 44 0E
Görlitz 106 51 10N 14 59E
Gorman, Calif., U.S.A. 81 34 47N 118 51W
Gorman, Tex., U.S.A. 75 32 15N 98 43W
Gormley 50 43 56N 79 23W
Gorna Oryakhovitsa 109 43 7N 25 40E
Gorno Filinskoye 120 60 5N 70 0E
Gorong, Kepulauan 127 4 5S 131 15E
Gorontalo 127 0 35N 123 13E
Gorron 100 48 25N 0 50W
Gort 97 53 4N 8 50W
Gorzów Wielkopolski 106 52 43N 15 15E
Gosainthan, Mt. 125 28 20N 85 45E
Goschen I. 62 53 48N 130 33W
Gosford 136 33 23N 151 18E
Goshen, Can. 39 45 23N 61 59W
Goshen, Calif., U.S.A. 80 36 21N 119 25W
Goshen, Ind., U.S.A. 77 41 36N 85 46W
Goshen, N.Y., U.S.A. 71 41 23N 74 21W
Goslar 106 51 55N 10 23E
Gospič 108 44 35N 15 23E
Gosport, U.K. 95 50 48N 1 8W
Gosport, U.S.A. 77 39 21N 86 40W
Göta Kanal 111 58 35N 14 15E
Götaland, reg. 111 58 0N 14 0E
Göteborg 111 57 43N 11 59E
Göteborg & Bohus □ 111 58 20N 11 50E
Gotha 106 50 56N 10 42E
Gothenburg 74 40 58N 100 8W
Gothenburg & Goteborg 111 57 43N 11 59E
Gotōr-rettō 132 32 55N 129 5E
Gotska Sandön 111 58 24N 19 15E
Göttingen 106 51 31N 9 55E
Gottwaldov (Zlin) 107 49 14N 17 40E
Gouda 105 52 1N 4 42E
Gough I. 13 40 10S 9 45W
Gough L. 61 52 2N 112 28W
Gouin Rés. 40 48 35N 74 40W
Goulais, R. 53 46 43N 84 27W
Goulburn, Austral. 136 34 44S 149 44E
Goulburn, N.S.W., Austral. 136 32 22S 149 31E
Goulburn Is. 134 11 40S 133 20E
Goulburn, R. 136 36 6S 144 55E
Goulds 37 47 29N 52 46W
Goundam 114 16 25N 3 45W
Gourdon 102 44 44N 1 23E
Gournay-en-Bray 101 49 29N 1 44E
Gourock Ra. 136 36 0S 149 25E
Gouverneur 71 44 18N 75 30W
Gouzon 102 46 12N 2 14E
Govan 56 51 20N 105 0W
Gove 135 12 25S 136 55E
Governador Valadares 87 18 15S 41 57W
Governor's Harbour 84 25 10N 76 14W
Gowanda 70 42 29N 78 58W
Gower, The 95 51 35N 4 10W
Gowna, L. 97 53 52N 7 35W
Gowrie 76 42 17N 94 17W
Goya 88 29 10S 59 10W
Goyelle, L. 50 47N 60 45W
Goyllarisquizga 86 10 19S 76 31W
Gozo, I. 108 36 0N 14 13E
Graaff-Reinet 117 32 13S 24 32E
Grabill 77 41 13N 84 57W
Gračac 108 44 18N 15 57E
Graçay 101 47 10N 1 50E
Grace 78 42 38N 111 46W
Gracefield 40 46 6N 76 3W
Graceville 74 45 36N 96 23W
Gracias a Dios, C. 84 15 0N 83 20W
Grado 104 43 23N 6 4W
Grady 75 34 52N 103 15W
Graénalon, L. 110 64 10N 17 20W
Grafton, Austral. 135 29 38S 152 58E
Grafton, Ill., U.S.A. 76 38 58N 90 26W
Grafton, N.Dak., U.S.A. 74 48 30N 97 25W
Grafton, C. 135 16 51S 146 0E
Graham, Can. 52 49 20N 90 30W
Graham, N.C., U.S.A. 73 36 5N 79 22W
Graham, Tex., U.S.A. 75 33 7N 98 38W
Graham Bell, Os. 120 80 5N 70 0E
Graham I., B.C., Can. 62 53 40N 132 30W
Graham I., N.W.T., Can. 65 77 25N 90 30W
Graham L. 60 56 35N 114 33W
Graham Land 91 65 0S 64 0W
Graham Mt. 79 32 46N 109 58W
Graham, R. 54 56 31N 122 17W
Grahamdale 57 51 23N 98 30W
Grahamstown 117 33 19S 26 31E
Grainland 56 50 59N 106 33W
Grajaú 87 5 50S 46 30W
Gramat 102 44 48N 1 43E
Grampian □ 96 57 0N 3 0W
Gramsh 96 40 52N 20 12E
Gran Chaco 130 25 0S 61 0W
Gran Paradiso 108 49 33N 7 17E
Gran Sabana, La 86 5 30N 61 30W
Gran Sasso d'Italia, Mt. 102 42 25N 13 30E
Granada, Nic. 84 11 58N 86 0W
Granada, Spain 104 37 10N 3 35W
Granada, U.S.A. 74 38 5N 102 13W
Granard 97 53 47N 7 30W
Granbury 75 32 28N 97 48W
Granby 41 45 25N 72 45W
Granby, R. 63 49 2N 118 27W
Grand Bahama I. 84 26 40N 78 30W
Grand Bank 37 47 6N 55 48W
Grand Bassam 114 5 10N 3 49W
Grand Bay 39 45 18N 66 12W
Grand Bend 46 43 19N 81 45W
Grand Blanc 46 42 56N 83 38W
Grand-Bourg 85 15 53N 61 19W
Grand Bruit 37 47 40N 58 14W
Grand Calumet, Île du 40 45 44N 76 41W
Grand Canal = Yun Ho 129 35 0N 117 0E
Grand Canyon National Park 79 36 15N 112 20W
Grand Cayman 84 19 20N 81 20W
Grand Centre 60 54 25N 110 13W
Grand Cess 114 4 40N 8 12W
Grand-Combe, La 103 44 13N 4 2E
Grand Coulee, Can. 56 50 26N 104 49W
Grand Coulee, U.S.A. 78 47 48N 119 1W
Grand Coulee Dam 78 48 0N 118 50W
Grand Falls 39 48 56N 55 40W
Grand Forks, Can. 63 49 0N 118 30W
Grand Forks, U.S.A. 74 48 0N 97 3W
Grand Fougeray, Le 100 47 44N 1 43W
Grand Harbour 39 44 41N 66 46W
Grand Haven 77 43 3N 86 13W
Grand I., Can. 57 52 51N 100 0W
Grand I., Mich., U.S.A. 53 46 30N 86 40W
Grand I., N.Y., U.S.A. 49 43 2N 78 59W
Grand Island 74 40 59N 98 25W
Grand Isle 75 29 15N 89 58W
Grand Junction, Colo., U.S.A. 79 39 0N 108 30W
Grand Junction, Iowa, U.S.A. 76 42 2N 94 14W
Grand L., N.B., Can. 39 45 57N 66 7W
Grand L., Newf., Can. 35 48 45N 57 45W
Grand L., Newf., Can. 36 53 40N 60 30W
Grand L., Newf., Can. 37 49 0N 57 30W
Grand L., Louis., U.S.A. 75 29 55N 92 45W
Grand L., Mich., U.S.A. 46 45 18N 83 30W
Grand L., Ohio, U.S.A. 77 40 32N 84 25W
Grand Lac 34 47 35N 77 35W
Grand Lake 78 40 20N 105 54W
Grand le Pierre 37 47 41N 54 47W
Grand Ledge 77 42 45N 84 45W
Grand-Lieu, Lac de 100 47 6N 1 40W
Grand Manan I. 39 44 45N 66 52W
Grand Marais, Can. 52 47 45N 90 25W
Grand Marais, U.S.A. 53 46 39N 85 59W
Grand Mère 41 46 36N 72 40W
Grand Motte, La 103 48 35N 1 4E
Grand Piles 41 46 40N 72 40W
Grand Portage 52 47 58N 89 41W
Grand Pressigny, Le 100 46 55N 0 48E
Grand, R., Can. 49 42 51N 79 34W
Grand, R., Mich., U.S.A. 77 43 4N 86 15W
Grand, R., Mo., U.S.A. 78 39 23N 93 27W
Grand, R., S.D., U.S.A. 78 45 45N 101 30W
Grand Rapids, Can. 57 53 12N 99 19W
Grand Rapids, Mich., U.S.A. 77 42 57N 85 40W
Grand Rapids, Minn., U.S.A. 52 47 15N 93 29W
Grand River 76 40 49N 93 58W
Grand Teton 78 43 54N 111 57W
Grand Valley, Can. 49 43 54N 80 19W
Grand Valley, U.S.A. 78 39 30N 108 2W
Grand View 57 51 10N 100 42W
Grande 87 11 30S 44 30W
Grande-Anse 39 47 48N 65 11W
Grande, B. 90 50 30S 68 20W
Grande Baie 41 48 19N 70 52W
Grande Baleine, R. de la 36 55 16N 77 47W
Grande Cache 60 53 53N 119 8W
Grande-Cascapédia 38 48 15N 65 54W
Grande, Coxilha 89 28 18S 51 30W
Grande de Santiago, R. 82 21 20N 105 50W
Grande-Entrée 39 47 30N 61 40W
Grande, Île 43 45 52N 73 14W
Grande, La 78 45 15N 118 0W
Grande, La, R. 36 53 50N 79 0W
Grande-Ligne 43 45 14N 73 22W
Grande Pointe 58 49 46N 97 3W
Grande Prairie 60 55 10N 118 50W
Grande, R., Jujuy, Argent. 88 23 9S 65 52W
Grande, R., Mendoza, Argent. 88 36 52S 69 45W
Grande R. 86 18 35S 63 0W
Grande, R., Brazil 87 20 0S 50 0W
Grande, R., U.S.A. 75 29 20N 100 40W
Grande-Rivière 38 48 26N 64 30W
Grande, Serra 87 4 30S 41 20W
Grande-Vallée 38 49 14N 65 8W
Grandes-Bergeronnes 41 48 16N 69 35W
Grandfalls 75 31 21N 102 51W
Grandmesnil, L. 38 51 19N 67 33W
Grandoe Mines 54 56 29N 129 54W
Grandpré 101 49 20N 4 50E
Grandview, Mo., U.S.A. 76 38 53N 94 32W
Grandview, Wash., U.S.A. 78 46 13N 119 58W
Grandview Heights 77 39 58N 83 2W
Grandville 77 42 54N 85 46W
Grandvilliers 101 49 40N 1 57E
Graneros 88 34 5S 70 45W
Granet, L. 40 47 47N 77 31W
Grange, La, Austral. 134 18 45S 121 43E
Grange, La, U.S.A. 80 37 42N 120 27W
Grange, La, Ga., U.S.A. 73 33 4N 85 0W
Grange, La, Ky., U.S.A. 72 38 20N 85 20W
Grange, La, Mo., U.S.A. 76 40 3N 91 35W
Grange, La, Tex., U.S.A. 75 29 54N 96 52W
Grangemouth 96 56 1N 3 43W
Granger 78 46 25N 120 5W
Grangeville 78 45 57N 116 4W
Granite, Pk. 78 45 8N 109 52W
Granite City 76 38 45N 90 3W
Granite Falls 74 44 45N 95 35W
Granite Mtn. 81 33 5N 116 28W
Granite Pt. 37 50 31N 56 17W
Granity 133 41 39S 171 51E
Granja 87 3 17S 40 50W
Granollers 104 41 39N 2 18E
Grant, Can. 34 50 6N 86 18W
Grant, U.S.A. 74 40 53N 101 42W
Grant City 76 40 30N 94 25W
Grant, Mt. 80 38 34N 118 48W
Grant, Pt. 136 38 32S 145 6E
Grant Range Mts. 79 38 30N 115 30W
Grantham 94 52 55N 0 39W
Grantown-on-Spey 96 57 19N 3 36W
Grants 79 35 14N 107 57W
Grants Pass 78 42 30N 123 22W
Grantsburg 74 45 46N 92 44W
Grantsville 78 40 35N 112 32W
Granville, France 100 48 50N 1 35W
Granville, N.D., U.S.A. 74 48 18N 100 48W
Granville, N.Y., U.S.A. 72 43 24N 73 16W
Granville L. 55 56 18N 100 30W
Grapeland 75 31 30N 95 25W
Gras, L. de 64 64 30N 110 30W
Grass, R. 55 56 3N 96 33W
Grass Range 78 47 0N 109 0W
Grass River Prov. Park 55 54 40N 100 50W
Grass Valley, Calif., U.S.A. 80 39 18N 121 0W
Grass Valley, Oreg., U.S.A. 78 45 28N 120 48W
Grasse 103 43 38N 6 56E
Grasset, L. 40 49 55N 78 10W
Grassie 49 43 9N 79 37W
Grassy Lake 61 49 49N 111 43W
Grate's Cove 35 48 8N 53 0W
Gratis 77 39 38N 84 32W
Gratz 77 38 28N 84 57W
Graulhet 102 43 45N 1 58E
Grave, Pte. de 102 45 34N 1 4W
Gravelbourg 56 49 50N 106 35W
Gravelines 101 51 0N 2 10E
's-Gravenhage 105 52 7N 4 17E
Gravenhurst 46 44 52N 79 20W
Gravesend 95 51 25N 0 22E
Gravois, Pointe-à 85 16 15N 73 45W
Gravone, R. 103 41 58N 8 45E
Gray 101 47 27N 5 35E
Grayling 46 44 40N 84 42W
Grayling, R. 54 59 21N 125 0W
Grays Harbor 78 46 55N 124 8W
Grays L. 78 43 8N 111 30W
Grays River 80 46 21N 123 37W
Grayson 56 50 45N 102 40W
Grayville 77 38 16N 88 0W
Graz 106 47 4N 15 27E
Greasy L. 54 62 55N 122 12W
Great Abaco I. 84 26 15N 77 10W
Great Australia Basin 135 26 0S 140 0E
Great Australian Bight 134 33 30S 130 0E
Great Barrier I. 133 36 11S 175 25E
Great Barrier Reef 135 19 0S 149 0E
Great Barrington 71 42 11N 73 22W
Great Basin 68 40 0N 116 30W
Great Bear L. 64 65 30N 120 0W
Great Bear, R. 64 65 0N 124 0W
Great Bena 71 41 57N 75 45W
Great Bend 74 38 25N 98 55W
Great Blasket, I. 97 52 5N 10 30W
Great Britain 93 54 0N 2 15W
Great Burnt L. 37 48 20N 56 20W
Great Central 62 49 20N 125 10W

Great Central L — Gunisao, R

Name	Page	Lat.	Long.
Great Central L.	62	49 22N	125 10W
Great Coco I.	128	14 10N	93 25E
Great Divide	135	23 0S	146 0E
Great Duck I.	46	45 40N	82 57W
Great Exuma I.	84	23 30N	75 50W
Great Falls, Can.	57	50 27N	96 1W
Great Falls, U.S.A.	78	47 27N	111 12W
Great Guana Cay	84	24 0N	76 20W
Great Harbour Deep	37	50 25N	56 25W
Great I.	55	58 53N	96 35W
Great Inagua I.	85	21 0N	73 20W
Gt. Indian Desert = Thar Desert	124	28 0N	72 0E
Great Jarvis	35	47 39N	57 12W
Great Karoo = Groot Karoo	117	32 30S	23 0E
Great Lake	135	41 50S	146 30E
Great Lakes	55	44 0N	82 0W
Great Orme's Head	94	53 20N	3 52W
Great Ouse, R.	94	52 20N	0 8E
Great Ruaha, R.	116	7 30S	35 0E
Gt. St. Bernard P.	106	45 50N	7 10E
Great Salt Lake	78	41 0N	112 30W
Great Salt Lake Desert	78	40 20N	113 50W
Great Salt Plains Res.	75	36 40N	98 15W
Great Sandy Desert	134	21 0S	124 0E
Great Sandy I. = Fraser I.	135	25 15S	153 0E
Great Sitkin I.	67	52 0N	176 10W
Great Slave L.	54	61 23N	115 38W
Great Stour, R.	95	51 21N	1 15E
Gt. Victoria Des.	134	29 30S	126 30E
Great Wall	130	38 30N	109 30E
Great Whale, R.	34	55 20N	75 30W
Great Whernside, mt.	85	54 9N	1 59W
Great Yarmouth	94	52 40N	1 45E
Greater Antilles	85	17 40N	74 0W
Greater Manchester □	94	53 30N	2 15W
Gredos, Sierra de	104	40 20N	5 0W
Greece ■	109	40 0N	23 0E
Greece's Point	43	45 36N	74 30W
Greeley, Colo., U.S.A.	74	40 30N	104 40W
Greeley, Nebr., U.S.A.	74	41 36N	98 32W
Greely Fd.	65	80 30N	85 0W
Green B., Can.	37	49 45N	55 55W
Green B., U.S.A.	72	45 0N	87 30W
Green Bay	72	44 30N	88 0W
Green C.	136	37 13S	150 1E
Green City	76	40 16N	92 57W
Green Cove Springs	73	29 59N	81 40W
Green Cr.	48	45 28N	75 34W
Green Island	133	45 55S	170 26E
Green Lake	56	54 17N	107 47W
Green Park	49	43 52N	80 27W
Green, R.	39	47 18N	68 9W
Green R., Ky., U.S.A.	77	37 54N	87 30W
Green R., Utah, U.S.A.	79	39 0N	110 6W
Green R., Wyo., U.S.A.	78	43 2N	110 2W
Green R., Wyo., U.S.A.	78	41 44N	109 28W
Green River	50	43 53N	79 11W
Greenbank	80	48 6N	122 34W
Greenbush, Mich., U.S.A.	46	44 35N	83 19W
Greenbush, Minn., U.S.A.	57	48 46N	96 10W
Greencastle	77	39 40N	86 48W
Greene, U.S.A.	76	42 54N	92 48W
Greene, N.Y., U.S.A.	71	42 20N	75 45W
Greenfield, Calif., U.S.A.	80	36 19N	121 15W
Greenfield, Calif., U.S.A.	81	35 15N	119 0W
Greenfield, Ill., U.S.A.	76	39 21N	90 12W
Greenfield, Ind., U.S.A.	77	39 47N	85 51W
Greenfield, Iowa, U.S.A.	76	41 18N	94 28W
Greenfield, Mass., U.S.A.	71	42 38N	72 38W
Greenfield, Miss., U.S.A.	75	37 28N	93 50W
Greenfield, Ohio, U.S.A.	77	39 21N	83 23W
Greenfield Park	45	45 29N	73 29W
Greenfields	49	43 18N	80 29W
Greenhills	77	39 16N	84 32W
Greening	34	48 10N	74 55W
Greenland	17	66 0N	45 0W
Greenland Sea	17	73 0N	10 0W
Greenock	96	55 57N	4 46W
Greenore	97	54 2N	6 8W
Greenore Pt.	97	52 15N	6 20W
Greenough Pt.	46	44 58N	81 26W
Greenport	71	41 5N	72 23W
Greensboro, Ga., U.S.A.	73	33 34N	83 12W
Greensboro, N.C., U.S.A.	73	36 7N	79 46W
Greensburg, Ind., U.S.A.	77	39 20N	85 30W
Greensburg, Kans., U.S.A.	75	37 38N	99 20W
Greensburg, Pa., U.S.A.	70	40 18N	79 31W
Greentown	77	40 29N	85 58W
Greenup	77	39 15N	88 10W
Greenville, Ala., U.S.A.	73	31 50N	86 37W
Greenville, Calif., U.S.A.	80	40 8N	121 0W
Greenville, Ill., U.S.A.	76	38 53N	89 22W
Greenville, Ind., U.S.A.	77	38 22N	85 59W
Greenville, Me., U.S.A.	35	45 30N	69 32W
Greenville, Mich., U.S.A.	77	43 12N	85 14W
Greenville, Miss., U.S.A.	75	33 25N	91 0W
Greenville, N.C., U.S.A.	73	35 37N	77 26W
Greenville, Ohio, U.S.A.	77	40 5N	84 38W
Greenville, Pa., U.S.A.	70	41 23N	80 22W
Greenville, S.C., U.S.A.	73	34 54N	82 24W
Greenville, Tenn., U.S.A.	73	36 13N	82 51W
Greenville, Tex., U.S.A.	75	33 5N	96 5W
Greenwater L.	52	48 34N	90 26W
Greenwater Lake	56	52 30N	103 31W
Greenwater Lake Prov. Park	56	52 32N	103 30W
Greenwich, U.K.	95	51 28N	0 0
Greenwich, N.Y., U.S.A.	71	43 2N	73 36W
Greenwich, Ohio, U.S.A.	70	41 1N	82 32W
Greenwood, B.C., Can.	63	49 10N	118 40W
Greenwood, Ont., Can.	51	43 56N	79 3W
Greenwood, Ind., U.S.A.	77	39 37N	86 7W
Greenwood, Miss., U.S.A.	75	33 30N	90 4W
Greenwood, S.C., U.S.A.	73	34 13N	82 13W
Gregory	74	43 14N	99 20W
Gregory, L.	135	28 55S	139 0E
Gregory Lake	134	20 10S	127 30E
Gregory Ra.	135	19 30S	143 40E
Greifswald	106	54 6N	13 23E
Gremikha	120	67 50N	39 40E
Grenada	75	33 45N	89 50W
Grenada I. ■	85	12 10N	61 40W
Grenade	102	43 47N	1 17E
Grenadines	85	12 40N	61 20W
Grenen	111	57 44N	10 40E
Grenfell, Austral.	136	33 52S	148 8E
Grenfell, Can.	56	50 30N	102 56W
Grenoble	103	45 12N	5 42E
Grenora	74	48 38N	103 54W
Grenville	43	45 37N	74 36W
Grenville, C.	135	12 0S	143 13E
Grenville Chan.	62	53 40N	129 46W
Gréoux-les-Bains	103	43 45N	5 52E
Gresham	80	45 30N	122 31W
Gresik	127	9 13S	112 38E
Gretna, Can.	57	49 1N	97 34W
Gretna, U.S.A.	75	30 0N	90 2W
Gretna Green	96	55 0N	3 3W
Grevenmacher	105	49 41N	6 26E
Greves, Les	43	45 59N	73 11W
Grey, C.	135	13 0S	136 35E
Grey Is.	37	50 50N	55 35W
Grey, Pt.	66	49 16N	123 16W
Grey, R., Can.	37	47 34N	57 6W
Grey, R., N.Z.	133	42 27S	171 12E
Grey Range	135	27 0S	143 30E
Grey Res.	37	48 20N	56 30W
Grey River	37	47 35N	57 6W
Greybull	78	44 30N	108 3W
Greytown, N.Z.	133	41 5S	175 29E
Greytown, S. Afr.	117	29 1S	30 36E
Gribbell I.	62	53 23N	129 0W
Gridley	80	39 27N	121 47W
Griffin	73	33 17N	84 14W
Griffith, Austral.	136	34 18S	146 2E
Griffith, Can.	47	45 15N	77 10W
Griffith I.	46	44 50N	80 55W
Griffith Mine	55	50 47N	93 25W
Grijalva, R.	82	16 20N	92 20W
Grim, C.	135	40 45S	144 45E
Grimari	116	5 43N	20 0E
Grimes	80	39 4N	121 54W
Grimsby, Can.	49	43 12N	79 34W
Grimsby, U.K.	94	53 35N	0 5W
Grimsby Beach	49	43 12N	79 32W
Grimsey	110	66 33N	18 0W
Grimshaw	60	56 10N	117 40W
Grimstad	111	58 22N	8 35E
Grindstone I.	47	44 43N	76 14W
Grindstone Island	35	47 25N	62 0W
Grinnell	76	41 45N	92 43W
Grise Fiord	65	76 25N	82 57W
Grisolles	102	43 49N	1 19E
Grita, La	86	8 8N	71 59W
Griz Nez, C.	101	50 50N	1 35E
Groais I.	37	50 55N	55 35W
Grodno	120	53 42N	23 52E
Grodzisk Wlkp.	106	52 15N	16 22E
Groesbeck	75	31 32N	96 34W
Groix	100	47 38N	3 29W
Groix, I. de	100	47 38N	3 28W
Grójec	107	51 50N	20 58E
Gronau	105	52 13N	7 2E
Grong	110	64 25N	12 8E
Groningen	105	53 15N	6 35E
Groningen □	105	53 16N	6 40E
Gronlid	56	53 6N	104 28W
Groom	75	35 12N	100 59W
Groot-Brakrivier	117	34 2S	22 18E
Groot Karoo	117	32 35S	23 0E
Groot Namakwaland = Namaland	117	26 0S	18 0E
Groote Eylandt	135	14 0S	136 50E
Grootfontein	117	19 31S	18 6E
Gros C.	54	61 59N	113 32W
Gros-Morne	38	49 15N	65 34W
Gros Morne Nat. Park	37	49 40N	57 50W
Grosne, R.	103	46 30N	4 40E
Gross Glockner	106	47 5N	12 40E
Grossa, Pta.	87	1 20N	50 0W
Grosse I.	46	42 8N	83 9W
Grosse Isle	57	50 4N	97 27W
Grossenhain	106	51 17N	13 32E
Grosses-Roches	38	48 57N	67 5W
Grosseto	108	42 45N	11 7E
Groswater B.	36	54 20N	57 40W
Groton	71	41 22N	72 12W
Grouard Mission	60	55 33N	116 9W
Grouin, Pointe du	100	48 43N	1 51W
Groundhog, R.	53	48 45N	82 20W
Grouse Creek	78	41 51N	113 57W
Grove City, Ohio, U.S.A.	77	39 53N	83 6W
Grove City, Pa., U.S.A.	70	41 10N	80 5W
Grovedale	60	55 3N	118 52W
Groveland	80	37 50N	120 14W
Grover City	81	35 7N	120 37W
Grover Hill	77	41 1N	84 29W
Groveton, N.H., U.S.A.	71	44 34N	71 30W
Groveton, Tex., U.S.A.	75	31 5N	95 4W
Groznyy	120	43 20N	45 45E
Grudziadz	107	53 30N	18 47E
Gruissan	102	43 8N	3 7E
Grünau	117	27 45S	18 26E
Grundy Center	76	42 22N	92 45W
Grundy Prov. Pk.	46	45 58N	80 30W
Grunthal	57	49 24N	96 51W
Gruver	75	36 19N	101 20W
Gryazi	120	52 30N	39 58E
Gryazovets	120	58 50N	40 20E
Grytviken	91	53 50S	37 10W
Gua	125	22 18N	85 20E
Guacanayabo, G. de	84	20 40N	77 20W
Guacara	86	10 14N	67 53W
Guachípas	88	25 40S	65 30W
Guachiria, R.	86	5 30N	71 30W
Guadalajara, Mexico	82	20 40N	103 20W
Guadalajara, Spain	104	40 37N	3 12W
Guadalcanal, I.	14	9 32S	160 12E
Guadales	88	34 30S	67 55W
Guadalete, R.	104	36 45N	5 47W
Guadalhorce, R.	104	36 50N	4 42W
Guadalquivir, R.	104	38 0N	4 0W
Guadalupe, Mexico	81	32 4N	116 32W
Guadalupe, U.S.A.	81	34 59N	120 33W
Guadalupe Bravos	82	31 20N	106 10W
Guadalupe de los Reyes	82	25 23N	104 15W
Guadalupe Pk.	79	31 50N	105 30W
Guadalupe, R., Mexico	81	32 6N	116 51W
Guadalupe, R., U.S.A.	75	29 25N	97 30W
Guadalupe, Sierra de	104	39 28N	5 30W
Guadalupe y Calvo	82	26 6N	106 58W
Guadarrama, Sierra de	104	41 0N	4 0W
Guadeloupe, I.	85	16 20N	61 40W
Guadeloupe, La	41	45 57N	70 56W
Guadeloupe Passage	85	16 50N	68 15W
Guadiana, R.	104	37 45N	7 35W
Guadix	104	37 18N	3 11W
Guafo, Boca del	90	43 35S	74 0W
Guaina	86	5 9N	63 36W
Guainía □	86	2 30N	69 00W
Guaira	89	24 5S	54 10W
Guaira, La	86	10 36N	66 56W
Guaitecas, Islas	90	44 0S	74 30W
Guajará-Mirim	86	10 50S	65 20W
Guajira, La □	86	11 30N	72 30W
Guajira, Pen. de la	85	12 0N	72 0W
Gualan	84	15 8N	89 22W
Gualeguay	88	33 10S	59 20W
Gualeguaychú	88	33 3S	58 31W
Guam I.	14	13 27N	144 45E
Guama	86	10 16N	68 49W
Guamareyes	86	0 30S	73 0W
Guamini	88	37 1S	62 28W
Guampí, Sierra de	86	6 0N	65 35W
Guamuchil	82	25 25N	108 3W
Guanabacoa	84	23 8N	82 18W
Guanabara □	89	23 0S	43 25W
Guanacaste	84	10 40N	85 30W
Guanacaste, Cordillera del	84	10 40N	85 4W
Guanacevío	82	25 40N	106 0W
Guanajay	84	22 56N	82 42W
Guanajuato	82	21 0N	101 20W
Guanajuato □	82	20 40N	101 20W
Guanare	86	8 42N	69 12W
Guanare, R.	86	8 50N	68 50W
Guandacol	88	29 30S	68 40W
Guane	84	22 10N	84 0W
Guanica	67	17 58N	66 55W
Guanipa, R.	86	9 20N	63 30W
Guanta	86	10 14N	64 36W
Guantánamo	85	20 10N	75 20W
Guapí	86	2 36N	77 54W
Guápiles	84	10 10N	83 46W
Guaporé	89	12 0S	64 0W
Guaporé, R.	86	13 0S	63 0W
Guaqui	86	16 41S	68 54W
Guarapari	89	20 40S	40 30W
Guarapuava	87	25 20S	51 30W
Guaratinguetá	89	22 49S	45 9W
Guaratuba	89	25 53S	48 38W
Guarda	104	40 32N	7 20W
Guardafui, C. = Asir, Ras	115	11 55N	51 10E
Guaria □	88	25 45N	56 30W
Guárico □	86	8 40N	66 35W
Guarujá	89	24 2S	46 25W
Guarus	89	21 30S	41 20W
Guasave	82	25 34N	108 27W
Guasdualito	86	7 15N	70 44W
Guasipati	86	7 28N	61 54W
Guatemala	84	14 40N	90 30W
Guatemala ■	84	15 40N	90 30W
Guatire	86	10 28N	66 32W
Guaviare, R.	86	3 30N	71 0W
Guaxupé	89	21 10S	47 5W
Guayabal	86	4 43N	71 37W
Guayama	85	17 59N	66 7W
Guayaquil	86	2 15S	79 52W
Guayaquil, G. de	86	3 10S	81 0W
Guaymallen	88	32 50S	68 45W
Guaymas	82	27 50N	111 0W
Guchil	128	5 35N	102 10E
Guchin-Us	130	45 28N	102 10E
Gudbransdal	111	61 33N	10 0E
Guddu Barrage	71	28 30N	69 50E
Gudivada	125	16 30N	81 15E
Gudur	124	14 12N	79 55E
Guebwiller	101	47 55N	7 12E
Guecho	104	43 21N	2 59W
Guéguen, L.	40	48 6N	77 13W
Guelph	49	43 35N	80 20W
Guéméné-Penfao	100	47 38N	1 50W
Guéméné-sur-Scorff	100	48 4N	3 13W
Güemes	88	24 50S	65 0W
Guer	100	47 54N	2 8W
Guérande	100	47 20N	2 26W
Guerche, La	100	47 57N	1 16W
Guerche-sur-l'Aubois, La	101	46 58N	2 56E
Guéret	102	46 11N	1 51E
Guérigny	101	47 6N	3 10E
Guerneville	80	38 30N	123 0W
Guernica	104	43 19N	2 40W
Guernsey, Can.	56	51 53N	105 11W
Guernsey, U.S.A.	74	42 19N	104 45W
Guernsey I.	100	49 30N	2 35W
Guerrero □	83	17 30N	100 0W
Gueugnon	103	45 36N	4 3E
Gueydan	75	30 3N	92 30W
Guhra	123	27 36N	56 8E
Guia Lopes da Laguna	89	21 26S	56 7W
Guiana Highlands	86	5 0N	60 0W
Guibes	117	26 41S	16 49E
Guigues	40	47 28N	79 26W
Guija	117	34 35S	33 15E
Guildford	95	51 14N	0 34W
Guilford	35	45 12N	69 25W
Guillaume-Delisle, L.	36	56 15N	76 17W
Guillaumes	103	44 5N	6 52E
Guillestre	103	44 39N	6 40E
Guilvinec	100	47 48N	4 17W
Guimarães	87	2 9S	44 35W
Guimaras I.	127	10 35N	122 37E
Guinda	80	38 50N	122 12W
Guinea ■	114	10 20N	10 0W
Guinea Bissau ■	114	12 0N	15 0W
Guinea, Gulf of	114	3 0N	2 30E
Guinea, Port. = Guinea Bissau	114	12 0N	15 0W
Güines	84	22 50N	82 0W
Guines, L.	38	52 8N	61 25W
Guingamp	100	48 34N	3 10W
Guipavas	100	48 26N	4 29W
Güiria	86	10 32N	62 18W
Guiscard	101	49 40N	3 0E
Guise	101	49 52N	3 35E
Guivan	127	11 5N	125 55E
Gujan-Mestras	102	44 38N	1 4W
Gujarat □	124	23 20N	71 0E
Gujranwala	124	32 10N	74 12E
Gujrat	124	32 40N	74 2E
Gukhothae	128	17 2N	99 50E
Gulargambone	136	31 20S	148 30E
Gulbahar	123	35 5N	69 10E
Gulbargâ	124	17 20N	76 50E
Gulf, The	123	27 0N	50 0E
Gulfport	75	30 28N	89 3W
Gulgong	136	32 20S	149 30E
Gulkana	67	62 15N	145 48W
Gull L., Can.	61	52 34N	114 0W
Gull L., U.S.A.	52	46 30N	94 21W
Gull Lake	56	50 10N	108 29W
Gull, R.	52	49 45N	89 0W
Gulpaigan	122	33 26N	50 20E
Gulshad	120	46 45N	74 25E
Gulu	116	2 48N	32 17E
Gum Lake	136	32 42S	143 9E
Guma	129	37 37N	78 18E
Gumma-ken □	132	36 30N	138 20E
Gummersbach	105	51 2N	7 32E
Gümüsane	122	40 30N	39 30E
Gumzai	127	5 28S	134 42E
Guna	124	24 40N	77 19E
Gundagai	136	35 3S	148 6E
Gundih	127	7 10S	110 56E
Gungu	116	5 43S	19 20E
Gunisao L.	57	53 33N	96 15W
Gunisao, R.	57	53 56N	97 53W

Gunnedah Harry S. Truman Res

Gunnedah 135 30 59 S 150 15 E
Gunning 136 34 47 S 149 14 E
Gunnison, Colo., U.S.A. 79 38 32N 106 56W
Gunnison, Utah, U.S.A. 78 39 11N 111 48W
Gunnison, R. 79 38 50N 108 30W
Guntakal 124 15 11N 77 27 E
Guntersville 73 34 18N 86 16W
Guntur 125 16 23N 80 30 E
Gunung-Sitoli 126 1 15N 97 30 E
Gunungap 127 6 45 S 126 30 E
Gunungsugih 126 4 58 S 105 7 E
Gunworth 55 51 20N 108 10W
Gupis 124 36 15N 73 20 E
Gürchañ 122 34 55N 49 25 E
Gurdaspur 124 32 5N 75 25 E
Gurdon 75 33 55N 93 10W
Gurgaon 124 28 33N 77 10 E
Gurkha 125 28 5N 84 40 E
Gurnee 77 42 22N 87 55W
Gurun 128 5 49N 100 27 E
Gürün 122 38 41N 37 22 E
Gurupá 87 1 20 S 51 45W
Gurupá, I. Grande de 87 1 0 S 51 45W
Gurupi, R. 87 3 20 S 47 20W
Gurvandzagal 130 49 35N 115 2 E
Guryev 120 47 5N 52 0 E
Gusau 114 12 18N 6 31 E
Gusinoczersk 130 51 16N 106 27 E
Gustavus 67 58 25N 135 58W
Gustine 80 37 21N 121 0W
Güstrow 106 53 47N 12 12 E
Guthega Dam 136 36 20 S 148 27 E
Guthrie 75 35 55N 97 30W
Guthrie Center 76 41 41N 94 30W
Guttenberg 76 42 46N 91 10W
Guyana ■ 86 5 0N 59 0W
Guyenne 102 44 30N 0 40 E
Guymon 75 36 45N 101 30W
Guysborough 39 45 23N 61 30W
Guzmán, Laguna de 82 31 25N 107 25W
Gwa 125 17 30N 94 40 E
Gwâdar 124 25 10N 62 18 E
Gwalior 124 26 12N 78 10 E
Gwanda 117 20 55 S 29 0 E
Gweebarra B. 97 54 52N 8 21W
Gweedore 97 55 4N 8 15W
Gwent □ 95 51 45N 2 55W
Gweru 117 19 28 S 29 45 E
Gwinn 53 46 15N 87 29W
Gwydir, R. 135 29 27 S 149 48 E
Gwynedd □ 94 53 0N 4 0W
Gya La 125 28 45N 84 45 E
Gyangtse 125 28 50N 89 33 E
Gydanskiy P-ov. 120 70 0N 78 0 E
Gympie 135 26 11 S 152 38 E
Gyoda 132 36 10N 139 30 E
Gyöngyös 107 47 48N 20 15 E
Györ 107 47 41N 17 40 E
Gypsum Pt. 54 61 53N 114 35W
Gypsumville 57 51 45N 98 40W

H

Ha Nam = Phu-Ly 128 20 35N 105 50 E
Haapamäki 110 62 18N 24 28 E
Haarlem 105 52 23N 4 39 E
Haast, R. 133 43 50 S 169 2 E
Hab Nadi Chauki 124 25 0N 66 50 E
Haba 122 27 10N 47 0 E
Habana, La 84 23 8N 82 22W
Habaswein 116 1 2N 39 30 E
Habay 54 58 50N 118 44W
Hachijō-Jima 132 33 5N 139 45 E
Hachinohe 132 40 30N 141 29 E
Hachiōji 132 35 30N 139 30 E
Hackensack 52 46 56N 94 29W
Hackett 54 52 9N 112 28W
Hadd, Ras al 123 22 35N 59 50 E
Haddington 96 55 57N 2 48W
Hadhramaut = Hadramawt 115 15 30N 49 30 E
Hadramawt 115 15 30N 49 30 E
Hadrians Wall 94 55 0N 2 30W
Haeju 130 38 3N 125 45 E
Hafar al Bātin 122 28 25N 46 50 E
Hafford 56 52 43N 107 21W
Hafizabad 124 32 5N 73 40 E
Haflong 125 25 10N 93 5 E
Hafnarfjörður 110 64 4N 21 57W
Haft-Gel 122 31 30N 49 32 E
Hagemeister I. 67 58 42N 161 0W
Hagen 105 51 21N 7 29 E
Hagensborg 62 52 23N 126 32W
Hagerman 75 33 5N 104 22W
Hagerstown, Ind., U.S.A. 77 39 55N 85 10W
Hagerstown, Md., U.S.A. 72 39 39N 77 46W
Hagersville 49 42 58N 80 3W
Hagetmau 102 43 39N 0 37W
Hagfors 111 60 3N 13 45 E
Hagi, Iceland 110 65 28N 23 25W
Hagi, Japan 132 34 30N 131 30 E
Hags Hd. 97 52 57N 9 30W
Hague, C. de la 100 49 44N 1 56W
Hague, The = s'-Gravenhage 105 52 7N 4 17 E
Haguenau 101 48 49N 7 47 E
Haicheng 130 40 56N 122 51 E
Haifa 115 32 46N 35 0 E
Haihang 131 20 55N 110 3 E
Haik'ou 131 20 5N 110 20 E
Haikow 131 20 0N 110 20 E
Hā'il 122 27 28N 42 2 E
Hailar 130 49 12N 119 37 E
Hailar Ho 130 49 30N 118 30 E
Hailey 78 43 30N 114 15W
Haileybury 34 47 30N 79 38W
Hailun 130 47 24N 127 0 E
Hailuoto 110 65 3N 24 45 E
Haimen 131 31 48N 121 8 E
Hainan, I. 131 19 0N 110 0 E
Hainan Str. = Ch'iungcho Haihsia 131 20 10N 110 15 E
Hainaut □ 105 50 30N 4 0 E
Haines, Alaska, U.S.A. 67 59 20N 135 36W
Haines, Oreg., U.S.A. 78 44 51N 117 59W
Haines City 73 28 6N 81 35W
Haines Junction 67 60 45N 137 30W
Haining 131 30 23N 120 30 E
Haiphong 128 20 47N 106 35 E
Haitan Tao 131 25 30N 119 45 E
Haiti ■ 85 19 0N 72 30W
Haiyen 131 30 28N 120 57 E
Haiyuan 130 36 32N 105 31 E
Haja 127 3 19 S 129 37 E
Hajdúböszörmény 107 47 40N 21 30 E
Haji Langar 124 35 50N 79 20 E
Hajnówka 107 52 45N 23 32 E
Hajr 123 24 0N 56 34 E
Hakken-Zan 132 34 10N 135 54 E
Hakodate 132 41 45N 140 44 E
Hala 124 25 43N 68 20 E
Halab = Aleppo 122 36 10N 37 15 E
Halabjah 122 35 10N 45 58 E
Halaib 115 22 5N 36 30 E
Halawa 67 21 9N 156 47W
Halberstadt 106 51 53N 11 2 E
Halbrite 56 49 30N 103 33W
Halcombe 133 40 8 S 175 30 E
Halcyon, Mt. 127 13 0N 121 30 E
Haldia 125 22 5N 88 3 E
Haldimand-Norfolk □ 49 42 57N 79 50W
Haldwani 124 29 25N 79 30 E
Hale, Mich., U.S.A. 46 44 18N 83 48W
Hale, Mo., U.S.A. 76 39 36N 93 20W
Haleakala Crater 67 20 43N 156 12W
Haleyville 73 34 15N 87 40W
Half Island Cove 39 45 21N 61 12W
Halfway 78 44 56N 117 8W
Halfway, R. 54 56 12N 121 32W
Haliburton 47 45 3N 78 30W
Halifax, Can. 39 44 38N 63 35W
Halifax, U.K. 94 53 43N 1 51W
Halifax B. 135 18 50 S 147 0 E
Halil, R. 123 27 40N 58 30 E
Halkirk 61 52 17N 112 9W
Hall Beach 65 68 46N 81 12W
Hall Land 17 81 20N 60 0W
Hall Pen. 65 63 30N 66 0W
Halland 111 56 55N 12 50 E
Halle 105 51 29N 12 0 E
Hallebourg 53 49 40N 83 31W
Hallettsville 75 29 28N 96 57W
Halley Bay 91 75 31 S 26 36W
Halliday 74 47 20N 102 25W
Halliday L. 55 61 21N 108 56W
Hallingdal, R. 111 60 34N 9 12 E
Hällnäs 110 64 19N 19 36 E
Hallock 57 48 47N 97 0W
Hall's Creek 134 18 16 S 127 46 E
Hallstead 71 41 56N 75 45W
Halmahera, I. 127 0 40N 128 0 E
Halmstad 111 56 41N 12 52 E
Hals 111 56 59N 10 18 E
Halstad 74 47 21N 96 41W
Halton □ 48 43 30N 79 53W
Hamā 122 35 5N 36 40 E
Hamada 132 34 50N 132 10 E
Hamadān 122 34 52N 48 32 E
Hamadān □ 122 35 0N 49 0 E
Hamamatsu 132 34 45N 137 45 E
Hamar 111 60 48N 11 7 E
Hamarøy 110 68 5N 15 38 E
Hambantota 124 6 10N 81 10 E
Hamber Prov. Park 63 52 20N 118 0W
Hamburg, Ger. 106 53 32N 9 59 E
Hamburg, Ark., U.S.A. 75 33 15N 91 47W
Hamburg, Iowa, U.S.A. 74 40 37N 95 38W
Hamburg, N.Y., U.S.A. 70 42 44N 78 50W
Hamburg, Pa., U.S.A. 71 40 33N 76 0W
Hame 111 61 30N 24 0 E
Hämeenlinna 111 61 0N 24 28 E
Hameln 106 52 7N 9 24 E
Hamer 71 42 38N 76 11W
Hamersley Ra. 134 22 0 S 117 45 E
Hamhung 130 40 0N 127 30 E
Hamilton, Austral. 136 37 45 S 142 2 E
Hamilton, Can. 48 43 15N 79 50W
Hamilton, N.Z. 133 37 47 S 175 19 E
Hamilton, U.K. 96 55 47N 4 2W
Hamilton, Alas., U.S.A. 67 62 55N 164 0W
Hamilton, Ill., U.S.A. 76 40 24N 91 21W
Hamilton, Ind., U.S.A. 77 41 33N 84 56W
Hamilton, Mo., U.S.A. 96 39 45N 93 59W
Hamilton, Mont., U.S.A. 78 46 20N 114 6W
Hamilton, N.Y., U.S.A. 71 42 49N 75 31W
Hamilton, Ohio, U.S.A. 77 39 20N 84 35W
Hamilton, Tex., U.S.A. 75 31 40N 98 5W
Hamilton, Wash., U.S.A. 63 48 31N 121 59W
Hamilton Beach 48 43 17N 79 47W
Hamilton City 80 39 45N 122 1W
Hamilton Harbour 48 43 18N 79 50W
Hamilton Inlet 35 54 0N 57 30W
Hamilton, R. 134 26 40 S 134 20 E
Hamilton Sound 37 49 35N 54 15W
Hamilton-Wentworth □ 48 43 15N 79 49W
Hamiota 57 50 11N 100 38W
Hamlet 73 34 56N 79 40W
Hamlin, N.Y., U.S.A. 70 43 17N 77 55W
Hamlin, Tex., U.S.A. 75 32 58N 100 8W
Hamm 105 51 40N 7 58 E
Hammenton 72 39 40N 74 47W
Hammerfest 110 70 39N 23 41 E
Hammond, Can. 71 45 26N 75 15W
Hammond, Ill., U.S.A. 77 39 48N 88 36W
Hammond, Ind., U.S.A. 77 41 40N 87 30W
Hammond, La., U.S.A. 75 30 32N 90 30W
Hammond B. 46 45 31N 84 0W
Hampden, Can. 37 49 33N 56 51W
Hampden, N.Z. 133 45 18 S 170 50 E
Hampshire □ 95 51 3N 1 20W
Hampshire Downs 95 51 10N 1 10W
Hampstead 39 45 37N 66 5W
Hampton, N.B., Can. 39 45 32N 65 51W
Hampton, Ont., Can. 47 43 58N 78 45W
Hampton, Ark., U.S.A. 75 33 35N 92 29W
Hampton, Iowa, U.S.A. 76 42 42N 93 12W
Hampton, N.H., U.S.A. 71 42 56N 70 48W
Hampton, S.C., U.S.A. 73 32 52N 81 2W
Hampton, Va., U.S.A. 72 37 4N 76 18W
Hampton Harbour 134 20 30 S 116 30 E
Hampton Tableland 134 32 0 S 127 0 E
Hamra 122 24 2N 38 55 E
Hamun Helmand 123 31 15N 61 15 E
Hamun-i-Lora 124 29 38N 64 58 E
Hamun-i-Mashkel 124 28 30N 63 0 E
Han K., Hupei, China 131 31 40N 112 20 E
Han K., Kwangtung, China 131 23 45N 116 35 E
Han Kiang R. 131 31 40N 112 20 E
Han Pijesak 109 44 0N 19 0 E
Hana 67 20 45N 155 59W
Hanau 106 50 8N 8 56 E
Hanbagd 130 43 12N 107 10 E
Hanceville 63 51 55N 123 2W
Hancheng 130 35 14N 110 22 E
Hanchow Wan 131 35 0N 119 0 E
Hancock, Mich., U.S.A. 52 47 10N 88 40W
Hancock, Minn., U.S.A. 74 45 26N 95 46W
Hancock, Pa., U.S.A. 71 41 57N 75 19W
Handa 132 34 53N 137 0 E
Handel 56 52 4N 108 42W
Handeni 116 5 25 S 38 2 E
Handlová 69 48 45N 18 35 E
Handshur 130 48 29N 118 2 E
Haney 63 49 12N 122 40W
Hanford 80 36 25N 119 39W
Hangchow 131 30 12N 120 1 E
Hangchow Wan 131 30 30N 121 30 E
Hangchwang 131 34 34N 117 27 E
Hangö (Hanko) 111 59 59N 22 57 E
Hanh 130 51 32N 100 35 E
Hankinson 74 46 9N 96 58W
Hanko = Hangö 111 59 59N 22 57 E
Hankow 131 30 32N 114 20 E
Hanksville 79 38 19N 110 45W
Hanku 130 39 16N 117 50 E
Hanlan 50 43 39N 79 39W
Hanle 124 32 42N 79 4 E
Hanley 56 51 38N 106 26W
Hanmer, Can. 46 46 39N 80 56W
Hanmer, N.Z. 133 42 32 S 172 50 E
Hann, Mt. 134 16 0 S 126 0 E
Hanna 61 51 40N 111 54W
Hannaford 74 47 23N 98 18W
Hannah 57 48 58N 98 42W
Hannah B. 34 51 40N 80 0W
Hannibal 76 39 42N 91 22W
Hannon 48 43 11N 79 50W
Hannover 106 52 23N 9 43 E
Hanoi 128 21 5N 105 55 E
Hanover, Can. 46 44 9N 81 2W
Hanover, U.S.A. 77 38 43N 85 28W
Hanover, N.H., U.S.A. 71 43 43N 72 17W
Hanover, Ohio, U.S.A. 70 40 5N 82 17W
Hanover, Pa., U.S.A. 72 39 46N 76 59W
Hanover = Hannover 106 52 23N 9 43 E
Hanover, I. 90 51 0 S 74 50W
Hansi 124 29 10N 75 57 E
Hanson Range 134 27 0 S 136 30 E
Hantan 130 36 42N 114 30 E
Hant's Harbour 37 48 1N 53 16W
Hantsport 39 45 4N 64 11W
Hanuy Gol 130 48 20N 101 30 E
Hanwood 136 34 22 S 146 2 E
Hanyang 131 30 32N 114 10 E
Haparanda 110 65 52N 24 8 E
Happy 75 34 47N 101 50W
Happy Camp 78 41 52N 123 30W
Happy Valley 36 53 15N 60 20W
Hapur 124 28 45N 77 45 E
Haql 122 29 10N 35 0 E
Har 127 5 16 S 133 14 E
Har-Ayrag 130 45 47N 109 16 E
Har Us Nuur 129 48 0N 92 0 E
Hara Narinula, (Lang Shan) 130 41 30N 107 0 E
Haraa Gol 129 49 0N 106 0 E
Harad 122 24 15N 49 0 E
Haradh 122 24 15N 49 0 E
Harare 117 17 50S 31 2 E
Harbin 130 45 46N 126 51 E
Harbor Beach 46 43 50N 82 38W
Harbor Springs 46 45 28N 85 0W
Harbour Breton 37 47 29N 55 50W
Harbour Deep 35 50 25N 56 30W
Harbour Grace 37 47 40N 53 22W
Harburg 106 53 27N 9 58 E
Harcourt 39 46 27N 65 15W
Hardangerfjorden. 111 60 15N 6 0 E
Hardap Dam 117 24 32 S 17 50 E
Hardenberg 105 52 34N 6 37 E
Harderwijk 105 52 21N 5 38 E
Hardin, Ill., U.S.A. 76 39 9N 90 37W
Hardin, Mont., U.S.A. 78 45 50N 107 35W
Harding 117 30 22 S 29 55 E
Hardinsburg 77 37 47N 86 28W
Hardinxveld 105 51 49N 4 53 E
Hardisty 61 52 40N 111 18W
Hardman 78 45 12N 119 49W
Hardoi 124 27 26N 80 15 E
Hardwar 124 29 58N 78 16 E
Hardwick 71 44 30N 72 20W
Hardwicke I. 62 50 27N 125 50W
Hardwicke Island 62 50 26N 125 55W
Hardwood Ridge 39 46 10N 66 1W
Hardy 75 36 20N 91 30W
Hardy, Pen. 90 55 30 S 68 20W
Hare B. 37 51 15N 55 45W
Hare Bay 37 48 51N 54 1W
Harelbeke 105 50 52N 3 20 E
Harer 115 9 20N 42 8 E
Harfleur 100 49 30N 0 10 E
Hargeisa 115 9 30N 44 2 E
Hargshamn 111 60 12N 18 30 E
Hari, R., Afghan. 124 34 20N 64 30 E
Hari, R., Indon. 126 1 10 S 101 50 E
Haringhata, R. 125 22 0N 89 58 E
Harirūd 123 35 0N 61 0 E
Harlan, Iowa, U.S.A. 74 41 37N 95 20W
Harlan, Tenn., U.S.A. 73 36 58N 83 20W
Harlech 94 52 52N 4 7W
Harlem 78 48 29N 108 39W
Harley 49 43 4N 80 29W
Harlingen, Neth. 105 53 11N 5 25 E
Harlingen, U.S.A. 75 26 20N 97 50W
Harlowton 78 46 30N 109 54W
Harmon L. 52 49 56N 90 13W
Harmony 49 43 54N 78 50W
Harney Basin 78 43 30N 119 0W
Harney L. 78 43 0N 119 0W
Harney Pk. 74 43 52N 103 33W
Harnösand 110 62 38N 18 5 E
Haro, C. 82 27 50N 110 55W
Haro Str. 63 48 30N 123 15W
Harp L. 36 55 5N 61 50W
Harpe, La 76 40 30N 91 0W
Harper Mt. 67 64 15N 143 57W
Harput 122 38 48N 39 15 E
Harrat al Kishb 122 22 30N 40 15 E
Harrat al Uwairidh 122 26 50N 38 0 E
Harricana, R. 40 50 56N 79 32W
Harriman 73 36 0N 84 35W
Harrington Harbour 38 50 31N 59 30W
Harris, Can. 56 51 44N 107 35W
Harris, U.K. 96 57 50N 6 55W
Harris L. 134 31 10 S 135 10 E
Harris Pt. 46 43 6N 82 9W
Harris, Sd. of 96 57 44N 7 6W
Harrisburg, Can. 49 43 14N 80 13W
Harrisburg, Ill., U.S.A. 77 37 42N 88 30W
Harrisburg, Nebr., U.S.A. 74 41 36N 103 46W
Harrisburg, Oreg., U.S.A. 78 44 25N 123 10W
Harrisburg, Pa., U.S.A. 70 40 18N 76 52W
Harrison, Ark., U.S.A. 75 36 10N 93 4W
Harrison, Idaho, U.S.A. 78 47 30N 116 51W
Harrison, Mich., U.S.A. 46 44 1N 84 48W
Harrison, Nebr., U.S.A. 74 42 42N 103 52W
Harrison, Ohio, U.S.A. 77 39 16N 84 49W
Harrison B. 67 70 25N 151 0W
Harrison, C. 36 54 55N 57 55W
Harrison Grove 49 43 18N 78 58W
Harrison Hot Springs 63 49 18N 121 47W
Harrison L. 63 49 33N 121 50W
Harrisonburg 72 38 28N 78 52W
Harrisonville 76 38 39N 94 21W
Harriston 46 43 57N 80 53W
Harrisville 46 44 40N 83 19W
Harrodsburg, Ind., U.S.A. 77 39 1N 86 33W
Harrodsburg, Ky., U.S.A. 77 37 46N 84 51W
Harrogate 94 53 59N 1 32W
Harrow, Can. 46 42 2N 82 55W
Harrow, U.K. 95 51 35N 0 15W
Harrowsmith 47 44 24N 76 40W
Harry S. Truman Res 76 38 14N 93 30W

Harstad	**110**	68 48N	16 30E
Hart	**72**	43 42N	86 21W
Hartell	**61**	50 36N	114 14W
Hartford, Conn., U.S.A.	**71**	41 47N	72 41W
Hartford, Ky., U.S.A.	**72**	37 26N	86 50W
Hartford, Mich., U.S.A.	**77**	42 13N	86 10W
Hartford, S.D., U.S.A.	**74**	43 40N	96 58W
Hartford, Wis., U.S.A.	**74**	43 18N	88 25W
Hartford City	**77**	40 22N	85 20W
Hartland, Can.	**39**	46 20N	67 32W
Hartland, U.S.A.	**77**	43 6N	88 21W
Hartland Pt.	**95**	51 2N	4 32W
Hartlepool	**94**	54 42N	1 11W
*Hartley	**117**	18 10S	30 7E
Hartley Bay	**62**	53 25N	129 15W
Hartney	**57**	49 30N	100 35W
Hartselle	**73**	34 25N	86 55W
Hartshorne	**75**	34 51N	95 30W
Hartsville	**73**	34 23N	80 2W
Hartwell	**73**	34 21N	82 52W
Harty	**53**	49 29N	82 41W
Harvard	**77**	42 25N	88 37W
Harvard, Mt.	**79**	39 0N	106 5W
Harvey, Can.	**39**	45 43N	67 1W
Harvey, Ill., U.S.A.	**77**	41 40N	87 40W
Harvey, N.D., U.S.A.	**74**	47 50N	99 58W
Harwich	**95**	51 56N	1 18E
Harwood	**70**	44 7N	78 11W
Haryana □	**124**	29 0N	76 10E
Harz	**106**	51 40N	10 40E
Hasa	**122**	26 0N	49 0E
Hasbaiya	**115**	33 25N	35 41E
Hashefela	**115**	31 30N	34 43E
Haskell, Okla., U.S.A.	**75**	35 51N	95 40W
Haskell, Tex., U.S.A.	**75**	33 10N	99 45W
Hasparren	**102**	43 24N	1 18W
Hassan	**122**	13 0N	76 5E
Hasselt, Belg.	**105**	50 56N	5 21E
Hasselt, Neth.	**105**	52 36N	6 6E
Hassi Messaoud	**114**	31 43N	6 8E
Hassi Taguenza	**88**	29 8N	0 23W
Hastings, Can.	**47**	44 18N	77 57W
Hastings, N.Z.	**133**	39 39S	176 52E
Hastings, U.K.	**95**	50 51N	0 36E
Hastings, Mich., U.S.A.	**77**	42 40N	85 20W
Hastings, Minn., U.S.A.	**74**	44 41N	92 51W
Hastings, Nebr., U.S.A.	**74**	40 34N	98 22W
Hastings, Pa., U.S.A.	**70**	40 40N	78 45W
Hastings Road	**66**	49 16N	122 56W
Hat Nhao	**128**	14 46N	106 32E
Hatch	**79**	32 45N	107 8W
Hatches Creek	**134**	20 56S	135 12E
Hatchet L.	**55**	58 36N	103 40W
Hatfield Post Office	**136**	33 54N	143 49E
Hathras	**124**	27 36N	78 6E
Hatia	**125**	22 30N	91 5E
Hato de Corozal	**86**	6 11N	71 45W
Hato Mayor	**85**	18 46N	69 15W
Hattem	**105**	52 28N	6 4E
Hatteras, C.	**73**	35 10N	75 30W
Hattiesburg	**75**	31 20N	89 20W
Hatton	**55**	50 2N	109 50W
Hattonford	**60**	53 46N	115 42W
Hatvan	**107**	47 40N	19 45E
Hau Bon (Cheo Reo)	**128**	13 25N	108 28E
Haubstadt	**77**	38 12N	87 34W
Hauchinango	**82**	20 12N	97 45W
Haugesund	**111**	59 23N	5 13E
Haultain, R.	**55**	55 51N	106 46W
Hauraki Gulf	**133**	36 35S	175 5E
Haut Atlas	**114**	32 0N	7 0W
Haut-Rhin □	**101**	48 0N	7 15E
Hauta Oasis	**122**	23 40N	47 0E
Hautah, Wahât al	**122**	23 40N	47 0E
Haute-Corse □	**103**	42 30N	9 30E
Haute-Garonne □	**102**	43 28N	1 30E
Haute-Loire □	**102**	45 5N	3 50E
Haute-Marne □	**101**	48 10N	5 20E
Haute-Saône □	**101**	47 45N	6 10E
Haute-Savoie □	**103**	46 0N	6 20E
Haute-Vienne □	**102**	45 50N	1 10E
Hauterive	**41**	49 10N	68 16W
Hautes-Alpes □	**103**	44 42N	6 20E
Hautes-Pyrénées □	**102**	43 0N	0 10E
Hauteville-Lompnes	**103**	45 59N	5 35E
Hautmont	**101**	50 15N	3 55E
Hauts-de-Seine □	**101**	48 52N	2 15E
Havana	**76**	40 19N	90 3W
Havana = La Habana	**84**	23 8N	82 22W
Havasu, L.	**81**	34 18N	114 28W
Havel, R.	**106**	52 40N	12 15E
Havelange	**105**	50 23N	5 15E
Havelock, N.B., Can.	**39**	46 2N	65 24W
Havelock, Ont., Can.	**47**	44 26N	77 53W
Havelock, Qué., Can.	**43**	45 3N	73 45W
Havelock, N.Z.	**133**	41 17S	173 48E
Havelock I.	**128**	11 55N	93 2E
Haverfordwest	**95**	51 48N	4 59W
Haverhill	**71**	42 50N	71 2W
Havering	**95**	51 33N	0 20E
Haverstraw	**71**	41 12N	73 58W
Havlíčkův Brod	**106**	49 36N	15 33E
Havre	**78**	48 40N	109 34W
Havre-St.-Pierre	**38**	50 18N	63 33W
Havre-Aubert	**39**	47 12N	61 56W
Havre Aubert, Î.	**39**	47 13N	61 57W
Havre-aux-Maisons, Î.	**39**	47 25N	61 47W
Havre, Le	**100**	49 30N	0 5E
Havza	**122**	41 0N	35 35E
Haw, R.	**73**	37 43N	80 52W
Hawaii □	**67**	20 30N	157 0W
Hawaii I.	**67**	20 0N	155 0W
Hawaiian Is.	**67**	20 30N	156 0W
Hawarden, Can.	**56**	51 25N	106 36W
Hawarden, U.S.A.	**74**	43 2N	96 28W
Hawea Lake	**133**	44 28S	169 19E
Hawera	**133**	39 35S	174 19E
Hawesville	**77**	37 54N	86 45W
Hawick	**96**	55 25N	2 48W
Hawk Junction	**53**	48 5N	84 38W
Hawk Lake	**52**	49 48N	93 59W
Hawk Point	**76**	38 58N	91 8W
Hawke B.	**133**	39 25N	177 20E
Hawke, C.	**136**	32 13S	152 34E
Hawker	**94**	31 59S	138 22E
Hawkes Bay	**37**	50 36N	57 10W
Hawke's Bay □	**133**	39 45S	176 35E
Hawkesbury	**43**	45 37N	74 37W
Hawkesbury I.	**62**	53 37N	129 3W
Hawkesbury River	**136**	33 50S	151 44W
Hawkestone	**70**	44 31N	79 27W
Hawkinsville	**73**	32 17N	83 30W
Hawley	**74**	46 58N	96 20W
Hawthorne	**78**	38 31N	118 37W
Haxtun	**74**	40 40N	102 39W
Hay, Austral.	**136**	34 30S	144 51E
Hay, U.K.	**95**	52 4N	3 9W
Hay, C.	**64**	74 25N	113 0W
Hay Cove	**39**	45 45N	60 44W
Hay I.	**46**	44 53N	80 58W
Hay L.	**54**	58 50N	118 50W
Hay Lakes	**61**	53 12N	113 2W
Hay, R., Austral.	**135**	24 10S	137 20E
Hay, R., Can.	**54**	60 0N	116 56W
Hay River	**54**	60 51N	115 44W
Hay Springs	**74**	42 40N	102 38W
Hayange	**101**	49 20N	6 2E
Haycock	**67**	65 10N	161 20W
Hayden, Ariz., U.S.A.	**79**	33 2N	110 54W
Hayden, Colo., U.S.A.	**78**	40 30N	107 22W
Haye Descartes, La	**100**	46 58N	0 42E
Haye-du-Puits, La	**100**	49 17N	1 33W
Hayes	**74**	44 22N	101 1W
Hayes Pen.	**17**	75 30N	65 0W
Hayes, R.	**55**	57 3N	92 12W
Haymana	**122**	39 30N	32 35E
Haynesville	**75**	33 0N	93 7W
Hays, Can.	**61**	50 6N	111 48W
Hays, U.S.A.	**74**	38 55N	99 25W
Haysboro	**59**	50 59N	114 5W
Haysville	**77**	38 28N	86 55W
Hayward, Calif., U.S.A.	**80**	37 40N	122 5W
Hayward, Wis., U.S.A.	**74**	46 2N	91 30W
Hayward's Heath	**95**	51 0N	0 5W
Hazard	**72**	37 18N	83 10W
Hazaribagh	**125**	23 58N	85 26E
Hazebrouck	**101**	50 42N	2 31E
Hazelmere	**66**	49 2N	122 43W
Hazelton, Can.	**54**	55 20N	127 42W
Hazelton, U.S.A.	**74**	46 30N	100 15W
Hazen	**78**	39 37N	119 2W
Hazenmore	**56**	49 42N	107 8W
Hazlehurst	**73**	31 50N	82 35W
Hazlet	**56**	50 24N	108 36W
Hazleton, Ind., U.S.A.	**77**	38 29N	87 34W
Hazleton, Pa., U.S.A.	**71**	40 58N	76 0W
Hazrat Imam	**123**	37 15N	68 50E
Head of Bay d'Espoir	**37**	47 56N	55 45W
Head of Bight	**134**	31 30S	131 25E
Head of St. Margarets Bay	**39**	44 41N	63 55W
Headingley	**58**	49 53N	97 24W
Healdsburg	**80**	38 33N	122 51W
Healdton	**75**	34 16N	97 31W
Healesville	**136**	37 35S	145 30E
Heanor	**94**	53 1N	1 20W
Heard I.	**16**	53 0S	74 0E
Hearne	**75**	30 54N	96 35W
Hearne B.	**55**	60 10N	99 10W
Hearne L.	**54**	62 20N	113 10W
Hearst	**53**	49 40N	83 41W
Heart, R.	**74**	46 40N	101 30W
Heart's Content	**37**	47 54N	53 27W
Heath Pt.	**38**	49 8N	61 40W
Heath Steele	**39**	47 17N	66 5W
Heatherton, Newf., Can.	**37**	48 17N	58 45W
Heatherton, N.S., Can.	**39**	45 35N	61 47W
Heavener	**75**	34 54N	94 36W
Hebbronville	**75**	27 20N	98 40W
Heber	**81**	32 44N	115 32W
Heber Springs	**75**	35 29N	91 59W
Hebert	**56**	50 30N	107 10W
Hebgen, L.	**78**	44 50N	111 15W
Hebrides, U.K.	**96**	57 30N	7 0W
Hebrides, Inner Is., U.K.	**96**	57 20N	6 40W
Hebrides, Outer Is., U.K.	**96**	57 50N	7 25W
Hebron, Newf., Can.	**36**	58 12N	62 38W
Hebron, N.S., Can.	**39**	43 53N	66 5W
Hebrón	**115**	31 32N	35 6E
Hebron, Ind., U.S.A.	**77**	41 19N	87 17W
Hebron, N.D., U.S.A.	**74**	46 56N	102 2W
Hebron, Nebr., U.S.A.	**74**	40 15N	97 33W
Hebron Fd.	**36**	58 9N	62 45W
Hecate I.	**62**	51 42N	128 0W
Hecate Str.	**62**	53 10N	130 30W
Hecks Corner	**43**	45 4N	73 12W
Hecla	**74**	45 56N	98 8W
Hecla I.	**57**	51 10N	96 43W
Hédé	**100**	48 18N	1 49W
Hede	**110**	62 23N	13 30E
Hedemora	**111**	60 18N	15 58E
Hedley, Can.	**63**	49 22N	120 4W
Hedley, U.S.A.	**75**	34 53N	100 39W
Hedley B.	**64**	73 0N	108 0W
Hedmark □	**111**	61 17N	11 40E
Hedrick	**76**	41 11N	92 19W
Heemstede	**105**	52 22N	4 37E
Heerenveen	**105**	52 57N	5 55E
Heerlen	**105**	50 55N	6 0E
Heidelberg	**106**	49 23N	8 41E
Heilbron	**117**	27 16S	27 59E
Heilbronn	**106**	49 8N	9 13E
Heilungkiang □	**130**	47 30N	129 0E
Heinola	**111**	61 13N	26 24E
Heinsburg	**55**	53 50N	110 30W
Heinze Is.	**128**	14 25N	97 45E
Heisler	**61**	52 41N	112 13W
Hejaz = Hijãz	**122**	26 0N	37 30E
Hekimhan	**122**	38 50N	38 0E
Hekla	**110**	63 56N	19 35W
Helena, Ark., U.S.A.	**75**	34 30N	90 35W
Helena, Mont., U.S.A.	**78**	46 40N	112 0W
Helendale	**81**	34 45N	117 19W
Helene L.	**56**	53 33N	108 12W
Helensburgh, Austral.	**136**	34 11S	151 1E
Helensburgh, U.K.	**96**	56 0N	4 44W
Helensville	**133**	36 41S	174 29E
Helgeland	**110**	66 20N	13 30E
Helgoland, I.	**106**	54 10N	7 51E
Heligoland = Helgoland	**106**	54 10N	7 51E
Hell-Ville	**117**	13 25S	48 16E
Hellick Kenyon Plateau	**91**	82 0S	110 0W
Hellin	**104**	38 31N	1 40W
Helmand □	**124**	31 20N	64 0E
Helmand, R.	**124**	34 0N	67 0E
Helmond	**105**	51 29N	5 41E
Helmsdale	**96**	58 7N	3 40W
Helmsdale, R.	**96**	58 10N	3 50W
Helper	**78**	39 44N	110 56W
Helsingborg	**111**	56 3N	12 42E
Helsingfors = Helsinki	**111**	60 15N	25 3E
Helsingør	**111**	56 2N	12 35E
Helsinki (Helsingfors)	**111**	60 15N	25 3E
Helvellyn	**94**	54 31N	3 1W
Hemet	**81**	33 45N	116 59W
Hemford	**39**	44 30N	64 47W
Hemingford	**74**	42 21N	103 4W
Hemmingford	**43**	45 3N	73 35W
Hemphill	**75**	31 21N	93 49W
Hempstead	**75**	30 5N	96 5W
Hemse	**111**	57 15N	18 22E
Henares, R.	**104**	40 55N	3 0W
Hendaye	**102**	43 23N	1 47W
Henderson, Argent.	**88**	36 18S	61 43W
Henderson, Ky., U.S.A.	**77**	37 50N	87 38W
Henderson, Nev., U.S.A.	**81**	36 2N	115 0W
Henderson, Pa., U.S.A.	**73**	35 25N	88 40W
Henderson, Tex., U.S.A.	**75**	32 5N	94 49W
Henderson, Mt.	**62**	54 16N	128 4W
Hendersonville	**73**	35 21N	82 28W
Hendrix Lake	**63**	52 5N	120 48W
Hengelo	**105**	52 16N	6 48E
Henghsien	**131**	22 36N	109 16E
Hengshan	**130**	27 10N	112 45E
Hengyang	**131**	26 51N	112 30E
Hénin-Beaumont	**101**	50 25N	2 58E
Henley Harbour	**37**	52 2N	55 51W
Henlopen, C.	**72**	38 48N	75 5W
Hennebont	**100**	47 49N	3 19W
Hennepin	**76**	41 15N	89 21W
Hennessy	**75**	36 8N	97 53W
Henribourg	**55**	53 25N	105 38W
Henrichemont	**101**	47 20N	2 21E
Henrietta	**75**	33 50N	98 15W
Henrietta Maria C.	**34**	55 9N	82 20W
Henry	**76**	41 5N	89 20W
Henry Kater, C.	**65**	69 8N	66 30W
Henryetta	**75**	35 30N	96 0W
Henrysburg	**43**	45 5N	73 27W
Henryville	**43**	45 8N	73 11W
Hensall	**46**	43 26N	81 30W
Hentiyn Nuruu	**130**	48 30N	108 30E
Henty	**136**	35 30N	147 0E
Henzada	**125**	17 38N	95 35E
Heppner	**78**	45 27N	119 34W
Hepworth	**46**	44 37N	81 9W
Héraðsflói	**110**	65 42N	14 12W
Héradsvötn	**110**	65 25N	19 5W
Herât	**124**	34 20N	62 7E
Herât □	**124**	35 0N	62 0E
Hérault □	**102**	43 34N	3 15E
Hérault, R.	**102**	43 20N	3 32E
Herbert I.	**67**	52 49N	170 10W
Herbert Inlet	**62**	49 20N	125 58W
Herbiers, Les	**100**	46 52N	1 0W
Herbignac	**100**	47 27N	2 18W
Hercegnovi	**109**	42 30N	18 33E
Herculaneum	**76**	38 16N	90 23W
Herðubreið	**110**	65 11N	16 21W
Herdman	**43**	45 2N	74 6W
Hereford, U.K.	**95**	52 4N	2 42W
Hereford, U.S.A.	**75**	34 50N	102 28W
Hereford and Worcester □	**95**	52 10N	2 30W
Hereford, Mt.	**41**	45 5N	71 36W
Herentals	**105**	51 12N	4 51E
Hereward	**49**	43 50N	80 19W
Herford	**106**	52 7N	8 40E
Héricourt	**101**	47 32N	6 55E
Herington	**74**	38 43N	97 0W
Heriot Bay	**62**	50 7N	125 13W
Hérisson	**102**	46 32N	2 42E
Herjehogna	**111**	61 43N	12 7E
Herkimer	**71**	43 0N	74 59W
Herlong	**80**	40 8N	120 8W
Herm I.	**100**	49 30N	2 28W
Herman	**74**	45 51N	96 8W
Hermandez	**80**	36 24N	120 46W
Hermann	**74**	38 40N	91 25W
Herment	**102**	45 45N	2 24E
Hermidale	**136**	31 30S	146 42E
Hermiston	**78**	45 50N	119 16W
Hermitage, Can.	**37**	47 33N	55 56W
Hermitage, N.Z.	**133**	43 44S	170 5E
Hermitage, U.S.A.	**76**	37 56N	93 19W
Hermitage B.	**35**	47 33N	56 10W
Hermite, Is.	**90**	55 50S	68 0W
Hermon, Mt.	**115**	33 20N	36 0E
Hermon, Mt. = Sheikh, J. ash	**115**	33 20N	36 0E
Hermosillo	**82**	29 10N	111 0W
Hernad, R.	**107**	48 20N	21 15E
Hernandarias	**89**	25 20S	54 40W
Hernando, Argent.	**88**	32 28S	63 40W
Hernando, U.S.A.	**75**	34 50N	89 59W
Herne	**105**	51 33N	7 12E
Herne Bay	**95**	51 22N	1 8E
Herning	**111**	56 8N	8 58E
Heroica Nogales	**82**	31 14N	110 56W
Heron Bay	**53**	48 40N	86 25W
Hérons, Ile aux	**44**	45 25N	73 35W
Herreid	**74**	45 53N	100 5W
Herrera	**104**	39 12N	4 50W
Herrero, Punta	**83**	19 17N	87 27W
Herrin	**76**	37 50N	89 0W
Herring Cove	**39**	44 34N	63 34W
Herschel	**56**	51 38N	108 21W
Herschel I.	**67**	69 35N	139 5W
Herstal	**105**	50 40N	5 38E
Hertford	**95**	51 47N	0 4W
Hertford □	**95**	51 51N	0 5W
's-Hertogenbosch	**105**	51 42N	5 17E
Hervey B.	**135**	25 0S	152 52E
*Hervey Is.	**15**	19 30S	159 0W
Hervey Junction	**34**	46 50N	72 29W
Herzliyya	**115**	32 10N	34 50E
Hesdin	**101**	50 21N	2 0E
Hespeler	**49**	43 26N	80 19W
Hesperia	**81**	34 25N	117 18W
Hesse = Hessen	**106**	50 40N	9 20E
Hessel	**46**	46 1N	84 28W
Hessen □	**106**	50 40N	9 20E
Hetch Hetchy Aqueduct	**80**	37 36N	121 25W
Hettinger	**74**	46 8N	102 38W
Hève, C. de la	**100**	49 30N	0 5E
Hewett, C.	**65**	70 16N	67 45W
Hexham	**94**	54 58N	2 7W
Heyfield	**136**	37 59S	146 47E
Heysham	**94**	54 5N	2 53W
Heywood	**136**	38 8S	141 37E
Hi-no-Misaki	**132**	35 26N	132 38E
Hi Vista	**81**	34 44N	117 46W
Hiawatha, Kans., U.S.A.	**74**	39 55N	95 33W
Hiawatha, Utah, U.S.A.	**78**	39 37N	111 1W
Hibben I.	**62**	53 0N	132 18W
Hibbing	**52**	47 30N	93 0W
Hickman	**75**	36 35N	89 8W
Hickmans Harbour	**37**	48 6N	53 44W
Hickory	**73**	35 46N	81 17W
Hicksville, N.Y., U.S.A.	**71**	40 46N	73 30W
Hicksville, Ohio, U.S.A.	**77**	41 18N	84 46W
Hida-Sammyaku	**132**	36 30N	137 40E
Hida-sammyaku	**132**	36 30N	137 40E
Hidalgo	**77**	39 9N	88 9W
Hidalgo □	**82**	20 30N	99 10W
Hidalgo del Parral	**82**	26 58N	105 40W
Hidalgo, Presa M.	**82**	26 30N	108 35W
Hifung	**131**	22 59N	115 17E
Higashiōsaka	**132**	34 40N	135 37E
Higbee	**76**	39 19N	92 31W
Higgins	**75**	36 9N	100 1W
Higgins Corner	**80**	39 2N	121 5W
Higgins L.	**46**	44 30N	84 45W
Higginsville	**76**	39 4N	93 43W
Higgs I. L.	**73**	36 20N	78 30W
High Atlas = Haut Atlas	**114**	32 30N	5 0W
High I., Newf., Can.	**35**	56 40N	61 10W
High I., Newf., Can.	**36**	52 28N	55 40W
High Island	**75**	29 32N	94 22W
High Level	**54**	58 31N	117 8W
High Point	**73**	35 57N	79 58W
High Prairie	**60**	55 30N	116 30W
High River	**61**	50 30N	113 50W
High Springs	**73**	29 50N	82 40W
High Wycombe	**95**	51 37N	0 45W
Highland, U.S.A.	**77**	41 33N	87 28W
Highland, Ill., U.S.A.	**76**	38 44N	89 41W

* *Renamed Chegutu*

* *Renamed Manuae*

Place	Page	Lat.	Long.
Highland, Wis., U.S.A.	76	43 6N	90 21W
Highland □	96	57 30N	5 0W
Highland Creek	50	43 47N	79 10W
Highland Park	59	51 6N	114 4W
Highland Pk., Ill., U.S.A.	77	42 10N	87 50W
Highland Pk., Mich., U.S.A.	70	42 25N	83 6W
Highmore	74	44 35N	99 26W
Highridge	60	54 3N	114 8W
Highrock L.	55	57 5N	105 32W
Higley	79	33 27N	111 46W
Higüay	85	18 37N	68 42W
Higüero, Pta.	85	18 22N	67 16W
Hiko	80	37 30N	115 13W
Hikone	132	35 15N	136 10E
Hikurangi	133	37 55S	178 4E
Hilda	61	50 28N	110 3W
Hilden	39	45 18N	63 18W
Hildesheim	106	52 9N	9 55E
Hill	47	45 40N	74 45W
Hill City, Idaho, U.S.A.	78	43 20N	115 2W
Hill City, Kans., U.S.A.	74	39 25N	99 51W
Hill City, Minn., U.S.A.	52	46 57N	93 35W
Hill City, S.D., U.S.A.	74	43 58N	103 35W
Hill Island L.	55	60 30N	109 50W
Hill Spring	61	49 17N	113 38W
Hilla, Iraq	122	32 30N	44 27E
Hilla, Si Arab.	122	23 35N	46 50E
Hillegom	105	52 18N	4 35E
Hillhurst	59	51 3N	114 7W
Hillingdon	95	51 33N	0 29W
Hillman	46	45 5N	83 52W
Hillmond	56	53 26N	109 41W
Hillsboro, Ill., U.S.A.	76	39 9N	89 29W
Hillsboro, Iowa, U.S.A.	76	40 50N	91 42W
Hillsboro, Kans., U.S.A.	74	38 28N	97 10W
Hillsboro, Mo., U.S.A.	76	38 14N	90 34W
Hillsboro, N. Mex., U.S.A.	79	33 0N	107 35W
Hillsboro, N.D., U.S.A.	74	47 23N	97 9W
Hillsboro, N.H., U.S.A.	71	43 8N	71 56W
Hillsboro, Ohio, U.S.A.	77	39 12N	83 37W
Hillsboro, Oreg., U.S.A.	80	45 31N	123 0W
Hillsboro, Tex., U.S.A.	75	32 0N	97 10W
Hillsborough	85	12 28N	61 28W
Hillsborough B.	39	46 8N	63 5W
Hillsburgh	49	43 47N	80 9W
Hillsdale, Can.	58	50 25N	104 37W
Hillsdale, Mich., U.S.A.	77	41 55N	84 40W
Hillsdale, N.Y., U.S.A.	71	42 11N	73 30W
Hillsport	53	49 27N	85 34W
Hillston	136	33 30S	145 31E
Hilo	67	19 44N	155 5W
Hilonghilong, mt.	127	9 10N	125 45E
Hilton	70	43 16N	77 48W
Hilton Beach	46	46 15N	83 53W
Hilversum	105	52 14N	5 10E
Himachal Pradesh □	124	31 30N	77 0E
Himalaya, mts.	124	29 0N	84 0E
Himatnagar	124	23 37N	72 57E
Himeji	132	34 50N	134 40E
Himi	132	36 50N	137 0E
Hims = Homs	122	34 40N	36 45E
Hinako, Kepulauan	126	0 50N	97 20E
Hinche	85	19 9N	72 1W
Hinckley, U.K.	95	52 33N	1 21W
Hinckley, U.S.A.	78	39 18N	112 41W
Hindmarsh L.	136	36 5S	141 55E
Hinds L.	37	48 58N	57 0W
Hindu Kush	124	36 0N	71 0E
Hindubagh	124	30 56N	67 57E
Hindupur	124	13 49N	77 32E
Hines Creek	60	56 20N	118 40W
Hingan	131	25 39N	110 43E
Hinganghat	124	20 30N	78 59E
Hingham	78	48 40N	110 29W
Hingi	131	25 4N	105 2E
Hingkwo	131	26 15N	115 13E
Hingning	131	24 2N	115 55E
Hingol, R.	124	25 30N	65 30E
Hingoli	124	19 41N	77 15E
Hinlopenstretet	17	79 35N	18 40E
Hinnøy	110	68 40N	16 28E
Hinojosa	104	38 30N	5 17W
Hinsdale	78	48 26N	107 2W
Hinton, Can.	60	53 26N	117 34W
Hinton, U.S.A.	72	37 40N	80 51W
Hirakud Dam	125	21 32N	83 45E
Hiratsuka	132	35 19N	139 21E
Hirosaki	132	40 34N	140 28E
Hiroshima	132	34 30N	132 30E
Hiroshima-ken □	132	34 50N	133 0E
Hirson	101	49 55N	4 4E
Hispaniola, I.	83	19 0N	71 0W
Hissar	124	29 12N	75 45E
Hita	132	33 20N	130 58E
Hitachi	132	16 40N	140 35E
Hitchcock	56	49 14N	103 7W
Hitchin	95	51 57N	0 16W
Hitoyoshi	132	32 13N	130 45E
Hitra	110	63 30N	8 45E
Hiungyao	130	40 10N	122 9E
Hixon	63	53 25N	122 35W
Hjalmar L.	55	61 33N	109 25W
Hjälmaren	111	59 18N	15 40E
Hjørring	111	57 29N	9 59E
Ho Chi Minh, Phanh Bho	128	10 58N	106 40E
Hoa Binh	128	20 50N	105 20E
Hoa Da (Phan Ri)	128	11 16N	108 40E
Hoadley	54	52 45N	114 30W
Hoai Nhon (Bon Son)	128	14 28N	109 1E
Hoare B.	65	65 17N	62 0W
Hobart, Austral.	135	42 50S	147 21E
Hobart, Ind., U.S.A.	77	41 32N	87 15W
Hobart, Okla., U.S.A.	75	35 0N	99 5W
Hobbs	75	32 40N	103 3W
Hobo	86	2 35N	75 30W
Hoboken, Belg.	105	51 11N	4 21E
Hoboken, U.S.A.	71	40 45N	74 4W
Hobro	111	56 39N	9 46E
Hobson L.	63	52 35N	120 15W
Hoburgen	111	56 55N	18 7E
Hochatown	75	34 11N	94 39W
Hochih	131	24 43N	107 43E
Hochwan	131	30 0N	106 15E
Hodeïda	115	14 50N	43 0E
Hodges Hill	37	49 4N	55 53W
Hodgeville	56	50 7N	106 58W
Hodgson	57	51 13N	97 36W
Hódmezóvásárhely	107	46 28N	20 22E
Hodonín	106	48 50N	17 0E
Hoëdic, I.	100	47 21N	2 52W
Hoek van Holland	105	52 0N	4 7E
Hof, Ger.	106	50 18N	11 55E
Hof, Iceland	110	64 33N	14 40W
Höfðakaupstaður	110	65 50N	20 19W
Hofei	131	31 52N	117 15E
Hofeng	131	29 55N	110 5E
Hofsjökull	110	64 49N	18 48W
Hofsós	110	65 53N	19 26W
Hōfu	132	34 3N	131 34E
Hofuf	122	25 20N	49 40E
Hog I.	46	45 48N	85 22W
Hogansville	73	33 14N	84 50W
Hogeland	56	48 51N	108 40W
Hogsty Reef	85	21 41N	73 48W
Hoh, R.	80	47 45N	124 29W
Hohenlimburg	105	51 21N	7 35E
Hohenwald	73	35 35N	87 30W
Hohpi	130	35 59N	114 13E
Hôi An	128	15 30N	108 19E
Hoi Xuan	128	20 25N	105 9E
Hoiping	131	22 30N	112 12E
Hoisington	74	38 33N	98 50W
Hokang	130	47 36N	130 28E
Hokiang	131	28 50N	105 50E
Hokianga Harbour	133	35 31S	173 22E
Hokitika	133	42 42S	171 0E
Hokkaidō	132	43 30N	143 0E
Hokow	128	22 39N	103 57E
Hokowchen	130	40 16N	111 4E
Holan Shan	130	38 40N	105 50E
Holberg	62	50 40N	128 0W
Holbrook, Austral.	136	35 42S	147 18E
Holbrook, U.S.A.	79	35 0N	110 0W
Holden, Can.	60	53 13N	112 11W
Holden, Mo., U.S.A.	76	38 43N	94 0W
Holden, Wash., U.S.A.	63	48 12N	120 47W
Holden Fillmore	78	39 0N	112 26W
Holdenville	75	35 5N	96 25W
Holderness	94	53 45N	0 5W
Holdfast	56	50 58N	105 25W
Holdrege	55	40 25N	99 30W
Holgate	77	41 15N	84 8W
Holguín	84	20 50N	76 20W
Holinshead L.	52	49 39N	89 40W
Hollams Bird I.	117	24 40S	14 30E
Holland, U.K.	94	52 50N	0 10W
Holland, U.S.A.	77	42 47N	86 7W
Holland Landing	70	44 7N	79 30W
Hollandia = Jayapura	127	2 28S	140 38E
Hollidaysburg	70	40 26N	78 25W
Hollis	75	34 45N	99 55W
Hollister, Calif., U.S.A.	80	36 51N	121 24W
Hollister, Idaho, U.S.A.	70	42 21N	114 36W
Holly, U.S.A.	46	42 48N	83 38W
Holly, Colo., U.S.A.	74	38 7N	102 7W
Holly Hill	73	29 15N	81 3W
Holly Springs	75	34 45N	89 25W
Hollywood, Calif., U.S.A.	68	34 7N	118 25W
Hollywood, Fla., U.S.A.	73	26 0N	80 9W
Holman	64	70 44N	117 44W
Hólmavík	110	65 42N	21 40W
Holmsund	110	63 41N	20 20E
Holroyd, R.	135	14 10S	141 36E
Holsteinsborg	65	66 40N	53 30W
Holt	110	63 33N	19 48W
Holton	36	54 31N	57 12W
Holtville	81	32 50N	115 27W
Holy Cross	67	62 10N	159 52W
Holy I., England, U.K.	94	55 42N	1 48W
Holy I., Wales, U.K.	94	53 17N	4 37W
Holyhead	94	53 18N	4 38W
Holyhead B.	94	53 20N	4 35W
Holyoke, Colo., U.S.A.	74	40 39N	102 18W
Holyoke, Mass., U.S.A.	71	42 14N	72 37W
Holyrood	37	47 27N	53 8W
Homalin	125	24 55N	95 0E
Homathko, R.	62	51 0N	124 56W
Hombori	114	15 20N	1 38W
Homburg	105	49 19N	7 21E
Home B.	65	68 40N	67 10W
Home Hill	135	19 43S	147 25E
Homedale	78	43 42N	116 59W
Homer, Can.	49	43 10N	79 11W
Homer, Alaska, U.S.A.	67	59 40N	151 35W
Homer, Ill, U.S.A.	77	40 4N	87 57W
Homer, La., U.S.A.	75	32 50N	93 4W
Homer, Mich., U.S.A.	77	42 9N	84 49W
Homestead, Can.	60	55 31N	119 22W
Homestead, Fla., U.S.A.	73	25 29N	80 27W
Homestead, Idaho, U.S.A.	70	45 3N	116 58W
Homewood, Calif., U.S.A.	80	39 4N	120 8W
Homewood, Ill., U.S.A.	77	41 34N	87 40W
Hominy	75	36 26N	96 24W
Homs (Hims)	122	34 40N	36 45E
Hon Chong	128	10 16N	104 38E
Honan □	131	33 50N	113 15E
Honcut	80	39 20N	121 32W
Honda	86	5 12N	74 45W
Hondeklipbaai	117	30 19S	17 17E
Hondo, Can.	60	55 4N	114 2W
Hondo, U.S.A.	75	29 22N	99 6W
Hondo, R.	83	18 25N	88 21W
Honduras ■	84	14 40N	86 30W
Honduras, Golfo de	84	16 50N	87 0W
Hönefoss	111	60 10N	10 12E
Honesdale	71	41 34N	75 17W
Honey Harbour	46	44 52N	79 49W
Honey L.	80	40 13N	120 14W
Honfleur	100	49 25N	0 13E
Hong Kong ■	131	22 11N	114 14E
Hongha, R.	128	22 0N	104 0E
Honghai B.	131	22 45N	115 15E
Hongkong ■	131	22 11N	114 14E
Honguedo, Détroit d'	38	49 15N	64 0W
Honiton	95	50 48N	3 11W
Honolulu	67	21 19N	157 52W
Honshū	132	36 0N	138 0E
Hood Mt.	78	45 30N	121 50W
Hood, Pt.	134	34 23S	119 34E
Hood River	78	45 45N	121 37W
Hoodsport	80	47 24N	123 7W
Hoogeveen	105	52 44N	6 30E
Hoogezand	105	53 11N	6 45E
Hooghly, R.	125	21 59N	88 10E
Hooglede	105	50 59N	3 5E
Hook Hd.	97	52 8N	6 57W
Hooker	75	36 55N	101 10W
Hooker L.	52	50 35N	91 1W
Hoonah	67	58 15N	135 30W
Hooper Bay	67	61 30N	166 10W
Hoopeston	77	40 30N	87 40W
Hoorn	105	52 38N	5 4E
Hoosick Falls	71	42 54N	73 21W
Hoover Dam	81	36 0N	114 45W
Hooversville	70	40 8N	78 57W
Hop Bottom	71	41 41N	75 47W
Hope, B.C., Can.	63	49 25N	121 25E
Hope, Ont., Can.	50	43 53N	79 31W
Hope, Ariz., U.S.A.	81	33 43N	113 42W
Hope, Ark., U.S.A.	75	33 40N	93 30W
Hope, Ind., U.S.A.	77	39 18N	85 46W
Hope, N.D., U.S.A.	74	47 21N	97 42W
Hope Bay	91	65 0S	55 0W
Hope I., B.C., Can.	62	50 55N	127 53W
Hope I., Ont., Can.	46	44 55N	80 11W
Hope Pt.	67	68 20N	166 50W
Hope Town	73	26 30N	76 30W
Hopedale	36	55 28N	60 13W
Hopelchén	83	19 46N	89 50W
Hopes Advance, C.	36	61 4N	69 34W
Hopetoun	136	33 57S	120 7E
Hopetown	117	29 34S	24 3E
Hopewell	39	45 29N	62 42W
Hopewell Cape	39	45 51N	64 35W
Hoping	131	24 31N	115 2E
Hopkins, Mich., U.S.A.	77	42 37N	85 46W
Hopkins, Mo., U.S.A.	76	40 31N	94 45W
Hopkins, R.	136	37 55S	142 40E
Hopkinsville	73	36 52N	87 26W
Hopland	80	39 0N	123 7W
Hoppo	131	21 32N	109 6E
Hoquiam	80	46 50N	123 55W
Hordaland fylke □	111	60 25N	6 15E
Hordern Hills	134	20 40S	130 20E
Horlick Mts.	91	84 0S	102 0W
Hormoz	123	27 35N	55 0E
Hormuz, I.	123	27 8N	56 28E
Hormuz Str.	123	26 30N	56 30E
Horn, Austria	106	48 39N	15 40E
Horn, Isafjarðarsýsla, Iceland	110	66 28N	22 28W
Horn, Suður-Múlasýsla, Iceland	110	65 10N	13 31W
Horn, Cape = Hornos, C. de	90	55 50S	67 30W
Horn Head	97	55 13N	8 0W
Horn, I.	73	30 17N	88 40W
Horn Mts.	54	62 15N	119 15W
Horn, R.	54	61 30N	118 1W
Hornaday, R.	64	69 19N	123 48W
Hornavan	110	66 15N	17 30E
Hornbeck	75	31 22N	93 20W
Hornbrook	78	41 58N	122 37W
Hornby	49	43 43N	79 50W
Horncastle	94	53 13N	0 8W
Hornell	70	42 23N	77 41W
Hornell L.	54	62 20N	119 25W
Hornepayne	53	49 14N	84 48W
Hornings Mills	46	44 9N	80 12W
Hornitos	80	37 30N	120 14W
Hornos, Cabo de	90	55 50S	67 30W
Hornoy	101	49 50N	1 54E
Hornsby	136	33 42S	151 2E
Hornsea	94	53 55N	0 10W
Hornu	105	50 26N	3 50E
Horoshiri Dake	132	42 40N	142 40E
Horqueta	88	23 15S	56 55W
Horse Cr.	74	41 33N	104 45W
Horse Is.	37	50 15N	55 50W
Horsefly	63	52 20N	121 25W
Horsefly L.	63	52 25N	121 0W
Horsens	111	55 52N	9 51E
Horseshoe Bay	66	49 22N	123 17W
Horseshoe Dam	79	33 45N	111 35W
Horsham, Austral.	136	36 44S	142 13E
Horsham, U.K.	95	51 4N	0 20W
Horten	111	59 25N	10 32E
Horton	74	39 42N	95 30W
Horton, R.	67	69 56N	126 52W
Horwood	37	49 27N	54 32W
Horwood, L.	53	48 5N	82 20W
Hose, Pegunungan	126	2 5N	114 6E
Hoshangabad	124	22 45N	77 45E
Hoshiarpur	124	31 30N	75 58E
Hosmer	74	45 36N	99 29W
Hospet	124	15 15N	76 20E
Hospitalet de Llobregat	104	41 21N	2 6E
Hospitalet, L'	102	42 36N	1 47E
Hoste, I.	90	55 0S	69 0W
Hostens	102	44 30N	0 40W
Hot	128	18 8N	98 29E
Hot Creek Ra.	78	39 0N	116 0W
Hot Springs, Ark, U.S.A.	75	34 30N	93 0W
Hot Springs, S.D., U.S.A.	74	43 25N	103 30W
Hotagen, L.	110	63 50N	14 30E
Hotchkiss	79	38 55N	107 47W
Hotchkiss, R.	60	57 2N	117 28W
Hotien (Khotan)	129	37 6N	79 59E
Hoting	110	64 8N	16 15E
Hottah L.	64	65 4N	118 30W
Hotte, Massif de la	85	18 30N	73 45W
Houat, I.	100	47 24N	2 58W
Houck	79	35 15N	109 15W
Houdan	101	48 48N	1 35E
Houffalize	105	50 8N	5 48E
Houghton	52	47 9N	88 39W
Houghton L.	46	44 20N	84 40W
Houghton Lake Heights	46	44 18N	84 51W
Houghton-le-Spring	94	54 51N	1 28W
Houhora	133	34 49S	173 9E
Houlton	35	46 5N	68 0W
Houma	75	29 35N	90 50W
Hourtin	102	45 11N	1 4W
Houston, Can.	54	54 25N	126 30W
Houston, Mo., U.S.A.	75	37 20N	92 0W
Houston, Tex., U.S.A.	75	29 50N	95 20W
Hovd (Jargalant)	129	48 2N	91 37E
Hove	95	50 50N	0 10W
Hövsgöl Nuur	130	51 0N	100 30E
Howard, Kans., U.S.A.	75	37 30N	96 16W
Howard, Penn., U.S.A.	70	41 0N	77 40W
Howard, S.D., U.S.A.	74	44 2N	97 30W
Howard L.	55	62 15N	105 57W
Howe	78	43 48N	113 0W
Howe, C.	136	37 30S	150 0E
Howe I.	47	44 16N	76 17W
Howe Sd.	63	49 35N	123 15W
Howell	46	42 38N	83 56W
Howick	43	45 11N	73 51W
Howley	37	49 12N	57 2W
Howrah	125	22 37N	88 27E
Howth Hd.	97	53 21N	6 0W
Hoy I.	96	58 50N	3 15W
Høyanger	111	61 25N	6 50E
Hpungan Pass	125	27 30N	96 55E
Hrádec Králové	106	50 15N	15 50E
Hron, R.	107	48 0N	18 4E
Hrvatska	108	45 20N	16 0E
Hsaichwan Shan	131	21 34N	112 30E
Hsaio Shan	131	34 0N	111 30E
Hsenwi	125	23 22N	97 55E
Hsiamen	131	24 30N	118 7E
Hsinchow	131	19 37N	109 17E
Hsinchu	131	24 48N	120 58E
Hsinhsing	131	22 45N	112 11E
Hua Hin	128	12 34N	99 58E
Huachacalla	82	18 45S	68 17W
Huachinera	82	30 9N	108 55W
Huachipato	88	36 45S	73 09W
Huacho	86	11 10S	77 35W
Huachón	86	10 35S	76 0W
Huacrachuco	86	8 35S	76 50W
Huaian	131	33 28N	119 5E
Huain	131	36 26N	119 12E
Huajuapan	83	17 50N	98 0W
Hualien	131	24 0N	121 30E
Huallaga, R.	86	5 30S	76 10W
Hualpai Pk.	79	35 8N	113 58W
Huancabamba	86	5 10S	79 15W
Huancané	86	15 10S	69 50W
Huancapi	86	13 25S	74 0W
Huancavelica	86	12 50S	75 5W
Huancayo	86	12 5S	75 0W
Huanglui	131	18 30N	108 46E

Huangnipo Incomáti, R

Huangnipo 131 27 40N 105 10 E
Huánuco 86 9 55 S 76 15W
Huaraz 86 9 30 S 77 32W
Huarmey 86 10 5 S 78 5W
Huasamota 82 22 30N 104 30W
Huascarán 86 9 0 S 77 30W
Huasco 88 28 24 S 71 15W
Huasco, R. 88 28 27 S 71 13W
Huasna 81 35 6N 120 24W
Huatabampo 82 26 50N 109 50W
Huauchinango 83 20 11N 98 3W
Huautla 82 18 20N 96 50W
Huautla de Jiménez 83 18 8N 96 51W
Huay Namota 82 21 56N 104 30W
Huayllay 86 11 03 S 76 21W
Hubbard, Can. 56 51 8N 103 22W
Hubbard, Iowa, U.S.A. 76 42 18N 93 18W
Hubbard, Tex., U.S.A. 75 31 50N 96 50W
Hubbard L. 46 44 49N 83 34W
Hubbards 39 44 38N 64 4W
Hubbart Pt. 55 59 21N 94 41W
Hubbell 52 47 11N 88 26W
Hubli-Dharwar 124 15 22N 75 15 E
Huchow 131 30 57N 120 1 E
Huchuetenango 82 15 25N 91 30W
Huddersfield 94 53 38N 1 49W
Hudiksvall 111 61 43N 17 10 E
Hudson, Ont., Can. 52 50 6N 92 09W
Hudson, Qué., Can. 44 45 27N 74 9W
Hudson, Mass., U.S.A. 71 42 23N 71 35W
Hudson, Mich., U.S.A. 77 41 50N 84 20W
Hudson, N.Y., U.S.A. 71 42 15N 73 46W
Hudson, Wis., U.S.A. 74 44 57N 92 45W
Hudson, Wyo., U.S.A. 78 42 54N 108 37W
Hudson B. 55 59 0N 91 0W
Hudson Bay, Can. 65 60 0N 86 0W
Hudson Bay, Sask., Can. 57 52 51N 102 23W
Hudson Falls 71 43 18N 73 34W
Hudson Heights 44 45 28N 74 10W
Hudson Hope 54 56 0N 121 54W
Hudson, R. 71 40 42N 74 2W
Hudson Str. 65 62 0N 70 0W
Hudsonville 77 42 52N 85 52W
Hudwin L. 57 53 12N 95 41W
Hué 128 16 30N 107 35 E
Huehuetenango 84 15 20N 91 28W
Huejúcar 82 22 21N 103 13W
Huelgoat 100 48 22N 3 46W
Huelva 104 37 18N 6 57W
Huentelauquén 88 31 38 S 71 33W
Huerta, Sa. de la 88 31 10 S 67 30W
Huesca 104 42 8N 0 25W
Huétamo 82 18 36N 100 54W
Hugh, R. 134 25 1 S 134 10 E
Hughenden 135 20 52 S 144 10 E
Hughes 67 66 0N 154 20W
Hugo, Colo., U.S.A. 74 39 12N 103 27W
Hugo, Okla., U.S.A. 75 34 0N 95 30W
Hugoton 75 37 18N 101 22W
Huhehot 130 40 52N 111 36 E
Huichapán 83 20 24N 99 40W
Huila □ 86 2 30N 75 45W
Huila, Nevado del 86 3 0N 76 0W
Huiling Shan 131 21 35N 111 57 E
Huinan 130 42 40N 126 5 E
Huinca Renancó 88 34 51 S 64 22W
Huixtla 83 15 9N 92 28W
Huiya 122 24 40N 49 15 E
Huizen 105 52 18N 5 14 E
Hukawng Valley 125 26 30N 96 30 E
Hukow 131 29 38N 116 25 E
Hulaifa 122 25 58N 41 0 E
Hulan 130 46 0N 126 44 E
Hulbert 46 46 21N 85 9W
Huld 130 45 5N 105 30 E
Hulin 130 45 45N 133 0 E
Hull, Can. 48 45 25N 75 44W
Hull, U.K. 94 53 45N 0 20W
Hull, U.S.A. 76 39 43N 91 13W
Hull, R. 94 53 55N 0 23W
Hulst 105 51 17N 4 2 E
Huma 130 51 44N 126 42 E
Humacao 67 18 9N 65 50W
Humahuaca 88 23 10 S 65 25W
Humaitá 86 7 35 S 62 40W
Humaita 88 27 2 S 58 31W
Humansville 76 37 48N 93 35W
Humber 49 43 54N 79 49W
Humber B. 50 43 38N 79 28W
Humber Bay 50 43 38N 79 27W
Humber, R., Can. 50 43 38N 79 28W
Humber, R., U.K. 94 53 40N 0 10W
Humberside □ 94 53 50N 0 30W
Humberstone 70 42 53N 79 16W
Humble 75 29 59N 95 10W
Humboldt, Can. 56 52 15N 105 9W
Humboldt, Iowa, U.S.A. 76 42 42N 94 15W
Humboldt, Minn., U.S.A. 57 48 53N 97 7W
Humboldt, Tenn., U.S.A. 73 35 50N 88 55W
Humboldt Gletscher 65 79 30N 62 0W
Humboldt, R. 78 40 55N 116 0W
Hume, Calif., U.S.A. 80 36 48N 118 54W
Hume, Kans., U.S.A. 76 38 5N 94 35W
Hume, L. 136 36 0 S 147 0 E
Humeston 76 40 51N 93 30W
Humphreys, Mt. 80 37 17N 118 40W
Humphreys Pk. 79 35 24N 111 38W
Humptulips 80 47 14N 123 57W
Huna Floi 110 65 50N 20 50W
Hunan □ 131 27 30N 111 30 E
Hunchun 130 42 49N 130 31 E
Hundred and Fifty Mile House 63 52 7N 121 57W
Hundred Mile House 63 51 38N 121 18W
Hunedoara 107 45 40N 22 50 E
Hung Ho, R. 131 32 25N 115 35 E
Hungary ■ 107 47 20N 19 20 E
Hungary, Plain of 93 47 0N 20 0 E
Hunghai Wan 131 22 45N 115 15 E
Hunghu (Sinti) 131 29 49N 113 30 E
Hungkiang 131 27 0N 109 49 E
Hŭngnam 130 39 55N 127 45 E
Hungshui Ho, R. 131 23 24N 110 12 E
Hungtze Hu 131 33 20N 118 35 E
Hunsrück, mts. 105 49 30N 7 0 E
Hunstanton 94 52 57N 0 30 E
Hunstsville 77 40 26N 83 48W
Hunter, N.D., U.S.A. 74 47 12N 97 17W
Hunter, N.Y., U.S.A. 71 42 13N 74 13W
Hunter, C. 65 71 42N 72 30W
Hunter, I. 135 40 30 S 144 54 E
Hunter I. 62 51 55N 128 0W
Hunter, R. 136 32 52 S 151 46 E
Hunter Ra. 136 32 45 S 150 15 E
Hunterville 133 39 56 S 175 35 E
Huntingburg 77 38 20N 86 58W
Huntingdon, Can. 43 45 6N 74 10W
Huntingdon, U.K. 95 52 20N 0 11W
Huntingdon, N.Y., U.S.A. 71 40 52N 73 25W
Huntingdon, Pa., U.S.A. 70 40 28N 78 1W
Huntingdon □ 43 45 5N 74 15W
Huntington, Ind., U.S.A. 77 40 52N 85 30W
Huntington, Oreg., U.S.A. 78 44 22N 117 21W
Huntington, Ut., U.S.A. 78 39 24N 111 1W
Huntington, W. Va., U.S.A. 72 38 20N 82 30W
Huntington Beach 81 33 40N 118 0W
Huntington Park 79 33 58N 118 15W
Huntington, Resr. 77 40 49N 85 25W
Huntley 77 42 10N 88 26W
Huntly, N.Z. 133 37 34 S 175 11 E
Huntly, U.K. 96 57 27N 2 48W
Huntsville, Can. 46 45 20N 79 14W
Huntsville, Ala., U.S.A. 73 34 45N 86 35W
Huntsville, Mo., U.S.A. 76 39 26N 92 33W
Huntsville, Tex., U.S.A. 75 30 45N 95 35W
Huonville 135 43 0 S 147 5 E
Hupei □ 131 31 5N 113 5 E
Hupel 63 50 37N 118 44W
Hurd C. 70 45 15N 81 40W
Hurley, N. Mex., U.S.A. 79 32 45N 108 7W
Hurley, Wis., U.S.A. 52 46 26N 90 10W
Huron, Calif., U.S.A. 80 36 12N 120 6W
Huron, Ohio, U.S.A. 70 41 22N 82 34W
Huron, S.D., U.S.A. 74 44 30N 98 20W
Huron B. 52 46 57N 88 9W
Huron, L. 46 45 0N 83 0W
Hurons, R. des 45 45 28N 73 16W
Hurricane 79 37 10N 113 12W
Hurstbridge 136 37 40 S 145 10 E
Hurunui, R. 133 42 54 S 173 18 E
Húsavik 110 66 3N 17 21W
Huskvarna 111 57 47N 14 15 E
Huslia 67 65 40N 156 30W
Hussar 61 51 3N 112 41W
Hutag 130 49 25N 102 34 E
Hutchinson, Kans., U.S.A. 75 38 3N 97 59W
Hutchinson, Minn, U.S.A. 74 44 50N 94 22W
Huto Ho 130 38 30N 113 45 E
Hutsonville 77 39 6N 87 40W
Hutte Sauvage, L. de la 36 56 15N 64 45W
Huttig 75 33 5N 92 10W
Huttonsville 49 43 38N 79 48W
Huy 105 50 31N 5 15 E
Hvammsfjörður 110 65 4N 22 5W
Hvammur 110 65 13N 21 49W
Hvar, I. 108 43 11N 16 28 E
Hvítá, Arnessýsla, Iceland 110 64 0N 20 58W
Hvítá, Mýrasýsla, Iceland 110 64 40N 21 5W
Hvítárvatn 110 63 37N 19 50W
Hwachwan 130 47 1N 130 50 E
Hwai Ho 131 32 20N 114 30 E
Hwainan 131 32 44N 117 1 E
Hwaiyang 131 33 50N 115 2 E
Hwan Ho 130 37 30N 117 30 E
Hwang-ho, R. 130 40 50N 107 30 E
Hwangan 131 31 30N 114 40 E
Hwangshih 131 30 27N 115 0 E
Hwangyen 131 28 34N 121 12 E
Hwanjen 130 41 24N 125 26 E
Hwateh 130 41 58N 113 58 E
Hwatien 130 43 0N 126 52 E
Hweian 131 25 2N 118 56 E
Hweichang 131 25 33N 115 41 E
Hweihsien 131 35 30N 113 46 E
Hweilai 131 23 0N 116 15 E
Hweimin 130 37 36N 117 30 E
Hweining 130 35 45N 105 0 E
Hweitseh 129 26 32N 103 6 E
Hwokiu 131 32 23N 116 16 E
Hyannis 74 42 0N 101 45W
Hyas 57 51 54N 102 16W
Hyattsville 72 38 59N 76 55W
Hydaburg 67 55 15N 132 45W
Hyde In. 65 75 2N 80 0W
Hyderabad, India 124 17 10N 78 29 E
Hyderabad, Pak. 124 25 23N 68 36 E
** Hyderabad □ 124 25 3N 68 24 E
Hyères 103 43 8N 6 9 E
Hyères, Is. d' 103 43 0N 6 28 E
Hyesan 130 41 20N 128 10 E
Hyland, R. 54 59 52N 128 12W
Hymers 52 48 18N 89 43W
Hyndman Pk. 78 43 50N 114 0W
Hyōgo-ken □ 132 35 15N 135 0 E
Hyrum 78 41 35N 111 56W
Hysham 78 46 21N 107 11W
Hythe, Can. 60 55 20N 119 33W
Hythe, U.K. 95 51 4N 1 5 E
Hyvinkä 111 60 38N 24 50 E

I

Iaco, R. 86 10 25 S 70 30W
Ialomiţa, R. 107 44 45N 27 57 E
Ian L. 62 53 50N 132 45W
Iaşi 107 47 10N 27 40 E
Iauaretê 86 0 30N 69 5W
Iba 127 15 22N 120 0 E
Ibadan 114 7 22N 3 58 E
Ibagué 86 4 27N 73 14W
Ibar, R. 109 43 15N 20 40 E
Ibaraki-ken □ 132 36 10N 140 10 E
Ibarra 86 0 21N 78 7W
Ibera, Laguna 88 28 30 S 57 9W
Iberia 76 38 5N 92 18W
Iberian Peninsula 93 40 0N 5 0W
Iberville 45 45 19N 73 17W
Iberville □ 45 45 15N 73 10W
Iberville, Lac d' 36 55 55N 73 15W
Iberville, Mt. d' 36 58 50N 63 50W
Ibiá 87 19 30 S 46 30W
Ibicuy 88 33 55 S 59 10W
Ibiracu 87 19 50 S 40 30W
Ibiza 104 38 54N 1 26 E
Ibiza, I. 104 39 0N 1 30 E
Ibo 117 12 22 S 40 32 E
Ibonma 127 3 22 S 133 31 E
Ibotirama 87 12 13 S 43 12W
Ibu 127 1 35N 127 25 E
Ica 86 14 0 S 75 30W
Ica, R. 86 2 55 S 69 0W
Icabarú 86 4 20N 61 45W
Içana 86 1 21N 69 0W
Iceland, I. ■ 110 65 0N 19 0W
Icha 121 55 30N 156 0 E
Ichang 131 30 48N 111 29 E
Ichchapuram 125 19 10N 84 40 E
Ichihara 132 35 28N 140 5 E
Ichikawa 132 35 44N 139 55 E
Ichilo, R. 86 16 30 S 64 45W
Ichinomiya 132 35 18N 136 48 E
Ichun, Heilungkiang, China 129 47 42N 129 8 E
Ichun, Kiangsi, China 131 27 51N 114 12 E
Ichun, Shensi, China 130 35 24N 109 9 E
Ichung 131 25 30N 112 29 E
Ichwan 130 36 9N 109 58 E
Icy C. 17 70 25N 162 0W
Icy Str. 54 58 20N 135 30W
Ida 77 41 55N 83 34W
Ida Grove 74 42 20N 95 25W
Idabel 75 33 53N 94 50W
Idaho □ 78 44 10N 114 0W
Idaho City 78 43 50N 115 52W
Idaho Falls 78 43 30N 112 10W
Idaho Springs 78 39 49N 105 30W
Idar-Oberstein 105 49 43N 7 19 E
Idhi Oros 109 35 15N 24 45 E
Idhra 109 37 20N 23 28 E
Idi 126 4 55N 97 45 E
* Idi Amin Dada, L. 116 0 25 S 29 40 E
Idiofa 116 4 55 S 19 42 E
Idria 80 36 25N 120 41W
Idutywa 117 32 8 S 28 18 E
Ieper 105 50 51N 2 53 E
Ierápetra 109 35 0N 25 44 E
Ierzu 108 39 48N 9 32 E
Ifanadiana 117 21 29 S 47 39 E
Ife 114 7 30N 4 31 E
Igarapava 87 20 3 S 47 47W
Igarapé Açu 87 1 4 S 47 33W
Igarka 121 67 30N 87 20 E
Igatimi 89 24 5 S 55 30W
Iggesund 111 61 39N 17 10 E
Iglésias 108 39 19N 8 27 E
Igloolik 65 69 20N 81 30W
Ignace 52 49 30N 91 40W
Igornachoix Bay 37 50 40N 57 25W
Iguaçu, Cat. del 89 25 41N 54 26W
Iguaçu, R. 89 25 30 S 53 10W
Iguala 83 18 20N 99 40W
Igualada 104 41 37N 1 37 E
Iguape, R. 89 24 40 S 48 0W
Iguassu = Iguaçu 89 25 41N 54 26W
Iguatu 87 6 20 S 39 18W
Iguéla 116 2 0 S 9 16 E
Ihing 131 31 21N 119 51 E
Ihosy 117 22 24 S 46 8 E
Ihsien 130 41 45N 121 3 E
Ihwang 131 27 30N 116 2 E
Ii 110 65 15N 25 30 E
Iida 132 35 35N 138 0 E
Iijoki 110 65 20N 26 15 E
Iisalmi 110 63 32N 27 10 E
Iizuka 132 33 38N 130 42 E
IJmuiden 105 52 28N 4 35 E
IJsselmeer 105 52 45N 5 20 E
IJsselstein 105 52 1N 5 2 E
Ijuí, R. 89 27 58 S 55 20W
Ikamatua 99 42 15 S 171 41 E
Ikaria, I. 109 37 35N 26 10 E
Ikela 116 1 0 S 23 35 E
Iki 132 33 45N 129 42 E
Ilan 130 46 14N 129 33 E
Ilanskiy 121 56 14N 96 3 E
Ile-à-la Crosse 55 55 27N 107 53W
Ile-à-la-Crosse, Lac 55 55 40N 107 45W
Île-aux-Noix 43 45 8N 73 17W
Île-Bizard 44 45 29N 73 53W
Île-Bouchard, L' 100 47 7N 0 26 E
Île-Cadieux 44 45 25N 74 1W
Île de France □ 101 49 0N 2 20 E
Ile d'Orleans, Chenal de l' 42 46 58N 71 0W
Île-Perrot 44 45 23N 73 57W
Île-Perrot-Sud 44 45 21N 73 54W
Île-Sainte-Thérèse 43 45 22N 73 15W
Ile-sur-le-Doubs, L' 101 47 26N 6 34 E
Ilebo 116 4 17 S 20 47 E
Ilek 120 51 32N 53 21 E
Ilek, R. 120 51 30N 53 22 E
Îles, L. des 40 46 20N 75 18W
Ilford 55 56 4N 95 35W
Ilfracombe, Austral. 135 23 30 S 144 30 E
Ilfracombe, U.K. 95 51 13N 4 8W
Ilheus 87 14 49 S 39 2W
Iliamna L. 67 59 35N 155 30W
Ilich 120 40 50N 68 27 E
Ilico 88 34 50 S 72 20W
Iliff 74 40 50N 103 3W
Ilio Pt. 67 21 13N 157 16W
Iliodhrómia 109 39 12N 23 50 E
Ilion 71 43 0N 75 3W
Iliysk 120 44 10N 77 20 E
Ilkeston 94 52 59N 1 19W
Ilkhuri Shan 130 51 30N 124 0 E
Ilkley 92 53 56N 1 49W
Illana B. 127 7 35N 123 45 E
Illapel 88 32 0 S 71 10W
Ille 102 42 40N 2 37 E
Ille-et-Vilaine □ 100 48 10N 1 30W
Iller, R. 106 47 53N 10 10 E
Illimani, Mte. 86 16 30 S 67 50W
Illinois □ 69 40 15N 89 30W
Illinois R. 76 38 5N 90 28W
Illiopolis 76 39 51N 89 15W
Illukotat, R. 36 60 48N 78 11W
Ilo 86 17 40 S 71 20W
Iloilo 127 10 45N 122 33 E
Ilorin 114 8 30N 4 35 E
Ilwaco 80 46 19N 124 3W
Ilwaki 127 7 55 S 126 30 E
Imabari 132 34 4N 133 0 E
Iman = Dalneretchensk 121 45 50N 133 40 E
Imandra, Oz. 120 67 45N 33 0 E
Imari 132 33 15N 129 52 E
Imbler 78 45 31N 118 0W
Imeni Poliny Osipenko 121 55 25N 136 29 E
Imeri, Serra 86 0 50N 65 25W
Imienpo 130 45 0N 128 16 E
Imlay 78 40 45N 118 9W
Imlay City 46 43 0N 83 2W
Immingham 94 53 37N 0 12W
Immokalee 73 26 25N 81 20W
Imola 108 44 20N 11 42 E
Imperatriz 87 5 30 S 47 29W
Impéria 108 43 52N 8 0 E
Imperial, Can. 56 51 21N 105 28W
Imperial, Calif., U.S.A. 81 32 52N 115 34W
Imperial, Nebr., U.S.A. 74 40 38N 101 39W
Imperial Beach 81 32 35N 117 8W
Imperial Dam 81 32 50N 114 30W
Imperial Res. 81 32 53N 114 28W
Imperial Valley 81 32 55N 115 30W
Impfondo 116 1 40N 18 0E
Imphal 125 24 48N 93 56 E
Imphy 101 46 56N 3 15 E
Imuruan B. 127 10 40N 119 10 E
In Salah 114 27 10N 2 32 E
Ina 132 35 50N 138 0 E
Inangahua Junc. 133 41 52 S 171 59 E
Inanwatan 127 2 10 S 132 5 E
Iñapari 86 11 0 S 69 40W
Inari 110 68 54N 27 5 E
Inari, L. 110 69 0N 28 0 E
Inawashir-Ko 132 37 28N 140 2 E
Inca 104 39 43N 2 54 E
Incaguasi 88 29 12 S 71 5W
Ince Burnu 122 42 2N 35 0 E
Inchŏn 130 37 32N 126 45 E
Incomáti, R. 117 25 15 S 32 35 E

* Renamed Edward, L.
** Now part of Sind

Incudine, Mte. I' Jacmel

Incudine, Mte. I'	103	41 50N	9 12 E
Indalsälven	110	62 36N	17 30 E
Indaw	125	24 15N	96 5 E
Independence, Calif., U.S.A.	80	36 51N	118 7W
Independence, Iowa, U.S.A.	76	42 27N	91 52W
Independence, Kans., U.S.A.	75	37 10N	95 50W
Independence, Ky., U.S.A.	77	38 57N	84 33W
Independence, Mo., U.S.A.	76	39 3N	94 25W
Independence, Oreg., U.S.A.	78	44 53N	123 6W
Independence Fjord	17	82 10N	29 0W
Independence Mts.	78	41 30N	116 2W
Independencia, La	83	16 31N	91 47W
Index	80	47 50N	121 33W
India ■	119	20 0N	80 0 E
Indian Arm	66	49 23N	122 53W
Indian Cabins	54	59 52N	117 2W
Indian Harbour	36	54 27N	57 13W
Indian Head	56	50 30N	103 35W
Indian L.	52	50 14N	94 5W
Indian Ocean	11	5 0S	75 0 E
Indian Springs	81	36 35N	115 40W
Indiana	70	40 38N	79 9W
Indiana □	72	40 0N	86 0W
Indianapolis	77	39 42N	86 10W
Indianola, Iowa, U.S.A.	76	41 20N	93 38W
Indianola, Miss., U.S.A.	75	33 27N	90 40W
Indiga	120	67 50N	48 50 E
Indigirka, R.	121	69 0N	147 0 E
Indio	81	33 46N	116 15W
Indonesia ■	126	5 0S	115 0 E
Indore	124	22 42N	75 53 E
Indramaju	127	6 21S	108 20 E
Indramaju, Tg.	127	6 20S	108 20 E
Indravati, R.	125	19 0N	81 15 E
Indre □	101	47 12N	1 39 E
Indre-et-Loire □	100	47 12N	0 40 E
Indre, R.	100	47 2N	1 8 E
Indus, R.	124	28 40N	70 10 E
Industry	76	40 20N	90 36W
İnebolu	122	41 55N	33 40 E
Infiernillo, Presa del	82	18 9N	102 0W
Ingelmunster	105	50 56N	3 16 E
Ingende	116	0 12S	18 57 E
Ingenio Santa Ana	88	27 25S	65 40W
Ingersoll	46	43 4N	80 55W
Ingham	135	18 43S	146 10 E
Ingleborough, mt.	94	54 11N	2 23W
Inglefield G.	65	77 30N	67 0W
Inglega	136	31 20S	147 50 E
Inglewood, Queensland, Austral.	136	28 25S	151 8 E
Inglewood, Vic., Austral.	136	36 29S	143 53 E
Inglewood, Can.	49	43 47N	79 56W
Inglewood, N.Z.	133	39 9S	174 14 E
Inglewood, U.S.A.	81	33 58N	118 21W
Ingólfshöfði	110	63 48N	16 39W
Ingolstadt	106	48 45N	11 26 E
Ingomar, Can.	39	43 34N	65 22W
Ingomar, U.S.A.	78	46 43N	107 37W
Ingonish	39	46 42N	60 18W
Ingonish Beach	39	46 38N	60 25W
Inhambane	117	23 54S	35 30 E
Inhaminga	117	18 26S	35 0 E
Inharrime	117	24 30S	35 0 E
Ining	131	25 8N	109 57 E
Ining (Kuldja)	129	43 57N	81 20 E
Inirida, R.	86	3 0N	68 40W
Inishbofin I.	97	53 35N	10 12W
Inishmore, I.	97	53 8N	9 45W
Inishowen, Pen.	97	55 14N	7 15W
Injune	135	25 46S	148 32 E
Inkerman	39	47 40N	64 49W
Inklin	54	58 56N	133 5W
Inklin, R.	54	58 50N	133 10W
Inkom	78	42 51N	112 7W
Inkpen Beacon	95	51 22N	1 28W
Inle Aing	125	20 30N	96 58 E
Inn, R.	106	48 35N	13 28 E
Inner Hebrides, Is.	96	57 0N	6 30W
Inner Mongolia □	130	44 50N	117 40 E
Inner Sound	96	57 30N	5 55W
Innerkip, Can.	70	43 12N	80 41W
Innerkip, Ont., Can.	46	43 13N	80 42W
Innetalling I.	36	56 0N	79 0W
Innisfail, Austral.	135	17 33S	146 5 E
Innisfail, Can.	61	52 0N	113 57W
Innisfree	60	53 22N	111 32W
Innsbruck	106	47 16N	11 23 E
Inongo	116	1 35S	18 30 E
Inosu	86	12 22N	71 38W
Inoucdjouac (Port Harrison)	36	58 27N	78 6W
Inowrocław	107	52 50N	18 20 E
Inquisivi	86	16 50S	66 45W
Intata Reach	62	53 38N	125 30W
Intendente Alvear	88	35 12S	63 32W
Interior	74	43 46N	101 59W
Interlaken	101	46 41N	7 50 E
International Falls	52	48 36N	93 25W
Interview I.	128	12 55N	92 42 E
Inthanon, Mt.	128	18 35N	98 29 E
Intiyaco	88	28 50S	60 0W
Inútil, B.	90	53 30S	70 15W
Inuvik	67	68 16N	133 40W
Inveraray	96	56 13N	5 5W
Inverbervie	96	56 50N	2 17W
Invercargill	133	46 24S	168 24 E
Inverell	135	29 45S	151 8 E
Invergordon	96	57 41N	4 10W
Invermay	56	51 48N	103 9W
Invermere	61	50 30N	116 2W
Inverness, Can.	39	46 15N	61 19W
Inverness, U.K.	96	57 29N	4 12W
Inverness, U.S.A.	73	28 50N	82 20W
Inverurie	96	57 15N	2 21W
Investigator Group	134	34 45S	134 20 E
Investigator Str.	135	35 30S	137 0 E
Invona	70	40 46N	78 35W
Inwood	57	50 30N	97 30W
Inyo Range	79	37 0N	118 0W
Inyokern	81	35 37N	117 54W
Inza	120	53 55N	46 25 E
Ioánnina (Janinà) □	109	39 39N	20 57 E
Ioco	66	49 18N	122 53W
Iola	75	38 0N	95 20W
Iona	39	45 58N	60 48W
Iona I.	96	56 20N	6 25W
Ione, Calif., U.S.A.	80	38 20N	121 0W
Ione, Wash., U.S.A.	63	48 44N	117 29W
Ionia	77	42 59N	85 7W
Ionian Is. = Ionioi Nisoi	109	38 40N	20 0 E
Ionian Sea	109	37 30N	17 30 E
Iónioi Nisoi	109	38 40N	20 8 E
Íos, I.	109	36 41N	25 20 E
Iowa □	74	42 18N	93 30W
Iowa City	76	41 40N	91 35W
Iowa Falls	76	42 30N	93 15W
Iowa, R.	76	41 10N	91 1W
Ipameri	87	17 44S	48 9W
Ipiales	86	0 50N	77 37W
Ipin	129	28 48N	104 33 E
Ipiros □	109	39 30N	20 30 E
Ipixuna	86	7 0S	71 40W
Ipoh	128	4 35N	101 5 E
Ippy	116	6 5N	21 7 E
Ipswich, Austral.	135	27 35S	152 46 E
Ipswich, U.K.	95	52 4N	1 9 E
Ipswich, N.H., U.S.A.	71	42 40N	70 50W
Ipswich, S.D., U.S.A.	74	45 28N	99 20W
Ipu	87	4 23S	40 44W
Iquique	86	20 19S	70 5W
Iquitos	86	3 45S	73 10W
Iracoubo	87	5 30N	53 10W
Iráklion	109	35 20N	25 12 E
Irala	89	25 55S	54 35W
Iran ■	123	33 0N	53 0 E
Iran, Pegunungan	126	2 20N	114 50 E
Iran, Plateau of	101	33 00N	55 0 E
Irānshahr	123	27 75N	60 40 E
Irapa	86	10 34N	62 35W
Irapuato	82	20 40N	101 40W
Iraq ■	122	33 0N	44 0 E
Irati	89	25 25S	50 38W
Irbid	115	32 35N	35 48 E
Irebu	116	0 40S	17 55 E
Ireland ■	97	53 0N	8 0W
Ireland's Eye	97	53 25N	6 4W
Irentala Steppe	130	43 45N	112 15 E
Iret	121	60 10N	154 5 E
Irian Jaya □	127	4 0S	137 0 E
Iringa	116	7 48S	35 43 E
Iriomote	131	24 25N	123 58 E
Iriona	84	15 57N	85 11W
Irish Republic ■	97	53 0N	8 0 E
Irish Sea	94	54 0N	5 0W
Irish Town	124	40 55S	145 9 E
Irkutsk	121	52 10N	104 20 E
Irma	61	52 55N	111 14W
Irmak	122	39 58N	33 25 E
Iroise, Mer d'	100	48 15N	4 45W
Iron Bridge	46	46 17N	83 14W
Iron Knob	135	32 46S	137 8 E
Iron Mountain	72	45 49N	88 4W
Iron River, Mich., U.S.A.	74	46 6N	88 40W
Iron River, Wis., U.S.A.	52	46 34N	91 24W
Iron Springs	61	49 56N	112 41W
Ironbridge	95	52 38N	2 29W
Irondale	70	44 51N	78 30W
Ironside	48	45 27N	75 45W
Ironton, Mo., U.S.A.	75	37 40N	90 40W
Ironton, Ohio, U.S.A.	72	38 35N	82 40W
Ironwood	52	46 30N	90 10W
Iroquois	47	44 51N	75 19W
Iroquois Falls	34	48 46N	80 41W
Iroquois, R.	77	41 5N	87 49W
Irrawaddy, R.	125	15 50N	95 6 E
Irshih	130	47 8N	119 57 E
Irtysh, R.	120	53 36N	75 30 E
Irumu	116	1 32N	29 53 E
Irún	104	43 20N	1 52W
Irvine, Can.	61	49 57N	110 16W
Irvine, U.K.	96	55 37N	4 40W
Irvine, U.S.A.	72	37 42N	83 58W
Irvine, R.	96	55 35N	4 40W
Irvinestown	97	54 28N	7 38W
Irvington	77	37 53N	86 17W
Irymple	136	34 14S	142 8 E
Is-sur-Tille	101	47 30N	5 10 E
Isaac, R.	135	22 55S	149 20 E
Isabel	74	45 27N	101 22W
Isabela, Dom. Rep.	85	19 58N	71 2W
Isabela, Pto Rico	67	18 30N	67 01W
Isabela, Cord.	84	13 30N	85 25W
Isabela, I.	82	21 51N	105 55W
Isachsen	65	78 47N	103 30W
Ísafjarðardjúp	110	66 10N	23 0W
Ísafjörður	110	66 5N	23 9W
Isangi	116	0 52N	24 10 E
Isar, R.	106	48 40N	12 30 E
Isbergues	101	50 36N	2 24 E
Ischia, I.	108	40 45N	13 51 E
Iscuandé	86	2 28N	77 59W
Ise	132	34 25N	136 45 E
Ise-Wan	132	34 43N	136 43 E
Isère □	103	45 15N	5 40 E
Isère, R.	102	45 15N	5 30 E
Iserlohn	105	51 22N	7 40 E
Ishan	130	24 30N	108 41 E
Ishigaki	131	24 26N	124 10 E
Ishikari-Wan	132	43 20N	141 20 E
Ishikawa-ken □	132	36 30N	136 30 E
Ishim	120	56 10N	69 18 E
Ishim, R.	120	57 45N	71 10 E
Ishinomaki	132	38 32N	141 20 E
Ishkuman	124	36 30N	73 50 E
Ishpeming	53	46 30N	87 40W
Isigny-sur-Mer	100	49 19N	1 6W
Isil Kul	120	54 55N	71 16 E
Isili	102	39 45N	9 6 E
Isiolo	116	0 24N	37 33 E
Isiro	116	2 53N	27 58 E
İskenderun	122	36 32N	36 10 E
Iskut, R.	54	56 45N	131 49W
Isla, La	86	6 51N	76 56W
Isla, R.	96	56 32N	3 20W
Islamabad	124	33 40N	73 0 E
Island Falls, Can.	53	49 35N	81 20W
Island Falls, U.S.A.	35	46 0N	68 25W
Island L., Can.	55	53 47N	94 25W
Island L., U.S.A.	52	47 7N	92 10W
Island Pond, Can.	37	48 25N	56 23W
Island Pond, U.S.A.	71	44 50N	71 50W
Island, R.	54	60 25N	121 12W
Islands, B. of, Can.	37	49 11N	58 15W
Islands, B. of, N.Z.	133	35 20S	174 20 E
Islay	60	53 24N	110 33W
Islay, I.	96	55 46N	6 10W
Islay Sound	96	55 45N	6 5W
Isle-Adam, L'	101	49 6N	2 14 E
Isle aux Morts	37	47 35N	59 0W
Isle-Jourdain, L', Gers, France	102	43 36N	1 5 E
Isle-Jourdain, L', Vienne, France	100	46 13N	0 31 E
Isle L.	60	53 38N	114 44W
Isle of Wight □	95	50 40N	1 20W
Isle Pierre	62	53 57N	123 16W
Isle Royale	52	48 0N	88 50W
Isle Royale Nat. Park	52	48 0N	89 0W
Isle-sur-la-Sorgue, L'	103	43 55N	5 2 E
Isle Verte, L'	41	48 1N	69 20W
Isle Vista	81	34 27N	119 52W
Isles, L. des	52	49 10N	89 40W
Islet, L'	35	47 4N	70 23W
Isleta	79	34 58N	106 46W
Isleton	80	38 10N	121 37W
Islington	50	43 38N	79 32W
Ismā'iliya	122	30 37N	32 18 E
Ismay	74	46 33N	104 44W
İsparta	122	37 47N	30 30 E
Ispica	108	36 47N	14 53 E
Israel ■	115	32 0N	34 50 E
Issoire	102	45 32N	3 15 E
Issoudun, Can.	41	46 35N	71 38W
Issoudun, France	101	46 57N	2 0 E
Issyk-Kul, Ozero	120	42 25N	77 15 E
İstanbul	122	41 0N	29 0 E
Istiaia	86	38 57N	23 10 E
Istmina	86	5 10N	76 39W
Istokpoga, L.	73	27 22N	81 14W
Istra	108	45 10N	14 0 E
Istres	103	43 31N	4 59 E
Istria = Istra	108	45 10N	14 0 E
Itá	88	25 29N	57 21W
Itabaiana	87	7 18S	35 19W
Itaberaba	87	12 32S	40 18W
Itabira	87	19 37S	43 13W
Itabirito	89	20 15S	43 48W
Itabuna	87	14 48S	39 16W
Itaete	87	13 0S	41 5W
Itaituba	87	4 10S	55 50W
Itajai	89	27 0S	48 45W
Itajubá	89	22 24S	45 30W
Italy ■	108	42 0N	13 0 E
Itambe, mt.	87	18 30S	43 15W
Itapecuru, R.	87	3 20S	44 15W
Itaperuna	87	21 10S	42 0W
Itapetininga	89	23 36S	48 7W
Itapeva	89	23 59S	48 59W
Itapicuru, R., Bahia, Brazil	87	10 50S	38 40W
Itapicuru, R., Maranhão, Brazil	87	5 40S	44 30W
Itapuá □	89	26 40S	55 40W
Itaquari	89	20 12S	40 25W
Itaquatiana	86	2 58S	58 30W
Itaqui	88	29 0S	56 30W
Itararé	89	24 6S	49 23W
Itati	88	27 16S	58 15W
Itatuba	86	5 40S	63 20W
Itbayat I.	131	20 45N	121 50 E
Itchen, R.	95	50 57N	1 20W
Ithaca, Mich., U.S.A.	46	43 18N	84 36W
Ithaca, N.Y., U.S.A.	71	42 25N	76 30W
Itháki	109	38 25N	20 43 E
Ito	132	34 58N	139 5 E
Itomamo, L.	41	49 11N	70 28W
Itoman	131	26 7N	127 40 E
Itonamas, R.	86	13 0S	64 25W
Itu	89	23 10S	47 15W
Ituaçu	87	13 50S	41 18W
Ituango	86	7 4N	75 45W
Ituiutaba	87	19 0S	49 25W
Ituliho	129	50 40N	121 30 E
Itumbiara	87	18 20S	49 10W
Ituna	56	51 10N	103 30W
Itung	130	43 25N	125 21 E
Iturbe	88	23 0S	65 25W
Iturup, Ostrov	121	45 0N	148 0 E
Ituyuro, R.	88	22 40S	63 50W
Iuka	77	38 37N	88 47W
Ivalo	110	68 38N	27 35 E
Ivalojoki	110	68 30N	27 0 E
Ivanhoe, Austral.	136	32 56S	144 20 E
Ivanhoe, U.S.A.	80	36 23N	119 13W
Ivanhoe L.	55	60 25N	106 30W
Ivano-Frankovsk, (Stanislav)	120	49 0N	24 40 E
Ivanovo	120	52 7N	25 29 E
Ivinheima, R.	89	21 48S	54 15W
Iviza = Ibiza	104	39 0N	1 30 E
Ivory Coast ■	114	7 30N	5 0W
Ivrea	108	45 30N	7 52 E
Ivugivik, (N.D. d'Ivugivic)	36	62 24N	77 55W
Iwahig	126	8 35N	117 32 E
Iwakuni	132	34 15N	132 8 E
Iwata	132	34 49N	137 59 E
Iwate-ken □	132	39 30N	141 30 E
Iwo	114	7 39N	4 9 E
Ixiamas	86	13 50S	68 5W
Ixtepec	83	16 40N	95 10W
Ixtlán de Juárez	83	17 23N	96 28W
Ixtlán del Rio	82	21 5N	104 28W
Iyang	131	28 36N	112 20 E
Izabal, L.	84	15 30N	89 10W
Izamal	83	20 56N	89 1W
Izegem	105	50 55N	3 12 E
*Izhevsk	120	56 51N	53 14 E
Izmail	120	45 22N	28 46 E
İzmir (Smyrna)	122	38 25N	27 8 E
İzmit	122	40 45N	29 50 E
Izumisano	132	34 40N	135 43 E
Izumo	132	35 20N	132 55 E

J

Jaab L.	53	51 10N	82 58W
Jabalpur	124	23 9N	79 58 E
Jablah	122	35 20N	36 0 E
Jablanica, Mt.	109	41 20N	20 30 E
Jablonec	106	50 43N	15 10 E
Jaboticabal	89	21 15S	48 17W
Jaburu	86	5 30S	64 0W
Jaca	104	42 35N	0 33W
Jacala	83	21 1N	99 11W
Jacarei	89	23 20S	46 0W
Jacarèzinho	89	23 5S	50 0W
Jáchal	88	30 5S	69 0W
Jack Lane B.	35	55 45N	60 35W
Jackfish	34	48 45N	87 0W
Jackfish L.	56	53 9N	108 29W
Jackman	35	45 35N	70 17W
Jacksboro	75	33 14N	98 15W
Jackson, Ala., U.S.A.	73	31 32N	87 53W
Jackson, Calif., U.S.A.	80	38 25N	120 47W
Jackson, Ky., U.S.A.	72	37 35N	83 22W
Jackson, Mich., U.S.A.	77	42 18N	84 25W
Jackson, Minn., U.S.A.	74	43 35N	95 0W
Jackson, Miss., U.S.A.	75	32 20N	90 10W
Jackson, Mo., U.S.A.	75	37 25N	89 42W
Jackson, Ohio, U.S.A.	72	39 0N	82 40W
Jackson, Tenn., U.S.A.	73	35 40N	88 50W
Jackson, Wyo., U.S.A.	78	43 30N	110 49W
Jackson Bay, Can.	54	50 32N	125 57W
Jackson Bay, N.Z.	133	43 58S	168 42 E
Jackson Center	77	40 27N	84 4W
Jackson, L.	78	43 55N	110 40W
Jacksons	133	42 46S	171 32 E
Jackson's Arm	37	49 52N	56 47W
Jacksonville, Ala., U.S.A.	73	33 49N	85 45W
Jacksonville, Calif., U.S.A.	80	37 52N	120 24W
Jacksonville, Fla., U.S.A.	73	30 15N	81 38W
Jacksonville, Ill., U.S.A.	76	39 42N	90 15W
Jacksonville, N.C., U.S.A.	73	34 50N	77 29W
Jacksonville, Oreg., U.S.A.	78	42 13N	122 56W
Jacksonville, Tex., U.S.A.	75	31 58N	95 12W
Jacksonville Beach	73	30 19N	81 26W
Jacmel	85	18 20N	72 40W

* Renamed Ustinov

Jacob Lake **Jundiaí**

Jacob Lake **79** 36 45N 112 12W
Jacobabad **124** 28 20N 68 29E
Jacobina **87** 11 11S 40 30W
Jacobs **52** 50 15N 89 50W
Jacques-Cartier **41** 45 31N 73 29W
Jacques Cartier, Dét. de **36** 50 0N 63 30W
Jacques-Cartier, L. **41** 47 35N 71 13W
Jacques-Cartier, Mt. **38** 48 57N 66 0W
Jacques Cartier Pass **35** 49 50N 62 30W
Jacques-Cartier, R. **41** 46 40N 71 45W
Jacquet River **39** 47 55N 66 0W
Jacuí, R. **89** 30 2S 51 15W
Jacuipe, R. **87** 12 30S 39 5W
Jacumba **81** 32 37N 116 11W
Jacundá, R. **87** 1 57S 50 26W
Jaén, Peru **86** 5 25S 78 40W
Jaén, Spain **104** 37 44N 3 43W
Jaffna **124** 9 45N 80 2E
Jagadhri **124** 30 10N 77 20E
Jagdalpur **125** 19 3N 82 6E
Jagersfontein **117** 29 44S 25 27E
Jagraon **124** 30 50N 75 25E
Jagtial **124** 18 50N 79 0E
Jaguariaíva **89** 24 10S 49 50W
Jaguaribe, R. **87** 6 0S 38 35W
Jagüey **84** 22 35N 81 7W
Jagungal, Mt. **136** 36 12S 148 28E
Jahrom **122** 28 30N 53 31E
Jainti **125** 26 45N 89 40E
Jaipur **124** 27 0N 76 10E
Jakarta **127** 6 9S 106 49E
Jakobshavn **65** 68 0N 51 0W
Jakobstad (Pietarsaari) **110** 63 40N 22 43E
Jal **75** 32 8N 103 8W
Jala **123** 27 30N 62 40E
Jalalabad **124** 34 30N 70 29E
Jalama **81** 34 29N 120 29W
Jalapa, Guat. **84** 14 45N 89 59W
Jalapa, Mexico **83** 19 30N 96 50W
Jalas, Jabal al **122** 27 30N 36 30E
Jalgaon, Maharashtra, India **124** 21 2N 76 31E
Jalgaon, Maharashtra, India **124** 21 0N 75 42E
Jalisco □ **82** 20 0N 104 0W
Jalna **124** 19 48N 75 57E
Jalón, R. **104** 41 20N 1 40W
Jalpa **82** 21 38N 102 58W
Jalpaiguri **125** 26 32N 88 46E
Jalq **123** 27 35N 62 33E
Jaluit I. **14** 6 0N 169 30E
Jamaica **76** 41 51N 94 18W
Jamaica, I. ■ **84** 18 10N 77 30W
Jamalpur, Bangla. **125** 24 52N 90 2E
Jamalpur, India **125** 25 18N 86 28E
Jamanxim, R. **87** 6 30S 55 50W
Jambe **127** 1 15S 132 10E
Jambi **126** 1 38S 103 30E
Jamdena, I. = Yamdena **127** 7 45S 131 20E
James B. **53** 51 30N 80 0W
James, R. **74** 44 50N 98 0W
James Ranges **134** 24 10S 132 0E
James River **39** 45 35N 62 7W
James Ross I. **91** 63 58S 50 94W
Jameson, C. **65** 72 5N 74 14W
Jamesport **76** 39 58N 93 48W
Jamestown, Austral. **135** 33 10S 138 32E
Jamestown, Ind., U.S.A. **77** 39 56N 86 38W
Jamestown, Ky., U.S.A. **72** 37 0N 85 5W
Jamestown, Mo., U.S.A. **76** 38 48N 92 30W
Jamestown, N.D., U.S.A. **74** 47 0N 98 45W
Jamestown, N.Y., U.S.A. **70** 42 5N 79 18W
Jamestown, Ohio, U.S.A. **77** 39 39N 83 44W
Jamestown, Penn., U.S.A. **70** 41 22N 80 27W
Jamestown, Tenn., U.S.A. **73** 36 25N 85 0W
Jamiltepec **83** 16 17N 97 49W
Jamkhandi **124** 16 30N 75 15E
Jammu **124** 32 43N 74 54E
Jammu & Kashmir □ **124** 34 25N 77 0E
Jamnagar **124** 22 30N 70 0E
Jamshedpur **125** 22 44N 86 20E
Jämtlands län □ **110** 62 40N 13 50E
Jan L. **55** 54 56N 102 55W
Jan Mayen Is. **17** 71 0N 11 0W
Jand **124** 33 30N 72 0E
Jandaq **122** 34 3N 54 22E
Janesville **76** 42 39N 89 1W
Jani Khel **123** 32 45N 68 25E
Janos **82** 30 45N 108 10W
Jansen **56** 51 54N 104 45W
Januária **87** 15 25S 44 25W
Janville **101** 48 10N 1 50E
Janzé **100** 47 55N 1 28W
Jaoho **130** 47 12N 134 15E
Jaora **124** 23 40N 75 10E
Japan ■ **132** 36 0N 136 0E
Japan, Sea of **132** 40 0N 135 0E
Japara **127** 6 30S 110 40E
Japen, I. = Yapen **127** 1 50S 136 0E
Japurá **86** 1 48S 66 30W
Japurá, R. **86** 3 8S 64 46W
Jaque **86** 7 27N 78 15W
Jaques-Cartier, Détroit de **38** 50 0N 63 30W
Jara, La **79** 37 16N 106 0W
Jarales **79** 34 39N 106 51W
Jarama, R. **104** 40 50N 3 20W
Jarbridge **78** 41 56N 115 27W
Jardim **88** 21 28S 56 9W
Jardines de la Reina, Is. **84** 20 50N 78 50W
Jargalant **130** 47 2N 115 1E
Jargalant (Kobdo) **129** 48 0N 91 43E
Jargeau **101** 47 50N 2 7E
Jarjarni **123** 37 5N 56 20E
Jarnac **102** 45 40N 0 11W
Jarny **101** 49 9N 5 53E
Jarosław **107** 50 2N 22 42E
Jarvis **46** 42 53N 80 6W
Jarvis I. **15** 0 15S 159 55W
Jarvis River **52** 48 7N 89 21W
Jarwa **125** 27 45N 82 30E
Jasin **128** 2 20N 102 26E
Jāsk **123** 25 38N 57 45E
Jasło **107** 49 45N 21 30E
Jasonville **77** 39 10N 87 13W
Jasper, Alta., Can. **61** 52 55N 118 5W
Jasper, Ont., Can. **47** 44 50N 75 56W
Jasper, Ont., Can. **71** 44 52N 75 57W
Jasper, Ala., U.S.A. **73** 33 48N 87 16W
Jasper, Fla., U.S.A. **73** 30 31N 82 58W
Jasper, Ind., U.S.A. **77** 38 24N 86 56W
Jasper, La., U.S.A. **75** 30 59N 93 58W
Jasper, Minn., U.S.A. **74** 43 52N 96 22W
Jasper Nat. Park **61** 52 50N 118 8W
Jasper Place **54** 53 33N 113 25W
Jászberény **107** 47 30N 19 55E
Jataí **87** 17 50S 51 45W
Jatibarang **127** 6 28S 108 18E
Jatinegara **127** 6 13S 106 52E
Játiva **104** 39 0N 0 32W
Jatobal **87** 4 35S 49 33W
Jaú **89** 22 10S 48 30W
Jauja **86** 11 45S 75 30W
Jaunpur **125** 25 46N 82 44E
Java = Jawa **127** 7 0S 110 0E
Java Sea **126** 4 35S 107 15E
Javhlant = Ulyasutay **129** 47 42N 13 10E
Javron **100** 48 25N 0 25W
Jawa **127** 7 0S 110 0E
Jay **75** 36 17N 94 46W
Jayapura **127** 2 28S 140 38E
Jayawijaya, Pegunungan **127** 7 0S 139 0E
Jaydot **55** 49 15N 110 15W
Jaynagar **125** 26 43N 86 9E
Jayton **75** 33 17N 100 35W
Jazminal **82** 24 56N 101 25W
Jean **81** 35 47N 115 20W
Jean Marie River **54** 61 32N 120 38W
Jean Rabel **85** 19 50N 73 30W
Jeanerette **75** 29 52N 91 38W
Jeanette L. **52** 51 5N 92 5W
Jeanne-d'Arc **48** 45 32N 75 38W
Jeannette **70** 40 20N 79 36W
Jedburgh **96** 55 28N 2 33W
Jedrzejów **107** 50 35N 20 15E
Jedway **62** 52 17N 131 14W
Jefferson, Iowa, U.S.A. **76** 42 3N 94 25W
Jefferson, Ohio, U.S.A. **70** 41 40N 80 46W
Jefferson, Tex., U.S.A. **75** 32 45N 94 23W
Jefferson, Wis., U.S.A. **77** 43 0N 88 49W
Jefferson City, Mo., U.S.A. **76** 38 34N 92 10W
Jefferson City, Tenn., U.S.A. **73** 36 8N 83 30W
Jefferson, Mt., Nev., U.S.A. **78** 38 51N 117 0W
Jefferson, Mt., Oreg., U.S.A. **78** 44 45N 121 50W
Jeffersontown **77** 38 17N 85 44W
Jeffersonville, Ind., U.S.A. **77** 38 20N 85 42W
Jeffersonville, Ohio, U.S.A. **77** 39 38N 83 34W
Jega **114** 12 15N 4 23E
Jelenia Góra **106** 50 50N 15 45E
Jelgava **111** 56 41N 22 49E
Jellicoe **53** 49 40N 87 30W
Jemaja **126** 3 5N 105 45E
Jemappes **105** 50 27N 3 54E
Jember **127** 8 11S 113 41E
Jembongan, I. **126** 6 45N 117 20E
Jemeppe **105** 50 37N 5 30E
Jemseg **39** 45 50N 66 7W
Jena, Ger. **106** 50 56N 11 33E
Jena, U.S.A. **75** 31 41N 92 7W
Jenhwai **131** 28 5N 106 10E
Jenin **115** 32 28N 35 18E
Jenkins **72** 37 13N 82 41W
Jenner **80** 38 27N 123 7W
Jennings, La., U.S.A. **75** 30 10N 92 45W
Jennings, Mo., U.S.A. **76** 38 43N 90 16W
Jennings, R. **54** 59 38N 132 5W
Jequié **87** 13 51S 40 5W
Jequitinhonha **87** 16 30S 41 0W
Jequitinhonha, R. **87** 15 51S 38 53W
Jerantut **128** 3 56N 102 22E
Jérémie **85** 18 40N 74 10W
Jerez de García Salinas **82** 22 39N 103 0W
Jerez de la Frontera **104** 36 41N 6 7W
Jerez de los Caballeros **104** 38 20N 6 45W
Jerez, Punta **83** 22 58N 97 40W
Jerico Springs **76** 37 37N 94 1W
Jerilderie **136** 35 20S 145 41E
Jermyn **71** 41 31N 75 31W
Jerome, Can. **53** 47 37N 82 14W
Jerome, U.S.A. **79** 34 50N 112 0W
Jersey City **71** 40 41N 74 8W
Jersey, I. **100** 49 13N 2 7W
Jersey Shore **70** 41 17N 77 18W
Jerseyside **37** 47 16N 53 58W
Jerseyville, Can. **49** 43 12N 80 7W
Jerseyville, U.S.A. **76** 39 5N 90 20W
Jerusalem **115** 31 47N 35 10E
Jervis B. **136** 35 8S 150 46E
Jervis Inlet **62** 50 0N 123 57W
Jesselton = Kota Kinabalu **126** 6 0N 116 12E
Jessore **125** 23 10N 89 10E
Jesup, U.S.A. **73** 31 30N 82 0W
Jesup, U.S.A. **76** 42 29N 92 4W
Jesús Carranza **83** 17 28N 95 1W
Jesus, Île **44** 45 35N 73 45W
Jesús María **88** 30 59S 64 5W
Jetmore **75** 38 10N 99 57W
Jewell **76** 42 20N 93 39W
Jewett, Ohio, U.S.A. **70** 40 22N 81 2W
Jewett, Tex., U.S.A. **75** 31 20N 96 8W
Jewett City **71** 41 36N 72 0W
Jeypore **125** 18 50N 82 38E
Jhal Jhao **124** 26 20N 65 35E
Jhalawar **124** 24 35N 76 10E
Jhang Maghiana **124** 31 15N 72 15E
Jhansi **124** 25 30N 78 36E
Jharsaguda **125** 21 50N 84 5E
Jhelum **124** 33 0N 73 45E
Jhelum, R. **124** 31 50N 72 10E
Jhunjhunu **124** 28 10N 75 20E
Jicarón, I. **84** 7 10N 81 50W
Jiddah **122** 21 29N 39 16E
Jido **125** 29 2N 94 58E
Jihchao **131** 35 18N 119 28E
Jihlava **106** 49 28N 15 35E
Jihlava R. **106** 49 21N 15 38E
Jiloca, R. **104** 41 0N 1 20W
Jima **115** 7 40N 36 55E
Jiménez **82** 27 10N 105 0W
Jindabyne **136** 36 25S 148 35E
Jindabyne L. **136** 36 20S 148 38E
Jinja **116** 0 25N 33 12E
Jinnah Barrage **124** 32 58N 71 33E
Jinné **130** 51 32N 121 25E
Jinotega **84** 13 6N 85 59W
Jinotepe **84** 11 50N 86 10W
Jiparaná (Machado), R. **86** 8 45S 62 20W
Jipijapa **86** 1 0S 80 40W
Jiquilpán **82** 19 57N 102 42W
Jis rash Shughur **122** 35 49N 36 18E
Jitra **128** 6 16N 100 25E
Jiu, R. **107** 44 50N 23 20E
Joaçaba **89** 27 5S 51 31W
*João de Almeida **117** 15 10S 13 50E
João Pessoa **87** 7 10S 34 52W
Joaquín V. González **88** 25 10S 64 0W
Jobourg, Nez de **100** 49 41N 1 57W
Jodhpur **124** 26 23N 73 2E
Joe Batt's Arm **37** 49 44N 54 10W
Jœuf **101** 49 12N 6 1E
Jofane **117** 21 15S 34 18E
Joffre, Mt. **61** 50 32N 115 13W
Joggins **39** 45 42N 64 27W
Jogjakarta = Yogyakarta **127** 7 49S 110 22E
Jogues, Ont., Can. **53** 49 36N 83 45W
Jogues, Qué., Can. **43** 45 29N 72 49W
Johannesburg, S. Afr. **117** 26 10S 28 8E
Johannesburg, U.S.A. **81** 35 22N 117 38W
John Days, R. **78** 45 0N 120 0W
John o' Groats **96** 58 39N 3 3W
Johnnie **81** 36 25N 116 5W
Johnson **75** 37 35N 101 48W
Johnson City, Ill., U.S.A. **76** 37 49N 88 56W
Johnson City, Tenn., U.S.A. **73** 36 18N 82 21W
Johnson City, Tex., U.S.A. **75** 30 15N 98 24W
Johnson Cy. **71** 42 9N 67 0W
Johnsonburg **70** 41 30N 78 40W
Johnsondale **81** 35 58N 118 32W
Johnson's Crossing **54** 60 29N 133 18W
Johnston I. **15** 17 10N 169 8E
Johnston Lakes **134** 32 20S 120 45E
Johnstone Str. **62** 50 28N 126 0W
Johnstown, N.Y., U.S.A. **71** 43 1N 74 20W
Johnstown, Pa., U.S.A. **70** 40 19N 78 53W
Johor □ **128** 2 5N 103 20E
Johor Baharu **128** 1 45N 103 47E
Joigny **101** 48 0N 3 20E
Joinvile **89** 26 15S 48 55E
Joinville **101** 48 27N 5 10E
Joinville I. **91** 63 15N 55 30W
Joir, R. **38** 51 59N 60 12W
Jojutla **83** 18 37N 99 11W
Jokkmokk **110** 66 35N 19 50E
Jökulsá á Brú **110** 65 40N 14 16W
Jökulsá Fjöllum **110** 65 30N 16 15W
Jökulsa R. **110** 65 30N 16 15W
Jolan **80** 35 58N 121 9W
Joliet **77** 41 30N 88 0W
Joliette **41** 46 3N 73 24W
Joliette, Parc. Prov. de **41** 46 30N 74 0W
Jolo I. **127** 6 0N 121 0E
Jome, I. **127** 1 16S 127 30E
Jones C. **34** 54 33N 79 35W
Jones Sound **65** 76 0N 89 0W
Jonesboro, Ark., U.S.A. **75** 35 50N 90 45W
Jonesboro, Ill., U.S.A. **75** 37 26N 89 18W
Jonesboro, La., U.S.A. **75** 32 15N 92 41W
Jonesburg **76** 38 51N 91 18W
Jonesport **35** 44 32N 67 38W
Jonesville, Ind., U.S.A. **77** 39 5N 85 54W
Jonesville, Mich., U.S.A. **77** 41 59N 84 40W
Jönköping **111** 57 45N 14 10E
Jönköpings län □ **111** 57 30N 14 30E
Jonquière **41** 48 27N 71 14W
Jonzac **102** 45 27N 0 28W
Joplin **75** 37 0N 94 25W
Jordan, Phil. **127** 10 41N 122 38E
Jordan, U.S.A. **78** 47 25N 106 58W
Jordan ■ **122** 31 0N 36 0E
Jordan Falls **39** 43 49N 65 14W
Jordan Harbour **49** 43 11N 79 23W
Jordan, L. **39** 44 5N 65 14W
Jordan, R. **115** 32 10N 35 32E
Jordan Valley **78** 43 0N 117 2W
Jorhat **125** 26 45N 94 20E
Jörn **110** 65 4N 20 1E
Jorquera, R. **88** 28 3S 69 58W
Jos **114** 9 53N 8 51E
José Batlle y OrdóPez **89** 33 20S 55 10W
Joseph **78** 45 27N 117 13W
Joseph City **79** 35 0N 110 16W
Joseph, L. **46** 45 10N 79 44W
Joseph, Lac **38** 52 45N 65 18W
Joseph, Petit lac **38** 52 36N 65 5W
Joshua Tree **81** 34 8N 116 19W
Joshua Tree Nat. Mon. **81** 33 56N 116 5W
Josselin **100** 47 57N 2 33W
Jostedal **111** 61 35N 7 15E
Jotunheimen **111** 61 35N 8 25E
Jounieh **122** 33 59N 35 30E
Jourdanton **75** 28 54N 98 32W
Joussard **60** 55 22N 115 57W
Jouzjan □ **123** 36 10N 66 0E
Jovellanos **84** 22 40N 81 10W
Joy B. **36** 61 30N 72 0W
Joyeuse **103** 44 29N 4 16E
Juan Aldama **82** 24 20N 103 23W
Juan Bautista **79** 36 55N 121 33W
Juan Bautista Alberdi **88** 34 26S 61 48W
Juan de Fuca Str. **80** 48 15N 124 0W
Juan de Nova, I. **117** 17 3S 42 45E
Juan Fernández, Arch. de **15** 33 50S 80 0W
Juan José Castelli **88** 25 57S 60 37W
Juan L. Lacaze **88** 34 26S 57 25W
Juan Perez Sd. **62** 52 32N 131 30W
Juárez, Argent. **88** 37 40S 59 43W
Juárez, Mexico **82** 27 37N 100 44W
Juárez, U.S.A. **81** 32 20N 115 57W
Juárez, Sierra de **82** 32 0N 116 0W
Juàzeiro **87** 9 30S 40 30W
Juàzeiro do Norte **87** 7 10S 39 18W
Jûbâ **115** 4 57N 31 35E
Juba, R. **115** 1 30N 42 35E
Jubaila **122** 24 55N 46 25E
Jubilee L. **37** 48 3N 55 11W
Juby, C. **114** 28 0N 12 59W
Júcar, R. **104** 40 8N 2 13W
Júcaro **84** 21 37N 78 51W
Juchitán **83** 16 27N 95 5W
Judaea = Yehuda **115** 31 35N 34 57E
Jude I. **37** 47 15N 54 49W
Judique **39** 45 52N 61 30W
Judith Gap **78** 46 48N 109 46W
Judith Pt. **71** 41 20N 71 30W
Judith, R. **78** 47 30N 109 30W
Juian **131** 27 45N 120 38E
Juigalpa **84** 12 6N 85 26W
Juillac **102** 45 20N 1 19E
Juiz de Fora **87** 21 43S 43 19W
Jujuy **88** 24 10S 65 25W
Jujuy □ **88** 23 20S 65 40W
Jukao **131** 32 24N 120 35E
Julesberg **74** 41 0N 102 20W
Juli **86** 16 10S 69 25W
Julia Creek **135** 20 39S 141 44E
Juliaca **86** 15 25S 70 10W
Julian **81** 33 4N 116 38W
Julian L. **54** 54 25N 77 57W
Julianehåb **17** 60 43N 46 0W
Julimes **82** 28 25N 105 27W
Jullundur **124** 31 20N 75 40E
Jumbo Pk. **81** 36 12N 114 11W
Jumento, Cayos **85** 23 0N 75 40E
Jumet **105** 50 27N 4 25E
Jumilla **104** 38 28N 1 19W
Jumla **125** 29 15N 82 13E
Jumna, R. = Yamuna **125** 27 0N 78 30E
Junagadh **124** 21 30N 70 30E
Junction, Tex., U.S.A. **75** 30 29N 99 48W
Junction, Utah, U.S.A. **79** 38 10N 112 15W
Junction B. **134** 11 52S 133 55E
Junction City, Kans., U.S.A. **74** 39 4N 96 55W
Junction City, Oreg., U.S.A. **78** 44 20N 123 12W
Jundah **135** 24 46S 143 2E
Jundiai **89** 23 10S 47 0W

** Renamed Chibia*

Juneau Kasenga

Juneau 67 58 26N 134 30W
Junee 136 34 53S 147 35E
Juniata, R. 70 40 30N 77 40W
Junin 88 34 33S 60 57W
Junin de los Andes 90 39 45S 71 0W
Juniper 39 46 33N 67 13W
Junkuren, R. 130 47 40N 113 0E
Junta, La 75 38 0N 103 30W
Juntura 78 43 44N 118 4W
Jupiter, R. 38 49 29N 63 37W
Jura 101 46 35N 6 5E
Jura □ 101 46 47N 5 45E
Jura, I. 96 56 0N 5 50W
Jura, Sd. of 96 55 57N 5 45W
Jurado 86 7 7N 77 46W
Jurien B. 134 30 17S 115 0E
Jurm 123 36 50N 70 45E
Juruá, R. 86 2 30S 66 0W
Juruena, R. 86 7 20S 58 3W
Juruti 87 2 9S 56 4W
Juskatla 62 53 37N 132 18W
Jussey 101 47 50N 5 55E
Justo Daract 88 33 52S 65 12W
Juticalpa 84 14 40N 85 50W
Jutland 93 56 0N 8 0E
Juvigny-sous-Andaine 100 48 32N 0 30W
Juvisy 101 48 43N 2 23E
Juwain 124 31 45N 61 30E
Juzennecourt 101 48 10N 5 0E
Jylland 111 56 15N 9 20E
Jyväskylä 110 62 14N 25 44E

K

K2, Mt. 124 36 0N 77 0E
Ka Lae (South C.) 67 18 55N 155 41W
Kaaia, Mt. 67 21 31N 158 9W
Kaap die Goeie Hoop 117 34 24S 18 30E
Kaap Plato 117 28 30S 24 0E
Kaapkruis 117 21 43S 14 0E
Kaapstad = Cape Town 117 33 56S 18 27E
Kabaena, I. 127 5 15S 122 0E
Kabale 116 1 15S 30 0E
Kabalo 116 6 0S 27 0E
Kabambare 116 4 41S 27 39E
Kabanjahe 126 8 2N 98 27E
Kabardino-Balkar, A.S.S.R. □ 120 43 30N 43 30E
Kabarega Falls 116 2 15N 31 38E
Kabasalan 127 7 47N 122 44E
Kabetogama L. 52 48 28N 92 59W
Kabinakagami L. 53 48 54N 84 25W
Kabinakagami, R. 53 50 25N 84 20W
Kabinda 116 6 23S 24 28E
Kabompo, R. 117 13 50S 24 10E
Kabongo 116 7 22S 25 33E
Kabūd Gonbad 123 37 5N 59 45E
Kabul 124 34 28N 69 18E
Kabul □ 124 34 0N 68 30E
Kaburuang 127 3 50N 126 30E
Kabwe 117 14 30S 28 29E
Kachin □ 125 26 0N 97 0E
Kachiry 120 53 10N 75 50E
Kaçkar 122 40 45N 41 30E
Kadan Kyun 128 12 30N 98 20E
Kadina 135 34 0S 137 43E
Kadoka 74 43 50N 101 31W
Kaduna 114 10 30N 7 21E
Kaedi 114 16 9N 13 28W
Kaegudeck L. 37 48 7N 55 12W
Kaelé 114 10 15N 14 15E
Kaena Pt. 67 21 35N 158 17W
Kaesŏng 130 37 58N 126 35E
Kāf 122 31 25N 37 20E
Kafakumba 116 9 38S 23 46E
Kafirévs, Ákra 109 38 9N 24 8E
Kafiristan 123 35 0N 70 30E
Kafue, R. 117 15 30S 26 0E
Kafulwe 116 9 0S 29 1E
Kagaki L. 52 49 13N 93 52W
Kagamil I. 67 53 0N 169 40W
Kagan 120 39 43N 64 33E
Kagawa-ken □ 132 34 15N 134 0E
Kagawong L. 46 45 54N 82 15W
Kagianagami L. 53 50 57N 87 50W
Kagiano L. 53 49 16N 86 26W
Kağizman 122 40 5N 43 10E
Kagoshima 132 31 36N 130 40E
Kagoshima-ken □ 132 30 0N 130 0E
Kagoshima-Wan 132 31 0N 130 40E
Kahajan, R. 126 2 10S 114 0E
Kahama 116 4 8S 32 30E
Kahemba 116 7 18S 18 55E
Kahniah, R. 54 58 15N 120 55W
Kahnūj 123 27 55N 57 40E
Kahoka 76 40 25N 91 42W
Kahoolawe, I. 67 20 33N 156 35W
Kahuku & Pt. 67 21 41N 157 57W
Kahulai 67 20 54N 156 28W
Kai, Kepulauan 127 5 55S 132 45W
Kaiapoi 133 42 24S 172 40E
Kaifeng 131 34 49N 114 30E
Kaihwa 131 29 0N 118 21E
Kaikohe 133 35 25S 173 49E
Kaikoura 133 42 25S 173 43E
Kaikoura Pen. 133 42 25S 173 43E
Kaikoura Ra. 133 41 59S 173 41E

Kailua 67 19 39N 156 0W
Kaimana 127 3 30S 133 45E
Kaimanawa Mts. 133 39 15S 175 56E
Kaingaroa Forest 133 38 30S 176 30E
Kainji Res. 114 10 1N 4 40E
Kaipara Harb. 133 36 25S 174 14E
Kaiping 130 40 28N 122 10E
Kaipokok B. 36 54 54N 59 47W
Kaironi 127 0 47S 133 40E
Kaiserslautern 105 49 30N 7 43E
Kaitaia 133 35 8S 173 17E
Kaitangata 133 46 17S 169 51E
Kaitung 130 44 58N 123 2E
Kaiwi Channel 67 21 13N 157 30W
Kaiyüan 130 42 40N 124 30E
Kaiyuh Mts. 67 63 40N 159 0W
Kajaani 110 64 17N 27 46E
Kajabbi 135 20 0S 140 1E
Kajan, R. 126 2 40N 116 40E
Kajang 128 2 59N 101 48E
Kajeli 127 3 20S 127 10E
Kajoa, I. 127 0 1N 127 28E
Kajuagung 126 3 2S 104 46E
Kakabeka Falls 52 48 24N 89 37W
Kakamas 117 28 45S 20 33E
Kakamega 116 0 20N 34 46E
Kakanui Mts. 133 45 10S 170 30E
Kake 67 57 0N 134 0W
Kakegawa 132 34 45N 138 1E
Kakinada = Cocanada 125 16 50N 82 11E
Kakisa L. 54 60 56N 117 43W
Kakisa, R. 54 61 3N 117 10W
Kaktovik 67 70 8N 143 50W
Kakwa, R. 60 54 37N 118 28W
Kalabagh 124 33 0N 71 28E
Kalabáka 109 39 42N 21 39E
Kalabo 117 14 58S 22 33E
Kaladan, R. 125 21 30N 92 45E
Kaladar 47 44 37N 77 5W
Kalahari, Des. 117 24 0S 22 0E
Kalakan 121 55 15N 116 45E
Kalama 80 46 0N 122 55W
Kalamata 109 37 3N 22 10E
Kalamazoo 77 42 20N 85 35W
Kalamazoo, R. 77 42 40N 86 12W
Kalao, I. 127 7 21S 121 0E
Kalaotoa, I. 127 7 20S 121 50E
Kalasin 128 16 26N 103 30E
Kalat 124 29 8N 66 31E
*Kalat □ 124 27 0N 64 30E
Kalat-i-Ghilzai 123 32 15N 66 58E
Kalaupapa 67 21 12N 156 59W
Kalegauk Kyun 125 15 33N 97 35E
Kalemie 116 5 55S 29 9E
Kalewa 125 22 41N 95 32E
Kálfafellsstaður 110 64 11N 15 53W
Kalgoorlie 134 30 40S 121 22E
Kalianda 126 5 50S 105 45E
Kalibo 127 11 43N 122 22E
Kalima 116 2 33S 26 32E
Kalimantan Barat □ 126 0 0 110 30E
Kalimantan Selatan □ 126 4 10S 115 30E
Kalimantan Tengah □ 126 2 0S 113 30E
Kalimantan Timur □ 126 1 30N 116 30E
Kálimnos, I. 109 37 0N 27 0E
Kalinin 120 56 55N 35 55E
Kaliningrad 120 54 42N 20 32E
Kalispell 78 48 10N 114 22W
Kalisz 107 51 45N 18 8E
Kaliua 116 5 5S 31 48E
Kalkaska 46 44 44N 85 11W
Kalkrand 117 24 1S 17 35E
Kallia 118 31 46N 35 30E
Kallsjön 110 63 38N 13 0E
Kalmar 111 56 40N 16 20E
Kalmthout 105 51 23N 4 29E
Kalmyk A.S.S.R. □ 120 46 5N 46 1E
Kalmykovo 120 49 0N 51 35E
Kalocsa 107 46 32N 19 0E
Kalomo 117 17 0S 26 30E
Kalona 76 41 29N 91 43W
Kaluga 120 54 35N 36 10E
Kalundborg 111 55 41N 11 5E
Kalutara 124 6 35N 80 0E
Kalyani 86 17 53N 76 59E
Kam Keut 128 18 20N 104 48E
Kama, R. 120 60 0N 53 0E
Kamaishi 132 39 20N 142 0E
Kamalino 67 21 50N 160 14W
Kamaran 115 15 28N 42 35E
Kamchatka, P-ov. 121 57 0N 160 0E
Kamen 120 53 50N 81 30E
Kamenets-Podolskiy 120 48 45N 26 10E
Kamenjak, Rt. 108 44 47N 13 55E
Kamensk-Uralskiy 120 56 25N 62 2E
Kamenskoye 121 62 45N 165 30E
Kamiah 78 46 12N 116 2W
Kamilukuak, L. 55 62 22N 101 40W
Kamina 116 8 45S 25 0E
Kaminak L. 55 62 10N 95 0W
Kaministikwia 52 48 32N 89 35W
Kamloops L. 63 50 45N 120 40W
Kamouraska 41 47 34N 69 52W
Kampala 116 0 20N 32 30E
Kampar 128 4 18N 101 9E
Kampar, R. 126 0 30N 102 0E
Kampen 105 52 33N 5 53E
Kampsville 76 39 18N 90 37W

Kampuchea ■ = Cambodia 128 12 15N 105 0E
Kamrau, Teluk 127 3 30S 133 45E
Kamsack 57 51 34N 101 54W
Kamuchawie L. 55 56 18N 101 59W
Kamyshin 120 50 10N 45 30E
Kanaaupscow 36 54 2N 76 30W
Kanaaupscow, R. 36 53 39N 77 9W
Kanab 79 37 3N 112 29W
Kanab Creek 79 37 0N 112 40W
Kanaga I. 67 51 45N 177 22W
Kanagawa-ken □ 132 35 20N 139 20E
Kanairiktok, R., Can. 35 54 30N 62 30W
Kanairiktok, R., Newf., Can. 36 55 2N 60 18W
Kanakanak 67 59 0N 158 58W
Kananchen 130 45 45N 121 55E
Kananga 116 5 55S 22 18E
Kanarraville 79 37 34N 113 12W
Kanaskat 80 47 19N 121 54W
Kanata 47 45 20N 75 59W
Kanawha, R. 72 39 40N 82 0W
Kanazawa 132 36 30N 136 38E
Kanchanaburi 128 14 8N 99 31E
Kanchenjunga, Mt. 125 27 50N 88 10E
Kanchipuram (Conjeeveram) 124 12 52N 79 45E
Kanchow 131 25 58N 114 55E
Kanchwan 130 36 29N 109 24E
Kanda Kanda 116 6 52S 23 48E
Kandahar 124 31 32N 65 30E
Kandahar □ 124 31 0N 65 0E
Kandalaksha 120 67 9N 32 30E
Kandalu 124 29 55N 63 20E
Kandangan 126 2 50S 115 20E
Kandi 114 11 7N 2 55E
Kandira 122 41 5N 30 10E
Kandla 124 23 0N 70 10E
Kandos 136 32 45S 149 58E
Kandy 124 7 18N 80 43E
Kane 70 41 39N 78 53W
Kane Basin 65 79 1N 73 0W
Kane Bassin 17 79 30N 68 0W
Kanen 131 18 46N 108 33E
Kaneohe 67 21 25N 157 48W
Kang 124 30 55N 61 55E
Kangar 128 6 27N 100 12E
Kangaroo Flat 136 36 45S 144 20E
Kangaroo I. 135 35 45S 137 0E
Kangavar 122 34 40N 48 0E
Kangean, Kepulauan 126 6 55S 115 23E
Kangerdlugsuaé 17 68 10N 32 20W
Kangnūng 130 37 45N 128 54E
Kango 116 0 11N 10 5E
Kangshan 131 22 43N 120 14E
Kangtissu Shan 125 31 0N 82 0E
Kangto, Mt. 125 27 50N 92 35E
Kaniapiskau L. 36 54 10N 69 55W
Kaniapiskau, R. 36 57 40N 69 30E
Kanin Nos, Mys 120 68 45N 43 20E
Kanin, P-ov. 120 68 0N 45 0E
Kaniva 136 36 22S 141 18E
Kankakee 77 41 6N 87 50W
Kankakee, R. 77 41 13N 87 0W
Kankan 114 10 30N 9 15W
Kanker 125 20 10N 81 40E
Kankunskiy 121 57 37N 126 8E
Kannapolis 73 35 32N 80 37W
Kannauj 124 27 3N 79 26E
Kannod 124 22 45N 76 40E
Kano 114 12 2N 8 30E
Kanowha 76 42 57N 93 47W
Kanowit 126 2 14N 112 20E
Kanowna 134 30 32S 121 31E
Kanoya 132 31 25N 130 50E
Kanpetlet 125 21 10N 93 59E
Kanpur 124 26 35N 80 20E
Kansas 77 39 33N 87 56W
Kansas □ 74 38 40N 98 0W
Kansas City, Kans., U.S.A. 76 39 0N 94 40W
Kansas City, Mo., U.S.A. 76 39 3N 94 30W
Kansas, R. 74 39 15N 96 20W
Kansk 121 56 20N 95 37E
Kansu □ 129 35 30N 104 30E
Kantishna 67 63 31N 151 5W
Kantse 129 31 30N 100 29E
Kanturk 97 52 10N 8 55W
Kanuma 132 36 44N 139 42E
Kanyu 131 34 56N 119 8E
Kaoan 131 28 20N 115 17E
Kaohsiung 131 22 35N 120 16E
Kaoko Otavi 117 18 12S 13 45E
Kaolack 114 14 5N 16 8W
Kaomi 130 36 25N 119 45E
Kaoping 130 35 57N 113 0E
Kaoyu Ho 131 32 50N 119 10E
Kapaa 67 22 5N 159 19W
Kapanga 116 8 30S 22 40E
Kapela, Mts. 108 44 40N 15 40E
Kapellen 105 51 19N 4 25E
Kapfenberg 106 47 26N 15 18E
Kapikotongwa, R. 53 50 39N 86 43W
Kapiri Mposhi 117 13 59S 28 43E
Kapiskau 34 52 50N 82 1W
Kapiskau, R. 34 52 47N 81 55W
Kapit 126 2 0N 113 5E
Kapiti I. 133 40 50S 174 56E

Kapoeta 115 4 50N 33 35E
Kaposvár 107 46 25N 17 47E
Kaposvar Cr. 56 50 31N 101 55W
Kapowsin 80 46 59N 122 13W
Kapuas Hulu, Pegunungan 126 1 30N 113 30E
Kapuas, R. 126 0 20N 111 40E
Kapuskasing 53 49 25N 82 30W
Kapuskasing, R. 53 49 49N 82 0W
Kaputir 116 2 5N 35 28E
Kara 120 69 10N 65 25E
Kara Bogaz Gol, Zaliv 120 41 0N 53 30E
Kara Kalpak A.S.S.R. □ 120 43 0N 60 0E
Kara Kum 120 39 30N 60 0E
Kara Nor 129 38 45N 98 0E
Kara Sea 120 75 0N 70 0E
Karabutak 120 49 59N 60 14E
Karachi, Austral. 136 36 58S 148 45E
Karachi, Pak. 124 24 53N 67 0E
Karad 124 17 15N 74 10E
Karadeniz Boğazı 122 41 10N 29 5E
Karadeniz Dağlari 122 41 30N 35 0E
Karagajly 120 49 26N 76 0E
Karaganda 120 49 50N 73 0E
Karaginskiy, Ostrov 121 58 45N 164 0E
Karaikkudi 124 10 0N 78 45E
Karaj 123 35 4N 51 0E
Karakas 120 48 20N 83 30E
Karakitang 127 3 14N 125 28E
Karakoram 124 35 20N 76 0E
Karakoram Pass 124 35 20N 78 0E
Karakorum 130 47 30N 102 20E
Karalon 121 57 5N 115 50E
Karamai 129 45 57N 84 30E
Karaman 122 37 14N 33 13E
Karambu 126 3 53S 116 6E
Karamea Bight 133 41 22S 171 40E
Karanganjar 127 7 38S 109 37E
Karasburg 117 28 0S 18 44E
Karasino 120 66 50N 86 50E
Karasjok 110 69 27N 25 30E
Karasuk 120 53 44N 78 2E
Karatau 120 43 10N 70 28E
Karatau, Khrebet 120 43 30N 69 30E
Karatsu 132 33 30N 130 0E
Karawa 116 3 18N 20 17E
Karawanken 108 46 30N 14 40E
Karazhal 120 48 2N 70 49E
Karbalā 122 32 47N 44 3E
Karcag 107 47 19N 21 1E
Kardhitsa 109 39 23N 21 54E
Kareeberge 117 30 50S 22 0E
Karelian A.S.S.R. □ 120 65 30N 32 30E
Karema 116 6 49S 30 24E
Karen 128 12 49N 92 53E
Kargānrūd 122 37 55N 49 0E
Kargasok 120 59 3N 80 53E
Kargat 120 55 10N 80 15E
Kariba Dam 117 16 30S 28 35E
Kariba Gorge 117 16 30S 28 35E
Kariba Lake 117 16 40S 28 25E
Karibib 117 21 0S 15 56E
Karikal 124 10 59N 79 50E
Karikkale 122 39 55N 33 30E
Karimata, Kepulauan 126 1 40S 109 0E
Karimata, Selat 126 2 0S 108 20E
Karimnagar 124 18 26N 79 10E
Karimundjawa, Kepulauan 126 5 50S 110 30E
Kariya 132 34 58N 137 1E
Karl-Marx-Stadt 106 50 50N 12 55E
Karlovac 108 45 31N 15 36E
Karlovy Vary 106 50 13N 12 51E
Karlsborg 111 58 33N 14 33E
Karlshamn 111 56 10N 14 51E
Karlskoga 111 59 22N 14 33E
Karlskrona 111 56 10N 15 35E
Karlsruhe 106 49 3N 8 23E
Karlstad, Sweden 111 59 23N 13 30E
Karlstad, U.S.A. 74 48 38N 96 30W
Karnal 124 29 42N 77 2E
Karnali, R. 125 29 0N 82 0E
Karnaphuli Res. 125 22 40N 92 20E
Karnataka □ 124 13 15N 77 0E
Karnes City 75 28 53N 97 53W
Karnische Alpen 106 46 36N 13 0E
Kärnten □ 106 46 52N 13 30E
Karonga 116 9 57S 33 55E
Kárpathos, I. 109 35 37N 27 10E
Kars 122 40 40N 43 5E
Karsakpay 120 47 55N 66 40E
Karshi 120 38 53N 65 48E
Kartaly 120 53 3N 60 40E
Karthaus 70 41 8N 78 9W
Karufa 127 3 50S 133 20E
Karungu 116 0 50S 34 10E
Karur 124 10 59N 78 2E
Karwar 124 14 55N 74 13E
Kas Kong 128 11 27N 102 12E
Kasai, R. 116 8 20S 22 0E
Kasama 116 10 16S 31 9E
Kasanga 116 8 30S 31 10E
Kasangulu 116 4 15S 15 15E
Kasaragod 124 12 30N 74 58E
Kasba L. 55 60 20N 102 10W
Kaschmar 123 35 16N 58 26E
Kasempa 117 13 30S 25 44E
Kasenga 116 10 20S 28 45E

* Now part of Baluchistan

Kashabowie Kiangyin

Kashabowie	52	48 40N	90 26W
Kāshān	123	34 5N	51 30E
Kashgar	129	39 46N	75 52E
Kashing	131	30 45N	120 41E
Kaskaskia, R.	76	37 58N	89 57W
Kaskattama, R.	55	57 3N	90 4W
Kaskinen (Kaskö)	110	62 22N	21 15E
Kaskö (Kaskinen)	110	62 22N	21 15E
Kaslo	63	49 55N	116 55W
Kasmere L.	55	59 34N	101 10W
Kasongo	116	4 30S	26 33E
Kasongo Lunda	116	6 35S	17 0E
Kásos, I.	109	35 20N	26 55E
Kassala	115	15 23N	36 26E
Kassala □	116	15 20N	36 26E
Kassel	106	51 19N	9 32E
Kassue	127	6 58S	139 21E
Kastamonu	122	41 25N	33 43E
Kastoría	109	40 30N	21 19E
Kasulu	116	4 37S	30 5E
Kasur	124	31 5N	74 25E
Kata	121	58 46N	102 40E
Katako Kombe	116	3 25S	24 20E
Katalla	67	60 10N	144 35W
Katangi	124	21 56N	79 50E
Katangli	121	51 42N	143 14E
Katanning	134	33 40S	117 33E
Katha	125	24 10N	96 30E
Katherina, Gebel	115	28 30N	33 57E
Katherine	134	14 27S	132 20E
Kathiawar, dist.	124	22 20N	71 0E
Katiet	126	2 21S	99 44E
Katihar	125	25 34N	87 36E
Katima Mulilo	117	17 28S	24 13E
Katimik L.	57	52 53N	99 21W
Katmai Nat. Monument	67	58 30N	155 0W
Katmai, vol.	67	58 20N	154 59W
Katmandu	125	27 45N	85 12E
Katompi	116	6 2S	26 23E
Katoomba	136	33 41S	150 19E
Katowice	107	50 17N	19 5E
Katrine L.	96	56 15N	4 30W
Katrineholm	111	59 9N	16 12E
Katsina	114	7 10N	9 20E
Katsuura	132	35 15N	140 20E
Kattawaz	124	32 48N	68 23E
*Kattawaz-Urgun □	124	32 10N	68 20E
Kattegat	111	57 0N	11 20E
Katwijk-aan-Zee	105	52 12N	4 24E
Kau Tao	128	10 6N	99 48E
Kauai Chan.	67	21 45N	158 50W
Kauai, I.	67	19 30N	155 30W
Kaufman	75	32 35N	96 20W
Kaukauna	72	44 20N	88 13W
Kaukonen	110	67 31N	24 53E
Kauliranta	110	66 27N	23 41E
Kaunas	120	54 54N	23 54E
Kaupulehu	67	19 43N	155 53W
Kautokeino	110	69 0N	23 4E
Kavacha	121	60 16N	169 51E
Kavali	124	14 55N	80 1E
Kavála	109	40 57N	24 28E
Kavanayén	86	5 38N	61 48W
Kaw = Caux	87	4 30N	52 15W
Kawagama L., Can.	70	45 18N	78 45W
Kawagama L., Ont., Can.	47	45 18N	78 45W
Kawagoe	132	35 55N	139 29E
Kawaguchi	132	35 52N	138 45E
Kawaihae	67	20 3N	155 50W
Kawaihoa Pt.	67	21 47N	160 12W
Kawaikini, Mt.	67	22 0N	159 30W
Kawambwa	116	9 48S	29 3E
Kawana	132	35 5N	135 27E
Kawardha	125	22 0N	81 17E
Kawasaki	132	35 35N	138 42E
Kawene	52	48 45N	91 15W
Kawerau	133	38 7S	176 42E
Kawhia Harbour	133	38 5S	174 51E
Kawinawl	57	52 50N	99 30W
Kawthaung	128	10 5N	98 36E
Kawthoolei □ = Kawthuk	125	18 0N	97 30E
Kawthuk □	125	18 0N	97 30E
Kayah □	125	19 15N	97 15E
Kayak I.	67	60 0N	144 30W
Kaycee	78	43 45N	106 46W
Kayenta	79	36 46N	110 15W
Kayes	114	14 25N	11 30W
Kayseri	122	38 45N	35 30E
Kaysville	78	41 2N	111 58W
Kazachinskoye	121	56 16N	107 36E
Kazachye	121	70 52N	135 58E
Kazakh S.S.R. □	120	50 0N	58 0E
Kazan	120	55 48N	49 3E
Kazan, R.	55	64 2N	95 30W
Kazanluk	109	42 38N	25 35E
Kāzerūn	123	29 38N	51 40E
Kazumba	116	6 25S	22 5E
Kazvin	122	36 15N	50 0E
Kazym, R.	120	63 40N	68 30E
Kéa	109	37 35N	24 22E
Keaau	67	19 37N	155 3W
Keams Canyon	79	35 53N	110 9W
Keanae	67	20 52N	156 9W
Kearney, Can.	46	45 33N	79 13W
Kearney, U.S.A.	76	39 22N	94 22W
Kearney, Nebr., U.S.A.	74	40 45N	99 3W
Keban	122	38 50N	38 50E

*Renamed Paktika

Kebnekaise, mt.	110	67 54N	18 33E
Kebumen	127	7 42S	109 40E
Kechika, R.	54	59 41N	127 12W
Kecskemét	107	46 57N	19 35E
Kedah □	128	5 50N	100 40E
Kedgwick	39	47 40N	67 20W
Kediri	127	7 51S	112 1E
Keefers	54	50 0N	121 40W
Keele, R.	67	64 15N	127 0W
Keeler	80	36 29N	117 52W
Keeley L.	55	54 54N	108 8W
Keeling Is. = Cocos Is.	16	12 12S	96 54E
Keelung = Chilung	131	25 3N	121 45E
Keene, Can.	47	44 15N	78 10W
Keene, Calif., U.S.A.	81	35 13N	118 33W
Keene, N.H., U.S.A.	71	42 57N	72 17W
Keeper, Mt.	97	52 46N	8 17W
Keer-Weer, C.	135	14 0S	141 32E
Keeseville	71	44 29N	73 30W
Keetmanshoop	117	26 35S	18 8E
Keewatin, Can.	52	49 46N	94 34W
Keewatin, U.S.A.	52	47 23N	93 0W
Keewatin □	55	63 20N	94 40W
Keewatin, R.	55	56 29N	100 46W
Keezhik L.	52	51 45N	88 30W
Kefallinía, I.	109	38 28N	20 30E
Kefamenanu	127	9 28S	124 38E
Keflavík	110	64 2N	22 35W
Keg River	54	57 54N	117 7W
Kegashka	38	50 9N	61 18W
Kégashka, L.	38	50 20N	61 25W
Keglo, B.	36	58 40N	66 0W
Keighley	94	53 52N	1 54W
Keith	96	57 33N	2 58W
Keith Arm	64	64 20N	122 15W
Keithsburg	76	41 6N	90 56W
Kejimkujik Nat. Park	39	44 25N	65 25W
Kekri	124	26 0N	75 10E
Kël	121	69 30N	124 10E
Kelang	128	3 2N	101 26E
Kelantan □	128	5 10N	102 0E
Kelantan, R.	128	6 13N	102 14E
Kellé	116	0 8S	14 38E
Keller	78	48 2N	118 44W
Kellerberrin	134	31 36S	117 38E
Kellett C.	64	72 0N	126 0W
Kellett Str.	64	75 45N	117 30W
Kelleys I.	70	41 35N	82 42W
Kelligrews	37	47 30N	53 1W
Kelliher	56	51 16N	103 44W
Kellogg	78	47 30N	116 5W
Kelloselkä	110	66 56N	28 53E
Kells = Ceanannas Mor	97	53 42N	6 53W
Kelowna	63	49 50N	119 25W
Kelsey Bay	62	50 25N	126 0W
Kelseyville	80	38 59N	122 50W
Kelso, N.Z.	133	45 54S	169 15E
Kelso, U.K.	96	55 36N	2 27W
Kelso, U.S.A.	80	46 10N	122 57W
Keluang	128	2 3N	103 18E
Kelvin I.	52	49 51N	88 40W
Kelvington	56	52 10N	103 30W
Kelwood	57	50 37N	99 28W
Kem	120	65 0N	34 38E
Kema	127	1 22N	125 8E
Kemah	122	39 32N	39 5E
Kemano	62	53 35N	128 0W
Kemerovo	120	55 20N	85 50E
Kemi	110	65 44N	24 34E
Kemi älv = Kemijoki	110	65 47N	24 32E
Kemijärvi	110	66 43N	27 22E
Kemijoki	110	65 47N	24 32E
Kemmerer	78	41 52N	110 30W
Kemmuna = Comino, I.	108	36 0N	14 20E
Kemp Coast	91	69 0S	55 0E
Kemp L.	75	33 45N	99 15W
Kempsey	135	31 1S	152 50E
Kempt, L.	41	47 25N	74 22W
Kempten	106	47 42N	10 18E
Kempton	77	40 56N	86 14W
Kemptown	39	45 28N	63 5W
Kemptville	47	45 0N	75 38W
Ken L.	96	55 0N	4 8W
Kenai	67	60 35N	151 20W
Kenai Mts.	67	60 0N	150 0W
Kenaston	56	51 30N	106 17W
Kendal, Indon.	127	6 56S	110 14E
Kendal, U.K.	94	54 19N	2 44W
Kendall	136	31 35S	152 44E
Kendallville	77	41 25N	85 15W
Kendari	127	3 50S	122 30E
Kendawangan	126	2 32S	110 17E
Kendrapara	125	20 35N	86 30E
Kendrick	78	46 43N	116 41W
Keng Tawng	125	20 45N	98 18E
Keng Tung	125	21 0N	99 30E
Kenge	116	4 50S	16 55E
Kenhardt	117	29 19S	21 12E
Kenho	130	50 43N	121 30E
Kenitra	114	34 15N	6 40W
Kenmare, Ireland	97	51 52N	9 35W
Kenmare, U.S.A.	74	48 40N	102 4W
Kenmare, R.	97	51 40N	10 0W
Kenmore	136	34 44S	149 45E
Kenn Reef	135	21 12S	155 46E
Kennaway	70	45 9N	78 11W
Kennebec	74	43 56N	99 54W
Kennebecasis, R.	39	45 19N	66 4W
Kennedy, B.C., Can.	66	49 10N	122 53W

Kennedy, Sask., Can.	57	50 1N	102 21W
Kennedy I.	62	54 3N	130 11W
Kennedy L.	62	49 3N	125 32W
Kennedy, Mt.	64	81 2N	78 55W
Kennedy Taungdeik	125	23 35N	94 4E
Kennet, R.	95	51 24N	1 7W
Kennetcook	39	45 11N	63 44W
Kennett	75	36 7N	90 0W
Kennewick	78	46 11N	119 2W
Keno Hill	96	63 57N	135 18W
Kénogami	41	48 25N	71 15W
Kénogami, L.	41	48 20N	71 23W
Kenogami, R.	53	51 6N	84 28W
Kenora	52	49 47N	94 29W
Kenosha	77	42 33N	87 48W
Kensington, P.E.I., Can.	39	46 28N	63 34W
Kensington, Qué., Can.	43	45 1N	74 18W
Kensington, U.S.A.	74	39 48N	99 2W
Kent, Ohio, U.S.A.	70	41 8N	81 20W
Kent, Oreg., U.S.A.	78	45 11N	120 45W
Kent, Tex., U.S.A.	75	31 5N	104 12W
Kent, Wash., U.S.A.	80	47 23N	122 14W
Kent □	95	51 12N	0 40E
Kent Junction	39	46 35N	65 20W
Kent Pen.	64	68 30N	107 0W
Kent, Vale of	98	51 12N	0 30E
Kentau	120	43 32N	68 36E
Kentland	77	40 45N	87 25W
Kenton	77	40 40N	83 35W
Kentucky □	72	37 20N	85 0W
Kentucky Dam	72	37 2N	88 15W
Kentucky L.	73	36 0N	88 0W
Kentucky, R.	77	38 41N	85 11W
Kentville	39	45 6N	64 29W
Kentwood	75	31 0N	90 30W
Kenville	57	52 0N	101 20W
Kenya ■	116	2 20N	38 0E
Kenya, Mt.	116	0 10S	37 18E
Keokuk	76	40 25N	91 24W
Keosauqua	76	40 44N	91 58W
Keota	76	41 22N	91 57W
Kepi	127	6 32S	139 19E
Keppel B.	135	23 21S	150 55E
Kepsut	122	39 40N	28 15E
Kepuhi	67	22 13N	159 21W
Kepulauan, R.	127	5 30S	139 0E
Kepulauan Sunda, Ketjil Barat □	126	8 50S	117 30E
Kepulauan Sunda, Ketjil Timor □	127	9 30S	122 0E
Kerala □	124	11 0N	76 15E
Kerang	136	35 40S	143 55E
Keray	123	26 15N	57 30E
Kerch	120	45 20N	36 20E
Keremeos	63	49 13N	119 50W
Kerguelen I.	16	48 15S	69 10E
Kericho	116	0 22S	35 15E
Kerinci	126	2 5S	101 0E
Kerki	120	37 50N	65 12E
Kérkira	109	39 38N	19 50E
Kermadec Is.	14	31 8S	175 16W
Kermān	123	30 15N	57 1E
Kerman	80	36 43N	120 4W
Kermān □	123	30 0N	57 0E
Kermānshāh	122	34 23N	47 0E
*Kermānshāh □	122	34 0N	46 30E
Kermit	75	31 56N	103 3W
Kern, R.	81	35 16N	119 18W
Kernville	81	35 45N	118 26W
Kerrobert	73	52 0N	109 11W
Kerrville	75	30 1N	99 8W
Kerry □	97	52 7N	9 35W
Kerry Hd.	97	52 26N	9 56W
Kersley	63	52 49N	122 25W
Kertosono	127	7 38S	112 9E
Kerulen, R.	130	48 48N	117 0E
Kesagami L.	34	50 23N	80 15W
Kesagami, R.	34	51 4N	79 45W
Keski Suomen □	110	62 45N	25 15E
Kessel-Lo	105	50 53N	4 43E
Kestenga	120	66 0N	31 50E
Keswick, Can.	46	44 15N	79 28W
Keswick, U.K.	94	54 35N	3 9W
Ketapang	126	1 55S	110 0E
Ketchikan	67	55 25N	131 40W
Ketchum	78	43 50N	114 27W
Kettering, U.K.	95	52 24N	0 44W
Kettering, U.S.A.	77	39 41N	84 10W
Kettle Falls	63	48 41N	118 2W
Kettle Pt.	46	43 13N	82 1W
Kettle, R., B.C., Can.	63	48 41N	118 7W
Kettle, R., Man., Can.	55	56 23N	94 34W
Kettle R.	52	46 22N	92 53W
Kettleman City	80	36 1N	119 58W
Kevin	61	48 45N	111 58W
Kewanee	76	41 18N	90 0W
Kewanna	77	41 1N	86 25W
Kewaunee	72	44 27N	87 30W
Keweenaw B.	52	46 56N	88 23W
Keweenaw Pen.	72	47 30N	88 0W
Keweenaw Pt.	72	47 26N	87 40W
Key Harbour	46	45 50N	80 45W
Key West	84	24 40N	82 0W
Keyesport	76	38 45N	89 17W
Keyport	71	40 26N	74 12W
Keyser	72	39 26N	79 0W
Keystone, S.D., U.S.A.	74	43 54N	103 27W
Keystone, W. Va., U.S.A.	72	37 30N	81 30W

*Renamed Bakhtaran

Keytesville	76	39 26N	92 56W
Kezhma	121	59 15N	100 57E
Khabarovo	120	69 30N	60 30E
Khabarovsk	121	48 20N	135 0E
Khaibar	122	25 38N	39 28E
Khairpur	124	27 32N	68 49E
Khairpur □	124	23 30N	69 8E
Khakhea	117	24 48S	23 22E
*Khalij-e-Fars □	123	28 20N	51 45E
Khalkis	109	38 27N	23 42E
Khalmer-Sede = Tazovskiy	120	67 30N	78 30E
Khalmer Yu	120	67 58N	65 1E
Khalturin	120	58 40N	48 50E
Khan Tengri	129	42 25N	80 10E
Khanabad	123	36 45N	69 5E
Khânaqin	122	34 23N	45 25E
Khandwa	124	21 49N	76 22E
Khandyga	121	62 30N	134 50E
Khanewal	124	30 20N	71 55E
Khaniá	109	35 30N	24 4E
Khanion Kólpos	109	35 33N	23 55E
Khanka, Oz.	120	45 0N	132 30E
Khanty-Mansiysk	120	61 0N	69 0E
Kharagpur	125	22 20N	87 25E
Kharan Kalat	124	28 34N	65 21E
Kharânaq	123	32 20N	54 45E
Kharda	124	18 40N	75 40E
Kharfa	122	22 0N	46 35E
Kharg, Jazireh	122	29 15N	50 28E
Khargon	124	21 45N	75 35E
Kharkov	120	49 58N	36 20E
Kharsaniya	122	27 10N	49 10E
Khartoum = El Khartûm	115	15 31N	32 35E
Khasab	123	26 14N	56 15E
Khâsh	124	28 15N	61 5E
Khashm el Girba	115	14 59N	35 58E
Khaskovo	109	41 56N	25 30E
Khatanga	121	72 0N	102 20E
Khatanga, Zaliv	17	66 0N	112 0E
Khatyrka	121	62 3N	175 15E
**Khavar □	122	37 20N	46 0E
Khed Brahma	124	24 7N	73 5E
Khedive	56	49 37N	104 31W
Khemmarat	128	16 10N	105 15E
Khenmarak Phouminville	126	11 40N	102 58E
Kherson	120	46 35N	32 35E
Khetinsiring	129	32 52N	92 21E
Khilok	121	51 30N	110 45E
Khingan, mts.	118	47 0N	119 30E
Khios	109	38 27N	26 9E
Khios, I.	109	38 20N	26 0E
Khiva	120	41 30N	60 18E
Khiyâv	122	38 30N	47 45E
Khlong, R.	128	15 30N	98 50E
Khmelnitsky	107	49 23N	27 0E
Khmer Republic ■ = Cambodia	128	12 15N	105 0E
Khoi	122	38 40N	45 0E
Khojak P.	124	30 55N	66 30E
Kholm	120	57 10N	31 15E
Kholmsk	121	35 5N	139 48E
Khomayn	122	33 40N	50 7E
Khon Kaen	128	16 30N	102 47E
Khong	128	13 55N	105 56E
Khong, R.	128	15 0N	106 50E
Khonh Hung (Soc Trang)	128	9 37N	105 50E
Khonu	121	66 30N	143 25E
Khoper, R.	120	52 0N	43 20E
Khorasan □	123	34 0N	58 0E
Khorat = Nakhon Ratchasima	128	14 59N	102 12E
Khorat, Cao Nguyen	128	15 30N	102 50E
Khorat Plat.	128	15 30N	102 50E
Khorog	120	37 30N	71 36E
Khorramābād	122	33 30N	48 25E
Khorromshahr	122	30 29N	48 15E
Khotan = Hotien	129	37 6N	79 59E
Khu Khan	128	14 42N	104 12E
Khufaifiya	122	24 50N	43 35E
Khugiani	124	31 28N	66 14E
Khulna	125	22 45N	89 34E
Khulna □	125	22 45N	89 35E
Khūr	123	32 55N	58 18E
Khurais	122	24 55N	48 5E
Khurma	122	21 58N	42 3E
Khush	124	32 55N	62 10E
Khushab	124	32 20N	72 20E
Khuzdar	124	27 52N	66 30E
Khuzestan □	122	31 0N	48 30E
Khvor	123	33 45N	55 0E
Khvormūj	123	28 40N	51 30E
Khvoy	122	38 35N	45 0E
Khwaja Muhammad	123	36 0N	70 0E
Khyber Pass	124	34 10N	71 8E
Kiahsien	130	38 10N	110 8E
Kiama	136	34 40S	150 50E
Kiamusze	130	46 45N	130 30E
Kian	131	27 1N	114 58E
Kianghwa	131	25 26N	111 29E
Kiangling	131	30 28N	113 16E
Kiangpeh	131	29 40N	106 30E
Kiangshan	131	28 51N	118 38E
Kiangsi □	131	27 20N	115 40E
Kiangsu □	131	33 0N	119 50E
Kiangyin	131	31 51N	120 0E

* Renamed Bushehr
** Now part of Āzarbāijān-e Sharqi

Kiangyu Kokand

Kiangyu	131	31 41N	104 26 E
Kiaochow Wan	130	36 10N	120 15 E
Kiaohsien	130	36 20N	120 0 E
Kiawang	131	34 23N	117 28 E
Kibangou	116	3 18 S	12 22 E
Kibombo	116	3 57 S	25 53 E
Kibondo	116	3 35 S	30 45 E
Kibwesa	116	6 30 S	29 58 E
Kibwezi	116	2 27 S	37 57 E
Kichiga	121	59 50N	163 5 E
Kichow	131	30 0N	115 30 E
Kicking Horse Pass	63	51 28N	116 16W
Kidderminster	95	52 24N	2 13W
Kidnappers, C.	133	39 38 S	177 5 E
Kiel	106	54 16N	10 8 E
Kielce	107	50 58N	20 42 E
Kieler Bucht	106	54 30N	10 30 E
Kienhinghsien	131	26 50N	116 50 E
Kienhsien	131	34 30N	108 16 E
Kienko	131	31 50N	105 30 E
Kienning	131	27 4N	118 21 E
Kienow	131	27 0N	118 16 E
Kienshui	129	23 57N	102 45 E
Kiensi	131	26 58N	106 0 E
Kienteh	131	29 30N	119 28 E
Kienyang, Fukien, China	131	27 30N	118 0 E
Kienyang, Hunan, China	131	27 10N	109 50 E
Kiev = Kiyev	120	50 30N	30 28 E
Kifri	122	34 45N	45 0 E
Kigali	116	1 5 S	30 4 E
Kiglapait Mts.	36	57 6N	61 22W
Kigoma-Ujiji	116	5 30 S	30 0 E
Kihsien	130	36 20N	110 35 E
Kii-Suido	132	33 40N	135 0 E
Kijik	67	60 20N	154 20W
Kikiang	131	28 58N	106 44 E
Kikinda	109	45 50N	20 30 E
Kikino	60	54 27N	112 8W
Kikkatla	62	53 47N	130 25W
Kikládhes □	109	37 0N	25 0 E
Kikládhes, Is.	109	37 20N	24 30 E
Kikwit	116	5 5 S	18 45 E
Kilauea	67	22 13N	159 25W
Kilauea Crater	67	19 24N	155 17W
Kilbride, Newf., Can.	37	47 32N	52 45W
Kilbride, Ont., Can.	49	43 25N	79 56W
Kilbuck Mts.	67	60 30N	160 0W
Kildala Arm	62	53 50N	128 29W
Kildare	97	53 10N	6 50W
Kildare □	97	53 10N	6 50W
Kilembe	116	0 15N	30 3 E
Kilgore	75	32 22N	94 55W
Kilimanjaro, Mt.	116	3 7 S	37 20 E
Kilindini	116	4 4 S	39 40 E
Kilis	122	36 50N	37 10 E
Kilkee	97	52 41N	9 40W
Kilkenny	97	52 40N	7 17W
Kilkenny □	97	52 35N	7 15W
Kilkieran B.	97	53 18N	9 45W
Killala	97	54 13N	9 12W
Killala B.	97	54 20N	9 12W
Killala L.	53	49 5N	86 32W
Killaloe	97	52 48N	8 28W
Killaloe Sta.	47	45 33N	77 25W
Killaly	56	50 45N	102 50W
Killam	61	52 47N	111 51W
Killarney, Man., Can.	34	49 10N	99 40W
Killarney, Ont., Can.	55	45 55N	81 30W
Killarney, Ireland	97	52 2N	9 30W
Killarney, L's. of	97	52 0N	9 30W
Killarney Prov. Park	46	46 2N	81 35W
Killary Harb.	97	53 38N	9 52W
Killbuck	70	40 29N	81 58W
Killdeer, Can.	56	49 6N	106 22W
Killdeer, U.S.A.	74	47 26N	102 48W
Killeen	75	31 7N	97 45W
Killiecrankie P.	96	56 44N	3 46W
Killinek I.	36	60 24N	64 37W
Killini, Mts.	109	37 54N	22 25 E
Killowen	43	45 36N	74 15W
Killybegs	97	54 38N	8 26W
Kilmar	43	45 46N	74 37W
Kilmarnock	96	55 36N	4 30W
Kilmore	136	37 25 S	144 53 E
Kilosa	116	6 48 S	37 0 E
Kilrush	97	52 39N	9 30W
Kilwa Kisiwani	116	8 58 S	39 32 E
Kilwa Kivinje	116	8 45 S	39 25 E
Kim	75	37 18N	103 20W
Kimba	134	33 8 S	136 23 E
Kimball, Nebr., U.S.A.	74	41 17N	103 40W
Kimball, S.D., U.S.A.	74	43 47N	98 57W
Kimberley, Austral.	134	16 20 S	127 0 E
Kimberley, Can.	61	49 40N	115 59W
Kimberley, S. Afr.	117	28 43 S	24 46 E
Kimberly	78	42 33N	114 25W
Kimbo	49	43 7N	79 36W
Kimchaek	130	40 40N	129 10 E
Kimiwan L.	60	55 45N	116 55W
Kimsquit	62	52 45N	126 57W
Kinabalu, mt.	126	6 0N	116 0 E
Kinaskan L.	54	57 38N	130 8W
Kincaid	56	49 40N	107 0W
Kincald	76	39 35N	89 25W
Kincardine	46	44 10N	81 40W
Kinchwan	130	42 28N	126 6 E
Kinde	46	43 56N	83 0W

Kindersley	56	51 30N	109 10W
Kindia	114	10 0N	12 52W
Kindu	116	2 55 S	25 50 E
King City, Can.	50	43 56N	79 32W
King City, U.S.A.	76	40 3N	94 31W
King City, Calif., U.S.A.	80	36 11N	121 8W
King Frederick VI Land	17	63 0N	43 0W
King Frederick VIII Land	17	77 30N	25 0W
King George B.	90	51 30 S	60 30W
King George I.	91	60 0 S	60 0W
King George Is.	36	57 20N	78 25W
King George Sd.	134	35 5 S	118 0 E
King I., Austral.	135	39 50 S	144 0 E
King I., Can.	62	52 10N	127 40W
King I. = Kadah Kyun	128	12 30N	98 20 E
King Leopold Ranges	134	17 20 S	124 20 E
King Sd.	134	16 50 S	123 20 E
King William I.	65	69 10N	97 25W
King William's Town	117	32 51 S	27 22 E
Kingaroy	135	26 32 S	151 51 E
Kingcome Inlet	62	50 56N	126 29W
Kingfisher	75	35 50N	97 55W
Kinghorn	50	43 55N	79 34W
Kingku	129	23 49N	100 30 E
Kingman, U.S.A.	77	39 58N	87 18W
Kingman, Ariz., U.S.A.	81	35 12N	114 2W
Kingman, Kans., U.S.A.	75	37 41N	98 9W
Kingmen	131	31 10N	112 15 E
Kingning	131	27 55N	119 30 E
Kingpeng	130	43 10N	117 25 E
Kings B.	17	78 0N	15 0 E
Kings Canyon National Park	80	37 0N	118 35W
King's Lynn	94	52 45N	0 25 E
Kings Mountain	73	35 13N	81 20W
King's Peak	78	40 46N	110 27W
King's Point	37	49 35N	56 11W
Kings, R.	80	36 10N	119 50W
Kingsburg	80	36 35N	119 36W
Kingsbury	77	41 31N	86 42W
Kingscourt	97	53 55N	6 48W
Kingsey Falls	41	45 51N	72 4W
Kingsgate	61	49 1N	116 11W
Kingsley	74	42 37N	95 58W
Kingsley Dam	74	41 20N	101 40W
Kingsmere L.	56	54 6N	106 27W
Kingsport	73	36 33N	82 36W
Kingston, N.S., Can.	39	44 59N	64 57W
Kingston, Ont., Can.	47	44 14N	76 30W
Kingston, Jamaica	84	18 0N	76 50W
Kingston, N.Z.	133	45 20 S	168 43 E
Kingston, Mich., U.S.A.	46	43 29N	83 11W
Kingston, Mo., U.S.A.	76	39 38N	94 2W
Kingston, N.Y., U.S.A.	71	41 55N	74 0W
Kingston, Pa., U.S.A.	71	41 19N	75 58W
Kingston, R.I., U.S.A.	71	41 29N	71 30W
Kingston, Wash., U.S.A.	80	47 48N	122 30W
Kingston Mines	76	40 34N	89 47W
Kingston Pk.	81	35 45N	115 54W
Kingstown	85	13 10N	61 10W
Kingstree	73	33 40N	79 48W
Kingsville, Can.	46	42 2N	82 45W
Kingsville, U.S.A.	75	27 30N	97 53W
Kingtai	130	37 4N	103 59 E
Kingtehchen (Fowliang)	131	29 8N	117 21 E
Kingtzekwan	131	33 25N	111 10 E
Kingussie	96	47 5N	4 2W
Kingyang	130	36 6N	107 49 E
Kinhsien	130	36 6N	107 49 E
Kinhwa	131	29 5N	119 32 E
Kinistino	56	52 57N	105 2W
Kinkala	116	4 18 S	14 49 E
Kinkora	39	46 19N	63 36W
Kinleith	133	38 20 S	175 56 E
Kinloch	133	44 51 S	168 20 E
Kinmen (Quemoy) Is.	131	24 25N	118 24 E
Kinmount	47	44 48N	78 45W
Kinmundy	77	38 46N	88 51W
Kinnaird	63	49 17N	117 39W
Kinnaird's Hd.	96	57 40N	2 0W
Kino	82	28 45N	111 59W
Kinoje Ls.	53	51 35N	81 48W
Kinoje, R.	34	52 8N	81 25W
Kinping	128	22 56N	103 15 E
Kinross	96	56 13N	3 25W
Kinsale, Can.	51	43 56N	79 2W
Kinsale, Ireland	97	51 42N	8 31W
Kinsale Harbour	97	51 40N	8 30W
Kinsale Old Hd.	97	51 37N	8 32W
Kinsha (Yangtze)	129	32 30N	98 30 E
Kinshasa	116	4 20 S	15 15 E
Kinsiang	131	35 4N	116 25 E
Kinsley	75	37 57N	99 30W
Kinston	73	35 18N	77 35W
Kintap	126	3 51 S	115 13 E
Kintyre, Mull of	96	55 17N	5 4W
Kintyre, pen.	96	55 30N	5 35W
Kinushseo, R.	34	55 15N	83 45W
Kinuso	60	55 20N	115 25W
Kinzua	70	41 52N	78 58W
Kinzua Dam	70	41 53N	79 0W
Kioshan	131	32 50N	114 0 E
Kiosk	47	46 6N	78 53W
Kiowa, Kans., U.S.A.	75	37 3N	98 30W
Kiowa, Okla., U.S.A.	75	34 45N	95 50W

Kipahigan L.	55	55 20N	101 55W
Kiparissia	109	37 15N	21 40 E
Kiparissiakós Kólpos	109	37 25N	21 25 E
Kipawa	40	46 47N	78 59W
Kipawa L.	40	46 50N	79 0W
Kipawa, Parc de	40	47 0N	78 50W
Kipawa Res. Prov. Park	34	47 0N	78 30W
Kipembawe	116	7 38 S	33 27 E
Kipili	116	7 28 S	30 32 E
Kipling	56	50 6N	102 38W
Kipnuk	67	59 55N	164 7W
Kippens	37	48 33N	58 38W
Kippure, Mt.	97	53 11N	6 23W
Kipushi	117	11 48 S	27 12 E
Kirensk	121	57 50N	107 55 E
Kirgiz S.S.R. □	120	42 0N	75 0 E
Kiribati ■	14	1 0 S	176 0 E
Kirikkale	122	39 51N	33 32 E
Kirin	130	43 58N	126 31 E
Kirin □	130	43 50N	125 45 E
Kirkcaldy	96	56 7N	3 10W
Kirkcudbright	96	54 50N	4 3W
Kirkee	124	18 34N	73 56 E
Kirkenes	110	69 40N	30 5 E
Kirkfield	47	44 34N	78 59W
Kirkfield Park	58	49 53N	97 17W
Kirkintilloch	96	55 57N	4 10W
Kirkjubæjarklaustur	110	63 47N	18 4W
Kirkland, Can.	44	45 27N	73 52W
Kirkland, U.S.A.	77	42 5N	88 51W
Kirkland, Ariz., U.S.A.	79	34 29N	112 46W
Kirkland, Wash., U.S.A.	78	47 40N	122 10W
Kirkland Lake	34	48 9N	80 2W
Kırklareli	109	41 44N	27 15 E
Kirklin	77	40 12N	86 22W
Kirksville	76	40 8N	92 35W
Kirkük	122	35 30N	44 21 E
Kirkwall, Can.	49	43 21N	80 10W
Kirkwall, U.K.	96	58 59N	2 59W
Kirkwood	76	38 35N	90 24W
Kirov, R.S.F.S.R., U.S.S.R.	120	58 35N	49 40 E
Kirov, R.S.F.S.R., U.S.S.R.	120	58 35N	49 40 E
Kirovabad	120	40 45N	46 10 E
Kirovograd	120	48 35N	32 20 E
Kirovsk	120	67 48N	33 50 E
Kirriemuir	55	51 56N	110 20W
Kirşehir	122	39 14N	34 5 E
Kirthar Range	124	27 0N	67 0 E
Kiruna	110	67 52N	20 15 E
Kirundu	116	0 50 S	25 35 E
Kiryū	132	36 24N	139 20 E
Kisalaya	84	14 40N	84 3W
Kisangani	116	0 35N	25 15 E
Kisar, I.	127	8 5 S	127 10 E
Kisaran	126	2 47N	99 29 E
Kisaratzu	132	35 25N	139 59 E
Kisbey	56	49 39N	102 40W
Kiselevsk	120	54 5N	86 6 E
Kishanganj	125	26 3N	88 14 E
Kishangarh	124	27 50N	70 30 E
Kishinev	120	47 0N	28 50 E
Kishiwada	132	34 28N	135 22 E
Kishow	131	28 16N	109 47 E
Kishtwar	124	33 20N	75 48 E
Kishwaukee, R.	77	42 12N	89 8W
Kisi	130	45 21N	131 0 E
Kisii	116	0 40 S	34 45 E
Kisiju	116	7 23 S	39 19 E
Kiska I.	67	52 0N	177 30 E
Kiskatinaw, R.	54	56 8N	120 10W
Kiskitto L.	57	54 16N	98 30W
Kiskittogisu L.	57	54 13N	98 20W
Kiskőrös	107	46 37N	19 20 E
Kiskunfelégyháza	107	46 42N	19 53 E
Kiskunhalas	107	46 28N	19 37 E
Kismayu	113	0 20 S	42 30 E
Kiso-Gawa	132	35 20N	137 0 E
Kiso-Sammyaku	132	35 30N	137 45 E
Kissimmee	73	28 18N	81 22W
Kissimmee, R.	73	27 20N	81 0W
Kississing L.	55	55 10N	101 10W
Kisumu	116	0 3 S	34 45 E
Kit Carson	74	38 48N	102 45W
Kita	114	13 5N	9 25W
Kitab	120	39 7N	66 52 E
Kitai	129	44 0N	89 27 E
Kitaibaraki	132	36 50N	140 45 E
Kitakami-Gawa	132	39 30N	141 15 E
Kitakyūshū	132	33 50N	130 50 E
Kitale	116	1 0N	35 12 E
Kitchener	49	43 27N	80 29W
Kitchigami, R.	34	50 35N	78 5W
Kitchioh	131	22 57N	116 2 E
Kitega = Citega	116	3 30 S	29 58 E
Kitgum Matidi	116	3 17N	32 52 E
Kíthira	109	36 9N	23 0 E
Kíthira, I.	109	36 15N	23 0 E
Kíthnos	109	37 26N	24 27 E
Kíthnos, I.	109	37 25N	24 25 E
Kitimat	62	54 3N	128 38W
Kitimat Arm	62	53 55N	128 42W
Kitimat Ranges	62	54 0N	129 15W
Kitinen, R.	110	67 34N	26 40 E
Kitscoty	60	53 20N	110 20W
Kittanning	70	40 49N	79 30W
Kittatinny Mts.	71	41 0N	75 0W
Kittertoksoak, I.	36	58 50N	65 50W

Kittery	71	43 7N	70 42W
Kitui	116	1 17 S	38 0 E
Kitwe	117	12 54 S	28 7 E
Kityang	131	23 30N	116 29 E
Kiuchuan	129	39 51N	98 30 E
Kiukiang	131	29 37N	116 2 E
Kiuling Shan, mts.	131	28 30N	114 30 E
Kiungchow	131	19 57N	110 17 E
Kiungchow Haihsia	131	20 40N	110 0 E
Kivalina	67	67 45N	164 40W
Kivalo	110	66 18N	26 0 E
Kivitoo	65	67 56N	64 52W
Kivu, L.	116	1 48 S	29 0 E
Kiyang	131	26 36N	111 42 E
Kiyev	120	50 30N	30 28 E
Kiyuanshan	131	28 6N	117 46 E
Kizil Kiya	120	40 20N	72 35 E
Kizlyar	120	43 51N	46 40 E
Kizyl-Arvat	120	38 58N	56 15 E
Klabat, Teluk	126	1 30 S	105 40 E
Kladno	106	50 10N	14 7 E
Klagenfurt	106	46 38N	14 20 E
Klaipeda	120	55 43N	21 10 E
Klamath Falls	78	42 20N	121 50W
Klamath Mts.	78	41 20N	123 0W
Klamath, R.	78	41 40N	123 30W
Klang = Kelang	128	3 1N	101 33 E
Klappan, R.	54	58 0N	129 43W
Klarälven	111	60 32N	13 15 E
Klaten	127	7 43 S	110 36 E
Klatovy	106	49 23N	13 18 E
Klawak	54	55 35N	133 0W
Klawer	117	31 44 S	18 36 E
Kleczkowski, L.	38	50 48N	63 27W
Kleena Kleene	62	52 0N	124 50W
Klein	78	46 26N	108 31W
Kleinburg	50	43 50N	79 38W
Kleindale	62	49 38N	123 58W
Klemtu	54	52 35N	128 55W
Klerksdorp	117	26 51 S	26 38 E
Kletskaïa Kletskiy	120	49 20N	43 0 E
Kletskiy	120	49 20N	43 0 E
Kleve	105	51 46N	6 10 E
Klickitat	78	45 50N	121 10W
Klickitat, R.	80	45 42N	121 17W
Klin	120	56 28N	36 48 E
Klinaklini, R.	62	51 21N	125 40W
Kłodzko	106	50 28N	16 38 E
Klondike	64	64 0N	139 26W
Klotz, L.	36	60 32N	73 40W
Kluane L.	64	61 15N	138 40W
Kluang = Keluang	128	1 59N	103 20 E
Knaresborough	94	54 1N	1 29W
Knee L., Man., Can.	55	55 3N	94 45W
Knee L., Sask., Can.	55	55 51N	107 0W
Knewstubb L.	62	53 33N	124 55W
Knight Inlet	62	50 45N	125 40W
Knighton	95	52 21N	3 2W
Knights Ferry	80	37 50N	120 40W
Knight's Landing	80	38 50N	121 43W
Knightstown	77	39 49N	85 32W
Knob, C.	134	34 32 S	119 16 E
Knockmealdown Mts.	97	52 16N	8 0W
Knokke	105	51 20N	3 17 E
Knossos	109	35 18N	25 10 E
Knowlton	41	45 13N	72 31W
Knox	77	41 18N	86 36W
Knox, C.	62	54 11N	133 5W
Knox City	75	33 26N	99 38W
Knox Coast	91	66 30 S	108 0 E
Knoxville, Iowa, U.S.A.	76	41 20N	93 5W
Knoxville, Pa., U.S.A.	73	41 57N	77 26W
Knoxville, Tenn., U.S.A.	73	35 58N	83 57W
Knud Rasmussen Land	65	79 0N	60 0W
Ko Chang	128	12 0N	102 20 E
Ko Kut	128	11 40N	102 32 E
Ko Phangan	128	9 45N	100 10 E
Ko Phra Thong	128	9 6N	98 15 E
Ko Samui	128	9 30N	100 0 E
Koartac (Notre Dame de Koartac)	36	61 5N	69 36 E
Koba, Aru, Indon.	127	6 37 S	134 37 E
Koba, Bangka, Indon.	126	2 26 S	106 14 E
Kobarid	108	46 15N	13 30 E
Kobayashi	132	31 56N	130 59 E
Kōbe	132	34 45N	135 10 E
København	111	55 41N	12 34 E
Koblenz	105	50 21N	7 36 E
Kobroor, Kepulauan	127	6 10 S	134 30 E
Kobuk	67	66 55N	157 0W
Kobuk, R.	67	66 55N	157 0W
Kočani	109	41 55N	22 25 E
Kočevje	108	45 39N	14 50 E
Kōchi	132	33 30N	133 35 E
Kōchi-ken □	132	33 40N	133 30 E
Kodiak	67	57 30N	152 45W
Kodiak I.	67	57 30N	152 45W
Kodiang	128	6 21N	100 18 E
Koes	117	26 0 S	19 15 E
Köflach	91	47 4N	15 4 E
Kōfu	132	35 40N	138 30 E
Kogaluk, R.	36	56 12N	61 44W
Koh-i-Baba, mts.	124	34 30N	67 0 E
Kohat	124	33 40N	71 29 E
Kohima	125	25 35N	94 10 E
Kohler Ra.	91	77 0N	110 0W
Kojabuti	127	2 36 S	140 37 E
Kokand	120	40 30N	70 57 E

Kokanee Glacier Prov. Park Kweiyang

Kokanee Glacier Prov. Park	63	49 47N	117 10W
Kokas	127	2 42S	132 26E
Kokchetav	120	53 20N	69 10E
Kokemäenjoki	111	61 32N	21 44E
Kokiu	129	23 30N	103 0E
Kokkola (Gamlakarleby)	110	63 50N	23 8E
Koko Kyunzu	128	14 10N	93 25E
Koko-Nor	129	37 0N	100 0E
Koko Shili	125	35 20N	91 0E
Kokomo	72	40 30N	86 6W
Kokoura	121	71 35N	144 50E
Kokstad	117	30 32S	29 29E
Kola	120	68 45N	33 8E
Kola, I.	127	5 35S	134 30E
Kola Pen. = Kolskiy P-ov.	120	67 30N	38 0E
Kolagede	127	7 54S	110 26E
Kolaka	127	4 3S	121 46E
Kolar	124	13 12N	78 15E
Kolar Gold Fields	124	12 58N	78 16E
Kolari	110	67 20N	23 48E
Kolarovgrad	109	43 27N	26 42E
Kolayat	124	27 50N	72 50E
Koldewey I.	17	77 0N	18 0W
Kolding	111	55 30N	9 29E
Kole	116	3 16S	22 42E
Kolepom, Pulau	127	8 0S	138 30E
Kolguyev, Ostrov	120	69 20N	48 30E
Kolhapur	124	16 43N	74 15E
Kolin	106	50 2N	15 9E
Köln	105	50 56N	9 58E
Koło	107	52 14N	18 40E
Kołobrzeg	106	54 10N	15 35E
Kolomna	120	55 8N	38 45E
Kolonodale	127	2 3S	121 25E
Kolosib	125	24 15N	92 45E
Kolpashevo	120	58 20N	83 5E
Kolskiy Poluostrov	120	67 30N	38 0E
Kolwezi	116	10 40S	25 25E
Kolyma, R.	121	64 40N	153 0E
Kolymskoye, Okhotsko	121	63 0N	157 0E
Komandorskiye Ostrava	121	55 0N	167 0E
Komárno	107	47 49N	18 5E
Komi, A.S.S.R. □	120	64 0N	55 0E
Kommunizma, Pik	120	39 0N	72 2E
Komodo	127	8 37S	119 20E
Komono	116	3 15S	13 20E
Komoran, Pulau	127	8 18S	138 45E
Komotiri	109	41 9N	25 26E
Kompong Cham	128	11 54N	105 30E
Kompong Chhnang	128	12 20N	104 35E
Kompong Speu	128	11 26N	104 32E
Kompong Thom	128	12 35N	104 51E
Komsomolets, Ostrov	121	80 30N	95 0E
Komsomolsk	121	50 30N	137 0E
Konawa	75	34 59N	96 46W
Kondoa	116	4 55S	35 50E
Kondratyevo	121	57 30N	98 30E
Kong	114	8 54N	4 36W
Kong Christian IX.s Land	17	68 0N	36 0W
Kong Christian X.s Land	17	74 0N	29 0W
Kong Frederik VIII.s Land	17	78 30N	26 0W
Kong Frederik VI.s Kyst	17	63 0N	43 0W
Kong, Koh	128	11 20N	103 0E
Kong Oscar Fjord	17	72 20N	24 0W
Kongmoon	131	22 35N	113 1E
Kongolo	116	5 22S	27 0E
Kongsberg	111	59 39N	9 39E
Kongsvinger	111	60 12N	12 2E
Konin	107	52 12N	18 15E
Konjic	109	43 42N	17 58E
Konosha	120	61 0N	40 5E
Konotop	120	51 12N	33 7E
Konskie	107	51 15N	20 23E
Konstanz	106	47 39N	9 10E
Kontagora	114	10 23N	5 27E
Kontum	128	14 24N	108 0E
Konya	122	37 52N	32 35E
Konza	116	1 45S	37 0E
Koo-wee-rup	136	38 13S	145 28E
Koocanusa, L.	61	49 20N	115 15W
Koog	17	52 27N	4 49E
Koolan I.	134	16 0S	123 45E
Kooloonong	136	34 48S	143 10E
Koorakee	136	34 27S	142 56E
Koorawatha	136	34 2S	148 33E
Kooskia	78	46 9N	115 59W
Koostatak	55	51 26N	97 26W
Kootenai, R.	78	48 30N	115 30W
Kootenay L.	63	49 45N	116 50W
Kootenay Nat. Park	61	51 0N	116 0W
Kootingal	89	31 1S	151 3E
Kopaonik Planina	109	43 10N	21 50E
Kópavogur	110	64 6N	21 55W
Koper	108	45 31N	13 44E
Kopervik	111	59 17N	5 17E
Kopeysk	120	55 7N	61 37E
Köping	111	59 31N	16 3E
Kopka, R.	52	50 4N	89 1W
Kopparberg	111	59 52N	15 0E
Kopparbergs län □	67	61 20N	14 15E
Koppeh Dāgh	123	38 0N	58 0E

Korab, mt.	109	41 44N	20 40E
Korça	109	40 37N	20 50E
Korčula, I.	108	42 57N	17 0E
Kordestān □	122	36 0N	47 0E
Kordestan, reg.	122	37 30N	42 0E
Korea, South ■	130	36 0N	128 0E
Korea Strait	118	34 0N	129 30E
Korea,North ■	130	40 0N	127 0E
Korhogo	114	9 29N	5 28W
Korim	127	0 58S	136 10E
Korinthiakós Kólpos	109	38 16N	22 30E
Kórinthos	109	37 56N	22 55E
Kōriyama	132	37 24N	140 23E
Korla	129	41 45N	86 4E
Kormack	53	47 38N	82 59W
Koro, I.	133	17 19S	179 23E
Koroc, R.	36	58 50N	65 50W
Korogwe	116	5 5S	38 25E
Koroit	136	38 18S	142 24E
Koror	127	7 20N	134 28E
Körös, R.	107	46 45N	20 20E
Korsakov	121	46 30N	142 42E
Korshunovo	121	58 37N	110 10E
Korsör	111	55 20N	11 9E
Kortrijk	105	50 50N	3 17E
Koryakskiy Khrebet	121	61 0N	171 0E
Kos	109	36 52N	27 19E
Kos, I.	109	36 50N	27 15E
Kosciusko	75	33 3N	89 34W
Kosciusko, I.	54	56 0N	133 40W
Kosciusko, Mt.	136	36 27S	148 16E
Koshkonong, L.	77	42 53N	88 58W
Košice	107	48 42N	21 15E
Kosônf	130	38 40N	128 22E
Kosovska-Mitrovica	109	42 54N	20 52E
Kosścian	106	52 5N	16 40E
Kôsti	115	13 8N	32 43E
Kostroma	120	57 50N	41 58E
Kostrzyn	106	52 24N	17 14E
Koszalin	106	54 12N	16 8E
Kota	124	25 14N	75 49E
Kota Baharu	128	6 7N	102 14E
Kota Kinabalu	126	6 0N	116 12E
Kota Tinggi	128	1 44N	103 53E
Kotaagung	126	5 38S	104 29E
Kotabaru	126	3 20S	116 20E
Kotabumi	126	4 49S	104 46E
Kotamobagu	127	0 57N	124 31E
Kotaneelee, R.	54	60 11N	123 42W
Kotawaringin	126	2 28S	111 27E
Kotcho L.	54	59 7N	121 12W
Kotelnich	120	58 20N	48 10E
Kotelnikovo	120	47 45N	43 15E
Kotelnyy, Ostrov	121	75 10N	139 0E
Kotka	111	60 28N	26 58E
Kotlas	120	61 15N	47 0E
Kotor	109	42 25N	18 47E
Kotri	124	25 22N	68 22E
Kottayam	124	9 35N	76 33E
Kotturu	124	14 45N	76 10E
Kotuy, R.	121	70 30N	103 0E
Kotzebue	67	66 50N	162 40W
Kotzebue Sd.	67	66 30N	164 0W
Kouango	116	5 0N	20 10E
Kouchibouguac Nat. Park	39	46 50N	65 20W
Koudougou	114	12 10N	2 20W
Kouilou, R.	116	4 10S	12 5E
Kouki	116	7 22N	17 3E
Koula Moutou	116	1 15S	12 25E
Koulen	128	13 50N	104 40E
Koulikoro	114	12 40N	7 50W
Koumradskiy	120	47 20N	75 0E
Kountze	75	30 20N	94 22W
Kouts	77	41 18N	87 2W
Kovel	120	51 10N	24 20E
Kovic, B.	36	61 35N	77 36W
Kowkash	53	50 20N	87 12W
Kowloon	131	22 20N	114 15E
Kowpangtze	130	41 24N	121 56E
Koyan, Pegunungan	126	3 15N	114 30E
Koyiu	131	23 2N	112 28E
Koyuk	67	64 55N	161 20W
Koyukuk, R.	67	65 45N	156 30W
Koza	131	26 20N	127 47E
Kozan	122	37 35N	35 50E
Kozàni	109	40 19N	21 47E
Kozhikode = Calicut	124	11 15N	75 43E
Kra Buri	128	10 22N	98 46E
Kra, Isthmus of = Kra, Kho Khot	128	10 15N	99 30E
Kra, Kho Khot	128	10 15N	99 30E
Kragan	127	6 43S	111 38E
Kragerø	111	58 52N	9 25E
Kragujevac	109	44 2N	20 56E
Krakatau = Rakata, Pulau	126	6 10S	105 20E
Kraków	107	50 4N	19 57E
Kraksaan	127	7 43S	113 23E
Kraljevo	109	43 44N	20 41E
Kramer	79	35 0N	117 38W
Kramfors	110	62 55N	17 48E
Kraskino	121	42 44N	130 48E
Krasnoarmeysk	120	50 32N	45 50E
Krasnodar	120	45 5N	38 50E
Krasnoiarsk	121	56 8N	93 0E
Krasnoperekopsk	120	46 0N	33 54E
Krasnoselkupsk	120	65 20N	82 10E
Krasnoturinsk	120	59 46N	60 12E

Krasnoufimsk	120	56 57N	57 46E
Krasnouralsk	120	58 21N	60 3E
Krasnovodsk	120	40 0N	52 52E
Krasnoyarsk	121	56 8N	93 0E
Kraśnik	107	50 55N	22 5E
Kratie	128	12 32N	106 10E
Kravanh, Chuor Phnum	128	12 0N	103 32E
Krawang	127	6 19N	107 18E
Krefeld	105	51 20N	6 22E
Kremenchug	120	49 5N	33 25E
Kremmling	78	40 10N	106 30W
Kremnica	107	48 45N	18 50E
Kribi	116	2 57N	9 56E
Krishna, R.	124	16 30N	77 0E
Krishnanagar	125	23 24N	88 33E
Kristiansand	111	58 9N	8 1E
Kristianstad	111	56 2N	14 9E
Kristianstad □	111	56 15N	14 0E
Kristiansund	110	63 7N	7 45E
Kristiinankaupunki	110	62 16N	21 21E
Kristinehamn	111	59 18N	14 13E
Kristinestad	110	62 16N	21 21E
Kriti, I.	109	35 15N	25 0E
Krivoy Rog	120	47 51N	33 20E
Krk, I.	108	45 8N	14 40E
Kroeng Krai	128	14 55N	98 30E
Kronobergs län □	111	56 45N	14 30E
Kronprins Harald Kyst	91	70 0S	35 1E
Kronprins Olav Kyst	91	69 0S	42 0E
Kronprinsesse Märtha Kyst	91	73 30S	10 0W
Kronshtadt	120	60 5N	29 35E
Kroonstad	117	27 43S	27 19E
Kropotkin	121	45 25N	40 35E
Krosno	107	49 35N	21 56E
Krotoszyn	107	51 42N	17 23E
Krugersdorp	117	26 5S	27 46E
Krung Thep(Bangkok)	128	13 45N	100 35E
Kruševac	109	43 35N	21 28E
Kruzof I.	54	57 10N	135 40W
Krydor	56	52 47N	107 4W
Krymskaya	120	45 0N	34 0E
Kuala	126	2 46N	105 47E
Kuala Kangsar	128	4 46N	100 56E
Kuala Kerai	128	5 30N	102 12E
Kuala Kubu Baharu	128	3 34N	101 39E
Kuala Lipis	128	4 10N	102 3E
Kuala Lumpur	128	3 9N	101 41E
Kuala Sedili Besar	128	1 55N	104 5E
Kuala Trengganu	128	5 20N	103 8E
Kualakahi Chan	67	22 2N	159 53W
Kualakapuas	126	2 55S	114 20E
Kualakurun	126	1 10S	113 50E
Kualapembuang, Indon.	126	2 52S	111 45E
Kualapembuang, Indon.	126	3 14S	112 38E
Kuandang	127	0 56N	123 1E
Kuantan	128	3 49N	103 20E
Kuba	120	41 21N	48 32E
Kucha	129	41 50N	82 30E
Kuchen	131	33 29N	117 27E
Kuching	126	1 33N	110 25E
Kuda	124	23 10N	71 15E
Kudat	126	6 55N	116 55E
Kudus	127	6 48S	110 51E
Kudymkar	120	59 1N	54 39E
Kufra, El Wâhât el	115	24 17N	23 15E
Kufstein	106	47 35N	12 11E
Kugaluk, B.	36	59 10N	78 40W
Kugmallit B.	67	29 0N	134 0W
Kugong, I.	36	56 18N	79 50W
Kūh-e-Aliju	123	31 30N	51 41E
Kūh-e-Dinar	123	30 10N	51 0E
Kūh-e-Hazārān	123	29 35N	57 20E
Kūh-e-Jebāl Bārez	123	29 0N	58 0E
Kūh-e-Sorkh	123	35 30N	58 45E
Kūh-e-Taftan	123	28 40N	61 0E
Kūhak	123	27 12N	63 10E
Kūhhā-ye-Bashākerd	123	26 45N	59 0E
Kūhhā-ye Sabalān	123	38 15N	47 45E
Kūhpāyeh	123	32 44N	52 20E
Kuinre	105	52 47N	5 51E
Kuiu I.	67	56 40N	134 15W
Kukukus L.	52	49 47N	91 41W
Kulai	128	1 44N	103 35E
Kulasekharapattanam	124	8 20N	78 0E
Kuldja = Ining	129	43 57N	81 20E
Kulm	74	46 22N	98 58W
Kulsary	120	46 59N	54 1E
Kulu	130	37 12N	115 2E
Kulunda	120	52 45N	79 15E
Kulunkai	130	42 46N	121 55E
Kulwin	136	35 0S	142 42E
Kulyab	120	37 55N	69 50E
Kum Darya	129	41 0N	89 0E
Kum Tekei	120	43 10N	79 30E
Kuma, R.	120	44 55N	45 57E
Kumagaya	132	36 9N	139 22E
Kumamoto	132	32 45N	130 45E
Kumamoto-ken □	132	32 30N	130 40E
Kumanovo	109	42 9N	21 42E
Kumara	133	42 37S	171 12E
Kumasi	114	6 41N	1 38W
Kumba	116	4 36N	9 24E
Kume-guntō	131	26 8N	126 45E
Kumla	111	59 8N	15 10E
Kumon Bum	125	26 30N	97 15E
Kumukahi, C.	67	19 31N	154 49W
Kunar	124	34 30N	71 3E
Kunashir, Ostrov	121	44 0N	146 0E

Kunch	124	26 0N	79 10E
Kunduz	123	36 50N	68 50E
Kunduz □	123	36 50N	68 50E
Kungan	131	30 0N	112 2E
Kungchuling	130	43 31N	124 58E
Kunghit I.	62	52 6N	131 3W
Kungho	129	36 28N	100 45E
Kungrad	120	43 6N	58 54E
Kungsbacka	111	57 30N	12 5E
Kungur	120	57 25N	56 57E
Kungyifow	131	22 24N	112 41E
Kunhsien	131	32 30N	111 17E
Kuningan	127	6 59S	108 29E
Kunlong	125	23 20N	98 50E
Kunlun Shan	129	36 0N	86 30E
Kunming	129	25 11N	102 37E
Kunsan	130	35 59N	126 45E
Kunshan	131	31 16N	121 0E
Kununurra	134	15 40S	128 39E
Kuopio	110	62 53N	27 35E
Kuopion Lääni □	110	63 25N	27 10E
Kupa, R.	108	45 30N	16 10E
Kupang	127	10 19S	123 39E
Kupreanof I.	67	56 50N	133 30W
Kupyansk	120	49 45N	37 35E
Kurashiki	132	34 40N	133 50E
Kurayoshi	132	35 26N	133 50E
Kure	132	34 14N	132 32E
Kurgaldzhino	120	50 35N	70 20E
Kurgan, R.S.F.S.R., U.S.S.R.	120	55 26N	65 18E
Kurgan, R.S.F.S.R., U.S.S.R.	121	64 5N	172 50W
Kurigram	125	25 49N	89 39E
Kurilskiye Ostrova	121	45 0N	150 0E
Kurnool	124	15 45N	78 0E
Kuroki	56	51 52N	103 29W
Kurow	133	44 4S	170 29E
Kurri Kurri	136	32 50S	151 28E
Kursk	120	51 42N	36 11E
Kuršumlija	109	43 9N	21 19E
Kurtalān	122	37 55N	41 40E
Kuruman	117	27 28S	23 28E
Kurume	132	33 15N	130 30E
Kurunegala	124	7 30N	80 18E
Kurya	121	61 15N	108 10E
Kusagaki	131	30 54N	129 28E
Kusawa L.	54	60 20N	136 13W
Kushan	130	39 58N	123 30E
Kushih	131	32 12N	115 43E
Kushiro	132	43 0N	144 25E
Kushirogawa	132	43 0N	144 30E
Kushk	124	34 55N	62 30E
Kushka	120	35 20N	62 18E
Kushtia	125	23 55N	89 5E
Kuskokwim Bay	67	59 50N	162 56W
Kuskokwim Mts.	67	63 0N	156 0W
Kuskokwim, R.	67	61 48N	157 0W
Kustanay	120	53 10N	63 35E
Kutahya	122	39 30N	30 2E
Kutaisi	120	42 19N	42 40E
Kutaradja = Banda Aceh	126	5 35N	95 20E
Kutatjane	126	3 45N	97 50E
Kutch, G. of	124	22 50N	69 15E
Kutch, Rann of	124	24 0N	70 0E
Kutno	107	52 15N	19 23E
Kutu	116	2 40S	18 11E
Kuwait = Al Kuwayt	122	29 30N	47 30E
Kuwait ■	122	29 30N	47 30E
Kuyang	130	41 8N	110 1E
Kuybyshev	120	55 27N	78 19E
Kuyung	131	32 0N	119 8E
Kvænangen	110	69 55N	21 15E
Kvarken	111	63 30N	21 0E
Kvarner	108	44 50N	14 10E
Kvarnerič	108	44 43N	14 37E
Kwadacha, R.	54	57 28N	125 38W
Kwakoegron	87	5 25N	55 25W
Kwando, R.	117	16 48S	22 45E
Kwangan	131	30 35N	106 40E
Kwangchow	131	23 10N	113 10E
Kwangchow Wan.	131	21 0N	111 0E
Kwangju	130	35 9N	126 55E
Kwangnan	129	24 10N	105 0E
Kwangping	130	36 40N	114 41E
Kwangshui	131	31 45N	114 0E
Kwangsi-Chuang □	131	23 30N	108 55E
Kwangtseh	131	27 30N	117 25E
Kwangtsi	131	30 2N	115 46E
Kwangtung	131	23 35N	114 0E
Kwangyuan	131	32 30N	105 49E
Kwanhsien	129	30 59N	103 40E
Kwantung	129	25 12N	101 37E
Kwanyun	131	34 28N	119 29E
Kwataboahegan, R.	53	51 9N	80 50W
Kwatisore	127	3 7S	139 59E
Kweichih	131	30 40N	117 30E
Kweichow = Fengkieh	131	31 0N	109 33E
Kweichow □	131	27 20N	107 0E
Kweihsien	131	22 59N	109 44E
Kweihwa = Mingki	131	26 10N	117 14E
Kweiki	131	28 10N	117 8E
Kweilin	131	25 16N	110 15E
Kweiping	131	23 12N	110 0E
Kweishun = Tsingsing	131	38 1N	114 4E
Kweitung	131	26 0N	113 35E
Kweiyang, Hunan, China	131	25 50N	112 25E

Name	Page	Lat.	Long.
Kweiyang, Kweichow, China	**131**	26 30N	106 35 E
Kwethluk	**67**	60 45N	161 34W
Kwidzyn	**107**	54 45N	18 58 E
Kwigillingok	**67**	59 50N	163 10W
Kwiguk	**67**	63 45N	164 35W
Kwinana	**134**	32 15 S	115 47 E
Kwinitsa	**62**	54 19N	129 22W
Kwo Ho	**131**	33 20N	116 50 E
Kwohwa	**131**	23 10N	107 0 E
Kwoyang	**131**	33 35N	116 15 E
Kyabram	**136**	36 19 S	145 4 E
Kyaikto	**128**	17 20N	97 3 E
Kyakhta	**121**	50 30N	106 25 E
Kyargas Nuur	**129**	49 0N	93 0 E
Kyaukpadaung	**125**	20 52N	95 8 E
Kyaukpyu	**125**	19 28N	93 30 E
Kyaukse	**125**	21 36N	96 10 E
Kyburz	**80**	38 47N	120 18W
Kyle	**56**	50 50N	108 2W
Kyle Dam	**117**	20 15 S	31 0 E
Kyle of Lochalsh	**96**	57 17N	5 43W
Kyneton	**136**	37 10 S	144 29 E
Kynoch Inlet	**62**	52 45N	128 0W
Kyō-ga-Saki	**132**	35 45N	135 15 E
Kyoga, L.	**116**	1 35N	33 0 E
Kyongju	**130**	35 50N	129 13 E
Kyongpyaw	**125**	17 12N	95 10 E
Kyōto	**132**	35 0N	135 45 E
Kyōto-fu □	**132**	35 15N	135 30 E
Kyrenia	**122**	35 20N	33 20 E
Kystatyam	**121**	67 20N	123 10 E
Kytalktakh	**121**	65 30N	123 40 E
Kyulyunken	**121**	64 10N	137 5 E
Kyunhla	**125**	23 25N	95 15 E
Kyuquot	**62**	50 3N	127 25W
Kyūshū	**132**	33 0N	131 0 E
Kyushu, I.	**132**	32 30N	131 0 E
Kyūshū-Sanchi	**132**	32 45N	131 40 E
Kyustendil	**109**	42 25N	22 41 E
Kyusyur	**121**	70 39N	127 15 E
Kywong	**136**	34 58 S	146 44 E
Kyzyl	**121**	51 50N	94 30 E
Kyzyl-Kiya	**120**	40 16N	72 8 E
Kyzyl Orda	**120**	44 56N	65 30 E
Kyzyl Rabat	**120**	37 45N	74 55 E
Kyzylkum	**120**	42 30N	65 0 E
Kzyl-orda	**120**	44 48N	65 28 E
L			
La Broquerie	**57**	49 25N	96 30W
La Havre, R.	**39**	44 14N	64 20W
La Push	**80**	47 55N	124 38W
Laau Pt.	**67**	21 57N	159 40W
Labastide	**102**	43 28N	2 39 E
Labastide-Murat	**102**	44 39N	1 33 E
Labe, R.	**106**	50 3N	15 20 E
Laberge, L.	**54**	61 11N	135 12W
Labis	**128**	2 22N	103 2 E
Laboa	**127**	8 6 S	122 50 E
Labouheyre	**102**	44 13N	0 55W
Laboulaye	**88**	34 10 S	63 30W
Labrador City	**38**	52 57N	66 55W
Labranzagrande	**86**	5 33N	72 34W
Lábrea	**86**	7 15 S	64 51W
Labrède	**102**	44 41N	0 32W
Labrie	**42**	46 48N	70 56W
Labrieville	**41**	49 18N	69 34W
Labuan, I.	**126**	5 15N	115 38W
Labuha	**127**	0 30 S	127 30 E
Labuhan	**127**	6 26 S	105 50 E
Labuhanbajo	**127**	8 28 S	120 1 E
Labuk, Telok	**126**	6 10N	117 50 E
Lac Allard	**38**	50 33N	63 24W
Lac-Alouette	**43**	45 49N	73 58W
Lac-au-Saumon	**38**	48 25N	67 22W
Lac-aux-Sables	**41**	46 51N	72 24W
Lac Bouchette	**41**	48 16N	72 11W
Lac-Brière	**43**	45 50N	73 58W
Lac Carré	**41**	46 7N	74 29W
Lac-des-Écorces	**40**	46 34N	75 22W
Lac du Bonnet	**57**	50 15N	96 4W
Lac du Flambeau	**74**	46 1N	89 51W
Lac Édouard	**41**	47 40N	72 16W
Lac-Etchemin	**41**	46 24N	70 30W
Lac la Biche	**60**	54 45N	111 58W
Lac la Hache	**63**	51 49N	121 27W
Lac la Martre	**64**	63 8N	117 16W
Lac-l'Achigan	**43**	45 57N	73 59W
Lac-Lapierre	**43**	45 56N	73 47W
Lac-Marois	**43**	45 51N	74 8W
Lac-Meach	**48**	45 32N	75 51W
Lac-Mégantic	**41**	45 35N	70 53W
Lac-Millette	**43**	45 58N	74 12W
Lac-Rémi	**40**	46 1N	74 46W
Lac-St-Charles	**42**	46 54N	71 23W
Lac-Ste-Marie	**40**	45 57N	75 57W
Lac Seul	**55**	50 28N	92 0W
Lacadie	**45**	45 19N	73 21W
Lacanau, Étang de	**102**	44 58N	1 7W
Lacanau Médoc	**102**	44 59N	1 5W
Lacantum, R.	**83**	16 36N	90 40W
Lacaune	**102**	43 43N	2 40 E
Lacaune, Mts. de	**102**	43 43N	2 50 E
Laccadive Is. = Lakshadweep Is.	**118**	10 0N	72 30 E
Lacepede Is.	**134**	16 55 S	122 0 E
Lacey	**80**	47 7N	122 49W
Lachenaie	**45**	45 42N	73 33W
Lachine	**44**	45 30N	73 40W
Lachlan, R.	**136**	34 22 S	143 55 E
Lachute	**43**	45 39N	74 21W
Lackawanna	**70**	42 49N	78 50W
Laclu	**52**	49 46N	94 41W
Lacolle	**43**	45 5N	73 22W
Lacombe	**61**	52 30N	113 44W
Lacon	**76**	41 2N	89 24W
Lacona, U.S.A.	**76**	41 11N	93 23W
Lacona, N.Y., U.S.A.	**71**	43 37N	76 5W
Laconia	**71**	43 32N	71 30W
Lacq	**102**	43 25N	0 35W
Lacrosse	**78**	46 51N	117 58W
Ladd	**76**	41 23N	89 13W
Laddonia	**76**	39 15N	91 39W
Lādiz	**123**	28 55N	61 15 E
Ladner	**66**	49 5N	123 4W
Ladon	**101**	48 0N	2 30 E
Ladozhskoye Ozero	**120**	61 15N	30 30 E
Ladrone Is. = Mariana Is.	**14**	17 0N	145 0 E
Lady Ann Str.	**65**	75 40N	79 50W
Lady Beatrix L.	**34**	5 20N	76 50W
Ladysmith, Can.	**62**	49 0N	123 49W
Ladysmith, S. Afr.	**117**	28 32 S	29 46 E
Ladysmith, U.S.A.	**74**	45 27N	91 4W
Lae	**14**	6 40 S	147 2 E
Læsø	**111**	57 15N	10 53 E
Lafayette, U.S.A.	**77**	40 25N	86 54W
Lafayette, Colo., U.S.A.	**74**	40 0N	105 2W
Lafayette, Ga., U.S.A.	**73**	34 44N	85 15W
Lafayette, La., U.S.A.	**75**	30 18N	92 0W
Lafayette, Tenn., U.S.A.	**73**	36 35N	86 0W
Laferté	**34**	48 37N	78 48W
Laferte, R.	**54**	61 53N	117 44W
Lafia	**114**	8 30N	8 34 E
Laflamme, R.	**40**	49 17N	77 9W
Laflèche	**43**	45 30N	73 28W
Lafleche	**56**	49 45N	106 40W
Lafontaine	**43**	45 48N	74 1W
Laforce	**40**	47 32N	78 44W
Laforest	**34**	47 4N	81 12W
Lagan, R.	**97**	54 35N	5 55W
Lagarfljót	**110**	65 40N	14 18W
Lagarto, Serra do	**89**	23 0 S	57 15W
Lågen, R.	**111**	61 30N	10 20 E
Laghman □	**123**	34 20N	70 0 E
Laghouat	**114**	33 50N	2 59 E
Lagnieu	**103**	45 55N	5 20 E
Lagny	**101**	48 52N	2 40 E
Lagonoy Gulf	**127**	13 50N	123 50 E
Lagoon	**63**	48 25N	123 28W
Lagos, Nigeria	**114**	6 25N	3 27 E
Lagos, Port.	**104**	37 5N	8 41W
Lagos de Moreno	**82**	21 21N	101 55W
Lagrange	**77**	41 39N	85 25W
Laguépie	**102**	44 8N	1 57 E
Laguna, Brazil	**89**	28 30 S	48 50W
Laguna, U.S.A.	**79**	35 3N	107 28W
Laguna Beach	**81**	33 31N	117 52W
Laguna Dam	**79**	32 55N	114 30W
Laguna Limpia	**88**	26 32 S	59 45W
Laguna Madre	**83**	27 0N	97 20W
Lagunas, Chile	**88**	21 0 S	69 45W
Lagunas, Peru	**86**	5 10 S	75 35W
Lagunillas	**86**	10 8N	71 16W
Laha	**130**	48 9N	124 30 E
Lahad Datu	**127**	5 0N	118 30 E
Lahaina	**67**	20 52N	156 41W
Lahat	**126**	3 45 S	103 30 E
Lahewa	**126**	1 22N	97 12 E
Lahijan	**122**	37 10N	50 6 E
Lahn, R.	**106**	50 52N	8 35 E
Laholm	**111**	56 30N	13 2 E
Lahontan Res.	**78**	39 28N	118 58W
Lahore	**124**	31 32N	74 22 E
*Lahore □	**124**	31 55N	74 5 E
Lahti	**111**	60 58N	25 40 E
Lai (Béhagle)	**114**	9 25N	16 30 E
Lai Chau	**128**	22 5N	103 3 E
Laichow Wan	**130**	37 30N	119 30 E
Laidlaw	**63**	49 20N	121 36W
Laifeng	**131**	29 30N	109 30 E
L'Aigle	**100**	48 46N	0 38 E
Laignes	**101**	47 50N	4 20 E
Laila	**122**	22 10N	46 40 E
Laillahue, Mt.	**86**	17 0 S	69 30W
Laipin	**131**	23 45N	109 10 E
Laird	**56**	52 43N	106 35W
Lairg	**96**	58 1N	4 24W
Lais	**126**	3 35 S	102 0 E
Laiyang	**130**	37 0N	120 42 E
Laja, R.	**82**	20 55N	100 46W
Lajes	**89**	27 48 S	50 20W
Lakar	**127**	8 15 S	128 17 E
Lake Alma	**56**	49 9N	104 12W
Lake Alpine	**80**	38 29N	120 0W
Lake Andes	**74**	43 10N	98 32W
Lake Anse	**72**	46 42N	88 25W
Lake Arthur	**75**	30 8N	92 40W
Lake Bluff	**77**	42 17N	87 50W
Lake Bronson	**57**	48 44N	96 49W
Lake Cargelligo	**136**	33 15 S	146 22 E
Lake Charles	**75**	30 15N	93 10W
Lake City, Colo, U.S.A.	**79**	38 3N	107 27W
Lake City, Fla., U.S.A.	**73**	30 10N	82 40W
Lake City, Iowa, U.S.A.	**77**	42 12N	94 42W
Lake City, Mich., U.S.A.	**46**	44 20N	85 10W
Lake City, Minn., U.S.A.	**74**	44 28N	92 21W
Lake City, Pa., U.S.A.	**70**	42 2N	80 20W
Lake City, S.C., U.S.A.	**73**	33 51N	79 44W
Lake Cowichan	**62**	48 49N	124 3W
Lake District	**98**	54 30N	3 10W
Lake Forest	**77**	42 15N	87 50W
Lake Geneva	**77**	42 36N	88 26W
Lake George	**71**	43 25N	73 43W
Lake Harbour	**65**	62 30N	69 50W
Lake Havasu City	**81**	34 25N	114 29W
Lake Hill	**63**	48 28N	123 22W
Lake Hughes	**81**	34 41N	118 26W
Lake Isabella	**81**	35 38N	118 28W
Lake Lenore	**56**	52 24N	104 59W
Lake Linden	**52**	47 11N	88 26W
Lake Louise	**61**	51 30N	116 10W
Lake Mead Nat. Rec. Area	**81**	36 0N	114 30W
Lake Michigan Beach	**77**	42 13N	86 25W
Lake Mills, U.S.A.	**77**	43 5N	88 55W
Lake Mills, Iowa, U.S.A.	**74**	43 23N	93 33W
Lake Nebagamon	**52**	46 30N	91 42W
Lake Odesse	**77**	42 47N	85 8W
Lake of the Woods	**69**	49 0N	95 0W
Lake Orion	**77**	42 47N	83 14W
Lake Providence	**75**	32 49N	91 12W
Lake River	**34**	54 22N	82 31W
Lake St. Peter	**47**	45 18N	78 2W
Lake Superior Prov. Park	**53**	47 45N	84 45W
Lake Traverse	**34**	45 56N	78 4W
Lake Tyers	**136**	37 52 S	148 5 E
Lake Victoria Res.	**136**	34 0 S	141 17 E
Lake View	**50**	43 34N	79 33W
Lake Villa	**77**	42 25N	88 5W
Lake Village	**75**	33 20N	91 19W
Lake Wales	**73**	27 55N	81 32W
Lake Worth	**73**	26 36N	80 3W
Lakefield, Ont., Can.	**47**	44 25N	78 16W
Lakefield, Qué., Can.	**43**	45 45N	74 15W
Lakeland	**73**	28 0N	82 0W
Lakemba, I.	**133**	18 13 S	178 47W
Lakeport, Calif., U.S.A.	**80**	39 1N	122 56W
Lakeport, Mich., U.S.A.	**46**	43 7N	82 30W
Lakes Entrance	**136**	37 50 S	148 0 E
Lakeside, Ariz., U.S.A.	**79**	34 12N	109 59W
Lakeside, Calif., U.S.A.	**81**	32 52N	116 55W
Lakeside, Nebr., U.S.A.	**74**	42 5N	102 24W
Lakeview, Ont., Can.	**48**	45 21N	75 50W
Lakeview, Qué., Can.	**44**	45 53N	74 34W
Lakeview, Sask., Can.	**58**	50 25N	104 38W
Lakeview, Mich., U.S.A.	**46**	43 27N	85 17W
Lakeview, N.Y., U.S.A.	**72**	42 43N	78 57W
Lakeview, Oreg., U.S.A.	**78**	42 15N	120 22W
Lakewood, U.S.A.	**80**	48 9N	122 12W
Lakewood, Calif., U.S.A.	**81**	33 51N	118 8W
Lakewood, N.J., U.S.A.	**71**	40 5N	74 13W
Lakewood, Ohio, U.S.A.	**70**	41 28N	81 50W
Laki	**110**	64 4N	18 14W
Lakin	**75**	37 58N	101 18W
Lakitusaki, R.	**34**	54 21N	82 25W
Lakonikós Kólpos	**109**	36 40N	22 40 E
Lakor, I.	**127**	8 15 S	128 17 E
Lakota	**74**	48 0N	98 22W
Laksefjorden	**110**	70 45N	26 50 E
Lakselv	**110**	70 2N	24 56 E
Lakshadweep Is.	**118**	10 0N	72 30 E
Lalín	**104**	42 40N	8 5W
Lalinde	**102**	44 50N	0 44 E
Lamaline	**37**	46 52N	55 49W
Lamar, Colo., U.S.A.	**74**	38 9N	102 35W
Lamar, Mo., U.S.A.	**75**	37 30N	94 20W
Lamas	**86**	6 28 S	76 31W
Lamastre	**103**	44 59N	4 35 E
Lamatientze	**130**	46 46N	124 46 E
Lamballe	**100**	48 29N	2 31W
Lambaréné	**116**	0 20 S	10 12 E
Lambay I.	**97**	53 30N	6 0W
Lambayeque □	**86**	6 45 S	80 0W
Lambert	**74**	47 44N	104 39W
Lambert Land	**17**	79 12N	20 30W
Lambesc	**103**	43 39N	5 16 E
Lambeth	**46**	42 54N	81 18W
Lambi Kyun, (Sullivan I.)	**128**	10 50N	98 20 E
Lambton	**41**	45 50N	71 5W
Lambton, C.	**64**	71 5N	123 9W
Lambton Mills	**50**	43 39N	79 31W
Lame Deer	**78**	45 45N	106 40W
Lamego	**104**	41 5N	7 52W
Lamèque	**39**	47 45N	64 38W
Lamesa	**75**	32 45N	101 57W
Lamía	**109**	38 55N	22 41 E
Lamitan	**127**	6 40N	122 10 E
Lammermuir Hills	**96**	55 50N	2 40W
Lamming Mills	**63**	53 20N	120 15W
Lamoille	**78**	40 47N	115 31W
Lamon Bay	**127**	14 30N	122 20 E
Lamoni	**76**	40 37N	93 56W
Lamont, Can.	**60**	53 46N	112 50W
Lamont, U.S.A.	**76**	42 35N	91 40W
Lamont, Calif., U.S.A.	**81**	35 15N	118 55W
Lampa	**86**	15 10 S	70 30W
Lampang	**128**	18 18N	99 31 E
Lampasas	**75**	31 5N	98 10W
Lampaul	**100**	48 28N	5 7W
Lampazos de Naranjo	**82**	27 2N	100 32W
Lampedusa, I.	**108**	35 36N	12 40 E
Lampeter	**95**	52 6N	4 6W
Lampman	**56**	49 25N	102 50W
Lamprey	**55**	58 33N	94 8W
Lampung	**126**	1 48 S	115 0 E
Lamu	**116**	2 10 S	40 55 E
Lamy	**79**	35 30N	105 58W
Lan Tsan Kiang (Mekong)	**119**	18 0N	104 15 E
Lan Yu, I.	**131**	22 0N	121 30 E
Lanai City	**67**	20 50N	156 56W
Lanai I.	**67**	20 50N	156 55W
Lanao, L.	**127**	7 52N	124 15 E
Lanark, Can.	**47**	45 1N	76 22W
Lanark, U.K.	**96**	55 40N	3 48W
Lancashire □	**94**	53 40N	2 30W
Lancaster, N.B., Can.	**35**	45 17N	66 10W
Lancaster, Ont., Can.	**47**	45 8N	74 30W
Lancaster, Ont., Can.	**71**	45 10N	74 30W
Lancaster, Qué., Can.	**43**	45 8N	74 30W
Lancaster, U.K.	**94**	54 3N	2 48W
Lancaster, Calif., U.S.A.	**81**	34 47N	118 8W
Lancaster, Ky., U.S.A.	**77**	37 40N	84 40W
Lancaster, Minn., U.S.A.	**57**	48 52N	96 48W
Lancaster, Mo., U.S.A.	**76**	40 31N	92 32W
Lancaster, N.H., U.S.A.	**71**	44 27N	71 33W
Lancaster, N.Y., U.S.A.	**70**	42 53N	78 43W
Lancaster, Pa., U.S.A.	**71**	40 4N	76 19W
Lancaster, S.C., U.S.A.	**73**	34 45N	80 47W
Lancaster, Wis., U.S.A.	**76**	42 48N	90 43W
Lancaster Sd.	**65**	74 13N	84 0W
Lancer	**56**	50 48N	108 53W
Lanchow	**130**	36 4N	103 44 E
Lanciano	**108**	42 15N	14 22 E
Lándana	**116**	5 11 S	12 5 E
Landau	**105**	49 12N	8 7 E
Landeck	**106**	47 9N	10 34 E
Landen	**105**	50 45N	5 3 E
Lander	**78**	42 50N	108 49W
Landerneau	**100**	48 28N	4 17W
Landes □	**102**	43 57N	0 48W
Landes, Les	**102**	44 20N	1 0W
Landis	**56**	52 12N	108 27W
Landivisiau	**100**	48 31N	4 6W
Landrecies	**101**	50 7N	3 40 E
Landrienne	**40**	48 30N	77 50W
Land's End, Can.	**17**	76 10N	123 0W
Land's End, U.K.	**95**	50 4N	5 43W
Landshut	**106**	48 31N	12 10 E
Landskrona	**111**	56 53N	12 50 E
Lanesboro	**71**	41 57N	75 34W
Lanett	**73**	33 0N	85 15W
Lanfeng	**131**	34 50N	114 58 E
Lang Bay	**62**	49 45N	124 21W
Langara I.	**62**	54 14N	133 1W
Langchung (Paoning)	**131**	31 30N	106 0 E
Langdon	**74**	48 47N	98 24W
Langeac	**102**	45 7N	3 29 E
Langenburg	**57**	50 51N	101 43W
Langfeng	**130**	48 4N	121 10 E
Langford	**63**	48 27N	123 29W
Langham	**56**	52 22N	106 58W
Langholm	**96**	55 9N	2 59W
Langjökull	**110**	64 39N	20 12W
Langkawi, P.	**128**	6 25N	99 45 E
Langkon	**126**	6 30N	116 40 E
Langlade, Can.	**34**	48 14N	76 10W
Langlade, St. P. & M.	**37**	46 50N	56 20W
Langley	**66**	49 7N	122 39W
Langlois	**78**	42 54N	124 26W
Langogne	**102**	44 43N	3 50 E
Langon	**102**	44 33N	0 16W
Langøya	**110**	68 45N	15 10 E
Langres	**101**	47 52N	5 20 E
Langres, Plateau de	**101**	47 45N	5 20 E
Langruth	**57**	50 23N	98 40W
Langsa	**126**	4 30N	97 57 E
Langson	**128**	21 52N	106 42 E
Langstaff	**50**	43 50N	79 25W
Langtry	**75**	29 50N	101 33W
Languedoc	**102**	43 58N	4 0 E
Lanigan	**56**	51 51N	105 2W
Lannemezan	**102**	43 8N	0 23 E
Lannilis	**100**	48 35N	4 32W
Lannion	**100**	48 46N	3 29W
Lanoraie	**43**	45 58N	73 13W
Lanouaille	**102**	45 24N	1 9 E
Lansdale	**71**	40 14N	75 18W
Lansdowne	**47**	44 24N	76 1W
Lansdowne House	**34**	52 14N	87 53W
Lansford	**71**	40 48N	75 55W
Lansing, Can.	**50**	43 45N	79 25W
Lansing, U.S.A.	**77**	42 47N	84 40W
Lanslebourg	**103**	45 17N	6 52 E
Lantuna	**127**	8 19 S	124 8 E
Lanus	**88**	34 44 S	58 27W
Lanz I.	**62**	50 49N	128 41W
Lanzville	**62**	49 15N	124 5W
Lao Cai	**128**	22 30N	103 57 E
Laoag	**127**	18 7N	120 34 E
Laoang	**127**	12 32N	125 8 E
Laois □	**97**	53 0N	7 20W

* *Now part of Punjab*

Laon Lewisburg

Laon	101	49 33N	3 35E
Laona	72	45 32N	88 41W
Laos ■	128	17 45N	105 0E
Lapa	89	25 46S	49 44W
Lapalisse	102	46 15N	3 44E
Laparan Cap, I.	127	6 0N	120 0E
Lapeer	46	43 3N	83 20W
Lapi □	110	67 0N	27 0E
Lapland = Lappland	110	68 7N	24 0E
Laporte	71	41 27N	76 30W
Lappland	110	68 7N	24 0E
Laprairie	44	45 20N	73 30W
Laprairie □	43	45 20N	73 30W
Laprida	88	37 34S	60 45W
Laptev Sea	121	76 0N	125 0E
Lapush	78	47 56N	124 33W
Lār	123	27 40N	54 14E
Lara □	86	10 10N	69 50W
Laragne-Monteglin	103	44 18N	5 49E
Laramie	74	41 15N	105 29W
Laramie Mts.	74	42 0N	105 30W
Laranjeiras do Sul	89	25 23S	52 23W
Larantuka	127	8 5S	122 55E
Larap	127	14 18N	122 39E
Larat, I.	127	7 0S	132 0E
Larder Lake	34	48 5N	79 40W
Laredo	75	27 34N	99 29W
Laredo Sd.	62	52 30N	128 53W
Laren	105	52 16N	5 14E
Largentière	103	44 34N	4 18E
Largs	96	55 48N	4 51W
Lariang	127	1 35S	119 25E
Larimore	74	47 55N	97 35W
Lárisa	109	39 38N	22 28E
Lark Harbour	37	49 6N	58 23W
Lark, R.	95	52 26N	0 18E
Larnaca	122	35 0N	33 35E
Lárnax	122	35 0N	33 35E
Larne	97	54 52N	5 50W
Larne □	97	54 55N	5 55W
Larned	74	38 15N	99 10W
Laroquebrou	102	44 58N	2 12E
Larrimah	134	15 35S	133 12E
Larrys River	39	45 13N	61 23W
Larsen Ice Shelf	91	67 0S	62 0W
Larus L.	52	51 17N	94 40W
Larvik	111	59 4N	10 0E
Laryak	120	61 15N	80 0E
Larzac, Causse du	102	44 0N	3 17E
Las Animas	75	38 8N	103 18W
Las Bonitas	86	7 50N	65 40W
Las Brenãs	88	27 5S	61 7W
Las Cascadas	84	9 5N	79 41W
Las Chimeneas	81	32 12N	116 5W
Las Cruces	79	32 25N	106 50W
Las Flores	88	36 0S	59 0W
Las Heras, Mendoza, Argent.	89	32 51S	68 49W
Las Heras, Santa Cruz, Argent.	90	46 30S	69 0W
Las Lajas	90	38 30S	70 25W
Las Lajitas	86	6 55N	65 39W
Las Lomitas	88	24 35S	60 50W
Las Mercedes	86	9 7N	66 24W
Las Palmas	88	27 8S	58 45W
Las Palmas □	114	28 10N	15 28W
Las Palmas, R.	81	32 8N	116 33W
Las Piedras	88	34 35S	56 20W
Las Plumas	90	43 40S	67 15W
Las Rosas	88	32 30S	61 40W
Las Tablas	84	7 49N	80 14W
Las Termas	88	27 29S	64 52W
Las Tres Marias, Is.	82	20 12N	106 30W
Las Varillas	88	32 0S	62 50W
Las Vegas, Nev., U.S.A.	81	36 10N	115 5W
Las Vegas, N.M., U.S.A.	79	35 35N	105 10W
Lasalle	44	45 26N	73 38W
Lascano	89	33 35S	54 18W
Lascaux	102	45 5N	1 10E
Lashburn	56	53 10N	109 40W
Lashio	125	22 56N	97 45E
Lasqueti	62	49 30N	124 21W
Lasqueti I.	62	49 29N	124 16W
Lassay	100	48 27N	0 30W
Lassen, Pk.	78	40 35N	121 40W
Last Mountain L.	56	51 5N	105 14W
Lastchance Cr.	80	40 2N	121 15W
Lastoursville	116	0 55S	12 38E
Lastovo, I.	108	42 46N	16 55E
Latacunga	86	0 50S	78 35W
Latakia = Al Lādhiquiyah	122	35 30N	35 45E
Latchford	34	47 20N	79 50W
Lathrop	76	39 33N	94 20W
Lathrop Wells	81	36 39N	116 24W
Latina	108	41 26N	12 53E
Lating	130	39 23N	118 55E
Laton	80	36 26N	119 41W
Latouche	67	60 0N	148 0W
Latouche Treville, C.	134	18 27S	121 49E
Latrobe, Austral.	136	38 8S	146 44E
Latrobe, U.S.A.	70	40 19N	79 21W
Latulipe	40	47 26N	79 2W
Lau (Eastern) Group	133	17 0S	178 30W
Lauchhammer	106	51 35N	13 40E
Lauenburg	106	53 23N	10 33E
Laugarbakki	110	65 20N	20 55W
Launceston, Austral.	135	41 24S	147 8E
Launceston, U.K.	95	50 38N	4 21W
Laune, R.	97	52 5N	9 40W
Launglon Bok	128	13 50N	97 54E
Laura	135	15 32S	144 32E
Laurel, Ont., Can.	49	43 57N	80 13W
Laurel, Qué., Can.	43	45 51N	74 28W
Laurel, U.S.A.	77	39 31N	85 11W
Laurel, Miss., U.S.A.	75	31 50N	89 0W
Laurel, Mont., U.S.A.	78	45 46N	108 49W
Laurencekirk	96	56 50N	2 30W
Laurens	73	34 32N	82 2W
Laurentian Plat.	36	52 0N	70 0W
Laurentides	43	45 51N	73 46W
Laurentides, Parc Prov. des	41	47 45N	71 15W
Laurie I.	91	60 0S	46 0W
Laurie L.	55	56 35N	101 57W
Laurier	57	50 53N	99 33W
Laurier-Station	41	46 32N	71 38W
Laurierville	41	46 18N	71 39W
Laurinburg	73	34 50N	79 25W
Laurium	52	47 14N	88 26W
Lausanne	106	46 32N	6 38E
Laut Kecil, Kepulauan	126	4 45S	115 40E
Laut, Kepulauan	126	4 45N	108 0E
Lautoka	133	17 37S	177 27E
Lauzon	42	46 48N	71 10W
Lava Hot Springs	78	42 38N	112 1W
Laval, Can.	44	45 35N	73 45W
Laval, France	100	48 4N	0 48W
Laval-des-Rapides	44	45 33N	73 42W
Laval-Ouest	44	45 33N	73 52W
Laval-sur-le-Lac	44	45 32N	73 52W
Lavalle	88	28 15S	65 15W
Lavaltrie	43	45 53N	73 17W
Lavandou, Le	103	43 8N	6 22E
Lavant Sta.	47	45 3N	76 42W
Lavardac	102	44 12N	0 20E
Lavaur	102	43 42N	1 49E
Lavaveix	102	46 5N	2 8E
Lavelanet	102	42 57N	1 51E
Laverendrye Prov. Park	34	46 15N	17 15W
Laverlochère	40	47 26N	79 18W
Laverne	75	36 43N	99 58W
Laverton	134	28 44S	122 29E
Lavieille, L.	47	45 51N	78 14W
Lavillètte	39	47 16N	65 18W
Lavoy	60	53 27N	111 52W
Lavras	89	21 20S	45 0W
Lavrentiya	121	65 35N	171 0W
Lávrion	109	37 40N	24 4E
Lawas	126	4 55N	115 40E
Lawele	127	5 16S	123 3E
Lawn	37	46 57N	55 35W
Lawrence, Austral.	89	29 30S	153 8E
Lawrence, U.S.A.	77	39 50N	86 2W
Lawrence, Kans., U.S.A.	74	39 0N	95 10W
Lawrence, Mass., U.S.A.	71	42 40N	71 9W
Lawrence Station	39	45 26N	67 11W
Lawrenceburg, Ind., U.S.A.	77	39 5N	84 50W
Lawrenceburg, Ky., U.S.A.	77	38 2N	84 54W
Lawrenceburg, Tenn., U.S.A.	73	35 12N	87 19W
Lawrencetown	39	44 53N	65 10W
Lawrenceville, U.S.A.	77	38 44N	87 41W
Lawrenceville, Ga., U.S.A.	73	33 55N	83 59W
Laws	80	37 24N	118 20W
Lawson	76	39 26N	94 12W
Lawton, U.S.A.	75	34 33N	98 25W
Lawton, U.S.A.	77	42 10N	85 50W
Lawu Mt.	127	7 40S	111 13E
Laxford, L.	96	58 25N	5 10W
Laytonville	78	39 44N	123 29W
Lazio □	108	42 10N	12 30E
Lea, R.	95	51 40N	0 3W
Leach I.	53	47 28N	84 57W
Lead	74	44 20N	103 40W
Leader	56	50 50N	109 30W
Leadhills	96	55 25N	3 47W
Leadville	79	39 17N	106 23W
Leaf L.	57	53 1N	102 8W
Leaf, R., Can.	36	58 47N	70 4W
Leaf, R., U.S.A.	75	31 45N	89 20W
Leakey	75	29 45N	99 45W
Leaksville	73	36 30N	79 49W
Lealui	117	15 10S	23 2E
Leamington, Can.	46	42 3N	82 36W
Leamington, N.Z.	14	37 55S	175 29E
Leamington, U.K.	95	52 18N	1 32W
Leamington, U.S.A.	78	39 37N	112 17W
Leandro Norte Alem	89	27 34S	55 15W
Learmonth	134	22 40S	114 10E
Leaside	50	43 42N	79 22W
Leask	56	53 5N	106 45W
Leavenworth, Mo., U.S.A.	74	39 25N	95 0W
Leavenworth, Wash., U.S.A.	78	47 44N	120 37W
Leavenworthth	77	38 12N	86 21W
Leawood	76	38 57N	94 37W
Lebak	127	6 32N	124 5E
Lebam	80	46 34N	123 33W
Lebanon, Ill., U.S.A.	76	38 38N	89 49W
Lebanon, Ind., U.S.A.	77	40 3N	86 20W
Lebanon, Kans., U.S.A.	74	39 50N	98 35W
Lebanon, Ky., U.S.A.	72	37 35N	85 15W
Lebanon, Mo., U.S.A.	76	37 40N	92 40W
Lebanon, N.H., U.S.A.	71	43 38N	72 15W
Lebanon, Ohio, U.S.A.	77	39 26N	84 13W
Lebanon, Oreg., U.S.A.	78	44 31N	122 57W
Lebanon, Pa., U.S.A.	71	40 20N	76 28W
Lebanon, Tenn., U.S.A.	73	36 15N	86 20W
Lebanon ■	122	34 0N	36 0E
Lebanon Junction	77	37 50N	85 44W
Lebbeke	105	51 0N	4 8E
Lebec	81	34 46N	118 59W
Lebel-sur-Quévillon	40	49 3N	76 59W
Lebrija	104	36 53N	6 5W
Lebu	88	37 40S	73 47W
Lecce	109	40 20N	18 10E
Lecco	108	45 50N	9 27E
Lectoure	102	43 56N	0 38E
Łeczyca	107	52 5N	19 45E
Ledbury	95	52 3N	2 25W
Leduc	60	53 15N	113 30W
Lee, Mass., U.S.A.	71	42 17N	73 18W
Lee, Nev., U.S.A.	78	40 35N	115 36W
Lee, R.	97	51 51N	9 2W
Lee Vining	80	37 58N	119 7W
Leech L., Can.	56	51 5N	102 28W
Leech L., U.S.A.	52	47 9N	94 23W
Leedey	75	35 53N	99 24W
Leeds, U.K.	94	53 48N	1 34W
Leeds, U.S.A.	73	33 32N	86 30W
Leek	94	53 7N	2 2W
Lee's Summit	76	38 55N	94 23W
Leesburg, U.S.A.	77	39 21N	83 33W
Leesburg, Fla., U.S.A.	73	28 47N	81 52W
Leesville	75	31 12N	93 15W
Leetonia	70	40 53N	80 45W
Leeuwarden	105	53 15N	5 48E
Leeuwin, C.	134	34 20S	115 9E
Leeward Is.	85	16 30N	63 30W
Lefebvre	41	47 12N	69 49W
Lefors	75	35 30N	100 50W
Lefroy	46	44 16N	79 34W
Lefroy, L.	134	31 21S	121 40E
Legal	60	53 55N	113 45W
Légère	39	47 25N	64 56W
Leghorn = Livorno	108	43 32N	10 18E
Legnica	106	51 12N	16 10E
Leh	124	34 15N	77 35E
Lehi	78	40 20N	112 0W
Lehighton	71	40 50N	75 44W
Lehua, I.	67	22 1N	160 6W
Leicester	95	52 39N	1 9W
Leicester □	95	52 40N	1 10W
Leichhardt, R.	135	17 50S	139 49E
Leichow = Haihang	131	20 55N	110 3E
Leichow Pantao	131	20 30N	110 0E
Leiden	105	52 9N	4 30E
Leie, R.	105	51 2N	3 45E
Leigh Creek	135	30 28S	138 24E
Leigh, R.	136	37 50S	144 0E
Leine, R.	106	52 35N	9 40E
Leinster □	97	53 0N	7 10W
Leinster Downs	70	27 52S	120 34E
Leinster, Mt.	97	52 38N	6 47W
Leipzig	106	51 20N	12 23E
Leiria	104	39 46N	8 53W
Leishan	131	25 55N	108 15E
Leith	96	55 59N	3 10W
Leith Hill	95	51 10N	0 23W
Leitrim, Can.	48	45 20N	75 36W
Leitrim, Ireland	97	54 0N	8 5W
Leitrim □	97	54 8N	8 0W
Leiyang	131	26 27N	112 50E
Lejeune	41	47 46N	68 34W
Lek, R.	105	51 54N	4 38E
Leksula	127	3 46S	126 31E
Leland	75	33 25N	90 52W
Leland Lakes	55	60 0N	110 59W
Leleque	90	42 15S	71 0W
Lelystad	105	52 30N	5 25E
Léman, Lac	106	46 26N	6 30E
Lemay	76	38 20N	90 16W
Lemberg	56	50 44N	103 12W
Lemery	127	13 58N	120 56E
Lemesós	122	34 42N	33 1E
Lemhi Ra.	78	44 30N	113 30W
Lemieux	41	46 18N	72 7W
Lemieux Is.	65	63 40N	64 20W
Lemieux, L.	40	50 19N	74 38W
Lemmer	105	52 51N	5 43E
Lemmon	74	45 59N	102 10W
Lemoine, L.	40	48 0N	78 0W
Lemon Grove	81	32 45N	117 2W
Lemont	77	41 40N	88 0W
Lemoore	80	36 23N	119 46W
Lemoyne	45	45 30N	73 30W
Lempdes	102	45 22N	3 17E
Lemvig	111	56 33N	8 20E
Lena, R.	121	64 30N	127 0E
Lencloître	100	46 50N	0 20E
Lengau de Vaca, Punta	88	30 14S	71 38W
Lenggong	128	5 6N	100 58E
Leninabad	120	40 17N	69 37E
Leninakan	120	41 0N	42 50E
Leningrad	120	59 55N	30 20E
Leninogorsk	120	50 20N	83 30E
Leninsk-Kuznetskiy	120	55 10N	86 10E
Leninskoye	121	47 56N	132 38E
Lenmalu	127	1 58S	130 0E
Lennoxville	41	45 22N	71 51W
Lenoir	73	35 55N	81 36W
Lenoir City	73	35 40N	84 20W
Lenora	74	39 39N	100 1W
Lenore L.	56	52 30N	104 59W
Lenox, U.S.A.	76	40 53N	94 34W
Lenox, Mass., U.S.A.	71	42 20N	73 18W
Lens	101	50 26N	2 50E
Lensk (Mukhtuya)	121	60 48N	114 55E
Lentini	108	37 18N	15 0E
Lenwood	81	34 53N	117 7W
Leoben	106	47 22N	15 5E
Leola	74	45 47N	98 58W
Leominster, U.K.	95	52 15N	2 43W
Leominster, U.S.A.	71	42 32N	71 45W
Léon	102	43 53N	1 18W
León, Mexico	82	21 7N	101 30W
León, Nic.	84	12 20N	86 51W
León, Spain	104	42 38N	5 34W
Leon	76	40 40N	93 40W
León □	104	42 40N	5 55W
León, Montañas de	104	42 30N	6 18W
Leonardtown	72	38 19N	76 39W
Leongatha	136	38 30S	145 58E
Leonora	134	28 49S	121 19E
Léopold II, Lac = Mai-Ndombe	116	2 0S	18 0E
Leopoldina	89	21 28S	42 40W
Leopoldsburg	105	51 7N	5 13E
Léopoldville = Kinshasa	116	4 20S	15 15E
Leoti	74	38 31N	101 19W
Leoville	56	53 39N	107 33W
Lepellé, R.	36	59 58N	72 24W
Lepikha	121	64 45N	125 55E
Lepreau	39	45 10N	66 28W
Lerdo	82	25 32N	103 32W
Lérida	104	41 37N	0 39E
Lérins, Is. de	103	43 31N	7 3E
Lérouville	101	48 50N	5 30E
Leroy	56	52 0N	104 44W
Leroy, L.	36	55 10N	67 15W
Lerwick	96	60 10N	1 10W
Léry	44	45 21N	73 48W
Leskov, I.	91	56 0S	28 0W
Leskovac	109	43 0N	21 58E
Leslie, U.S.A.	77	42 27N	84 26W
Leslie, Ark., U.S.A.	75	35 50N	92 35W
Leslieville	61	52 23N	114 36W
Lesneven	100	48 35N	4 20W
Lesotho ■	117	29 40S	28 0E
Lesozavodsk	121	45 30N	133 20E
Lesparre-Médoc	102	45 18N	0 57W
Lessay	100	49 14N	1 30W
Lesse, R.	105	50 15N	4 54E
Lesser Antilles	85	12 30N	61 0W
Lesser Slave L.	60	55 30N	115 25W
Lesser Slave Lake Prov. Park	60	55 26N	114 49W
Lessines	105	50 42N	3 50E
Lester	80	47 12N	121 29W
Lestock	56	51 19N	103 59W
Lésvos, I.	109	39 0N	26 20E
Leszno	106	51 50N	16 30E
Letchworth	95	51 58N	0 13W
Lethbridge, Alta., Can.	61	49 45N	112 45W
Lethbridge, Newf., Can.	37	48 22N	53 52W
Leti	127	8 10S	127 40E
Leti, Kepulauan	127	8 10S	128 0E
Leticia	86	4 0S	70 0W
Letsôk-aw-Kyun (Domel I.)	128	11 30N	98 25E
Letterkenny	97	54 57N	7 42W
Leucadia	81	33 4N	117 18W
Leucate	102	42 56N	3 3E
Leucate, Étang de	102	42 50N	3 0E
Leuser, G.	126	4 0N	96 51E
Leuven (Louvain)	105	50 52N	4 42E
Leuze	105	50 36N	3 37E
Levack	46	46 38N	81 23W
Levan	78	39 37N	111 32W
Levanger	110	63 45N	11 19E
Levelland	75	33 38N	102 17W
Leven	96	56 12N	3 0W
Leven, L.	96	56 12N	3 22W
Levens	103	43 50N	7 12E
Leveque C.	134	16 20S	123 0E
Levering	46	45 38N	84 47W
Leverkusen	105	51 2N	6 59E
Levet	101	46 56N	2 22E
Levick, Mt.	91	75 0S	164 0E
Levie	103	41 40N	9 7E
Levier	101	46 58N	6 8E
Levin	133	40 37S	175 18E
Lévis	42	46 48N	71 9W
Levis, L.	54	62 37N	117 58W
Levittown	71	40 10N	74 51W
Levkás, I.	109	38 40N	20 43E
Levkôsia = Nicosia	122	35 10N	33 25E
Levroux	101	47 0N	1 38E
Lewellen	74	41 22N	102 5W
Lewes, U.K.	95	50 53N	0 2E
Lewes, U.S.A.	72	38 45N	75 8W
Lewis, Butt of	96	58 30N	6 12W
Lewis Hills	37	48 48N	58 30W
Lewis, I.	96	58 10N	6 40W
Lewis, R.	80	45 51N	122 48W
Lewis Range	78	48 0N	113 15W
Lewisburg, U.S.A.	77	39 51N	84 33W

Lewisburg Lobstick L

Lewisburg, Pa., U.S.A. 70 40 57N 76 57W
Lewisburg, Tenn., U.S.A. 73 35 29N 86 46W
Lewisport 77 37 56N 86 54W
Lewisporte 37 49 15N 55 3W
Lewiston, Idaho, U.S.A. 78 46 30N 117 0W
Lewiston, Mich., U.S.A. 46 44 53N 84 18W
Lewiston, N.Y., U.S.A. 49 43 12N 79 2W
Lewiston, Utah, U.S.A. 78 41 58N 111 56W
Lewistown, Ill., U.S.A. 76 40 24N 90 9W
Lewistown, Mont., U.S.A. 78 47 0N 109 25W
Lewistown, Pa., U.S.A. 70 40 37N 77 33W
Lewisville 39 46 6N 64 46W
Lexington, Ill., U.S.A. 77 40 37N 88 47W
Lexington, Ky., U.S.A. 77 38 6N 84 30W
Lexington, Mich., U.S.A. 46 43 15N 82 30W
Lexington, Miss., U.S.A. 75 33 8N 90 2W
Lexington, Mo., U.S.A. 76 39 7N 93 55W
Lexington, N.C., U.S.A. 73 35 50N 80 13W
Lexington, Nebr., U.S.A. 74 40 48N 99 45W
Lexington, Ohio, U.S.A. 70 40 39N 82 35W
Lexington, Oreg., U.S.A. 78 45 29N 119 46W
Lexington, Tenn., U.S.A. 73 35 38N 88 25W
Leyte, I. 127 11 0N 125 0E
Lezay 102 46 17N 0 0E
Lèze, R. 102 43 28N 1 25E
Lézignan-Corbières 102 43 13N 2 43E
Lezoux 102 45 49N 3 21E
Lhasa 129 29 50N 91 3E
Lhatse Dzong 129 29 10N 87 45E
Lhokseumawe 126 5 20N 97 10E
Liang Liang 127 5 58N 121 30E
Lianga 127 8 38N 126 6E
Liangpran, Gunong 126 1 0N 114 23E
Liangsiang 130 39 55N 116 15E
Liao Ho, R. 130 41 0N 121 55E
Liaocheng 130 36 30N 115 59E
Liaochung 130 41 35N 122 45E
Liaoning □ 130 41 40N 122 30E
Liaotung 130 40 10N 123 0E
Liaotung Wan 130 40 0N 120 45E
Liaoyang 130 41 15N 123 10E
Liaoyüan 130 42 55N 125 10E
Liard, R. 54 61 51N 121 18W
Libby 78 48 20N 115 10W
Libenge 116 3 40N 18 55E
Liberal, Kans., U.S.A. 75 37 4N 101 0W
Liberal, Mo., U.S.A. 75 37 35N 94 30W
Liberec 106 50 47N 15 7E
Liberia 84 10 40N 85 30W
Liberia ■ 114 6 30N 9 30W
Libertad 86 8 20N 69 37W
Libertad, La 84 16 47N 90 7W
Liberty, Can. 56 51 8N 105 26W
Liberty, U.S.A. 77 39 38N 84 56W
Liberty, Mo., U.S.A. 76 39 15N 94 24W
Liberty, N.Y., U.S.A. 71 41 48N 74 45W
Liberty, Tex., U.S.A. 75 30 5N 94 50W
Liberty Center 77 41 27N 84 1W
Libertyville 77 42 18N 87 57W
Libiya, Sahrâ' 112 27 35N 25 0E
Libourne 102 44 55N 0 14W
Libreville 116 0 25N 9 26E
Libya ■ 114 28 30N 17 30E
Licantén 88 34 55S 72 0W
Licata 108 37 6N 13 55E
Lichfield 94 52 40N 1 50W
Lichtenburg 117 26 8S 26 8E
Lida 79 37 30N 117 30W
Liddon Gulf 64 75 3N 113 0W
Lidköping 111 58 31N 13 14E
Liechtenstein ■ 106 47 8N 9 35E
Liège 105 50 38N 5 35E
Liège □ 105 50 32N 5 35E
Lienhua 131 26 58N 113 59E
Lienkiang 131 26 11N 119 30E
Lienshankwan 130 41 0N 123 59E
Lienyunkang 131 34 45N 119 30E
Lienz 106 46 50N 12 46E
Liepāja 120 56 30N 21 0E
Lier 105 51 7N 4 34E
Lieshankwan 130 40 56N 124 51E
Liévin 101 50 24N 2 47E
Lièvre, R. 40 45 31N 75 26W
Liffey, R. 97 53 21N 6 20W
Lifford 97 54 50N 7 30W
Liffré 100 48 12N 1 30W
Ligny-en-Barrois 101 48 36N 5 20E
Ligny-le-Châtel 101 47 54N 3 45E
Ligua, La 88 32 30S 71 16W
Liguria □ 108 44 30N 9 0E
Ligurian Sea 108 43 20N 9 0E
Lihou Reefs and Cays 135 17 25S 151 40E
Lihue 67 21 59N 159 24W
Likasi 116 10 55S 26 48E
Likati 116 3 20N 24 0E
Likely 63 52 37N 121 35W
Likiang 129 26 50N 100 15E
Likunpu 130 36 31N 106 12E
Liling 131 27 47N 113 30E
Lille 101 50 38N 3 3E
Lille Bælt 111 55 30N 9 45E
Lillebonne 100 49 30N 0 32E
Lillehammer 111 61 8N 10 30E
Lillers 101 50 35N 2 28E
Lillesand 111 58 15N 8 23E
Lillestrøm 111 59 58N 11 5E
Lillian L. (Daré, Le, L.) 38 51 17N 61 23W
Lillooet 63 50 44N 121 57W
Lillooet L. 63 50 18N 122 35W
Lillooet, R. 63 49 15N 121 57W
Lilongwe 117 14 0S 33 48E
Liloy 127 8 4N 122 39E
Lima, Austral. 136 36 44S 146 10E
Lima, Indon. 127 3 37S 128 4E
Lima, Peru 86 12 0S 77 0W
Lima, Mont., U.S.A. 78 44 41N 112 38W
Lima, Ohio, U.S.A. 77 40 42N 84 5W
Limages 71 45 20N 75 16W
Limassol 122 34 42N 33 1E
Limavady 97 55 3N 6 58W
Limavady □ 97 55 0N 6 55W
Limay Mahuida 88 37 10S 66 45W
Limay, R. 90 39 40S 69 45W
Limbang 126 4 42N 115 6E
Limbour 48 45 29N 75 45W
Limbourg □ 105 51 2N 5 25E
Limburg □ 108 51 20N 5 55E
Limehouse 49 43 38N 79 58W
Limeira 89 22 35S 47 28W
Limerick, Can. 56 49 39N 106 16W
Limerick, Ireland 97 52 40N 8 38W
Limerick □ 97 52 30N 8 50W
Limestone 70 42 2N 78 39W
Limestone B. 57 53 50N 98 53W
Limestone, R. 55 56 31N 94 7W
Limfjorden 111 56 55N 9 0E
Limia, R. 104 41 55N 8 8W
Limko 131 20 57N 109 43E
Limmen Bight 134 14 40S 135 35E
Limnos, I. 109 39 50N 25 5E
Limoeiro do Norte 87 5 5S 38 0W
Limoges, Can. 47 45 20N 75 15W
Limoges, France 102 45 50N 1 15E
Limón 85 10 0N 83 2W
Limon, Panama 84 9 20N 79 45W
Limon, U.S.A. 74 39 18N 103 38W
Limon B. 84 9 22N 79 56W
Limousin 102 46 0N 1 0E
Limousin, Plateau du 102 46 0N 1 0E
Limoux 102 43 4N 2 12E
Limpopo, R. 117 23 15S 32 5E
Limuru 116 1 2S 36 35E
Linares 88 35 50S 71 40W
Linàres 86 1 23N 77 31W
Linares, Mexico 83 24 50N 99 40W
Linares, Spain 104 38 10N 3 40W
Linares □ 88 36 0S 71 0W
Linaria 60 54 19N 114 8W
Linch'eng 130 37 26N 114 34E
Lincheng 131 37 20N 114 30E
Lincoln, Argent. 88 34 55N 61 30W
Lincoln, Can. 49 43 10N 79 29W
Lincoln, N.Z. 133 43 38S 172 30E
Lincoln, U.K. 94 53 14N 0 32W
Lincoln, Calif., U.S.A. 80 38 54N 121 17W
Lincoln, Ill., U.S.A. 76 40 10N 89 20W
Lincoln, Kans., U.S.A. 74 39 6N 98 9W
Lincoln, Maine, U.S.A. 35 45 27N 68 29W
Lincoln, Mich., U.S.A. 46 44 41N 83 25W
Lincoln, N. Mex., U.S.A. 79 33 30N 105 26W
Lincoln, Nebr., U.S.A. 74 40 50N 96 42W
Lincoln □ 94 53 14N 0 32W
Lincoln Park 77 42 15N 83 11W
Lincoln Sea 17 84 0N 55 0W
Lincoln Wolds 94 53 20N 0 5W
Lincolnton 73 35 30N 81 15W
Lincolnville 39 45 30N 61 33W
Lind 78 47 0N 118 33W
Linda 80 39 6N 121 34W
Lindell Beach 63 49 2N 122 1W
Linden, Can. 61 51 36N 113 28W
Linden, Guyana 86 6 0N 58 10W
Linden, U.S.A. 77 40 11N 86 54W
Linden, Calif., U.S.A. 80 38 1N 121 5W
Linden, Mich., U.S.A. 46 42 49N 83 47W
Linden, Tex., U.S.A. 75 33 0N 94 20W
Lindi 116 9 58S 39 38E
Lindsay, Can. 47 44 22N 78 43W
Lindsay, Calif., U.S.A. 80 36 14N 119 6W
Lindsay, Okla., U.S.A. 75 34 51N 97 37W
Lindsborg 74 38 35N 97 40W
Linea de la Concepción, La 104 36 15N 5 23W
Lineville 76 40 35N 93 31W
Linfen 130 36 0N 111 30E
Lingayer 127 16 1N 120 14E
Lingayer G. 127 16 10N 120 15E
Lingen 105 52 32N 7 21E
Lingga, Kepulauan 126 0 10S 104 30E
Linghsien, Hunan, China 130 26 26N 113 45E
Linghsien, Shantung, China 130 37 21N 116 34E
Lingle 74 42 10N 104 18W
Lingling 131 26 15N 111 40E
Linglo 131 24 20N 105 25E
Lingshan 131 22 26N 109 17E
Lingshih 130 36 55N 111 45E
Lingshui 131 18 27N 110 0E
Lingt'ai 131 35 4N 107 37E
Linguéré 114 15 25N 15 5W
Linh Cam 128 18 31N 105 31E
Linhai 131 28 50N 121 8E
Linho 130 40 50N 107 30E
Linhsien 130 37 57N 110 57E
Lini 131 35 5N 118 20E
Linière 41 46 4N 70 32W
Link L. 62 52 25N 127 40W
Linkian 130 41 57N 126 59E
Linkiang 129 46 2N 133 56E
Linköping 111 58 28N 15 36E
Linkow 130 45 16N 130 18E
Linlithgow 96 55 58N 3 38W
Linn 76 38 29N 91 51W
Linn, Mt. 78 40 0N 123 0W
Linneus 76 39 53N 93 11W
Linney Head 95 51 37N 5 4W
Linnhe, L. 96 56 36N 5 25W
Linping 131 24 25N 114 32E
Lins 89 21 40S 49 44W
Linsi 130 43 30N 118 5E
Linsia 129 35 50N 103 0E
Lintan 129 34 37N 103 40E
Lintao 130 35 16N 103 38E
Lintien 129 46 8N 124 58E
Lintlaw 56 52 4N 103 14W
Linton, Ont., Can. 50 43 56N 79 40W
Linton, Qué., Can. 41 47 15N 72 16W
Linton, Ind., U.S.A. 77 39 0N 87 10W
Linton, N. Dak., U.S.A. 74 46 21N 100 12W
Lintsing 130 36 50N 115 45E
Lintung 130 43 59N 119 8E
Linwood 46 43 35N 80 43W
Linwu 131 25 25N 112 10E
Linxe 102 43 56N 1 13W
Linyi 130 37 10N 116 50E
Linz, Austria 106 48 18N 14 18E
Linz, Ger. 106 50 33N 7 18E
Lion-d'Angers, Le 100 47 37N 0 43W
Lion, G. du 102 43 0N 4 0E
Lion's Head 34 44 58N 81 15W
Lioyang 131 33 30N 106 0E
Lipari, Is. 108 38 40N 15 0E
Lipetsk 120 52 45N 39 35E
Liping 131 26 12N 109 0E
Lipo 131 25 33N 107 45E
Lippe, R. 105 51 40N 7 20E
Lipscomb 75 36 16N 100 28W
Lipton 56 50 54N 103 51W
Liptrap C. 136 38 50S 145 55E
Lira 116 2 17N 32 57E
Liria 104 39 37N 0 35W
Lisala 116 2 12N 21 38E
Lisboa 104 38 42N 9 10W
Lisbon, N. Dak., U.S.A. 74 46 30N 97 46W
Lisbon, N.H., U.S.A. 71 44 13N 71 52W
Lisbon, Ohio, U.S.A. 70 40 45N 80 42W
Lisbon = Lisboa 104 38 42N 9 10W
Lisburn 97 54 30N 6 9W
Lisburn □ 97 54 30N 6 5W
Lisburne, C. 67 68 50N 166 0W
Liscannor 97 52 57N 9 24W
Liscannor, B. 97 52 57N 9 24W
Liscomb 35 45 2N 62 0W
Lishih 130 37 30N 111 7E
Lishui 131 28 27N 119 54E
Lisianski I. 14 25 30N 174 0W
Lisieux 100 49 10N 0 12E
Lisle-sur-Tarn 102 43 52N 1 49E
Lismore, Austral. 135 37 58S 143 21E
Lismore, Ireland 97 52 8N 7 58W
Lisse 105 52 16N 4 33E
Lista, Norway 111 58 7N 6 39E
Lista, Sweden 111 59 19N 16 16E
Lister, Mt. 91 78 0S 162 0E
Listowel, Can. 46 43 44N 80 58W
Listowel, Ireland 97 52 27N 9 30W
Lit-et-Mixe 102 44 2N 1 15W
Litang, China 131 23 6N 109 2E
Litang, Malay. 127 5 27N 118 31E
Litchfield, Calif., U.S.A. 80 40 24N 120 23W
Litchfield, Conn., U.S.A. 71 41 44N 73 12W
Litchfield, Ill., U.S.A. 76 39 10N 89 40W
Litchfield, Minn., U.S.A. 74 45 5N 94 40W
Lithgow 136 33 25S 150 8E
Lithinon, Ákra 109 34 55N 24 44E
Lithuania S.S.R. □ 120 55 30N 24 0E
Litoměrice 106 50 33N 14 10E
Little Abaco I. 73 26 50N 77 30W
Little Abitibi, R. 53 50 29N 81 32W
Little America 91 79 0N 160 0W
Little Andaman I. 128 10 40N 92 15E
Little Barrier I. 133 36 12S 175 8E
Little Bay 37 49 36N 55 57W
Little Belt Mts. 78 46 50N 111 0W
Little Blue, R. 74 40 18N 97 45W
Little Bow, R. 61 49 53N 112 29W
Little Burnt Bay 37 49 25N 55 5W
Little Cadotte, R. 60 56 41N 117 6W
Little Cayman, I. 84 19 41N 80 3W
Little Churchill, R. 55 57 30N 95 22W
Little Coco I. 128 14 0N 93 15E
Little Colorado, R. 79 36 0N 111 31W
Little Corners 49 43 20N 80 17W
Little Current 46 45 55N 82 0W
Little Current, R. 53 50 57N 84 36W
Little Dover 39 45 15N 61 3W
Little Falls, Minn., U.S.A. 74 45 58N 94 19W
Little Falls, N.Y., U.S.A. 71 43 3N 74 50W
Little Fork, R. 52 48 31N 93 35W
Little Fort 63 51 26N 120 13W
Lit. Grand Rapids 57 52 0N 95 29W
Lit. Humboldt, R. 78 41 20N 117 27W
Lit. Inagua I. 85 21 40N 73 50W
Little Lake 81 35 58N 117 58W
Little Longlac 34 49 42N 86 58W
Little Marais 74 47 24N 91 8W
Little Mecatinà I. 35 50 30N 59 25W
Little Minch 96 57 35N 6 45W
Lit. Missouri R. 74 46 40N 103 50W
Little Narrows 39 45 59N 60 59W
Little Ouse, R. 95 52 25N 0 50E
Little Pic, R. 53 48 48N 86 37W
Little Quill L. 56 51 55N 104 5W
Little Red, R. 75 35 40N 92 15W
Little River 133 43 45S 172 49E
Little Rock 75 34 41N 92 10W
Little Rouge, R. 51 43 48N 79 8W
Little Sable Pt. 72 43 40N 86 32W
Little Sioux, R. 67 42 20N 95 55W
Little Smoky, R. 60 54 44N 117 11W
Little Snake, R. 78 40 45N 108 15W
Little Valley 70 42 15N 78 48W
Little Wabash, R. 77 38 40N 88 20W
Little Whale, R. 34 55 50N 75 0W
Little White, R. 46 46 23N 83 20W
Little York 76 41 1N 90 45W
Littlefield 75 33 57N 102 17W
Littlefork 74 48 24N 93 35W
Littlehampton 95 50 48N 0 32W
Littleton 71 44 19N 71 47W
Liuan 131 31 49N 116 29E
Liucheng 131 24 5N 109 3E
Liuchow 131 24 10N 109 10E
Liupa 131 33 40N 107 0E
Liupan Shan 130 35 40N 106 10E
Liuwa Plain 117 14 20S 22 30E
Livarot 100 49 0N 0 9E
Live Oak, Calif., U.S.A. 80 39 17N 121 40W
Live Oak, Fla., U.S.A. 73 30 17N 83 0W
Lively 46 46 26N 81 9W
Livermore 80 37 41N 121 47W
Livermore, Mt. 75 30 45N 104 8W
Liverpool, Austral. 136 33 54S 150 58E
Liverpool, Can. 39 44 5N 64 41W
Liverpool, U.K. 94 53 25N 3 0W
Liverpool Bay, Can. 67 70 0N 128 0W
Liverpool Bay, U.K. 98 53 30N 3 20W
Liverpool, C. 65 73 38N 78 6W
Liverpool Plains 136 31 15S 150 15E
Liverpool Ra. 136 31 50S 150 30E
Livingston, Guat. 84 15 50N 88 50W
Livingston, U.S.A. 76 42 54N 90 26W
Livingston, Calif., U.S.A. 80 37 23N 120 43W
Livingston, Mont., U.S.A. 78 45 40N 110 40W
Livingstone 75 30 44N 94 54W
Livingstone I. 91 63 0S 60 15W
Livingstone (Maramba) 117 17 46S 25 52E
Livingstonia 116 10 38S 34 5E
Livny 120 52 30N 37 30E
Livonia 46 42 25N 83 23W
Livorno 108 43 32N 10 18E
Livramento 89 30 55S 55 30W
Livron-sur-Drôme 103 44 46N 4 51E
Liwale 116 9 48S 37 58E
Lizard Pt. 95 49 57N 5 11W
Ljubljana 108 46 4N 14 33E
Ljungan, R. 110 62 30N 14 30E
Ljungby 111 56 49N 13 55E
Ljusdal 111 61 46N 16 3E
Ljusnan, R. 111 62 0N 15 20E
Ljusne 111 61 13N 17 7E
Llancanelo, Salina 88 35 40S 69 8W
Llandovery 95 51 59N 3 49W
Llandrindod Wells 95 52 15N 3 23W
Llandudno 94 53 19N 3 51W
Llanelli 95 51 41N 4 11W
Llanes 104 43 25N 4 50W
Llangollen 94 52 58N 3 10W
Llanidloes 95 52 28N 3 31W
Llano Estacado 68 34 0N 103 0W
Llano R. 75 30 50N 99 0W
Llanos 86 3 25N 71 35W
Llaoyang 130 41 14N 123 6E
Llera 83 23 19N 99 1W
Llico 88 34 46S 72 5W
Llobregat, R. 104 41 19N 2 9E
Lloret de Mar 104 41 41N 2 53E
Lloyd L. 55 57 22N 108 57W
Lloydminster 56 53 17N 110 0W
Lloyds, R. 37 48 35N 57 15W
Lloydtown 50 43 59N 79 42W
Llullaillaco, volcán 88 24 30S 68 30W
Lo Ho 131 34 15N 111 10E
Loa 79 38 18N 111 46W
Loa, R. 88 21 30S 70 0W
Lobatse 117 25 12S 25 40E
Lobería 88 38 10S 58 40W
Lobito 117 12 18S 13 35E
Lobos 88 35 2S 59 0W
Lobos, I. 82 21 27N 97 13W
Lobstick L. 36 54 0N 65 12W

Loc Binh **Lufkin**

Loc Binh 128 21 46N 106 54 E
Loc Ninh 128 11 50N 106 34 E
Locarno 106 46 10N 8 47 E
Lochaber 96 56 55N 5 0W
Lochdale 66 49 17N 122 58W
Loche, La 55 56 29N 109 26W
Loche, La, L. 55 56 40N 109 30W
Lochem 105 52 9N 6 26 E
Loches 100 47 7N 1 0 E
Lochgelly 96 56 7N 3 18W
Lochgilphead 96 56 2N 5 37W
Lochnagar, Mt. 96 56 57N 3 14W
Lochwan 130 35 59N 109 30 E
Lochy, R. 96 56 52N 5 3W
Lock Haven 70 41 7N 77 31W
Lockeford 80 38 10N 121 9W
Lockeport 39 43 47N 65 4W
Lockerbie 96 55 7N 3 21W
Lockhart 75 29 55N 97 40W
Lockport, U.S.A. 77 41 35N 88 3W
Lockport, N.Y., U.S.A. 70 43 12N 78 42W
Locminé 100 47 54N 2 51W
Locronan 100 48 7N 4 15W
Loctudy 100 47 50N 4 12W
Locust Cr. 76 39 40N 93 17W
Lod 115 31 57N 34 54 E
Loddon, R. 136 35 31 S 143 51 E
Lodève 102 43 44N 3 19 E
Lodge Grass 78 45 21N 107 27W
Lodgepole, Can. 61 53 6N 115 19W
Lodgepole, U.S.A. 74 41 12N 102 40W
Lodgepole Cr. 74 41 20N 104 30W
Lodhran 124 29 32N 71 30 E
Lodi 80 38 12N 121 16W
Lodja 116 3 30 S 23 23 E
Lodji 127 1 38 S 127 28 E
Lodwar 116 3 10N 35 40 E
Łodz 107 51 45N 19 27 E
Lofoten Is. 110 68 30N 15 0 E
Logan, Kans., U.S.A. 74 39 40N 99 35W
Logan, Ohio, U.S.A. 72 39 25N 82 22W
Logan, Utah, U.S.A. 78 41 45N 111 50W
Logan I. 52 50 7N 88 27W
Logan, Mount 38 48 53N 66 38W
Logan, Mt. 67 60 41N 140 22W
Logan Pass 61 48 41N 113 44W
Logandale 81 36 36N 114 29W
Logansport, U.S.A. 77 40 45N 86 22W
Logansport, La., U.S.A. 72 31 58N 93 58W
Loggieville 39 47 4N 65 23W
Logroño 104 42 28N 2 32W
Logy Bay 37 47 38N 52 40W
Lohardaga 125 23 27N 84 45 E
Loho 131 33 33N 114 5 E
Lohrville 76 42 17N 94 33W
Loikaw 125 19 40N 97 17 E
Loimaa 111 60 50N 23 5 E
Loir-et-Cher □ 101 47 40N 1 20 E
Loire □ 103 45 40N 4 5 E
Loire-Atlantique □ 100 47 25N 1 40W
Loire, R. 100 47 16N 2 10W
Loiret □ 101 47 58N 2 10 E
Loja, Ecuador 86 3 59 S 79 16W
Loja, Spain 104 37 10N 4 10W
Lokandu 116 2 30 S 25 45 E
Lokchong 131 25 15N 113 0 E
Lokeren 105 51 6N 3 59 E
Lokitaung 116 4 12N 35 48 E
Lokka 110 67 49N 27 45 E
Løkken 110 63 8N 9 45 E
Lokoja 114 7 47N 6 45 E
Lokolama 116 2 35 S 19 50 E
Loktung 131 18 41N 109 5 E
Lokwei 131 19 12N 110 30 E
Lola, Mt. 80 39 26N 120 22W
Loliondo 116 2 2 S 35 39 E
Lolland 111 54 45N 11 30 E
Lolo 78 46 50N 114 8W
Lom 109 43 48N 23 20 E
Loma 78 47 59N 110 29W
Loma Linda 81 34 3N 117 16W
Lomami, R. 116 1 0 S 24 40 E
Lomas de Zamóra 88 34 45 S 58 25W
Lombard, U.S.A. 77 41 53N 88 1W
Lombard, Mont., U.S.A. 78 46 7N 111 28W
Lombardia □ 108 45 35N 9 45 E
Lombardy = Lombardia 108 45 35N 9 45 E
Lombez 102 43 29N 0 55 E
Lomblen, I. 127 8 30 S 123 32 E
Lombok, I. 126 8 35 S 116 20 E
Lomé 114 6 9N 1 20 E
Lomela 116 2 5 S 23 52 E
Lomela, R. 116 1 30 S 22 50 E
Lometa 75 31 15N 98 25W
Lomie 116 3 13N 13 38 E
Lommel 105 51 14N 5 19 E
Lomond 61 50 24N 112 36W
Lomond, L. 96 56 8N 4 38W
Lompobatang, mt. 127 5 24 S 119 56 E
Lompoc 81 34 41N 120 32W
Łomza 107 53 10N 22 2 E
Loncoche 90 39 20 S 72 50W
Londa 124 15 30N 74 30 E
Londe, La 103 43 8N 6 14 E
Londinières 100 49 50N 1 25 E
London, Can. 46 42 59N 81 15W
London, U.K. 95 51 30N 0 5W
London, Ky., U.S.A. 72 37 11N 84 5W
London, Ohio, U.S.A. 77 39 54N 83 28W
London □ 95 51 30N 0 5W
London Mills 76 40 43N 90 11W
Londonderry, Can. 39 45 29N 63 36W
Londonderry, U.K. 97 55 0N 7 20W
Londonderry, C. 134 13 45 S 126 55 E
Londonderry, Co. 97 55 0N 7 20W
Londonderry, I. 90 55 0 S 71 0W
Londrina 89 23 0 S 51 10W
Lone Butte 63 51 33N 121 12W
Lone Pine, Can. 60 54 18N 115 7W
Lone Pine, U.S.A. 80 36 35N 118 2W
Lone Rock 56 53 3N 109 53W
Lonely I. 46 45 34N 81 28W
Long Beach, Can. 62 49 1N 125 40W
Long Beach, Calif., U.S.A. 81 33 46N 118 12W
Long Beach, N.Y., U.S.A. 71 40 35N 73 40W
Long Beach, Wash., U.S.A. 80 46 20N 124 1W
Long Branch, Can. 50 43 35N 79 32W
Long Branch, U.S.A. 71 40 19N 74 0W
Long Cr. 56 49 7N 102 59W
Long Eaton 94 52 54N 1 16W
Long I., Bahamas 85 23 20N 75 10W
Long I., Newf., Can. 37 47 34N 55 59W
Long I., N.W.T., Can. 36 54 50N 79 20W
Long I., U.S.A. 71 40 50N 73 20W
Long I. Sd. 71 41 10N 73 0W
Long L., Alta., Can. 60 54 22N 112 46W
Long L., Ont., Can. 53 49 30N 86 50W
Long L., U.S.A. 71 43 57N 74 25W
Long Lake, Can. 39 44 36N 63 38W
Long Lake, U.S.A. 46 44 25N 83 52W
Long Mynd 98 52 35N 2 50W
Long Pine 74 42 33N 99 50W
Long Pt., Man., Can. 57 53 2N 98 25W
Long Pt., Newf., Can. 37 48 47N 58 46W
Long Pt., Ont., Can. 46 42 38N 80 8W
Long Pt., Ont., Can. 46 42 35N 80 2W
Long Point B. 46 42 40N 80 10W
Long Pt. Bay 70 42 40N 80 20W
Long Range Mts 37 48 0N 58 30W
Long Range Mts. 37 49 30N 57 30W
Long Reach 39 45 28N 66 5W
Long Str. 17 70 0N 175 0 E
Long Xuyen 128 10 19N 105 28 E
Longeau 101 47 47N 5 20 E
Longford 97 53 43N 7 50W
Longford □ 97 53 42N 7 45W
Longhawan 126 2 15N 114 55 E
Longiram 126 0 5 S 115 45 E
Longlac 53 49 45N 86 25W
Longlegged L. 52 50 46N 94 8W
Longmont 74 40 10N 105 4W
Longnawan 126 21 50N 114 55 E
Longreach 135 23 28 S 144 14 E
Longs Peak 78 40 20N 105 50W
Longué 100 47 22N 0 8W
Longue-Pointe-de-Mingan 38 50 16N 64 9W
Longueuil, Can. 71 45 32N 73 28W
Longueuil, Qué., Can. 45 45 32N 73 30W
Longueuil-St-Hubert 43 45 29N 73 26W
Longuyon 101 49 27N 5 35 E
Longview, Can. 61 50 32N 114 10W
Longview, Tex., U.S.A. 75 32 30N 94 45W
Longview, Wash., U.S.A. 80 46 9N 122 58W
Longwy 101 49 30N 5 45 E
Loning 131 34 28N 111 42 E
Löningen 105 54 43N 7 44 E
Lonoke 75 34 48N 91 57W
Lonouaille 102 46 30N 1 35 E
Lons-le-Saunier 101 46 40N 5 31 E
Lønsdal 110 66 46N 15 26 E
Looc 127 12 20N 112 5 E
Loogootee 77 38 41N 86 55W
Lookout, C., Can. 34 55 18N 83 56W
Lookout, C., U.S.A. 73 34 30N 76 30W
Loomis 55 49 15N 108 45W
Loon L. 55 44 50N 77 15W
Loon Lake 56 54 2N 109 10W
Loon, R., Alta., Can. 60 57 8N 115 3W
Loon, R., Man., Can. 55 55 53N 101 59W
Loop Hd. 97 52 34N 9 55W
Lop Nor 129 40 20N 90 10 E
Lopatina, G. 121 50 0N 143 30 E
Lopei 130 47 40N 131 12 E
Lopez C. 116 0 47 S 8 40 E
Lopez I. 63 48 30N 122 54W
Lopphavet 110 70 27N 21 15 E
Lora, R. 124 32 0N 67 15 E
Lorain 70 41 20N 82 55W
Loraine 76 40 9N 91 13W
Loralai 124 30 29N 68 30 E
Lorca 104 37 41N 1 42W
Lord Howe I. 14 31 33 S 159 6 E
Lord Selkirk 58 49 56N 97 11W
Lord's Cove 37 46 53N 55 40W
Lordsburg 79 32 15N 108 45W
Loreburn 56 51 13N 106 36W
Loreto, Brazil 87 7 5 S 45 30W
Loreto, Italy 108 43 26N 13 36 E
Loreto, Mexico 82 26 1N 111 21W
Lorette 57 49 44N 96 52W
Loretteville 42 46 51N 71 21W
Lorgues 103 43 28N 6 22 E
Lorica 86 9 14N 75 49W
Lorient 100 47 45N 3 23W
Lorimor 76 41 7N 94 3W
Lorne, Austral. 136 38 33 S 143 59 E
Lorne, Can. 39 47 53N 66 8W
Lorne, U.K. 96 56 26N 5 10W
Lorne, Firth of 96 56 20N 5 40W
Lorne Park 50 43 32N 79 36W
Lorraine, Can. 44 45 41N 73 47W
Lorraine, France 101 49 0N 6 0 E
Lorrainville 40 47 21N 79 23W
Los Alamos, Calif., U.S.A. 81 34 44N 120 17W
Los Alamos, N. Mex., U.S.A. 79 35 57N 106 17W
Los Altos 80 37 23N 122 7W
Los Andes 88 32 50 S 70 40W
Los Ángeles 88 37 28 S 72 23W
Los Angeles 81 34 0N 118 10W
Los Angeles Aqueduct 81 35 25N 118 0W
Los Banos 80 37 8N 120 56W
Los Blancos 88 23 45 S 62 30W
Los Gatos 80 37 15N 121 59W
Los Lamentos 82 30 36N 105 50W
Los Lunas 79 34 55N 106 47W
Los Mochis 82 25 45N 109 5W
Los Olivos 81 34 40N 120 7W
Los Palacios 84 22 35N 83 15W
Los Reyes 82 19 21N 99 7W
Los Roques, Is. 85 11 50N 66 45W
Los Testigos, Is. 86 11 23N 63 6W
Los Vilos 88 32 0 S 71 30W
Loshing 131 24 45N 108 58 E
Loshkalakh 121 62 45N 147 20 E
Lošinj, I. 108 44 30N 14 30 E
Lossiemouth 96 57 43N 3 17W
Lost River 43 45 50N 74 33W
Lot □ 102 44 39N 1 40 E
Lot-et-Garonne □ 102 44 22N 0 30 E
Lot, R. 102 44 18N 0 20 E
Lota 88 37 5 S 73 10W
Lothiers 101 46 42N 1 33 E
Loting 131 22 46N 111 34 E
Lott Cr. 59 51 0N 114 13W
Loudéac 100 48 11N 2 47W
Loudon 73 35 35N 84 22W
Loudonville 70 40 40N 82 15W
Loudun 100 47 0N 0 5 E
Loué 100 47 59N 0 9W
Loue, R. 100 47 4N 6 10 E
Loughborough 94 52 46N 1 11W
Lougheed 61 52 44N 111 33W
Lougheed I. 64 77 26N 105 6W
Loughrea 97 53 11N 8 33W
Loughros More, B. 97 54 48N 8 30W
Louhans 103 46 38N 5 12 E
Louis Creek 63 51 8N 120 7W
Louis Trichardt 117 23 0 S 29 55 E
Louis XIV, Pte. 36 54 37N 79 45W
Louisa 72 38 5N 82 40W
Louisa, L. 43 45 46N 74 25W
Louisbourg 39 45 55N 60 0W
Louisbourg Nat. Historic Park 39 45 58N 60 20W
Louisburg 76 38 37N 94 41W
Louisdale 39 45 36N 61 4W
Louise I. 62 52 55N 131 40W
Louiseville 41 46 20N 72 56W
Louisiade Arch. 14 11 10 S 153 0 E
Louisiana 76 39 25N 91 0W
Louisiana □ 75 30 50N 92 0W
Louisville, Ky., U.S.A. 77 38 15N 85 45W
Louisville, Miss., U.S.A. 75 33 7N 89 3W
Loulay 102 46 3N 0 30W
Loulé 104 37 9N 8 0W
Lount L. 55 50 10N 94 20W
Loup City 74 41 19N 98 57W
Loupe, La 100 48 29N 1 1 E
Loups Marins, Lacs des 36 56 30N 73 45W
Lourdes, Can. 37 48 39N 59 0W
Lourdes, France 102 43 6N 0 3W
Lourdus-du-Blanc-Sablon 37 51 24N 57 12W
Lourenço-Marques = Maputo 117 25 58 S 32 32 E
Louroux Béconnais, Le 100 47 30N 0 55W
Louth, Ireland 97 53 47N 6 33W
Louth, U.K. 94 53 23N 0 0W
Louth □ 97 53 55N 6 30W
Louvière, La 105 50 27N 4 10 E
Louviers 100 49 12N 1 10 E
Love 56 53 29N 104 10W
Loveland, U.S.A. 77 39 16N 84 16W
Loveland, Colo., U.S.A. 74 40 27N 105 4W
Lovell 78 44 51N 108 20W
Lovelock 78 40 17N 118 25W
Loverna 56 51 40N 110 0W
Loves Park 76 42 19N 89 3W
Loviisa = Lovisa 111 60 31N 26 20 E
Lovilia 76 41 8N 92 55W
Loving 75 32 17N 104 4W
Lovington, U.S.A. 77 39 43N 88 38W
Lovington, N.Mex., U.S.A. 75 33 0N 103 20W
Low 40 45 50N 76 0W
Low, C. 65 63 7N 85 18W
Low L. 36 55 54N 67 5W
Low Rocky Pt. 135 42 59 S 145 29 E
Lowa 116 1 25 S 25 47 E
Lowden 76 41 52N 90 56W
Lowe Farm 57 49 21N 97 35W
Lowell, Ind., U.S.A. 77 41 18N 87 25W
Lowell, Mass., U.S.A. 71 42 38N 71 19W
Lowell, Mich., U.S.A. 77 42 56N 85 20W
Lower Arrow L. 63 49 40N 118 5W
Lower Capilano 66 49 19N 123 7W
Lower Hutt 133 41 10 S 174 55 E
Lower L. 78 41 17N 120 3W
Lower Lake 80 38 56N 122 36W
Lower Manitou L. 52 49 15N 93 0W
Lower Neguac 35 47 20N 65 10W
Lower Nicola 63 50 12N 120 54W
Lower Post 54 59 58N 128 30W
Lower Red L. 52 48 0N 94 50W
Lower Sackville 35 44 45N 63 43W
Lower Seal, L. 34 56 30N 74 23W
Lower West Pubnico 39 43 38N 65 48W
Lower Wood Harbour 39 43 31N 65 44W
Lowestoft 95 52 29N 1 44 E
Łowicz 107 52 6N 19 55 E
Lowry City 76 38 8N 93 44W
Lowther 53 49 32N 83 2W
Lowville 71 43 48N 75 30W
Loxton 135 34 28 S 140 31 E
Loyalton 80 39 41N 120 14W
Loyalty Is. 14 21 0 S 167 30 E
Loyang 131 34 41N 112 28 E
Loyauté, Îles 14 21 0 S 167 30 E
Loyüan 131 26 25N 119 33 E
Loyung 131 24 25N 109 25 E
Lozère □ 102 44 35N 3 30 E
Lu-ta 130 39 0N 121 31 E
Lü-ta (Dairen-P. Arthur) 130 39 0N 121 31 E
Lü-Tao 131 22 47N 121 20 E
Luabo 85 18 30 S 36 10 E
Luacano 116 11 15 S 21 37 E
Lualaba, R. 116 5 45 S 26 50 E
Luan 127 6 10N 124 25 E
Luan Chau 128 21 38N 103 24 E
Luanda 116 8 58 S 13 9 E
Luang Prabang 128 19 45N 102 10 E
Luangwa, R. 117 14 25 S 30 25 E
Luanshya 117 13 3 S 28 28 E
Luapula, R. 116 12 0 S 28 50 E
Luarca 104 43 32N 6 32W
Luashi 116 10 50 S 23 36 E
Lubalo 116 9 10 S 19 15 E
Lubang Is. 127 13 50N 120 12 E
Lubbock 75 33 40N 101 55W
Lübeck 106 53 52N 10 41 E
Lubefu 116 4 47 S 24 27 E
Lubicon L. 60 56 23N 115 56W
Lubicon Lake 60 56 22N 115 52W
Lublin 107 51 12N 22 38 E
Lubny 120 50 3N 32 58 E
Lubok Antu 126 1 3N 111 50 E
Lubuagan 127 17 21N 121 10 E
Lubudi 116 6 50 S 21 20 E
Lubuhanbilik 126 2 33N 100 14 E
Lubuk Linggau 126 3 15 S 102 55 E
Lubuk Sikaping 126 0 10N 100 15 E
Lubumbashi 117 11 32 S 27 28 E
Lubutu 116 0 45 S 26 30 E
Luc-en-Diois 103 44 36N 5 28 E
Luc, Le 103 43 23N 6 21 E
Lucan 46 43 11N 81 24W
Lucania, Mt. 67 60 48N 141 25W
Lucca 108 43 50N 10 30 E
Luce Bay 96 54 45N 4 48W
Lucea 84 18 25N 78 10W
Lucedale 73 30 55N 88 34W
Lucena, Phil. 127 13 56N 121 37 E
Lucena, Spain 104 37 27N 4 31W
Lučenec 107 48 18N 19 42 E
Lucerne, Can. 63 52 52N 118 33W
Lucerne, Calif., U.S.A. 80 39 6N 122 48W
Lucerne, Wash., U.S.A. 63 48 12N 120 36W
Lucerne = Luzern 106 47 3N 8 18 E
Lucerne Valley 81 34 27N 116 57W
Lucero 82 30 49N 106 30W
Luceville 41 48 32N 68 22W
Luchow 131 28 57N 105 26 E
Lucira 117 14 0 S 12 35 E
Luck L. 56 51 5N 107 5W
Luckenwalde 106 52 5N 13 11 E
Luckey 77 41 27N 83 29W
Lucknow, Can. 46 43 57N 81 31W
Lucknow, India 125 26 50N 81 0 E
Lucky Lake 56 50 59N 107 8W
Luçon 102 46 28N 1 10W
Lüdenscheid 105 51 13N 7 38 E
Lüderitz 117 26 41 S 15 8 E
Ludhiana 124 30 57N 75 56 E
Ludington 72 43 58N 86 27W
Ludlow, Can. 39 46 29N 66 21W
Ludlow, U.K. 95 52 23N 2 42W
Ludlow, Calif., U.S.A. 81 34 43N 116 10W
Ludlow, Vt., U.S.A. 71 43 25N 72 40W
Ludvika 111 60 8N 15 14 E
Ludwigsburg 106 48 53N 9 11 E
Ludwigshafen 106 49 27N 8 27 E
Luebo 116 5 21 S 21 17 E
Luepa 86 5 43N 61 31W
Lufira R. 116 9 30 S 27 0 E
Lufkin 75 31 25N 94 40W

Luga Madre de Dios, R

Luga 120 58 40N 29 55 E
Lugano 106 46 0N 8 57 E
Lugansk = Voroshilovgrad 120 48 35N 39 29 E
Lugnaquilla, Mt. 97 52 48N 6 28W
Lugo 104 43 2N 7 35W
Lugoj 107 45 42N 21 57 E
Lugovoy 120 43 0N 72 20 E
Luiana 117 17 25 S 22 30W
Luichow = Haihang 131 20 55N 110 3 E
Luichow Pantao 131 20 30N 110 0 E
Luipa 131 33 43N 107 2 E
Luis 82 26 36N 109 11W
Luis Correia 87 3 0 S 41 35W
Luiza 116 7 40 S 22 30 E
Luján 88 34 45 S 59 5W
Lukang 131 24 0N 120 19 E
Lukanga Swamp 117 14 30 S 27 40 E
Lukenie, R. 116 3 0 S 18 50 E
Luki 131 28 10N 109 58 E
Lukolela 116 1 10 S 17 12 E
Łukow 107 51 58N 22 22 E
Lukulu 117 14 35 S 23 25 E
Lule, R. 110 65 35N 22 10 E
Luleå 110 65 35N 22 10 E
Lüleburgaz 122 41 23N 27 28 E
Luling 75 29 45N 97 40W
Lulonga, R. 116 1 0N 19 0 E
Lulu I. 66 49 10N 123 5W
Lulua, R. 117 6 30 S 22 50 E
Luluabourg = Kananga 116 5 55 S 22 18 E
Lulung 130 39 55N 118 57 E
Lumai 117 13 20 S 21 25 E
Lumajang 127 8 8 S 113 16 E
Lumbala N'guimbo 117 12 36 S 22 30 E
Lumberton, Miss., U.S.A. 75 31 4N 89 28W
Lumberton, N. Mex., U.S.A. 79 36 58N 106 57W
Lumberton, N.C., U.S.A. 73 34 37N 78 59W
Lumbres 101 50 40N 2 5 E
Lumby 54 50 10N 118 50W
Lumege 117 11 45 S 20 50 E
Lummi I. 63 48 42N 122 40W
Lumsden, Newf., Can. 37 49 19N 53 37W
Lumsden, Sask., Can. 56 50 39N 104 52W
Lumsden, N.Z. 133 45 44 S 168 27 E
Lumut 128 4 13N 100 37 E
Lumut, Tg. 126 3 50 S 105 58 E
Lun 130 47 55N 105 1 E
Lund, Can. 62 49 59N 124 45W
Lund, U.S.A. 78 38 53N 115 0W
Lundar 57 50 42N 98 2W
Lundazi 117 12 20 S 33 7 E
Lundbreck 61 49 35N 114 10W
Lundu 126 1 40N 109 50 E
Lundy, I. 95 51 10N 4 41W
Lune, R. 94 54 0N 2 51W
Lüneburg 106 53 15N 10 23 E
Lüneburg Heath = Lüneburger Heide 106 53 0N 10 0 E
Lüneburger Heide 106 53 0N 10 0 E
Lunel 103 43 39N 4 9 E
Lünen 105 51 36N 7 31 E
Lunenburg 39 44 22N 64 18W
Lunéville 101 48 36N 6 30 E
Lungan 131 23 10N 107 42 E
Lungchuan 131 24 1N 116 8 E
Lungch'uan 131 24 6N 115 15 E
Lungholt 110 63 35N 18 10 E
Lunghsien 131 34 47N 107 0 E
Lunghwa 130 41 15N 117 51 E
Lungkiang 130 47 22N 123 4 E
Lungkow 130 37 40N 120 25 E
Lungleh 125 22 55N 92 45 E
Lunglin 131 24 43N 105 26 E
Lungmoon 131 23 50N 114 18 E
Lungshan 131 29 26N 109 31 E
Lungsheng 131 25 58N 110 0 E
Lungsi 130 35 0N 104 35 E
Lungteh 130 35 30N 106 5 E
Lungtsin 131 22 20N 106 52 E
Lungyan 131 25 6N 117 2 E
Luni 124 26 0N 73 6 E
Luni, R. 124 25 40N 72 20 E
Luning 78 38 30N 118 10W
Luofu 116 0 1 S 29 15 E
Luozi 116 4 54 S 14 0 E
Luqa 108 35 48N 14 27 E
Luque 88 25 19 S 57 25W
Luray 72 38 39N 78 26W
Lure 101 47 40N 6 30 E
Luremo 116 8 30 S 17 50 E
Lurgan 97 54 28N 6 20W
Luristan 122 33 20N 47 0 E
Lusaka 117 15 28 S 28 16 E
Lusambo 116 4 58 S 23 28 E
Luscar 61 53 4N 117 24W
Luseland 56 52 5N 109 24W
Lushan, Kweichow, China 131 26 33N 107 58 E
Lushan, Szechwan, China 131 30 10N 102 59 E
Lushih 131 34 4N 110 2 E
Lushoto 116 4 47 S 38 20 E
Lüshun 130 38 48N 121 16 E
Lusignan 102 46 26N 0 8 E
Lusigny-sur-Barse 101 48 16N 4 15 E
Lusk 74 42 47N 104 27W
Lussac-les-Châteaux 102 46 24N 0 43 E
Luther, L. 49 43 56N 80 26W
Luton 95 51 53N 0 24W
Lutong 126 4 30N 114 0 E
Lutsk 120 50 50N 25 15 E
Luverne 76 43 35N 96 12W
Luwingu, Mt. 116 10 15 S 30 2 E
Luwuk 127 10 0 S 122 40 E
Luxembourg 105 49 37N 6 9 E
Luxembourg □ 105 49 58N 5 30 E
Luxembourg ■ 105 50 0N 6 0 E
Luxeuil-les-Bains 101 47 49N 6 24 E
Luy-de-Béarn, R. 102 43 39N 0 48W
Luy-de-France, R. 102 43 39N 0 48W
Luy, R. 102 43 39N 1 9W
Luz-St-Sauveur 102 42 53N 0 1 E
Luzern 106 47 3N 8 18 E
Luziânia 87 16 20 S 48 0W
Luzon, I. 127 16 0N 121 0 E
Luzy 101 46 47N 3 58 E
Lvov 120 49 40N 24 0 E
Lwanhsien 130 39 45N 118 45 E
Lyakhovskiye, Ostrova 121 73 40N 141 0 E
Lyal I. 46 44 57N 81 24W
*Lyallpur 124 31 30N 73 5 E
Lycksele 110 64 38N 18 40 E
Lydda = Lod 115 31 57N 34 54 E
Lydenburg 117 25 10 S 30 29 E
Lyell 133 41 48 S 172 4 E
Lyell I. 62 52 40N 131 35W
Lyell Range 133 41 38 S 172 20 E
Lyman 78 41 24N 110 15W
Lymburn 60 55 21N 119 47W
Lyme Bay 98 50 36N 2 55W
Lyme Regis 95 50 44N 2 57W
Lymington 95 50 46N 1 32W
Lyn 71 44 36N 75 47W
Lyna, R. 107 54 17N 21 0 E
Lynchburg, U.S.A. 77 39 15N 83 48W
Lynchburg, Va., U.S.A. 72 37 23N 79 10W
Lynden, Can. 49 43 14N 80 9W
Lynden, U.S.A. 80 48 56N 122 32W
Lyndonville, N.Y., U.S.A. 70 43 19N 78 25W
Lyndonville, Vt., U.S.A. 71 44 32N 72 1W
Lynn, U.S.A. 77 40 3N 84 56W
Lynn, Mass., U.S.A. 71 42 28N 70 57W
Lynn Canal 54 58 50N 135 20W
Lynn Cr. 66 49 18N 123 2W
Lynn Creek 66 49 20N 123 2W
Lynn L. 55 56 30N 101 40W
Lynn Lake 55 56 51N 101 3W
Lynnmour 66 49 19N 123 3W
Lynton 95 51 14N 3 50W
Lynwood 80 47 49N 122 19W
Lynx L. 55 62 25N 106 15W
Lyon 103 45 46N 4 50 E
Lyonnais 103 45 45N 4 15 E
Lyons, Colo., U.S.A. 74 40 17N 105 15W
Lyons, Ga., U.S.A. 73 32 10N 82 15W
Lyons, Kans., U.S.A. 74 38 24N 98 13W
Lyons, N.Y., U.S.A. 70 43 3N 77 0W
Lyons = Lyon 103 45 46N 4 50 E
Lyons, R. 134 25 2 S 115 9 E
Lyster 41 46 22N 71 37W
Lytle 75 29 14N 98 46W
Lyttelton 133 43 35 S 172 44 E
Lytton 63 50 13N 121 31W

M

Ma-Me-O Beach 61 52 58N 113 59W
Ma'an 122 30 12N 35 44 E
Maanshan 131 31 40N 118 30 E
Maarianhamina 111 60 5N 19 55 E
Maas, R. 106 51 48N 4 55 E
Maaseik 105 51 6N 5 45 E
Maassluis 105 51 56N 4 16 E
Maastricht 105 50 50N 5 40 E
Mabel L. 63 50 35N 118 43W
Maberly 47 44 50N 76 32W
Mablethorpe 94 53 21N 0 14 E
Mabou 39 46 4N 61 29W
Mc Grath 67 62 58N 155 40W
Mac Tier 70 45 9N 79 46W
Macachin 88 37 10 S 63 43W
McAdam 39 45 36N 67 20W
McAdoo 71 40 54N 76 0W
Macaé 89 22 20 S 41 55W
Macaguane 86 6 35N 71 43W
McAlester 75 34 57N 95 40W
Macalister 63 52 27N 122 24W
Macallister, R. 136 38 2 S 146 59 E
Macamic 40 48 45N 79 0W
Macao = Macau 131 22 16N 113 35 E
Macapá 87 0 5N 51 10W
Macarena, Serrania de la 86 2 45N 73 55W
McArthur, R. 135 16 45 S 136 0 E
Macau 87 5 0 S 36 40W
Macau ■ 131 22 16N 113 35 E
Macaulay Pt. 63 48 25N 123 24W
McAuley 57 50 16N 101 23W
McBride 63 53 20N 120 10W
McCallum 37 47 38N 56 14W
McCamey 75 31 8N 102 15W
McCammon 78 42 41N 112 11W
Maccan 39 45 43N 64 15W
McCarthy 67 61 25N 143 0W
McCauley I. 62 53 40N 130 15W
McClelland L. 60 57 29N 111 20W
Macclesfield 94 53 16N 2 9W
McClintock 55 57 50N 94 10W
McCloud 78 41 14N 122 5W
McCluer Gulf 127 2 20 S 133 0 E
McClure 70 40 42N 77 20W
McClure, L. 80 37 35N 120 16W
McClusky 74 47 30N 100 31W
McComb 75 31 20N 90 30W
McConnell Creek 54 56 53N 126 30W
McCook 74 40 15N 100 35W
McCormick 43 45 21N 74 33W
McCreary 57 50 46N 99 29W
McCulloch 54 49 45N 119 15W
McCullough Mtn. 81 35 35N 115 13W
McCusker, R. 55 55 32N 108 39W
McDame 54 59 44N 128 59W
McDermitt 78 42 0N 117 45W
Macdiarmid 52 49 26N 88 8W
McDonald I. 16 54 0 S 73 0 E
Macdonald L. 134 23 30 S 129 0 E
McDonald, L. 43 45 52N 74 35W
Macdonald, R. 136 33 22 S 151 0 E
Macdonald Ra. 136 15 35 S 124 50 E
Macdonnell Ranges 134 23 40 S 133 0 E
Macdougall L. 22 66 00N 98 27W
MacDowell L. 34 52 15N 92 45W
Macduff 96 57 40N 2 30W
Macdun 56 49 19N 103 16W
Mace 34 48 55N 80 0W
**Macedo de Cavaleiros 116 41 31N 6 57W
Maceió 87 9 40 S 35 41W
Macerata 108 43 19N 13 28 E
Maces Bay 39 45 6N 66 29W
McFarland 81 35 41N 119 14W
Macfarlane, L. 135 32 0 S 136 40 E
McFarlane, R. 55 59 12N 107 58W
McGehee 75 33 40N 91 25W
McGill 78 39 27N 114 50W
Macgillycuddy's Reeks, mts. 97 52 2N 9 45W
McGrath 52 46 11N 93 18W
MacGregor 57 49 57N 98 48W
McGregor, Iowa, U.S.A. 76 42 58N 91 15W
McGregor, Minn., U.S.A. 52 46 37N 93 17W
McGregor L. 61 50 25N 112 52W
McGregor, R. 54 55 10N 122 0W
Mach 124 29 50N 67 20 E
Machachi 86 0 30 S 78 15W
Machado, R. = Jiparana 86 8 45 S 62 20W
Machagai 88 26 56 S 60 2W
Machakos 116 1 30 S 37 15 E
Machala 86 3 10 S 79 50W
Machattie, L. 135 24 50 S 139 48 E
Machecoul 100 47 0N 1 49W
Macheng 131 31 0N 114 40 E
Machevna 121 61 20N 172 20 E
Machias 35 44 40N 67 34W
Machichi, R. 55 57 3N 92 6W
Machilipatnam 125 16 12N 131 15 E
Machine, La 101 46 54N 3 27 E
Mchinji 117 13 47 S 32 58 E
Machiques 86 10 4N 72 34W
Machupicchu 86 13 8 S 72 30W
Machynlleth 95 52 36N 3 51W
†Macias Nguema Biyoga 113 3 30N 8 40 E
McIlwraith Ra. 135 13 50 S 143 20 E
McIntosh, Can. 52 49 57N 93 36W
McIntosh, U.S.A. 74 45 57N 101 20W
McIntosh L. 55 55 45N 105 0W
McIntyre B. 62 54 5N 132 0W
Macintyre, R. 135 28 37 S 149 40 E
Mackay, Austral. 135 21 8 S 149 11 E
Mackay, Can. 60 53 39N 115 35W
Mackay, U.S.A. 78 43 58N 113 37W
Mackay, L. 134 22 30 S 129 0 E
McKay L. 53 49 37N 86 25W
Mackay, R. 60 57 10N 111 38W
McKees Rock 70 40 27N 80 3W
McKeesport 70 40 21N 79 50W
McKellar 46 45 30N 79 55W
McKenna 80 46 56N 122 33W
Mackenzie 54 55 20N 123 05W
McKenzie 73 36 10N 88 31W
*Mackenzie □ 64 64 0N 120 0W
Mackenzie Bay 67 69 0N 137 30W
Mackenzie City = Linden 86 6 0N 58 10W
Mackenzie Highway 54 58 0N 117 15W
Mackenzie King I. 64 77 45N 111 0W
McKenzie L. 56 54 12N 102 30W
Mackenzie Mts. 67 64 0N 130 0W
Mackenzie, R., Austral. 135 23 38 S 149 46 E
Mackenzie, R., Can. 64 69 10N 134 20W
McKenzie, R. 78 44 2N 122 30W
Mackenzie, Terr. 64 62 0N 115 0W
Mackinac I. 46 45 51N 84 37W
Mackinac, Straits of 46 45 49N 84 42W
Mackinaw 76 40 32N 89 21W
Mackinaw City 46 45 47N 84 44W
Mackinaw, R. 76 40 33N 89 44W
McKinley, Mt. 67 63 10N 151 0W
McKinley Sea 17 84 0N 10 0W
McKinney 75 33 10N 96 40W
McKittrick 81 35 18N 119 39W
Macklin 56 52 20N 109 56W
McLaughlin 74 45 50N 100 50W
Maclean 135 29 26 S 153 16 E
McLean, Can. 56 50 31N 104 4W
McLean, U.S.A. 76 40 19N 89 10W
McLean, Tex., U.S.A. 75 35 15N 100 35W
Maclean Str. 65 77 30N 103 30W
McLeansboro 77 38 5N 88 30W
Maclear 117 31 2 S 28 23 E
McLeary 80 47 3N 123 16W
Macleay, R. 135 30 56 S 153 0 E
McLennan 60 55 42N 116 50W
MacLeod, B. 54 62 53N 110 0W
McLeod L. 134 24 9 S 113 47 E
MacLeod Lake 54 54 58N 123 0W
McLeod, R. 60 54 9N 115 42W
McLoughlin, Mt. 78 42 10N 122 30W
McLure 63 51 2N 120 13W
McMasterville 45 45 33N 73 15W
McMechen 70 39 57N 80 44W
McMillan L. 75 32 40N 104 20W
McMinnville, Oreg., U.S.A. 78 45 16N 123 11W
McMinnville, Tenn., U.S.A. 73 35 43N 85 45W
McMorran 56 51 19N 108 42W
McMurdo Sd. 91 77 0 S 170 0 E
McMurray 80 48 19N 122 19W
McMurray = Fort McMurray 54 56 45N 111 27W
McNabs I 39 44 37N 63 32W
McNary 79 34 4N 109 53W
*McNaughton L. 63 52 0N 118 10W
MacNutt 57 51 5N 101 36W
Macomb 76 40 25N 90 40W
Mâcon 103 46 19N 4 50 E
Macon, Ga., U.S.A. 73 32 50N 83 37W
Macon, Ill., U.S.A. 76 39 43N 89 0W
Macon, Miss., U.S.A. 73 33 7N 88 31W
Macon, Mo., U.S.A. 76 39 40N 92 26W
Macondo 117 12 37 S 23 46 E
Macoun L. 55 56 32N 103 50W
Macoupin Cr. 76 39 11N 90 38W
McPherson 74 38 25N 97 40W
McPherson Pk. 81 34 53N 119 53W
Macquarie Harbour 135 42 15 S 145 15 E
Macquarie Is. 14 50 0 S 160 0 E
Macquarie, L. 136 33 4 S 151 36 E
Macquarie, R. 135 30 50 S 147 30 E
MacRobertson Coast 91 68 30 S 63 0 E
Macroom 97 51 54N 8 57W
MacTier 46 45 8N 79 47W
Macu 86 0 25N 69 15W
Macujer 86 0 24N 73 0W
Macumba, R. 135 27 11 S 136 0 E
Macuspana 83 17 46N 92 36W
Mácuzari, Presa 82 27 10N 109 10W
Madagascar ■ 117 20 0 S 47 0 E
Madagascar, I. 117 20 0 S 47 0 E
Madame I. 39 45 30N 60 58W
Madang 14 5 12 S 145 49 E
Madaripur 125 23 2N 90 15 E
Madauk 125 17 56N 96 52 E
Madawaska 70 45 30N 77 55W
Madawaska, R. 47 45 27N 76 21W
Madaya 125 22 20N 96 10 E
Maddalena, I. 108 41 15N 9 23 E
Madden Dam 84 9 13N 79 37W
Madden Lake 84 9 20N 79 37W
Maddox Cove 37 47 28N 52 42W
Made 105 51 41N 4 49 E
Madeira 77 39 11N 84 22W
Madeira, Is. 114 32 50N 17 0W
Madeira Park 62 49 37N 124 0W
Madeira, R. 86 5 30 S 61 20W
Madeleine-Centre 38 49 15N 65 22W
Madeleine, Îs. de la 39 47 30N 61 40W
Madeleine, R. 38 49 15N 65 19W
Madeline I. 52 46 47N 90 40W
Madera 80 37 0N 120 1W
Madha 124 18 0N 75 55 E
Madhya Pradesh □ 124 21 50N 81 0 E
Madill 75 34 5N 96 49W
Madimba 116 5 0 S 15 0 E
Madinat al Shaab 115 12 50N 45 0 E
Madingou 116 4 10 S 13 33 E
Madison, Calif., U.S.A. 80 38 41N 121 59W
Madison, Fla., U.S.A. 73 30 29N 83 26W
Madison, Ind., U.S.A. 77 38 42N 85 20W
Madison, Mo., U.S.A. 76 39 28N 92 13W
Madison, Nebr., U.S.A. 74 41 53N 97 25W
Madison, Ohio, U.S.A. 70 41 45N 81 4W
Madison, S.D., U.S.A. 74 44 0N 97 8W
Madison, Wis., U.S.A. 76 43 5N 89 25W
Madison Junc. 78 44 42N 110 56W
Madison, R. 78 45 0N 111 48W
Madisonville 72 37 42N 87 30W
Madiun 127 7 38 S 111 32 E
Madoc 47 44 30N 77 28W
Madoonga 86 26 56 S 117 35 E
Madras, India 124 13 8N 80 19 E
Madras, U.S.A. 78 44 40N 121 10W
Madras = Tamil Nadu □ 124 11 0N 77 0 E
Madre de Dios, I. 90 50 20N 75 10W
Madre de Dios, R. 86 11 30 S 67 30W

* Renamed Faisalabad

† Renamed Bioko

* Now Inuvik Region and Fort Smith Region

** Renamed Andulo

* Renamed Kinbasket L.

Madre del Sur, Sierra Manitoba, L

Madre del Sur, Sierra 83 17 30N 100 0W
Madre, Laguna 83 25 0N 97 30W
Madre Occidental, Sierra 82 27 0N 107 0W
Madre Oriental, Sierra 82 25 0N 100 0W
Madre, Sierra, Mexico 83 16 0N 93 0W
Madre, Sierra, Phil. 127 17 0N 122 0E
Madrid, Spain 104 40 25N 3 45W
Madrid, U.S.A. 76 41 53N 93 49W
Madsen 52 50 58N 93 55W
Madura, Selat 127 7 30S 113 20E
Madurai 124 9 55N 78 10E
Madurantakam 124 12 30N 79 50E
Mae Hong Son 128 19 16N 98 8E
Mae Sot 128 16 43N 98 34E
Maebashi 132 36 24N 139 4E
Maesteg 95 51 36N 3 40W
Maestra, Sierra 84 20 15N 77 0W
Maestrazgo, Mts. del 104 40 30N 0 25W
Maevatanana 117 16 56N 46 49E
Mafeking, Can. 57 52 40N 101 10W
*Mafeking, S. Afr. 117 25 50S 25 38E
Maffra 136 37 53S 146 58E
Mafia I. 116 7 45S 39 50E
Mafra, Brazil 89 26 10N 50 0W
Mafra, Port. 104 38 55N 9 20W
Magadan 121 59 30N 151 0E
Magadi 116 1 54S 36 19E
Magaguadavic 39 45 42N 67 12W
Magaguadavic L. 39 45 43N 67 12W
Magaguadavic, R. 39 45 7N 66 54W
Magallanes, Estrecho de 90 52 30S 75 0W
Magangué 86 9 14N 74 45W
Magdalen Is. = Madeleine, Is. de la 35 47 30N 61 40W
Magdalena, Argent. 88 35 5S 57 30W
Magdalena, Boliv. 86 13 13S 63 57W
Magdalena, Mexico 82 30 50N 112 0W
Magdalena, U.S.A. 79 34 10N 107 20W
Magdalena □ 86 10 0N 74 0W
Magdalena, B. 82 24 30N 112 10W
Magdalena, I. 82 24 40N 112 15W
Magdalena, Llano de la 82 25 0N 111 30W
Magdalena, mt. 126 4 25N 117 55E
Magdalena, R., Colomb. 86 8 30N 74 0W
Magdalena, R., Mexico 82 30 50N 112 0W
Magdeburg 106 52 8N 11 36E
Magee 75 31 53N 89 45W
Magee, I. 97 54 48N 5 44W
Magelang 127 7 29S 110 13E
Magellan's Str. 90 52 30S 75 0W
Magellan's Str. = Magallanes, Est. de 90 52 30S 75 0W
Maggiore, L. 108 46 0N 8 35E
Magherafelt 97 54 44N 6 37W
Magherafelt □ 97 54 50N 6 40W
Magnac-Laval 102 46 13N 1 11E
Magnetawan 46 45 40N 79 39W
Magnetic Pole, 1980, (South) 91 65 36S 139 24E
Magnetic Pole, 1980 (North) 17 77 18N 101 48W
Magnitogorsk 120 53 27N 59 4E
Magnolia, Ark., U.S.A. 75 33 18N 93 12W
Magnolia, Miss., U.S.A. 75 31 8N 90 28W
Magny-en-Vexin 101 49 9N 1 47E
Magog 41 45 18N 72 9W
Magosa = Famagusta 122 35 8N 33 55E
Magpie 38 50 19N 64 30W
Magpie L. 38 51 0N 64 41W
Magpie, R., Ont., Can. 53 47 56N 84 50W
Magpie, R., Qué., Can. 38 50 19N 64 27W
Magrath 61 49 25N 112 50W
Maguarinho, C. 87 0 15S 48 30W
Maguse L. 55 61 40N 95 10W
Maguse Pt. 55 61 20N 93 50W
Maguse River 55 61 20N 94 25W
Magwe 125 20 10N 95 0E
Mahābād 122 36 50N 45 45E
Mahabo 117 20 23S 44 40E
Mahagi 116 2 20N 31 0E
Mahajamba, B. de la 117 15 24S 47 5E
Mahakam, R. 126 1 0N 114 40E
Mahalapye 117 23 1S 26 51E
Mahallāt 123 33 55N 50 30E
Mahanadi R. 125 20 33N 85 0E
Mahanoro 117 19 54S 48 48E
Mahanoy City 71 40 48N 76 10W
Maharashtra □ 124 19 30N 75 30E
Mahatta River 62 50 22N 127 47W
Mahbubnagar 124 16 45N 77 59E
Mahd Dhahab 122 25 55N 45 30E
Mahdia 114 35 28N 11 0E
Mahé, I. 16 5 0S 55 30E
Mahenge 116 8 45S 36 35E
Maheno 133 45 10S 170 50E
Mahia Pen. 133 39 9S 177 55E
Mahnomen 74 47 22N 95 57W
Mahomet 77 40 12N 88 24W
Mahón 104 39 50N 4 18E
Mahone Bay 35 44 30N 64 20W
Mahood Falls 63 51 50N 120 38W
Mahood L. 63 51 50N 120 23W
Mahukona 67 20 11N 155 52W
Mai-Ndombe, L. 116 2 0S 18 0E
Maicasagi, R. 40 49 58N 76 33W
Maîche 101 47 16N 6 48E
Maicuru, R. 87 1 0S 54 30W

* *Renamed Mafikeng*

Maidenhead 95 51 31N 0 42W
Maidstone, Can. 56 53 5N 109 20W
Maidstone, U.K. 95 51 16N 0 31E
Maiduguri 114 12 0N 13 20E
Maignelay 101 49 32N 2 30E
Maigualida, Sierra 86 5 30N 65 10W
Maijdi 125 22 48N 91 10E
Maikala Ra. 125 22 0N 81 0E
Maillardville 66 49 15N 122 52W
Mailly-le-Camp 101 48 41N 4 12E
Maimana 124 35 53N 64 38E
Main-à-Dieu 39 46 0N 59 51W
Main Barrier Ra. 136 31 10S 141 20E
Main Brook 37 51 11N 56 1W
Main Centre 56 50 35N 107 21W
Main Channel 70 45 22N 81 45W
Main, R., Ger. 106 50 13N 11 0E
Main, R., U.K. 97 54 49N 6 20W
Maine 100 48 0N 0 0E
Maine □ 35 45 20N 69 0W
Maine-et-Loire □ 100 47 31N 0 30W
Maine, R. 97 52 10N 9 40W
Maingkwan 125 26 15N 96 45E
Mainit, L. 127 9 31N 125 30E
Mainland, I., Orkneys, U.K. 96 59 0N 3 10W
Mainland, I., Shetlands, U.K. 96 60 15N 1 22W
Maintenon 101 48 35N 1 35E
Maintirano 117 18 3S 44 1E
Mainz 106 50 0N 8 17E
Maipú 88 37 0S 58 0W
Maipures 86 5 11N 67 49W
Maiquetía 86 10 36N 66 57W
Mairabari 125 26 30N 92 30E
Maisi 85 20 17N 74 9W
Maisi, C. 85 20 10N 74 10W
Maisonnette 39 47 49N 65 0W
Maisse 101 48 24N 2 21E
Maitland, Austral. 136 32 44S 151 36E
Maitland, Can. 39 45 19N 63 30W
Maitland Bridge 39 44 27N 65 12W
Maitland, R. 70 43 45N 81 33W
Maíz, Islas del 84 12 15N 83 4W
Maizuru 132 35 25N 135 22E
Majagual 86 8 33N 74 38W
Majalengka 127 6 55S 108 14E
Majene 127 3 27S 118 57E
Major 56 51 52N 109 37W
Majorca, I. = Mallorca, I. 104 39 30N 3 0E
*Majunga 117 15 40S 46 25E
Makale 127 3 6S 119 51E
Makamik 34 48 45N 79 0W
Makapuu Hd. 67 21 19N 157 39W
Makarikari = Makgadikgadi 117 20 40S 25 45E
Makarovo 121 57 40N 107 45E
Makasar = Ujung Pandang 127 5 10S 119 20E
Makasar, Selat 127 1 0S 118 20E
Makat 120 47 39N 53 19E
Makedhona □ 109 40 39N 22 0E
Makedonija □ 109 41 53N 21 40E
Makena 67 20 39N 156 27W
Makeyevka 120 48 0N 38 0E
Makgadikgadi Salt Pans 117 20 40S 25 45E
Makhachkala 120 43 0N 47 15E
Makian, I. 127 0 12N 127 20E
†Makin, I. 14 3 30N 174 0E
Makindu 116 2 7S 37 40E
Makinsk 120 52 37N 70 26E
Makkah 122 21 30N 39 54E
Makkovik 36 55 10N 59 10W
Makklakovo 121 58 16N 92 29E
Makó 107 46 14N 20 33E
Makokibatan L. 53 51 17N 87 20W
Makoua 116 0 5S 15 50E
Makrai 124 22 2N 77 0E
Makran 123 26 13N 61 30E
Makran Coast Range 124 25 40N 4 0E
Maksimkin Yar 120 58 58N 86 50E
Mākū 122 39 15N 44 31E
Makumbi 116 5 50S 20 43E
Makurazaki 132 31 15N 130 20E
Makurdi 114 7 43N 8 28E
Mal B. 97 52 50N 9 30W
Mala, Pta. 84 7 28N 80 2W
Malabang 127 7 36N 124 3E
Malabar Coast 124 11 0N 75 0E
Malacca = Melaka 128 2 15N 102 15E
Malacca, Str. of 128 3 0N 101 0E
Malachi 52 49 56N 94 59W
Malad City 78 42 15N 112 20E
Maladetta, Mt. 104 42 40N 0 30E
Málaga 86 6 42N 72 44W
Malaga 75 32 12N 104 2W
Málaga 104 36 38N 4 58W
Malagasy Rep. ■ = Madagascar ■ 117 20 0S 47 0E
Malakal 115 9 33N 31 50E
Malakand 124 34 40N 71 55E
Malakoff 75 32 10N 95 55W
Malakwa 54 50 55N 118 50W
Malamyzh 121 50 0N 136 50E
Malang 127 7 59S 112 35E
Malanje 116 9 30S 16 17E
Mälaren 111 59 30N 17 10E
Malargüe 88 35 40S 69 30W

* *Renamed Mahajunga*
† *Renamed Butaritari*

Malartic 40 48 9N 78 9W
Malartic, L. 40 48 15N 78 5W
Malatya 122 38 25N 38 20E
Malawi ■ 117 13 0S 34 0E
Malawi, L. (Lago Niassa) 117 12 30S 34 30E
Malay Peninsula 128 7 25N 100 0E
Malaybalay 127 8 5N 125 15E
Malayer 122 34 19N 48 51E
Malaysia ■ 126 5 0N 110 0E
Malaysia, Peninsular □ 128 5 0N 102 0E
Malazgirt 122 39 10N 42 33E
Malbaie, La 41 47 40N 70 10W
Malbork 107 54 3N 19 10E
Malcolm 134 28 51S 121 25E
Malcolm I. 62 50 38N 127 0W
Maldegem 105 51 14N 3 26E
Malden, Mass., U.S.A. 71 42 26N 71 5W
Malden, Mo., U.S.A. 75 36 35N 90 0W
Maldive Is. ■ 16 2 0N 73 0W
Maldonado 89 35 0S 55 0W
Maldonado, Punta 83 16 19N 98 35W
Malé Karpaty 106 48 30N 17 20E
Malea, Ákra 109 36 28N 23 7E
Malegaon 124 20 30N 74 30E
Malesherbes 101 48 15N 2 24E
Malestroit 100 47 49N 2 25W
Malgomaj L. 110 64 40N 16 30E
Malhão, Sa. do 104 37 25N 8 0W
Malheur L. 78 43 19N 118 42W
Malheur, R. 78 43 55N 117 55W
Mali ■ 114 15 0N 10 0W
Mali Kyun, I. 128 13 0N 98 20E
Mali, R. 125 26 20N 97 40E
Malibu 81 34 2N 118 41W
Maligne L. 61 52 40N 117 31W
Malik 127 0 39S 123 16E
Malili 127 2 42S 121 23E
Malin Hd. 97 55 18N 7 16W
Malinau 126 3 35N 116 30E
Malindi 116 3 12S 40 5E
Maling, Mt. 127 1 0N 121 0E
Malingping 127 6 45S 106 2E
Malita 127 6 19N 125 39E
Mallacoota 136 37 40S 149 40E
Mallacoota Inlet 136 37 40S 149 40E
Mallaig, Can. 60 54 13N 111 22W
Mallaig, U.K. 96 57 0N 5 50W
Mallard 76 42 56N 94 41W
Mallee 136 35 10S 142 20E
Mallemort 103 43 44N 5 11E
Mallorca, I. 104 39 30N 3 0E
Mallorytown, Can. 71 44 29N 75 53W
Mallorytown, Ont., Can. 47 44 29N 75 53W
Mallow 97 52 8N 8 40W
Malmberget 110 67 11N 20 40E
Malmö 111 55 36N 12 59E
Malmöhus län □ 111 55 45N 13 30E
Malolos 127 14 50N 121 2E
Malone 71 44 50N 74 19W
Malott 63 48 19N 119 39W
Malpelo I. 86 4 3N 80 35W
Malta, Idaho, U.S.A. 78 42 15N 113 30W
Malta, Mont., U.S.A. 78 48 20N 107 55W
Malta ■ 108 35 50N 14 30E
Maltahöhe 117 24 55S 17 0E
Malton, Ont., Can. 49 43 42N 79 38W
Malton, Ont., Can. 50 43 42N 79 38W
Malton, U.K. 94 54 9N 0 48W
Maluku □ 127 3 0S 128 0E
Maluku, Is. 127 1 0S 127 0E
Maluku, Kepulauan 127 3 0S 128 0E
Malung 57 48 45N 95 45W
Malvan 124 16 2N 73 30E
Malvern, Can. 50 43 48N 79 14W
Malvern, U.K. 95 52 7N 2 19W
Malvern, Ark., U.S.A. 75 34 22N 92 50W
Malvern, Ohio, U.S.A. 70 40 31N 31 12W
Malvern Hills 95 52 0N 2 19W
Malvinas Is. = Falkland Is. 86 51 30S 59 0W
Mama 121 58 18N 112 54E
Mamaia 107 44 18N 28 37E
Mamanguape 87 6 50S 35 4W
Mamasa 127 2 55S 119 20E
Mamberamo, R. 127 2 0S 137 50E
Mameigwess L., Can. 34 52 35N 87 50W
Mameigwess L., Ont., Can. 52 49 34N 91 49W
Mamers 100 48 21N 0 22E
Mammamattawa 34 50 25N 84 23W
Mammoth 79 32 46N 110 43W
Mamoi 131 26 0N 119 25E
Mamoré, R. 87 9 55S 65 20W
Mamou 114 10 15N 12 0W
Mampawah 126 0 30N 109 5E
Mamuju 127 2 50S 118 50E
Man 114 7 30N 7 40W
Man, I. of 94 54 15N 4 30W
Man Na 125 23 27N 97 19E
Man O' War Peak 35 56 58N 61 40W
Mana, Fr. Gui. 87 5 45N 53 55W
Mana, U.S.A. 67 22 3N 159 45W
Manaar, Gulf of 124 8 30N 79 0E
Manacacías, R. 86 4 23N 72 4W
Manacapuru 86 3 10S 60 50W
Manacor 104 39 32N 3 12E
Managua 84 12 0N 86 20W
Managua, L. 84 12 20N 86 30W
Manakara 117 22 8S 48 1E
Manamāh, Al 123 26 11N 50 35E
Mananara 117 16 10S 49 30E
Mananjary 117 21 13S 48 20E
Manantenina 117 24 17S 47 19E
Manaos = Manaus 86 3 0S 60 0W
Manapouri 133 45 34S 167 39E
Manapouri, L. 133 45 32S 167 32E
Manas, R. 125 26 12N 90 40E
Manasalowo Chih 129 30 45N 81 20E
Manasir 123 24 30N 51 10E
Manasquan 71 40 7N 74 3W
Manass 129 44 20N 86 21E
Manassa 79 37 12N 105 58W
Manati 67 18 26N 66 29W
Manaung Kyun 125 18 45N 93 40E
Manaus 86 3 0S 60 0W
Manawan L. 55 55 24N 103 14W
Manay 127 7 17N 126 33E
Mancelona 46 44 54N 85 5W
Mancha, La 104 39 10N 2 54W
Manche □ 100 49 10N 1 20W
Manchester, U.K. 94 53 30N 2 15W
Manchester, U.S.A. 77 42 9N 84 2W
Manchester, Calif., U.S.A. 80 38 58N 123 41W
Manchester, Conn., U.S.A. 71 41 47N 72 30W
Manchester, Ga., U.S.A. 73 32 53N 84 32W
Manchester, Iowa, U.S.A. 76 42 28N 91 27W
Manchester, Ky., U.S.A. 72 37 15N 83 45W
Manchester, N.H., U.S.A. 71 42 58N 71 29W
Manchester, N.Y., U.S.A. 70 42 56N 77 16W
Manchester Depot 71 43 10N 73 5W
Manchester L. 55 61 28N 107 29W
Manchouli 129 49 46N 117 24E
Mand, R. 123 28 20N 52 30E
Manda 116 10 30S 34 40E
Mandabé 117 21 0S 44 55E
Mandaguari 89 23 32S 51 42W
Mandal 111 58 2N 7 25E
Mandal Gobi 130 45 47N 106 15E
Mandalay 125 22 0N 96 10E
Mandalgovi 130 45 40N 106 22E
Mandali 122 33 52N 45 28E
Mandan 74 46 50N 101 0W
Mandar, Teluk 127 3 35S 119 4E
Mandasaur 124 24 3N 75 8E
Mandawai (Katingan), R. 126 1 30S 113 0E
Mandelieu-la-Napoule 103 43 34N 6 57E
Mandi 124 31 39N 76 58E
Mandimba 117 14 20S 35 40E
Mandioli 127 0 40S 127 20E
Mandla 125 22 39N 80 30E
Mandritsara 117 15 50S 48 49E
Mandvi 124 22 51N 69 22E
Mandya 124 12 30N 77 0E
Manfredónia 108 41 40N 15 55E
Mangabeiras, Chapada das 87 10 0S 46 30W
Mangaia, I. 133 21 55S 157 55W
Mangalia 107 43 50N 28 35E
Mangalore 124 12 55N 74 47E
Manggar 126 2 50S 108 10E
Manggawitu 127 4 8S 133 32E
Mangla Dam 124 33 32N 73 50E
Mangoche 117 14 25S 35 16E
Mangole I. 127 1 50S 125 55E
Mangonui 133 35 1S 173 32E
Mangueira, Lagoa da 89 33 0S 52 50W
Mangum 75 34 50N 99 30W
Mangyai 129 38 6N 91 37E
Mangyshlak P-ov. 120 43 40N 52 30E
Manhattan, U.S.A. 77 41 26N 87 59W
Manhattan, Kans., U.S.A. 74 39 10N 96 40W
Manhattan, Nev., U.S.A. 78 38 31N 117 3W
Manhuaçu 87 20 15S 42 2W
Mani 86 4 49N 72 17W
Manicoré 86 6 0S 61 10W
Manicouagan L. 38 51 25N 68 15W
Manicouagan, R. 41 49 30N 68 30W
Manicouagan, Rés. 36 51 5N 68 40W
Manifah 122 27 30N 49 0E
Manigotagan 57 51 6N 96 8W
Manigotagan L. 57 50 52N 95 37W
Manihiki I. 15 10 24S 161 1W
Manila, Phil. 127 14 40N 121 3E
Manila, U.S.A. 78 41 0N 109 44W
Manila B. 127 14 0N 120 0E
Manipur □ 125 24 30N 94 0E
Manipur, R. 125 23 45N 93 40E
Manisa 122 38 38N 27 30E
Manistee 72 44 15N 86 20W
Manistee, R. 46 44 15N 86 21W
Manistique 72 45 59N 86 18W
Manito 76 40 25N 89 47W
Manito L. 56 52 43N 109 43W
Manitoba □ 57 55 30N 97 0W
Manitoba, L. 57 51 0N 98 45W

Manitou **Masi**

Manitou, Man., Can. **57** 49 15N 98 32W
Manitou, Qué., Can. **38** 50 18N 65 15W
Manitou Beach **77** 41 58N 84 19W
Manitou I. **53** 47 22N 87 30W
Manitou Is. **72** 45 8N 86 0W
Manitou L., Ont., Can. **46** 45 51N 82 0W
Manitou L., Ont., Can. **55** 49 15N 93 0W
Manitou L., Qué., Can. **36** 50 55N 65 17W
Manitou, R. **38** 50 18N 65 15W
Manitoulin I. **46** 45 40N 82 30W
Manitouwadge **53** 49 8N 85 48W
Manitowaning **46** 45 46N 81 49W
Manitowoc **72** 44 8N 87 40W
Maniwaki **40** 46 23N 75 58W
Manizales **86** 5 5N 75 32W
Manja **117** 21 26S 44 20E
Manjacaze **117** 24 45S 34 0E
Manjhand **124** 25 50N 68 10E
Manjil **122** 36 46N 49 30E
Manjimup **134** 34 15S 116 6E
Manjra, R. **124** 18 20N 77 20E
Mankato, Kans., U.S.A. **74** 39 49N 98 11W
Mankato, Minn., U.S.A. **74** 44 8N 93 59W
Mankota **56** 49 25N 107 5W
Manlius **58** 50 0N 97 2W
Manly **136** 33 48S 151 17E
Manmad **124** 20 18N 74 28E
Manna **126** 4 25S 102 55E
Mannar **124** 9 1N 79 54E
Mannar, G. of **124** 8 30N 79 0E
Mannar I. **124** 9 5N 79 45E
Mannheim, Can. **49** 43 24N 80 33W
Mannheim, Ger. **106** 49 28N 8 29E
Manning, Can. **60** 56 53N 117 39W
Manning, Oreg., U.S.A. **80** 45 45N 123 13W
Manning, S.C., U.S.A. **73** 33 40N 80 9W
Manning Park **63** 49 4N 120 47W
Manning Prov. Park **63** 49 5N 120 45W
Manning, R. **136** 31 52S 152 43E
Mannington **72** 39 35N 80 25W
Mannville **60** 53 20N 111 10W
Manokwari **127** 0 54S 134 0E
Manombo **117** 22 57S 43 28E
Manono **116** 7 15S 27 25E
Manor **57** 49 36N 102 5W
Manosque **103** 43 49N 5 47E
Manotick **47** 45 13N 75 41W
Manouane L. **36** 50 45N 70 45W
Manouane, L. **41** 47 33N 74 6W
Manresa **104** 41 48N 1 50E
Mans, Le **100** 48 0N 0 10E
Mansa **116** 11 13S 28 55E
Manseau **41** 46 22N 72 0W
Mansel I. **36** 62 0N 79 50W
Mansfield, Austral. **136** 37 4S 146 6E
Mansfield, U.K. **94** 53 8N 1 12W
Mansfield, La., U.S.A. **75** 32 2N 93 40W
Mansfield, Mass., U.S.A. **71** 42 2N 71 12W
Mansfield, Ohio, U.S.A. **70** 40 45N 82 30W
Mansfield, Pa., U.S.A. **70** 41 48N 77 4W
Mansfield, Wash., U.S.A. **78** 47 51N 119 44W
Mansle **102** 45 52N 0 9E
Manso, R. **87** 14 0S 52 0W
Manson **76** 42 32N 94 32W
Manson Creek **54** 55 37N 124 25W
Manta **86** 1 0S 80 40W
Mantalingajan, Mt. **126** 8 55N 117 45E
Manteca **80** 37 50N 121 12W
Mantecal **86** 7 34N 69 17W
Manteno **77** 41 15N 87 50W
Manteo **73** 35 55N 75 41W
Mantes-la-Jolie **101** 49 0N 1 41E
Manthani **124** 18 40N 79 35E
Manthelan **100** 47 9N 0 47E
Manti **78** 39 23N 111 32W
Mantiqueira, Serra da **89** 22 0S 44 0W
Manton **46** 44 23N 85 25W
Mántova **108** 45 10N 10 47E
Mänttä **110** 62 0N 24 40E
Mantua **70** 41 15N 81 14W
Mantua = Mántova **108** 45 10N 10 47E
Manu **86** 12 10S 71 0W
Manua Is. **133** 14 13S 169 35W
Manucan **127** 8 14N 123 3E
Manuel Alves, R. **87** 11 19S 48 28W
Manuels **39** 47 3N 64 59W
Manui I. **127** 3 35S 123 5E
Manville **74** 42 48N 104 36W
Many **75** 31 36N 93 28W
Many Island L. **61** 50 8N 110 3W
Manyara L. **116** 3 40S 35 50E
Manyberries **61** 49 24N 110 42W
Manyoni **116** 5 45S 34 55E
Manzai **124** 32 20N 70 15E
Manzanares **104** 39 0N 3 22W
Manzanillo, Cuba **84** 20 20N 77 10W
Manzanillo, Mexico **82** 19 0N 104 20W
Manzanillo, Pta. **84** 9 30N 79 40W
Manzano Mts. **79** 34 30N 106 45W
Maoke, Pengunungan **126** 3 40S 137 30E
Mapastepec **83** 15 26N 92 54W
Mapia, Kepulauan **127** 0 50N 134 20E
Mapimí **82** 25 50N 103 31W
Mapimí, Bolsón de **82** 27 30N 103 15W
Maple **50** 43 51N 79 31W
Maple Bay **63** 48 48N 123 37W
Maple Creek **56** 49 55N 109 29W
Maple Falls **63** 48 56N 122 5W
Maple Grove **44** 45 19N 73 50W
Maple, R. **77** 42 58N 84 56W
Maple Valley **80** 47 25N 122 3W
Maples, The **49** 43 52N 80 10W
Mapleton **78** 44 4N 123 58W
Maplewood **74** 38 33N 90 18W
Mapuera, R. **86** 0 30S 58 25W
Maputo **117** 25 58S 32 32E
Maqnā **122** 28 25N 34 50E
Maquinchao **90** 41 15S 68 50W
Maquoketa **76** 42 4N 90 40W
Mar Chiquita, L. **88** 30 40S 62 50W
Mar del Plata **88** 38 0S 57 30W
Mar, Serra do **89** 25 30S 49 0W
Maraã **86** 1 43S 65 25W
Marabá **87** 5 20S 49 5W
Maracá, I. de **87** 2 10N 50 30W
Maracaibo **86** 10 40N 71 37W
Maracaibo, Lago de **86** 9 40N 71 30W
Maracaju **89** 21 38S 55 9W
Maracay **86** 10 15N 67 36W
Marâgheh **122** 37 30N 46 12E
Marajó, Ilha de **87** 1 0S 49 30W
Maralal **116** 1 0N 36 38E
Marana **79** 32 30N 111 9W
Marand **122** 38 30N 45 45E
Marandellas **117** 18 5S 31 42E
Maranguape **87** 3 55S 38 50W
Maranhão = São Luis **87** 2 31S 44 16W
Maranhão □ **87** 5 0S 46 0W
Marañón, R. **86** 4 50S 75 35W
Maranoa R. **135** 27 50S 148 37E
Maraş **122** 37 37N 36 53E
Marathon **53** 48 44N 86 23W
Marathón **109** 38 11N 23 58E
Marathon, U.S.A. **76** 42 52N 94 59W
Marathon, N.Y., U.S.A. **71** 42 25N 76 3W
Marathon, Tex., U.S.A. **75** 30 15N 103 15W
Maratua, I. **127** 2 10N 118 35E
Marbella **104** 36 30N 4 57W
Marble **52** 47 19N 93 18W
Marble Bar **134** 21 9S 119 44E
Marble Falls **75** 30 30N 98 15W
Marblehead, Can. **63** 50 15N 116 58W
Marblehead, U.S.A. **71** 42 29N 70 51W
Marblemount **63** 48 32N 121 26W
Marbleton **41** 45 37N 71 35W
Marburg **106** 50 49N 8 44E
Marceau, L. **38** 51 25N 66 41W
Marcelin **56** 52 55N 106 47W
Marceline **76** 39 43N 92 57W
March **95** 52 33N 0 5E
Marché **102** 46 0N 1 20E
Marche □ **108** 43 22N 13 10E
Marche-en-Famenne **105** 50 14N 5 19E
Marchin **105** 50 28N 5 14E
Marcigny **103** 46 17N 4 2E
Marcillac-Vallon **102** 44 29N 2 27E
Marcillat **102** 46 12N 2 38E
Marck **101** 50 57N 1 57E
Marckolsheim **101** 48 10N 7 30E
Marconi **58** 49 55N 97 6W
Marcos Juárez **88** 32 42S 62 5W
Marcus I. **14** 24 0N 153 45E
Marcy Mt. **71** 44 7N 73 55W
Mardan **124** 34 20N 72 0E
Marden **49** 43 36N 80 18W
Mardin **122** 37 20N 40 36E
Maree L. **96** 57 40N 5 30W
Mareeba **135** 16 59S 145 28E
Marek **127** 4 41S 120 24E
Marek = Stanke Dimitrov **109** 42 17N 23 9E
Marelan **43** 45 38N 74 33W
Maremma **108** 42 45N 11 15E
Maremma, reg. **108** 42 30N 11 0E
Marengo, Can. **56** 51 29N 109 47W
Marengo, U.S.A. **76** 41 42N 92 5W
Marenisco **52** 46 23N 89 40W
Mareuil-sur-Lay **102** 46 32N 1 14W
Marfa **75** 30 15N 104 0W
Margaree Forks **39** 46 20N 61 5W
Margaree Harbour **35** 46 26N 61 8W
Margaret Bay **62** 51 20N 127 20W
Margaret L. **54** 58 56N 115 25W
Margarita **84** 9 20N 79 55W
Margarita, Isla de **86** 11 0N 64 0W
Margate **95** 51 23N 1 24E
Margeride, Mts. de la **102** 44 43N 3 38E
Margo **56** 51 49N 103 20W
Marguerite **63** 52 30N 122 25W
Mari, A.S.S.R. □ **120** 56 30N 48 0E
Maria **38** 48 10N 65 59W
María Elena **88** 22 18S 69 40W
María Grande **88** 31 45S 59 55W
Maria, I. **134** 14 52S 135 45E
Maria I. **134** 42 35S 148 0E
Maria van Diemen, C. **133** 34 29S 172 40E
Marian L. **54** 63 0N 116 15W
Mariana Is. **14** 17 0N 145 0E
Mariana Trench **14** 13 0N 145 0W
Marianao **84** 23 8N 82 24W
Marianna, Ark., U.S.A. **75** 34 48N 90 48W
Marianna, Fla., U.S.A. **73** 30 45N 85 15W
Marias, R. **78** 48 26N 111 40W
Mariato, Punta **84** 7 12N 80 52W
Maribor **108** 46 36N 15 40E
Maricopa, Ariz., U.S.A. **79** 33 5N 112 2W
Maricopa, Calif., U.S.A. **81** 35 7N 119 27W
Maricourt **36** 56 34N 70 49W
Marie Galante, I. **85** 15 56N 61 16W
Marie L. **60** 54 38N 110 18W
Mariehamn (Maarianhamina) **111** 60 5N 19 57E
Marienberg **105** 52 30N 6 35E
Marienbourg **105** 50 6N 4 31E
Mariental **117** 24 36S 18 0E
Marienville **70** 41 27N 79 8W
Mariestad **111** 58 43N 13 50E
Marietta, Ga., U.S.A. **73** 34 0N 84 30W
Marietta, Ohio, U.S.A. **72** 39 27N 81 27W
Marieville **45** 45 26N 73 10W
Marignane **103** 43 25N 5 13E
Mariinsk **120** 56 10N 87 20E
Marilia **89** 22 0S 50 0W
Marin **104** 42 23N 8 42W
Marina **80** 36 41N 121 48W
Marinduque, I. **127** 13 25N 122 0E
Marine City **46** 42 45N 82 29W
Marinel, Le **116** 10 25S 25 17E
Marinette, Ariz., U.S.A. **79** 33 41N 112 16W
Marinette, Wis., U.S.A. **72** 45 4N 87 40W
Maringá **89** 23 35S 51 50W
Marion, Ala., U.S.A. **73** 32 33N 87 20W
Marion, Ill., U.S.A. **76** 37 45N 88 55W
Marion, Ind., U.S.A. **77** 40 35N 85 40W
Marion, Iowa, U.S.A. **76** 42 2N 91 36W
Marion, Kans., U.S.A. **74** 38 25N 97 2W
Marion, Mich., U.S.A. **46** 44 7N 85 8W
Marion, N.C., U.S.A. **73** 35 42N 82 0W
Marion, Ohio, U.S.A. **77** 40 38N 83 8W
Marion, S.C., U.S.A. **73** 34 11N 79 22W
Marion, Va., U.S.A. **73** 36 51N 81 29W
Marion I. **16** 47 0S 38 0E
Marion, L. **73** 33 30N 80 15W
Marion Reef **135** 19 10S 152 17E
Maripa **86** 7 26N 65 9W
Mariposa **80** 37 31N 119 59W
Mariscal Estigarribia **88** 22 3S 60 40W
Maritsa, R. **109** 42 15N 24 0E
Marjan **123** 32 5N 68 20E
Markdale **46** 44 19N 80 39W
Marked Tree **75** 35 35N 90 24W
Markerville **61** 52 7N 114 10W
Market Drayton **94** 52 55N 2 30W
Market Harborough **95** 52 29N 0 55W
Markham **50** 43 52N 79 16W
Markham I. **17** 84 0N 0 45W
Markham L. **55** 62 30N 102 35W
Markham Mts. **91** 83 0S 164 0E
Markleeville **80** 38 42N 119 47W
Markovo **121** 64 40N 169 40E
Markstay **46** 46 29N 80 32W
Marksville **75** 31 10N 92 2W
Marl **105** 51 39N 7 4E
Marlbank **47** 44 26N 77 6W
Marlboro, Can. **54** 53 30N 116 50W
Marlboro, U.S.A. **71** 42 19N 71 33W
Marlborough □ **133** 41 45S 173 33E
Marlborough Downs **95** 51 25N 1 55W
Marle **101** 49 43N 3 47E
Marlin **75** 31 25N 96 50W
Marlow **75** 34 40N 97 58W
Marmagao **124** 15 25N 73 56E
Marmande **102** 44 30N 0 10E
Marmara Denizi **122** 40 45N 28 15E
Marmara, I. **109** 40 35N 27 38E
Marmara, Sea of = Marmara Denizi **122** 40 45N 28 15E
Marmaris **122** 36 50N 28 14E
Marmarth **74** 46 21N 103 52W
Marmion L. **52** 48 55N 91 30W
Marmolada, Mte. **108** 46 25N 11 55E
Marmora **47** 44 28N 77 41W
Marnay **101** 47 20N 5 48E
Marne □ **101** 49 0N 4 10E
Marne, R. **101** 48 53N 2 25E
Marnoo **136** 36 40S 142 54E
Maroa **86** 2 43N 67 33W
Maroantsetra **117** 15 26S 49 44E
Maroni, R. **87** 4 0N 52 0W
Marovoay **117** 16 6S 46 39E
Marquesas Is. = Marquises **15** 9 30S 140 0W
Marquette, Can. **57** 50 4N 97 44W
Marquette, U.S.A. **53** 46 30N 87 21W
Marquette I. **46** 45 58N 84 18W
Marquette, L. **41** 48 54N 73 54W
Marquise **101** 50 50N 1 40E
Marquises, Is. **15** 9 30S 140 0W
Marrakech **114** 31 40N 8 0W
Marrat **122** 25 0N 45 35E
Marree **135** 29 39S 138 1E
Marromeu **117** 18 40S 36 25E
Marrupa **117** 13 8S 37 30E
Mars, Le **74** 43 0N 96 0W
Marsabit **116** 2 18N 38 0E
Marsala **108** 37 48N 12 25E
Marsaxlokk (Medport) **108** 35 47N 14 32E
Marsden **56** 52 51N 109 49W
Marseillan **102** 43 23N 3 31E
Marseille **103** 43 18N 5 23E
Marseilles **77** 41 20N 88 43W
Marseilles = Marseille **103** 43 18N 5 23E
Marsh I. **75** 29 35N 91 50W
Marshall, Can. **56** 53 11N 109 47W
Marshall, Ark., U.S.A. **75** 35 58N 92 40W
Marshall, Ill., U.S.A. **77** 39 23N 87 42W
Marshall, Mich., U.S.A. **77** 42 17N 84 59W
Marshall, Minn., U.S.A. **74** 44 25N 95 45W
Marshall, Mo., U.S.A. **76** 39 8N 93 15W
Marshall, Tex., U.S.A. **75** 32 29N 94 20W
Marshall Is. **14** 9 0N 171 0E
Marshalltown **76** 42 5N 92 56W
Marshfield, Mo., U.S.A. **75** 37 20N 92 58W
Marshfield, Wis., U.S.A. **74** 44 42N 90 10W
Marsoui **38** 49 13N 66 4W
Marstrand **111** 57 53N 11 35E
Marsville **49** 43 50N 80 13W
Mart **75** 31 34N 96 51W
Martaban **125** 16 30N 97 35E
Martagne **100** 46 59N 0 57W
Martapura **126** 3 22S 114 56E
Martelange **105** 49 49N 5 43E
Marten River **46** 46 44N 79 49W
Martensdale **76** 41 23N 93 45W
Martensville **56** 52 17N 106 40W
Martha's Vineyard **71** 41 25N 70 35W
Martigné Ferchaud **100** 47 50N 1 20W
Martigues **103** 43 24N 5 4E
Martin, S.D., U.S.A. **74** 43 11N 101 45W
Martin, Tenn., U.S.A. **75** 36 23N 88 51W
Martin, L. **73** 32 45N 85 50W
Martinborough **133** 41 14S 175 29E
Martinez **80** 38 1N 122 8W
Martinique, I. **85** 14 40N 61 0W
Martinique Passage **85** 15 15N 61 0W
Martinópolis **89** 22 11S 51 12W
Martins Ferry **71** 40 5N 80 46W
Martinsburg, Pa., U.S.A. **70** 40 18N 78 21W
Martinsburg, W. Va., U.S.A. **72** 39 30N 77 57W
Martinsville, Ill., U.S.A. **77** 39 20N 87 53W
Martinsville, Ind., U.S.A. **77** 39 29N 86 23W
Martinsville, N.Y., U.S.A. **49** 43 2N 78 50W
Martinsville, Va., U.S.A. **73** 36 41N 79 52W
Marton **133** 40 4S 175 23E
Martos **104** 37 44N 3 58W
Martre, L., La **64** 63 0N 118 0W
Marudi **126** 4 10N 114 25E
Maruf **124** 31 30N 67 0E
Marugame **132** 34 15N 133 55E
Marvejols **102** 44 33N 3 19E
Marvine Mt. **79** 38 44N 111 40W
Marwar **124** 25 43N 73 45E
Marwayne **60** 53 32N 110 20W
Mary **120** 37 40N 61 50E
Mary Frances L. **55** 63 19N 106 13W
Mary Kathleen **135** 20 35S 139 48E
Maryborough, Queens., Austral. **135** 25 31S 152 37E
Maryborough, Vic., Austral. **136** 37 0S 143 44E
Maryborough = Port Laoise **97** 53 2N 7 20W
Maryen, L. **38** 51 20N 60 28W
Maryfield **57** 49 50N 101 35W
Maryhill **49** 43 32N 80 23W
Maryland □ **72** 39 10N 76 40W
Maryport **94** 54 43N 3 30W
Mary's Harbour **36** 52 18N 55 51W
Marystown **37** 47 10N 55 10W
Marysvale **79** 38 25N 112 17W
Marysville, B.C., Can. **61** 49 35N 116 0W
Marysville, N.B., Can. **39** 45 59N 66 35W
Marysville, Calif., U.S.A. **80** 39 14N 121 40W
Marysville, Kans., U.S.A. **74** 39 50N 96 38W
Marysville, Mich., U.S.A. **46** 42 55N 82 29W
Marysville, Ohio, U.S.A. **77** 40 15N 83 20W
Marysville, Wash., U.S.A. **80** 48 3N 122 11W
Maryville, U.S.A. **76** 40 21N 94 52W
Maryville, Tenn., U.S.A. **73** 35 50N 84 0W
Marzo, Punta **86** 6 50N 77 42W
Marzuq **114** 25 53N 14 10E
Masaka **116** 0 21S 31 45E
Masalima, Kepulauan **126** 5 10S 116 50E
Masamba **127** 2 30S 120 15E
Masan **130** 35 11N 128 32E
Masandam, Ras **123** 26 30N 56 30E
Masasi **116** 10 45S 38 52E
Masaya **84** 12 0N 86 7W
Mascarene Is. **16** 22 0S 55 0E
Mascota **82** 20 30N 104 50W
Mascouche **44** 45 45N 73 36W
Mascouche, R. **44** 45 41N 73 37W
Mascoutah **76** 38 29N 89 48W
Masela **127** 8 9S 129 51E
Maseme **85** 18 46S 25 3E
Maseru **117** 29 18S 27 30E
Mashābih **122** 25 35N 36 30E
Mashhad **123** 36 20N 59 35E
Mashike **132** 43 31N 141 30E
Mashki Chah **124** 29 5N 62 30E
Mashkode **34** 47 2N 84 7W
Masi **110** 69 26N 23 50E

Masi-Manimba Mendota

Masi-Manimba 116 4 40S 18 5E
Masindi 116 1 40N 31 43E
Masisea 86 8 35S 74 15W
Masjed Soleyman 122 31 55N 49 25E
Mask, L. 97 53 36N 9 24W
Maskinongé 41 46 14N 73 1W
Masoala, C. 117 15 59S 50 13E
Masohi 127 3 2S 128 15E
Mason, Mich., U.S.A. 77 42 35N 84 27W
Mason, Nev., U.S.A. 80 38 56N 119 8W
Mason, Ohio, U.S.A. 77 39 22N 84 19W
Mason, S.D., U.S.A. 74 45 12N 103 27W
Mason, Tex., U.S.A. 75 30 45N 99 15W
Mason City, Ill., U.S.A. 76 40 12N 89 42W
Mason City, Iowa, U.S.A. 76 43 9N 93 12W
Mason City, Wash., U.S.A. 78 48 0N 119 0W
Masqat 123 23 37N 58 36E
Massa 108 44 2N 10 7E
Massachusetts □ 71 42 25N 72 0W
Massachusetts B. 72 42 30N 70 0W
Massangena 117 21 34S 33 0E
Massat 102 42 53N 1 21E
Massena 71 44 52N 74 55W
Masset 62 54 2N 132 10W
Masset Inlet 62 53 43N 132 20W
Massey 46 46 12N 82 5W
Massiac 102 45 15N 3 11E
Massif Central 102 45 30N 2 21E
Massillon 70 40 47N 81 30W
Massinga 117 23 15S 35 22E
Masson 40 45 32N 75 25W
Masson I. 91 66 10S 93 20E
Massueville 43 45 55N 72 56W
Mastanli = Momchilgrad 92 41 33N 25 23E
Masterton 133 40 56S 175 39E
Mastigouche, Parc 41 46 33N 73 41W
Mastuj 124 36 20N 72 36E
Mastung 124 29 50N 66 42E
Masuda 132 34 40N 131 51E
Mataboor 127 1 41S 138 3E
Matachewan 34 47 56N 80 39W
Matad 129 47 11N 115 27E
Matadi 116 5 52S 13 31E
Matador 55 50 49N 107 56W
Matagalpa 84 13 10N 85 40W
Matagami 40 49 45N 77 34W
Matagami, L. 40 49 50N 77 40W
Matagorda 75 28 43N 96 0W
Matagorda, B. 75 28 30N 96 15W
Matagorda I. 75 28 10N 96 40W
Matak, P. 126 3 18N 106 16E
Matakana, I. 136 37 32S 176 5E
Matamec, L. 38 50 21N 65 58W
Matamoros, Campeche, Mexico 83 25 53N 97 30W
Matamoros, Coahuila, Mexico 82 25 45N 103 1W
Matamoros, Puebla, Mexico 83 18 2N 98 17W
Matamoros, Tamaulipas, Mexico 83 25 50N 97 30W
Matana, D. 127 2 30S 121 25E
Matane 38 48 50N 67 33W
Matane, Parc Prov. de 38 48 40N 67 0W
Matane, R. 38 48 50N 67 35W
Matanzá 86 7 22N 73 2W
Matanzas 84 23 0N 81 40W
Matapédia 39 48 0N 66 59W
Matapédia, L. 38 48 35N 67 35W
Matara 124 5 58N 80 30E
Mataram 126 8 41S 116 10E
Matarani 86 16 50S 72 10W
Mataranka 134 14 55S 133 4E
Mataura 133 46 11S 168 51E
Matawin, R. 41 46 54N 72 56W
Matawin, Rés. 41 46 46N 73 50W
Matchi-Manitou, L. 40 48 0N 77 4W
Matehuala 82 23 40N 100 50W
Matera 108 40 40N 16 37E
Matha 102 45 52N 0 20W
Matheson Island 57 51 45N 96 56W
Mathis 75 28 4N 97 48W
Mathura 124 27 30N 77 48E
Mati 127 6 55N 126 15E
Matías Romero 83 16 53N 95 2W
Matinenda L. 46 46 22N 82 57W
Matlock 94 53 8N 1 32W
Mato Grosso □ 87 14 0S 55 0W
Mato Grosso, Planalto do 86 15 0S 54 0W
Matochkin Shar 120 73 10N 56 40E
Matour 103 46 19N 4 29E
Matozinhos 104 41 11N 8 42W
Matrah 123 23 37N 58 30E
Matrûh 115 31 19N 27 9E
Matsang Tsangpo (Brahmaputra), R. 125 29 25N 88 0E
Matsue 132 35 25N 133 10E
Matsumoto 132 36 15N 138 0E
Matsuyama 132 33 45N 132 45E
Mattagami L. 53 47 54N 81 35W
Mattagami, R. 53 50 43N 81 29W
Mattancheri 124 9 50N 76 15E
Mattawa 34 46 20N 78 45W
Mattawamkeag 35 45 30N 68 30W
Mattawitchewan, R. 53 49 52N 83 12W
Matterhorn, mt. 106 45 58N 7 39E
Matteson 77 41 30N 87 42W
Matthew Town 85 20 57N 73 40W
Matthews 77 40 23N 85 31W
Matthew's Ridge 86 7 37N 60 10W
Mattice 53 49 40N 83 20W
Mattituck 71 40 58N 72 32W
Mattoon 77 39 30N 88 20W
Matua 126 2 58S 110 52E
Matucana 86 11 55S 76 15W
Matun 124 33 22N 69 58E
Maturín 86 9 45N 63 11W
*Mau-é-ele 117 24 18S 34 2E
Mau Ranipur 124 25 16N 79 8E
Mauagami, R. 34 49 30N 82 0W
Maubeuge 101 50 17N 3 57E
Maubourguet 102 43 29N 0 1E
Maudheim 91 71 5S 11 0W
Maudin Sun 125 16 0N 94 30E
Maués 86 3 20S 57 45W
Mauganj 125 24 50N 81 55E
Maugerville 39 45 52N 66 27W
Maui I. 67 20 45N 156 20E
Mauke, I. 133 20 09S 157 20W
Maulamyaing 125 16 30N 97 40E
Maule □ 88 36 5S 72 30W
Mauléon-Licharre 102 43 14N 0 54W
Maumee 77 41 35N 83 40W
Maumee, R. 77 41 42N 83 28W
Maumere 127 8 38S 122 13E
Maun 117 20 0S 23 26E
Mauna Kea, Mt. 67 19 50N 155 28W
Mauna Loa, Mt. 67 19 50N 155 28W
Maungmagan Is. 125 14 0S 97 48E
Maungmagan Kyunzu 128 14 0N 97 48E
Maunoir, L. 64 67 30N 124 55W
Maupin 78 45 12N 121 9W
Maure-de-Bretagne 100 47 53N 2 0W
Maurepas L. 75 30 18N 90 35W
Maures, mts. 103 43 15N 6 15E
Mauriac 102 45 13N 2 19E
Maurice L. 134 29 30S 131 0E
Mauricie, Parc Nat. de la 41 46 45N 73 0W
Maurienne 103 45 15N 6 20E
Mauritania ■ 114 20 50N 10 0W
Mauritius ■ 16 20 0S 57 0E
Mauron 100 48 9N 2 18W
Maurs 102 44 43N 2 12E
Mauston 74 43 48N 90 5W
Mauvezin 102 43 44N 0 53E
Mauzé-sur-le-Mignon 102 46 12N 0 41W
Mavillette 39 44 6N 66 11W
Mavinga 117 15 50S 20 10E
Mawcook 43 45 27N 72 47W
Mawer 55 50 46N 106 22W
Mawkmai 125 20 14N 97 50E
Mawlaik 125 23 40N 94 26E
Mawson Base 91 67 30N 65 0E
Max 74 47 50N 101 20W
Maxcanú 83 20 40N 90 10W
Maxhamish L. 54 59 50N 123 17W
Maxixe 117 23 54S 35 17E
Maxville 47 45 17N 74 51W
Maxwell 80 39 17N 122 11W
May Pen 84 17 58N 77 15W
Maya Mts. 83 16 30N 89 0W
Maya, R. 121 58 20N 135 0E
Mayaguana Island 85 21 30N 72 44W
Mayagüez 85 18 12N 67 9W
Mayapán 83 20 38N 89 27W
Mayarí 85 20 40N 75 39W
Mayarí 85 20 40N 75 41W
Maybell 78 40 30N 108 4W
Mayenne 100 48 20N 0 38W
Mayenne □ 100 48 10N 0 40W
Mayer 79 34 28N 112 17W
Mayerthorpe 60 53 57N 115 8W
Mayfair 56 52 58N 107 36W
Mayfield 73 36 45N 88 40W
Mayhill 79 32 58N 105 30W
Maykop 120 44 35N 40 25E
Mayland 59 51 3N 114 0W
Maymont 56 52 34N 107 42W
Maymyo 128 22 2N 96 28E
Maynard 80 47 59N 122 55W
Mayne 63 48 52N 123 17W
Mayne, Le, L. 35 57 5N 68 30W
Maynooth, Can. 34 45 14N 77 56W
Maynooth, Ireland 97 53 22N 6 38W
Mayo 67 63 38N 135 57W
Mayo □ 97 53 47N 9 7W
Mayo L. 67 63 45N 135 0W
Mayo, R. 82 26 45N 109 47W
Mayon, Mt. 127 13 15N 123 42E
Mayor I. 133 37 16S 176 17E
Mayson L. 55 57 55N 107 10W
Maysville, U.S.A. 76 39 53N 94 21W
Maysville, U.S.A. 77 38 39N 83 46W
Mayu, I. 127 1 30N 126 30E
Mayville, N.D., U.S.A. 74 47 30N 97 23W
Mayville, N.Y., U.S.A. 70 42 14N 79 31W
Maywood 77 41 53N 87 51W
Mayya 121 61 44N 130 18E
Mazabuka 117 15 52S 27 44E
Mazagão 87 0 20S 51 50W
Mazama, Can. 54 49 43N 120 8W
Mazama, U.S.A. 63 48 37N 120 25W
Mazamet 102 43 30N 2 20E
Mazán 86 3 15S 73 0W
Mazapil 82 24 38N 101 34W
Mazar-i-Sharif 123 36 41N 67 0E
Mazarredo 90 47 10S 66 50W
Mazarrón 104 37 38N 1 19W
Mazaruni, R. 86 6 15N 60 0W
Mazatán 82 29 0N 110 8W
Mazatenango 84 14 35N 91 30W
Mazatlán 82 23 10N 106 30W
Mazenod 56 49 52N 106 13W
Mazhabong L. 53 46 58N 82 30W
Māzhān 123 32 30N 59 0E
Mazinān 123 36 25N 56 48E
Mazoe R. 117 16 45S 32 30E
Mazomanie 76 43 11N 89 48W
Mazon 77 41 14N 88 25W
Mbabane 117 26 18S 31 6E
M'Baiki 116 3 53N 18 1E
Mbala 116 8 46S 31 17E
Mbale 116 1 8N 34 12E
Mbalmayo 116 3 33N 11 33E
Mbamba Bay 116 11 13S 34 49E
Mbandaka 116 0 1S 18 18E
Mbanza Ngungu 116 5 12S 14 53E
Mbarara 116 0 35S 30 25E
Mbeya 116 8 54S 33 29E
Mbini □ 114 1 30N 10 0E
Mbuji-Mayi 116 6 9S 23 40E
Mbulu 116 3 45S 35 30E
Mburucuyá 88 28 1S 58 14W
M'Clintock Chan. 64 72 0N 102 0W
M'Clure Str., Can. 22 75 0N 118 0W
M'Clure Str., N.W.T., Can. 64 75 0N 119 0W
Mdina 108 35 51N 14 25E
Meacham 56 52 6N 105 45W
Meachen 61 49 38N 116 17W
Mead L. 81 36 1N 114 44W
Meade, Can. 34 49 26N 83 51W
Meade, U.S.A. 75 37 18N 100 25W
Meadow L. 56 54 7N 108 20W
Meadow Lake 56 54 10N 108 26W
Meadow Lake Prov. Park 55 54 27N 109 0W
Meadow Valley Wash 81 36 30N 114 24W
Meadowlands 52 47 7N 92 49W
Meadville, U.S.A. 76 39 47N 93 18W
Meadville, Pa., U.S.A. 70 41 39N 80 9W
Meaford 46 44 36N 80 35W
Meaghers Grant 39 44 55N 63 15W
Mealy Mts. 35 53 10N 59 30W
Meander, R. = Menderes, Büyük 122 37 45N 27 40E
Meander River 54 59 2N 117 42W
Meares, C. 78 45 37N 124 0W
Meares I. 62 49 12N 125 50W
Mearim, R. 87 3 4S 44 35W
Meath □ 97 53 32N 6 40W
Meath Park 56 53 27N 105 22W
Meaulne 102 46 36N 2 28E
Meaux 101 48 58N 2 50E
Mecatina, Little, R. 38 52 10N 60 40W
Mécatina, Petit-, R. 38 50 40N 59 30W
Mecca 81 33 37N 116 3W
Mechanicsburg 70 40 12N 77 0W
Mechanicsville 76 41 54N 91 16W
Mechanicville 71 42 54N 73 41W
Mechelen 105 51 2N 4 29E
Mechernich 105 50 35N 6 39E
Méchins, Les 38 48 59N 66 59W
Mecklenburger Bucht 106 54 20N 11 40E
Meconta 117 14 59S 39 50E
Meda, R. 134 17 20S 124 30E
Medan 126 3 40N 98 38E
Medanosa, Pta. 90 48 0S 66 0W
Medaryville 77 41 4N 86 55W
Medellín 86 6 15N 75 35W
Medford, Oreg., U.S.A. 78 42 20N 122 52W
Medford, Wis., U.S.A. 74 45 9N 90 21W
Media Agua 88 31 58S 68 25W
Media Luna 88 34 45S 66 44W
Mediapolis 76 41 0N 91 10W
Mediaş 107 46 9N 24 22E
Medical Lake 78 47 41N 117 42W
Medicine Bow 78 41 56N 106 11W
Medicine Hat 61 50 0N 110 45W
Medicine Lake 74 48 30N 104 30W
Medicine Lodge 75 37 20N 98 37W
Medina, Colomb. 86 4 30N 73 21W
Medina, N.D., U.S.A. 74 46 57N 99 20W
Medina, N.Y., U.S.A. 70 43 15N 78 27W
Medina, Ohio, U.S.A. 70 41 9N 81 50W
Medina = Al Madīnah 122 24 35N 39 52E
Medina del Campo 104 41 18N 4 55W
Medina L. 75 29 35N 98 58W
Medina, R. 75 29 10N 98 20W
Medina-Sidonia 104 36 28N 5 57W
Mediterranean Sea 93 35 0N 15 0E
Medley 60 54 25N 110 16W
Médoc 102 45 10N 0 56W
Medora 77 38 49N 86 10W
Medstead 56 53 19N 108 5W
Meductic 39 46 0N 67 29W
Medvezhi, Ostrava 121 71 0N 161 0E
Medvezhyegorsk 120 63 0N 34 25E
Medway, R., Can. 39 44 8N 64 36W
Medway, R., U.K. 95 51 12N 0 23E
Meekatharra 134 26 32S 118 29E
Meeker 78 40 1N 107 58W
Meelpaeg L. 35 48 18N 56 35W
Meerut 124 29 1N 77 50E
Meeteetsa 78 44 10N 108 56W
Mégantic 35 45 36N 70 56W
Mégantic, L. 41 45 32N 70 53W
Mégantic, Mt. 41 45 28N 71 9W
Mégara 109 37 58N 23 22E
Mégève 103 45 51N 6 37E
Meghalaya □ 125 25 50N 91 0E
Mégiscane, L. 40 48 35N 75 55W
Mégiscane, R. 40 48 29N 75 38W
Mehadia 107 44 56N 22 23E
Meharry, Mt. 134 22 59S 118 35E
Mehsana 124 23 39N 72 26E
Mehun-sur-Yèvre 101 47 10N 2 13E
Meighen I. 65 80 0N 99 30W
Meihokow 130 42 37N 125 46E
Meihsien 131 24 18N 116 7E
Meiktila 125 21 0N 96 0E
Meissen 106 51 10N 13 29E
Meit'an 131 27 45N 107 28E
Méjean, Causse 102 44 15N 3 30E
Mejillones 88 23 10S 70 30W
Mekambo 116 1 2N 14 5E
Mekhtar 124 30 30N 69 15E
Mékinac, L. 41 47 3N 72 41W
Meklong = Samut Songkhram 128 13 24N 100 1E
Meknès 114 33 57N 5 33W
Mekong, R. 128 18 0N 104 15E
Mekongga 127 3 50S 121 30E
Mekoryok 67 60 20N 166 20W
Melagiri Hills 124 12 20N 77 30E
Melaka 128 2 15N 102 15E
Melaka □ 128 2 20N 102 15E
Melalap 126 5 10N 116 5E
Melanesia 14 4 0S 155 0E
Melbourne, Austral. 136 37 50S 145 0E
Melbourne, U.S.A. 76 41 57N 93 6W
Melbourne, Fla., U.S.A. 73 28 13N 80 35W
Melcher 76 41 13N 93 15W
Melchor Múzquiz 82 27 50N 101 40W
Melchor Ocampo (San Pedro Ocampo) 82 24 52N 101 40W
Meldrum Bay 46 45 56N 83 6W
Meldrum Creek 63 52 6N 122 21W
Mêle-sur-Sarthe, Le 100 48 31N 0 22E
Mélèzes, R. 36 57 40N 69 29W
Melfort 56 52 50N 104 37W
Melilla 114 35 21N 2 57W
Melilot 100 31 22N 34 37E
Melipilla 88 33 42S 71 15W
Melita 57 49 15N 101 0W
Melitopol 120 46 50N 35 22E
Melk 106 48 13N 15 20E
Mellansel 110 63 25N 18 17E
Melle 102 46 14N 0 10W
Mellen 52 46 19N 90 36W
Mellerud 111 58 41N 12 28E
Mellette 74 45 11N 98 29W
Mellish Reef 135 17 25S 155 50E
Melo 89 32 20S 54 10W
Melochville 44 45 19N 73 56W
Melolo 127 9 53S 120 40E
Melones Res. 80 37 57N 120 31W
Melrose, U.K. 96 55 35N 2 44W
Melrose, U.S.A. 76 40 59N 93 3W
Melrose, N.Mex., U.S.A. 75 34 27N 103 33W
Melstone 78 46 40N 107 55W
Melton Mowbray 94 52 46N 0 52W
Melun 101 48 32N 2 39E
Melville 56 50 55N 102 50W
Melville B. 135 12 0S 136 45E
Melville Bugt 65 75 30N 63 0W
Melville, C. 135 14 11S 144 30E
Melville I., Austral. 134 11 30S 131 0E
Melville I., Can. 64 75 30N 111 0W
Melville, L. 35 53 45N 59 40W
Melville Pen. 65 68 0N 84 0W
Melvin, R. 54 59 11N 117 31W
Memba 117 14 11S 40 30E
Memboro 127 9 30S 119 30E
Memmingen 106 47 59N 10 12E
Memphis, U.S.A. 76 40 28N 92 10W
Memphis, Mich., U.S.A. 46 42 54N 82 46W
Memphis, Tenn., U.S.A. 75 35 7N 90 0W
Memphis, Tex., U.S.A. 75 34 45N 100 30W
Memphrémagog, L. 41 45 8N 72 17W
Mena 75 34 40N 94 15W
Menai Strait 94 53 7N 4 20W
Ménaka 114 15 59N 2 18E
Menard 75 30 57N 99 58W
Ménardville 45 45 17N 73 4W
Ménascouagama, L. 38 51 13N 61 52W
Menasha 72 44 13N 88 27W
Menate 126 0 12S 112 47E
Mencheng 131 33 27N 116 45E
Mendawai, R. 126 1 30S 113 0E
Mende 102 44 31N 3 30E
Mendenhall, C. 67 59 44N 166 10W
Menderes, R. 122 37 25N 28 45E
Mendez 83 25 7N 98 34W
Mendham 56 50 46N 109 40W
Mendip Hills 95 51 17N 2 40W
Mendocino 78 39 26N 123 50W
Mendon 77 42 0N 85 27W
Mendota, Calif., U.S.A. 80 36 46N 120 24W

* Renamed Marão

Mendota **Mindanao Trench**

Mendota, Ill., U.S.A.	**76**	41 35N	89 5W
Mendoza	**88**	32 50S	68 52W
Mendoza □	**88**	33 0S	69 0W
Mene Grande	**86**	9 49N	70 56W
Menemen	**122**	38 18N	27 10E
Menfi	**108**	37 36N	12 57E
Meng-so	**128**	22 33N	99 31E
Meng Wang	**128**	22 18N	100 31E
Menggala	**126**	4 20S	105 15E
Mengshan	**131**	24 2N	110 32E
Mengtsz	**129**	23 20N	103 20E
Mengyin	**130**	35 40N	117 55E
Menihek	**36**	54 28N	56 36W
Menihek L.	**36**	54 0N	67 0W
Menin	**105**	50 47N	3 7E
Menindee	**136**	32 20S	142 25E
Ménistouc, L.	**38**	52 52N	66 29W
Menlo Park	**80**	37 27N	122 12W
Menominee	**72**	45 9N	87 39W
Menominee, R.	**72**	45 30N	87 50W
Menomonee Falls	**77**	43 11N	88 7W
Menomonie	**74**	44 50N	91 54W
Menor, Mar	**104**	37 43N	0 48W
Menorca, I.	**104**	40 0N	4 0E
Mentawai, Kepulauan	**126**	2 0S	99 0E
Menton	**103**	43 50N	7 29E
Mentone	**77**	41 10N	86 2W
Mentor	**70**	41 40N	81 21W
Menzies	**134**	29 40S	120 58E
Meoqui	**82**	28 17N	105 29W
Meota	**56**	53 2N	108 27W
Meppel	**105**	52 42N	6 12E
Meppen	**105**	52 41N	7 20E
Mequon	**77**	43 14N	87 59W
Mer Rouge	**75**	32 47N	91 48W
Merabéllou, Kólpos	**109**	35 10N	25 50E
Merak	**127**	5 55S	106 1E
Meramec, R.	**76**	38 23N	91 21W
Merano (Meran)	**108**	46 40N	11 10E
Merasheen I.	**37**	47 25N	54 15W
Merauke	**127**	8 29S	140 24E
Merbabu, Mt.	**127**	7 30S	110 40E
Merbein	**136**	34 10S	142 2E
Merca	**115**	1 48N	44 50E
Mercara	**124**	12 30N	75 45E
Merced	**80**	37 18N	120 30W
Merced Pk.	**80**	37 36N	119 24W
Mercedes, Buenos Aires, Argent.	**88**	34 40S	59 30W
Mercedes, Corrientes, Argent.	**88**	29 10S	58 5W
Mercedes, San Luis, Argent.	**88**	33 5S	65 21W
Mercedes, Uruguay	**88**	33 12S	58 0W
Merceditas	**88**	28 20S	70 35W
Mercer, N.Z.	**133**	37 16S	175 5E
Mercer, U.S.A.	**76**	40 31N	93 32W
Mercer, Pa., U.S.A.	**70**	41 14N	80 13W
Mercier	**44**	45 19N	73 45W
Mercoal	**60**	53 10N	117 5W
Mercury	**81**	36 40N	116 0W
Mercy C.	**65**	65 0N	62 30W
Merdrignac	**100**	48 11N	2 27W
Meredith C.	**90**	52 15S	60 40W
Meredith, L.	**75**	35 30N	101 35W
Meredosia	**76**	39 50N	90 34W
Méréville	**101**	48 20N	2 5E
Mergui Arch.	**128**	12 30N	98 35E
Mergui Arch. = Myeik Kyunzu	**128**	11 30N	97 30E
Mérida, Mexico	**83**	20 50N	89 40W
Mérida, Spain	**104**	38 55N	6 25W
Mérida, Venez.	**86**	8 36N	71 8W
Mérida □	**86**	8 30N	71 10W
Mérida, Cord. de	**86**	9 0N	71 0W
Meriden	**71**	41 33N	72 47W
Meridian, Calif., U.S.A.	**80**	39 9N	121 55W
Meridian, Idaho, U.S.A.	**78**	43 41N	116 25W
Meridian, Miss., U.S.A.	**73**	32 20N	88 42W
Meridian, Tex., U.S.A.	**75**	31 55N	97 37W
Merigomish	**39**	45 38N	62 26W
Merimula	**136**	36 54S	149 54E
Meringur	**136**	34 20S	141 19E
Merirumã	**87**	1 15N	54 50W
Merivale	**48**	45 19N	75 43W
Merkel	**75**	32 30N	100 0W
Merksem	**105**	51 16N	4 25E
Merlebach	**101**	49 5N	6 52E
Merlerault, Le	**100**	48 41N	0 16E
Merowe	**115**	18 29N	31 46E
Merredin	**134**	31 28S	118 18E
Merrick, Mt.	**96**	55 8N	4 30W
Merrickville	**47**	44 55N	75 50W
Merrill, Mich., U.S.A.	**46**	43 25N	84 20W
Merrill, Oregon, U.S.A.	**78**	42 2N	121 37W
Merrill, Wis., U.S.A.	**74**	45 11N	89 41W
Merriton	**70**	43 12N	79 13W
Merritt	**63**	50 10N	120 45W
Merry I.	**36**	55 29N	77 31W
Merrygoen	**136**	31 51S	149 12E
Merryville	**75**	30 47N	93 31W
Mersch	**105**	49 44N	6 7E
Merseburg	**106**	51 20N	12 0E
Mersey, R., Can.	**39**	44 2N	64 43W
Mersey, R., U.K.	**94**	53 20N	2 56W
Merseyside □	**94**	53 25N	2 55W
Mersin	**122**	36 51N	34 36E
Mersing	**128**	2 25N	103 50E
Merthyr Tydfil	**95**	51 45N	3 23W
Mertoa	**136**	36 33S	142 29E
Mértola	**104**	37 40N	7 40E
Merton	**49**	43 25N	79 44W
Mertzon	**75**	31 17N	100 48W
Méru	**101**	49 13N	2 8E
Meru	**116**	0 3N	37 40E
Merville, Can.	**62**	49 48N	125 3W
Merville, France	**101**	50 38N	2 38E
Mervin	**56**	53 20N	108 53W
Méry-sur-Seine	**101**	48 31N	3 54E
Merzig	**105**	49 26N	6 37E
Mesa	**79**	33 20N	111 56W
Mesa, La, Colomb.	**86**	4 38N	74 28W
Mesa, La, Calif., U.S.A.	**81**	32 48N	117 5W
Mesa, La, N. Mex., U.S.A.	**79**	32 6N	106 48W
Mesgouez, L.	**36**	51 20N	75 0W
Meshed = Mashhad	**123**	36 20N	59 35E
Meshoppen	**71**	41 36N	76 3W
Mesick	**72**	44 24N	85 42W
Mesilinka, R.	**54**	56 6N	124 30W
Mesilla	**79**	32 20N	106 50W
Meslay-du-Maine	**100**	47 58N	0 33W
Mesolóngion	**109**	38 27N	21 28E
Mesopotamia, reg.	**122**	33 30N	44 0E
Mess Cr.	**54**	57 55N	131 14W
Messac	**100**	47 49N	1 50W
Messeix	**102**	45 37N	2 33E
Messina, Italy	**108**	38 10N	15 32E
Messina, S. Afr.	**117**	22 20S	30 12E
Messina, Str. di	**108**	38 5N	15 35E
Messine	**40**	46 14N	76 2W
Messini	**109**	37 4N	22 1E
Messiniakós, Kólpos	**109**	36 45N	22 5E
Mesta, R.	**109**	41 30N	24 0E
Meta	**76**	38 19N	92 10W
Meta □	**86**	3 30N	73 0W
Meta, R.	**86**	6 20N	68 5W
Metagama	**34**	47 0N	81 55W
Metaline Falls	**63**	48 52N	117 22W
Metamora	**76**	40 47N	89 22W
Metán	**88**	25 30S	65 0W
Metchosin	**54**	48 15N	123 37W
Meteghan	**39**	44 11N	66 10W
Methuen	**71**	42 43N	71 10W
Methven	**133**	43 38S	171 40E
Methy L.	**55**	56 28N	109 30W
Metil	**117**	16 24S	39 0E
Métis-sur-Mer	**38**	48 40N	67 59W
Metlakatla	**67**	55 10N	131 33W
Metropolis	**75**	37 10N	88 47W
Mettur Dam	**124**	11 45N	77 45E
Metz	**101**	49 8N	6 10E
Meulaboh	**126**	4 11N	96 3E
Meulan	**101**	49 0N	1 52E
Meung-sur-Loire	**101**	47 50N	1 40E
Meureudu	**126**	5 19N	96 10E
Meurthe-et-Moselle □	**101**	48 52N	6 0E
Meurthe, R.	**101**	48 47N	6 9E
Meuse □	**101**	49 8N	5 25E
Meuse, R.	**105**	50 45N	5 41E
Mexborough	**94**	53 29N	1 18W
Mexia	**75**	31 38N	96 32W
Mexiana, I.	**87**	0 0	49 30W
Mexicali	**82**	32 40N	115 30W
México	**83**	19 20N	99 10W
Mexico, Me., U.S.A.	**71**	44 35N	70 30W
Mexico, Mo., U.S.A.	**76**	39 10N	91 55W
Mexico ■	**82**	20 0N	100 0W
México □	**82**	19 20N	99 10W
Mexico, G. of	**83**	25 0N	90 0W
Meymac	**102**	45 32N	2 10E
Meyrargues	**103**	43 38N	5 32E
Meyronne	**56**	49 39N	106 50W
Meyrueis	**102**	44 12N	3 27E
Meyssac	**102**	45 3N	1 40E
Mèze	**102**	43 27N	3 36E
Mezen	**120**	65 50N	44 20E
Mezen, R.	**120**	64 34N	46 30E
Mézidon	**100**	49 5N	0 1W
Mézilhac	**103**	44 49N	4 21E
Mézin	**102**	44 4N	0 16E
Mezökövesd	**107**	47 49N	20 35E
Mézos	**102**	44 5N	1 10W
Mezötúr	**107**	47 0N	20 41E
Mezquital	**82**	23 29N	104 23W
Mhow	**124**	22 33N	75 50E
Miahuatlán	**83**	16 21N	96 36W
Miami, Ariz., U.S.A.	**79**	33 25N	111 0W
Miami, Fla., U.S.A.	**73**	25 52N	80 15W
Miami, Tex., U.S.A.	**75**	35 44N	100 38W
Miami Beach	**73**	25 49N	80 6W
Miami, R.	**72**	39 20N	84 40W
Miamisburg	**77**	39 40N	84 11W
Miandowāb	**122**	37 0N	46 5E
Miandrivazo	**117**	19 50S	45 56E
Mīāneh	**122**	37 30N	47 40E
Mianwali	**124**	32 38N	71 28E
Miao Tao	**130**	38 10N	120 50E
Miaoli	**131**	24 33N	120 42E
Miarinarivo	**117**	18 57S	46 55E
Miass	**120**	54 59N	60 6E
Mica Creek	**63**	52 2N	118 35W
Mica Dam	**63**	52 5N	118 32W
Mica Res.	**54**	51 55N	118 00W
Michaudville	**43**	45 50N	73 4W
Michelson, Mt.	**67**	69 20N	144 20W
Michigan □	**69**	44 40N	85 40W
Michigan Center	**46**	42 14N	84 20W
Michigan City	**77**	41 42N	86 56W
Michigan, L.	**72**	44 0N	87 0W
Michih	**130**	37 58N	110 0E
Michipicoten	**53**	47 55N	84 55W
Michipicoten B.	**53**	47 53N	84 53W
Michipicoten I.	**53**	47 40N	85 50W
Michoacan □	**82**	19 0N	102 0W
Michurinsk	**120**	52 58N	40 27E
Micmac Lake	**39**	44 41N	63 33W
Micronesia	**14**	17 0N	160 0E
Mid Glamorgan □	**95**	51 40N	3 25W
Midai, P.	**126**	3 0N	107 47E
Midale	**56**	49 25N	103 20W
Midas	**78**	41 14N	116 56W
Middelburg, Neth.	**105**	51 30N	3 36E
Middelburg, S. Afr.	**117**	31 30S	25 0E
Middle Alkali L.	**78**	41 30N	120 3W
Middle Andaman I.	**128**	12 30N	92 30E
Middle Brook	**35**	48 40N	54 20W
Middle Church	**58**	49 59N	97 4W
Middle Fork Feather, R.	**80**	39 35N	121 25W
Middle Lake	**56**	52 29N	105 18W
Middle Musquodoboit	**39**	45 3N	63 9W
Middle, R.	**76**	41 26N	93 30W
Middle Raccoon, R.	**76**	41 35N	93 35W
Middleboro	**71**	41 56N	70 52W
Middleburg, N.Y., U.S.A.	**71**	42 36N	74 19W
Middleburg, Pa., U.S.A.	**70**	40 46N	77 5W
Middlebury, Ind., U.S.A.	**77**	41 41N	85 42W
Middlebury, Vt., U.S.A.	**71**	44 0N	73 9W
Middleport	**72**	39 0N	82 5W
Middlesbrough	**94**	54 35N	1 14W
Middlesex, Belize	**83**	17 2N	88 31W
Middlesex, U.S.A.	**71**	40 36N	74 30W
Middleton, Can.	**39**	44 57N	65 4W
Middleton, U.S.A.	**76**	43 6N	89 30W
Middleton I.	**67**	59 30N	146 28W
Middletown, Calif., U.S.A.	**80**	38 45N	122 37W
Middletown, Conn., U.S.A.	**71**	41 37N	72 40W
Middletown, N.Y., U.S.A.	**71**	41 28N	74 28W
Middletown, Ohio, U.S.A.	**77**	39 30N	84 21W
Middletown, Pa., U.S.A.	**71**	40 12N	76 44W
Middleville	**77**	42 43N	85 28W
Middlewood	**39**	44 14N	64 34W
Midi, Canal du	**102**	43 45N	1 21E
Midland, Man., Can.	**58**	49 54N	97 11W
Midland, Ont., Can.	**46**	44 45N	79 50W
Midland, Calif., U.S.A.	**81**	33 52N	114 48W
Midland, Mich., U.S.A.	**46**	43 37N	84 17W
Midland, Pa., U.S.A.	**70**	40 39N	80 27W
Midland, Tex., U.S.A.	**75**	32 0N	102 3W
Midland Junction	**134**	31 50S	115 58E
Midleton	**97**	51 52N	8 12W
Midlothian	**75**	32 30N	97 0W
Midnapore, Can.	**59**	50 55N	114 5W
Midnapore, India	**125**	22 25N	87 21E
Midvale	**78**	40 39N	111 58W
Midway	**63**	49 1N	118 48W
Midway Is.	**14**	28 13N	177 22W
Midway Wells	**81**	32 41N	115 7W
Midwest	**78**	43 27N	106 11W
Mie-ken □	**132**	34 30N	136 10E
Miedzychód	**106**	52 35N	15 53E
Miedzyrzec Podlaski	**107**	51 58N	22 45E
Miélan	**102**	43 27N	0 19E
Mienchih	**131**	34 47N	111 49E
Mienhsien	**131**	33 11N	106 35E
Mienyang, Hupei, China	**131**	30 10N	113 20E
Mienyang, Szechwan, China	**131**	31 18N	104 26E
Miercurea Ciuc	**107**	46 21N	25 48E
Mieres	**104**	43 18N	5 48W
Miette Hotsprings	**60**	53 8N	117 46W
Migennes	**101**	47 58N	3 31E
Miguel Alemán, Presa	**83**	18 15N	96 40W
Miguel Alves	**87**	4 11S	42 55W
Mihara	**132**	34 24N	133 5E
Milntown	**70**	40 34N	77 24W
Mikardo	**46**	44 34N	83 28W
Mikinai	**109**	37 43N	22 46E
Mikindani	**116**	10 15S	40 2E
Mikkeli	**111**	61 43N	27 25E
Mikkeli □	**110**	62 0N	28 0E
Mikkwa, R.	**60**	58 25N	114 46W
Míkonos, I.	**109**	37 30N	25 25E
Mikura-Jima	**132**	33 52N	139 36E
Milaca	**74**	45 45N	93 40W
Milagro	**86**	2 0S	79 30W
Milan, U.S.A.	**46**	42 5N	83 40W
Milan, Ill., U.S.A.	**76**	41 27N	90 34W
Milan, Mo., U.S.A.	**76**	40 10N	93 5W
Milan, Tenn., U.S.A.	**73**	35 55N	88 45W
Milan = Milano	**108**	45 28N	9 10E
Milano	**108**	45 28N	9 10E
Milâs	**122**	37 20N	27 50E
Milazzo	**108**	38 13N	15 13E
Milbank	**74**	45 17N	96 38W
Milden	**56**	51 29N	107 32W
Mildmay	**46**	44 3N	81 7W
Mildura	**136**	34 13S	142 9E
Miles, Austral.	**135**	26 40S	150 23E
Miles, U.S.A.	**75**	31 39N	100 11W
Miles City	**74**	46 30N	105 50W
Milestone	**56**	49 59N	104 31W
Milford, U.S.A.	**77**	42 35N	83 36W
Milford, U.S.A.	**77**	41 40N	87 43W
Milford, Conn., U.S.A.	**71**	41 13N	73 4W
Milford, Del., U.S.A.	**72**	38 52N	75 27W
Milford, Mass., U.S.A.	**71**	42 8N	71 30W
Milford, Pa., U.S.A.	**71**	41 20N	74 47W
Milford, Utah, U.S.A.	**79**	38 20N	113 0W
Milford Haven	**95**	51 43N	5 2W
Milford Haven, B.	**95**	51 40N	5 10W
Milford Sd.	**133**	44 34S	167 47E
Milford Station	**39**	45 3N	63 26W
Milk, R., Can.	**61**	49 0N	110 33W
Milk, R., U.S.A.	**78**	48 40N	107 15W
Milk River	**61**	49 10N	112 5W
Mill City	**78**	44 45N	122 28W
Mill Cr.	**59**	53 33N	113 29W
Mill Grove	**48**	43 20N	79 58W
Mill, I.	**91**	66 0S	101 30E
Mill Shoals	**77**	38 15N	88 21W
Mill Valley	**80**	37 54N	122 32W
Mill Village	**39**	44 9N	64 39W
Millau	**102**	44 8N	3 4E
Millbridge	**47**	44 41N	77 36W
Millbrook	**47**	44 10N	78 29W
Mille	**73**	33 7N	83 15W
Mille Îles, R. des	**44**	45 42N	73 32W
Mille Isles	**43**	45 49N	74 14W
Mille Lacs, L.	**52**	46 10N	93 30W
Mille Lacs, L. des	**52**	48 45N	90 35W
Milledgeville	**76**	41 58N	89 46W
Millen	**73**	32 50N	81 57W
Miller	**74**	44 35N	98 59W
Millerand	**39**	47 13N	61 59W
Millersburg, U.S.A.	**77**	41 32N	85 42W
Millersburg, Mich., U.S.A.	**46**	45 20N	84 4W
Millersburg, Ohio, U.S.A.	**70**	40 32N	81 52W
Millersburg, Pa., U.S.A.	**70**	40 32N	76 58W
Millerton	**71**	41 57N	73 32W
Millerton, L.	**80**	37 0N	119 42W
Millertown	**37**	48 49N	56 33W
Millet	**61**	53 6N	113 28W
Millevaches, Plat. de	**102**	45 45N	2 0E
Millicent	**135**	37 34S	140 21E
Milliken	**50**	43 49N	79 18W
Millington	**46**	43 17N	83 32W
Millinocket	**35**	45 45N	68 45W
Mills L.	**54**	61 30N	118 20W
Millsboro	**70**	40 0N	80 0W
Millstream	**39**	48 2N	67 2W
Milltown, N.B., Can.	**39**	45 10N	67 18W
Milltown, Newf., Can.	**37**	47 54N	55 46W
Milltown Malbay	**97**	52 51N	9 25W
Millview	**39**	44 43N	63 40W
Millville, Can.	**39**	46 8N	67 12W
Millville, U.S.A.	**72**	39 22N	75 0W
Millwood Res.	**75**	33 45N	94 0W
Milly	**101**	48 24N	2 20E
Milnesville	**50**	43 55N	79 16W
Milnor	**74**	46 19N	97 29W
Milo	**61**	50 34N	112 53W
Milolii	**67**	22 8N	159 42W
Milos	**109**	36 44N	24 25E
Milot	**41**	48 54N	71 49W
Milroy	**77**	39 30N	85 28W
Milton, N.S., Can.	**39**	44 4N	64 45W
Milton, Ont., Can.	**49**	43 31N	79 53W
Milton, N.Z.	**133**	46 7S	169 59E
Milton, U.S.A.	**76**	40 41N	92 10W
Milton, U.S.A.	**77**	42 47N	88 56W
Milton, Calif., U.S.A.	**80**	38 3N	120 51W
Milton, Fla., U.S.A.	**73**	30 38N	87 0W
Milton, Pa., U.S.A.	**70**	41 0N	76 53W
Milton-Freewater	**78**	45 57N	118 24W
Milton Heights	**49**	43 31N	79 56W
Milton Keynes	**95**	52 3N	0 42W
Milton West	**70**	43 33N	79 53W
Milverton	**46**	43 34N	80 55W
Milwaukee	**77**	43 9N	87 58W
Milwaukie	**80**	45 27N	122 39W
Mimico Cr.	**50**	43 37N	79 30W
Mimingash	**39**	46 53N	64 14W
Miminiska L.	**52**	51 35N	88 37W
Mimizan	**102**	44 12N	1 13W
Mimosa	**49**	43 44N	80 13W
Min K.	**131**	26 0N	119 20E
Mina	**79**	38 21N	118 9W
Mina Pirquitas	**88**	22 40S	66 40W
Mina Saud	**122**	28 45N	48 20E
Minā'al Ahmadī	**122**	29 5N	48 10E
Mīnāb	**123**	27 10N	57 1E
Minago, R.	**57**	54 33N	98 59W
Minaki	**52**	49 59N	94 40W
Minamata	**132**	32 10N	130 30E
Minas Basin	**39**	45 20N	64 12W
Minas Channel	**39**	45 15N	64 45W
Minas de Rio Tinto	**104**	37 42N	6 22W
Minas Gerais □	**87**	18 50S	46 0W
Minas, Sierra de las	**84**	15 9N	89 31W
Minatitlán	**83**	17 58N	94 35W
Minbu	**125**	20 10N	95 0E
Mindanao, I.	**127**	8 0N	125 0E
*Mindanao Sea	**127**	9 0N	124 0E
Mindanao Trench	**127**	8 0N	128 0E

* *Renamed Bohol Sea*

Name	Page	Lat.	Long.
Mindemoya	46	45 44N	82 10W
Minden, Can.	47	44 55N	78 43W
Minden, Ger.	106	52 18N	8 54 E
Minden, La., U.S.A.	75	32 40N	93 20W
Minden, Nev., U.S.A.	80	38 57N	119 48W
Mindiptana	127	5 45 S	140 22 E
Mindona, L.	136	33 6 S	142 6 E
Mindoro, I.	127	13 0N	121 0 E
Mindoro Strait	127	12 30N	120 30 E
Mindouli	116	4 12 S	14 28 E
Mine Centre	52	48 45N	92 37W
Mine, L.	38	50 51N	64 43W
Minegan, Îles de	38	50 12N	63 35W
Minehead	95	51 12N	3 29W
Mineola	75	32 40N	95 30W
Mineral King	80	36 27N	118 36W
Mineral Point	76	42 52N	90 11W
Mineral Wells	75	32 50N	98 5W
Minersville, Pa., U.S.A.	71	40 40N	76 17W
Minersville, Utah, U.S.A.	79	38 14N	112 58W
Minerva	70	40 43N	81 8W
Minette	73	30 54N	87 43W
Minetto	71	43 24N	76 28W
Mingan	38	50 20N	64 0W
Mingan = Pangkiang	130	43 4N	112 30 E
Mingan, R.	38	50 18N	63 59W
Mingechaurskoye Vdkhr.	120	40 56N	47 20 E
Mingin	125	22 50N	94 30 E
Mingki (Kweihwa)	131	26 10N	117 14 E
Minho □	104	41 25N	8 20W
Minho, R.	104	41 58N	8 40W
Minhow = Foochow	131	26 2N	119 12 E
Minhsien	131	34 26N	104 2 E
Minidoka	78	42 47N	113 34W
Minier	76	40 26N	89 19W
Minilya	134	23 55 S	114 0 E
Minipi, L.	38	52 25N	60 45W
Miniss L.	52	50 48N	90 50W
Minitonas	57	52 5N	101 2W
Mink L.	54	61 54N	117 40W
Minkiang	131	32 30N	114 10 E
Minneapolis, Kans., U.S.A.	74	39 11N	97 40W
Minneapolis, Minn., U.S.A.	74	44 58N	93 20W
Minnedosa	57	50 14N	99 50W
Minnesota □	74	46 40N	94 0W
Minnitaki L.	52	49 57N	91 55W
Miño, R.	104	41 58N	8 40W
Minonk	76	40 54N	89 2W
Minooka	77	41 27N	88 16W
Minorca = Menorca	104	40 0N	4 0 E
Minot	74	48 10N	101 15W
Minquiers, Les	100	48 58N	2 8W
Minsk	120	53 52N	27 30 E
Minsk Mazowiecki	107	52 10N	21 33 E
Minster	77	40 24N	84 23W
Minstrel Island	62	50 37N	126 18W
Mintaka Pass	124	37 0N	74 58 E
Minto, Can.	39	46 5N	66 5W
Minto, U.S.A.	67	64 55N	149 20W
Minto, L.	36	57 13N	75 0W
Minton	56	49 10N	104 35W
Mintsing	131	26 8N	118 57 E
Minturn	78	39 45N	106 25W
Minusinsk	121	53 50N	91 20 E
Minutang	125	28 15N	96 30 E
Minvoul	116	2 9N	12 8 E
Minya Konka, mt.	129	29 36N	101 50 E
Mio	46	44 39N	84 8W
Mios Num, I.	127	1 30 S	135 10 E
Miquelon, Can.	40	49 25N	76 27W
Miquelon, St. P. & M.	37	47 3N	56 20W
Miquelon, I.	37	47 1N	56 20W
Miquelon, St. Pierre et, □	37	47 8N	56 24W
Mira	39	46 2N	59 58W
Mira, R.	39	46 2N	59 58W
Mirabel	44	45 40N	74 10W
Mirabel Airport	44	45 41N	74 2W
Miraflores	82	23 21N	109 45W
Miraflores Locks	84	8 59N	79 36W
Miraj	124	16 50N	74 45 E
Miram Shah	124	33 0N	70 0 E
Miramar	88	38 15 S	57 50W
Miramas	103	43 33N	4 59 E
Mirambeau	102	45 23N	0 35W
Miramichi B.	39	47 15N	65 0W
Miramichi, Little S.W., R.	39	46 58N	65 38W
Miramichi, N.W., R.	39	46 57N	65 55W
Miramichi, S.W., R.	39	46 58N	65 38W
Miramont-de-Guyenne	102	44 37N	0 21 E
Miranda	87	20 10 S	56 15W
Miranda de Ebro	104	42 41N	2 57W
Mirando City	75	27 28N	98 59W
Mirandópolis	89	21 9 S	51 6W
Miraporvos, I.	85	22 9N	74 30W
Mirassol	89	20 46 S	49 28W
Mirebeau, Côte d'Or, France	101	47 25N	5 20 E
Mirebeau, Vienne, France	100	46 49N	0 10 E
Mirecourt	101	48 20N	6 10 E
Miri	126	4 18N	114 0 E
Mirim, Lagoa	89	32 45 S	52 50W
Mirimire	86	11 10N	68 43W
Mirny	91	66 0 S	95 0 E
Mirnyy	121	62 33N	113 53 E
Mirond L.	55	55 6N	102 47W
Mirool	136	34 24 S	147 5 E
Mirpur Khas	124	25 30N	69 0 E
Mirror	61	52 30N	113 7W
Miryang	130	35 34N	128 42 E
Mirzapur	125	25 10N	82 45 E
Misantla	83	19 56N	96 50W
Miscou Centre	39	47 57N	64 34W
Miscou I.	39	47 57N	64 31W
Miscouche	39	46 26N	63 52W
Misehkow, R.	52	51 26N	89 11W
Mish'āb, Ra'as al	122	28 15N	48 43 E
Mishan	129	45 31N	132 2 E
Mishawaka	77	41 40N	86 8W
Mishima	132	35 10N	138 52 E
Misión	81	32 6N	116 53W
Misión, La	82	32 5N	116 50W
Misiones □, Argent.	89	27 0 S	55 0W
Misiones □, Parag.	88	27 0 S	56 0W
Miskīn	123	23 44N	56 52 E
Miskitos, Cayos	84	14 26N	82 50W
Miskolc	107	48 7N	20 50 E
Misoöl, I.	127	2 0 S	130 0 E
Misrâtah	114	32 18N	15 3 E
Missanabie	53	48 20N	84 6W
Missinaibi L.	53	48 23N	83 40W
Missinaibi Lake Prov. Park	53	48 25N	83 30W
Missinaibi, R.	53	50 43N	81 29W
Mission, S.D., U.S.A.	74	43 21N	100 36W
Mission, Tex., U.S.A.	75	26 15N	98 30W
Mission City	63	49 10N	122 15W
Missipuskiow, R.	56	53 53N	103 18W
Missisa L.	34	52 20N	85 7W
Missisicabi, R.	36	51 14N	79 31W
Missisquoi □	45	45 5N	73 0W
Missisquoi, B.	43	45 2N	73 9W
Mississagi Prov. Park	46	46 30N	82 40W
Mississagi, R.	46	46 15N	83 9W
Mississauga	50	43 32N	79 35W
Mississinewa, R.	77	40 46N	86 3W
Mississippi, Delta of the	75	29 15N	90 30W
Mississippi L.	47	45 5N	76 10W
Mississippi, R.	75	35 29N	89 15W
Mississippi Sd.	75	30 25N	89 0W
Missoula	78	47 0N	114 0W
Missouri □	74	38 25N	92 30W
Missouri, Little, R.	78	46 0N	111 35W
Missouri, R.	72	40 20N	95 40W
Mist	80	45 59N	123 15W
Mistake B.	55	62 8N	93 0W
Mistanipisipou, R.	38	51 32N	61 50W
Mistaouac, L.	40	49 25N	78 41W
Mistassibi Nord-Est., R.	41	49 31N	71 56W
Mistassibi, R.	41	48 53N	72 13W
Mistassini	41	48 53N	72 12W
Mistassini L.	36	51 0N	73 40W
Mistassini, Parc. Prov. de	41	50 20N	74 0W
Mistassini, R.	41	48 42N	72 20W
Mistastin L.	35	55 57N	63 20W
Mistatim	56	52 52N	103 22W
Mistretta	108	37 56N	14 20 E
Misty L.	55	58 53N	101 40W
Mitchell, Austral.	135	26 29 S	147 58 E
Mitchell, Can.	46	43 28N	81 12W
Mitchell, Ind., U.S.A.	77	38 42N	86 25W
Mitchell, Nebr., U.S.A.	74	41 58N	103 45W
Mitchell, Oreg., U.S.A.	78	44 31N	120 8W
Mitchell, S.D., U.S.A.	74	43 40N	98 0W
Mitchell Corners, Ont., Can.	49	43 55N	78 53W
Mitchell Corners, Qué., Can.	43	45 2N	73 1W
Mitchell I.	66	49 12N	123 5W
Mitchell L.	63	52 52N	120 37W
Mitchell, Mt.	73	35 40N	82 20W
Mitchell, R.	135	15 12 S	141 35 E
Mitchelstown	97	52 16N	8 18W
Mitchelton	97	27 25 S	152 59 E
Mitchinamécus, Rés.	40	47 19N	75 9W
Mitiaro, I.	133	19 49 S	157 43W
Mitilini = Lesvos	109	39 0N	26 20 E
Mitla	83	16 55N	96 24W
Mito	132	36 20N	140 30 E
Mitsinjo	117	16 1 S	45 52 E
Mitsiwa Channel	115	15 30N	40 0 E
Mitta Mitta, R.	136	36 14 S	147 10 E
Mittagong	136	34 28 S	150 29 E
Mitú	86	1 8N	70 3W
Mituas	86	3 52N	68 49W
Mitumba, Chaîne des	116	10 0 S	26 20 E
Mitwaba	116	8 2N	27 17 E
Mitzick	116	0 45N	11 40 E
Mixteco, R.	83	18 11N	98 30W
Miyagi-Ken □	132	38 15N	140 45 E
Miyake-Jima	132	34 0N	139 30 E
Miyako	132	39 40N	141 75 E
Miyako-rettō	131	24 47N	125 20 E
Miyakonojō	132	31 32N	131 5 E
Miyazaki	132	31 56N	131 30 E
Miyazaki-ken □	132	32 0N	131 30 E
Miyazu	132	35 35N	135 10 E
Miyet, Bahr el	115	31 30N	35 30 E
Miyun	130	40 25N	116 50 E
Mizamis = Ozamiz	127	8 15N	123 50 E
Mizen Hd., Cork, Ireland	97	51 27N	9 50W
Mizen Hd., Wick., Ireland	97	52 52N	6 4W
Mizoram □	125	23 0N	92 40 E
Mjölby	111	58 20N	15 10 E
Mjøsa	111	60 40N	11 0 E
Mkushi	117	14 25 S	29 15 E
Mladá Boleslav	106	50 27N	14 53 E
Mława	107	53 9N	20 25 E
Mo i Rana	110	66 15N	14 7 E
Moa, I.	127	8 0 S	128 0 E
Moab	79	38 40N	109 35W
Moabi	116	2 24 S	10 59 E
Moala, I.	133	18 36 S	179 53 E
Moama	136	36 3 S	144 45 E
Moamba	136	25 34 S	32 16 E
Moapo	81	36 45N	114 37W
Moba	116	7 0 S	29 48 E
Mobaye	116	4 25N	21 5 E
Mobayi	116	4 15N	21 8 E
Moberley	76	39 25N	92 25W
Moberly, R.	54	56 12N	120 55W
Mobert	34	48 41N	85 40W
Mobile	73	30 41N	88 3W
Mobile B.	73	30 30N	88 0W
Mobile, Pt.	73	30 15N	88 0W
Mobridge	74	45 40N	100 28W
Mobutu Sese Seko, L.	116	1 30N	31 0 E
Moçambique	117	15 3 S	40 42 E
Mochudi	117	24 27 S	26 7 E
Mocimboa da Praia	116	11 25 S	40 20 E
Moclips	80	47 14N	124 10W
*Moçamedes □	117	16 35 S	12 30 E
Mocoa	86	1 15N	76 45W
Mococa	89	21 28 S	47 0W
Mocorito	82	25 20N	108 0W
Moctezuma	82	30 12N	106 26W
Moctezuma, R.	83	21 59N	98 34W
Mocuba	117	16 54 S	37 25 E
Modane	103	45 12N	6 40 E
Módena	108	44 39N	10 55 E
Modena	79	37 55N	113 56W
Modesto	80	37 43N	121 0W
Módica	108	36 52N	14 45 E
Modjokerto	127	7 29 S	112 25 E
Moe	135	38 12 S	146 19 E
Moei, R.	128	17 25N	98 10 E
Moëlan-sur-Mer	100	47 49N	3 38W
Moengo	87	5 45N	54 20W
Moffat, Can.	49	43 31N	80 3W
Moffat, U.K.	96	55 20N	3 27W
Mogadiscio = Mogadishu	115	2 2N	45 25 E
Mogadishu	115	2 2N	45 25 E
Mogami-gawa, R.	132	38 45N	140 0 E
Mogaung	125	25 20N	97 0 E
Mogi das Cruzes	89	23 45 S	46 20W
Mogi-Guaçu, R.	89	20 53 S	48 10W
Mogi-Mirim	89	22 20 S	47 0W
Mogilev	120	53 55N	30 18 E
Mogilla	136	36 41 S	149 38 E
Mogincual	117	15 35 S	40 25 E
Mogocha	121	53 40N	119 50 E
Mogoi	127	1 55 S	133 10 E
Mogok	125	23 0N	96 40 E
Mogollon	79	33 25N	108 55W
Mogollon Mesa	79	35 0N	111 0W
Mohács	107	45 58N	18 41 E
Mohall	74	48 46N	101 30W
Mohammadābād	123	37 30N	59 5 E
Mohave Desert	79	35 0N	117 30W
Mohave L.	81	35 25N	114 36W
Mohawk, Ariz., U.S.A.	79	32 45N	113 50W
Mohawk, Mich., U.S.A.	52	47 18N	88 26W
Mohembo	117	18 15 S	21 43 E
Mohican, C.	67	60 10N	167 30W
Möhne, R.	105	51 29N	8 10 E
Moho	129	53 15N	122 27 E
Mohon	101	49 45N	4 44 E
Mohoro	116	8 6 S	39 8 E
Moidart, L.	96	56 47N	5 40W
Moille, La	76	41 32N	89 17W
Moine, R. La	76	39 58N	90 32W
Mointy	120	47 40N	73 45 E
Moira, R.	47	44 21N	77 24W
Moirans	103	45 20N	5 33 E
Moirans-en-Montagne	103	46 26N	5 43 E
Moisie	38	50 12N	66 1W
Moisie, R.	38	50 14N	66 5W
Moissac	102	44 7N	1 5 E
Mojave	81	35 8N	118 8W
Mojave Desert	81	35 0N	116 30W
Mojikit L.	52	50 40N	88 15W
Mojo	88	21 48 S	65 33W
Mojo, I.	126	8 10 S	117 40 E
Mokai	133	38 32 S	175 56 E
Mokane	76	38 41N	91 53W
Mokelumne Hill	80	38 18N	120 43W
Mokelumne, R.	80	38 23N	121 25W
Mokokchung	125	26 15N	94 30 E
Mokpo	131	34 50N	126 30 E
Mol	105	51 11N	5 5 E
Molchanovo	120	57 40N	83 50 E
Mold	94	53 10N	3 10W
Moldavian S.S.R. □	120	47 0N	28 0 E
Molde	110	62 45N	7 9 E
Molepolole	117	24 28 S	25 28 E
Molfetta	108	41 12N	16 35 E
Moline	76	41 30N	90 30W
Molinos	88	25 28 S	66 15W
Moliro	116	8 12 S	30 30 E
Molise □	108	41 45N	14 30 E
Mollendo	86	17 0 S	72 0W
Mölndal	111	57 40N	12 3 E
Molokai, I.	67	21 8N	157 0W
Molong	136	33 5 S	148 54 E
Molopo, R.	117	25 40 S	24 30 E
Molotov, Mys	121	81 10N	95 0 E
Moloundou	116	2 8N	15 15 E
Molsheim	101	48 33N	7 29 E
Molson L.	57	54 22N	95 32W
Molu, I.	127	6 45 S	131 40 E
Molucca Sea	127	4 0 S	124 0 E
Moluccas = Maluku, Is.	127	1 0 S	127 0 E
Moma	117	16 47 S	39 4 E
Mombasa	116	4 2 S	39 43 E
Momchilgrad	109	41 33N	25 23 E
Momence	77	41 10N	87 40W
Mompós	86	9 14N	74 26W
Møn	111	54 57N	12 15 E
Mon, R.	125	20 25N	94 30 E
Mona, Canal de la	85	18 30N	67 45W
Mona, I.	85	18 5N	67 54W
Mona Passage	85	18 0N	67 40W
Mona, Punta	84	9 37N	82 36W
Monach Is.	96	57 32N	7 40W
Monaco ■	103	43 46N	7 23 E
Monadhliath Mts.	96	57 10N	4 4W
Monagas □	86	9 20N	63 0W
Monaghan	97	54 15N	6 58W
Monaghan □	97	54 10N	7 0W
Monahans	75	31 35N	102 50W
Monarch	61	49 48N	113 7W
Monarch Mt.	54	51 55N	125 57W
Monaro Ra.	136	36 20 S	149 0 E
Monashee Prov. Park	63	50 30N	118 15W
Monastier-sur-Gazeille, Le	102	44 57N	3 59 E
Monastir = Bitola	109	41 5N	21 21 E
Moncayo, Sierra del	104	41 48N	1 50W
Mönchengladbach	105	51 12N	6 23 E
Monchique	104	37 19N	8 38W
Monchique, Sa. de.	104	37 18N	8 39W
Monck	49	43 58N	80 29W
Monclova	82	26 50N	101 30W
Moncontour	100	48 22N	2 38W
Moncouche, L.	41	48 45N	70 42W
Moncton	39	46 7N	64 51W
Mondego, R.	104	40 28N	8 0W
Mondeodo	127	3 21 S	122 9 E
Mondonac, L.	41	47 24N	73 58W
Mondovi	108	44 23N	7 56 E
Mondovi	74	44 37N	91 40W
Mondragon	103	44 13N	4 44 E
Monessen	70	40 9N	79 50W
Monestier-de-Clermont	103	44 55N	5 38 E
Monet	34	48 10N	75 40W
Monêtier-les-Bains, Le	103	44 58N	6 30 E
Monett	75	36 55N	93 56W
Monflanquin	102	44 32N	0 47 E
Monforte	104	39 6N	7 25W
Mong Cai	128	21 27N	107 54 E
Möng Hsu	125	21 54N	98 30 E
Möng Kung	125	21 35N	97 35 E
Mong Lang	128	20 29N	97 52 E
Möng Nai	125	20 32N	97 55 E
Möng Pai	125	19 40N	97 15 E
Mong Pawk	125	22 4N	99 16 E
Mong Ton	125	20 25N	98 45 E
Mong Wa	125	21 26N	100 27 E
Mong Yai	125	22 28N	98 3 E
Mongalla	115	5 8N	31 55 E
Monger, L.	134	29 25 S	117 5 E
Monghyr	125	25 23N	86 30 E
Mongolia	49	43 56N	79 13W
Mongolia ■	129	47 0N	103 0 E
Mongolia, Inner □	130	44 15N	117 0 E
Mongoumba	116	3 33N	18 40 E
Mongpang	128	23 5N	100 25 E
Mongu	117	15 16 S	23 12 E
Monistrol-St.-Loire	103	45 17N	4 11 E
Monitor	61	51 58N	110 34W
Monk	55	47 7N	69 59W
Monkey River	83	16 22N	88 29W
Monkoto	116	1 38 S	20 35 E
Monkstown	37	47 35N	54 26W
Monkton	46	43 35N	81 5W
Monmouth, U.K.	95	51 48N	2 43W
Monmouth, U.S.A.	76	40 50N	90 40W
Monmouth Mt.	62	51 0N	123 47W
Mono, L.	80	38 0N	119 9W
Mono Mills	49	43 57N	79 58W
Mono, Punta del	84	12 0N	83 30W
Mono Road Station	49	43 51N	79 51W
Monolith	81	35 7N	118 22W
Monon	77	40 52N	86 53W
Monona, Iowa, U.S.A.	76	43 3N	91 24W
Monona, Wis., U.S.A.	76	43 4N	89 20W
Monongahela	70	40 12N	79 56W
Monópoli	108	40 57N	17 18 E
Monroe, Iowa, U.S.A.	76	41 31N	93 6W
Monroe, La., U.S.A.	75	32 32N	92 4W
Monroe, Mich., U.S.A.	46	41 55N	83 26W
Monroe, N.C., U.S.A.	73	35 2N	80 37W
Monroe, N.Y., U.S.A.	71	41 19N	74 11W
Monroe, Ohio, U.S.A.	77	39 27N	84 22W
Monroe, Utah, U.S.A.	79	38 45N	112 5W

* Renamed Namibe

Monroe **Mouchalagane, R**

Monroe, Wash., U.S.A.	**80**	47 51N	121 58W
Monroe, Wis., U.S.A.	**76**	42 38N	89 40W
Monroe City	**76**	39 40N	91 40W
Monroe, Res.	**77**	39 1N	86 31W
Monroeville, U.S.A.	**77**	40 59N	84 52W
Monroeville, Ala., U.S.A.	**73**	31 33N	87 15W
Monrovia, Liberia	**114**	6 18N	10 47W
Monrovia, U.S.A.	**79**	34 7N	118 1W
Mons	**105**	50 27N	3 58E
Monse	**127**	4 0S	123 10E
Monségur	**102**	44 38N	0 4E
Mont-Carmel	**41**	47 26N	69 52W
Mont-de-Marsan	**102**	43 54N	0 31W
Mont d'Or, Tunnel	**101**	46 45N	6 18E
Mont-Dore, Le	**102**	45 35N	2 50E
Mont-Gabriel	**43**	45 55N	74 10W
Mont-Joli	**41**	48 37N	68 10W
Mont Laurier	**40**	46 35N	75 30W
Mont-Louis	**38**	49 15N	65 44W
Mont Luis	**35**	42 31N	2 6E
Mont-Rolland	**43**	45 57N	74 7W
Mont-Royal	**44**	45 31N	73 39W
Mont-St-Grégoire	**45**	45 20N	73 10W
Mont-St-Hilaire	**43**	45 34N	73 12W
Mont St-Pierre	**38**	49 13N	65 49W
Mont-St-Michel, Le	**100**	48 40N	1 30W
Mont-Tremblant	**40**	46 13N	74 36W
Mont Tremblant Prov. Park	**41**	46 30N	74 30W
Montagnac	**102**	43 29N	3 28E
Montagu, I.	**82**	58 30S	26 15W
Montague, Can.	**39**	46 10N	62 39W
Montague, Calif., U.S.A.	**78**	41 47N	122 30W
Montague, Mass., U.S.A.	**71**	42 31N	72 33W
Montague, I.	**82**	31 40N	144 46W
Montague I.	**67**	60 0N	147 0W
Montague Sd.	**134**	14 28S	125 20E
Montaigu	**100**	46 59N	1 18W
Montalbán	**104**	40 50N	0 45W
Montalvo	**81**	34 15N	119 12W
Montaña	**86**	6 0S	73 0W
Montana □	**68**	47 0N	110 0W
Montañita	**86**	1 30N	75 28W
Montargis	**101**	48 0N	2 43E
Montauban	**102**	44 0N	1 21E
Montauk	**71**	41 3N	71 57W
Montbard	**101**	47 38N	4 20E
Montbéliard	**101**	47 31N	6 48E
Montbrison	**103**	45 36N	4 3E
Montcalm □	**43**	45 59N	73 45W
Montcalm, Pic de	**102**	42 40N	1 25E
Montceau-les-Mines	**101**	46 40N	4 23E
Montcerf	**40**	46 32N	76 3W
Montcevelles, L.	**38**	51 7N	60 38W
Montclair	**71**	40 53N	74 49W
Montcornet	**101**	49 40N	4 0E
Montcuq	**102**	44 21N	1 13E
Montdidier	**101**	49 38N	2 35E
Monte Albán	**83**	17 2N	96 45W
Monte Alegre	**87**	2 0S	54 0W
Monte Bello Is.	**134**	20 30S	115 45E
Monte-Carlo	**103**	43 46N	7 23E
Monte Caseros	**88**	30 10S	57 50W
Monte Comán	**88**	34 40S	68 0W
Monte Cristi	**85**	19 52N	71 39W
Monte, Le	**76**	38 47N	93 27W
Monte Libano	**93**	8 5N	75 29W
Monte Lindo, R.	**88**	25 30S	58 40W
Monte Quemado	**88**	25 53S	62 41W
Monte Rio	**80**	38 28N	123 0W
Monte Sant' Ángelo	**108**	41 42N	15 59E
Monte Santu, C. di	**108**	40 5N	9 42E
Monte Visto	**79**	37 40N	106 8W
Monteagudo	**89**	27 14S	54 8W
Montebello	**40**	45 40N	74 55W
Montebourg	**100**	49 30N	1 20W
Montecito	**81**	34 26N	119 40W
Montecristi	**86**	1 0S	80 40W
Montego B.	**84**	18 30N	78 0W
Montelibano	**86**	8 5N	75 29W
Montélimar	**103**	44 33N	4 45E
Montello	**74**	43 49N	89 21W
Montemorelos	**83**	25 11N	99 42W
Montendre	**102**	45 16N	0 26W
Montenegro	**89**	29 39S	51 29W
Montepuez	**117**	13 8S	38 59E
Montereau	**101**	48 22N	2 57E
Monterey, U.S.A.	**77**	41 11N	86 30W
Monterey, Calif., U.S.A.	**80**	36 35N	121 57W
Monterey, B.	**80**	36 50N	121 55W
Monteria	**86**	8 46N	75 53W
Monteros	**88**	27 11S	65 30W
Monterrey	**82**	25 40N	100 30W
Montes Claros	**87**	16 30S	43 50W
Montesano	**80**	47 0N	123 39W
Monteverde	**116**	8 45S	16 45E
Montevideo	**89**	34 50S	56 11W
Montezuma, U.S.A.	**76**	41 32N	92 35W
Montezuma, U.S.A.	**77**	39 47N	87 22W
Montfaucon, Haute-Loire, France	**103**	45 11N	4 20E
Montfaucon, Meuse, France	**101**	49 16N	5 8E
Montfort	**43**	45 53N	74 20W
Montfort-l'Amaury	**101**	48 47N	1 49E
Montfort-sur-Meu	**100**	48 8N	1 58W
Montgenèvre	**103**	44 56N	6 42E
Montgomery, Can.	**59**	51 4N	114 10W
Montgomery, U.K.	**95**	52 34N	3 9W
Montgomery, U.S.A.	**77**	41 44N	88 21W
Montgomery, Ala., U.S.A.	**73**	32 20N	86 20W
Montgomery, W. Va., U.S.A.	**72**	38 9N	81 21W
Montgomery = Sahiwal	**124**	30 45N	73 8E
Montgomery City	**76**	38 59N	91 30W
Montguyon	**102**	45 12N	0 12W
Monticello, Can.	**49**	43 59N	80 24W
Monticello, U.S.A.	**76**	40 7N	91 43W
Monticello, U.S.A.	**76**	42 13N	91 11W
Monticello, Ark., U.S.A.	**75**	33 40N	91 48W
Monticello, Fla., U.S.A.	**73**	30 35N	83 50W
Monticello, Ill., U.S.A.	**77**	40 1N	88 34W
Monticello, Ind., U.S.A.	**77**	40 40N	86 45W
Monticello, Iowa, U.S.A.	**74**	42 18N	91 18W
Monticello, Ky., U.S.A.	**73**	36 52N	84 50W
Monticello, Minn., U.S.A.	**74**	45 17N	93 52W
Monticello, Miss., U.S.A.	**75**	31 35N	90 8W
Monticello, N.Y., U.S.A.	**71**	41 37N	74 42W
Monticello, Utah, U.S.A.	**79**	37 55N	109 27W
Montier	**101**	48 30N	4 45E
Montignac	**102**	45 4N	1 10E
Montigny-les-Metz	**101**	49 7N	6 10E
Montigny-sur-Aube	**101**	47 57N	4 45E
Montijo	**104**	38 52N	6 39W
Montilla	**104**	37 36N	4 40W
Montivideo	**74**	44 55N	95 40W
Montlhéry	**101**	48 39N	2 15E
Montluçon	**102**	46 22N	2 36E
Montmagny	**41**	46 58N	70 34W
Montmartre	**56**	50 14N	103 27W
Montmédy	**101**	49 30N	5 20E
Montmélian	**103**	45 30N	6 4E
Montmirail	**101**	48 51N	3 30E
Montmoreau-St.-Cybard	**102**	45 23N	0 8E
Montmorency	**42**	46 53N	71 11W
Montmorency, R.	**42**	46 53N	71 7W
Montmorillon	**102**	46 26N	0 50E
Montmort	**101**	48 55N	3 49E
Monto	**135**	24 52S	151 12E
Montoro	**104**	38 1N	4 27W
Montour Falls	**70**	42 20N	76 51W
Montpelier, Idaho, U.S.A.	**78**	42 15N	111 20W
Montpelier, Ind., U.S.A.	**77**	40 33N	85 17W
Montpelier, Ohio, U.S.A.	**77**	41 34N	84 40W
Montpelier, Vt., U.S.A.	**71**	44 15N	72 38W
Montpellier	**102**	43 37N	3 52E
Montpezat-de-Quercy	**102**	44 15N	1 30E
Montpon-Ménestrol	**102**	45 2N	0 11E
Montréal, Can.	**44**	45 31N	73 34W
Montréal, France	**102**	43 13N	2 8E
Montreal I.	**53**	47 19N	84 44W
Montréal, Île de	**44**	45 30N	73 40W
Montreal L.	**56**	54 20N	105 45W
Montreal Lake	**56**	54 3N	105 46W
Montréal-Nord	**44**	45 36N	73 38W
Montreal, R.	**53**	47 14N	84 39W
Montredon-Labessonnié	**102**	43 45N	2 18E
Montréjeau	**102**	43 6N	0 35E
Montrésor	**100**	47 10N	1 10E
Montreuil	**101**	50 27N	1 45E
Montreuil-Bellay	**100**	47 8N	0 9W
Montreuil, L.	**40**	50 12N	77 40W
Montreux	**106**	46 26N	6 55E
Montrevault	**100**	47 17N	1 2W
Montrevel-en-Bresse	**103**	46 21N	5 8E
Montrichard	**100**	47 20N	1 10E
Montrose, B.C., Can.	**63**	49 5N	117 35W
Montrose, Ont., Can.	**49**	43 3N	79 8W
Montrose, U.K.	**96**	56 43N	2 28W
Montrose, Col., U.S.A.	**79**	38 30N	107 52W
Montrose, Mich., U.S.A.	**46**	43 11N	83 54W
Montrose, Pa., U.S.A.	**71**	41 50N	75 55W
Montrose, L.	**76**	38 18N	93 50W
Monts, Pte des	**38**	49 20N	67 12W
Montsalvy	**102**	44 41N	2 30E
Montsauche	**101**	47 13N	4 0E
Montserrat, I.	**85**	16 40N	62 10W
Monveda	**116**	2 52N	21 30E
Mônywa	**125**	22 7N	95 11E
Monze	**117**	16 17S	27 29E
Monze, C.	**124**	24 47N	66 37E
Monzón	**104**	41 52N	0 10E
Moonbeam	**53**	49 20N	82 10W
Moonie, R.	**136**	27 45S	150 0E
Moorcroft	**74**	44 17N	104 58W
Moore, L.	**134**	29 50S	117 35E
Moore Pt.	**51**	43 48N	79 3W
Moorefield	**72**	39 5N	78 59W
Moores Mill	**39**	45 18N	67 17W
Moores Res.	**71**	44 45N	71 50W
Mooresville, U.S.A.	**77**	39 37N	86 22W
Mooresville, N.C., U.S.A.	**73**	35 36N	80 45W
Moorfoot Hills	**96**	55 44N	3 8W
Moorhead	**74**	47 0N	97 0W
Mooroopna	**136**	36 25S	145 22E
Moorpark	**81**	34 17N	118 53W
Moose Creek	**47**	45 15N	74 58W
Moose Factory	**53**	51 16N	80 40W
Moose Heights	**63**	53 4N	122 31W
Moose Hill	**52**	48 15N	89 29W
Moose I.	**57**	51 42N	97 10W
Moose Jaw	**56**	50 24N	105 30W
Moose Jaw, R.	**56**	50 34N	105 18W
Moose L.	**57**	53 46N	100 8W
Moose Lake, Can.	**57**	53 43N	100 20W
Moose Lake, U.S.A.	**52**	46 27N	92 48W
Moose Mountain Cr.	**56**	49 13N	102 12W
Moose Mtn. Prov. Park	**57**	49 48N	102 25W
Moose, R.	**53**	51 20N	80 25W
Moose River	**53**	50 48N	81 17W
Moosehead L.	**35**	45 40N	69 40W
Moosomin	**57**	50 9N	101 40W
Moosonee	**53**	51 17N	80 39W
Moosup	**71**	41 44N	71 52W
Mopeia	**117**	17 30S	35 40E
Mopti	**114**	14 30N	4 0W
Moquegua	**86**	17 15S	70 46W
Mora, Sweden	**111**	61 2N	14 38E
Mora, Minn., U.S.A.	**74**	45 52N	93 19W
Mora, N. Mex., U.S.A.	**79**	35 58N	105 21W
Moradabad	**124**	28 50N	78 50E
Morafenobe	**117**	17 50S	44 53E
Morales	**86**	2 45N	76 38W
Moramanga	**117**	18 56S	48 12E
Moran, Kans., U.S.A.	**75**	37 53N	94 35W
Moran, Mich., U.S.A.	**46**	46 0N	84 50W
Moran, Wyo., U.S.A.	**78**	43 53N	110 37W
Morant Cays	**84**	17 22N	76 0W
Morant Pt.	**84**	17 55N	76 12W
Morar L.	**96**	56 57N	5 40W
Moratuwa	**124**	6 45N	79 55E
Morava, R.	**106**	49 50N	16 50E
Moravatio	**82**	19 51N	100 25W
Moravia	**76**	40 50N	92 50W
Morawhanna	**86**	8 30N	59 40W
Moray Firth	**96**	57 50N	3 30W
Morbihan □	**100**	47 55N	2 50W
Morcenx	**102**	44 0N	0 55W
Mordelles	**100**	48 5N	1 52W
Morden	**57**	49 15N	98 10W
Mordialloc	**136**	38 1S	145 6E
Mordovian S.S.R. □	**120**	54 20N	44 30E
Mordvinske A.S.S.R.	**96**	54 20N	44 30E
More L.	**96**	58 18N	4 52W
Møre og Romsdal □	**110**	63 0N	9 0E
Moreau, R.	**74**	45 15N	102 45W
Morecambe	**94**	54 5N	2 52W
Morecambe B.	**94**	54 7N	3 0W
Moree	**135**	29 28S	149 54E
Morehead	**72**	38 12N	83 22W
Morehead City	**73**	34 46N	76 44W
Moreira	**86**	0 34S	63 26W
Morelia	**82**	19 40N	101 11W
Morell	**39**	46 25N	62 42W
Morella	**104**	40 35N	0 5W
Morelos	**82**	26 42N	107 40W
Morelos □	**83**	18 40N	99 10W
Morena, Sierra	**104**	38 20N	4 0W
Morenci, U.S.A.	**77**	41 43N	84 13W
Morenci, Ariz., U.S.A.	**79**	33 7N	109 20W
Mores, I.	**73**	26 15N	77 35W
Moresby I.	**62**	52 30N	131 40W
Morestel	**103**	45 40N	5 28E
Moret	**101**	48 22N	2 58E
Moreton B.	**135**	27 10S	153 10E
Moreton, I.	**135**	27 10S	153 25E
Moreuil	**101**	49 46N	2 30E
Morez	**103**	46 31N	6 2E
Morgan	**78**	41 3N	111 44W
Morgan City	**75**	29 40N	91 15W
Morgan Hill	**80**	37 8N	121 39W
Morganfield	**72**	37 40N	87 55W
Morganton	**73**	35 46N	81 48W
Morgantown, U.S.A.	**77**	39 22N	86 16W
Morgantown, W. Va., U.S.A.	**72**	39 39N	79 58W
Morgat	**100**	48 15N	4 32W
Morhange	**101**	48 55N	6 38E
Moriarty	**79**	35 3N	106 2W
Morice L.	**62**	53 50N	127 40W
Morice, R.	**62**	54 12N	127 5W
Morichal	**86**	2 10N	70 34W
Morichal Largo, R.	**86**	8 55N	63 0W
Morin-Heights	**43**	45 54N	74 15W
Morinville	**60**	53 49N	113 41W
Morioka	**132**	39 45N	141 8E
Moris	**82**	28 8N	108 32W
Moriston, Glen	**96**	57 10N	5 0W
Moriston, R.	**96**	57 10N	5 0W
Morlaàs	**102**	43 21N	0 18W
Morlaix	**100**	48 36N	3 52W
Mormant	**101**	48 37N	2 52E
Mornington	**136**	38 15S	145 5E
Mornington I.	**135**	16 30S	139 30E
Mornington, I.	**90**	49 50S	75 30W
Moro G.	**127**	6 30N	123 0E
Morocco	**77**	40 57N	87 27W
Morocco ■	**114**	32 0N	5 50W
Morococha	**86**	11 40S	76 5W
Morogoro	**116**	6 50S	37 40E
Morokweng	**117**	26 12S	23 45E
Moroleón	**82**	20 8N	101 32W
Morombé	**117**	21 45S	43 22E
Moron	**88**	34 39S	58 37W
Morón	**84**	22 0N	78 30W
Morón de la Frontera	**104**	37 6N	5 28W
Morondava	**117**	20 17S	44 17E
Morongo Valley	**81**	34 3N	116 37W
Morotai, I.	**127**	2 10N	128 30E
Moroto	**116**	2 28N	34 42E
Morpeth	**94**	55 11N	1 41W
Morrilton	**75**	35 10N	92 45W
Morrin	**61**	51 40N	112 47W
Morrinhos	**87**	17 45S	49 10W
Morrinsville	**133**	37 40S	175 32E
Morris, Can.	**57**	49 25N	97 22W
Morris, Ill., U.S.A.	**77**	41 20N	88 20W
Morris, Minn., U.S.A.	**74**	45 33N	95 56W
Morris L.	**39**	44 39N	63 30W
Morris, R.	**57**	49 21N	97 21W
Morrisburg	**47**	44 55N	75 7W
Morrison	**76**	41 47N	90 0W
Morrisonville	**76**	39 25N	89 27W
Morriston	**49**	43 27N	80 7W
Morristown, U.S.A.	**77**	39 40N	85 42W
Morristown, Ariz., U.S.A.	**79**	33 54N	112 45W
Morristown, N.J., U.S.A.	**71**	40 48N	74 30W
Morristown, S.D., U.S.A.	**74**	45 57N	101 44W
Morristown, Tenn., U.S.A.	**73**	36 18N	83 20W
Morro Bay	**80**	35 27N	120 54W
Morro, Pta.	**88**	27 6S	71 0W
Morrosquillo, Golfo de	**85**	9 35N	75 40W
Morrow	**77**	39 21N	84 8W
Morrumbene	**117**	23 31S	35 16E
Morse	**56**	50 25N	107 3W
Morson	**52**	49 6N	94 19W
Mortagne	**102**	45 28N	0 49W
Mortagne-au-Perche	**100**	48 31N	0 33E
Mortagne, R.	**101**	48 30N	6 30E
Mortain	**100**	48 40N	0 57W
Morteau	**101**	47 3N	6 35E
Morteros	**88**	30 50S	62 0W
Mortes, R. das	**87**	11 45S	50 44W
Mortlach	**56**	50 27N	106 4W
Mortlake	**136**	38 5S	142 50E
Morton, U.S.A.	**76**	40 37N	89 28W
Morton, Tex., U.S.A.	**75**	33 39N	102 49W
Morton, Wash., U.S.A.	**80**	46 33N	122 17W
Morvan, Mts. du	**101**	47 5N	4 0E
Morven, dist.	**96**	56 38N	5 44W
Morvern	**96**	56 38N	5 44W
Morwell	**136**	38 10S	146 22E
Moscos Is.	**128**	14 0N	97 30E
Moscow	**78**	46 45N	116 59W
Moscow = Moskva	**120**	55 45N	37 35E
Mosel, R.	**105**	50 22N	7 36E
Moselle □	**101**	48 59N	6 33E
Moselle, R.	**105**	50 22N	7 36E
Moses Inlet	**62**	51 47N	127 23W
Moses Lake	**78**	47 16N	119 17W
Mosgiel	**133**	45 53S	170 21E
Mosher	**53**	48 42N	84 12W
Moshi	**116**	3 22S	37 18E
Mosjøen	**110**	65 51N	13 12E
Moskenesøya	**110**	67 58N	13 0E
Moskenstraumen	**110**	67 47N	13 0E
Moskva	**120**	55 45N	37 35E
Mosley Cr.	**62**	51 18N	124 50W
Mosquera	**86**	2 35N	78 30W
Mosquero	**75**	35 48N	103 57W
Mosquitia	**84**	15 20N	84 10W
Mosquito B.	**36**	61 10N	78 0W
Mosquitos, Golfo de los	**84**	9 15N	81 10W
Moss	**111**	59 27N	10 40E
Moss Vale	**136**	34 32S	150 25E
Mossaka	**116**	1 15S	16 45E
Mossbank	**56**	49 56N	105 56W
Mossburn	**133**	45 41S	168 15E
Mosselbaai	**117**	34 11S	22 8E
Mossendjo	**116**	2 55S	12 42E
Mossman	**135**	16 28S	145 23E
Mossoró	**87**	5 10S	37 15W
Mossuril	**117**	14 58S	40 42E
Mossy, R.	**56**	54 5N	102 58W
Most	**106**	50 31N	13 38E
Mosta	**108**	35 54N	14 24E
Mostaganem	**114**	35 54N	0 5E
Mostar	**109**	43 22N	17 50E
Mostardas	**89**	31 2S	50 51W
Mosul = Al Mawsil	**122**	36 20N	43 5E
Mosun	**131**	23 35N	109 30E
Motagua, R.	**84**	15 44N	88 14W
Motala	**111**	58 32N	15 1E
Mothe-Achard, La	**100**	46 37N	1 40W
Mothe, La, Rés.	**41**	48 46N	71 9W
Motherwell	**96**	55 48N	4 0W
Motihari	**125**	26 37N	85 1E
Motocurunya	**86**	4 24N	64 5W
Motozintea de Mendoza	**83**	15 21N	92 14W
Mott	**74**	46 25N	102 14W
Motte-Chalançon, La	**103**	44 30N	5 21E
Motte, L. la	**40**	48 20N	78 2W
Motte, La	**103**	44 20N	6 3E
Motueka	**133**	41 7S	173 1E
Motul	**83**	21 0N	89 20W
Mouchalagane, R.	**36**	50 56N	68 41W

Moucontant Myanaung

Moucontant 100 46 43N 0 36W
Moúdhros 109 39 50N 25 18E
Mouila 116 1 50S 11 0E
Moulamein Cr. 136 35 6S 144 3E
Mould Bay 64 76 12N 119 25W
Moule, Le 85 16 20N 61 22W
Moulins 102 46 35N 3 19E
Moulmein 125 16 30N 97 40E
Moulton, U.S.A. 76 40 41N 92 41W
Moulton, Tex., U.S.A. 75 29 35N 97 8W
Moultrie 73 31 11N 83 47W
Moultrie, L. 73 33 25N 80 10W
Mound City, Mo., U.S.A. 74 40 2N 95 25W
Mound City, S.D., U.S.A. 74 45 46N 100 3W
Moundsville 70 39 53N 80 43W
Mount Airy 73 36 31N 80 37W
Mount Albert, Can. 70 44 10N 79 20W
Mount Albert, Ont., Can. 46 44 8N 79 19W
Mount Angel 78 45 4N 122 46W
Mount Assiniboine Prov. Park 61 50 53N 115 39W
Mount Ayr 76 40 43N 94 14W
Mount Baker 63 48 50N 121 40W
Mount Barker 134 34 38S 117 40E
Mount Brydges 46 42 54N 81 29W
Mount Carleton Prov. Park 39 47 25N 66 55W
Mount Carmel, Can. 37 47 9N 53 29W
Mount Carmel, Ill., U.S.A. 77 38 20N 87 48W
Mount Carmel, Pa., U.S.A. 71 40 46N 76 25W
Mount Carroll 76 42 6N 89 59W
Mount Clemens 46 42 35N 82 50W
Mount Darwin 117 16 47S 31 38E
Mount Dennis 50 43 41N 79 29W
Mount Desert I. 35 44 25N 68 25W
Mount Dora 73 28 49N 81 32W
Mount Eden 77 38 3N 85 9W
Mount Edgecumbe 67 57 8N 135 22W
Mount Enid 134 21 42S 116 26E
Mount Forest 46 43 59N 80 43W
Mount Gambier 136 37 50S 140 46E
Mount Goldsworthy 134 20 25S 119 39E
Mount Hamilton 48 43 14N 79 51W
Mount Henry 77 42 21N 88 16W
Mount Hope, Can. 48 43 9N 79 55W
Mount Hope, U.S.A. 72 37 52N 81 9W
Mount Horeb 76 43 0N 89 42W
Mount Hotham 136 37 2S 146 52E
Mount Isa 135 20 42S 139 26E
Mount Joy 71 40 6N 76 30W
Mount Laguna 81 32 52N 116 25W
Mount Lavinia 124 6 50N 79 50E
Mount Lofty Ra. 135 34 35S 139 5E
Mount McKinley Nat. Pk. 67 64 0N 150 0W
Mount Magnet 134 28 2S 117 47E
Mount Maunganui 133 37 40S 176 14E
Mount Morgan 135 23 40S 150 25E
Mount Moriah 37 48 58N 58 2W
Mount Morris, Mich., U.S.A. 46 43 8N 83 42W
Mount Morris, N.Y., U.S.A. 70 42 43N 77 50W
Mount Nicholas 134 22 54S 120 27E
Mount Olive 76 39 4N 89 44W
Mount Olivet 77 38 32N 84 2W
Mount Orab 77 39 5N 83 56W
Mount Pearl 37 47 31N 52 47W
Mount Pleasant, Alta., Can. 59 51 4N 114 5W
Mount Pleasant, Ont., Can. 49 43 5N 80 19W
Mount Pleasant, Iowa, U.S.A. 76 41 0N 91 35W
Mount Pleasant, Mich., U.S.A. 46 43 35N 84 47W
Mount Pleasant, Pa., U.S.A. 70 40 9N 79 31W
Mount Pleasant, S.C., U.S.A. 73 32 45N 79 48W
Mount Pleasant, Tenn., U.S.A. 73 35 31N 87 11W
Mount Pleasant, Tex., U.S.A. 75 33 5N 95 0W
Mount Pleasant, Ut., U.S.A. 78 39 40N 111 29W
Mount Pocono 71 41 8N 75 21W
Mount Pulaski 76 40 1N 89 17W
Mount Rainier Nat. Park. 80 46 50N 121 43W
Mount Revelstoke Nat. Park 63 51 5N 118 30W
Mount Robson 54 52 56N 119 15W
Mount Robson Prov. Park 63 53 0N 119 0W
Mount Royal 58 50 27N 104 40W
Mount Seymour Prov. Park 66 49 24N 122 55W
Mount Shasta 78 41 20N 122 18W
Mount Signal 81 32 39N 115 37W
Mount Singleton 136 32 30S 151 3E
Mount Sterling, Ill., U.S.A. 76 40 0N 90 40W
Mount Sterling, Ky., U.S.A. 77 38 0N 84 0W
Mount Sterling, Ohio, U.S.A. 77 39 43N 83 16W
Mount Stewart 39 46 22N 62 52W
Mount Tolmie 63 48 28N 123 20W
Mount Tom Price 134 22 50S 117 40E
Mount Uniacke 39 44 54N 63 50W
Mount Union 70 40 22N 77 51W
Mount Vernon, Can. 49 43 6N 80 24W
Mount Vernon, Ill., U.S.A. 77 38 19N 88 55W
Mount Vernon, Ind., U.S.A. 77 38 17N 88 57W
Mount Vernon, Iowa, U.S.A. 76 41 55N 91 23W
Mount Vernon, N.Y., U.S.A. 71 40 57N 73 49W
Mount Vernon, Ohio, U.S.A. 72 40 20N 82 30W
Mount Vernon, Wash., U.S.A. 63 48 25N 122 20W
Mount Vernon, Wash., U.S.A. 80 48 27N 122 18W
Mount Washington 77 38 3N 85 33W
Mount Whaleback 134 23 18S 119 44E
Mount Zion 77 39 46N 88 53W
Mountain Center 81 33 42N 116 44W
Mountain City, Nev., U.S.A. 78 41 54N 116 0W
Mountain City, Tenn., U.S.A. 73 36 30N 81 50W
Mountain Grove 75 37 5N 92 20W
Mountain Home, Ark., U.S.A. 75 36 20N 92 25W
Mountain Home, Idaho, U.S.A. 78 43 11N 115 45W
Mountain Iron 74 47 30N 92 37W
Mountain Park. 61 52 50N 117 15W
Mountain Pass 81 35 29N 115 35W
Mountain View, Can. 61 49 8N 113 36W
Mountain View, Ark., U.S.A. 75 35 52N 92 10W
Mountain View, Calif., U.S.A. 79 37 26N 122 5W
Mountain Village 67 62 10N 163 50W
Mountainair 79 34 35N 106 15W
Mountmellick 97 53 7N 7 20W
Mountnorris 97 54 15N 6 29W
Moura 86 1 25S 61 45W
Moure, La 74 46 27N 98 17W
Mourenx 102 43 23N 0 36W
Mourmelon-le-Grand 101 49 8N 4 22E
Mourne Mts. 97 54 10N 6 0W
Mourne, R. 97 54 45N 7 39W
Mouscron 105 50 45N 3 12E
Mouthe 101 46 44N 6 12E
Moûtiers 103 45 29N 6 31E
Moutong 127 0 28N 121 13E
Mouy 101 49 18N 2 20E
Movas 82 28 10N 109 25W
Moville 97 55 11N 7 3W
Moweaqua 76 39 37N 89 1W
Mowming 131 21 50N 110 32E
Mowping 130 37 25N 121 34E
Moy, R. 97 54 5N 8 50W
Moyahua 82 21 16N 103 10W
Moyale 116 3 30N 39 0E
Moyie 54 49 17N 115 50W
Moyie Springs 61 48 43N 116 11W
Moyle □ 97 55 10N 6 15W
Moyobamba 86 6 0S 77 0W
Mozambique = Moçambique 117 15 3S 40 42E
Mozambique ■ 117 19 0S 35 0E
Mozambique Chan. 117 20 0S 39 0E
Mozdok 120 43 45N 44 48E
Mozyr 120 52 0N 29 15E
Mpanda 116 6 23S 31 40E
Mpika 117 11 51S 31 25E
Mpwapwa 116 6 30S 36 30E
Msoro 117 13 35S 31 50E
Mtwara 116 10 20S 40 20E
Muaná 87 1 25S 49 15W
Muang Chiang Rai 128 19 52N 99 50E
Muang Kalasin 128 16 26N 103 30E
Muang Lampang 128 18 16N 99 32E
Muang Lamphun 128 18 40N 98 53E
Muang Nan 128 18 52N 100 42E
Muang Phetchabun 128 16 23N 101 12E
Muang Phichit 128 16 29N 100 21E
Muang Ubon 128 15 15N 104 50E
Muang Yasothon 128 15 50N 104 10E
Muar 128 2 3N 102 34E
Muar, R. 128 2 15N 102 48E
Muarabungo 126 1 40S 101 10E
Muaradjuloi 126 0 12S 114 3E
Muaraenim 126 3 40S 103 50E
Muarakaman 126 0 2S 116 45E
Muaratebo 126 1 30S 102 26E
Muaratembesi 126 1 42S 103 2E
Muaratewe 126 0 50S 115 0E
Mubairik 122 23 22N 39 8E
Mubende 116 0 33N 31 22E
Mucajai, Serra do 86 2 23N 61 10W
Muchalat Inlet 62 49 38N 126 15W
Muchikan 129 53 2N 120 27E
Muck, I. 96 56 50N 6 15W
Mucuri 87 18 0S 40 0W
Mud B. 66 49 5N 122 53W
Mud L. 78 40 15N 120 15W
Muddy L. 56 52 19N 109 6W
Muddy, R. 79 38 30N 110 55W
Mudgee 136 32 32S 149 31E
Mudhnib 122 25 50N 44 18E
Mudjatik, R. 55 56 1N 107 36W
Muenster 56 52 12N 105 0W
Muerto, Mar 83 16 10N 94 10W
Mufulira 117 12 32S 28 15E
Muğla 122 37 15N 28 28E
Mugu 125 29 45N 82 30E
Mühlig-Hofmann-fjella 91 72 30S 5 0E
Mui Bai Bung 128 8 35N 104 42E
Mui Ron 128 18 7N 106 27E
Muine Bheag 97 52 42N 6 59W
Mukah 126 2 55N 112 5E
Mukalla 115 14 33N 49 2E
Mukden = Shenyang 130 41 35N 123 30E
Mukomuko 126 2 20S 101 10E
Muktsar 124 30 30N 74 30E
Mukur 124 32 50N 67 50E
Mukutawa, R. 57 53 10N 97 24W
Mukwonago 77 42 52N 88 20W
Mulanay 127 13 30N 122 30E
Mulatas, Arch. de las 84 6 51N 78 31W
Mulberry Grove 76 38 55N 89 16W
Mulchén 88 37 45S 72 20W
Mulde, R. 106 50 55N 12 42E
Muldraugh 77 37 56N 85 59W
Mule Creek 74 43 19N 104 8W
Mulegé 82 26 53N 112 1W
Muleshoe 75 34 17N 102 42W
Mulgrave 39 45 38N 61 31W
Mulhacén 104 37 4N 3 20W
Mülheim 105 51 26N 6 53W
Mulhouse 101 47 40N 7 20E
Mull I. 96 56 27N 6 0W
Mull, Sound of 96 56 30N 5 50W
Mullaittvu 124 9 15N 80 55E
Mullen 74 42 5N 101 0W
Mullens 72 37 34N 81 22W
Muller, Pegunungan 126 0 30N 113 30E
Mullet Pen. 97 54 10N 10 2W
Mullett L. 46 45 30N 84 30W
Mullewa 134 28 29S 115 30E
Mullin 75 31 33N 98 38W
Mullingar 97 53 31N 7 20W
Mullins 73 34 12N 79 15W
Mullion Creek 136 33 9S 148 7E
Multan 124 30 15N 71 30E
*Multan □ 124 30 29N 72 29E
Mulvane 75 37 30N 97 15W
Mulwala 136 35 59S 146 0E
Mumbwa 117 15 0S 27 0E
Mun 128 15 17N 103 0E
Muna, I. 127 5 0S 122 30E
Muna Sotuta 83 20 29N 89 43W
München 106 48 8N 11 33E
Munchen-Gladbach = Mönchengladbach 105 51 12N 6 23E
Muncho Lake 54 59 0N 125 50W
Muncie 77 40 10N 85 20W
Mundala, Puncak 127 4 30S 141 0E
Mundare 60 53 35N 112 20W
Munday 75 33 26N 99 39W
Münden 106 51 25N 9 42E
Mundo Novo 87 11 50S 40 29W
Mungbere 116 2 36N 28 28E
Mungindi 135 28 58S 149 1E
Munhango R. 117 11 30S 19 30E
Munich = München 106 48 8N 11 35E
Munising 53 46 25N 86 39W
Muñoz Gamero, Pen. 90 52 30S 73 5E
Munroe L. 55 59 13N 98 35W
Munson 61 51 34N 112 45W
Munster 101 48 2N 7 8E
Münster, Ger. 105 52 59N 10 5E
Münster, Switz. 106 46 30N 8 17E
Munster □ 97 52 20N 8 40W
Muntok 126 2 5S 105 10E
Muon Pak Beng 128 19 51N 101 4E
Muong La 128 20 52N 102 5E
Muonio 110 67 57N 23 40E
Muonio älv 110 67 48N 23 25E
Mur-de-Bretagne 100 48 12N 3 0W
Múr, R. 106 47 7N 13 55E
Murallón, Cuerro 90 49 55S 73 30W
Murang'a 116 0 45S 37 9E
Murashi 120 59 30N 49 0E
Murat 102 45 7N 2 53E
Murchison I. 52 50 0N 88 21W
Murchison, R. 134 26 45S 116 15E
Murchison Ra. 134 20 0S 134 10E
Murcia 104 38 2N 1 10W
Murcia □ 104 37 50N 1 30W
Murdo 74 43 56N 100 43W
Murdochville 38 48 58N 65 30W
Murdock 58 49 56N 97 4W
Mure, La 103 44 55N 5 48E
Mures R. 107 46 0N 22 0E
Muret 102 43 30N 1 20E
Murfreesboro 73 35 50N 86 21W
Murgab 120 38 10N 73 59E
Murgon 135 26 15S 151 54E
Muriaé 89 21 8S 42 23W
Muriel L. 60 54 9N 110 40W
Müritz-see 106 53 25N 12 40E
Murjo Mt. 127 6 36S 110 53E
Murmansk 120 68 57N 33 10E
Muro 103 42 34N 8 54E
Muro, C. de 103 41 44N 8 37E
Murom 120 55 35N 42 3E
Muroran 132 42 25N 141 0E
Muroto-Misaki 132 33 15N 134 10E
Murphy 78 43 11N 116 33W
Murphy L. 63 52 3N 121 15W
Murphys 80 38 8N 120 28W
Murphysboro 76 37 50N 89 20W
Murray, U.S.A. 76 41 3N 93 57W
Murray, Ky., U.S.A. 73 36 40N 88 20W
Murray, Utah, U.S.A. 78 40 41N 111 58W
Murray Bridge 135 35 6S 139 14E
Murray Harbour 39 46 0N 62 28W
Murray, L. 73 34 8N 81 30W
Murray, R., S. Australia, Austral. 136 35 20S 139 22E
Murray, R., W. Australia, Austral. 135 32 33S 115 45E
Murray, R., Can. 54 56 11N 120 45W
Murray River 39 46 1N 62 37W
Murraysburg 117 31 58S 23 47E
Murrayville, Austral. 136 35 16S 141 11E
Murrayville, U.S.A. 76 39 35N 90 15W
Murree 124 33 56N 73 28E
Murrieta 81 33 33N 117 13W
Murrumbidgee, R. 136 34 40S 143 0E
Murrumburrah 136 34 32S 148 22E
Murrurundi 136 31 42S 150 51E
Murtle L. 63 52 8N 119 38W
Murtoa 136 36 35S 142 28E
Murwara 125 23 46N 80 28E
Murwillumbah 135 28 18S 153 27E
Mürzzuschlag 106 47 36N 15 41E
Muş 122 38 45N 41 30E
Musa Khel 124 30 29N 69 52E
Musa Qala (Musa Kala) 124 32 20N 64 50E
Musaffargarh 124 30 10N 71 10E
Musala, I. 126 1 41N 98 28E
Musalla, mt. 109 42 13N 23 37E
Musan 130 42 12N 129 12E
Muscat = Masqat 123 23 37N 58 36E
Muscatine 76 41 25N 91 5W
Muscoda 76 43 11N 90 27W
Musgrave Harbour 37 49 27N 53 58W
Musgrave Ras. 134 26 0S 132 0E
Mushaboom 39 44 51N 62 32W
Mushie 116 2 56S 17 4E
Musi, R. 126 2 55S 103 40E
Muskeg B. 52 48 59N 95 5W
Muskeg L. 52 49 0N 90 2W
Muskeg, R. 54 60 20N 123 20W
Muskeg River 60 53 55N 118 39W
Muskego 77 42 54N 88 8W
Muskegon 46 43 15N 86 17W
Muskegon Hts. 77 43 12N 86 17W
Muskegon, R. 72 43 25N 86 0W
Muskogee 75 35 50N 95 25W
Muskoka, L. 46 45 0N 79 25W
Muskwa L. 60 56 9N 114 38W
Muskwa, R., Alta., Can. 60 56 15N 113 48W
Muskwa, R., B.C., Can. 54 58 47N 122 48W
Musoma 116 1 30S 33 48E
Musquanousse, L. 38 50 22N 61 5W
Musquaro 38 50 10N 61 3W
Musquaro, L. 36 50 38N 61 5W
Musquash 39 45 11N 66 19W
Musquodoboit Harbour 39 44 50N 63 9W
Mussel Inlet 62 52 53N 128 7W
Musselburgh 96 55 57N 3 3W
Musselshell, R. 78 46 30N 108 15W
Mussidan 102 45 2N 0 22E
Mussooree 124 30 27N 78 6E
Mustafa Kemalpaşa 122 40 3N 28 25E
Mustajidda 122 26 30N 41 50E
Mustang 125 29 10N 83 55E
Musters, L. 90 45 20S 69 25W
Muswellbrook 135 32 16S 150 56E
Mut 122 36 40N 33 28E
Mutan Kiang 130 46 18N 129 31E
Mutankiang 130 44 35N 129 30E
Mutis 86 1 4N 77 25W
Mutshatsha 116 10 35S 24 20E
Muttaburra 135 22 38S 144 29E
Mutton Bay 35 50 50N 59 2W
Muxima 116 9 25S 13 52E
Muy, Le 103 43 28N 6 34E
Muy Muy 84 12 39N 85 36W
Muya 121 56 27N 115 39E
Muzaffarabad 124 34 25N 73 30E
Muzaffarnagar 124 29 26N 77 40E
Muzaffarpur 125 26 7N 85 32E
Muzhi 120 65 25N 64 40E
Muzillac 100 47 35N 2 30W
Muzo 86 5 32N 74 6W
Muzon C. 54 54 40N 132 40W
Muztagh P. 129 36 30N 87 22E
Mwanza, Congo 116 7 55S 26 43E
Mwanza, Tanz. 116 2 30S 32 58E
Mwaya 116 9 32S 33 55E
Mweelrea, Mt. 97 53 37N 9 48W
Mweka 116 4 50S 21 40E
Mwenga 116 3 1S 28 21E
Mweru, L. 116 9 0S 29 0E
Mwinilunga 117 11 43S 24 25E
My Tho 128 10 29N 106 23E
Myall, R. 136 32 30S 152 15E
Myanaung 125 18 25N 95 10E

* Now part of Punjab

Myaungmya Negra Pt

Myaungmya	**125**	16 30N	95 0 E
Mycenæ	**109**	37 44N	22 45 E
Myerstown	**71**	40 22N	76 18W
Myingyan	**125**	21 30N	95 30 E
Myitkyina	**125**	25 30N	97 26 E
Mymensingh	**125**	24 45N	90 24 E
Myndmere	**74**	46 23N	97 7W
Myogi	**128**	21 24N	96 28 E
Mýrdalsjökull	**110**	63 40N	19 6W
Myrnam	**60**	53 40N	111 14W
Myrtle Beach	**73**	33 43N	78 50W
Myrtle Creek	**78**	43 0N	123 9W
Myrtle Point	**78**	43 0N	124 4W
Myrtleford	**136**	36 34 S	146 44 E
Mysore	**124**	12 17N	76 41 E
Mysore □ = Karnataka	**124**	13 15N	77 0 E
Mystery Lake	**60**	54 10N	114 55W
Mystic, U.S.A.	**76**	40 47N	92 57W
Mystic, Conn., U.S.A.	**71**	41 21N	71 58W
Myton	**78**	40 10N	110 2W
Mývatn	**110**	65 36N	17 0W

N

Naab, R.	**106**	49 10N	12 0 E
Naaldwijk	**105**	51 59N	4 13 E
Naalehu	**67**	19 4N	155 35W
Naantali	**111**	60 29N	22 2 E
Naas	**97**	53 12N	6 40W
Nabadwip	**125**	23 34N	88 20 E
Nabas	**127**	11 47N	122 6 E
*Naberezhnyye Chelny	**120**	55 42N	52 19 E
Nabesna	**67**	62 33N	143 10W
Nabire	**127**	3 15 S	136 27 E
Nabisipi, R.	**36**	50 14N	62 13W
Nablus = Nâbulus	**115**	32 14N	35 15 E
Nâbulus	**115**	32 14N	35 15 E
Nacala-Velha	**117**	14 32 S	40 34 E
Nacaome	**84**	13 31N	87 30W
Naches	**78**	46 48N	120 49W
Naches, R.	**80**	46 38N	120 31W
Nachi	**131**	28 50N	105 25 E
Nachicapau, L.	**36**	56 40N	68 5W
Nachingwea	**116**	10 49 S	38 49 E
Nachvak Fd.	**36**	59 3N	63 45W
Nacimento Res.	**80**	35 46N	120 53W
Nackawic	**39**	45 59N	67 17W
Nacmine	**61**	51 28N	112 47W
Naco, Mexico	**82**	31 20N	109 56W
Naco, U.S.A.	**79**	31 24N	109 58W
Nacogdoches	**75**	31 33N	95 30W
Nácori Chico	**82**	29 39N	109 1W
Nacozari	**82**	30 30N	109 50W
Nadern Harb.	**62**	54 0N	132 36W
Nadiad	**124**	22 41N	72 56 E
Nadina L.	**62**	53 53N	127 2W
Nadina, R.	**62**	53 58N	126 30W
Nadûshan	**123**	32 2N	53 35 E
Nadym	**120**	63 35N	72 42 E
Nadym, R.	**120**	65 30N	73 0 E
Naft Shâh	**122**	34 0N	45 30 E
Nafûd ad Dahy	**122**	22 0N	45 0 E
Naga, Japan	**131**	26 34N	127 43 E
Naga, Phil.	**127**	13 38N	123 15 E
Naga Hills	**130**	26 0N	94 30 E
Nagagami L.	**53**	49 25N	85 1W
Nagagami, R.	**53**	49 40N	84 40W
Nagagamisis L.	**53**	49 28N	84 40W
Nagaland □	**125**	26 0N	94 30 E
Nagano	**132**	36 40N	138 10 E
Nagano-ken □	**132**	36 15N	138 0 E
Nagaoka	**132**	37 27N	138 50 E
Nagappattinam	**124**	10 46N	79 51 E
Nagar Parkar	**124**	24 30N	70 35 E
Nagas Pt.	**62**	52 12N	131 22W
Nagasaki	**132**	32 47N	129 50 E
Nagasaki-ken □	**132**	32 50N	129 40 E
Nagasin L.	**53**	47 48N	83 37W
Nagaur	**124**	27 15N	73 45 E
Nagercoil	**124**	8 12N	77 33 E
Nagineh	**123**	34 20N	57 15 E
Nago	**131**	26 36N	128 0 E
Nagoya	**132**	35 10N	136 50 E
Nagpur	**124**	21 8N	79 10 E
Nagua	**85**	19 23N	69 50W
Nagykanizsa	**106**	46 28N	17 0 E
Nagykörös	**107**	46 55N	19 48 E
Naha	**131**	26 12N	127 40 E
Nahanni Butte	**54**	61 2N	123 20W
Nahanni Nat. Pk.	**54**	61 15N	125 0W
Nahariya	**115**	33 1N	35 5 E
Nahâvand	**122**	34 10N	48 30 E
Nahlin	**54**	58 55N	131 38W
Naicá	**82**	27 53N	105 31W
Naicam	**56**	52 30N	104 30W
Naikoon Prov. Park	**62**	53 55N	131 55W
Nain	**36**	56 34N	61 40W
Nâ'in	**123**	32 54N	53 0 E
Nainpur	**124**	22 30N	80 10 E
Naintré	**100**	46 46N	0 29 E
Naira, I.	**127**	4 28 S	130 0 E
Nairn, Can.	**46**	46 20N	81 35W
Nairn, U.K.	**96**	57 35N	3 54W
Nairobi	**116**	1 17 S	36 48 E
Naivasha	**116**	0 40 S	36 30 E
Najac	**102**	44 14N	1 58 E
Najafâbâd	**123**	32 40N	51 15 E
Najd	**122**	26 30N	42 0 E
Najibabad	**124**	29 40N	78 20 E
Najin	**130**	42 12N	130 15 E
Nakamura	**132**	33 0N	133 0 E
Nakano Shima	**132**	29 50N	130 0 E
Nakelele Pt.	**67**	21 2N	156 35W
Nakhi Mubarak	**122**	24 10N	38 10 E
Nakhichevan A.S.S.R. □	**120**	39 14N	45 30 E
Nakhodka	**121**	43 10N	132 45 E
Nakhon Phanom	**128**	17 23N	104 43 E
Nakhon Ratchasima (Khorat)	**128**	14 59N	102 12 E
Nakhon Sawan	**128**	15 35N	100 10 E
Nakhon Si Thammarat	**128**	8 29N	100 0 E
Nakina, B.C., Can.	**54**	59 12N	132 52W
Nakina, Ont., Can.	**53**	50 10N	86 40W
Naknek	**67**	58 45N	157 0W
Nakskov	**111**	54 50N	11 8 E
Naktong, R.	**130**	35 7N	128 57 E
Nakuru	**116**	0 15 S	35 5 E
Nakusp	**63**	50 20N	117 45W
Nal, R.	**124**	27 0N	65 50 E
Nalayh	**129**	47 43N	107 22 E
Nalchik	**120**	43 30N	43 33 E
Nalgonda	**124**	17 6N	79 15 E
Nallamalai Hills	**124**	15 30N	78 50 E
Nalón, R.	**104**	43 35N	6 10W
Nam Dinh	**128**	20 25N	106 5 E
Nam-Phan	**128**	10 30N	106 0 E
Nam Phong	**128**	16 42N	102 52 E
Nam Tha	**128**	20 58N	101 30 E
Nam Tso	**129**	30 40N	90 30 E
Nama	**131**	23 45N	108 1 E
Namacurra	**117**	17 30 S	36 50 E
Namakan L.	**52**	48 27N	92 35W
Namaland	**117**	26 0 S	18 0 E
Naman	**131**	25 0N	118 30 E
Namangan	**120**	41 0N	71 40 E
Namapa	**117**	13 43 S	39 50 E
Namber	**127**	1 2 S	134 57 E
Nambour	**135**	26 32 S	152 58 E
Namcha Barwa	**129**	29 40N	95 10 E
Nameh	**126**	2 34N	116 21 E
Namew L., Can.	**57**	54 10N	102 0W
Namew L., Sask., Can.	**55**	54 14N	101 56W
Namib Desert = Namib Woestyn	**117**	22 30 S	15 0 E
Namib-Woestyn	**117**	22 30 S	15 0 E
Namibia □	**117**	22 0 S	18 9 E
Namiquipa	**82**	29 15N	107 25W
Namja Pass	**125**	30 0N	82 25 E
Namlea	**127**	3 10 S	127 5 E
Namoa tao	**131**	23 30N	117 0 E
Nampa	**78**	43 40N	116 40W
Nampula	**117**	15 6 S	39 7 E
Namrole	**127**	3 46 S	126 46 E
Namsen, R.	**110**	64 40N	12 45 E
Namsos	**110**	64 28N	11 0 E
Namtu	**125**	23 5N	97 28 E
Namu	**62**	51 52N	127 50W
Namur, Belg.	**105**	50 27N	4 52 E
Namur, Can.	**40**	45 54N	74 56W
Namur □	**105**	50 17N	5 0 E
Namutoni	**117**	18 49 S	16 55 E
Namwala	**117**	15 44 S	26 30 E
Namyung	**131**	25 15N	114 5 E
Nan Shan	**129**	38 30N	99 0 E
Nanaimo	**62**	49 10N	124 0W
Nanam	**130**	41 44N	129 40 E
Nanango	**135**	26 40 S	152 0 E
Nanao	**132**	37 0N	137 0 E
Nanchang, Hupei, China	**131**	31 50N	111 50 E
Nanchang, Kiangsi, China	**131**	28 34N	115 48 E
Nancheng	**131**	27 30N	116 28 E
Nancheng = Hanchung	**131**	33 10N	107 2 E
Nanchung	**131**	30 47N	105 59 E
Nanchwan	**131**	29 10N	107 15 E
Nancy	**101**	48 42N	6 12 E
Nanda Devi, Mt.	**129**	30 30N	80 30 E
Nander	**124**	19 10N	77 20 E
Nandi	**133**	17 25 S	176 50 E
Nandurbar	**124**	21 20N	74 15 E
Nandyal	**124**	15 30N	78 30 E
Nanga Eboko	**116**	4 41N	12 22 E
Nanga Parbat, mt.	**124**	35 10N	74 35 E
Nangapinoh	**126**	0 20 S	111 14 E
Nangarhar □	**124**	34 20N	70 0 E
Nangatajap	**126**	1 32 S	110 34 E
Nangfeng	**131**	27 10N	116 20 E
Nangis	**101**	48 33N	3 0 E
Nanika L.	**62**	53 47N	127 38W
Nanisivik	**65**	73 2N	84 33W
Nankang	**131**	25 42N	114 35 E
Nankiang	**131**	32 20N	106 50 E
Nanking	**131**	32 10N	118 50 E
Nannine	**134**	26 51 S	118 18 E
Nanning	**131**	22 48N	108 20 E
Nanpi	**130**	38 0N	116 40 E
Nanping, Fukien, China	**131**	26 45N	118 5 E
Nanping, Szechwan, China	**131**	33 20N	103 56 E
Nanpu	**131**	31 17N	105 59 E
Nansei-Shotô, Japan	**132**	26 0N	128 0 E
Nansei-Shotô, Japan	**132**	29 0N	129 0 E
Nansen Sd.	**65**	81 0N	91 0W
Nant	**102**	44 1N	3 18 E
Nantan	**131**	25 0N	107 35 E
Nantes	**100**	47 12N	1 33W
Nanteuil-le-Haudouin	**101**	49 9N	2 48 E
Nantiat	**102**	46 1N	1 11 E
Nanticoke	**71**	41 12N	76 1W
Nanton	**61**	50 21N	113 46W
Nantou	**131**	23 57N	120 35 E
Nantua	**103**	46 10N	5 35 E
Nantucket I.	**69**	41 16N	70 3W
Nantung	**131**	32 0N	120 50 E
Nanuque	**87**	17 50 S	40 21W
Nanyang	**131**	33 0N	112 32 E
Nanyuan	**130**	39 45N	116 30 E
Nanyuki	**116**	0 2N	37 4 E
Nao, C. de la	**104**	38 44N	0 14 E
Naococane L.	**36**	52 50N	70 45W
Naoetsu	**132**	37 12N	138 10 E
Napa	**80**	38 18N	122 17W
Napa, R.	**80**	38 10N	122 19W
Napamute	**67**	61 30N	158 45W
Napanee	**47**	44 15N	77 0W
Napanoch	**71**	41 44N	74 2W
Napartokh B.	**36**	58 1N	62 19W
Naperville	**77**	41 46N	88 9W
Napier	**133**	39 30 S	176 56 E
Napierville	**45**	45 11N	73 25W
Napierville □	**44**	45 10N	73 30W
Napinka	**57**	49 19N	100 50W
Naples, Fla., U.S.A.	**73**	26 10N	81 45W
Naples, N.Y., U.S.A.	**70**	42 35N	77 25W
Naples = Nápoli	**108**	40 50N	14 5 E
Napo □	**86**	0 30 S	77 0W
Napo, R.	**86**	3 5 S	73 0W
Napoleon, N. Dak., U.S.A.	**74**	46 32N	99 49W
Napoleon, Ohio, U.S.A.	**77**	41 24N	84 7W
Nápoli	**108**	40 50N	14 5 E
Nappanee	**77**	41 27N	86 0W
Nara, Japan	**132**	34 40N	135 49 E
Nara, Mali	**114**	15 25N	7 20W
Nara-ken □	**132**	34 30N	136 0 E
Nara Visa	**75**	35 39N	103 10W
Naracoorte	**136**	36 58 S	140 45 E
Naradhan	**136**	33 34 S	146 17 E
Narasapur	**125**	16 26N	81 50 E
Narathiwat	**128**	6 40N	101 55 E
Narayanganj	**125**	23 31N	90 33 E
Narayanpet	**124**	16 45N	77 30 E
Narbonne	**102**	43 11N	3 0 E
Nardò	**109**	40 10N	18 0 E
Narin	**124**	36 5N	69 0 E
Narinda, B. de	**117**	14 55 S	47 30 E
Narino □	**86**	1 30N	78 0W
Narmada, R.	**124**	22 40N	77 30 E
Narooma	**136**	36 14 S	150 4 E
Narrabri	**135**	30 19 S	149 46 E
Narrandera	**136**	34 42 S	146 31 E
Narraway, R.	**60**	55 44N	119 55W
Narriah	**136**	33 56 S	146 43 E
Narrogin	**134**	32 58 S	117 14 E
Narromine	**136**	32 12 S	148 12 E
Narsinghpur	**124**	22 54N	79 14 E
Narva	**120**	59 10N	28 5 E
Narvik	**110**	68 28N	17 26 E
Naryan-Mar	**120**	68 0N	53 0 E
Narym	**120**	59 0N	81 58 E
Narymskoye	**120**	49 10N	84 15 E
Naryn	**120**	41 26N	75 58 E
Nasa, mt.	**110**	66 32N	15 23 E
Naseby	**133**	45 1 S	170 10 E
Naselle	**80**	46 22N	123 49W
Naser, Buheirat en	**115**	23 0N	32 30 E
Nash Creek	**39**	47 56N	66 6W
Nashua, Iowa, U.S.A.	**76**	42 55N	92 34W
Nashua, Mont., U.S.A.	**78**	48 10N	106 25W
Nashua, N.H., U.S.A.	**71**	42 50N	71 25W
Nashville, Ark., U.S.A.	**75**	33 56N	93 50W
Nashville, Ga., U.S.A.	**73**	31 13N	83 15W
Nashville, Ill., U.S.A.	**76**	38 21N	89 23W
Nashville, Ind., U.S.A.	**77**	39 12N	86 14W
Nashville, Mich., U.S.A.	**77**	42 36N	85 5W
Nashville, Tenn., U.S.A.	**73**	36 12N	86 46W
Nashwaak Bridge	**39**	46 14N	66 37W
Nashwaaksis	**39**	45 59N	66 38W
Nasik	**124**	20 2N	73 50 E
Nasirabad, Bangla.	**125**	24 42N	90 30 E
Nasirabad, India	**124**	26 15N	74 45 E
Naskaupi, R.	**36**	53 47N	60 51W
Nass, R.	**54**	55 0N	129 40W
Nassau, Bahamas	**84**	25 0N	77 30W
Nassau, U.S.A.	**71**	42 30N	73 34W
Nassau, Bahia	**90**	55 20 S	68 0W
Nasser, L. = Naser, Buheiret en	**115**	23 0N	32 30 E
Nässjö	**111**	57 38N	14 45 E
Nastapoka, Is.	**36**	56 55N	76 50W
Nastapoka, R.	**36**	56 55N	76 33W
Nastopoka Is.	**34**	57 0N	77 0W
Nata	**131**	19 37N	109 17 E
Natâ	**122**	27 15N	48 35 E
Nata	**117**	2 0 S	34 25 E
Natagaima	**86**	3 37N	75 6W
Natal, Brazil	**87**	5 47 S	35 13W
Natal, Can.	**61**	49 43N	114 51W
Natal, Indon.	**126**	0 35N	99 0 E
Natal □	**117**	28 30 S	30 30 E
Natalkuz L.	**62**	53 36N	125 20W
Natanz	**123**	33 30N	51 55 E
Natashquan	**38**	50 14N	61 46W
Natashquan-Est, R.	**38**	51 20N	61 40W
Natashquan Pt.	**38**	50 8N	61 40W
Natashquan, R.	**38**	50 7N	61 50W
Natchez	**75**	31 35N	91 25W
Natchitoches	**75**	31 47N	93 4W
Nathdwara	**124**	24 55N	73 50 E
Natick	**71**	42 16N	71 19W
Natih	**123**	22 25N	56 30 E
Nation, R.	**54**	55 30N	123 32W
National City	**80**	32 45N	117 7W
National Mills	**55**	52 52N	101 40W
Natividad, I. de	**82**	27 50N	115 10W
Natkyizin	**128**	14 57N	97 59 E
Natoma	**74**	39 14N	99 0W
Natron L.	**116**	2 20 S	36 0 E
Natrona	**70**	40 39N	79 43W
Natuna Besar, Kepulauan	**126**	4 0N	108 15 E
Natuna Selatan, Kepulauan	**126**	2 45N	109 0 E
Natural Bridge	**71**	44 5N	75 30W
Naturaliste, C.	**134**	33 32 S	115 0 E
Naturaliste Channel	**134**	25 20 S	113 0 E
Naubinway	**46**	46 7N	85 27W
Naucelle	**102**	44 13N	2 20 E
Naugatuck	**71**	41 28N	73 4W
Naughton	**46**	46 24N	81 12W
Naumburg	**106**	51 10N	11 48 E
Nauru I.	**14**	0 25N	166 0 E
Naushahra	**124**	34 0N	72 0 E
Nauta	**86**	4 20 S	73 35W
Nautanwa	**125**	27 20N	83 25 E
Nautla	**83**	20 20N	96 50W
Nauvoo	**76**	40 33N	91 23W
Nava	**82**	28 25N	100 46W
Navalcarnero	**104**	40 17N	4 5W
Navan = An Uaimh	**97**	53 39N	6 40W
Navarino, I.	**90**	55 0 S	67 30W
Navarra □	**104**	42 40N	1 40W
Navarre, France	**102**	43 15N	1 20 E
Navarre, U.S.A.	**70**	40 43N	81 31W
Navarrenx	**102**	43 20N	0 47W
Navarro	**80**	39 10N	123 32W
Navasota	**75**	30 20N	96 5W
Navassa I.	**85**	18 30N	75 0W
Naver, R.	**96**	58 34N	4 15W
Navidad	**88**	33 57 S	71 50W
Navin	**58**	49 51N	97 0W
Navoi	**120**	40 9N	65 22 E
Navojoa	**82**	27 0N	109 30W
Navolato	**82**	24 47N	107 42W
Návpaktos	**109**	38 23N	21 42 E
Návplion	**109**	37 33N	22 50 E
Navsari	**124**	20 57N	72 59 E
Nawabshah	**124**	26 15N	68 25 E
Nawakot	**125**	28 0N	85 10 E
Nawalgarh	**124**	27 50N	75 15 E
Náxos	**109**	37 8N	25 25 E
Nay	**102**	43 10N	0 18W
Nây Band	**123**	27 20N	52 40 E
Naya	**86**	3 13N	77 22W
Naya, R.	**86**	3 13N	77 22W
Nayakhan	**121**	62 10N	159 0 E
Nayarit □	**82**	22 0N	105 0W
Nazaré	**87**	13 0 S	39 0W
Nazaré da Mata	**87**	7 44 S	35 14W
Nazareth	**115**	32 42N	35 17 E
Nazas	**82**	25 10N	104 0W
Nazas, R.	**82**	25 20N	104 4W
Naze, The	**95**	51 43N	1 19 E
Nazir Hat	**125**	22 35N	91 55 E
Nazko	**62**	53 1N	123 37W
Nazko, R.	**62**	53 7N	123 34W
Ncheu	**117**	14 50 S	34 37 E
Ndélé	**116**	8 25N	20 36 E
Ndendeé	**116**	2 29 S	10 46 E
Ndjamena	**114**	12 4N	15 8 E
Ndjolé	**116**	0 10 S	10 45 E
Ndola	**117**	13 0 S	28 34 E
Neagh, Lough	**97**	54 35N	6 25W
Neah Bay	**80**	48 25N	124 40W
Near Is.	**67**	53 0N	172 0W
Neath	**95**	51 39N	3 49W
Neath, R.	**98**	51 46N	3 35W
Nebraska □	**74**	41 30N	100 0W
Nebraska City	**74**	40 40N	95 52W
Nébrodi, Monti	**108**	37 55N	14 45 E
Necedah	**74**	44 2N	90 7W
Nechako, R.	**63**	53 30N	122 44W
Neche	**57**	48 59N	97 39W
Neches, R.	**75**	31 80N	94 20W
Neckar, R.	**106**	48 43N	9 15 E
Necochea	**88**	38 30 S	58 50W
Needles	**81**	34 50N	114 35W
Needles, The	**95**	50 48N	1 19W
Ñeembucú □	**88**	27 0 S	58 0W
Neemuch (Nimach)	**124**	24 30N	74 50 E
Neenah	**72**	44 10N	88 30W
Neepawa	**57**	50 15N	99 30W
Negaunee	**53**	46 30N	87 36W
Negeri Sembilan □	**128**	2 50N	102 10 E
Negoiu, Vf.	**107**	43 35N	24 31 E
Negombo	**124**	7 12N	79 50 E
Negotin	**109**	44 16N	22 37 E
Negra, La	**88**	23 46 S	70 18W
Negra Pt.	**127**	18 40N	120 50 E

* *Renamed Brezhnev*

Negro, R **Niemur**

Negro, R., Argent. **90** 40 0S 64 0W
Negro, R., Brazil **86** 0 25S 64 0W
Negro, R., Uruguay **89** 32 30S 55 30W
Negros, I. **127** 10 0N 123 0E
Neguac **39** 47 15N 65 5W
Nehalem **80** 45 40N 123 56W
Nehbandān **123** 31 35N 60 5E
Neidpath **56** 50 12N 107 20W
Neihart **78** 47 0N 110 52W
Neikiang **131** 29 35N 105 10E
Neila Gaari Post Office **136** 32 1S 142 48E
Neilburg **56** 52 50N 109 38W
Neil's Harbour **39** 46 48N 60 20W
Neilton **78** 47 24N 123 59W
Neisiang **131** 33 10N 112 0E
Neisse, R. **106** 51 0N 15 0E
Neiva **86** 2 56N 75 18W
Nejanilini L. **55** 59 33N 97 48W
Neksø **111** 55 4N 15 8E
Neligh **74** 42 11N 98 2W
Nelkan **121** 57 50N 136 15E
Nellore **124** 14 27N 79 59E
Nelma **121** 47 30N 139 0E
Nelson, Austral. **136** 38 3S 141 2E
Nelson, B.C., Can. **63** 49 30N 117 20W
Nelson, Ont., Can. **48** 43 23N 79 50W
Nelson, N.Z. **133** 41 18S 173 16E
Nelson, U.K. **94** 53 50N 2 14W
Nelson, Ariz., U.S.A. **79** 35 35N 113 24W
Nelson, Nev., U.S.A. **81** 35 46N 114 55W
Nelson □ **133** 42 11S 172 15E
Nelson, C. **136** 38 26S 141 32E
Nelson, Estrecho **90** 51 30S 75 0W
Nelson Forks **54** 59 30N 124 0W
Nelson House **55** 55 47N 98 51W
Nelson I. **67** 60 40N 164 40W
Nelson L. **55** 55 48N 100 7W
Nelson-Miramichi **39** 46 59N 65 34W
Nelson, R. **55** 54 33N 98 2W
Nelspruit **117** 25 29S 30 59E
Néma **114** 16 40N 7 15W
Neman (Nemunas), R. **120** 53 30N 25 10E
Nemegos **34** 47 40N 83 15W
Nemegosenda L. **53** 48 0N 83 7W
Nemeiben L. **55** 55 20N 105 20W
Némiscachingue, L. **40** 47 25N 74 30W
Nemiscau **36** 51 18N 76 54W
Nemiscau, L. **36** 51 25N 76 40W
Nemours **101** 48 16N 2 40E
Nemunas, R. **120** 55 25N 21 10E
Nemuro **132** 43 20N 145 35E
Nemuro-Kaikyō **132** 43 30N 145 30E
Nemuy **121** 55 40N 135 55E
Nenagh **97** 52 52N 8 11W
Nenana **67** 64 30N 149 0W
Nene, R. **94** 52 38N 0 7E
Nenusa, Kepulauan **127** 4 45N 127 1E
Neodesha **75** 37 30N 95 37W
Neoga **77** 39 19N 88 27W
Neosho **75** 36 56N 94 28W
Neosho, R. **75** 35 59N 95 10W
Neoskweskau **36** 51 52N 74 17W
Nepal ■ **125** 28 0N 84 30E
Nepalganj **125** 28 0N 81 40E
Nephi **78** 39 43N 111 52W
Nephin, Mt. **97** 54 1N 9 21W
Nepisiguit, R. **39** 47 37N 65 38W
Neptune **56** 49 22N 104 4W
Neptune City **71** 40 13N 74 4W
Nérac **102** 44 10N 0 20E
Nerchinsk **121** 52 0N 116 39E
Nerchinskiy Zavod **121** 51 10N 119 30E
Neret L. **36** 54 45N 70 44W
Neretva, R. **109** 43 30N 17 50E
Nerva **104** 37 42N 6 30W
Nes **110** 65 53N 17 24W
Neskaupstaður **110** 65 9N 13 42W
Nesle **101** 49 45N 2 53E
Nespelem **63** 48 10N 118 58W
Ness, Loch **96** 57 15N 4 30W
Nestaocano, R. **41** 49 38N 73 28W
Nestor Falls **52** 49 7N 93 56W
Nesttun **111** 60 19N 5 21E
Nèthe, R. **105** 51 5N 4 55E
Netherby **49** 42 57N 79 8W
Netherdale **135** 21 10S 148 33E
Netherlands ■ **105** 52 0N 5 30E
Netherlands Antilles **85** 12 20N 69 0W
Nett L. **52** 48 6N 93 10W
Nettancourt **101** 48 51N 4 57E
Nettilling L. **65** 66 30N 71 0W
Netzahualcoyotl, Presa **83** 17 10N 93 30W
Neubrandenburg **106** 53 33N 13 17E
Neuchâtel **106** 47 0N 6 55E
Neuchâtel, Lac de **106** 46 53N 6 50E
Neudorf **56** 50 43N 103 1W
Neuf-Brisach **101** 48 0N 7 30E
Neufchâteau, Belg. **105** 49 50N 5 25E
Neufchâteau, France **101** 48 21N 5 40E
Neufchâtel, Can. **42** 46 51N 71 23W
Neufchâtel, France **101** 49 43N 1 30E
Neufchâtel-sur-Aisne **101** 49 26N 4 0E
Neuillé-Pont-Pierre **100** 47 33N 0 33E
Neuilly-St-Front **101** 49 10N 3 15E
Neumünster **106** 54 4N 9 58E
Neung-sur-Beuvron **101** 47 30N 1 50E
Neunkirchen **105** 49 23N 7 6E
Neuquén **90** 38 0S 68 0E
Neuquén □ **88** 38 0S 69 50W
Neuruppin **106** 52 56N 12 48E
Neuse, R. **73** 35 5N 77 40W
Neusiedler See **106** 47 50N 16 47E
Neuss **105** 51 12N 6 39E
Neussargues-Moissac **102** 45 9N 3 1E
Neustadt **46** 44 5N 81 0W
Neustrelitz **106** 53 22N 13 4E
Neuvic **102** 45 23N 2 16E
Neuville **101** 45 52N 4 51E
Neuville-aux-Bois **101** 48 4N 2 3E
Neuvy-St.-Sépulchure **102** 46 35N 1 48E
Neuvy-sur-Barangeon **101** 47 20N 2 15E
Neuwied **105** 50 26N 7 29E
Nevada, Iowa, U.S.A. **76** 42 1N 93 27W
Nevada, Mo., U.S.A. **76** 37 51N 94 22W
Nevada □ **78** 39 20N 117 0W
Nevada City **80** 39 20N 121 0W
Nevada de Sta. Marta, Sa. **86** 10 55N 73 50W
Nevada, Sierra, Spain **104** 37 3N 3 15W
Nevada, Sierra, U.S.A. **78** 39 0N 120 30W
Nevado, Cerro **88** 35 30S 68 20W
Nevado de Colima, Mt. **82** 19 35N 103 45W
Nevanka **121** 56 45N 98 55E
Nevers **101** 47 0N 3 9E
Nevertire **136** 31 50S 147 44E
Neville **56** 49 58N 107 39W
Nevis I. **85** 17 0N 62 30W
Nevşehir **122** 38 33N 34 40E
New Albany, Ind., U.S.A. **77** 38 20N 85 50W
New Albany, Miss., U.S.A. **75** 34 30N 89 0W
New Albany, Pa., U.S.A. **71** 41 35N 76 28W
New Amsterdam **86** 6 15N 57 30W
New Athens **76** 38 19N 89 53W
New Baltimore **46** 42 41N 82 44W
New Bedford **71** 41 40N 70 52W
New Berlin, U.S.A. **76** 39 44N 89 55W
New Berlin, U.S.A. **77** 42 59N 88 6W
New Bern **73** 35 8N 77 3W
New Bethlehem **70** 41 0N 79 22W
New Bloomfield **70** 40 24N 77 12W
New Boston **75** 33 27N 94 21W
New Braunfels **75** 29 43N 98 9W
New Brigden **61** 51 42N 110 29W
New Brighton **133** 43 29S 172 43E
New Britain **71** 41 41N 72 47W
New Brunswick **71** 40 30N 74 28W
New Brunswick □ **35** 46 50N 66 30W
New Buffalo **77** 41 47N 86 45W
New Byrd **91** 80 0S 120 0W
New Caledonia, I. **14** 21 0S 165 0E
New Canton **76** 39 37N 91 8W
New Carlisle, Can. **39** 48 1N 65 20W
New Carlisle, Ind., U.S.A. **77** 41 45N 86 32W
New Carlisle, Ohio, U.S.A. **77** 39 56N 84 2W
New Castile = Castilla La Neuva **104** 39 45N 3 20W
New Castle, Ind, U.S.A. **77** 39 55N 85 22W
New Castle, Ind., U.S.A. **77** 39 55N 85 23W
New Castle, Ky., U.S.A. **77** 38 26N 85 10W
New Castle, Pa., U.S.A. **70** 41 0N 80 20W
New City **71** 41 8N 74 0W
New Cristóbal **84** 9 25N 79 40W
New Cumberland **70** 40 30N 80 36W
New Cuyama **81** 34 57N 119 38W
New Delhi **124** 28 37N 77 13E
New Denmark **39** 47 2N 67 38W
New Denver **63** 50 0N 117 25W
New Dundee **49** 43 21N 80 31W
New Durham **49** 43 3N 80 34W
New England **74** 46 36N 102 47W
New England Ra. **135** 30 20S 151 45E
New Forest **95** 50 53N 1 40W
New Franklin **76** 39 1N 92 44W
New Germany **39** 44 33N 64 43W
New Glarus **76** 42 49N 89 38W
New Glasgow, N.S., Can. **39** 45 35N 62 36W
New Glasgow, Qué., Can. **43** 45 50N 73 53W
New Guinea, I. **14** 4 0S 136 0E
New Hamburg **46** 43 23N 80 42W
New Hampshire □ **71** 43 40N 71 40W
New Hampton **76** 43 2N 92 20W
New Harbour **39** 45 13N 61 29W
New Harmony **77** 38 7N 87 56W
New Haven, Conn., U.S.A. **71** 41 20N 72 54W
New Haven, Ill., U.S.A. **77** 37 55N 88 8W
New Haven, Ind., U.S.A. **77** 41 4N 85 1W
New Haven, Mich., U.S.A. **46** 42 44N 82 46W
New Haven, Mo., U.S.A. **76** 38 37N 91 13W
New Hazelton **54** 55 20N 127 30W
† New Hebrides, Is. **14** 15 0S 168 0E
New Iberia **75** 30 2N 91 54W
New Ireland, I. **14** 3 20S 151 50E
New Jersey □ **71** 39 50N 74 10W
New Kensington **70** 40 36N 79 43W
New Lexington **72** 39 40N 82 15W
New Liskeard **34** 47 31N 79 41W
New London, Conn., U.S.A. **71** 41 23N 72 8W
New London, Iowa, U.S.A. **76** 40 55N 91 24W
New London, Minn., U.S.A. **74** 45 17N 94 55W
New London, Mo., U.S.A. **76** 39 35N 91 24W
New London, Ohio, U.S.A. **70** 41 4N 82 25W
New London, Wis., U.S.A. **74** 44 23N 88 43W
New Madison **77** 39 58N 84 43W
New Madrid **75** 36 40N 89 30W
New Market **71** 43 4N 70 57W
New Meadows **78** 45 0N 116 10W
New Mexico □ **68** 34 30N 106 0W
New Miami **77** 39 26N 84 32W
New Milford, Conn., U.S.A. **71** 41 35N 73 25W
New Milford, Pa., U.S.A. **71** 41 50N 75 45W
New Norfolk **135** 42 46S 147 2E
New Norway **61** 52 52N 112 57W
New Orleans **75** 30 0N 90 5W
New Palestine **77** 39 45N 85 52W
New Paris **77** 39 5N 84 48W
New Pekin **77** 38 31N 86 2W
New Philadelphia **70** 40 29N 81 25W
New Plymouth, Bahamas **84** 26 56N 77 20W
New Plymouth, N.Z. **133** 39 4S 174 5E
New Providence I. **84** 25 0N 77 30W
New Radnor **95** 52 15N 3 10W
New Richmond, Can. **38** 48 15N 65 45W
New Richmond, U.S.A. **77** 38 57N 84 17W
New Richmond, Wis., U.S.A. **74** 45 6N 92 34W
New Roads **75** 30 43N 91 30W
New Rochelle **71** 40 55N 73 46W
New Rockford **74** 47 44N 99 7W
New Ross, Can. **39** 44 44N 64 27W
New Ross, Ireland **97** 52 24N 6 58W
New Salem **74** 46 51N 101 25W
New Sarepta **60** 53 16N 113 8W
New Sharon **76** 41 28N 92 39W
New Siberian Is. = Novosibirskiye Os. **121** 75 0N 140 0E
New Smyrna Beach **73** 29 0N 80 50W
New South Wales □ **135** 33 0S 146 0E
New Toronto **50** 43 36N 79 30W
New Ulm **74** 44 15N 94 30W
New Vienna **77** 39 19N 83 42W
New Virginia **76** 41 11N 93 44W
New Waterford **39** 46 13N 60 4W
New Westminster **66** 49 13N 122 55W
New World I. **37** 49 35N 54 40W
New York □ **71** 42 40N 76 0W
New York City **71** 40 45N 74 0W
New Zealand ■ **14** 40 0S 176 0E
Newala **116** 10 58S 39 10E
Newark, U.K. **94** 53 6N 0 48W
Newark, Del., U.S.A. **72** 39 42N 75 45W
Newark, N.J., U.S.A. **71** 40 41N 74 12W
Newark, N.Y., U.S.A. **70** 43 2N 77 10W
Newark, Ohio, U.S.A. **70** 40 5N 82 30W
Newberg, U.S.A. **76** 37 55N 91 54W
Newberg, Oreg., U.S.A. **78** 45 22N 123 0W
Newberry **46** 46 20N 85 32W
Newberry Springs **81** 34 50N 116 41W
Newboro L. **47** 44 38N 76 20W
Newbrook **60** 54 24N 112 57W
Newburgh, Can. **47** 44 19N 76 52W
Newburgh, U.S.A. **77** 37 57N 87 24W
Newburgh, N.Y., U.S.A. **71** 41 30N 74 1W
Newbury, U.K. **95** 51 24N 1 19W
Newbury, U.S.A. **71** 44 7N 72 6W
Newburyport **71** 42 48N 70 50W
Newcastle, Austral. **136** 33 0S 151 40E
Newcastle, N.B., Can. **39** 47 1N 65 38W
Newcastle, Ont., Can. **70** 43 54N 78 34W
Newcastle, S. Afr. **117** 27 45S 29 58E
Newcastle, U.K. **97** 54 13N 5 54W
Newcastle, Calif., U.S.A. **80** 38 53N 121 8W
Newcastle, Me., U.S.A. **71** 43 4N 70 41W
Newcastle, Wyo., U.S.A. **74** 43 50N 104 12W
Newcastle Bridge **39** 46 5N 66 3W
Newcastle Emlyn **95** 52 2N 4 29W
Newcastle Ra. **135** 15 45S 130 15E
Newcastle-under-Lyme **94** 53 2N 2 15W
Newcastle-upon-Tyne **94** 54 59N 1 37W
Newcastle Waters **134** 17 30S 133 28E
Newcastle West **97** 52 27N 9 3W
Newdegate **134** 33 6S 119 0E
Newell **74** 44 48N 103 25W
Newell, L. **61** 50 26N 111 55W
Newenham, C. **67** 58 40N 162 15W
Newfoundland **35** 48 30N 56 0W
Newfoundland □ **35** 48 28N 56 0W
Newgate **61** 49 2N 115 12W
Newhalem **63** 48 41N 121 16W
Newhalen **67** 59 40N 155 0W
Newhall **81** 34 23N 118 32W
Newham **95** 51 31N 0 2E
Newhaven **95** 50 47N 0 4E
Newkirk **75** 36 52N 97 3W
Newman, U.S.A. **77** 39 48N 87 59W
Newman, U.S.A. **80** 37 19N 121 1W
Newman, Mt. **134** 23 20S 119 34E
Newmarket, Can. **46** 44 3N 79 28W
Newmarket, Ireland **97** 52 13N 9 0W
Newmarket, U.K. **95** 52 15N 0 23E
Newmarket, U.S.A. **71** 43 4N 70 57W
Newnan **73** 33 22N 84 48W
Newport, Austral. **136** 33 40S 151 20E
Newport, Can. **38** 48 16N 64 45W
Newport, Ont., Can. **49** 43 6N 80 14W
Newport, Gwent, U.K. **95** 51 35N 3 0W
Newport, I. of W., U.K. **95** 50 42N 1 18W
Newport, Salop, U.K. **95** 52 47N 2 22W
Newport, U.S.A. **77** 42 2N 83 22W
Newport, Ark., U.S.A. **75** 35 38N 91 15W
Newport, Ind., U.S.A. **77** 39 53N 87 26W
Newport, Ky., U.S.A. **77** 39 5N 84 23W
Newport, N.H., U.S.A. **71** 43 23N 72 8W
Newport, Oreg., U.S.A. **78** 44 41N 124 2W
Newport, Pa., U.S.A. **70** 40 28N 77 8W
Newport, R.I., U.S.A. **71** 41 30N 71 19W
Newport, Tenn., U.S.A. **73** 35 59N 83 12W
Newport, Vt., U.S.A. **71** 44 57N 72 17W
Newport, Wash., U.S.A. **63** 48 11N 117 2W
Newport Beach **81** 33 40N 117 58W
Newport News **72** 37 2N 76 30W
Newquay **95** 50 24N 5 6W
Newry **97** 54 10N 6 20W
Newry & Mourne □ **97** 54 10N 6 15W
Newton, Can. **66** 49 8N 122 51W
Newton, Ill., U.S.A. **77** 38 59N 88 10W
Newton, Iowa, U.S.A. **76** 41 40N 93 3W
Newton, Mass., U.S.A. **72** 42 21N 71 10W
Newton, N.C., U.S.A. **73** 35 42N 81 10W
Newton, N.J., U.S.A. **71** 41 3N 74 46W
Newton, Texas, U.S.A. **75** 30 54N 93 42W
Newton Abbot **95** 50 32N 3 37W
Newton Brook **50** 43 48N 79 24W
Newton Stewart **96** 54 57N 4 30W
Newtonabbey □ **97** 54 45N 6 0W
Newtown, Austral. **136** 37 38S 143 40E
Newtown, Can. **37** 49 12N 53 31W
Newtown, U.K. **95** 52 31N 3 19W
Newtown, U.S.A. **76** 40 22N 93 20W
Newtownabbey **97** 54 40N 5 55W
Newtownabbey □ **105** 54 45N 6 0W
Newtownards **97** 54 37N 5 40W
Newville **70** 40 10N 77 24W
Neyrīz **123** 29 15N 54 55E
Neyshābūr **123** 36 10N 58 20E
Nezhin **120** 51 5N 31 55E
Nezperce **78** 46 13N 116 15W
Ngabang **126** 0 30N 109 55E
Ngami Depression **117** 20 30S 22 46E
Ngandjuk **127** 7 32S 111 55E
Ngaoundéré **114** 7 15N 13 35E
Ngapara **133** 44 57S 170 46E
Ngau, I. **133** 18 2S 179 18E
Ngawi **127** 7 24S 111 26E
Ngha Lo **128** 21 33N 104 28E
Ngoring Nor **129** 34 50N 98 0E
Ngudu **116** 2 58S 33 25E
Nguru **114** 12 56N 10 29E
Nha Trang **128** 12 16N 109 10E
Nhill **136** 36 18S 141 40E
Nhulunbuy **135** 12 10S 136 45E
Niagara **72** 45 45N 88 0W
Niagara □, Can. **49** 43 15N 79 4W
Niagara □, U.S.A. **49** 43 16N 78 55W
Niagara Falls, Can. **49** 43 7N 79 5W
Niagara Falls, N. Amer. **34** 43 5N 79 5W
Niagara Falls, U.S.A. **49** 43 5N 79 0W
Niagara-on-the-Lake **49** 43 15N 79 4W
Niagara, R. **49** 43 16N 79 3W
Niah **126** 3 58N 113 46E
Nialia, L. **136** 33 20S 141 42E
Niamey **114** 13 27N 2 6E
Niangara **116** 3 50N 27 50E
Niangua, R. **76** 38 0N 92 48W
Nias, I. **126** 1 0N 97 40E
Nibong Tebal **128** 5 10N 100 29E
Nicaragua ■ **84** 11 40N 85 30W
Nicaragua, Lago de **84** 12 50N 85 30W
Nicastro **108** 39 0N 16 18E
Nice **103** 43 42N 7 14E
Niceville **73** 30 30N 86 30W
Nichinan **132** 31 38N 131 23E
Nicholas, Chan. **84** 23 30N 80 30W
Nicholasville **72** 37 54N 84 31W
Nichols **71** 42 1N 76 22W
Nicholson, Can. **34** 47 58N 83 47W
Nicholson, U.S.A. **71** 41 37N 75 47W
Nicobar Is. **118** 9 0N 93 0E
Nicoclí **86** 8 25N 76 48W
Nicola **63** 50 12N 120 40W
Nicola L. **63** 50 10N 120 32W
Nicolasville **77** 37 53N 84 34W
Nicolet **41** 46 17N 72 35W
Nicolls Town **84** 25 8N 78 0W
Nicomekl, R. **66** 49 3N 122 52W
Nicosia **122** 35 10N 33 25E
Nicoya **84** 10 9N 85 27W
Nicoya, G. de **84** 10 0N 85 0W
Nicoya, Pen. de **84** 9 45N 85 40W
Nidd, R. **94** 54 1N 1 32W
Niederbronn **101** 48 57N 7 39E
Niemur **136** 35 17S 144 9E

† *Renamed Vanuatu* ■

Nienburg Nosratābād

Nienburg 106 52 38N 9 15 E
Nientzeshan 130 47 38N 122 58 E
Nieuw Nickerie 87 6 0N 57 10W
Nieuwpoort 105 51 8N 2 45 E
Nièvre □ 101 47 10N 3 40 E
Niğde 122 38 0N 34 40 E
Nigel I. 62 50 53N 127 43W
Niger ■ 114 13 30N 10 0 E
Niger, R. 114 10 0N 4 40 E
Nigeria ■ 114 8 30N 8 0 E
Nightcaps 133 45 57 S 168 14 E
Nii-Jima 132 34 20N 139 15 E
Niigata 132 37 58N 139 0 E
Niigata-ken □ 132 37 15N 138 45 E
Niihama 132 33 55N 133 10 E
Niihau, I. 67 21 55N 160 10W
Nijkerk 105 52 13N 5 30 E
Nijmegen 105 51 50N 5 52 E
Nikel 110 69 30N 30 5 E
Nikiniki 127 9 40 S 124 30 E
Nikki 114 9 58N 3 21 E
Nikkō 132 36 45N 139 35 E
Nikolayev 120 46 58N 32 7 E
Nikolayevsk-na-Amur 121 53 40N 140 50 E
Nikolayevski 120 50 10N 45 35 E
Nikolski 67 53 0N 168 50W
Nikolskoye, Amur, U.S.S.R. 121 47 50N 131 5 E
Nikolskoye, Kamandorskiye, U.S.S.R. 121 55 12N 166 0 E
Nīkshahr 123 26 15N 60 10 E
Nikšić 115 42 50N 18 57 E
Nîl el Abyad, Bahr 115 9 30N 31 40 E
Nîl el Azraq □ 114 12 30N 34 30 E
Nîl el Azraq, Bahr 115 10 30N 35 0 E
Nîl, Nahr el 115 27 30N 30 30 E
Nila 127 8 24 S 120 29 E
Niland 81 33 16N 115 30W
Nile, R. = Nîl, Nahr el 115 27 30N 30 30 E
Niles 70 41 8N 80 40W
Nimach = Neemuch 124 24 30N 74 50 E
Nimba, Mt. 114 7 39N 8 30W
Nîmes 103 43 50N 4 23 E
Nimingarra 134 20 31 S 119 55 E
Nimneryskiy 121 58 0N 125 10 E
Nimpkish L. 62 50 25N 126 59W
Nimpkish, R. 62 50 34N 126 58W
Nimpo L. 62 52 20N 125 10W
Nimule 116 3 32N 32 3 E
Ninemile 54 56 0N 130 7W
Ninette 57 49 24N 99 38W
Ninety Mile Beach 14 34 45 S 173 0 E
Ninety Mile Beach, The 135 38 15 S 147 24 E
Nineveh 122 36 25N 43 10 E
Ningan 130 44 23N 129 26 E
Ninghsien 130 35 35N 107 58 E
Ninghwa 131 32 58N 119 59 E
Ningkiang 131 32 52N 106 17 E
Ningming 131 22 10N 107 59 E
Ningpo 131 29 53N 121 33 E
Ningshan 131 33 12N 108 29 E
Ningsia Hui A.R. □ 130 37 45N 106 0 E
Ningteh 131 26 45N 120 0 E
Ningtsin 130 37 40N 115 0 E
Ningtu 131 26 30N 115 58 E
Ningwu 130 39 2N 112 15 E
Ningyüan 131 25 36N 111 54 E
Ninh Binh 128 20 15N 105 55 E
Ninkiang 131 32 50N 106 20 E
Ninove 105 50 51N 4 2 E
Nioaque 89 21 5 S 55 50W
Niobrara 74 42 48N 97 59W
Niobrara R. 74 42 30N 103 0W
Nioki 116 2 47 S 17 40 E
Nioman 36 50 25N 66 5W
Nioro du Sahel 114 15 30N 9 30W
Niort 102 46 19N 0 29W
Nipawin 56 53 20N 104 0W
Nipawin Prov. Park 56 54 0N 104 37W
Nipekamew, R. 56 54 59N 104 52W
Nipigon 52 49 0N 88 17W
Nipigon B. 53 48 53N 87 50W
Nipigon, L. 52 49 50N 88 30W
Nipin, R. 55 55 46N 109 2W
Nipishish L. 36 54 12N 60 45W
Nipisi L. 60 55 47N 114 57W
Nipissing L. 46 46 20N 80 0W
Nipissis, L. 38 51 2N 66 10W
Nipissis, R. 36 50 30N 66 5W
Nipisso, L. 38 50 52N 65 50W
Nipomo 81 35 4N 120 29W
Nipper's Harbour 37 49 48N 55 52W
Nipton 81 35 28N 115 16W
Nirmal 124 19 3N 78 20 E
Nirmali 125 26 20N 86 35 E
Niš 109 43 19N 21 58 E
Nishinomiya 132 34 45N 135 20 E
Niskibi, R. 34 56 29N 88 9W
Nisqually, R. 80 47 6N 122 42W
Nisswa 52 46 31N 94 17W
Nisutlin, R. 54 60 14N 132 34W
Nitchequon 36 53 10N 70 58W
Niterói 89 22 52 S 43 0W
Nith, R., Can. 46 43 12N 80 23W
Nith, R., U.K. 96 55 20N 3 5W
Nitinat 62 48 56N 124 29W
Nitinat L. 62 48 45N 124 45W
Nitra 107 48 19N 18 4 E
Nitra, R. 107 48 30N 18 7 E
Niuafo'ou, I. 133 15 30 S 175 58W
Niue I. (Savage I.) 14 19 2 S 169 54W
Niut, Mt. 126 0 55N 109 30 E
Nivelles 105 50 35N 4 20 E
Nivernais 101 47 0N 3 40 E
Niverville 57 49 36N 97 3W
Nixon, Nev., U.S.A. 78 39 54N 119 22W
Nixon, Tex., U.S.A. 75 29 17N 97 45W
Nizamabad 124 18 45N 78 7 E
Nizamghat 125 28 20N 95 45 E
Nizhanaya Tunguska 121 64 20N 93 0 E
Nizhne Kolymsk 121 68 40N 160 55 E
Nizhne-Vartovskoye 120 60 56N 76 38 E
Nizhneangarsk 121 56 0N 109 30 E
Nizhneudinsk 121 55 0N 99 20 E
Nizhniy Tagil 120 57 55N 59 57 E
Nizip 122 37 5N 37 50 E
Nizké Tatry 107 48 55N 20 0 E
Njombe 116 9 20 S 34 50 E
Nkhata Bay 116 11 33 S 34 16 E
Nkhota Kota 117 12 56 S 34 15 E
Nkongsamba 116 4 55N 9 55 E
Nmai, R. 125 25 30N 98 0 E
Noakhali = Maijdi 125 22 50N 90 45 E
Noatak 67 67 32N 163 10W
Noatak, R. 67 68 0N 161 0W
Nobel 46 45 25N 80 6W
Nobeoka 132 32 36N 131 41 E
Noble 77 38 42N 88 14W
Nobleford 61 49 53N 113 3W
Noblesville 77 40 1N 85 59W
Nobleton 50 43 54N 79 40W
Nocera Inferiore 108 40 45N 14 37 E
Nochixtlán 83 17 28N 97 14W
Nocona 75 33 48N 97 45W
Noda 121 47 30N 142 5 E
Noel, Can. 39 45 18N 63 45W
Noel, U.S.A. 75 36 36N 94 29W
Noelville 46 46 8N 80 26W
Nogales, Mexico 82 31 36N 94 29W
Nogales, U.S.A. 79 31 33N 115 50W
Nōgata 132 33 48N 130 54 E
Nogent-en-Bassigny 101 48 0N 5 20 E
Nogent-le-Rotrou 100 48 20N 0 50 E
Nogent-sur-Seine 101 48 30N 3 30 E
Noginsk 121 64 30N 90 50 E
Nogoa, R. 135 23 33 S 148 32 E
Nogoyá 88 32 24 S 59 48W
Noi, R. 128 14 50N 100 15 E
Noirclair, L. 38 50 38N 60 23W
Noire, Mt. 100 48 11N 3 40W
Noire, R. 40 45 54N 76 57W
Noirétable 102 45 48N 3 46 E
Noirmoutier 100 47 0N 2 15W
Noirmoutier, Î. de 100 46 58N 2 10W
Nok Kundi 124 28 50N 62 45 E
Nokhtuysk 121 60 0N 117 45 E
Nokomis, Can. 56 51 35N 105 0W
Nokomis, U.S.A. 76 39 18N 89 18W
Nokomis L. 55 57 0N 103 0W
Nola 116 3 35N 16 10 E
Nolay 101 46 58N 4 35 E
Noman L. 55 62 15N 108 55W
Nombinnie 136 32 56 S 145 53 E
Nombre de Dios 84 9 34N 79 28W
Nome 67 64 30N 165 30W
Nominingue 40 46 24N 75 2W
Nominingue, L. 40 46 26N 74 59W
Nonacho L. 55 61 57N 109 28W
Nonancourt 100 48 47N 1 11 E
Nonant-le-Pin 100 48 42N 0 12 E
Nong Khae 128 14 29N 100 53 E
Nong Khai 128 17 50N 102 46 E
Nonoava 82 27 22N 106 38W
Nonopapa 67 21 50N 160 15W
Nontron 102 45 31N 0 40 E
Noonan 56 48 51N 102 59W
Noonkanbah 126 18 30 S 124 50 E
Noorvik 67 66 50N 161 14W
Nootka 62 49 38N 126 38W
Nootka I. 62 49 40N 126 50W
Noqui 116 5 55 S 13 30 E
Nora Springs 76 43 9N 92 1W
Norah Head 136 33 15 S 151 35 E
Noranda 40 48 20N 79 0W
Norborne 76 39 18N 93 40W
Norco 81 33 56N 117 33W
Nord □ 101 50 15N 3 30 E
Nord, Grand L. du 38 50 54N 67 6W
Nord-Ostee Kanal 106 54 5N 9 15 E
Nord, Petit L. du 38 50 50N 67 10W
Nord, R. 43 45 31N 74 20W
Nord-Trondelag Fylke □ 110 64 20N 12 0 E
Nordaustlandet 17 79 55N 23 0 E
Nordegg 61 52 29N 116 5W
Nordhausen 106 51 29N 10 47 E
Nordhorn 105 52 27N 7 4 E
Nordkapp, Norway 110 71 10N 25 44 E
Nordkapp, Svalb. 17 80 31N 20 0 E
Nordkinn 93 71 3N 28 0 E
Nordland Fylke □ 110 65 40N 13 0 E
Nordrhein-Westfalen □ 106 51 45N 7 30 E
Nordvik 121 73 40N 110 57 E
Nore R. 97 52 40N 7 20W
Norembega 34 48 59N 80 43W
Norfolk, Nebr., U.S.A. 74 42 3N 97 25W
Norfolk, N.Y., U.S.A. 71 44 47N 75 1W
Norfolk, Va., U.S.A. 72 36 52N 76 15W
Norfolk □ 94 52 39N 1 0 E
Norfolk Broads 94 52 30N 1 15 E
Norfolk I. 14 28 58 S 168 3 E
Norfork Res. 75 36 25N 92 0W
Norg 105 53 4N 6 28 E
Norilsk 121 69 20N 88 0 E
Normal 76 40 30N 89 0W
Norman 75 35 12N 97 30W
Norman, R. 135 19 20 S 142 35 E
Norman Wells 64 65 17N 126 45W
Normanby, R. 135 14 23 S 144 10 E
Normandie 100 48 45N 0 10 E
Normandie, Collines de 100 48 55N 0 45W
Normandin 41 48 49N 72 31W
Normandy = Normandie 100 48 45N 0 10 E
Norman's Cove 37 47 33N 53 40W
Normanton 135 17 40 S 141 10 E
Normanview 58 50 28N 104 40W
Normétal 40 49 0N 79 22W
Norquay 57 51 53N 102 5W
Ñorquinco 90 41 51 S 70 55W
Norrby 110 64 55N 18 15 E
Nørresundby 111 57 5N 9 52 E
Norris 78 45 40N 111 48W
Norris Arm 37 49 5N 55 15W
Norris City 77 37 59N 88 20W
Norris Point 37 49 31N 57 53W
Norristown 71 40 9N 75 15W
Norrköping 111 58 37N 16 11 E
Norrland □ 110 66 50N 18 0 E
Norrtälje 111 59 46N 18 42 E
Norsk 121 52 30N 130 0 E
Norte de Santander □ 86 8 0N 73 0W
North Adams 71 42 42N 73 6W
North Andaman I. 128 13 15N 92 40 E
North Atlantic Ocean 12 30 0N 50 0W
North Aulatsivik I. 36 59 46N 64 5W
North Baltimore 77 41 11N 83 41W
North Battleford 56 52 50N 108 17W
North Bay 46 46 20N 79 30W
North Belcher Is. 36 56 50N 79 50W
North Bend, Can. 63 49 50N 121 35W
North Bend, Oreg., U.S.A. 78 43 28N 124 7W
North Bend, Pa., U.S.A. 70 41 20N 77 42W
North Bend, Wash., U.S.A. 80 47 30N 121 47W
North Berwick, U.K. 96 56 4N 2 44W
North Berwick, U.S.A. 71 43 18N 70 43W
North Buck L. 60 54 41N 112 32W
North Burnaby 66 49 17N 123 0W
North Canadian, R. 75 36 48N 103 0W
North C., Antarct. 91 71 0N 166 0 E
North C., Can. 35 47 2N 60 20W
North, Cape 39 47 2N 60 25W
North C., N.Z. 133 34 23 S 173 4 E
North C., Spitsbergen 17 80 40N 20 0 E
North Caribou L. 34 52 50N 90 40W
North Carolina □ 73 35 30N 80 0W
North Cascades Nat. Park 63 48 45N 121 14W
North Channel, Br. Is. 96 55 0N 5 30W
North Channel, Can. 46 46 0N 83 0W
North Chicago 77 42 19N 87 50W
North College Hill 77 39 13N 84 33W
North Dakota □ 74 47 30N 100 0W
North Down □ 97 54 40N 5 45W
North Downs 95 51 17N 0 30W
North East 70 42 17N 79 50W
North English 76 41 31N 92 5W
North Esk, R. 96 56 44N 2 25W
North European Plain 93 55 0N 20 0 E
North Fabius, R. 76 39 54N 91 28W
N. Foreland, Pt. 95 51 22N 1 28 E
North Fork 80 37 14N 119 29W
North Fork, American, R. 80 38 45N 121 8W
North Fork, Feather, R. 80 39 17N 121 38W
North Fork, Salt R. 76 39 26N 91 5W
North French, R. 53 51 10N 80 50W
North Glanford 48 43 11N 79 54W
North Gower 47 45 8N 75 43W
North Grant 39 45 40N 62 2W
North Hatley 41 45 17N 71 58W
North Head, N.B., Can. 39 44 46N 66 45W
North Head, Newf., Can. 37 47 29N 52 38W
North Henik L. 55 61 45N 97 40W
North Highlands 80 38 40N 121 25W
North I. 133 38 0 S 175 0 E
North Judson 77 41 13N 86 46W
North Kamloops 54 50 40N 120 25W
North Kansas City 76 39 9N 94 35W
North Kingsville 70 41 53N 80 42W
North Knife, R. 55 58 53N 94 45W
North Korea ■ 130 40 0N 127 0 E
N. Lakhimpur 125 27 15N 94 10 E
North Lancaster 43 45 13N 74 30W
N. Las Vegas 81 36 15N 115 6W
North Liberty 77 41 32N 86 26W
North Lonsdale 66 49 20N 123 4W
North Magnetic Pole 65 77 18N 101 48W
North Manchester 77 41 0N 85 46W
North Minch 96 58 5N 5 55W
North Nahanni, R. 54 62 15N 123 20W
North Ossetian A.S.S.R. □ 120 43 30N 44 30 E
North Palisade 80 37 6N 118 32W
North Platte 74 41 10N 100 50W
North Platte, R. 78 42 50N 106 50W
North Pt. 39 47 5N 64 0W
North Pole 17 90 0N 0 0 E
North Portal 57 49 0N 102 33W
North Powder 78 45 2N 117 59W
North, R. 36 57 30N 61 50W
North Ram, R. 61 52 16N 114 38W
North Ronaldsay, I. 96 59 20N 2 30W
North Rustico 39 46 27N 63 19W
N. Saskatchewan R. 56 53 15N 105 5W
North Sea 93 56 0N 4 0 E
North Seneca 49 43 7N 79 56W
North Sentinel, I. 128 11 35N 92 15 E
North Star 60 56 51N 117 38W
North Stradbroke I. 135 27 35 S 153 28 E
North Sydney 39 46 12N 60 21W
North Thompson, R. 63 50 40N 120 20W
N. Tonawanda 49 43 5N 78 50W
North Troy 71 44 59N 72 24W
N. Truchas Pk. 79 36 0N 105 30W
North Twin I. 36 53 20N 80 0W
North Twin L. 37 49 16N 55 56W
North Tyne, R. 94 54 59N 2 7W
North Uist I. 96 57 40N 7 15W
North Vancouver 66 49 2N 123 3W
North Vermilion 54 58 25N 116 0W
North Vernon 77 39 0N 85 35W
North Wabasca L. 60 56 0N 113 55W
North Walsham 94 52 49N 1 22 E
North Webster 77 41 25N 85 48W
North West Highlands 96 57 35N 5 2W
North West River 36 53 30N 60 10W
North York 50 43 46N 79 30W
North York Moors 94 54 25N 0 50W
North Yorkshire □ 94 54 15N 1 25W
Northallerton 94 54 20N 1 26W
Northam 134 31 35 S 116 42 E
Northampton, Austral. 134 28 21 S 114 33 E
Northampton, U.K. 95 52 14N 0 54W
Northampton, Mass., U.S.A. 71 42 22N 72 39W
Northampton, Pa., U.S.A. 71 40 38N 75 24W
Northampton □ 95 52 16N 0 55W
Northbridge 71 42 12N 71 40W
N.E. Land 17 80 0N 24 0 E
N.E. Providence Chan. 84 26 0N 76 0W
Northeast Providence Channel 84 26 0N 76 0W
Northern Circars 125 17 30N 82 30 E
Northern Group 133 10 00 S 160 00W
Northern Indian L. 55 57 20N 97 20W
Northern Ireland □ 97 54 45N 7 0W
Northern Light, L. 52 48 15N 90 39W
Northern Territory □ 134 16 0 S 133 0 E
Northfield 74 44 30N 93 10W
Northland □ 133 35 30 S 173 30 E
Northmount 50 43 46N 79 24W
Northome 52 47 53N 94 15W
Northport, Can. 39 45 56N 63 52W
Northport, Ala., U.S.A. 73 33 15N 87 35W
Northport, Mich., U.S.A. 72 45 8N 85 39W
Northport, Wash., U.S.A. 63 48 55N 117 48W
Northumberland □ 94 55 12N 2 0W
Northumberland, C. 135 38 5 S 140 40 E
Northumberland Str. 39 46 20N 64 0W
Northville 72 43 13N 74 11W
Northway Junction 67 63 0N 141 55W
Northwest Gander, R. 37 48 55N 55 2W
N.W. Providence Chan. 84 26 0N 78 0W
Northwest Terr. □ 64 65 0N 100 0W
N.W. Frontier □ 134 35 0N 72 0 E
Northwich 94 53 16N 2 30W
Northwood, Iowa, U.S.A. 74 43 27N 93 0W
Northwood, N.D., U.S.A. 74 47 44N 97 30W
Norton, Can. 39 45 38N 65 42W
Norton, U.S.A. 74 39 50N 100 0W
Norton B. 67 64 40N 162 0W
Norton Sd. 67 64 0N 165 0W
Norton Shores 77 43 8N 86 15W
Norwalk, Calif., U.S.A. 81 33 54N 118 5W
Norwalk, Conn., U.S.A. 71 41 9N 73 25W
Norwalk, Ohio, U.S.A. 70 41 13N 82 38W
Norway 72 45 46N 87 57W
Norway ■ 111 67 0N 11 0 E
Norway House 57 53 59N 97 50W
Norwegian B. 65 77 30N 90 0W
Norwegian Dependency 91 66 0N 15 0 E
Norwegian Sea 12 66 0N 1 0 E
Norwich, Can. 46 42 59N 80 36W
Norwich, U.K. 94 52 38N 1 17 E
Norwich, Conn., U.S.A. 71 41 33N 72 5W
Norwich, N.Y., U.S.A. 71 42 32N 75 30W
Norwood, Can. 47 44 23N 77 59W
Norwood, Mass., U.S.A. 71 42 10N 71 10W
Norwood, Ohio, U.S.A. 77 39 10N 89 27W
Nos Kaliakra, C. 109 43 21N 28 30 E
Nose Cr. 59 51 3N 114 1W
Noshiro 132 40 12N 140 0 E
Noshiro, R. 132 40 15N 140 15 E
Nosok 120 70 10N 82 20 E
Nosratābād 123 29 55N 60 0 E

Noss Hd.	**96**	58 29N	3 4W
Nossob, R.	**117**	25 15S	20 30E
Nosy Bé, I.	**117**	13 25S	48 15E
Nosy Mitsio, I.	**117**	12 54S	48 36E
Nosy Varika	**117**	20 35S	48 32E
Notigi Dam	**55**	56 40N	99 10W
Notikewin	**54**	56 55N	117 50W
Notikewin, R.	**60**	57 2N	117 38W
Notituchow	**131**	24 25N	107 20E
Noto	**108**	36 52N	15 4E
Noto-Hanto	**132**	37 0N	137 0E
Notre-Dame, N.B., Can.	**39**	46 18N	64 46W
Notre-Dame, Qué., Can.	**45**	45 28N	73 28W
Notre Dame B.	**37**	49 45N	55 30W
Notre Dame de Koartac	**36**	60 55N	69 40W
Notre-Dame-de-la-Doré	**41**	48 43N	72 39W
Notre-Dame-de-l'Île-Perrot	**44**	45 23N	73 56W
Notre Dame de Lourdes	**57**	49 32N	98 33W
Notre-Dame-de-Stanbridge	**43**	45 8N	73 2W
Notre-Dame-des-Bois	**41**	45 24N	71 4W
Notre-Dame-des-Laurentides	**42**	46 55N	71 18W
Notre-Dame-du-Bon-Conseil	**41**	46 0N	72 21W
Notre Dame du Lac	**46**	46 18N	80 11W
Notre-Dame-du-Lac	**41**	47 36N	68 48W
Notre-Dame-du-Laus	**40**	46 5N	75 37W
Notre-Dame-du-Nord	**40**	47 36N	79 30W
Notre-Dame-du-Portage	**41**	47 46N	69 37W
Notre-Dame, Les	**38**	48 10N	68 0W
Nottawasaga B.	**46**	44 35N	80 15W
Nottaway, R.	**36**	51 22N	78 55W
Nottingham	**94**	52 57N	1 10W
Nottingham □	**94**	53 10N	1 0W
Nottingham I.	**65**	63 20N	77 55W
Nottingham Island	**65**	63 6N	77 50W
Nottoway, R.	**72**	37 0N	77 45W
Notukeu Cr.	**56**	49 56N	106 29W
Nouadhibou	**114**	21 0N	17 0W
Nouakchott	**114**	18 20N	15 50W
Nouméa	**14**	22 17S	166 30E
Noupoort	**117**	31 10S	24 57E
Nouveau Comptoir (Paint Hills)	**36**	53 0N	78 49W
Nouveau-Quebec, Reg.	**36**	56 0N	71 0W
Nouvelle	**39**	48 8N	66 19W
Nouvelle France, C. de	**36**	62 27N	73 42W
Nouvelle, R.	**39**	48 7N	66 19W
Nouzonville	**101**	49 48N	4 44E
*Nova Chaves	**116**	10 50S	21 15E
Nova Cruz	**87**	6 28S	35 25W
Nova Esperança	**89**	23 8S	52 13W
Nova Friburgo	**89**	22 10S	42 30W
Nova Gaia	**116**	10 10S	17 35E
Nova Iguaçu	**89**	22 45S	43 28W
Nova Iorque	**87**	7 0S	44 5W
Nova Lima	**89**	19 59S	43 51W
Nova Lisboa = Huambo	**117**	12 42S	15 54E
Nova Mambone	**117**	21 0S	35 3E
Nova Preixo	**117**	14 45S	36 22E
Nova Scotia □	**35**	45 10N	63 0W
Nova Sofala	**117**	20 7S	34 48E
Nova Venécia	**87**	18 45S	40 24W
Nova Zembla I.	**65**	72 11N	74 50W
Novalorque	**87**	6 48S	44 0W
Novar	**46**	45 27N	79 15W
Novara	**108**	45 27N	8 36E
Novato	**80**	38 6N	122 35W
Novaya Lyalya	**120**	58 50N	60 35E
Novaya Sibir, O.	**121**	75 10N	150 0E
Novaya Zemlya	**120**	75 0N	56 0E
Nové Zámky	**107**	48 2N	18 8E
Novelty	**76**	40 1N	92 12W
Novgorod	**120**	58 30N	31 25E
Novi-Pazar	**109**	43 25N	27 15E
Novi Sad	**109**	45 18N	19 52E
Novinger	**76**	40 14N	92 43W
Nôvo Hamburgo	**89**	29 37S	51 7W
Novo Luso	**127**	4 3S	126 6E
Novoataysk	**120**	53 30N	84 0E
Novocherkassk	**120**	47 27N	40 5E
Novokazalinsk	**120**	45 40N	61 40E
Novokuznetsk	**120**	54 0N	87 10E
Novomoskovsk	**120**	54 5N	38 15E
Novorossiysk	**120**	44 43N	37 52E
Novosibirsk	**120**	55 0N	83 5E
Novosibirskiye Ostrava	**121**	75 0N	140 0E
Novska	**108**	45 19N	17 0E
Novyy Port	**120**	67 40N	72 30E
Now Shahr	**123**	36 40N	51 40E
Nowgong	**125**	26 20N	92 50E
Nowingi	**136**	34 33S	142 15E
Nowra	**136**	34 53S	150 35E
Nowy Sącz	**107**	49 40N	20 41E
Nowy Tomyssl	**106**	52 19N	16 10E
Noxen	**71**	41 25N	76 4W
Noxon	**78**	48 0N	115 54W
Noyant	**100**	47 30N	0 6E
Noyers	**101**	47 40N	4 0E
Noyes, I.	**54**	55 30N	133 40W
Noyon	**101**	49 34N	3 0E
Nriquinha	**117**	16 0S	21 25E
Nsanje	**117**	16 55S	35 12E

* *Renamed Muconda*

*Nuanetsi	**117**	21 15S	30 48E
Nubian Desert	**115**	21 30N	33 30E
Nûbîya, Es Sahrâ En	**115**	21 30N	33 30E
Ñuble □	**88**	37 0S	72 0W
Nuboai	**127**	2 10S	136 30E
Nudo Ausangate, Mt.	**86**	13 45S	71 10W
Nudo de Vilcanota	**86**	14 30S	70 0W
Nueces, R.	**75**	28 18N	98 39W
Nueltin L.	**55**	60 30N	99 30W
Nueva Antioquia	**86**	6 5N	69 26W
Nueva Casas Grandes	**82**	30 25N	107 55W
Nueva Esparta □	**86**	11 0N	64 0W
Nueva Gerona	**84**	21 53N	82 49W
Nueva Imperial	**90**	38 45S	72 58W
Nueva Palmira	**88**	33 52S	58 20W
Nueva Rosita	**82**	28 0N	101 20W
Nueva San Salvador	**84**	13 40N	89 25W
Nuéve de Julio	**88**	35 30S	61 0W
Nuevitas	**84**	21 30N	77 20W
Nuevo, Golfo	**90**	43 0S	64 30W
Nuevo Guerrero	**83**	26 34N	99 15W
Nuevo Laredo	**83**	27 30N	99 40W
Nuevo León □	**82**	25 0N	100 0W
Nuevo Rocafuerte	**86**	0 55S	76 50W
Nugget Pt.	**133**	46 27S	169 50E
Nugssuaq Pen.	**65**	70 30N	53 0W
Nuhaka	**133**	39 3S	177 45E
Nuhurowa, I.	**127**	5 30S	132 45E
Nuits-St.-Georges	**101**	47 10N	4 56E
Nukey Bluff, Mt.	**134**	32 32S	135 40E
Nukus	**120**	42 20N	59 40E
Nulato	**67**	64 40N	158 10W
Nulki L.	**62**	53 55N	124 7W
Nulla Nulla	**136**	33 47S	141 28E
Nullagine	**134**	21 53S	120 6E
Nullarbor Plain	**134**	30 45S	129 0E
Numan	**114**	9 29N	12 3E
Numata	**132**	36 45N	139 4E
Numazu	**132**	35 7N	138 51E
Numfoor, I.	**127**	1 0S	134 50E
Numurkah	**136**	36 0S	145 26E
Nunaksaluk I.	**36**	55 49N	60 20W
Nuneaton	**95**	52 32N	1 29W
Nungan	**130**	44 29N	125 10E
Nungesser L.	**52**	51 28N	93 30W
Nunivak I.	**67**	60 0N	166 0W
Nunkiang	**129**	49 11N	125 12E
Nunkun, Mt.	**124**	33 57N	76 8E
Nunspeet	**105**	52 21N	5 45E
Nuorgam	**108**	70 5N	27 51E
Nuqui	**86**	5 42N	77 17W
Nurcoung	**136**	36 45S	141 42E
Nuremburg = Nürnberg	**106**	49 26N	11 5E
Nuri	**82**	28 2N	109 22W
Nürnberg	**106**	49 26N	11 5E
Nusa Barung	**127**	8 22S	113 20E
Nusa Kambangan	**127**	7 47S	109 0E
Nusa Tenggara □	**126**	7 30S	117 0E
Nusa Tenggara Barat	**126**	8 50S	117 30E
Nusa Tenggara Timur	**127**	9 30S	122 0E
Nushki	**124**	29 35N	65 65E
Nut L.	**56**	52 22N	103 42W
Nutak	**36**	57 28N	61 52W
Nuvuk Is.	**36**	62 24N	78 3W
Nuwakot	**125**	28 10N	83 55E
Nuweveldberge	**117**	32 10S	21 45E
Nuyts Arch.	**134**	32 12S	133 20E
Nuyts, Pt.	**134**	35 4S	116 38E
Nyaake (Webo)	**114**	4 52N	7 37W
Nyabing	**134**	33 30S	118 7E
Nyack	**71**	41 5N	73 57W
Nyagyn	**120**	62 8N	63 36E
Nyah West	**136**	35 11S	143 21E
Nyahanga	**116**	2 20S	33 37E
Nyahururu	**116**	0 2N	36 27E
Nyâlâ	**115**	12 2N	24 58E
Nyarling, R.	**54**	60 41N	113 23W
Nyasa, L. = Malawi, L.	**117**	12 0S	34 30E
Nybro	**111**	56 44N	15 55E
Nyda	**120**	66 40N	73 10E
Nyenchen Tanglha Shan	**129**	30 30N	95 0E
Nyeri	**116**	0 23S	36 56E
Nyíregyháza	**107**	48 0N	21 47E
Nykarleby (Uusikaarlepyy)	**110**	63 32N	22 31E
Nykøbing	**111**	54 56N	11 52E
Nylstroom	**117**	24 42S	28 22E
Nynäshamn	**111**	58 54N	17 57E
Nyngan	**136**	31 30S	147 8E
Nyons	**103**	44 22N	5 10E
Nysa	**107**	50 40N	17 22E
Nysa, R.	**106**	52 4N	14 46E
Nyssa	**78**	43 56N	117 2W
Nyurba	**121**	63 17N	118 20E
Nzega	**116**	4 10S	33 12E

O

O-Shima	**132**	34 44N	139 24E
Oacoma	**74**	43 50N	99 26W
Oahe	**74**	44 33N	100 29W
Oahe Dam	**74**	44 28N	100 25W
Oahe Res	**74**	45 30N	100 15W
Oahu I.	**67**	21 30N	158 0W
Oak Bay, B.C., Can.	**63**	48 26N	123 18W
Oak Bay, N.B., Can.	**39**	45 14N	67 12W

* *Renamed Mwenezi*

Oak Bluff	**58**	49 46N	97 19W
Oak Creek, U.S.A.	**77**	42 52N	87 55W
Oak Creek, Colo., U.S.A.	**78**	40 15N	106 59W
Oak Harb.	**80**	48 20N	122 38W
Oak Hill, Can.	**39**	45 20N	67 20W
Oak Hill, U.S.A.	**72**	38 0N	81 7W
Oak I.	**52**	46 57N	90 51W
Oak Lake	**57**	49 46N	100 38W
Oak Lawn	**77**	41 43N	87 44W
Oak Park	**72**	41 55N	87 45W
Oak Point	**57**	50 30N	98 1W
Oak Ridge	**73**	36 1N	84 5W
Oak Ridges	**50**	43 57N	79 28W
Oak River	**57**	50 8N	100 26W
Oak View	**81**	34 24N	119 18W
Oakbank	**58**	49 57N	96 51W
Oakdale, Calif., U.S.A.	**80**	37 49N	120 56W
Oakdale, La., U.S.A.	**75**	30 50N	92 38W
Oakengates	**94**	52 42N	2 29W
Oakes	**74**	46 14N	98 4W
Oakesdale	**78**	47 11N	117 9W
Oakford	**76**	40 6N	89 58W
Oakham	**94**	52 40N	0 43W
Oakhurst	**80**	37 19N	119 40W
Oakland, Can.	**49**	43 2N	80 20W
Oakland, Calif., U.S.A.	**80**	37 50N	122 18W
Oakland, Ill., U.S.A.	**77**	39 39N	88 2W
Oakland City	**77**	38 20N	87 20W
Oakleigh	**136**	37 54S	145 6E
Oakley	**78**	42 14N	113 55W
Oakridge	**78**	43 47N	122 31W
Oaktown	**77**	38 52N	87 27W
Oakville, Can.	**50**	43 27N	79 41W
Oakville, U.S.A.	**80**	46 50N	123 14W
Oakville, R.	**49**	43 27N	79 41W
Oakwood, Ohio, U.S.A.	**77**	39 43N	84 11W
Oakwood, Ohio, U.S.A.	**77**	41 6N	84 23W
Oakwood, Tex., U.S.A.	**75**	31 35N	95 47W
Oamaru	**133**	45 5S	170 59E
Oasis, Calif., U.S.A.	**81**	33 28N	116 6W
Oasis, Nev., U.S.A.	**80**	37 29N	117 55W
Oates Coast	**91**	69 0S	160 0E
Oatman	**81**	35 1N	114 19W
Oaxaca	**83**	17 2N	96 40W
Oaxaca □	**83**	17 0N	97 0W
Ob, R.	**120**	62 40N	66 0E
Oba	**53**	49 4N	84 7W
Oba L.	**53**	48 40N	84 16W
Obakamiga L.	**53**	49 9N	85 9W
Obalski, L.	**40**	48 43N	77 58W
Obamsca, L.	**40**	50 24N	78 16W
Oban, N.Z.	**133**	46 55S	168 10E
Oban, U.K.	**96**	56 25N	5 30W
Obatanga Prov. Park	**53**	48 20N	85 10W
Obatogamau L.	**34**	49 34N	74 26W
Obbia	**115**	5 25N	48 30E
Obed	**60**	53 30N	117 10W
Obedjwan	**40**	48 40N	74 56W
Obeh	**124**	34 28N	63 10E
Obera	**89**	27 21S	55 2W
Oberhausen	**105**	51 28N	6 50E
Oberlin, Kans., U.S.A.	**74**	39 52N	100 31W
Oberlin, La., U.S.A.	**75**	30 42N	92 42W
Oberlin, Ohio, U.S.A.	**70**	41 15N	82 10W
Obernai	**101**	48 28N	7 30E
Oberon	**136**	33 45S	149 52E
Obi, Kepulauan	**127**	1 30S	127 30E
Óbidos	**87**	1 50S	55 30W
Obihiro	**132**	42 25N	143 12E
Objat	**102**	45 16N	1 24E
Oblong	**77**	39 0N	87 55W
Obluchye	**121**	49 10N	130 50E
Obo	**116**	5 20N	26 32E
Obonga L.	**52**	49 57N	89 22W
Oboyan	**120**	51 20N	36 28E
Obozerskaya	**120**	63 20N	40 15E
Observatory Inlet	**54**	55 25N	129 45W
Obshchi Syrt	**93**	52 0N	53 0E
Obskaya Guba	**120**	70 0N	73 0E
Ocala	**73**	29 11N	82 5W
Ocampo	**82**	28 9N	108 8W
Ocaña	**104**	39 55N	3 30W
Ocanomowoc	**74**	43 7N	88 30W
Ocate	**75**	36 12N	104 59W
Occidental, Cordillera	**86**	5 0N	76 0W
Ocean City, N.J., U.S.A.	**72**	39 18N	74 34W
Ocean City, Wash., U.S.A.	**80**	47 4N	124 10W
Ocean Falls	**62**	52 18N	127 48W
*Ocean I.	**14**	0 45S	169 50E
Ocean Park, Can.	**66**	49 2N	122 52W
Ocean Park, U.S.A.	**80**	46 30N	124 2W
Oceanlake	**78**	45 0N	124 0W
Oceano	**81**	35 6N	120 37W
Oceanport	**71**	40 20N	74 3W
Oceanside	**81**	33 13N	117 26W
Ochil Hills	**96**	56 14N	3 40W
Ochre River	**57**	51 4N	99 47W
Ocilla	**73**	31 35N	83 12W
Ocmulgee, R.	**73**	32 0N	83 19W
Oconee, R.	**73**	32 30N	82 55W
Oconomowoc	**77**	43 6N	88 30W
Oconto	**72**	44 52N	87 53W
Oconto Falls	**72**	44 52N	88 10W
Ocós	**84**	14 31N	92 11W
Ocosingo	**83**	18 4N	92 15W
Ocotal	**84**	13 41N	86 41W

* *Renamed Banaba*

Ocotlán	**82**	20 21N	102 42W
Octave	**79**	34 10N	112 43W
Octeville	**100**	49 38N	1 40W
Octyabrskoy Revolyutsii, Os.	**121**	79 30N	97 0E
Ocumare del Tuy	**86**	10 7N	66 46W
Ocussi	**127**	9 20S	124 30E
Odanah	**52**	46 38N	90 41W
Ódáoahraun	**110**	65 5N	17 0W
Odawara	**132**	35 20N	139 6E
Odda	**111**	60 3N	6 35E
Odei, R.	**55**	56 6N	96 54W
Odell	**77**	41 0N	88 31W
Ödemiş	**122**	38 15N	28 0E
Odense	**111**	55 22N	10 23E
Oder, R.	**106**	53 0N	14 12E
Odessa, Ont., Can.	**47**	44 17N	76 43W
Odessa, Sask., Can.	**56**	50 17N	103 47W
Odessa, U.S.A.	**76**	39 0N	93 57W
Odessa, Tex., U.S.A.	**75**	31 51N	102 23W
Odessa, Wash., U.S.A.	**78**	47 25N	118 35W
O'Donnell	**75**	33 0N	101 48W
Odorheiul Secuiesc	**107**	46 21N	25 21E
Odra, R.	**106**	52 40N	14 28E
Odžak	**109**	45 3N	18 18E
Odzi	**117**	19 0S	32 20E
Oeiras	**87**	7 0S	42 8W
Oelrichs	**74**	43 11N	103 14W
O'Fallon	**76**	38 50N	90 43W
Ofanto, R.	**108**	41 8N	15 50E
Offaly □	**97**	53 15N	7 30W
Offenbach	**106**	50 6N	8 46E
Offranville	**100**	49 52N	1 0E
Ofotfjorden	**110**	68 27N	16 40E
Ogahalla	**53**	50 6N	85 51W
Ōgaki	**132**	35 21N	136 37E
Ogallala	**74**	41 12N	101 40W
Ogascanane, L.	**40**	47 5N	78 25W
Ogbomosho	**114**	8 1N	3 29E
Ogden, Can.	**59**	51 0N	114 0W
Ogden, Iowa, U.S.A.	**76**	42 3N	94 0W
Ogden, Utah, U.S.A.	**78**	41 13N	112 1W
Ogdensburg	**71**	44 40N	75 27W
Ogeechee, R.	**73**	32 30N	81 32W
Ogema	**56**	49 35N	104 55W
Ogilby	**81**	32 49N	114 50W
Ogilvie Mts.	**64**	65 0N	140 0W
Oglesby	**76**	41 21N	89 3W
Oglio, R.	**108**	45 15N	10 15E
Ogmore Vale	**95**	51 35N	3 32W
Ognon, R.	**101**	47 16N	5 28E
Ogoki	**53**	51 38N	85 58W
Ogoki L.	**53**	50 50N	87 10W
Ogoki, R.	**53**	51 38N	85 57W
Ogoki Res.	**52**	50 45N	88 15W
Ogooué, R.	**116**	1 0S	10 0E
Ogowe, R. = Ogooué, R.	**116**	1 0S	10 0E
Ohai	**133**	44 55S	168 0E
Ohakune	**133**	39 24S	175 24E
Ohau, L.	**133**	44 15S	169 53E
Oheida	**76**	41 4N	90 13W
Ohey	**105**	50 26N	5 8E
O'Higgins □	**88**	34 15S	71 1W
Ohio □	**72**	40 20N	83 0W
Ohio City	**77**	40 46N	84 37W
Ohio, R.	**72**	38 0N	86 0W
Ohre, R.	**106**	50 10N	12 30E
Ohridsko, Jezero	**109**	41 8N	20 52E
Ohsweken	**49**	43 4N	80 7W
Oil City	**70**	41 26N	79 40W
Oil Springs	**46**	42 47N	82 7W
Oildale	**81**	35 25N	119 1W
Oise □	**101**	49 28N	2 30E
Oise, R.	**101**	49 53N	3 50E
Oisterwijk	**105**	51 35N	5 12E
Oita	**132**	33 14N	131 36E
Oita-ken □	**132**	33 15N	131 30E
Oiticica	**87**	5 3S	41 5W
Ojai	**81**	34 28N	119 16W
Ojinaga	**82**	29 34N	104 25W
Ojocaliente	**82**	30 25N	106 30W
Ojos del Salado	**88**	27 0S	68 40W
Oka	**44**	45 28N	74 5W
Oka, R.	**120**	56 20N	43 59E
Oka-sur-le-Lac	**44**	45 28N	74 6W
Okahandja	**117**	22 0S	16 59E
Okak	**36**	57 33N	61 58W
Okak Is.	**36**	57 30N	61 30W
Okanagan L.	**63**	50 0N	119 30W
Okanagan Mission	**63**	49 45N	119 30W
Okanagan Mountain Prov. Park	**63**	49 45N	119 30W
Okanogan	**63**	48 22N	119 35W
Okanogan, R.	**78**	48 40N	119 24W
Okarito	**133**	43 15S	170 9E
Okaukuejo	**117**	19 10S	16 0E
Okavango, R. = Cubango, R.	**117**	16 15S	18 0E
Okavango Swamp	**117**	19 30S	23 0E
Okawville	**76**	38 26N	89 33W
Okaya	**132**	36 0N	138 10E
Okayama	**132**	34 40N	133 54E
Okayama-ken □	**132**	35 0N	133 50E
Okazaki	**132**	34 57N	137 10E
Okeechobee	**73**	27 16N	80 46W
Okeechobee L.	**73**	27 0N	80 50W
Okefenokee Swamp	**73**	30 50N	82 15W
Okehampton	**95**	50 44N	4 1W

Okha Otago □

Okha 121 53 40N 143 0 E
Okhotsk 121 59 20N 143 10 E
Okhotsk, Sea of 121 55 0N 145 0 E
Okhotskiy Perevoz 121 61 52N 135 35 E
Okhotsko Kolymskoy 121 63 0N 157 0 E
Oki no Erabu 131 27 15N 128 45 E
Oki-Shotō 132 36 15N 133 15 E
Okiep 117 29 39 S 17 53 E
Okinawa 131 26 40N 128 0 E
Okinawa-guntō 131 26 0N 127 30 E
Oklahoma □ 75 35 20N 97 30W
Oklahoma City 75 35 25N 97 30W
Okmulgee 75 35 38N 96 0W
Okolona, U.S.A. 75 34 0N 88 45W
Okolona, U.S.A. 77 38 8N 85 41W
Okondja 116 0 35 S 13 45 E
Oku 131 26 35N 127 50 E
Okuru 133 43 55 S 168 55 E
Okushiri-Tō 132 42 15N 139 30 E
Ola 75 35 2N 93 10W
Ólafsfjörður 110 66 4N 18 39W
Ólafsvík 110 64 53N 23 43W
Olancha 81 36 15N 118 1W
Olancha Pk. 81 36 15N 118 7W
Olanchito 85 15 30N 86 30W
Öland 111 56 45N 16 50 E
Olargues 102 43 34N 2 53 E
Olascoaga 88 35 15 S 60 39W
Olathe 74 38 50N 94 50W
Olavarría 88 36 55 S 60 20W
Ólbia 108 40 55N 9 30 E
Old Bahama Chan. 84 22 10N 77 30W
Old Baldy Pk = San Antonio, Mt. 81 34 17N 117 38W
Old Castile = Castilla la Vieja 104 41 55N 4 0W
Old Castle 97 53 46N 7 10W
Old Chelsea 48 45 30N 75 49W
Old Crow 64 67 30N 140 5 E
Old Dale 81 34 8N 115 47W
Old Factory 34 52 36N 78 43W
Old Forge, N.Y., U.S.A. 71 43 43N 74 58W
Old Forge, Pa., U.S.A. 71 41 20N 75 46W
Old Fort, R. 55 58 36N 110 24W
Old Harbor 67 57 12N 153 22W
Old Perlican 37 48 5N 53 1W
Old Speckle, Mt. 71 44 35N 70 57W
Old Town 35 45 0N 68 50W
Old Wives L. 56 50 5N 106 0W
Oldcastle 97 53 46N 7 10W
Oldenburg 105 53 10N 8 10 E
Oldham 94 53 33N 2 8W
Oldman, R. 61 49 57N 111 42W
Olds 61 51 50N 114 10W
Olean 70 42 8N 78 25W
O'Leary 39 46 42N 64 13W
Olekma, R. 121 58 0N 121 30 E
Olekminsk 121 60 40N 120 30 E
Olema 80 38 3N 122 47W
Olenek 121 68 20N 112 30 E
Olenek, R. 121 71 0N 123 50 E
Oléron, I. d' 102 45 55N 1 15W
Oleśnica 107 51 13N 17 22 E
Olga 121 43 50N 135 0 E
Olga, L. 40 49 47N 77 15W
Olga, Mt. 134 25 20 S 130 40 E
Olgastretet 17 78 35N 25 0 E
Olifants, R. 117 24 5 S 31 20 E
Ólimbos, Óros 109 40 6N 22 23 E
Olímpia 89 20 44 S 48 54W
Olimpo□ 88 20 30 S 58 45W
Olin 76 42 0N 91 9W
Oliva 88 32 0 S 63 38W
Olive Hill 77 38 18N 83 13W
Olivehurst 80 39 6N 121 34W
Oliveira 87 20 50 S 44 50W
Olivenza 104 38 41N 7 9W
Oliver 63 49 13N 119 30W
Oliver L. 55 56 56N 103 22W
Ollagüe 88 21 15 S 68 10W
Olmos, L. 88 33 25 S 63 19W
Olney, Ill., U.S.A. 77 38 40N 88 0W
Olney, Tex., U.S.A. 75 33 25N 98 45W
Olomane, R. 36 50 14N 60 37W
Olomouc 106 49 38N 17 12 E
Olongapo 127 14 50N 120 18 E
Oloron-Ste.-Marie 102 43 11N 0 38W
Olovyannaya 121 50 50N 115 10 E
Olsztyn 107 53 48N 20 29 E
Olt, R. 107 43 50N 24 40 E
Olteniţa 107 44 7N 26 42 E
Olton 75 34 16N 102 7W
Oltu 122 40 35N 41 50 E
Olympia, Greece 109 37 39N 21 39 E
Olympia, U.S.A. 80 47 0N 122 58W
Olympic Mts. 80 47 50N 123 45W
Olympic Nat. Park 80 47 48N 123 30W
Olympus, Mt. 80 47 52N 123 40W
Olympus, Mt. = Olimbos, Oros 109 40 6N 22 23 E
Olyphant 71 41 27N 75 36W
Omachi 132 36 30N 137 50 E
Omagh 97 54 36N 7 20W
Omagh □ 97 54 35N 7 15W
Omaha 74 41 15N 96 0W
Omak 63 48 24N 119 31W
Omak L. 63 48 16N 119 23W
Oman ■ 122 23 0N 58 0 E
Oman, G. of 123 24 30N 58 30 E
Omaruru 117 21 26 S 16 0 E
Omate 86 16 45 S 71 0W
Ombai, Selat 127 8 30 S 124 50 E
Omboué 116 1 35 S 9 15 E
Ombrone, R. 108 42 48N 11 15 E
Omdurmân 115 15 40N 32 28 E
Omemee 47 44 18N 78 33W
Ometepe, Isla de 84 11 32N 85 35W
Ometepec 83 16 39N 98 23W
Omineca, R. 54 56 3N 124 16W
Ōmiya 132 35 54N 139 38 E
Ommanney B. 65 73 0N 101 0W
Ommen 105 52 31N 6 26 E
Omsk 120 55 0N 73 38 E
Omsukchan 121 62 32N 155 48 E
Omu 130 43 48N 128 10 E
Omul, Vf. 107 45 27N 25 29 E
Omura 132 33 8N 130 0 E
Omuramba, R. 117 19 10 S 19 20 E
Ōmuta 132 33 0N 130 26 E
Onaga 74 39 32N 96 12W
Onakawana 53 50 36N 81 27W
Onalaska 74 43 53N 91 14W
Onaman L. 53 50 0N 87 26W
Onaman, R. 53 49 59N 88 0W
Onamia 74 46 4N 93 38W
Onancock 72 37 42N 75 49W
Onang 127 3 2 S 118 55 E
Onanole 57 50 37N 99 58W
Onaping 46 46 37N 81 25W
Onaping L. 53 47 3N 81 30W
Onaping, R. 46 46 37N 81 18W
Onarga 77 40 43N 88 1W
Onatchiway, L. 41 49 3N 71 5W
Onavas 82 28 28N 109 30W
Onawa 74 42 2N 96 2W
Onaway 46 45 21N 84 11W
Oncocua 117 16 30 S 13 40 E
Onda 104 39 55N 0 17W
Öndörhaan 129 47 19N 110 39 E
Ondorhaan 130 47 22N 110 31 E
Ondverdarnes 110 64 52N 24 0W
One Tree 136 34 13 S 144 42 E
Onega 120 64 0N 38 10 E
Onega, G. of = Onezhskaya G. 120 64 30N 37 0 E
Onega, L. = Onezhskoye Oz. 120 62 0N 35 30 E
Onehunga 133 36 55N 174 30 E
Oneida 71 43 5N 75 40W
Oneida L. 71 43 12N 76 0W
O'Neill 74 42 30N 98 38W
Onekotan, Ostrov 121 49 59N 154 0 E
Oneonta, Ala., U.S.A. 73 33 58N 86 29W
Oneonta, N.Y., U.S.A. 71 42 26N 75 5W
Onezhskoye Ozero 120 62 0N 35 30 E
Ongarue 133 38 42 S 175 19 E
Ongiyn Gol 130 45 56N 103 0 E
Ongole 124 15 33N 80 2 E
Onida 74 44 42N 100 5W
Onilahy, R. 117 23 30 S 44 0 E
Onion Lake 56 53 43N 110 0W
Onitsha 114 6 6N 6 42 E
Onoda 132 33 59N 131 11 E
Onondaga 49 43 7N 80 7W
Onoway 60 53 42N 114 12W
Onslow 134 21 40 S 115 0 E
Onslow B. 73 34 30N 77 0W
Onstwedde 105 52 2N 7 4 E
Ontake-San 132 35 53N 137 29 E
Ontario, Calif., U.S.A. 81 34 2N 117 40W
Ontario, Oreg., U.S.A. 78 44 1N 117 1W
Ontario □ 34 52 0N 88 10W
Ontario, L. 48 43 40N 78 0W
Ontonagon 52 46 52N 89 19W
Onyx 81 35 41N 118 14W
Oodnadatta 134 27 33 S 135 30 E
Ooglaamie 17 72 1N 157 0W
Ookala 67 20 1N 155 17W
Ooldea 134 30 27 S 131 50 E
Oona River 62 53 57N 130 16W
Oostende 105 51 15N 2 50 E
Oosterhout 105 51 39N 4 52 E
Oosterschelde 105 51 33N 4 0 E
Ootacamund 124 11 30N 76 44 E
Ootmarsum 105 52 24N 6 54 E
Ootsa L. 62 53 50N 126 20W
Ootsa Lake 62 53 50N 126 5W
Opala, U.S.S.R. 121 52 15N 156 15 E
Opala, Zaïre 116 1 11 S 24 45 E
Opanake 124 6 35N 80 40 E
Opasatica, L. 40 48 5N 79 18W
Opasatika 53 49 30N 82 50W
Opasatika L. 53 49 4N 83 6W
Opasatika, R. 53 50 25N 82 25W
Opasquia 55 53 16N 93 34W
Opataca, L. 40 50 22N 74 55W
Opava 107 49 57N 17 58 E
Opawica, L. 40 49 35N 75 55W
Opelousas 75 30 35N 92 0W
Opémisca L. 36 50 0N 75 0W
Opémisca, L. 40 49 56N 74 52W
Opeongo L. 47 45 42N 78 23W
Opheim 56 48 52N 106 30W
Ophir 67 63 10N 156 40W
Ophthalmia Ra. 134 23 15 S 119 30 E
Opinaca L. 36 52 39N 76 20W
Opinaca, R. 36 52 15N 78 2W
Opiscoteo, L. 36 53 10N 68 10W
Opiskotish, L. 36 53 10N 67 50W
Opladen 105 51 4N 7 2 E
Opocopa, L. 38 52 38N 66 35W
Opole 107 50 42N 17 58 E
Oporto = Porto 104 41 8N 8 40W
Opotiki 133 38 1 S 177 19 E
Opp 73 31 19N 86 13W
Oppland fylke □ 111 61 15N 9 30 E
Opua 133 35 19 S 174 9 E
Opunake 133 39 26 S 173 52 E
Oquawka 76 40 56N 90 57W
Oracle 79 32 45N 110 46W
Oradea 107 47 2N 21 58 E
Öræfajökull 110 64 2N 16 39W
Orai 124 25 58N 79 30 E
Oraison 103 43 55N 5 55 E
Oran, Alg. 114 35 37N 0 39W
Oran, Argent. 88 23 10 S 64 20W
Orange, Austral. 136 33 15 S 149 7 E
Orange, France 103 44 8N 4 47 E
Orange, Calif., U.S.A. 81 33 47N 117 51W
Orange, Mass., U.S.A. 71 42 35N 72 15W
Orange, Tex., U.S.A. 75 30 10N 93 50W
Orange, Va., U.S.A. 72 38 17N 78 5W
Orange, C. 87 4 20N 51 30W
Orange Cove 80 36 38N 119 19W
Orange Free State □ 117 28 30 S 27 0 E
Orange Grove 75 27 57N 97 57W
Orange, R. = Oranje, R. 117 28 30 S 18 0 E
Orange Walk 83 18 6N 88 33W
Orangeburg 73 33 35N 80 53W
Orangeville, Can. 49 43 55N 80 5W
Orangeville, U.S.A. 76 42 28N 89 39W
Oranienburg 106 52 45N 13 15 E
Oranje, R. 117 28 30 S 18 0 E
Oranje Vrystaat □ 117 28 30 S 27 0 E
Oranjemund (Orange Mouth) 117 28 32 S 16 29 E
Orapa 117 21 13 S 25 25 E
Oras 127 12 9N 125 22 E
Orb, R. 102 43 17N 3 17 E
Orbec 100 49 1N 0 23 E
Orbetello 108 42 26N 11 11 E
Orbost 136 37 40 S 148 29 E
Orcas 63 48 36N 122 57W
Orchies 101 50 28N 3 14 E
Orchila, Isla 85 11 48N 66 10W
Orchy, Bridge of 96 56 30N 4 46W
Orchy, Glen 96 56 27N 4 52W
Orcutt 81 34 52N 120 27W
Ord, Mt. 134 17 20 S 125 34 E
Ord, R. 134 15 33 S 128 35 E
Orderville 79 37 18N 112 43W
Ordos 130 39 25N 108 45 E
Ordu 122 40 55N 37 53 E
Ordway 74 38 15N 103 42W
Ordzhonikidze 120 43 0N 44 35 E
Örebro 111 59 20N 15 18 E
Örebro län □ 111 59 27N 15 0 E
Oregon, U.S.A. 77 41 38N 83 25W
Oregon, Ill., U.S.A. 76 42 1N 89 20W
Oregon, Wis., U.S.A. 76 42 56N 89 23W
Oregon □ 78 44 0N 120 0W
Oregon City 80 45 21N 122 35W
Orel 120 52 57N 36 3 E
Orem 78 40 27N 111 45W
Orenburg 120 51 45N 55 6 E
Orense 104 42 19N 7 55W
Orepuki 133 46 19 S 167 46 E
Orford Ness 95 52 6N 1 31 E
Orgon 103 43 47N 5 3 E
Orhon Gol 129 49 30N 106 0 E
Orient 76 41 12N 94 25W
Orient Bay 34 49 20N 88 10W
Oriente 88 38 44 S 60 37W
Origny-Ste.-Benoîte 101 49 50N 3 30 E
Orihuela 104 38 7N 0 55W
Orillia 46 44 40N 79 24W
Orinoco, Delta del 85 8 30N 61 0W
Orinoco, R. 86 5 45N 67 40W
Orion, Can. 55 49 28N 110 49W
Orion, U.S.A. 76 41 21N 90 23W
Orissa □ 125 21 0N 85 0 E
Oristano 108 39 54N 8 35 E
Oristano, Golfo di 108 39 50N 8 22 E
Orizaba 83 18 50N 97 10W
Orkanger 110 63 18N 9 52 E
Orkla, R. 110 63 18N 9 51 E
Orkney □ 96 59 0N 3 0W
Orkney Is. 96 59 0N 3 0W
Orland, U.S.A. 77 41 47N 85 12W
Orland, Calif., U.S.A. 80 39 46N 122 12W
Orlando 73 28 30N 81 25W
Orléanais 101 48 0N 2 0 E
Orléans 101 47 54N 1 52 E
Orleans 71 44 49N 72 10W
Orléans, Î. d' 42 46 54N 70 58W
Ormara 124 25 16N 64 33 E
Ormiston 56 49 44N 105 24W
Ormoc 127 11 0N 124 37 E
Ormond, N.Z. 133 38 33 S 177 56 E
Ormond, U.S.A. 73 29 13N 81 5W
Ormstown 43 45 8N 74 0W
Ornans 101 47 7N 6 10 E
Orne □ 100 48 40N 0 0 E
Örnsköldsvik 110 63 17N 18 40 E
Oro Grande 81 34 36N 117 20W
Oro, R. 82 26 8N 105 58W
Orocué 86 4 48N 71 20W
Orogrande 79 32 20N 106 4W
Oromocto 39 45 54N 66 29W
Oromocto, L. 39 45 36N 67 0W
Oron, R. 121 69 21N 95 43 E
Orono 47 43 59N 78 37W
Oroquieta 127 8 32N 123 44 E
Orós 87 6 15 S 38 55W
Orosei 108 40 20N 9 40 E
Orotukan 121 62 16N 151 42 E
Oroville, Calif., U.S.A. 80 39 31N 121 30W
Oroville, Wash., U.S.A. 63 48 58N 119 30W
Oroville, Res. 80 39 33N 121 29W
Orr 52 48 3N 92 48W
Orrick 76 39 13N 94 7W
Orrville 70 40 50N 81 46W
Orsainville 42 46 51N 71 14W
Orsha 120 54 30N 30 25 E
Orsk 120 51 12N 58 34 E
Orşova 107 44 41N 22 25 E
Ortegal, C. 104 43 43N 7 52W
Orthez 102 43 29N 0 48W
Ortigueira 104 43 40N 7 50W
Orting 80 47 6N 122 12W
Ortles, mt. 108 46 31N 10 33 E
Ortón, R. 86 10 50 S 67 0W
Ortona 108 42 21N 14 24 E
Oruro 86 18 0 S 67 19W
Orvault 100 47 17N 1 38W
Orvieto 108 42 43N 12 8 E
Orwell 70 41 32N 80 52W
Orwell, R. 95 52 2N 1 12 E
Oryakhovo 109 43 40N 23 57 E
Osa, Pen. de 84 8 0N 84 0W
Osage, Iowa, U.S.A. 74 43 15N 92 50W
Osage, Wyo., U.S.A. 74 43 59N 104 25W
Osage City 74 38 43N 95 51W
Osage, R. 76 38 15N 92 30W
Ōsaka 132 34 30N 135 30 E
Osaka-fu □ 132 34 40N 135 30 E
Osawatomie 74 38 30N 94 55W
Osawin, R. 53 49 45N 85 19W
Osborne 74 39 30N 98 45W
Osborne Corners 49 43 13N 80 16W
Osceola, Ark., U.S.A. 75 35 40N 90 0W
Osceola, Iowa, U.S.A. 76 41 0N 93 20W
Osceola, Mo., U.S.A. 76 38 3N 93 42W
Oscoda-Au-Sable 46 44 26N 83 20W
Osgood 77 39 8N 85 18W
Osgoode 47 45 8N 75 36W
Osh 120 40 37N 72 49 E
Oshawa 51 43 50N 78 50W
Oshawa Cr. 51 43 52N 78 50W
Oshikango 117 17 9 S 16 10 E
Oshkosh, Nebr., U.S.A. 72 41 27N 102 20W
Oshkosh, Wis., U.S.A. 72 44 3N 88 35W
Oshogbo 114 7 48N 4 37 E
Oshwe 116 3 25 S 19 28 E
Osijek 109 45 34N 18 41 E
Oskaloosa 76 41 18N 92 40W
Oskarshamn 111 57 15N 16 27 E
Oskélanéo 40 48 5N 75 15W
Osler 56 52 22N 106 33W
Oslo 111 59 55N 10 45 E
Oslob 127 9 31N 123 26 E
Oslofjorden 111 59 20N 10 35 E
Osmanabad 124 18 5N 76 10 E
Osmaniye 122 37 5N 36 10 E
Osnabrück 105 52 16N 8 2 E
Osnaburgh L. 52 51 12N 90 9W
Osorio 89 29 53 S 50 17W
Osorno 90 40 25 S 73 0W
Osorno, Vol. 90 41 0N 72 30W
Osoyoos 63 49 0N 119 30W
Osoyoos L. 63 49 0N 119 27W
Ospika, R. 54 56 20N 124 0W
Osprey Reef 135 13 52 S 146 36 E
Ospringe 49 43 42N 80 7W
Oss 105 51 46N 5 32 E
Ossa, Mt. 135 41 52 S 146 3 E
Ossa, Oros 109 39 47N 22 42 E
Ossabaw I. 73 31 45N 81 8W
Ossineke 46 44 55N 83 26W
Ossining 71 41 9N 73 50W
Ossipee 71 43 41N 71 9W
Ossokmanuan L. 36 53 25N 65 0W
Ossora 121 59 20N 163 13 E
Ostaboningue, L. 40 47 9N 78 53W
Ostend = Oostende 105 51 15N 2 50 E
Österdalälven 111 61 30N 13 45 E
Östergötlands Län □ 111 58 35N 15 45 E
Östersund 110 63 10N 14 38 E
Østfold fylke □ 111 59 25N 11 25 E
Ostfriesische Inseln 106 53 45N 7 15 E
Ostfriesland 105 53 18N 7 30 E
Ostia 108 41 40N 12 20 E
Ostrava 107 49 51N 18 18 E
Ostróda 107 53 42N 19 58 E
Ostrołeka 107 53 4N 21 38 E
Ostrów Mazowiecka 107 52 50N 21 51 E
Ostrów Wielkopolski 107 51 36N 17 44 E
Ostrowiec-Swietokrzyski 107 50 55N 21 22 E
O'Sullivan L. 53 50 25N 87 2W
Osumi-Kaikyō 132 30 55N 131 0 E
Osumi-Shotō 132 30 30N 130 45 E
Osuna 104 37 14N 5 8W
Oswego 71 43 29N 76 30W
Oswestry 94 52 52N 3 3W
Otago □ 133 45 20 S 169 20 E

Otago Harb Panhandle

Otago Harb.	**133**	45 47 S	170 42 E
Otake	**132**	34 12 N	132 13 E
Otaki	**133**	40 45 S	175 10 E
Otaru	**132**	43 10 N	141 0 E
Otaru-Wan	**132**	43 25 N	141 1 E
Otavalo	**86**	0 20 N	78 20 W
Otavi	**117**	19 40 S	17 24 E
Otelnuk L.	**36**	56 9 N	68 12 W
Othello	**78**	46 53 N	119 8 W
Otira Gorge	**133**	42 53 S	171 33 E
Otis	**74**	40 12 N	102 58 W
Otish, Mts.	**36**	52 22 N	70 30 W
Otjiwarongo	**117**	20 30 S	16 33 E
Otorohanga	**133**	38 12 S	175 14 E
Otoskwin, R.	**34**	52 13 N	88 6 W
Otosquen	**57**	53 17 N	102 1 W
Otranto	**109**	40 9 N	18 28 E
Otranto, C.d'	**109**	40 7 N	18 30 E
Otranto, Str. of	**109**	40 15 N	18 40 E
Otsego	**77**	42 27 N	85 42 W
Ottawa, Can.	**48**	45 27 N	75 42 W
Ottawa, Ill., U.S.A.	**77**	41 20 N	88 55 W
Ottawa, Kans., U.S.A.	**74**	38 40 N	95 10 W
Ottawa, Ohio, U.S.A.	**77**	41 1 N	84 3 W
Ottawa □	**48**	45 23 N	75 40 W
Ottawa International Airport	**48**	45 19 N	75 40 W
Ottawa Is.	**23**	59 35 N	80 16 W
Ottawa, R.	**44**	45 20 N	73 55 W
Otter L.	**55**	55 35 N	104 39 W
Otter Lake	**46**	43 13 N	83 28 W
Otter Rapids, Ont., Can.	**53**	50 11 N	81 39 W
Otter Rapids, Sask., Can.	**55**	55 38 N	104 44 W
Otterbein	**77**	40 29 N	87 6 W
Otterburn Park	**45**	45 32 N	73 13 W
Otterville, Can.	**46**	42 55 N	80 36 W
Otterville, U.S.A.	**76**	38 42 N	93 0 W
Ottoville	**77**	40 57 N	84 22 W
Ottumwa	**76**	41 0 N	92 25 W
Otway, Bahia	**90**	53 30 S	74 0 W
Otway, C.	**136**	38 52 S	143 30 E
Otwock	**107**	52 5 N	21 20 E
Ötztaler Alpen	**106**	46 58 N	11 0 E
Ou, R.	**128**	20 4 N	102 13 E
Ou-Sammyaku	**132**	39 20 N	140 35 E
Ouachita Mts.	**75**	34 50 N	94 30 W
Ouachita, R.	**75**	33 0 N	92 15 W
Ouadda	**116**	8 15 N	22 20 E
Ouagadougou	**114**	12 25 N	1 30 W
Ouanda Djallé	**116**	8 55 N	22 53 E
Ouango	**116**	4 19 N	22 30 E
Ouareau, L., Rés.	**41**	46 17 N	74 9 W
Ouargla	**114**	31 59 N	5 25 E
Ouasiemsca, R.	**41**	49 0 N	72 30 W
Oubangi, R.	**116**	1 0 N	17 50 E
Ouche, R.	**101**	47 11 N	5 10 E
Oude Rijn, R.	**105**	52 12 N	4 24 E
Oudenaarde	**105**	50 50 N	3 37 E
Oudenbosch	**105**	51 35 N	4 32 E
Oudon	**100**	47 22 N	1 19 W
Oudon, R.	**100**	47 47 N	1 2 W
Oudtshoorn	**117**	33 35 S	22 14 E
Ouessant, Île d'	**100**	48 28 N	5 6 W
Ouesso	**116**	1 37 N	16 5 E
Ouest, Pte.	**38**	49 52 N	64 40 W
Ougrée	**105**	50 36 N	5 32 E
Ouimet	**34**	48 43 N	88 35 W
Ouistreham	**100**	49 17 N	0 18 W
Oulu	**110**	65 1 N	25 29 E
Oulu □	**110**	65 10 N	27 20 E
Oulujärvi	**110**	64 25 N	27 0 E
Oulujoki	**110**	64 45 N	26 30 E
Ouray	**79**	38 3 N	107 48 W
Ouricuri	**87**	7 53 S	40 5 W
Ourinhos	**89**	23 0 S	49 54 W
Ouro Fino	**89**	22 16 S	46 25 W
Ouro Prêto	**89**	20 20 S	43 30 W
Ourthe, R.	**105**	50 29 N	5 35 E
Ouse, Great, R.	**94**	52 12 N	0 7 E
Ouse, Little, R.	**95**	52 25 N	0 20 E
Ouse, R., Sussex, U.K.	**95**	50 58 N	0 3 E
Ouse, R., Yorks., U.K.	**94**	54 3 N	0 7 E
Oust	**102**	42 52 N	1 13 E
Oust, R.	**100**	48 8 N	2 49 W
Oustic	**49**	43 42 N	80 15 W
Outaouais, R.	**48**	45 28 N	75 38 W
Outardes	**41**	50 20 N	69 10 W
Outardes, R.	**41**	49 24 N	69 30 W
Outer Hebrides, Is.	**96**	57 30 N	7 40 W
Outer I., Can.	**36**	51 10 N	58 35 W
Outer I., U.S.A.	**52**	47 5 N	90 30 W
Outjo	**117**	20 5 S	16 7 E
Outlook, Can.	**56**	51 30 N	107 0 W
Outlook, U.S.A.	**56**	48 53 N	104 46 W
Outreau	**101**	50 40 N	1 36 E
Outremount	**44**	45 31 N	73 37 W
Ouyen	**136**	35 1 S	142 22 E
Ouzouer-le-Marché	**100**	47 54 N	1 32 E
Ovalau, I.	**133**	17 40 S	178 48 E
Ovalle	**88**	30 33 S	71 18 W
Ovamboland = Owambo	**117**	17 20 S	16 30 E
Ovar	**104**	40 51 N	8 40 W
Ovejas	**86**	9 32 N	75 14 W
Ovens, R.	**136**	36 2 S	146 12 E
Overflakkee	**105**	51 44 N	4 10 E
Overflowing, R.	**57**	53 8 N	101 5 W
Overijssel □	**105**	52 25 N	6 35 E
Overland	**76**	38 41 N	90 23 W
Overland Park	**76**	38 58 N	94 40 W
Overton	**81**	36 32 N	114 31 W
Övertorneå	**110**	66 23 N	23 40 E
Ovid, Colo., U.S.A.	**74**	41 0 N	102 17 W
Ovid, Mich., U.S.A.	**46**	43 1 N	84 22 W
Oviedo	**104**	43 25 N	5 50 W
Ovruch	**120**	51 25 N	28 45 E
Owaka	**133**	46 27 S	169 40 E
Owambo	**117**	17 20 S	16 30 E
Owase	**132**	34 7 N	136 5 E
Owatonna	**74**	44 3 N	93 17 W
Owego	**71**	42 6 N	76 17 W
Owen Sound	**46**	44 35 N	80 55 W
Owendo	**116**	0 17 N	9 30 E
Owens L.	**81**	36 20 N	118 0 W
Owens, R.	**80**	36 32 N	117 59 W
Owensboro	**77**	37 40 N	87 5 W
Owensville, U.S.A.	**77**	38 16 N	87 41 W
Owensville, Mo., U.S.A.	**76**	38 20 N	91 30 W
Owenton	**77**	38 32 N	84 50 W
Owikeno L.	**62**	51 40 N	126 50 W
Owingsville	**77**	38 9 N	83 46 W
Owl, R.	**55**	57 51 N	92 44 W
Owosso	**77**	43 0 N	84 10 W
Owyhee	**78**	42 0 N	116 3 W
Owyhee, R.	**78**	43 10 N	117 37 W
Owyhee Res.	**78**	43 30 N	117 30 W
Ox Mts.	**97**	54 6 N	9 0 W
Oxbow	**57**	49 14 N	102 10 W
Oxelösund	**111**	58 43 N	17 15 E
Oxford, Can.	**39**	45 44 N	63 52 W
Oxford, N.Z.	**133**	43 18 S	172 11 E
Oxford, U.K.	**95**	51 45 N	1 15 W
Oxford, U.S.A.	**76**	41 43 N	91 47 W
Oxford, Mich., U.S.A.	**46**	42 49 N	83 16 W
Oxford, Mich., U.S.A.	**77**	42 49 N	83 16 W
Oxford, Miss., U.S.A.	**75**	34 22 N	89 30 W
Oxford, N.C., U.S.A.	**73**	36 19 N	78 36 W
Oxford, Ohio, U.S.A.	**77**	39 30 N	84 40 W
Oxford □	**95**	51 45 N	1 15 W
Oxford L.	**55**	54 51 N	95 37 W
Oxleys Pk.	**136**	31 51 S	150 22 E
Oxnard	**81**	34 10 N	119 14 W
Oya	**126**	2 55 N	111 55 E
Oyama	**63**	50 7 N	119 22 W
Oyem	**116**	1 42 N	11 43 E
Oyen	**61**	51 22 N	110 28 W
Oykell, R.	**96**	57 55 N	4 26 W
Oymyakon	**121**	63 25 N	143 10 E
Oyo	**114**	7 46 N	3 56 E
Oyonnax	**103**	46 16 N	5 40 E
Oyster B.	**71**	40 52 N	73 32 W
Oyster River	**62**	49 53 N	125 7 W
Ozaka	**132**	34 40 N	135 30 E
Ozamis (Mizamis)	**127**	8 15 N	123 50 E
Ozark, Ala., U.S.A.	**73**	31 29 N	85 39 W
Ozark, Ark., U.S.A.	**75**	35 30 N	93 50 W
Ozark, Mo., U.S.A.	**75**	37 0 N	93 15 W
Ozark Plateau	**75**	37 20 N	91 40 W
Ozarks, L. of	**76**	38 10 N	93 0 W
Ozette, L.	**80**	48 6 N	124 38 W
Ozona	**75**	30 43 N	101 11 W
Ozuluama	**83**	21 40 N	97 50 W

P

Pa-an	**125**	16 45 N	97 40 E
Pa Sak, R.	**128**	15 30 N	101 0 E
Paan (Batang)	**129**	30 0 N	99 3 E
Paarl	**117**	33 45 S	18 56 E
Paatsi, R.	**110**	68 55 N	29 0 E
Paauilo	**67**	20 3 N	155 22 W
Pab Hills	**124**	26 30 N	66 45 E
Pabna	**124**	24 1 N	89 18 E
Pabos Mills	**38**	48 19 N	64 42 W
Pacajá, R.	**87**	1 56 S	50 50 W
Pacasmayo	**86**	7 20 S	79 35 W
Pacaudière, La	**101**	46 11 N	3 52 E
Pacho	**86**	5 8 N	74 10 W
Pachpadra	**124**	25 58 N	72 10 E
Pachuca	**83**	20 10 N	98 40 W
Pachung	**131**	31 58 N	106 40 E
Pacific, Can.	**54**	54 48 N	128 28 W
Pacific, U.S.A.	**76**	38 29 N	90 45 W
Pacific Grove	**80**	36 38 N	121 58 W
Pacific Ocean	**14**	10 0 N	140 0 W
Pacific Rim Nat. Park	**62**	48 40 N	124 45 W
Pacifica	**80**	37 36 N	122 30 W
Packenham	**47**	45 22 N	76 25 W
Packwood	**80**	46 36 N	121 40 W
Pacofi	**54**	53 0 N	132 30 W
Pacquet	**37**	50 0 N	55 53 W
Pacy-sur-Eure	**100**	49 1 N	1 23 E
Padaido, Kepulauan	**127**	1 5 S	138 0 E
Padalarang	**127**	7 50 S	107 30 E
Padang	**126**	1 0 S	100 20 E
Padang, I.	**126**	1 0 S	100 10 E
Padangsidimpuan	**126**	1 30 N	99 15 E
Paddockwood	**56**	53 30 N	105 30 W
Paderborn	**106**	51 42 N	8 44 E
Padlei	**55**	62 10 N	97 5 W
Padloping Island	**65**	67 0 N	63 0 W
Pádova	**108**	45 24 N	11 52 E
Padre I.	**75**	27 0 N	97 20 W
Padstow	**95**	50 33 N	4 57 W
Padua = Pádova	**108**	45 24 N	11 52 E
Paducah, Ky., U.S.A.	**72**	37 0 N	88 40 W
Paducah, Tex., U.S.A.	**75**	34 3 N	100 16 W
Paeroa	**133**	37 23 S	175 41 E
Pag, I.	**108**	44 30 N	14 50 E
Pagadian	**127**	7 55 N	123 30 E
Pagai Selatan, I.	**126**	3 0 S	100 15 W
Pagai Utara, I.	**126**	2 35 S	100 0 E
Pagalu = Annobón	**112**	1 35 S	3 35 E
Pagaralam	**126**	4 0 S	103 17 E
Pagastikós Kólpos	**109**	39 15 N	23 12 E
Pagatan	**126**	3 33 S	115 59 E
Page	**74**	47 11 N	97 37 W
Pagny-sur-Moselle	**101**	48 59 N	6 2 E
Pago Pago	**133**	14 16 S	170 43 W
Pagosa Springs	**79**	37 16 N	107 4 W
Pagwa River	**53**	50 2 N	85 14 W
Pagwachuan, R.	**53**	50 12 N	84 43 W
Pahala	**67**	20 25 N	156 0 W
Pahang □	**128**	3 40 N	102 20 E
Pahang, R.	**128**	3 30 N	103 9 E
Pahiatua	**133**	40 27 S	175 50 E
Pahoa	**67**	19 30 N	154 57 W
Pahokee	**73**	26 50 N	80 30 W
Pahrump	**81**	36 15 N	116 0 W
Paia	**67**	20 54 N	156 22 W
Paicheng	**130**	45 50 N	122 53 E
Paicines	**80**	36 44 N	121 17 W
Paignton	**95**	50 26 N	3 33 W
Päijänne	**111**	61 30 N	25 30 E
Pailin	**128**	12 46 N	102 36 E
Pailolo Chan.	**67**	21 5 N	156 42 W
Paimbœuf	**100**	47 17 N	2 0 W
Paimpol	**100**	48 48 N	3 4 W
Paimpont, L.	**38**	50 28 N	61 34 W
Painan	**126**	1 15 S	100 40 E
Painesdale	**52**	47 2 N	88 41 W
Painesville	**70**	41 42 N	81 18 W
Paint I.	**55**	55 28 N	97 57 W
Paint Rock	**75**	31 30 N	99 56 W
Painted Desert	**79**	36 40 N	111 30 W
Paintsville	**72**	37 50 N	82 50 W
Paipa	**86**	5 47 N	73 7 W
Paisley, Can.	**46**	44 18 N	81 16 W
Paisley, U.K.	**96**	55 51 N	4 27 W
Paisley, U.S.A.	**78**	42 43 N	120 40 W
Paita	**86**	5 5 S	81 0 W
Paix, Îles de la	**44**	45 20 N	73 51 W
Paiyin	**130**	36 45 N	104 4 E
Paiyü Shan, mts.	**130**	37 20 N	107 30 E
Paiyunopo	**130**	41 46 N	109 58 E
Pajares	**104**	39 57 N	1 48 W
Pak Lay	**128**	18 15 N	101 27 E
Pakanbaru	**126**	0 30 N	101 15 E
Pakaraima, Sierra	**86**	6 0 N	60 0 W
Pakashkan L.	**52**	49 21 N	90 15 W
Pakenham	**71**	45 18 N	76 18 W
Pakhoi	**131**	21 30 N	109 10 E
Pakistan ■	**124**	30 0 N	70 0 E
Pakokku	**125**	21 30 N	95 0 E
Pakonghow	**131**	23 50 N	113 0 E
Pakowi L.	**61**	49 20 N	111 0 W
Pakse	**128**	15 5 N	105 52 E
Paktya □	**124**	33 0 N	69 15 E
Pakwash L.	**52**	50 45 N	93 30 W
Pala	**81**	33 22 N	117 5 W
Palacios	**75**	28 44 N	96 12 W
Palagruza	**108**	42 24 N	16 15 E
Palais, Le	**100**	47 20 N	3 10 W
Palam	**124**	19 0 N	77 0 E
Palamós	**104**	41 50 N	3 10 E
Palampur	**124**	32 10 N	76 30 E
Palana	**121**	59 10 N	160 10 E
Palanan	**127**	17 8 N	122 29 E
Palanpur	**124**	24 10 N	72 25 E
Palapye	**117**	22 30 S	27 7 E
Palatine	**77**	42 7 N	88 3 W
Palatka	**73**	29 40 N	81 40 W
*Palau Is.	**14**	7 30 N	134 30 E
Palauig	**127**	15 26 N	119 54 E
Palauk	**128**	13 10 N	98 40 E
Palavas	**102**	43 32 N	3 56 E
Palawan, I.	**126**	10 0 N	119 0 E
Palayancottai	**124**	8 45 N	77 45 E
Palchewoflock	**136**	35 20 S	142 15 E
Paleleh	**127**	1 10 N	121 50 E
Palembang	**126**	3 0 S	104 50 E
Palencia	**104**	42 1 N	4 34 W
Palermo, Can.	**49**	43 26 N	79 47 W
Palermo, Colomb.	**86**	2 54 N	75 26 W
Palermo, Italy	**108**	38 8 N	13 20 E
Palermo, U.S.A.	**78**	39 30 N	121 37 W
Palestine, Asia	**115**	32 0 N	35 0 E
Palestine, U.S.A.	**75**	31 42 N	95 35 W
Paletwa	**125**	21 30 N	92 50 E
Palghat	**124**	10 46 N	76 42 E
Palgrave	**49**	43 57 N	79 50 W
Pali	**124**	25 50 N	73 20 E
Palinyuch'i (Tapanshang)	**130**	43 40 N	118 20 E
Palisade	**74**	40 35 N	101 10 W
Palitana	**124**	21 32 N	71 49 E
Palizada	**83**	18 18 N	92 8 W
Palk Bay	**124**	9 30 N	79 30 E
Palk Strait	**124**	10 0 N	80 0 E
Palm Beach	**73**	26 46 N	80 0 W
Palm Desert	**81**	33 43 N	116 22 W
Palm Is.	**135**	18 40 S	146 35 E
Palm Springs	**81**	33 51 N	116 35 W
Palma, Canary Is.	**93**	28 40 N	17 50 W
Palma, Mozam.	**116**	10 46 S	40 29 E
Palma, Bahía de	**104**	39 30 N	2 39 E
Palma, La, Panama	**84**	8 15 N	78 0 W
Palma, La, Spain	**104**	37 21 N	6 38 W
Palma, R.	**87**	10 10 N	71 50 W
Palma Soriano	**84**	20 15 N	76 0 W
Palmares	**87**	8 41 S	35 36 W
Palmarito	**86**	7 37 N	70 10 W
Palmarolle	**40**	48 40 N	79 12 W
Palmas	**89**	26 29 S	52 0 W
Palmas, C.	**114**	4 27 N	7 46 W
Pálmas, G. di	**108**	39 0 N	8 30 E
Palmdale	**81**	34 36 N	118 7 W
Palmeira dos Índios	**87**	9 25 S	36 37 W
Palmer, Alaska, U.S.A.	**67**	61 35 N	149 10 W
Palmer, Mass., U.S.A.	**71**	42 9 N	72 21 W
Palmer Arch	**91**	64 15 S	65 0 W
Palmer Lake	**74**	39 10 N	104 52 W
Palmer Pen.	**91**	73 0 S	60 0 W
Palmer, R., N. Terr., Austral.	**134**	24 30 S	133 0 E
Palmer, R., Queens., Austral.	**134**	16 5 S	142 43 E
Palmerston, Can.	**70**	43 50 N	80 40 W
Palmerston, Ont., Can.	**46**	43 50 N	80 51 W
Palmerston, N.Z.	**133**	45 29 S	170 43 E
Palmerston, C.	**135**	21 32 S	149 29 E
Palmerston North	**133**	40 21 S	175 39 E
Palmerton	**71**	40 47 N	75 36 W
Palmetto	**73**	27 33 N	82 33 W
Palmi	**108**	38 21 N	15 51 E
Palmira, Argent.	**88**	32 59 S	68 25 W
Palmira, Colomb.	**86**	3 32 N	76 16 W
Palms	**46**	43 37 N	82 47 W
Palmyra, U.S.A.	**77**	42 52 N	88 36 W
Palmyra, Ill., U.S.A.	**76**	39 26 N	90 0 W
Palmyra, Mo., U.S.A.	**76**	39 45 N	91 30 W
Palmyra, N.Y., U.S.A.	**70**	34 5 N	77 18 W
Palmyra = Tadmor	**122**	34 30 N	37 55 E
Palni Hills	**124**	10 14 N	77 33 E
Palo Alto	**80**	37 25 N	122 8 W
Palo Verde	**81**	33 26 N	114 45 W
Paloe	**127**	8 20 S	121 43 E
Paloma, La	**88**	30 35 S	71 0 W
Palomar	**53**	48 10 N	82 16 W
Palopo	**127**	3 0 S	120 16 E
Palos, Cabo de	**104**	37 38 N	0 40 W
Palos Verdes	**81**	33 48 N	118 23 W
Palos Verdes, Pt.	**81**	33 43 N	118 26 W
Palouse	**78**	46 59 N	117 5 W
Palu, Indon.	**127**	1 0 S	119 59 E
Palu, Turkey	**122**	38 45 N	40 0 E
Paluan	**127**	13 35 N	120 29 E
Pamamaroo, L.	**136**	32 17 S	142 28 E
Pamanukan	**127**	6 16 S	107 49 E
Pamekasan	**127**	7 10 S	113 29 E
Pameungpeuk	**127**	7 38 S	107 44 E
Pamiencheng	**130**	43 16 N	124 4 E
Pamiers	**102**	43 7 N	1 39 E
Pamirs, Ra.	**120**	37 40 N	73 0 E
Pamlico, R.	**73**	35 25 N	76 40 W
Pamlico Sd.	**73**	35 20 N	76 0 W
Pampa	**75**	35 35 N	100 58 W
Pampa de las Salinas	**88**	32 1 S	66 58 W
Pampa, La □	**88**	36 50 S	66 0 W
Pampanua	**127**	4 22 S	120 14 E
Pampas, Argent.	**88**	34 0 S	64 0 W
Pampas, Peru	**86**	12 20 S	74 50 W
Pamplona, Colomb.	**86**	7 23 N	72 39 W
Pamplona, Spain	**104**	42 48 N	1 38 W
Pana	**76**	39 25 N	89 10 W
Panaca	**79**	37 51 N	114 50 W
Panache, L.	**46**	46 15 N	81 20 W
Panaitan, I.	**127**	6 35 S	105 10 E
Panaji (Panjim)	**124**	15 25 N	73 50 E
Panamá	**84**	9 0 N	79 25 W
Panama ■	**84**	8 48 N	79 55 W
Panama Canal	**84**	9 10 N	79 56 W
* Panama Canal Zone	**84**	9 10 N	79 56 W
Panama City	**73**	30 10 N	85 41 W
Panamá, Golfo de	**84**	8 4 N	79 20 W
Panamint Mts.	**79**	36 15 N	117 20 W
Panamint Springs	**81**	36 20 N	117 28 W
Panão	**86**	9 55 S	75 55 W
Panarukan	**127**	7 40 S	113 52 E
Panay, G.	**127**	11 0 N	122 30 E
Panay I.	**127**	11 10 N	122 30 E
Pancake Ra.	**79**	38 30 N	116 0 W
Pančevo	**109**	44 52 N	20 41 E
Pancorbo, Paso	**104**	42 32 N	3 5 W
Pandan	**127**	11 45 N	122 10 E
Pandangpanjang	**126**	0 40 S	100 20 E
Pandeglang	**127**	6 25 S	106 0 E
Pandharpur	**124**	17 41 N	75 20 E
Pando	**89**	34 30 S	56 0 W
Panfilov	**120**	44 30 N	80 0 E
Pang-Long	**125**	23 11 N	98 45 E
Pangani	**116**	5 25 S	38 58 E
Pangi	**116**	3 10 S	26 35 E
Pangkalanberandan	**126**	4 1 N	98 20 E
Pangkalansusu	**126**	4 2 N	98 42 E
Pangkiang (Mingan)	**130**	43 4 N	112 30 E
Pangkoh	**126**	3 5 S	114 8 E
Pangmar	**56**	49 39 N	104 40 W
Pangong Tso, L.	**124**	34 0 N	78 20 E
Pangrango	**127**	6 46 S	107 1 E
Panguitch	**79**	37 52 N	112 30 W
Pangutaran Group	**127**	6 18 N	120 34 E
Panhandle	**75**	35 23 N	101 23 W

* *Renamed Belau* □

* *Now part of Panama*

Panjgur Pelican Rapids

Panjgur	**124**	27 0N	64 5 E
Panjim = Panaji	**124**	15 25N	73 50 E
Panjinad Barrage	**124**	29 22N	71 15 E
Pankadjene	**127**	4 46 S	119 34 E
Pankal Pinang	**126**	2 0 S	106 0 E
Panna	**124**	24 40N	80 15 E
Panny, R.	**60**	57 8N	114 51W
Panora	**76**	41 41N	94 22W
Panorama	**89**	21 21 S	51 51W
Panshan	**130**	41 15N	122 0 E
Panshih	**130**	42 59N	126 0 E
Pantano	**79**	32 0N	110 32W
Pantar, I.	**127**	8 28 S	124 10 E
Pantelleria, I.	**108**	36 52N	12 0 E
Pantjo	**127**	8 42 S	118 40 E
Pantukan	**127**	7 17N	125 58 E
Panuco	**83**	22 0N	98 25W
Paochang	**130**	41 46N	115 30 E
Paocheng	**131**	33 12N	107 0 E
Paokang	**131**	31 57N	111 21 E
Paoki	**131**	34 25N	107 15 E
Paoko	**131**	34 22N	107 12 E
Paola	**74**	38 36N	94 50W
Paoii	**77**	31 33N	86 28W
Paonia	**79**	38 56N	107 37W
Paoshan	**125**	25 7N	99 9 E
Paoteh	**130**	39 0N	110 45 E
Paoting	**130**	38 50N	115 30 E
Paotow	**130**	40 45N	110 0 E
Paotsing	**131**	28 35N	109 35 E
Paoua	**116**	7 25N	16 30 E
Papá	**107**	47 22N	17 30 E
Papagayo, Golfo de	**84**	10 4N	85 50W
Papagayo, R., Brazil	**82**	12 30 S	58 10W
Papagayo, R., Mexico	**83**	16 36N	99 43W
Papaikou	**67**	19 47N	155 6W
Papakura	**133**	37 4 S	174 59 E
Papaloapan, R.	**82**	18 2N	96 51W
Papantla	**83**	20 45N	97 21W
Papar	**126**	5 45N	116 0 E
Papenburg	**105**	53 7N	7 25 E
Papigochic, R.	**82**	29 9N	109 40W
Papineau-Labelle, Parc Prov.	**40**	46 10N	75 15W
Papineauville	**40**	45 37N	75 1W
Paposo	**88**	25 0 S	70 30W
Papua New Guinea ■	**14**	8 0 S	145 0 E
Papudo	**88**	32 29 S	71 27W
Papun	**125**	18 0N	97 30 E
Pará = Belém	**87**	1 20 S	48 30W
Pará □	**87**	3 20 S	52 0W
Paracatú	**87**	17 10 S	46 50W
Paracel Is.	**126**	16 49N	111 2 E
Paradip	**125**	20 15N	86 35 E
Paradis	**40**	48 15N	76 35W
Paradise, Calif., U.S.A.	**80**	39 46N	121 37W
Paradise, Mich., U.S.A.	**46**	46 38N	85 3W
Paradise, Mont., U.S.A.	**78**	47 27N	114 54W
Paradise, Nev., U.S.A.	**81**	36 4N	115 7W
Paradise Hill	**56**	53 32N	109 28W
Paradise, R.	**36**	53 27N	57 19W
Paradise Valley, Can.	**61**	53 2N	110 17W
Paradise Valley, U.S.A.	**78**	41 30N	117 28W
Parado	**127**	8 42 S	118 30 E
Paragould	**75**	36 5N	90 30W
Paragua, La	**86**	6 50N	63 20W
Paragua, R.	**86**	6 30N	63 30W
Paraguaçu Paulista	**89**	22 22 S	50 35W
Paraguaçu, R.	**87**	12 45 S	38 54W
Paraguai, R.	**86**	16 0 S	57 52W
Paraguaipoa	**86**	11 21N	71 57W
Paraguana, Pen. de	**86**	12 0N	70 0W
Paraguarí	**88**	25 36 S	57 0W
Paraguarí □	**88**	26 0 S	57 10W
Paraguay ■	**88**	23 0 S	57 0W
Paraguay, R.	**88**	27 18 S	58 38W
Paraíba = Joao Pessoa	**82**	7 10 S	35 0W
Paraiba □	**87**	7 0 S	36 0W
Paraíba do Sul, R.	**89**	21 37 S	41 3W
Parainen	**111**	60 18N	22 18 E
Paraíso	**83**	19 3 S	52 59W
Paraiso	**83**	18 24N	93 14W
Parakou	**114**	9 25N	2 40 E
Paramaribo	**87**	5 50N	55 10W
Paramillo, Nudo del	**86**	7 4N	75 55W
Paramushir, Ostrov	**121**	40 24N	156 0 E
Paraná	**88**	32 0 S	60 30W
Paranã	**87**	12 30 S	47 40W
Paraná □	**89**	24 30 S	51 0W
Paraná, R.	**88**	33 43 S	59 15W
Paranã, R.	**87**	22 25 S	53 1W
Paranaguá	**89**	25 30 S	48 30W
Paranaíba, R.	**87**	18 0 S	49 12W
Paranapanema, R.	**89**	22 40 S	53 9W
Paranapiacaba, Serra do	**89**	24 31 S	48 35W
Paranavaí	**89**	23 4 S	52 28W
Parang, Jolo, Phil.	**127**	5 55N	120 54 E
Parang, Mindanao, Phil.	**127**	7 23N	124 16 E
Paratinga	**87**	12 40 S	43 10W
Paray-le-Monial	**103**	46 27N	4 7 E
Parbhani	**124**	19 8N	76 52 E
Parchim	**106**	53 25N	11 50 E
Pardee Res.	**80**	38 16N	120 51W
Pardo, R., Bahia, Brazil	**87**	15 40 S	39 0W
Pardo, R., Mato Grosso, Brazil	**87**	21 0 S	53 25W
Pardo, R., São Paulo, Brazil	**87**	20 45 S	48 0W
Pardubice	**106**	50 3N	15 45 E
Pare	**127**	7 43 S	112 12 E
Pare Pare	**127**	4 0 S	119 45 E
Parecis, Serra dos	**86**	13 0 S	60 0W
Paren	**121**	62 45N	163 0 E
Parent	**40**	47 55N	74 35W
Parent, Lac.	**40**	48 31N	77 1W
Parentis-en-Born	**102**	44 21N	1 4W
Parepare	**127**	4 0 S	119 40 E
Parfuri	**117**	22 28 S	31 17 E
Parham, Can.	**71**	44 40N	76 40W
Parham, Ont., Can.	**47**	44 39N	76 43W
Paria, Golfo de	**86**	10 20N	62 0W
Paria, Pen. de	**86**	10 50N	62 30W
Pariaguán	**86**	8 51N	64 43W
Pariaman	**126**	0 47 S	100 11 E
Paricutín, Cerro	**82**	19 28N	102 15W
Parigi	**127**	0 50 S	120 5 E
Parika	**86**	6 50N	58 20W
Parima, Serra	**86**	2 30N	64 0W
Parinari	**86**	4 35 S	74 25W
Parîngul-Mare, mt.	**107**	45 20N	23 37 E
Parintins	**87**	2 40 S	56 50W
Pariparit Kyun	**125**	14 55 S	93 45 E
Paris, Can.	**49**	43 12N	80 25W
Paris, France	**101**	48 50N	2 20 E
Paris, U.S.A.	**76**	39 29N	92 0W
Paris, Idaho, U.S.A.	**78**	42 13N	111 30W
Paris, Ill., U.S.A.	**77**	39 36N	87 42W
Paris, Ky., U.S.A.	**77**	38 12N	84 12W
Paris, Tenn., U.S.A.	**73**	36 20N	88 20W
Paris, Tex., U.S.A.	**75**	33 40N	95 30W
Parish	**71**	43 24N	76 9W
Pariti	**127**	9 55 S	123 30 E
Park	**80**	48 45N	122 18W
Park City	**78**	40 42N	111 35W
Park Falls	**74**	45 58N	90 27W
Park Head	**70**	44 36N	81 10W
Park Range	**78**	40 0N	106 30W
Park Rapids	**74**	46 56N	95 0W
Park Ridge	**77**	42 2N	87 51W
Park River	**74**	48 25N	97 50W
Park Royal	**66**	49 20N	123 8W
Park View	**79**	36 45N	106 37W
Parker, Can.	**49**	43 46N	80 35W
Parker, Ariz., U.S.A.	**81**	34 8N	114 16W
Parker, S.D., U.S.A.	**74**	43 25N	97 7W
Parker Dam	**81**	34 13N	114 5W
Parkersburg, U.S.A.	**76**	42 35N	92 47W
Parkersburg, W. Va., U.S.A.	**72**	39 18N	81 31W
Parkerview	**56**	51 21N	103 18W
Parkes, A.C.T., Austral.	**135**	35 18 S	149 8 E
Parkes, N.S.W., Austral.	**136**	33 9 S	148 11 E
Parkfield	**80**	35 54N	120 26W
Parkhill	**46**	43 15N	81 38W
Parkland	**80**	47 9N	122 26W
Parks L.	**53**	49 27N	87 38W
Parkside	**56**	53 10N	106 33W
Parkston	**74**	43 25N	98 0W
Parksville	**62**	49 20N	124 21W
Parma, Italy	**108**	44 50N	10 20 E
Parma, Idaho, U.S.A.	**78**	43 49N	116 59W
Parma, Ohio, U.S.A.	**70**	41 25N	81 42W
Parnaguá	**87**	10 10 S	44 10W
Parnaíba, Piauí, Brazil	**87**	3 0 S	41 40W
Parnaíba, São Paulo, Brazil	**87**	19 34 S	51 14W
Parnaíba, R.	**87**	3 35 S	43 0W
Parnassós, mt.	**109**	38 17N	21 30 E
Pärnu	**120**	58 12N	24 33 E
Paroo Chan.	**135**	30 50 S	143 35 E
Paroo, R.	**135**	30 0 S	144 5 E
Paropamisus Range = Fī roz Kohi	**123**	34 45N	63 0 E
Páros, I.	**109**	37 5N	25 12 E
Parowan	**79**	37 54N	112 56W
Parpaillon, mts.	**103**	44 30N	6 40 E
Parral	**88**	36 10 S	72 0W
Parramatta	**136**	33 48 S	151 1 E
Parras	**82**	25 30N	102 20W
Parrett, R.	**95**	51 7N	2 58W
Parris I.	**73**	32 20N	80 30W
Parrsboro	**39**	45 30N	64 25W
Parry	**55**	49 47N	104 41W
Parry, C.	**67**	70 20N	123 38W
Parry Is.	**64**	77 0N	110 0W
Parry Sound	**46**	45 20N	80 0W
Parshall	**74**	47 56N	102 11W
Parsnip, R.	**54**	55 10N	123 2W
Parson	**63**	51 5N	116 37W
Parsons	**75**	37 20N	95 10W
Parsons Pond	**37**	49 59N	57 37W
Parson's Pond	**37**	50 2N	57 43W
Parthenay	**100**	46 38N	0 16W
Partridge Pt.	**37**	50 10N	56 10W
Partridge, R.	**53**	51 19N	80 18W
Paru, R.	**87**	0 20 S	53 30W
Paruro	**86**	13 45 S	71 50W
Parvatipuram	**125**	18 50N	83 25 E
Parwan □	**124**	35 0N	69 0 E
Pas-de-Calais □	**101**	50 30N	2 30 E
Pasadena, Can.	**37**	49 1N	57 36W
Pasadena, Calif., U.S.A.	**81**	34 5N	118 9W
Pasadena, Tex., U.S.A.	**75**	29 45N	95 14W
Pasaje	**86**	3 10 S	79 40W
Pasaje, R.	**88**	25 35 S	64 57W
Pascagoula	**75**	30 30N	88 30W
Pascagoula, R.	**75**	30 40N	88 35W
Pasco	**78**	46 10N	119 0W
Pasco, Cerro de	**86**	10 45 S	76 10W
Pasfield L.	**55**	58 24N	105 20W
Pasir Mas	**128**	6 2N	102 8 E
Pasir Puteh	**128**	5 50N	102 24 E
Pasirian	**127**	8 13 S	113 8 E
Pasley, C.	**134**	33 52 S	123 35 E
Pasni	**124**	25 15N	63 27 E
Paso Cantinela	**81**	32 33N	115 47W
Paso de Indios	**90**	43 55 S	69 0W
Paso de los Libres	**88**	29 44 S	57 10W
Paso de los Toros	**88**	32 36 S	56 37W
Paso Robles	**79**	35 40N	120 45W
Paspébiac	**39**	48 3N	65 17W
Pass Island	**37**	47 30N	56 12W
Passage Pt.	**64**	73 29N	115 16W
Passage West	**97**	51 52N	8 20W
Passaic	**71**	40 50N	74 8W
Passau	**106**	48 34N	13 27 E
Passero, C.	**108**	36 42N	15 8 E
Passo Fundo	**89**	28 10 S	52 30W
Passos	**87**	20 45 S	46 37W
Passy	**101**	45 55N	6 41 E
Pastaza, R.	**86**	2 45 S	76 50W
Pasteur, L.	**38**	50 13N	66 58W
Pasto	**86**	1 13N	77 17W
Pasuruan	**127**	7 40 S	112 53 E
Patagonia, Argent.	**90**	45 0 S	69 0W
Patagonia, U.S.A.	**79**	31 35N	110 45W
Patan	**124**	23 54N	72 14 E
Patan (Lalitapur)	**125**	27 40N	85 20 E
Patani	**127**	0 20N	128 50 E
Pataokiang	**130**	41 58N	126 30 E
Patay	**101**	48 2N	1 40 E
Patchewollock	**136**	35 22 S	142 12 E
Patchogue	**71**	40 46N	73 1W
Patea	**133**	39 45 S	174 30 E
Paternò	**108**	37 34N	14 53 E
Paternoster, Kepulauan	**126**	7 5 S	118 15 E
Pateros	**78**	48 4N	119 58W
Paterson, Austral.	**136**	32 37 S	151 39 E
Paterson, U.S.A.	**71**	40 55N	74 10W
Pathankot	**124**	32 18N	75 45 E
Pathfinder Res.	**78**	42 30N	107 0W
Páti	**127**	6 45 S	111 3 E
Patiala	**124**	30 23N	76 26 E
Patjitan	**127**	8 12 S	111 8 E
Patkai Bum	**125**	27 0N	95 30 E
Pátmos, I.	**109**	37 21N	26 36 E
Patna	**125**	25 35N	85 18 E
Patos de Minas	**87**	18 35 S	46 32W
Patos, Lag. dos	**89**	31 20 S	51 0 E
Patquía	**88**	30 0 S	66 55W
Pátrai	**109**	38 14N	21 47 E
Pátraikos, Kólpos	**109**	38 17N	21 30 E
Patrick's Cove	**37**	47 3N	54 7W
Patrie, La	**41**	45 24N	71 15W
Patrocínio	**87**	18 57 S	47 0W
Pattani	**128**	6 48N	101 15 E
Patten	**35**	45 59N	68 28W
Patterson, Can.	**50**	43 54N	79 28W
Patterson, Calif., U.S.A.	**80**	37 30N	121 9W
Patterson, La., U.S.A.	**75**	29 44N	91 20W
Patterson, Mt.	**80**	38 29N	119 20W
Patti	**108**	38 8N	14 57 E
Patton	**70**	40 38N	78 40W
Pattonsburg	**76**	40 3N	94 8W
Patuakhali	**125**	22 20N	90 25 E
Patuca, Punta	**84**	15 49N	84 14W
Patuca, R.	**84**	15 20N	84 40W
Patung	**131**	31 0N	110 30 E
Pátzcuaro	**82**	19 30N	101 40W
Pau	**102**	43 19N	0 25W
Pauillac	**102**	45 11N	0 46W
Pauini, R.	**86**	1 42 S	62 50W
Pauk	**125**	21 55N	94 30 E
Paul I.	**36**	56 30N	61 20W
Paul-Sauvé, L.	**40**	50 15N	78 20W
Paulatuk	**67**	69 25N	124 0W
Paulding	**77**	41 8N	84 35W
Paulhan	**102**	43 33N	3 28 E
Paulistana	**87**	8 9 S	41 9W
Paullina	**74**	42 55N	95 40W
Paulo Afonso	**87**	9 21 S	38 15W
Paul's Valley	**75**	34 40N	97 17W
Pauma Valley	**81**	33 16N	116 58W
Pavia	**108**	45 10N	9 10 E
Pavlodar	**120**	52 33N	77 0 E
Pavlof Is.	**67**	55 30N	161 30W
Pavlovo	**121**	63 5N	115 25 E
Paw-Paw	**76**	41 41N	88 59W
Paw Paw	**77**	42 13N	85 53W
Pawhuska	**75**	36 40N	96 25W
Pawling	**71**	41 35N	73 37W
Pawnee, U.S.A.	**76**	39 35N	89 35W
Pawnee, Okla., U.S.A.	**75**	36 24N	96 50W
Pawnee City	**74**	40 8N	96 10W
Pawtucket	**71**	41 51N	71 22W
Paxton, Ill., U.S.A.	**77**	40 25N	88 0W
Paxton, Nebr., U.S.A.	**74**	41 12N	101 27W
Paya Bakri	**128**	2 3N	102 44 E
Payakumbah	**126**	0 20 S	100 35 E
Payen	**129**	45 57N	127 58 E
Payette	**78**	44 0N	117 0W
Payne	**77**	41 5N	84 44W
Payne = Bellin	**36**	60 1N	70 1W
Paynesville	**74**	45 21N	94 44W
Paysandú	**88**	32 19 S	58 8W
Payson, Ariz., U.S.A.	**79**	34 17N	111 15W
Payson, Utah, U.S.A.	**78**	40 8N	111 41W
Paz, Bahía de la	**82**	24 15N	110 25W
Paz Centro, La	**84**	12 20N	86 41W
Paz, La, Entre Ríos, Argent.	**88**	30 50 S	59 45W
Paz, La, San Luis, Argent.	**88**	33 30 S	67 20W
Paz, La, Boliv.	**86**	16 20 S	68 10W
Paz, La, Hond.	**84**	14 20N	87 47W
Paz, La, Mexico	**82**	24 10N	110 20W
Paz, La, Bahía de	**82**	24 20N	110 40W
Paz, R.	**84**	13 44N	90 10W
Pazar	**122**	41 10N	40 50 E
Pazardzhik	**109**	42 12N	24 20 E
Pe Ell	**80**	46 30N	123 18W
Peabody	**71**	42 31N	70 56W
Peace Point	**54**	59 7N	112 27W
Peace, R.	**54**	59 0N	111 25W
Peace River	**60**	56 15N	117 18W
Peace River Res.	**54**	55 40N	123 40W
Peach Springs	**79**	35 36N	113 30W
Peachland	**63**	49 47N	119 45W
Peak Hill	**134**	32 39 S	148 11 E
Peak Range	**135**	22 50 S	148 20 E
Peak, The	**94**	53 24N	1 53W
Peale Mt.	**79**	38 25N	109 12W
Pearblossom	**81**	34 30N	117 55W
Pearce	**79**	31 57N	109 56W
Pearl, Can.	**52**	48 40N	88 40W
Pearl, U.S.A.	**76**	39 28N	90 38W
Pearl City, U.S.A.	**76**	42 16N	89 50W
Pearl City, Hawaii, U.S.A.	**67**	21 24N	158 0W
Pearl Harbor	**67**	21 20N	158 0W
Pearl, R.	**75**	31 50N	90 0W
Pearsall	**75**	28 55N	99 8W
Pearse I.	**54**	54 52N	130 14W
Peary Land	**17**	82 40N	33 0W
Pease, R.	**75**	34 18N	100 15W
Pebane	**117**	17 10 S	38 8 E
Pebas	**86**	3 10 S	71 55W
Pebble Beach	**80**	36 34N	121 57W
Pec	**109**	42 40N	20 17 E
Pecatonica	**76**	42 19N	89 22W
Pecatonica, R.	**76**	42 26N	89 17W
Pechenga	**120**	69 30N	31 25 E
Pechora, R.	**120**	62 30N	56 30 E
Pechorskaya Guba	**120**	68 40N	54 0 E
Peck	**46**	43 16N	82 49W
Pecos	**75**	31 25N	103 35W
Pecos, R.	**75**	31 22N	102 30W
Pécs	**107**	46 5N	18 15 E
Pedasí	**84**	7 32N	80 3W
Pedernales	**85**	18 2N	71 44W
Pedjantan, I.	**126**	0 5 S	106 15 E
Pedra Azul	**87**	16 2 S	41 17W
Pedreiras	**87**	4 32 S	44 40W
Pedrera, La	**86**	1 18 S	69 43W
Pedro Afonso	**87**	9 0 S	48 10W
Pedro Antonio Santos	**83**	18 54N	88 15W
Pedro Cays	**84**	17 5N	77 48W
Pedro Chico	**86**	1 4N	70 25W
Pedro de Valdivia	**88**	22 33 S	69 38W
Pedro Juan Caballero	**89**	22 30 S	55 40W
Pedro Miguel Locks	**84**	9 1N	79 36W
Peebles, U.K.	**96**	55 40N	3 12W
Peebles, U.S.A.	**77**	38 57N	83 23W
Peekshill	**71**	41 18N	73 57W
Peel	**94**	54 14N	4 40W
Peel □	**50**	43 45N	79 47W
Peel, R.	**64**	67 0N	135 0W
Peerless L.	**60**	56 37N	114 40W
Peerless Lake	**60**	56 40N	114 35W
Peers	**60**	53 40N	116 0W
Pegasus Bay	**133**	43 20 S	173 10 E
Peggy's Cove	**39**	44 30N	63 55W
Pegu	**125**	17 20N	96 29 E
Pegu Yoma, mts.	**125**	19 0N	96 0 E
Peh K.	**131**	24 20N	113 20 E
Pehan	**129**	48 17N	120 31 E
Pehpei	**131**	29 44N	106 29 E
Pehtaiho	**130**	39 50N	119 30 E
Pehuajó	**88**	36 0 S	62 0W
Peine	**88**	23 45 S	68 8W
Peiping = Peking	**130**	39 50N	116 20 E
Peixe	**87**	12 0 S	48 40W
Pekalongan	**127**	6 53 S	109 40 E
Pekan	**128**	3 30N	103 25 E
Pékans, R.	**38**	52 12N	66 49W
Pekin	**76**	40 35N	89 40W
Peking (Beijing)	**130**	39 50N	116 20 E
Pelabuhan Ratu, Teluk	**127**	7 5 S	106 30 E
Pelabuhanratu	**127**	7 0 S	106 32 E
Pelaihari	**126**	3 55 S	114 45 E
Peleaga, mt.	**107**	45 22N	22 55 E
Pelee I.	**46**	41 47N	82 40W
Pelée, Mt.	**85**	14 40N	61 0W
Pelee, Pt.	**46**	41 54N	82 31W
Peleng, I.	**127**	1 20 S	123 30 E
Pelham, Can.	**49**	43 3N	79 21W
Pelham, U.S.A.	**73**	31 5N	84 6W
Pelham Union	**49**	43 5N	79 23W
Pelican	**67**	58 12N	136 28W
Pelican L.	**57**	52 28N	100 20W
Pélican, L.	**36**	59 47N	73 35W
Pelican L., U.S.A.	**52**	48 4N	92 58W
Pelican L., U.S.A.	**52**	46 36N	94 5W
Pelican Narrows	**55**	55 10N	102 56W
Pelican Portage	**54**	55 51N	113 0W
Pelican Rapids	**57**	52 45N	100 42W

Peligre, L. de Pine Flat Res

Peligre, L. de 85 19 1N 71 58W
Pelkosenniemi 110 67 6N 27 28E
Pella 76 41 30N 93 0W
Pelletier Sta. 41 47 33N 69 26W
Pellston 46 45 33N 84 47W
Pelly 57 51 52N 101 56W
Pelly Bay 65 68 0N 89 50W
Pelly Crossing 64 62 49N 136 34W
Pelly L. 64 66 0N 102 0W
Pelly Pt. 66 49 7N 123 12W
Pelly, R. 64 62 15N 133 30W
Peloponnese = Pelóponnisos 109 37 10N 22 0E
Pelopónnisos Kai Dhitikti Iprotiki Ellas □ 109 37 10N 22 0E
Peloro, C. 108 38 15N 15 40E
Pelorus Sound 133 40 59S 173 59E
Pelotas 89 31 42S 52 23W
Pelvoux, Massif de 103 44 52N 6 20E
Pemalang 127 6 53S 109 23E
Pematang Siantar 126 2 57N 99 5E
Pemba 117 16 30S 27 28E
Pemba, I. 117 5 0S 39 45E
Pemberton, Austral. 134 34 30S 116 0E
Pemberton, Can. 63 50 25N 122 50W
Pembina 57 48 58N 97 15W
Pembina, R., Alta., Can. 60 54 45N 114 17W
Pembina, R., Man., Can. 57 49 0N 98 12W
Pembine 72 45 38N 87 59W
Pembroke, Can. 47 45 50N 77 7W
Pembroke, N.Z. 133 44 33S 169 9E
Pembroke, U.K. 95 51 41N 4 57W
Pembroke, U.S.A. 73 32 5N 81 32W
Pen-y-Ghent 94 54 10N 2 15W
Peña de Francia, Sierra de 104 40 32N 6 10W
Peñalara, Pico 104 40 51N 3 57W
Penang = Pinang 128 5 25N 100 15E
Penápolis 89 21 30S 50 0W
Peñas, C. de 104 43 42N 5 52W
Peñas, G. de 90 47 0S 75 0W
Peñas, Pta. 86 11 17N 70 28W
Pend Oreille, L. 63 48 0N 116 30W
Pend Oreille, R. 78 49 4N 117 37W
Pendembu 114 9 7N 12 14W
Pendleton, U.S.A. 77 40 0N 85 45W
Pendleton, Calif., U.S.A. 81 33 16N 117 23W
Pendleton, Oreg., U.S.A. 78 45 35N 118 50W
Penedo 87 10 15S 36 36W
Penetanguishene, Newf., Can. 37 47 36N 52 45W
Penetanguishene, Ont., Can. 46 44 50N 79 55W
Pengalengan 127 7 9S 107 30E
Pengan 131 31 0N 106 18E
Pengchia Yu (Agincourt) Is. 131 25 4N 122 2E
Penghu (Pescadores) 131 23 34N 119 30E
Penglai (Tengchowfu) 130 37 50N 120 50E
Pengpu 131 33 0N 117 25E
Pengshui 131 29 20N 108 15E
Penhold 61 52 8N 113 52W
Peniche 104 39 19N 9 22W
Penida, I. 126 8 45S 115 30E
Penki 130 41 20N 132 50E
Penmarch 100 47 49N 4 21W
Penmarch, Pte. de 100 47 48N 4 22W
Pennant 56 50 32N 108 14W
Penner, R. 124 14 50N 78 20E
Penniac 39 46 2N 66 34W
Pennines 94 54 50N 2 20W
Pennington 80 39 15N 121 47W
Pennsylvania □ 72 40 50N 78 0W
Pennville 77 40 30N 85 9W
Penny 63 53 51N 121 20W
Penny Highland 65 67 19N 66 20W
Penny Str. 65 76 30N 97 0W
Pennyan 70 42 39N 77 7W
Penola 136 37 25S 140 47E
Penong 134 31 59S 133 5E
Penonomé 84 8 31N 80 21W
Penrhyn Is. 15 9 0S 150 30W
Penrith, Austral. 136 33 43S 150 38E
Penrith, U.K. 94 54 40N 2 45W
Pensacola 73 30 30N 87 10W
Pensacola Mts. 91 84 0S 40 0W
Pense 56 50 25N 104 59W
Pentecôte, L. 38 49 53N 67 20W
Pentecôte, R. 38 49 46N 67 10W
Penticton 63 49 30N 119 30W
Pentland 135 20 32S 145 25E
Pentland Corners 49 43 40N 80 30W
Pentland Firth 96 58 43N 3 10W
Pentland Hills 96 55 48N 3 25W
Penylan L. 55 61 50N 106 20W
Penza 120 53 15N 45 5E
Penzance 95 50 7N 5 32W
Penzhinskaya Guba 121 61 30N 163 0E
Peoria, Ariz., U.S.A. 79 33 40N 112 15W
Peoria, Ill., U.S.A. 76 40 40N 89 40W
Peoria Heights 76 40 45N 89 35W
Peotone 77 41 20N 87 48W
Pepperwood 78 40 23N 124 0W
Perabumilih 126 3 27S 104 15E
Peraki, R. 128 5 10N 101 4E
Percé 38 48 31N 64 13W
Perche 100 48 31N 1 1E
Perche, Collines de la 100 42 30N 2 5E
Percy, France 100 48 55N 1 11W
Percy, U.S.A. 76 38 5N 89 41W
Perdido, Mte. 104 42 40N 0 50E
Perdue 56 52 4N 107 33W
Pereira 86 4 49N 75 43W
Perez, I. 83 22 24N 89 42W
Pérgamino 88 33 52S 60 30W
Perham 74 46 36N 95 36W
Perhentian, Kepulauan 128 5 54N 102 42E
Péribonca, L. 41 50 1N 71 10W
Péribonca, R. 36 48 45N 72 5W
Peribonka 41 48 46N 72 3W
Perico 88 24 20S 65 5W
Pericos 82 25 3N 107 42W
Périers 100 49 11N 1 25W
Périgord 102 45 0N 0 40E
Périgueux 102 45 10N 0 42E
Perija, Sierra de 86 9 30N 73 3W
Perkam, Tg. 127 1 35S 137 50E
Perlas, Arch. de las 84 8 41N 79 7W
Perlas, Punta de 84 11 30N 83 30W
Perlis □ 128 6 30N 100 15E
Perm (Molotov) 120 58 0N 57 10E
Pernambuco = Recife 87 8 0S 35 0W
Pernambuco □ 87 8 0S 37 0W
Péronne 101 49 55N 2 57E
Perouse Str., La 118 45 40N 142 0E
Perow 54 54 35N 126 10W
Perpignan 102 42 42N 2 53E
Perrington 77 43 12N 84 42W
Perris 81 33 47N 117 14W
Perros-Guirec 100 48 49N 3 28W
Perrot, Île 44 45 22N 73 57W
Perry, U.S.A. 77 42 50N 84 13W
Perry, Fla., U.S.A. 73 30 9N 83 40W
Perry, Ga., U.S.A. 73 32 25N 83 41W
Perry, Iowa, U.S.A. 76 41 48N 94 5W
Perry, Maine, U.S.A. 73 44 59N 67 20W
Perry, Mo., U.S.A. 76 39 26N 91 40W
Perry, N.Y., U.S.A. 70 42 44N 77 59W
Perry, Okla., U.S.A. 75 36 20N 97 20W
Perry River 65 67 43N 102 14W
Perrysburg 77 41 34N 83 38W
Perryton 75 36 28N 100 48W
Perryville, Alas., U.S.A. 67 55 54N 159 10W
Perryville, Mo., U.S.A. 76 37 42N 89 50W
Persepolis 123 29 55N 52 50E
Persia = Iran 123 35 0N 50 0E
*Persian Gulf 123 27 0N 50 0E
Perth, Austral. 134 31 57S 115 52E
Perth, N.B., Can. 34 46 43N 67 42W
Perth, N.B., Can. 39 46 44N 67 42W
Perth, Ont., Can. 47 44 55N 76 15W
Perth, U.K. 96 56 24N 3 27W
Perth, U.S.A. 71 40 33N 74 36W
Perth Amboy 72 40 30N 74 25W
Perthus, Le 102 42 30N 2 53E
Pertuis 103 43 42N 5 30E
Peru, Ill., U.S.A. 76 41 18N 89 12W
Peru, Ind., U.S.A. 77 40 42N 86 0W
Peru ■ 86 8 0S 75 0W
Perúgia 108 43 6N 12 24E
Péruwelz 105 50 31N 3 36E
Pervouralsk 120 56 55N 60 0E
Pésaro 108 43 55N 12 53E
Pesca, La 83 23 46N 97 47W
Pescadores = Penghu 131 23 34N 119 30E
Pescara 108 42 28N 14 13E
Peshawar 124 34 2N 71 37E
†Peshawar □ 124 35 0N 72 50E
Peshtigo 72 45 4N 87 46W
Pesqueira 87 8 20S 36 42W
Pesquieria 82 29 23N 110 54W
Pesquieria, R. 82 25 54N 99 11W
Pessac 102 44 48N 0 37W
Petaling Jaya 128 3 4N 101 42E
Petaluma 80 38 13N 122 39W
Petange 105 49 33N 5 55E
Petatlán 82 17 31N 101 16W
Petauke 117 14 14S 31 12E
Petawawa 47 45 54N 77 17W
Petén Itza, Lago 84 16 58N 89 50W
Peter 1st, I. 91 69 0S 91 0W
Peter Pond L. 55 55 55N 108 44W
Peterbell 53 48 36N 83 21W
Peterboro 71 42 55N 71 59W
Peterborough, S. Australia, Austral. 135 32 58S 138 51E
Peterborough, Victoria, Austral. 135 38 37S 142 50E
Peterborough, Can. 47 44 20N 78 20W
Peterborough, U.K. 95 52 35N 0 14W
Peterhead 96 57 30N 1 49W
Peters, L. 36 59 41N 70 53W
Petersburg, U.S.A. 76 40 1N 89 51W
Petersburg, Alas., U.S.A. 54 56 50N 133 0W
Petersburg, Ind., U.S.A. 77 38 30N 87 15W
Petersburg, Va., U.S.A. 72 37 17N 77 26W
Petersburg, W. Va., U.S.A. 72 38 59N 79 10W
Petersfield 57 50 18N 96 58W
Petit Bois I. 73 30 16N 88 25W
Petit-Brûlé 44 45 35N 74 2W
Petit-Cap 38 48 3N 64 30W
Petit-de-Grat 39 45 30N 60 58W
Petit Étang 39 46 39N 60 58W
Petit Goâve 85 18 27N 72 51W
Petit-Mécatina, I. du 36 50 30N 59 25W
Petit-Quevilly, Le 100 49 26N 1 0E
Petit-Rocher 39 47 46N 65 43W
Petitcodiac 39 45 57N 65 11W
Petite Baleine, R. 36 56 0N 76 45W
Petite-Cascapédia, Parc Prov. de la 38 48 30N 65 45W
Petite-Rivière 41 47 20N 70 33W
Petite Rivière Bridge 39 44 14N 64 27W
Petite Saguenay 41 48 15N 70 4W
Petitsikapau, L. 36 54 37N 66 25W
Petlad 124 22 30N 72 45E
Peto 83 20 10N 89 0W
Petone 133 41 13S 174 53E
Petoskey 46 45 22N 84 57W
Petra, Ostrova 17 76 15N 118 30E
Petrich 109 41 24N 23 13E
Petrolândia 87 9 5S 38 20W
Petrolia 46 42 54N 82 9W
Petrolina 87 9 24S 40 30W
Petropavlovsk 120 55 0N 69 0E
Petropavlovsk-Kamchatskiy 121 53 16N 159 0E
Petrópolis 89 22 33S 43 9W
Petroşeni 107 45 28N 23 20E
Petrovaradin 109 45 16N 19 55E
Petrovsk-Zabaykalskiy 121 51 26N 108 30E
Petrozavodsk 120 61 41N 34 20E
Petty Harbour Long Pond 37 47 31N 52 58W
Peumo 88 34 21S 71 19W
Peureulak 126 4 48N 97 45E
Pevek 121 69 15N 171 0E
Peyrehorade 102 43 34N 1 7W
Peyruis 103 44 1N 5 56E
Pézenas 102 43 28N 3 24E
Pforzheim 106 48 53N 8 43E
Phagwara 124 31 10N 75 40E
Phala 117 23 45S 26 50E
Phalodi 124 27 12N 72 24E
Phalsbourg 101 48 46N 7 15E
Phan Rang 128 11 40N 109 9E
Phan Thiet 128 11 1N 108 9E
Phangnga 128 8 28N 98 30E
Phanh Bho Ho Chi Minh 128 10 58N 106 40E
Phanom Dang Raek, mts. 128 14 45N 104 0E
Pharo Dzong 129 27 45N 89 14E
Phatthalung 128 7 39N 100 6E
Phelps, N.Y., U.S.A. 70 42 57N 77 5W
Phelps, Wis., U.S.A. 74 46 2N 89 2W
Phelps L. 55 59 15N 103 15W
Phenix City 73 32 30N 85 0W
Phetchabun 128 16 25N 101 8E
Phetchaburi 128 13 1N 99 55E
Phichai 128 17 22N 100 10E
Philadelphia, Miss., U.S.A. 75 32 47N 89 5W
Philadelphia, N.Y., U.S.A. 71 44 9N 75 40W
Philadelphia, Pa., U.S.A. 72 40 0N 75 10W
Philip 74 44 4N 101 42W
Philip Smith Mts. 67 68 0N 146 0W
Philippeville 105 50 12N 4 33E
Philippines ■ 127 12 0N 123 0E
Philipsburg, Can. 43 45 2N 73 5W
Philipsburg, Mont., U.S.A. 78 46 20N 113 21W
Philipsburg, Pa., U.S.A. 70 40 53N 78 10W
Phillip, I. 136 38 30S 145 12E
Phillips, Texas, U.S.A. 75 35 48N 101 17W
Phillips, Wis., U.S.A. 74 45 41N 90 22W
Phillipsburg, Kans., U.S.A. 74 39 48N 99 20W
Phillipsburg, Penn., U.S.A. 71 40 43N 75 12W
Philmont 71 42 14N 73 37W
Philomath 78 44 28N 123 21W
Phitsanulok 128 16 50N 100 12E
Phnom Penh 128 11 33N 104 55E
Phnom Thbeng 128 13 50N 104 56E
Phoenix, Ariz., U.S.A. 79 33 30N 112 10W
Phoenix, N.Y., U.S.A. 71 43 13N 76 18W
Phoenix Is. 14 3 30S 172 0W
Phoenixville 71 40 12N 75 29W
Phong Saly 128 21 42N 102 9E
Phra Chedi Sam Ong 128 15 16N 98 23E
Phra Nakhon Si Ayutthaya 128 14 25N 100 30E
Phrae 128 18 7N 100 9E
Phrao 128 19 23N 99 15E
Phu Doan 128 21 40N 105 10E
Phu Loi 128 20 14N 103 14E
Phu Ly (Ha Nam) 128 20 35N 105 50E
Phu Qui 128 19 20N 105 20E
Phuket 128 8 0N 98 28E
Phuoc Le (Baria) 128 10 39N 107 19E
Pi Ho 131 32 0N 116 20E
Piacenza 108 45 2N 9 42E
Pialba 135 25 20S 152 45E
Piana 103 42 15N 8 34E
Piapot 56 49 59N 109 8W
Piashti, L. 38 50 29N 62 52W
Piatra Neamţ 107 46 56N 26 21E
Piauí □ 87 7 0S 43 0W
Piave, R. 108 45 50N 13 9E
Piazza Armerina 108 37 21N 14 20E
Pic I. 53 48 43N 86 37W
Pic, R. 53 48 36N 86 18W
Pica 86 20 35S 69 25W
Picardie 101 50 0N 2 15E
Picardie, Plaine de 101 50 0N 2 0E
Picardy = Picardie 101 50 0N 2 15E
Picayune 75 30 40N 89 40W
Piccadilly 37 48 34N 58 55W
Pichieh 131 27 20N 105 20E
Pichilemu 88 34 22S 72 9W
Pickerel L. 52 48 40N 91 25W
Pickering 51 43 52N 79 2W
Pickering Beach 51 43 50N 78 59W
Pickford 46 46 10N 84 22W
Pickle Lake 52 51 30N 90 12W
Pico 93 38 28N 28 18W
Pico Truncado 90 46 40S 68 10W
Picquigny 101 49 56N 2 10E
Picton, Austral. 136 34 12S 150 34E
Picton, Can. 47 44 1N 77 9W
Picton, N.Z. 133 41 18S 174 3E
Pictou 39 45 41N 62 42W
Pictou I. 39 45 49N 62 33W
Picture Butte 61 49 55N 112 45W
Picún-Leufú 90 39 30S 69 5W
Pidurutalagala, mt. 124 7 10N 80 50E
Pie I. 52 48 15N 89 6W
Piedad, La 82 20 20N 102 1W
Piedecuesta 86 6 59N 73 3W
Piedmont, Can. 43 45 54N 74 8W
Piedmont, U.S.A. 73 33 55N 85 39W
Piedmont = Piemonte 108 45 0N 7 30E
Piedmont Plat. 73 34 0N 81 30W
Piedras Blancas Pt. 79 35 45N 121 18W
Piedras Negras 82 28 35N 100 35W
Piedras, R. de las 86 11 40S 70 50W
Piemonte □ 108 45 0N 7 30E
Pierce 78 46 46N 115 53W
Piercefield 71 44 13N 74 35W
Pierceland 56 54 20N 109 46W
Pierre, France 101 46 54N 5 13E
Pierre, U.S.A. 74 44 23N 100 20W
Pierrefeu 103 43 8N 6 9E
Pierrefonds, Can. 44 45 29N 73 52W
Pierrefonds, France 101 49 20N 3 0E
Pierrefontaine 101 47 14N 6 32E
Pierrefort 102 44 55N 2 50E
Pierrelatte 103 44 23N 4 43E
Pierreville 41 46 4N 72 49W
Pierson 57 49 11N 101 15W
Piestany 69 48 35N 17 50E
Piet Retief 117 27 1S 30 50E
Pietarsaari 110 63 41N 22 40E
Pietermaritzburg 117 29 35S 30 25E
Pietersburg 117 23 54S 29 25E
Pietrosul 107 47 35N 24 43E
Pigeon 46 43 50N 83 17W
Pigeon Hill 43 45 3N 72 56W
Pigeon L., Alta., Can. 61 53 1N 114 2W
Pigeon L., Ont., Can. 47 44 27N 78 30W
Pigeon, R. 34 48 1N 89 42W
Piggott 75 36 20N 90 10W
Pigü 88 37 36S 62 25W
Pike River 43 45 4N 73 6W
Pikes Peak 74 38 50N 105 10W
Piketberg 117 32 55S 18 40E
Pikeville 72 37 30N 82 30W
Pikwitonei 55 55 35N 97 9W
Pilar, Brazil 87 9 36S 35 56W
Pilar, Parag. 88 26 50S 58 10W
Pilas, I. 127 6 39N 121 37E
Pilbara Cr. 134 21 15S 118 22E
Pilcomayo, R. 88 25 21S 57 42W
Pilibhit 124 28 40N 79 50E
Pilica, R. 107 51 25N 20 45E
Pilos 109 36 55N 21 42E
Pilot Butte 56 50 28N 104 25W
Pilot Grove 76 38 53N 92 55W
Pilot Mound 57 49 15N 98 54W
Pilot Point 75 33 26N 97 0W
Pilot Rock 78 45 30N 118 58W
Pilsen = Plzen 106 49 45N 13 22E
Pimba 135 31 18S 136 46E
Pimenta Bueno 86 11 35S 61 10W
Pimentel 86 6 45S 79 55W
Pin-Blanc, L. 40 46 45N 78 8W
Pinacle, Le, mt. 43 45 2N 72 45W
Pinang, I. 128 5 25N 100 15E
Pinar del Rio 84 22 26N 83 40W
Pinawa 57 50 9N 95 50W
Pincher Creek 61 49 30N 113 57W
Pinchi L. 54 54 38N 124 30W
Pinckneyville 76 38 5N 89 20W
Pinconning 46 43 52N 83 57W
Pincourt 44 45 23N 74 0W
Pinczów 107 50 30N 20 35E
Pindos Óros 109 40 0N 21 0E
Pindus Mts. = Pindos Óros 109 40 0N 21 0E
Pine 79 34 27N 111 30W
Pine Bluff 75 34 10N 92 0W
Pine, C. 37 46 37N 53 32W
Pine City 74 45 46N 93 0W
Pine Creek 134 13 50S 131 49E
Pine Dock 57 51 38N 96 48W
Pine Falls 57 50 34N 96 11W
Pine Flat Res. 80 36 50N 119 20W

* *Also known as The Gulf*
† *Renamed N.W. Frontier Province*

Pine Grove Pontian Kechil

Pine Grove **50** 43 48N 79 35W
Pine Hill **43** 45 44N 74 29W
Pine, La **78** 40 53N 80 45W
Pine Pass **54** 55 25N 122 42W
Pine Point **54** 60 50N 114 28W
Pine Portage **52** 49 20N 88 26W
Pine, R. **55** 58 50N 105 38W
Pine Ridge, Can. **58** 50 0N 96 50W
Pine Ridge, U.S.A. **74** 43 0N 102 35W
Pine River, Can. **57** 51 45N 100 30W
Pine River, U.S.A. **52** 46 43N 94 24W
Pine Valley **81** 32 50N 116 32W
Pinecrest **80** 38 12N 120 1W
Pinedale, Ariz., U.S.A. **79** 34 23N 110 16W
Pinedale, Calif., U.S.A. **80** 36 50N 119 48W
Pinega, R. **120** 64 20N 43 0E
Pinerolo **108** 44 47N 7 21E
Pinetop **79** 34 10N 109 57W
Pinetown **117** 29 48S 30 54E
Pinetree **74** 43 42N 105 52W
Pineview **63** 53 50N 122 38W
Pineville, Ky., U.S.A. **73** 36 42N 83 42W
Pineville, La., U.S.A. **75** 31 22N 92 30W
Pinewood **55** 48 45N 94 10W
Piney, Can. **55** 49 5N 96 10W
Piney, France **101** 48 22N 4 21E
Ping, R. **128** 15 42N 100 9E
Pinghua **131** 24 14N 117 2E
Pingkiang **131** 28 45N 113 30E
Pingliang **130** 35 20N 106 40E
Pinglo, Kwangsi-Chuang, China **131** 24 30N 110 45E
Pinglo, Ningsia Hui, China **130** 38 58N 106 30E
Pingnam **131** 23 30N 110 15E
Pingsiang, Kiangsi, China **131** 27 43N 113 50E
Pingsiang, Kwangsi-Chuang, China **131** 22 2N 106 55E
Pingtung **131** 22 36N 120 30E
Pingyang **131** 27 45N 120 25E
Pingyao **130** 37 12N 112 0E
Pingyuan **130** 37 5N 106 40E
Pinhal **89** 22 10S 46 46W
Pinhel **104** 40 18N 7 0W
Pini, I. **126** 0 10N 98 40E
Piniós, R. **109** 39 55N 22 10E
Pinjarra **134** 32 37S 115 52E
Pink, R. **55** 56 50N 103 50W
Pinnacles **80** 36 33N 121 8W
Pinnaroo **136** 35 13S 140 56E
Pinon Hills **81** 34 26N 117 39W
Pinos **82** 22 20N 101 40W
*Pinos, I. de **84** 21 40N 82 40W
Pinos, Mt **81** 34 49N 119 8W
Pinos Pt. **79** 36 50N 121 57W
Pinotepa Nacional **83** 16 25N 97 55W
Pinrang **127** 3 46S 119 34E
Pins, Pte. aux **46** 42 15N 81 51W
Pinsk **120** 52 10N 26 8E
Pintados **86** 20 35S 69 40W
Pintendre **42** 46 45N 71 8W
Pinting **130** 37 45N 113 34E
Pinto Butte Mt. **55** 49 22N 107 27W
Pinware **37** 51 37N 56 42W
Pinware R. **37** 51 39N 56 42W
Pinyang **131** 23 17N 108 47E
Pinyug **120** 60 5N 48 0E
Pioche **79** 38 0N 114 35W
Piombino **108** 42 54N 10 30E
Pioner, I. **121** 79 50N 92 0E
Piorini, L. **86** 3 15S 62 35W
Piotrków Trybunalski **107** 51 23N 19 43E
Pip **123** 26 45N 60 10E
Pipestone **74** 44 0N 96 20W
Pipestone Cr., Man., Can. **57** 49 38N 100 15W
Pipestone Cr., Sask., Can. **55** 53 37N 109 46W
Pipestone, R. **34** 52 53N 89 23W
Pipinas **88** 35 30S 57 19W
Pipmuacan, Rés. **41** 49 45N 70 30W
Pipriac **100** 47 49N 1 58W
Piqua **77** 40 10N 84 10W
Piquiri, R. **89** 24 3S 54 14W
Piracicaba **89** 22 45S 47 30W
Piracuruca **87** 3 50S 41 50W
Piræus = Piraiévs **109** 37 57N 23 42E
Piraiévs **109** 37 57N 23 42E
Pirajui **89** 21 59S 49 29W
Pirane **88** 25 25S 59 30W
Pirapora **87** 17 20S 44 56W
Pirgos **109** 37 40N 21 27E
Piriac-sur-Mer **100** 47 22N 2 33W
Piribebuy **88** 25 26S 57 2W
Pirin Planina **109** 41 40N 23 30E
Pirineos, mts. **104** 42 40N 1 0E
Piripiri **87** 4 15S 41 46W
Piritu **86** 9 23N 69 12W
Pirmasens **105** 49 12N 7 30E
Pirot **109** 43 9N 22 39E
Pirtleville **79** 31 25N 109 35W
Piru **81** 34 25N 118 48W
Pisa **108** 43 43N 10 23E
Pisagua **86** 19 40S 70 15W
Pisco **86** 13 50S 76 5W
Pisek **106** 49 19N 14 10E
Pising **127** 5 8S 121 53E
Pismo Beach **81** 35 9N 120 38W
Pissos **102** 44 19N 0 49W
Pistoia **108** 43 57N 10 53E
Pistol B. **55** 62 25N 92 37W
Pistolet B. **37** 51 35N 55 45W
Pisuerga, R. **104** 42 10N 4 15W
Pitalito **86** 1 51N 76 2W
Pitcairn I. **15** 25 5S 130 5W
Pite älv **110** 65 44N 20 50W
Piteå **110** 65 20N 21 25E
Piteşti **107** 44 52N 24 54E
Pithapuram **125** 17 10N 82 15E
Pithiviers **101** 48 10N 2 13E
Pitiquito **82** 30 42N 112 2W
Pitlochry **96** 56 43N 3 43W
Pitt I. **62** 53 30N 129 50W
Pitt L. **63** 49 25N 122 32W
Pitt Meadows **66** 49 13N 122 42W
Pitt, R. **66** 49 13N 122 46W
Pittsburg, Calif., U.S.A. **80** 38 1N 121 50W
Pittsburg, Kans., U.S.A. **75** 37 21N 94 43W
Pittsburg, Tex., U.S.A. **75** 32 59N 94 58W
Pittsburgh **70** 40 25N 79 55W
Pittsfield, Ill., U.S.A. **76** 39 35N 90 46W
Pittsfield, Mass., U.S.A. **71** 42 28N 73 17W
Pittsfield, N.H., U.S.A. **71** 43 17N 71 18W
Pittston **71** 41 19N 75 50W
Piura **86** 5 5S 80 45W
Pivabiska, R. **53** 50 13N 82 52W
Pivijay **86** 10 28N 74 37W
Pixley **80** 35 58N 119 18W
Pizarro **86** 4 58N 77 22W
Pizzo **108** 38 44N 16 10E
Placentia **37** 47 20N 54 0W
Placentia B. **37** 47 0N 54 40W
Placerville **80** 38 47N 120 51W
Placetas **84** 22 15N 79 44W
Plage-St-Blaise **43** 45 12N 73 16W
Plain **76** 43 17N 90 3W
Plain Dealing **75** 32 56N 93 41W
Plaine, La **44** 45 47N 73 46W
Plainfield, U.S.A. **77** 41 37N 88 12W
Plainfield, N.J., U.S.A. **71** 40 37N 74 28W
Plains, Kans., U.S.A. **75** 37 20N 100 35W
Plains, Mont., U.S.A. **78** 47 27N 114 57W
Plains, Tex., U.S.A. **75** 33 11N 102 50W
Plainview, Nebr., U.S.A. **74** 42 25N 97 48W
Plainview, Tex., U.S.A. **75** 34 10N 101 40W
Plainville **74** 39 18N 99 19W
Plainwell **72** 42 28N 85 40W
Plaisance **102** 43 36N 0 3E
Pláka **109** 36 45N 24 26E
Plakhino **120** 67 45N 86 5E
Plamondon **60** 54 51N 112 32W
Plana Cays **85** 22 38N 73 30W
Planada **80** 37 18N 120 19W
Planaltina **87** 15 30S 47 45W
Plancoët **100** 48 32N 2 13W
Planeta Rica **86** 8 25N 75 36W
Plankinton **74** 43 45N 98 27W
Plano **75** 33 0N 96 45W
Plant City **73** 28 0N 82 15W
Plant, La **74** 45 11N 100 40W
Plaquemine **75** 30 20N 91 15W
Plasencia **104** 40 3N 6 8W
Plaster City **81** 32 47N 115 51W
Plaster Rock **39** 46 53N 67 22W
Plata, La, Argent. **88** 35 0S 57 55W
Plata, La, U.S.A. **76** 40 2N 92 29W
Plata, La, Río de **88** 35 0S 56 40W
Platani, R. **108** 37 28N 13 23E
Plateau **91** 70 55S 40 0E
Plateau du Coteau du Missouri **74** 47 9N 101 5W
Plati, Ákra **109** 40 27N 24 0E
Platinum **67** 59 2N 161 50W
Plato **86** 9 47N 74 47W
Platte **74** 43 28N 98 50W
Platte City **76** 39 22N 94 47W
Platte, R., Minn., U.S.A. **52** 45 47N 94 17W
Platte, R., Nebr., U.S.A. **76** 41 04N 95 53W
Platteville, U.S.A. **76** 42 44N 90 29W
Platteville, Colo., U.S.A. **74** 40 18N 104 47W
Plattsburg **76** 39 34N 94 27W
Plattsburgh **71** 44 41N 73 30W
Plattsmouth **74** 41 0N 95 50W
Plauen **106** 50 29N 12 9E
Playa Azul **82** 17 59N 102 24W
Playgreen L. **57** 54 0N 98 15W
Pleasant Bay **35** 46 51N 60 48W
Pleasant Hill, Ill., U.S.A. **76** 39 27N 90 52W
Pleasant Hill, Mo., U.S.A. **76** 38 48N 94 14W
Pleasant Ridge Park **77** 38 9N 85 50W
Pleasantdale **56** 52 35N 104 30W
Pleasanton **75** 29 0N 98 30W
Pleasantville, U.S.A. **76** 41 23N 93 18W
Pleasantville, N.J., U.S.A. **72** 39 25N 74 30W
Pléaux **102** 45 8N 2 13E
Pledger L. **53** 50 53N 83 42W
Pleiku (Gia Lai) **128** 14 3N 108 0E
Plélan-le-Grand **100** 48 0N 2 7W
Plémet **100** 48 11N 2 36W
Pléneuf-Val-André **100** 48 35N 2 32W
Plenty **56** 51 47N 108 38W
Plenty, Bay of **133** 37 45S 177 0E
Plentywood **74** 48 45N 104 35W
Plessisville **41** 46 14N 71 47W
Plestin-les-Grèves **100** 48 40N 3 39W
Pletipi L. **36** 51 44N 70 6W
Pleven **109** 43 26N 24 37E
Plevlja **109** 43 21N 19 21E
Plevna **47** 44 58N 76 59W
Ploëmeur **100** 47 44N 3 26W
Ploërmel **100** 47 55N 2 26W
Ploieşti **107** 44 57N 26 5E
Plomb du Cantal **102** 45 2N 2 48E
Plombières **101** 47 59N 6 27E
Plonge, Lac La **55** 55 8N 107 20W
Plouay **100** 47 55N 3 21W
Ploudalmézeau **100** 48 34N 4 41W
Plougasnou **100** 48 42N 3 49W
Plouha **100** 48 41N 2 57W
Plouhinec **100** 48 0N 4 29W
Plovdiv **109** 42 8N 24 44E
Plum Coulee **57** 49 11N 97 45W
Plum I. **71** 41 10N 72 12W
Plumas, Can. **57** 50 23N 99 5W
Plumas, U.S.A. **80** 39 45N 119 4W
Plummer **78** 47 21N 116 59W
Plumtree **117** 20 27S 27 55E
Plunkett **56** 51 55N 105 27W
Pluvigner **100** 47 46N 3 1W
Plymouth, U.K. **95** 50 23N 4 9W
Plymouth, U.S.A. **76** 40 29N 90 58W
Plymouth, Calif., U.S.A. **80** 38 29N 120 51W
Plymouth, Ind., U.S.A. **77** 41 20N 86 19W
Plymouth, Mass., U.S.A. **71** 41 58N 70 40W
Plymouth, Mich., U.S.A. **46** 42 22N 83 28W
Plymouth, N.C., U.S.A. **73** 35 54N 76 55W
Plymouth, N.H., U.S.A. **71** 43 44N 71 41W
Plymouth, Pa., U.S.A. **71** 41 17N 76 0W
Plymouth, Wis., U.S.A. **72** 43 42N 87 58W
Plymouth Sd. **95** 50 20N 4 10W
Plympton **39** 44 30N 65 55W
Plynlimon = Pumlumon Fawr **95** 52 29N 3 47W
Plzen **106** 49 45N 13 22E
Po Hai **130** 38 30N 119 0E
Po, R. **108** 45 0N 10 45E
Pobedino **120** 49 51N 142 49E
Pobedy Pik **120** 40 45N 79 58E
Pocahontas, Arkansas, U.S.A. **75** 36 18N 91 0W
Pocahontas, Ill., U.S.A. **76** 38 50N 89 33W
Pocahontas, Iowa, U.S.A. **76** 42 41N 94 42W
Pocatello **78** 42 50N 112 25W
Pocatière, La **41** 47 22N 70 2W
Pochontas **54** 53 10N 117 51W
Pochutla **83** 15 50N 96 31W
Pocita Casas **82** 28 32N 111 6W
Pocomoke City **72** 38 4N 75 32W
Poços de Caldas **89** 21 50S 46 45W
Podensac **102** 44 40N 0 22W
Podgorica = Titograd **109** 42 30N 19 19E
Podkamennaya Tunguska **121** 61 50N 90 26E
Pofadder **117** 29 10S 19 22E
Pogamasing **53** 46 55N 81 50W
Pogranichnyy **130** 44 21N 131 23E
Poh **127** 0 46S 122 51E
Pohang **130** 36 1N 129 23E
Pohsien **131** 33 53N 115 48E
Poile, La **37** 47 41N 58 24W
Point Baker **67** 56 20N 133 35W
Point-du-Jour **45** 45 41N 72 59W
Point Edward **46** 43 0N 82 30W
Point Fortin **85** 10 9N 61 46W
Point Gatineau **40** 45 28N 75 42W
Point Hope **67** 68 20N 166 50W
Point L. **64** 65 15N 113 4W
Point Lay **67** 69 45N 163 10W
Point Leamington **37** 49 20N 55 24W
Point Pedro **124** 9 50N 80 15E
Point Pelee Nat. Park **46** 41 57N 82 31W
Point Pleasant, Can. **39** 44 37N 63 34W
Point Pleasant, U.S.A. **72** 38 50N 82 7W
Point Roberts **66** 48 59N 123 13W
Point Sapin **39** 46 58N 64 50W
Pointe-à-la-Frégate **38** 49 12N 64 55W
Pointe-à-la Hache **75** 29 35N 89 55W
Pointe-à-Maurier **38** 50 20N 59 48W
Pointe-à-Pitre **85** 16 10N 61 30W
Pointe au Baril Sta. **46** 45 35N 80 23W
Pointe-au-Pic **41** 47 38N 70 9W
Pointe-aux-Anglais **38** 49 41N 67 10W
Pointe-aux-Outardes **41** 49 3N 68 26W
Pointe-Aux-Trembles **43** 45 39N 73 30W
Pointe-aux-Trembles **45** 45 40N 73 30W
Pointe-Calumet **44** 45 30N 73 58W
Pointe-Cavagnal **44** 45 27N 74 4W
Pointe-Claire **44** 45 26N 73 50W
Pointe-des-Cascades **44** 45 20N 73 58W
Pointe du Bois **57** 50 18N 95 33W
Pointe-Fortune **43** 45 34N 74 23W
Pointe-Gatineau **48** 45 28N 75 42W
Pointe-Lebel **41** 49 10N 68 12W
Pointe-Noire **116** 4 48S 12 0E
Pointe-Parent **38** 50 8N 61 47W
Pointe Verte **39** 47 51N 65 46W
Poisson-Blanc, L. du **40** 46 0N 75 45W
Poissy **101** 48 55N 2 0E
Poitiers **100** 46 35N 0 20E
Poitou, Plaines du **102** 46 30N 0 1W
Poix **101** 49 47N 2 0E
Poix-Terron **101** 49 38N 4 38E
Pojoaque **79** 35 55N 106 0W
Pokaran **124** 27 0N 71 50E
Pokegama Res. **52** 47 12N 93 39W
Poko **116** 5 41N 31 55E
Pokotu **129** 48 47N 122 7E
Pokpak **131** 22 20N 109 45E
Pokrovsk **121** 61 29N 129 6E
Pola **129** 57 30N 32 0E
Polacca **79** 35 52N 110 25W
Polan **123** 25 30N 61 10E
Poland ■ **107** 52 0N 20 0E
Polar Bear Prov. Park **34** 54 30N 83 20W
Polcura **88** 37 10S 71 50W
Polden Hills **95** 51 7N 2 50W
Polewali, Sulawesi, Indon. **127** 4 8S 119 43E
Polewali, Sulawesi, Indon. **127** 3 21S 119 31E
Poli **129** 45 43N 130 28E
Poligny **101** 46 50N 5 42E
Polillo I. **127** 14 56N 122 0E
Polis **122** 35 3N 32 30E
Políyiros **109** 40 23N 23 25E
Polk **70** 41 22N 79 57W
Pollachi **124** 10 35N 77 0E
Pollock **74** 45 58N 100 18W
Polnovat **120** 63 50N 66 5E
Polo, Ill., U.S.A. **76** 42 0N 89 38W
Polo, Mo., U.S.A. **76** 39 33N 94 3W
Polotsk **120** 55 30N 28 50E
Polson **78** 47 45N 114 12W
Poltava **120** 49 35N 34 35E
Poltimore **40** 45 47N 75 43W
Polynesia **15** 10 0S 162 0W
Pomaro **82** 18 20N 103 18W
Pombal, Brazil **87** 6 55S 37 50W
Pombal, Port. **104** 39 55N 8 40W
Pomeroy, Ohio, U.S.A. **72** 39 0N 82 0W
Pomeroy, Wash., U.S.A. **78** 46 30N 117 33W
Pomme de Terre, Res. **76** 37 54N 93 19W
Pomona **81** 34 2N 117 49W
Pompano Beach **73** 26 12N 80 6W
Pompey **101** 48 50N 6 2E
Pompeys Pillar **78** 46 0N 108 0W
Ponape I. **14** 6 55N 158 10E
Ponask, L. **34** 54 0N 92 41W
Ponass L. **56** 52 16N 103 58W
Ponca **74** 42 38N 96 41W
Ponca City **75** 36 40N 97 5W
Ponce **85** 18 1N 66 37W
Ponchatoula **75** 30 27N 90 25W
Poncheville, L. **40** 50 10N 76 55W
Poncin **103** 46 6N 5 25E
Pond **81** 35 43N 119 20W
Pond Inlet **65** 72 30N 77 0W
Pondicherry **124** 11 59N 79 50E
Ponds, I. of **36** 53 27N 55 52W
Ponferrada **104** 42 32N 6 35W
Ponnani **124** 10 45N 75 59E
Ponnyadaung **125** 22 0N 94 10E
Ponoi, R. **120** 67 10N 39 0E
Ponoka **61** 52 42N 113 40W
Ponorogo **127** 7 52S 111 29E
Pons **102** 45 35N 0 34W
Ponsonby **49** 43 38N 80 22W
Pont-à-Mousson **101** 45 54N 6 1E
Pont Audemer **100** 49 21N 0 30E
Pont Aven **100** 47 51N 3 47W
Pont-Château **44** 45 20N 74 12W
Pont-de-Roide **101** 47 23N 6 45E
Pont-de-Salars **102** 44 18N 2 44E
Pont-de-Vaux **101** 46 26N 4 56E
Pont-de-Veyle **103** 46 17N 4 53E
Pont-l'Abbé **100** 47 52N 4 15W
Pont Lafrance **35** 47 40N 64 58W
Pont-l'Evêque **100** 49 18N 0 11E
Pont-Mousseau **43** 45 52N 73 39W
Pont-Rouge **41** 46 45N 71 42W
Pont-St.-Esprit **103** 44 16N 4 40E
Pont-sur-Yonne **101** 48 18N 3 10E
Pont-Viau **44** 45 34N 73 41W
Ponta Grossa **89** 25 0S 50 10W
Ponta Pora **89** 22 20S 55 35W
Pontacq **102** 43 11N 0 8W
Pontailler **101** 47 18N 5 24E
Pontarlier **101** 46 54N 6 20E
Pontaubault **100** 48 40N 1 20W
Pontaumur **102** 45 52N 2 40E
Pontcharra **103** 45 26N 6 1E
Pontchartrain, L. **75** 30 12N 90 0W
Pontchâteau **100** 47 25N 2 5W
Ponte Leccia **103** 42 28N 9 13E
Ponte Nova **89** 20 25S 42 54W
Pontedera **108** 43 40N 10 37E
Pontefract **94** 53 42N 1 19W
Ponteix **56** 49 46N 107 29W
Pontemacassar Naikliu **127** 9 30S 123 58E
Pontevedra **104** 42 26N 8 40W
Pontiac, Ill., U.S.A. **77** 40 50N 88 40W
Pontiac, Mich., U.S.A. **77** 42 40N 83 20W
Pontiac, Parc **40** 46 30N 76 30W
Pontian Kechil **128** 1 29N 103 23E

* *Renamed Isla de la Juventud*

Pontianak **Presidio**

Pontianak **126** 0 3 S 109 15 E
Pontine Mts. = Karadeniz D. **122** 41 30N 35 0 E
Pontivy **100** 48 5N 3 0W
Pontoise **101** 49 3N 2 5 E
Ponton, R. **54** 58 27N 116 11W
Pontorson **100** 48 34N 1 30W
Ponts-de Cé, Les **100** 47 25N 0 30W
Pontypool, Can. **47** 44 6N 78 38W
Pontypool, U.K. **95** 51 42N 3 1W
Pontypridd **95** 51 36N 3 21W
Ponziane, Isole **108** 40 55N 13 0 E
Poole **95** 50 42N 2 2W
Pooley I. **62** 52 45N 128 15W
Poona = Pune **124** 18 29N 73 57 E
Pooncarie **136** 33 22 S 142 31 E
Poopelloe, L. **136** 31 40 S 144 0 E
Poopó, Lago de **86** 18 30 S 67 35W
Poorman **67** 64 5N 155 48W
Popak **128** 22 15N 109 56 E
Popakai, Austral. **87** 32 12 S 141 46 E
Popakai, Surinam **87** 3 20N 55 30W
Popayán **86** 2 27N 76 36W
Poperinge **105** 50 51N 2 42 E
Popigay **121** 71 55N 110 47 E
Poplar, Mont., U.S.A. **74** 48 3N 105 9W
Poplar, Wis., U.S.A. **52** 46 35N 91 48W
Poplar Bluff **75** 36 45N 90 22W
Poplar Point **57** 50 4N 97 59W
Poplar, R., Man., Can. **57** 53 0N 97 19W
Poplar, R., N.W.T., Can. **54** 61 22N 121 52W
Poplarfield **57** 50 53N 97 36W
Poplarville **75** 30 55N 89 30W
Popocatepetl, vol. **83** 19 10N 98 40W
Popokabaka **116** 5 49 S 16 40 E
Porbandar **124** 21 44N 69 43 E
Porcher I. **62** 53 50N 130 30W
Porcupine **53** 48 30N 81 11W
Porcupine Plain **56** 52 36N 103 15W
Porcupine, R., Can. **55** 59 11N 104 46W
Porcupine, R., U.S.A. **67** 67 0N 143 0W
Pore **86** 5 43N 72 0W
Pori **111** 61 29N 21 48 E
Porjus **110** 66 57N 19 50 E
Porkkala **111** 59 59N 24 26 E
Porlamar **86** 10 57N 63 51W
Pornic **100** 47 7N 2 5W
Poronaysk **121** 49 20N 143 0 E
Porreta Pass **108** 44 0N 11 10 E
Porsangen **110** 70 40N 25 40 E
Port **101** 47 43N 6 4 E
Port Alberni **62** 49 40N 124 50W
Port Albert **136** 38 42 S 146 42 E
Port Albert Victor **124** 21 0N 71 30 E
Port Alexander **67** 56 13N 134 40W
Port Alfred, Can. **41** 48 18N 70 53W
Port Alfred, S. Afr. **117** 33 36 S 26 55 E
Port Alice **62** 50 20N 127 25W
Port Allegany **70** 41 49N 78 17W
Port Allen **75** 30 30N 91 15W
Port Angeles **80** 48 7N 123 30W
Port Antonio **84** 18 10N 76 30W
Port Aransas **75** 27 49N 97 4W
Port Arthur, Austral. **135** 43 7 S 147 50 E
Port Arthur, U.S.A. **75** 30 0N 94 0W
Port Arthur = Lüshun **130** 38 51N 121 20 E
Port Arthur = Thunder Bay **52** 48 25N 89 10W
Port au Choix **37** 50 43N 57 22W
Port au Port **37** 48 33N 58 43W
Port au Port B. **37** 48 40N 58 50W
Port-au-Prince **85** 18 40N 72 20W
Port Augusta **135** 32 30 S 137 50 E
Port Augusta West **135** 32 29 S 137 47 E
Port Austin **46** 44 3N 82 59W
Port Bergé Vaovao **117** 15 33 S 47 40 E
Port Blair **128** 11 40N 92 30 E
Port Blandford **37** 48 20N 54 10W
Port Bolivar **75** 29 20N 94 40W
Port Burwell **46** 42 40N 80 48W
Port Canning **125** 22 17N 88 48 E
Port Carling **46** 45 7N 79 35W
Port-Cartier **38** 50 2N 66 50W
Port-Cartier-Ouest **38** 50 1N 66 52W
Port Chalmers **133** 45 49 S 170 30 E
Port Chester **71** 41 0N 73 41W
Port Clements **62** 53 40N 132 10W
Port Clinton **77** 41 30N 83 0W
Port Colborne **46** 42 50N 79 10W
Port Coquitlam **66** 49 15N 122 45W
Port Credit **50** 43 33N 79 35W
Port Dalhousie **49** 43 13N 79 16W
Port-Daniel, Parc Prov. de **38** 48 11N 64 58W
Port Darwin **90** 51 50 S 59 0W
Port-de-Bouc **103** 43 24N 4 59 E
Port de Paix **85** 19 50N 72 50W
Port Dickson **128** 2 30N 101 49 E
Port Dover **46** 42 47N 80 12W
Port Dufferin **39** 44 55N 62 23W
Port Edward **62** 54 12N 130 10W
Port Elgin, N.B., Can. **39** 46 3N 64 5W
Port Elgin, Ont., Can. **34** 44 25N 81 25W
Port Elizabeth **117** 33 58 S 25 40 E
Port Erin **94** 54 5N 4 45W
Port Fairy **136** 38 22 S 142 12 E
Port Gamble **80** 47 51N 122 35W
Port-Gentil **116** 0 47 S 8 40 E
Port Gibson **75** 31 57N 91 0W
Port Glasgow **96** 55 57N 4 40W
Port Greville **39** 45 24N 64 33W
Port Guichon **66** 49 5N 123 7W
Port Hammond **66** 49 12N 122 39W
Port Harcourt **114** 4 40N 7 10 E
Port Hardy **62** 50 41N 127 30W
Port Hastings **39** 45 39N 61 24W
Port Hawkesbury **39** 45 36N 61 22W
Port Hedland **134** 20 25 S 118 35 E
Port Heiden **67** 57 0N 158 40W
Port Henry **71** 44 0N 73 30W
Port Hood **39** 46 0N 61 32W
Port Hope, Can. **47** 43 56N 78 20W
Port Hope, U.S.A. **46** 43 57N 82 43W
Port Howe **39** 45 51N 63 45W
Port Hueneme **81** 34 7N 119 12W
Port Huron **46** 43 0N 82 28W
Port Isabel **75** 26 12N 97 9W
Port Jackson **135** 33 50 S 151 18 E
Port Jefferson **71** 40 58N 73 5W
Port Jervis **71** 41 22N 74 42W
Port-Joinville **100** 46 45N 2 23W
Port Kaituma **86** 8 3N 59 58W
Port Kelang **128** 3 0N 101 23 E
Port Kells **66** 49 10N 122 42W
Port Kembla **136** 34 29 S 150 56 E
Port-la-Nouvelle **102** 43 1N 3 3 E
Port Laoise **97** 53 2N 7 20W
Port Lavaca **75** 28 38N 96 38W
Port Lewis **43** 45 10N 74 17W
Port Lincoln **134** 34 42 S 135 52 E
Port Loring **46** 45 55N 80 0W
Port Lorne **39** 44 57N 65 16W
Port Louis, France **100** 47 42N 3 22W
Port Louis, Maur. **16** 20 10 S 57 30 E
Port McNeill **62** 50 35N 127 5W
Port Macquarie **135** 31 25 S 152 54 E
Port Maitland **70** 42 53N 79 35W
Port Mann **66** 49 12N 122 49W
Port Maria **84** 18 25N 76 55W
Port Medway **39** 44 8N 64 35W
Port Mellon **63** 49 32N 123 31W
Port-Menier **38** 49 51N 64 15W
Port Moody **66** 49 17N 122 51W
Port Morant **84** 17 54N 76 19W
Port Moresby **14** 9 24 S 147 8 E
Port Mouton **39** 43 58N 64 50W
Port-Navalo **100** 47 34N 2 54W
Port Nelson, Man., Can. **55** 57 3N 92 36W
Port Nelson, Ont., Can. **48** 43 20N 79 46W
Port Nolloth **117** 29 17 S 16 52 E
* Port Nouveau-Quebec (George R.) **36** 58 30N 65 50W
Port O'Connor **75** 28 26N 96 24W
Port of Spain **85** 10 40N 61 20W
Port Orchard **80** 47 31N 122 38W
Port Oxford **78** 42 45N 124 28W
Port Pegasus **133** 47 12 S 167 41 E
Port Perry **47** 44 6N 78 56W
Port Phillip B. **136** 38 10 S 144 50 E
Port Pirie **135** 33 10 S 137 58 E
Port Pleasant **71** 40 5N 74 4W
Port Renfrew **62** 48 30N 124 20W
Port Robinson **49** 43 2N 79 13W
Port Rowan **46** 42 40N 80 30W
Port Royal **39** 44 43N 65 36W
Port Ryerse **70** 42 47N 80 15W
Port Said = Bûr Sa'îd **115** 31 16N 32 18 E
Port St. Joe **73** 29 49N 85 20W
Port-St.-Louis-du-Rhône **103** 43 23N 4 49 E
Port St. Servain **35** 51 21N 58 0W
Port Sanilac **46** 43 26N 82 33W
Port Saunders **37** 50 40N 57 18W
Port Severn **46** 44 48N 79 43W
Port Shepstone **117** 30 44 S 30 28 E
Port Simpson **54** 54 30N 130 20W
Port Stanley **46** 42 40N 81 10W
Port Stephens **136** 32 38 S 152 12 E
Port Talbot **95** 51 35N 3 48W
Port Townsend **80** 48 7N 122 50W
Port-Vendres **102** 42 32N 3 8 E
Port Wallace **39** 44 42N 63 33W
Port Washington **72** 43 25N 87 52W
Port Weld **128** 4 50N 100 38 E
Port Weller East **49** 43 14N 79 13W
Port Whitby **51** 43 51N 78 56W
Port Wing **52** 46 47N 91 23W
Portachuelo **86** 17 10 S 63 20W
Portadown (Craigavon) **97** 54 27N 6 26W
Portage, Can. **35** 46 40N 64 5W
Portage, U.S.A. **74** 43 31N 89 25W
Portage B. **57** 51 33N 98 50W
Portage L. **52** 47 3N 88 30W
Portage La Prairie **57** 49 58N 98 18W
Portage Mt. Dam **54** 56 0N 122 0W
Portage, R. **77** 41 32N 82 58W
Portageville **75** 36 25N 89 40W
Portalegre **104** 39 19N 7 25W
Portalegre □ **104** 39 20N 7 40W
Portales **75** 34 12N 103 25W
Portarlington **97** 53 10N 7 10W
Porte City, La **76** 42 19N 92 12W
Porte, La **77** 41 36N 86 43W
Porter **77** 41 36N 87 4W
Porter L., N.W.T., Can. **55** 61 41N 108 5W
Porter L., Sask., Can. **55** 56 20N 107 20W
Porterville **80** 36 5N 119 0W

** Renamed Kangiqsualujjuaq*

Portet **102** 43 34N 0 11W
Porthill **61** 49 0N 116 30W
Portile de Fier **107** 44 42N 22 30 E
Portimão **104** 37 8N 8 32W
Portland, N.S.W., Austral. **136** 33 20 S 150 0 E
Portland, Victoria, Austral. **136** 38 20 S 141 35 E
Portland, Can. **47** 44 42N 76 12W
Portland, Conn., U.S.A. **71** 41 34N 72 39W
Portland, Ind., U.S.A. **77** 40 26N 84 59W
Portland, Me., U.S.A. **35** 43 40N 70 15W
Portland, Mich., U.S.A. **77** 42 52N 84 58W
Portland, Oreg., U.S.A. **80** 45 35N 122 40W
Portland B. **136** 38 15 S 141 45 E
Portland Bill **95** 50 31N 2 27W
Portland, C. **135** 40 46 S 148 0 E
Portland Creek Pond **37** 50 11N 57 32W
Portland, I. of **95** 50 32N 2 25W
Portland Prom. **36** 58 40N 78 33W
Portneuf **42** 46 43N 71 55W
Portneuf, Parc Prov. de **41** 47 10N 72 25W
Portneuf, R. **41** 48 38N 69 5W
Pôrto **104** 41 8N 8 40W
Pôrto Alegre, Mato Grosso, Brazil **87** 21 40 S 53 30W
Pôrto Alegre, Rio Grande do Sul, Brazil **89** 30 5 S 51 3W
* Porto Alexandre **117** 15 55 S 11 55 E
Pôrto de Moz **87** 1 41 S 52 22W
Porto Empédocle **108** 37 18N 13 30 E
Pôrto Esperança **86** 19 37 S 57 29W
Pôrto Franco **87** 6 20 S 47 24W
Porto, G. de **103** 42 17N 8 34 E
Porto Mendes **89** 24 30 S 54 15W
Pôrto Murtinho **86** 21 45 S 57 55W
Pôrto Nacional **87** 10 40 S 48 30W
Porto Novo **114** 6 23N 2 42 E
Pôrto São José **89** 22 43 S 53 10W
Pôrto Seguro **87** 16 26 S 39 5W
Porto Tórres **108** 40 50N 8 23 E
Pôrto União **89** 26 10 S 51 10W
Pôrto Válter **86** 8 5 S 72 40W
Porto-Vecchio **103** 41 35N 9 16 E
Pôrto Velho **86** 8 46 S 63 54W
Portobelo **84** 9 35N 79 42W
Portoferráio **108** 42 50N 10 20 E
Portola **80** 39 49N 120 28W
Portoscuso **108** 39 12N 8 22 E
Portoviejo **86** 1 0 S 80 20W
Portpatrick **96** 54 50N 5 7W
Portree **96** 57 25N 6 11W
Portrush **97** 55 13N 6 40W
Portsall **100** 48 37N 4 45W
Portsmouth, Can. **71** 44 14N 76 34W
Portsmouth, Domin. **85** 15 34N 61 27W
Portsmouth, U.K. **95** 50 48N 1 6W
Portsmouth, N.H., U.S.A. **71** 43 5N 70 45W
Portsmouth, Ohio, U.S.A. **72** 38 45N 83 0W
Portsmouth, R.I., U.S.A. **71** 41 35N 71 44W
Portsmouth, Va., U.S.A. **72** 36 50N 76 20W
Porttipahta **110** 68 5N 26 30 E
Portugal ■ **104** 40 0N 7 0W
Portuguesa □ **86** 9 10N 69 15W
Portuguese Timor = Timor **127** 8 0 S 126 30 E
Portumna **97** 53 5N 8 12W
Portville **70** 42 3N 78 21W
Porvenir **90** 53 10 S 70 30W
Porvoo **111** 60 24N 25 40 E
Posadas **89** 27 30 S 56 0W
Poseh **131** 23 50N 106 0 E
Posen **46** 45 16N 83 42W
Poseyville **77** 38 10N 87 47W
Poso **127** 1 20 S 120 55 E
Poso Colorado **88** 23 30 S 58 45W
Poso, D. **127** 1 20 S 120 55 E
Posse **87** 14 4 S 46 18W
Possel **116** 5 5N 19 10 E
Possession I. **91** 72 4 S 172 0 E
Post **75** 33 13N 101 21W
Post Falls **78** 47 50N 116 59W
† Poste de la Baleine **36** 55 17N 77 45W
Postiljon, Kepulauan **127** 6 30 S 118 50 E
Postojna **107** 45 46N 14 12 E
Poston **81** 34 0N 114 24W
Postville **76** 43 5N 91 34W
Potchefstroom **117** 26 41 S 27 7 E
Poteau **75** 35 5N 94 37W
Poteet **75** 29 4N 98 35W
Potenza **108** 40 40N 15 50 E
Poteriteri, L. **133** 46 5 S 167 10 E
Potgietersrus **117** 24 10 S 29 3 E
Potomac, R. **72** 38 0N 76 23W
Potosí **86** 19 38 S 65 50W
Potosi **76** 37 56N 90 47W
Potosí □ **86** 20 31 S 67 0W
Potosi Mt. **81** 35 57N 115 29W
Potow **130** 38 8N 116 31 E
Potrerillos **88** 26 20 S 69 30W
Potros, Cerro del **88** 28 32 S 69 0W
Potsdam, Ger. **106** 52 23N 13 4 E
Potsdam, U.S.A. **71** 44 40N 74 59W
Pottageville **50** 43 59N 79 37W
Potter **74** 41 15N 103 20W
Pottstown **71** 40 17N 75 40W

** Renamed Tombua*
† Renamed Kuujjuarapik

Pottsville **71** 40 39N 76 12W
Pottuvil **124** 6 55N 81 50 E
Pouancé **100** 47 44N 1 10W
Pouce Coupé **54** 55 40N 120 10W
Pouch Cove **37** 47 46N 52 46W
Poughkeepsie **71** 41 40N 73 57W
Pouilly **101** 47 18N 2 57 E
Poulaphouca Res. **97** 53 8N 6 30W
Pouldu, Le **100** 47 41N 3 36W
Poulin-de-Courval, L. **41** 48 52N 70 27W
Poulsbo **80** 47 45N 122 39W
Pouso Alegre, Mato Grosso, Brazil **87** 11 55 S 57 0W
Pouso Alegre, Minas Gerais, Brazil **89** 22 14 S 45 57W
Poutrincourt, L. **41** 49 11N 74 7W
Pouzages **102** 46 40N 0 50W
Povenets **120** 62 50N 34 50 E
Poverty Bay **133** 38 43 S 178 2 E
Póvoa de Varzim **104** 41 25N 8 46W
Povungnituk **36** 60 2N 77 10W
Povungnituk, B. **36** 60 0N 77 30W
Povungnituk, Mts. de **36** 61 22N 75 5W
Povungnituk, R. **36** 60 3N 77 15W
Powassan **46** 46 5N 79 25W
Poway **81** 32 58N 117 2W
Powder, R. **74** 46 47N 105 12W
Powell **78** 44 45N 108 45W
Powell Creek **134** 18 6 S 133 46 E
Powell L. **62** 50 2N 124 25W
Powell River **62** 49 50N 124 35W
Powers, Mich., U.S.A. **72** 45 40N 87 32W
Powers, Oreg., U.S.A. **78** 42 53N 124 2W
Powers Lake **74** 48 37N 102 38W
Powis, Vale of **98** 52 40N 3 10W
Powys □ **95** 52 20N 3 20W
Poyang **131** 28 59N 116 40 E
Poyang Hu **131** 29 10N 116 10 E
Poyarkovo **121** 49 36N 128 41 E
Poza Rica **83** 20 33N 97 27W
Požarevac **109** 44 35N 21 18 E
Poznan **106** 52 25N 17 0 E
Pozo **81** 35 20N 120 24W
Pozo Almonte **86** 20 10 S 69 50W
Pozoblanco **104** 38 23N 4 51W
Prachin Buri **128** 14 0N 101 25 E
Prachuap Khiri Khan **128** 11 49N 99 48 E
Pradelles **102** 44 46N 3 52 E
Pradera **86** 3 25N 76 15W
Prades **102** 42 38N 2 23 E
Prado **87** 17 20 S 39 13W
Prague = Praha **106** 50 5N 14 22 E
Praha **106** 50 5N 14 22 E
Prahecq **102** 46 19N 0 26W
Praid **107** 46 32N 25 10 E
Prainha, Amazonas, Brazil **86** 7 10 S 60 30W
Prainha, Pará, Brazil **87** 1 45 S 53 30W
Prairie City **78** 44 27N 118 44W
Prairie du Chien **76** 43 1N 91 9W
Prairie du Rocher **76** 38 5N 90 6W
Prairie, La **45** 45 25N 73 30W
Prairie, R. **75** 34 45N 101 15W
Prairies, R. des **44** 45 42N 73 29W
Praja **126** 8 39 S 116 27 E
Prapat **126** 2 41N 98 58 E
Prata, Minas Gerais, Brazil **87** 19 25 S 49 0W
Prata, Pará, Brazil **87** 1 10 S 47 35W
Prato **108** 43 53N 11 5 E
Prats-de-Mollo **102** 42 25N 2 27 E
Pratt **75** 37 40N 98 45W
Prattville **73** 32 30N 86 28W
Pravia **104** 43 30N 6 12W
Pré-en-Pail **100** 48 28N 0 12W
Precordillera **88** 30 0 S 69 1W
Preeceville **56** 51 57N 102 40W
Préfailles **100** 47 9N 2 11W
Pregonero **86** 8 1N 71 46W
Preissac, L. **40** 48 20N 78 20W
Prelate **56** 50 51N 109 24W
Premier **54** 56 4N 129 56W
Premier Downs **134** 30 30 S 126 30 E
Premont **75** 27 19N 98 8W
Prentice **74** 45 31N 90 19W
Prenzlau **106** 53 19N 13 51 E
Prepansko Jezero **109** 40 45N 21 0 E
Preparis North Channel **128** 15 12N 93 40 E
Preparis South Channel **128** 14 36N 93 40 E
Prerov **107** 49 28N 17 27 E
Prescott, Can. **47** 44 45N 75 30W
Prescott, Ariz., U.S.A. **79** 34 35N 112 30W
Prescott, Ark., U.S.A. **75** 33 49N 93 22W
Prescott □ **43** 45 32N 74 30W
Prescott I. **62** 54 6N 130 37W
Présentation, La **45** 45 39N 73 3W
Preservation Inlet **133** 46 8 S 166 35 E
Presho **74** 43 56N 100 4W
Presidencia de la Plaza **88** 27 0 S 60 0W
Presidencia Roque Sáenz Peña **88** 26 45 S 60 30W
Presidente Dutra **82** 5 15 S 44 30W
Presidente Hayes □ **88** 24 0 S 59 0W
Presidente Hermes **86** 11 0 S 61 55W
Presidente Prudente **89** 22 5 S 51 25W
Presidente Rogue Saena Peña **88** 34 33 S 58 30W
Presidio, Mexico **82** 29 29N 104 23W
Presidio, U.S.A. **75** 29 30N 104 20W

Presque Isle

Quilán, C

Presque Isle 35 46 40N 68 0W
Presteigne 95 52 17N 3 0W
Preston, Can. 49 43 23N 80 21W
Preston, U.K. 94 53 46N 2 42W
Preston, U.S.A. 76 42 6N 90 24W
Preston, Idaho, U.S.A. 78 42 10N 111 55W
Preston, Minn., U.S.A. 74 43 39N 92 3W
Preston, Nev., U.S.A. 78 38 59N 115 2W
Preston, C. 134 20 51S 116 12E
Prestonpans 96 55 58N 3 0W
Prestwick 96 55 30N 4 38W
Pretoria 117 25 44S 28 12E
Preuilly-sur-Claise 100 46 51N 0 56E
Préveza 109 38 57N 20 47E
Préville 45 45 29N 73 30W
Prevost 43 45 52N 74 5W
Prey-Veng 128 11 35N 105 29E
Pribilov Is. 17 56 0N 170 0W
Pribram 106 49 41N 14 2E
Price, Can. 38 48 36N 68 7W
Price, U.S.A. 78 39 40N 110 48W
Price I. 62 52 23N 128 41W
Prieska 117 29 40S 22 42E
Priest L. 63 48 30N 116 55W
Priest River 78 48 11N 116 55W
Priest Valley 80 36 10N 120 39W
Priestly 54 54 8N 125 20W
Prilep 109 41 21N 21 37E
Primrose L. 55 54 55N 109 45W
Prince 56 52 58N 108 23W
Prince Albert 56 53 15N 105 50W
Prince Albert Nat. Park 56 54 0N 106 25W
Prince Albert Pen. 64 72 30N 116 0W
Prince Albert Sd. 64 70 25N 115 0W
Prince Alfred C. 64 74 20N 124 40W
Prince Charles I. 64 67 47N 76 12W
Prince Edward I. □. 39 46 30N 63 30W
Prince Edward Is. 16 45 15S 39 0E
Prince Edward Island Nat. Pk. 39 46 26N 63 12W
Prince Edward Pt. 47 43 56N 76 52W
Prince George 63 53 55N 122 50W
Prince Gustav Adolf Sea 64 78 30N 107 0W
Prince of Wales, C. 67 65 50N 168 0W
Prince of Wales I. 67 73 0N 99 0W
Prince of Wales, I. 67 53 30N 131 30W
Prince of Wales Is. 135 10 40S 142 10E
Prince of Wales Str. 64 73 0N 117 0W
Prince Patrick I. 64 77 0N 120 0W
Prince Regent Inlet 65 73 0N 90 0W
Prince Rupert 62 54 20N 130 20W
Prince William Sd. 67 60 20N 146 30W
Princess Charlotte B. 135 14 25S 144 0E
Princess Margaret Range 65 80 30N 92 0W
Princess Royal Chan. 62 53 0N 128 31W
Princess Royal I. 62 53 0N 128 40W
Princeton, B.C., Can. 63 49 27N 120 30W
Princeton, Ont., Can. 49 43 10N 80 32W
Princeton, Calif., U.S.A. 80 39 24N 122 1W
Princeton, Ill., U.S.A. 76 41 23N 89 28W
Princeton, Ill., U.S.A. 76 41 25N 89 25W
Princeton, Ind., U.S.A. 77 38 20N 87 35W
Princeton, Ky., U.S.A. 72 37 6N 87 55W
Princeton, Mo., U.S.A. 76 40 23N 93 35W
Princeton, N.J., U.S.A. 71 40 18N 74 40W
Princeton, W. Va., U.S.A. 72 37 21N 81 8W
Princeville, Can. 41 46 10N 71 53W
Princeville, U.S.A. 76 40 56N 89 46W
Principe Chan. 62 53 28N 130 0W
Principe da Beira 86 12 20S 64 30W
Principe, I. de 112 1 37N 7 27E
Prineville 78 44 17N 120 57W
Prins Harald Kyst 91 70 0S 35 1E
Prinzapolca 84 13 20N 83 35W
Pripet, R. = Pripyat, R. 120 51 30N 30 0E
Pripyat, R. 120 51 30N 30 0E
Priština 109 42 40N 21 13E
Pritchard 73 30 47N 88 5W
Privas 103 44 45N 4 37E
Prizren 109 42 13N 20 45E
Probolinggo 127 7 46S 113 13E
Procter 63 49 37N 116 57W
Proddatur 124 14 45N 78 30E
Progreso 83 21 20N 89 40W
Prokopyevsk 120 54 0N 87 3E
Prome = Pyè 125 18 45N 95 30E
Prophet, R. 54 58 48N 122 40W
Prophetstown 76 41 40N 89 56W
Propriá 87 10 13S 36 51W
Propriano 103 41 41N 8 52E
Proserpine 135 20 21S 148 36E
Prosser 78 46 11N 119 52W
Prostějov 106 49 30N 17 9E
Protection 75 37 16N 99 30W
Prøven 65 72 10N 55 8W
Provence 103 43 40N 5 46E
Providence, Ky., U.S.A. 72 37 25N 87 46W
Providence, R.I., U.S.A. 71 41 41N 71 15W
Providence Bay 46 45 41N 82 15W
Providence, La 45 45 37N 72 57W
Providence Mts. 79 35 0N 115 30W
Providencia 86 0 28S 76 28W
Providencia, I. de 84 13 25N 81 26W
Provideniya 121 64 23N 173 18E
Province Wellesley 128 5 15N 100 20E
Provincetown 72 42 5N 70 11W
Provins 101 48 33N 3 15E
Provo 78 40 16N 111 37W
Provost 61 52 25N 110 20W
Prudhoe Bay 67 70 20N 148 20W
Prudhoe Land 17 78 1N 65 0W
Prud'homme 56 52 20N 105 54W
Pruszków 107 52 9N 20 49E
Prut, R. 107 46 3N 28 10E
Prydz B. 91 69 0S 74 0E
Pryor 75 36 17N 95 20W
Przemyśl 107 49 50N 22 45E
Przeworsk 107 50 6N 22 32E
Przhevalsk 120 42 30N 78 20E
Pskov 120 57 50N 28 25E
Puán 88 37 30S 63 0W
Pubnico 35 43 47N 65 50W
Pucallpa 86 8 25S 74 30W
Pucheng 131 28 0N 118 30E
Puchi 131 29 42N 113 54E
Pudukkottai 124 10 28N 78 47E
Puebla 83 19 0N 98 10W
Puebla □ 83 18 30N 98 0W
Pueblo 74 38 20N 104 40W
Pueblo Bonito 79 36 4N 107 57W
Pueblo Hundido 88 26 20S 69 30W
Pueblo Nuevo 86 8 26N 71 26W
Pueblonuevo 104 38 16N 5 16W
Puelches 88 38 5S 66 0W
Puelén 88 37 32S 67 38W
Puente Alto 88 33 32S 70 35W
Puente Genil 104 37 22N 4 47W
Puerco, R. 79 35 10N 109 45W
Puerh 129 23 11N 100 56E
Puerto Aisén 90 45 10S 73 0W
Puerto Angel 83 15 40N 96 29W
Puerto Arista 83 15 56N 93 48W
Puerto Armuelles 84 8 20N 83 10W
Puerto Ayacucho 86 5 40N 67 35W
Puerto Barrios 84 15 40N 88 40W
Puerto Belgrano 131 38 50S 62 0W
Puerto Bermejo 88 26 55S 58 34W
Puerto Bermúdez 86 10 20S 75 0W
Puerto Bolívar 86 3 10S 79 55W
Puerto Cabello 86 10 28N 68 1W
Puerto Cabezas 84 14 0N 83 30W
Puerto Cabo Gracias a Dios 84 15 0N 83 10W
Puerto Carreño 86 6 12N 67 22W
Puerto Casado 88 22 19S 57 56W
Puerto Castilla 84 16 0N 86 0W
Puerto Chicama 86 7 45S 79 20W
Puerto Coig 90 50 54S 69 15W
Puerto Columbia 86 10 59N 74 58W
Puerto Cortés, C. Rica 84 8 20N 82 20W
Puerto Cortés, Hond. 84 15 51N 88 0W
Puerto Cuemani 86 0 5N 73 21W
Puerto Cumarebo 86 11 29N 69 21W
Puerto de Morelos 83 20 49N 86 52W
Puerto de Santa María 104 36 36N 6 13W
Puerto Deseado 90 47 45S 66 0W
Puerto Heath 86 12 25S 68 45W
Puerto Huitoto 86 0 18N 74 3W
Puerto Juárez 83 21 11N 86 49W
Puerto La Cruz 86 10 13N 64 38W
Puerto Leguizamo 86 0 12S 74 46W
Puerto Libertad 82 29 55N 112 41W
Puerto Limón, Meta, Colomb. 86 3 23N 73 30W
Puerto Limón, Putumayo, Colomb. 86 1 3N 76 30W
Puerto Lobos 90 42 0S 65 3W
Puerto López 86 4 5N 72 58W
Puerto Madryn 90 42 48S 65 4W
Puerto Maldonado 86 12 30S 69 10W
Puerto Manotí 84 21 22N 76 50W
Puerto Mercedes 86 1 11N 72 53W
Puerto Montt 90 41 22S 72 40W
Puerto Natales 90 51 45S 72 25W
Puerto Nuevo 86 5 53N 69 56W
Puerto Ordaz 86 8 16N 62 44W
Puerto Padre 84 21 13N 76 35W
Puerto Páez 86 6 13N 67 28W
Puerto Peñasco 82 31 20N 113 33W
Puerto Pinasco 88 22 43S 57 50W
Puerto Pirámides 90 42 35S 64 20W
Puerto Plata 85 19 40N 70 45W
Puerto Quellón 90 43 7S 73 37W
Puerto Quepos 84 9 29N 84 6W
Puerto Rico 86 1 54N 75 10W
Puerto Rico ■ 85 18 15N 66 45W
Puerto Rico Trough 12 20 0N 63 0W
Puerto Sastre 88 22 25S 57 55W
Puerto Suárez 86 18 58S 57 52W
Puerto Tejada 86 3 14N 76 24W
Puerto Umbria 86 0 52N 76 33W
Puerto Vallarta 82 20 26N 105 15W
Puerto Villamizar 86 8 25N 72 30W
Puerto Wilches 86 7 21N 73 54W
Puertollano 104 38 43N 4 7W
Pueyrredón, L. 90 47 20S 72 0W
Pugachev 120 52 0N 48 55E
Puget Sd. 78 47 15N 122 30W
Puget-Théniers 103 43 58N 6 53E
Púglia □ 108 41 0N 16 30E
Pugwash 39 45 51N 63 40W
Puhute Mesa 80 37 25N 116 50W
Puigcerdá 104 42 24N 1 50E
Puisaye, Collines de 101 47 34N 3 28E
Puiseaux 101 48 11N 2 30E
Pukaki L. 133 44 4S 170 1E
Pukaskwa Nat. Park 53 48 20N 86 0W
Pukatawagan 55 55 45N 101 20W
Pukekohe 133 37 12S 174 55E
Pukoo 67 21 4N 156 48W
Pukow 131 32 15N 118 45E
Pula 108 39 0N 9 0E
Pulantien 130 39 25N 122 0E
Pulaski, N.Y., U.S.A. 71 43 32N 76 9W
Pulaski, Tenn., U.S.A. 73 35 10N 87 0W
Pulaski, Va., U.S.A. 72 37 4N 80 49W
Pulga 80 39 48N 121 29W
Pulicat, L. 124 13 40N 80 15E
Pullman 78 46 49N 117 10W
Pulog, Mt. 127 16 40N 120 50E
Puloraja 126 4 55N 95 24E
Pumlumon Fawr 95 52 29N 3 47W
Puna 86 19 45S 65 28W
Puna de Atacama 88 25 0S 67 0W
Puná, I. 86 2 55S 80 5W
Punakha 125 27 42N 89 52E
Punata 86 17 25S 65 50W
Punch 124 33 48N 74 4E
Pune 124 18 29N 73 57E
Punjab □ 124 31 0N 76 0E
Punnichy 56 51 23N 104 18W
Puno 86 15 55S 70 3W
Punta Alta 90 38 53S 62 4W
Punta Arenas 90 53 0S 71 0W
Punta de Diaz 88 28 0S 70 45W
Punta de Piedras 86 10 54N 64 6W
Punta del Lago Viedma 90 49 45S 72 0W
Punta Gorda, Belize 83 16 10N 88 45W
Punta Gorda, U.S.A. 73 26 55N 82 0W
Punta Prieta 82 28 58N 114 17W
Puntarenas 84 10 0N 84 50W
Punto Fijo 86 11 42N 70 13W
Puntzi L. 62 52 12N 124 2W
Punxsutawney 70 40 56N 79 0W
Punyu 131 22 58N 113 16E
Puquio 86 14 45S 74 10W
Pur, R. 120 65 30N 77 40E
Purace, vol. 86 2 21N 76 23W
Purbeck, Isle of 95 50 40N 2 5W
Purcell 75 35 0N 97 25W
Puri 125 19 50N 85 58E
Purificación 86 3 51N 74 55W
Purísima, La 82 26 10N 112 4W
Purmerend 105 52 30N 4 58E
Purnea 125 25 45N 87 31E
Pursat 128 12 34N 103 50E
Puruey 86 7 35N 64 48W
Purukcahu 126 0 35S 114 35E
Purulia 125 23 17N 86 33E
Purus, R. 86 5 25S 64 0W
Purwakarta 127 6 35S 107 29E
Purwodadi, Jawa, Indon. 127 7 51S 110 0E
Purwodadi, Jawa, Indon. 127 7 7S 110 55E
Purworejo 127 7 43S 110 2E
Pusan 130 35 5N 129 0E
Pushchino 121 54 20N 158 10E
Puskitamika L. 34 49 20N 76 30W
Puslinch 49 43 26N 80 5W
Puslinch, L. 49 43 25N 80 16W
Putahow L. 55 59 54N 100 40W
Putao 125 27 28N 97 30E
Putaruru 133 38 2S 175 50E
Putehachi (Chalantun) 129 48 4N 122 45E
Puthein Myit, R. 125 15 56N 94 18E
Putien 131 25 28N 119 0E
Putignano 108 40 50N 17 5E
Putnam 71 41 55N 71 55W
Putorana, Gory 121 69 0N 95 0E
Puttalam 124 8 1N 79 55E
Putten 105 52 16N 5 36E
Puttgarden 106 54 28N 11 15E
Putumayo □ 86 1 30S 70 0W
Putumayo, R. 86 1 30S 70 0W
Putussibau, G. 126 0 45N 113 50E
Puy-de-Dôme 102 45 46N 2 57E
Puy-de-Dôme □ 102 45 47N 3 0E
Puy-de-Sancy 102 45 32N 2 41E
Puy Guillaume 102 45 57N 3 28E
Puy, Le 102 45 3N 3 52E
Puy l'Évêque 102 44 31N 1 9E
Puyallup 80 47 10N 122 22W
Puyang 130 35 45N 115 22E
Puyjalon, L. 38 50 30N 63 25W
Puylaurens 102 43 35N 2 0E
Puyôo 102 43 33N 0 56W
Pweto 116 8 25S 28 51E
Pwllheli 94 52 54N 4 26W
Pyapon 125 16 5N 95 50E
Pyasina, R. 121 72 30N 90 30E
Pyatigorsk 120 44 2N 43 0E
Pyinmana 125 19 45N 96 20E
Pyŏngyang 130 39 0N 125 30E
Pyote 75 31 34N 103 5W
Pyramid L. 78 40 0N 119 30W
Pyramid Pk. 81 36 25N 116 37W
Pyrénées 102 42 45N 0 18E
Pyrenees = Pyrénées 102 42 45N 0 18E
Pyrénées-Atlantiques □ 102 43 15N 1 0W
Pyrénées-Orientales □ 102 42 35N 2 26E
Pyu 125 18 30N 96 35E

Q

Qadam 123 32 55N 66 45E
Qadhimah 122 22 20N 39 13E
Qala-i-Kirta 123 32 15N 63 0E
Qala Nau 123 35 0N 63 5E
Qala Punja 123 37 0N 72 40E
Qal'at al Akhdar 122 28 0N 37 10E
Qal'eh Shaharak 124 34 10N 64 20E
Qamruddin Karez 124 31 45N 68 20E
Qarachuk 122 37 0N 42 2E
Qarah 122 29 55N 40 3E
Qasr-e-Qand 123 26 15N 60 45E
Qatar ■ 123 25 30N 51 15E
Qattara Depression = Q. Munkhafed el 115 29 30N 27 30E
Qattâra, Munkhafed el 115 29 30N 27 30E
Qāyen 123 33 40N 59 10E
Qazvin 122 36 15N 50 0E
Qeisari, (Caesarea) 115 32 30N 34 53E
Qena 115 26 10N 32 43E
Qesari 115 32 30N 34 53E
Qeshm 123 26 55N 56 10E
Qeshm, I. 123 26 50N 56 0E
Qila Saifulla 124 30 45N 68 17E
Qom 123 34 40N 51 0E
Quadra I. 62 50 10N 125 15W
Quakerstown 71 40 27N 75 20W
Qualicum Beach 62 49 22N 124 26W
Quan Long 128 9 7N 105 8E
Quanan 75 34 20N 99 45W
Quang Nam 128 15 55N 108 15E
Quang Ngai 128 15 13N 108 58E
Quang Yen 128 21 3N 106 52E
Quantock Hills, The 95 51 8N 3 10W
Qu'Appelle 56 50 33N 103 53W
Qu'Appelle, R. 56 50 26N 101 19W
Quaraí 88 30 15S 56 20W
Quarré les Tombes 101 47 21N 4 0E
Quarryville 39 46 50N 65 47W
Quartzsite 81 33 44N 114 16W
Quathiaski Cove 62 50 3N 125 12W
Quatsino 62 50 30N 127 40W
Quatsino Sd. 62 50 25N 127 58W
Qūchān 123 37 10N 58 27E
* Que Que 117 18 58S 29 48E
Queanbeyan 136 35 17S 149 14E
Québec 42 46 52N 71 13W
Québec □ 35 50 0N 70 0W
Queen Alexandra Ra. 91 85 0S 170 0E
Queen Bess Mt. 54 51 13N 124 35W
Queen Charlotte 62 53 15N 132 2W
Queen Charlotte Is. 62 53 20N 132 10W
Queen Charlotte Mts. 62 53 5N 132 15W
Queen Charlotte Sd. 62 51 30N 130 0W
Queen Charlotte Str. 62 51 0N 128 0W
Queen City 76 40 25N 92 34W
Queen Elizabeth Is. 10 76 0N 95 0W
Queen Mary Coast 91 70 0S 95 0E
Queen Maud G. 64 68 15N 102 30W
Queen's Chan. 134 15 0S 129 30E
Queens Sd. 62 51 57N 128 20W
Queensborough 66 49 12N 122 56W
Queenscliff 136 38 16S 144 39E
Queensland □ 135 15 0S 142 0E
Queenston 49 43 10N 79 3W
Queenstown, Austral. 135 42 4S 145 35E
Queenstown, Can. 39 45 41N 66 7W
Queenstown, N.Z. 133 45 1S 168 40E
Queenstown, S. Afr. 117 31 52S 26 52E
Queets 80 47 32N 124 20W
Queguay Grande, R. 88 32 9S 58 9W
Queimadas 87 11 0S 39 38W
Quela 116 9 10S 16 56E
Quelimane 117 17 53S 36 58E
Quelpart = Cheju Do 131 33 29N 126 34E
Quemado, N. Mex., U.S.A. 79 34 17N 108 28W
Quemado, Tex., U.S.A. 75 28 58N 100 35W
Quemoy = Kinmen 131 24 25N 118 24E
Quemú-Quemú 88 36 3S 63 36W
Quequén 88 38 30S 58 30W
Querétaro 82 20 40N 100 23W
Querétaro □ 82 20 30N 100 30W
Quesnel 63 53 0N 122 30W
Quesnel L. 63 52 30N 121 20W
Quesnel, R. 63 52 58N 122 29W
Questa 79 36 45N 105 35W
Questembert 100 47 40N 2 28W
Quetico 34 48 45N 90 55W
Quetico Prov. Park 52 48 30N 91 45W
Quetta 124 30 15N 66 55E
** Quetta □ 124 30 15N 66 55E
Quévillon, L. 40 49 4N 76 57W
Quezaltenango 84 14 40N 91 30W
Quezon City 127 14 38N 121 0E
Qui Nhon 128 13 40N 109 13E
Quiaca, La 88 22 5S 65 35W
Quibaxi 116 8 24S 14 27E
Quibdó 86 5 42N 76 40W
Quiberon 100 47 29N 3 9W
Quíbor 86 9 56N 69 37W
Quick 54 54 36N 126 54W
Quidi Vidi 37 47 35N 52 41W
Quiet L. 54 61 5N 133 5W
Quiindy 88 25 58S 14 5W
Quila 82 24 23N 107 13W
Quilán, C. 90 43 15S 74 30W

* Renamed Kwekwe
** Now part of Baluchistan

Quilcene Reefton

Name	Map	Lat.	Long.
Quilcene	**80**	47 49N	122 53W
Quilchena	**63**	50 10N	120 30W
Quilengues	**117**	14 12S	14 12E
Quilimarí	**88**	32 5S	70 30W
Quilino	**88**	30 14S	64 29W
Quill Lake	**56**	52 4N	104 15W
Quillabamba	**86**	12 50S	72 50W
Quillagua	**88**	21 40S	69 40W
Quillaicillo	**88**	31 17S	71 40W
Quillan	**102**	42 53N	2 10E
Quillebeuf	**100**	49 28N	0 30E
Quillota	**88**	32 54S	71 16W
Quilmes	**88**	34 43S	58 15W
Quilon	**124**	8 50N	76 38E
Quilpie	**135**	26 35S	144 11E
Quilpué	**88**	33 5S	71 33W
Quimili	**88**	27 40S	62 30W
Quimper	**100**	48 0N	4 9W
Quimperlé	**100**	47 53N	3 33W
Quinault, R.	**80**	47 23N	124 18W
Quincy, Calif., U.S.A.	**80**	39 56N	121 0W
Quincy, Fla., U.S.A.	**73**	30 34N	84 34W
Quincy, Ill., U.S.A.	**74**	39 55N	91 20W
Quincy, Mass., U.S.A.	**72**	42 14N	71 0W
Quincy, Wash., U.S.A.	**78**	47 22N	119 56W
Quines	**88**	32 13S	65 48W
Quinga	**117**	15 49S	40 15E
Quingey	**101**	47 7N	5 52E
Quinhagak	**67**	59 45N	162 0W
Quintana Roo □	**83**	19 0N	88 0W
Quintanar de la Orden	**104**	39 36N	3 5W
Quintanar de la Sierra	**104**	41 57N	2 55W
Quintero	**88**	32 45S	71 30W
Quintin	**100**	48 26N	2 56W
Quinton	**56**	51 23N	104 24W
Quinze, L. des	**40**	47 35N	79 5W
Quirihue	**88**	36 15S	72 35W
Quiriquire	**86**	9 59N	63 13W
Quisiro	**86**	10 53N	71 17W
Quissac	**103**	43 55N	4 0E
Quissanga	**117**	12 24S	40 28E
Quitilipi	**88**	26 50S	60 13W
Quitman, Ga., U.S.A.	**73**	30 49N	83 35W
Quitman, Miss., U.S.A.	**73**	32 2N	88 42W
Quitman, Tex., U.S.A.	**75**	32 48N	95 25W
Quito	**86**	0 15S	78 35W
Quixadá	**87**	4 55S	39 0W
Quneitra	**115**	33 7N	35 48E
Quorn, Austral.	**135**	32 25S	138 0E
Quorn, Can.	**34**	49 25N	90 55W
Quruq Tagh, mts.	**129**	41 30N	90 0E
Quseir	**115**	26 7N	34 16E
Quyon	**40**	45 31N	76 14W

R

Name	Map	Lat.	Long.
Raahe	**110**	64 40N	24 28E
Raanes Pen.	**65**	78 30N	85 45W
Raasay I.	**96**	57 25N	6 4W
Raasay, Sd. of	**96**	57 30N	6 8W
Raba	**127**	8 36S	118 55E
Rabastens, Hautes Pyrénées, France	**102**	43 25N	0 10E
Rabastens, Tarn, France	**102**	43 50N	1 43E
Rabat, Malta	**108**	35 53N	14 25E
Rabat, Moroc.	**114**	34 2N	6 48W
Rabaul	**14**	4 24S	152 18E
Rabbit L.	**55**	47 0N	79 38W
Rabbit Lake	**56**	53 8N	107 46W
Rabbit, R.	**54**	59 41N	127 12W
Rabbitskin, R.	**54**	61 47N	120 42W
Rabigh	**122**	22 50N	39 5E
Raccoon Cr.	**77**	39 47N	87 23W
Raccoon, R.	**76**	41 35N	93 37W
Race, C.	**37**	46 40N	53 5W
Rach Gia	**128**	10 5N	105 5E
Rachaya	**115**	33 30N	35 50E
Racine	**77**	42 41N	87 51W
Racine L.	**53**	48 2N	83 20W
Rackerby	**80**	39 26N	121 22W
Radauti	**107**	47 53N	25 48E
Radcliff	**77**	37 51N	85 57W
Radford	**72**	37 8N	80 32W
Radisson	**56**	52 30N	107 20W
Radium Hill	**135**	32 30S	140 42E
Radium Hot Springs	**61**	50 35N	116 2W
Radnor Forest	**95**	52 17N	3 10W
Radom	**107**	51 23N	21 12E
Radomir	**109**	42 37N	23 4E
Radomsko	**107**	51 5N	19 28E
Radstock	**95**	51 17N	2 25W
Radstock, C.	**134**	33 12S	134 20E
Radville	**56**	49 30N	104 15W
Radway	**60**	54 4N	112 57W
Rae	**54**	62 50N	116 3W
Rae Bareli	**125**	26 18N	81 20E
Rae Isthmus	**65**	66 40N	87 30W
Raeside, L.	**134**	29 20S	122 0E
Raetihi	**133**	39 25S	175 17E
Rafaela	**88**	31 10S	61 30W
Rafai	**116**	4 59N	23 58E
Rafhã	**122**	29 35N	43 35E
Rafsanjān	**123**	30 30N	56 5E
Ragama	**124**	7 0N	79 50E
Raglan	**133**	37 55S	174 55E
Ragueneau	**35**	49 11N	68 18W
Ragusa	**108**	36 56N	14 42E
Raha	**127**	8 20S	118 40E
Raichur	**124**	16 10N	77 20E
Raigarh	**125**	21 56N	83 25E
Raiis	**122**	23 33N	38 43E
Raijua	**127**	10 37S	121 36E
Rainbow Lake	**54**	58 30N	119 23W
Rainier	**80**	46 4N	123 0W
Rainier, Mt.	**80**	46 50N	121 50W
Rainy L.	**52**	48 42N	93 10W
Rainy, R.	**52**	48 43N	94 29W
Rainy River	**52**	48 43N	94 29W
Raipur	**125**	21 17N	81 45E
Raith	**34**	48 50N	90 0W
Raj Nandgaon	**125**	21 0N	81 0E
Raja Empat, Kepulauan	**127**	0 30S	129 40E
Raja, Ujung	**126**	3 40N	96 25E
Rajahmundry	**125**	17 1N	81 48E
Rajang, R.	**126**	2 30N	113 30E
Rajapalaiyarm	**124**	9 25N	77 35E
Rajasthan □	**124**	26 45N	73 30E
Rajasthan Canal	**124**	30 31N	71 0E
Rajgarh	**124**	24 2N	76 45E
Rajkot	**124**	22 15N	70 56E
Rajojooseppi	**110**	68 25N	28 30E
Rajpipla	**124**	21 50N	73 30E
Rajshahi	**125**	24 22N	88 39E
Rajshahi □	**125**	25 0N	89 0E
Rakaia	**133**	43 45S	172 1E
Rakaia, R.	**133**	43 26S	171 47E
Rakan, Ras	**123**	26 10N	51 20E
Rakaposhi, mt.	**124**	36 20N	74 30E
Raleigh, Can.	**37**	51 34N	55 44W
Raleigh, U.S.A.	**34**	35 46N	78 38W
Raleigh B.	**73**	34 50N	76 15W
Ralls	**75**	33 40N	101 20W
Ralston	**61**	50 15N	111 10W
Rām Allāh	**115**	31 55N	35 10E
Ram Hd.	**136**	37 47S	149 30E
Ram, R., Alta., Can.	**61**	52 23N	115 25W
Ram, R., N.W.T., Can.	**54**	62 1N	123 41W
Rama, Can.	**56**	51 46N	103 0W
Rama, Nic.	**84**	12 9N	84 15W
Ramadi	**122**	33 28N	43 15E
Ramah	**36**	58 52N	63 15W
Ramah B.	**36**	58 52N	63 13W
Ramanathapuram	**124**	9 25N	78 55E
Rambervillers	**101**	48 20N	6 38E
Rambipudji	**127**	8 12S	113 37E
Rambouillet	**101**	48 40N	1 48E
Rambre Kyun	**125**	19 0N	94 0E
Ramea, Can.	**35**	47 28N	57 4W
Ramea, Newf., Can.	**37**	47 31N	57 23W
Ramea Is.	**37**	47 31N	57 22W
Ramechhap	**125**	27 25N	86 10E
Ramelau, Mte.	**127**	8 55S	126 22E
Ramgarh, Bihar, India	**125**	23 40N	85 35E
Ramgarh, Rajasthan, India	**124**	27 30N	70 36E
Rāmhormoz	**122**	31 15N	49 35E
Ramla	**115**	31 55N	34 52E
Ramnad = Ramanathapuram	**124**	9 25N	78 55E
Ramona	**81**	33 1N	116 56W
Ramore	**34**	48 30N	80 25W
Ramos Arizpe	**82**	23 35N	100 59W
Ramos, R.	**82**	25 35N	105 3W
Rampart	**67**	65 0N	150 15W
Rampur	**124**	28 50N	79 5E
Rampurhat	**125**	24 10N	87 50E
Ramsay I.	**62**	52 33N	131 23W
Ramsayville	**48**	45 23N	75 34W
Ramsey, Can.	**53**	47 25N	82 20W
Ramsey, U.K.	**94**	54 20N	4 21W
Ramsey, U.S.A.	**76**	39 8N	89 7W
Ramsey L.	**53**	47 13N	82 15W
Ramsgate	**95**	51 20N	1 25E
Ramtek	**124**	21 20N	79 15E
Ranaghat	**125**	23 15N	88 35E
Ranau	**126**	6 2N	116 40E
Rancagua	**88**	34 10S	70 50W
Rance, R.	**100**	48 34N	1 59W
Rancheria, R.	**54**	60 13N	129 7W
Ranchester	**78**	44 57N	107 12W
Ranchi	**125**	23 19N	85 27E
Rand	**136**	35 33S	146 32E
Randall	**52**	46 9N	94 28W
Randan	**102**	46 2N	3 21E
Randers	**111**	56 29N	10 1E
Randle	**80**	46 32N	121 57W
Randolph, N.Y., U.S.A.	**70**	42 10N	78 59W
Randolph, Utah, U.S.A.	**78**	41 43N	111 10W
Randolph, Vt., U.S.A.	**71**	43 55N	72 39W
Random I.	**37**	48 8N	53 44W
Randsburg	**81**	35 26N	117 44W
Råne älv	**110**	66 26N	21 10E
Råneå	**110**	65 53N	22 18E
Ranfurly	**60**	53 25N	111 41W
Rang-des-Dusseau	**40**	45 11N	73 9W
Rangaunu B.	**133**	34 51S	173 15E
Rangeley	**71**	44 58N	70 33W
Rangely	**78**	40 3N	108 53W
Ranger	**75**	32 30N	98 42W
Ranger L.	**53**	46 52N	83 35W
Rangia	**125**	26 15N	91 20E
Rangiora	**133**	43 19S	172 36E
Rangitaiki	**14**	38 52S	176 23E
Rangitaiki, R.	**133**	37 54S	176 49E
Rangitata, R.	**133**	43 45S	171 15E
Rangkasbitung	**127**	6 22S	106 16E
Rangon, R.	**125**	16 28N	96 40E
Rangoon	**125**	16 45N	96 20E
Rangpur	**125**	25 42N	89 22E
Ranibennur	**124**	14 35N	75 30E
Raniganj	**125**	23 40N	87 15E
Raniwara	**124**	24 50N	72 10E
Rankin, U.S.A.	**77**	40 28N	87 54W
Rankin, Tex., U.S.A.	**75**	31 16N	101 56W
Rankin Inlet	**65**	62 30N	93 0W
Rankin's Springs	**136**	33 49S	146 14E
Rannoch	**96**	56 41N	4 20W
Rannoch L.	**96**	56 41N	4 20W
Ranohira	**117**	22 29S	45 24E
Ranoke	**53**	50 26N	81 35W
Ranong	**128**	9 56N	98 40E
Ransom	**77**	41 9N	88 39W
Ransomville	**49**	43 15N	78 55W
Rantau	**126**	4 15N	98 5E
Rantauprapat	**126**	2 15N	99 50E
Rantemario	**127**	3 15S	119 57E
Rantoul	**77**	40 18N	88 10W
Raon-l'Étape	**101**	48 24N	6 50E
Rapa Iti, I.	**15**	27 35S	144 20W
Rapang	**127**	3 45S	119 55E
Rāpch	**123**	25 40N	59 15E
Raper, C.	**65**	69 44N	67 6W
Rapid City, Can.	**57**	50 7N	100 2W
Rapid City, Mich., U.S.A.	**46**	44 50N	85 17W
Rapid City, S.D., U.S.A.	**74**	44 0N	103 0W
Rapid, R., Can.	**54**	59 15N	129 5W
Rapid, R., U.S.A.	**52**	48 42N	94 26W
Rapid River	**72**	45 55N	87 0W
Rapide-Blanc	**41**	47 48N	73 2W
Rapide-Mascouche	**44**	45 46N	73 40W
Rapide-Sept	**40**	47 46N	78 19W
Rapides des Joachims	**40**	46 13N	77 43W
Rarotonga, I.	**15**	21 30S	160 0W
Ras al Khaima	**123**	25 50N	56 5E
Ra's at Tannūrah	**122**	26 40N	50 10E
Ras Dashan, mt.	**116**	13 8N	37 45E
Rasa, Punta	**90**	40 50S	62 15W
Rasht	**122**	37 20N	49 40E
Raso, C.	**87**	1 50N	50 0W
Rason, L.	**134**	28 45S	124 25E
Rat Buri	**128**	13 30N	99 54E
Rat, Is.	**67**	51 50N	178 15E
Rat, R., Man., Can.	**54**	56 0N	99 30W
Rat, R., Man., Can.	**57**	49 35N	97 10W
Rat River	**54**	61 7N	112 36W
Ratangarh	**124**	28 5N	74 35E
Rath Luirc (Charleville)	**97**	52 21N	8 40W
Rathbun Res.	**76**	40 49N	93 53W
Rathdrum, Ireland	**97**	52 57N	6 13W
Rathdrum, U.S.A.	**78**	47 50N	116 58W
Rathenow	**106**	52 38N	12 23E
Rathkeale	**97**	52 32N	8 57W
Rathlin I.	**97**	55 18N	6 14W
Rathlin O'Birne I.	**97**	54 40N	8 50W
Ratlam	**124**	23 20N	75 0E
Ratnagiri	**124**	16 57N	73 18E
Raton	**75**	37 0N	104 30W
Rats, R. aux	**41**	48 53N	72 14W
Rattray Hd.	**96**	57 38N	1 50W
Ratz, Mt.	**54**	57 23N	132 12W
Raub	**128**	3 47N	101 52E
Rauch	**88**	36 45S	59 5W
Raufarhöfn	**110**	66 27N	15 57W
Raukumara Ra.	**133**	38 5S	177 55E
Rauma	**111**	61 10N	21 30E
Raung, Mt.	**127**	8 8S	114 4E
Rāvar	**123**	31 20N	56 51E
Ravena	**71**	42 28N	73 49W
Ravenna, Italy	**108**	44 28N	12 15E
Ravenna, U.S.A.	**77**	43 11N	85 56W
Ravenna, U.S.A.	**77**	37 42N	83 55W
Ravenna, Nebr., U.S.A.	**74**	41 3N	98 58W
Ravenna, Ohio, U.S.A.	**70**	41 11N	81 15W
Ravensburg	**106**	47 48N	9 38E
Ravenshoe	**135**	17 37S	145 29E
Ravensthorpe	**134**	33 35S	120 2E
Ravenswood	**72**	38 58N	81 47W
Raventasón	**86**	6 10S	81 0W
Ravenwood	**76**	40 23N	94 41W
Ravi, R.	**124**	31 0N	73 0E
Rawalpindi	**124**	33 38N	73 8E
* Rawalpindi □	**124**	33 10N	72 50E
Rawāndūz	**122**	36 40N	44 30E
Rawang	**128**	3 20N	101 35E
Rawdon	**41**	46 3N	73 40W
Rawene	**133**	35 25S	173 32E
Rawlinna	**134**	30 58S	125 28E
Rawlins	**78**	41 50N	107 20W
Rawlinson Range	**134**	24 40S	128 30E
Rawson	**90**	43 15S	65 0W
Ray	**74**	48 21N	103 6W
Ray, C.	**37**	47 33N	59 15W
Ray Mts.	**67**	66 0N	152 10W
Rayadrug	**124**	14 40N	76 50E
Rayagada	**125**	19 15N	83 20E
Raychikhinsk	**121**	49 46N	129 25E
Rayin	**123**	29 40N	57 22E
Rayleigh	**63**	50 49N	120 17W
Raymond, Can.	**61**	49 30N	112 35W
Raymond, U.S.A.	**76**	39 19N	89 34W
Raymond, Calif., U.S.A.	**80**	37 13N	119 54W
Raymond, Wash., U.S.A.	**80**	46 45N	123 48W
Raymondville	**75**	26 30N	97 50W
Raymore	**56**	51 25N	104 31W
Rayne	**75**	30 16N	92 16W
Rayón	**82**	29 43N	110 35W
Rayong	**128**	12 40N	101 20E
Raytown	**76**	39 1N	94 28W
Rayville	**75**	32 30N	91 45W
Raz, Pte. du	**100**	48 2N	4 47W
Razgrad	**109**	43 33N	26 34E
Razor Back Mt.	**54**	51 32N	125 0W
Ré, Île de	**102**	46 12N	1 30W
Read Island	**64**	69 12N	114 31W
Reading, Can.	**49**	43 50N	80 13W
Reading, U.K.	**95**	51 27N	0 57W
Reading, Mich., U.S.A.	**77**	41 50N	84 45W
Reading, Ohio, U.S.A.	**77**	39 13N	84 26W
Reading, Pa., U.S.A.	**71**	40 20N	75 53W
Realicó	**88**	35 0S	64 15W
Réalmont	**102**	43 48N	2 10E
Ream	**128**	10 34N	103 39E
Reata	**82**	26 8N	101 5W
Reay	**96**	58 33N	3 48W
Rebais	**101**	48 50N	3 10E
Rebi	**127**	5 30S	134 7E
Rebun-jima	**132**	45 20N	142 45E
Recherche, Arch. of the	**134**	34 15S	122 50E
Recife	**87**	8 0S	35 0W
Recklinghausen	**105**	51 36N	7 10E
Reconquista	**88**	29 10S	59 45W
Recreo	**88**	29 25S	65 10W
Red Bank	**71**	40 21N	74 4W
Red Bay, Newf., Can.	**36**	51 44N	56 25W
Red Bay, Newf., Can.	**37**	51 44N	56 25W
Red Bluff	**78**	40 11N	122 11W
Red Bluff L.	**75**	31 59N	103 58W
Red Bud	**76**	38 13N	90 0W
Red Cloud	**74**	40 8N	98 33W
Red Deer	**61**	52 20N	113 50W
Red Deer L., Alta., Can.	**61**	52 43N	113 2W
Red Deer L., Man., Can.	**57**	52 55N	101 20W
Red Deer, R.	**61**	50 58N	110 0W
Red Deer R.	**57**	52 53N	101 1W
Red Hill South	**136**	38 25S	145 2E
Red I.	**37**	47 23N	54 10W
Red Indian L.	**37**	48 35N	57 0W
Red L.	**52**	51 3N	93 49W
Red Lake	**52**	51 3N	93 49W
Red Lake Falls	**74**	47 54N	96 15W
Red Lake Road	**52**	49 59N	93 25W
Red Lodge	**78**	45 10N	109 10W
Red Mountain	**81**	35 37N	117 38W
Red Oak	**74**	41 0N	95 10W
Red Pass	**63**	53 0N	119 0W
Red, R., Can.	**58**	50 24N	96 48W
Red, R., Minn., U.S.A.	**74**	48 10N	97 0W
Red, R., Tex., U.S.A.	**75**	33 57N	95 30W
Red River Floodway	**58**	49 50N	96 57W
Red Rock, B.C., Can.	**63**	53 42N	122 40W
Red Rock, Ont., Can.	**52**	48 55N	88 15W
Red Rock, L.	**76**	41 30N	93 15W
Red Sea	**115**	25 0N	36 0E
Red Slate Mtn.	**80**	37 31N	118 52W
Red Sucker L	**55**	54 9N	93 40W
Red Tower Pass = Turnu Rosu P.	**107**	45 33N	24 17E
Red Wing	**74**	44 32N	92 35W
Redberry L.	**56**	52 45N	107 14W
Redbridge	**95**	51 35N	0 7E
Redcar	**94**	54 37N	1 4W
Redcliff	**61**	50 10N	110 50W
Redding	**78**	40 30N	122 25W
Redditch	**95**	52 18N	1 57W
Redditt	**52**	49 59N	94 24W
Redfield	**74**	45 0N	98 30W
Redkey	**77**	40 21N	85 9W
Redknife, R.	**54**	61 14N	119 22W
Redlands	**81**	34 0N	117 11W
Redmond, Oreg., U.S.A.	**78**	44 19N	121 11W
Redmond, Wash., U.S.A.	**80**	47 40N	122 7W
Redon	**100**	47 40N	2 6W
Redonda, I.	**85**	16 58N	62 19W
Redonda Is.	**62**	50 15N	124 50W
Redondela	**104**	42 15N	8 38W
Redondo	**104**	38 39N	7 37W
Redondo Beach	**81**	33 52N	118 26W
Redondz Bay	**62**	50 17N	124 57W
Redrock Pt.	**54**	62 11N	115 2W
Redruth	**95**	50 14N	5 14W
Redvers	**57**	49 35N	101 40W
Redwater	**60**	53 55N	113 6W
Redwillow, R.	**60**	55 2N	119 18W
Redwood	**71**	44 18N	75 48W
Redwood City	**80**	37 30N	122 15W
Redwood Falls	**74**	44 30N	95 2W
Ree, L.	**97**	53 35N	8 0W
Reed City	**72**	43 52N	85 30W
Reed, L	**55**	54 38N	100 30W
Reed, Mt.	**35**	52 5N	68 5W
Reeder	**74**	46 7N	102 52W
Reedley	**80**	36 36N	119 27W
Reedsburg	**74**	43 34N	90 5W
Reedsport	**78**	43 45N	124 4W
Reef Pt.	**133**	35 10S	173 5E
Reefton	**133**	42 6S	171 51E

* *Now part of Punjab*

Reese Robe-Noire

Reese 46 43 27N 83 42W
Refugio 75 28 18N 97 17W
Regensburg 106 49 1N 12 7E
Regent Park 58 50 28N 104 39W
Réggio di Calábria 108 38 7N 15 38E
Réggio nell' Emilia 108 44 42N 10 38E
Regina 58 50 27N 104 35W
Regina Beach 56 50 47N 105 0W
Registan □ 124 30 15N 65 0E
Registro 89 24 29S 47 49W
Rehoboth 117 23 15S 17 4E
Reichenbach 106 50 36N 12 19E
Reid L. 56 50 0N 108 9W
Reid Lake 62 53 58N 123 6W
Reidsville 73 36 21N 79 40W
Reigate 95 51 14N 0 11W
Reims 101 49 15N 4 0E
Reina Adelaida, Arch. 90 52 20S 74 0W
Reinbeck 76 42 18N 92 0W
Reindeer I. 57 52 30N 98 0W
Reindeer L. 55 57 15N 102 15W
Reindeer, R. 55 55 36N 103 11W
Reine, La 40 48 50N 79 30W
Reinga, C. 133 34 25S 172 43E
Reinland 57 49 2N 97 52W
Reliance 55 63 0N 109 20W
Remanso 87 9 41S 42 4W
Rembang 127 6 42S 111 21E
Remedios, Colomb. 86 7 2N 74 41W
Remedios, Panama 84 8 15N 81 50W
Remer 52 47 3N 93 55W
Remeshk 123 26 55N 58 50E
Remi Lake Prov. Park 53 49 30N 82 15W
Rémigny 40 47 46N 79 12W
Remington 77 40 45N 87 8W
Remiremont 101 48 0N 6 36E
Remoulins 103 43 55N 4 35E
Remscheid 105 51 11N 7 12E
Remus 46 43 36N 85 9W
Renata 63 49 27N 118 7W
Rencontre East 37 47 38N 55 12W
Rend L. 76 38 2N 88 58W
Rendsburg 106 54 18N 9 41E
Rene 121 66 2N 179 25W
Renews 37 46 56N 52 56W
Renfrew, Can. 47 45 30N 76 40W
Renfrew, U.K. 96 55 52N 4 24W
Rengat 126 0 30S 102 45E
Rengo 88 34 24S 70 50W
Renison 53 50 58N 81 7W
Renkum 105 51 58N 5 43E
Renmark 135 34 11S 140 43E
Rennell Sd. 62 53 23N 132 35W
Renner Springs Teleg. Off. 134 18 20S 133 47E
Rennes 100 48 7N 1 41W
Rennie 57 49 51N 95 33W
Rennison I. 62 52 50N 129 20W
Reno 80 39 30N 119 50W
Reno, R. 108 44 45N 11 40E
Renovo 70 41 20N 77 47W
Rens 104 54 54N 9 5E
Rensselaer, Ind., U.S.A. 77 41 0N 87 10W
Rensselaer, N.Y., U.S.A. 71 42 38N 73 41W
Renton 80 47 30N 122 9W
Réole, La 102 44 35N 0 1W
Repentigny 45 45 44N 73 28W
Republic, Mich., U.S.A. 53 46 25N 87 59W
Republic, Wash., U.S.A. 63 48 38N 118 42W
Republican City 74 40 9N 99 20W
Republican, R. 74 40 0N 98 30W
Repulse B., Antarct. 91 64 30S 99 30E
Repulse B., Austral. 135 20 31S 148 45E
Repulse Bay 65 66 30N 86 30W
Requena, Peru 86 5 5S 73 52W
Requena, Spain 104 39 30N 1 4W
Reserve, Can. 56 52 28N 102 39W
Reserve, U.S.A. 79 33 50N 108 54W
Resht = Rasht 122 37 20N 49 40E
Resistencia 88 27 30S 59 0W
Reşiţa 107 45 18N 21 53E
Resolute 65 74 42N 94 54W
Resolution I., Can. 23 61 30N 65 0W
Resolution I., N.Z. 133 45 40S 166 40E
Restigouche, R. 39 47 50N 67 0W
Reston 57 49 33N 101 6W
Restrepo 86 4 15N 73 33W
Retalhuleu 84 14 33N 91 46W
Rethel 101 49 30N 4 20E
Réthimnon 109 35 15N 24 40E
Rétiers 100 47 55N 1 25W
Retiro 88 35 59S 71 47W
Réunion, Î. 16 22 0S 56 0E
Reutlingen 106 48 28N 9 13E
Revel 102 43 28N 2 0E
Revelstoke 63 51 0N 118 10W
Revigny 101 48 50N 5 0E
Revilla Gigedo, Is. de 15 18 40N 112 0W
Revillagigedo I. 54 55 50N 131 20W
Revin 101 49 55N 4 39E
Rewa 125 24 33N 81 25E
Rewari 124 28 15N 76 40E
Rex 67 64 10N 149 20W
Rexburg 78 43 55N 111 50W
Rexdale 50 43 43N 79 33W
Rexton, Can. 39 46 39N 64 52W
Rexton, U.S.A. 46 46 10N 85 14W
Rey Malabo 116 3 45N 8 50E
Reyes, Pt. 80 37 59N 123 2W
Reykjahlið 110 65 40N 16 55W
Reykjanes 110 63 48N 22 40W
Reykjavík 110 64 10N 21 57E
Reynolds, Can. 57 49 40N 95 55W
Reynolds, U.S.A. 76 41 20N 90 40W
Reynolds Ra. 134 22 30S 133 0E
Reynoldsville 70 41 5N 78 58W
Reynosa 83 26 5N 98 18W
*Rezā'iyeh, Daryācheh-ye 122 37 30N 45 30E
Rhayader 95 52 19N 3 30W
Rhein 57 51 25N 102 15W
Rhein, R. 106 51 42N 6 20E
Rheine 105 52 17N 7 25E
Rheinland-Pfalz □ 105 50 50N 7 0E
Rheydt 105 51 10N 6 24E
Rhinau 101 48 19N 7 43E
Rhine, R. = Rhein 106 51 42N 6 20E
Rhinelander 74 45 38N 89 29W
Rhode Island □ 71 41 38N 71 37W
Rhodes = Ródhos 109 36 15N 28 10E
Rhodesia = Zimbabwe ■ 117 20 0S 30 0E
Rhodope Mts. = Rhodopi Planina 109 41 40N 24 20E
Rhodopi Planina 109 41 40N 24 20E
Rhön, mts. 106 50 24N 9 58E
Rhondda 95 51 39N 3 30W
Rhône □ 103 45 54N 4 35E
Rhône, R. 103 43 28N 4 42E
Rhum, I. 96 57 0N 6 20W
Rhyl 94 53 19N 3 29W
Riachão 87 7 20S 46 37W
Rialto 81 34 6N 117 22W
Rians 103 43 37N 5 44E
Riasi 124 33 10N 74 50E
Riau □ 126 0 0 102 35E
Riau, Kepulauan 126 0 30N 104 20E
Ribadeo 104 43 35N 7 5W
Ribat 117 29 50N 60 55E
Ribatejo □ 104 39 15N 8 30W
Ribble, R. 94 54 13N 2 20W
Ribe 111 55 19N 8 44E
Ribeauvillé 101 48 10N 7 20E
Ribécourt 101 49 30N 2 55E
Ribeirão Prêto 89 21 10S 47 50W
Ribémont 101 49 47N 3 27E
Ribérac 102 45 15N 0 20E
Riberalta 86 11 0S 66 0W
Ribstone Cr. 61 52 52N 110 5W
Riccarton 133 43 32S 172 37E
Rice 81 34 5N 114 51W
Rice L., Can. 47 44 12N 78 10W
Rice L., U.S.A. 52 46 30N 93 22W
Rice Lake 74 45 30N 91 42W
Riceburg 43 45 8N 72 56W
Riceton 56 50 7N 104 19W
Rich, C. 46 44 43N 80 38W
Rich Hill 75 38 5N 94 22W
Rich Valley 60 53 51N 114 21W
Richan 52 49 59N 92 49W
Richards Deep 13 25 0S 73 0W
Richards I. 64 68 0N 135 0W
Richards L. 55 59 10N 107 10W
Richardson 58 50 23N 104 27W
Richardson Mts. 64 68 20N 135 45W
Richardson Pt. 51 43 50N 78 59W
Richardson, R. 55 58 25N 111 14W
Richardson Springs 80 39 51N 121 46W
Richardton 74 46 56N 102 22W
Riche, Pte. 37 50 42N 57 25W
Richelieu, Can. 45 45 27N 73 15W
Richelieu, France 100 47 0N 0 20E
Richelieu □ 43 45 55N 73 0W
Richelieu, R. 45 45 28N 73 18W
Richey 74 47 42N 105 5W
Richfield, Idaho, U.S.A. 78 43 2N 114 5W
Richfield, Utah, U.S.A. 78 38 50N 112 0W
Richford 71 45 0N 72 40W
Richibucto 39 46 42N 64 54W
Richland, Ga., U.S.A. 73 32 7N 84 40W
Richland, Iowa, U.S.A. 76 41 13N 91 58W
Richland, Mo., U.S.A. 76 37 51N 92 26W
Richland, Oreg., U.S.A. 78 44 49N 117 9W
Richland, Wash., U.S.A. 78 46 15N 119 15W
Richland Center 74 43 21N 90 22W
Richlands 72 37 7N 81 49W
Richmond, N.S.W., Austral. 136 33 35S 150 42E
Richmond, Queens., Austral. 135 20 43S 143 8E
Richmond, N.S., Can. 39 44 40N 63 36W
Richmond, Ont., Can. 47 45 11N 75 50W
Richmond, Qué., Can. 41 45 40N 72 9W
Richmond, N.Z. 133 41 4S 173 12E
Richmond, S. Afr. 117 29 51S 30 18E
Richmond, N. Yorks., U.K. 94 54 24N 1 43W
Richmond, Surrey, U.K. 95 51 28N 0 18W
Richmond, Calif., U.S.A. 80 38 0N 122 21W
Richmond, Ind., U.S.A. 77 39 50N 84 50W
Richmond, Ky., U.S.A. 77 37 40N 84 20W
Richmond, Mich., U.S.A. 46 42 47N 82 45W
Richmond, Mo., U.S.A. 74 39 15N 93 58W
Richmond, N.Y., U.S.A. 71 40 35N 74 6W
Richmond, Tex., U.S.A. 75 29 32N 95 42W
Richmond, Va., U.S.A. 72 37 33N 77 27W
Richmond □ 66 49 9N 123 7W
Richmond Gulf 34 56 20N 75 50W
Richmond Hill 50 43 52N 79 27W
Richmound 56 50 27N 109 45W
Richton 73 31 23N 88 58W
Richvale 50 43 51N 79 26W
Richwood, U.S.A. 77 40 26N 83 18W
Richwood, W. Va., U.S.A. 72 38 17N 80 32W
Rideau Canal 48 44 53N 76 0W
Rideau, R. 48 45 27N 75 42W
Ridge Farm 77 39 54N 87 39W
Ridge, R. 53 50 25N 84 20W
Ridgecrest 81 35 38N 117 40W
Ridgedale 56 53 0N 104 10W
Ridgefield 80 45 49N 122 45W
Ridgeland 73 32 30N 80 58W
Ridgetown 46 42 26N 81 52W
Ridgeville 77 40 18N 85 2W
Ridgway, Ill., U.S.A. 77 37 48N 88 16W
Ridgway, Pa., U.S.A. 70 41 25N 78 43W
Riding Mt. Nat. Park 57 50 50N 100 0W
Ried 106 48 14N 13 30E
Rietfontein 117 26 44S 20 1E
Rieti 108 42 23N 12 50E
Rieupeyroux 102 44 19N 2 12E
Riez 103 43 49N 6 6E
Rifle 78 39 40N 107 50W
Rifstangi 110 66 32N 16 12W
Riga 120 56 53N 24 8E
Rigaud 43 45 29N 74 18W
Rigby 78 43 41N 111 58W
Riggins 78 45 29N 116 26W
Rignac 102 44 25N 2 16E
Rigolet 36 54 10N 58 23W
Riihimäki 111 60 45N 24 48E
Riiser-Larsen halvøya 91 68 0S 35 0E
Riishiri-Tō 132 45 11N 141 15E
Rijeka (Fiume) 108 45 20N 14 21E
Rijkevorsel 105 51 21N 4 46E
Rijssen 105 52 19N 6 30E
Rijswijk 105 52 4N 4 22E
Rilly 101 49 11N 4 3E
Rimbey 61 52 35N 114 15W
Rímini 108 44 3N 12 33E
Rîmnicu Sărat 107 45 26N 27 3E
Rîmnicu Vîlcea 107 45 9N 24 21E
Rimouski 41 48 27N 68 30W
Rimouski-Est 41 48 28N 68 31W
Rimouski, Parc Prov. de 41 48 0N 68 15W
Rimouski, R. 41 48 27N 68 32W
Rimrock 80 46 38N 121 10W
Rinca 127 8 45S 119 35E
Rincón de Romos 82 22 14N 102 18W
Rinconada 88 22 26S 66 10W
Rineanna 97 52 42N 85 7W
Ringkøbing 111 56 5N 8 15E
Ringling 78 46 16N 110 56W
Ringvassøy 110 69 36N 19 15E
Ringwood 50 43 58N 79 17W
Rinía, I. 109 37 23N 25 13E
Rio Arica 86 1 35S 75 30W
Rio Branco 86 9 58S 67 49W
Río Branco 89 32 40S 53 40W
Rio Brilhante 89 21 48S 54 33W
Río Chico 86 10 19N 65 59W
Rio Claro, Brazil 89 22 19S 47 35W
Rio Claro, Trin. 85 10 20N 61 25W
Río Colorado 90 39 0S 64 0W
Río Cuarto 88 33 10S 64 25W
Rio de Janeiro 89 23 0S 43 12W
Rio de Janeiro □ 89 22 50S 43 0W
Rio do Sul 89 27 95S 49 37W
Río Gallegos 90 51 35S 69 15W
Río Grande 90 53 50S 67 45W
Rio Grande 89 32 0S 52 20W
Río Grande, Mexico 82 23 50N 103 2W
Río Grande, Nic. 84 12 54N 83 33W
Rio Grande City 75 26 30N 98 55W
Río Grande del Norte, R. 68 26 0N 97 0W
Río Grande do Norte □ 87 5 40S 36 0W
Rio Grande do Sul □ 89 30 0S 53 0W
Rio Grande, R. 79 37 47N 106 15W
Río Hato 84 8 22N 80 10W
Rio Lagartos 83 21 36N 88 10W
Rio Largo 87 9 28S 35 50W
Río Mulatos 86 19 40S 66 50W
Rio Muni □ = Mbini □ 114 1 30N 10 0E
Rio Negro 89 26 0S 50 0W
Río Oriente 84 22 17N 81 13W
Rio Pardo, Minas Gerais, Brazil 87 15 55S 42 30W
Rio Pardo, Rio Grande do Sul, Brazil 89 30 0S 52 30W
Río Segundo 88 31 40S 63 59W
Río Tercero 88 32 15S 64 8W
Río Verde 83 21 56N 99 59W
Rio Vista 80 38 11N 121 44W
Ríobamba 86 1 50S 78 45W
Riohacha 86 11 33N 72 55W
Rioja, La, Argent. 88 29 20S 67 0W
Rioja, La, Spain 104 42 20N 2 20W
Rioja, La □ 88 29 30S 67 0W
Riom 102 45 54N 3 7E
Riom-ès-Montagnes 102 45 17N 2 39E
Rion-des-Landes 102 43 55N 0 56W
Riondel 63 49 46N 116 51W
Rionegro 86 6 9N 75 22W
Riosucio, Caldas, Colomb. 86 5 30N 75 40W
Riosucio, Choco, Colomb. 86 7 27N 77 7W
Riou L. 55 59 7N 106 25W
Ripley, Can. 46 44 4N 81 35W
Ripley, U.S.A. 77 38 45N 83 51W
Ripley, Calif., U.S.A. 81 33 32N 114 39W
Ripley, N.Y., U.S.A. 70 42 16N 79 44W
Ripley, Tenn., U.S.A. 75 35 43N 89 34W
Ripon, Can. 40 45 45N 75 10W
Ripon, U.K. 94 54 8N 1 31W
Ripon, Calif., U.S.A. 80 37 44N 121 7W
Ripon, Wis., U.S.A. 72 43 51N 88 50W
Riscle 102 43 39N 0 5W
Rising Sun 77 38 57N 84 51W
Risle, R. 100 48 55N 0 41E
Rison 75 33 57N 92 11W
Risør 111 58 43N 9 13E
Ritchie L. 38 52 58N 66 1W
Ritchie's Archipelago 128 12 5N 94 0E
Rittman 70 40 57N 81 48W
Ritzville 78 47 10N 118 21W
Riva Bella 100 49 17N 0 18W
Rivadavia, Buenos Aires, Argent. 88 35 29S 62 59W
Rivadavia, Mendoza, Argent. 88 33 13S 68 30W
Rivadavia, Salta, Argent. 88 24 5S 63 0W
Rivadavia, Chile 88 29 50S 70 35W
Rivas 84 11 30N 85 50W
Rive-de-Gier 103 45 32N 4 37E
River Hébert 39 45 42N 64 23W
River John 39 45 45N 63 3W
River Jordan 62 48 26N 124 3W
River of Ponds 37 50 32N 57 24W
River of Ponds L. 37 50 30N 57 20W
River Rouge 77 42 16N 83 9W
River Valley 46 46 35N 80 11W
Rivera 89 31 0S 55 50W
Rivercrest 58 50 0N 97 3W
Riverdale 80 36 26N 119 52W
Riverfield 43 45 9N 73 49W
Riverhead, Can. 37 46 58N 53 31W
Riverhead, U.S.A. 71 40 53N 72 40W
Riverhurst 56 50 55N 106 50W
Riverina 135 35 30S 145 20E
Riverport 39 44 18N 64 20W
Rivers 57 50 2N 100 14W
Rivers Inl. 62 51 40N 127 20W
Rivers Inlet 62 51 42N 127 15W
Rivers, L. of the 56 49 49N 105 44W
Riversdal 117 34 7S 21 15E
Riverside, Can. 70 42 17N 82 59W
Riverside, Calif., U.S.A. 81 34 0N 117 22W
Riverside, Wash., U.S.A. 63 48 29N 119 30W
Riverside, Wyo., U.S.A. 78 41 12N 106 57W
Riverside-Albert 39 45 42N 64 45W
Riverton, Can. 57 51 1N 97 0W
Riverton, N.Z. 133 46 21S 168 0E
Riverton, U.S.A. 76 39 51N 89 33W
Riverton, Wyo., U.S.A. 78 43 1N 108 27W
Riverview Heights 39 46 4N 64 48W
Rives 103 45 21N 5 31E
Rivesaltes 102 42 47N 2 50E
Rivière-Ste.-Marguerite 38 50 8N 66 37W
Rivière-à-la-Chaloupe 38 50 17N 65 6W
Rivière-à-Pierre 41 46 59N 72 11W
Rivière-au-Renard 38 48 59N 64 23W
Rivière-aux-Rats 41 47 13N 72 53W
Rivière-Beaudette 43 45 14N 74 20W
Rivière-Bersimis 41 48 56N 68 42W
Rivière-Bleue 35 47 26N 69 2W
Rivière-de-la-Chaloupe 38 49 8N 62 32W
Rivière-des-Hurons 45 45 30N 73 9W
Rivière-des-Prairies 44 45 39N 73 33W
Rivière-du-Loup 41 47 50N 69 30W
Rivière-Ouelle 41 47 26N 70 1W
Rivière-Pigou 38 50 16N 65 35W
Rivière-Pontecôte 38 49 57N 67 1W
Rivière-Portneuf 41 48 38N 69 6W
Rivière-St-Jean 38 50 17N 64 19W
Rivière Verte 39 47 19N 68 9W
Rivierre-au-Tonnère 38 50 16N 64 47W
Riyadh = Ar Riyād 122 24 41N 46 42E
Rize 122 41 0N 40 30E
Rizzuto, C. 108 38 54N 17 5E
Rjukan 111 59 54N 8 33E
Roachdale 77 39 51N 86 48W
Road Town 85 18 27N 64 37W
Roag, L. 96 58 10N 6 55W
Roanne 103 46 3N 4 4E
Roanoke, U.S.A. 77 40 58N 85 22W
Roanoke, Ala., U.S.A. 73 33 9N 85 23W
Roanoke, Va., U.S.A. 72 37 19N 79 55W
Roanoke I. 73 35 55N 75 40W
Roanoke, R. 73 36 15N 77 20W
Roanoke Rapids 73 36 36N 77 42W
Roatán 84 16 18N 86 35W
Robb 60 53 13N 116 58W
Robe, Mt. 136 31 40S 141 20E
Robe-Noire, L. de la 38 50 42N 62 42W

** Renamed Orūmīyeh, Daryācheh -ye*

Robe, R **Ruel**

Robe, R.	**97**	53 38N	9 10W
Robert Lee	**75**	31 55N	100 26W
Roberts, U.S.A.	**77**	40 37N	88 11W
Roberts, Idaho, U.S.A.	**78**	43 44N	112 8W
Robert's Arm	**37**	49 29N	55 49W
Roberts Bank Superport	**66**	49 1N	123 9W
Roberts Creek	**63**	49 26N	123 38W
Roberts, Pt.	**63**	49 0N	123 6W
Robertson, Austral.	**134**	34 37S	150 36E
Robertson, S. Afr.	**117**	33 46S	19 50E
Robertson I.	**91**	68 0S	75 0W
Robertsonville	**41**	46 9N	71 13W
Robertville	**39**	47 42N	65 46W
Roberval	**41**	48 32N	72 15W
Robeson Kanal	**17**	82 0N	61 30W
Robinson	**77**	39 0N	87 44W
Robinson Ranges	**134**	25 40S	118 0E
Robinvale	**136**	34 40S	142 45E
Robla, La	**104**	42 50N	5 41W
Roblin	**57**	51 14N	101 21W
Roblin Park	**58**	49 52N	97 17W
Roboré	**86**	18 10S	59 45W
Robsart	**56**	49 23N	109 17W
Robson, Mt.	**63**	53 10N	119 10W
Robstown	**75**	27 47N	97 40W
Roca, C. da	**104**	38 40N	9 31W
Roca Partida, I.	**82**	19 1N	112 2W
* Roçadas	**117**	16 45S	15 0E
Rocanville	**57**	50 23N	101 42W
Rocas, I.	**87**	4 0S	34 1W
Rocha	**89**	34 30S	54 25W
Rochdale	**94**	53 36N	2 10W
Roche-Bernard, La	**100**	47 31N	2 19W
Roche-Canillac, La	**102**	45 12N	1 57E
Roche, La	**103**	46 4N	6 19E
Roche Percée	**56**	49 4N	102 48W
Roche-sur-Yon, La	**100**	46 40N	1 25W
Rochebaucourt	**40**	48 41N	77 30W
Rochechouart	**102**	45 50N	0 49E
Rochefort, Belg.	**105**	50 9N	5 12E
Rochefort, France	**102**	45 56N	0 57W
Rochefort-en-Terre	**100**	47 42N	2 22W
Rochefoucauld, La	**102**	45 44N	0 24E
Rochelle	**76**	41 55N	89 5W
Rochelle, La	**102**	46 10N	1 9W
Rocher River	**54**	61 23N	112 44W
Roches, R.	**38**	50 2N	66 55W
Rocheservière	**100**	46 57N	1 30W
Rochester, Austral.	**136**	36 22S	144 41E
Rochester, Can.	**60**	54 22N	113 27W
Rochester, U.K.	**95**	51 22N	0 30E
Rochester, Ind., U.S.A.	**77**	41 5N	86 15W
Rochester, Mich., U.S.A.	**77**	42 41N	83 8W
Rochester, Minn., U.S.A.	**74**	44 1N	92 28W
Rochester, N.H., U.S.A.	**71**	43 19N	70 57W
Rochester, N.Y., U.S.A.	**70**	43 10N	77 40W
Rochester, Pa., U.S.A.	**70**	40 41N	80 17W
Rock Creek	**63**	49 4N	119 0W
Rock Falls	**76**	41 47N	89 41W
Rock Hill	**73**	34 55N	81 2W
Rock Island, Can.	**41**	45 26N	73 34W
Rock Island, U.S.A.	**76**	41 30N	90 35W
Rock Lake	**74**	48 50N	99 13W
Rock Port	**74**	40 26N	95 30W
Rock, R.	**54**	60 7N	127 7W
Rock Rapids	**74**	43 25N	96 10W
Rock River	**78**	41 49N	106 0W
Rock Sound	**84**	24 54N	76 12W
Rock Sprs., Ariz., U.S.A.	**79**	34 2N	112 11W
Rock Sprs., Mont., U.S.A.	**78**	46 55N	106 11W
Rock Sprs., Tex., U.S.A.	**75**	30 2N	100 11W
Rock Sprs., Wyo., U.S.A.	**78**	41 40N	109 10W
Rock Valley	**74**	43 10N	96 17W
Rockall I.	**93**	57 37N	13 42W
Rockburn	**43**	45 1N	74 1W
Rockcliffe Park	**48**	45 27N	75 41W
Rockdale, Tex., U.S.A.	**75**	30 40N	97 0W
Rockdale, Wash., U.S.A.	**80**	47 22N	121 28W
Rockefeller Plat.	**91**	84 0S	130 0W
Rockford, Ill., U.S.A.	**76**	42 20N	89 0W
Rockford, Iowa, U.S.A.	**76**	43 3N	92 57W
Rockford, Mich., U.S.A.	**77**	43 7N	85 34W
Rockford, Ohio, U.S.A.	**77**	40 41N	84 39W
Rockglen	**56**	49 11N	105 57W
Rockhampton	**135**	23 22S	150 32E
Rockingham	**39**	44 41N	63 39W
Rockingham For.	**95**	52 28N	0 42W
Rocklake	**57**	48 47N	99 15W
Rockland, Can.	**47**	45 33N	75 17W
Rockland, Idaho, U.S.A.	**78**	42 37N	112 57W
Rockland, Me., U.S.A.	**35**	44 0N	69 0W
Rockland, Mich., U.S.A.	**52**	46 40N	89 10W
Rocklands Reservoir	**136**	37 15S	142 5E
Rocklin	**80**	38 48N	121 14W
Rockmart	**73**	34 1N	85 2W
Rockport, U.S.A.	**77**	37 53N	87 3W
Rockport, Tex., U.S.A.	**75**	28 2N	97 3W
Rockport, Wash., U.S.A.	**63**	48 30N	121 38W
Rockton	**49**	43 17N	80 7W
Rockville, U.S.A.	**77**	39 46N	87 14W
Rockville, Conn., U.S.A.	**71**	41 51N	72 27W
Rockville, Md., U.S.A.	**72**	39 7N	77 10W
Rockwall	**75**	32 55N	96 30W
Rockway	**49**	43 6N	79 20W
Rockwell	**136**	32 3S	141 32E
Rockwell City	**76**	42 20N	94 35W
Rockwood, Can.	**49**	43 37N	80 8W
Rockwood, U.S.A.	**77**	42 4N	83 15W
Rockwood, Tenn., U.S.A.	**73**	35 52N	84 40W
Rocky Ford	**74**	38 7N	103 45W
Rocky Fork Lake	**77**	39 12N	83 23W
Rocky Harbour	**37**	49 36N	57 55W
Rocky Island L.	**53**	46 55N	83 0W
Rocky Lane	**54**	58 31N	116 22W
Rocky Mount	**73**	35 55N	77 48W
Rocky Mountain House	**61**	52 22N	114 55W
Rocky Mts.	**54**	55 0N	121 0W
Rocky Pt.	**134**	33 30S	123 57E
Rocky, R.	**61**	53 8N	117 59W
Rockyford	**61**	51 14N	113 10W
Rocroi	**101**	49 55N	4 30E
Rod	**124**	28 10N	63 5E
Roda, La	**104**	39 13N	2 15W
Rødby Havn	**111**	54 39N	11 22E
Roddickton	**37**	50 51N	56 8W
Roden	**105**	53 8N	6 26E
Roderick I.	**62**	52 38N	128 22W
Rodez	**102**	44 21N	2 33E
Ródhos	**109**	36 15N	28 10E
Ródhos, I.	**109**	36 15N	28 10E
Rodney	**46**	42 34N	81 41W
Rodney, C.	**133**	36 17S	174 50E
Rodoni, C.	**109**	41 32N	19 30E
Rodriguez, I.	**16**	20 0S	65 0E
Roe, R.	**97**	55 0N	6 56W
Roebling	**71**	40 7N	74 45W
Roebourne	**134**	20 44S	117 9E
Roebuck B.	**134**	18 5S	122 20E
Roermond	**105**	51 12N	6 0E
Roes Welcome Sd.	**65**	65 0N	87 0W
Roeselare	**105**	50 57N	3 7E
Rogagua, L.	**86**	14 0S	66 50W
Rogaland fylke □	**111**	59 12N	6 20E
Roger, L.	**40**	47 50N	78 59W
Rogers	**75**	36 20N	94 0W
Rogers City	**46**	45 25N	83 49W
Rogerson	**78**	42 10N	114 40W
Rogersville, Can.	**39**	46 44N	65 26W
Rogersville, U.S.A.	**73**	36 27N	83 1W
Roggan	**36**	54 25N	79 32W
Roggan L.	**36**	54 8N	77 50W
Rogliano	**103**	42 57N	9 30E
Rogoaguado, L.	**86**	13 0S	65 30W
Rogue, R.	**78**	42 30N	124 0W
Rohan	**100**	48 4N	2 45W
Rohault, L.	**41**	49 23N	74 20W
Rohnert Park	**80**	38 16N	122 40W
Rohrbach	**101**	49 3N	7 15E
Rohri	**124**	27 45N	68 51E
Rohtak	**124**	28 55N	76 43E
Roi Et	**128**	15 56N	103 40E
Roisel	**101**	49 58N	3 6E
Rojas	**88**	34 10S	60 45W
Rojo, C., Mexico	**83**	21 33N	97 20W
Rojo, C., W. Indies	**67**	17 56N	67 11W
Rokan, R.	**126**	1 30N	100 50E
Roland	**57**	49 22N	97 56W
Rolândia	**89**	23 5S	52 0W
Rolette	**74**	48 42N	99 50W
Rolfe	**76**	42 49N	94 31W
Rolla, Kansas, U.S.A.	**75**	37 10N	101 40W
Rolla, Missouri, U.S.A.	**76**	37 56N	91 42W
Rolla, N. Dak., U.S.A.	**57**	48 50N	99 36W
Rollet	**40**	47 55N	79 15W
Rolling Hills	**61**	50 13N	111 46W
Rolling, R.	**77**	38 0N	85 56W
Roma, Austral.	**135**	26 32S	148 49E
Roma, Italy	**108**	41 54N	12 30E
Roma, Sweden	**111**	57 32N	18 26E
Romaine, R.	**36**	50 18N	63 47W
Roman	**107**	43 8N	23 54E
Romana, La	**85**	18 27N	68 57W
Romania ■	**107**	46 0N	25 0E
Romano, Cayo	**84**	22 0N	77 30W
Romanzof, C.	**67**	62 0N	165 50W
Rome, Ga., U.S.A.	**73**	34 20N	85 0W
Rome, N.Y., U.S.A.	**71**	43 14N	75 29W
Rome = Roma	**108**	41 54N	12 30E
Romenay	**103**	46 30N	5 1E
Romilly	**101**	48 31N	3 44E
Romney, Can.	**70**	42 9N	82 23W
Romney, U.S.A.	**72**	39 21N	78 45W
Romney Marsh	**95**	51 0N	1 0E
Romorantin-Lanthenay	**101**	47 21N	1 45E
Romsdalen	**110**	62 25N	7 50E
Ronan	**78**	47 30N	114 11W
Roncador Cay	**84**	13 40N	80 4W
Roncador, Serra do	**87**	12 30S	52 30W
Ronceverte	**72**	37 45N	80 28W
Ronda	**104**	36 46N	5 12W
Rondane	**111**	61 57N	9 50E
Rondeau Prov. Park	**46**	42 19N	81 51W
Rondón	**86**	6 17N	71 6W
Rondônia □	**86**	11 0S	63 0W
Rong, Koh	**128**	10 45N	103 15E
Ronge, La	**55**	55 5N	105 20W
Ronge,Lac La	**55**	55 6N	105 17W
Rønne	**111**	55 6N	14 44E
Ronne Land	**91**	83 0S	70 0W
Ronse	**105**	50 45N	3 35E
Roodepoort-Maraisburg	**117**	26 8S	27 52E
Roodhouse	**76**	39 29N	90 24W
Roof Butte	**79**	36 29N	109 5W
Roorkee	**124**	29 52N	77 59E
Roosendaal	**105**	51 32N	4 29E
Roosevelt, Minn., U.S.A.	**74**	48 51N	95 2W
Roosevelt, Utah, U.S.A.	**78**	40 19N	110 1W
Roosevelt I.	**91**	79 0S	161 0W
Roosevelt, Mt.	**54**	58 20N	125 20W
Roosevelt Res.	**79**	33 46N	111 0W
Roosville	**61**	49 0N	115 3W
Roper, R.	**134**	14 43S	135 27E
Ropesville	**75**	33 25N	102 10W
Roque Pérez	**88**	35 25S	59 24W
Roquefort	**102**	44 2N	0 20W
Roquefort-sur-Soulzon	**102**	43 58N	2 59E
Roquemaure	**103**	44 3N	4 48E
Roquevaire	**103**	43 20N	5 36E
Roraima □	**86**	2 0N	61 30W
Roraima, Mt.	**86**	5 10N	60 40W
Rorketon	**57**	51 24N	99 35W
Røros	**110**	62 35N	11 23E
Rosa, U.S.A.	**78**	38 15N	122 16W
Rosa, Zambia	**116**	9 33S	31 15E
Rosa, Monte	**106**	45 57N	7 53E
Rosalia	**78**	47 26N	117 25W
Rosalind	**61**	52 47N	112 27W
Rosamund	**81**	34 52N	118 10W
Rosans	**103**	44 24N	5 29E
Rosario	**88**	33 0S	60 50W
Rosário, Maran., Brazil	**87**	3 0S	44 15W
Rosário, Rio Grande do Sul, Brazil	**90**	30 15S	55 0W
Rosario, Baja California, Mexico	**82**	30 0N	116 0W
Rosario, Durango, Mexico	**82**	26 30N	105 35W
Rosario, Sinaloa, Mexico	**82**	23 0N	106 0W
Rosario, Venez.	**86**	10 19N	72 19W
Rosario de la Frontera	**88**	25 50S	65 0W
Rosario de Lerma	**88**	24 59S	65 35W
Rosario del Tala	**88**	32 20S	59 10W
Rosário do Sul	**89**	30 15S	54 55W
Rosarito, Mexico	**82**	28 38N	114 4W
Rosarito, U.S.A.	**81**	32 18N	117 4W
Rosas	**104**	42 19N	3 10E
Rosas, G. de,	**104**	42 10N	3 15E
Roscoe	**76**	37 58N	93 48W
Roscoff	**100**	48 44N	4 0W
Roscommon, Ireland	**97**	53 38N	8 11W
Roscommon, U.S.A.	**46**	44 27N	84 35W
Roscommon □	**97**	53 40N	8 15W
Roscrea	**97**	52 57N	7 50W
Rose Blanche	**37**	47 38N	58 45W
Rose City	**46**	44 25N	84 7W
Rose Harbour	**62**	52 15N	131 10W
Rose Pt.	**62**	54 11N	131 39W
Rose Valley	**56**	52 19N	103 49W
Roseau, Domin.	**85**	15 20N	61 30W
Roseau, U.S.A.	**57**	48 51N	95 46W
Rosebud, Austral.	**136**	38 21S	144 54E
Rosebud, U.S.A.	**75**	31 5N	97 0W
Rosebud, R.	**61**	51 25N	112 38W
Roseburg	**78**	43 10N	123 10W
Rosedale, Can.	**63**	49 10N	121 48W
Rosedale, U.S.A.	**77**	39 38N	87 17W
Rosedale, Miss., U.S.A.	**75**	33 51N	91 0W
Roseisle	**57**	49 30N	98 20W
Roseland	**80**	38 25N	122 43W
Rosemary	**61**	50 46N	112 5W
Rosemère	**44**	45 38N	73 48W
Rosemont	**58**	50 27N	104 39W
Rosenberg	**75**	29 30N	95 48W
Rosendaël	**101**	51 3N	2 24E
Rosendale	**76**	40 4N	94 51W
Rosenheim	**106**	47 51N	12 9E
Rosetown	**56**	51 35N	107 59W
Roseville, U.S.A.	**76**	40 44N	90 40W
Roseville, Calif., U.S.A.	**80**	38 46N	121 17W
Roseville, Mich., U.S.A.	**46**	42 30N	82 56W
Rosières	**101**	48 36N	6 20E
Rosignol	**86**	6 15N	57 30W
Roskilde	**111**	55 38N	12 3E
Roslavl	**120**	53 57N	32 55E
Rosporden	**100**	47 57N	3 50W
Ross, N.Z.	**133**	42 53S	170 49E
Ross, U.K.	**95**	51 55N	2 34W
Ross Dependency	**91**	70 0S	170 5W
Ross I.	**91**	77 30S	168 0E
Ross Ice Shelf	**91**	80 0S	180 0W
Ross L.	**63**	48 50N	121 5W
Ross on Wye	**95**	51 55N	2 34W
Ross Pt.	**51**	43 51N	78 54W
Ross River	**67**	62 30N	131 30W
Ross Sea	**91**	74 0S	178 0E
Rossan Pt.	**97**	54 42N	8 47W
Rossburn	**57**	50 40N	100 49W
Rosseau, Can.	**70**	45 26N	79 39W
Rosseau, Ont., Can.	**46**	45 16N	79 39W
Rosseau L.	**46**	45 10N	79 35W
Rosser	**58**	49 59N	97 27W
Rossford	**77**	41 36N	83 34W
Rossignol, L., N.S., Can.	**39**	44 12N	65 0W
Rossignol, L., Qué., Can.	**36**	52 43N	73 40W
Rossland	**63**	49 6N	117 50W
Rosslare	**97**	52 17N	6 23W
Rossmore	**47**	44 8N	77 23W
Rossosh	**120**	50 15N	39 20E
Rossport	**53**	48 50N	87 30W
Røssvatnet	**110**	65 45N	14 5E
Rossville	**77**	40 25N	86 35W
Rosthern	**56**	52 40N	106 20W
Rostock	**106**	54 4N	12 9E
Rostov	**120**	47 15N	39 45E
Rostrenen	**100**	48 14N	3 21W
Roswell	**75**	33 26N	104 32W
Rosyth	**96**	56 2N	3 26W
Rotan	**75**	32 52N	100 30W
Rothaargebirge	**106**	51 0N	8 20E
Rother, R.	**95**	50 59N	0 40W
Rotherham	**94**	53 26N	1 21W
Rothes	**96**	57 31N	3 12W
Rothesay, Can.	**39**	45 23N	66 0W
Rothesay, U.K.	**96**	55 50N	5 3W
Roti, I.	**127**	10 50S	123 0E
Roto	**136**	33 0S	145 30E
Rotoroa Lake	**133**	41 55S	172 39E
Rotorua	**133**	38 9S	176 16E
Rotorua, L.	**133**	38 5S	176 18E
Rotterdam	**105**	51 55N	4 30E
Rottweil	**106**	48 9N	8 38E
Rotuma, I.	**14**	12 25S	177 5E
Roubaix	**101**	50 40N	3 10E
Rouen	**100**	49 27N	1 4E
Rouergue	**103**	44 20N	2 20E
Rouge Hill	**51**	43 48N	79 8W
Rouge, R., Ont., Can.	**51**	43 48N	79 7W
Rouge, R., Qué., Can.	**40**	45 17N	74 10W
Rougemont	**45**	45 26N	73 3W
Rouillac	**102**	45 47N	0 4W
Rouleau	**56**	50 10N	104 56W
Round Hill, Alta., Can.	**61**	53 10N	112 38W
Round Hill, N.S., Can.	**39**	44 46N	65 24W
Round L., Newf., Can.	**37**	51 15N	56 32W
Round L., Ont., Can.	**47**	45 38N	77 30W
Round Mt.	**135**	30 26S	152 16E
Round Mountain	**78**	38 46N	117 3W
Round Pond	**37**	48 11N	56 0W
Round Valley	**60**	53 21N	116 57W
Roundup	**78**	46 25N	108 35W
Rousay, I.	**96**	59 10N	3 2W
Rouses Point	**43**	44 58N	73 22W
Rousse, L'Île	**103**	42 27N	8 57E
Roussillon, Can.	**43**	45 41N	74 26W
Roussillon, France	**103**	45 24N	4 49E
Routhierville	**38**	48 11N	67 9W
Rouville □	**45**	45 33N	73 10W
Rouvray, L.	**41**	49 18N	70 49W
Rouyn	**40**	48 20N	79 0W
Rovaniemi	**110**	66 29N	25 41E
Rovereto	**108**	45 53N	11 3E
Rovigo	**108**	45 4N	11 48E
Rovinj	**108**	45 5N	13 40E
Rovira	**86**	4 15N	75 20W
Rovno	**120**	50 40N	26 10E
Rowan L.	**52**	49 18N	93 32W
Rowatt	**58**	50 20N	104 37W
Rowley I.	**65**	69 6N	77 52W
Rowley Shoals	**134**	17 40S	119 20E
Rowood	**79**	32 18N	112 54W
Roxas	**127**	11 36N	122 49E
Roxboro, Can.	**44**	45 31N	73 48W
Roxboro, U.S.A.	**73**	36 24N	78 59W
Roxburgh, N.Z.	**133**	45 33S	169 19E
Roxburgh, U.K.	**96**	55 34N	2 30W
Roxton Falls	**41**	45 34N	72 31W
Roy, U.S.A.	**78**	47 17N	109 0W
Roy, N. Mex., U.S.A.	**75**	35 57N	104 8W
Roy, Le, U.S.A.	**77**	40 21N	88 46W
Roy, Le, Kans., U.S.A.	**75**	38 8N	95 35W
Royal Center	**77**	40 52N	86 30W
Royal Oak, Can.	**63**	48 29N	123 23W
Royal Oak, U.S.A.	**77**	42 30N	83 5W
Royan	**102**	45 37N	1 2W
Roye	**101**	47 40N	6 31E
Rozay	**101**	48 40N	2 56E
Rozier, Le	**102**	44 13N	3 12E
Rozoy-sur-Serre	**101**	49 40N	4 8E
Rtishchevo	**120**	52 35N	43 50E
Ruahine Ra.	**133**	39 55S	176 2E
Ruapehu	**133**	39 17S	175 35E
Ruapuke I.	**133**	46 46S	168 31E
Rub 'al Khali	**115**	21 0N	51 0E
Rubicon, R.	**80**	38 53N	121 4W
Rubicone, R.	**108**	44 0N	12 20E
Rubio	**86**	7 43N	72 22W
Rubtsovsk	**120**	51 30N	80 50E
Ruby	**67**	64 40N	155 35W
Ruby L.	**78**	40 10N	115 28W
Ruby Mts.	**78**	40 30N	115 30W
Rudbar	**123**	30 0N	62 30E
Rudh a'Mhail, C.	**96**	55 55N	6 25W
Rudnogorsk	**121**	57 15N	103 42E
Rudnyy	**120**	52 57N	63 7E
Rudok	**129**	33 30N	79 40E
Rudyard	**46**	46 14N	84 35W
Rue	**101**	50 15N	1 40E
Rue, La	**77**	40 35N	83 23W
Ruel	**53**	47 15N	81 28W

** Renamed Xangongo*

Ruelle St-Eustache

Ruelle	102	45 41N	0 14E
Ruffec Charente	102	46 2N	0 12E
Rufiji, R.	116	7 50S	38 15E
Rufino	88	34 20S	62 50W
Rugby, U.K.	95	52 23N	1 16W
Rugby, U.S.A.	74	48 21N	100 0W
Rügen, I.	106	54 22N	13 25E
Rugles	100	48 50N	0 40E
Ruhr, R.	105	51 25N	7 15E
Ruidosa	75	29 59N	104 39W
Ruidoso	79	33 19N	105 39W
Ruisseau-des-Anges	43	45 48N	73 40W
Ruisseau-Vert	41	49 4N	68 28W
Rukwa L.	116	7 50S	32 10E
Rully	85	46 52N	4 44E
Rum Jungle	134	13 0S	130 59E
Rumāh	122	25 35N	47 10E
Rumania ■	107	46 0N	25 0E
Rumford	71	44 30N	70 30W
Rumilly	103	45 53N	5 56E
Rummelhardt	49	43 27N	80 34W
Rumoi	132	43 56N	141 39W
Rumorosa, La	81	32 33N	116 4W
Rumsey	61	51 51N	112 48W
Runanga	133	42 25S	171 15E
Runaway, C.	133	37 32S	178 2E
Runcorn	94	53 20N	2 44W
Rungwa	116	6 55S	33 32E
Runton Ra.	136	23 35S	123 15E
Rupa	125	27 15N	92 30E
Rupat, I.	126	1 45N	101 40E
Rupert B.	36	51 35N	79 0W
Rupert House = Fort Rupert	36	51 30N	78 40W
Rupert, R.	36	51 29N	78 45W
Rupununi, R.	87	3 30N	59 30W
Rurrenabaque	86	14 30S	67 32W
Rusagonis	39	45 48N	66 37W
Rusape	117	18 35S	32 8E
Ruschuk = Ruse	109	43 48N	25 59E
Ruse	109	43 48N	25 59E
Rush L.	53	47 47N	82 11W
Rush Lake	56	50 24N	107 24W
Rushden	95	52 17N	0 37W
Rushford	74	43 48N	91 46W
Rushoon	37	47 21N	54 55W
Rushville, Ill., U.S.A.	76	40 6N	90 35W
Rushville, Ind., U.S.A.	77	39 38N	85 22W
Rushville, Nebr., U.S.A.	74	42 43N	102 20W
Rushworth	136	36 32S	145 1E
Russell, Man., Can.	55	50 50N	101 20W
Russell, Que., Can.	71	45 16N	75 21W
Russell, N.Z.	133	35 16S	174 10E
Russell, U.S.A.	74	38 56N	98 55W
Russell I.	65	74 0N	98 25W
Russell L., Man., Can.	55	56 15N	101 30W
Russell L., N.W.T., Can.	54	63 5N	115 44W
Russellkonda	125	19 57N	84 42E
Russelltown	43	45 4N	73 45W
Russellville, Ala., U.S.A.	73	34 30N	87 44W
Russellville, Ark., U.S.A.	75	35 15N	93 0W
Russellville, Ky., U.S.A.	73	36 50N	86 50W
Russian Mission	67	61 45N	161 25W
Russian, R.	80	38 27N	123 8W
Russian S.F.S.R. □	121	62 0N	105 0E
Russiaville	77	40 25N	86 16W
Russkoye Ustie	17	71 0N	149 0E
Rustenburg	117	25 41S	27 14E
Ruston	75	32 30N	92 58W
Rutba	122	33 4N	40 15E
Ruteng	127	8 26S	120 30E
Ruth, Mich., U.S.A.	46	43 42N	82 45W
Ruth, Nev., U.S.A.	78	39 15N	115 1W
Rutherford	80	38 26N	122 24W
Rutherglen, Austral.	136	36 5S	146 29E
Rutherglen, U.K.	96	55 50N	4 11W
Rutland	71	43 38N	73 0W
Rutland I.	128	11 25N	92 40E
Rutledge L.	55	61 33N	110 47W
Rutledge, R.	55	61 4N	112 0W
Rutshuru	116	1 13S	29 25E
Rutter	46	46 6N	80 40W
Ruvuma, R.	116	11 30S	36 10E
Ruwaidha	122	23 40N	44 40E
Ruwandiz	122	36 40N	44 32E
Ruwenzori Mts.	116	0 30N	29 55E
Ruwenzori, mt.	116	0 30N	29 55E
Ruzomberok	107	49 3N	19 17E
Rwanda ■	116	2 0S	30 0E
Ryan, L.	96	55 0N	5 2W
Ryans B.	36	59 35N	64 3W
Ryazan	120	54 50N	39 40E
Rybache	120	46 40N	81 20E
*Rybinsk	120	58 5N	38 50E
Ryckman	48	43 15N	79 54W
Rycroft	60	55 45N	118 40W
Ryde	95	50 44N	1 9W
Ryderwood	80	46 23N	123 3W
Rye	95	50 57N	0 46E
Rye Patch Res.	78	40 45N	118 20W
Rye, R.	94	54 12N	0 53W
Ryegate	78	46 21N	109 27W
Ryley	60	53 17N	112 26W
Rypin	107	53 3N	19 32E
Ryūkyū Is. = Ryūkyū-rettō	131	26 0N	127 0E
Rzeszów	107	50 5N	21 58E
Rzhev	120	56 20N	34 20E

S

Sa Dec	128	10 20N	105 46E
Sa'ādatābād	123	30 10N	53 5E
Saale, R.	106	51 25N	11 56E
Saanich	63	48 28N	123 22W
Saar, R.	106	49 25N	6 35E
Saar (Sarre), □	101	49 20N	6 45E
Saarbrücken	105	49 15N	6 58E
Saaremaa	120	58 30N	22 30E
Saariselkä	110	68 16N	28 15E
Saarland □	15	49 20N	6 45E
Saarlouis	105	49 19N	6 45E
Saba I.	85	17 30N	63 10W
Sabadell	104	41 28N	2 7E
Sabagalel	126	1 36S	98 40E
Sabah □	126	6 0N	117 0E
Sabak	128	3 46N	100 58E
Sábana de la Mar	85	19 7N	69 40W
Sábanalarga	86	10 38N	74 55W
Sabang	126	5 50N	95 15E
Sabará	87	19 55S	43 55W
Sabarania	127	2 5S	138 18E
Sabattis	71	44 6N	74 40W
Sabaudia	108	41 17N	13 2E
Sabhah	114	27 9N	14 29E
Sabina	77	39 29N	83 38W
Sabinal, Mexico	82	30 50N	107 25W
Sabinal, U.S.A.	75	29 20N	99 27W
Sabinas	82	27 50N	101 10W
Sabinas Hidalgo	82	26 40N	100 10W
Sabinas, R.	82	27 37N	100 42W
Sabine	75	29 42N	93 54W
Sabine, R.	75	31 30N	93 35W
Sablayan	127	12 5N	120 50E
Sable	100	47 50N	0 21W
Sable, C., Can.	39	43 29N	65 38W
Sable, C., U.S.A.	84	25 5N	81 0W
Sable I.	35	44 0N	60 0W
Sable River	39	43 51N	65 3W
Sablé-sur-Sarthe	100	47 50N	0 20W
Sables-D'Olonne, Les	102	46 30N	1 45W
Sables, R. aux	46	46 13N	82 3W
Sabourin, L.	40	47 58N	77 41W
Sabrevois	43	45 12N	73 14W
Sabrina Coast	91	67 0S	120 0E
Sabtang I.	131	20 15N	121 30E
Sabula	76	42 26N	90 23W
Sabzevār	123	36 15N	57 40E
Sabzvāran	123	28 45N	57 50E
Sac City	76	42 26N	95 0W
Sachigo, L.	34	53 50N	92 12W
Sachigo, R.	34	55 6N	88 58W
Sachs Harbour	64	71 59N	125 15W
Sackett's Harbor	71	43 56N	72 38W
Sackville	39	45 54N	64 22W
Saco, Me., U.S.A.	73	43 30N	70 27W
Saco, Mont., U.S.A.	78	48 28N	107 19W
Sacramento	80	38 39N	121 30E
Sacramento Mts.	79	32 30N	105 30W
Sacramento, R.	80	38 3N	121 56W
Sacramento Valley	80	39 0N	122 0W
Sacré-Coeur-de-Jésus	41	48 14N	69 48W
Sadaba	104	42 19N	1 12W
Sa'dani	116	5 58S	38 35E
Sadao	128	6 38N	100 26E
Saddle Mt.	80	45 58N	123 41W
Sadieville	77	38 23N	84 32W
Sado	132	38 0N	138 25E
Sado, Shima	132	38 15N	138 30E
Saegerstown	70	80 10N	41 42W
Safaniya	122	28 5N	48 42E
Saffron Walden	95	52 2N	0 15E
Safi	114	32 18N	9 14W
Safiah	100	31 27N	34 46E
Sag Harbor	71	40 59N	72 17W
Saga	127	2 40S	132 55E
Saga-ken □	132	33 15N	130 20E
Sagaing	125	23 30N	95 30E
Saganaga L.	52	48 14N	90 52W
Saganash L.	53	49 4N	82 35W
Sagar	124	23 50N	78 50E
Sagil	129	50 15N	91 15E
Saginaw	46	43 26N	83 55W
Saginaw B.	46	43 50N	83 40W
Sagleipie	103	45 25N	7 0E
Saglek B.	36	58 30N	63 0W
Saglek Fd.	36	58 29N	63 15W
Saglouc	36	62 14N	75 38W
Sagone	103	42 7N	8 42E
Sagone, G. de	103	42 4N	8 40E
Sagra, La, Mt.	104	38 0N	2 35W
Sagres	104	37 0N	8 58W
Sagua la Grande	84	22 50N	80 10W
Saguache	79	38 10N	106 4W
Saguenay, R.	41	48 22N	71 0W
Sagunto	104	39 42N	0 18W
Sahagún, Colomb.	86	8 57N	75 27W
Sahagún, Spain	104	42 18N	5 2W
Sahara	114	23 0N	5 0W
Saharanpur	124	29 58N	77 33E
Sahiwal	124	30 45N	73 8E
Sahtaneh, R.	54	59 2N	122 28W
Sahuaripa	82	29 30N	109 0W
Sahuarita	79	31 58N	110 59W
Sahuayo	82	20 4N	102 43W
Sa'idabad	123	29 30N	55 45E
Saidapet	124	13 0N	80 15E
Saidu	124	34 50N	72 15E
Säie	111	59 8N	12 55E
Sāighan	123	35 10N	67 55E
Saignes	102	45 20N	2 31E
Saigon = Phanh Bho Ho Chi Minh	128	10 58N	106 40E
Saih-al-Malih	123	23 37N	58 31E
Saijō	132	34 0N	133 5E
Saikhoa Ghat	125	27 50N	95 40E
Saiki	132	32 58N	131 57E
Saillans	103	44 42N	5 12E
Sailolof	127	1 7S	130 46E
St-Hyacinthe	45	45 40N	72 58W
St-Jean-Port-Joli	41	47 15N	70 13W
St Jovite	40	46 8N	74 38W
St.-Julien-du-Sault	101	48 1N	3 17E
St. Abb's Head	96	55 55N	2 10W
St-Adalbert	41	46 51N	69 53W
St-Adolphe-d'Howard	43	45 58N	74 20W
St-Affrique	102	43 57N	2 53E
St-Agapitville	41	46 34N	71 26W
St-Agrève	103	45 0N	4 23E
St.-Aignan	100	47 16N	1 22E
St. Alban's	37	47 51N	55 50W
St. Albans, U.K.	95	51 44N	0 19W
St. Albans, Vt., U.S.A.	71	44 49N	73 7W
St. Albans, W. Va., U.S.A.	72	38 21N	81 50W
St. Alban's Head	95	50 34N	2 3W
St. Albert	60	53 37N	113 40W
St-Alexandre, Qué., Can.	41	47 41N	69 38W
St-Alexandre, Qué., Can.	45	45 14N	73 7W
St-Alexis	43	45 56N	73 37W
St-Alexis-des-Monts	41	46 28N	73 8W
St-Amable	45	45 39N	73 18W
St-Amand	101	50 25N	3 6E
St-Amand-en-Puisaye	101	47 32N	3 5E
St-Amand-Mont-Rond	102	46 43N	2 30E
St-Amarin	101	47 54N	7 0E
St-Ambroise	41	48 33N	71 20W
St-Amour	103	46 26N	5 21E
St-Anaclet	41	48 29N	68 26W
St-André	39	47 8N	67 45W
St-André-Avellin	40	45 43N	75 3W
St-André-de-Cubzac	102	44 59N	0 26W
St-André de l'Eure	100	48 54N	1 16E
St-André-Est	43	45 34N	74 20W
St-André-les-Alpes	103	43 58N	6 30E
St. Andrews	39	45 7N	67 5W
St. Andrew's	37	47 45N	59 15W
St. Andrews	96	56 20N	2 48W
St-Angèle-de-Monnoir	45	45 23N	73 6W
St-Anicet	43	45 8N	74 22W
St. Ann B.	39	46 22N	60 25W
St. Anne	100	49 43N	2 11W
St Anne	77	41 1N	87 43W
St. Annes	57	49 40N	96 39W
St. Anns	49	43 5N	79 30W
St. Ann's Bay	84	18 26N	77 15W
St-Anselme, N.B., Can.	39	46 4N	64 43W
St-Anselme, Qué., Can.	41	46 37N	70 58W
St. Anthony, N.B., Can.	39	46 22N	64 45W
St. Anthony, Newf., Can.	37	51 22N	55 35W
St. Anthony, U.S.A.	78	44 0N	111 49W
St-Antoine	44	45 46N	73 59W
St-Antoine-des-Laurentides	44	45 46N	73 59W
St-Antoine-sur-Richelieu	45	45 46N	73 11W
St-Antonin	41	47 46N	69 29W
St-Antonin-Noble-Val	102	44 10N	1 45E
St-Apolline	41	46 48N	70 12W
St. Arnaud	136	36 32S	143 16E
St. Arthur	39	47 33N	67 46W
St. Asaph	94	53 15N	3 27W
St-Astier	102	45 8N	0 31E
St-Aubert	41	47 11N	70 13W
St-Aubin-du-Cormier	100	48 15N	1 26W
St-Augustin	44	45 38N	73 59W
St-Augustin-de-Desmaures	42	46 45N	71 30W
St-Augustin, L.	42	46 45N	71 23W
St-Augustin, R.	36	51 16N	58 40W
St-Augustin-Saguenay	37	51 13N	58 38W
St. Augustine	73	29 52N	81 20W
St. Austell	95	50 20N	4 48W
St-Avold	101	49 6N	6 43E
St-Barnabé-Sud	45	45 44N	72 55W
St-Barthélémy	41	46 11N	73 8W
St. Barthélemy, I.	85	17 50N	62 50W
St-Basile	39	47 21N	68 14W
St-Basile-le-Grand	45	45 32N	73 17W
St-Basile-Sud	41	46 45N	71 49W
St. Bee's Hd.	94	54 30N	3 38E
St. Benedict	56	52 34N	105 23W
St-Benoît	44	45 34N	74 6W
St-Benoît-du-Sault	102	46 26N	1 24E
St-Bernard-de-Lacolle	43	45 5N	73 25W
St-Blaise	43	45 13N	73 17W
St. Boniface	58	49 53N	97 5W
St-Bonnet	103	44 40N	6 5E
St. Brendan's	37	48 52N	53 40W
St-Brévin-les-Pins	100	47 14N	2 10W
St-Brice-en-Coglès	100	48 25N	1 22W
St. Bride's	37	46 56N	54 10W
St. Bride's B.	95	51 48N	5 15W
St-Brieuc	100	48 30N	2 46W
St. Brieux	56	52 38N	104 54W
St-Bruno	41	48 28N	71 39W
St-Bruno-de-Montarville	45	45 32N	73 21W
St-Calais	100	47 55N	0 45E
St-Calixte-de-Kilkenny	43	45 57N	73 51W
St-Calixte-Nord	43	45 59N	73 55W
St-Canut	44	45 43N	74 5W
St-Casimir	41	46 40N	72 8W
St-Cast	100	48 37N	2 18W
St. Catharines	49	43 10N	79 15W
St. Catherines I.	73	31 35N	81 10W
St. Catherine's Pt.	95	50 34N	1 18W
St-Céré	102	44 51N	1 54E
St-Cernin	102	45 5N	2 25E
St-Césaire	45	45 25N	73 0W
St-Chamond	103	45 28N	4 31E
St. Charles	58	49 53N	97 19W
St-Charles	42	46 46N	70 57W
St. Charles, Ill., U.S.A.	77	41 55N	88 21W
St. Charles, Mich., U.S.A.	46	43 18N	84 9W
St. Charles, Mo., U.S.A.	76	38 46N	90 30W
St-Charles, L.	42	46 55N	71 23W
St-Charles, R.	42	46 49N	71 13W
St-Charles-sur-Richelieu	45	45 41N	73 11W
St-Chély-d'Apcher	102	44 48N	3 17E
St-Chinian	102	43 25N	2 56E
St. Christopher -Nevis ■	85	17 20N	62 40W
St-Chrysostôme	43	45 6N	73 46W
St-Ciers-sur-Gironde	102	45 17N	0 37W
Saint Clair	76	38 21N	90 59W
St. Clair, Mich, U.S.A.	46	42 47N	82 27W
St. Clair, Pa., U.S.A.	71	40 42N	76 12W
St. Clair, L.	46	42 30N	82 45W
St. Clair, R.	70	42 40N	82 20W
St. Clairsville	70	40 5N	80 53W
St-Claud	102	45 54N	0 28E
St. Claude	57	49 40N	98 20W
St-Claude	103	46 22N	5 52E
St-Clet	43	45 21N	74 13W
St-Cloud	100	48 51N	2 12E
St. Cloud, Fla., U.S.A.	73	28 15N	81 15W
St. Cloud, Minn., U.S.A.	74	45 30N	94 11W
St-Coeur de Marie	41	48 39N	71 43W
St-Colomban	44	45 44N	74 8W
St-Côme	41	46 16N	73 47W
St-Constant	44	45 22N	73 37W
St-Croix	39	45 34N	67 26W
St. Croix Falls	74	45 18N	92 22W
St. Croix, I.	85	17 45N	64 45W
St. Croix, R., Canada	39	45 5N	67 6W
St. Croix, R., U.S.A.	74	45 20N	92 50W
St-Cyprien	102	42 37N	3 0E
St-Cyr	103	43 11N	5 43E
St-Cyrille-de-L'Islet	41	47 2N	70 17W
St. Cyrus	96	56 47N	2 25W
St-Damase	45	45 31N	73 1W
St. David	76	40 30N	90 3W
St-David-de-l'Auberivière	42	46 47N	71 12W
St-David-d'Yamaska	43	45 57N	72 51W
St. David's	37	48 12N	58 52W
St. Davids	49	43 10N	79 6W
St. David's	95	51 54N	5 16W
St. David's Head	95	51 54N	5 16W
St-Denis, Can.	45	45 47N	73 9W
St-Denis, France	101	48 56N	2 22E
St.-Denis	16	20 52S	55 27E
St-Denis-d'Orques	100	48 2N	0 17W
St-Dié	101	48 17N	6 56E
St-Dizier	101	48 40N	5 0E
St-Dominique	44	45 20N	74 8W
St-Donat-de-Montcalm	41	46 19N	74 13W
St-Edouard-de-Napierville	43	45 14N	73 31W
St-Egrève	103	45 14N	5 41E
St-Eleanors	39	46 25N	63 49W
St. Elias, Mt.	67	60 20N	141 59W
St.Elias Mts.	54	60 33N	139 28W
Saint Elmo	77	39 2N	88 51W
St-Éloi	41	48 2N	69 14W
St-Élouthère	41	47 30N	69 15W
St.-Eloy-les-Mines	102	46 10N	2 51E
St-Émile	42	46 52N	71 20W
St-Émilion	102	44 53N	0 9W
St-Éphrem-de-Tring	41	46 2N	70 59W
St-Esprit	43	45 54N	73 40W
St-Étienne	103	45 27N	4 22E
St-Étienne-de-Tinée	103	44 16N	6 56E
St-Étienne-de-Beauharnois	44	45 15N	73 55W
St. Eugène	47	45 30N	74 28W
St-Eugène	43	45 30N	74 29W
St-Eusèbe	41	47 33N	68 55W
St. Eustache	57	49 59N	97 47W
St-Eustache	44	45 33N	73 54W

* *Renamed Andropov*

St-Sulpice
San Gabriel

St-Sulpice 43 45 50N 73 21W
St-Sulpice-Laurière 102 46 3N 1 29E
St-Sulpice-la-Pointe 102 43 46N 1 41E
St-Télesphore 43 45 17N 74 23W
St-Thégonnec 100 48 31N 3 57W
St. Thomas 46 42 45N 81 10W
St-Thomas-d'Aquin 45 45 39N 72 59W
St. Thomas, I. 85 18 21N 64 55W
St-Timothée 44 45 18N 74 2W
St-Tite 41 46 45N 72 40W
St-Tite-des-Caps 41 47 8N 70 47W
St-Tropez 103 43 17N 6 38E
St-Ulric 38 48 47N 67 42W
St-Urbain 41 47 33N 70 32W
St-Urbain-de-Châteauguay 43 45 13N 73 44W
St-Vaast-la-Hougue 100 49 35N 1 17W
St-Valérien 43 45 34N 72 43W
St-Valéry 101 50 10N 1 38E
St-Valéry-en-Caux 100 49 52N 0 43E
St.-Vallier 103 45 11N 4 50E
St-Vallier-de-Thiey 103 43 42N 6 51E
St.-Varent 100 46 53N 0 13W
St-Vianney 38 48 37N 67 25W
St. Victor 56 49 26N 105 52W
St. Vincent 12 18 0N 26 1W
St. Vincent C. 117 21 58S 43 20E
St-Vincent-de-Tyrosse 102 43 39N 1 18W
St-Vincent-de-Paul 44 45 37N 73 39W
St. Vincent, G. 135 35 0S 138 0E
St. Vincent and the Grenadines ■ 85 13 10N 61 10W
St. Vincent's 37 46 48N 53 38W
St. Vital 58 49 51N 97 7W
St-Vith 105 50 17N 6 9E
St. Walburg 56 53 39N 109 12W
St-Yrieux-la-Perche 102 45 31N 1 12E
St-Yvon 38 49 10N 64 48W
St-Zotique 43 45 15N 74 15W
Ste-Adèle 43 45 57N 74 7W
Ste-Adresse 100 49 31N 0 5E
Ste. Agathe 57 49 34N 97 11W
Ste-Agathe 41 46 23N 71 25W
Ste-Agathe-des-Monts 41 46 3N 74 17W
Ste-Agnès-de-Dundee 43 45 1N 74 25W
Ste-Angèle-de-Mérici 38 48 32N 68 5W
Ste-Angèle-de-Monnoir 43 45 23N 73 6W
Ste. Anne 85 14 26N 60 53W
Ste Anne de Beaupré 41 47 2N 70 58W
Ste-Anne-de-Bellevue 44 45 24N 73 57W
Ste-Anne-de-Madawaska 39 47 15N 68 2W
Ste. Anne de Portneuf 35 48 38N 69 8W
Ste-Anne-de-Prescott 43 45 26N 74 29W
Ste-Anne-des-Monts 38 49 8N 66 30W
Ste-Anne-des-Plaines 44 45 47N 73 49W
Ste-Anne-du-Lac 40 46 48N 75 25W
Ste-Anne, L. 38 50 0N 67 42W
Ste. Anne, Lac 60 53 42N 114 25W
Ste-Blandine 41 48 22N 68 28W
Ste-Brigide-d'Iberville 45 45 19N 73 4W
Ste. Cecile 35 47 56N 64 34W
Ste-Cécile-de-Milton 43 45 29N 72 44W
Ste-Claire 41 46 36N 70 51W
Ste-Clothilde-de-Châteauguay 43 45 10N 73 41W
Ste-Croix, Can. 41 46 38N 71 44W
Ste-Croix, Switz. 101 46 49N 6 34W
Ste-Dorothée 44 45 32N 73 49W
Ste-Enimie 102 44 22N 3 26E
Ste-Famille 41 46 58N 70 58W
Ste-Félicité 38 48 54N 67 20W
Ste-Florence 38 48 16N 67 14W
Ste-Foy 42 46 47N 71 17W
Ste-Foy-la-Grande 102 44 50N 0 13E
Ste-Françoise 41 48 6N 69 4W
Ste-Geneviève 44 45 29N 73 52W
Ste. Genevieve 76 37 59N 90 2W
Ste. Germaine 35 46 24N 70 24W
Ste-Hélène-de-Bagot 43 45 44N 72 44W
Ste-Hermine 102 46 32N 1 4W
Ste-Julie 45 45 35N 73 19W
Ste-Julienne 43 45 58N 73 43W
Ste-Justine-de-Newton 43 45 22N 74 25W
Ste-Livrade-sur-Lot 102 44 24N 0 36E
Ste-Madeleine 45 45 36N 73 6W
Ste-Marguerite, R. 36 50 9N 66 36W
Ste. Marie 85 14 48N 61 1W
Ste-Marie-aux-Mines 101 48 10N 7 12E
Ste-Marie de la Madeleine 41 46 26N 71 0W
*Ste. Marie, I. 117 16 50S 49 55E
Ste-Marie-Salomé 43 45 56N 73 30W
Ste-Marthe 43 45 24N 74 18W
Ste-Marthe-de-Gaspé 38 49 12N 66 10W
Ste-Marthe-sur-le-Lac 44 45 32N 73 57W
Ste-Martine 44 45 15N 73 48W
Ste-Maure-de-Touraine 100 47 7N 0 37E
Ste-Maxime 103 43 19N 6 39E
Ste-Menehould 101 49 5N 4 54E
Ste-Mère-Église 100 49 24N 1 19W
Ste-Monique 41 48 44N 71 51W
Ste-Monique-des-Deux-Montagnes 44 45 40N 74 0W
Ste-Pudentienne 41 45 28N 72 40W
Ste-Rosalie 43 45 38N 72 54W
Ste-Rose 43 45 37N 73 48W
Ste. Rose 85 16 20N 61 45W
Ste.-Rose du lac 57 51 4N 99 30W

** Renamed Nosy Boraha*

Ste-Sabine 43 45 15N 73 2W
Ste-Scholastique 44 45 39N 74 5W
Ste. Teresa 88 33 33S 60 54W
Ste-Thècle 41 46 49N 72 31W
Ste-Thérèse 44 45 38N 73 51W
Ste-Thérèse-de-Lisieux 42 46 56N 71 12W
Ste-Thérèse, Île, Qué., Can. 45 45 40N 73 29W
Ste-Thérèse, Île, Qué., Can. 45 45 41N 73 28W
Ste-Thérèse-Ouest 44 45 37N 73 50W
Ste-Victoire 43 45 57N 73 5W
Saintes 102 45 45N 0 37W
Saintes, I. des 85 15 50N 61 35W
Saintes-Maries-de-la-Mer 103 43 26N 4 26E
Saintonge 102 45 40N 0 50W
Sairang 125 23 50N 92 45E
Sairecábur, Cerro 88 22 43S 67 54W
Sairs, L. 40 46 49N 78 26W
Saitama-ken □ 132 36 25N 137 0E
Sajama, Nevada 86 18 0S 68 55W
Sâkahka 122 30 0N 40 8E
Sakai 132 34 30N 135 30E
Sakai Shimane 132 35 30N 133 25E
Sakaimachi 132 35 30N 133 15E
Sakami, L. 36 53 15N 76 45W
Sakania 117 12 43S 28 30E
Sakata 132 36 38N 138 19E
Sakhalin, Ostrov 121 51 0N 143 0E
Sakishima-guntō 131 24 30N 124 0E
Sakon Nakhon 128 17 10N 104 9E
Sala 111 59 58N 16 35E
Sala-y-Gomez, I. 15 26 28S 105 28W
Salaberry-de-Valleyfield 44 45 15N 74 8W
Salaberry, Île de 44 45 17N 74 7W
Salada, La 82 24 30N 111 30W
Saladas 88 28 15S 58 40W
Saladillo 88 35 40S 59 55W
Salado, R., Buenos Aires, Argent. 88 35 40S 58 10W
Salado, R., Santa Fe, Argent. 88 27 0S 63 40W
Salado, R., Mexico 82 26 52N 99 19W
Salamanca, Chile 88 32 0S 71 25W
Salamanca, Spain 104 40 58N 5 39W
Salamanca, U.S.A. 70 42 10N 78 42W
Salamina 86 5 25N 75 29W
Salamis 109 37 56N 23 30E
Salamonie, R. 77 40 47N 85 40W
Salamonie, Resvr. 77 40 45N 85 35W
Salar de Atacama 90 23 30S 68 25W
Salar de Uyuni 86 20 30S 67 45W
Salatu 130 44 25N 107 58E
Salaverry 86 8 15S 79 0W
Salayar, I. 127 6 15S 120 30E
Salbris 101 47 25N 2 3E
Saldaña 104 42 32N 4 48W
Saldanha 117 33 0S 17 58E
Sale, Austral. 136 38 6S 147 6E
Sale, U.K. 94 53 26N 2 19W
Salebabu 127 3 45N 125 55E
Sālehābād 123 35 40N 61 2E
Salekhard 120 66 30N 66 25E
Salem, Can. 49 43 42N 80 27W
Salem, India 124 11 40N 78 11E
Salem, U.S.A. 76 38 38N 88 57W
Salem, Ind., U.S.A. 77 38 38N 86 0W
Salem, Mass., U.S.A. 71 42 29N 70 53W
Salem, Mo., U.S.A. 75 37 40N 91 30W
Salem, N.J., U.S.A. 72 39 34N 75 29W
Salem, Ohio, U.S.A. 70 40 52N 80 50W
Salem, Oreg., U.S.A. 78 45 0N 123 0W
Salem, Va., U.S.A. 72 37 19N 80 8W
Salembu, Kepulauan 126 5 35S 114 30E
Salen 111 64 41N 11 27E
Salernes 103 43 34N 6 15E
Salerno 108 40 40N 14 44E
Salford 94 53 30N 2 17W
Salies-de-Béarn 102 43 28N 0 56W
Salima 117 13 47S 34 28E
Salina 74 38 50N 97 40W
Salina Cruz 83 16 10N 95 10W
Salina, I. 108 38 35N 14 50E
Salina, La 86 10 22N 71 27W
Salinas, Brazil 87 16 20S 42 10W
Salinas, Chile 88 23 31S 69 29W
Salinas, Ecuador 86 2 10S 80 50W
Salinas, Mexico 82 23 37N 106 8W
Salinas, U.S.A. 80 36 40N 121 31W
Salinas Ambargasta 88 29 0S 65 30W
Salinas, B. de 84 11 4N 85 45W
Salinas (de Hidalgo) 82 22 30N 101 40W
Salinas Grandes 88 30 0S 65 0W
Salinas, Pampa de las 88 31 58S 66 42W
Salinas, R., Mexico 83 16 28N 90 31W
Salinas, R., U.S.A. 80 36 45N 121 48W
Saline 46 42 12N 83 49W
Saline, R. 74 39 10N 99 5W
Salinópolis 87 0 40S 47 20W
Salins-les-Bains 101 46 58N 5 52E
Salisbury, Can. 39 46 2N 65 3W
*Salisbury, Zimbabwe 117 17 50S 31 2E
Salisbury, U.K. 95 51 4N 1 48W
Salisbury, U.S.A. 76 39 25N 92 48W
Salisbury, Md., U.S.A. 72 38 20N 75 38W
Salisbury, N.C., U.S.A. 73 35 42N 80 29W
Salisbury I. 65 63 30N 77 0W
Salisbury Plain 95 51 13N 1 50W

** Renamed Harare*

Salle, La 76 41 20N 89 6W
Salles-Curan 102 44 11N 2 48E
Sallisaw 75 35 26N 94 45W
Sally's Cove 37 49 44N 57 56W
Salmo 63 49 10N 117 20W
Salmon 78 45 12N 113 56W
Salmon Arm 63 50 40N 119 15W
Salmon Falls 78 42 55N 114 59W
Salmon, R., B.C., Can. 54 54 3N 122 40W
Salmon, R., N.B., Can. 39 46 6N 65 56W
Salmon, R., Qué., Can. 38 49 25N 62 15W
Salmon, R., U.S.A. 78 46 0N 116 30W
Salmon Res. 37 48 05N 56 00W
Salmon River 39 44 3N 66 10W
Salmon River Mts. 78 45 0N 114 30W
Salo 111 60 22N 23 3E
Salome 81 33 51N 113 37W
Salon-de-Provence 103 43 39N 5 6E
Salonta 107 46 49N 21 42E
Salop □ 95 52 36N 2 45W
Salsacate 88 31 20S 65 5W
Salses 102 42 50N 2 55E
Salso, R. 108 37 6N 13 55E
Salt Fork R. 75 37 25N 98 40W
Salt Lake City 78 40 45N 111 58W
Salt, R., Can. 54 60 0N 112 25W
Salt, R., U.S.A. 76 39 29N 91 5W
Salt, R., U.S.A. 77 37 54N 85 51W
Salt, R., Ariz., U.S.A. 79 33 50N 110 25W
Salta 88 24 47S 65 25W
Salta □ 88 24 48S 65 30W
Saltair 62 48 57N 123 46W
Saltcoats, Can. 57 51 5N 102 15W
Saltcoats, U.K. 96 55 38N 4 47W
Saltee Is. 97 52 7N 6 37W
Saltery Bay 62 49 47N 124 10W
Saltfjorden 110 67 15N 14 20E
Salthólmavík 110 65 24N 21 57W
Saltillo 82 25 30N 100 57W
Salto, Argent. 88 34 20S 60 15W
Salto, Uruguay 88 31 20S 57 59W
Salto □ 88 31 20S 57 59W
Salto Augusto, falls 88 8 30S 58 0W
Salton City 81 33 21N 115 59W
Salton Sea 81 33 20N 115 50W
Saltspring 54 48 54N 123 37W
Salula, R. 73 34 12N 81 45W
Salûm 115 31 31N 25 7E
Salur 125 18 27N 83 18E
Saluzzo 108 44 39N 7 29E
Salvador, Brazil 87 13 0S 38 30W
Salvador, Can. 56 52 10N 109 25W
Salvador ■ 82 13 50N 89 0W
Salvador, L. 75 29 46N 90 16W
Salvail 45 45 40N 73 4W
Salvail, R. 45 45 49N 73 58W
Salvisa 77 37 54N 84 51W
Salwa 123 24 45N 50 55E
Salween, R. 125 16 31N 97 37E
Salzburg 106 47 48N 13 2E
Salzburg □ 106 47 15N 13 0E
Salzgitter 106 52 2N 10 22E
Sam Neua 128 20 29N 104 0E
Sam Ngao 128 17 18N 99 0E
Sam Rayburn Res. 75 31 15N 94 20W
Sama 120 60 12N 60 22E
Sama de Langreo 104 43 18N 5 40W
Samales Group 127 6 0N 122 0E
Samana Cay 85 23 3N 73 45W
Samanco 86 9 10S 78 30W
Samangan □ 123 36 15N 67 40E
Samar, I. 127 12 0N 125 0E
Samarkand 120 39 40N 67 0E
Samarra 122 34 16N 43 55E
Samatan 102 43 29N 0 55E
Sambalpur 125 21 28N 83 58E
Sambas, S. 126 1 20N 109 20E
Sambava 117 14 16S 50 10E
Sambhal 124 28 35N 78 37E
Sambhar 124 26 52N 75 10E
Sambiase 108 38 58N 16 16E
Sambor 128 12 46N 106 0E
Sambre, R. 105 50 27N 4 52E
Sambro 39 44 28N 63 36W
Samchŏk 130 37 30N 129 10E
Same 116 4 2S 37 38E
Samer 101 50 38N 1 44E
Samo Alto 88 30 22S 71 0W
Samoan Is. 10 14 0S 171 0W
Samoëns 103 46 5N 6 45E
Samoorombón, Bahía 88 36 5S 57 20W
Sámos, I. 109 37 45N 26 50E
Samosir, P. 126 2 35N 98 50E
Samothráki, I. 109 40 25N 25 40E
Sampacho 88 33 20S 64 50W
Sampang 127 7 11S 113 13E
Sampit 126 2 20S 113 0E
Samra 122 25 35N 41 0E
Samshui 131 23 7N 112 58E
Samsun 122 41 15N 36 15E
Samut Prakan 128 13 32N 100 40E
Samut Sakhon 128 13 31N 100 20E
Samut Songkhram (Mekong) 128 13 24N 100 1E
San Agustin 86 1 53N 76 16W
San Agustin, C. 127 6 20N 126 13E
San Agustin de Valle Fértil 88 30 35S 67 30W
San Ambrosio, I. 15 26 35S 79 30W
San Andreas 80 38 17N 120 39W
San Andrés, I. de 84 12 42N 81 46W
San Andres Mts. 79 33 0N 106 45W
San Andrés Tuxtla 83 18 30N 95 20W
San Angelo 75 31 30N 100 30W
San Anselmo 80 37 49N 122 34W
San Antonio, Belize 83 16 15N 89 2W
San Antonio, Chile 88 33 40S 71 40W
San Antonio, N. Mex., U.S.A. 79 33 58N 106 57W
San Antonio, Tex., U.S.A. 75 29 30N 98 30W
San Antonio, Venez. 86 3 30N 66 44W
San Antonio, C., Argent. 88 36 15S 56 40W
San Antonio, C., Cuba 84 21 50N 84 57W
San Antonio de Caparo 86 7 35N 71 27W
San Antonio de los Baños 84 22 54N 82 31W
San Antonio de los Cobres 88 24 16S 66 2W
*San Antonio do Zaire 116 6 8S 12 11E
San Antonio, Mt. (Old Baldy Pk.) 81 34 17N 117 38W
San Antonio Oeste 90 40 40S 65 0W
San Antonio, R. 75 28 30N 97 14W
San Ardo 80 36 1N 120 54W
San Augustine 75 31 30N 94 7W
San Benedetto 108 45 2N 10 57E
San Benedicto, I. 82 19 18N 110 49W
San Benito 75 26 5N 97 32W
San Benito Mt. 80 36 22N 120 37W
San Benito, R. 80 36 53N 121 50W
San Bernardino 81 34 7N 117 18W
San Bernardo 88 33 40S 70 50W
San Bernardo, I. de 86 9 45N 75 50W
San Blas 82 26 10N 108 40W
San Blas, C. 73 29 40N 85 25W
San Blas, Cord. de 84 9 15N 78 30W
San Borja 86 15 0S 67 12W
San Buenaventura 82 27 5N 101 32W
San Buenaventura = Ventura 81 34 17N 119 18W
San Carlos, Argent. 88 33 50S 69 0W
San Carlos, Chile 130 36 25S 72 0W
San Carlos, Mexico 82 29 0N 101 10W
San Carlos, Nic. 84 11 12N 84 50W
San Carlos, Phil. 127 10 29N 123 25E
San Carlos, Uruguay 89 34 46S 54 58W
San Carlos, U.S.A. 79 33 24N 110 27W
San Carlos, Amazonas, Venez. 86 1 55N 67 4W
San Carlos, Cojedes, Venez. 86 9 40N 68 36W
San Carlos de Bariloche 90 41 10S 71 25W
San Carlos del Zulia 86 9 1N 71 55W
San Carlos L. 79 33 20N 110 10W
San Clara 57 51 29N 101 26W
San Clemente, Chile 88 35 30S 71 39W
San Clemente, U.S.A. 81 33 29N 117 45W
San Clemente I. 81 32 53N 118 30W
San Cristóbal, Argent. 88 30 20S 61 10W
San Cristóbal, Dom. Rep. 85 18 25N 70 6W
San Cristóbal, Venez. 86 7 46N 72 14W
San Cristóbal de las Casas 83 16 50N 92 33W
San Diego, Calif., U.S.A. 81 32 43N 117 10W
San Diego, Tex., U.S.A. 75 27 47N 98 15W
San Diego, C. 90 54 40S 65 10W
San Diego de la Unión 82 21 28N 100 52W
San Estanislao 88 24 39S 56 26W
San Felipe, Chile 88 32 43S 70 50W
San Felipe, Mexico 82 31 0N 114 52W
San Felipe, Venez. 86 10 20N 68 44W
San Felipe, R. 81 33 12N 115 49W
San Feliu de Guixols 104 41 45N 3 1E
San Félix 86 8 20N 62 35W
San Felix, I. 15 26 30S 80 0W
San Fernando, Chile 88 34 30S 71 0W
San Fernando, Mexico 82 30 0N 115 10W
San Fernando, Luzon, Phil. 127 16 40N 120 23E
San Fernando, Luzon, Phil. 127 15 5N 120 37E
San Fernando, Spain 104 36 22N 6 17W
San Fernando, Trin 85 10 20N 61 30W
San Fernando, U.S.A. 81 34 15N 118 29W
San Fernando de Apure 86 7 54N 67 28W
San Fernando de Atabapo 86 4 3N 67 42W
San Fernando, R. 82 25 0N 99 0W
San Francisco, Córdoba, Argent. 88 31 30S 62 5W
San Francisco, San Luis, Argent. 88 32 45S 66 10W
San Francisco, U.S.A. 80 37 47N 122 30W
San Francisco de Macorís 85 19 19N 70 15W
San Francisco del Monte de Oro 88 32 36S 66 8W
San Francisco del Oro 82 26 52N 105 50W
San Francisco, Paso de 88 35 40S 70 24W
San Francisco, R. 79 33 30N 109 0W
San Francisco Solano, Pta. 86 6 18N 77 29W
San Francisville 75 30 48N 91 22W
San Gabriel 86 0 36N 77 49W

** Renamed Soyo*

San German Santa Rosa

San German	**67**	18 5N	67 3W
San Gil	**86**	6 33N	73 8W
San Gorgonio Mt.	**81**	34 7N	116 51W
San Gottardo, Paso del	**106**	46 33N	8 33 E
San Gregorio, Uruguay	**89**	32 37 S	55 40W
San Gregorio, U.S.A.	**80**	37 20N	122 23W
San Ignacio, Boliv.	**86**	16 20 S	60 55W
San Ignacio, Mexico	**82**	27 27N	112 51W
San Ignacio, Parag.	**88**	26 52 S	57 3W
San Ignacio, Laguna	**82**	26 50N	113 11W
San Ildefonso, C.	**127**	16 0N	122 10 E
San Isidro	**88**	34 29 S	58 31W
San Jacinto, Colomb.	**86**	9 50N	75 8W
San Jacinto, U.S.A.	**81**	33 47N	116 57W
San Javier, Misiones, Argent.	**89**	27 55 S	55 5W
San Javier, Santa Fe, Argent.	**88**	30 40 S	59 55W
San Javier, Boliv.	**86**	16 18 S	62 30W
San Javier, Chile	**88**	35 40 S	71 45W
San Jerónimo, Sa. de	**86**	8 0N	75 50W
San Joaquin	**80**	36 36N	120 11W
San Joaquín	**86**	10 16N	67 47W
San Joaquin R.	**80**	37 4N	121 51W
San Joaquin Valley	**80**	37 0N	120 30W
San Jorge	**88**	31 54 S	61 50W
San Jorge, Bahía de	**82**	31 20N	113 20W
San Jorge, Golfo de	**90**	46 0 S	66 0W
San Jorge, G. de	**104**	40 50N	0 55W
San José, Boliv.	**86**	17 45 S	60 50W
San José, C. Rica	**84**	10 0N	84 2W
San José, Guat.	**82**	14 0N	90 50W
San José, Luzon, Phil.	**127**	15 45N	120 55 E
San José, Mindoro, Phil.	**127**	10 50N	122 5 E
San Jose, U.S.A.	**76**	40 18N	89 36W
San Jose, Calif., U.S.A.	**80**	37 20N	121 53W
San Jose, N. Mex., U.S.A.	**75**	35 26N	105 30W
San José Carpizo	**83**	19 26N	90 32W
San José de Feliciano	**88**	30 26 S	58 46W
San José de Jáchal	**88**	30 5 S	69 0W
San José de Mayo	**88**	34 27 S	56 27W
San José de Ocuné	**86**	4 15N	70 20W
San José del Cabo	**82**	23 0N	109 50W
San José del Guaviare	**86**	2 35N	72 38W
San José, I.	**82**	25 0N	110 50W
San Juan, Argent.	**88**	31 30 S	68 30W
San Juan, Antioquía, Colomb.	**86**	8 46N	76 32W
San Juan, Meta, Colomb.	**86**	3 26N	73 50W
San Juan, Dom. Rep.	**67**	18 49N	71 12W
San Juan, Coahuila, Mexico	**82**	29 34N	101 53W
San Juan, Jalisco, Mexico	**82**	21 20N	102 50W
San Juan, Querétaro, Mexico	**82**	20 25N	100 0W
San Juan, Phil.	**127**	8 35N	126 20 E
San Juan, Pto Rico	**85**	18 28N	66 37W
San Juan □	**88**	31 9 S	69 0W
San Juan Bautista, Parag.	**88**	26 37 S	57 6W
San Juan Bautista, U.S.A.	**80**	36 51N	121 32W
San Juan, C.	**67**	18 23N	65 37W
San Juan Capistrano	**81**	33 29N	117 40W
San Juan de Guadalupe	**82**	24 38N	102 44W
San Juan de los Cayos	**86**	11 10N	68 25W
San Juan de los Morros	**86**	9 55N	67 21W
San Juan de Norte, B. de	**84**	11 30N	83 40W
San Juan del Norte	**84**	10 58N	83 40W
San Juan del Río	**83**	24 47N	104 27W
San Juan del Sur	**84**	11 20N	86 0W
San Juan I.	**80**	48 32N	123 5W
San Juan Mts.	**79**	38 30N	108 30W
San Juan, Presa de	**82**	17 45N	95 15W
San Juan, R., Argent.	**88**	32 20 S	67 25W
San Juan, R., Colomb.	**86**	4 0N	77 20W
San Juan, R., Nic.	**84**	11 0N	84 30W
San Juan, R., Calif., U.S.A.	**80**	36 14N	121 9W
San Juan, R., Utah, U.S.A.	**79**	37 20N	110 20W
San Julián	**90**	49 15 S	68 0W
San Justo	**88**	30 55 S	60 30W
San Lázaro, C.	**82**	24 50N	112 18W
San Lázaro, Sa. de	**82**	23 25N	110 0W
San Leandro	**80**	37 40N	122 6W
San Lorenzo, Argent.	**88**	32 45 S	60 45W
San Lorenzo, Ecuador	**86**	1 15N	78 50W
San Lorenzo, Parag.	**88**	25 20 S	57 32W
San Lorenzo, Venez.	**86**	9 47N	71 4W
San Lorenzo, I., Mexico	**82**	28 35N	112 50W
San Lorenzo, I., Peru	**86**	12 20 S	77 35W
San Lorenzo, Mt.	**90**	47 40 S	72 20W
San Lorenzo, R.	**82**	24 15N	107 24W
San Lucas, Boliv.	**86**	20 5 S	65 0W
San Lucas, Baja California S., Mexico	**82**	22 53N	109 54W
San Lucas, Baja California S., Mexico	**82**	27 10N	112 14W
San Lucas, U.S.A.	**80**	36 8N	121 1W
San Lucas, C. de	**82**	22 50N	110 0W
San Luis, Argent.	**88**	33 20 S	66 20W
San Luis, Cuba	**84**	22 17N	83 46W
San Luis, Guat.	**84**	16 14N	89 27W

San Luis, U.S.A.	**79**	37 14N	105 26W
San Luis, Venez.	**86**	11 7N	69 42W
San Luis □	**88**	34 0 S	66 0W
San Luis de la Loma	**82**	17 18N	100 55W
San Luis de la Paz	**82**	21 19N	100 32W
San Luis de Potosí	**82**	22 9N	100 59W
San Luis de Potosí □	**82**	22 10N	101 0W
San Luis, I.	**82**	29 58N	114 26W
San Luis Obispo	**79**	35 21N	120 38W
San Luis Res.	**80**	37 4N	121 5W
San Luis Río Colorado	**82**	32 29N	114 48W
San Luis, Sierra de	**88**	37 25N	66 10W
San Marcos, Guat.	**84**	14 59N	91 52W
San Marcos, U.S.A.	**75**	29 53N	98 0W
San Marcos, I.	**82**	27 13N	112 6W
San Marino	**108**	43 56N	12 25 E
San Marino ■	**108**	43 56N	12 25 E
San Martín, Argent.	**88**	33 5 S	68 28W
San Martín, Colomb.	**86**	3 42N	73 42W
San Martín, L.	**90**	48 50 S	72 50W
San Mateo	**80**	37 32N	122 19W
San Matías	**86**	16 25 S	58 20W
San Matías, Golfo de	**90**	41 30 S	64 0W
San Miguel, El Sal.	**84**	13 30N	88 12W
San Miguel, Panama	**84**	8 27N	78 55W
San Miguel, U.S.A.	**80**	35 45N	120 42W
San Miguel, Venez.	**86**	9 40N	65 11W
San Miguel de Tucumán	**88**	26 50 S	65 20W
San Miguel del Monte	**88**	35 23 S	58 50W
San Miguel I.	**81**	34 2N	120 23W
San Miguel, R., Boliv.	**86**	16 0 S	62 45W
San Miguel, R., Ecuador/Ecuador	**86**	0 25N	76 30W
San Narcisco	**127**	15 2N	120 3 E
San Nicolás de los Arroyas	**88**	33 17 S	60 10W
San Nicolas I.	**68**	33 16N	119 30W
San Onafre	**81**	33 22N	117 34W
San Onofre	**86**	9 44N	75 32W
San Pablo, Boliv.	**88**	21 43 S	66 38W
San Pablo, Colomb.	**86**	5 27N	70 56W
San Pedro, Buenos Aires, Argent.	**89**	33 43 S	59 45W
San Pedro, Jujuy, Argent.	**88**	24 12 S	64 55W
San Pedro, Chile	**88**	21 58 S	68 30W
San Pedro, Colomb.	**86**	4 56N	71 53W
San Pedro, Dom. Rep.	**85**	18 30N	69 18W
San Pedro, Mexico	**82**	23 55N	110 17W
San Pedro □	**88**	24 0 S	57 0W
San Pedro Channel	**81**	33 35N	118 25W
San Pedro de Arimena	**86**	4 37N	71 42W
San Pedro de Atacama	**88**	22 55 S	68 15W
San Pedro de Jujuy	**88**	24 12 S	64 55W
San Pedro de las Colonias	**82**	25 50N	102 59W
San Pedro de Lloc	**86**	7 15 S	79 28W
San Pedro del Norte	**84**	13 4N	84 33W
San Pedro del Paraná	**88**	26 43 S	56 13W
San Pedro Mártir, Sierra	**82**	31 0N	115 30W
San Pedro Mixtepec	**83**	16 2N	97 0W
San Pedro Ocampo = Melchor Ocampo	**82**	24 52N	101 40W
San Pedro, Pta.	**88**	25 30 S	70 38W
San Pedro, R., Chihuahua, Mexico	**82**	28 20N	106 10W
San Pedro, R., Michoacan, Mexico	**82**	19 23N	103 51W
San Pedro, R., Nayarit, Mexico	**82**	21 45N	105 30W
San Pedro, R., U.S.A.	**79**	32 45N	110 35W
San Pedro Sula	**84**	15 30N	88 0W
San Pedro Tututepec	**83**	16 9N	97 38W
San Pedro,Pta.	**88**	25 30 S	70 38W
San Quintín, Mexico	**82**	30 29N	115 57W
San Quintín, Phil.	**127**	16 1N	120 56 E
San, R.	**107**	50 25N	22 20 E
San Rafael, Argent.	**88**	34 40 S	68 30W
San Rafael, Colomb.	**86**	6 2N	69 45W
San Rafael, Calif., U.S.A.	**80**	38 0N	122 32W
San Rafael, N. Mex., U.S.A.	**79**	35 6N	107 58W
San Rafael, Venez.	**86**	10 42N	71 46W
San Rafael Mt.	**81**	34 41N	119 52W
San Ramón de la Nueva Orán	**88**	23 10 S	64 20W
San Remo	**108**	43 48N	7 47 E
San Román, C.	**86**	12 12N	70 0W
San Roque	**88**	28 15 S	58 45W
San Rosendo	**88**	37 10 S	72 50W
San Saba	**75**	31 12N	98 45W
San Salvador	**84**	13 40N	89 20W
San Salvador de Jujuy	**88**	23 30 S	65 40W
San Salvador (Watlings) I.	**85**	24 0N	74 40W
San Sebastián, Argent.	**90**	53 10 S	68 30W
San Sebastián, Spain	**104**	43 17N	1 58W
San Sebastián, Venez.	**86**	9 57N	67 11W
San Severo	**108**	41 41N	15 23 E
San Simeon	**80**	35 39N	121 11W
San Simon	**79**	32 14N	109 16W
San Telmo	**82**	30 58N	116 6W
San Tiburcio	**82**	24 8N	101 32W
San Valentin, Mte.	**90**	46 30 S	73 30W
San Vicente de la Barquera	**104**	43 30N	4 29W
San Vicente del Caguán	**86**	2 7N	74 46W

San Vicenzo	**123**	43 9N	10 32 E
San Yanaro	**86**	2 47N	69 42W
San Ygnacio	**75**	27 6N	99 24W
San Ysidro	**79**	32 33N	117 5W
San'a	**115**	15 27N	44 12 E
Sana, R.	**108**	44 40N	16 43 E
Sanaga, R.	**116**	3 35N	9 38 E
Sanak I	**67**	53 30N	162 30W
Sanaloa, Presa	**82**	24 50N	107 20W
Sanana	**127**	2 5 S	125 50 E
Sanandaj	**122**	35 25N	47 7 E
Sanandita	**88**	21 40 S	63 35W
Sanary	**103**	43 7N	5 48 E
Sancergues	**101**	47 10N	2 54 E
Sancerre	**101**	47 20N	2 50 E
Sancha Ho	**131**	26 20N	105 30 E
Sánchez	**85**	19 15N	69 36W
Sanco, Pt.	**127**	8 15N	126 24 E
Sancoins	**101**	46 47N	2 55 E
Sancti-Spiritus	**84**	21 52N	79 33W
Sand Creek, R.	**77**	39 5N	85 52W
Sand I.	**52**	46 59N	91 0W
Sand L.	**52**	50 10N	94 35W
Sand Lake	**34**	47 46N	84 31W
Sand Pt.	**46**	43 54N	83 27W
Sand Point	**67**	55 20N	160 32W
Sand, R.	**60**	54 23N	111 2W
Sand Springs	**75**	36 12N	96 5W
Sandakan	**126**	5 53N	118 10 E
Sandan	**128**	12 46N	106 0 E
Sanday, I.	**96**	59 15N	2 30W
Sandbank L.	**53**	51 8N	82 41W
Sanders, U.S.A.	**77**	38 40N	84 56W
Sanders, Ariz., U.S.A.	**79**	35 12N	109 25W
Sanderson	**75**	30 5N	102 30W
Sandfell	**110**	63 57N	16 48W
Sandfly L.	**55**	55 43N	106 6W
Sandhill	**49**	43 50N	79 52W
Sandía	**86**	14 10 S	69 30W
Sandikli	**122**	38 30N	30 20 E
Sandnes	**111**	58 50N	5 45 E
Sandoa	**116**	9 48 S	23 0 E
Sandomierz	**107**	50 40N	21 43 E
Sandona	**86**	1 17N	77 28W
Sandoval	**76**	38 37N	89 7W
Sandover, R.	**135**	21 43 S	136 32 E
Sandoway	**125**	18 20N	94 30 E
Sandpoint	**78**	48 20N	116 40W
Sandringham	**94**	52 50N	0 30 E
Sandspit	**62**	53 14N	131 49W
Sandstone	**134**	27 59 S	119 16 E
Sandusky, Mich., U.S.A.	**46**	43 26N	82 50W
Sandusky, Ohio, U.S.A.	**70**	41 25N	82 40W
Sandusky, R.	**77**	41 27N	83 0W
Sandviken	**111**	60 38N	16 46 E
Sandwich	**77**	41 39N	88 37W
Sandwich B.	**36**	53 40N	57 15W
Sandwich Group	**91**	57 0 S	27 0W
Sandwip Chan.	**125**	22 35N	91 35 E
Sandy, Nev., U.S.A.	**81**	35 49N	115 36W
Sandy, Oreg., U.S.A.	**80**	45 24N	122 16W
Sandy Beach	**49**	43 4N	78 59W
Sandy C., Queens., Austral.	**135**	24 42 S	153 15 E
Sandy C., Tas., Austral.	**135**	41 25 S	144 45 E
Sandy Cay	**85**	23 13N	75 18W
Sandy Cove	**37**	51 21N	56 40W
Sandy Cr.	**78**	42 20N	109 30W
Sandy Hook	**76**	38 5N	83 8W
Sandy L., Alta., Can.	**60**	53 47N	114 2W
Sandy L., Newf., Can.	**37**	49 15N	57 0W
Sandy L., Ont., Can.	**34**	53 2N	93 0W
Sandy Lake	**34**	53 0N	93 15W
Sandy Narrows	**55**	55 5N	103 4W
Sandy Point	**39**	43 42N	65 19W
Sandy, R.	**36**	55 30N	68 21W
Sandybeach L.	**52**	49 49N	92 21W
Sanford, Fla., U.S.A.	**73**	28 45N	81 20W
Sanford, Me., U.S.A.	**71**	43 28N	70 47W
Sanford, N.C., U.S.A.	**73**	35 30N	79 10W
Sanford, R.	**134**	27 22 S	115 53 E
Sanga Tolon	**121**	61 50N	149 40 E
Sangamner	**124**	19 30N	74 15 E
Sangamon R.	**76**	40 2N	90 21W
Sangar	**121**	63 55N	127 31 E
Sangasanga	**126**	0 29 S	117 13 E
Sangchih	**131**	29 25N	109 30 E
Sangeang, I.	**127**	8 12 S	119 6 E
Sanger	**80**	36 47N	119 35W
Sanggau	**126**	0 5N	110 30 E
Sangihe, Kep.	**127**	3 0N	126 0 E
Sangihe, P.	**127**	3 45N	125 30 E
Sangkan Ho	**130**	40 24N	115 19 E
Sangkapura	**126**	5 52 S	112 40 E
Sangli	**124**	16 55N	74 33 E
Sangmélina	**116**	2 57N	12 1 E
Sangonera, R.	**104**	37 39N	2 0W
Sangre de Cristo Mts.	**75**	37 0N	105 0W
Sangsang	**129**	29 30N	86 0 E
Sangudo	**60**	53 50N	114 54W
Sanguinaires, Is.	**103**	41 51N	8 36 E
Sanish	**74**	48 0N	102 30W
Sankiang	**131**	25 39N	109 30 E
Sankt Moritz	**106**	46 30N	9 50 E
Sankuru, R.	**116**	4 17 S	20 25 E
Sanlúcar de Barrameda	**104**	37 26N	6 18W
Sanmaur	**41**	47 54N	73 47W
Sanmen Hu	**131**	34 40N	111 0 E

Sanmen Wan	**131**	29 10N	121 45 E
Sanmenhsia	**131**	34 46N	111 30 E
Sannicandro Gargánico	**108**	41 50N	15 34 E
Sanok	**107**	49 35N	22 10 E
Sanquhar	**96**	55 21N	3 56W
Santa Ana, Ecuador	**86**	1 10 S	80 20W
Santa Ana, El Sal.	**84**	14 0N	89 40W
Santa Ana, Mexico	**82**	30 31N	111 8W
Santa Ana, U.S.A.	**81**	33 48N	117 55W
Santa Ana, El Beni	**86**	13 50 S	65 40W
Santa Bárbara, Brazil	**87**	16 0 S	59 0W
Santa Bárbara, Colomb.	**86**	5 53N	75 35W
Santa Barbara	**84**	14 53N	88 14W
Santa Bárbara	**82**	26 48N	105 50W
Santa Barbara	**81**	34 25N	119 40W
Santa Bárbara	**86**	7 47N	71 10W
Santa Barbara Channel	**81**	34 20N	120 0W
Santa Barbara I.	**81**	33 29N	119 2W
Santa Barbara Is.	**79**	33 31N	119 0W
Santa Catalina	**86**	10 36N	75 17W
Santa Catalina, G. of	**81**	33 0N	118 0W
Santa Catalina, I., Mexico	**82**	25 40N	110 50W
Santa Catalina, I., U.S.A.	**81**	33 20N	118 30W
Santa Catarina □	**89**	27 25 S	48 30W
Santa Catarina, I. de	**89**	27 30 S	48 40W
Santa Cecília	**89**	26 56 S	50 27W
Santa Clara, Cuba	**84**	22 20N	80 0W
Santa Clara, Calif., U.S.A.	**80**	37 21N	122 0W
Santa Clara, Utah, U.S.A.	**79**	37 10N	113 38W
Santa Clara de Olimar	**89**	32 50 S	54 54W
Santa Clotilde	**86**	2 25 S	73 45W
Santa Cruz, Argent.	**90**	50 0 S	68 50W
Santa Cruz, Boliv.	**86**	17 43 S	63 10W
Santa Cruz, Canary Is.	**114**	28 29N	16 26W
Santa Cruz, Chile	**88**	34 38 S	71 27W
Santa Cruz, C. Rica	**84**	10 15N	85 41W
Santa Cruz, Phil.	**127**	14 20N	121 30 E
Santa Cruz, Calif., U.S.A.	**80**	36 55N	122 1W
Santa Cruz, N. Mexico, U.S.A.	**79**	35 59N	106 1W
Santa Cruz □	**86**	17 43 S	63 10W
Santa Cruz de Barahona	**85**	18 12N	71 6W
Santa Cruz del Norte	**84**	23 9N	81 55W
Santa Cruz del Sur	**84**	20 50N	78 0W
Santa Cruz do Rio Pardo	**89**	22 54 S	49 37W
Santa Cruz do Sul	**89**	29 42 S	52 25W
Santa Cruz I.	**68**	34 0N	119 45W
Santa Cruz, Is.	**14**	10 30 S	166 0 E
Santa Cruz, R.	**90**	50 10 S	70 0W
Santa Elena, Argent.	**88**	30 58 S	59 47W
Santa Elena, Ecuador	**86**	2 16 S	80 52W
Santa Elena C.	**85**	10 54N	85 56W
Santa Fe, Argent.	**88**	31 35 S	60 41W
Santa Fe, U.S.A.	**79**	35 40N	106 0W
Santa Fé □	**88**	31 50 S	60 55W
Santa Filomena	**87**	9 0 S	45 50W
Santa Genoveva, Mt.	**82**	23 18N	109 52W
Santa Inés, I.	**90**	54 0 S	73 0W
Santa Isabel, Argent.	**88**	36 10 S	67 0W
Santa Isabel, Brazil	**87**	13 45 S	56 30W
Santa Lucía, Corrientes, Argent.	**88**	28 58 S	59 5W
Santa Lucía, San Juan, Argent.	**88**	31 30 S	68 45W
Santa Lucia	**88**	34 27 S	56 24W
Santa Lucia Range	**80**	36 0N	121 20W
Santa Magdalena, I.	**82**	24 50N	112 15W
Santa Margarita, Argent.	**88**	38 18 S	61 35W
Santa Margarita, U.S.A.	**80**	35 23N	120 37W
Santa Margarita, I.	**82**	24 30N	112 0W
Santa Margarita, R.	**81**	33 13N	117 23W
Santa María, Argent.	**88**	26 40 S	66 0W
Santa Maria, Brazil	**89**	29 40 S	53 40W
Santa María, Mexico	**82**	27 40N	114 40W
Santa Maria	**81**	34 58N	120 29W
Santa María, Bahía de	**82**	25 10N	108 40W
Santa Maria da Vitória	**87**	13 24 S	44 12W
Santa María del Oro	**82**	25 30N	105 20W
Santa Maria di Leuca, C.	**109**	39 48N	18 20 E
Santa María, R.	**82**	31 0N	107 14W
Santa Marta	**86**	11 15N	74 13W
Santa Marta Grande, C.	**89**	28 43 S	48 50W
Santa Marta, Sierra Nevada de	**67**	10 55N	73 50W
Santa Monica	**81**	34 0N	118 30W
Santa Napa	**78**	38 28N	122 45W
Santa Paula	**81**	34 20N	119 2W
Santa Rita, U.S.A.	**79**	32 50N	108 0W
Santa Rita, Guarico, Venez.	**86**	8 8N	66 16W
Santa Rita, Zulia, Venez.	**86**	10 32N	71 32W
Santa Rosa, La Pampa, Argent.	**88**	36 40 S	64 30W
Santa Rosa, San Luis, Argent.	**88**	32 30 S	65 10W
Santa Rosa, Boliv.	**86**	10 25 S	67 20W
Santa Rosa, Brazil	**89**	27 52 S	54 29W
Santa Rosa, Colomb.	**86**	3 32N	69 48W
Santa Rosa, Hond.	**82**	14 40N	89 0W

Santa Rosa Sebastopol

Santa Rosa, Calif., U.S.A. 80 38 26N 122 43W
Santa Rosa, N. Mexico, U.S.A. 75 34 58N 104 40W
Santa Rosa, Amazonas, Venez. 86 1 29N 66 55W
Santa Rosa, Apure, Venez. 86 6 37N 67 57W
Santa Rosa de Cabal 86 4 52N 75 38W
Santa Rosa de Copán 84 14 47N 88 46W
Santa Rosa de Osos 86 6 39N 75 28W
Santa Rosa de Río Primero 88 31 8S 63 20W
Santa Rosa de Viterbo 86 5 53N 72 59W
Santa Rosa I., Calif., U.S.A. 81 34 0N 120 6W
Santa Rosa I., Fla., U.S.A. 73 30 23N 87 0W
Santa Rosa Mts. 78 41 45N 117 30W
Santa Rosalía 82 27 20N 112 30W
Santa Sylvina 88 27 50S 61 10W
Santa Tecla = Nueva San Salvador 82 13 40N 89 25W
Santa Teresa, Argent. 88 33 25S 60 47W
Santa Teresa, Mexico 83 25 17N 97 51W
Santa Teresa, Venez. 86 4 43N 61 4W
Santa Vitória do Palmar 89 33 32S 53 25W
Santa Ynez 81 34 37N 120 5W
Santa Ynez, R. 81 34 37N 120 41W
Santa Ysabel 81 33 7N 116 40W
Santana, Coxilha de 89 30 50S 55 35W
Santana do Livramento 89 30 55S 55 30W
Santander, Colomb. 86 3 1N 76 28W
Santander, Spain 104 43 27N 3 51W
Santander Jiménez 83 24 11N 98 29W
Santaquin 78 40 0N 111 51W
Santarém, Brazil 87 2 25S 54 42W
Santarém, Port. 104 39 12N 8 42W
Santaren Channel 84 24 0N 79 30W
Santiago, Brazil 89 29 11S 54 52W
Santiago, Chile 88 33 24S 70 50W
Santiago, Dom. Rep. 85 19 30N 70 40W
Santiago, Panama 84 8 0N 81 0W
Santiago □ 88 33 30S 70 50W
Santiago de Compostela 104 42 52N 8 37W
Santiago de Cuba 84 20 0N 75 49W
Santiago del Estero 88 27 50S 64 15W
Santiago del Estero □ 88 27 50S 64 20W
Santiago Ixcuintla 82 21 50N 105 11W
Santiago Papasquiaro 82 25 0N 105 20W
Santiaguillo, L. de 82 24 50N 104 50W
Santo Amaro 87 12 30S 38 50W
Santo Anastácio 89 21 58S 51 39W
Santo André 89 23 39S 46 29W
Santo Ângelo 89 28 15S 54 15W
Santo Antonio 87 15 50S 56 0W
Santo Corazón 86 18 0S 58 45W
Santo Domingo, Dom. Rep. 85 18 30N 70 0W
Santo Domingo, Baja Calif. N., Mexico 82 30 43N 115 56W
Santo Domingo, Baja Calif. S., Mexico 82 25 32N 112 2W
Santo Domingo, Nic. 84 12 14N 84 59W
Santo Tomas 82 31 33N 116 24W
Santo Tomás 86 14 34S 72 30W
Santo Tomé 89 28 40S 56 5W
Santoña 104 43 29N 3 20W
Santos 89 24 0S 46 20W
Santos Dumont 89 22 55S 43 10W
Santu 131 25 59N 107 52E
Santuaho 131 26 36N 119 42E
Sanvignes-les-Mines 101 46 40N 4 18E
Sanyüan 131 34 39N 108 59E
Sanza Pombo 116 7 18S 15 56E
São Anastacio 89 22 0S 51 40W
São Borja 89 28 45S 56 0W
São Carlos 89 22 0S 47 50W
São Cristóvão 87 11 15S 37 15W
São Domingos, Brazil 87 13 25S 46 10W
São Domingos, Guin.-Biss. 87 12 22N 16 8W
Sao Francisco 87 16 0S 44 50W
São Francisco do Sul 89 26 15S 48 36W
São Francisco, R. 87 10 30S 36 24W
São Gabriel 89 30 10S 54 30W
São Gonçalo 89 22 48S 43 5W
São João da Boa Vista 89 22 0S 46 52W
São João del Rei 89 21 8S 44 15W
São João do Araguaia 87 5 23S 48 46W
São João do Piaui 87 8 10S 42 15W
São José do Rio Prêto 89 20 50S 49 20W
São José dos Campos 89 23 7S 45 52W
São Leopoldo 89 29 50S 51 10W
São Lourenço 89 16 30S 55 5W
São Lourenço, R. 87 16 40S 56 0W
São Luís Gonzaga 89 28 25S 55 0W
São Luís (Maranhão) 87 2 39S 44 15W
São Marcelino 86 1 0N 67 12W
Sao Marcelino 86 1 0N 67 12W
São Marcos, B. de 87 2 0S 44 0W
São Marcos, R. 87 18 15S 47 37W
São Mateus 87 18 44S 39 50W
São Miguel 93 37 33N 25 27W
São Paulo 89 23 40S 46 50W
São Paulo □ 89 22 0S 49 0W
São Romão 86 5 53S 67 50W
São Roque, C. de 87 5 30S 35 10W
São Sebastião do Paraíso 89 20 54S 46 59W
São Sebastião, I. 89 23 50S 45 18W
São Tomé, C. de 89 22 0S 41 10W
Sao Tomé & Principe ■ 112 0 10N 7 0E
São Vicente 89 23 57S 46 23W
São Vicente, Cabo de 104 37 0N 9 0W
Saona, I. 85 18 10N 68 40W
Saône-et-Loire □ 101 46 25N 4 50E
Saône, R. 101 46 25N 4 50E
Saonek 127 0 28S 130 47E
Saparua, I. 127 3 33S 128 40E
Sapelo I. 73 31 28N 81 15W
Sapodnyy Sayan 121 52 30N 94 0E
Saposoa 86 6 55S 76 30W
Sappho 80 48 4N 124 16W
Sapporo 132 43 0N 141 15E
Sapudi, I. 127 7 2S 114 17E
Sapulpa 75 36 0N 96 10W
Saqqez 122 36 15N 46 20E
Sar-i-Pul 123 36 10N 66 0E
Sar Planina 109 42 10N 21 0E
Sarāb 122 38 0N 47 30E
Sarada, R. 125 28 15N 80 30E
Saragossa = Zaragoza 104 41 39N 0 53W
Saraguro 86 3 35S 79 16W
Sarajevo 109 43 52N 18 26E
Saran, G. 126 0 30S 111 25E
Saranac 77 42 56N 85 13W
Saranac Lake 71 44 20N 74 10W
Sarandí del Yi 89 33 18S 55 38W
Sarandí Grande 88 33 20S 55 50W
Sarangani B. 127 6 0N 125 13E
Sarangani Is. 127 5 25N 125 25E
Sarangarh 125 21 30N 82 57E
Saransk 120 54 10N 45 10E
Sarapul 120 56 28N 53 48E
Sarasota 73 27 10N 82 30W
Saratoga, Calif., U.S.A. 80 37 16N 122 2W
Saratoga, Wyo., U.S.A. 78 41 30N 106 56W
Saratoga Springs 71 43 5N 73 47W
Saratok 126 3 5S 110 50E
Saratov 120 51 30N 46 2E
Saravane 128 15 43N 106 25E
Sarawak □ 126 2 0N 113 0E
Sarbāz 123 26 38N 61 19E
Sarbisheh 123 32 30N 59 40E
Sardarshahr 124 28 30N 74 29E
Sardegna, I. 108 39 57N 9 0E
Sardinata 86 8 5N 72 48W
Sardinia 77 39 0N 83 49W
Sardinia = Sardegna 108 39 57N 9 0E
Sardis 63 49 8N 121 58W
Sarektjåkkå 110 67 27N 17 43E
Sargasso Sea 12 27 0N 72 0W
Sargent 74 41 42N 99 24W
Sargodha 124 32 10N 72 40E
* Sargodha □ 124 31 50N 72 0E
Sarh 114 9 5N 18 23E
Sārī 123 36 30N 53 11E
Sarichef C. 67 54 38N 164 59W
Sarikamiş 122 40 22N 42 35E
Sarikei 126 2 8N 111 30E
Sarina 135 21 22S 149 13E
Sarita 75 27 14N 97 49W
Sariwŏn 130 38 31N 125 44E
Sark, I. 100 49 25N 2 20W
Sarlat-la-Canéda 102 44 54N 1 13E
Sarles 57 48 58N 99 0W
Sarmi 127 1 49S 138 38E
Sarnia 46 42 58N 82 23W
Sarny 120 51 17N 26 40E
Sarolangun 126 2 30S 102 30E
Saronikós Kólpos 109 37 45N 23 45E
Saros Körfezi 109 40 30N 26 15E
Sarpsborg 111 59 16N 11 12E
Sarralbe 101 48 55N 7 1E
Sarre, La 40 48 45N 79 15W
Sarre, R. 101 48 49N 7 0E
Sarre-Union 101 48 55N 7 4E
Sarrebourg 101 48 43N 7 3E
Sarreguemines 101 49 1N 7 4E
Sartène 103 41 38N 9 0E
Sarthe □ 100 47 58N 0 10E
Sarthe, R. 100 47 33N 0 31W
Sartilly 100 48 45N 1 28W
Sartynya 120 63 30N 62 50E
Sarūr 123 23 17N 58 4E
Sarvestān 123 29 20N 53 10E
Sary-Tash 120 39 44N 73 15E
Saryshagan 120 46 12N 73 48E
Sarzeau 100 47 31N 2 48W
Sasaginnigak L. 57 51 36N 95 39W
Sasaram 125 24 57N 84 5E
Sasebo 132 33 10N 129 43E
Saseginaga, L. 40 47 6N 78 35W
Saser Mt. 124 34 50N 77 50E
Saskatchewan □ 55 54 40N 106 0W
Saskatchewan Landing Prov. Park 56 50 38N 107 59W
Saskatchewan, R. 57 53 12N 99 16W
Saskatoon 56 52 10N 106 38W
Sassandra 114 5 0N 6 8W
Sássari 108 40 44N 8 33E
Sassnitz 106 54 29N 13 39E
Sata-Misaki 132 30 59N 130 40E
Satanta 75 37 30N 101 0W
Satara 94 17 44N 73 58E
Satilla, R. 73 31 15N 81 50W

* *Now part of Punjab*

Satmala Hills 124 20 15N 74 40E
Satna 125 24 35N 80 50E
Sátoraljaújhely 107 48 25N 21 41E
Satpura Ra. 124 21 40N 75 0E
Satu Mare 107 47 46N 22 55E
Satui 126 3 50S 115 20E
Satun 128 6 43N 100 2E
Saturna 63 48 47N 123 11W
Saturnina, R. 86 12 15S 58 10W
Saubosq, L. 38 51 30N 64 53W
Sauce 88 30 5S 58 46W
Sauceda 82 25 46N 101 19W
Saucillo 82 28 1N 105 17W
Sauda 111 59 38N 6 21E
Sauðarkrókur 110 65 45N 19 40W
Saudi Arabia ■ 122 26 0N 44 0E
Sauerland 105 51 0N 8 0E
Saugatuck 77 42 40N 86 12W
Saugeen, R. 46 44 30N 81 22W
Saugerties 71 42 4N 73 58W
Saugues 102 44 58N 3 32E
Saujon 102 45 41N 0 55W
Sauk Center 74 45 42N 94 56W
Sauk City 76 43 17N 89 43W
Sauk Rapids 74 45 35N 94 10W
Saulieu 101 47 17N 4 14E
Saulnierville 39 44 16N 66 8W
Sault 103 44 6N 5 24E
Sault-au-Moulton 41 48 33N 69 15W
Sault aux Cochons, R. 41 48 44N 69 4W
Sault Ste. Marie, Can. 46 46 30N 84 20W
Sault Ste. Marie, U.S.A. 46 46 27N 84 22W
Saumlaki 127 7 55S 131 20E
Saumur 100 47 15N 0 5W
Saumur, L. 38 51 16N 62 49W
Saunders 54 52 58N 115 40W
Saunders C. 133 45 53S 170 45E
Saunders I. 91 57 30S 27 30W
Saunemin 77 40 54N 88 24W
Saurbær, Borgarfjarðarsýsla, Iceland 110 64 24N 21 35W
Saurbær, Eyjafjarðarsýsla, Iceland 110 65 27N 18 13W
Sausalito 80 37 51N 122 29W
Sautatá 86 7 50N 77 4W
Sauvage, L. 40 50 6N 74 30W
Sauveterre, B. 102 43 25N 0 57W
Sauzé-Vaussais 102 46 8N 0 8E
Savá 84 15 32N 86 15W
Sava, R. 109 44 40N 19 50E
Savage 74 47 43N 104 20W
Savanna 76 42 5N 90 10W
Savanna la Mar 84 18 10N 78 10W
Savannah, Ga., U.S.A. 73 32 4N 81 4W
Savannah, Mo., U.S.A. 76 39 55N 94 46W
Savannah, Tenn., U.S.A. 73 35 12N 88 18W
Savannah, R. 73 33 0N 81 30W
Savannakhet 128 16 30N 104 49E
Savant L. 52 50 30N 90 25W
Savant Lake 52 50 14N 90 40W
Savanur 124 14 59N 75 28E
Save R. 117 21 16S 34 0E
Saveh 122 35 2N 50 20E
Savenay 100 47 20N 1 55W
Saverdun 102 43 14N 1 34E
Saverne 101 48 39N 7 20E
Savigny-sur-Braye 100 47 53N 0 49E
Savoie □ 103 45 26N 6 35E
Savona, Can. 63 50 45N 120 50W
Savona, Italy 108 44 19N 8 29E
Sawahlunto 126 0 52S 100 52E
Sawai 127 3 0S 129 5E
Sawai Madhopur 124 26 0N 76 25E
Sawara 132 35 55N 140 30E
Sawatch Mts. 79 38 30N 106 30W
Sawel, Mt. 97 54 48N 7 5W
Sawmills 117 19 30S 28 2E
Sawu, I. 127 10 35S 121 50E
Sawu Sea 127 9 30S 121 50E
Sawyerville 41 45 20N 71 34W
Saxon 52 46 29N 90 25W
Saxton 70 40 12N 79 18W
Sayabec 38 48 35N 67 41W
Sayán 86 11 0S 77 25W
Sayan, Vostochnyy 121 54 0N 96 0E
Sayan, Zapadnyy 121 52 30N 94 0E
Sayda 115 33 35N 35 25E
Saylorville Res. 76 41 43N 93 41W
Saynshand 130 44 55N 110 11E
Sayre, Okla., U.S.A. 75 35 20N 99 40W
Sayre, Pa., U.S.A. 71 42 0N 76 30W
Sayula 82 19 50N 103 40W
Sayville 71 40 45N 73 7W
Sazan 109 40 30N 19 20E
Sázava, R. 106 49 50N 15 0E
Sazin 124 35 35N 73 30E
Sca Fell 94 54 27N 3 14W
Scaër 100 48 2N 3 42W
Scammon Bay 67 62 0N 165 49W
Scandia 61 50 20N 112 0W
Scandinavia 93 64 0N 12 0E
Scapa Flow 96 58 52N 3 6W
Scappoose 80 45 45N 122 53W
Scarborough, Can. 50 43 45N 79 12W
Scarborough, Trin 85 11 11N 60 42W
Scarborough, U.K. 94 54 17N 0 24W
Scarpe, R. 101 50 31N 3 27E
Scatarie I. 39 46 0N 59 44W
Scenic 74 43 49N 102 32W
Sceptre 56 50 51N 109 15W
Schaffhausen 106 47 42N 8 39E
Schefferville 36 54 48N 66 50W
Schelde, R. 105 51 10N 4 20E
Schell City 76 38 1N 94 7W
Schenectady 71 42 50N 73 58W
Scheveningen 105 52 6N 4 16E
Schiedam 105 51 55N 4 25E
Schiermonnikoog, I. 105 53 30N 6 15E
Schiltigheim 101 48 35N 7 45E
Schio 108 45 42N 11 21E
Schirmeck 101 48 29N 7 12E
Schleswig 106 54 32N 9 34E
Schleswig-Holstein □ 106 54 10N 9 40E
Schneider 77 41 13N 87 28W
Schofield 74 44 54N 89 39W
Scholls 80 45 24N 122 56W
Schoolcraft 77 42 7N 85 38W
Schouten, Kepulauan 127 1 0S 136 0E
Schouwen, I. 105 51 43N 3 45E
Schraumberg 77 42 0N 88 15W
Schreiber 53 48 45N 87 20W
Schuler 61 50 20N 110 6W
Schumacher 53 48 30N 81 16W
Schurz 78 38 57N 118 48W
Schuyler 74 41 30N 97 3W
Schuylkill Haven 71 40 37N 76 11W
Schwäbischer Alb 106 48 30N 9 30E
Schwangcheng 130 45 27N 126 27E
Schwangyashan 129 46 35N 131 15E
Schwarzwald 106 48 0N 8 0E
Schweinfurt 106 50 3N 10 12E
Schwerin 106 53 37N 11 22E
Schwyz 106 47 2N 8 39E
Sciacca 108 37 30N 13 3E
Scie, La 37 49 57N 55 36W
Scilla 108 38 18N 15 44E
Scilly, Isles of 95 49 55N 6 15W
Scioto, R. 72 39 0N 83 0W
Scobey 74 48 47N 105 30W
Scone, Austral. 136 32 0S 150 52E
Scone, U.K. 96 56 25N 3 26W
Scoresby Sund 17 70 20N 23 0W
Scotia, Calif., U.S.A. 78 40 36N 124 4W
Scotia, N.Y., U.S.A. 71 42 50N 73 58W
Scotia Sea 91 56 5S 56 0W
Scotland, Can. 49 43 1N 80 22W
Scotland, U.S.A. 74 43 10N 97 45W
Scotland □ 96 57 0N 4 0W
Scotland Neck 73 36 6N 77 24W
Scotstown 41 45 32N 71 17W
Scott, Antarct. 91 77 0S 165 0E
Scott, Can. 56 52 22N 108 50W
Scott, C. 91 71 30S 168 0E
Scott Chan. 62 50 45N 128 30W
Scott City 74 38 30N 100 52W
Scott, I. 91 67 0S 179 0E
Scott Inlet 65 71 0N 71 0W
Scott Is. 62 50 48N 128 40W
Scott-Jonction 41 46 30N 71 4W
Scott L. 55 59 55N 106 18W
Scott Reef 134 14 0S 121 50E
Scottdale 70 40 8N 79 35W
Scottsbluff 74 41 55N 103 35W
Scottsboro 73 34 40N 86 0W
Scottsburg 77 38 40N 85 46W
Scottsdale 135 41 9S 147 31E
Scottsville, Ky., U.S.A. 73 36 48N 86 10W
Scottsville, N.Y., U.S.A. 70 43 2N 77 47W
Scottville 72 43 57N 86 18W
Scranton, Iowa, U.S.A. 76 42 1N 94 33W
Scranton, Pa., U.S.A. 71 41 22N 75 41W
Screggan 100 53 15N 7 32W
Scugog, L. 47 44 10N 78 55W
Scunthorpe 94 53 35N 0 38W
Scutari (Üsküdar) 109 41 0N 29 5E
Sea Breeze 70 43 12N 77 32W
Sea I. 66 49 12N 123 10W
Seaford, Austral. 136 38 10S 145 11E
Seaford, U.S.A. 72 38 37N 75 36W
Seaforth 46 43 35N 81 25W
Seager Wheeler L. 56 54 17N 103 31W
Seagraves 75 32 56N 102 30W
Seahorse L. 38 52 12N 65 48W
Seal Cove, N.B., Can. 39 44 39N 66 51W
Seal Cove, Newf., Can. 37 47 29N 56 4W
Seal Cove, Newf., Can. 37 49 57N 56 22W
Seal L. 36 54 20N 61 30W
Seal, R. 55 58 50N 97 30W
Sealy 75 29 46N 96 9W
Seaman 77 38 57N 83 34W
Searchlight 81 35 31N 114 55W
Searchmont 53 46 47N 84 3W
Searcy 75 35 15N 91 45W
Searle 58 49 51N 97 15W
Searles, L. 81 35 47N 117 17W
Seaside, Calif., U.S.A. 80 36 37N 121 50W
Seaside, Oreg., U.S.A. 80 46 0N 123 55W
Seattle 80 47 41N 122 15W
Seaview Ra. 135 18 40S 145 45E
Seba Beach 60 53 35N 114 47W
Sebastián Vizcaíno, Bahía 82 28 0N 114 30W
Sebastopol 80 38 24N 122 49W
Sebastopol = Sevastopol 120 44 35N 33 30E

Sebewaing **Sheldon**

Sebewaing 46 43 45N 83 27W
Sebinkarahisar 122 40 22N 38 28E
Sebring, Fla., U.S.A. 73 27 36N 81 20W
Sebring, Ohio, U.S.A. 70 40 55N 81 2W
Sebringville 46 43 24N 81 4W
Sebuku, I. 126 3 30S 116 25E
Sebuku, Teluk 126 4 0N 118 10E
Sechelt 62 49 25N 123 42W
Sechura, Desierto de 86 6 0S 80 30W
Seclin 101 50 33N 3 2E
Second Narrows 66 49 18N 123 2W
Secondigny 100 46 37N 0 26W
Secretary I. 133 45 15S 166 56E
Secunderabad 124 17 28N 78 30E
Sedalia 76 38 40N 93 18W
Sedan, France 101 49 43N 4 57E
Sedan, U.S.A. 75 37 10N 96 11W
Seddon 133 41 40S 174 7E
Seddonville 133 41 33S 172 1E
Sedgewick 61 52 48N 111 41W
Sedley 56 50 10N 104 0W
Sedova, Pik 120 73 20N 55 10E
Sedro Woolley 80 48 30N 122 15W
Seeheim 117 26 32S 17 52E
Seeley's Bay 47 44 29N 76 14W
Sées 100 48 38N 0 10E
Seg-ozero 120 63 0N 33 10E
Segamat 128 2 30N 102 50E
Seget 127 1 24S 130 58E
Segonzac 102 45 36N 0 14W
Ségou 114 13 30N 6 10W
Segovia 104 40 57N 4 10W
Segré 100 47 40N 0 52W
Segre, R. 104 41 40N 0 43E
Seguam 67 52 0N 172 30W
Seguam Pass. 67 53 0N 175 30W
Séguéla 114 7 55N 6 40W
Segula I. 67 52 0N 178 5W
Segundo 75 37 12N 104 50W
Segundo, R. 88 30 53S 62 44W
Segura, R. 104 38 9N 0 40W
Sehithwa 117 20 30S 22 30E
Sehore 124 23 10N 77 5E
Seilandsjøkelen 110 70 25N 23 16E
Seiling 75 36 10N 99 5W
Seille, R. 103 46 31N 4 57E
Sein, I. de 100 48 2N 4 52W
Sein, R. 58 49 54N 97 7W
Seinäjoki 110 62 48N 22 43E
Seine-Maritime □ 100 49 40N 1 0E
Seine □ 101 49 0N 3 0E
Seine-et-Marne □ 101 48 45N 3 0E
Seine, R. 100 49 28N 0 15E
Seine-Saint-Denis □ 101 48 58N 2 24E
Seistan 123 30 50N 61 0E
Sejal 86 2 45N 68 0W
Sekaju 126 2 58S 103 58E
Sekibi-shō 131 25 45N 124 35E
Sekiu 78 48 30N 124 29W
Sekondi-Takoradi 114 5 0N 1 48W
Selah 78 46 40N 120 30W
Selama 128 5 12N 100 42E
Selangor □ 128 3 20N 101 30E
Selaru, I. 127 8 18S 131 0E
Selawik 67 66 55N 160 10W
Selby, U.K. 94 53 47N 1 5W
Selby, U.S.A. 74 45 34N 99 55W
Selby Lake 43 45 6N 72 48W
Selden 74 39 24N 100 39W
Seldovia 67 59 30N 151 45W
Sele, R. 108 40 27N 15 0E
Selenga, R. = Selenge Mörön 130 52 16N 106 16E
Selenge 129 49 25N 103 59E
Selenge Mörön, R. 130 52 16N 106 16E
Sélestat 101 48 10N 7 26E
Seletan, Tg. 126 4 10S 114 40E
Selfridge 74 46 3N 100 57W
Sélibaby 114 15 20N 12 15W
Seligman 79 35 17N 112 56W
Selkirk, Man., Can. 57 50 10N 96 55W
Selkirk, Ont., Can. 46 42 49N 79 56W
Selkirk, U.K. 96 55 33N 2 50W
Selkirk I. 57 53 20N 99 6W
Selkirk Mts. 54 51 15N 117 40W
Selles-sur-Cher 101 47 16N 1 33E
Sellières 101 46 50N 5 32E
Sells 79 31 57N 111 57W
Selma, Ala., U.S.A. 73 32 30N 87 0W
Selma, Calif., U.S.A. 80 36 39N 119 39W
Selma, N.C., U.S.A. 73 35 32N 78 15W
Selmer 73 35 9N 88 36W
Selongey 101 47 36N 5 10E
Selpele 127 0 1S 130 5E
Selsey Bill 95 50 44N 0 47W
Seltz 101 48 48N 8 4E
Selu, I. 127 7 26S 130 55E
Selukwe 117 19 40S 30 0E
Sélune, R. 100 48 38N 1 22W
Selva 88 29 50S 62 0W
Selva Beach, La 80 36 56N 121 51W
Selvas 86 6 30S 67 0W
Selwyn 135 21 30S 140 29E
Selwyn L. 55 60 0N 104 30W
Selwyn Mts. 67 63 0N 130 0W
Selwyn Ra. 135 21 10S 140 0E
Semani, R. 109 40 45N 19 50E
Semans 56 51 25N 104 44W
Semarang 127 7 0S 110 26E
Semeru, Mt. 127 8 4S 113 3E
Semiahmoo B. 66 49 1N 122 50W
Seminoe Res. 78 42 0N 107 0W
Seminole, Okla., U.S.A. 75 35 15N 96 45W
Seminole, Tex., U.S.A. 75 32 41N 102 38W
Semiozernoye 120 52 22N 64 8E
Semipalatinsk 120 50 30N 80 10E
Semirara Is. 127 12 0N 121 20E
Semisopochnoi I. 67 52 0N 179 40W
Semitau 126 0 29N 111 57E
Semiyarskoye 120 50 55N 78 30E
Semmering Pass. 106 47 41N 15 45E
Semnān 123 35 55N 53 25E
Semnan □ 123 36 0N 54 0E
Semois, R. 105 49 53N 4 44E
Semporna 127 4 30N 118 33E
Semuda 126 2 51S 112 58E
Semur-en-Auxois 101 47 30N 4 20E
Sen, R. 128 13 45N 105 12E
Sena Madureira 86 9 5S 68 45W
Senai 128 1 38N 103 38E
Senaja 126 6 49S 117 2E
Senanga 117 16 2S 23 14E
Senatobia 75 34 38N 89 57W
Sendai, Kagoshima, Japan 132 31 50N 130 20E
Sendai, Miyagi, Japan 132 38 15N 141 0E
Seneca, Oreg., U.S.A. 78 44 10N 119 2W
Seneca, S.C., U.S.A. 73 34 43N 82 59W
Seneca Falls 70 42 55N 76 50W
Seneca L. 70 42 40N 76 58W
Sénécal, L. 38 52 5N 63 20W
Senegal ■ 114 14 30N 14 30W
Senegal, R. 114 16 30N 15 30W
Seney 53 46 25N 86 0W
Senge Khambab (Indus), R. 125 28 40N 70 10E
Senhor-do-Bonfim 87 10 30S 40 10W
Senigállia 108 43 42N 13 12E
Senj 108 45 0N 14 58E
Senja 110 69 25N 17 20E
Senkaku-guntō 131 25 50N 123 30E
Senlis 101 49 13N 2 35E
Senmonorom 128 12 27N 107 12E
Sennâr 115 13 30N 33 35E
Senneterre 40 48 25N 77 15W
Senneville 44 45 27N 73 57W
Senonches 100 48 34N 1 2E
Sens 101 48 11N 3 15E
Senta 109 45 55N 20 3E
Sentein 102 42 53N 0 58E
Sentinel 79 32 56N 113 13W
Sentolo 127 7 55S 110 13E
Seo de Urgel 104 42 22N 1 23E
Seoul = Sŏul 130 37 31N 127 6E
Separation Point 36 53 37N 57 25W
Sepone 128 16 45N 106 13E
Sept-Îles 36 50 13N 66 22W
Sequart L. 38 52 26N 63 47W
Sequim 80 48 3N 123 9W
Sequoia Nat. Park 80 36 30N 118 30W
Seraing 105 50 35N 5 32E
Seram, I. 127 3 10S 129 0E
Seram Sea 127 2 30S 128 30E
Serampore 125 22 44N 88 30E
Serang 127 6 8S 106 10E
Serasan, I. 126 2 29N 109 4E
Serbia = Srbija 109 43 30N 21 0E
Seremban 128 2 43N 101 53E
Serena, La 88 29 55S 71 10W
Serenje 117 13 14S 30 15E
Sergipe □ 87 10 30S 37 30W
Seria 126 4 37N 114 30E
Serian 126 1 10N 110 40E
Sérifontaine 101 49 20N 1 45E
Sérignan 102 43 17N 3 17E
Sérigny, R. 36 56 47N 66 0W
Serik 122 36 55N 31 10E
Sermaize-les-Bains 101 48 47N 4 54E
Sermata, I. 127 8 15S 128 50E
Sernovdsk 120 61 20N 73 28E
Serov 120 59 36N 60 35E
Serowe 117 22 25S 26 43E
Serpentine, R. 66 49 5N 122 51W
Serpent's Mouth 86 10 0N 61 30W
Serpukhov 120 54 55N 37 28E
Serrai 109 41 0N 23 30E
Serres 103 44 26N 5 43E
Serrezuela 88 30 40S 65 20W
Sertânia 87 8 5S 37 20W
Sertanópolis 89 23 4S 51 2W
Sertão 87 10 0S 40 20W
Serua, P. 127 6 18S 130 1E
Serui 127 1 45S 136 10E
Serule 117 21 57S 27 11E
Serviceton 136 36 25S 141 55E
Sesajap Lama 126 3 32N 117 11E
Sesepe 127 1 30S 127 59E
Sesfontein 117 19 7S 13 39E
Sesheke 117 17 29S 24 13E
Sesser 76 38 7N 89 3W
Sessy 130 42 40N 110 30E
Sestao 104 43 18N 3 0W
Sète 102 43 25N 3 42E
Sete Lagoas 87 19 27S 44 16W
Seto Naikai 132 34 20N 133 30E
Seton L. 63 50 42N 122 8W
Seton Portage 63 50 42N 122 17W
Setté Cama 116 2 32S 9 57E
Setting L. 55 55 0N 98 38W
Settle 94 54 5N 2 18W
Settlement Pt. 73 26 40N 79 0W
Setúbal 104 38 30N 8 58W
Setúbal, B. de 104 38 40N 8 56W
Seul L. 34 50 25N 92 30W
Seul Réservoir, Lac 52 50 25N 92 30W
Seulimeum 126 5 27N 95 15E
Sevastopol 120 44 35N 33 30E
Seven Islands B. 36 59 25N 63 45W
Seven Sisters Falls 57 50 7N 96 2W
Seven Sisters, mt 54 54 56N 128 10W
Seventy Mile House 63 51 18N 121 23W
Sévérac-le-Château 102 44 20N 3 5E
Severn L. 34 53 54N 90 48W
Severn, R., Can. 34 56 2N 87 36W
Severn, R., U.K. 95 51 35N 2 38W
Severnaya Zemlya 121 79 0N 100 0E
Severo-Kurilsk 121 50 40N 156 8E
Severodvinsk 120 64 27N 39 58E
Sevier 79 38 39N 112 11W
Sevier L. 78 39 0N 113 20W
Sevier, R. 79 39 10N 112 50W
Sevilla, Colomb. 86 4 16N 75 57W
Sevilla, Spain 104 37 23N 6 0W
Seville = Sevilla 104 37 23N 6 0W
Seward 67 60 0N 149 40W
Seward Pen. 67 65 0N 164 0W
Sewell, Can. 62 53 47N 132 16W
Sewell, Chile 88 34 10S 70 45W
Sewer 127 5 46S 134 40E
Sewickley 70 40 33N 80 12W
Sexsmith 60 55 21N 118 47W
Seychelles, Is. 16 5 0S 56 0E
Seyðisfjörður 110 65 16N 14 0W
Seymchan 121 62 40N 152 30E
Seymour, Austral. 136 37 0S 145 10E
Seymour, U.S.A. 76 40 45N 93 7W
Seymour, Conn., U.S.A. 71 41 23N 73 5W
Seymour, Ind., U.S.A. 77 39 0N 85 50W
Seymour, Tex., U.S.A. 75 33 35N 99 18W
Seymour, Wis., U.S.A. 72 44 30N 88 20W
Seymour Arm 63 51 15N 118 57W
Seymour Heights 66 49 19N 123 0W
Seymour Inlet 62 51 3N 127 0W
Seymour L. 66 49 27N 122 57W
Seymour, Mt. 66 49 24N 122 57W
Seymour, R. 66 49 18N 123 1W
Seyne 103 44 21N 6 22E
Seyne-sur-Mer, La 103 43 7N 5 52E
Sézanne 101 48 40N 3 40E
Sfax 114 34 49N 10 48E
Sfintu Gheorghe 107 45 52N 25 48E
Shaba 116 8 0S 25 0E
*Shabani 117 20 17S 30 2E
Shabogamo L., Can. 35 48 40N 77 0W
Shabogamo L., Newf., Can. 36 53 15N 66 30W
Shabunda 116 2 40S 27 16E
Shabuskwia L. 52 51 15N 89 0W
Shackleton 91 78 30S 36 1W
Shackleton Inlet 91 83 0S 160 0E
Shadrinsk 120 56 5N 63 58E
Shafer, L. 77 40 46N 86 46W
Shafter 81 35 32N 119 14W
Shaftesbury 95 51 0N 2 12W
**Shāhābād 123 37 40N 56 50E
†Shāhbād 122 34 10N 46 30E
Shahcheng 130 40 18N 115 27E
Shahdād 123 30 30N 57 40E
Shahdadkot 124 27 50N 67 55E
Shahgarh 124 27 15N 69 50E
Shāhī 123 36 30N 52 55E
Shaho 131 28 29N 113 2E
Shahpūr 122 38 12N 44 45E
Shahr Kord 123 32 15N 50 55E
Shahraban 122 34 0N 45 0E
‡‡Shahrezā 123 32 0N 51 55E
Shahrig 124 30 15N 67 40E
Shahriza 123 32 0N 51 50E
††Shāhrūd 123 36 30N 55 0E
Shahrukh 123 33 50N 60 10E
‡Shahsavār 123 36 45N 51 12E
Shahsien 131 26 25N 117 50E
Shajapur 124 23 20N 76 15E
Shakespeare I. 52 49 38N 88 25W
Shakhty 120 47 40N 40 10E
Shakhunya 120 57 40N 47 0E
Shaki 114 8 41N 3 21E
Shakopee 74 44 45N 93 30W
Shaktolik 67 64 30N 161 15W
Shalalth 63 50 43N 122 13W
Shallow Lake 46 44 36N 81 5W
Shalu 131 24 24N 120 26E
Sham, J. ash 123 23 10N 57 5E
Shamattawa 55 55 51N 92 5W
Shamattawa, R. 34 55 1N 85 23W
Shamil 123 27 30N 56 55E
Shammar, Jabal 122 27 40N 41 0E
Shamo (Gobi) 129 44 0N 111 0E
Shamokin 71 40 47N 76 33W
Shamrock, Can. 56 50 10N 106 37W
Shamrock, U.S.A. 75 35 15N 100 15W
Shamva 117 17 20S 31 32E
Shan □ 125 21 30N 98 30E
Shanchengtze 130 42 29N 125 30E
Shandon 80 35 39N 120 23W
Shangani, R. 117 18 35S 27 45E
Shangch'eng 131 31 44N 115 22E
Shangchih, (Chuho) 130 45 10N 127 59E
Shangchwan Shan 131 21 35N 112 45E
Shanghai 131 31 10N 121 25E
Shanghsien 131 33 30N 109 58E
Shangjao 131 28 25N 117 57E
Shangkao 131 28 16N 114 50E
Shangkiu 131 34 28N 115 42E
Shangpancheng 130 40 52N 118 4E
Shangshui 131 33 42N 114 34E
Shangsze 131 22 0N 107 45E
Shangtu 130 41 31N 113 35E
Shangyu 131 25 59N 114 29E
Shanh 129 47 5N 103 5E
Shaniko 78 45 0N 120 50W
Shannon, Greenl. 17 75 10N 18 30W
Shannon, N.Z. 133 40 33S 175 25E
Shannon I. 17 75 0N 18 0W
Shannon L., Can. 53 49 48N 83 24W
Shannon L., U.S.A. 63 48 37N 121 42W
Shannon, R. 97 53 10N 8 10W
Shansi □ 130 37 30N 112 15E
Shantar, Ostrov Bolshoi 121 55 9N 137 40E
Shantou (Chan-t'eou) 131 23 23N 116 41E
Shantow (Swatow) 131 23 25N 116 40E
Shantung □ 130 36 0N 117 30E
Shanyang 131 33 39N 110 2E
Shaohing 131 30 0N 120 32E
Shaowu 131 27 25N 117 30E
Shaoyang 131 27 10N 111 30E
Shapinsay, I. 96 59 2N 2 50W
Shaqra 122 25 15N 45 16E
Sharbot Lake 47 44 46N 76 41W
Sharhjui 123 32 30N 67 22E
Shari 122 27 20N 43 45E
Sharin Gol 129 49 12N 106 27E
Sharjah 123 25 23N 55 26E
Shark B. 134 11 20S 130 35E
Sharon, U.S.A. 77 42 30N 88 44W
Sharon, Mass., U.S.A. 71 42 5N 71 11W
Sharon, Pa., U.S.A. 70 41 18N 80 30W
Sharpe, L. 34 54 10N 93 21W
Sharpe L. 55 54 5N 93 40W
Sharpsburg 70 40 30N 79 56W
Sharpsville 70 41 16N 80 28W
Shashi 117 21 15S 27 27E
Shasi 131 30 16N 112 20E
Shasta, Mt. 78 41 30N 122 0W
Shasta Res. 78 40 50N 122 15W
Shattuck 75 36 17N 99 55W
Shaunavon 56 49 35N 108 25W
Shaver Lake 80 37 9N 119 18W
Shaw, R. 134 20 21S 119 17E
Shawan 129 44 21N 85 37E
Shawanaga 46 45 31N 80 17W
Shawano 72 44 45N 88 38W
Shawbridge 43 45 52N 74 5W
Shawinigan 41 46 35N 72 50W
Shawinigan Sud 41 46 31N 72 45W
Shawnee, U.S.A. 76 39 1N 94 43W
Shawnee, N.Y., U.S.A. 49 43 9N 78 53W
Shawnee, Okla., U.S.A. 75 35 15N 97 0W
Shawville 40 45 36N 76 30W
Shcherbakov = Rybinsk 120 58 5N 38 50E
Shchuchinsk 120 52 56N 70 12E
Shebandowan 52 48 38N 90 4W
Sheboygan 72 43 46N 87 45W
Shediac 39 46 14N 64 32W
Sheelin, Lough 97 53 48N 7 20W
Sheep Haven 97 55 12N 7 55W
Sheerness 95 51 26N 0 47E
Sheet Harbour 39 44 56N 62 31W
Sheffield, Can. 49 43 19N 80 12W
Sheffield, N.Z. 94 43 23S 172 2E
Sheffield, U.K. 94 53 23N 1 28W
Sheffield, Ala., U.S.A. 73 34 45N 87 42W
Sheffield, Ill., U.S.A. 76 41 21N 89 44W
Sheffield, Iowa, U.S.A. 76 42 54N 93 13W
Sheffield, Mass., U.S.A. 71 42 6N 73 23W
Sheffield, Pa., U.S.A. 71 41 42N 79 3W
Sheffield, Tex., U.S.A. 75 30 42N 101 49W
Sheffield L. 37 49 20N 56 34W
Sheguiandah 46 45 54N 81 55W
Sheho 56 51 35N 103 13W
Sheila 39 47 29N 64 55W
Shekhupura 124 31 42N 73 58E
Shekichen 131 33 10N 113 0E
Shekki 131 22 30N 113 15E
Sheklung 131 23 5N 113 55E
Shelbina 76 39 47N 92 2W
Shelburn 77 39 10N 87 24W
Shelburne, N.S., Can. 39 43 47N 65 20W
Shelburne, Ont., Can. 46 44 4N 80 15W
Shelburne, U.S.A. 71 44 23N 73 15W
Shelburne B. 135 11 50S 143 0E
Shelburne Falls 71 42 36N 72 45W
Shelby, Mich., U.S.A. 72 43 34N 86 27W
Shelby, Mont., U.S.A. 78 48 30N 111 59W
Shelby, N.C., U.S.A. 73 35 18N 81 34W
Shelby, Ohio, U.S.A. 70 40 52N 82 40W
Shelbyville, U.S.A. 76 39 48N 92 2W
Shelbyville, Ill., U.S.A. 77 39 25N 88 45W
Shelbyville, Ind., U.S.A. 77 39 30N 85 42W
Shelbyville, Ky., U.S.A. 77 38 13N 85 14W
Shelbyville, Tenn., U.S.A. 73 35 30N 86 25W
Shelbyville, Res. 77 39 26N 88 46W
Sheldon, U.S.A. 76 37 40N 94 18W
Sheldon, Iowa, U.S.A. 74 43 6N 95 51W

†† *Renamed Emamrud*
‡ *Renamed Tonekabon*
‡‡ *Renamed Qomsheh*
* *Renamed Zvishavane*
** *Renamed Ashkhaneh*
† *Renamed Eslamabad-e-Gharb*

Sheldon Point **Sinkiang-Uighur**

Sheldon Point	**67**	62 30N	165 0W
Sheldrake	**36**	50 20N	64 51W
Shelikef, Str.	**67**	58 0N	154 0W
Shelikhova, Zaliv	**121**	59 30N	157 0E
Shell Lake	**56**	53 19N	107 2W
Shellbrook	**56**	53 13N	106 24W
Shelley	**63**	54 0N	122 37W
Shellharbour	**136**	34 31S	150 51E
Shellmouth	**57**	50 56N	101 29W
Shellsburg	**76**	42 6N	91 52W
Shelter Bay	**35**	50 30N	67 20W
Shelton, Conn., U.S.A.	**71**	41 18N	73 7W
Shelton, Wash., U.S.A.	**80**	47 15N	123 6W
Shenandoah, Iowa, U.S.A.	**74**	40 50N	95 25W
Shenandoah, Pa., U.S.A.	**71**	40 49N	76 13W
Shenandoah, Va., U.S.A.	**72**	38 30N	78 38W
Shenandoah, R.	**72**	38 30N	78 38W
Shenchih	**130**	39 12N	112 2E
Shenmu	**130**	38 56N	110 19E
Shensi □	**131**	34 50N	109 25E
Shentsa	**129**	30 56N	88 25E
Shenyang (Mukden)	**130**	41 35N	123 30E
Sheopur Kalan	**124**	25 40N	76 40E
Shepard	**59**	50 57N	113 55W
Shepherd	**46**	43 32N	84 41W
Shepherdsville	**77**	37 59N	85 43W
Shepparton	**136**	36 23S	145 26E
Sheppton	**71**	40 52N	76 10W
Sher Khan Qala	**124**	29 55N	66 10E
Sherborne	**95**	50 56N	2 31W
Sherbro I.	**114**	7 30N	12 40W
Sherbrooke	**39**	45 28N	71 57W
Sheridan, Can.	**50**	43 31N	79 40W
Sheridan, U.S.A.	**76**	40 31N	94 37W
Sheridan, Ark., U.S.A.	**75**	34 20N	92 25W
Sheridan, Col., U.S.A.	**74**	39 44N	105 3W
Sheridan, Ill., U.S.A.	**77**	41 32N	88 41W
Sheridan, Ind., U.S.A.	**77**	40 8N	86 13W
Sheridan, Wyo., U.S.A.	**78**	44 50N	107 0W
Sheridan L.	**63**	51 31N	120 54W
Sherman, Can.	**66**	49 21N	123 14W
Sherman, U.S.A.	**75**	33 40N	96 35W
Sherridon	**55**	55 8N	101 5W
Sherrington	**43**	45 10N	73 31W
Sherwood, U.S.A.	**77**	41 17N	84 33W
Sherwood, N.D., U.S.A.	**57**	48 59N	101 36W
Sherwood, Tex., U.S.A.	**75**	31 18N	100 45W
Sherwood For.	**94**	53 5N	1 5W
Sherwood Park	**59**	53 31N	113 19W
Shesheke	**117**	17 14S	24 22E
Sheslay	**54**	58 17N	131 45W
Sheslay, R.	**54**	58 48N	132 5W
Shethanei L.	**55**	58 48N	97 50W
Shetland □	**96**	60 30N	1 30W
Shetland Is.	**96**	60 30N	1 30W
Shevchenko	**120**	44 25N	51 20E
Sheyenne	**75**	47 52N	99 8W
Sheyenne, R.	**74**	47 40N	98 15W
Shiawassea, R.	**46**	43 38N	83 50W
Shibeli, R.	**115**	2 0N	44 0E
Shiberghan □	**123**	35 45N	66 0E
Shibogama L.	**34**	53 35N	88 15W
Shibushi	**132**	31 25N	131 0E
Shiel, L.	**96**	56 48N	5 32W
Shifnal	**96**	52 40N	2 23W
Shiga-ken □	**132**	35 20N	136 0E
Shigatse	**129**	29 10N	89 0E
Shih Ho	**131**	31 45N	115 50E
Shihchwan	**131**	33 5N	108 30E
Shihkiachwang	**130**	38 0N	114 32E
Shihkwaikow	**130**	40 59N	110 4E
Shihlu	**131**	19 15N	109 0E
Shihpu	**131**	29 12N	121 58E
Shihtao	**130**	36 55N	122 25E
Shihtsien	**131**	27 28N	108 3E
Shihwei	**129**	51 28N	119 59E
Shikarpur	**124**	27 57N	68 39E
Shikohabad	**123**	27 6N	78 38E
Shikoku	**132**	33 30N	133 30E
Shikoku □	**132**	33 30N	133 30E
Shikoku-Sanchi	**132**	33 30N	133 30E
Shilka	**121**	52 0N	115 55E
Shilka, R.	**121**	57 30N	93 18E
Shillelagh	**97**	52 46N	6 32W
Shillong	**125**	25 35N	91 53E
Shilo	**57**	49 49N	99 38W
Shimabara	**132**	32 48N	130 20E
Shimada	**132**	34 49N	138 19E
Shimane-ken □	**132**	35 0N	132 30E
Shimano-gawa	**132**	36 50N	138 30E
Shimenovsk	**121**	52 15N	127 30E
Shimizu	**132**	35 0N	138 30E
Shimodate	**132**	36 20N	139 55E
Shimoga	**124**	13 57N	75 32E
Shimonoseki	**132**	33 58N	131 0E
Shin Dand	**124**	33 12N	62 8E
Shin, L.	**96**	58 7N	4 30W
Shinankow	**129**	48 40N	121 32E
Shingleton	**53**	46 25N	86 33W
Shingu	**132**	33 40N	135 55E
Shinkiachwang	**130**	38 0N	114 31E
Shinyanga	**116**	3 45S	33 27E
Shio-no-Misaki	**132**	33 25N	135 45E
Ship I.	**75**	30 16N	88 55W
Shipka	**109**	42 46N	25 33E
Shipki La	**124**	31 45N	78 40E
Shippegan	**39**	47 45N	64 45W
Shippegan I.	**39**	47 50N	64 38W
Shippensburg	**70**	40 4N	77 32W
Shiprock	**79**	36 51N	108 45W
Shir Kūh	**123**	31 45N	53 30E
Shirāz	**123**	29 42N	52 30E
Shire, R.	**117**	16 30S	35 0E
Shiriya-Zaki	**132**	41 25N	141 30E
Shirley	**77**	39 53N	85 35W
Shirvan	**123**	37 30N	57 50E
Shirwa L. = Chilwa L.	**117**	15 15S	35 40E
Shishmaref	**67**	66 15N	166 10W
Shiukwan	**131**	24 58N	113 3E
Shively	**77**	38 12N	85 49W
Shivpuri	**124**	25 18N	77 42E
Shizuoka	**132**	35 0N	138 30E
Shizuoka-ken □	**132**	35 15N	138 40E
Shkoder = Shkodra	**109**	42 6N	19 20E
Shkodra	**109**	42 6N	19 20E
Shkumbini, R.	**109**	41 5N	19 50E
Shmidt, O.	**121**	81 0N	91 0E
Shoal Cr.	**76**	39 39N	93 35W
Shoal L.	**52**	49 33N	95 1W
Shoal Lake	**57**	50 30N	100 35W
Shoalhaven, R.	**136**	34 54S	150 42E
Shoals	**77**	38 40N	86 47W
Shoals Prov. Park	**53**	47 50N	83 50W
Shoeburyness	**95**	51 31N	0 49E
Shohsien	**130**	39 30N	112 25E
Sholapur	**124**	17 43N	75 56E
Shologontsy	**121**	66 13N	114 14E
Shongopovi	**79**	35 49N	110 37W
Shoshone, Calif., U.S.A.	**81**	35 58N	116 16W
Shoshone, Idaho, U.S.A.	**78**	43 0N	114 27W
Shoshone L.	**78**	44 30N	110 40W
Shoshone Mts.	**78**	39 30N	117 30W
Shoshong	**117**	22 56S	26 31E
Shoshoni	**78**	43 13N	108 5W
Show Low	**79**	34 16N	110 0W
Showyang	**130**	38 0S	113 4E
Shreveport	**75**	32 30N	93 50W
Shrewsbury	**94**	52 42N	2 45W
Shropshire □	**95**	52 36N	2 45W
Shubenacadie	**39**	45 5N	63 24W
Shucheng	**131**	31 25N	117 2E
Shuikiahu	**131**	32 14N	117 4E
Shulan	**130**	44 27N	126 57E
Shullsburg	**76**	42 35N	90 15W
Shumagin Is.	**67**	55 0N	159 0W
Shumikha	**120**	55 10N	63 15E
Shunan	**131**	29 37N	119 0E
Shunchang	**131**	26 52N	117 48E
Shungnak	**67**	66 55N	157 10W
Shuntak	**131**	22 54N	113 8E
Shur, R.	**123**	28 30N	55 0E
Shūsf	**123**	31 50N	60 5E
Shūshtar	**122**	32 0N	48 50E
Shuswap L.	**63**	50 55N	119 3W
Shuyak I.	**67**	58 35N	152 30W
Shuyang	**131**	34 9N	118 51E
Shwangcheng	**130**	45 30N	126 20E
Shwangliao	**130**	43 39N	123 40E
Shwebo	**125**	22 30N	95 45E
Shwegu	**125**	18 49N	95 26E
Shweli, R.	**125**	23 45N	96 45E
Shyok	**124**	34 15N	78 5E
Shyok, R.	**124**	34 30N	78 15E
Si Racha	**128**	13 10N	100 56E
Siah	**122**	22 0N	47 0E
Siahan Range	**124**	27 30N	64 40E
Siahoyen	**130**	42 30N	120 30E
Siaksriinderapura	**126**	0 51N	102 0E
Siakwan	**129**	25 45N	100 10E
Sialkot	**124**	32 32N	74 30E
*Siam, G. of	**128**	11 30N	101 0E
Sian	**131**	34 2N	109 0E
Siang K., Hunan, China	**131**	27 10N	112 45E
Siang K., Kwangsi-chuang, China	**131**	23 20N	107 40E
Siangcheng	**131**	33 16N	115 2E
Siangfan	**131**	32 15N	112 2E
Siangning	**130**	36 0N	110 50E
Siangsiang	**131**	27 50N	112 30E
Siangtan	**131**	28 0N	112 55E
Siangyang	**131**	32 18N	111 0E
Siangyin	**131**	28 45N	113 0E
Siantan, P.	**126**	3 10N	106 15E
Siao Hingan Ling	**129**	49 0N	127 0E
Siaohaotze	**129**	46 52N	124 22E
Siapu	**131**	26 53N	120 0E
Siāreh	**123**	28 5N	60 20E
Siargao, I.	**127**	9 52N	126 3E
Siasi	**127**	5 34N	120 50E
Siau, I.	**127**	2 50N	125 25E
Sibbald	**55**	51 24N	110 10W
Sibenik	**108**	43 48N	15 54E
Siberia	**121**	60 0N	100 0E
Siberut, I.	**126**	1 30S	99 0E
Sibi	**124**	29 30N	67 48E
Sibil	**127**	4 59S	140 35E
Sibiti	**116**	3 38S	13 19E
Sibiu	**107**	45 45N	24 9E
Sibley, U.S.A.	**77**	40 35N	88 23W
Sibley, Iowa, U.S.A.	**74**	43 21N	95 43W
Sibley, La., U.S.A.	**75**	32 34N	93 16W
Sibley Prov. Park	**52**	48 30N	88 45W
Sibolga	**126**	1 50N	98 45E
Sibsagar	**125**	27 0N	94 36E
Sibuco	**127**	7 20N	122 10E
Sibuguey B.	**127**	7 50N	122 45E
Sibuko	**127**	7 20N	122 10E
Sibut	**116**	5 52N	19 10E
Sibutu, I.	**127**	4 45N	119 30E
Sibutu Passage	**127**	4 50N	120 0E
Sibuyan, I.	**127**	12 25N	122 40E
Sicamous	**63**	50 49N	119 0W
Sicapoo	**127**	18 9N	121 34E
Sicasica	**68**	17 20S	67 45W
Sichang	**129**	28 0N	102 10E
Sichwan	**131**	33 6N	111 30E
Sicilia □	**108**	37 30N	14 30E
Sicilia, I.	**108**	37 30N	14 30E
Sicily = Sicilia	**108**	37 30N	14 30E
Sicuani	**86**	14 10S	71 10W
Siddipet	**124**	18 0N	79 0E
Sideburned L.	**53**	47 45N	83 15W
Sidell	**77**	39 55N	87 49W
Sidi-Bel-Abbès	**114**	35 13N	0 10W
Sidlaw Hills	**96**	56 32N	3 10W
Sidmouth	**95**	50 40N	3 13W
Sidnaw	**52**	46 30N	88 43W
Sidney, B.C., Can.	**63**	48 39N	123 24W
Sidney, Man., Can.	**57**	49 54N	99 4W
Sidney, Mont., U.S.A.	**74**	47 51N	104 7W
Sidney, N.Y., U.S.A.	**71**	42 18N	75 20W
Sidney, Ohio, U.S.A.	**77**	40 18N	84 6W
Sidoardjo	**127**	7 30S	112 46E
Sidon = Saydā	**115**	33 35N	35 25E
Sidon, (Saida)	**122**	33 38N	35 28E
Siedlce	**107**	52 10N	22 20E
Siegburg	**105**	50 48N	7 12E
Siegen	**105**	50 52N	8 2E
Siem Reap	**128**	13 20N	103 52E
Siena	**108**	43 20N	11 20E
Sienfeng	**131**	29 45N	109 10E
Sienyang	**131**	34 20N	108 48E
Sierck-les-Bains	**101**	49 26N	6 20E
Sierpe, Bocas de la	**86**	10 0N	61 30W
Sierra Blanca	**79**	31 11N	105 17W
Sierra Blanca, mt.	**79**	33 20N	105 54W
Sierra City	**80**	39 34N	120 42W
Sierra Colorado	**90**	40 35S	67 50W
Sierra Gorda	**88**	23 0S	69 15W
Sierra Leone ■	**114**	9 0N	12 0W
Sierra Majada	**82**	27 19N	103 42W
Sierraville	**80**	39 36N	120 22W
Sifnos	**109**	37 0N	24 45E
Sifton	**57**	51 21N	100 8W
Sifton Pass	**54**	57 52N	126 15W
Sigaboy	**127**	6 39N	126 10E
Sigean	**102**	43 2N	2 58E
Sighetul Marmatiei	**107**	47 57N	23 52E
Sighişoara	**107**	46 12N	24 50E
Sigli	**126**	5 25N	96 0E
Siglufjörður	**110**	66 12N	18 55W
Sigma	**127**	11 29N	122 40E
Signal	**81**	34 30N	113 38W
Signal Hill	**37**	47 35N	52 41W
Signal Pk.	**81**	33 25N	114 4W
Signy I.	**91**	60 45S	46 30W
Signy-l'Abbaye	**101**	49 40N	4 25E
Sigourney	**76**	41 20N	92 12W
Sigsig	**86**	3 0S	78 50W
Sigtuna	**111**	59 36N	17 44E
Sigüenza	**104**	41 3N	2 40W
Siguiri	**114**	11 31N	9 10W
Sigurd	**79**	38 57N	112 0W
Sigutlat L.	**62**	52 57N	126 12W
Sihanoukville = Kompong Som	**128**	10 40N	103 30E
Siho	**131**	34 0N	105 0E
Sihsien, Anwhei, China	**130**	29 55N	118 23E
Sihsien, Shansi, China	**131**	36 54N	111 0E
Siirt	**122**	37 57N	41 55E
Sijsele	**91**	51 12N	3 20E
Sikandra Rao	**123**	27 43N	78 24E
Sikar	**124**	27 39N	75 10E
Sikeston	**75**	36 52N	89 35W
Sikhote Alin, Khrebet	**121**	46 0N	136 0E
Sikinos, I.	**109**	36 40N	25 8E
Sikkani Chief, R.	**54**	57 47N	122 15W
Sikkim □	**125**	27 50N	88 50E
Siku	**131**	33 48N	104 18E
Sil, R.	**104**	42 23N	7 30W
Silacayoapán	**83**	17 30N	98 9W
Silamulun Ho	**130**	43 30N	123 35E
Silchar	**125**	24 49N	92 48E
Silcox	**55**	57 12N	94 10W
Siler City	**73**	35 44N	79 30W
Silesia	**106**	51 0N	16 30E
Silesia = Slask	**106**	51 0N	16 30E
Silgarhi Doti	**125**	29 15N	82 0E
Silghat	**125**	26 35N	93 0E
Silifke	**122**	36 22N	33 58E
Siliguri	**125**	26 45N	88 25E
Silin	**131**	24 10N	105 36E
Silinhot	**130**	43 16N	116 0E
Silistra	**109**	44 6N	27 19E
Siljan, L.	**111**	60 55N	14 45E
Silkeborg	**111**	56 10N	9 32E
Sillajhuay, Cordillera	**86**	19 40S	68 40W
Sillé-le Guillaume	**100**	48 10N	0 8W
Sillery	**42**	46 46N	71 15W
Siloam Springs	**75**	36 15N	94 31W
Silogui	**126**	1 10S	98 46E
Silsbee	**75**	30 20N	94 8W
Silver Bay	**52**	47 17N	91 16W
Silver City, Pan. C. Z.	**84**	9 21N	79 53W
Silver City, Calif., U.S.A.	**78**	36 19N	119 44W
Silver City, N. Mex., U.S.A.	**79**	32 50N	108 18W
Silver Cr., R.	**78**	43 30N	119 30W
Silver Creek	**70**	42 33N	79 9W
Silver Grove	**77**	39 2N	84 24W
Silver Islet	**52**	48 20N	88 45W
Silver L.	**80**	38 39N	120 6W
Silver Lake, Calif., U.S.A.	**81**	35 21N	116 7W
Silver Lake, Ind., U.S.A.	**77**	41 4N	85 53W
Silver Lake, Oreg., U.S.A.	**78**	43 9N	121 4W
Silver Lake, Wis., U.S.A.	**77**	42 33N	88 13W
Silver Ridge	**57**	50 48N	98 52W
Silver Star Prov. Park	**63**	50 23N	119 5W
Silver Water	**46**	45 52N	82 52W
Silverlake	**80**	38 38N	120 7W
Silvertip Mt.	**63**	49 10N	121 13W
Silverton, Austral.	**136**	31 52S	141 10E
Silverton, Can.	**63**	49 57N	117 21W
Silverton, Colo., U.S.A.	**79**	37 51N	107 45W
Silverton, Tex., U.S.A.	**75**	34 30N	101 16W
Silverton, Wash., U.S.A.	**63**	48 5N	121 34W
Silvia	**86**	2 37N	76 21W
Silvies, R.	**78**	43 57N	119 5W
Silvis	**76**	41 33N	90 28W
Silwani	**123**	23 18N	78 27E
Simanggang	**126**	1 15N	111 25E
Simard, L.	**40**	47 40N	78 40W
Simarun	**123**	31 16N	51 40E
Simcoe	**46**	42 50N	80 20W
Simcoe Co.	**50**	43 59N	79 49W
Simcoe, L.	**46**	44 25N	79 20W
Simenga	**121**	62 50N	107 55E
Simeulue, I.	**126**	2 45N	95 45E
Simferopol	**120**	44 55N	34 3E
Simi Valley	**81**	34 16N	118 47W
Simikot	**125**	30 0N	81 50E
Simiti	**86**	7 58N	73 57W
Simla	**124**	31 2N	77 15E
Simmie	**56**	49 56N	108 6W
Simmler	**81**	35 21N	119 59W
Simmons	**48**	45 26N	75 49W
Simmons Pen.	**65**	76 40N	89 7W
Simojärvi	**110**	66 5N	27 10E
Simojoki	**110**	65 46N	25 15E
Simojovel	**83**	17 12N	92 38W
Simonette, R.	**60**	55 9N	118 15W
Simonhouse	**57**	54 26N	101 23W
Simpang	**128**	4 50N	100 40E
Simplon Pass	**106**	46 15N	8 0E
Simpson	**56**	51 27N	105 27W
Simpson Des.	**135**	25 0S	137 0E
Simpson I.	**53**	48 46N	87 41W
Simpson Pen.	**65**	68 34N	88 45W
Simpsons Corners	**49**	43 46N	80 18W
Simunjan	**126**	1 25N	110 45E
Simushir, Ostrov	**121**	46 50N	152 30E
Sinabang	**126**	2 30N	46 30E
Sinaloa	**82**	25 50N	108 20W
Sinaloa □	**82**	25 0N	107 30W
Sinamaica	**86**	11 5N	71 51W
Sincé	**86**	9 15N	75 9W
Sincelejo	**86**	9 18N	75 24W
Sincheng, Honan, China	**131**	34 25N	113 56E
Sincheng, Kwangsi, China	**131**	24 1N	108 35E
Sinchengtu	**131**	23 55N	108 30E
Sinclair	**78**	41 47N	107 35W
Sinclair Mills	**54**	54 5N	121 40W
Sinclair Pass	**61**	50 40N	115 58W
Sincorá, Serra do	**87**	13 30S	41 0W
Sind Sagar Doab	**124**	32 0N	71 30E
Sindangan	**127**	8 10N	123 5E
Sindangbarang	**127**	7 27S	107 9E
Sindjai	**127**	5 0S	120 20E
Sines	**104**	37 56N	8 51W
Sinfeng, Kiangsi, China	**131**	25 28N	114 40E
Sinfeng, Kweichow, China	**131**	26 59N	106 55E
Singa	**115**	13 10N	33 57E
Singaparna	**127**	7 23S	108 4E
Singapore ■	**128**	1 17N	103 51E
Singapore, Straits of	**128**	1 15N	104 0E
Singaraja	**126**	8 15S	115 10E
Singida	**116**	4 49S	34 48E
Singitikós, Kólpos	**109**	40 6N	24 0E
Singkang	**127**	4 8S	120 1E
Singkawang	**126**	1 0N	109 5E
Singkep, I.	**126**	0 30S	104 20E
Singleton	**136**	32 33S	151 10E
Singleton, Mt.	**134**	29 27S	117 15E
Singtai	**130**	37 2N	114 30E
Singtze	**131**	29 30N	116 4E
Singyang	**131**	32 10N	114 0E
Sinhailien	**131**	34 31N	119 0E
Sinhsien	**130**	38 25N	112 45E
Sinhwa	**131**	27 36N	111 6E
Sining	**129**	36 35N	101 50E
Sinkan	**131**	27 45N	115 30E
Sinkiang	**130**	35 35N	111 25E
Sinkiang-Uighur □	**129**	42 0N	86 0E

* *Renamed Thailand, G. of*

Sinkin South Bend

Sinkin 130 39 30N 122 29 E
Sinlo 130 38 25N 114 50 E
Sinmak 130 38 25N 126 15 E
Sinmin 130 42 0N 122 50 E
Sinni, R. 108 40 6N 16 15 E
Sinoia 117 17 20S 30 8 E
Sinop 122 42 1N 35 11 E
Sinpin 130 41 50N 125 0 E
Sinsiang 131 35 15N 113 55 E
Sinskoye 121 61 8N 126 48 E
Sint Eustatius, I. 85 17 30N 62 59W
Sint Maarten, I. 85 18 4N 63 4W
Sintai 131 30 59N 105 0 E
Sintaluta 56 50 29N 103 27W
Sintang 126 0 5N 111 35 E
Sinti (Hunghu) 131 29 49N 113 30 E
Sinton 75 28 1N 97 30W
Sintra 104 38 47N 9 25W
Sinŭiju 130 40 5N 124 24 E
Sinuk 67 64 42N 166 22W
Sinyang 131 32 6N 114 2 E
Sióma 117 16 25S 23 28 E
Sion 106 46 14N 7 20 E
Sioux City 74 42 32N 96 25W
Sioux Falls 74 43 35N 96 40W
Sioux Lookout 52 50 10N 91 50W
Sioux Narrows 52 49 25N 94 10W
Sipa 131 33 34N 118 59 E
Sipera, I. 126 2 18S 99 40 E
Siping 131 33 25N 114 10 E
Sipiwesk L. 55 55 5N 97 35W
Siquia, R. 84 12 30N 84 30W
Siquijor, I. 127 9 12N 123 45 E
Siquirres 84 10 6N 83 30W
Siquisique 86 10 34N 69 42W
Sir Edward Pellew Group 135 15 40S 137 10 E
Sir Francis Drake, Mt. 62 50 49N 124 48W
Sir Sandford, Mt. 63 51 40N 117 52W
Siracusa 108 37 4N 15 17 E
Sirajganj 125 24 25N 89 47 E
Siret, R. 107 47 58N 26 5 E
Sirohi 124 24 52N 72 53 E
Sironj 124 24 5N 77 45 E
Síros, I. 109 37 28N 24 57 E
Sirretta Pk. 81 35 56N 118 19W
Sirsa 124 29 33N 75 4 E
Sisak 108 45 30N 16 21 E
Sisaket 128 15 8N 104 23 E
Sisiang 131 33 2N 107 48 E
Sisipuk I. 55 55 40N 102 0W
Sisipuk L. 55 55 45N 101 50W
Sisophon 128 13 31N 102 59 E
Sisseton 74 45 43N 97 3W
Sissonne 101 49 34N 3 51 E
Sistan-Baluchistan □ 123 27 0N 62 0 E
Sisteron 103 44 12N 5 57 E
Sisters 78 44 21N 121 32W
Sitapur 125 27 38N 80 45 E
Sitges 104 41 17N 1 47 E
Sitka 67 57 9N 134 58W
Sittang Myit, R. 125 18 20N 96 45 E
Sittard 105 51 0N 5 52 E
Situbondo 127 7 45S 114 0 E
Siuna 84 13 37N 84 45W
Siuwu 131 35 10N 113 30 E
Siuyen 130 40 20N 123 15 E
Sivand 123 30 5N 52 55 E
Sivas 122 39 43N 36 58 E
Siverek 122 37 50N 39 25 E
Sivrihisar 122 39 30N 31 35 E
Sivry 105 50 10N 4 12 E
Siwalik Range 125 28 0N 83 0 E
Siwan 125 26 13N 84 27 E
Sixteen Island Lake 43 45 56N 74 28W
Sizewell 95 52 13N 1 38 E
Sjaelland 111 55 30N 11 30 E
Sjiptjenski P. 109 42 46N 25 33 E
Sjumen = Kolarovgrad 109 43 27N 26 42 E
Skagafjörður 110 65 54N 19 35W
Skagastölstindane, mt. 111 61 25N 8 10 E
Skagen 111 68 37N 14 27 E
Skagerrak 111 57 30N 9 0 E
Skagit, R. 80 48 20N 122 25W
Skagway 67 59 30N 135 20W
Skaidi 110 70 26N 24 30 E
Skandia 53 46 25N 87 16W
Skanee 52 46 53N 88 20W
Skara 111 58 25N 13 30 E
Skaraborgs län □ 111 58 20N 13 30 E
Skardu 124 35 20N 75 35 E
Skeena Mts. 54 56 40N 128 30W
Skeena, R. 62 54 9N 130 5W
Skeggjastadir 110 66 3N 14 50W
Skegness 94 53 9N 0 20 E
Skeldon 86 6 0N 57 20W
Skellefte älv 110 65 30N 18 30 E
Skellefteå 110 64 45N 20 58 E
Skelleftehamn 110 64 41N 21 14 E
Skellig Rocks 97 51 47N 10 32W
Skerries, The 94 53 27N 4 40W
Skibbereen 97 51 33N 9 16W
Skiddaw, Mt. 94 54 39N 3 9W
Skidegate 62 53 15N 132 1W
Skien 111 59 12N 9 35 E
Skierniewice 107 51 58N 20 19 E
Skihist, Mt. 63 50 12N 121 54W
Skikda 114 36 50N 6 58 E
Skillett Fork, Little Wabash, R. 77 38 6N 88 9W
Skipton 94 53 57N 2 1W
Skiros, I. 109 38 55N 24 34 E
Skive 111 56 33N 9 2 E
Skjálfandafljót 110 65 15N 17 25W
Skjálfandi 110 66 5N 17 30W
Skoghall 111 59 20N 13 30 E
Skopje 109 42 1N 21 32 E
Skövde 111 58 15N 13 59 E
Skovorodino 121 54 0N 125 0 E
Skowhegan 35 44 49N 69 40W
Skownan 57 51 58N 99 35W
Skudeneshavn 111 59 10N 5 10 E
Skull 97 51 32N 9 40W
Skunk, R. 76 40 42N 91 7W
Skwaner, Pegunungan 126 1 0S 112 30 E
Skwierzyna 106 52 46N 15 30 E
Skye, I. 96 57 15N 6 10W
Skykomish 78 47 43N 121 16W
Slamet, G. 126 7 16S 109 8 E
Slaney, R. 97 52 52N 6 45W
Slaokan 131 30 57N 114 2 E
Slask 106 51 25N 16 0 E
Slate Is. 34 48 40N 87 0W
Slater 76 39 13N 93 4W
Slatina 107 44 28N 24 22 E
Slaton 75 33 27N 101 38W
Slave Lake 60 55 17N 114 50W
Slave Pt. 54 61 11N 115 56W
Slave, R. 54 61 18N 113 39W
Slavgorod 120 53 10N 78 50 E
Slavkov (Austerlitz) 106 49 10N 16 52 E
Sleaford 94 53 0N 0 22W
Sleat, Sd. of 96 57 5N 5 47W
Sleepy Eye 74 44 15N 94 45W
Sleman 127 7 40S 110 20 E
Slemon L. 54 63 13N 116 4W
Slidell 75 30 20N 89 48W
Sliedrecht 105 51 50N 4 45 E
Slieve Aughty 97 53 4N 8 30W
Slieve Bloom 97 53 4N 7 40W
Slieve Donard 97 54 10N 5 57W
Slieve Gullion 97 54 8N 6 26W
Slieve Mish 97 52 12N 9 50W
Slievenamon Mt. 97 52 25N 7 37W
Sligo 97 54 17N 8 28W
Sligo □ 97 54 10N 8 35W
Sligo B. 97 54 20N 8 40W
Slite 111 57 42N 18 48 E
Sliven 109 42 42N 26 19 E
Sloan 81 35 57N 115 13W
Sloansville 71 42 45N 74 22W
Slocan 63 49 48N 117 28W
Slocan L. 63 49 50N 117 23W
Slochteren 105 53 12N 6 48 E
Slough 95 51 30N 0 35W
Sloughhouse 80 38 26N 121 12W
Slovakia □ 107 48 30N 19 0 E
Slovenia = Slovenija 108 45 58N 14 30 E
Slovenija □ 108 45 58N 14 30 E
Slovenské Rhudhorie 107 48 45N 19 0 E
Slyne Hd. 97 53 25N 10 10W
Slyudyanka 121 51 40N 103 30 E
Smalltree L. 55 61 0N 105 0W
*Smallwood Reservoir 35 54 20N 63 10W
Smartville 80 39 13N 121 18W
Smeaton 56 53 30N 104 49W
Smederevo 109 44 40N 20 57 E
Smethport 70 41 50N 78 28W
Smidovich 121 48 36N 133 49 E
Smilde 105 52 58N 6 28 E
Smiley 56 51 38N 109 29W
Smith 60 55 10N 114 0W
Smith Arm 54 66 15N 123 0W
Smith Center 74 39 50N 98 50W
Smith I. 36 54 13N 58 18W
Smith Pen. 65 77 12N 78 50W
Smith, R. 54 59 34N 126 30W
Smith Sund 65 78 30N 74 0W
Smithers 54 54 45N 127 10W
Smithfield 73 35 31N 78 16W
Smiths Cove 39 44 37N 65 42W
Smiths Falls 47 44 55N 76 0W
Smithville, Can. 49 43 6N 79 33W
Smithville, U.S.A. 76 39 23N 94 35W
Smithville, Tex., U.S.A. 75 30 2N 97 12W
Smjörfjöll 110 65 30N 15 42W
Smoky Falls 53 50 4N 82 10W
Smoky Hill, R. 74 38 45N 98 0W
Smoky Lake 60 54 10N 112 30W
Smoky, R. 60 56 10N 117 21W
Smola 110 63 23N 8 3 E
Smolensk 120 54 45N 32 0 E
Smolikas, Óros 109 40 9N 20 58 E
Smolyan 109 41 36N 24 38 E
Smooth Rock Falls 53 49 17N 81 37W
Smoothrock L. 52 50 30N 89 30W
Smoothstone L. 55 54 40N 106 50W
Smyrna = İzmir 122 38 25N 27 8 E
Snaefell 94 54 18N 4 26W
Snaefells Jökull 110 64 45N 23 25W
Snake I. 136 38 47S 146 33 E
Snake L. 55 55 32N 106 35W
Snake, R. 78 46 31N 118 50W
Snake Ra., Mts. 78 39 0N 114 30W
Snake River Plain 78 43 13N 113 0W
Snaring 61 53 5N 118 4W
Sneek 105 53 2N 5 40 E
Snelgrove 49 43 44N 79 49W
Snelling 80 37 31N 120 26W
Snĕzka 106 50 14N 15 50 E
Snipe L. 60 55 7N 116 47W
Snizort, L. 96 57 33N 6 28W
Snohetta 110 62 19N 9 16 E
Snohomish 80 47 53N 122 6W
Snow Hill 72 38 10N 75 21W
Snow L. 55 54 52N 100 3W
Snow Mt. 80 39 22N 122 44W
Snowbird L. 55 60 45N 103 0W
Snowdon, Mt. 94 53 4N 4 8W
Snowdrift 55 62 24N 110 44W
Snowdrift, R. 55 62 24N 110 44W
Snowflake, Can. 57 49 3N 98 39W
Snowflake, U.S.A. 79 34 30N 110 4W
Snowshoe 54 53 43N 121 0W
Snowville 78 41 59N 112 47W
Snowy Mts. 136 36 30S 148 20 E
Snowy, R. 136 37 46S 148 30 E
Snug Corner 85 22 33N 73 52W
Snyder, Can. 49 42 57N 79 3W
Snyder, Okla., U.S.A. 75 34 40N 99 0W
Snyder, Tex., U.S.A. 75 32 45N 100 57W
Soacha 86 4 35N 74 13W
Soalala 117 16 6S 45 20 E
Soap Lake 78 47 29N 119 31W
Sobat, R. 115 8 32N 32 40 E
Sobral 87 3 50S 40 30W
Soc Trang = Khonh Hung 128 9 37N 105 50 E
Socha 86 6 0N 72 41W
Soche (Yarkand) 129 38 24N 77 20 E
Sochi 120 43 35N 39 40 E
Société, Is. de la 15 17 0S 151 0W
Society Is. = Société, Is. de la 15 17 0S 151 0W
Socompa, Portezuelo de 88 24 27S 68 18W
Socorro, Colomb. 86 6 29N 73 16W
Socorro, U.S.A. 71 34 3N 106 58W
Socorro, I. 82 18 45N 110 58W
Socotra, I. 115 12 30N 54 0 E
Soda Creek 54 52 25N 122 10W
Soda L. 79 35 7N 116 2W
Soda Springs 78 42 40N 111 40W
Söderhamn 111 61 18N 17 10 E
Söderköping 111 58 31N 16 35 E
Södermanlands län □ 111 59 10N 16 30 E
Södertälje 111 59 12N 17 50 E
Sodo 115 7 0N 37 57 E
Sodus 70 43 13N 77 5W
Sodus Pt. 70 43 15N 77 0W
Soest 105 51 34N 8 7 E
Soeurs, Île des 45 45 28N 73 33W
Sofia = Sofiya 109 42 45N 23 20 E
Sofia, R. 117 15 25S 48 40 E
Sofiya 109 42 45N 23 20 E
Sogad 127 10 30N 125 0 E
Sogamoso 86 5 43N 72 56W
Sogn og Fjordane fylke □ 111 61 40N 6 0 E
Sogndalsfjøra 111 61 14N 7 5 E
Sognefjorden 111 61 10N 5 50 E
Sohâg 115 26 27N 31 43 E
Soignies 105 50 35N 4 5 E
Sointula 62 50 38N 127 0W
Soissons 101 49 25N 3 19 E
Söke 122 37 48N 27 28 E
Sokhta Chinar 123 35 5N 67 35 E
Sokó'ka 107 53 25N 23 30 E
Sokoto 114 13 2N 5 16 E
Sol Iletsk 120 51 10N 55 0 E
Solano 127 16 25N 121 15 E
Soledad, Colomb. 86 10 55N 74 46W
Soledad, U.S.A. 80 36 27N 121 16W
Soledad, Venez. 86 8 10N 63 34W
Solemint 81 34 25N 118 27W
Solent, The 95 50 45N 1 25W
Solenzara 103 41 53N 9 23 E
Solesmes 101 50 10N 3 30 E
Solfonn, Mt. 111 60 2N 6 57 E
Solikamsk 120 59 38N 56 50 E
Solimões, R. 86 2 15S 66 30W
Solina 49 43 58N 78 47W
Solingen 105 51 10N 7 4 E
Sollefteå 110 63 12N 17 20 E
Soller 104 39 43N 2 45 E
Solok 126 0 55S 100 40 E
Sololá 84 14 49N 91 10 E
Solomon Is. 14 6 0S 155 0 E
Solomon, N. Fork, R. 74 39 45N 99 0W
Solomon, S. Fork, R. 74 39 25N 99 12W
Solon Springs 52 46 19N 91 47W
Solor, I. 127 8 27S 123 0 E
Solothurn 106 47 13N 7 32 E
Soltanābād 123 36 29N 58 5 E
Soltāniyeh 122 36 20N 48 55 E
Solun 129 46 40N 120 40 E
Solunska Glava 109 41 44N 21 31 E
Solvang 81 34 36N 120 8W
Solvay 71 43 5N 76 17W
Solvesborg 111 56 5N 14 35 E
Solway Firth 96 54 45N 3 38W
Solwezi 117 12 20S 26 21 E
Somali Rep. ■ 115 7 0N 47 0 E
Sombernon 101 47 20N 4 40 E
Sombor 109 45 46N 19 17 E
Sombra 46 42 43N 82 29W
Sombrerete 82 23 40N 103 40W
Sombrero I. 85 18 30N 63 30W
Somers 78 48 4N 114 18W
Somerset, Can. 57 49 25N 98 39W
Somerset, Colo., U.S.A. 79 38 55N 107 30W
Somerset, Ky., U.S.A. 72 37 5N 84 40W
Somerset, Mass., U.S.A. 71 41 45N 71 10W
Somerset, Pa., U.S.A. 70 40 1N 79 4 E
Somerset □ 95 51 9N 3 0W
Somerset East 117 32 42S 25 35 E
Somerset, I. 65 73 30N 93 0W
Somersworth 71 43 15N 70 51W
Somerton 79 32 41N 114 47W
Somerville 71 40 34N 74 36W
Someş, R. 107 47 15N 23 45 E
Somme □ 101 50 0N 2 20 E
Somme, B. de la 100 5 22N 1 30 E
Sommepy-Tahure 101 49 15N 4 31 E
Sommesous 101 48 44N 4 12 E
Sommières 103 43 47N 4 6 E
Somoto 84 13 28N 86 37W
Somovit 109 43 40N 24 45 E
Somport, Puerto de 104 42 48N 0 31W
Son La 128 21 20N 103 50 E
Soná 84 8 0N 81 10W
Sønderborg 111 54 55N 9 49 E
Söndre Stromfjord 17 66 30N 50 52W
Sonepat 124 29 0N 77 5 E
Sonepur 125 20 55N 83 50 E
Song Cau 128 13 20N 109 18 E
Songea 116 10 40S 35 40 E
Songeons 101 49 32N 1 50 E
Songkhla 128 7 13N 100 37 E
Sonmiani 124 25 25N 66 40 E
Sonningdale 56 52 23N 107 44W
Sono, R. 87 8 58S 48 11W
Sonora, Can. 39 45 4N 61 54W
Sonora, Calif., U.S.A. 80 37 59N 120 27W
Sonora, Texas, U.S.A. 75 30 33N 100 37W
Sonora □ 82 28 0N 111 0W
Sonora I. 62 50 22N 125 15W
Sonora P. 78 38 17N 119 35W
Sonora, R. 82 28 30N 111 33W
Sonoyta 82 31 51N 112 50W
Sonsonate 84 13 43N 89 44W
Soo Junction 72 46 20N 85 14W
Soochow 131 31 18N 120 41 E
Sooke 63 48 13N 123 43W
Sopi 127 2 40N 128 28 E
Sopot 107 54 27N 18 31 E
Sopron 106 47 41N 16 37 E
Sop's Arm 37 49 46N 56 56W
Sør-Rondane 91 72 0S 25 0 E
Sør Trøndelag fylke □ 110 63 0N 11 0 E
Sorata 86 15 50S 68 50W
Sorel 41 46 0N 73 10W
Sorento 76 39 0N 89 34W
Sorgono 108 40 0N 9 0 E
Sorgues 103 44 1N 4 53 E
Soria 104 41 43N 2 32W
Soriano 88 33 24S 58 19W
Soriano □ 90 33 30S 58 0W
Sorocaba 89 23 31S 47 35W
Sorong 127 0 55S 131 15 E
Sororoca 86 0 43N 61 31W
Soroti 116 1 43N 33 35 E
Soröy Sundet 110 70 25N 23 0 E
Soröya 110 70 35N 22 45 E
Sorrento 108 40 38N 14 23 E
Sorsele 110 65 31N 17 30 E
Sorsogon 127 13 0N 124 0 E
Soscumica, L. 40 50 15N 77 27W
Sosnowiec 107 50 20N 19 10 E
Sospel 103 43 52N 7 27 E
Soto la Marina, R. 83 23 40N 97 40W
Sotteville-lès-Rouen 100 49 24N 1 5 E
Souanké 116 2 10N 14 10 E
Soucy 40 48 10N 75 30W
Soúdhas, Kólpos 109 35 31N 24 10 E
Soufrière 85 13 51N 61 4W
Soufrière, vol. 85 13 10N 61 10W
Souillac 102 44 53N 1 29 E
Sŏul 130 37 31N 127 6 E
Soulac-sur-Mer 102 45 30N 1 7W
Soulanges □ 44 45 18N 74 3W
Soulanges, Canal de 44 45 20N 73 58W
Soultz 101 48 57N 7 52 E
Sound, The 111 56 7N 12 30 E
Sounding Cr. 61 52 6N 110 28W
Sounding L. 61 52 8N 110 29W
Sources, Mt. aux 117 28 45S 28 50 E
Sourdeval 100 48 43N 0 55W
Soure 87 0 35S 48 30W
Souris, Man., Can. 55 49 40N 100 20W
Souris, P.E.I., Can. 39 46 21N 62 15W
Souris, R. 57 49 40N 99 34W
Sousa 87 6 45S 38 10W
Sousel 87 2 38S 52 29W
Soustons 102 43 45N 1 19W
Souterraine, La 102 46 15N 1 30 E
South Africa, Rep. of, ■ 117 30 0S 25 0 E
South Aulatsivik I. 36 56 45N 61 30W
South Australia □ 134 32 0S 139 0 E
South Baldy, Mt. 79 34 6N 107 27W
South Baymouth 46 45 33N 82 1W
South Beloit 76 42 29N 89 2W
South Bend, Indiana, U.S.A. 77 41 38N 86 20W
South Bend, Wash., U.S.A. 80 46 44N 123 52W

* Renamed Michikamau L.

South Bentinck Arm	**62**	52 7N	126 47W
South Berwick	**71**	43 15N	70 47W
South Boston	**73**	36 42N	78 58W
South Branch	**37**	47 55N	59 2W
South Brook	**37**	49 26N	56 5W
South Burnaby	**66**	49 13N	123 0W
South Cape	**67**	18 58N	155 24E
South Carolina □	**73**	33 45N	81 0W
South Charleston	**72**	38 20N	81 40W
South China Sea	**128**	7 0N	107 0E
South Dakota □	**74**	45 0N	100 0W
South Downs	**95**	50 53N	0 10W
South East C.	**135**	43 40S	146 50E
South East Passage	**39**	44 36N	63 28W
South Esk, R.	**96**	56 44N	3 3W
South Foreland	**95**	51 7N	1 23E
S. Fork, American, R.	**80**	38 45N	121 5W
South Fork, Feather, R.	**80**	39 17N	121 36W
South Fork, Lucking R.	**77**	38 40N	84 19W
South Fork, R.	**78**	47 54N	113 15W
South Gamboa	**82**	9 4N	79 40W
South Gate	**81**	33 57N	118 12W
South Georgia	**91**	54 30S	37 0W
South Gillies	**52**	48 14N	89 42W
South Glamorgan □	**95**	51 30N	3 20W
South Granby	**43**	45 19N	72 43W
South Grand, R.	**76**	38 17N	94 25W
South Haven	**77**	42 22N	86 20W
South Hd.	**37**	49 9N	58 22W
South Heart, R.	**60**	55 34N	116 11W
South Henik, L.	**55**	61 30N	97 30W
South Horr	**116**	2 12N	36 56E
South I.	**133**	43 0S	170 0E
South International Falls	**52**	48 35N	93 24W
South Invercargill	**133**	46 26N	168 23E
South Knife, R.	**55**	58 55N	94 37W
South Korea ■	**130**	36 0N	128 0E
South Lake Tahoe	**80**	38 57N	119 59W
South Lancaster	**43**	45 8N	74 30W
South Lyon	**46**	42 28N	83 39W
South Magnetic Pole (1980)	**91**	65 36S	139 24E
South Milwaukee	**77**	42 50N	87 52W
South Monroe	**46**	41 54N	83 25W
South Nahanni, R.	**54**	61 3N	123 21W
South Nation, R.	**47**	45 34N	75 6W
South Orkney Is.	**91**	63 0S	45 0W
South Pass	**78**	42 20N	108 58W
South Pekin	**76**	40 30N	89 39W
South Pines	**73**	35 10N	79 25W
South Platte, R.	**74**	40 50N	102 45W
South Pt.	**46**	44 54N	83 19W
South Pole	**91**	90 0S	0 0E
South Porcupine	**53**	48 30N	81 12W
South River	**46**	45 52N	79 29W
South Ronaldsay, I.	**96**	58 46N	2 58W
S. Sandwich Is.	**13**	57 0S	27 0W
South Saskatchewan, R.	**56**	53 15N	105 5W
South Seal, R.	**55**	58 48N	98 8W
South Sentinel, I.	**128**	11 1N	92 16E
South Shetland Is.	**91**	62 0S	59 0W
South Shields	**94**	54 59N	1 26W
South Sioux City	**74**	42 30N	96 30W
South Taranaki Bight	**133**	39 40S	174 5E
South Thompson, R.	**63**	50 40N	120 20W
South Twin I.	**36**	53 7N	79 52W
South Twin L.	**37**	49 16N	55 47W
South Tyne, R.	**94**	54 46N	2 25W
South Uist, I.	**96**	57 4N	7 21W
South Wabasca L.	**60**	55 55N	113 45W
South Wayne	**76**	42 34N	89 53W
South West Africa ■ = Namibia	**117**	22 0S	18 9E
South West Cape	**133**	47 16S	167 31E
South West Port Moulton	**39**	43 54N	64 49W
South Westminster	**66**	49 12N	122 53W
South Whitley	**77**	41 5N	85 38W
South Yemen ■	**115**	15 0N	48 0E
South Yorkshire □	**94**	53 30N	1 20W
Southampton, N.S., Can.	**39**	45 35N	64 15W
Southampton, Ont., Can.	**46**	44 30N	81 25W
Southampton, U.K.	**95**	50 54N	1 23W
Southampton, U.S.A.	**71**	40 54N	72 22W
Southampton I.	**65**	64 30N	84 0W
Southbank	**62**	54 2N	125 46W
Southbridge, N.Z.	**133**	43 48S	172 16E
Southbridge, U.S.A.	**71**	42 4N	72 2W
Southdate	**39**	44 40N	63 34W
Southeast C.	**67**	62 55N	169 40W
Southend	**55**	56 19N	103 14W
Southend-on-Sea	**95**	51 32N	0 42E
Southern Alps	**133**	43 41S	170 11E
Southern Cross	**134**	31 12S	119 15E
Southern Indian L.	**55**	57 10N	98 30W
Southern Indian Lake	**55**	57 0N	99 0W
Southern Ocean	**91**	62 0S	160 0W
Southern Uplands	**96**	55 30N	3 3W
Southey	**56**	50 56N	104 30W
Southington	**71**	41 37N	72 53W
Southold	**71**	41 4N	72 26W
Southport, Austral.	**135**	27 58S	153 25E
Southport, U.K.	**94**	53 38N	3 1W
Southport, U.S.A.	**73**	33 55N	78 0W
Southwold	**95**	52 19N	1 41E
Soutpansberge	**117**	23 0S	29 30E
Souvigny	**102**	46 33N	3 10E
Sovereign	**56**	51 31N	107 43W
Sovetskaya Gavan	**121**	48 50N	140 0E
Soviet Union ■	**121**	47 0N	100 0E
Sōya-Misaki	**132**	45 30N	142 0E
Soyopa	**82**	28 41N	109 37W
Spa	**105**	50 29N	5 53E
Spain ■	**104**	40 0N	5 0W
Spalding, Can.	**56**	52 20N	104 30W
Spalding, U.K.	**94**	52 47N	0 9W
Spalding, U.S.A.	**74**	41 45N	98 27W
Spandau	**106**	52 35N	13 7E
Spangler	**70**	40 39N	78 48W
Spaniard's Bay	**37**	47 38N	53 20W
Spanish	**46**	46 12N	82 20W
Spanish Fork	**78**	40 10N	111 37W
Spanish, R.	**46**	46 11N	82 19W
Spanish Town	**84**	18 0N	77 20W
Sparks	**80**	39 30N	119 45W
Sparta, U.S.A.	**76**	38 7N	89 42W
Sparta, U.S.A.	**77**	43 10N	85 42W
Sparta, Ga., U.S.A.	**73**	33 18N	82 59W
Sparta, Wis., U.S.A.	**74**	43 55N	91 10W
Sparta = Spárti	**109**	37 5N	22 25E
Spartanburg, Pa., U.S.A.	**70**	41 48N	79 43W
Spartanburg, S.C., U.S.A.	**73**	35 0N	82 0W
Spárti	**109**	37 5N	22 25E
Spartivento, C., Calabria, Italy	**108**	37 56N	16 4E
Spartivento, C., Sard., Italy	**108**	38 52N	8 50E
Sparwood	**61**	49 44N	114 53W
Spassk-Dalniy	**121**	44 40N	132 40E
Spatha Ákra.	**109**	35 42N	23 43E
Spatsizi, R.	**54**	57 42N	128 7W
Spear, C.	**37**	47 31N	52 37W
Spearfish	**74**	44 32N	103 52W
Spearman	**75**	36 15N	101 10W
Speed, R.	**49**	43 23N	80 22W
Speedway	**77**	39 47N	86 15W
Speers	**56**	52 43N	107 34W
Speightstown	**85**	13 15N	59 39W
Spenard	**67**	61 5N	149 50W
Spencer, U.S.A.	**77**	39 17N	86 46W
Spencer, Idaho, U.S.A.	**78**	44 18N	112 8W
Spencer, Iowa, U.S.A.	**74**	43 5N	95 3W
Spencer, Nebr., U.S.A.	**74**	42 52N	98 43W
Spencer, N.Y., U.S.A.	**71**	42 14N	76 30W
Spencer, W. Va., U.S.A.	**72**	38 47N	81 24W
Spencer Bay	**65**	69 32N	93 32W
Spencer, C.	**135**	35 20S	136 45E
Spencer G.	**135**	34 0S	137 20E
Spencerville, Can.	**47**	44 51N	75 33W
Spencerville, U.S.A.	**77**	40 43N	84 21W
Spences Bridge	**63**	50 25N	121 20W
Spenser Mts.	**133**	42 15S	172 45E
Sperling	**57**	49 30N	97 42W
Sperrin Mts.	**97**	54 50N	7 0W
Spessart	**106**	50 0N	9 20E
Spey, R.	**96**	57 26N	3 25W
Speyer	**106**	49 19N	8 26E
Speyer, R.	**99**	49 18N	7 52E
Spezia = La Spézia	**108**	44 7N	9 49E
Spézia, La	**108**	44 8N	9 50E
Spickard	**76**	40 14N	93 36W
Spillimacheen	**54**	51 6N	117 0W
Spin Baldak	**123**	31 3N	66 16E
Spinazzola	**108**	40 58N	16 5E
Spincourt	**101**	49 20N	5 39E
Spirit Lake, Idaho, U.S.A.	**78**	47 56N	116 56W
Spirit Lake, Wash., U.S.A.	**80**	46 15N	122 9W
Spirit River	**60**	55 45N	118 50W
Spiritwood	**56**	53 24N	107 33W
Spithead	**95**	50 43N	0 56W
Spitzbergen (Svalbard)	**17**	78 0N	17 0E
Split	**108**	43 31N	16 26E
Split L.	**55**	56 8N	96 15W
Splügenpass	**106**	46 30N	9 20E
Spoffard	**75**	29 10N	100 27W
Spokane	**78**	47 45N	117 25W
Spoleto	**108**	42 46N	12 47E
Spoon, R.	**76**	40 19N	90 4W
Spooner	**74**	45 49N	91 51W
Sporyy Navolok, Mys	**120**	75 50N	68 40E
Spragge	**46**	46 15N	82 40W
Sprague, Can.	**57**	49 2N	95 38W
Sprague, U.S.A.	**78**	47 25N	117 59W
Sprague River	**78**	42 28N	121 31W
Spratly, I.	**126**	8 20N	112 0E
Spray	**78**	44 56N	119 46W
Spree, R.	**106**	52 23N	13 52E
Spremberg	**106**	51 33N	14 21E
Sprigg's Pt.	**37**	47 33N	52 40W
Spring City	**78**	39 31N	111 28W
Spring Coulee	**61**	49 20N	113 3W
Spring Garden	**80**	39 52N	120 47W
Spring Green	**76**	43 11N	90 4W
Spring Mts.	**79**	36 20N	115 43W
Spring Valley, Can.	**56**	49 56N	105 24W
Spring Valley, U.S.A.	**76**	41 20N	89 14W
Spring Valley, Minn., U.S.A.	**74**	43 40N	92 30W
Spring Valley, N.Y., U.S.A.	**71**	41 7N	74 4W
Springbok	**117**	29 42S	17 54E
Springbrook	**49**	43 39N	79 47W
Springburn	**133**	43 40S	171 32E
Springdale, Can.	**37**	49 30N	56 6W
Springdale, Ark., U.S.A.	**75**	36 10N	94 5W
Springdale, Wash., U.S.A.	**63**	48 1N	117 50W
Springerville	**79**	34 10N	109 16W
Springfield, Man., Can.	**58**	49 56N	96 56W
Springfield, N.S., Can.	**39**	44 38N	64 52W
Springfield, Ont., Can.	**46**	42 50N	80 56W
Springfield, N.Z.	**133**	43 19S	171 56E
Springfield, Colo., U.S.A.	**75**	37 26N	102 40W
Springfield, Ill., U.S.A.	**76**	39 48N	89 40W
Springfield, Ky., U.S.A.	**77**	37 41N	85 13W
Springfield, Mass., U.S.A.	**71**	42 8N	72 37W
Springfield, Mo., U.S.A.	**75**	37 15N	93 20W
Springfield, Ohio, U.S.A.	**72**	39 58N	83 48W
Springfield, Oreg., U.S.A.	**78**	44 2N	123 0W
Springfield, Tenn., U.S.A.	**73**	36 35N	86 55W
Springfield, Vt., U.S.A.	**71**	43 20N	72 30W
Springfield, L.	**76**	39 46N	89 36W
Springfontein	**117**	30 15S	25 40E
Springhill	**35**	45 40N	64 4W
Springhouse	**63**	51 56N	122 7W
Springs	**117**	26 13S	28 25E
Springside	**56**	51 21N	102 44W
Springsure	**135**	24 8S	148 6E
Springvale, Can.	**48**	43 13N	79 59W
Springvale, U.S.A.	**71**	43 28N	70 48W
Springville, Calif., U.S.A.	**80**	36 8N	118 49W
Springville, N.Y., U.S.A.	**70**	42 31N	78 41W
Springville, Utah, U.S.A.	**78**	40 14N	111 35W
Springwater	**56**	51 58N	108 23W
Sproat L.	**62**	49 17N	125 2W
Spruce-Creek	**70**	40 36N	78 9W
Spruce Grove	**60**	53 32N	113 55W
Spruce I.	**57**	53 5N	100 40W
Spruce Woods Prov. Park	**57**	49 43N	99 5W
Sprucedale	**46**	45 29N	79 28W
Spryfield	**39**	44 37N	63 37W
Spur	**75**	33 28N	100 50W
Spurgeon	**77**	38 14N	87 15W
Spurn Hd.	**94**	53 34N	0 8E
Spuzzum	**63**	49 37N	121 23W
Squamish	**63**	49 45N	123 10W
Squamish, R.	**63**	49 45N	123 8W
Square Islands	**36**	52 47N	55 47W
Squatec	**41**	47 53N	68 43W
Squaw Rapids	**56**	53 41N	103 21W
Squillace	**108**	38 50N	16 26E
Sragen	**127**	7 28S	110 59E
Srbija □	**109**	43 30N	21 0E
Sre Umbell	**128**	11 8N	103 46E
Sredinyy Khrebet	**121**	57 0N	160 0E
Sredne Tambovskoye	**121**	50 55N	137 45E
Srednekolymsk	**121**	67 20N	154 40E
Srednevilyuysk	**121**	63 50N	123 5E
Sredniy Ural, mts.	**84**	59 0N	59 0E
Sremska Mitrovica	**109**	44 59N	19 35E
Sretensk	**121**	52 10N	117 40E
Sri Lanka ■	**124**	7 30N	80 50E
Srikakulam	**125**	18 14N	84 4E
Srinagar	**124**	34 12N	74 50E
Srnetica	**108**	44 25N	16 35E
Staðarhólskirkja	**110**	65 23N	21 58W
Stadlandet	**110**	62 10N	5 10E
Stadskanaal	**105**	53 4N	6 48E
Stafafell	**110**	64 25N	14 52W
Staffa, I.	**96**	56 26N	6 21W
Stafford, U.K.	**96**	52 49N	2 9W
Stafford, U.S.A.	**75**	38 0N	98 35W
Stafford □	**94**	52 53N	2 10W
Stafford Springs	**71**	41 58N	72 20W
Staines	**95**	51 26N	0 30W
Stalingrad = Volgograd	**120**	48 40N	44 25E
Stalybridge	**94**	53 29N	1 56W
Stamford, Can.	**49**	43 8N	79 6W
Stamford, U.K.	**95**	52 39N	0 29W
Stamford, Conn., U.S.A.	**71**	41 5N	73 30W
Stamford, Tex., U.S.A.	**75**	32 58N	99 50W
Stamping Ground	**77**	38 16N	84 41W
Stamps	**75**	33 22N	93 30W
Stanberry	**74**	40 12N	94 32W
Stanbridge East	**43**	45 7N	72 55W
Standard	**61**	51 7N	112 59W
Standerton	**117**	26 55S	29 13E
Standish	**72**	43 58N	83 57W
Stanford	**78**	47 11N	110 10W
Stanhope	**76**	42 17N	93 48W
Stanislaus, R.	**80**	37 40N	121 15W
Stanke Dimitrov	**109**	42 17N	23 9E
Stanley, N.B., Can.	**39**	46 20N	66 50W
Stanley, Sask., Can.	**55**	55 24N	104 22W
Stanley, Falk. Is.	**90**	51 40S	58 0W
Stanley, Idaho, U.S.A.	**78**	44 10N	114 59W
Stanley, N.D., U.S.A.	**74**	48 20N	102 23W
Stanley, N.Y., U.S.A.	**70**	42 48N	77 6W
Stanley, Wis., U.S.A.	**74**	44 57N	91 0W
Stanleyville = Kisangani	**116**	0 35N	25 15E
*Stann Creek	**83**	17 0N	88 20W
Stanovoy Khrebet	**121**	55 0N	130 0E
Stanthorpe	**135**	28 36S	151 59E
Stanton, Can.	**67**	69 45N	128 52W
Stanton, Mich., U.S.A.	**46**	43 18N	85 5W
Stanton, Tex., U.S.A.	**75**	32 8N	101 45W
Stanwood	**80**	48 15N	122 23W
Stapleton	**74**	41 30N	100 31W
Star City	**56**	52 50N	104 20W
Stara Planina	**109**	43 15N	23 0E
Stara Zagora	**109**	42 26N	25 39E
Staraya Russa	**120**	57 58N	31 10E
Starbuck	**57**	49 46N	97 37W
Starbuck I.	**15**	5 37S	155 55W
Stargard	**106**	53 29N	13 19E
Starke	**73**	30 0N	82 10W
Starkville, Colo., U.S.A.	**75**	37 10N	104 31W
Starkville, Miss., U.S.A.	**73**	33 26N	88 48W
Starogard	**107**	53 55N	18 30E
Start Pt., Devon, U.K.	**95**	50 13N	3 38W
Start Pt., Orkney, U.K.	**95**	59 17N	2 25W
Staryy Kheydzhan	**121**	60 0N	144 50E
State Center	**76**	42 1N	93 10W
State College	**70**	40 47N	77 49W
State Is.	**53**	48 40N	87 0W
Stateline	**80**	38 57N	119 56W
Staten I.	**71**	40 35N	74 10W
Staten, I. = Los Estados, I. de	**90**	54 40S	64 0W
Statesboro	**73**	32 26N	81 46W
Statesville	**73**	35 48N	80 51W
Station-du-Côteau, La	**43**	45 17N	74 14W
Stauffer	**81**	34 45N	119 3W
Staunton, Ill., U.S.A.	**76**	39 0N	89 49W
Staunton, Va., U.S.A.	**72**	38 7N	79 4W
Stavanger	**75**	58 57N	5 40E
Stave Falls	**63**	49 13N	122 22W
Stave L.	**63**	49 22N	122 17W
Stavelot	**105**	50 23N	5 55E
Stavely	**61**	50 10N	113 38W
Staveren	**105**	52 53N	5 22E
Stavern	**111**	59 0N	10 1E
Stavropol	**120**	45 5N	42 0E
Stawell	**136**	37 5S	142 47E
Stayner, Can.	**70**	44 25N	80 5W
Stayner, Ont., Can.	**46**	44 25N	80 5W
Steamboat Springs	**78**	40 30N	106 58W
Steele	**74**	46 56N	99 52W
Steele, Mt.	**64**	61 6N	140 23W
Steelton	**70**	40 17N	76 50W
Steelville	**76**	37 57N	91 21W
Steen, R.	**54**	59 35N	117 10W
Steen River	**54**	59 40N	117 12W
Steensby Inl.	**65**	70 15N	78 35W
Steenvoorde	**101**	50 48N	2 33E
Steenwijk	**105**	52 47N	6 7E
Steep Pt.	**134**	26 08S	113 8E
Steep Rock	**57**	51 30N	98 48W
Steep Rock Lake	**34**	48 50N	91 38W
Stefanie L. = Chew Bahir	**116**	4 40N	30 50E
Stefansson I.	**64**	73 20N	105 45W
Steger	**77**	41 28N	87 38W
Stehekin	**63**	48 19N	120 39W
Steiermark □	**106**	47 26N	15 0E
Steilacoom	**80**	47 10N	122 36W
Steinbach	**57**	49 32N	96 40W
Steinkjer	**110**	63 59N	11 31E
Steinkopf	**117**	29 15S	17 48E
Stellarton	**39**	45 32N	62 45W
Stellenbosch	**117**	33 58S	18 50E
Stelvio, Paso dello	**108**	46 32N	10 27E
Stendal	**106**	52 36N	11 50E
Stephan	**74**	48 30N	96 53W
Stephens I.	**62**	54 10N	130 45W
Stephenville, Can.	**37**	48 31N	58 35W
Stephenville, U.S.A.	**75**	32 12N	98 12W
Stephenville Crossing	**37**	48 30N	58 26W
Sterlego, Mys	**17**	80 30N	90 0E
Sterling, Colo., U.S.A.	**74**	40 40N	103 15W
Sterling, Ill., U.S.A.	**76**	41 45N	89 45W
Sterling, Kans., U.S.A.	**74**	38 17N	98 13W
Sterling City	**75**	31 50N	100 59W
Sterling Run	**70**	41 25N	78 12W
Sterlitamak	**120**	53 40N	56 0E
Stettin = Szczecin	**106**	53 27N	14 27E
Stettler	**61**	52 19N	112 40W
Steubenville	**70**	40 21N	80 39W
Stevens	**53**	49 33N	85 49W
Stevens Port	**74**	44 32N	89 34W
Stevens Village	**67**	66 0N	149 10W
Stevenson	**80**	45 42N	121 53W
Stevenson L.	**57**	53 55N	96 0W
Steveston	**66**	49 8N	123 11W
Steward	**76**	41 51N	89 1W
Stewardson	**77**	39 16N	88 38W
Stewart, B.C., Can.	**54**	55 56N	129 57W
Stewart, N.W.T., Can.	**67**	63 19N	139 26W
Stewart, U.S.A.	**80**	39 5N	119 46W
Stewart, I.	**90**	54 50S	71 30W
Stewart I.	**133**	46 58S	167 54E
Stewart Valley	**56**	50 36N	107 48W
Stewarts Point	**80**	38 39N	123 20W
Stewartsville	**76**	39 45N	94 30W
Stewiacke	**39**	45 9N	63 22W
Steyr	**106**	48 3N	14 25E
Stickney	**39**	46 23N	67 34W

** Renamed Dangriga*

Stigler **Sussex, W. □**

Stigler **75** 35 19N 95 6W
Stikine, R. **67** 58 0N 131 12W
Stillwater, Minn., U.S.A. **74** 45 3N 92 47W
Stillwater, N.Y., U.S.A. **71** 42 55N 73 41W
Stillwater, Okla., U.S.A. **75** 36 5N 97 3W
Stillwater Mts. **78** 39 45N 118 6W
Stilwell **75** 35 52N 94 36W
Stimson **34** 48 58N 80 30W
Štip **109** 41 42N 22 10E
Stiring Wendel **101** 49 12N 6 57E
Stirling, Alta., Can. **61** 49 30N 112 30W
Stirling, Ont., Can. **47** 44 18N 77 33W
Stirling, U.K. **96** 56 17N 3 57W
Stirling Ra. **134** 34 0S 118 0E
Stittsville **47** 45 15N 75 55W
Stockbridge **46** 42 27N 84 11W
Stockerau **106** 48 24N 16 12E
Stockett **78** 47 23N 111 7W
Stockholm, Can. **57** 50 39N 102 18W
Stockholm, Sweden **111** 59 20N 18 3E
Stockinbingal **136** 34 30S 147 53E
Stockport **94** 53 25N 2 11W
Stockton, Austral. **136** 32 56S 151 47E
Stockton, Calif., U.S.A. **80** 38 0N 121 20W
Stockton, Ill., U.S.A. **76** 42 21N 90 1W
Stockton, Kans., U.S.A. **74** 39 30N 99 20W
Stockton, Mo., U.S.A. **76** 37 40N 93 48W
Stockton I. **52** 46 57N 90 35W
Stockton-on-Tees **94** 54 34N 1 20W
Stockton, Reservoir **76** 37 42N 93 46W
Stoke-on-Trent **94** 53 1N 2 11W
Stokes Bay, Can. **34** 45 0N 81 22W
Stokes Bay, Can. **46** 45 0N 81 28W
Stokkseyri **110** 63 50N 20 58W
Stokksnes **110** 64 14N 14 58W
Stolac **109** 43 8N 17 59E
Stolberg **105** 50 48N 6 13E
Stolbovaya **121** 64 50N 153 50E
Stonecliffe **34** 46 13N 77 56W
Stoneham **41** 47 0N 71 22W
Stonehaven **96** 56 58N 2 11W
Stonehenge **95** 51 9N 1 45W
Stoner **63** 53 38N 122 40W
Stonewall **57** 50 10N 97 19W
Stoney Creek **48** 43 14N 79 45W
Stonington **76** 39 44N 89 12W
Stony L., Man., Can. **55** 58 51N 98 40W
Stony L., Ont., Can. **47** 44 30N 78 0W
Stony Mountain **57** 50 5N 97 13W
Stony Plain **60** 53 32N 114 0W
Stony Rapids **55** 59 16N 105 50W
Stony River **67** 61 48N 156 48W
Stony Tunguska = Tunguska, Nizhmaya **121** 64 0N 95 0E
Stonyford **80** 39 23N 122 33W
Stora Lulevatten **110** 67 10N 19 30E
Stora Sjøfallet **110** 67 29N 18 40E
Storavan **110** 65 45N 18 10E
Store Bælt **111** 55 20N 11 0E
Storen **110** 63 3N 10 18E
Storkerson B. **64** 72 56N 124 50W
Storm B. **135** 43 10S 147 30E
Storm Lake **74** 42 35N 95 5W
Stormberg **117** 31 16S 26 17E
Stormy L. **52** 49 23N 92 18W
Stornoway **96** 58 12N 6 23W
Storsjön **110** 62 50N 13 8E
Storuman, L. **110** 65 5N 17 10E
Story City **76** 42 11N 93 36W
Stouffville **50** 43 58N 79 15W
Stoughton, Can. **56** 49 40N 103 0W
Stoughton, U.S.A. **76** 42 55N 89 13W
Stour, R., Dorset, U.K. **95** 50 48N 2 7W
Stour, R., Heref. & Worcs., U.K. **94** 52 25N 2 13W
Stour, R., Kent, U.K. **95** 51 15N 0 57E
Stour, R., Suffolk, U.K. **95** 51 55N 1 5E
Stourbridge **95** 52 28N 2 8W
Stout, L. **55** 52 0N 94 40W
Stove Pipe Wells Village **81** 36 35N 117 11W
Stowmarket **95** 52 11N 1 0E
Strabane **97** 54 50N 7 28W
Strabane □ **97** 54 45N 7 25W
Strachan, Mt. **66** 49 25N 123 12W
Strahan **135** 42 9S 145 20E
Stralsund **106** 54 17N 13 5E
Strand **117** 34 9S 18 48E
Strangford **97** 54 23N 5 34W
Strangford, L. **97** 54 30N 5 37W
Stranraer, Can. **56** 51 43N 108 29W
Stranraer, U.K. **96** 54 54N 5 0W
Strasbourg, Can. **56** 51 4N 104 55W
Strasbourg, France **101** 48 35N 7 42E
Strasburg **74** 46 12N 100 9W
Stratford, Austral. **136** 37 59S 147 7E
Stratford, Can. **46** 43 23N 81 0W
Stratford, N.Z. **133** 39 20S 174 19E
Stratford, Calif., U.S.A. **80** 36 10N 119 49W
Stratford, Conn., U.S.A. **71** 41 13N 73 8W
Stratford, Tex., U.S.A. **75** 36 20N 102 3W
Stratford-on-Avon **95** 52 12N 1 42W
Strath Spey **96** 57 15N 3 40W
Strathclyde □ **96** 56 0N 4 50W
Strathcona Prov. Park **62** 49 38N 125 40W
Strathmore, Can. **61** 51 5N 113 25W
Strathmore, U.K. **96** 56 40N 3 4W
Strathmore, U.S.A. **80** 36 9N 119 4W
Strathnaver **63** 53 20N 122 33W
Strathroy **46** 42 58N 81 38W
Strathy Pt. **96** 58 35N 4 0W
Stratton, Can. **52** 48 41N 94 10W
Stratton, U.S.A. **74** 39 20N 102 36W
Straumnes **110** 66 26N 23 8W
Strawberry Hill **66** 49 8N 122 53W
Strawberry Point **76** 42 41N 91 32W
Strawberry Res. **78** 40 0N 111 0W
Strawn **75** 32 36N 98 30W
Streaky Bay **134** 32 48S 134 13E
Streator **77** 41 9N 88 52W
Streetsville **50** 43 35N 79 42W
Strelka **121** 58 5N 93 10E
Strezhevoy **120** 60 42N 77 34E
Strezhnoye **120** 57 45N 84 2E
Strezlecki **136** 38 16S 145 50E
Strómboli, I. **108** 38 48N 15 12E
Strome **61** 52 48N 112 4W
Stromeferry **96** 57 20N 5 33W
Ströms Vattudal L. **110** 64 0N 15 30E
Strömstad **111** 58 55N 11 15E
Stromsund **110** 63 51N 15 35E
Strongfield **56** 51 20N 106 35W
Stronghurst **76** 40 45N 91 55W
Strongs Corners **46** 46 18N 84 55W
Stronsay, I. **96** 59 8N 2 38W
Stroud, Can. **46** 44 19N 79 37W
Stroud, U.K. **95** 51 44N 2 12W
Stroud Road **136** 32 18S 151 57E
Stroudsberg **71** 40 59N 75 15W
Struer **111** 56 30N 8 35E
Struma, R. **109** 41 50N 23 18E
Strumica **109** 41 28N 22 41E
Struthers, Can. **53** 48 41N 85 51W
Struthers, U.S.A. **70** 41 6N 80 38W
Stryker **61** 48 40N 114 44W
Strzelecki Creek **135** 29 37S 139 59E
Stuart, U.S.A. **76** 41 30N 94 19W
Stuart, Fla., U.S.A. **73** 27 11N 80 12W
Stuart, Nebr., U.S.A. **74** 42 39N 99 8W
Stuart I. **67** 63 55N 164 50W
Stuart L. **54** 54 30N 124 30W
Stuart, R. **54** 54 0N 123 35W
Stuart Range **134** 29 10S 134 56E
Stuart Town **136** 32 44S 149 4E
Stull, L. **55** 54 24N 92 34W
Stung-Treng **128** 13 31N 105 58E
Stupart, R. **55** 56 0N 93 25W
Sturgeon B. **57** 52 0N 97 50W
Sturgeon Bay **72** 44 52N 87 20W
Sturgeon Cr. **58** 49 52N 97 16W
Sturgeon Falls **46** 46 25N 79 57W
Sturgeon L., Alta., Can. **60** 55 6N 117 32W
Sturgeon L., Ont., Can. **47** 44 28N 78 43W
Sturgeon L., Ont., Can. **52** 50 0N 90 45W
Sturgeon L., Ont., Can. **52** 48 29N 91 38W
Sturgeon, R., Alta., Can. **59** 53 46N 113 10W
Sturgeon, R., Ont., Can. **46** 46 35N 80 11W
Sturgeon, R., Sask., Can. **56** 53 12N 105 52W
Sturgis, Can. **56** 51 56N 102 36W
Sturgis, Mich., U.S.A. **77** 41 50N 85 25W
Sturgis, S.D., U.S.A. **74** 44 25N 103 30W
Sturt, R. **134** 34 58S 138 31E
Stutterheim **117** 32 33S 27 28E
Stuttgart, Ger. **106** 48 46N 9 10E
Stuttgart, U.S.A. **75** 34 30N 91 33W
Stuyvesant **71** 42 23N 73 45W
Stykkishólmur **110** 65 2N 22 40W
Suakin **115** 19 0N 37 20E
Suancheng **131** 30 58N 118 57E
Süanen **131** 30 0N 109 30E
Suanhan **131** 31 17N 107 46E
Suanhwa **130** 40 35N 115 0E
Suao **131** 24 32N 121 42E
Suaqui **82** 29 12N 109 41W
Suay Rieng **128** 11 9N 105 45E
Subang **127** 7 30S 107 45E
Subansiri, R. **125** 26 48N 93 50E
Subi, I. **126** 2 58N 108 50E
Subotica **109** 46 6N 19 29E
Success **56** 50 28N 108 6W
Suceava **107** 47 38N 26 16E
Suchil **82** 23 38N 103 55W
Suchitoto **84** 13 56N 89 0W
Süchow **131** 34 10N 117 20E
Sucio, R. **86** 6 40N 77 0W
Suck, R. **97** 53 17N 8 10W
Sucre, Boliv. **86** 19 0S 65 15W
Sucre, Venez. **86** 10 25N 64 5W
Sucre □, Colomb. **86** 8 50N 75 40W
Sucre □, Venez. **86** 10 25N 63 30W
Sucunduri, R. **86** 6 20N 58 35W
Sud-Ouest, Pte. du **38** 49 23N 63 36W
Sud, Pte. **38** 49 3N 62 14W
Sudan ■ **115** 15 0N 30 0E
Sudan, The **112** 11 0N 9 0E
Sudbury **46** 46 30N 81 0W
Sudetan Mts. = Sudety **106** 50 20N 16 45E
Sudety **106** 50 20N 16 45E
Sudirman, Pengunungan **127** 4 30N 137 0E
Sueca **104** 39 12N 0 21W
Sueur, Le **74** 44 25N 93 52W
Suez = El Suweis **115** 29 58N 32 31E
Suez Canal **115** 31 0N 32 20E
Sufaina **122** 23 6N 40 44E
Suffield **61** 50 12N 111 10W
Suffolk **72** 36 47N 76 33W
Suffolk □ **95** 52 16N 1 0E
Suffolk, East **95** 52 16N 1 10E
Suffolk, West **95** 52 16N 0 45E
Sufu **129** 39 44N 75 53E
Sufuk **123** 23 50N 51 50E
Sugar City **74** 38 18N 103 38W
Sugar Cr. **76** 40 12N 89 41W
Sugar L. **63** 50 24N 118 30W
Sugar, R., Ill., U.S.A. **76** 42 25N 89 15W
Sugar, R., Ind., U.S.A. **77** 39 50N 87 23W
Sugarloaf Head **37** 47 37N 52 39W
Sugarloaf Pt. **136** 32 22S 152 30E
Suggi L. **56** 54 22N 102 47W
Suhār **123** 24 20N 56 40E
Suhbaatar **130** 50 17N 106 10E
Suhsien **131** 33 40N 117 0E
Suichung **130** 40 20N 120 20E
Suichwan **131** 26 26N 114 32E
Suifenho **130** 44 30N 131 2E
Suihsien **131** 31 58N 113 20E
Suihwa **130** 46 40N 126 57E
Suiknai **131** 21 17N 110 19E
Suining **131** 26 11N 109 5E
Suiping **131** 33 15N 114 6E
Suippes **101** 49 8N 4 30E
Suir, R. **97** 52 31N 7 59W
Suiteh **130** 37 35N 110 5E
Sukabumi **127** 6 56S 106 57E
Sukadana **126** 1 10S 110 0E
Sukandja **126** 2 28S 110 25E
Sukarnapura = Jayapura **127** 2 28N 140 38E
Sukarno, G. = Jaya Puncak **127** 3 57S 137 17E
Sukhona, R. **120** 60 30N 45 0E
Sukhumi **120** 43 0N 41 0E
Sukkur **124** 27 50N 68 46E
Sukkur Barrage **124** 27 50N 68 45E
Sukunka, R. **54** 55 45N 121 15W
Sula, Kepulauan **127** 1 45S 125 0E
Sulaco, R. **84** 15 2N 87 44W
Sulaiman Range **124** 30 30N 69 50E
Sulawesi □ **127** 2 0S 120 0E
Sulawesi, I. **127** 2 0S 120 0E
Sulina **107** 45 10N 29 40E
Sulitälma **110** 67 17N 17 28E
Sulitjelma **110** 61 7N 16 8E
Sullanà **86** 5 0S 80 45W
Sullivan, B.C., Can. **66** 49 7N 122 48W
Sullivan, Qué., Can. **40** 48 7N 77 50W
Sullivan, Ill., U.S.A. **77** 39 40N 88 40W
Sullivan, Ind., U.S.A. **77** 39 5N 87 26W
Sullivan, Mo., U.S.A. **76** 38 10N 91 10W
Sullivan Bay **62** 50 55N 126 50W
Sullivan L. **61** 52 0N 112 0W
Sully **76** 41 34N 92 50W
Sully-sur-Loire **101** 47 45N 2 20E
Sulphur, La., U.S.A. **75** 30 20N 93 22W
Sulphur, Okla., U.S.A. **75** 34 35N 97 0W
Sulphur Pt. **54** 60 56N 114 48W
Sulphur Springs **75** 33 5N 95 30W
Sulphur Springs, Cr. **75** 32 50N 102 8W
Sultan, Can. **53** 47 36N 82 47W
Sultan, U.S.A. **80** 47 51N 121 49W
Sultanpur **125** 26 18N 82 10E
Sulu Arch. **127** 6 0N 121 0E
Sulu Sea **127** 8 0N 120 0E
Suluq **115** 31 44N 20 14E
Sulzbach-Rosenburg **105** 49 30N 11 46E
Sumalata **127** 1 0N 122 37E
Sumampa **88** 29 25S 63 29W
Sumatera, I. **126** 0 40N 100 20E
Sumatera Selatan □ **126** 3 30S 104 0E
Sumatera Tengah □ **126** 1 0S 100 0E
Sumatera Utara □ **126** 2 0N 99 0E
Sumatra **78** 46 45N 107 37W
Sumatra = Sumatera **126** 0 40N 100 20E
Sumba, I. **127** 9 45S 119 35E
Sumba, Selat **127** 9 0S 118 40E
Sumbawa **126** 8 26S 117 30E
Sumbawa, I. **127** 8 34S 117 17E
Sumber **129** 46 21N 108 25E
Sumbing, mt. **127** 7 19S 110 3E
Sumburgh Hd. **96** 59 52N 1 17W
Sumedang **127** 6 49S 107 56E
Sumenep **127** 7 3S 113 51E
Summer L. **78** 42 50N 120 50W
Summerford **37** 49 29N 54 47W
Summerland **63** 49 32N 119 41W
Summerside, Newf., Can. **37** 48 59N 57 59W
Summerside, P.E.I., Can. **39** 46 24N 63 47W
Summerstown **43** 45 4N 74 32W
Summerville, Newf., Can. **37** 48 27N 53 33W
Summerville, Ont., Can. **50** 43 37N 79 34W
Summerville, Ga., U.S.A. **73** 34 30N 85 20W
Summerville, S.C., U.S.A. **73** 33 2N 80 11W
Summit, Can. **34** 47 50N 72 20W
Summit, U.S.A. **67** 63 20N 149 20W
Summit Lake **54** 54 20N 122 40W
Summit Pk. **79** 37 20N 106 48W
Summitt **77** 41 48N 87 48W
Sumner, U.S.A. **77** 38 42N 87 53W
Sumner, Iowa, U.S.A. **76** 42 49N 92 7W
Sumner, Wash., U.S.A. **80** 47 12N 122 14W
Sumperk **106** 49 59N 17 0E
Sumter **73** 33 55N 80 10W
Sumy **120** 50 57N 34 50E
Sun City **81** 33 41N 117 11W
Sun Prairie **76** 43 11N 89 13W
Sunart, L. **96** 56 42N 5 43W
Sunburst **61** 48 56N 111 59W
Sunbury, Can. **66** 49 9N 122 59W
Sunbury, U.S.A. **71** 40 50N 76 46W
Sunchales **88** 30 58S 61 35W
Suncho Corral **88** 27 55S 63 14W
Sunchŏn **131** 34 52N 127 31E
Suncook **71** 43 8N 71 27W
Sunda Ketjil, Kepulauan **126** 7 30S 117 0E
Sunda, Selat **126** 6 20S 105 30E
Sundance **74** 44 27N 104 27W
Sundarbans, The **125** 22 0N 89 0E
Sundargarh **125** 22 10N 84 5E
Sunderland, Can. **47** 44 16N 79 4W
Sunderland, U.K. **94** 54 54N 1 22W
Sunderland, U.S.A. **71** 42 27N 72 36W
Sundown **57** 49 6N 96 16W
Sundre **61** 51 49N 114 38W
Sundridge **46** 45 45N 79 25W
Sundsvall **110** 62 23N 17 17E
Sung-hua Hu **130** 43 0N 127 0E
Sung-hua Kiang (Sungari) **130** 47 0N 130 50E
Sungaipakning **126** 1 19N 102 0E
Sungaipenuh **126** 2 1S 101 20E
Sungaitiram **126** 0 45S 117 8E
Sungari = Sung-hua Kiang **130** 47 0N 130 50E
Sungei Lembing **128** 2 53N 103 4E
Sungei Patani **128** 5 38N 100 29E
Sungei Siput **128** 4 51N 101 6E
Sungguminasa **127** 5 17S 119 30E
Sunghsien **131** 34 10N 112 10E
Sungkiang **131** 31 0N 121 20E
Sungpan **129** 32 50N 103 20E
Sungtao **131** 28 12N 109 12E
Sungtzu **131** 30 25N 111 46E
Sungtzu Hu **131** 30 10N 111 45E
Sungurlu **122** 40 12N 34 21E
Sungyang **131** 28 16N 119 29E
Sunny Corner **39** 46 57N 65 49W
Sunnybrae **39** 45 24N 62 30W
Sunnyside, Can. **37** 47 51N 53 55W
Sunnyside, Utah, U.S.A. **78** 39 40N 110 24W
Sunnyside, Wash., U.S.A. **78** 46 24N 120 2W
Sunnyvale **80** 37 23N 122 2W
Sunray **75** 36 1N 101 47W
Sunshine **136** 37 48S 144 52E
Suntar **121** 62 15N 117 30E
Sunwapta Pass **61** 52 13N 117 10W
Supai **79** 36 14N 112 44W
Supaul **125** 26 10N 86 40E
Superior, Ariz., U.S.A. **79** 33 19N 111 9W
Superior, Mont., U.S.A. **78** 47 15N 114 57W
Superior, Nebr., U.S.A. **74** 40 3N 98 2W
Superior, Wis., U.S.A. **52** 46 45N 92 5W
Superior, L. **69** 47 40N 87 0W
Suphan Buri **128** 14 30N 100 10E
Supu **131** 27 57N 110 15E
Supung Hu **130** 40 40N 125 0E
Sūr, Leb. **115** 33 19N 35 16E
Sūr, Oman **123** 22 34N 59 32E
Sur, Pt. **80** 36 18N 121 54W
Sura, R. **120** 55 30N 46 20E
Surabaja = Surabaya **127** 7 17S 112 45E
Surabaya **127** 7 17S 112 45E
Surakarta **127** 7 35S 110 48E
Surat **124** 21 12N 72 55E
Surat Thani **128** 9 6N 99 14E
Suratgarh **124** 29 18N 73 55E
Sûre, R. **105** 49 51N 6 6E
Surf **81** 34 41N 120 36W
Surf Inlet **54** 53 8N 128 50W
Surgères **102** 46 7N 0 47W
Suri **125** 23 50N 87 34E
Suriapet **124** 17 10N 79 40E
Surin **128** 14 50N 103 34E
Surinam ■ **87** 4 0N 56 15W
Suriname, R. **87** 4 30N 55 30W
Surprise L. **54** 59 40N 133 15W
Surprise, L. **40** 49 20N 74 55W
Surrey **66** 49 12N 122 51W
Surrey □, Can. **66** 49 9N 122 46W
Surrey □, U.K. **95** 51 16N 0 30W
Surrey Centre **66** 49 7N 122 45W
Surtsey **110** 63 20N 20 30W
Suruga-Wan **132** 34 45N 138 30E
Surup **127** 6 27N 126 17E
Surur **123** 23 20N 58 10E
Susa **108** 45 8N 7 3E
Süsangerd **122** 31 35N 48 20E
Susanino **121** 52 50N 140 14E
Susanville **78** 40 28N 120 40W
Susquehanna Depot **71** 41 55N 75 36W
Susquehanna, R. **71** 41 50N 76 20W
Susques **88** 23 35S 66 25W
Sussex, Can. **45** 45 45N 65 37W
Sussex, U.S.A. **71** 41 12N 74 38W
Sussex, E. □ **95** 51 0N 0 0E
Sussex, W. □ **95** 51 0N 0 30W

Sustut, R — Taohsien

Sustut, R. **54** 56 20N 127 30W
Susuman **121** 62 47N 148 10E
Susuna **127** 3 20S 133 25E
Sutherland, Can. **55** 52 15N 106 40W
Sutherland, S. Afr. **117** 32 33S 20 40E
Sutherland, U.S.A. **74** 41 12N 101 11W
Sutherland Falls **133** 44 48S 167 46E
Sutherland Pt. **135** 28 15S 153 35E
Sutherlin **78** 43 28N 123 16W
Sutlej, R. **124** 30 0N 73 0E
Sutter **80** 39 10N 121 45W
Sutter Creek **80** 38 24N 120 48W
Sutton, Can. **71** 45 8N 72 36W
Sutton, Ont., Can. **46** 44 18N 79 22W
Sutton, Qué., Can. **41** 45 6N 72 37W
Sutton, U.S.A. **74** 40 40N 97 50W
Sutton-in-Ashfield **94** 52 8N 1 16W
Sutton, R. **34** 55 15N 83 45W
Sutwik I. **67** 56 35N 157 10W
Suva **133** 17 40S 178 8E
Suva Planina **109** 43 10N 22 5E
Suvorov Is. **15** 13 15S 163 30W
Suwałki **107** 54 8N 22 59E
Suwannee, R. **73** 30 0N 83 0W
Suwanose Jima **132** 29 26N 129 30E
Suwen **131** 20 27N 110 2E
Suwŏn **130** 37 17N 127 1E
Suyung **131** 28 12N 105 10E
Suze, La **100** 47 54N 0 2E
Suzuka **132** 34 55N 136 36E
Svalbard, Arctica **17** 78 0N 17 0E
Svalbard, Iceland **110** 66 12N 15 43W
Svanvik **110** 69 38N 30 3E
Svappavaari **110** 67 40N 21 03E
Svartenhuk Pen. **65** 71 50N 54 30W
Svartisen **110** 66 40N 14 16E
Svealand □ **111** 59 55N 15 0E
Sveg **111** 62 2N 14 21E
Svendborg **111** 55 4N 10 35E
Sverdlovsk **120** 56 50N 60 30E
Sverdrup Chan. **65** 79 56N 96 25W
Sverdrup Is. **65** 79 0N 97 0W
Svishov **109** 43 36N 25 23E
Svobodnyy **121** 51 20N 128 0E
Svolvær **110** 68 15N 14 34E
Swain Reefs **135** 21 45S 152 20E
Swainsboro **73** 32 38N 82 22W
Swakopmund **117** 22 37S 14 30E
Swale, R. **94** 54 18N 1 20W
Swan Hill **136** 35 20S 143 33E
Swan Hills **60** 54 42N 115 24W
Swan Islands **84** 17 22N 83 57W
Swan L. **57** 52 30N 100 40W
Swan, R., Austral. **134** 32 3S 115 35E
Swan, R., Alta., Can. **60** 55 30N 115 18W
Swan, R., Man., Can. **57** 52 30N 100 45W
Swan River **57** 52 10N 101 16W
Swanage **95** 50 36N 1 59W
Swansea, Austral. **136** 33 3S 151 35E
Swansea, Can. **50** 43 38N 79 28W
Swansea, U.K. **95** 51 37N 3 57W
Swartz Creek **46** 42 58N 83 50W
Swastika **34** 48 7N 80 6W
Swatow = Shantow **131** 23 25N 116 40E
Swaziland ■ **117** 26 30S 31 30E
Sweden ■ **111** 67 0N 15 0E
Sweet Home **78** 44 26N 122 38W
Sweet Springs **76** 38 58N 93 25W
Sweetwater, Nev., U.S.A. **80** 38 27N 119 9W
Sweetwater, Tex., U.S.A. **75** 32 30N 100 28W
Sweetwater, R. **78** 42 31N 107 30W
Swellendam **117** 34 1S 20 26E
Swidnica **106** 50 50N 16 30E
Swiebodzin **106** 52 15N 15 37E
Swift Current, Newf., Can. **37** 47 53N 54 12W
Swift Current, Sask., Can. **56** 50 20N 107 45W
Swiftcurrent Cr. **56** 50 38N 107 44W
Swilly L. **97** 55 12N 7 35W
Swindle, I. **62** 52 30N 128 35W
Swindon **95** 51 33N 1 47W
Swinemünde = Świnouścje **106** 53 54N 14 16E
Świnouścje **106** 53 54N 14 16E
Switzerland ■ **106** 46 30N 8 0E
Swords **97** 53 27N 6 15W
Sydenham, R. **46** 42 33N 82 25W
Sydney, Austral. **136** 33 53S 151 10E
Sydney, Can. **39** 46 7N 60 7W
Sydney, U.S.A. **74** 41 12N 103 0W
Sydney L. **52** 50 41N 94 25W
Sydney Mines **39** 46 18N 60 15W
Sydney River **39** 46 7N 60 13W
Sydproven **17** 60 30N 45 35W
Syktyvkar **120** 61 45N 50 40E
Sylacauga **73** 33 10N 86 15W
Sylarna, Mt. **110** 63 2N 12 11E
Sylhet **125** 24 54N 91 52E
Sylvan L. **61** 52 21N 114 10W
Sylvan Lake **61** 52 20N 114 10W
Sylvania, Can. **56** 52 42N 104 0W
Sylvania, U.S.A. **77** 41 43N 83 42W
Sylvania, Ga., U.S.A. **73** 32 45N 81 37W
Sylvester, Can. **60** 55 0N 119 41W
Sylvester, U.S.A. **73** 31 31N 83 50W
Sym **120** 60 20N 87 50E
Symón **82** 24 42N 102 35W
Syr Darya **120** 45 0N 65 0E
Syracuse, U.S.A. **77** 41 28N 85 47W
Syracuse, Kans., U.S.A. **75** 38 0N 101 40W
Syracuse, N.Y., U.S.A. **71** 43 4N 76 11W
Syria ■ **122** 35 0N 38 0E
Syrian Des. **122** 31 30N 40 0E
Syuldzhyukyor **121** 63 25N 113 40E
Syzran **120** 53 12N 48 30E
Szczecin **106** 53 27N 14 27E
Szczecinek **106** 53 43N 16 41E
Szechwan □ **129** 30 15N 103 15E
Szeged **107** 46 16N 20 10E
Székesfehérvár **107** 47 15N 18 25E
Szekszárd **107** 46 22N 18 42E
Szemao **129** 22 50N 101 0E
Szenan **131** 27 50N 108 25E
Szengen, Kwangsi-Chuang, China **131** 23 20N 108 5E
Szengen, Kwangsi-Chuang, China **131** 24 50N 108 0E
Szentes **107** 46 39N 20 21E
Szeping **130** 43 10N 124 18E
Szeshui **94** 34 50N 113 20E
Szewui **131** 23 30N 112 35E
Szolnok **107** 47 10N 20 15E
Szombathely **106** 47 14N 16 38E

T

Ta Fengman **130** 43 45N 126 35E
Ta Hinghan Ling **129** 48 0N 121 0E
Ta Liang Shan **129** 28 0N 103 0E
Tabacal **88** 23 15S 64 15W
Tabaco **127** 13 22N 123 44E
Tābah **122** 26 55N 42 30E
Tabas, Khorasan, Iran **123** 32 48N 60 12E
Tabas, Khorasan, Iran **123** 33 35N 56 55E
Tabasará, Serranía de **84** 8 35N 81 40W
Tabasco □ **83** 17 45N 93 30W
Tabatière, La **37** 50 50N 58 58W
Tabatinga **86** 4 11S 69 58W
Tabatinga, Serra da **87** 10 30S 44 0W
Taber **61** 49 47N 112 8W
Tablas, I. **127** 12 25N 122 2E
Table B. **36** 53 40N 56 25W
Table Grove **76** 40 20N 90 27W
Table Mt. **117** 34 0S 18 22E
Tábor **106** 49 25N 14 39E
Tabora **116** 5 2S 32 57E
Tabrīz **122** 38 7N 46 20E
Tabūk **122** 28 30N 36 25E
Tacámbaro **82** 19 14N 101 28W
Tacarigua, L. de **86** 11 3N 68 25W
Tachick L. **62** 53 57N 124 12W
Tachintala **130** 45 13N 121 37E
Tachira **86** 8 7N 72 21W
Tachira □ **86** 8 7N 72 15W
Tachu **131** 30 45N 107 13E
Tacloban **127** 11 15N 124 58E
Tacna **86** 18 0S 70 20W
Tacoma **80** 47 15N 122 30W
Tacuarembó **89** 31 45S 56 0W
Tademaït, Plateau du **114** 28 30N 2 30E
Tadmor, N.Z. **133** 41 27S 172 45E
Tadmor, Syria **122** 34 30N 37 55E
Tado **86** 5 16N 76 32W
Tadoule, L. **55** 58 36N 98 20W
Tadoussac **41** 48 11N 69 42W
Tadzhik S.S.R. □ **120** 35 30N 70 0E
Taegu **130** 35 50N 128 37E
Taejŏn **130** 36 20N 127 28E
Taerh Hu **130** 43 25N 116 40E
Taf, R. **95** 51 55N 4 36W
Tafalla **104** 42 30N 1 41W
Tafermaar **127** 6 47S 134 10E
Tafí Viejo **88** 26 43S 65 17W
Taft, Phil. **127** 11 57N 125 30E
Taft, Calif., U.S.A. **81** 35 10N 119 28W
Taft, Tex., U.S.A. **75** 27 58N 97 23W
Taga Dzong **125** 27 5N 90 0E
Taganrog **120** 47 12N 38 50E
Tagbilaran **127** 9 39N 123 51E
Tagish **54** 60 19N 134 16W
Tagish L. **67** 60 10N 134 20W
Tagliamento, R. **108** 45 38N 13 5E
Tagua, La **86** 0 3N 74 40W
Taguatinga **87** 12 26S 46 26W
Tagum (Hijo) **127** 7 33N 125 53E
Tagus = Tajo, R. **104** 39 44N 5 50W
Tahahbala, I. **126** 0 30S 98 30E
Tahakopa **133** 46 30S 169 23E
Tahan, Gunong **128** 4 45N 102 25E
Tahcheng **129** 46 50N 83 1E
Taheiho **130** 50 10N 127 20E
Tāherī **123** 27 43N 52 20E
Tahiti, I. **15** 17 37S 149 27W
Tahoe **80** 39 12N 120 9W
Tahoe, L. **80** 39 0N 120 9W
Taholah **80** 47 21N 124 17W
Tahoua **114** 14 57N 5 16E
Tahsien **131** 31 17N 107 30E
Tahsis **62** 49 55N 126 40W
Tahulandang, I. **127** 2 27N 125 23E
Tahuna **127** 3 45N 125 30E
Tai Hu **131** 31 10N 120 0E
Taian **130** 36 20N 117 0E
Taichow **131** 32 30N 119 50E
Taichow Wan. **131** 28 55N 121 10E
Taichung **131** 24 10N 120 35E
Taieri, R. **133** 46 3S 170 12E
Taihan Shan **130** 36 0N 114 0E
Taihape **133** 39 41S 175 48E
Taiho **131** 26 50N 114 54E
Taihsien **130** 39 9N 112 58E
Taihu **131** 30 30N 116 25E
Taikang **131** 34 3N 115 0E
Taikiang **131** 26 45N 108 44E
Taiku **130** 37 46N 112 28E
Taikung **131** 26 50N 108 40E
Tailagein Shara **130** 44 10N 106 0E
Tailai **129** 46 28N 123 18E
Taïma **122** 27 35N 38 45E
Taimyr = Taymyr **121** 75 0N 100 0E
Taimyr, Oz. **121** 74 20N 102 0E
Tain **96** 57 49N 4 4W
Tainan **131** 23 0N 120 15E
Taínaron, Ákra **109** 36 22N 22 27E
Taining **131** 27 0N 117 15E
Taipei **131** 25 2N 121 30E
Taiping **128** 4 51N 100 44E
Taishan **131** 27 29N 119 34E
Taitao, Pen. de **90** 46 30S 75 0W
Taitung **131** 22 43N 121 4E
Taivalkoski **110** 65 33N 28 12E
Taiwan (Formosa) ■ **131** 23 30N 121 0E
Taiwara **123** 33 30N 64 24E
Taïyetos Óros **109** 37 0N 22 23E
Taiyüan **130** 38 0N 112 30E
Tajicaringa **82** 23 15N 104 44W
Tajitos **82** 30 58N 112 18W
Tajo, R. **104** 40 35N 1 52W
Tajumulco, Volcán de **83** 15 20N 91 50W
Tak **128** 16 52N 99 8E
Takada **132** 37 7N 138 15E
Takaka **133** 40 51N 172 50E
Takamatsu **132** 34 20N 134 5E
Takanabe **132** 32 8N 131 30E
Takaoka **132** 36 40N 137 0E
Takapuna **133** 36 47S 174 47E
Takasaki **132** 36 20N 139 0E
Takatsuki **132** 34 51N 135 37E
Takaungu **116** 3 38S 39 52E
Takayama **132** 36 18N 137 11E
Takefu **132** 35 50N 136 10E
Takeo **128** 10 59N 104 47E
Tākestān **122** 36 0N 49 50E
Takhing **131** 23 10N 111 45E
Takingeun **126** 4 45N 96 50E
Takiyuak L. **64** 65 30N 113 5W
Takla L. **54** 55 15N 125 45W
Takla Landing **54** 55 30N 125 50W
Takla Makan **129** 39 0N 83 0E
Taku, R. **54** 58 30N 133 50W
Takushan **130** 39 55N 123 30E
Takysie Lake **62** 53 53N 125 53W
Tala, Uruguay **89** 34 21S 55 46W
Tala, U.S.S.R. **121** 72 40N 113 30E
Talachih **130** 36 45N 105 0E
Talagante **88** 33 40S 70 50W
Talai **130** 45 30N 124 20W
Talamanca, Cordillera de **84** 9 20N 83 20W
Talara **86** 4 30S 81 10E
Talas **120** 42 45N 72 0E
Talaud, Kepulauan **127** 4 30N 127 10E
Talavera de la Reina **104** 39 55N 4 46W
Talayan **127** 6 52N 124 24E
Talbot, C. **134** 13 48S 126 43E
Talbot L. **57** 54 0N 99 55W
Talbragar, R. **136** 32 5S 149 15E
Talca **88** 35 20S 71 46W
Talca □ **88** 35 20S 71 46W
Talcahuano **88** 36 40S 73 10W
Talcher **125** 20 55N 85 3E
Taldy Kurgan **120** 45 10N 78 45E
Talesh, Kūhā-Ye **122** 39 0N 48 30E
Talguppa **124** 14 10N 74 45E
Tali, Shensi, China **131** 34 48N 109 48E
Tali, Yunnan, China **129** 25 45N 100 5E
Taliabu, I. **127** 1 45S 125 0E
Taliang Shan **129** 28 0N 103 0E
Talien, (Dairen) **130** 38 53N 121 37E
Talihina **75** 34 45N 95 1W
Taling Sung **128** 15 5N 99 11E
Taliwang **126** 8 50S 116 55E
Talkeetna **67** 62 20N 150 0W
Talkeetna Mts. **67** 62 20N 149 0W
Talladega **73** 33 28N 86 2W
Tallahassee **73** 30 25N 84 15W
Tallangatta **136** 36 15S 147 10E
Tallering Pk **134** 28 6S 115 37E
Tallinn (Reval) **120** 59 29N 24 58E
Tallulah **75** 32 25N 91 12W
Talmage **55** 49 46N 103 40W
Talmont **102** 46 27N 1 37W
Talpa de Allende **82** 20 23N 104 51W
Taltal **88** 25 23S 70 40W
Taltson L. **55** 61 30N 110 15W
Taltson R. **54** 61 24N 112 46W
Talunkwan I. **62** 52 50N 131 45W
Talyawalka Cr. **136** 32 28S 142 22E
Tama **76** 41 56N 92 37W
Tama Abu, Pegunungan **126** 3 10N 115 0E
Tamalameque **86** 8 52N 73 49W
Tamale **114** 9 22N 0 50W
Tamano **132** 34 35N 133 59E
Tamanrasset **114** 22 56N 5 30E
Tamaqua **71** 40 46N 75 58W
Tamar, R. **95** 50 33N 4 15W
Támara **86** 5 50N 72 10W
Tamaroa **76** 38 8N 89 14W
*Tamatave **117** 18 10S 49 25E
Tamaulipas □ **83** 24 0N 99 0W
Tamaulipas, Sierra de **83** 23 30N 98 20W
Tamazula **82** 24 55N 106 58W
Tamazunchale **83** 21 16N 98 47W
Tambelan, Kepulauan **126** 1 0N 107 30E
Tambo de Mora **86** 13 30S 76 20W
Tambora, G. **126** 8 12S 118 5E
Tambov **120** 52 45N 41 20E
Tambuku, G. **127** 7 8S 113 40E
Tame **86** 6 28N 71 44W
Tamega, R. **104** 41 12N 8 5W
Tamenglong **125** 25 0N 93 35E
Tamerfors **111** 61 30N 23 50E
Tamgak, Mts. **114** 19 12N 8 35E
Tamiahua, Laguna de **83** 21 30N 97 30W
Tamil Nadu □ **124** 11 0N 77 0E
Taming **130** 36 20N 115 10E
Tammisaari (Ekenäs) **111** 60 0N 23 26E
Tampa **73** 27 57N 82 30W
Tampa B. **73** 27 40N 82 40W
Tampere **111** 61 30N 23 50E
Tampico, Mexico **83** 22 20N 97 50W
Tampico, U.S.A. **76** 41 38N 89 47W
Tampin **128** 2 28N 102 13E
Tamsagbulag **130** 47 15N 117 5E
Tamu **125** 24 13N 94 12E
Tamworth, Austral. **135** 31 0S 150 58E
Tamworth, Can. **47** 44 29N 77 0W
Tamworth, U.K. **95** 52 38N 1 41W
Tan Kiang **131** 33 25N 111 0E
Tana **110** 70 7N 28 5E
Tana, L. **115** 13 5N 37 30E
Tana, R. **116** 0 50S 39 45E
Tanacross **67** 63 40N 143 30W
Tanafjorden **110** 70 45N 28 25E
Tanahdjampea, I. **127** 7 10S 120 35E
Tanahgrogot **126** 1 55S 116 15E
Tanahmasa, I. **126** 0 5S 98 29E
Tanahmerah **127** 6 0S 140 7E
Tanami Des. **134** 18 50S 132 0E
Tanana **67** 65 10N 152 15W
Tanana, R. **67** 64 25N 145 30W
Tananarive = Antananarivo **117** 18 55S 47 31E
Tánaro, R. **108** 44 9N 7 50E
Tancarville **100** 49 29N 0 28E
Tanchai **131** 25 58N 107 49E
Tanchŏn **130** 40 27N 128 54E
Tanchow **131** 19 33N 109 22E
Tandag **127** 9 4N 126 9E
Tandil **88** 37 15S 59 6W
Tandjungpandan **126** 2 43S 107 38E
Tando Adam **124** 25 45N 68 40E
Tandou L. **136** 32 40S 142 5E
Tane-ga-Shima **132** 30 30N 131 0E
Taneatua **133** 38 4S 177 1E
Tanen Range **128** 19 40N 99 0E
Tanen Tong Dan **125** 16 30N 98 30E
Tanezrouft **114** 23 9N 0 11E
Tanga **116** 5 5S 39 2E
Tanganyika, L. **116** 6 40S 30 0E
Tanger **114** 35 50N 5 49W
Tangerang **127** 6 12S 106 39E
Tanghing **131** 21 30N 108 2E
Tangho **131** 32 47N 113 2E
Tanghsien **130** 38 48N 114 54E
Tangier **39** 44 48N 62 42W
Tangkak **128** 2 18N 102 34E
Tangku **130** 39 0N 117 40E
Tanglha Shan **129** 33 0N 90 0E
Tangshan, Anhwei, China **131** 34 17N 116 25E
Tangshan, Hopei, China **130** 39 40N 118 10E
Tangtu **131** 31 37N 118 39E
Tangyang **131** 30 50N 111 45E
Tanhsien (Nata) **131** 19 30N 109 17E
Tanimbar, Kepulauan **127** 7 30S 131 30E
Taning = Wuki **131** 31 27N 109 46E
Tanjay **127** 9 30N 123 5E
Tanjore = Thanjavur **124** 10 48N 79 12E
Tanjung **126** 2 10S 115 25E
Tanjungbalai **126** 2 55N 99 44E
Tanjungbatu **126** 2 23N 118 3E
Tanjungkarang **126** 5 20S 105 10E
Tanjungpinang **126** 1 5N 104 30E
Tanjungpriok **127** 6 8S 106 55E
Tanjungredeb **126** 2 9N 117 29E
Tanjungselor **126** 2 55N 117 25E
Tannin **34** 49 40N 91 0W
Tannu Ola **129** 51 0N 94 0E
Tanout **114** 14 50N 8 55E
Tanshui **131** 25 10N 121 28E
Tansley **49** 43 25N 79 48W
Tanta **115** 30 45N 30 57E
Tantallon **57** 50 32N 101 50W
Tantoyuca **83** 21 21N 98 10W
Tanu I. **62** 52 46N 131 40W
Tanus **102** 44 8N 2 19E
Tanzania ■ **116** 6 40S 34 0E
Tanzilla, R. **54** 58 8N 130 43W
Taohsien **131** 25 37N 111 24E

** Renamed Toamasina*

Taokow Teulon

Taokow 130 35 30N 114 30E
Taolaihao 130 44 51N 125 57E
Taonan 130 45 30N 122 20E
Taos 79 36 28N 105 35W
Taoyuan, Hunan, China 131 29 8N 111 15E
Taoyuan, Taiwan, China 131 25 0N 121 4E
Tapa Shan 131 31 45N 109 30E
Tapachula 83 14 54N 92 17W
Tapah 128 4 12N 101 15E
Tapajós, R. 87 4 30S 56 10W
Tapaktuan 126 3 30N 97 10E
Tapanshang = Palinyuchi 130 43 40N 118 20E
Tapanui 133 45 56S 169 18E
Tapauá 86 5 40S 64 20W
Tapauá, R. 86 6 0S 65 40W
Tapirapecó, Serra 86 1 10N 65 0W
Tapleytown 48 43 11N 79 44W
Tappahannock 72 37 56N 76 50W
Tapti, R. 124 21 25N 75 0E
Tapuaenuku, Mt. 133 41 55S 173 50E
Tapul Group, Is. 127 5 35N 120 50E
Taquara 89 29 36N 50 46W
Taquari, R. 89 18 10S 56 0W
Tar Island 54 57 03N 111 40W
Tara, Can. 46 44 28N 81 9W
Tara, U.S.S.R. 120 56 55N 74 30E
Tara, R. 109 43 5N 19 20E
Tarabagatay, Khrebet 121 48 0N 83 0E
Tarābulus, Leb. 122 34 31N 33 52E
Tarābulus, Libya 114 32 49N 13 7E
Tarakan 126 3 20N 117 35E
Taranaki □ 133 39 5S 174 51E
Taranga Hill 124 24 0N 72 40E
Táranto 108 40 30N 17 11E
Táranto, G. di 108 40 0N 17 15E
Tarapacá 86 2 56S 69 46W
Tarapacá □ 88 20 45S 69 30W
Tarare 103 45 54N 4 26E
Tararua Range 133 40 45S 175 25E
Tarascon, Ariège, France 102 42 50N 1 37E
Tarascon, Bouches-du-Rhône, France 103 43 48N 4 39E
Tarauacá 86 8 6S 70 48W
Tarauacá, R. 86 7 30S 70 30W
Taravo, R. 103 41 48N 8 52E
Tarawera 133 39 2S 176 36E
Tarawera L. 133 38 13S 176 27E
Tarbagatai 129 48 30N 99 0E
Tarbat Ness 96 57 52N 3 48W
Tarbela Dam 124 34 0N 72 52E
Tarbert, Can. 49 43 56N 80 20W
Tarbert, U.K. 96 57 54N 6 49W
Tarbes 102 43 15N 0 3E
Tarboro 73 35 55N 77 30W
Tarcoola 134 30 44S 134 36E
Tardets-Sorholus 102 43 8N 0 52W
Tardin 129 37 16N 92 30E
Taree 136 31 50S 152 30E
Tarentaise 103 45 30N 6 35E
Tarfaya 114 27 55N 12 55W
Targon 102 44 44N 0 16W
Tari Nur 130 43 25N 116 40E
Táriba 86 7 49N 72 13W
Tarifa 104 36 1N 5 36W
Tarija 88 21 30S 64 40W
Tarija □ 88 21 30S 63 30W
Tarim, R. 129 41 5N 86 40E
Taritoe, R. 127 3 0S 138 5E
Tarko Sale 120 64 55N 77 50E
Tarlac 127 15 29N 120 35E
Tarma 86 11 25S 75 45W
Tarn □ 102 43 49N 2 8E
Tarn-et-Garonne □ 102 44 8N 1 20E
Tarn, R. 102 44 5N 1 2E
Tarnów 107 50 3N 21 0E
Tarnowskie Góry 107 50 27N 18 54E
Taroom 135 25 36S 149 48E
Tarpon Springs 73 28 8N 82 42W
Tarragona 104 41 5N 1 17E
Tarrasa 104 41 26N 2 1E
Tarrytown 71 41 5N 73 52W
Tarsus 122 36 58N 34 55E
Tartagal 88 22 30S 63 50W
Tartas 102 43 50N 0 49W
Tartūs 122 34 55N 35 55E
Tarutao, Ko 128 6 33N 99 40E
Tarutung 126 2 0N 99 0E
Taschereau 40 48 40N 78 40W
Taseko L. 62 51 15N 123 35W
Taseko, R. 62 52 4N 123 9W
Tashauz 120 42 0N 59 20E
Tashi Chho Dzong 125 27 31N 89 45E
Tashigong 129 33 0N 79 30E
Tashihkao 130 40 47N 122 29E
Tashkent 120 41 20N 69 10E
Tashkumyr 120 41 40N 72 10E
Tashkurgan 129 37 51N 74 57E
Tashkurghan 123 36 45N 67 40E
Tashtagol 120 52 47N 87 53E
Tasi Ho 131 28 20N 119 40E
Tasikmalaya 127 7 18S 108 12E
Tasin (Yangli) 131 22 57N 107 15E
Tasjön 110 64 15N 15 45E
Tasman Bay 133 40 59S 173 25E
Tasman Glacier 133 43 45S 170 20E
Tasman Mts. 133 41 3S 172 25E
Tasman Pen. 135 43 10S 148 0E
Tasman Sea 135 36 0S 160 0E
Tasmania, I., □ 135 49 0S 146 30E
Tassialuk, L. 36 59 3N 74 0W
Tasu 62 52 45N 132 5W
Tasu Sd. 62 52 47N 132 2W
Tatamagouche 39 45 43N 63 18W
Tatar A.S.S.R. □ 120 55 30N 51 30E
Tatarsk 120 55 20N 75 50E
Tatarskiy Proliv 121 54 0N 141 0E
Tateyama 132 35 0N 139 50E
Tathlina L. 54 60 33N 117 39W
Tatien 131 25 45N 118 0E
Tating 131 27 0N 105 35E
Tatinnai L. 55 60 55N 97 40W
Tatla L. 62 52 0N 124 20W
Tatlayoko L. 62 51 35N 124 24W
Tatnam, C. 55 57 16N 91 0W
Tatsaitan 129 37 55N 95 0E
Tatsu 131 29 40N 105 45E
Tatta 124 24 42N 67 55E
Tatton 63 51 43N 121 22W
Tatuī 89 23 25S 48 0W
Tatuk, L. 62 53 32N 124 14W
Tatum 75 33 16N 103 16W
Tatung 130 30 50N 117 45E
Tatungkow 130 39 55N 124 10E
Tatura 136 36 29S 145 16E
Tatvan 122 37 28N 42 27E
Taubaté 89 23 5S 45 30W
Tauern, mts. 106 47 15N 12 40E
Taumarunui 133 38 53S 175 15E
Taumaturgo 86 9 0S 73 50W
Taungdwingyi 125 20 1N 95 40E
Taunggyi 125 20 50N 97 0E
Taungup Taunggya 125 18 20N 93 40E
Taunton, Can. 49 43 56N 78 49W
Taunton, U.K. 95 51 1N 3 7W
Taunus 106 50 15N 8 20E
Taupo 133 38 41S 176 7E
Taupo, L. 133 38 46S 175 55E
Tauq 122 35 12N 44 29E
Tauramena 86 5 1N 72 45W
Tauranga 133 37 35S 176 11E
Tauranga Harb. 133 37 30S 176 5E
Taureau, Lac 34 46 50N 73 40W
Taurianova 108 38 22N 16 1E
Taurus Mts. = Toros Dağlari 122 37 0N 35 0E
Tava Wan 131 22 35N 114 35E
Tavani 55 62 10N 93 30W
Tavas 122 37 35N 29 8E
Tavda 120 58 7N 65 8E
Tavda, R. 120 59 30N 63 0E
Taverny 101 49 2N 2 13E
Taveta 116 3 31N 37 37E
Taviche 83 16 38N 96 32W
Tavignano, R. 103 42 7N 9 33E
Tavira 104 37 8N 7 40W
Tavistock, Can. 46 43 19N 80 50W
Tavistock, U.K. 95 50 33N 4 9W
Tavoy 128 14 7N 98 18E
Tavoy, I. = Mali Kyun 125 13 0N 98 20E
Taw, R. 95 50 58N 3 58W
Tawas City 46 44 16N 83 31W
Tawau 126 4 20N 117 55E
Tawu 131 22 30N 120 50E
Tay, Firth of 96 56 25N 3 8W
Tay, L. 96 56 30N 4 10W
Tay Ninh 128 11 20N 106 5E
Tay, R. 96 56 37N 3 38W
Tayabamba 86 8 15S 77 10W
Tayen 131 30 4N 115 0E
Taylor, Can. 54 56 13N 120 40W
Taylor, Alaska, U.S.A. 67 65 40N 164 50W
Taylor, Pa., U.S.A. 71 41 23N 75 43W
Taylor, Tex., U.S.A. 75 30 30N 97 30W
Taylor Mt. 79 35 16N 107 50W
Taylorsville 77 38 2N 85 21W
Taylorville 77 39 32N 89 20W
Taymyr, Oz. 121 74 50N 102 0E
Taymyr, P-ov. 121 75 0N 100 0E
Tayport 96 56 27N 2 52W
Tayshet 121 55 58N 97 25E
Tayside □ 96 56 25N 3 30W
Taytay 127 10 45N 119 30E
Tayu 131 25 38N 114 9E
Tayulehsze 129 29 15N 98 1E
Tayung 131 29 8N 110 30E
Taz, R. 120 65 40N 82 0E
Tazin L. 55 59 44N 108 42W
Tazin, R. 55 60 26N 110 45W
Tazovskiy 120 67 30N 78 30E
Tbilisi (Tiflis) 120 41 50N 44 50E
Tchad, Lac 114 13 30N 14 30E
Tchentlo L. 54 55 15N 125 0W
Tchibanga 116 2 45S 11 12E
Tchpao (Tienpao) 131 23 25N 106 47E
Te Anau L. 133 45 15S 167 45E
Te Aroha 133 37 32S 175 44E
Te Awamutu 133 38 1S 175 20E
Te Horo 133 40 48S 175 6E
Te Kuiti 133 38 20S 175 11E
Te Puke 133 37 46S 176 22E
Te Waewae B. 133 46 13S 167 33E
Teague 75 31 40N 96 20W
Teapa 83 17 35N 92 56W
Tebicuary, R. 88 26 36S 58 16W
Tebing Tinggi 126 3 38S 102 1E
Tecapa 81 35 51N 116 14W
Tecate 82 32 34N 116 38W
Tecomán 82 18 55N 103 53W
Tecoripa 82 28 37N 109 57W
Tecuci 107 45 51N 27 27E
Tecumseh, Can. 46 42 19N 82 54W
Tecumseh, U.S.A. 77 42 1N 83 59W
Tedzhen 120 37 23N 60 31E
Tee Lake 40 46 40N 79 0W
Teepee Creek 60 55 22N 118 24W
Tees B. 94 54 37N 1 10W
Tees, R. 94 54 36N 1 25W
Teesside 94 54 37N 1 13W
Teeswater 46 43 59N 81 17W
Tefé 86 3 25S 64 50W
Tegal 127 6 52S 109 8E
Tegid, L. 94 52 53N 3 38W
Tegucigalpa 84 14 10N 87 0W
Tehachapi 81 35 11N 118 29W
Tehachapi Mts. 81 35 0N 118 40W
Tehchow 130 37 29N 116 11E
Tehping 130 37 26N 117 0E
Tehrān 123 35 44N 51 30E
*Tehrān □ 123 35 0N 49 30E
Tehtsin (Atuntze) 129 28 45N 98 58E
Tehuacán 83 18 20N 97 30W
Tehuantepec 83 16 10N 95 19W
Tehuantepec, Golfo de 83 15 50N 95 0W
Tehuantepec, Istmo de 83 17 0N 94 30W
Teich, Le 102 44 38N 0 59W
Teifi, R. 95 52 4N 4 14W
Teign, R. 95 50 41N 3 42W
Teignmouth 95 50 33N 3 30W
Teil, Le 103 44 33N 4 40E
Teilleul, Le 100 48 32N 0 53W
Tejo, R. 104 39 15N 8 35W
Tejon Pass 81 34 49N 118 53W
Tekamah 74 41 48N 96 14W
Tekapo, L. 133 43 53S 170 33E
Tekax 83 20 20N 89 30W
Tekeli 120 44 50N 79 0E
Tekirdağ 122 40 58N 27 30E
Tekkali 125 18 43N 84 24E
Tekoa 78 47 19N 117 4W
Tel Aviv-Jaffa = Tel Aviv-Yafo 115 32 4N 34 48E
Tela 84 15 40N 87 28W
Telanaipura = Jambi 126 1 38S 103 30E
Telegraph Cove 62 50 32N 126 50W
Telegraph Cr. 54 58 0N 131 10W
Telemark fylke □ 111 59 25N 8 30E
Telén 88 36 15S 65 31W
Teles Pires (São Manuel), R. 86 8 40S 57 0W
Telescope Peak, Mt. 81 36 6N 117 7W
Telford 94 52 42N 2 31W
Telisze 130 39 50N 112 0E
Telkwa 54 54 41N 126 56W
Tell City 77 38 0N 86 44W
Teller 67 65 12N 166 24W
Tellicherry 124 11 45N 75 30E
Telluride 79 37 58N 107 54W
Telok Anson 128 4 3N 101 0E
Teloloapán 83 18 21N 99 51W
Telom, R. 128 4 20N 101 46E
Telsen 90 42 30S 66 50W
Telukbetung 126 5 29S 105 17E
Telukdalem 126 0 45N 97 50E
Tema 114 5 41N 0 0E
Temagami L. 34 47 0N 80 10W
Temanggung 127 7 18S 110 10E
Temapache 83 21 4N 97 38W
Temax 83 21 10N 88 50W
Tembeling, R. 128 4 20N 102 23E
Temblor Ra, mts. 81 35 30N 120 0W
Teme, R. 95 52 23N 2 15W
Temecula 81 33 26N 117 6W
Temerloh 128 3 27N 102 25E
Temir Tau 120 53 10N 87 20E
Temirtau 120 50 5N 72 56E
Temiscamie, R. 36 50 59N 73 5W
Témiscaming 40 46 44N 79 5W
Témiscamingue, L. 40 47 10N 79 25W
Temora 136 34 30S 147 30E
Temosachic 82 28 58N 107 50W
Tempe, S. Afr. 79 29 1S 26 13E
Tempe, U.S.A. 79 33 26N 111 59W
Temperance Vale 39 46 4N 67 15W
Temperanceville 50 43 56N 79 28W
Tempestad 86 1 20S 74 56W
Tempino 126 1 55S 103 23E
Tempiute 80 37 39N 115 38W
Temple 75 31 5N 97 28W
Temple B. 135 12 15S 143 3E
Temple Sowerby 95 54 38N 2 33W
Templeman, Mt. 63 50 42N 117 12W
Templemore 97 52 48N 7 50W
Templeton, Can. 48 45 29N 75 35W
Templeton, U.S.A. 80 35 33N 120 42W
Tempoal 83 21 31N 98 23W
Temuco 90 38 50S 72 50W
Temuka 133 44 14S 171 17E
Ten Mile L. 37 51 6N 56 42W
Tena 86 0 59S 77 49W
Tenabo 83 20 2N 90 12W
Tenaha 75 31 57N 94 15W
Tenali 124 16 15N 80 35E
Tenancingo 83 19 0N 99 33W
Tenango 83 19 0N 99 40W
Tenasserim 128 12 6N 99 3E
Tenasserim □ 128 14 0N 98 30E
Tenay 103 45 55N 5 30E
Tenby 95 51 40N 4 42W
Tende 103 44 5N 7 35E
Tende, Col de 103 44 9N 7 32E
Tenerife, I. 114 28 20N 16 40W
Teng, R. 128 20 30N 98 10E
Tengah □ 127 2 0S 122 0E
Tengah Kepulauan 126 7 5S 118 15E
Tengchowfu = Penglai 130 37 50N 120 50E
Tenggara □ 127 3 0S 122 0E
Tenghsien, Kwangsi-Chuang, China 131 23 20N 111 0E
Tenghsien, Shantung, China 131 35 10N 117 10E
Tengiz, Ozero 120 50 30N 69 0E
Tengkow 130 39 45N 106 40E
Tenille 73 32 58N 82 50W
Tenino 80 46 51N 122 51W
Tenkasi 124 8 55N 77 20E
Tenke 116 10 32S 26 7E
Tennant Creek 134 19 30S 134 0E
Tennessee □ 69 36 0N 86 30W
Tennyson 77 38 5N 87 7W
Tenom 126 5 4N 115 38E
Tenosique 83 17 30N 91 24W
Tenryū-gawa, R. 132 35 39N 137 48E
Tent L. 55 62 25N 107 54W
Tenterfield 135 29 0S 152 0E
Teófilo Otôni 87 17 50S 41 30W
Tepalcatepec, R. 82 18 35N 101 59W
Tepehuanes 82 25 21N 105 44W
Tepetongo 82 22 28N 103 9W
Tepic 82 21 30N 104 54W
Teplice 106 50 39N 13 50E
Tepoca, C. 82 29 20N 112 25W
Tequila 82 20 54N 103 47W
Ter Apel 105 52 53N 7 5E
Ter, R. 104 42 0N 2 30E
Téramo 108 42 40N 13 40E
Terang 136 38 15S 142 55E
Tercan 122 39 50N 40 30E
Terceira 93 38 43N 27 13W
Tercero, R. 88 32 58S 61 47W
Terence Bay 39 44 28N 63 43W
Terengganu □ 128 4 55N 103 0E
Teresina 87 5 2S 42 45W
Terezinha 86 0 44N 69 27W
Tergnier 101 49 40N 3 17E
Termas de Chillan 88 36 50S 71 31W
Termez 120 37 0N 67 15E
Términi Imerese 101 37 59N 13 51E
Términos, Laguna de 83 18 35N 91 30W
Térmoli 108 42 0N 15 0E
Ternate 127 0 45N 127 25E
Terneuzen 105 51 20N 3 50E
Terney 121 45 3N 136 37E
Terni 108 42 34N 12 38E
Terra Bella 81 35 58N 119 3W
Terra Cotta 49 43 43N 79 56W
Terra Nova 37 48 30N 54 13W
Terra Nova B. 91 74 50S 164 40E
Terra Nova Nat. Park 37 48 33N 53 58W
Terra Nova, R. 37 48 40N 54 0W
Terrace 54 54 30N 128 35W
Terrace Bay 53 48 47N 87 5W
Terracina 108 41 17N 13 12E
Terralba 108 39 42N 8 38E
Terranova = Ólbia 108 40 55N 9 30E
Terrasse-Vaudreuil 44 45 24N 73 59W
Terrasson 102 45 7N 1 19E
Terre Haute 77 39 28N 87 25W
Terrebonne 44 45 42N 73 38W
Terrebonne □ 44 45 50N 74 0W
Terrebonne B. 75 29 15N 90 28W
Terrebonne Heights 44 45 44N 73 38W
Terrell 75 32 44N 96 19W
Terrenceville 37 47 40N 54 44W
Terry 74 46 47N 105 20W
Terschelling, I. 105 53 25N 5 20E
Teruel 104 40 22N 1 8W
Tervola 110 66 6N 24 49E
Tešanj 109 44 38N 17 59E
Teshio-Gawa, R. 132 44 53N 141 45E
Tesiyn Gol 129 50 40N 93 20E
Teslin 67 60 10N 132 43W
Teslin L. 54 60 15N 132 57W
Teslin, R. 54 61 34N 134 35W
Tessenderlo 105 51 4N 5 5E
Tessier 55 51 48N 107 26W
Test, R. 95 51 7N 1 30W
Teste, La 102 44 37N 1 8W
Tetachuck L. 62 53 18N 125 55W
Tetas, Pta. 88 23 31S 70 38W
Tete 117 16 13S 33 33E
Tête-à-la-Baleine 37 50 41N 59 20W
Teteven 109 42 58N 24 17E
Tethull, R. 54 60 35N 112 12W
Tetlin 67 63 14N 142 50W
Tetlin Junction 67 63 29N 142 55W
Teton, R. 78 47 58N 111 0W
Tétouan 114 35 35N 5 21W
Tetovo 109 42 1N 21 2E
Tetu L. 52 50 11N 95 2W
Tetuán = Tétouan 114 35 30N 5 25W
Tetyukhe 121 44 45N 135 40E
Teuco, R. 88 25 30S 60 25W
Teulon 57 50 23N 97 16W

* *Now part of Marzaki*

Teutoburger Wald Togo

Teutoburger Wald	106	52 5N	8 20E
Tevere, R.	108	42 30N	12 20E
Teviot, R.	96	55 21N	2 51W
Tewkesbury	95	51 59N	2 8W
Texada I.	62	49 40N	124 25W
Texarkana, Ark., U.S.A.	75	33 25N	94 0W
Texarkana, Tex., U.S.A.	75	33 25N	94 3W
Texas □	75	31 40N	98 30W
Texas City	75	29 20N	95 20W
Texel, I.	105	53 5N	4 50E
Texhoma	75	36 32N	101 47W
Texline	75	36 26N	103 0W
Texoma L.	75	34 0N	96 38W
Teziutlán	83	19 50N	97 30W
Tezpur	125	26 40N	92 45E
Tezzeron L.	54	54 43N	124 30W
Tha-anne, R.	55	60 31N	94 37W
Tha Nun	128	8 12N	98 17E
Thabana Ntlenyana, Mt.	117	29 30S	29 9E
Thabazimbi	117	24 40S	26 4E
Thai Nguyen	128	21 35N	105 46E
Thailand (Siam) ■	128	16 0N	102 0E
Thakhek	128	17 25N	104 45E
Thal	124	33 28N	70 33E
Thal Desert	124	31 0N	71 30E
Thala La	125	28 25N	97 23E
Thame	95	51 44N	0 58W
Thame, R.	95	51 52N	0 47W
Thames	70	42 35N	82 1W
Thames, R., Can.	46	42 20N	82 25W
Thames, R., N.Z.	133	37 32S	175 45E
Thames, R., U.K.	95	51 30N	0 35E
Thames, R., U.S.A.	71	41 18N	72 9W
Thamesford	46	43 4N	81 0W
Thamesville	46	42 33N	81 59W
Thana	124	19 12N	72 59E
Thanet, I. of	95	51 21N	1 20E
Thang Binh	128	15 50N	108 20E
Thanh Hoa	128	19 48N	105 46E
Thanjavur (Tanjore)	124	10 48N	79 12E
Thann	101	47 48N	7 5E
Thaon	101	48 15N	6 25E
Thar (Great Indian) Desert	124	28 25N	72 0E
Tharad	124	24 30N	71 30E
Thargomindah	135	27 58S	143 46E
Tharrawaddy	125	17 38N	95 48E
Tharthār, Bahr ath	122	34 0N	43 0E
Thásos, I.	109	40 40N	24 40E
Thatcher, Ariz., U.S.A.	79	32 54N	109 46W
Thatcher, Colo., U.S.A.	79	37 38N	104 6W
Thaton	125	16 55N	97 22E
Thau, Étang de	102	43 23N	3 36E
Thaungdut	125	24 30N	94 40E
Thayer	75	36 34N	91 34W
Thayetmyo	125	19 20N	95 18E
Thazi	125	21 0N	96 5E
The Bight	85	24 19N	75 24W
The Dalles	78	45 40N	121 11W
The Grampians, Mts.	136	37 0S	142 30E
The Great Divide	136	35 0S	149 17E
The Grenadines, Is.	85	12 30N	61 30W
The Hague = 's-Gravenhage	106	52 7N	7 14E
The Lake	85	21 5N	73 34W
The Pas	57	53 45N	101 15W
The Rock	136	35 15S	147 2E
The Vale	136	33 34S	143 49E
Thedford, Can.	46	43 9N	81 51W
Thedford, U.S.A.	74	41 59N	100 31W
Thekulthili L.	55	61 3N	110 0W
Thelon, R.	55	62 35N	104 3W
Thénezay	100	46 44N	0 2W
Thenon	102	45 9N	1 4E
Theodore, Austral.	135	24 55S	150 3E
Theodore, Can.	56	51 26N	102 55W
Thérain, R.	101	49 15N	2 27E
Theresa	71	44 13N	75 50W
Thermaïkos Kólpos	109	40 15N	22 45E
Thermopilai P.	109	38 48N	22 45E
Thermopolis	78	43 35N	108 10W
Thesiger B.	64	71 30N	124 5W
Thessalía □	109	39 30N	22 0E
Thessalon	46	46 20N	83 30W
Thessaloníki	109	40 38N	23 0E
Thessaly = Thessalía	109	39 30N	22 0E
Thetford	95	52 25N	0 44E
Thetford Mines	41	46 8N	71 18W
Theux	105	50 32N	5 49E
Thévet, L.	38	51 50N	64 12W
Thiberville	100	49 8N	0 27E
Thicket Portage	55	55 19N	97 42W
Thief River Falls	75	48 15N	96 10W
Thiérache	101	49 51N	3 45E
Thiers	102	45 52N	3 33E
Thies	114	14 50N	16 51W
Thika	116	1 1S	37 5E
Thikombia, I.	133	15 44S	179 55W
Thillot, Le	101	47 53N	6 46E
Thimphu (Tashi Chho Dzong)	125	27 31N	89 45E
þingvallavatn	110	64 11N	21 9W
Thionville	101	49 20N	6 10E
Thirá	109	36 23N	25 27E
Thirsk	94	54 15N	1 20W
Thisted	111	56 58N	8 40E
Thistle I.	134	35 0S	136 8E
Thistletown	50	43 44N	79 33W
Thiu Khao Phetchabun	128	16 20N	100 55E
Thívai	109	38 19N	23 19E
Thiviers	102	45 25N	0 54E
Thizy	103	46 2N	4 18E
þjorsa	110	63 47N	20 48W
Thlewiaza, R., Man., Can.	55	59 43N	100 5W
Thlewiaza, R., N.W.T., Can.	55	60 29N	94 40W
Thoa, R.	55	60 31N	109 47W
Thoissey	103	46 12N	4 48E
Thom Bay	65	70 9N	92 25W
Thomas, Okla., U.S.A.	75	35 48N	98 48W
Thomas, W. Va., U.S.A.	72	39 10N	79 30W
Thomas Hubbard, C.	65	82 0N	94 25W
Thomas Resr.	76	39 34N	92 39W
Thomastown	97	52 32N	7 10W
Thomasville, Ala., U.S.A.	73	31 55N	87 42W
Thomasville, Ga.., U.S.A.	73	30 50N	84 0W
Thomasville, N.C., U.S.A.	73	35 55N	80 4W
Thompson, B.C., Can.	63	50 15N	121 24W
Thompson, Man., Can.	55	55 45N	97 52W
Thompson Falls	78	47 37N	115 26W
Thompson Landing	55	62 56N	110 40W
Thompson, R., Can.	63	50 15N	121 24W
Thompson, R., U.S.A.	74	39 46N	93 37W
Thompsons	79	39 0N	109 50W
Thompsonville, U.S.A.	77	37 55N	88 46W
Thompsonville, Vt., U.S.A.	71	42 0N	72 37W
Thomson	76	41 58N	90 6W
Thomson, R.	135	25 11S	142 53E
Thonburi	128	13 50N	100 36E
Thônes	103	45 54N	6 18E
Thonon-les-Bains	103	46 22N	6 29E
Thorburn	39	45 34N	62 33W
Thorhild	60	54 10N	113 7W
þorlákshöfn	110	63 51N	21 22W
Thornaby on Tees	94	54 36N	1 19W
Thornburn Road	37	47 35N	52 51W
Thornbury	46	44 34N	80 26W
Thorne Glacier	91	87 30S	150 0E
Thornhill, Man., Can.	57	49 12N	98 14W
Thornhill, Ont., Can.	50	43 48N	79 25W
Thornton	76	42 57N	93 23W
Thorntown	77	40 8N	86 36W
Thorold	49	43 7N	79 12W
Thorold South	49	43 6N	79 12W
Thorsby	60	53 14N	114 3W
Thouarcé	101	47 17N	0 30W
Thousand Oakes	81	34 10N	118 50W
Thrace = Thráki	109	41 10N	25 30E
Thráki	109	41 9N	25 30E
Three Forks	78	45 55N	111 40W
Three Hills	61	51 43N	113 15W
Three Kings Is.	133	34 10S	172 10E
Three Lakes	74	45 41N	89 10W
Three Mile Plains	39	44 58N	64 7W
Three Oaks	77	41 48N	86 36W
Three Rivers, Calif., U.S.A.	80	36 26N	118 54W
Three Rivers, Mich., U.S.A.	77	41 57N	85 38W
Three Rivers, Tex., U.S.A.	75	28 30N	98 10W
Three Sisters, Mt.	78	44 10N	121 52W
Throop	71	41 24N	75 39W
Throssell Ra.	134	17 24S	126 4E
þ órshöfn	110	66 12N	15 20W
Thrumster	96	58 24N	3 8W
Thubun Lakes	55	61 30N	112 0W
Thuddungra	136	34 8S	148 8E
Thueyts	103	44 41N	4 9E
Thuin	105	50 20N	4 17E
Thuir	102	42 38N	2 45E
Thule	65	77 30N	69 0W
Thun	106	46 45N	7 38E
Thunder B., Can.	52	48 20N	89 0W
Thunder B., U.S.A.	70	45 0N	83 20W
Thunder Bay	52	48 25N	89 15W
Thunder Cr.	56	50 23N	105 32W
Thunder River	54	52 13N	119 20W
Thung Song	128	8 10N	99 40E
Thunkar	125	27 55N	91 0E
Thüringer Wald	106	50 35N	11 0E
Thurles	97	52 40N	7 53W
Thursday I.	135	10 30S	142 3E
Thurso, Can.	40	45 36N	75 15W
Thurso, U.K.	96	58 34N	3 31W
Thurso, R.	96	58 36N	3 30W
Thurston	70	39 50N	82 33W
Thurston I.	91	72 0S	100 0W
Thury-Harcourt	100	49 0N	0 30W
Thutade L.	54	57 0N	126 55W
Tiahualilo	82	26 20N	103 30W
Tiaret	114	30 52N	10 10E
Tibagi	89	24 30S	50 24W
Tibagi, R.	89	22 47S	51 1W
Tibati	114	6 22N	12 30E
Tiber = Tevere, R.	108	42 30N	12 20E
Tiber Res.	78	48 20N	111 15W
Tiberias	115	32 47N	35 32E
Tibesti	114	21 0N	17 30E
Tibet □	129	32 30N	86 0E
Tibooburra	135	29 26S	142 1E
Tibugá, Golfo de	86	5 45N	77 20W
Tiburón, I.	82	29 0N	112 30W
Ticino □	106	46 20N	8 45E
Ticino, R.	108	45 23N	8 47E
Ticonderoga	71	43 50N	73 28W
Ticul	83	20 20N	89 50W
Tiddim	125	23 20N	93 45E
Tide Head	39	47 59N	66 47W
Tidore	127	0 40N	127 25E
Tiehling	130	42 25N	123 51E
Tiel	105	51 53N	5 26E
Tielt	105	51 0N	3 20E
Tien Shan	129	42 0N	80 0E
Tienchen	130	40 32N	114 0E
Tienen	105	50 48N	4 57E
Tienho	131	24 58N	108 35E
Tieno	131	25 3N	107 3E
Tienpao	131	23 25N	106 47E
Tienshui	131	34 30N	105 34E
Tientsin	130	39 10N	117 0E
Tientu	131	18 12N	109 33E
Tientung	131	23 47N	107 2E
Tierra Alta	86	8 11N	76 4W
Tierra Amarilla	88	27 28S	70 18W
Tierra Colorada	83	17 10N	99 35W
Tierra de Campos	104	42 10N	4 50W
Tierra del Fuego, I. Gr. de	90	54 0S	69 0W
Tiétar, R.	104	39 55N	5 50W
Tieté, R.	87	20 40S	51 35W
Tiffin	77	41 8N	83 10W
Tiffin, R.	77	41 20N	84 24W
Tiflis = Tbilisi	120	41 50N	44 50E
Tifton	73	31 28N	83 32W
Tifu	127	3 39S	126 18E
Tigalda I.	67	54 9N	165 0W
Tigil	121	58 0N	158 10E
Tignish	39	46 58N	64 2W
Tigre, R.	86	3 30S	74 58W
Tigyaing	125	23 45N	96 10E
Tihua	129	43 40N	87 50E
Tijiamis	127	7 16S	108 29E
Tijibadok	127	6 53S	106 47E
Tijuana	82	32 30N	117 3W
Tikal	84	17 2N	89 35W
Tikamgarh	124	24 44N	78 57E
Tikang	131	31 7N	118 2E
Tikhoretsk	120	45 56N	40 5E
Tikrit	122	34 35N	43 37E
Tiksi	121	71 50N	129 0E
Tilamuta	127	0 40N	122 15E
Tilburg	105	51 31N	5 6E
Tilbury, Can.	46	42 17N	82 23W
Tilbury, U.K.	95	51 27N	0 24E
Tilcara	88	23 30S	65 23W
Tilden	74	42 3N	97 45W
Tilichiki	121	61 0N	166 5E
Till, R.	94	55 35N	2 3W
Tillamook	78	45 29N	123 55W
Tilley	54	50 28N	111 38W
Tillsonburg	46	42 53N	80 44W
Tilos, I.	109	36 27N	27 27E
Tilston	57	49 23N	101 19W
Tilt, R.	96	56 50N	3 50W
Tilton	71	43 25N	71 36W
Timaru	133	44 23S	171 14E
Timber Lake	74	45 29N	101 0W
Timber Mtn.	80	37 6N	116 28W
Timberlea	39	44 40N	63 45W
Timbilica	136	37 22S	149 42E
Timbio	86	2 20N	76 40W
Timbiqui	86	2 46N	77 42W
Timboon	136	38 30S	142 58E
Timbuktu = Tombouctou	114	16 50N	3 0W
Timişoara	107	45 43N	21 15E
Timmins	53	48 28N	81 25W
Timok, R.	109	44 10N	22 40E
Timon	87	5 8S	42 52W
Timor, I.	127	9 0S	125 0E
Timor Sea	135	10 0S	127 0E
Timur □	127	9 0S	125 0E
Tin Mtn.	80	36 54N	117 28W
Tinaca Pt.	127	5 30N	125 25E
Tinaco	86	9 42N	68 26W
Tinambacan	127	12 5N	124 32E
Tinaquillo	86	9 55N	68 18W
Tinchebray	100	48 47N	0 45W
Tindouf	114	27 50N	8 4W
Tingan	131	19 42N	110 18E
Tinghai	131	30 0N	122 10E
Tingnan	131	24 45N	114 50E
Tingo María	86	9 10S	76 0W
Tingpien	130	37 30N	107 50E
Tingsi	130	35 50N	104 17E
Tinnia	88	27 0S	62 45W
Tinnoset	111	59 45N	9 3E
Tinogasta	88	28 0S	67 40W
Tinos	109	37 33N	25 8E
Tinpak	131	21 40N	111 15E
Tintagel	62	54 12N	125 35W
Tintina	88	27 2S	62 45W
Tioga	70	41 54N	77 9W
Tioman, I.	128	2 50N	104 10E
Tioman, Pulau, Is.	128	2 50N	104 10E
Tionaga	34	48 0N	82 0W
Tionesta	70	41 29N	79 28W
Tipongpani	125	27 20N	95 55E
Tipp City	77	39 58N	84 11W
Tippecanoe, R.	77	40 31N	86 47W
Tipperary	97	52 28N	8 10W
Tipperary □	97	52 37N	7 55W
Tipton, U.K.	95	52 32N	2 4W
Tipton, Calif., U.S.A.	80	36 3N	119 19W
Tipton, Ind., U.S.A.	77	40 17N	86 0W
Tipton, Iowa, U.S.A.	76	41 45N	91 12W
Tipton, Mo., U.S.A.	76	38 41N	92 48W
Tipton, Mt.	81	35 32N	114 16W
Tiptonville	75	36 22N	89 30W
Tīrān	123	32 45N	51 0E
Tirana	109	41 18N	19 49E
Tiraspol	120	46 55N	29 35E
Tire	122	38 5N	27 50E
Tirebolu	122	40 58N	38 45E
Tiree, I.	96	56 31N	6 55W
Tîrgovişte	107	44 55N	25 27E
Tîrgu-Jiu	107	45 5N	23 19E
Tîrgu Mureş	107	46 31N	24 38E
Tirich Mir Mt.	124	36 15N	71 35E
Tirodi	124	21 35N	79 35E
Tirol □	106	47 3N	10 43E
Tirso, R.	108	40 33N	9 12E
Tiruchchirappalli	124	10 45N	78 45E
Tirunelveli (Tinnevelly)	124	8 45N	77 45E
Tirupati	124	13 45N	79 30E
Tiruvannamalai	124	12 10N	79 12E
Tisa, R.	107	45 30N	20 20E
Tisdale	56	52 50N	104 0W
Tishomingo	75	34 14N	96 38W
Tit-Ary	121	71 50N	126 30E
Titicaca, L.	86	15 30S	69 30W
Titograd	109	42 30N	19 19E
Titov Veles	109	41 46N	21 47E
Titovo Užice	109	43 55N	19 50E
Tittabawassee, R.	46	43 23N	83 59W
Titule	116	3 15N	25 31E
Titumate	86	8 19N	77 5W
Titusville	70	41 35N	79 39W
Tiverton, N.S., Can.	39	44 23N	66 13W
Tiverton, Ont., Can.	46	44 16N	81 32W
Tiverton, U.K.	95	50 54N	3 30W
Tívoli	108	41 58N	12 45E
Tiwī	123	22 45N	59 12E
Tizmin	83	21 0N	88 1W
Tiznados, R.	86	8 50N	67 50W
Tiznit	114	29 48N	9 45W
Tjalang	127	4 30N	95 43E
Tjangkuang, Tg.	126	7 0S	105 0E
Tjareme, G.	127	6 55S	108 27E
Tjeggelvas	110	66 37N	17 45E
Tjepu	127	7 12S	111 31E
Tjiandjur	127	6 51S	107 7E
Tjibatu	127	7 8S	107 59E
Tjikadjang	127	7 25S	107 48E
Tjimahi	127	6 53S	107 33E
Tjirebon = Cirebon	127	6 45S	108 32E
Tjörnes	110	66 12N	17 9W
Tjurup	126	4 26S	102 13E
Tlacolula	83	16 57N	96 29W
Tlacotalpán	83	18 37N	95 40W
Tlaquepaque	82	20 39N	103 19W
Tlaxcala	83	19 20N	98 14W
Tlaxcala □	83	19 30N	98 20W
Tlaxiaco	83	17 10N	97 40W
Tlell	62	53 34N	131 56W
Tlemcen	114	34 52N	1 15W
Toad, R.	54	59 25N	124 57W
Toay	88	36 50S	64 30W
Toba	132	34 30N	136 45E
Toba Inlet	62	50 25N	124 35W
Toba Kakar	124	31 30N	69 0E
Toba, L.	126	2 40N	98 50E
Tobago, I.	85	11 10N	60 30W
Tobelo	127	1 25N	127 56E
Tobermory, Can.	46	45 12N	81 40W
Tobermory, U.K.	96	56 37N	6 4W
Tobin	80	39 55N	121 19W
Tobin L.	56	53 35N	103 30W
Tobique, R.	39	46 46N	67 42W
Toboali	126	3 0S	106 25E
Tobol	120	52 40N	62 39E
Toboli	127	0 38S	120 12E
Tobolsk	120	58 0N	68 10E
Tobruk = Tubruq	115	32 7N	23 55E
Toby Creek	63	50 20N	116 25W
Tobyhanna	71	41 10N	75 15W
Tocantinópolis	87	6 20S	47 25W
Tocantins, R.	87	14 30S	49 0W
Tocca	73	34 32N	83 17W
Tochigi	132	36 25N	139 45E
Tochigi-ken □	132	36 45N	139 45E
Toconao	88	34 35N	83 19W
Tocópero	86	11 30N	69 16W
Tocopilla	88	22 5S	70 10W
Tocumwal	136	35 45S	145 31E
Tocuyo, R.	86	10 50N	69 0W
Todeli	127	1 38S	124 34E
Todenyang	116	4 35N	35 56E
Todjo	127	1 20S	121 15E
Todos os Santos, Baia de	87	12 48S	38 38W
Todos Santos	82	23 27N	110 13W
Todos Santos, Bahia de	82	31 48N	116 42W
Tofield	60	53 25N	112 40W
Tofua I.	133	19 45S	175 05W
Toghral Ombo	129	35 10N	81 40E
Togian, Kepulauan	127	0 20S	121 50E
Togliatti	120	53 37N	49 18E
Togo	57	51 24N	101 35W

Name	Page	Lat.	Long.
Togo ■	114	6 15N	1 35E
Tōhoku □	132	39 50N	141 45E
Toirim	130	46 0N	106 50E
Tokaj	107	48 8N	21 27E
Tokala, G.	127	1 30S	121 40E
Tokamachi	132	37 8N	138 43E
Tokanui	133	46 34S	168 56E
Tokara-gunto	132	29 0N	129 0E
Tokara Kaikyō	132	30 0N	130 0E
Tokarahi	133	44 56S	170 39E
Tokat	122	40 22N	36 35E
Tokeland	80	46 42N	123 59W
Tokelau Is.	14	9 0S	172 0W
Tokong	128	5 27N	100 23E
Tokoto	130	40 18N	111 0E
Tokuno-shima	131	27 50N	129 2E
Tokushima	132	34 4N	134 34E
Tokushima-ken □	132	35 50N	134 30E
Tokuyama	132	34 0N	131 50E
Tōkyō	132	35 45N	139 45E
Tōkyō-to □	132	35 40N	139 30E
Tolaga Bay	133	38 21S	178 20E
Tolageak	67	70 2N	162 50W
Tolbukhin	109	43 37N	27 49E
Toledo, Spain	104	39 50N	4 2W
Toledo, U.S.A.	76	42 0N	92 35W
Toledo, U.S.A.	77	39 16N	88 15W
Toledo, Ohio, U.S.A.	72	41 37N	83 33W
Toledo, Oreg., U.S.A.	78	44 40N	123 59W
Toledo, Wash., U.S.A.	78	46 29N	122 58W
Toledo, Montes de	104	39 33N	4 20W
Tolfino	62	49 11N	125 55W
Tolga	114	34 46N	5 22E
Tolima □	86	3 45N	75 15W
Tolima, Vol.	86	4 40N	75 19W
Tolitoli	127	1 5N	120 50E
Tolleson	79	33 29N	112 10W
Tollhouse	80	37 1N	119 24W
Tolo	116	2 50S	18 40E
Tolo, Teluk	127	2 20S	122 10E
Tolono	77	39 59N	88 16W
Tolosa	104	43 8N	2 5W
Tolstoi	57	49 5N	96 49W
Toluca	83	19 20N	99 50W
Tolun	130	42 22N	116 30E
Tomahawk	74	45 28N	89 40W
Tomales	80	38 15N	122 53W
Tomales B.	80	38 15N	123 58W
Tomar	104	39 36N	8 25W
Tomaszów Mazowiecki	107	51 30N	19 57E
Tomatlán	82	19 56N	105 15W
Tombigbee, R.	73	32 0N	88 6W
Tombodor, Serra do	87	12 0S	41 30W
Tombouctou	114	16 50N	3 0W
Tombstone	79	31 40N	110 4W
Tomé	88	36 36S	73 6W
Tomelloso	104	39 10N	3 2W
Tomiko L.	46	46 32N	79 49W
Tomini	127	0 30N	120 30E
Tomini, Teluk	127	0 10S	122 0E
Tommot	121	58 50N	126 20E
Tomo	86	2 38N	67 32W
Tomorong	136	35 0S	151 9E
Tomorrit, mt.	109	40 40N	20 30E
Tompkins	56	50 4N	108 47W
Toms Place	80	37 34N	118 41W
Toms River	71	39 59N	74 12W
Tomsk	120	56 30N	85 12E
Tonalá	83	16 8N	93 41W
Tonalea	79	36 17N	110 58W
Tonantins	86	2 45S	67 45W
Tonasket	63	48 45N	119 30W
Tonawanda	49	43 0N	78 54W
Tonbridge	95	51 12N	0 18E
Tondano	127	1 35N	124 54E
Tone-Gawa, R.	132	35 44N	140 51E
Tonga Is. ■	133	20 0S	173 0W
Tonga Trench	133	18 0S	175 0W
Tongatapu, I.	133	21 10S	174 0W
Tongeren	105	50 47N	5 28E
Tongking = Bac-Phan	128	21 30N	105 0E
Tongking, G. of	128	20 0N	108 0E
Tongoy	88	30 25S	71 40W
Tongsa Dzong	125	27 31N	90 31E
Tongue, R.	78	48 30N	106 30W
Tonica	76	41 13N	89 4W
Tonk	124	26 6N	75 54E
Tonkawa	75	36 44N	67 22W
Tonlé Sap	128	13 0N	104 0E
Tonnay-Charente	102	45 56N	0 55W
Tonneins	102	44 24N	0 20E
Tonnerre	101	47 51N	3 59E
Tonopah	79	38 4N	117 12W
Tonosí	84	7 20N	80 20W
Tonsberg	111	59 19N	10 25E
Tooele	78	40 30N	112 20W
Toora-Khem	121	52 28N	96 9E
Toowoomba	135	27 32S	151 56E
Top	124	34 15N	68 35E
Top of the World Prov. Park	61	50 0N	115 35W
Topaz	80	38 41N	119 30W
Topeka	74	39 3N	95 40W
Topki	120	55 25N	85 20E
Topley	54	54 32N	126 5W
Topocalma, Pta.	88	34 10S	72 2W
Topock	81	34 46N	114 29W
Topolobampo	82	25 40N	109 10W
Toppenish	78	46 27N	120 16W

Name	Page	Lat.	Long.
Tor Bay, Austral.	134	35 5S	117 50E
Tor Bay, U.K.	98	50 26N	3 31W
Torata	86	17 3S	70 1W
Torbat-e Heydārīyeh	123	35 15N	59 12E
Torbat-e Jām	123	35 8N	60 35E
Torbay, Can.	37	47 40N	52 42W
Torbay, U.K.	95	50 26N	3 31W
Torch, R.	56	53 50N	103 5W
Tordesillas	104	41 30N	5 0W
Torfajökull	110	63 54N	19 0W
Torgau	106	51 32N	13 0E
Torhout	105	51 5N	3 7E
Torigni-sur-Vire	100	49 3N	0 58W
Torin	82	27 33N	110 5W
Torino	108	45 4N	7 40E
Tormentine	35	46 6N	63 46W
Tormes, R.	104	41 7N	6 0W
Tormore	50	43 51N	79 42W
Tornado Mt.	54	49 55N	114 40W
Torne älv	110	65 50N	24 12E
Torneträsk	110	68 24N	19 15E
Torngat Mts.	36	59 0N	63 40W
Tornio	110	65 50N	24 12E
Tornionjoki	110	65 50N	24 12E
Tornquist	88	38 0S	62 15W
Toro, Cerro del	88	29 0S	69 50W
Toro Pk.	81	33 34N	116 24W
Toro, Pta.	84	9 22N	79 57W
Toronátos Kólpos	109	40 5N	23 30E
Toronto, Austral.	136	33 0S	151 30E
Toronto, Can.	50	43 39N	79 20W
Toronto, U.S.A.	70	40 27N	80 36W
Toronto □	50	43 39N	79 23W
Toronto Harbour	50	43 38N	79 22W
Toronto I.	50	43 37N	79 23W
*Toronto International Airport	50	43 42N	79 38W
Toronto, L.	82	27 40N	105 30W
Toropets	120	56 30N	31 40E
Tororo	116	0 45N	34 12E
Toros Dağlari	122	37 0N	35 0E
Torquay, Can.	56	49 9N	103 30W
Torquay, U.K.	95	50 27N	3 31W
Torrance	81	33 50N	118 19W
Torre Annunziata	108	40 45N	14 26E
Tôrre de Moncorvo	104	41 12N	7 8W
Torrelavega	104	43 20N	4 5W
Torremolinos	104	36 38N	4 30W
Torrens, L.	135	31 0S	137 50E
Torreón	82	25 33N	103 25W
Torres	82	28 46N	110 47W
Torres Strait	135	9 50S	142 20E
Torres Vedras	104	39 5N	9 15W
Torrevieja	104	37 59N	0 42W
Torrey	79	38 12N	111 30W
Torridge, R.	95	50 51N	4 10W
Torridon, L.	96	57 35N	5 50W
Torrington, Can.	61	51 48N	113 35W
Torrington, Conn., U.S.A.	71	41 50N	73 9W
Torrington, Wyo., U.S.A.	74	42 5N	104 8W
Torrowangee	136	31 22S	141 30E
Torsill Mts.	65	65 0N	84 30W
Tortola, I.	85	18 19N	65 0W
Tortosa	104	40 49N	0 31E
Tortosa C.	104	40 41N	0 52E
Tortue, I. de la	85	20 5N	72 57W
Tortue, R. de la	45	45 27N	73 56W
Tortuga, Isla la	85	11 8N	67 2W
Torūd	123	35 25N	55 5E
Torun	107	53 0N	18 39E
Tory Hill	70	44 56N	78 18W
Tory I.	97	55 17N	8 12W
Tosa-Wan	132	33 15N	133 30E
Toscana	108	43 30N	11 5E
Tostado	88	29 15S	61 50W
Toteng	117	20 22S	22 58E
Tôtes	100	49 41N	1 3E
Totma	120	60 0N	42 40E
Totonicapán	84	14 50N	91 20W
Tottenham, Austral.	136	32 14S	147 21E
Tottenham, Can.	46	44 1N	79 49W
Tottori	132	35 30N	134 15E
Tottori-ken □	132	35 30N	134 12E
Touamotou, Archipel de (Tuamotu Arch.)	15	17 0S	144 0W
Toubkal, Djebel	114	31 0N	8 0W
Toubouai, Îles	15	25 0S	150 0W
Touchwood	56	51 21N	104 9W
Toucy	101	47 44N	3 15E
Touggourt	114	33 6N	6 4E
Toul	101	48 40N	5 53E
Toulnustouc Nord-Est., R.	38	50 56N	67 44W
Toulnustouc, R.	38	49 35N	68 24W
Toulon, France	103	43 10N	5 55E
Toulon, U.S.A.	76	41 6N	89 52W
Toulouse	102	43 37N	1 27E
Touques, R.	100	49 22N	0 8E
Touquet, Le	101	50 30N	1 36E
Tour-du-Pin, La	103	45 33N	5 27E
Touraine	100	47 20N	0 30E
Tourcoing	101	50 42N	3 10E
Tournai	105	50 35N	3 25E
Tournan-en-Brie	101	48 44N	2 46E
Tournay	102	43 13N	0 13E
Tournon	103	45 4N	4 50E
Tournon-St.-Martin	100	46 45N	0 58E

Name	Page	Lat.	Long.
Tournus	103	46 35N	4 54E
Tours	100	47 22N	0 40E
Tovar	86	8 20N	71 46W
Towanda, U.S.A.	77	40 36N	88 53W
Towanda, N.Y., U.S.A.	71	41 46N	76 30W
Tower	52	47 49N	92 17W
Towner	74	48 25N	100 26W
Townsend	78	46 25N	111 32W
Townshend, C.	135	22 18S	150 30E
Townshend, I.	135	22 16S	150 31E
Townsville	135	19 15S	146 45E
Towshan	131	22 5N	112 50E
Towson	72	39 26N	76 34W
Toyah	75	31 20N	103 48W
Toyahvale	75	30 58N	103 45W
Toyama	132	36 40N	137 15E
Toyama-ken □	132	36 45N	137 30E
Toyama-Wan	132	37 0N	137 30E
Toyohashi	132	34 45N	137 25E
Toyokawa	132	34 48N	137 27E
Toyonaka	132	34 50N	135 28E
Toyooka	132	35 35N	134 55E
Toyota	132	35 3N	137 7E
Trabzon	122	41 0N	39 45E
Tracadie	39	47 30N	64 55W
Tracy, N.B., Can.	39	45 41N	66 41W
Tracy, Qué., Can.	41	46 1N	73 9W
Tracy, Calif., U.S.A.	80	37 46N	121 27W
Tracy, Minn., U.S.A.	74	44 12N	95 30W
Tradom	129	30 0N	83 59E
Traer	76	42 12N	92 28W
Trafalgar, Austral.	136	38 14S	146 12E
Trafalgar, Can.	50	43 29N	79 43W
Trafalgar, C.	104	36 10N	6 2W
Trail	63	49 5N	117 40W
Trainor L.	54	60 24N	120 17W
Tralee	97	52 16N	9 42W
Tralee B.	97	52 17N	9 55W
Tramore	97	52 10N	7 10W
Tramping Lake	56	52 8N	108 57W
Tran Ninh, Cao Nguyen	128	19 30N	103 10E
Tranas	111	58 3N	14 59E
Trancas	88	26 20S	65 20W
Tranche-sur-Mer, La	100	46 20N	1 27W
Trang	128	7 33N	99 38E
Trangan, I.	127	6 40S	134 20E
Trangie	136	32 4S	148 0E
Trani	108	41 17N	16 24E
Tranqueras	89	31 8S	56 0W
Transcona	58	49 55N	97 0W
Transilvania	107	46 19N	25 0E
Transkei □	117	32 15S	28 15E
Transvaal □	117	25 0S	29 0E
Transylvania = Transilvania	107	46 19N	25 0E
Trápani	108	38 1N	12 30E
Trappe, La	44	45 29N	74 2W
Trappe Peak, Mt.	78	45 56N	114 29W
Traralgon	135	38 12S	146 34E
Tras os Montes e Alto-Douro □	104	41 25N	7 20W
Trasimeno, L.	108	43 10N	12 5E
Trat	128	12 14N	102 33E
Travers, Mt.	133	42 1S	172 45E
Travers Res.	61	50 12N	112 51W
Traverse City	72	44 45N	85 39W
Traverse I.	91	48 0S	28 0E
Travnik	109	44 17N	17 39E
Traynor	55	52 20N	108 32W
Trebbia, R.	108	44 52N	9 30E
Trebinje	109	42 44N	18 22E
Třebon	106	48 59N	14 48E
Tredegar	95	51 47N	3 16W
Trégastel-Plage	100	48 49N	3 31W
Tréguier	100	48 47N	3 16W
Trégune	100	47 51N	3 51W
Treherne	57	49 38N	98 42W
Treignac	102	45 32N	1 48E
Treinta y Tres	89	33 10S	54 50W
Trelew	90	43 10S	65 20W
Trélissac	102	45 11N	0 47E
Trelleborg	111	55 20N	13 10E
Trélon	101	50 5N	4 6E
Tremblade, La	102	45 46N	1 8W
Tremblant, Mt.	40	46 16N	74 35W
Trementina	75	35 27N	105 30W
Tremonton	78	41 45N	112 10W
Tremp	104	42 10N	0 52E
Trenary	72	46 12N	86 59W
Trenche, R.	41	47 46N	72 53W
Trend Village	48	45 19N	75 48W
Trenggalek	127	8 5S	111 44E
Trenque Lauquen	88	36 0S	62 45W
Trent, R., Can.	47	44 6N	77 34W
Trent, R., U.K.	94	53 33N	0 44W
Trente et un Milles, L. des	40	46 12N	75 49W
Trentino-Alto Adige □	108	46 5N	11 0E
Trento	108	46 5N	11 8E
Trenton, N.S., Can.	39	45 37N	62 38W
Trenton, Ont., Can.	47	44 10N	77 40W
Trenton, U.S.A.	77	42 8N	83 11W
Trenton, Mo., U.S.A.	76	40 5N	93 37W
Trenton, Nebr., U.S.A.	74	40 14N	101 4W
Trenton, N.J., U.S.A.	71	40 15N	74 41W
Trenton, Tenn., U.S.A.	75	35 58N	88 57W
Trepassey	37	46 43N	53 25W
Trepassey B.	37	46 37N	53 30W
Tréport, Le	100	50 3N	1 20E

Name	Page	Lat.	Long.
Tres Arroyos	88	38 20S	60 20W
Três Corações	89	21 30S	45 30W
Três Lagoas	87	20 50S	51 50W
Tres Marías, Is.	82	21 25N	106 28W
Tres Montes, C.	90	47 0S	75 35W
Tres Pinos	80	36 48N	121 19W
Três Pontas	89	21 23S	45 29W
Tres Puentes	88	27 50S	70 15W
Três Puntas, C.	90	47 0S	66 0W
Tres Rios	89	22 20S	43 30W
Tres-St-Redempteur	43	45 26N	74 23W
Tres Valles	83	18 15N	96 8W
Trets	103	43 27N	5 41E
Treungen	111	59 1N	8 31E
Treuter Mts.	65	75 42N	82 30W
Trêve, L. la	40	49 56N	75 30W
Treviso	108	45 40N	12 15E
Trévoux	103	45 57N	4 47E
Triang	128	3 13N	102 27E
Triaucourt-en-Argonne	101	48 59N	5 2E
Tribulation, C.	135	16 5S	145 29E
Tribune, Can.	56	49 15N	103 49W
Tribune, U.S.A.	74	38 30N	101 45W
Trichur	124	10 30N	76 18E
Trier	105	49 45N	6 37E
Trieste	108	45 39N	13 45E
Triglav	108	46 25N	13 45E
Tríkkala	109	39 34N	21 47E
Trikora, G.	127	4 11S	138 0E
Trilby	77	41 39N	83 37W
Trim	97	53 34N	6 48W
Trincomalee	124	8 38N	81 15E
Trindade, I.	13	20 20S	29 50W
Tring-Jonction	41	46 16N	70 59W
Trinidad, Boliv.	86	14 54S	64 50W
Trinidad, Colomb.	86	5 25N	71 40W
Trinidad, Cuba	84	21 40N	80 0W
Trinidad, Uruguay	88	33 30S	56 50W
Trinidad, U.S.A.	75	37 15N	104 30W
Trinidad & Tobago ■	85	10 30N	61 20W
Trinidad, I., Argent.	90	39 10S	62 0W
Trinidad, I., S. Amer.	85	10 30N	61 15W
Trinidad, R.	83	17 49N	95 9W
Trinity, Can.	37	48 59N	53 55W
Trinity, U.S.A.	75	30 59N	95 20W
Trinity B., Austral.	135	16 30S	146 0E
Trinity B., Can.	37	48 20N	53 10W
Trinity Mts.	75	40 20N	118 50W
Trinity R.	75	30 30N	95 0W
Trion	73	34 35N	85 18W
Tripoli	76	42 49N	92 16W
Tripoli = Tarābulus	122	34 31N	33 52E
Tripolis	109	37 31N	22 25E
Tripp	74	43 16N	97 58W
Tripura □	125	24 0N	92 0E
Triquet, L.	38	50 42N	59 47W
Tristan da Cunha, I.	13	37 6S	12 20W
Trivandrum	124	8 31N	77 0E
Trnava	107	48 23N	17 35E
Trochu	61	51 50N	113 13W
Trodely I.	36	52 15N	79 26W
Troglav, mt.	108	43 56N	16 36E
Troilus, L.	36	50 50N	74 35W
Trois-Pistoles	41	48 5N	69 10W
Trois-Rivières	41	46 25N	72 40W
Troitsk	120	54 10N	61 35E
Troitsko-Pechorsk	120	62 40N	56 10E
Trolladyngja	110	64 49N	17 29W
Tröllladyngja	110	64 54N	17 15W
Trollhättan	111	58 17N	12 20E
Tromelin I.	16	15 52S	54 25E
Troms fylke □	110	68 56N	19 0E
Tromsø	110	69 40N	18 56E
Trona	81	35 46N	117 23W
Tronador, Mt.	90	41 53S	71 0W
Trondheim	110	63 25N	10 25E
Trondheimsfjorden	110	63 35N	10 30E
Troodos, mt.	122	34 58N	32 55E
Tropic	79	37 44N	112 4W
Trossachs, The	96	56 14N	4 24W
Trostan Mt.	97	55 4N	6 10W
Troup	75	32 10N	95 3W
Trout Creek, Can.	46	45 59N	79 22W
Trout Creek, U.S.A.	52	46 28N	89 1W
Trout L., N.W. Terr., Can.	54	60 40N	121 40W
Trout L., Ont., Can.	52	51 20N	93 15W
Trout Lake, Can.	63	50 35N	117 25W
Trout Lake, Mich., U.S.A.	46	46 10N	85 2W
Trout Lake, Wash., U.S.A.	80	45 60N	121 32W
Trout, R.	54	61 19N	119 51W
Trout River, Newf., Can.	37	49 29N	58 8W
Trout River, Qué., Can.	43	45 3N	74 17W
Trouville	100	49 21N	0 5E
Trowbridge	95	51 18N	2 12W
Troy, N.S., Can.	39	45 42N	61 26W
Troy, Ont., Can.	49	43 16N	80 11W
Troy, Turkey	122	39 55N	26 20E
Troy, Alabama, U.S.A.	73	31 50N	85 58W
Troy, Ill., U.S.A.	76	38 44N	89 54W
Troy, Ind., U.S.A.	77	38 0N	86 48W
Troy, Kans., U.S.A.	74	39 47N	95 2W
Troy, Mo., U.S.A.	76	38 56N	90 59W
Troy, Montana, U.S.A.	78	48 30N	115 58W
Troy, N.Y., U.S.A.	71	42 45N	73 39W
Troy, Ohio, U.S.A.	77	40 0N	84 10W

* *Renamed Lester B. Pearson International Airport*

Troyes Udmurt, A.S.S.R. □

Troyes 101 48 19N 4 3 E
Trucial States = Utd. Arab Emirates ■ 123 24 0N 54 30 E
Truckee 80 39 20N 120 11W
Truite, L. à la 40 47 20N 78 20W
Trujillo, Colomb. 86 4 10N 76 19W
Trujillo, Hond. 84 16 0N 86 0W
Trujillo, Peru 86 8 0S 79 0W
Trujillo, Spain 104 39 28N 5 55W
Trujillo, U.S.A. 75 35 34N 104 44W
Trujillo, Venez. 86 9 22N 70 26W
Truk Is. 15 7 25N 151 46 E
Trumann 75 35 42N 90 32W
Trumbull, Mt. 79 36 25N 113 32W
Trun 100 48 50N 0 2 E
Trundle 136 32 53S 147 42 E
Truro, Can. 39 45 21N 63 14W
Truro, U.K. 95 50 17N 5 2W
Truth or Consequences 79 33 9N 107 16W
Trutnov 106 50 37N 15 54 E
Truyère, R. 102 44 38N 2 34 E
Tryon 73 35 15N 82 16W
Tryonville 70 41 42N 79 48W
Tsacha L. 62 53 3N 124 50W
Tsagaan 129 50 20N 105 3 E
Tsaidam 129 37 0N 95 0 E
Tsamkong = Chan Kiang 131 21 15N 110 20 E
Tsanghsien 130 38 24N 116 57 E
Tsangpo 129 29 40N 89 0 E
Tsaochwang 86 35 11N 115 28 E
Tsaohsien 131 34 50N 115 45 E
Tsaratanana 117 16 47S 47 39 E
Tsaring Nor 129 34 40N 97 20 E
Tsau 117 20 8S 22 29 E
Tsawassen 66 49 1N 123 6W
Tselinograd 120 51 10N 71 30 E
Tsenkung 131 27 3N 108 40 E
Tsetserleg 129 47 36N 101 32 E
Tsetserling 130 47 29N 101 10 E
Tshabong 117 26 2S 22 29 E
Tshane 117 24 5S 21 54 E
Tshela 116 5 4S 13 0 E
Tshikapa 116 6 17S 21 0 E
Tshofa 116 5 8S 25 8 E
Tshwane 117 22 24S 22 1 E
Tsian 130 41 12N 126 5 E
Tsiaotso 131 35 11N 113 37 E
Tsihombe 117 25 10S 45 41 E
Tsimlyanskoye Vdkhr. 120 48 0N 43 0 E
Tsimo 130 36 25N 120 29 E
Tsin Ling Shan 131 34 0N 107 30 E
Tsinan 130 34 50N 105 40 E
Tsincheng 130 35 30N 113 0 E
Tsinghai 129 35 10N 96 0 E
Tsinghsien 131 26 30N 109 30 E
Tsingkiang 131 27 50N 114 38 E
Tsingliu 131 26 0N 116 50 E
Tsinglo 130 38 40N 112 0 E
Tsingning 130 35 25N 105 50 E
Tsingshih 131 29 43N 112 13 E
Tsingshuiho 130 39 56N 111 55 E
Tsingsi 130 38 1N 114 4 E
Tsingsi (Kweishun) 131 23 6N 106 25 E
Tsingtao 130 36 0N 120 25 E
Tsingtung Hu 130 37 34N 105 40 E
Tsingyuan 130 37 43N 104 35 E
Tsingyun 131 23 45N 112 55 E
Tsining 131 35 30N 116 35 E
Tsitsihar 129 47 20N 124 0 E
Tsitsutl Pk. 62 52 43N 125 47W
Tsivory 117 24 4S 46 5 E
Tsowhsien 131 35 29N 117 0 E
Tsu 132 34 45N 136 25 E
Tsu L. 54 60 40N 111 52W
Tsuchiura 132 36 12N 140 15 E
Tsugaru-Kaikyō 132 41 35N 141 0 E
Tsuiluan 130 47 58N 128 27 E
Tsumeb 117 19 9S 17 44 E
Tsumis 117 23 39S 17 29 E
Tsungfa 131 23 35N 113 35 E
Tsungming Tao 131 31 40N 121 40 E
Tsungsin 130 35 2N 107 0 E
Tsungtso 131 22 26N 107 34 E
Tsunhwa 130 40 10N 117 57 E
Tsuniah L. 62 51 33N 124 4W
Tsuruga 132 35 45N 136 2 E
Tsushima, I. 132 34 20N 129 20 E
Tsushima-kaikyō 132 34 20N 130 0 E
Tsuyama 132 35 0N 134 0 E
Tual 127 5 30S 132 50 E
Tuam 97 53 30N 8 50W
Tuamotu Arch = Touamotou 15 17 0S 144 0W
Tuan 131 23 59N 108 3 E
Tuao 127 17 47S 121 30 E
Tuatapere 133 46 8S 167 41 E
Tuba City 79 36 8N 111 12W
Tubac 79 31 45N 111 2W
Tubai Is. = Toubouai, Îles 15 25 0S 150 0W
Tuban 126 6 57S 112 4 E
Tubarão 89 28 30S 49 0W
Tubau 126 3 10N 113 40 E
Tubbergen 105 52 24N 6 48 E
Tübingen 106 48 31N 9 4 E
Tubruq (Tobruk) 115 32 7N 23 55 E
Tucacas 86 10 48N 68 19W
Tuchang 131 29 15N 116 15 E
Tuchodi, R. 54 58 17N 123 42W
Tucson 79 32 14N 110 59W
Tucumán 88 26 50S 65 20W
Tucumán □ 88 26 48S 66 2W
Tucumcari 75 35 12N 103 45W
Tucupido 86 9 17N 65 47W
Tucupita 86 9 14N 62 3W
Tucuracas 86 11 45N 72 22W
Tucuruí 87 3 42S 49 27W
Tudela 104 42 4N 1 39W
Tudor, Lac 36 55 50N 65 25W
Tugaske 56 50 52N 106 17W
Tugidak I. 67 56 30N 154 40W
Tuguegarao 127 17 35N 121 42 E
Tugur 121 53 50N 136 45 E
Tuhshan 131 25 40N 107 30 E
Tukangbesi, Kepulauan 127 6 0S 124 0 E
Tukarak I. 36 56 15N 78 45W
Tuktoyaktuk 64 69 27N 133 2W
Tukuyu 116 9 17S 33 35 E
Tukzar 124 35 55N 66 25 E
Tula, Hidalgo, Mexico 83 20 0N 99 20W
Tula, Tamaulipas, Mexico 83 23 0N 99 40W
Tula, U.S.S.R. 120 54 13N 37 32 E
Tulak 123 33 55N 63 40 E
Tulan 129 37 24N 98 1 E
Tulancingo 83 20 5N 98 22W
Tulare 80 36 15N 119 26W
Tulare Basin 80 36 0N 119 48W
Tulare Lake 79 36 0N 119 53W
Tularosa 79 33 4N 106 1W
Tulbagh 117 33 16S 19 6 E
Tulcán 86 0 48N 77 43W
Tulcea 107 45 13N 28 46 E
*Tuléar 117 23 21S 43 40 E
Tulemalu L. 55 62 58N 99 25W
Tuli, Indon. 127 1 24S 122 26 E
Tuli, Zimbabwe 117 21 58S 29 13 E
Tulkarm 115 32 19N 35 10 E
Tulla 75 34 35N 101 44W
Tullahoma 73 35 23N 86 12W
Tullamore, Can. 50 43 47N 79 46W
Tullamore, Ireland 97 53 17N 7 30W
Tulle 102 45 16N 1 47 E
Tullins 103 45 18N 5 29 E
Tullow 97 52 48N 6 45W
Tulsa 75 36 10N 96 0W
Tulsequah 54 58 39N 133 35W
Tulua 86 4 6N 76 11W
Tulun 121 54 40N 100 10 E
Tulungagung 127 8 5S 111 54 E
Tum 127 3 28S 130 21 E
Tuma, R. 84 13 18N 84 50W
Tumaco 86 1 50N 78 45W
Tumatumari 86 5 20N 58 55W
Tumba, L. 116 0 50S 18 0 E
Tumbarumba 136 35 44S 148 0 E
Tumbaya 88 23 50S 65 20W
Tumbes 86 3 30S 80 20W
Tumen 130 42 58N 129 49 E
Tumen K. 130 42 30N 130 0 E
Tumeremo 86 7 18N 61 30W
Tumkur 124 13 18N 77 12 E
Tummel, L. 96 56 43N 3 55W
Tummo 114 22 45N 14 8 E
Tump 124 26 7N 62 16 E
Tumpat 128 6 11N 102 10 E
Tumucumaque, Serra de 87 2 0N 55 0W
Tumut 136 35 16S 148 13 E
Tumwater 78 47 0N 122 58W
Tuna, Pta. 67 17 59N 65 53W
Tunas de Zaza 84 21 39N 79 34W
Tunbridge Wells 95 51 7N 0 16 E
Tunduru 116 11 0S 37 25 E
Tundzha, R. 109 42 0N 26 35 E
Tung-Pei 121 44 0N 126 0 E
Tung-Shan 131 23 40N 117 25 E
Tungabhadra, R. 124 15 30N 77 0 E
Tungcheng 131 31 0N 117 3 E
Tungchow 130 39 58N 116 50 E
Tungchuan 131 35 4N 109 2 E
Tungfanghsien 131 18 50N 108 33 E
Tunghwa 130 41 46N 126 0 E
Tungien 131 27 45N 109 3 E
Tungjen 131 27 40N 109 10 E
Tungkang 131 22 18N 120 29 E
Tungkiang, Heilungkiang, China 130 47 40N 132 30 E
Tungkiang, Szechwan, China 131 31 55N 107 30 E
Tungkingcheng 130 44 5N 129 15 E
Tungkun 131 23 0N 113 45 E
Tungkwan 131 34 40N 110 10 E
Tungla 84 13 24N 84 15W
Tunglan 131 24 30N 107 23 E
Tungliao 130 43 42N 122 11 E
Tungliu 131 31 0N 117 54 E
Tunglu 131 29 50N 119 35 E
Tungnafellsjökull 110 64 45N 17 55W
Tungping 130 35 50N 116 20 E
Tungshan, Fukien, China 131 23 40N 117 31 E
Tungshan, Hupeh, China 131 29 36N 114 28 E
Tungsheng 130 39 57N 110 0 E
Tungsten, Can. 54 61 57N 128 16W
Tungsten, U.S.A. 78 40 50N 118 10W

** Renamed Toliary*

Tungtai 131 32 55N 120 15 E
Tungtao 131 26 15N 109 25 E
Tungting Hu 131 29 15N 112 30 E
Tungtze 131 27 59N 106 56 E
Tunguska, Nizhmaya, R. 121 64 0N 95 0 E
Tunguska, Podkammenaya, R. 121 61 0N 98 0 E
Tungyang 131 29 12N 120 12 E
Tunhwa 130 43 27N 128 16 E
Tunhwang 129 40 5N 94 46 E
Tunia 86 2 41N 76 31W
Tunica 75 34 43N 90 23W
Tunis 114 36 50N 10 11 E
Tunisia ■ 114 33 30N 9 10 E
Tunja 86 5 40N 73 25W
Tunkhannock 71 41 32N 75 56W
Tunki 131 29 44N 118 4 E
Tunliu 130 36 15N 112 54 E
Tunnsjøen 110 64 45N 13 25 E
Tuntatuliag 67 60 20N 162 45W
Tunulic, R. 36 58 57N 66 50W
Tunungayualok I. 36 56 0N 61 0W
Tunuyán 88 33 55S 69 0W
Tunuyán, R. 88 33 33S 67 30W
Tuolumne 80 37 59N 120 16W
Tuolumne, R. 80 37 36N 121 13W
Tuoy-Khaya 121 62 32N 111 18 E
Tupã 89 21 57S 50 28W
Tuparro, R. 86 5 0N 68 40W
Tupelo 73 34 15N 88 42W
Tupik 121 54 26N 119 57 E
Tupinambaranas, I. 86 3 0S 58 0W
Tupiza 88 21 30S 65 40W
Tupman 81 35 18N 119 21W
Tupper 54 55 32N 120 1W
Tupper L. 71 44 18N 74 30W
Tupungato, Cerro 88 33 15S 69 50W
Tuque, La 41 47 30N 72 50W
Túquerres 86 1 5N 77 37W
Tura 121 64 20N 99 30 E
Turagua, Serrania 86 7 20N 64 35W
Tūrān 123 35 45N 56 50 E
Turan 121 51 38N 101 40 E
Turek 107 52 3N 18 30 E
Turen 86 9 17N 69 6W
Turfan 129 43 6N 89 24 E
Turfan Depression 129 42 45N 89 0 E
Turgeon, L. 40 49 2N 79 4W
Turgeon, R. 40 50 0N 78 56W
Turgutlu 122 38 30N 27 48 E
Turhal 122 40 24N 36 19 E
Turia, R. 104 39 43N 1 0W
Turiaçí 87 1 40S 45 28W
Turiaçí, R. 87 3 0S 46 0W
Turin, Can. 54 49 47N 112 24W
Turin, Alta., Can. 61 49 58N 112 31W
Turin = Torino 108 45 3N 7 40 E
Turiy Rog 130 45 5N 131 45 E
Turkana, L. 116 4 10N 32 10 E
Turkestan 120 43 10N 68 10 E
Turkey ■ 122 39 0N 36 0 E
Turkey, R. 76 42 43N 91 2W
Turkmen S.S.R. □ 120 39 0N 59 0 E
Turks Is. 85 21 20N 71 20W
Turks Island Passage 85 21 30N 71 20W
Turku (Åbo) 111 60 30N 22 19 E
Turlock 80 37 30N 120 55W
Turnagain, C. 133 40 28S 176 38 E
Turnagain, R. 54 59 12N 127 35W
Turnberry 55 53 25N 101 45W
Turneffe Is. 83 17 20N 87 50W
Turner 78 48 52N 108 25W
Turner Valley 61 50 40N 114 17W
Turners Falls 71 42 36N 72 34W
Turnhout 105 51 19N 4 57 E
Turnor L. 55 56 35N 108 35W
Turnour I. 62 50 36N 126 27W
Turnovo 109 43 5N 25 41 E
Turnu Măgurele 107 43 46N 24 56 E
Turnu Rosu Pasul 107 45 33N 24 17 E
Turnu-Severin 107 44 39N 22 41 E
Turon 75 37 48N 98 27W
Turriff 96 57 32N 2 28W
Turtle L., Can. 56 53 36N 108 38W
Turtle L., U.S.A. 74 45 22N 92 10W
Turtle Lake 74 47 30N 100 55W
Turtle Mt. Prov. Park 57 49 3N 100 15W
Turtle, R. 52 48 51N 92 45W
Turtleford 56 53 23N 108 57W
Turūbah 122 28 20N 43 15 E
Turukhansk 121 65 50N 87 50 E
Turun ja Porin □ 111 60 27N 22 15 E
Tuscaloosa 73 33 13N 87 31W
Tuscar Rock 97 52 10N 6 15W
Tuscola, Ill., U.S.A. 77 39 48N 88 15W
Tuscola, Tex., U.S.A. 75 32 15N 99 48W
Tuscumbia, U.S.A. 76 38 14N 92 28W
Tuscumbia, Ala., U.S.A. 73 34 42N 87 42W
Tushikow 130 41 25N 115 55 E
Tuskar Rock 97 52 12N 6 10W
Tuskegee 73 32 24N 85 39W
Tusket 39 43 52N 65 58W
Tusket, R. 39 43 41N 65 57W
Tutóia 87 2 45S 42 20W
Tutong 126 4 47N 114 34 E
Tutrakan 109 44 2N 26 40 E
Tutshi L. 54 59 56N 134 30W
Tuttlingen 106 47 59N 8 50 E
Tutuaia 127 8 25S 127 15 E
Tutuila, I. 133 14 19S 170 50W
Tuul Gol, R. 130 48 30N 104 25 E
Tuva, A.S.S.R. □ 121 51 30N 95 0 E
Tuxedo 58 49 52N 97 13W
Tuxford 56 50 34N 105 35W
Tuxpan 83 20 50N 97 30W
Tuxtla Gutiérrez 83 16 50N 93 10W
Tuy 104 42 3N 8 39W
Tuy Hoa 128 13 5N 109 17 E
Tuya L. 54 59 7N 130 35W
Tuyen Hoa 128 17 50N 106 10 E
Tuyun 131 26 15N 107 32 E
Tuz Gölü 122 38 45N 33 30 E
Tuz Khurmātu 122 34 50N 44 45 E
Tuzla 109 44 34N 18 41 E
Twain 80 40 1N 121 3W
Twain Harte 80 38 2N 120 14W
Tweed 47 44 29N 77 19W
Tweed, R. 94 55 42N 2 10W
Tweedmuir 56 53 34N 105 57W
Tweedside, N.B., Can. 39 45 38N 67 1W
Tweedside, Ont., Can. 49 43 10N 79 41W
Tweedsmuir Prov. Park 62 53 0N 126 20W
Twelve Mile L. 56 49 29N 106 14W
Twelve Pins 97 53 32N 9 50W
Twenty Mile Creek, R. 49 43 10N 79 22W
Twentynine Palms 81 34 10N 116 4W
Twillingate 37 49 42N 54 45W
Twin Bridges 78 45 33N 112 23W
Twin City 52 48 22N 89 25W
Twin Falls 78 42 30N 114 30W
Twin Valley 74 47 18N 96 15W
Twisp 63 48 21N 120 5W
Two Creeks 60 54 18N 116 21W
Two Harbors 52 47 1N 91 40W
Two Hills 60 53 43N 111 45W
Two Rivers 72 44 10N 87 31W
Twofold B. 136 37 8S 149 59 E
Tyler, Minn., U.S.A. 74 44 18N 96 15W
Tyler, Tex., U.S.A. 75 32 18N 94 58W
Tyndall 57 50 5N 96 40W
Tyndinskiy 121 55 10N 124 43 E
Tyne & Wear □ 94 54 55N 1 35W
Tyne, R. 94 54 58N 1 28W
Tyne Valley 39 46 35N 63 56W
Tynemouth 94 55 1N 1 27W
Tyre = Sūr 115 33 19N 35 16 E
Tyrell Creek 136 35 22S 143 0 E
Tyrell L. 136 35 22S 143 0 E
Tyrifjorden 111 60 2N 10 8 E
Tyrma 130 50 0N 132 2 E
Tyrol = Tirol 106 46 50N 11 20 E
Tyrone 70 40 39N 78 10W
Tyrone □ 97 54 40N 7 15W
Tyrone, Co. 97 54 40N 7 15W
Tyrrell Arm 55 62 27N 97 30W
Tyrrell, L. 136 35 20S 142 50 E
Tyrrell L. 55 63 7N 105 27W
Tyrrell, R. 136 35 26S 142 51 E
Tyrrhenian Sea 108 40 0N 12 30 E
Tysfjörden 110 68 10N 16 10 E
Tyumen 120 57 0N 65 18 E
Tywi, R. 95 51 48N 4 20W
Tzaneen 117 23 47S 30 9 E
Tzechung 131 29 47N 104 50 E
Tzehsien 130 36 25N 114 24 E
Tzeki 131 27 40N 117 5 E
Tzekwei 131 31 0N 110 46 E
Tzepo 130 36 28N 117 58 E
Tzetung 131 31 31N 105 1 E
Tzuyang 131 35 44N 116 51 E

U

Uainambi 86 1 43N 69 51W
Uasadi-jidi, Sierra 86 4 54N 65 18W
Uato-Udo 127 4 3S 126 6 E
Uatumã, R. 86 1 30S 59 25W
Uaupés 86 0 8S 67 5W
Uaxactún 84 17 25N 89 29W
Ubá 89 21 0S 43 0W
Ubaitaba 87 14 18S 39 20W
Ubangi, R. = Oubangi 116 1 0N 17 50 E
Ubaté 86 5 19N 73 49W
Ubauro 124 28 15N 69 45 E
Ube 132 33 56N 131 15 E
Ubeda 104 38 3N 3 23W
Uberaba 87 19 50S 47 55W
Uberlândia 87 19 0S 48 20W
Ubon Ratchathani 128 15 15N 104 50 E
Ubundi 116 0 22S 25 30 E
Ucayali, R. 86 6 0S 75 0W
Uchi Lake 52 51 5N 92 35W
Uchiura-Wan 132 42 25N 140 40 E
Ucluelet 62 48 57N 125 32W
Uda, R. 121 54 42N 135 14 E
Udaipur 124 24 36N 73 44 E
Udaipur Garhi 125 27 0N 86 35 E
Uddevalla 111 58 21N 11 55 E
Uden 105 51 40N 5 37 E
Udgir 124 18 25N 77 5 E
Udhampur 124 33 0N 75 5 E
Údine 108 46 5N 13 10 E
Udipi 124 13 25N 74 42 E
Udmurt, A.S.S.R. □ 120 57 30N 52 30 E

Udon Thani **Valrita**

Udon Thani **128** 17 29N 102 46 E
Ueda **132** 36 24N 138 16 E
Uedineniya, Os. **17** 78 0N 85 0 E
Uelen **121** 66 10N 170 0W
Uelzen **106** 53 0N 10 33 E
Uere, R. **116** 3 45N 24 45 E
Ufa **120** 54 45N 55 55 E
Ugad R. **117** 20 55 S 14 30 E
Ugalla, R. **116** 6 0 S 32 0 E
Uganda ■ **116** 2 0N 32 0 E
Ugine **103** 45 45N 6 25 E
Uhrichsville **70** 40 23N 81 22W
Uiju **130** 40 15N 124 35 E
Uinta Mts. **78** 40 45N 110 30W
Uitenhage **117** 33 40 S 25 28 E
Uithuizen **105** 53 24N 6 41 E
Uivuk, C. **36** 58 29N 62 34W
Uji-guntō **131** 31 15N 129 25 E
Ujjain **124** 23 9N 75 43 E
Ujpest **107** 47 22N 19 6 E
Ujung Pandang **127** 5 10 S 119 20 E
Uka **121** 57 50N 162 0 E
Ukerewe Is. **116** 2 0 S 33 0 E
Ukhrul **125** 25 10N 94 25 E
Ukhta **120** 63 55N 54 0 E
Ukiah **80** 39 10N 123 9W
Ukraine S.S.R. □ **120** 48 0N 35 0 E
Ulaan Nuur **130** 44 30N 103 40 E
Ulaanbaatar **130** 47 54N 106 52 E
Ulaangom **129** 50 0N 92 10 E
Ulak I. **67** 51 24N 178 58W
Ulan-Bator = Ulaanbaatar **130** 47 54N 106 52 E
Ulan Ude **121** 52 0N 107 30 E
Ulanhot **130** 46 5N 122 1 E
Ulcinj **109** 41 58N 19 10 E
Uldz Gol **130** 49 30N 114 0 E
Ulhasnagar **124** 19 15N 73 10 E
Ulladulla **136** 35 21 S 150 29 E
Ullapool **96** 57 54N 5 10W
Ullswater, L. **94** 54 35N 2 52W
Ullŭng Do **130** 37 30N 130 30 E
Ulm **106** 48 23N 10 0 E
Ulricehamn **111** 57 46N 13 26 E
Ulster □ **97** 54 45N 6 30W
Ulverston **94** 54 13N 3 7W
Ulverstone **135** 41 11 S 146 11 E
Ulya **121** 59 10N 142 0 E
Ulyanovsk **120** 54 25N 48 25 E
Ulyasutay, (Javhlant) **129** 47 56N 97 28 E
Ulysses **75** 37 39N 101 25W
Umala **86** 17 25 S 68 5W
Umánaé **17** 70 40N 52 10W
Umánaé Fjord **10** 70 40N 52 0W
Umanak **65** 70 58N 52 0W
Umaria **125** 23 35N 80 50 E
Umarkot **70** 25 15N 69 40 E
Umatilla **78** 45 58N 119 17W
Umba **120** 66 50N 34 20 E
Umbrella Mts. **133** 45 35 S 169 5 E
Umbria □ **108** 42 53N 12 30 E
Ume, R. **110** 64 45N 18 30 E
Umeå **110** 63 45N 20 20 E
Umera **127** 0 12 S 129 30 E
Umfreville L. **52** 50 18N 94 45W
Umiat **67** 69 25N 152 20W
Umm al Qaiʻvain **123** 25 30N 55 35 E
Umm az Zamul **123** 22 35N 55 18 E
Umm Lajj **122** 25 0N 37 23 E
Umm Said **123** 25 0N 51 40 E
Umnak. **67** 53 20N 168 20W
Umnak I. **67** 53 0N 168 0W
Umniati, R. **117** 18 0 S 29 0 E
Umpang **128** 16 3N 98 54 E
Umpqua, R. **78** 43 30N 123 30W
*Umtali **117** 18 58 S 32 38 E
Umtata **117** 31 36 S 28 49 E
†Umvuma **117** 19 16 S 30 30 E
Umzimvubu, R. **117** 31 38 S 29 33 E
Unac, R. **108** 44 42N 16 15 E
Unadilla **71** 42 20N 75 17W
Unalanaska I. **67** 54 0N 164 30W
Uncia **86** 18 25 S 66 40W
Uncompahgce Pk., Mt. **79** 38 5N 107 32W
Underbool **136** 35 10 S 141 51 E
Ungarie **136** 33 38 S 146 56 E
Ungava B. **36** 59 30N 67 30W
Ungava Pen. **36** 60 0N 75 0W
Unggi **130** 42 16N 130 28 E
União **87** 4 50 S 37 50W
União da Vitória **89** 26 5 S 51 0W
Unimak I. **67** 54 30N 164 30W
Unimak Pass. **67** 53 30N 165 15W
Union, Mo., U.S.A. **76** 38 25N 91 0W
Union, N.J., U.S.A. **71** 40 47N 74 3W
Union, S.C., U.S.A. **73** 34 49N 81 39W
Union Bay **62** 49 35N 124 53W
Union City, N.J., U.S.A. **71** 40 47N 74 5W
Union City, Ohio, U.S.A. **77** 40 11N 84 49W
Union City, Pa., U.S.A. **70** 41 53N 79 50W
Union City, Tenn., U.S.A. **71** 36 25N 89 0W
Union Gap **73** 46 38N 120 29W
Union Grove **77** 42 41N 88 3W
Union I. **62** 50 0N 127 16W
Unión, La, Chile **90** 40 10 S 73 0W
Unión, La, Colomb. **86** 1 35N 77 5W
Unión, La, El Sal. **83** 13 20N 87 50W
Union, La **82** 17 58N 101 49W
Unión, La **86** 7 28N 67 53W
Union, Mt. **79** 34 34N 112 21W
Union of Soviet Soc. Rep. ■ **121** 47 0N 100 0 E
Union Springs **73** 32 9N 85 44W
Union Star **76** 39 59N 94 36W
Uniontown, U.S.A. **77** 37 47N 87 56W
Uniontown, Pa., U.S.A. **72** 39 54N 79 45W
Unionville, Can. **50** 43 52N 79 18W
Unionville, U.S.A. **76** 40 29N 93 1W
Unionville, Mich., U.S.A. **46** 43 39N 83 28W
United Arab Emirates ■ **123** 23 50N 54 0 E
United Arab Republic = Egypt ■ **113** 27 5N 30 0 E
United States of America ■ **69** 37 0N 96 0W
United States Range **65** 82 25N 68 0W
Unity **56** 52 30N 109 5W
University City **76** 38 40N 90 20W
University, R. **53** 47 55N 85 12W
Unnao **125** 26 35N 80 30 E
Unst, I. **96** 60 50N 0 55W
Unturán, Sierra de **86** 1 35N 64 40W
Unuk, R. **54** 56 5N 131 3W
Ünye **122** 41 5N 37 15 E
Upata **86** 8 1N 62 24W
Upemba, L. **116** 8 30 S 26 20 E
Upernavik **65** 72 49N 56 20W
Upington **117** 28 25 S 21 15 E
Uplands, B.C., Can. **63** 48 27N 123 17W
Uplands, Sask., Can. **58** 50 29N 104 36W
Upolu, I. **133** 13 58 S 172 0W
Upolu Pt. **67** 20 16N 155 52W
Upper Alkali Lake **78** 41 47N 120 0W
Upper Arlington **77** 40 0N 83 4W
Upper Arrow L. **63** 50 30N 117 50W
Upper Blackville **39** 46 39N 65 52W
Upper Campbell L. **62** 49 55N 125 39W
Upper Foster L. **55** 56 47N 105 20W
Upper Goose L. **52** 51 43N 92 43W
Upper Humber R. **37** 49 11N 57 28W
Upper Hutt **133** 41 8 S 175 5 E
Upper Klamath L. **78** 42 16N 121 55W
Upper L. Erne **97** 54 14N 7 22W
Upper Lachute **43** 45 40N 74 14W
Upper Lake **80** 39 10N 122 55W
Upper Manitou L. **52** 49 24N 92 48W
Upper Musquodoboit **39** 45 10N 62 58W
Upper Red L., U.S.A. **52** 48 10N 94 40W
Upper Red L., U.S.A. **74** 48 0N 95 0W
Upper Sandusky **77** 40 50N 83 17W
Upper Stewiacke **39** 45 13N 63 0W
*Upper Volta ■ **114** 12 0N 0 30W
Uppsala **111** 59 53N 17 38 E
Uppsala län □ **111** 60 0N 17 30 E
Upsala **52** 49 3N 90 28W
Upton, Can. **41** 45 39N 72 41W
Upton, U.S.A. **74** 44 8N 104 35W
Ur **122** 30 55N 46 25 E
Urabá, Golfo de **86** 8 25N 76 53W
Uracará **86** 2 20 S 57 50W
Ural Mts. = Uralskie Gory **120** 60 0N 59 0 E
Ural, R. **120** 49 0N 52 0W
Uralsk **120** 51 20N 51 20 E
Uralskie Gory **120** 60 0N 59 0 E
Urana **136** 35 15 S 146 21 E
Urandangi **135** 21 32 S 138 14 E
Uranium City **55** 59 34N 108 37W
Uraricaá, R. **86** 3 20N 61 56W
Urawa **132** 35 50N 139 40 E
Uray **120** 60 5N 65 15 E
Urbana, U.S.A. **76** 37 51N 93 10W
Urbana, Ill., U.S.A. **77** 40 7N 88 12W
Urbana, Ohio, U.S.A. **77** 40 9N 83 44W
Urbana, La **86** 7 8N 66 56W
Urbandale **76** 41 38N 93 43W
Urbino **108** 43 43N 12 38 E
Urbión, Picos de **104** 42 1N 2 52W
Urcos **86** 13 30 S 71 30W
Urdinarrain **88** 32 37 S 58 52W
Urdos **102** 42 51N 0 35W
Urdzhar **120** 47 5N 81 38 E
Ure, R. **94** 54 20N 1 25W
Ures **82** 29 30N 110 30W
Urfa **122** 37 12N 38 50 E
Urfahr **106** 48 19N 14 17 E
Urgench **120** 41 40N 60 30 E
Urgun **123** 32 55N 69 12 E
Uribante, R. **86** 7 25N 71 50W
Uribe **86** 3 13N 74 24W
Uribia **86** 11 43N 72 16W
Uriondo **88** 21 41 S 64 41W
Urique **82** 27 13N 107 55W
Urique, R. **82** 26 29N 107 58W
Urk **105** 52 39N 5 36 E
Urla **122** 38 20N 26 55 E
Urmia, L. **122** 37 30N 45 30 E
Urmia (Rezā'iyeh) **122** 37 40N 45 0 E
Urrao **86** 6 20N 76 11W
Ursula Chan. **62** 53 25N 128 55W
Uruaca **87** 15 30 S 49 41W
Uruapán **82** 19 30N 102 0W
Urubamba **86** 13 5 S 72 10W
Urubamba, R. **86** 11 0 S 73 0W
Uruçuí **87** 7 20 S 44 28W
Uruguai, R. **89** 24 0 S 53 30W
Uruguaiana **88** 29 50 S 57 0W
Uruguay ■ **88** 32 30 S 55 30W
Uruguay, R. **88** 28 0 S 56 0W
Urumchi = Wulumuchi **129** 43 40N 87 50 E
Urungu **129** 46 30N 88 50 E
Urup, I. **121** 43 0N 151 0 E
Uruyén **86** 5 41N 62 25W
Uruzgan □ **124** 33 30N 66 0 E
Usa **120** 2 23 S 36 52 E
Uşak **122** 38 43N 29 28 E
Usakos **117** 22 0 S 15 31 E
Usedom **106** 53 50N 13 55 E
Useko **116** 5 8 S 32 24 E
Ush-Tobe **120** 45 16N 78 0 E
Ushakova, O. **17** 82 0N 80 0 E
Ushant = Ouessant, Île d' **100** 48 25N 5 5W
Ushuaia **90** 54 50 S 68 23W
Ushumun **121** 52 47N 126 32 E
Usk, R. **95** 51 37N 2 56W
Üsküdar **122** 41 0N 29 5 E
Usolye Sibirskoye **121** 52 40N 103 40 E
Uspallata, P. de **88** 32 30 S 69 28W
Uspenskiy **120** 48 50N 72 55 E
Ussel **102** 45 32N 2 18 E
Ussuriysk **130** 43 40N 131 50 E
Ust Aldan = Batamay **121** 63 30N 129 15 E
Ust Amginskoye = Khandyga **121** 62 30N 134 50 E
Ust-Bolsheretsk **121** 52 40N 156 30 E
Ust Ilga **121** 55 5N 104 55 E
Ust Ilimpeya = Yukti **121** 63 20N 105 0 E
Ust-Ilimsk **121** 58 3N 102 39 E
Ust Ishim **120** 57 45N 71 10 E
Ust Kamchatsk **121** 56 10N 162 0 E
Ust Kamenogorsk **120** 50 0N 82 20 E
Ust Karenga **121** 54 40N 116 45 E
Ust Khayryuzova **121** 57 15N 156 55 E
Ust Kut **121** 56 50N 105 10 E
Ust Kuyga **121** 70 1N 135 36 E
Ust Maya **121** 60 30N 134 20 E
Ust Mil **121** 59 50N 133 0 E
Ust Nera **121** 64 35N 143 15 E
Ust Olenek **121** 73 0N 120 10 E
Ust-Omchug **121** 61 9N 149 38 E
Ust Port **120** 70 0N 84 10 E
Ust Tsilma **120** 65 25N 52 0 E
Ust-Tungir **121** 55 25N 120 15 E
Ust Urt = Ustyurt **120** 44 0N 55 0 E
Ust Vorkuta **120** 67 7N 63 35 E
Ustaritz **102** 43 24N 1 27W
Ustí nad Labem **106** 50 41N 14 3 E
Ustica, I. **108** 38 42N 13 10 E
Ustye **121** 55 30N 97 30 E
Ustyurt, Plato **120** 44 0N 55 0 E
Usuki **132** 33 8N 131 49 E
Usulután **84** 13 25N 88 28W
Usumacinta, R. **83** 17 0N 91 0W
Utah □ **78** 39 30N 111 30W
Utah, L. **78** 40 10N 111 58W
Ute Cr. **75** 36 5N 103 45W
Utete **116** 8 0 S 38 45 E
Uthai Thani **128** 15 22N 100 3 E
Uthmaniyah **122** 25 5N 49 6 E
Utiariti **86** 13 0 S 58 10W
Utica, Mich., U.S.A. **46** 42 38N 83 2W
Utica, N.Y., U.S.A. **71** 43 5N 75 18W
Utica, Ohio, U.S.A. **70** 40 13N 82 26W
Utik L. **55** 55 15N 96 0W
Utikuma L. **60** 55 50N 115 30W
Utrecht, Neth. **105** 52 3N 5 8 E
Utrecht, S. Afr. **117** 27 38 S 30 20 E
Utrecht □ **105** 52 6N 5 7 E
Utrera **104** 37 12N 5 48W
Utsjoki **110** 69 51N 26 59 E
Utsunomiya **132** 36 30N 139 50 E
Uttar Pradesh □ **124** 27 0N 80 0 E
Uttaradit **128** 17 36N 100 5 E
Utterson **70** 45 13N 79 20W
Uttoxeter **94** 52 53N 1 50W
Uudenmaan lääni □ **111** 60 25N 25 0 E
Uuldza **130** 49 8N 112 10 E
Uusikaarlepyy **110** 63 32N 22 31 E
Uusikaupunki **111** 60 47N 21 25 E
Uvalde **75** 29 15N 99 48W
Uvat **120** 59 5N 68 50 E
Uvinza **116** 5 5 S 30 24 E
Uvira **116** 3 22 S 29 3 E
Uvs Nuur **129** 50 20N 92 30 E
Uwainid **122** 24 50N 46 0 E
Uwajima **132** 33 10N 132 35 E
Uxbridge **46** 44 6N 79 7W
Uxmal **83** 20 22N 89 46W
Uyuni **88** 20 35 S 66 55W
Uyuni, Salar de **88** 20 10 S 68 0W
Uzbekistan S.S.R. □ **120** 40 5N 65 0 E
Uzerche **102** 45 25N 1 35 E
Uzès **103** 44 1N 4 26 E

V

Vaal, R. **117** 27 40 S 25 30 E
Vaasan lääni □ **110** 63 2N 22 50 E
Vabre **102** 43 42N 2 24 E
Vác **107** 47 49N 19 10 E
Vacaria **89** 28 31 S 50 52W
Vacaville **80** 38 21N 122 0W
Vach, R. **120** 60 56N 76 38 E
Vache, I.-à **85** 18 2N 73 35W
Vadodara **124** 22 20N 73 10 E
Vadsø **110** 70 3N 29 50 E
Vaerøy **110** 67 40N 12 40 E
Vagney **101** 48 1N 6 43 E
Váh, R. **107** 49 10N 18 20 E
Vaigach **120** 70 10N 59 0 E
Vaiges **100** 48 2N 0 30W
Vaihsel B. **91** 75 0 S 35 0W
Vailly Aisne **101** 49 25N 3 30 E
Vaison **103** 44 14N 5 4 E
Val-Alain **41** 46 24N 71 45W
Val-Barrette **40** 46 30N 75 21W
Val Brillant **38** 48 32N 67 33W
Val Caron **46** 46 37N 81 1W
Val d' Ajol, Le **101** 47 55N 6 30 E
Val-de-Marne □ **101** 48 45N 2 28 E
Val-des-Bois **40** 45 54N 75 35W
Val-d'Espoir **38** 48 31N 64 24W
Val-d'Oise □ **101** 49 5N 2 0 E
Val d'Or **40** 48 7N 77 47W
Val Marie **56** 49 15N 107 45W
Val-St-Michael **42** 46 52N 71 27W
Valahia **107** 44 35N 25 0 E
Valcheta **90** 40 40 S 66 20W
Valcourt **41** 45 29N 72 18W
Valdahon, Le **101** 47 8N 6 20 E
Valdepeñas **104** 38 43N 3 25W
Valdes I. **63** 49 4N 123 39W
Valdes Pen. **90** 42 30 S 63 45W
Valdez **67** 61 14N 146 10W
Valdezia **97** 23 5 S 30 14 E
Valdivia **90** 39 50 S 73 14W
Valdivia □ **90** 40 0 S 73 0W
Valdivia, La **88** 34 43 S 72 5W
Valdosta **73** 30 50N 83 20W
Vale **78** 44 0N 117 15W
Valemount **63** 52 50N 119 15W
Valença **87** 13 20 S 39 5W
Valença do Piaui **87** 6 20 S 41 45W
Valence **103** 44 57N 4 54 E
Valence-d'Agen **102** 44 8N 0 54 E
Valencia, Spain **104** 39 27N 0 23W
Valencia, Venez. **86** 10 11N 68 0W
Valencia □ **104** 39 20N 0 40W
Valencia, Albufera de **104** 39 20N 0 27W
Valencia de Alcántara **104** 39 25N 7 14W
Valencia, G. de **104** 39 30N 0 20 E
Valencia, L. de **85** 10 13N 67 40W
Valenciennes **101** 50 20N 3 34 E
Valensole **103** 43 50N 5 59 E
Valentia Hr. **97** 51 56N 10 17W
Valentia I. **97** 51 54N 10 22W
Valentine, Nebr., U.S.A. **74** 42 50N 100 35W
Valentine, Tex., U.S.A. **75** 30 36N 104 28W
Valenton **78** 48 45N 2 28 E
Valera **86** 9 19N 70 37W
Valier **78** 48 25N 112 9W
Valinco, G. de **103** 41 40N 8 52 E
Valjevo **109** 44 18N 19 53 E
Valkeakoski **111** 61 16N 24 2 E
Valkenswaard **105** 51 21N 5 29 E
Valladolid, Mexico **83** 20 30N 88 20W
Valladolid, Spain **104** 41 38N 4 43W
Valle d'Aosta □ **108** 45 45N 7 22 E
Valle de la Pascua **86** 9 13N 66 0W
Valle de las Palmas **81** 32 20N 116 43W
Valle de Santiago **82** 20 25N 101 15W
Valle de Zaragoza **82** 27 28N 105 49W
Valle del Cauca □ **86** 3 45N 76 30W
Valle Fértil, Sierra del **88** 30 20 S 68 0W
Valle Hermosa **83** 25 35N 102 25 E
Valle Nacional **83** 17 47N 96 19W
Vallecas **104** 40 23N 3 41W
Valledupar **86** 10 29N 73 15W
Vallée-Jonction **41** 46 22N 70 55W
Vallejo **80** 38 12N 122 15W
Vallenar **88** 28 30 S 70 50W
Valleraugue **102** 44 6N 3 39 E
Vallet **100** 47 10N 1 15W
Valletta **108** 35 54N 14 30 E
Valley Center **81** 33 13N 117 2W
Valley City **74** 46 57N 98 0W
Valley Falls **78** 42 33N 120 8W
Valley Park **76** 38 33N 90 29W
Valley Springs **80** 38 11N 120 50W
Valley Station **77** 38 10N 85 50W
Valley Wells **81** 35 27N 115 46W
Valleyfield **34** 45 15N 74 8W
Valleyview, Alta., Can. **60** 55 5N 117 17W
Valleyview, B.C., Can. **63** 50 10N 120 13W
Vallimanca, Arroyo **88** 35 40 S 59 10W
Vallon **103** 44 25N 4 23 E
Valls **104** 41 18N 1 15 E
Valmeyer **76** 38 18N 90 19W
Valmont **100** 49 45N 0 30 E
Valmy **101** 49 5N 4 45 E
Valognes **100** 49 30N 1 28W
Valora **52** 49 46N 91 13W
Valparaiso, Chile **88** 33 2 S 71 40W
Valparaiso, Mexico **82** 22 50N 103 32W
Valparaiso **77** 41 27N 87 2W
Valparaiso □ **88** 33 2 S 71 40W
Valréas **103** 44 24N 5 0 E
Valrita **53** 49 27N 82 33W

* Renamed Mutare
† Renamed Mvuma

* Renamed Burkina Faso ■

Vals-les-Bains Villa Guillermina

Vals-les-Bains	103	44 42N	4 24 E
Vals, Tanjung	127	8 32 S	137 32 E
Valsbaai	117	34 15 S	18 40 E
Valverde del Camino	104	37 35N	6 47W
Van	122	38 30N	43 20 E
Van Alstyne	75	33 25N	96 36W
Van Bruyssel	41	47 56N	72 9W
Van Buren, Can.	39	47 10N	67 55W
Van Buren, Ark., U.S.A.	75	35 28N	94 18W
Van Buren, Me., U.S.A.	73	47 10N	68 1W
Van Buren, Mo., U.S.A.	75	37 0N	91 0W
Van Diemen, C.	135	11 9 S	130 24 E
Van Diemen G.	134	11 45 S	131 50 E
Van Gölü	122	38 30N	43 0 E
Van Horn	79	31 3N	104 55W
Van Horne	76	42 1N	92 4W
Van Tassell	74	42 40N	104 3W
Van Wert	77	40 52N	84 31W
Vananda	62	49 46N	124 33W
Vanavara	121	60 22N	102 16 E
Vanceburg	77	38 36N	83 19W
Vancouver, Can.	66	49 15N	123 10W
Vancouver, U.S.A.	80	45 44N	122 41W
Vancouver Harb.	66	49 18N	123 5W
Vancouver I.	62	49 50N	126 0W
Vancouver I. Ranges	62	49 30N	125 40W
Vancouver International Airport	66	48 12N	123 11W
Vandalia, Ill., U.S.A.	76	38 57N	89 4W
Vandalia, Mo., U.S.A.	76	39 19N	91 29W
Vandalia, Mo., U.S.A.	76	39 18N	91 30W
Vandalia, Ohio, U.S.A.	77	39 54N	84 12W
Vandenburg	81	34 35N	120 44W
Vanderbijlpark	118	26 42 S	27 54 E
Vanderbilt	46	45 9N	84 40W
Vandergrift	70	40 36N	79 33W
Vanderhoof	62	54 0N	124 0W
Vanderlin I.	135	15 44 S	137 2 E
Vandry	41	47 52N	73 34W
Vänern	111	58 47N	13 30 E
Vänersborg	111	58 26N	12 27 E
Vanessa	49	42 58N	80 24W
Vang Vieng	128	18 58N	102 32 E
Vanga	116	4 35 S	39 12 E
Vangaindrano	117	23 21 S	47 36 E
Vanguard	56	49 55N	107 20W
Vanier, Ont., Can.	48	45 27N	75 40W
Vanier, Qué., Can.	42	46 49N	71 15W
Vankleek Hill	47	45 32N	74 40W
Vanna	110	70 6N	19 50 E
Vannas	110	63 58N	19 48 E
Vannes	100	47 40N	2 47W
Vanoise, Massif de la	103	45 25N	6 40 E
Vanrhynsdorp	117	31 36 S	18 44 E
Vans, Les	103	44 25N	4 7 E
Vansbro	111	60 32N	14 15 E
Vanscoy	56	52 0N	106 59W
Vansittart B.	134	14 3 S	126 17 E
Vansittart I.	65	65 50N	84 0W
Vanua Levu, I.	133	16 33 S	178 8 E
Vanua Mbalavu, I.	133	17 40 S	178 57W
Var □	103	43 27N	6 18 E
Varades	100	47 25N	1 1W
Varanasi (Benares)	125	25 22N	83 8 E
Varangerfjorden	110	70 3N	29 25 E
Varazdin	108	46 20N	16 20 E
Varberg	111	57 17N	12 20 E
Vardar, R.	109	41 25N	22 20 E
Varennes	43	45 39N	73 28W
Varennes-sur-Allier	102	46 19N	3 24 E
Varese	108	45 49N	8 50 E
Varginha	89	21 33 S	45 25W
Varillas	88	24 0 S	70 10W
Värmlands län □	111	59 45N	13 20 E
Varna, Bulg.	109	43 13N	27 56 E
Varna, U.S.A.	76	41 2N	89 14W
Varnamo	111	57 10N	14 3 E
Vars	47	45 21N	75 21W
Varto	122	39 10N	41 28 E
Varzaneh	123	32 25N	52 40 E
Varzy	101	47 22N	3 20 E
Vasa	110	63 6N	21 38 E
Vasa Barris, R.	87	11 10 S	37 10W
Vascongadas	104	42 50N	2 45W
Vasht = Khāsh	123	28 20N	61 6 E
Vaslui	107	46 38N	27 42 E
Vassa	110	63 6N	21 38 E
Vassar, Can.	57	49 10N	95 55W
Vassar, U.S.A.	46	43 23N	83 33W
Västerås	111	59 37N	16 38 E
Västerbottens län □	110	64 58N	18 0 E
Västerdalälven	111	60 50N	13 25 E
Västernorrlands län □	110	63 30N	17 40 E
Västervik	111	57 43N	16 43 E
Västmanland □	111	59 55N	16 30 E
Vasto	108	42 8N	14 40 E
Vatan	101	47 4N	1 50 E
Vatnajökull	110	64 30N	16 48W
Vatneyri	110	65 35N	24 0W
Vatoa, I.	133	19 50 S	178 13W
Vatomandry	117	19 20 S	48 59 E
Vatra-Dornei	107	47 22N	25 22 E
Vättern, L.	111	58 25N	14 30 E
Vaucluse	43	45 54N	73 26W
Vaucluse □	103	44 3N	5 10 E
Vaucouleurs	101	48 37N	5 40 E
Vaudreuil	44	45 24N	74 1W
Vaudreuil □	44	45 25N	74 15W
Vaudreul-sur-le-Lac	44	45 25N	74 3W
Vaughan	79	34 37N	105 12W
Vaughn	78	47 37N	111 36W
Vaupés □	86	1 0N	71 0W
Vaupés, R.	86	1 0N	71 0W
Vauvert	103	43 42N	4 17 E
Vauxhall	61	50 5N	112 9W
Vavàu, I.	133	18 36 S	174 0W
Vavenby	63	51 36N	119 43W
Vavincourt	101	48 49N	5 12 E
Växjö	111	56 52N	14 50 E
Vaygach, Ostrov	120	70 0N	60 0 E
Vaza Barris, R.	87	10 0 S	37 30W
Vedea, R.	107	44 0N	25 20 E
Vedia	88	34 30 S	61 31W
Vedrin	105	50 30N	4 52 E
Veendam	105	53 5N	6 52 E
Vefsna	110	65 48N	13 10 E
Vega	75	35 18N	102 26W
Vega Baja	67	18 27N	66 23W
Vega Fd.	110	65 37N	12 0 E
Vega, I.	110	65 42N	11 50 E
Vega, La	85	19 20N	70 30W
Veghel	105	51 37N	5 32 E
Vegreville	60	53 30N	112 5W
Veinticino de Mayo	88	38 0 S	67 40W
Vejer de la Frontera	104	36 15N	5 59W
Vejle	111	55 43N	9 30 E
Velarde	79	36 11N	106 1W
Velas, C.	84	10 21N	85 52W
Velasco	75	29 0N	95 20W
Velasco, Sierra de.	88	29 20 S	67 10W
Velay, Mts. du	102	45 0N	3 40 E
Velebit Planina	108	44 50N	15 20 E
Vélez	86	6 1N	73 41W
Vélez Málaga	104	36 48N	4 5W
Vélez Rubio	104	37 41N	2 5W
Velhas, R.	87	17 13 S	44 49W
Velikiye Luki	120	56 25N	30 32 E
Velikonda Range	124	14 45N	79 10 E
Velletri	108	41 43N	12 43 E
Vellir	110	65 55N	18 28W
Vellore	124	12 57N	79 10 E
Velsen-Noord	105	52 27N	4 40 E
Velva	74	48 6N	100 56W
Venado	82	22 50N	101 10W
Venado Tuerto	88	33 50 S	62 0W
Venarey-les-Laumes	101	47 32N	4 26 E
Vence	103	43 43N	7 6 E
Vendée □, France	100	46 50N	1 35W
Vendée □, France	102	46 40N	1 20W
Vendée, Collines de	100	46 35N	0 45W
Vendée, R.	100	46 30N	0 45W
Vendeuvre-sur-Barse	101	48 14N	4 28 E
Vendôme	100	47 47N	1 3 E
Venetie	67	67 0N	146 30W
Véneto □	108	45 40N	12 0 E
Venézia	108	45 27N	12 20 E
Venézia, Golfo di	108	45 20N	13 0 E
Venezuela ■	86	8 0N	65 0W
Venezuela, Golfo de	86	11 30N	71 0W
Vengurla	124	15 53N	73 45 E
Venice = Venézia	108	45 27N	12 20 E
Venise	43	45 5N	73 8W
Vénissieux	103	45 43N	4 53 E
Venkatapuram	125	18 20N	80 30 E
Venlo	105	51 22N	6 11 E
Venosta	40	45 52N	76 1W
Venraij	105	51 31N	6 0 E
Venta, La	83	18 8N	94 3W
Ventana, Punta de la	82	24 4N	109 48W
Ventnor	95	50 35N	1 12W
Ventspils	111	57 25N	21 32 E
Ventuari, R.	86	5 20N	66 0W
Ventucopa	81	34 50N	119 29W
Ventura	81	34 16N	119 18W
Ventura, La	82	24 38N	100 54W
Venturosa, La	86	6 8N	68 48W
Vera, Argent.	88	29 30 S	60 20W
Vera, Spain	104	37 15N	1 15W
Veracruz	83	19 10N	96 10W
Veracruz □	83	19 0N	96 15W
Veraval	124	20 53N	70 27 E
Vercelli	108	45 19N	8 25 E
Verchères	45	45 47N	73 21W
Verchères □	43	45 45N	73 15W
Verdalsøra	110	63 48N	11 30 E
Verde, R., Argent.	90	41 55 S	66 0W
Verde, R., Chihuahua, Mexico	82	26 59N	107 58W
Verde, R., Oaxaca, Mexico	82	15 59N	97 50W
Verde, R., Veracruz, Mexico	83	21 10N	102 50W
Verde, R., Parag.	88	23 9 S	57 37W
Verden	107	52 58N	9 18 E
Verdi	80	39 31N	119 59W
Verdigre	74	42 38N	98 0W
Verdon-sur-Mer, Le	102	45 33N	1 4W
Verdun, Can.	44	45 27N	73 34W
Verdun, France	101	49 12N	5 24 E
Verdun-sur-le Doubs	101	46 54N	5 0 E
Vereeniging	117	26 38 S	27 57 E
Veregin	57	51 35N	102 5W
Vérendrye, Parc Prov. de la	40	47 20N	76 40W
Vergennes	71	44 9N	73 15W
Vergt	102	45 2N	0 43 E
Verkhoyansk	121	67 50N	133 50 E
Verkhoyanskiy Khrebet	121	66 0N	129 0 E
Verlo	56	50 19N	108 35W
Vermenton	101	47 40N	3 42 E
Vermeulle, L.	36	54 43N	69 24W
Vermilion	60	53 20N	110 50W
Vermilion, B.	75	29 45N	91 55W
Vermilion Bay	52	49 51N	93 34W
Vermilion Chutes	54	58 22N	114 51W
Vermilion L.	52	50 3N	92 13W
Vermilion Pass	63	51 15N	116 2W
Vermilion, R., Alta., Can.	60	53 22N	110 51W
Vermilion, R., Qué., Can.	41	47 38N	72 56W
Vermilion, R., Ill., U.S.A.	77	41 19N	89 5W
Vermilion, R., Ind., U.S.A.	77	39 57N	87 27W
Vermillion	74	42 50N	96 56W
Vermillion L.	52	47 53N	92 25W
Vermont	76	40 18N	90 26W
Vermont □	71	43 40N	72 50W
Vernal	78	40 28N	109 35W
Vernalis	80	37 36N	121 17W
Verner	46	46 25N	80 8W
Verneuil-sur-Avre	100	48 45N	0 55 E
Vernon, Can.	63	50 20N	119 15W
Vernon, France	100	49 5N	1 30 E
Vernon, U.S.A.	75	34 10N	99 20W
Vernon, U.S.A.	76	38 48N	89 5W
Vernon, U.S.A.	77	38 59N	85 36W
Vernonia	80	45 52N	123 11W
Vero Beach	73	27 39N	80 23W
Véroia	109	40 34N	22 18 E
Véron, L.	38	51 48N	65 7W
Verona, Can.	47	44 29N	76 42W
Verona, Italy	108	45 27N	11 0 E
Verona, U.S.A.	76	42 59N	89 32W
Veropol	121	66 0N	168 0 E
Versailles, France	101	48 48N	2 8 E
Versailles, Ill., U.S.A.	76	39 53N	90 39W
Versailles, Ind., U.S.A.	77	39 4N	85 15W
Versailles, Ky., U.S.A.	77	38 3N	84 44W
Versailles, Mo., U.S.A.	76	38 26N	92 51W
Versailles, Ohio, U.S.A.	77	40 13N	84 29W
Vert I.	52	48 55N	88 3W
Verte, I.	41	48 2N	69 26W
Vertou	100	47 10N	1 28W
Vertus	101	48 54N	4 0 E
Verviers	105	50 37N	5 52 E
Vervins	101	49 50N	3 53 E
Verwood	55	49 30N	105 40W
Vesle, R.	101	49 17N	3 50 E
Vesoul	101	60 40N	6 11 E
Vest-Agder fylke □	111	58 30N	7 15 E
Vesta	84	9 43N	83 3W
Vesterålen	110	68 45N	14 30 E
Vestfjorden	110	67 55N	14 0 E
Vestfold fylke □	111	59 15N	10 0 E
Vestmannaeyjar	110	63 27N	20 15W
Vestspitsbergen	17	78 40N	17 0 E
Vestvågøy	110	68 18N	13 50 E
Vesuvio	108	40 50N	14 22 E
Vesuvius, Mt. = Vesuvio	108	40 50N	14 22 E
Veszprém	107	47 8N	17 57 E
Veteran	61	52 0N	111 7W
Vetlanda	111	57 24N	15 3 E
Vetlugu, R.	120	57 0N	45 25 E
Vettore, Mte.	108	44 38N	7 5 E
Vevay	77	38 45N	85 4W
Veys	122	31 30N	49 0 E
Vézelise	101	48 30N	6 5 E
Vezhen, mt.	109	42 50N	24 20 E
Viacha	86	16 30 S	68 5W
Viana, Brazil	87	3 0 S	44 40W
Viana, Port.	104	38 20N	8 0W
Viana do Castelo	104	41 42N	8 50W
Vianópolis	87	16 40 S	48 35W
Vibank	56	50 20N	103 56W
Viborg	111	56 27N	9 23 E
Vic-en-Bigorre	102	43 24N	0 3 E
Vic-Fézensac	102	43 47N	0 19 E
Vic-sur-Cère	102	44 59N	2 38 E
Vic-sur-Seille	101	48 45N	6 33 E
Vicenza	108	45 32N	11 31 E
Viceroy	56	49 28N	105 22W
Vich	104	41 58N	2 19 E
Vichada □	86	5 0N	69 30W
Vichy	102	46 9N	3 26 E
Vicksburg, Ariz., U.S.A.	81	33 45N	113 45W
Vicksburg, Mich., U.S.A.	77	42 10N	85 30W
Vicksburg, Miss., U.S.A.	75	32 22N	90 56W
Viçosa, Min. Ger., Brazil	87	20 45 S	42 53W
Viçosa, Pernambuco, Brazil	87	9 28 S	36 14W
Victor, Colo., U.S.A.	74	38 43N	105 7W
Victor, N.Y., U.S.A.	70	42 58N	77 24W
Victor Harbour	135	35 30 S	138 37 E
Victor, L.	38	50 35N	61 50W
Victoria, Argent.	88	32 40 S	60 10W
‡ Victoria, Camer.	116	4 1N	9 10 E
Victoria, B.C., Can.	63	48 30N	123 25W
Victoria, Newf., Can.	37	47 46N	53 14W
Victoria, Ont., Can.	49	43 46N	79 53W
Victoria, Chile	90	38 13 S	72 20W
Victoria, H. K.	131	22 25N	114 15 E
Victoria, Malay.	126	5 20N	115 20 E
Victoria, Seychelles	16	5 0 S	55 40 E
Victoria, U.S.A.	76	41 2N	90 6W
Victoria, Kans., U.S.A.	74	38 52N	99 8W
Victoria, Tex., U.S.A.	75	28 50N	97 0W
Victoria & Albert Mts.	65	80 45N	72 0W
Victoria □	136	37 0 S	144 0 E
Victoria Beach	57	50 40N	96 35W
Victoria de las Tunas	84	20 58N	76 59W
Victoria Falls	117	17 58 S	25 45 E
Victoria, Grand L.	40	47 31N	77 30W
Victoria Harbour	46	44 45N	79 45W
Victoria I.	64	71 0N	111 0W
Victoria, L., Austral.	136	38 2 S	147 34 E
Victoria, L., E. Afr.	116	1 0 S	33 0 E
Victoria, La	86	10 14N	67 20W
Victoria Ld.	91	75 0 S	160 0 E
Victoria Pk.	61	49 18N	114 8W
Victoria Pk	62	50 3N	126 5W
Victoria, R.	134	15 10 S	129 40 E
Victoria Res.	37	48 20N	57 27W
Victoria Square	50	43 54N	79 22W
Victoria Taungdeik	125	21 15N	93 55 E
Victoria West	117	31 25 S	23 4 E
Victoriaville	41	46 4N	71 56W
Victorica	88	36 20 S	65 30W
Victorino	86	2 48N	67 50W
Victorville	81	34 32N	117 18W
Vicuña	88	30 0 S	70 50W
Vicuña Mackenna	88	33 53 S	64 25W
Vidal	81	34 7N	114 31W
Vidalia	73	32 13N	82 25W
Vidauban	103	43 25N	6 27 E
Vidin	109	43 59N	22 28 E
Vidisha (Bhilsa)	124	23 28N	77 53 E
Viedma	90	40 50 S	63 0W
Viedma, L.	90	49 30 S	72 30W
Viejo Canal de Bahama	84	22 10N	77 30W
Vien Pou Kha	128	20 45N	101 5 E
Vienna, Can.	46	42 41N	80 48W
Vienna, U.S.A.	76	38 11N	91 57W
Vienna, Illinois, U.S.A.	75	37 29N	88 54W
Vienna = Wien	106	48 12N	16 22 E
Vienne	103	45 31N	4 53 E
Vienne □	102	46 30N	0 42 E
Vienne, R.	100	47 5N	0 30 E
Vientiane	128	17 58N	102 36 E
Vieques, I.	67	18 8N	65 25W
Viersen	105	51 15N	6 23 E
Vierzon	101	47 13N	2 5 E
Vietnam ■	128	19 0N	106 0 E
Vieux-Boucau-les-Bains	102	43 48N	1 23W
Vif	103	45 5N	5 41 E
Vigan	127	17 35N	120 28 E
Vigan, Le	102	44 0N	3 36 E
Vigia	87	0 50 S	48 5W
Vigia Chico	83	19 46N	87 35W
Vignacourt	101	50 1N	2 15 E
Vignemale, Pic du	102	42 47N	0 10W
Vigneulles	101	48 59N	5 40 E
Vigo	104	42 12N	8 41W
Vihiers	100	47 10N	0 30W
Vijayawada (Bezwada)	125	16 31N	80 39 E
Viking	61	53 7N	111 50W
Vikna	111	64 52N	10 57 E
Vikulovo	120	56 50N	70 40 E
* Vila Arriaga	117	14 35 S	13 30 E
Vila Bittencourt	86	1 20 S	69 20W
Vila Coutinho	117	14 37 S	34 19 E
Vila da Maganja	117	17 18 S	37 30 E
Vila de Aljustrel	117	13 30 S	19 45 E
Vila de Liquica	127	8 40 S	125 20 E
** Vila de Manica	117	18 58 S	32 59 E
† Vila Fontes	117	17 51 S	35 24 E
Vila Franca de Xira	104	38 57N	8 59W
Vila Machado	117	19 15 S	34 14 E
Vila Marechal Carmona = Uige	116	7 30 S	14 40 E
Vila Murtinho	86	10 20 S	65 20W
Vila Nova do Seles	117	11 35 S	14 22 E
Vila Real	104	41 17N	7 48W
Vila Real de Santo Antonio	104	37 10N	7 28W
Vila Salazar	127	5 25 S	123 50 E
Vila Velha	89	20 20 S	40 17W
†† Vila Verissimo Sarmento	116	8 15 S	20 50 E
Vilaine, R.	100	47 35N	2 10W
Vilanculos	117	22 1 S	35 17 E
Vilhelmina	110	64 35N	16 39 E
Vilhena	86	12 30 S	60 0W
Viliga	121	60 2N	156 56 E
Villa Abecia	88	21 0 S	68 18W
Villa Ahumada	82	30 30N	106 40W
Villa Ana	88	28 28 S	59 40W
Villa Ángela	88	27 34 S	60 45W
Villa Bella	86	10 25 S	65 30W
Villa Cañas	88	34 0 S	61 35W
Villa Cisneros = Dakhla	114	23 50N	15 53W
Villa Colón	88	31 38 S	68 20W
Villa Constitución	88	33 15 S	60 20W
Villa de Cura	86	10 2N	67 29W
Villa de María	88	30 0 S	63 43W
Villa de Rosario	88	24 30 S	57 35W
Villa Dolores	88	31 58 S	65 15W
Villa Franca	88	26 14 S	58 20W
Villa Frontera	82	26 56N	101 27W
Villa Grove	77	39 52N	88 10W
Villa Guillermina	88	28 15 S	59 29W

‡ *Renamed Limbe*

* *Renamed Bibala*
** *Renamed Manica*
† *Renamed Caia*
†† *Renamed Camissombo*

Villa Hayes — Walton

Villa Hayes	**88**	25 0S	57 20W
Villa Iris	**88**	38 12S	63 12W
Villa Julia Molina	**85**	19 5N	69 45W
Villa Madero	**82**	24 28N	104 10W
Villa María	**88**	32 20S	63 10W
Villa Mazán	**88**	28 40S	66 30W
Villa Mentes	**88**	21 10S	63 30W
Villa Montes	**88**	21 10S	63 30W
Villa Ocampo, Argent.	**88**	28 30S	59 20W
Villa Ocampo, Mexico	**82**	26 29N	105 30W
Villa Ojo de Agua	**88**	29 30S	63 44W
Villa San Agustín	**88**	30 35S	67 30W
Villa San José	**88**	32 12S	58 15W
Villa San Martín	**88**	28 9S	64 9W
Villa Unión	**82**	23 12N	106 14W
Villach	**106**	46 37N	13 51E
Villagarcía de Arosa	**104**	42 34N	8 46W
Villagrán	**83**	24 29N	99 29W
Villaguay	**88**	32 0S	58 45W
Villahermosa	**83**	17 45N	92 50W
Villaines-la-Juhel	**100**	48 21N	0 20W
Villalba	**104**	40 36N	3 59W
Villamblard	**102**	45 2N	0 32E
Villanueva, Colomb.	**86**	10 37N	72 59W
Villanueva, U.S.A.	**79**	35 16N	105 31W
Villanueva de la Serena	**104**	38 59N	5 50W
Villard	**103**	45 4N	5 33E
Villard-Bonnet	**103**	45 14N	5 53E
Villard-de-Lans	**103**	45 3N	5 33E
Villarreal	**104**	39 55N	0 3W
Villarrica, Chile	**90**	39 15S	72 30W
Villarrica, Parag.	**88**	25 40S	56 30W
Villarrobledo	**104**	39 18N	2 36W
Villars	**103**	46 0N	5 2E
Villavicencio, Argent.	**88**	32 28S	69 0W
Villavicencio, Colomb.	**86**	4 9N	73 37W
Villaviciosa	**104**	43 32N	5 27W
Villazón	**88**	22 0S	65 35W
Ville de Paris □	**101**	48 50N	2 20E
Ville-Guay	**42**	46 50N	71 5W
Ville-Marie	**40**	47 20N	79 30W
Ville Platte	**75**	30 45N	92 17W
Villebon, L.	**40**	47 58N	77 17W
Villedieu	**100**	48 50N	1 12W
Villefort	**102**	44 28N	3 56E
Villefranche	**101**	47 19N	1 46E
Villefranche-de-Lauragais	**102**	43 25N	1 44E
Villefranche-de-Rouergue	**102**	44 21N	2 2E
Villefranche-du-Périgord	**102**	44 38N	1 5E
Villefranche-sur-Saône	**103**	45 59N	4 43E
Villemaur	**101**	48 14N	3 40E
Villemontel	**40**	48 38N	78 22W
Villemur-sur-Tarn	**102**	43 51N	1 31E
Villena	**104**	38 39N	0 52W
Villenauxe	**101**	48 36N	3 30E
Villenave	**102**	44 46N	0 33W
Villeneuve	**101**	48 42N	2 25E
Villeneuve-l'Archevêque	**101**	48 14N	3 32E
Villeneuve-lès-Avignon	**103**	43 57N	4 49E
Villeneuve-sur-Allier	**102**	46 40N	3 13E
Villeneuve-sur-Lot	**102**	44 24N	0 42E
Villeréal	**102**	44 38N	0 45E
Villers Bocage	**100**	49 3N	0 40W
Villers Bretonneux	**101**	49 50N	2 30E
Villers-Cotterêts	**101**	49 15N	3 4E
Villers-sur-Mer	**100**	49 21N	0 2W
Villersexel	**101**	47 33N	6 26E
Villerupt	**101**	49 28N	5 55E
Villerville	**100**	49 26N	0 5E
Villieu	**42**	46 44N	71 17W
Villisca	**76**	40 55N	94 59W
Vilna	**60**	54 7N	111 55W
Vilnius	**120**	54 38N	25 25E
Vilvoorde	**105**	50 56N	4 26E
Vilyuy, R.	**121**	63 58N	125 0E
Vilyuysk	**121**	63 40N	121 20E
Vimont	**44**	45 36N	73 43W
Vimoutiers	**100**	48 57N	0 10E
Viña del Mar	**88**	33 0S	71 30W
Vinaroz	**104**	40 30N	0 27E
Vincennes	**77**	38 42N	87 29W
Vincent	**81**	34 33N	118 11W
Vinchina	**88**	28 45S	68 15W
Vindel älv	**110**	64 20N	19 20E
Vindeln	**110**	64 12N	19 43E
Vindhya Ra.	**124**	22 50N	77 0E
Vine Grove	**77**	37 49N	85 59W
Vineland, Can.	**49**	43 9N	79 24W
Vineland, U.S.A.	**72**	39 30N	75 0W
Vinh	**128**	18 45N	105 38E
Vinita	**75**	36 40N	95 12W
Vinkovci	**109**	45 19N	18 48E
Vinnitsa	**120**	49 15N	28 30E
Vinton, Calif., U.S.A.	**80**	39 48N	120 10W
Vinton, Iowa, U.S.A.	**76**	42 8N	92 1W
Vinton, La., U.S.A.	**75**	30 13N	93 35W
Viola	**76**	41 12N	90 35W
Viqueque	**127**	8 42S	126 30E
Virac	**127**	13 30N	124 20E
Virago Sd.	**62**	54 0N	132 30W
Viramgam	**124**	23 5N	72 0E
Virden, Can.	**57**	49 50N	100 56W
Virden, U.S.A.	**76**	39 30N	89 46W
Vire	**100**	48 50N	0 53W
Vírgenes, C.	**90**	52 19S	68 21W
Virgil	**49**	43 13N	79 8W
Virgin Gorda, I.	**85**	18 45N	64 26W
Virgin Is.	**85**	18 40N	64 30W
Virgin, R., Can.	**55**	57 2N	108 17W
Virgin, R., U.S.A.	**79**	36 50N	114 10W
Virginia, U.S.A.	**76**	39 57N	90 13W
Virginia, Minn., U.S.A.	**52**	47 30N	92 32W
Virginia □	**72**	37 45N	78 0W
Virginia Beach	**72**	36 54N	75 58W
Virginia City, Mont., U.S.A.	**78**	45 25N	111 58W
Virginia City, Nev., U.S.A.	**80**	39 19N	119 39W
Virginia Falls	**54**	61 38N	125 42W
Virginiatown	**34**	48 9N	79 36W
Virgins, C.	**90**	52 10S	68 30W
Virieu-le-Grand	**103**	45 51N	5 39E
Viroqua	**74**	43 33N	90 57W
Virton	**105**	49 35N	5 32E
Virudhunagar	**124**	9 30N	78 0E
Vis, I.	**108**	43 0N	16 10E
Visalia	**80**	36 25N	119 18W
Visayan Sea	**127**	11 30N	123 30E
Visby	**111**	57 37N	18 18E
Viscount	**56**	51 57N	105 39W
Viscount Melville Sd.	**64**	74 10N	108 0W
Visé	**105**	50 44N	5 41E
Višegrad	**109**	43 47N	19 17E
Viseu, Brazil	**87**	1 10S	46 20W
Viseu, Port.	**104**	40 40N	7 55W
Vishakhapatnam	**125**	17 45N	83 20E
Visikoi I.	**91**	56 30S	26 40E
Viso, Mte.	**108**	44 38N	7 5E
Vista	**81**	33 12N	117 14W
Vistula, R. = Wisła, R.	**107**	53 38N	18 47E
Vitebsk	**120**	55 10N	30 15E
Viterbo	**108**	42 25N	12 8E
Viti Levu, I.	**133**	17 30S	177 30E
Vitim	**121**	59 45N	112 25E
Vitim, R.	**121**	58 40N	112 50E
Vitlal Junction	**81**	34 11N	114 34W
Vitória	**87**	20 20S	40 22W
Vitoria	**104**	42 50N	2 41W
Vitória da Conquista	**87**	14 51S	40 51W
Vitória de São Antão	**87**	8 10S	37 20W
Vitré	**100**	48 8N	1 12W
Vitry-le-François	**101**	48 43N	4 33E
Vitteaux	**101**	47 24N	4 30E
Vittel	**101**	48 12N	5 57E
Vittoria	**70**	42 48N	81 21W
Vittória	**108**	36 58N	14 30E
Vittório Véneto	**108**	45 59N	12 18E
Vivero	**104**	43 39N	7 38W
Viviers	**103**	44 30N	4 40E
Vivonne	**102**	46 36N	0 15E
Vizcaíno, Desierto de	**82**	27 40N	113 50W
Vizcaíno, Sierra	**82**	27 30N	114 0W
Vizianagaram	**125**	18 6N	83 10E
Vizille	**103**	45 5N	5 46E
Vlaardingen	**105**	51 55N	4 21E
Vladimir	**120**	56 0N	40 30E
Vladivostok	**130**	43 10N	131 53E
Vlieland, I.	**105**	53 30N	4 55E
Vlissingen	**105**	51 26N	3 34E
Vlonë = Vlórë	**109**	40 32N	19 28E
Vlórë	**109**	40 32N	19 28E
Vltava, R.	**106**	49 35N	14 10E
Vogar	**57**	50 57N	98 39W
Vogelkop = Doberai, Jazirah	**127**	1 25S	133 0E
Vogelsberg	**106**	50 37N	9 30E
Vohimarina	**117**	13 25S	50 0E
Vohipeno	**117**	22 22S	47 51E
Voi	**116**	3 25S	38 32E
Void	**101**	48 40N	5 36E
Voiron	**103**	45 22N	5 35E
Voisey B.	**36**	56 15N	61 50W
Vojmsjön	**110**	64 55N	16 40E
Volborg	**74**	45 50N	105 44W
Volda	**110**	62 9N	6 5E
Volendam	**105**	52 30N	5 4E
Volga, R.	**120**	52 20N	48 0E
Volgograd	**120**	48 40N	44 25E
Völklingen	**105**	49 15N	6 50E
Vollenhove	**105**	52 40N	5 58E
Volochayevka	**121**	48 40N	134 30E
Vologda	**120**	59 25N	40 0E
Vólos	**109**	39 24N	22 59E
Volsk	**120**	52 5N	47 28E
Volta, L.	**114**	7 30N	0 15E
Volta, R.	**114**	8 0N	0 10W
Volta Redonda	**89**	22 31S	44 5W
Volterra	**108**	43 24N	10 50E
Volturno, R.	**108**	41 18N	14 20E
Vonda	**56**	52 19N	106 6W
Voorburg	**105**	52 5N	4 24E
Vopnafjörður	**110**	65 45N	14 40W
Vorarlberg □	**106**	47 20N	10 0E
Voreppe	**103**	45 18N	5 39E
Voríai Sporádhes	**109**	39 15N	23 30E
Vorkuta	**120**	67 48N	64 20E
Voronezh	**120**	51 40N	39 10E
Voroshilovgrad	**120**	48 38N	39 15E
Vorovskoye	**121**	54 30N	155 50E
Vosges	**101**	48 20N	7 10E
Vosges □	**101**	48 12N	6 20E
Voss	**111**	60 38N	6 26E
Vostok I.	**15**	10 5S	152 23W
Vostotnyy Sayan	**121**	54 0N	96 0E
Votkinsk	**120**	57 0N	53 55E
Vouga, R.	**104**	40 46N	8 10W
Voulte-sur-Rhône, La	**103**	44 48N	4 46E
Vouziers	**101**	49 22N	4 40E
Voves	**101**	48 15N	1 38E
Voyageurs Nat. Park	**52**	48 30N	92 55W
Voznesenye	**120**	61 0N	35 45E
Vrangelja, Ostrov	**121**	71 0N	180 0E
Vranje	**109**	42 34N	21 54E
Vratsa	**109**	43 13N	23 30E
Vrbas, R.	**109**	44 30N	17 10E
Vrede	**117**	27 24S	29 6E
Vredenburg	**117**	32 51S	18 0E
Vršac	**109**	45 8N	21 18E
Vryburg	**117**	26 55S	24 45E
Vryheid	**117**	27 54S	30 47E
Vught	**105**	51 38N	5 20E
Vulcan, Can.	**61**	50 25N	113 15W
Vulcan, U.S.A.	**72**	45 46N	87 51W
Vulcano, I.	**108**	38 25N	14 58E
Vung Tau	**128**	10 21N	107 4E
Vyazemskiy	**121**	47 32N	134 45E
Vyazma	**120**	55 10N	34 15E
Vychegda R.	**120**	61 50N	52 30E
Vychodné Beskydy	**107**	49 30N	22 0E
Vyrnwy, L.	**94**	52 48N	3 30W
Vyshniy Volochek	**120**	57 30N	34 30E
Vyssi Brod	**122**	48 36N	14 20E
Vytegra	**120**	61 15N	36 40E

W

Wa	**114**	10 7N	2 25W
Waal, R.	**105**	51 59N	4 8E
Waalwijk	**105**	51 42N	5 4E
Wabakimi L.	**52**	50 38N	89 45W
Wabamun	**60**	53 33N	114 28W
Wabana	**35**	47 40N	53 0W
Wabano, R.	**41**	48 20N	74 3W
Wabasca	**54**	55 57N	113 45W
Wabasca, R.	**60**	58 22N	115 20W
Wabash	**77**	40 48N	85 46W
Wabash, R.	**72**	39 10N	87 30W
Wabaskang L.	**52**	50 26N	93 13W
Wabassi, R.	**53**	51 45N	86 20W
Wabatongushi L.	**53**	48 26N	84 13W
Wabeno	**72**	45 25N	88 40W
Wabigoon	**52**	49 43N	92 35W
Wabigoon L.	**52**	49 44N	92 44W
Wabimeig L.	**53**	51 28N	85 36W
Wabinosh L.	**52**	50 5N	89 0W
Wabowden	**55**	54 55N	98 38W
Wabrzezno	**107**	53 16N	18 57E
Wabuk Pt.	**34**	55 20N	85 5W
Wabush	**38**	52 55N	66 52W
Wabuska	**78**	39 16N	119 13W
W.A.C. Bennett Dam	**54**	56 2N	122 6W
Waco, Can.	**36**	51 27N	65 37W
Waco, U.S.A.	**75**	31 33N	97 5W
Waconichi, L.	**41**	50 8N	74 0W
Wacouno, R.	**38**	50 54N	65 57W
Wad ar Rima	**122**	26 5N	41 30E
Wâd Medanî	**115**	14 28N	33 30E
Waddenzee	**105**	53 6N	5 10E
Waddington	**71**	44 51N	75 12W
Waddington, Mt.	**62**	51 23N	125 15W
Waddinxveen	**105**	52 2N	4 40E
Wadena, Can.	**56**	51 57N	103 38W
Wadena, U.S.A.	**74**	46 25N	95 2W
Wadesboro	**73**	35 2N	80 2W
Wadhams	**62**	51 30N	127 30W
Wadi Halfa	**115**	21 53N	31 19E
Wadi Sabha	**122**	23 50N	48 30E
Wadlin L.	**60**	57 44N	115 35W
Wadsley	**66**	49 21N	123 13W
Wadsworth	**78**	39 44N	119 22W
Wafra	**122**	28 33N	48 3E
Wageningen	**105**	51 58N	5 40E
Wager B.	**65**	65 26N	88 40W
Wager Bay	**65**	65 56N	90 49W
Wagga Wagga	**136**	35 7S	147 24E
Waghete	**127**	4 10S	135 50E
Wagin	**134**	33 17S	117 25E
Wagon Mound	**75**	36 10N	104 50W
Wagoner	**75**	36 0N	95 20W
Wahai	**127**	2 48S	129 35E
Wahiawa	**67**	21 30N	158 2W
Wahoo	**74**	41 15N	96 35W
Wahpeton	**74**	46 20N	96 35W
Waianae	**67**	21 25N	158 8W
Waiau, R.	**133**	42 47S	173 22E
Waibeem	**127**	0 30S	132 50E
Waigeo, I.	**127**	0 20S	130 40E
Waihi	**133**	37 23S	175 52E
Waihou, R.	**133**	37 15S	175 40E
Waikabubak	**127**	9 45S	119 25E
Waikaoti	**15**	45 36S	170 41E
Waikaremoana	**133**	38 42S	177 12E
Waikari	**133**	42 58S	172 41E
Waikato, R.	**133**	37 23S	174 43E
Waikawa Harbour	**133**	46 39S	169 9E
Waikokopu	**133**	39 3S	177 52E
Waikouaiti	**133**	45 36S	170 41E
Wailuku	**67**	20 53N	156 26W
Waimakariri, R.	**133**	42 23S	172 42E
Waimanola	**67**	21 19N	157 43W
Waimarino	**133**	40 40S	175 20E
Waimate	**133**	44 53S	171 3E
Waimea	**67**	21 57N	159 39W
Wainganga, R.	**124**	21 0N	79 45E
Waingapu	**127**	9 35S	120 11E
Wainiha	**67**	22 9N	159 34W
Wainwright, Can.	**61**	52 50N	110 50W
Wainwright, U.S.A.	**67**	70 39N	160 10W
Waiouru	**133**	39 28S	175 41E
Waipahu	**67**	21 23N	158 1W
Waipara	**133**	43 3S	172 46E
Waipawa	**133**	39 56S	176 38E
Waipiro	**133**	38 2S	176 22E
Waipori	**15**	45 50S	169 52E
Waipu	**133**	35 59S	174 29E
Waipukurau	**133**	40 1S	176 33E
Wairakei	**133**	38 37S	176 6E
Wairarapa I.	**133**	41 14S	175 15E
Wairoa	**133**	39 3S	177 25E
Waitaki, R.	**133**	44 23S	169 55E
Waitara	**133**	38 59S	174 15E
Waitsburg	**78**	46 15N	118 0W
Waiuku	**133**	37 15S	174 45E
Waiyeung	**131**	23 12N	114 32E
Wajima	**132**	37 30N	137 0E
Wajir	**116**	1 42N	40 20E
Wakamatsu	**132**	33 50N	130 45E
Wakasa-Wan	**132**	34 45N	135 30E
Wakatipu, L.	**133**	45 5S	168 33E
Wakaw	**56**	52 39N	105 44W
Wakayama	**132**	34 15N	135 15E
Wakayama-ken □	**132**	33 50N	135 30E
Wake Forest	**73**	35 58N	78 30W
Wake I.	**14**	19 18N	166 36E
Wakefield, Can.	**40**	45 38N	75 56W
Wakefield, N.Z.	**133**	41 24S	173 5E
Wakefield, U.K.	**94**	53 41N	1 31W
Wakefield, Mass., U.S.A.	**71**	42 30N	71 3W
Wakefield, Mich., U.S.A.	**52**	46 28N	89 53W
Wakeham	**38**	48 50N	64 34W
Wakeham Bay = Maricourt	**36**	61 36N	71 58W
Wakerusa	**77**	41 32N	86 1W
Wakhan □	**123**	37 0N	73 0E
Wakkanai	**132**	45 28N	141 35E
Wako	**34**	49 50N	91 22W
Wakomata L.	**46**	46 34N	83 22W
Wakre	**127**	0 30S	131 5E
Wakuach L.	**36**	55 34N	67 32W
Wałbrzych	**106**	50 45N	16 18E
Walcheren, I.	**105**	51 30N	3 35E
Walcott	**78**	41 50N	106 55W
Waldeck	**56**	50 22N	107 36W
Walden, Colo., U.S.A.	**78**	40 47N	106 20W
Walden, N.Y., U.S.A.	**71**	41 32N	74 13W
Waldheim	**56**	52 39N	106 37W
Waldo	**77**	40 28N	83 5W
Waldport	**78**	44 30N	124 2W
Waldron, Can.	**55**	50 53N	102 35W
Waldron, U.S.A.	**75**	34 52N	94 4W
Wales, Alas., U.S.A.	**67**	65 38N	168 10W
Wales, N.Dak., U.S.A.	**57**	48 55N	98 35W
Wales □	**95**	52 30N	3 30W
Wales I.	**36**	62 0N	72 30W
Walgett	**135**	30 0S	148 5E
Walhachin	**63**	50 45N	120 59W
Walhalla	**57**	48 55N	97 55W
Walker, U.S.A.	**76**	37 54N	94 14W
Walker, Minn., U.S.A.	**52**	47 4N	94 35W
Walker L., Man., Can.	**55**	54 42N	95 57W
Walker L., Qué., Can.	**36**	50 20N	67 11W
Walker L., U.S.A.	**78**	38 56N	118 46W
Walkerton, Can.	**46**	44 10N	81 10W
Walkerton, U.S.A.	**77**	41 28N	86 29W
Wall	**74**	44 0N	102 14W
Wall Lake	**76**	42 16N	95 5W
Walla Walla	**78**	46 3N	118 25W
Wallace, N.S., Can.	**39**	45 48N	63 29W
Wallace, Ont., Can.	**70**	45 12N	78 9W
Wallace, Idaho, U.S.A.	**78**	47 30N	116 0W
Wallace, N.C., U.S.A.	**73**	34 50N	77 59W
Wallace, Nebr., U.S.A.	**74**	40 51N	101 12W
Wallaceburg	**46**	42 40N	82 23W
Wallachia = Valahia	**107**	44 35N	25 0E
Wallaroo	**135**	33 56S	137 39E
Wallasey	**94**	53 26N	3 2W
Wallowa	**78**	45 40N	117 35W
Wallowa, Mts.	**78**	45 20N	117 30W
Wallsend, Austral.	**136**	32 55S	151 40E
Wallsend, U.K.	**94**	54 59N	1 30W
Wallula	**78**	46 3N	118 59W
Walmore	**49**	43 7N	78 55W
Walmsley, L.	**55**	63 25N	108 36W
Walney, Isle of	**94**	54 5N	3 15W
Walnut	**76**	41 33N	89 36W
Walnut Ridge	**75**	36 7N	90 58W
Walsall	**95**	52 36N	1 59W
Walsenburg	**75**	37 42N	104 45W
Walsh, Can.	**61**	49 57N	110 3W
Walsh, U.S.A.	**75**	37 28N	102 15W
Walterboro	**73**	32 53N	80 40W
Walters	**75**	34 25N	98 20W
Waltham	**71**	42 22N	71 12W
Waltham Sta.	**40**	45 57N	76 57W
Waltman	**78**	43 8N	107 15W
Walton, Can.	**39**	45 14N	64 0W
Walton, U.S.A.	**77**	38 52N	84 37W
Walton, Mich., U.S.A.	**46**	44 30N	85 14W

Walton Wendesi

Walton, N.Y., U.S.A. 71 42 12N 75 9W
Waltonville 76 38 13N 89 2W
Walvis Ridge 13 30 0S 3 0E
Walvisbaai 117 23 0S 14 28E
Wamba 116 2 10N 27 57E
Wamego 74 39 14N 96 22W
Wamena 127 3 58S 138 50E
Wampsville 71 43 4N 75 42W
Wamsasi 127 3 27S 126 7E
Wan Ta Shan 130 46 20N 132 20E
Wana 124 32 20N 69 32E
Wanaka L. 133 44 33S 169 7E
Wanan 131 26 25N 114 50E
Wanapiri 127 4 30S 135 50E
Wanapitei 34 46 30N 80 45W
Wanapitei L. 46 46 45N 80 40W
Wanapitei, R. 46 46 2N 80 51W
Wanchuan 130 40 53N 114 32E
Wang Saphung 128 17 18N 101 46E
Wangal 127 6 8S 134 9E
Wanganui 133 39 35S 175 3E
Wangaratta 136 36 21S 146 19E
Wangching 130 43 15N 129 37E
Wangerooge I. 106 53 47N 7 52E
Wangiwangi, I. 127 5 22S 123 37E
Wangkiang 131 30 6N 116 45E
Wanham 60 55 44N 118 24W
Wanhsien, Kansu, China 130 36 45N 107 24E
Wanhsien, Szechwan, China 131 30 50N 108 30E
*Wankie 117 18 18S 26 30E
Wanless 57 54 11N 101 21W
Wanning 131 18 45N 110 28E
Wannon, R. 136 37 38S 141 25E
Wantsai 131 28 5N 114 22E
Wanyang Shan, mts. 131 26 30N 113 45E
Wanyüan 131 32 4N 108 5E
Wapakoneta 77 40 35N 84 10W
Wapato 78 46 30N 120 25W
Wapawekka L. 55 54 55N 104 40W
Wapella 57 50 16N 101 58W
Wapello 76 41 11N 91 11W
Wapikopa L. 34 42 50N 88 10W
Wapiti, R. 34 55 5N 118 18W
Wappingers Fs. 71 41 35N 73 56W
Wapsipinicon, R. 76 41 44N 90 19W
Waranga Res. 136 36 32S 145 5E
Warangal 124 17 58N 79 45E
Waratah B. 136 38 54S 146 5E
Warba 52 47 9N 93 16W
Warburg 61 53 11N 114 19W
Warburton 136 37 47S 145 42E
Warburton, R. 133 27 30S 138 30E
Ward 133 41 49S 174 11E
Ward Cove 54 55 25N 132 10W
Ward Mt. 80 37 12N 118 54W
Wardha 124 20 45N 78 39E
Wardha, R. 124 19 57N 79 11E
Wardlow 61 50 56N 111 31W
Wardner 61 49 25N 115 26W
Wardoan 135 25 59S 149 59E
Ware, Can. 54 57 26N 125 41W
Ware, U.S.A. 71 42 16N 72 15W
Wareham 71 41 45N 70 44W
Warendorf 105 51 57N 8 0E
Warfield 63 49 6N 117 46W
Warialda 135 29 29S 150 33E
Wariap 127 1 30S 134 5E
Warkopi 127 1 12S 134 9E
Warley 95 52 30N 2 0W
Warm Springs, Mont., U.S.A. 78 46 11N 112 56W
Warm Springs, Nev., U.S.A. 79 38 16N 116 32W
Warman 56 52 19N 106 30W
Warmbad, Namibia 117 19 14S 13 51E
Warmbad, S. Afr. 117 24 51S 28 19E
Warmeriville 101 49 20N 4 13E
Warncoort 136 38 30S 143 45E
Warnemünde 106 54 9N 12 5E
Warner 61 49 17N 112 12W
Warner Range, Mts. 78 41 30S 120 20W
Warner Robins 73 32 41N 83 36W
Warracknabeal 136 36 9S 142 26E
Warragul 136 38 10S 145 58E
Warrego, R. 135 30 24S 145 21E
Warrego Ra. 135 25 15S 146 0E
Warren, Austral. 136 31 42S 147 51E
Warren, Can. 46 46 27N 80 18W
Warren, U.S.A. 77 42 31N 83 2W
Warren, Ark., U.S.A. 75 33 35N 92 3W
Warren, Ill., U.S.A. 76 42 30N 89 59W
Warren, Ohio, U.S.A. 70 41 18N 80 52W
Warren, Pa., U.S.A. 70 41 52N 79 10W
Warren, R.I., U.S.A. 71 41 43N 71 19W
Warrender, C. 65 74 28N 81 46W
Warrenpoint 97 54 7N 6 15W
Warrens Corners 49 43 13N 78 45W
Warren's Landing 55 53 40N 98 0W
Warrensburg, Ill., U.S.A. 76 39 56N 89 4W
Warrensburg, Mo., U.S.A. 74 38 45N 93 45W
Warrenton, S. Afr. 117 28 9S 24 47E
Warrenton, U.S.A. 76 38 49N 91 9W
Warrenton, Oreg., U.S.A. 80 46 11N 123 59W
Warrina 134 28 12S 135 50E
Warrington, U.K. 94 53 25N 2 38W
Warrington, U.S.A. 73 30 22N 87 16W
Warrnambool 136 38 25S 142 30E
Warroad 52 48 54N 95 19W
Warsaw, Ill., U.S.A. 76 40 22N 91 26W
Warsaw, Ind., U.S.A. 77 41 14N 85 50W
Warsaw, Ky., U.S.A. 77 38 47N 84 54W
Warsaw, Mo., U.S.A. 76 38 15N 93 23W
Warsaw, N.Y., U.S.A. 70 42 46N 78 10W
Warsaw, Ohio, U.S.A. 70 40 20N 82 0W
Warsaw = Warszawa 107 52 13N 21 0E
Warszawa 107 52 13N 21 0E
Warta, R. 106 52 40N 16 10E
Warthe, R. = Warta, R. 106 52 40N 16 10E
Waru 127 3 30S 130 36E
Warwick, Austral. 135 28 10S 152 1E
Warwick, U.K. 95 52 17N 1 36W
Warwick, U.S.A. 71 41 43N 71 25W
Warwick □ 95 52 20N 1 30W
Wasa 54 49 45N 115 50W
Wasaga Beach 46 44 31N 80 1W
Wasatch, Mt., Ra. 78 40 30N 111 15W
Wascana Cr. 58 50 39N 104 55W
Wascana L. 58 50 26N 104 36W
Wasco, Calif., U.S.A. 81 35 37N 119 16W
Wasco, Oreg., U.S.A. 78 45 45N 120 46W
Waseca, Can. 56 53 6N 109 28W
Waseca, U.S.A. 74 44 3N 93 31W
Wasekamio L. 55 56 45N 108 45W
Wash, The 94 52 58N 0 20W
Washago 46 44 45N 79 20W
Washburn, U.S.A. 76 40 55N 89 17W
Washburn, N.D., U.S.A. 74 47 23N 101 0W
Washburn, Wis., U.S.A. 52 46 38N 90 55W
Washi L. 53 51 24N 87 2W
Washington, Can. 49 43 18N 80 35W
Washington, Calif., U.S.A. 80 39 22N 120 48W
Washington, D.C., U.S.A. 72 38 52N 77 0W
Washington, Ga., U.S.A. 73 33 45N 82 45W
Washington, Ind., U.S.A. 77 38 40N 87 8W
Washington, Iowa, U.S.A. 76 41 20N 91 45W
Washington, Mo, U.S.A. 76 38 35N 91 20W
Washington, N.C., U.S.A. 73 35 35N 77 1W
Washington, N.J., U.S.A. 71 40 45N 74 59W
Washington, Pa., U.S.A. 70 40 10N 80 20W
Washington, Utah, U.S.A. 79 37 10N 113 30W
Washington □ 78 47 45N 120 30W
Washington Court House 77 39 34N 83 26W
*Washington I., Pac. Oc. 15 4 43N 160 25W
Washington I., U.S.A. 72 45 24N 86 54W
Washington Mt. 71 44 15N 71 18W
Washir 124 32 15N 63 50E
Washougal 80 45 35N 122 21W
Wasian 127 1 47S 133 19E
Wasior 127 2 43S 134 30E
Waskada 57 49 6N 100 48W
Waskaiowaka, L. 55 56 33N 96 23W
Waskateena Beach 56 53 45N 105 15W
Waskatenau 60 54 7N 112 47W
Waskesiu L. 56 53 58N 106 12W
Waskesiu Lake 56 53 55N 106 5W
Waskish 52 48 11N 94 28W
Wassenaar 105 52 8N 4 24E
Wassy 101 48 30N 4 58E
Waswanipi 40 49 40N 75 59W
Waswanipi, L. 40 49 35N 76 40W
Waswanipi, R. 40 49 40N 76 25W
Watangpone 127 4 29S 120 25E
Watawaha, P. 127 6 30S 122 20E
Water Valley 75 34 9N 89 38W
Waterberg 117 20 30S 17 18E
Waterbury, Conn., U.S.A. 71 41 32N 73 0W
Waterbury, Vt., U.S.A. 71 44 22N 72 44W
Waterbury L. 55 58 10N 104 22W
Waterdown 48 43 20N 79 53W
Waterford, Can. 46 42 56N 80 17W
Waterford, Ireland 97 52 16N 7 8W
Waterford, U.S.A. 77 42 46N 88 13W
Waterford, Calif., U.S.A. 80 37 38N 120 46W
Waterford □ 97 51 10N 7 40W
Waterford Harb. 97 52 10N 6 58W
Waterford, R. 37 47 33N 52 43W
Waterhen L., Man., Can. 57 52 10N 99 40W
Waterhen L., Sask., Can. 55 54 28N 108 25W
Waterloo, Belg. 105 50 43N 4 25E
Waterloo, Ont., Can. 49 43 30N 80 32W
Waterloo, Ont., Can. 52 43 25N 80 30W
Waterloo, Qué., Can. 41 45 21N 72 31W
Waterloo, Que., Can. 71 45 22N 72 32W
Waterloo, U.S.A. 77 41 24N 85 2W
Waterloo, Ill., U.S.A. 76 38 22N 90 6W
Waterloo, Iowa, U.S.A. 76 42 27N 92 20W
Waterloo, N.Y., U.S.A. 70 42 54N 76 53W
Waterloo, Wis., U.S.A. 76 43 11N 88 59W
Waterman 77 41 46N 88 47W
Watermeet 74 46 15N 89 12W
Waterpoint 70 43 19N 78 15W
Waterton Lakes Nat. Park 61 49 5N 114 15W
Waterton Park 61 49 3N 113 55W
Watertown, Conn., U.S.A. 71 41 36N 73 7W
Watertown, N.Y., U.S.A. 71 43 58N 75 57W
Watertown, S.D., U.S.A. 74 44 57N 97 5W
Watertown, Wis., U.S.A. 77 43 15N 88 45W
Waterville, N.S., Can. 39 45 3N 64 41W
Waterville, Qué., Can. 41 45 16N 71 54W
Waterville, Me., U.S.A. 35 44 35N 69 40W
Waterville, N.Y., U.S.A. 71 42 56N 75 23W
Waterville, Pa., U.S.A. 70 41 19N 77 21W
Waterville, Wash., U.S.A. 78 47 45N 120 1W
Watervliet, U.S.A. 77 42 11N 86 18W
Watervliet, N.Y., U.S.A. 71 42 46N 73 43W
Wates 127 7 53S 110 6E
Watford, Can. 46 42 57N 81 53W
Watford, U.K. 95 51 38N 0 23W
Watford City 74 47 50N 103 23W
Wathaman, R. 55 57 16N 102 59W
Watkins Glen 70 42 25N 76 55W
Watlings I. 85 24 0N 74 35W
Watonga 75 35 51N 98 24W
Watrous, Can. 56 51 40N 105 25W
Watrous, U.S.A. 75 35 50N 104 55W
Watsa 116 3 4N 29 30E
Watseka 77 40 45N 87 45W
Watshishou, L. 38 50 20N 60 50W
Watson 56 52 10N 104 30W
Watson Lake 67 60 6N 128 49W
Watsonville 80 36 55N 121 49W
Wattle Hill 136 38 42S 143 17E
Watubela, Kepulauan 127 4 28S 131 54E
Waubamik 46 45 27N 80 1W
Waubaushene 46 44 45N 79 42W
Waubay 74 45 42N 97 17W
Waubra 136 37 21S 143 39E
Wauchope 136 31 28S 152 45E
Wauchula 73 27 35N 81 50W
Waugh 57 49 40N 95 2W
Waukegan 77 42 22N 87 54W
Waukesha 77 43 0N 88 15W
Waukon 74 43 14N 91 33W
Wauneta 74 40 27N 101 25W
Waupaca 74 44 22N 89 8W
Waupun 74 43 38N 88 44W
Waurika 75 34 12N 98 0W
Wausau 74 44 57N 89 40W
Wauseon 77 41 33N 84 8W
Wautoma 74 44 3N 89 20W
Wauwatosa 77 43 6N 87 59W
Wave Hill 134 17 32S 131 0E
Waveland 77 39 53N 87 3W
Waveney, R. 95 52 24N 1 20E
Waverley, Can. 39 44 47N 63 36W
Waverley, N.Z. 133 39 46S 174 37E
Waverly, Ill., U.S.A. 76 39 36N 89 57W
Waverly, Iowa, U.S.A. 76 42 40N 92 30W
Waverly, Mo., U.S.A. 76 39 13N 93 31W
Waverly, N.Y., U.S.A. 71 42 0N 76 33W
Wavre 105 50 43N 4 38E
Wâw 115 7 45N 28 1E
Wawa 53 47 59N 84 47W
Wawagosic, R. 40 49 58N 79 6W
Wawanesa 57 49 36N 99 40W
Wawang L. 52 49 25N 90 34W
Wawasee, L. 77 41 24N 85 42W
Wawona 80 37 32N 119 39W
Waxahachie 75 32 22N 96 53W
Way Way 136 33 30S 151 18E
Wayabula Rau 127 2 29N 128 17E
Wayagamac, L. 41 47 21N 72 39W
Waycross 73 31 12N 82 25W
Wayland 77 42 40N 85 39W
Wayne, Mich., U.S.A. 46 42 17N 83 23W
Wayne, Nebr., U.S.A. 76 42 16N 97 0W
Wayne, W. Va., U.S.A. 72 38 15N 82 27W
Wayne City 77 38 21N 88 35W
Waynesboro, Miss., U.S.A. 73 31 40N 88 39W
Waynesboro, Pa., U.S.A. 72 39 46N 77 32W
Waynesboro, Va., U.S.A. 72 38 4N 78 57W
Waynesburg 72 39 54N 80 12W
Waynesville, U.S.A. 76 37 50N 92 12W
Waynesville, U.S.A. 77 39 32N 84 5W
Waynesville, N.C., U.S.A. 73 35 31N 83 0W
Waynoka 75 36 38N 98 53W
Waza 124 33 22N 69 22E
Wazirabad, Afghan. 123 36 44N 66 47E
Wazirabad, Pak. 124 32 30N 74 8E
We 126 6 3N 95 56E
Weald, The 95 51 7N 0 9E
Wear, R. 94 54 55N 1 22W
Weatherford, Okla., U.S.A. 75 35 30N 98 45W
Weatherford, Tex., U.S.A. 75 32 45N 97 48W
Weaubleau 76 37 54N 93 32W
Webb 56 50 11N 108 12W
Webb City 75 37 9N 94 30W
Webbwood 46 46 16N 81 52W
Webster, Mass., U.S.A. 71 42 4N 71 54W
Webster, N.Y., U.S.A. 70 43 11N 77 27W
Webster, S.D., U.S.A. 74 45 24N 97 33W
Webster, Wis., U.S.A. 74 45 53N 92 25W
Webster City 76 42 30N 93 50W
Webster Green 74 38 38N 90 20W
Webster Springs 72 38 30N 80 25W
Weda 127 0 30N 127 50E
Weda, Teluk 127 0 30N 127 50E
Weddell I. 90 51 50S 61 0W
Weddell Sea 91 72 30S 40 0W
Wedge I. 134 30 50S 115 11E
Wedgeport 39 43 44N 65 59W
Weed 78 41 29N 122 22W
Weed Heights 80 38 59N 119 13W
Weedon-Centre 41 45 42N 71 27W
Weedsport 71 43 3N 76 35W
Weedville 70 41 17N 78 28W
Weekes 56 52 34N 102 52W
Weert 105 51 15N 5 43E
Weesp 105 52 18N 5 2E
Wei Ho, R. 131 34 38N 110 20E
Weichow Tao 131 21 0N 109 1E
Weifang 130 36 47N 119 10E
Weihai 130 37 30N 122 10E
Weimar 106 51 0N 11 20E
Weinan 131 34 30N 109 35E
Weipa 135 12 24S 141 50E
Weir, R. 55 56 54N 93 21W
Weir River 55 56 49N 94 6W
Weirdale 56 53 27N 105 15W
Weirton 70 40 22N 80 35W
Weiser 78 44 10N 117 0W
Weiyüan 130 35 10N 104 10E
Wejherowo 107 54 35N 18 12E
Wekusko 55 54 30N 99 45W
Wekusko L. 55 54 40N 99 50W
Welby 55 50 33N 101 29W
Welch 72 37 29N 81 36W
Weldon 56 53 1N 105 8W
Welkom 117 28 0S 26 50E
Welland 49 43 0N 79 15W
Welland Canal 49 43 3N 79 13W
Welland, R., Can. 49 43 4N 79 3W
Welland, R., U.K. 94 52 43N 0 10W
Wellandport 49 43 0N 79 29W
Weller Park 49 43 14N 79 13W
Wellesley Is. 135 17 20S 139 30E
Wellin 105 50 5N 5 6E
Wellingborough 95 52 18N 0 41W
Wellington, Austral. 136 32 35S 148 59E
Wellington, B.C., Can. 62 49 13N 123 58W
Wellington, Newf., Can. 37 48 53N 53 58W
Wellington, Ont., Can. 43 43 57N 77 20W
Wellington, P.E.I., Can. 39 46 27N 64 0W
Wellington, N.Z. 133 41 19S 174 46E
Wellington, U.K. 94 50 58N 3 13W
Wellington, U.S.A. 76 39 8N 93 59W
Wellington, Col., U.S.A. 74 40 43N 105 0W
Wellington, Kans., U.S.A. 75 37 15N 97 25W
Wellington, Nev., U.S.A. 80 38 47N 119 28W
Wellington, Ohio, U.S.A. 70 41 9N 82 12W
Wellington, Tex., U.S.A. 75 34 55N 100 13W
Wellington □, Can. 49 43 50N 80 30W
Wellington □, N.Z. 133 40 8S 175 36E
Wellington Chan. 65 75 0N 93 0W
Wellington, I. 90 49 30S 75 0W
Wellington, L. 136 38 6S 147 20E
Wellington (Telford) 94 52 42N 2 31W
Wells, Can. 63 53 6N 121 36W
Wells, Norfolk, U.K. 94 52 57N 0 51E
Wells, Somerset, U.K. 95 51 12N 2 39W
Wells, Me., U.S.A. 71 43 18N 70 35W
Wells, Minn., U.S.A. 74 43 44N 93 45W
Wells, Nev., U.S.A. 78 41 8N 115 0W
Wells Gray Prov. Park 63 52 30N 120 15W
Wells L. 134 26 44S 123 15E
Wells River 71 44 9N 72 4W
Wellsboro 70 41 46N 77 20W
Wellsburg 70 40 15N 80 36W
Wellsville, Mo., U.S.A. 76 39 4N 91 30W
Wellsville, N.Y., U.S.A. 70 42 9N 77 53W
Wellsville, Ohio, U.S.A. 70 40 36N 80 40W
Wellsville, Utah, U.S.A. 78 41 35N 111 59W
Wellton 79 32 46N 114 6W
Wels 106 48 9N 14 1E
Welsford 39 45 27N 66 20W
Welshpool 95 52 40N 3 9W
Welwyn 55 50 20N 101 30W
Wem 94 52 52N 2 45W
Wembley 60 55 9N 119 8W
Wenasaga, R. 52 50 38N 93 10W
Wenatchee 78 47 30N 120 17W
Wenchang 131 19 45N 110 50E
Wenchow 131 28 0N 120 38E
Wendell 78 42 50N 114 51W
Wenden 81 33 49N 113 33W
Wendesi 127 2 30S 134 10E

* Renamed Hwange

* Renamed Teraina

Wendover **Williamston**

Wendover	**78**	40 49N	114 1W
Wenebegon L.	**53**	47 23N	83 6W
Wenebegon, R.	**53**	46 53N	83 12W
Wengniu	**130**	43 2N	118 54E
Wengteng	**130**	37 15N	122 10E
Wenlock Edge	**98**	52 30N	2 43W
Wenlock, R.	**135**	12 2S	141 55E
Wenona	**76**	41 3N	89 3W
Wensi	**131**	35 25N	111 7E
Wensiang	**131**	34 35N	110 40E
Wensu	**129**	41 15N	80 14E
Wenteng	**130**	37 10N	122 0E
Wentworth, Austral.	**136**	34 2S	141 54E
Wentworth, Can.	**39**	45 38N	63 33W
Wentzville	**76**	38 49N	90 51W
Wenut	**127**	3 11S	133 19E
Weott	**78**	40 19N	123 56W
Wepener	**117**	29 42S	27 3E
Werda	**117**	25 24S	23 15E
Weri	**127**	3 10S	132 30E
Werne	**105**	51 38N	7 38E
Werra, R.	**105**	51 0N	10 0E
Werribee	**136**	37 54S	144 40E
Werris Creek	**136**	31 18S	150 38E
Wersar	**127**	1 30S	131 55E
Wesel	**105**	51 39N	6 34E
Weser, R.	**106**	53 33N	8 30E
Wesiri	**127**	7 30S	126 30E
Weslemkoon L.	**47**	45 2N	77 25W
Wesleyville, Can.	**37**	49 8N	53 36W
Wesleyville, U.S.A.	**70**	42 9N	80 1W
Wessel Is.	**135**	11 10S	136 45E
Wessington	**74**	44 30N	98 40W
Wessington Springs	**74**	44 10N	98 35W
West	**75**	31 50N	97 5W
West Allis	**77**	43 1N	87 0W
West, B.	**75**	29 5N	89 27W
West Bend	**72**	43 25N	88 10W
West Bengal □	**125**	25 0N	90 0E
West Branch	**46**	44 16N	84 13W
West Bromwich	**95**	52 32N	2 1W
West Carrollton	**77**	39 33N	84 17W
West Chazy	**71**	44 49N	73 28W
West Chester	**72**	39 58N	75 36W
West Chicago	**77**	41 53N	88 12W
West Columbia	**75**	29 10N	95 38W
West Covina	**81**	34 4N	117 54W
West Des Moines	**76**	41 30N	93 45W
West Don, R.	**50**	43 42N	79 20W
West Duffin, R.	**51**	43 51N	79 4W
West End	**84**	26 41N	78 58W
West Falkland Island	**90**	51 30S	60 0W
West Fork, Cuivre, R.	**76**	39 2N	90 58W
West Frankfort	**76**	37 56N	89 0W
West Glamorgan □	**95**	51 40N	3 55W
West Harbour	**15**	45 51S	170 33E
West Hartford	**71**	41 45N	72 45W
West Haven	**71**	41 18N	72 57W
West Helena	**75**	34 30N	90 40W
West Hill	**50**	43 47N	79 12W
West Humber, R.	**50**	43 44N	79 33W
West Indies	**74**	15 0N	70 0W
West Kildonan	**58**	49 56N	97 8W
West Lafayette	**77**	40 27N	86 55W
West Liberty, Iowa, U.S.A.	**76**	41 34N	91 16W
West Liberty, Ky., U.S.A.	**77**	37 55N	83 16W
West Liberty, Ohio, U.S.A.	**77**	40 15N	83 45W
West Lorne	**46**	42 36N	81 36W
West Louisville	**77**	37 42N	87 17W
West Magpie, R., Can.	**38**	51 2N	64 42W
West Magpie, R., Qué., Can.	**36**	52 0N	65 0W
West Manchester	**77**	39 55N	84 38W
West Memphis	**75**	35 5N	90 3W
West Midlands □	**95**	52 30N	1 55W
West Milton	**77**	39 58N	84 20W
West Monroe	**75**	32 32N	92 7W
West Montrose	**49**	43 35N	80 29W
West Newton	**70**	40 14N	79 46W
West Nicholson	**117**	21 2S	29 20E
West Palm Beach	**73**	26 44N	80 3W
West Paris	**128**	44 18N	70 30W
West Pittston	**71**	41 19N	75 49W
West Plains	**75**	36 45N	91 50W
West Point, Jamaica	**84**	18 14N	78 30W
West Point, Ga., U.S.A.	**73**	32 54N	85 10W
West Point, Ill., U.S.A.	**76**	40 15N	91 11W
West Point, Iowa, U.S.A.	**76**	40 43N	91 27W
West Point, Ky., U.S.A.	**77**	37 59N	85 57W
West Point, Miss., U.S.A.	**73**	33 36N	88 38W
West Point, Nebr., U.S.A.	**74**	41 50N	96 43W
West Point, Va., U.S.A.	**72**	37 35N	76 47W
West Poplar	**56**	49 0N	106 22W
West Road R.	**63**	53 18N	122 53W
West Salem	**77**	38 31N	88 1W
West Spitsbergen	**17**	78 40N	17 0E
West Sussex □	**95**	50 55N	0 30W
West Terre Haute	**77**	39 27N	87 27W
West Thurlow I.	**62**	50 25N	125 35W
West Union, Iowa, U.S.A.	**76**	42 57N	91 49W
West Union, Ohio, U.S.A.	**77**	38 48N	83 33W
West Unity	**77**	41 35N	84 26W
West Vancouver	**66**	49 21N	123 8W
West Virginia □	**72**	39 0N	81 0W
West Walker, R.	**80**	38 54N	119 9W
West Wyalong	**136**	33 56S	147 10E
West Yellowstone	**78**	44 47N	111 4W
West Yorkshire □	**94**	53 45N	1 40W
Westbank	**54**	49 50N	119 40W
Westbourne	**57**	50 8N	98 35W
Westbrook, Maine, U.S.A.	**72**	43 40N	70 22W
Westbrook, Tex., U.S.A.	**75**	32 25N	101 0W
Westby, Austral.	**136**	35 30S	147 24E
Westby, U.S.A.	**74**	48 52N	104 3W
Westdale	**48**	43 17N	79 53W
Westend	**81**	35 42N	117 24W
Western Australia □	**134**	25 0S	118 0E
Western Duck I.	**46**	45 45N	83 0W
Western Ghats	**124**	15 30N	74 30E
Western Isles □	**96**	57 30N	7 10W
Western Pen.	**52**	49 30N	94 50W
Western Samoa ■	**133**	14 0S	172 0W
Western Shore	**39**	44 32N	64 19W
Westernport	**72**	39 30N	79 5W
Westerschelde, R.	**105**	51 25N	4 0E
Westerwald, mts.	**105**	50 39N	8 0E
Westfield, Can.	**39**	45 22N	66 14W
Westfield, Ill., U.S.A.	**77**	39 27N	88 0W
Westfield, Ind., U.S.A.	**77**	40 2N	86 8W
Westfield, Mass., U.S.A.	**71**	42 9N	72 49W
Westfield, N.Y., U.S.A.	**70**	42 20N	79 38W
Westfield, Pa., U.S.A.	**70**	41 54N	77 32W
Westfriesche Eilanden	**105**	53 20N	5 10E
Westham I.	**66**	49 5N	123 10W
Westhope	**57**	48 55N	101 0W
Westland □	**133**	43 33S	169 59E
Westland Bight	**133**	42 55S	170 5E
Westlock	**60**	54 9N	113 55W
Westmeath □	**97**	53 30N	7 30W
Westminster	**72**	39 34N	77 1W
Westmorland	**79**	33 2N	115 42W
Westmount	**44**	45 29N	73 36W
Weston, Can.	**50**	43 43N	79 31W
Weston, Malay.	**126**	5 10N	115 35E
Weston, Ohio, U.S.A.	**77**	41 21N	83 47W
Weston, Oreg., U.S.A.	**78**	45 50N	118 30W
Weston, W. Va., U.S.A.	**72**	39 3N	80 29W
Weston I.	**36**	52 33N	79 36W
Weston-super-Mare	**95**	51 20N	2 59W
Westover	**49**	43 19N	80 5W
Westphalia	**76**	38 26N	92 0W
Westport, Newf., Can.	**37**	49 47N	56 38W
Westport, N.S., Can.	**39**	44 15N	66 22W
Westport, Ont., Can.	**47**	44 40N	76 25W
Westport, Ireland	**97**	53 44N	9 31W
Westport, N.Z.	**133**	41 46S	171 37E
Westport, U.S.A.	**77**	39 11N	85 34W
Westport, Ore., U.S.A.	**80**	46 10N	123 23W
Westport, Wash., U.S.A.	**78**	46 48N	124 4W
Westray	**57**	53 36N	101 24W
Westray, I.	**96**	59 18N	3 0W
Westree	**53**	47 26N	81 34W
Westsyde	**63**	50 47N	120 21W
Westview	**54**	49 50N	124 31W
Westville, Can.	**39**	45 34N	62 43W
Westville, Calif., U.S.A.	**80**	39 8N	120 42W
Westville, Ill., U.S.A.	**77**	40 3N	87 36W
Westville, Ind., U.S.A.	**77**	41 35N	86 55W
Westville, N.Y., U.S.A.	**43**	44 58N	74 20W
Westville, Okla., U.S.A.	**75**	36 0N	94 33W
Westwood	**78**	40 26N	121 0W
Wetar, I.	**127**	7 30S	126 30E
Wetaskiwin	**61**	52 55N	113 24W
Wetteren	**105**	51 0N	3 53E
Wetupoa	**136**	35 16S	143 46E
Wetzlar	**106**	50 33N	8 30E
Wewaka	**75**	35 10N	96 35W
Wexford, Can.	**50**	43 45N	79 18W
Wexford, Ireland	**97**	52 20N	6 28W
Wexford □	**97**	52 20N	6 25W
Wexford Harb.	**97**	52 20N	6 25W
Weyburn	**56**	49 40N	103 50W
Weyburn L.	**54**	63 0N	117 59W
Weymouth, Can.	**39**	44 30N	66 1W
Weymouth, U.K.	**95**	50 36N	2 28W
Weymouth, U.S.A.	**71**	42 13N	70 53W
Weymouth, C.	**135**	12 37S	143 27E
Wezep	**105**	52 28N	6 0E
Whakatane	**133**	37 57S	177 1E
Whale Cove	**55**	62 11N	92 36W
Whale, R.	**36**	58 15N	67 40W
Whales	**91**	78 0S	165 0W
Whaletown	**62**	50 7N	125 2W
Whalsay, I.	**96**	60 22N	1 0W
Whampoa	**131**	23 5N	113 20E
Whangamomona	**133**	39 8S	174 44E
Whangarei	**133**	35 43S	174 21E
Whangarei Harbour	**133**	35 45S	174 28E
Wharfe, R.	**94**	53 55N	1 30W
Wharton, N.J., U.S.A.	**71**	40 53N	74 36W
Wharton, Pa., U.S.A.	**70**	41 31N	78 1W
Wharton, Tex., U.S.A.	**75**	29 20N	96 6W
Whatcom, L.	**63**	48 43N	122 20W
Wheatfield	**77**	41 13N	87 4W
Wheatland, Calif., U.S.A.	**80**	39 1N	121 25W
Wheatland, Ind., U.S.A.	**77**	38 40N	87 19W
Wheatland, Wyo., U.S.A.	**74**	42 4N	105 58W
Wheatley	**46**	42 6N	82 27W
Wheaton, U.S.A.	**77**	41 52N	88 6W
Wheaton, Minn., U.S.A.	**74**	45 50N	96 29W
Wheelbarrow Pk.	**80**	37 26N	116 5W
Wheeler, Oreg., U.S.A.	**78**	45 45N	123 57W
Wheeler, Tex., U.S.A.	**75**	35 29N	100 15W
Wheeler Peak, Mt.	**78**	38 57N	114 15W
Wheeler, R., Qué., Can.	**36**	57 2N	67 13W
Wheeler, R., Sask., Can.	**55**	57 34N	104 15W
Wheeler Ridge	**81**	35 0N	118 57W
Wheeling	**70**	40 2N	80 41W
Whernside, Mt.	**94**	54 14N	2 24W
Whidbey I.	**63**	48 15N	122 40W
Whidbey Is.	**134**	34 30S	135 3E
Whiskey Gap	**61**	49 0N	113 3W
Whiskey Jack L.	**55**	58 23N	101 55W
Whistler	**73**	30 50N	88 10W
Whitbourne	**37**	47 25N	53 32W
Whitby, Can.	**51**	43 52N	78 56W
Whitby, U.K.	**94**	54 29N	0 37W
Whitcombe, Mt.	**15**	43 12S	171 0E
Whitcombe, P.	**15**	43 12S	171 0E
White B.	**37**	50 0N	56 35W
White Bear	**56**	50 53N	108 13W
White Bear Res.	**37**	48 10N	57 5W
White Bird	**78**	45 46N	116 21W
White Butte	**72**	46 23N	103 25W
White City	**74**	38 50N	96 45W
White Cliffs	**133**	43 26S	171 55E
White Deer	**75**	35 30N	101 8W
White Fox	**56**	53 27N	104 5W
White Hall	**76**	39 25N	90 27W
White Haven	**71**	41 3N	75 47W
White I.	**133**	37 30S	177 13E
White L., Ont., Can.	**47**	45 18N	76 31W
White L., Ont., Can.	**53**	48 47N	85 37W
White L., U.S.A.	**75**	29 45N	92 30W
White Mts.	**80**	37 30N	118 15W
White, Mts.	**71**	44 15N	71 15W
White Nile = Nîl el Abyad, Bahr	**115**	9 30N	31 40E
White Otter L.	**52**	49 5N	91 55W
White Owl L.	**53**	47 10N	82 35W
White Pass, Can.	**67**	59 40N	135 3W
White Pass, U.S.A.	**80**	46 38N	121 24W
White Pigeon	**77**	41 48N	85 39W
White Pine	**52**	46 44N	89 35W
White Plains	**71**	41 2N	73 44W
White, R., Can.	**53**	48 33N	86 16W
White, R., U.S.A.	**77**	38 25N	87 45W
White, R., Ark., U.S.A.	**75**	36 28N	93 55W
White, R., Colo., U.S.A.	**78**	40 8N	108 52W
White, R., Ind., U.S.A.	**72**	39 25N	86 30W
White, R., S.D., U.S.A.	**74**	43 10N	102 52W
White, R., Wash., U.S.A.	**80**	47 12N	122 15W
White River, Can.	**53**	48 35N	85 20W
White River, U.S.A.	**74**	43 48N	100 45W
White River Junc.	**71**	43 38N	72 20W
White Rock	**66**	49 2N	122 48W
White Sulphur Springs, Mont., U.S.A.	**78**	46 35N	111 0W
White Sulphur Springs, W. Va., U.S.A.	**78**	37 50N	80 16W
White Swan	**80**	46 23N	120 44W
Whiteclay L.	**52**	50 53N	88 45W
Whitecourt	**60**	54 10N	115 45W
Whiteface	**75**	33 35N	102 40W
Whiteface R.	**52**	46 58N	92 48W
Whitefield	**71**	44 23N	71 37W
Whitefish, Can.	**46**	46 23N	81 19W
Whitefish, U.S.A.	**78**	48 25N	114 22W
Whitefish Bay	**77**	43 23N	87 54W
Whitefish Falls	**46**	46 7N	81 44W
Whitefish L., Can.	**55**	62 41N	106 48W
Whitefish L., U.S.A.	**52**	46 40N	94 10W
Whitefish Pt.	**53**	46 45N	85 0W
Whitegull, L.	**36**	55 27N	64 17W
Whitehall, Mich., U.S.A.	**72**	43 21N	86 20W
Whitehall, Mont., U.S.A.	**78**	45 52N	112 4W
Whitehall, N.Y., U.S.A.	**71**	43 32N	73 28W
Whitehall, Wis., U.S.A.	**74**	44 20N	91 19W
Whitehaven	**94**	54 33N	3 35W
Whitehorse	**67**	60 43N	135 3W
Whitehorse, Vale of	**95**	51 37N	1 30W
Whiteman	**76**	38 45N	93 40W
Whitemouth	**57**	49 57N	95 58W
Whitemouth L.	**57**	49 15N	95 40W
Whitemouth, R.	**57**	50 7N	96 2W
Whitemud Cr.	**59**	53 31N	113 34W
Whitesail, L.	**54**	53 35N	127 45W
Whitesand, R.	**56**	51 34N	102 56W
Whitesboro, N.Y., U.S.A.	**71**	43 8N	75 20W
Whitesboro, Tex., U.S.A.	**75**	33 40N	96 58W
Whiteshell Prov. Park	**57**	50 0N	95 40W
Whiteside	**76**	39 12N	91 2W
Whiteswan Ls.	**56**	54 5N	105 10W
Whitetail	**56**	48 54N	105 15W
Whitevale	**50**	43 53N	79 9W
Whiteville	**73**	34 20N	78 40W
Whitewater	**77**	42 50N	88 45W
Whitewater Baldy, Mt.	**79**	33 20N	108 44W
Whitewater, Cr.	**56**	49 0N	108 0W
Whitewater L.	**52**	50 50N	89 10W
Whitewood	**57**	50 20N	102 20W
Whithorn	**96**	54 55N	4 25W
Whitianga	**133**	36 47S	175 41E
Whiting	**77**	41 41N	87 29W
Whitman	**71**	42 4N	70 55W
Whitmire	**73**	34 33N	81 40W
Whitney	**47**	45 31N	78 14W
Whitney, Mt.	**80**	36 35N	118 14W
Whitney Pt.	**71**	42 19N	75 59W
Whitstable	**95**	51 21N	1 2E
Whitsunday I.	**135**	20 15S	149 4E
Whittemore	**76**	43 4N	94 26W
Whittier	**67**	60 46N	148 48W
Whittington	**49**	43 59N	80 23W
Whitwell	**73**	35 15N	85 30W
Wholdaia L.	**55**	60 43N	104 20W
Whyalla	**135**	33 2S	137 30E
Whycocomagh	**39**	45 59N	61 7W
Wiarton	**46**	44 40N	81 10W
Wibaux	**74**	47 0N	104 13W
Wichita	**75**	37 40N	97 29W
Wichita Falls	**75**	33 57N	98 30W
Wick	**96**	58 26N	3 5W
Wicked Pt.	**47**	43 52N	77 15W
Wickenburg	**79**	33 58N	112 45W
Wickett	**75**	31 37N	102 58W
Wickham	**41**	45 45N	72 30W
Wickliffe	**70**	41 46N	81 29W
Wicklow	**97**	53 0N	6 2W
Wicklow □	**97**	52 59N	6 25W
Wicklow Hd.	**97**	52 59N	6 3W
Wicklow Mts.	**97**	53 0N	6 30W
Widnes	**94**	53 22N	2 44W
Wieliczka	**107**	50 0N	20 5E
Wielun	**107**	51 15N	18 40E
Wien	**106**	48 12N	16 22E
Wiener Neustadt	**106**	47 49N	16 16E
Wiesbaden	**105**	50 7N	8 17E
Wigan	**94**	53 33N	2 38W
Wiggins, Colo., U.S.A.	**74**	40 16N	104 3W
Wiggins, Miss., U.S.A.	**75**	30 53N	89 9W
Wight, I. of	**95**	50 40N	1 20W
Wigtown	**96**	54 52N	4 27W
Wigtown B.	**96**	54 46N	4 15W
Wikwemikong	**46**	45 48N	81 43W
Wilber	**74**	40 34N	96 59W
Wilberforce, Can.	**47**	45 2N	78 13W
Wilberforce, U.S.A.	**77**	39 43N	83 52W
Wilburton	**75**	34 55N	95 15W
Wilcannia	**136**	31 30S	143 26E
Wilcock Lake	**50**	43 56N	79 25W
Wilcocks L.	**50**	43 57N	79 26W
Wilcox, Can.	**56**	50 6N	104 44W
Wilcox, U.S.A.	**70**	41 34N	78 43W
Wildcat Creek, R.	**77**	40 28N	86 48W
Wildfield	**50**	43 49N	79 44W
Wildgoose L.	**53**	49 44N	87 11W
Wildhay, R.	**60**	53 59N	117 20W
Wildrose, Calif., U.S.A.	**81**	36 14N	117 11W
Wildrose, N. Dak., U.S.A.	**74**	48 36N	103 17W
Wildwood, Can.	**60**	53 37N	115 14W
Wildwood, U.S.A.	**72**	38 59N	74 46W
Wilhelm II Coast	**91**	67 0S	90 0E
Wilhelmina, Mt.	**87**	3 50N	56 30W
Wilhelmshaven	**106**	53 30N	8 9E
Wilkes-Barre	**71**	41 15N	75 52W
Wilkes Land	**91**	69 0S	120 0E
Wilkesboro	**73**	36 10N	81 9W
Wilkie	**56**	52 27N	108 42W
Wilkinsburg	**70**	40 26N	79 50W
Willamina	**78**	45 9N	123 32W
Willandra Billabong Creek	**136**	33 22S	145 52E
Willapa, B.	**78**	46 44N	124 0W
Willapa Hills	**80**	46 35N	123 25W
Willard, N. Mex., U.S.A.	**79**	34 35N	106 1W
Willard, Utah, U.S.A.	**78**	41 28N	112 1W
Willcox	**79**	32 13N	109 53W
Willebroek	**105**	51 4N	4 22E
Willemstad	**85**	12 5N	69 0W
William A. Switzer Prov. Park	**60**	53 30N	117 48W
William L.	**57**	53 54N	99 21W
William, R.	**55**	59 8N	109 19W
Williams, Ariz., U.S.A.	**79**	35 16N	112 11W
Williams, Calif., U.S.A.	**80**	39 9N	122 9W
Williams, Minn., U.S.A.	**52**	48 45N	94 54W
Williams L.	**52**	51 48N	90 45W
Williams Lake	**63**	52 10N	122 10W
Williamsburg, Can.	**49**	43 24N	80 30W
Williamsburg, Ky., U.S.A.	**73**	36 45N	84 10W
Williamsburg, Pa., U.S.A.	**70**	40 27N	78 14W
Williamsburg, Va., U.S.A.	**72**	37 17N	76 44W
Williamsfield	**76**	40 55N	90 1W
Williamson, N.Y., U.S.A.	**70**	43 14N	77 15W
Williamson, W. Va., U.S.A.	**72**	37 46N	82 17W
Williamsport, Ind., U.S.A.	**77**	40 17N	87 17W
Williamsport, Pa., U.S.A.	**70**	41 18N	77 1W
Williamston, U.S.A.	**77**	42 41N	84 17W

Williamston — Xique-Xique

Williamston, S.C., U.S.A. 73 35 50N 77 5W
Williamstown, Austral. 136 37 51S 144 52E
Williamstown, Can. 43 45 9N 74 34W
Williamstown, U.S.A. 77 38 38N 84 34W
Williamstown, Mass., U.S.A. 71 42 41N 73 12W
Williamstown, N.Y., U.S.A. 71 43 25N 75 54W
Williamsville, U.S.A. 76 39 57N 89 33W
Williamsville, Mo., U.S.A. 75 37 0N 90 33W
Willimantic 71 41 45N 72 12W
Willingdon 60 53 50N 112 8W
Willisburg 77 37 49N 85 8W
Williston, Fla, U.S.A. 73 29 25N 82 28W
Williston, N.D., U.S.A. 74 48 10N 103 35W
Williston L. 54 56 0N 124 0W
Willits 78 39 28N 123 17W
Willmar 74 45 5N 95 0W
Willmore Wilderness Park 60 53 45N 119 30W
Willoughby 70 41 38N 81 26W
Willow Bunch 56 49 20N 105 35W
Willow Bunch L. 56 49 27N 105 27W
Willow L. 54 62 10N 119 8W
Willow Lake 74 44 40N 97 40W
Willow River 54 54 6N 122 28W
Willow Springs 75 37 0N 92 0W
Willowbrook 56 51 12N 102 48W
Willowdale 50 43 47N 79 26W
Willowlake, R. 54 62 42N 123 8W
Willowmore 117 33 15S 23 30E
Willows 80 39 30N 122 10W
Wills Pt. 75 32 42N 95 57W
Wilmette 72 42 6N 87 44W
Wilmington, U.S.A. 77 39 27N 83 50W
Wilmington, Del., U.S.A. 72 39 45N 75 32W
Wilmington, Ill., U.S.A. 77 41 19N 88 10W
Wilmington, N.C., U.S.A. 73 34 14N 77 54W
Wilmot 39 46 2N 62 30W
Wilsall 78 45 59N 110 40W
Wilson, N.C., U.S.A. 73 35 44N 77 54W
Wilson, N.Y., U.S.A. 49 43 19N 78 50W
Wilson Creek 62 49 27N 123 43W
Wilson Landing 63 50 0N 119 30W
Wilson, Mt. 79 37 55N 108 3W
Wilsons Beach 39 44 56N 66 56W
Wilson's Promontory 136 38 55S 146 25E
Wilsonvale 44 45 18N 74 11W
Wilsonville 49 42 58N 80 19W
Wilton, U.K. 95 51 5N 1 52W
Wilton, U.S.A. 74 47 12N 100 53W
Wiltshire □ 95 51 20N 2 0W
Wiltz 105 49 57N 5 55E
Wiluna 134 26 36S 120 14E
Wimereux 101 50 45N 1 37E
Wimmera 135 36 30S 142 0E
Wimmera, R. 136 36 8S 141 56E
Winagami L. 60 55 37N 116 44W
Winagami Lake Prov. Park 60 55 37N 116 39W
Winamac 77 41 3N 86 36W
Winch 71 42 26N 71 9W
Winchendon 71 42 40N 72 3W
Winchester, Can. 47 45 6N 75 21W
Winchester, U.K. 95 51 4N 1 19W
Winchester, U.S.A. 76 39 38N 90 27W
Winchester, U.S.A. 77 38 57N 83 40W
Winchester, Conn., U.S.A. 71 41 53N 73 9W
Winchester, Idaho, U.S.A. 78 46 11N 116 32W
Winchester, Ind., U.S.A. 77 40 10N 84 56W
Winchester, Ky., U.S.A. 77 38 0N 84 8W
Winchester, Nev., U.S.A. 81 36 6N 115 10W
Winchester, N.H., U.S.A. 71 42 47N 72 22W
Winchester, Tenn., U.S.A. 73 35 11N 86 8W
Winchester, Va., U.S.A. 72 39 14N 78 8W
Wind Pt. 77 42 47N 87 46W
Wind, R. 78 43 30N 109 30W
Wind River Range, Mts. 78 43 0N 109 30W
Windber 70 40 14N 78 50W
Windemere L. 53 47 58N 83 47W
Winder 73 34 0N 83 40W
Windermere, Can. 61 50 28N 115 59W
Windermere, U.K. 94 54 24N 2 56W
Windermere, L. 94 54 20N 2 57W
Windfall, Can. 60 54 12N 116 13W
Windfall, U.S.A. 77 40 22N 85 57W
Windflower L. 54 62 52N 118 30W
Windhoek 117 22 35S 17 4E
Windigo, R. 41 47 46N 73 19W
Windom 74 43 48N 95 3W
Windorah 135 25 24S 142 36E
Window Rock 79 35 47N 109 4W
Windrush, R. 95 51 48N 1 35W
Windsor, Austral. 136 33 37S 150 50E
Windsor, Newf., Can. 37 48 57N 55 40W
Windsor, N.S., Can. 39 44 59N 64 5W
Windsor, Ont., Can. 46 42 18N 83 0W
Windsor, Qué., Can. 41 45 34N 72 0W
Windsor, U.K. 95 51 28N 0 36W
Windsor, U.S.A. 77 39 26N 88 36W
Windsor, Col., U.S.A. 74 40 33N 104 45W
Windsor, Conn., U.S.A. 71 41 50N 72 40W
Windsor, Mo., U.S.A. 76 38 32N 93 31W
Windsor, N.Y., U.S.A. 71 42 5N 75 37W
Windsor, Vt., U.S.A. 71 43 30N 72 25W
Windsor Heights 37 47 36N 52 49W
Windsor L. 37 47 36N 52 48W
Windthorst 56 50 6N 102 50W
Windward Is. 85 13 0N 63 0W
Windward Passage 85 20 0N 74 0W
Windy L., N.W.T., Can. 55 60 20N 100 2W
Windy L., Sask., Can. 56 54 22N 102 35W
Winefred L. 60 55 30N 110 30W
Winfield, Can. 61 52 58N 114 26W
Winfield, Ill., U.S.A. 76 41 5N 91 30W
Winfield, Kans., U.S.A. 75 37 15N 97 0W
Winfield, Mo., U.S.A. 76 39 0N 90 44W
Wingen Mt. 136 31 50S 150 58E
Wingham, Austral. 136 31 48S 152 22E
Wingham, Can. 46 43 55N 81 20W
Winifred 78 47 30N 109 28W
Winisk 34 55 20N 85 15W
Winisk L. 34 52 55N 87 22W
Winisk, R. 34 55 17N 85 5W
Wink 75 31 49N 103 9W
Winkler 57 49 10N 97 56W
Winlock 80 46 29N 122 56W
Winnebago, Ill., U.S.A. 76 42 15N 89 18W
Winnebago, Minn., U.S.A. 74 43 43N 94 8W
Winnebago L. 72 44 0N 88 20W
Winnemucca 78 41 0N 117 45W
Winnemucca, L. 78 40 25N 19 21W
Winner 74 43 23N 99 52W
Winnetka 72 42 8N 87 46W
Winnett 78 47 2N 108 28W
Winnfield 75 31 57N 92 38W
Winnibigoshish L. 52 47 25N 94 12W
Winnipeg 58 49 54N 97 9W
Winnipeg Beach 57 50 30N 96 58W
Winnipeg International Airport 58 49 55N 97 15W
Winnipeg, L. 57 52 0N 97 0W
Winnipeg, R. 57 50 38N 96 19W
Winnipegosis 57 51 39N 99 55W
Winnipegosis L. 57 52 30N 100 0W
Winnsboro, La., U.S.A. 75 32 10N 91 41W
Winnsboro, S.C., U.S.A. 73 34 23N 81 5W
Winnsboro, Tex., U.S.A. 74 32 56N 95 15W
Winokapau, L. 36 53 15N 62 50W
Winona, Can. 49 43 12N 79 39W
Winona, Miss., U.S.A. 75 33 30N 89 42W
Winona, Wis., U.S.A. 52 46 53N 88 55W
Winona, Wis., U.S.A. 74 44 2N 91 45W
Winooski 71 44 31N 73 11W
Winschoten 105 53 9N 7 3E
Winslow, U.S.A. 77 38 23N 87 13W
Winslow, Ariz., U.S.A. 79 35 2N 110 41W
Winslow, Wash., U.S.A. 80 47 37N 122 31W
Winstead 71 41 55N 73 5W
Winston-Salem 73 36 7N 80 15W
Winter Garden 73 28 33N 81 35W
Winter Harbour 62 50 31N 128 2W
Winter Haven 73 28 0N 81 42W
Winter Park 73 28 34N 81 19W
Winterbourne 49 43 33N 80 28W
Winterhaven 81 32 47N 114 39W
Wintering L. 53 49 26N 87 16W
Winters, Calif., U.S.A. 80 38 32N 121 58W
Winters, Tex., U.S.A. 75 31 58N 99 58W
Winterset 76 41 18N 94 0W
Wintersville 70 40 23N 80 38W
Winterswijk 105 51 58N 6 43E
Winterthur 106 47 30N 8 44E
Winterton 37 47 58N 53 20W
Winthrop, Minn., U.S.A. 74 44 31N 94 25W
Winthrop, Wash., U.S.A. 63 48 27N 120 6W
Winton, Austral. 135 22 24S 143 3E
Winton, N.Z. 133 46 8S 168 20E
Winton, N.C., U.S.A. 73 36 25N 76 58W
Winton, Pa., U.S.A. 71 41 27N 75 33W
Wirral 94 53 25N 3 0W
Wisbech 94 52 39N 0 10E
Wisconsin □ 74 44 30N 90 0W
Wisconsin Dells 74 43 38N 89 45W
Wisconsin, R. 74 45 25N 89 45W
Wisconsin Rapids 74 44 25N 89 50W
Wisdom 67 45 36N 113 1W
Wiserman 67 67 25N 150 15W
Wiseton 56 51 19N 107 39W
Wishart 56 51 33N 103 59W
Wishaw 96 55 46N 3 55W
Wishek 74 46 20N 99 35W
Wisła, R. 107 53 38N 18 47E
Wismar 106 53 53N 11 23E
Wisner 74 42 0N 96 46W
Wissant 101 50 52N 1 40E
Wissembourg 101 48 57N 7 57E
Wistaria 62 53 52N 126 22W
Witbank 117 25 51S 29 14E
Witham, R. 94 53 3N 0 8W
Withernsea 94 53 43N 0 2W
Withrow 61 52 23N 114 30W
Witney 95 51 47N 1 29W
Witten 105 51 26N 7 19E
Wittenberg 106 51 51N 12 39E
Wittenberge 106 53 0N 11 44E
Wittenoom 134 22 15S 118 20E
Wkra, R. 107 52 45N 20 30E
Wlen 78 51 0N 15 39E
Wlingi 127 8 5S 112 25E
Woburn, Can. 50 43 46N 79 13W
Woburn, U.S.A. 71 42 31N 71 7W
Wodonga 136 36 5S 146 50E
Woerth 101 48 57N 7 45E
Woëvre 101 49 15N 5 45E
Wokam, I. 127 5 45S 134 28E
Woking 54 55 35N 118 50W
Wolcottville 77 41 32N 85 22W
Wolf Bay 38 50 16N 60 8W
Wolf Creek 78 47 1N 112 2W
Wolf L. 54 60 24N 131 40W
Wolf Point 74 48 6N 105 40W
Wolf, R. 54 60 17N 132 33W
Wolfe I. 47 44 7N 76 20W
Wolfenden 54 52 0N 119 25W
Wolfville 39 45 5N 64 22W
Wolin 106 53 40N 14 37E
Wollaston, Islas 90 55 40S 67 30W
Wollaston L. 55 58 7N 103 10W
Wollaston Pen. 64 69 30N 115 0W
Wollondilly, R. 136 34 12S 150 18E
Wollongong 136 34 25S 150 54E
Wolseley 56 50 25N 103 15W
Wolstenholme, C. 36 62 35N 77 30W
Wolstenholme Fjord 65 76 0N 70 0W
Wolvega 105 52 52N 6 0E
Wolverhampton 95 52 35N 2 6W
Wolverine 46 45 16N 84 36W
Won Wron 136 38 23S 146 45E
Wondai 135 26 20S 151 49E
Wŏnju 130 37 22N 127 58E
Wonosari 127 7 38S 110 36E
Wŏnsan 130 39 11N 127 27E
Wonthaggi 136 38 37S 145 37E
Wood Buffalo Nat. Park 54 59 0N 113 41W
Wood L. 55 55 17N 103 17W
Wood Lake 74 42 38N 100 14W
Wood Mt. 55 49 14N 106 30W
Wood, R. 56 50 8N 106 13W
Wood River 76 38 52N 90 5W
Woodbridge 50 43 47N 79 36W
Woodburn 49 43 8N 79 45W
Woodchopper 67 65 25N 143 30W
Woodend 136 37 20N 144 33E
Woodfibre 63 49 41N 123 15W
Woodfords 80 38 47N 119 50W
Woodhill 50 43 45N 79 41W
Woodlake 80 36 25N 119 6W
Woodland 80 38 40N 121 50W
Woodlands 57 50 12N 97 40W
Woodpecker 63 53 30N 122 40W
Woodridge 57 49 20N 96 9W
Woodroffe, Mt. 134 26 20S 131 45E
Woodruff, Ariz., U.S.A. 79 34 51N 110 1W
Woodruff, Utah, U.S.A. 78 41 30N 111 4W
Woods, L., Austral. 134 17 50S 133 30E
Woods, L., Can. 36 54 30N 65 13W
Woods, L. of the 52 49 15N 94 45W
Woodside, Austral. 136 38 31S 146 52E
Woodside, Can. 39 44 39N 63 33W
Woodstock, N.B., Can. 39 46 11N 67 37W
Woodstock, Ont., Can. 46 43 10N 80 45W
Woodstock, U.K. 95 51 51N 1 20W
Woodstock, Ill., U.S.A. 77 42 17N 88 30W
Woodstock, Vt., U.S.A. 71 43 37N 72 31W
Woodsville 71 44 10N 72 0W
Woodville, N.Z. 133 40 20S 175 53E
Woodville, U.S.A. 77 41 27N 83 22W
Woodville, Tex., U.S.A. 75 30 45N 94 25W
Woodward 75 36 24N 99 28W
Woody 81 35 42N 118 50W
Woody Point 37 49 30N 57 55W
Woombye 136 26 40S 152 55E
Woomera 135 31 11S 136 47E
Woonona 136 34 21S 150 54E
Woonsocket 71 42 0N 71 30W
Woonsockett 74 44 5N 98 15W
Wooramel, R. 134 25 30S 114 30E
Wooster 70 40 38N 81 55W
Worcester, S. Afr. 117 33 39S 19 27E
Worcester, U.K. 95 52 12N 2 12W
Worcester, Mass., U.S.A. 71 42 14N 71 49W
Worcester, N.Y., U.S.A. 71 42 35N 74 45W
Worden 76 38 56N 89 50W
Workington 94 54 39N 3 34W
Worksop 94 53 19N 1 9W
Workum 105 52 59N 5 26E
Worland 78 44 0N 107 59W
Wormerveer 105 52 30N 4 46E
Wormhoudt 101 50 52N 2 28E
Worms 106 49 37N 8 21E
Worsley 60 56 31N 119 8W
Wortham 75 31 48N 96 27W
Worthing 95 50 49N 0 21W
Worthington, Ind., U.S.A. 77 39 7N 86 59W
Worthington, Minn., U.S.A. 74 43 35N 95 30W
Worthington, Ohio, U.S.A. 77 40 5N 83 1W
Wosi 127 0 15S 128 0E
Woss Camp 62 50 13N 126 35W
Woss L. 62 50 7N 126 36W
Wota (Shoa Ghimirra) 115 7 4N 35 51E
Wottonville 41 45 44N 71 48W
Wowoni, I. 127 4 5S 123 5E
Wrangell 67 56 30N 132 25W
Wrangell, I. 54 56 20N 132 10W
Wrangell Mts. 67 61 40N 143 30W
Wrath, C. 96 58 38N 5 0W
Wray 74 40 8N 102 18W
Wrekin, The, Mt. 94 52 41N 2 35W
Wrens 73 33 13N 82 23W
Wrexham 94 53 5N 3 0W
Wright, Can. 63 51 52N 121 40W
Wright, Phil. 127 11 42N 125 2E
Wright, Mt. 35 52 40N 67 25W
Wrightson, Mt. 79 31 49N 110 56W
Wrightwood 81 34 21N 117 38W
Wrigley 64 63 16N 123 27W
Wrigley Corners 49 43 17N 80 22W
Wrocław 106 51 5N 17 5E
Wrottesley, C. 64 74 32N 121 33W
Wroxton 57 51 14N 101 53W
Września 107 52 21N 17 36E
Wu K. 131 27 30N 107 45E
Wuchai 130 39 10N 111 36E
Wuchan 131 28 30N 108 10E
Wuchang 130 44 51N 127 10E
Wuchen 130 41 10N 108 32E
Wuchow 131 23 26N 111 19E
Wuchung 130 38 4N 106 12E
Wuhan 131 30 35N 114 15E
Wuhu 131 31 18N 118 20E
Wukang, Chekiang, China 131 30 35N 119 50E
Wukang, Hunan, China 131 26 50N 110 15E
Wuki (Taning) 131 31 27N 109 46E
Wukung Shan, mts. 131 27 20N 114 0E
Wuliaru, I. 127 7 10S 131 0E
Wulumuchi 129 43 40N 87 50E
Wuning 131 29 16N 115 0E
Wunnummin L. 34 52 55N 89 10W
Wuntho 125 23 55N 95 45E
Wuping 131 25 5N 116 20E
Wuppertal 105 51 15N 7 8E
Würzburg 106 49 46N 9 55E
Wushan 131 31 3N 109 57E
Wusih 131 31 30N 120 30E
Wusu 129 44 27N 84 37E
Wutai 130 41 16N 113 59E
Wuting Ho 130 37 8N 110 31E
Wutu 131 33 27N 104 37E
Wutunghliao 129 29 25N 104 0E
Wuwei 129 37 55N 102 48E
Wuyi, China 130 37 54N 116 0E
Wuyi, China 131 28 45N 119 56E
Wuyi Shan 131 26 40N 116 30E
Wuying 130 48 10N 129 20E
Wuyuan 130 41 15N 108 30E
Wuyun 129 46 16N 129 37E
Wyalong 136 33 54S 147 16E
Wyalusing 71 41 40N 76 16W
Wyandotte 77 42 14N 83 13W
Wyandra 135 27 12S 145 56E
Wyangala Res. 136 33 54S 149 0E
Wycheproof 136 36 0N 143 17E
Wye, R. 95 52 0N 2 36W
Wymark 56 50 7N 107 44W
Wymlet 136 34 52S 142 10E
Wymondham, Leicester, U.K. 95 52 45N 0 42W
Wymondham, Norfolk, U.K. 95 52 34N 1 7E
Wymore 74 40 10N 96 40W
Wynadotte 46 42 11N 83 14W
Wyndham, Austral. 134 15 33S 128 3E
Wyndham, N.Z. 133 46 20S 168 51E
Wyndham Hills 49 43 10N 80 17W
Wyniatt B. 64 72 45N 110 30W
Wynndel 61 49 11N 116 33W
Wynne 75 35 15N 90 50W
Wynyard 56 51 45N 104 10W
Wyoming, Can. 46 42 57N 82 7W
Wyoming, U.S.A. 77 42 53N 85 42W
Wyoming, Ill., U.S.A. 76 41 4N 89 47W
Wyoming, Iowa, U.S.A. 76 42 4N 91 3W
Wyoming, N.Y., U.S.A. 70 42 46N 78 4W
Wyoming □ 68 42 48N 109 0W
Wyong 136 33 14S 151 24E
Wytheville 72 37 0N 81 3W

X

Xanthi 109 41 10N 24 58E
Xapuri 86 10 35S 68 35W
Xavantina 89 21 15S 52 48W
Xenia, Ill., U.S.A. 77 38 38N 88 38W
Xenia, Ohio, U.S.A. 77 39 42N 83 57W
Xieng Khouang 128 19 17N 103 25E
Xinavane 117 25 2S 32 47E
Xingu, R. 87 2 25S 52 35W
Xique-Xique 87 10 50S 42 40W

Yaan Zeeland □

Y

Yaan 129 30 0N 102 59 E
Yaapeet 136 35 45 S 142 3 E
Yablonovyy Khrebet 121 53 0N 114 0 E
Yabrīn 122 23 7N 48 52 E
Yacuiba 88 22 0 S 63 25W
Yadgir 124 16 45N 77 5 E
Yadkin, R. 73 36 15N 81 0W
Yahatahama 132 33 25N 132 40 E
Yahk 61 49 6N 116 10W
Yahuma 116 1 0N 22 5 E
Yaicheng 131 18 14N 109 7 E
Yakataga 67 60 5N 142 32W
Yakima 78 46 42N 120 30W
Yakima, R. 78 47 0N 120 30W
Yakoshih 129 49 13N 120 35 E
Yakut A.S.S.R. □ 121 62 0N 130 0 E
Yakutat 67 59 50N 139 44W
Yakutsk 121 62 5N 129 40 E
Yala 128 6 33N 101 18 E
Yalabusha, R. 75 33 53N 89 50W
Yale, Can. 80 49 34N 121 25W
Yale, U.S.A. 46 43 9N 82 47W
Yalgoo 134 28 16 S 116 39 E
Yalinga 116 6 20N 23 10 E
Yalkubul, Punta 83 21 32N 88 37W
Yallourn 136 38 10 S 146 18 E
Yalu K. 130 41 30N 126 30 E
Yalung K. 129 32 0N 100 0 E
Yalutorovsk 120 56 30N 65 40 E
Yam Kinneret (L. Tiberias) 115 32 49N 35 36 E
Yamagata 132 38 15N 140 15 E
Yamagata-ken □ 132 38 30N 140 0 E
Yamaguchi 132 34 10N 131 32 E
Yamaguchi-ken □ 132 34 20N 131 40 E
Yamal, Poluostrov 120 71 0N 70 0 E
Yamana 122 24 5N 47 30 E
Yamanashi-ken □ 132 35 40N 138 40 E
Yamantau 120 54 20N 57 40 E
Yamantau, Gora 120 54 15N 58 6 E
Yamaska 41 46 0N 72 55W
Yamaska □ 43 46 50N 72 50W
Yamaska, Mt. 43 45 27N 72 52W
Yamaska, R. 45 45 17N 72 55W
Yambol 109 42 30N 26 36 E
Yamdena 127 7 45 S 131 20 E
Yamdrok Tso 129 29 0N 90 40 E
Yamethin 125 20 29N 96 18 E
Yamhsien 131 21 45N 108 31 E
Yamma-Yamma L. 135 26 16 S 141 20 E
Yampa, R. 78 40 37N 108 0W
Yampi Sd. 134 16 8 S 123 38 E
Yamuna (Jumna), R. 125 27 0N 78 30 E
Yana, R. 121 69 0N 134 0 E
Yanac 136 36 8 S 141 25 E
Yanaul 120 56 25N 55 0 E
Yanbu 'al Bahr 122 24 0N 38 5 E
Yanco 136 34 38 S 146 27 E
Yandoon 125 17 0N 95 40 E
Yangambi 116 0 47N 24 20 E
Yangchow 131 32 25N 119 25 E
Yangchuan 130 38 0N 113 29 E
Yangi-Yer 120 40 17N 68 48 E
Yangkao 130 40 20N 113 40 E
Yangshui (Hinghwa) 131 29 53N 115 3 E
Yangso 131 24 36N 110 32 E
Yangtsun 130 39 29N 117 4 E
Yangtze Kiang 131 31 40N 122 0 E
Yanhee Res. 128 17 30N 98 45 E
Yankton 74 42 55N 97 25W
Yanping 131 22 25N 112 0 E
Yao Shan 131 24 0N 110 0 E
Yaomen 130 44 31N 125 8 E
Yaoundé 116 3 50N 11 35 E
Yap Is. 127 9 30N 138 10 E
Yapen 127 1 50 S 136 0 E
Yapen, Selat 127 1 20 S 136 10 E
Yapero 127 4 59 S 137 11 E
Yapo, R. 86 0 30 S 77 0W
Yaqui, R. 82 28 28N 109 30W
Yar-Sale 120 66 50N 70 50 E
Yaracuy □ 86 10 20N 68 45W
Yaraka 135 24 53 S 144 3 E
Yare, R. 95 52 36N 1 28 E
Yarensk 120 61 10N 49 8 E
Yarí, R. 86 1 0N 73 40W
Yarkand (Soche) 129 38 24N 77 20 E
Yarker 47 44 23N 76 46W
Yarkhun, R. 124 36 30N 72 45 E
Yarmouth 39 43 50N 66 7W
Yaroslavl 120 57 35N 39 55 E
Yarra, R. 136 37 50 S 144 53 E
Yarrawonga 136 36 0 S 146 0 E
Yarrow 63 49 5N 122 2W
Yartsevo 121 60 20N 90 0 E
Yarumal 86 6 58N 75 24W
Yasawa Group 133 17 00 S 177 23 E
Yasinski, L. 36 53 16N 77 35W
Yasothon 128 15 50N 104 10 E
Yass 136 34 49 S 148 54 E
Yass, Res. 136 34 50 S 149 0 E
Yates Center 75 37 53N 95 45W
Yathkyed L. 55 62 40N 98 0W
Yatsushiro 132 32 30N 130 40 E
Yauyos 86 12 10 S 75 50W
Yavari R. 86 4 50 S 72 0W
Yayama-rettō 131 24 30N 123 40 E
Yazd (Yezd) 123 31 55N 54 27 E
Yazdan 123 33 30N 60 50 E
Yazoo City 75 32 48N 90 28W
Yazoo, R. 75 32 35N 90 50W
Yding Skovhøj 111 55 59N 9 46 E
Yebyu 125 14 15N 98 13 E
Yecla 104 38 35N 1 5W
Yécora 82 28 20N 108 58W
Yegros 88 26 20 S 56 25W
Yehsien 130 37 12N 119 58 E
Yehuda, Midbar 115 31 35N 34 57 E
Yelanskoye 121 61 25N 128 0 E
Yelets 120 52 40N 38 30 E
Yell, I. 96 60 35N 1 5W
Yell Sd. 96 60 33N 1 15W
Yellow Creek 56 52 45N 105 15W
Yellow Grass 56 49 48N 104 10W
Yellow Mt. 136 32 31 S 146 52 E
Yellow River = Hwang Ho 131 38 0N 117 20 E
Yellow Sea 130 35 0N 123 0 E
Yellowhead P. 63 52 53N 118 25W
Yellowknife 54 62 27N 114 21W
Yellowknife, R. 54 62 31N 114 19W
Yellowstone L. 78 44 30N 110 20W
Yellowstone National Park 78 44 35N 110 0W
Yellowstone, R. 74 46 35N 105 45W
Yemen ■ 115 15 0N 44 0 E
Yemen, South ■ 115 15 0N 48 0 E
Yenangyaung 125 20 30N 95 0 E
Yenchang 130 36 44N 110 2 E
Yencheng, Honan, China 131 33 43N 114 10 E
Yencheng, Kiangsu, China 131 33 22N 120 12 E
Yenchwan 130 37 0N 110 5 E
Yenda 136 34 13 S 146 14 E
Yengchun 131 22 10N 111 27 E
Yenisey, R. 120 68 0N 86 30 E
Yeniseysk 121 58 39N 92 4 E
Yeniseyskiy Zaliv 120 72 20N 81 0 E
Yenki, Kirin, China 130 43 12N 129 30 E
Yenki, Sinkiang, China 129 42 12N 86 30 E
Yenking 130 40 30N 116 0 E
Yenne 103 45 43N 5 44 E
Yenshih 131 34 42N 112 50 E
Yentai 130 37 30N 121 22 E
Yenyuka 121 58 20N 121 30 E
Yeo, L. 134 28 0 S 124 30 E
Yeo, R. 95 51 1N 2 46W
Yeola 124 20 0N 74 30 E
Yeotmal 124 20 20N 78 15 E
Yeovil 95 50 57N 2 38W
Yeppoon 135 23 5 S 150 47 E
Yerbent 120 39 30N 58 50 E
Yerbogachen 121 61 16N 108 0 E
Yerevan 120 40 10N 44 20 E
Yerington 80 38 59N 119 10W
Yermakovo 121 52 35N 126 20 E
Yermo 81 34 58N 116 50W
Yerofey Pavlovich 121 54 0N 122 0 E
Yershov 120 51 15N 48 27 E
Yerville 100 49 40N 0 53 E
Yes Tor, Mt. 95 50 41N 3 59W
Yeso 75 34 29N 104 37W
Yeu, I. d' 100 46 42N 2 20W
Yeungchun 131 22 15N 111 40 E
Yeungkong 131 21 55N 112 0 E
Yeungshan 131 24 27N 112 15 E
Yeysk Staro 120 46 40N 38 12 E
Yhati 88 25 45 S 56 35W
Yhú 89 25 0 S 56 0W
Yi, R. 88 33 7 S 57 8W
Yiannitsa 109 40 46N 22 24 E
Yihsien 131 34 50N 117 50 E
Yilan 131 24 47N 121 44 E
Yin Shan, mts. 130 41 0N 112 0 E
Yincheng 131 31 0N 113 40 E
Yinchwan 130 38 30N 106 20 E
Yingcheng 131 31 0N 113 44 E
Yingchow 130 39 45N 113 30 E
Yingkiang 131 28 10N 108 40 E
Yingkow 130 40 43N 122 9 E
Yingshan 131 30 50N 115 45 E
Yingtak 131 24 10N 113 5 E
Yingtan 131 28 12N 117 0 E
Yinmabin 125 22 10N 94 55 E
Yipang 128 22 15N 101 26 E
Yíthion 109 36 46N 22 34 E
Yitu 130 36 40N 118 25 E
Yixian 131 41 32N 121 15 E
Yiyang 131 28 45N 112 16 E
Ylitornio 110 66 19N 23 39 E
Ylivieska 110 64 4N 24 28 E
Ynykchanskiy 121 60 15N 137 43 E
Yoakum 75 29 20N 97 10W
Yog Pt. 127 13 55N 124 20 E
Yogyakarta 127 7 49 S 110 22 E
Yoho Nat. Park 63 51 25N 116 30W
Yojoa, L. de 84 14 53N 88 0W
Yokadouma 116 3 35N 14 50 E
Yōkaichi 132 35 6N 136 12 E
Yokkaichi 132 35 0N 136 30 E
Yokohama 132 35 27N 139 39 E
Yokosuka 132 35 20N 139 40 E
Yola 114 9 10N 12 29 E
Yolaina, Cordillera de 84 11 30N 84 0W
Yolgali 136 34 20 S 146 7 E
Yom Mae Nam 128 15 15N 100 20 E
Yonago 132 35 25N 133 19 E
Yonaguni 131 24 28N 122 59 E
Yong Peng 128 2 0N 103 3 E
Yŏngchŏn 130 35 55N 128 55 E
Yŏngwŏl 130 37 18N 128 20 E
Yonker 55 52 40N 109 40W
Yonkers 71 40 57N 73 51W
Yonne □ 101 47 50N 3 40 E
Yonne, R. 101 48 23N 2 58 E
York, Austral. 134 31 52 S 116 47 E
York, Ont., Can. 50 43 1N 79 53W
York, Ont., Can. 50 43 42N 79 27W
York, U.K. 94 53 58N 1 7W
York, Ala., U.S.A. 73 32 30N 88 18W
York, Nebr., U.S.A. 74 40 55N 97 35W
York, Pa., U.S.A. 72 39 57N 76 43W
York □ 49 43 55N 79 30W
York, C., Austral. 135 10 42 S 142 31 E
York, C., Can. 65 76 30N 68 0W
York Factory 55 57 0N 92 18W
York, Kap 17 75 55N 66 25W
York Mills 50 43 45N 79 25W
York, R. 38 48 49N 64 34W
York Sd. 134 14 50 S 125 5 E
York, Vale of 98 54 15N 1 25W
Yorke Pen. 135 34 50 S 137 40 E
Yorkshire, reg. 94 54 54N 1 0W
Yorkshire Wolds 94 54 0N 0 30W
Yorkton 57 51 11N 102 28W
Yorktown 75 29 0N 97 29W
Yorkville, U.S.A. 77 41 38N 88 27W
Yorkville, Calif., U.S.A. 80 38 52N 123 13W
Yoro 84 15 9N 87 7W
Yosemite National Park 80 38 0N 119 30W
Yosemite Village 80 37 45N 119 35W
Yŏsu 131 34 47N 127 45 E
Yotsing 131 28 10N 120 55 E
Youbou 62 48 53N 124 13W
Youghal 97 51 58N 7 51W
Youghal B. 97 51 55N 7 50W
Youghal Har. 97 51 55N 7 50W
Young, Austral. 136 34 19 S 148 18 E
Young, Can. 56 51 47N 105 45W
Young, Uruguay 88 32 44 S 57 36W
Young, U.S.A. 79 34 9N 110 56W
Youngstown, Can. 61 51 35N 111 10W
Youngstown, N.Y., U.S.A. 49 43 16N 79 2W
Youngstown, Ohio, U.S.A. 70 41 7N 80 41W
Youngsville 70 41 51N 79 21W
Yoyang 131 29 27N 113 10 E
Yozgat 122 39 51N 34 47 E
Ypané, R. 88 23 29 S 57 19W
Yport 100 49 45N 0 15 E
Ypsilanti 77 42 18N 83 40W
Yreka 78 41 44N 122 40W
Ysleta 79 31 45N 106 24W
Yssingeaux 103 45 9N 4 8 E
Ystad 111 55 26N 13 50 E
Ythan, R. 96 57 26N 2 12W
Ytyk-Kel 121 62 20N 133 28 E
Yu Shan, Mt. 131 23 30N 121 0 E
Yuan Kiang 131 28 40N 110 30 E
Yuanling 131 28 30N 110 5 E
Yuanyang 129 23 10N 102 58 E
Yuba City 80 39 12N 121 37W
Yuba, R. 80 39 8N 121 36W
Yūbetsu 132 43 13N 144 5 E
Yucatán □ 83 21 30N 86 30W
Yucatán Basin 12 20 0N 84 0W
Yucatán Channel 84 22 0N 86 30W
Yucca 81 34 56N 114 6W
Yucca Valley 81 34 8N 116 30W
Yucheng 130 36 55N 116 40 E
Yudino 120 55 10N 67 55 E
Yugoslavia ■ 109 44 0N 20 0 E
Yühsien 130 34 10N 113 30 E
Yuhsien 131 39 45N 114 33 E
Yuhwan 131 28 1N 121 12 E
Yukan 131 28 43N 116 35 E
Yukikow 131 31 29N 118 17 E
Yukon, R. 67 65 30N 150 0W
Yukon Territory □ 64 63 0N 135 0W
Yukti 121 63 20N 105 0 E
Yule, R. 134 20 24 S 118 12 E
Yülin 130 18 10N 109 31 E
Yülin (Watlam) 131 22 30N 110 50 E
Yuma, Ariz., U.S.A. 81 32 45N 114 37W
Yuma, Colo., U.S.A. 74 40 10N 102 43W
Yuma, B. de 85 18 20N 68 35W
Yumbo 86 3 35N 76 28W
Yumen 129 41 13N 96 55 E
Yun Ho 129 35 0N 117 0 E
Yün Ho, R. 131 33 15N 119 45 E
Yunaska I. 67 52 40N 170 40W
Yundamindra 136 29 4 S 122 3 E
Yungan 131 25 50N 117 25 E
Yungas 86 17 0 S 66 0W
Yungay 88 37 10 S 72 5W
Yungchun 131 25 20N 118 15 E
Yungfu 131 24 59N 109 59 E
Yunghing 131 26 12N 113 3 E
Yunghwo 130 36 58N 110 56 E
Yungshun 131 29 3N 109 50 E
Yungsin 131 26 55N 114 10 E
Yungtsi 131 34 50N 110 25 E
Yungyun 131 24 31N 113 28 E
Yunhsien 131 32 30N 111 0 E
Yunhwo 131 28 0N 119 32 E
Yunlin 131 23 45N 120 30 E
Yunnan □ 129 25 0N 102 30 E
Yunsiao 131 24 0N 117 20 E
Yur 121 59 52N 137 49 E
Yurga 120 55 42N 84 51 E
Yuribei 120 71 20N 76 30 E
Yurimaguas 86 5 55 S 76 0W
Yuscarán 84 13 58N 86 51W
Yushu = Fyekundo 129 33 6N 96 48 E
Yütu 131 26 0N 115 24 E
Yutze 130 37 45N 112 45 E
Yuyang 131 28 44N 108 46 E
Yuyao 131 30 0N 121 20 E
Yuyu 130 40 20N 112 30 E
Yuzhno-Sakhalinsk 121 47 5N 142 5 E
Yvelines □ 101 48 40N 1 45 E
Yvetot 100 49 37N 0 44 E

Z

Zaandam 105 52 26N 4 49 E
Zabaykalskiy 121 49 40N 117 10 E
Zābol 123 31 0N 61 25 E
Zābolī 123 27 10N 61 35 E
Zabrze 107 50 18N 18 46 E
Zacapa 84 14 59N 89 31W
Zacapu 82 19 50N 101 43W
Zacatecas 82 22 49N 102 34W
Zacatecas □ 82 23 30N 103 0W
Zacatecolua 84 13 29N 88 51W
Zacaultipán 83 20 39N 98 36W
Zacoalco 82 20 10N 103 40W
Zadar 108 44 8N 15 8 E
Zadetkyi Kyun 128 10 0N 98 25 E
Zafra 104 38 26N 6 30W
Zagan 106 51 39N 15 22 E
Zagreb 108 45 50N 16 0 E
Zāgros, Kudhā-ye 123 33 45N 47 0 E
Zāhedān 123 29 30N 60 50 E
Zahlah 115 33 52N 35 50 E
Zaïre, R. 116 1 30N 28 0 E
Zaïre, Rep. of ■ 116 3 0 S 23 0 E
Zaječar 109 43 53N 22 18 E
Zakamensk 121 50 23N 103 17 E
Zakhū 122 37 10N 42 50 E
Zákinthos 109 37 47N 20 54 E
Zákinthos, I. 109 37 45N 27 45 E
Zambèze, R. 117 18 46 S 36 16 E
Zambezi, R. 117 18 46 S 36 16 E
Zambia ■ 117 15 0 S 28 0 E
Zamboanga 127 6 59N 122 3 E
Zambrano 86 9 45N 74 49W
Zamora, Mexico 82 20 0N 102 21W
Zamora, Spain 104 41 30N 5 45W
Zamość 107 50 50N 23 22 E
Zamuro, Sierra del 86 4 0N 62 30W
Zanaga 116 2 48 S 13 48 E
Zandvoort 105 52 22N 4 32 E
Zanesville 70 39 56N 82 2W
Zanjan 122 36 40N 48 35 E
Zanthus 134 31 2 S 123 34 E
Zanzibar 116 6 12 S 39 12 E
Zanzibar I. 116 6 12 S 39 12 E
Zaouiet El Kahla 114 27 10N 6 40 E
Zaouiet Reggane 114 26 32N 0 3 E
Zapadnaya Dvina 120 56 15N 32 3 E
Západné Beskydy 107 49 30N 19 0 E
Zapala 90 39 0 S 70 5W
Zapaleri, Cerro 88 22 49 S 67 11W
Zapata 75 26 56N 99 17W
Zaporozhye 120 47 50N 35 10 E
Zara 122 39 58N 37 43 E
Zaragoza, Colomb. 86 7 30N 74 52W
Zaragoza, Coahuila, Mexico 82 28 30N 101 0W
Zaragoza, Nuevo León, Mexico 83 24 0N 99 36W
Zaragoza □ 104 41 35N 1 0W
Zarand 123 30 46N 56 34 E
Zarate 88 34 7 S 59 0W
Zaraza 86 9 21N 65 19W
Zarembo I. 54 56 20N 132 50W
Zaria 114 11 0N 7 40 E
Zaruma 86 3 40 S 79 30W
Zary 106 51 37N 15 10 E
Zarzal 86 4 24N 76 4W
Zashiversk 121 67 25N 142 40 E
Zaskar Mountains 124 33 15N 77 30 E
Zavareh 123 33 35N 52 28 E
Zavitinsk 121 50 10N 129 20 E
Zavodoski, I. 91 56 0 S 27 45W
Zawiercie 107 50 30N 19 13 E
Zāyandeh, R. 123 32 35N 32 0 E
Zayarsk 121 56 20N 102 55 E
Zaysan 120 47 28N 84 52 E
Zaysan, Oz. 120 48 0N 83 0 E
Zdunska Wola 107 51 37N 18 59 E
Zealand Station 39 46 3N 66 56W
Zealandia 56 51 37N 107 45W
Zearing 76 42 10N 93 20W
Zeballos 62 49 59N 126 50W
Zeebrugge 105 51 19N 3 12 E
Zeeland 77 42 49N 86 1W
Zeeland □ 105 51 30N 3 50 E

Geographical Terms

This is a list of some of the geographical words from foreign languages which are found in the place names on the maps and in the index. Each is followed by the language and the English meaning.

Afr. afrikaans
Alb. albanian
Amh. amharic
Ar. arabic
Ber. berber
Bulg. bulgarian
Bur. burmese

Chin. chinese
Cz. czechoslovakian
Dan. danish
Dut. dutch
Fin. finnish
Flem. flemish
Fr. french

Gae. gaelic
Ger. german
Gr. greek
Heb. hebrew
Hin. hindi
I.-C. indo-chinese
Ice. icelandic

It. italian
Jap. japanese
Kor. korean
Lapp. lappish
Lith. lithuanian
Mal. malay
Mong. mongolian

Nor. norwegian
Pash. pashto
Pers. persian
Pol. polish
Port. portuguese
Rum. rumanian
Russ. russian

Ser.-Cr. serbo-croat
Siam. siamese
Sin. sinhalese
Som. somali
Span. spanish
Swed. swedish
Tib. tibetan
Turk. turkish

A. (Ain) *Ar.* spring
–á *Ice.* river
a *Dan., Nor., Swed.* stream
–abad *Pers., Russ.* town
Abyad *Ar.* white
Ad. (Adrar) *Ar., Ber.* mountain
Ada, Adasi *Tur.* island
Addis *Amh.* new
Adrar *Ar., Ber.* mountain
Ain *Ar.* spring
Äkra *Gr.* cape
Akrotíri *Gr.* cape
Alb *Ger.* mountains
Albufera *Span.* lagoon
–álen *Nor.* islands
Alpen *Ger.* mountain pastures
Alpes *Fr.* mountains
Alpi *It.* mountains
Alto *Port.* high
–älv, –älven *Swed.* stream, river
Amt *Dan.* first-order administrative division
Appennino *It.* mountain range
Arch. (Archipiélago) *Span.* archipelago
Arcipélago *It.* archipelago
Arq. (Arquipélago) *Port.* archipelago
Arr. (Arroyo) *Span.* stream
–Ås, –åsen *Nor., Swed.* hill
Autonomna Oblast *Ser.-Cr.* autonomous region
Ayios *Gr.* island
Ayn *Ar.* well, waterhole

B(a). (Baía) *Port.* bay
B. (Baie) *Fr.* bay
B. (Bahía) *Span.* bay
B. (Ben) *Gae.* mountain
B. (Bir) *Ar.* well
B. (Bucht) *Ger.* bay
B. (Bugt.) *Dan.* bay
Baai, –baai *Afr.* bay
Bāb *Ar.* gate
Bäck, –bäcken *Swed.* stream
Back, backen, *Swed.* hill
Bad, –baden *Ger.* spa
Bādiya,-t *Ar.* desert
Baek *Dan.* stream
Baelt *Dan.* strait
Bahía *Span.* bay
Bahr *Ar.* sea, river
Bahra *Ar.* lake
Baía *Port.* bay
Baie *Fr.* bay
Bajo, –a, *Span.* lower
Bakke *Nor.* hill
Bala *Pers.* upper
Baltă *Rum.* marsh, lake
Banc *Fr.* bank
Bander *Ar., Mal.* port
Bandar *Pers.* bay
Banja *Ser. Cr.* spa. resort
Barat *Mal.* western
Barr. (Barrage) *Fr.* dam
Barracão *Port.* dam, waterfall
Bassin *Fr.* bay
Bayt *Heb.* house, village
Bazar *Hin.* market, bazaar
Be'er *Heb.* well
Beit *Heb.* village
Belo-, Belyy, Belaya,

Beloye, *Russ.* white
Ben *Gae.* mountain
Bender *Somal.* harbour
Berg, (e) –berg(e) *Afr.* mountain(s)
Berg, –berg *Ger.* mountain
–berg, –et *Nor., Swed.* hill, mountain, rock
Bet *Heb.* house, village
Bir, Bîr *Ar.* well
Birket *Ar.* lake, bay, marsh
Bj. (Bordj) *Ar.* port
–bjerg *Dan.* hill, point
Boca *Span.* river mouth
Bodden *Ger.* bay, inlet
Bogaz, Boğaz, –ı *Tur.* strait
Boka *Ser.-Cr.* gulf, inlet
Bol. (Bolshoi) *Russ.* great, large
Bordj *Ar.* fort
–borg *Dan., Nor., Swed.* castle, fort
–botn *Nor.* valley floor
bouche(s) *Fr.* mouth
Br. (Burnu) *Tur.* cape
Braţul *Rum.* distributary stream
–breen *Nor.* glacier
–bruck *Ger.* bridge
–brunn *Swed.* well, spring
Bucht *Ger.* bay
Bugt, –bugt *Dan.* bay
Buheirat *Ar.* lake
Bukit *Mal.* hill
Bukten *Swed.* bay
–bulag *Mong.* spring
Bûr *Ar.* port
Burg. *Ar.* fort
Burg, –burg *Ger.* castle
Burnu *Tur.* cape
Burun *Tur.* cape
Butt *Gae.* promontory
–by *Dan., Nor., Swed.* town
–byen *Nor., Swed.* town

C. (Cabo) *Port., Span.* headland, cape
C. (Cap) *Fr.* cape
C. (Capo) *It.* cape
Cabeza *Span.* peak, hill
Camp *Port., Span.* land, field
Campo *Span.* plain
Campos *Span.* upland
Can. (Canal) *Fr., Span.* canal
Canale *It.* canal
Canalul *Ser.-Cr.* canal
Cao Nguyên *Thai.* plateau, tableland
Cap *Fr.* cape
Capo *It.* cape
Cataracta *Sp.* cataract
Cauce *Span.* intermittent stream
Causse *Fr.* upland (limestone)
Cayi *Tur.* river
Cayo(s) *Span.* rock(s), islet(s)
Cerro *Span.* hill, peak
Ch. (Chaîne(s)) *Fr.* mountain range(s)
Ch. (Chott) *Ar.* salt lake
Chaco *Span.* jungle
Chaîne(s) *Fr.* mountain range(s)
Chap. (Chapada) *Port.* hills, upland

Chapa *Span.* hills, upland
Chapada *Port.* hills, upland
Chaung *Bur.* stream, river
Chen *Chin.* market town
Ch'eng *Chin.* town
Chiang *Chin.* river
Ch'ih *Chin.* pool
Ch'ŏn *Kor.* river
–chŏsuji *Kor.* reservoir
Chott *Ar.* salt lake, swamp
Chou *Chin.* district
Chu *Tib.* river
Chung *Chin.* middle
Chute *Fr.* waterfall
Co. (Cerro) *Span.* hill, peak
Coch. (Cochilla) *Port.* hills
Col *Fr., It.* Pass
Colline(s) *Fr.* hill(s)
Conca *It.* plain, basin
Cord. (Cordillera) *Span.* mountain chain
Costa *It., Span.* coast
Côte *Fr.* coast, slope, hill
Cuchillas *Spain* hills
Cu-Lao *I.-C.* island

D. (Dolok) *Mal.* mountain
Dágh *Pers.* mountain
Dağ(ı) *Tur.* mountain(s)
Dağları *Tur.* mountain range
Dake *Jap.* mountain
–dal *Nor.* valley
–dal, –e *Dan., Nor.* valley
–dal, –en *Swed.* valley, stream
Dalay *Mong.* sea, large lake
–dalir *Ice.* valley
–dalur *Ice.* valley
–damm, –en *Swed.* lake
Danau *Mal.* lake
Dao *I.-O.* island
Dar *Ar.* region
Darya *Russ.* river
Daryācheh *Pers.* marshy lake, lake
Dasht *Pers.* desert, steppe
Daung *Bur.* mountain, hill
Dayr *Ar.* depression, hill
Debre *Amh.* hill
Deli *Ser.-Cr.* mountain(s)
Denizi *Tur.* sea
Dépt. (Département) *Fr.* first-order administrative division
Desierto *Span.* desert
Dhar *Ar.* region, mountain chain
Dj. (Djebel) *Ar.* mountain
Dō *Jap., Kor.* island
Dong *Kor.* village, town
Dong *Thai.* jungle region
–dorf *Ger.* village
–dorp *Afr.* village
–drif *Afr.* ford
–dybet *Dan.* marine channel
Dzong *Tib.* town, settlement

Eil.-eiland(en) *Afr., Dut.* island(s)
–elv *Nor.* river
–'emeq *Heb.* plain, valley
'erg *Ar.* desert with dunes
Estrecho *Span.* strait
Estuario *Span.* estuary

Étang *Fr.* lagoon
–ey(jar) *Ice.* island(s)

F. (Fiume) *It.* river
F. Folyó *Hung.* river
Fd. (Fjord) *Nor.* Inlet of sea
–feld *Ger.* field
–fell *Ice.* mountain, hill
–feng *Chin.* mountain
Fiume *It.* river
Fj. (–fjell) *Nor.* mountain
–fjall *Ice.* mountain(s), hill(s)
–fjäll(et) *Swed.* hill(s), mountain(s), ridge
–fjällen *Swed.* mountains
–fjard(en) *Swed.* fjord, bay, lake
Fjeld *Dan.* mountain
–fjell *Nor.* mountain, rock
–fjord(en) *Nor.* inlet of sea
–fjörður *Ice.* fjord
Fl. (Fleuve) *Fr.* river
Fl. (Fluss) *Ger.* river
–flói *Ice.* bay, marshy country
Fluss *Ger.* river
foce, –en *It.* mouth(s)
Folyó *Hung.* river
–fontein *Afr.* fountain, spring
–fors, –en, *Swed.* rapids, waterfall
Foss *Ice., Nor.* waterfall
–furt *Ger.* ford
Fylke *Nor.* first-order administrative division

G. (Gebel) *Ar.* mountain
G. (Gebirge) *Ger.* hills, mountains
G. (Golfe) *Fr.* gulf
G. (Golfo) *It.* gulf
G. (Gora) *Bulg., Russ., Ser.-Cr.* mountain
G. (Gunong) *Mal.* mountain
–gang *Kor.* river
Ganga *Hin., Sin.* river
–gat *Dan.* sound
–gau *Ger.* district
Gave *Fr.* stream
–gawa *Jap.* river
Geb. (Gebirge) *Ger.* hills, mountains
Gebel *Ar.* mountain
Geziret *Ar.* island
Ghat *Hin.* range of hills
Ghiol *Rum.* lake
Ghubbat *Ar.* bay, inlet
Gji *Alb.* bay
Gjol *Alb.* lagoon, lake
Gl. (Glava) *Ser.-Cr.* mountain, peak
Glen. *Gae.* valley
Gletscher *Ger.* glacier
Gobi *Mong.* desert
Gol *Mong.* river
Golfe *Fr.* gulf
Golfo *It., Span.* gulf
Gomba *Tib.* settlement
Gora *Bulg., Russ., Ser.-Cr.* mountain(s)
Góry *Pol., Russ.* mountain
Gölü *Tur.* lake
–gorod *Russ.* small town
Grad *Bulg., Russ., Ser.-Cr.* town, city

Grada *Russ.* mountain range
Guba *Russ.* bay
–Guntō *Jap.* island group
Gunong *Mal.* mountain
Gurā *Rum.* passage

H. Hadabat *Ar.* plateau
–hafen *Ger.* harbour, port
Haff *Ger.* bay
Hai *Chin.* sea
Haihsia *Chin.* strait
–hale *Dan.* spit, peninsula
Hals *Dan., Nor.* peninsula, isthmus
Halvø *Dan.* peninsula
Halvøya *Nor.* peninsula
Hāmad, Hamada, Hammādah *Ar.* stony desert, plain
–hamn *Swed., Nor.* harbour, anchorage
Hāmūn *Ar.* plain
Hāmūn *Pers.* low-lying marshy area
–Hantō *Jap.* peninsula
Harju *Fin.* hill
Hassi *Ar.* well
–haug *Nor.* hill
Hav *Swed.* gulf
Havet *Nor.* sea
–havn *Dan., Nor.* harbour
Hegyseg *Hung.* forest
Heide *Ger.* heath
Hi. (hassi) *Ar.* well
Ho *Chin.* river
–hø *Nor.* peak
Hochland *Afr.* highland
Hoek, –hoek *Afr., Dut.* cape
Höfn *Ice.* harbour, port
–hög, –en, –högar, –högarna *Swed.* hill(s), peak, mountain
Höhe *Ger.* hills
Holm *Dan.* island
–holm, –holme, –holzen, *Swed.* island
Hon *I.-C.* island
Hora *Cz.* mountain
–horn *Nor.* peak
Hory *Cz.* mountain range, forest
–hoved *Dan.* point, headland, peninsula
Hráun *Ice.* lava
–hsi *Chin.* mountain, stream
–hsiang *Chin.* village
–hsien *Chin.* district
Hu *Chin.* lake
Huk *Dan., Ger.* point
Huken *Nor.* head

I. (Île) *Fr.* island
I. (Ilha) *Port.* island
I. (Insel) *Ger.* island
I. (Isla) *Span.* island
I. (Isola) *It.* island
Idehan *Ar., Ber.* sandy plain
Île(s) *Fr.* island(s)
Ilha *Port.* island
Insel(n) *Ger.* island(s)
Irmak *Tur.* river
Is. (Inseln) *Ger.* islands
Is. (Islas) *Span.* islands
Is. (Isola) *It.* island
Isola, –e *It.* island(s)
Istmo *Span.* isthmus

J. (Jabal) *Ar.* mountain
J. (Jazira) *Ar.* island
J. (Jebel) *Ar.* mountain
J. (Jezioro) *Pol.* lake
Jabal *Ar.* mountain, range
–jaur *Swed.* lake
–järvi *Fin.* lake, bay, pond
Jasovir *Bulg.* reservoir
Jazā'ir *Ar.* islands
Jazira *Ar.* island
Jazireh *Pers.* island
Jebel *Ar.* mountain
Jezero *Ser.-Cr.* lake
Jezioro *Pol.* lake
–Jima *Jap.* island
Jøkelen *Nor.* glacier
–joki *Fin.* stream
–jökull *Ice.* glacier
Jūras Līcis *Lat.* bay, gulf

K. (Kap) *Dan.* cape
K (Khalig) *Ar.* gulf
K. (Kiang) *Chin.* river
K. (Kuala) *Mal.* confluence, estuary
Kaap *Afr.* cape
Kai *Jap.* sea
Kaikyō *Jap.* strait
Kamennyy *Russ.* stony
Kampong *Mal.* village
Kan. (Kanal) *Ser.-Cr.* channel, canal
Kanaal *Dut., Flem.* canal
Kanal *Dan.* channel, gulf
Kanal *Ger., Swed.* canal, stream
kanal *Ser.-Cr.* channel, canal
Kang *Kor.* river, bay
Kangri *Tib.* mountain glacier
Kap *Dan., Ger.* cape
Kapp *Nor.* cape
Kas *I.-C.* island
–kaupstaður *Ice.* market town
–kaupunki *Fin.* town
Kavir *Pers.* salt desert
Kébir *Ar.* great
Kéfar *Heb.* village, hamlet
–ken *Jap.* first-order administrative division
Kep *Alb.* cape
Kepulauan *Mal.* archipelago
Ketjil *Mal.* lesser, little
Khalig, Khalij *Ar.* gulf
khamba, –ldg *Tib.* source, spring
Khawr *Ar.* wadi
Khirbat *Ar.* ruins
Kho Khot *Thai.* isthmus
Khōr *Pers.* creek, estuary
Khrebet *Russ.* mountain range
Kiang *Chin.* river
–klint *Dan.* cliff
–Klintar *Swed.* hills
Kloof *Afr.* gorge
Knude *Dan.* point
Ko *Jap.* lake
Ko *Thai.* island
Kohi *Pash.* mountains
Kol *Russ.* lake
Kolymskoye *Russ.* mountain range
Kólpos *Gr., Tur.* gulf, bay
Kompong *Mal.* landing place
–kop *Afr.* hill

–köping *Swed.* market town
Körfezi *Tur.* gulf
Kosa *Russ.* spit
–koski *Fin.* cataract, rapids
–kraal *Afr.* native village
Krasnyy *Russ.* red
Kryash *Russ.* ridge, hills
Kuala *Mal.* confluence, estuary
kuan *Chin.* pass
Kuh –hha *Pers.* mountains
Kul *Russ.* lake
Kulle *Swed.* hill, shoal
Kum *Russ.* sandy desert
Kumpu *Fin.* hill
Kurgan *Russ.* mound
Kwe *Bur.* bay, gulf
Kyst *Dan.* coast
Kyun, –zu, –umya *Bur.* island(s)

L. (Lac) *Fr.* lake
L. (Lacul) *Rum.* lake
L. (Lago) *It., Span.* lake, lagoon
L. (Lagoa) *Port.* lagoon
L. (Límni) *Gr.* lake
L. (Loch) *Gae.* (lake, inlet)
L. (Lough) *Gae.* (lake, inlet)
La *Tib.* pass
La (Lagoa) *Port.* lagoon
–laagte *Afr.* watercourse
Läani *Fin.* first-order administrative division
Län *Swed.* first-order administrative division
Lac *Fr.* lake
Lacul *Rum.* lake, lagoon
Lago *It., Span.* lake, lagoon
Lagoa *Port.* lagoon
Laguna *It., Span.* lagoon, intermittent lake
Lagune *Fr.* lake
Lahti *Fin.* bay, gulf, cove
Lakhti *Russ.* bay, gulf
Lampi *Fin.* lake
Land *Ger.* first-order administrative division
–land *Dan.* region
–land *Afr., Nor.* land, province
Lido *It.* beach, shore
Liehtao *Chin.* islands
Lilla *Swed.* small
Límni *Gr.* lake
Ling *Chin.* mountain range, ice
Linna *Fin.* historical fort
Llano *Span.* prairie, plain
Loch *Gae.* (lake)
Lough *Gae.* (lake)
Lum *Alb.* river
Lund *Dan.* forest
–lund, –en *Swed.* wood(s)

M. (Maj, Mai) *Alb.* mountain, peak
M. (Mont) *Fr.* mountain peak
M. (Mys) *Russ.* cape
Madīna(h) *Ar.* town, city
Madiq *Ar.* strait
Maj *Alb.* peak
Mäki *Fin.* hill, hillside
Mal *Alb.* mountain
Mal *Russ.* little, small
Mal/a, –i, –o *Ser.-Cr.* small, little
Man *Kor.* bay
Mar *Span.* lagoon, sea
Mare *Rum.* great
Marisma *Span.* marsh
–mark *Dan., Nor.* land
Marsâ *Ar.* anchorage, bay, inlet
Masabb *Ar.* river mouth
Massif *Fr.* upland, plateau
Mato *Port.* forest
Mazar *Pers.* shrine, tomb
Meer *Afr., Dut., Ger.* lake sea

Mi., Mti. (Monti) *It.* mountains
Miao *Chin.* temple, shrine
Midbar *Heb.* wilderness
Mif. (Massif) *Fr.* upland, plateau
Misaki *Jap.* cape, point
–mo *Nor., Swed.* heath, island
–mon *Swed.* heath
Mong *Bur.* town
Mont *Fr.* hill, mountain
Montagna *It.* mountain
Montagne *Fr.* hill, mountain
Montaña *Span.* mountain
Monte *It., Port., Span.* mountain
Monti *It.* mountains
More *Russ.* sea
Mörön *Hung.* river
Mt. (Mont) *Fr.* mountain
Mt. (Monti) *It.* mountain
Mt. (Montaña) *Span.* mountain range
Mte. (Monte) *It., Port., Span.* mountain
Mţi. (Munţi) *Rum.* mountain
Mts. (Monts) *Fr.* mountains
Muang *Mal.* town
Mui *Ar., I.-C.* cape
Mull *Gae.* (promontory)
Mund, –mund *Afr.* mouth
Munkhafed *Ar.* depression
Munte *Rum.* mount
Munţi(i) *Rum.* mountain(s)
Muong *Mal.* village
Myit *Bur.* river
Myitwanya *Bur.* mouths of river
–mýri *Ice.* bog
Mys *Russ.* cape

N. (Nahal) *Heb.* river
Naes *Dan.* point, cape
Nafūd *Ar.* sandy desert
Nahal *Heb.* river
Nahr *Ar.* river, stream
Najd *Ar.* plateau, pass
Nakhon *Thai.* town
Nam *I.-C.* river
–nam *Kor.* south
–näs *Swed.* cape
–nes *Ice., Nor.* cape
Ness, –ness *Gae.* promontory, cape
Nez *Fr.* cape
–niemi *Fin.* cape, point, peninsula, island
Nizhne, –iy *Russ.* lower
Nizmennost *Russ.* plain, lowland
Nísos, Nísoi *Gr.* island(s)
Nor *Chin.* lake
Nor *Tib.* peak
Nos *Bulg., Russ.* cape, point
Nudo *Span.* mountain
Nuruu *Mong.* mountain range
Nuur *Mong.* lake

O. (Ostrov) *Russ.* island
O (Ouâdi, Oued) *Ar.* wadi
–ö *Swed.* island, peninsula, point
–öar, (–na) *Swed.* islands
Oblast *Russ.* administrative division
Öbor *Mong.* inner
Occidental *Fr., Span.* western
Odde *Dan., Nor.* point, peninsula, cape
Oji *Alb.* bay
Ojo *Span.* spring
Oki *Jap.* bay
–ön *Swed.* island peninsula
Ondör *Mong.* high, tall

–ör *Swed.* island, peninsula, point
Oraşul *Rum.* city
Ord *Gae.* point
Óri *Gr.* mountains
Oriental *Span.* eastern
Órmos *Gr.* bay
Óros *Gr.* mountain
Ort *Ger.* point, cape
Ostrov(a) *Russ.* island(s)
Otok(–i) *Ser.-Cr.* island(s)
Ouadi, –edi *Ar.* dry watercourse, wadi
Ouzan *Pers.* river
Ova (–si) *Tur.* plains, lowlands
–øy, (–a) *Nor.* island(s)
Oya *Hin.* point
Oya *Sin.* river
Oz. (Ozero, a) *Russ.* lake(s)

P. (Passo) *It.* pass
P. (Pasul) *Rum.* pass
P. (Pico) *Span.* peak
P. (Prokhod) *Bulg.* pass
–pää *Fin.* hill(s), mountain
Pahta *Lapp.* hill
Pampa, –s *Span.* plain(s) salt flat(s)
Pan. (Pantano) *Span.* Reservoir
Pantao *Chin.* peninsula
Parbat *Urdu* mountain
Pas *Fr.* gap
Paso *Span.* pass, marine channel
Pass *Ger.* pass
Passo *It.* pass
Pasul *Rum.* pass
Patam *Hin.* small village
Patna, –patnam *Hin.* small village
Pegunungan *Mal.* mountain, range
Pei, –pei *Chin.* north
Pélagos *Gr.* sea
Pen. (Península) *Span.* peninsula
Peña *Span.* rock, peak
Península *Span.* peninsula
Per. (Pereval) *Russ.* pass
Pertuis *Fr.* channel
Peski *Russ.* desert, sands
Phanom *I.-C., Thai.* mountain
Phnom *I.-C.* mountain
Phu *I.-C.* mountain
Pic *Fr.* peak
Pico(s) *Span.* peak(s)
Pik *Russ.* peak
Piz., pizzo *It.* peak
Pl. (Planina) *Ser.-Cr.* mountain, range
Plage *Fr.* beach
Plaine *Fr.* plain
Planalto *Span.* plateau
Planina *Bulg., Ser.-Cr.* mountain, range
Plat. (Plateau) *Fr.* level upland
Plato *Russ.* plateau
Playa *Span.* beach
P-ov. (Poluostrov) *Russ.* peninsula
Pointe *Fr.* point, cape
Pojezierze *Pol.* lakes plateau
Polder *Dut.* reclaimed farmland
–pólis *Gr.* city, town
Poluostrov *Russ.* peninsula
Połwysep *Pol.* peninsula
Pont *Fr.* bridge
Ponta *Port.* point, cape
Ponte *It.* bridge
Poort *Afr.* passage, gate
–poort *Dut.* port
Porta *Port.* pass
Porţil, –e *Rum.* gate
Portillo *Span.* pass
Porto *It.* port
Porto *Port., Span.* port

Pot. (Potámi, Potamós) *Gr.* river
Poulo *I.-C.* island
Pr. (Průsmyk) *Cz.* pass
Pradesh *Hin.* state
Presa *Span.* reservoir
Presqu'île *Fr.* peninsula
Prokhod *Bulg.* pass
Proliv *Russ.* strait
Prusmyk *Cz.* pass
Pso. (Passo) *It.* pass
Pta. (Ponta) *Port.* point, cape
Pta. (Punta) *It., Span.* point, cape, peak
Pte. (Pointe) *Fr.* point cape
Puerto *Span.* port, pass
Puig *Cat.* peak
Pulau *Mal.* island
Puna *Span.* desert plateau
Punta *It., Span.* point, peak
Puy *Fr.* hill

Qal'at *Ar.* fort
Qanal *Ar.* canal
Qasr *Ar.* fort
Qiryat *Heb.* town
Qolleh *Pers.* mountain

Ramla *Ar.* sand
Rann *Hin.* swampy region
Rao *I.-C.* river
Ras *Amh.* cape, headland
Rās *Ar.* cape, headland
Recife(s) *Port.* reef(s)
Reka *Bulg., Cz., Russ.* river
Repede *Rum.* rapids
Represa *Port.* dam
Reshteh *Pers.* mountain range
–Rettō *Jap.* group of islands
Ría *Span.* estuary, bay
Ribeirão *Port.* river
Rijeka *Ser.-Cr.* river
Rio *Port.* river
Río *Span.* river
Riv. (Riviera) *It.* coastal plain, coast, river
Rivier *Afr.* river
Riviera *It.* coast
Rivière *Fr.* river
Roche *Fr.* rock
Rog *Russ.* horn
–rück *Ger.* ridge
Rūd *Pers.* stream, river
Rudohorie *Cz.* ore mountains
Rzeka *Pol.* river

S. (Sungei) *Mal.* river
Sa. (Serra) *It., Port.* range of hills
Sa. (Sierra) *Span.* range of hills
–saari *Fin.* island
Sadd *Ar.* dam
Sagar, –ara *Hin., Urdu* lake
Saharā *Ar.* desert
Sahrâ *Ar.* desert
Sa'id *Ar.* highland
Sakar *Fin.* mountain
–Saki *Jap.* point
Sal. (Salar) *Span.* salt pan
Salina(s) *Span.* salt flat(s)
–salmi *Fin.* strait, sound, lake, channel
Saltsjöbad *Swed.* resort
Sammyaku *Jap.* mountain, range
Samut *Thai.* gulf
–San *Jap.* hill, mountain
Sap. (Sapadno) *Russ.* west
Sasso *It.* mountain
Se, Sé *I.-C.* river
Sebkha, –kra *Ar.* salt flats
See *Ger.* lake
–see *Ger.* sea
–şehir *Turk.* town
Selat *Mal.* strait
–selkä *Fin.* bay, lake, sound, ridge, hills

Selva *Span.* forest, wood
Seno *Span.* bay, sound
Serír *Ar.* desert of small stones
Serra *It., Port.* range of hills
Serranía *Span.* mountains
Sev. (Severo) *Russ.* north
–shahr *Pers.* city, town
Shan *Chin.* hills, mountains, pass
Shan-mo *Chin.* mountain range
Shatt *Ar.* river
–Shima *Jap.* island
Shimāli *Ar.* northern
–Shotō *Jap.* group of islands
Shuik'u *Chin.* reservoir
Sierra *Span.* hill, range
Sjö, sjön *Swed.* lake, bay, sea
Sjøen *Dan.* sea
Skär *Swed.* island, rock, cape
Skog *Nor.* forest
–skog, –skogen *Swed.* wood(s)
–skov *Dan.* forest
Slieve *Gae.* range of hills
–sø *Dan., Nor.* lake
Sør *Nor.* south, southern
Solonchak *Russ.* salt lake, marsh
Souk *Ar.* market
Spitze *Ger.* peak, mountain
–spruit *Afr.* stream
–stad *Afr., Nor., Swed.* town
–stadt *Ger.* town
Staður *Ice.* town
Stausee *Ger.* reservoir
Stenón *Gr.* strait, pass
Step *Russ.* plain
Str. (Stretto) *It.* strait
–strand *Dan., Nor.* beach
–strede *Nor.* straits
Strelka *Russ.* spit
–strete *Nor.* straits
Stretto *It.* strait
Stroedet *Dan.* strait
–ström, –strömmen *Swed.* stream(s)
–stroom *Afr.* large river
Suidō *Jap.* strait, channel
Sûn *Bur.* cape
Sund *Dan.* sound
–sund, –sundet *Swed.* sound, estuary, inlet
–sund(et) *Nor.* sound
Sungai, –ei *Mal.* river
Sungei *Mal.* river
Sur *Span.* south, southern
Sveti *Bulg.* pass
Syd *Dan., Swed.* south

Tai –tai *Chin.* tower
Tal *Mong.* plain, steppe
–tal *Ger.* valley
Tall *Ar.* hills, hummocks
Tandjung *Mal.* cape, headland
Tao *Chin.* island
Tassili *Ar.* rocky plateau
Tau *Russ.* mountain, range
Taung *Bur.* mountain, south
Taunggya *Bur.* pass
Tělok *I.-C., Mal.* bay bight
Teluk *Mal.* bay, gulf
Tg. (Tandjung) *Mal.* cape, headland
–thal *Ger.* valley
Thok *Tib.* town
Tierra *Span.* land, country
–tind *Nor.* peak
Tjärn, –en, –et *Swed.* lake
Tong *Nor.* village, town
Tong *Bur., Thai.* mountain range
Tonle *I.-C.* large river, lake
–träsk *Swed.* bog, swamp
Tsangpo *Tib.* large river
Tso *Tib.* lake

Tsu *Jap.* entrance, bay
Tulur *Ar.* hill
T'un *Chin.* village
Tung *Chin.* east
Tunnel *Fr.* tunnel
Tunturi *Fin.* hill(s), mountain(s), ridge

Uad *Ar.* dry watercourse, wadi
Udjung *Mal.* cape
Udd, udde, udden *Swed.* point, peninsula
Uebi *Somal.* river
Us *Mong.* water
Ust *Russ.* river mouth
Uul *Mong., Russ.* mountain, range

V. (Volcán) *Span.* volcano
–vaara *Fin.* hill, mountain, ridge, peak
–våg *Nor.* bay
Val *Fr., It.* valley
Valea *Rum.* valley
–vall, –vallen *Swed.* mountain
Valle *Span.* valley
Vallée *Fr.* valley
Valli *It.* lake, lagoon
Väst *Swed.* west
–vatn *Ice., Nor.* lake
Vatten *Swed.* lake
Vdkhr. (Vodokhranilishche) *Russ.* reservoir
–ved, –veden *Swed.* range, hills
Veld, –veld *Afr.* field
Velik/a, –e, –i, –o *Ser.Cr.* large
–vesi *Fin.* water, lake, bay sound, strait
Vest *Dan., Nor.* west
Vf. (vîrful) *Rum.* peak, mountain
–vidda *Nor.* plateau
Vig *Dan.* bay, inlet, cove, lagoon, lake, bight
–vik, –vika, –viken *Nor., Swed.* bay, cove, gulf, inlet, lake
Vila *Port.* small town
Villa *Span.* town
Ville *Fr.* town
Vinh *I.-C.* bay
Vîrful *Rum.* peak, mountain
–vlei *Afr.* pond, pool
Vodokhranilishche *Russ.* reservoir
Vol. (Volcán) *Span.* volcano, mountain
Vorota *Russ.* gate
Vostochnyy *Russ.* eastern
Vozyshennost *Russ.* heights, uplands
Vrata *Bulg.* gate, pass
Vrchovina *Cz.* mountainous country
Vrchy *Cz.* mountain range
Vung *I.-C.* gulf
–vuori *Fin.* mountain, hill

W. (Wādī) *Ar.* dry watercourse
Wâhât *Ar.* oasis
Wald *Ger.* wood, forest
Wan *Chin., Jap.* bay
Webi *Amh.* river
Woestyn *Afr.* desert

Yam *Heb.* sea
Yang *Chin.* ocean
Yazovir *Bulg.* reservoir
Yoma *Bur.* mountain range
–yüan *Chin.* spring

–**Z**aki *Jap.* peninsula
Zalew *Pol.* lagoon, swamp
Zaliv *Russ.* bay
Zan *Jap.* mountain
Zatoka *Pol.* bay
Zee *Dut.* sea
Zemlya *Russ.* land, island(s)

Principal Cities of the World

The population figures used are from censuses or more recent estimates and are given in thousands for towns and cities over 200 000 (over 500 000 in China and India and 250 000 in Brazil, Japan, United States and U.S.S.R.). Where possible the population of the metropolitan areas is given e.g. Greater London. Greater New York, etc.

AFRICA

ALGERIA (1974)
Algiers 1 503
Oran 485
Constantine 350
Annaba 313
Tizi-Ouzou 224

ANGOLA (1970)
Luanda 475

CAMEROON (1976)
Douala 458
Yaoundé 314

CANARY ISLANDS (1981)
Las Palmas 360

CONGO (1980)
Brazzaville 422

EGYPT (1976)
Cairo 5 074
Alexandria 2 318
El Giza 1 230
Shubra el Kheima 394
El Mahalla el Kubra 292
Tanta 285
Port Said 263
El Mansura 259
Asyut 214
Zagazig 203

ETHIOPIA (1980)
Addis Abeba 1 277
Asmera 443

GABON (1976)
Libreville 186

GHANA (1970)
Accra 738
Kumasi 345

GUINEA (1972)
Conakry 526

IVORY COAST (1976)
Abidjan 850
Bouaké 318

KENYA (1979)
Nairobi 835
Mombasa 312

LIBYA (1973)
Tripoli 551
Benghazi 282

MADAGASCAR (1978)
Antananarivo 400

MALAWI (1977)
Blantyre 229

MALI (1976)
Bamako 419

MOROCCO (1973)
Casablanca 1 753
Rabat-Salé 596
Marrakesh 436
Fès 426
Meknès 403
Oujda 349
Kénitra 341
Tétouan 308
Safi 215
Tanger 208

MOZAMBIQUE (1970)
Maputo 384

NIGERIA (1975)
Lagos 1 477
Ibadan 847
Ogbomosho 432
Kano 399
Oshogbo 282
Ilorin 282
Abeokuta 253
Port Harcourt 242
Zaria 224
Ilesha 224
Onitsha 220
Iwo 214
Ado-Ekiti 213
Kaduna 202

SENEGAL (1976)
Dakar 799

SIERRA LEONE (1974)
Freetown 214

SOMALI REP. (1980)
Mogadishu 400

SOUTH AFRICA (1970)
Johannesburg 1 441
Cape Town 1 107
Durban 851
Pretoria 563
Port Elizabeth 476
Germiston 222

SUDAN (1980)
Khartoum 561
Omdurman 454
Khartoum North 249
Port Sudan 205

TANZANIA (1978)
Dar-es-Salaam 757

TUNISIA (1976)
Tunis 944
Sfax 475
Sousse 255

UGANDA (1975)
Kampala 332

ZAIRE (1975)
Kinshasa 2 242
Lubumbashi 481
Kananga 377
Kisangani 298
Mbuji Mayi 283

ZAMBIA (1980)
Lusaka 641
Kitwe 341
Ndola 323

ZIMBABWE (1981)
Harare 686
Bulawayo 400

ASIA

AFGHANISTAN (1979)
Kabul 1036

BANGLADESH (1982)
Dhaka 3 459
Chittagong 1 388
Khulna 623
Narayanganj 298

BURMA (1977)
Rangoon 2 276
Mandalay 458
Kanbe 254

CAMBODIA (1981)
Phnom Penh 400

CHINA (1970)
Shanghai 11 860
Peking 9 231
Tientsin 7 764
Shenyang 2 800
Wuhan 2 560
Canton 2 500
Chungking 2 400
Nanking 1 750
Harbin 1 670
Luta 1 650
Sian 1 600
Lanchow 1 450
Taiyuan 1 350
Tsingtao 1 300
Chengtu 1 250
Changchun 1 200
Kunming 1 100
Tsinan 1 100
Fushun 1 080
Anshan 1 050
Chengchow 1 050
Hangchow 960
Tangshan 950
Paotow 920
Tzepo 850
Changsha 825
Shihkiachwang 800
Tsitsihar 760
Soochow 730
Kirin 720
Suchow 700
Foochow 680
Nanchang 675
Kweiyang 660
Wusih 650
Hofei 630
Hwainan 600
Penki 600
Loyang 580
Nanning 550
Huhehot 530
Sining 500
Wulumuchi 500

HONG KONG (1981)
Kowloon 2 450
Hong Kong 1 184
Tsuen Wan 599

INDIA (1981)
Calcutta 9 194
Bombay 8 243
Delhi 5 729
Madras 4 289
Bangalore 2 922
Ahmedabad 2 548
Hyderabad 2 546
Pune 1 686
Kanpur 1 639
Nagpur 1 302
Jaipur 1 015
Lucknow 1 008
Coimbatore 920
Patna 919
Surat 914
Madurai 908
Indore 829
Varanasi 797
Jabalpur 757
Agra 747
Vadodara 744
Cochin 686
Dhanbad 678
Bhopal 671
Jamshedpur 670
Allahabad 650
Ulhasnagar 649
Tiruchchirapalli 610
Ludhiana 606
Srinagar 606
Vishakhapatnam 604
Amritsar 595
Gwalior 556
Calicut 546
Vijawada 543
Meerut 537
Dharwad 527
Trivandrum 520
Salem 519
Solapur 515
Jodhpur 506
Ranchi 503

INDONESIA (1971)
Jakarta 4 576
Surabaya 1 556
Bandung 1 202
Semarang 647
Medan 636
Palembang 583
Ujung Pandang 435
Malang 422
Surakarta 414
Yogyakarta 342
Banjarmasin 282
Pontianak 218

IRAN (1976)
Tehran 4 496
Esfahan 672
Mashhad 670
Tabriz 599
Shiraz 416
Ahvaz 329
Abadan 296
Qahremanshahr 291
Qom 247

IRAQ (1970)
Baghdad 2 969
Basra 371
Mosul 293
Kirkuk 208

ISRAEL (1981)
Jerusalem 407
Tel Aviv-Jaffa 335
Haifa 230

JAPAN (1980)
Tokyo 8 349
Yokohama 2 774
Osaka 2 648
Nagoya 2 088
Kyoto 1 473
Sapporo 1 402
Kobe 1 367
Fukuoka 1 089
Kitakyushu 1 065
Kawasaki 1 041
Hiroshima 899
Sakai 810
Chiba 746
Sendai 665
Okayama 546
Kumamoto 526
Amagasaki 524
Higashiosaka 522
Kagoshima 505
Hamamatsu 491
Funabashi 479
Niigata 458
Shizuoka 458
Nagasaki 447
Himeji 446
Sagamihara 439
Yokosuka 421
Kanazawa 418
Gifu 410
Nishinoyama 410
Kurashiki 404
Toyonaka 403
Matsuyama 402
Matsudo 401
Wakayama 401
Hachioji 387
Kawaguchi 379
Utsunomiya 378
Ichikawa 364
Oita 360
Urawa 358
Omiya 354
Asahikawa 353
Hirakata 353
Fukuyama 346
Iwaki 342
Takatsuki 341
Suita 332
Nagano 324
Hakodate 320
Takamatsu 317
Toyama 305
Toyohashi 304
Kochi 301
Fujisawa 300
Nara 298
Naha 296
Machida 295
Aomori 288
Koriyama 286
Akita 285
Toyota 282
Yao 273
Shimonoseki 269
Maebashi 265
Miyazaki 265
Fukushima 263
Okazaki 262
Kawagoe 259
Neyagawa 256
Akashi 255
Yokkaichi 255
Ichinomiya 253
Sasebo 251

JORDAN (1979)
Amman 649
Az Zarqa 216

KOREA, NORTH (1967-70)
Pyongyang 1 500
Chongjin 265

KOREA, SOUTH (1980)
Seoul 8 367
Pusan 3 160
Taegu 1 607
Inchon 1 085
Kwangju 728
Taejon 652
Masan 387
Seongnam 376
Chonju 367
Suweon 311
Ulsan 253

KUWAIT (1975)
Kuwait 775

LEBANON (1980)
Beirut 702

MACAU (1981)
Macau 250

MALAYSIA (1980)
Kuala Lumpur 938
Ipoh 301
Georgetown 251

MONGOLIA (1980)
Ulan Bator 419

NEPAL (1971)
Katmandu 210

PAKISTAN (1972)
Karachi 3 499
Lahore 2 165
Faisalabad 822
Hyderabad 628
Rawalpindi 615
Multan 542
Gujranwala 360
Peshawar 268
Sialkot 204
Sargodha 201

PHILIPPINES (1975)
Manila 1 479
Quezon City 957
Davao 485
Cebu 413
Caloocan 397
Iloilo 265
Pasay 255
Zamboanga 227

SAUDI ARABIA (1974)
Riyadh 667
Jedda 561
Mecca 367
Taif 205

SINGAPORE (1981)
Singapore 2 443

SRI LANKA (1981)
Colombo 1 412

SYRIA (1979)
Damascus 1 156
Aleppo 919
Homs 326
Latakia 204

TAIWAN (1981)
Taipei 2 271
Kaohsiung 1 227
Taichung 607
Tainan 595
Chilung 348
Sanchung 335
Chiai 252
Hsinchu 243

THAILAND (1979)
Bangkok 4 871

TURKEY (1980)
Istanbul 2 854
Ankara 2 204
Izmir 754
Adana 569
Bursa 466
Gaziantep 371
Konya 326
Ekisehir 309
Kayseri 273

UNITED ARAB EMIRATES (1980)
Abu Dhabi 449
Dubai 278

VIETNAM (1973-79)
Ho Chi Minh City 3 420
Hanoi 2 571
Haiphong 1 279
Da-Nang 492
Nha-trang 216
Qui-Nhon 214
Hue 209

YEMEN, SOUTH (1977)
Aden 285

AUSTRALASIA

AUSTRALIA (1981)
Sydney 3 205
Melbourne 2 723
Brisbane 1 029
Adelaide 932
Perth 899
Newcastle 389
Wollongong 223
Canberra 220

NEW ZEALAND (1981)
Auckland 770
Wellington 321
Christchurch 290

EUROPE

AUSTRIA (1981)
Vienna 1 516
Graz 243

BELGIUM (1983)
Brussels 989
Gent 237
Charleroi 216
Liège 207

BULGARIA (1980)
Sofia 1 052
Plovdiv 346
Varna 289

CZECHOSLOVAKIA (1982)
Prague 1 184
Bratislava 392
Brno 377
Ostrava 323
Kosice 209

DENMARK (1981)
Copenhagen 1 382

FINLAND (1981)
Helsinki 483

FRANCE (1975)
Paris 9 863
Lyon 1 152
Marseille 1 004
Lille 929
Bordeaux 591
Toulouse 495
Nantes 438
Nice 433
Rouen 389
Grenoble 389
Toulon 379
Strasbourg 355
St-Etienne 335
Lens 313
Nancy 279
Le Havre 264
Grasse-Cannes 255
Tours 235
Clermont-Ferrand 225
Valenciennes 224
Mulhouse 219
Rennes 213
Montpellier 205
Orléans 205
Dijon 203
Douai 203

GERMANY, EAST (1981)
East Berlin 1 158
Leipzig 562
Dresden 517
Karl-Marx-Stadt 318
Magdeburg 289
Rostock 234
Halle 232
Erfurt 212

GERMANY, WEST (1980)
West Berlin 1 896
Hamburg 1 645
München 1 299
Cologne 977
Essen 648
Frankfurt am Main 629
Dortmund 608
Düsseldorf 590
Stuttgart 581
Duisburg 558

Bremen	555
Hannover	535
Nürnberg	484
Bochum	401
Wuppertal	393
Bielefeld	313
Gelsenkirchen	304
Mannheim	304
Bonn	288
Wiesbaden	274
Karlsruhe	272
Münster	270
Braunschweig	261
Mönchengladbach	258
Kiel	250
Augsburg	248
Aachen	244
Oberhausen	229
Krefeld	224
Lübeck	221
Hagen	219

GREECE (1981)

Athens	3 027
Thessaloniki	706

HUNGARY (1980)

Budapest	2 060
Miskolc	207

IRISH REPUBLIC (1981)

Dublin	525

ITALY (1981)

Rome	2 831
Milano	1 635
Napoli	1 211
Torino	1 104
Genova	760
Palermo	700
Bologna	456
Firenze	453
Catánia	379
Bari	371
Venézia	333
Verona	261
Messina	256
Trieste	251
Táranto	243
Cágliari	233
Padova	231
Bréscia	206

NETHERLANDS (1983)

Rotterdam	1 025
Amsterdam	936
s'Gravenhage	674
Utrecht	499
Eindhoven	374
Arnhem	291
Heerlen-Kerkrade	265
Enschede-Hengelo	248
Nijmegen	229
Tilburg	221
Haarlem	219
Groningen	206

NORWAY (1980)

Oslo	624
Bergen	208

POLAND (1981)

Warsaw	1 612
Lódz	843
Kraków	723
Wroclaw	622
Poznań	558
Gdańsk	459
Szczecin	390
Katowice	364
Bydgoszcz	352
Lublin	309
Sosnowiec	252
Bytom	238
Czestochowa	238
Gdynia	237
Bialystok	230
Gliwice	202

PORTUGAL (1981)

Lisbon	818
Oporto	330

ROMANIA (1980)

Bucharest	2 090
Brasov	305
Timisoara	287
Cluj	284
Constanta	284
Iasi	271
Galati	261
Craiova	227
Braila	215
Ploiesti	212

SPAIN (1981)

Madrid	3 159
Barcelona	1 753
Valencia	745
Sevilla	646
Zaragoza	572
Málaga	502
Bilbao	433
Valladolid	320
Hospitalet	295
Palma de Mallorca	290
Murcia	285
Córdoba	279
Vigo	261
Gijón	256
Granada	247
Alicante	246
La Coruña	232
Badalona	230

SWEDEN (1980)

Stockholm	1 387
Göteborg	693
Malmö	453

SWITZERLAND (1982)

Zürich	705
Basel	363
Genève	339
Berne	289
Lausanne	226

U.S.S.R. (1981)

Moskva	8 203
Leningrad	4 676
Kiyev	2 248
Tashkent	1 858
Kharkov	1 485
Gorkiy	1 367
Novosibirsk	1 343
Minsk	1 333
Sverdlovsk	1 239
Kuybyshev	1 238
Dnepropetrovsk	1 100
Tbilisi	1 095
Odessa	1 072
Chelyabinsk	1 055
Yerevan	1055
Baku	1 046
Omsk	1 044
Donetsk	1 040
Perm	1 018
Kazan	1 011
Ufa	1 009
Alma-Ata	975
Rostov	957
Volgograd	948
Saratov	873
Riga	850
Krasnoyarsk	820
Zaporozhye	812
Voronezh	809
Lvov	688
Krivoy Rog	663
Yaroslavl	608
Karaganda	583
Krasnodar	581
Novokuznetsk	581
Ustinov	574
Irkutsk	568
Vladivostok	565
Frunze	552
Barnaul	549
Khabarovsk	545
Kishinev	539
Togliatti	533
Tula	521
Zhdanov	511
Dushanbe	510
Vilnius	503
Penza	500
Samarkand	489
Kemerovo	486
Ulyanovsk	485
Orenburg	482
Voroshilovgrad	474
Ivanovo	470
Astrakhan	470
Ryazan	470
Nikolayev	458
Makeyevka	442
Tallinn	442
Tomsk	439
Kalinin	422
Lipetsk	415
Magnitogorsk	413
Bryansk	407
Gomel	405
Nizhniy Tagil	404
Kirov	396
Murmansk	394
Arkhangelsk	391
Kursk	390
Kaunas	383
Groznyy	379
Tyumen	378
Kaliningrad (Kaliningrad region)	366
Brezhnev	346
Cheboksary	340
Gorlovka	338
Chimkent	334
Vinnitsa	332
Kherson	329
Ashkhabad	325
Kurgan	322
Orel	315
Chita	315
Sevastopol	315
Simferopol	314
Smolensk	311
Ulan Ude	310
Vitebsk	310
Mogilev	308
Vladimir	307
Sochi	295
Semipalatinsk	291
Pavlodar	288
Ordzhonikidze	287
Ust-Kamenogorsk	286
Poltava	284
Taganrog	281
Saransk	280
Cherepovets	279
Tambov	277
Dzhambul	277
Kaluga	276
Komsomolsk-na-Amur	274
Stavropol	271
Makhachkala	269
Prokopyevsk	267
Dzerzhinsk	263
Kostroma	259
Dneprodzerzhinsk	257
Belgorod	255
Orsk	254
Zhitomir	254
Chernigov	252

UNITED KINGDOM (1981)

London	6 696
Birmingham	920
Glasgow	762
Liverpool	510
Sheffield	477
Leeds	449
Manchester	449
Edinburgh	419
Bristol	388
Belfast	374
Coventry	314
Bradford	281
Leicester	280
Cardiff	274
Nottingham	271
Hull	268
Wolverhampton	252
Stoke-on-Trent	252
Plymouth	244
Derby	216
Southampton	204

YUGOSLAVIA (1971)

Belgrade	775
Zagreb	602
Skopje	388
Sarajevo	271
Ljubljana	213

NORTH AMERICA

CANADA (1981)

Toronto	2 999
Montréal	2 828
Vancouver	1 268
Ottawa	718
Edmonton	657
Calgary	593
Winnipeg	585
Québec	576
Hamilton	542
St. Catherines	304
Kitchener	288
London	284
Halifax	278
Windsor	246
Victoria	233

COSTA RICA (1982)

San José	265

CUBA (1981)

Havana	1 924
Santiago de Cuba	345
Camagüey	345

DOMINICAN REPUBLIC (1978)

Santo Domingo	1 103
Santiago de los Caballeros	242

EL SALVADOR (1974)

San Salvador	366

GUATEMALA (1979)

Guatemala City	793

HAITI (1982)

Port-au-Prince	888

HONDURAS (1980)

Tegucigalpa	473
San Pedro Sula	343

JAMAICA (1980)

Kingston	671

MEXICO (1979)

Mexico City	14 750
Guadalajara	2 468
Netzahualcóyotl	2 331
Monterrey	2 019
Puebla de Zaragoza	711
Ciudad Juárez	625
León de los Aldamas	625
Tijuana	566
Acapulco	462
Torreón	407
Tampico	390
Chihuahua	386
Mexicali	349
San Luis Potosi	327
Culiacán	324
Hermosillo	319
Veracruz Llave	307
Mérida	270
Saltillo	258
Aguascalientes	257
Morelia	251
Toluca	242
Cuernavaca	241
Reynosa	231
Durango	229
Nuevo Laredo	224
Jalapa	201

NICARAGUA (1979)

Managua	608

PANAMA (1981)

Panama	655

PUERTO RICO (1980)

San Juan	1 086
Ponce	253
Bayamón	209

UNITED STATES (1980)

New York	16 121
Los Angeles	11 498
Chicago	7 870
Philadelphia	5 548
San Francisco	5 180
Detroit	4 618
Boston	3 448
Houston	3 101
Washington	3 061
Dallas	2 975
Cleveland	2 834
Miami	2 644
St. Louis	2 356
Pittsburgh	2 264
Baltimore	2 174
Minneapolis-St Paul	2 114
Seattle	2 093
Atlanta	2 030
San Diego	1 817
Cincinnati	1 660
Denver	1 621
Milwaukee	1 570
Tampa	1 569
Phoenix	1 509
Kansas City	1 327
Indianapolis	1 306
Portland	1 243
Buffalo	1 243
New Orleans	1 187
Providence	1 096
Columbus	1 093
San Antonio	1 072
Sacramento	1 014
Dayton	1 014
Rochester	971
Salt Lake City	936
Memphis	913
Louisville	906
Nashville	851
Birmingham	847
Oklahoma	834
Greensboro	827
Norfolk	807
Albany	795
Toledo	792
Honolulu	763
Jacksonville	738
Hartford	726
Orlando	700
Tulsa	689
Syracuse	643
Scranton	640
Charlotte	637
Allentown	635
Richmond	632
Grand Rapids	602
Omaha	570
Greenville	569
West Palm Beach	577
Austin	537
Tucson	531
Springfield	531
Youngstown	531
Raleigh	531
Flint	522
Fresno	515
Baton Rouge	494
El Paso	480
Knoxville	477
Lansing	472
Las Vegas	463
Albuquerque	454
Harrisburg	447
Mobile	444
Johnson City	434
Charleston (S.C.)	430
Chattanooga	427
New Haven	418
Wichita	411
Columbia	410
Canton	404
Bakersfield	403
Bridgeport	395
Little Rock	394
Davenport	384
Fort Wayne	383
York	381
Shreveport	377
Beaumont	375
Worcester	373
Peoria	366
Newport News	364
Lancaster	362
Stockton	347
Spokane	342
Des Moines	338
Augusta	327
Corpus Christi	326
Madison	324
Lakeland	322
Jackson	320
Utica	320
Lexington-Fayette	318
Colorado Springs	317
Reading	313
Huntingdon	311
Huntsville	309
Evansville	309
Binghamton	301
Santa Barbara	299
Santa Rosa	292
Appleton	291
Salinas	290
Pensacola	290
McAllen	283
South Bend	281
Erie	280
Rockford	280
Kalamazoo	279
Eugene	275
Montgomery	273
Melbourne	273
Charleston (W. Va.)	270
Duluth	267
Modesto	266
Johnstown	265
Newburgh	260
Daytona Beach	259
Macon	254
Salem	250

SOUTH AMERICA

ARGENTINA (1980)

Buenos Aires	9 927
Córdoba	982
Rosario	955
Mendoza	597
La Plata	560
San Miguel de Tucuman	497
Mar del Plata	407
San Juan	290
Santa Fé	287
Salta	260
Bahía Blanca	221
Resistencia	218

BOLIVIA (1980)

La Paz	720
Santa Cruz	255
Cochabamba	205

BRAZIL (1980)

São Paulo	8 732
Rio de Janeiro	5 539
Belo Horizonte	1 937
Salvador	1 502
Recife	1 433
Fortaleza	1 307
Brasilia	1 306
Pôrto Alegre	1 221
Nova Iguaçu	1 184
Curitiba	943
Belém	934
Goiânia	680
Duque de Caxias	666
São Gonçalo	660
Santo André	634
Campinas	587
Osasco	492
Manaus	483
Santos	453
Sào João de Meriti	442
Niterói	433
São Luiz	405
Guarulhos	404
Natal	401
Maceió	390
Campos	357
Londrina	349
Teresina	349
São Bernardo do Campo	348
Juiz de Fora	334
João Pessoa	332
Jaboatao	321
Ribeirão Preto	309
Olinda	308
Feira de Santana	274
Aracaju	273
Campina Grande	266
Pelotas	256

CHILE (1982)

Santiago	3 831
Viña del Mar	306
Valparaiso	272
Concepción	245
Talcahuano	233

COLOMBIA (1973)

Bogotá	2 855
Medellin	1 159
Cali	990
Barranquilla	692
Cartagena	355
Bucaramanga	323
Cucuta	279
Manizales	232
Pereira	227
Ibagué	223

ECUADOR (1981)

Guayaquil	1 169
Quito	844

PARAGUAY (1978)

Asunción	602

PERU (1981)

Lima	4 601
Arequipa	447
Callao	441
Trujillo	355
Chiclayo	280
Chimbote	216

URUGUAY (1975)

Montevideo	1 173

VENEZUELA (1979)

Caracas	2 849
Maracaibo	874
Valencia	488
Barquisimeto	474
Maracay	333
Barcelona-Puerto La Cruz	267
San Cristóbal	264

Principal Countries of the World

Country	Area in thousands of square km	Population in thousands	Density of population per sq. km.	Capital Population in thousands
Afghanistan	647	16 786	26	Kabul (1036)
Albania	29	2 858	99	Tiranë (198)
Algeria	2 382	20 293	9	Algiers (1 503)
Angola	1 247	7 452	6	Luanda (475)
Argentina	2 767	28 432	10	Buenos Aires (9 927)
Australia	7 687	15 175	2	Canberra (220)
Austria	84	7 571	90	Vienna (1 516)
Bangladesh	144	92 619	643	Dhaka (3 459)
Belgium	31	9 845	318	Brussels (995)
Belize	23	171	7	Belmopan (3)
Benin	113	3 618	32	Porto-Novo (132)
Bhutan	47	1 355	29	Thimphu (60)
Bolivia	1 099	5 916	5	Sucre (63) La Paz (635)
Botswana	600	859	1	Gaborone (60)
Brazil	8 512	126 806	15	Brasilia (1 306)
Brunei	6	250	42	Bandar Seri Begawan (58)
Bulgaria	111	9 107	82	Sofia (1 052)
Burma	677	37 065	55	Rangoon (2 276)
Burundi	28	4 460	159	Bujumbura (157)
Cambodia	181	6 981	39	Phnom Penh (400)
Cameroon	475	8 865	19	Yaoundé (314)
Canada	9 976	24 625	2	Ottawa (718)
Central African Rep.	623	2 405	4	Bangui (302)
Chad	1 284	4 643	4	Ndjamena (303)
Chile	757	11 487	15	Santiago (3 831)
China	9 597	1 020 673	106	Peking (9 231)
Colombia	1 139	28 776	25	Bogota (2 855)
Congo	342	1 621	5	Brazzaville (422)
Costa Rica	51	2 324	46	San José (265)
Cuba	115	9 782	85	Havana (1 924)
Cyprus	9	645	72	Nicosia (161)
Czechoslovakia	128	15 369	120	Prague (1 184)
Denmark	43	5 118	119	Copenhagen (1 382)
Djibouti	22	332	15	Djibouti (150)
Dominican Republic	49	5 744	117	Santo Domingo (1 103)
Ecuador	284	8 945	31	Quito (844)
Egypt	1 001	44 673	45	Cairo (5 074)
El Salvador	21	4 999	238	San Salvador (366)
Equatorial Guinea	28	381	14	Rey Malabo (37)
Ethiopia	1 222	32 775	27	Addis Abeba (1 277)
Fiji	18	658	37	Suva (68)
Finland	337	4 824	14	Helsinki (483)
France	547	54 221	99	Paris (9 863)
French Guiana	91	64	1	Cayenne (39)
Gabon	268	563	2	Libréville (186)
Gambia	11	635	58	Banjul (109)
Germany, East	108	16 864	156	East Berlin (1 158)
Germany, West	249	61 638	248	Bonn (288)
Ghana	239	12 244	51	Accra (738)
Greece	132	9 793	74	Athens (3 027)
Greenland	2 176	52	0.02	Godthåb (10)
Guatemala	109	7 699	71	Guatemala (793)
Guinea	246	5 285	21	Conakry (526)
Guinea-Bissau	36	594	17	Bissau (109)
Guyana	215	922	4	Georgetown (187)
Haiti	28	5 201	186	Port-au-Prince (888)
Honduras	112	3 955	35	Tegucigalpa (473)
Hong Kong	1	5 233	5 233	Hong Kong (1 184)
Hungary	93	10 702	115	Budapest (2 060)
Iceland	103	236	2	Reykjavik (84)
India	3 288	711 664	216	Delhi (5 729)
Indonesia	2 027	153 032	75	Jakarta (4 576)
Iran	1 648	40 240	24	Tehran (4 496)
Iraq	435	13 997	32	Baghdad (2 969)
Irish Republic	70	3 483	50	Dublin (525)
Israel	21	4 022	192	Jerusalem (407)
Italy	301	56 276	187	Rome (2 831)
Ivory Coast	322	8 568	27	Abidjan (850)
Jamaica	11	2 253	205	Kingston (671)
Japan	372	118 449	318	Tokyo (8 349)
Jordan	98	3 489	36	Amman (649)
Kenya	583	17 864	31	Nairobi (835)
Korea, North	121	18 747	155	Pyongyang (1 500)
Korea, South	98	39 331	401	Seoul (8 367)
Kuwait	18	1 562	87	Kuwait (775)
Laos	237	3 902	16	Vientiane (90)
Lebanon	10	2 739	274	Beirut (702)
Lesotho	30	1 409	47	Maseru (45)
Liberia	111	2 113	19	Monrovia (204)
Libya	1 760	3 224	2	Tripoli (551)
Luxembourg	3	357	119	Luxembourg (79)
Madagascar	587	9 233	16	Antananarivo (400)
Malawi	118	6 267	53	Lilongwe (103)
Malaysia	330	14 765	45	Kuala Lumpur (938)
Mali	1 240	7 342	6	Bamako (419)
Malta	0.3	360	1 200	Valletta (14)
Mauritania	1 031	1 730	2	Nouakchott (135)
Mauritius	2	983	492	Port Louis (146)
Mexico	1 973	73 011	37	Mexico (14 750)
Mongolia	1 565	1 764	1	Ulan Bator (419)
Morocco	447	21 667	48	Rabat (597)
Mozambique	783	11 052	14	Maputo (384)
Namibia	824	852	1	Windhoek (61)
Nepal	141	15 020	107	Katmandu (210)
Netherlands	41	14 310	349	Amsterdam (936)
New Zealand	269	3 158	12	Wellington (321)
Nicaragua	130	2 918	22	Managua (608)
Niger	1 267	5 646	4	Niamey (130)
Nigeria	924	82 392	89	Lagos (1 477)
Norway	324	4 115	13	Oslo (624)
Oman	212	948	4	Muscat (25)
Pakistan	804	87 125	108	Islamabad (77)
Panama	76	2 043	27	Panama (655)
Papua New Guinea	462	3 094	7	Port Moresby (123)
Paraguay	407	3 370	8	Asunción (602)
Peru	1 285	18 790	15	Lima (4 601)
Philippines	300	50 740	169	Manila (1 479)
Poland	313	36 227	116	Warsaw (1 612)
Portugal	92	10 056	109	Lisbon (818)
Puerto Rico	9	3 952	439	San Juan (1 086)
Romania	238	22 638	95	Bucharest (2 090)
Rwanda	26	5 276	203	Kigali (90)
Saudi Arabia	2 150	9 684	5	Riyadh (667)
Senegal	196	5 968	30	Dakar (799)
Sierra Leone	72	3 672	51	Freetown (214)
Singapore	0.6	2 472	4 120	Singapore (2 443)
Somali Republic	638	5 116	8	Mogadishu (400)
South Africa	1 221	31 008	25	Pretoria (563) Cape Town (1 107)
Spain	505	37 935	75	Madrid (3 159)
Sri Lanka	66	15 189	230	Colombo (1 412)
Sudan	2 506	19 451	8	Khartoum (561)
Surinam	163	407	2	Paramaribo (151)
Swaziland	17	585	34	Mbabane (23)
Sweden	450	8 325	19	Stockholm (1 387)
Switzerland	41	6 478	158	Berne (289)
Syria	185	9 660	52	Damascus (1 156)
Taiwan	36	18 458	513	Taipei (2 271)
Tanzania	945	19 111	20	Dar-es-Salaam (757)
Thailand	514	48 450	94	Bangkok (4 871)
Togo	56	2 747	49	Lomé (247)
Trinidad and Tobago	5	1 202	240	Port of Spain (66)
Tunisia	164	6 672	41	Tunis (944)
Turkey	781	46 312	59	Ankara (2 204)
Uganda	236	14 057	60	Kampala (332)
United Arab Emirates	84	790	9	Abu Dhabi (449)
U.S.S.R.	22 402	269 994	12	Moscow (8 203)
United Kingdom	245	55 782	228	London (6 696)
United States	9 363	232 057	25	Washington (3 061)
*Upper Volta	274	6 360	23	Ouagadougou (173)
Uruguay	178	2 947	17	Montevideo (1 173)
Venezuela	912	14 714	16	Caracas (2 849)
Vietnam	330	56 205	170	Hanoi (2 571)
Western Samoa	3	159	53	Apia (32)
Yemen, North	195	6 077	31	Sana (448)
Yemen, South	288	2 093	7	Aden (285)
Yugoslavia	256	22 646	88	Belgrade (775)
Zaire	2 345	26 377	11	Kinshasa (2 242)
Zambia	753	6 163	8	Lusaka (641)
Zimbabwe	391	7 540	19	Harare (686)

* Renamed Burkina Faso

Great Slave Lake

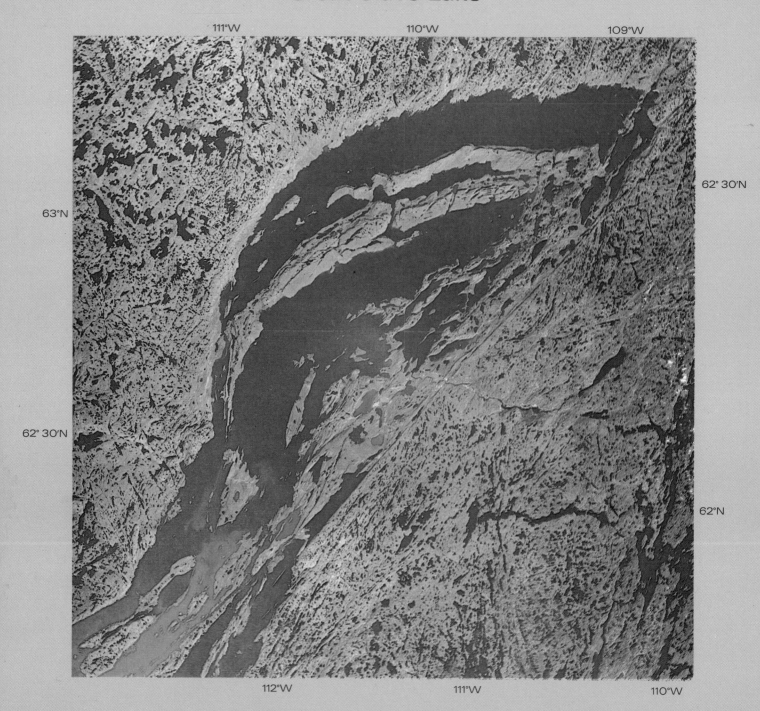

This image, depicting the eastern arm of the Great Slave Lake, shows two major geological regions – the Canadian Shield, with folded and faulted Archaean crystalline rocks, and a Proterozoic basin (in which the arm of the lake lies) with flat-lying sedimentary rocks and igneous instrusions. Running along the southern side of the lake is the distinctive McDonald fault system – one of the major structures of the Shield, having been identified on the surface for a total length of 560 km. The vegetation of the area is characteristically sparse on the thin covering of peat and sub-arctic soils, although there is a little open woodland. Several scars from forest fires are visible as dark green or grey patches within the reddish background of the healthy vegetation. In the southwest of the area, part of the sediment from the mouth of the Slave river to the south is visible as light-blue within the otherwise dark waters of the lake.

(20 October 1973)